CONTENTS

MAPS

ABOUT THIS GUIDE

Fodor's Ratings

Everything in this guide is worth doing—we don't cover what isn't—but exceptional sights, hotels, and restaurants are recognized with additional accolades. **Fodor's Choice★** indicates our top recommendations; ★ highlights places we deem **Highly Recommended**; and **Best Bets** call attention to notable hotels and restaurants in various categories. Care to nominate a new place? Visit Fodors.com/contact-us.

Trip Costs

We list prices wherever possible to help you budget well. Hotel and restaurant price categories from **$** to **$$$$** are noted alongside each recommendation. For hotels, we include the lowest cost of a standard double room in high season. For restaurants, we cite the average price of a main course at dinner or, if dinner isn't served, at lunch. For attractions, we always list adult admission fees; discounts are usually available for children, students, and senior citizens.

Hotels

Our local writers vet every hotel to recommend the best overnights in each price category, from budget to expensive. Unless otherwise specified, you can expect private bath, phone, and TV in your room. For expanded hotel reviews, facilities, and deals visit Fodors.com.

TripAdvisor ⊙⊙

Our expert hotel picks are reinforced by high ratings on TripAdvisor. Look for representative quotes in this guide, and the latest TripAdvisor ratings and feedback at Fodors.com.

Restaurants

Unless we state otherwise, restaurants are open for lunch and dinner daily. We mention dress code only when there's a specific requirement and reservations only when they're essential or not accepted. To make restaurant reservations, visit Fodors.com.

Credit Cards

The hotels and restaurants in this guide typically accept credit cards. If not, we'll say so.

Ratings	Hotels & Restaurants
★ Fodor's Choice	
★ Highly recommended	🏨 Hotel
☾ Family-friendly	⤴ Number of rooms
Listings	ⅠⓄⅠ Meal plans
✉ Address	✕ Restaurant
✉ Branch address	☌ Reservations
ⅆ Mailing address	🏛 Dress code
☏ Telephone	▭ No credit cards
✄ Fax	⑤ Price
⊕ Website	**Other**
✍ E-mail	⇨ See also
✇ Admission fee	☞ Take note
☉ Open/closed times	⅄ Golf facilities
Ⓜ Subway	
⊹ Directions or Map coordinates	

Experience
the Caribbean

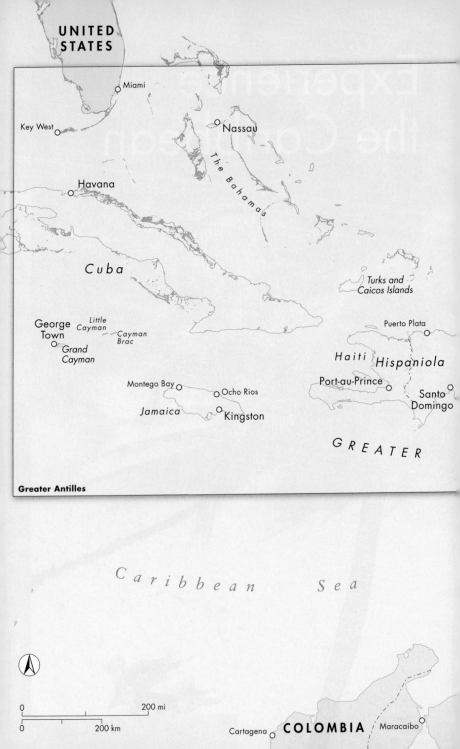

UNITED
STATES

Miami

Key West

Nassau

Havana

The Bahamas

C u b a

*Turks and
Caicos Islands*

George
Town
*Little
Cayman*
*Cayman
Brac*
Puerto Plata

*Grand
Cayman*

H a i t i *Hispaniola*

Montego Bay Ocho Rios Port-au-Prince

Jamaica Kingston

Santo
Domingo

G R E A T E R

Greater Antilles

C a r i b b e a n   *S e a*

0 _____ 200 mi

0 _____ 200 km

Cartagena **COLOMBIA** Maracaibo

The Caribbean

ATLANTIC OCEAN

Dominican Republic

San Juan

St. Thomas
St. John
Tortola
Virgin Gorda
Puerto Rico
St. Croix

ANTILLES

Anguilla
St. Maarten/St. Martin
St. Barthélemy
Saba
St. Eustatius
St. Kitts
Nevis
Montserrat
Guadeloupe

LEEWARD ISLANDS

Barbuda
Antigua

Marie Galante

Leeward Islands

Dominica

Martinique
Fort-de-France

LESSER ANTILLES

WINDWARD ISLANDS

St. Lucia

St. Vincent

Bequia
The Grenadines
Carriacou
St. George's
Grenada

Barbados
Bridgetown

Tobago

Aruba
Curaçao
Bonaire
Willemstad

Islas Los Roques

La Guaira
Caracas

Port of Spain

Trinidad

Windward Islands

VENEZUELA

U.S.A.

West Palm Beach

Little Abaco

Marsh Harbor

Grand Bahama

Miami

Bimini Islands

Abaco

Florida Keys

Key West

Nassau

Eleuthera

Cat Island

Andros

Cay Sal Bank

San Salvaador

Exuma Cays

Rum Cay

The Bahamas

Havana

Lond Island

Ragged Islands

Crooked Islands

Acklins

Cuba

Santiago de Cuba

Guantanamo

Grand Cayman

Little Cayman

Cayman Brac

George Town

Cayman Islands

0   100 mi

0   100 km

Jamaica

Montego Bay

Negril

Ocho Rios

Black River

Kingston

G R E A T E R

C a r i b b e a n

Cayman Islands ⇨ Ch. 8

Vacationers appreciate the mellow civility of the islands, and Grand Cayman's exceptional Seven Mile Beach has its share of fans. Divers come to explore the pristine reefs or perhaps to swim with friendly stingrays. Go if you want a safe, family-friendly vacation spot. Don't go if you're trying to save money, because there are few real bargains here.

Jamaica ⇨ Ch. 14

Easy to reach and with resorts in every price range, Jamaica is also an easy choice for many travelers. Go to enjoy the music, food, beaches, and sense of hospitality that's made it one of the Caribbean's most popular destinations. Don't go if you can't deal with the idea that a Caribbean paradise still has problems of its own to solve.

THE GREATER ANTILLES

The islands closest to the United States mainland—composed of Cuba, Jamaica, Haiti, the Dominican Republic, and Puerto Rico—are also the largest in the chain that stretches in an arc from the southern coast of Florida down to Venezuela. Haiti and Cuba aren't covered in this book. The Cayman Islands, just south of Cuba, are usually included in this group.

Dominican Republic ⇨ Ch. 11
Dominicans have beautiful smiles and warm hearts and are proud of their island, which is blessed with pearl-white beaches and a vibrant, Latin culture. Go for the best-priced resorts in the Caribbean and a wide range of activities that will keep you moving day and night. Don't go if you can't go with the flow. Things don't always work here, and not everyone speaks English.

Turks and Caicos Islands ⇨ Ch. 26
Miles of white-sand beaches surround this tiny island chain, only eight of which are inhabited. The smaller islands seem to come from some long-forgotten era of Caribbean life. Go for deserted beaches and excellent diving on one of the world's largest coral reefs. Don't go for nightlife and a fast pace. And don't forget your wallet. This isn't a budget destination.

Puerto Rico ⇨ Ch. 17
San Juan is hopping day and night; beyond the city, you'll find a sunny escape and slower pace. Party in San Juan, relax on the beach, hike the rain forest, or play some of the Caribbean's best golf courses. You have the best of both worlds here, with natural and urban thrills alike. So go for both. Just don't expect to do it in utter seclusion.

WHAT'S WHERE

LESSER ANTILLES: THE EASTERN CARIBBEAN

The Lesser Antilles are larger in number but smaller in size than the Greater Antilles, and they make up the bulk of the Caribbean arc. Beginning with the Virgin Islands but going all the way to Grenada, the islands of the Eastern Caribbean form a barrier between the Atlantic Ocean and the Caribbean Sea. The best beaches are usually on the Caribbean side.

U.S. Virgin Islands ⇨ Ch. 27

A perfect combination of the familiar and the exotic, the U.S. Virgin Islands are a little bit of America set in an azure sea. Go to St. Croix if you like history and interesting restaurants. Go to St. John if you crave a back-to-nature experience. Go to St. Thomas if you want a shop-'til-you-drop experience and a big selection of resorts, activities, and nightlife.

British Virgin Islands ⇨ Ch. 7

The lure of the British Virgins is exclusivity and personal attention, not lavish luxury. Even the most expensive resorts are selling a state of mind rather than state-of-the-art. So go with an open mind, and your stress may very well melt away. Don't go if you expect glitz or stateside efficiency. These islands are about getting away, not getting it all.

Montserrat ⇨ Ch. 16

Montserrat has staged one of the best comebacks of the new century, returning to the tourism scene after a disastrous volcanic eruption in 1995. Go for exciting volcano ecotourism and great diving or just to taste what the Caribbean used to be like. Don't go for splashy resorts or nightlife. You'll be happier here if you can appreciate simpler pleasures.

Anguilla ⇨ Ch. 2

With miles of brilliant beaches and a range of luxurious resorts (even a few that mere mortals can afford), Anguilla is where the rich, powerful, and famous go to chill out. Go for the fine cuisine in elegant surroundings, great snorkeling, and funky late-night music scene. Don't go for shopping and sightseeing. This island is all about relaxing and reviving.

St. Maarten/St. Martin ⇨ Ch. 23

Two nations (Dutch and French), many nationalities, one small island, a lot of development. But there are also more white, sandy beaches than days in a month. Go for the awesome restaurants, excellent shopping, and wide range of activities. Don't go if you're not willing to get out and search for the really good stuff.

St. Barthélemy ⇨ Ch. 19

If you come to St. Barth for a taste of European village life, not for a conventional full-service resort experience, you will be richly rewarded. Go for excellent dining and wine, great boutiques with the latest hip fashions, and an active, on-the-go vacation. Don't go for big resorts, and make sure your credit card is platinum-plated.

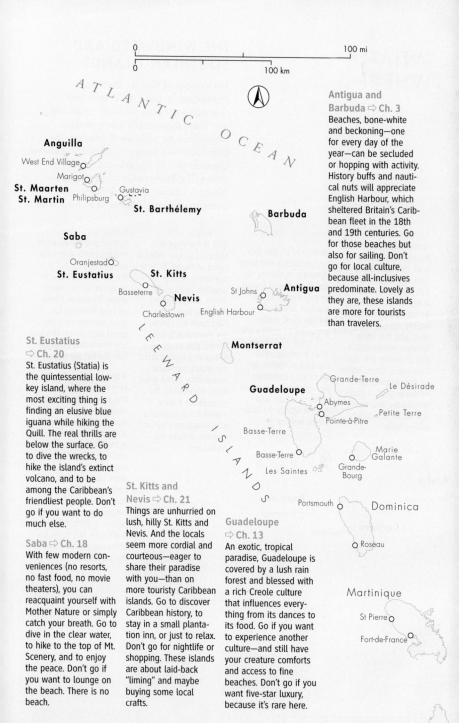

ATLANTIC OCEAN

100 mi

100 km

Anguilla

West End Village

Marigot

St. Maarten
St. Martin   Philipsburg   Gustavia

St. Barthélemy

Barbuda

Saba

Oranjestad

St. Eustatius   St. Kitts

Basseterre   Nevis

Charlestown   English Harbour

St Johns   Antigua

Montserrat

L E E W A R D   I S L A N D S

Grande-Terre   Le Désirade

Guadeloupe   Abymes

Pointe-à-Pitre   Petite Terre

Basse-Terre

Basse-Terre   Marie
Galante

Les Saintes   Grande-
Bourg

Portsmouth   Dominica

Roseau

Martinique

St Pierre

Fort-de-France

Antigua and Barbuda ⇨ Ch. 3

Beaches, bone-white and beckoning—one for every day of the year—can be secluded or hopping with activity. History buffs and nautical nuts will appreciate English Harbour, which sheltered Britain's Caribbean fleet in the 18th and 19th centuries. Go for those beaches but also for sailing. Don't go for local culture, because all-inclusives predominate. Lovely as they are, these islands are more for tourists than travelers.

St. Eustatius ⇨ Ch. 20

St. Eustatius (Statia) is the quintessential low-key island, where the most exciting thing is finding an elusive blue iguana while hiking the Quill. The real thrills are below the surface. Go to dive the wrecks, to hike the island's extinct volcano, and to be among the Caribbean's friendliest people. Don't go if you want to do much else.

Saba ⇨ Ch. 18

With few modern conveniences (no resorts, no fast food, no movie theaters), you can reacquaint yourself with Mother Nature or simply catch your breath. Go to dive in the clear water, to hike to the top of Mt. Scenery, and to enjoy the peace. Don't go if you want to lounge on the beach. There is no beach.

St. Kitts and Nevis ⇨ Ch. 21

Things are unhurried on lush, hilly St. Kitts and Nevis. And the locals seem more cordial and courteous—eager to share their paradise with you—than on more touristy Caribbean islands. Go to discover Caribbean history, to stay in a small plantation inn, or just to relax. Don't go for nightlife or shopping. These islands are about laid-back "liming" and maybe buying some local crafts.

Guadeloupe ⇨ Ch. 13

An exotic, tropical paradise, Guadeloupe is covered by a lush rain forest and blessed with a rich Creole culture that influences everything from its dances to its food. Go if you want to experience another culture—and still have your creature comforts and access to fine beaches. Don't go if you want five-star luxury, because it's rare here.

WHAT'S WHERE

THE WINDWARD AND SOUTHERN ISLANDS

The Windward Islands—Dominica, Martinique, St. Lucia, St. Vincent, and Grenada—complete the main Caribbean arc. These dramatically scenic southern islands face the trade winds head-on. The Grenadines—a string of small islands between Grenada and St. Vincent—are heaven for sailors. The Southern Caribbean islands—Trinidad, Tobago, Aruba, Bonaire, and Curaçao—are rarely bothered by hurricanes.

Aruba ⇨ Ch. 4
Some Caribbean travelers seek an undiscovered paradise, some seek the familiar and safe: Aruba is for the latter. On the smallest of the ABC islands, the waters are peacock blue, and the white beaches are beautiful and powdery soft. For Americans, Aruba offers all the comforts of home: English is spoken universally, and the U.S. dollar is accepted everywhere.

Bonaire ⇨ Ch. 6
With only 15,000 year-round citizens and huge numbers of visiting divers, Bonaire still seems largely untouched by tourism. Divers come for the clear water, profusion of marine life, and great dive shops. With a surreal, arid landscape, immense flamingo population, and gorgeous turquoise vistas, you can also have a wonderful land-based holiday.

Curaçao ⇨ Ch. 9
Rich in heritage and history, Curaçao offers a blend of island life and city savvy, wonderful weather, spectacular diving, and charming beaches. Dutch and Caribbean influences are everywhere, but there's also an infusion of touches from around the world, particularly noteworthy in the great food. Willemstad, the picturesque capital, is a treat for pedestrians, with shopping clustered in areas around the waterfront.

Dominica ⇨ Ch. 10
Dominica is the island to find your bliss exploring nature's bounty, not in the sun and surf. Go to be active, either diving under the sea or hiking on land. Don't go for great beaches or a big-resort experience. This is one island that's delightfully behind the times.

Martinique ⇨ Ch. 15
Excellent cuisine, fine service, highly touted rum, and lilting Franco-Caribbean music are the main draws in Martinique. Go if you're a Francophile drawn to fine food, wine, and sophisticated style. Don't go if you are looking for a bargain and don't have patience. Getting here is a chore, but there are definitely rewards for the persistent.

Caribbean   Sea

Aruba
○Oranjestad

Bonaire
○Kralendijk

Curaçao ○
Willemstad

Islas Los Roques

La Guaira

Isla La Tortuga

○ Caracas

0   100 mi

0   100 km

VENEZUELA

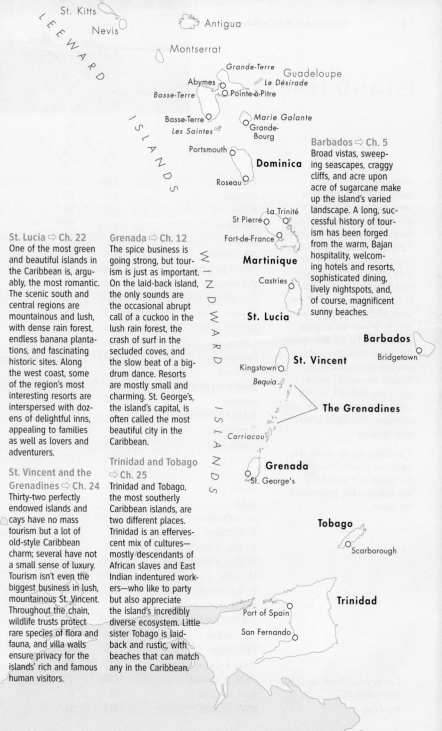

L E E W A R D   I S L A N D S

St. Kitts
Nevis
Antigua
Montserrat

Guadeloupe
Grande-Terre
Le Désirade
Abymes
Basse-Terre
Pointe-à-Pitre
Basse-Terre
Les Saintes
Marie Galante
Grande-Bourg

Portsmouth
Dominica
Roseau

La Trinité
St Pierre
Fort-de-France
Martinique

Castries
St. Lucia

W I N D W A R D   I S L A N D S

Kingstown
St. Vincent
Bequia

The Grenadines

Carriacou

St. George's
Grenada

Tobago
Scarborough

Port of Spain
Trinidad
San Fernando

Bridgetown
Barbados

Barbados ⇨ Ch. 5

Broad vistas, sweeping seascapes, craggy cliffs, and acre upon acre of sugarcane make up the island's varied landscape. A long, successful history of tourism has been forged from the warm, Bajan hospitality, welcoming hotels and resorts, sophisticated dining, lively nightspots, and, of course, magnificent sunny beaches.

St. Lucia ⇨ Ch. 22

One of the most green and beautiful islands in the Caribbean is, arguably, the most romantic. The scenic south and central regions are mountainous and lush, with dense rain forest, endless banana plantations, and fascinating historic sites. Along the west coast, some of the region's most interesting resorts are interspersed with dozens of delightful inns, appealing to families as well as lovers and adventurers.

St. Vincent and the Grenadines ⇨ Ch. 24

Thirty-two perfectly endowed islands and cays have no mass tourism but a lot of old-style Caribbean charm; several have not a small sense of luxury. Tourism isn't even the biggest business in lush, mountainous St. Vincent. Throughout the chain, wildlife trusts protect rare species of flora and fauna, and villa walls ensure privacy for the islands' rich and famous human visitors.

Grenada ⇨ Ch. 12

The spice business is going strong, but tourism is just as important. On the laid-back island, the only sounds are the occasional abrupt call of a cuckoo in the lush rain forest, the crash of surf in the secluded coves, and the slow beat of a big-drum dance. Resorts are mostly small and charming. St. George's, the island's capital, is often called the most beautiful city in the Caribbean.

Trinidad and Tobago ⇨ Ch. 25

Trinidad and Tobago, the most southerly Caribbean islands, are two different places. Trinidad is an effervescent mix of cultures—mostly descendants of African slaves and East Indian indentured workers—who like to party but also appreciate the island's incredibly diverse ecosystem. Little sister Tobago is laid-back and rustic, with beaches that can match any in the Caribbean.

ISLAND FINDER

To help you decide which island is best for you, we've rated each island in several areas that might influence your decision on choosing the perfect Caribbean vacation spot. Each major island covered in this book has been rated in terms of cost from $ (very inexpensive) to $$$$$ (very expensive), and since prices often vary a great deal by season, we've given you a rating for the high season (December through mid-April) and low season (mid-April through November). We've also compared each island's relative strength in several other categories that might influence your decision.

If an island has no marks in a particular column (under "Golf" for example), it means that the activity is not available on the island.

	Cost High Season	Cost Low Season
Anguilla	$$$$	$$$
Antigua	$$$	$$
Aruba	$$$	$$
Barbados	$$$$	$$$$
Bonaire	$$	$$
BVI: Tortola	$$$	$$
BVI: Virgin Gorda	$$$$$	$$$$
BVI: Anegada	$$$$	$$$
BVI: Jost Van Dyke	$$$$	$$$
Cayman Islands: Grand Cayman	$$$$	$$$
Cayman Islands: Little Cayman	$$$	$$$
Cayman Islands: Cayman Brac	$$	$$
Curaçao	$$$$	$$$
Dominica	$$	$
Dominican Republic	$$	$
Grenada	$$$	$$$
Grenada: Carriacou	$$	$
Guadeloupe	$$	$$
Jamaica	$$$	$$
Martinique	$$$	$$
Montserrat	$	$
Puerto Rico	$$$	$$
Saba	$$	$
St. Barthélemy	$$$$$	$$$$
St. Eustatius	$$	$
St. Kitts & Nevis: St. Kitts	$$$	$$
St. Kitts & Nevis: Nevis	$$$$	$$$
St. Lucia	$$$$	$$$
St. Maarten/St. Martin	$$$	$$$
SVG: St. Vincent	$$	$$
SVG: The Grenadines	$$$$	$$$
T&T: Trinidad	$$$	$$
T&T: Tobago	$$$	$$
Turks & Caicos Islands	$$$$*	$$$*
USVI: St. Thomas	$$$$	$$$
USVI: St. Croix	$$	$
USVI: St. John	$$$	$$

* Cost for Provo (Parrot Cay $$$$$, other islands $$)

** Provo Only

Beautiful Beaches	Fine Dining	Shopping	Casinos	Nightlife	Diving	Golf	Eco-tourism	Good for Families
▲▲▲▲▲	▲▲▲▲	▲▲		▲▲	▲	▲▲▲	▲	▲▲
▲▲▲▲▲	▲▲▲▲▲	▲▲▲▲	▲▲▲	▲▲▲	▲▲	▲▲▲	▲▲▲	▲▲▲
▲▲▲▲	▲▲▲▲	▲▲▲	▲▲▲▲	▲▲▲▲▲	▲▲▲	▲▲	▲▲	▲▲▲▲
▲▲▲	▲▲▲▲▲	▲▲▲		▲▲▲	▲▲	▲▲▲▲▲	▲▲	▲▲▲▲
▲▲▲	▲▲▲	▲▲	▲	▲	▲▲▲▲▲		▲▲▲▲	▲▲▲▲
▲▲	▲▲▲	▲▲		▲▲	▲▲▲		▲▲▲	▲▲▲
▲▲▲▲▲	▲▲▲	▲		▲	▲▲▲		▲▲▲▲	▲▲▲
▲▲▲▲▲	▲▲▲			▲	▲▲▲		▲▲▲▲	▲▲▲
▲▲▲▲	▲▲▲	▲▲		▲▲▲▲	▲▲▲		▲▲▲	▲▲
▲▲▲▲▲	▲▲▲▲	▲▲▲▲▲		▲▲	▲▲▲	▲▲▲	▲▲	▲▲▲▲
					▲▲▲	▲▲▲▲▲	▲▲▲	▲▲▲
▲▲					▲▲▲		▲▲▲	▲▲▲
▲▲▲▲	▲▲▲▲	▲▲▲	▲▲▲	▲▲▲▲	▲▲▲	▲▲▲	▲▲▲▲	▲▲▲
▲	▲▲▲	▲▲▲		▲▲	▲▲▲▲▲		▲▲▲▲▲	▲▲▲
▲▲▲▲▲	▲▲▲	▲▲	▲▲▲	▲▲▲	▲▲▲	▲▲▲▲▲	▲▲▲	▲▲▲
▲▲▲▲	▲▲▲	▲▲		▲	▲▲▲	▲	▲▲▲▲	▲▲▲
▲▲▲	▲		▲				▲▲▲	▲▲▲
▲▲▲	▲▲	▲▲▲	▲▲▲	▲▲▲	▲▲▲	▲▲▲	▲▲▲▲▲	▲▲▲
▲▲▲	▲▲▲	▲▲	▲	▲▲	▲▲▲	▲▲▲▲▲	▲▲▲▲▲	▲▲▲▲▲
▲▲▲▲	▲▲▲▲	▲▲▲	▲▲	▲▲▲	▲▲▲	▲▲▲	▲▲▲	▲▲
▲	▲	▲		▲	▲▲▲▲		▲▲▲▲	▲▲▲
▲▲▲	▲▲▲▲	▲▲		▲	▲▲▲▲▲		▲▲▲▲	▲
▲▲▲▲	▲▲▲▲▲	▲▲▲▲▲		▲▲	▲▲▲			▲
▲	▲	▲▲		▲	▲▲▲▲▲		▲▲▲▲▲	▲▲▲
▲▲▲	▲▲▲	▲▲▲	▲▲▲▲	▲▲▲	▲▲▲	▲▲▲▲	▲▲▲▲▲	▲▲▲▲▲
▲▲▲	▲▲▲▲	▲▲		▲▲▲	▲▲▲	▲▲▲▲▲	▲▲▲▲▲	▲▲▲▲▲
▲▲▲	▲▲▲	▲▲		▲▲▲	▲▲▲	▲	▲▲▲▲▲	▲▲▲
▲▲▲▲	▲▲▲▲▲	▲▲▲▲	▲▲▲	▲▲▲▲	▲▲▲	▲	▲▲	▲▲▲
▲	▲▲	▲	▲	▲	▲▲▲▲		▲▲▲▲▲	▲▲▲
▲▲▲▲▲	▲▲▲	▲		▲	▲▲▲▲▲	▲▲▲▲▲	▲▲▲	▲▲▲
▲▲▲	▲▲▲	▲▲	▲▲▲	▲▲▲▲	▲▲▲	▲▲▲▲	▲▲▲	▲▲▲
▲▲▲▲	▲▲▲	▲▲	▲▲▲	▲▲▲	▲▲▲	▲▲▲	▲▲▲	▲▲▲
▲▲▲▲▲	▲▲**	▲	▲	▲	▲▲▲▲▲	▲▲▲▲**	▲▲▲▲	▲▲▲**
▲▲▲	▲▲▲▲	▲▲▲▲▲		▲▲	▲▲▲	▲▲▲▲	▲▲	▲▲▲▲
▲▲▲	▲▲▲	▲▲	▲▲	▲▲	▲▲▲	▲▲▲	▲▲▲	▲▲▲
▲▲▲▲▲	▲▲▲	▲▲		▲		▲▲▲	▲▲▲	▲▲▲▲▲

CARIBBEAN LODGING

When to Reserve

School vacation periods, especially in high season, generally require advance booking at most hotels. The most popular properties book as much as a year in advance because of their high numbers of repeat clientele, many of whom request the same room every year. Many respected chain resorts, such as the Ritz-Carlton and the Four Seasons, also book well in advance during peak periods. The most difficult time to find a well-priced room is typically around the Christmas holidays and New Year's, when minimum-stay requirements of one to two weeks may be common and room rates typically double.

But for the typical Caribbean resort, two months is usually sufficient notice. In popular mass-market destinations such as Punta Cana or Negril, you could probably find something even a couple of weeks in advance. Paradoxically, it's easier to find an acceptable room in the busiest destinations by sheer virtue of the number of rooms available at any given time. Although waiting until the last minute doesn't net as many bargains as cruises, flexibility can pay off either in a deep discount (usually at a larger resort) or a room category upgrade.

Fees and Add-Ons

Every island charges an accommodations tax, whether on private villa rentals, bed-and-breakfast stays, or megaresorts. This ranges from 7% to 15%, depending on the destination (you can find the exact surcharge listed in the individual chapters' hotel and restaurant price chart). In addition, most Caribbean hotels and resorts tack on a service fee, usually around 10%. The service fee isn't quite the same as a tip for service, and it is customary at most non-all-inclusive resorts to tip the staff. Generally, expect to pay at least 20% above and beyond the base rate for a Caribbean resort room. The latest growing trend—though it's hardly unique to the Caribbean—is the "resort fee." You can encounter this almost anywhere, though resort fees are almost universal in San Juan, Puerto Rico. The fee presumably covers costs such as housekeeping (though you might sometimes see this on your bill, too, especially for villa rentals), utilities, and use of resort facilities. Figure $5 to $50 per night, but know that this is generally restricted to larger hotels and defies generalization because it depends more on the individual resort or hotel chain than the island itself. These additional costs aren't always mentioned when you book, so be sure to inquire.

Picking the Best Room

On virtually every island, especially at beachfront lodgings, the better the beach access or ocean view, the higher the price. If you're the active type who really uses a room only to sleep, then you can save $100 or more per night by choosing a garden-, mountain-, or town-view room. But regardless of view, be sure to ask about the property's layout. For example, if you want to be close to the "action" at many larger resorts, whether you have mobility concerns or just need to satisfy your gambling or beach-gamboling itch, the trade-off might be noise, whether from screaming kids jumping in the pool or DJs pumping and thumping reggae in the bar. Likewise, saving that $100 may not be worth it if your room faces a busy thoroughfare. This is your vacation, so if you have any specific desires or dislikes, discuss them thoroughly with the reservations staff.

Types of Lodgings

Inclusive or Not?

1

Most islands offer the gamut of glitzy resorts, boutique-chic hotels, historic hostelries, family-run B&Bs, condo resorts, self-catering apartments, and private villas that are typical throughout the Caribbean.

Condos and Time-Shares Condo resorts are increasingly popular and can offer both extra space and superior savings for families, with kitchens, sofa beds, and more. In fact, they dominate the sensuous sweeps of Grand Cayman's Seven-Mile Beach and Provo's amazing Grace Bay in the Turks and Caicos. Some of these are time-share properties, but not all time-shares require you to sit through a sales pitch.

Inns and B&Bs Historic inns come in all shapes and sizes. The old Spanish colonial capitals of Santo Domingo and San Juan have converted monasteries. Puerto Rico also offers affordable lodgings in its paradors, patterned after the Spanish system, most of them historically and/or culturally significant buildings such as old-time thermal baths or working coffee plantations. Longtime sailing and whaling destinations such as Antigua or Bequia in the Grenadines offer their own pieces of history adapted to modern comfort, and Guadeloupe and Martinique feature converted sugar plantations. St. Kitts and Nevis are also prized by Caribbean connoisseurs for their restored great-house plantation inns, often with a resident eccentric expat owner who lives on-site and enhances your experience with amusing anecdotes and insider insights.

Private Villas Another increasingly popular option for families or those seeking a surprising bargain: private villas. Self-catering means saving on dining out on more expensive islands, such as St. Barth (where villas usually cost much less than hotels), though a car is usually necessary except in mini-villages such as Cayman Kai on Grand Cayman. Many villas have private pools with stunning sea views and/or beachfront access. Montserrat offers exceptional value for anyone.

Resorts Most prevalent are large resorts, including all-inclusives, usually strategically positioned on the beach. These include golf/spa resorts and name-brand chain hotels in various price categories from Ritz-Carlton to Comfort Suites. Jamaica and the Dominican Republic specialize in the all-inclusive experience. Some islands abound in cookie-cutter tour-group hotels that look like they could be plonked down anywhere, including Aruba (along one of the Caribbean's most alluring beaches) and Guadeloupe, though both also offer distinctive properties as well.

The AI (which stands for "all-inclusive") concept is especially prominent on islands such as Jamaica, the Dominican Republic, Antigua, and St. Lucia. For those who have only a week for vacation, the allure is obvious: a hassle-free, pay-one-price vacation including accommodations, meals, unlimited drinks, entertainment, and most activities. And you tend to get what you pay for: AIs range from hedonistic high-tech luxury to barebones beachfront bang-for-the-buck, with prices to match. It pays to do your homework: some of these resorts are intimate romantic hideaways, some emphasize sporting options, others cater to families, and still others cater to singles ready to mingle in a nonstop frat-party atmosphere.

But there are caveats. Few AIs offer *everything* for free. That sybaritic spa treatment, the scuba trip (and instruction), the sunset cruise, or the tour of the nearby plantation generally won't be included. Moreover, there can be surcharges for dining in some restaurants (which must be reserved).

AI resorts appeal most to travelers who just need to get away and bask in the sun, piña colada within easy reach. They're not for more adventuresome types who seek genuine interaction with the locals and immersion in their culture, nor are they good for people who want to eat local food, since most AI travelers rarely leave their resort boundaries.

CARIBBEAN LOGISTICS

Time

The Cayman Islands, Cuba, Haiti, Jamaica, and the Turks and Caicos Islands are all in the Eastern Standard Time zone. All other Caribbean islands are in the Atlantic Standard Time zone, which is one hour later than Eastern Standard. Caribbean islands don't observe daylight saving time, so during that period (March through October) Eastern Standard is one hour behind, and Atlantic Standard is the same time as Eastern Daylight Time.

Driving

Your own valid driver's license works in some countries. However, temporary local driving permits are required in several Caribbean destinations (Anguilla, Antigua, Barbados, the British Virgin Islands, Cayman Islands, Dominica, Grenada, Nevis, St. Kitts, St. Lucia, and St. Vincent and the Grenadines), which you can get at rental agencies or local police offices upon presentation of a valid license and a small fee. St. Lucia and St. Vincent and the Grenadines require a temporary permit only if you don't have an International Driving Permit (available from AAA).

Flights

Many carriers fly nonstop or direct routes to the Caribbean from major international airports in the United States, including Atlanta, Boston, Charlotte, Chicago, Dallas, Fort Lauderdale, Houston, Miami, New York (JFK), Newark, Philadelphia, Phoenix, and Washington (Dulles). If you live somewhere else in the United States, you'll probably have to make a connection to get to your Caribbean destination. It's also not uncommon to make a connection in the Caribbean, most often in San Juan, Montego Bay, Barbados, or St. Maarten.

Some flights will be on small planes operated by local or regional carriers, which may have code-share arrangements with major airlines from the United States. Or you can confidently book directly with the local carrier, using a major credit card, sometimes online but more often by phone.

Some smaller airlines may make multiple stops, accepting and discharging passengers and/or cargo at each small airport or airstrip along the way. This is not unusual. What is also not unusual is the sometimes erratic schedules these smaller airlines can have. Be sure to confirm your flights on interisland carriers, and make sure that the carrier has a local contact telephone number for you, as you may be subject to a small carrier's whims: if no other passengers are booked on your flight, particularly if the carrier operates "scheduled charters," you'll be rescheduled on another flight or at a different departure time (earlier or later than your original reservation) that is more convenient for the airline. If you're connecting from an interisland flight to a major airline, be sure to include a substantial buffer of time for these kinds of delays.

Typical Travel Times by Air

	NEW YORK	MIAMI
Puerto Rico	3½ hours	2½ hours
Jamaica	4½ hours	1½ hours
St. Lucia	4½ hours	3½ hours
Trinidad	5 hours	3½ hours
Aruba	4¾ hours	2½ hours

Airlines

Major Airlines Air Jamaica (☎ 800/523–5585 ⊕ www. airjamaica.com). **American Airlines/American Eagle** (☎ 800/433–7300 or 800/223–5436 for automated flight information ⊕ www.aa.com). **Caribbean Airlines** (☎ 800/920–4225 ⊕ www.caribbean-airlines.com). **Delta Airlines** (☎ 800/241–4141 ⊕ www.delta.com). **JetBlue** (☎ 800/538–2583 ⊕ www.jetblue.com). **Spirit Airlines** (☎ 800/772–7117 ⊕ www.spiritair.com). **United Airlines** (☎ 800/538–2929 ⊕ www.united.com). **US Airways** (☎ 800/622–1015 ⊕ www.usairways.com).

Smaller/Regional Airlines Air Antilles Express (☎ 0890/648–648 in Guadeloupe ⊕ www.airantilles. com). **Air Caraïbes** (☎ 877/772–1005 ⊕ www. aircaraibes.com). **Air Sunshine** (☎ 800/327–8900, 800/435–8900 in Florida ⊕ www.airsunshine. com). **Air Turks & Caicos** (☎ 954/323–4949 ⊕ www. airturksandcaicos.com). **Bahamas Air** (☎ 242/702–4140 in Nassau, 800/222–4262 in U.S. ⊕ bahamasair. com). **Caicos Express** (☎ 649/243–0237 ⊕ caicos-expressairways.com).**Cape Air** (☎ 866/227–3247 or 508/771–6944 ⊕ www.flycapeair.com). **Cayman Airways** (☎ 345/949–8200 or 800/422–9626 ⊕ www.caymanairways.com). **Dutch Antilles Express** (☎ 599/461–3009 ⊕ www.flydae.com). **Grenadine Air Alliance (Mustique Air, SVG Air, TIA)** (☎ 246/418–1654 for shared-charter flights, 784/456–6793 for intra-Grenadines flights). **Insel Air** (☎ 800/386–4800 ⊕ www. fly-inselair.com). **LIAT** (☎ 866/549–5428, 888/844–5428 within the Caribbean ⊕ www.liatairline.com). **Mustique Airways** (☎ 718/618–4492 in U.S., 784/458–4380 in St. Vincent ⊕ www.mustique.com). **Seaborne Airlines** (☎ 340/773–6442 or 866/359–8784 ⊕ www. seaborneairlines.com). **St. Barths Commuter** (☎ 599/546–7698 ⊕ www.stbarthcommuter.com)**SVG Air** (☎ 784/457–5124 or 800/744–7285 ⊕ www.svgair.com). **Winair** (Windward Island Airways ☎ 866/466–0410 ⊕ www. fly-winair.com). **Windward Express Airways** (☎ 599/545–2001 in St. Maarten ⊕ www.windwardexpress.com).

Ferries

Interisland ferries are an interesting and often less expensive way to travel around certain areas of the Caribbean, but they are not offered everywhere. A few destinations are reached only by ferry (St. John, for example). In most cases, where service is offered it is frequent (either daily or several times daily).

MAJOR FERRY ROUTES

Ferries connect Puerto Rico with the outlying islands of Vieques and Culebra; St. Thomas with Water Island, St. John, St. Croix, and the British Virgin Islands; St. Croix with St. Thomas; the various islands of the British Virgin Islands with each other and with the U.S. Virgin Islands; St. Martin/St. Maarten with Anguilla, St. Barth, and Saba; St. Kitts with Nevis; Antigua with Barbuda and Montserrat; Guadeloupe with La Désirade, Marie-Galante, and Les Saintes, as well as Dominica, Martinique, and St. Lucia; St. Lucia with Guadeloupe, Martinique, Dominica, and Barbados; St. Vincent with Bequia and the other islands of the Grenadines; Grenada with Carriacou and Petite Martinique; and Trinidad with Tobago; there's limited ferry service in the Turks and Caicos Islands (Provo and North Caicos, Grand Turk and Salt Cay). In most cases, service is frequent—either daily or several times daily.

RENTING A VILLA

In the Caribbean the term villa can be used to describe anything from a traditional cottage to a luxurious architectural wonder, but what it almost always means is a stand-alone accommodation, often privately owned. Villa rentals provide some of the region's most desirable accommodations, both from a comfort and an economic point of view. We recommend considering this option, especially if you're a group of friends or a family: you get a lot more space, much more privacy, and a better sense of the island than you would get at a hotel, usually at a fraction of the cost.

Factor in the ability to fix simple meals, snacks, and drinks, and the savings really add up. An additional advantage to Americans is that villa rates are generally negotiated in dollars, thus bypassing unfavorable euro fluctuations in St. Martin, St. Barth, and Martinique.

What Does It Cost?

Rental rates vary widely by island and by season. In-season rates range anywhere from $1,200 for a simple one-bedroom cottage to more than $40,000 a week for a multiroom luxury home. Many full-service resorts also offer villas of varying sizes on their property, and although pricey, these can be an excellent choice if you want the best of both worlds—full service and facilities but also space and privacy. In many cases, renting a villa at a resort will cost less than renting three or four "normal" rooms, and you can still have a waiter deliver your 'ti punch to a beach chair or enjoy access to a high-tech fitness room.

What's Included?

Units are generally furnished nicely and have updated bathrooms and usable kitchens. They are equipped with linens, kitchen utensils, CD and DVD players, a phone, satellite TV, and, increasingly, Wi-Fi access to the Internet. The sophistication of all of the above is factored into the price, so the more luxurious the digs, the higher the price.

Upscale rental villas generally have small, private swimming pools (rather few are beachfront), and housekeeping service a few hours daily except Sunday included in the quoted price. On some islands, including the Dominican Republic, Jamaica, and Barbados, two or even three staff members are common. Inquire about the villa's staff, and specify particular needs or expectations right from the start, including start times and specific duties such as laundry, cooking, or child care.

How Do You Rent?

Some owners rent their properties directly (⊕ www.vrbo.com), but in general, we recommend renting a villa through a reputable local agency that both manages and maintains the properties and has an office with local staff to facilitate and troubleshoot on your behalf if something goes wrong. Lavish catalogs or websites with detailed descriptions and photographs of each villa can help to assuage your fears about what to expect. The agent will meet you at the airport, bring you to the villa, explain and demonstrate the household systems, and even stock the kitchen with starter groceries (for a fee). Some agencies provide comprehensive concierge services and will arrange or recommend car rentals and help you find additional staff such as chefs or babysitters or yoga instructors. Some of the larger companies even host a weekly cocktail party so renters can meet each other and form a community to share local information or socialize.

Specific villa-rental companies are listed and recommended throughout this guide.

Choosing a Villa

These days, your hunt will no doubt start on the Internet. A simple search for "villa rental [island name]" will get you started, and the tourist board of each island can provide a list of reputable local rental agents.

Villa-rental websites allow you to see pictures of the places you may wish to rent. And, via the website, you can talk to a knowledgeable representative who can help you sort through the listings according to your requirements. But use caution, warns Peg Walsh of St. Barths Properties: "There are a lot of websites and listings [from] people who say they do villa rentals, but in many cases, they don't actually know the villa they are renting." Instead, they consolidate listings from other sources. It pays to seek out reputable companies, especially if you are a first-time renter.

Things to Think About When Searching for a Villa

How many people are you? How many bedrooms will you want? Do they have to be equal? Do they all have to be attached to the house? If you are two couples, you might want to specify that there be two master suites. If you are traveling with young children, you might not want them in a separate bedroom pavilion. Definitely confirm what types of beds are in each room; couples may prefer queens or kings, whereas kids would be better in single beds. Those looking for a bit more privacy might prefer to be in a guesthouse or small cottage that's separate from the main house.

What location do you prefer? Do you need to be right on a beach? Do you want to walk to town? Will proximity to a particular activity such as golf or scuba diving enhance your vacation? Are you willing to rent a car to get around?

What are your requirements for electronics and appliances? Do you require satellite TV? Internet service (and if so, does it need to be Wi-Fi)? Or would you be okay with something less connected? Do you need a dishwasher? A microwave? How about an outdoor gas grill, or is charcoal sufficient?

Is the villa child-friendly? Ask whether rooms have direct access to the pool area; this might not be a safe choice for younger kids who could open a sliding door and enter the pool area unsupervised. Are you comfortable at all having a pool? Most Caribbean villas don't have child-proof security gates around pools, or pool alarms. If the villa has two floors, are the rooms best suited for kids on a floor separate from the master suite?

What specific issues about your destination will affect your villa choice? There are realities about personal security in many areas of the Caribbean. Evaluate the location of potential rentals in relation to known problem areas, and ask if the villa has an alarm system. A surprisingly low rental rate on an otherwise expensive island might be a red flag.

Will you really be comfortable on your own? The final thing to consider is your relative hardiness and that of your traveling companions. Is this your first time in the destination? Do you relish or dread the idea of navigating local markets? Will you miss having a concierge to help arrange things for you? Do you really want to be faced with a sink full of dishes a few times a day? Will your kids be happy without a hotel full of peers? What about you?

CARIBBEAN
TOP EXPERIENCES

Diving in Bonaire

(A) Nautical nuts love Bonaire for the kaleidoscopic profusion of marine life, dramatic underwater-scape, excellent environmental stewardship, and accessibility of its pyrotechnic reefs: the majority explode with color just 5–25 minutes from shore in currents mild enough for snorkeling, too.

Hiking in Dominica

(B) Morne Trois Pitons National Park, a UNESCO World Heritage Site, explains Dominica's nickname "The Nature Isle." The island is so green that you can practically see plants grow during rainfall, with mountains filigreed by waterfalls, crater lakes, and natural pools—contrasted with the blast furnace Valley of Desolation, including the world's second-largest Boiling Lake belching sulfurously.

Snorkeling the Cayman Islands

(C) Swimming at Stingray City, even wading at the adjacent sandbar, you can interact with gracefully balletic stingrays, so tame you can feed them as they nuzzle you, practically begging petlike for handouts. Numerous boats take you out for the ray-diant experience. Shore diving and snorkeling excels throughout all three islands.

Shopping St. Thomas

(D) The Caribbean has colorful historic capitals known for duty-free shopping, including Curaçao's Willemstad and St. Maarten's Philipsburg, but Charlotte Amalie on St. Thomas is like an elegant bazaar, with name-brand luxury boutiques tucked away in its charming arcaded Danish alleys.

Birding in Trinidad

(E) Trinidad is noted for Carnival, calypso, oil, and asphalt production—and bountiful birdlife. More than 200 species flutter flirtatiously through the Asa Wright Nature Centre, a glorious old plantation also home to bats and giant lizards. Flocks of scarlet ibis turn the mangroves at Caroni Bird Sanctuary into a Christmas decoration come sunset.

Whale-Watching in the Dominican Republic

(F) Samaná in the northeast D.R. is revered for shimmering water, champagne-hue strands, and superior sportfishing. But its signature aquatic activity is world-class whale-watching in season (January through March) as pods of humpbacks mate and calve, the male's signature song echoing across the water.

Eating Well in St. Martin

(G) Few places rival the French West Indies for fine food and exotic ambience. One small St. Martin fishing village, Grand Case, has become the Caribbean's Restaurant Row. More than 40 eateries line the main beachfront drag, from humble lolos (shacks serving heaping helpings of creole fare at fair prices) to Michelin-worthy haute kitchens.

Boating in the Grenadines

(H) Yachties forever debate the merits of the British Virgin Islands versus the Grenadines for calm waters, exquisite anchorages, warm islanders, boisterous beach bars (such as Basil's on Mustique), and splendid diving and snorkeling (and beachcombing) at such spots as the deserted Tobago Cays.

Viewing Colonial Architecture in Puerto Rico

(I) Old San Juan is a majestic maze of narrow cobblestone alleys opening into broad tree-shaded plazas; beautifully preserved 18th-century Spanish buildings range from stone mansions with wrought-iron balconies (now housing chic boutiques and restaurants) to the UNESCO World Heritage El Morro fortress guarding the bay.

IF YOU LIKE

Great Beaches

What makes a great beach can depend on personal preference. You might dream of sifting your toes in soft white sand with just a hint of warmth. You may love to walk along a virgin beach with nothing but the occasional palm tree. You may be charmed by that cute little crescent that's reachable by a precipitous climb down an almost-sheer rock cliff. You may want to be surrounded by a hundred pairs of beautiful limbs, all smelling slightly of coconut oil. The Caribbean can give you all these. Part of the fun of taking a tropical vacation is discovering your own favorites, which are sometimes the ones you'd least suspect. Here are a few of the beaches we like:

■ **Baie Orientale, St. Maarten/St. Martin.** Often crowded, but considered by many to be the island's most beautiful beach.

■ **The Baths, Virgin Gorda, British Virgin Islands.** Giant boulders form grottoes filled with seawater that you can explore.

■ **Eagle Beach, Aruba.** Once undeveloped, this beach on Aruba's southwestern coast is now hopping and happening.

■ **Half Moon Bay, Providenciales, Turks and Caicos Islands.** A natural ribbon of ivory sand joins two tiny, uninhabited cays.

■ **Macaroni Beach, Mustique, St. Vincent and the Grenadines.** The most famous beach on the most famous Grenadine.

■ **Negril Beach, Jamaica.** Seven miles of sand lined by bars, restaurants, and hotels in westernmost Jamaica.

■ **Seven Mile Beach, Grand Cayman, Cayman Islands.** Free of litter and peddlers, the best northern sections are a sight to behold.

■ **Shoal Bay, Anguilla.** Sand or talcum powder? You decide.

Diving and Snorkeling

Many people would rather spend their days under the sea than on the beach. Generally, the best conditions for diving—clear water and lots of marine life—are also good for snorkelers, though you won't see as much from the surface looking down. If you haven't been certified yet, take a resort course. After learning the basics in a pool, you can often do a short dive from shore. Here are some of the Caribbean's best dive destinations:

■ **Anegada, British Virgin Islands.** The reefs surrounding this flat coral-and-limestone atoll are a sailor's nightmare but a scuba diver's dream.

■ **Bonaire.** The current is mild, the reefs often begin just offshore, visibility is generally 60 feet to 100 feet, and the marine life is magnificent.

■ **Dominica.** Serious divers know that the pristine, bubbly waters around Dominica's submerged volcanic crater are among the best in the world.

■ **Little Cayman, Cayman Islands.** The drop-off at Bloody Bay Wall goes from 18 feet to more than 1,000 feet—diving doesn't get much better than this.

■ **Saba.** Beside one of the lively Caribbean reefs, the diving on Saba is some of the best in the world.

■ **St. Eustatius.** The waters here are tops for wreck diving.

■ **Tobago Cays, St. Vincent and the Grenadines.** A group of five uninhabited islands surrounds a beautiful lagoon studded with sponges, coral formations, and countless colorful fish.

■ **Turks and Caicos Islands.** The world's third-largest coral reef is visible from the air and packed with exotic marine life, dramatic wall drop-offs, colorful fans, and pristine coral formations.

Shopping

Almost as many people go to the Caribbean to shop as to lie on the beach. Whether it's jewelry in St. Maarten, fragrant spices in Grenada, high-end designer fashions in St. Barth, or island crafts almost anywhere, you're likely to come home with a bag full of treasures.

■ **Grenada.** Visit a historic spice plantation, tour a nutmeg-processing plant, and replenish your spice rack with nutmeg, cinnamon sticks, cocoa, and cloves at an outdoor market.

■ **Puerto Rico.** From the boutiques of Old San Juan to ateliers of the young designers elsewhere in metro San Juan to galleries scattered all over the island, there's plenty to see and buy. You may also consider picking up some of the santos created in San Germán.

■ **St. Barthélemy.** Without a doubt, the shopping here for luxury goods and fashion is the best in the Caribbean. The variety and quality are astounding. The unfavorable exchange rates mean fewer bargains for Americans, but the prices here—all duty-free—are still less than what you'd pay in Paris or St. Tropez.

■ **St. Maarten/St. Martin.** Hundreds of duty-free shops in Philipsburg make the island the best in the Caribbean for bargain hunters, especially for high-quality jewelry and perfumes. Marigot has its fair share of nice boutiques.

■ **St. Thomas, U.S. Virgin Islands.** Main Street in Charlotte Amalie is well known for numerous duty-free shops, selling everything from rum to designer fashions and gems. The Caribbean's biggest cruise port also has several malls.

Staying Active

There's much more to do in the Caribbean than simply lie on the beach, sip rum punches, or play a round of golf. Try hiking through rain forests, kayaking through mangroves, or sailing on a board through a windswept bay.

■ **Bird-Watching, Trinidad and Tobago.** So the watching part isn't so active, but hiking through the rain forests and savannas on these sister islands will give you the opportunity to see more bird species than any other place in the Caribbean.

■ **Hiking the Quill, St. Eustatius.** The crater of Statia's extinct volcano is filled with a primeval rain forest and is a top hiking destination.

■ **Horseback Riding at Chukka Cove, Jamaica.** Headquartered at the Ocho Rios polo fields, Chukka Caribbean Adventures is now Jamaica's top soft-adventure outfitter, having added canopy tours, river rafting, and more to its excellent horseback-riding program.

■ **Kayaking Through Bahía Mosquito, Puerto Rico.** Vieques's bioluminescent bay is best experienced on a kayak tour on a moonless night, when every stroke makes the water light up.

■ **Tennis at Casa de Campo, Dominican Republic.** Casa de Campo isn't just for golfers. With 13 courts (10 lighted for night play) and a staff of more than 25 pros and instructors, this is one place where you can enjoy your game, whether you're an experienced player or a beginner.

■ **Trekking to Boiling Lake, Dominica.** This bubbly, brackish cauldron is actually a flooded fumarole. A trek here is an unforgettable trip into an otherworldly place.

IF YOU WANT

To Take It Easy on Your Wallet

The Caribbean isn't all about five-star resorts. Often, you may want to save a bit of your vacation cash to eat in elegant restaurants or to shop for the perfect gift. Saving money in the Caribbean doesn't have to mean sacrificing comfort. Sometimes it just means going to a cheaper island, such as the Dominican Republic, Saba, or Dominica. But there are some unique inns and resorts in the Caribbean where you can sleep for much less and still have a great time.

■ **Bayaleau Point Cottages, Carriacou.** Owner Dave Goldhill built four colorful gingerbread guest cottages on this peaceful Windward hillside overlooking the Grenadines, as well as a 28-foot boat to take his guests on snorkeling trips.

■ **Bay Gardens Beach Resort, St. Lucia.** One of three Bay Gardens properties in Rodney Bay known for their friendly hospitality, this family-friendly hotel has a prime location on beautiful Reduit Beach.

■ **Beachcombers Hotel, St. Vincent.** Cheryl Hornsey's family home, once a tiny B&B, has morphed into a popular, 31-room beachfront hotel overlooking the sea at Villa Beach.

■ **Bellafonte Chateau de la Mer, Bonaire.** An oceanfront room at this chic, palazzo-style hotel will remind you why you came to the Caribbean.

■ **Carringtons Inn, St. Croix, U.S. Virgin Islands.** A stay at this spacious B&B harks back to a gentler time, when people spent the winter, rather than a week, in the Caribbean.

■ **Coco Palm, St. Lucia.** Rodney Bay is a beehive of activity, and this stylish boutique hotel is definitely the honey—beautiful rooms, amenities you'd expect at

pricier resorts, a great restaurant, and nightly entertainment.

■ **Frangipani Hotel, Bequia.** Luxurious guest rooms, built of local stone and hardwoods, are tucked into a gentle slope filled with fragrant frangipani trees and overlook Admiralty Bay.

■ **The Horny Toad, St. Maarten/St. Martin.** A marvelous little oceanfront guesthouse with a funky name offers the island's best value for those who want to keep costs down.

■ **La Sagesse Nature Centre, Grenada.** At this secluded country inn on La Sagesse Bay, 10 miles from town, guest rooms are 30 feet from the beach and a hop, skip, and jump from surrounding nature trails.

■ **Peach and Quiet, Barbados.** This small seaside inn on the southeast coast is the sweetest deal on Barbados.

■ **Rockhouse Hotel, Jamaica.** Perched on the cliffs of Negril's West End, unique bungalows blend comfort and rustic style. Regular rooms keep costs down, but if you want to spend a bit more, the dramatic villas are worth every penny.

To Have the Perfect Honeymoon

Swaying palms, moonlight strolls on the beach, candlelit dinners: no wonder the Caribbean is a favorite honeymoon destination. Whatever you are looking for in a honeymoon—seclusion, privacy, or more active fun—you can certainly find it, and it will usually be on a perfect beach. You can be pampered or just left alone, stay up late or get up with the sun, get out and stay active or simply rest and relax. Our favorites run the gamut, so if you need a place with easy access, or if you want to really get away from it all, we have the perfect spot.

■ **Horned Dorset Primavera, Puerto Rico.** Whisk your beloved to this sunset-kissed hotel and just disappear. You may never leave your elegant oceanfront room. When you do, the restaurant is one of the best in Puerto Rico.

■ **Palm Island, Grenadines.** Enjoy five dazzling beaches for water sports, nature trails for quiet walks, a pool with waterfall, sophisticated dining, impeccable service, exquisite accommodations—and privacy.

■ **Sandals Grande St. Lucian Spa & Beach Resort, St. Lucia.** Big, busy, and all-inclusive, this resort is a favorite of young honeymooners—particularly for its complimentary weddings.

■ **The Somerset, Turks and Caicos Islands.** Provo's most beautiful resort is more focused on your comfort than on attracting a celebrity clientele, so regular folks will still feel at home.

■ **Spice Island Beach Resort, Grenada.** Grenada's best resort has impeccable service, placing it among the Caribbean's finest small resorts.

To Eat Well

Caribbean food is a complex blend of indigenous, African, and colonial influences. Native tubers such as yuca and taro, leafy vegetables like callaloo, and herbs such as cilantro recur in most island cuisines. Africans brought plantains, yams, pigeon peas, and assorted peppers. The Spanish introduced rice, and the British brought breadfruit from the South Pacific. Here are some of our favorite Caribbean restaurants:

Banana Tree Grille, St. Thomas, U.S. Virgin Islands. The eagle's-eye view of the Charlotte Amalie harbor from this breeze-cooled restaurant is as fantastic as the food.

■ **Blue by Eric Ripert, Cayman Islands.** Grand Cayman's best restaurant is brought to you by one of New York's finest chefs.

■ **Boston Jerk Centre, Port Antonio, Jamaica.** To enjoy the best Jamaican jerk in the place where it was invented, these simple beach huts are the place to head.

■ **Coral Grill, Nevis, St. Kitts and Nevis.** The steak house at the Four Seasons Nevis is stunning and wildly successful—and a memorable place to eat.

■ **The Cliff, Barbados.** Chef Paul Owens's mastery is the foundation of one of the finest dining experiences in the Caribbean, with prices to match.

■ **Coyaba Restaurant, Providenciales, Turks and Caicos Islands.** This posh eatery serves nostalgic favorites in a palm-fringed setting, one of the island's most romantic and inviting places to dine.

■ **Iguane Café, Guadeloupe.** Unquestionably original cuisine with influences from around the world is daring and dramatic, not to mention delicious.

■ **KoalKeel, Anguilla.** One of the island's best new restaurants mixes French and West Indian styles to excellent effect.

■ **Le Tastevin, St. Martin.** In the heart of Grand Case, Le Tastevin is on everyone's list of favorites.

■ **Le Ti St. Barth Caribbean Tavern, St. Barthélemy.** Chef-owner Carole Gruson captures the funky, sexy spirit of the island in her wildly popular hilltop hot spot.

■ **The Verandah, Trinidad.** Phyllis Vieira's free-style Caribbean cuisine is one of the best-kept secrets in Trinidad—well, we can't keep this secret any longer.

WHEN TO GO

The Caribbean high season is traditionally winter—from December 15 to April 14. During this season you're guaranteed the most entertainment at resorts and the most people with whom to enjoy it. It's also the most fashionable, the most expensive, and the most popular time to visit—and most hotels are heavily booked. You must make reservations at least two or three months in advance for the very best places (sometimes a year in advance for the most exclusive spots). Hotel prices drop 20% to 50% after April 15; airfares and cruise prices also fall. Saving money isn't the only reason to visit the Caribbean during the off-season. Temperatures are only a few degrees warmer than at other times of the year, and many islands now schedule their carnivals, music festivals, and other events during the off-season. Late August, September, October, and early November are the least crowded.

Climate

The Caribbean climate is fairly constant. The average year-round temperatures for the region are 78°F to 88°F. The temperature extremes are 65°F low, 95°F high; but, as everyone knows, it's the humidity, not the heat, that makes you suffer, especially when the two go hand in hand.

As part of the late-fall rainy season, hurricanes occasionally sweep through the Caribbean. Check the news daily and keep abreast of brewing tropical storms. The southernmost Caribbean islands (from St. Vincent to Trinidad, along with Aruba, Bonaire, and Curaçao) are generally spared the threat of hurricanes. The rainy season consists mostly of brief showers interspersed with sunshine. You can watch the clouds thicken, feel the rain, then have brilliant sunshine dry you off, all while remaining on your lounge chair.

A spell of overcast days or heavy rainfall is unusual, as everyone will tell you.

HURRICANE SEASON

The Atlantic hurricane season lasts from June 1 through November 30, but it's fairly rare to see a large storm in either June or November. Most major hurricanes occur between August and October, with the peak season in September.

Avoiding the Storms: Keep in mind that hurricanes are rarer the farther south you go. The ABC Islands (Aruba, Bonaire, and Curaçao) as well as Trinidad and Tobago are the least likely to see a direct hit by a hurricane, but all these islands have had their run-ins, so it's not a certainty that you'll avoid storms by going south. Similarly, Barbados is less likely to be adversely affected by a strong storm because it lies 100 miles farther east than the rest of the Antilles.

Airlines: Airports are usually closed during hurricanes and many flights canceled, which results in a disruption of the steady flow of tourists in and out of affected islands. If you are scheduled to fly into an area where a hurricane is expected, check with your airline regularly and often. If flights are disrupted, airlines will usually allow you to rebook at a later date, but you will not get a refund if you have booked a nonrefundable ticket, nor in most cases will you be allowed to change your ticket to a different destination; rather, you will be expected to reschedule your trip for a later date.

Hotels and Resorts: If a hurricane warning is issued and flights to your destination are disrupted, virtually every Caribbean resort will waive cancellation and change penalties and allow you to rebook your trip for a later date; some will allow you to cancel even if a hurricane threatens to strike, even if flights aren't canceled. Some will give you a refund if you have prepaid for your stay; others will expect you to rebook your trip for a later date. Some large resort companies—including Sandals and SuperClubs—have "hurricane guarantees," but they apply only when flights have been canceled or when a hurricane is sure to strike.

Travel Insurance: If you plan to travel to the Caribbean during the hurricane season, it is wise to buy travel insurance that allows you to cancel for any reason. This kind of coverage can be expensive (up to 10% of the value of the trip), but if you have to prepay far in advance for an expensive vacation package, the peace of mind may be worth it. Just be sure to read the fine print; some policies don't kick in unless flights are canceled and the hurricane strikes, something you may not be assured of until the day you plan to travel. To get a complete cancellation policy, you must usually buy your insurance within a week of booking your trip. If you wait until after the hurricane warning is issued to purchase insurance, it will be too late.

Track Those Hurricanes: The obsessive and naturally curious keep a close eye on the Caribbean during hurricane season. You can, too. Several websites track hurricanes during the season, including ⊕ *www.weather.com*, ⊕ *hurricanetrack.com*, and ⊕ *www.accuweather.com*.

WEDDINGS

Destination weddings, once the exclusive domain of celebs and the superrich, are becoming more affordable in the Caribbean. Many resorts offer attractive packages that couples are taking advantage of to create their ultimate island-paradise wedding. As an added bonus, many islands and resorts provide a plethora of experienced wedding planners. So whether you picture an intimate beachfront ceremony for two or a full-blown affair, you can confidently leave the details to a professional and simply concentrate on exchanging your vows.

Finding a Wedding Planner

Hiring a planner to handle all of the logistics—from the preliminary paperwork right down to final toast—allows you to relax and truly enjoy your big day. The best of the bunch will advise you about legalities (like any residency requirements), help organize the marriage license, and hire the officiant, plus arrange for venues, flowers, music, refreshments, or anything else your heart desires. Planners typically have established relationships with local vendors and can bundle packages with them—which can save you money. Most resorts have on-site coordinators. But there are also many independents available, including those who specialize in certain types of ceremonies—by locale, size, religious affiliation, and so on. Island tourism boards often maintain an online list of names, and a simple "Caribbean weddings" Google search will yield scores more. What's important is that you feel comfortable with your coordinator. Ask for references—and call them. Share your budget. Ask how long they've been in business, how much they charge, how often you'll meet with them, and how they select vendors. Above all, request a detailed, written list of what they'll provide. If your vision of the dream wedding doesn't match their services, try someone else. If you can afford it, you might even want to schedule a preliminary trip to meet the planner in person.

Making It Legal

Your goal is to tie the knot, not get tied up in red tape. So it is important to be mindful of the legalities involved. Specifics vary widely, depending on the type of ceremony you want (civil ones are invariably less complicated than religious services) and the island where you choose to wed. In the Dominican Republic, for example, key documents must be submitted in Spanish: unless you enlist a translator, your wedding will be conducted in Spanish, too. On the French-speaking islands (Guadeloupe, Martinique, St. Barth, and St. Martin) language issues are further compounded by stringent residency requirements, which can make marrying there untenable.

There are, however, **standard rules** that apply throughout the islands:

■ Most places will expect you to produce a valid passport as proof of identification when applying for a marriage license (the exceptions being Puerto Rico and the U.S. Virgin Islands, where official government-issued picture ID will suffice for American citizens).

■ If you are under 18 years old, parental consent is also needed unless otherwise stated in the chart that follows.

■ If you are divorced, the original divorce or annulment decree is required.

■ If you are a widow or widower, original marriage and death certificates are required. (In certain locales, an apostille stamp confirming the authenticity of such documents must be attached.)

ISLAND	COSTS	WAITING PERIOD	GOOD TO KNOW
Anguilla http://ivisitan-guilla.com/weddings	License $284	At least 2 business days to process license	Special rules apply here for religious weddings. Couples marrying in church must allow extra time; some churches require prenuptial consultation and extra documentation.
Antigua www.antigua-barbuda.org/Agmarr01.htm	License $150; marriage officer's fee $50	None	Couples landing in Antigua after 3 pm won't have enough time to get a license from the Ministry of Justice and wed the same day. If you're really in a rush, catch an earlier flight.
Aruba www.aruba.com/SpecializedVacations/Weddings_and_Honeymoons	License $80 during office hours; $200 on Sat. or after hours	None, provided all documents are submitted at least one month in advance	Civil ceremonies may take place in Oranjestad's historic City Hall, on the beach, or at your venue of choice.
Barbados http://idobarba-dos.com	License $75 plus a $12.50 stamp fee; separate magistrate and court fees for civil ceremonies	None	Couples must apply in person to the Ministry of Home Affairs in Bridgetown for a license. A letter from the person performing your ceremony must be presented at this time.
Bonaire www.tourismbo-naire.com/en/vacation-planner/specialized-vacations/wedding-honeymoons	License $150	One partner must be on-island 7 days to establish residency; license takes 4 business days to process.	One partner must get a temporary residency permit before applying for a license. Official witnesses must do the same, but most wedding coordinators can arrange for local ones.
British Virgin Islands www.bvito-urism.com/rules-requirements	License $110 for those in the territory less than 15 days before the ceremony; $50 if in the BVI more than 15 days; registrar's fee $35 for weddings in the office and $100 at other locations	Minimum of 3 business days to process license	It is standard practice to have 2 witnesses at your ceremony. In BVI you also need 2 different witnesses present when you sign your license application.

ISLAND	COSTS	WAITING PERIOD	GOOD TO KNOW
Cayman Islands www.cayman-vows.ky	License $200	None	When applying for a license, you must present a letter from the marriage officer who will be officiating (a list can be obtained from the deputy chief secretary's office).
Curaçao www.curacao.com/Plan-Your-Trip/Get-Married-A-True-Caribbean-Wedding	License $197	3 days before applying for license; 14-day waiting period	Curaçao is a stickler for paperwork, so hiring a wedding pro helps. Documents, which must be original, recent, and apostille, are to be with your planner at least 2 months in advance.
Dominica www.dominica.dm/site/weddings.cfm	License $112; statutory declaration fee $187; registrar's fee $11 for weddings at the office and $37 at other locations	One partner must be on-island 2 days before the wedding.	Couples must sign a statutory declaration of marital status in the presence of a local lawyer. You must also complete an application form and have it witnessed by a magistrate.
Dominican Republic www.godominicanrepublic.com/en	Combined fees $400 for civil ceremonies in the registry office; $600 elsewhere	Notice of intended marriage must be published before ceremony	Both partners must provide proof of single status that has been translated into Spanish at a Dominican Consulate. All paperwork should be submitted at least 6 months in advance.
Grenada www.grenadagrenadines.com/wedding	License $2.50; registration and stamp fees $10	Couples must be on-island 3 days before applying for a license; 2 business days needed for processing.	If you are under the age of 21, parental consent (in the form of an affidavit) is required. If you've been married before, it may take a bit longer for your license to be processed.
Jamaica www.visitjamaica.com/vacation-themes/weddings.aspx	License $50; marriage officer's fee $50–$250	24 hours	Accommodating laws and upscale couples-only resorts make Jamaica a top pick. Some all-inclusives even offer complimentary weddings, complete with officiant and license.
Nevis www.nevisisland.com/Weddings.htm	License $80 if on-island for a minimum of 2 business days; $20 if on-island for 15 days beforehand	Both parties must be on-island at least 2 business days.	You'll pay $20 to complete your application before a justice of the peace. If you've never been married, also be prepared to pop $20 for a notarized affidavit of single status.
Puerto Rico www.seepuertorico.com/romance	License and stamp fees $30	None	Blood tests and a health license are needed (the former done within 14 days of the wedding, the latter within 10). These can be obtained from your own physician, then certified by one in Puerto Rico.

1

ISLAND	COSTS	WAITING PERIOD	GOOD TO KNOW
St. Eustatius www.statia-tourism.com/weddings.html	License, stamp fees, and marriage book $300	14 days after document registration	Marriages performed outside the marriage hall require 6 witnesses.
St. Kitts www.stkitts-tourism.kn/Weddings/Tying_Knot.asp	License $200	Both parties must be on-island a minimum of 2 business days.	Thinking of a casual sunrise or sunset ceremony on the beach? Consider this: Civil weddings are performed only from 8 to 6. Church weddings may be held 6 to 6.
St. Lucia www.stlucia.org/planner/weddings.asp	License $125 for standard or $200 for special; registrar fees $37; marriage certificate $3	None with a special license, 3 days with a standard license	St. Lucia, a leader in the destination wedding biz, has a streamlined process that makes marrying easy. Most lodgings have enticing packages and on-site planners.
St. Maarten www.st-maarten.com/index.php/intro/weddings/legal-requirements	Combined cost of civil ceremony, marriage book, certificate, and stamps $410	Couples must submit requests 14 days before the wedding and be on-island 7 days beforehand.	It is much easier to marry in St. Maarten than in St. Martin. The French side of the island requires translated documents and a monthlong residency period for 1 partner.
St. Vincent and the Grenadines www.discoversvg.com/index.php/en/whattodo	License $185 plus approximately $8 for stamp fees	1 day	Blessed with camera-ready beaches, gorgeous gardens, private island resorts, and historic buildings, these 32 islands boast a broader-than-average range of venues.
Trinidad and Tobago www.gotrinidadandtobago.com/tobago/weddings.php	License $55	3 days	To obtain a license both partners must be nonresidents. Documents, such as airline tickets, are required to confirm your dates of entry and onward passage.
Turks and Caicos www.turksandcaicostourism.com/tci-weddings.html	License $150	24 hours, but licenses may take 2–3 days to process	The marriage is registered here. To have it registered in your home country, you must make special arrangements. Parental consent needed if under 21.
U.S. Virgin Islands www.visitusvi.com/plan_events/weddings_honeymoons	Marriage application and license fee $100; officiating fee $200 if not married in court by a judge	8 days from receipt of application	Licenses must be picked up in person on weekdays, but you can shorten the wait by applying from home.

KIDS AND FAMILIES

Traveling with kids to the Caribbean is fun and easy. Many resorts, except for those that are exclusively couples-only, offer kids free promotions, special restaurant menus, and programs for tots on up to teens.

Choosing a Place to Stay

Everything from brand-name resorts to independent hotels, condominiums, and even campgrounds can offer a great family vacation. It just depends what you're looking for.

Let them entertain you. If you prefer to relax while the kids are entertained, choose a major resort with all-inclusive meal plan and kids' program. A few best bets are **Beaches Resorts** (Beaches Turks and Caicos, Beaches Negril, and Beaches Sandy Bay in Jamaica). The Sandals-owned chain (Antigua, Jamaica, St. Lucia) has kids' programs to match all ages, outdoor playgrounds, gaming centers, trips for ages 12 and up such as snorkeling and scuba diving, and Sesame Street character appearances. **Hyatt Regency Aruba Beach Resort & Casino** features Camp Hyatt, where kids ages 3 to 12 can participate in a variety of activities and adventures. **Club Med Punta Cana**, in the Dominican Republic, offers a baby gym, Crayola arts-and-crafts programs, hip-hop dance instruction, Petite Chef (ages 3 to 7) cooking classes, and The Ramp, an interactive club for 14- to 17-year-olds.

DIY. If you'd prefer more of a home base from which to explore the island on your own, choose a hotel, condo, or villa near the attractions you'd most like to visit. Condos and villas provide more of an at-home atmosphere with full kitchens and separate bedrooms, and many include home entertainment systems. **Maho Bay**

Camps on St. John, in the U.S. Virgin Islands, is a great kid-friendly option. You stay in screened cottages or canvas tents. There are cooking facilities in each unit, and a cafeteria-style restaurant gives Mom the night off. Lifeguards are on duty, there are water-sports rentals, and there's plenty of white-sand beach for sand castles and swimming.

Top Attractions

The Caribbean offers an abundance of family attractions. Museums, forts, caves, zoos, and aquariums are sure to keep tots, teens, adults, and seniors happy when it's time to take a break from the sun, sand, and sea.

Momentous Museums. Many kids have read about Christopher Columbus in history books, but at **El Faro a Colón** (Columbus Lighthouse), just outside Santo Domingo in the Dominican Republic, they can visit his tomb. The huge pyramid-shape complex has six museums that trace the history of the area from the ancient Indian days to the construction of this modern, multimillion-dollar structure. Kids will marvel over ancient maps, jewelry-studded royal crowns, and replicas of dugout canoes. For a real treat, visit at night when the 688-foot-tall lighthouse projects a cross-shape beam of light some 44 miles into the sky. In Jamaica, teenagers may enjoy the **Bob Marley Museum**. This former home of the late great king of reggae music—painted Rastafarian red, yellow, and green—is filled with Marley's personal memorabilia. A 15-minute video presents the life story of Marley along with familiar music clips. Younger kids will love the **Anancy Family Fun & Nature Park**. Located near Negril, the park boasts three small museums—crafts-, conservation-, and heritage-oriented—along with a nature trail, fishing pond, go-kart riding track, and miniature-golf course. The park is named for Anancy, a mischievous spider in Jamaican folk stories.

Fantastic Fortresses. A long grassy walk leads up to the 500-year-old **Castillo del Morro** (El Morro) Castle, an imposing structure in Puerto Rico's Old San Juan that looks like the Wicked Witch's scary fortress. Venture inside the thick walls and cruise the ramparts, tunnels, and dungeons. Wax mannequins model historic battle uniforms, and a video shows the history of building and defending this stronghold. Equally imposing is St. Kitts's **Brimstone Hill**, known as the Gibraltar of the West Indies. Ft. George, which sits atop the hill, is built of 7-foot-thick walls of black volcanic stone. Kids can woefully imagine being imprisoned here during a "time-out." From high atop the fort's cannon ways, kids can search the horizon for the islands of Nevis, Montserrat, Saba, St. Maarten/St. Martin, and St. Barth. It's also fun to try spotting the scampering green monkeys that play along the nature trails that wind around this 38-acre site.

Cool Caves. Don a bright yellow hard hat and ride a tramcar into Barbados's **Harrison's Cave**. Specially lighted caverns illuminate the stalactites, stalagmites, and underground waterfalls so the caves don't seem too spooky. The **Hato Caves** in Curaçao were made during the Ice Age, but today the inhabitants are not cavemen but long-nosed bats. Puerto Rico's **Rio Camuy Cave Park** tour begins with a short video and then a trolley ride right to the mouth of the cave. Though 200 feet high, the cave is only half a mile long. The walking tour is level and flat, allowing kids' eyes to roam all over without fear of stumbling.

Zany Zoos. Roam freely with the animals at the **Barbados Wildlife Reserve**. This outdoor zoo keeps kids engaged as they walk along shady pathways and spot exotic animals, reptiles, and birds in their natural habitat. There are land turtles, fine-feathered peacocks, green monkeys, parrots, and even an otter. Some species here are threatened with extinction. After exploring outside, kids can check out the walk-in aviary and the many natural-history exhibits. The **Emperor Valley Zoo**, named for Trinidad's native blue butterflies, is one of the best in the Caribbean. The island's president and prime minister have houses on this site, but most intriguing for kids is the 8-acre zoo that is filled with birds and other wildlife from the region, ranging from blue-and-gold macaws and small red brocket deer to giant anacondas.

Awesome Aquariums. **Curaçao Sea Aquarium** boasts more than 400 species of sea life. Some of the most fascinating creatures are the sharks—hand-fed daily, to the delight of kids of all ages. Sharks are another big draw to the **Acuario National** outside Santa Domingo in the Dominican Republic. The huge creatures sometimes nap across glass-tunnel walkways where kids can check out the vibrating gills of these sleeping demons. Coral World's shark encounter is also a draw, as is a baby shark pond where park staff will let kids feel this fearsome fish's sandpaper skin.

FLAVORS OF THE
CARIBBEAN

by Charyn Pfeuffer

As an entry point to the New World, the Caribbean has a rich culinary tradition reflecting the diversity of its immigrants. This melting pot of Spanish, African, French, English, and Dutch influences has created dishes packed with fresh ingredients and bold, spicy flavors and seasonings.

Local produce is varied and includes lima beans, black-eyed peas, corn, yams, sweet potatoes, cassava, and taro. Rice and beans are ever-present staples, commonly seasoned with ingredients like curry, cilantro, soy sauce, and ginger. The spice-forward "jerk" style of marinated and rubbed meat, fish, and fowl is prevalent. Jamaica, Haiti, Guadeloupe, and other French Caribbean islands savor goat meat in dishes like goat water, a tomato-based stew, which is the official national dish of Montserrat and a speciality on St. Kitts and Nevis. Fresh-caught seafood from local waters also figures prominently into the cuisine.

Modern menus don't stray too far from tradition, opting instead for clever twists rather than reinvention, like flavoring black beans with tequila and olive oil, or serving rice spiked with coconut and ginger. No matter where your culinary curiosities take you in the islands, plan on a well-seasoned eating adventure.

(opposite) Dasheene Restaurant at Ladera Resort, St. Lucia, (top) Jerk pork, a signature Jamaican dish, (bottom) scotch bonnet peppers.

THE ISLANDS' GLOBAL FLAVORS

Island cuisine developed through waves of wars, immigration, and natives' innovations from the 15th century through the mid-19th century. Early Amerindian native peoples, the Arawaks and the Caribs, are said to have introduced the concept of spicing food with chili peppers, a preparation that remains a hallmark of Caribbean cuisine. Pepper pot stew was a staple for the Caribs, who would make the dish with *cassareep*, a savory sauce made from cassava. The stew featured wild meats (possum, wild pig, or armadillo), squash, beans, and peanuts, which were added to the cassareep and simmered in a clay pot. The dish was traditionally served to guests as a gesture of hospitality. Today's recipes substitute meats like pig trotters, cow heel, or oxtail.

Caribbean-style curried goat

After Columbus' discovery of the New World, European traders and settlers brought new fruits, vegetables, and meats. Their arrival coincided with that of African slaves en route to the Americas. Every explorer, settler, trader, and slave brought something to expand the palette of flavors. Although Caribbean cooking varies from island to island, trademark techniques and spices unite the cuisine.

SPANISH INFLUENCES

The Caribbean islands were discovered by Christopher Columbus in 1492, while he was working for the Spanish crown. When he returned to colonize the islands a year later, he brought ships laden with coconut, chickpeas, cilantro, eggplant, onions, and garlic. The Bahamas, Hispaniola, and Cuba were among Columbus' first findings, and as a result, Cuba and nearby Puerto Rico have distinctly Spanish-accented cuisine, including *paella* (a seafood- or meat-studded rice dish), *arroz con pollo* or *pilau* (chicken cooked with yellow rice), and white-bean Spanish stews.

Arroz con Pollo

FRENCH TECHNIQUE

As tobacco and sugar crops flourished and the Caribbean became a center of European trade and colonization, the French settled Martinique and Guadeloupe in 1635 and later expanded to St. Barthélemy, St. Martin, Grenada, St. Lucia, and western Hispaniola. French culinary technique meets the natural resources of the islands to create dishes like whelk (sea snail) grilled in garlic butter, fish cooked *en papillote* (baked in parchment paper), and *crabs farcis*, land crab meat that is steamed, mixed with butter, breadcrumbs, ham, chilis, and garlic, then stuffed back into the crab shells and grilled.

DUTCH INGENUITY

Beginning in the 1620s, traders from the Dutch East India Company brought Southeast Asian ingredients like soy sauce to the islands of Curaçao and St. Maarten. Dutch influence is also evident throughout Aruba and Bonaire (all have been under Dutch rule since the early 19th century), where dishes like *keshi yeni*, or "stuffed cheese," evolved from stuffing discarded rinds of Edam cheese with minced meat, olives, and capers. Another Dutch-influenced dish is *boka dushi* (Indonesian-style chicken satay), which translates to "sweet mouth" in the islands' Papiamento dialect.

Paella

Boka dushi

Jerk meat

Roti

Whelk

ENGLISH IMPORTS

British settlers brought pickles, preserves, and chutneys to the Caribbean, and current-day chefs take advantage of the islands' indigenous fruits to produce these items. British influence also is evidenced by the Indian and Chinese contributions to Caribbean cuisine. British (and Dutch) colonists brought over indentured laborers from India and China to work on sugar plantations, resulting in the introduction of popular dishes like curry goat and *roti,* an Indian flatbread stuffed with vegetables or chicken curry.

AFRICAN INGREDIENTS

The African slave trade that began in the early 1600s brought foods from West Africa, including yams, okra, plantains, breadfruit, pigeon peas, and oxtail to the islands. Slave cooks often had to make do with plantation leftovers and scraps, yielding dishes like cow heel soup and pigfoot souse (a cool soup with pickled cucumber and meat), both of which are still popular today. One of the most significant African contributions to the Caribbean table is "jerking," the process of dry-rubbing meat with allspice, Scotch bonnet peppers, and other spices. Although the cooking technique originated with native Amerindians, it was the Jamaican Maroons, a population of runaway African slaves living in the island's mountains during the years of slavery, who developed and perfected it, resulting in the style of jerk meat familiar in restaurants today.

CARIBBEAN'S NATURAL BOUNTY

Soursop

Despite its spicy reputation, Caribbean food isn't always fiery; the focus is on enhancing and intensifying flavors with herbs and spices. Food plays a major role in island culture, family life, and traditions, and no holiday would be complete without traditional dishes prepared from the island's natural products.

TANTALIZING TROPICAL FRUIT

Breadfruit, a versatile starch with potato-like flavor, can be served solo—baked or grilled—or added to soups and stews.

With its rich, refreshing milk, **coconut** frequently appears in soups, stews, sauces, and drinks to help temper hot, spicy flavors with its rich, refreshing milk.

The bright orange tropical fruit **guava** tastes somewhat like a tomato when it's not fully ripe, but is pleasantly sweet when mature. It is used in compotes, pastes, and jellies.

The pungent smell of **jackfruit** may be off-putting for some, but its sweet fleshy meat is popular in milkshakes.

Papaya is sweet and floral when ripe; unripe, it can be shredded and mixed with spices and citrus for a refreshing salad. It is often

used in fruit salsas that are served with seafood.

The brightly flavored **passion fruit** is commonly puréed and used in sauces, drinks, and desserts.

The dark-green skinned, creamy fleshed **soursop** is known for its sweet-tart juice used in drinks, sorbets, and ice creams.

The fibrous stalks of **sugarcane**, a giant grass native to India, are rich with sugar, which can be consumed in several forms, including freshly extracted juice and processed sugar.

Tamarind is the fruit of a large tree. The sticky pulp of its pod is used in chutneys and curries to impart a slightly sweet, refreshingly sour flavor.

FARM-FRESH VEGETABLES

Cassava (also called yucca) can be used much like a potato in purées, dumplings, soups, and stews. The flour of its roots is made into tapioca.

Chayote is a versatile member of the squash and melon family, often used raw in salads or stuffed with cheese and tomatoes and baked.

Dasheen (taro) is much like a potato, but creamier. It can be

Jackfruit

sliced thinly and fried like a potato chip.

Fitweed (or French thistle) is a tropical herb related to coriander (cilantro), and is popular in Caribbean seasonings.

Pod-like **okra** is commonly used in *callaloo*, the national dish of Trinidad and Tobago. The creamy, spicy stew is made of leafy greens, okra, and crabmeat.

Green plantain is a cooking staple across the Caribbean, often sliced, pounded, dipped in a seasoned batter, and deep-fried.

The leafy green **sorrel** is typically pureed in soups

Tamarind

Chayote

Curry powder

and stews, or used in salads.

SWEET AND SAVORY SPICES

Native **allspice**, also called Jamaican pepper, is commonly added to Caribbean curries. It is the dried unripe berry of the evergreen pimento tree. Native Jamaicans once used it to preserve meats. It is an essential ingredient in jerk preparations.

Curries are intensely seasoned gravy-based dishes originating from India—they are most prevalent on the islands of Jamaica, Trinidad, and Tobago.

Native Carib people pioneered the use of **chili peppers** in the islands for hot, spicy flavoring, using primarily habaneros and Scotch bonnet peppers.

Ginger can be used raw or dried and ground into a powder that adds flavor

and heat to ginger beer, sweet potatoes, or coconut milk-based sauces.

The mix of spices in **jerk** seasoning vary, but typically include scallions, thyme, allspice, onions, and garlic.

The tiny island of Grenada is the second largest exporter of **nutmeg** in the world. It often accents sweet dishes, and is frequently added to vegetables in Dutch preparations.

ISLAND FISH AND SEAFOOD

Bonito is a medium-sized fish in the mackerel family. Atlantic bonito is moderately fatty, with a firm texture and darker color. It is served blackened, grilled (sometimes with fruit-based salsas), or Jamaican jerk style.

On many islands, including the Bahamas, **conch**—a large shellfish—are made into conch fritters, a mix of conch meat, corn meal, and spices that are deep fried and make an excellent snack.

Cascadura fish is a small fish found in the freshwater swamps of Trinidad and Tobago. It is typically served in curry with a side of rice or dumplings.

Conch salad

Flying fish are named for the wing-like fins that enable them to glide or "fly" over water. Firm in texture, it is typically served steamed or fried. Flying fish is a staple in Bajan cuisine and is found in abundance off the coast of Barbados.

Kingfish is another word for wahoo, a delicate white fish commonly fished off the coasts of St. Croix and Barbados. It's served *escabeche* style, marinated in a vinegar mixture, then fried or poached.

Land crab is found throughout the islands. Delicate in flavor, its common preparations include curried crab stewed in coconut milk, stuffed crab, and crab soup.

Mahi mahi is fished off the coast of St. Croix. With a subtle, sweet flavor, its firm, dark flesh lends itself to soy sauce glazes and Asian preparations.

Salt fish is a dish made from dried cod, often seasoned with tomatoes, onions, and thyme. Stir-fried ackee (a tropical fruit with nutty-flavored flesh) and saltfish is Jamaica's national dish.

Allspice

Salt fish

THE RISE OF RUM

The Caribbean is the world center for rum production, with many islands making their own brands and styles of rum. Dozens of rum companies operate throughout the islands. Although larger, mainstream brands like Bacardi, Captain Morgan, and Mount Gay are available on every island, you may have to look harder for the smaller brands. The best-quality rums are dark, aged rums meant for sipping, priced from $30 to $700 a bottle. For excellent sipping rum at the lower end of the spectrum, try Appleton or Rhum Barbancourt. For mixed drinks, use clear or golden-colored rums that are less expensive and pair well with fruit juices or cola. Spiced and flavored rums are also popular in cocktails. Here are some of the best rums you'll encounter at an island bar:

Appleton Estate (Jamaica) The Estate VX is an amber-colored rum with subtle brown sugar aromas and a smooth, toasted honey finish. Excellent mixer for classic cocktails.

Bacardi (Bermuda, PR) Superior is a clear, mild rum with subtle hints of vanilla and fresh fruits. It is smooth and light on the palate. Best in mixed drinks.

Captain Morgan (PR) Its Black Label Jamaica Rum is dark, rich, and smooth, with strong notes of vanilla. Sip it iced, or with a splash of water.

Clarke's Court (Grenada) The Original White is clear with a touch of sweetness

Ron Barceló

and a hint of heat, best used as a mixer.

Cruzan (VI) Less strong and sweet than most rums, the White Rum is smooth, and best suited for mixing.

Havana Club (Cuba) The Añejo 3 Años is deceiving—light in color and body and delicate in flavor. It is a nice rum to sip neat.

Mount Gay Rum (Barbados) Eclipse, the brand's flagship rum, has a golden color with a butterscotch caramel nose and sweet taste on the palate with mouth-warming flavor.

Pusser's (BVI) Self-described as "the single malt of rum," the aged 15-year variety boasts notes of cinnamon, woody spice, and citrus. A good sipping rum.

Rhum Barbancourt (Haiti) Aged 15-years, this premium dark rum is distilled twice in copper pot stills and often called the "Cognac of Rum." Sip it neat.

Ron Barceló (DR) The Añejo is dark copper in color, with a rich flavor, while the aged Imperial boasts notes of toffee on the nose, and a buttery smooth finish.

Shillingford Estates (Dominica) Its most popular product, Macoucherie Spiced is a blend of rum, the bark of the Bois Bande tree, and spices.

Mount Gay Rum

(left) Pusser's Rum, (right) Havana Club

ISLANDS' BEST BREWS

IN FOCUS FLAVORS OF THE CARIBBEAN

Beer in the Caribbean was largely home-made for centuries, a tradition inherited from British colonial rulers. The first commercial brewery in the islands was founded in Trinidad and Tobago in 1947.

In the islands, do what the locals do: drink local beer. Whatever brand is brewed on-island is the one you'll find at every restaurant and bar. And no matter where you go in the Caribbean, there's a local island brew worth trying. Another plus: local brands are almost always cheaper than imports like Corona or Heineken. Most island beers are pale lagers, though you'll find a smattering of Dutch-style pilsners and English-style pale ales. The beers listed below are our top picks for beachside sipping:

Kalik

Banks Beer (Banks Breweries, Barbados) A straw-colored lager that is light tasting with a touch of maltiness on the nose and tongue.

Blackbeard Ale (Virgin Islands Brewing Co., Virgin Islands) This English pale ale-style beer is bright amber in color with a creamy white head. Well-crafted beer with a nice hoppy bite at the finish.

Balashi Beer (Brouwerij Nacional Balashi N.V., Aruba) Refreshingly light, this Dutch pilsner boasts mild flavor, slight sweetness, and subtle hop bitterness.

Legends Premium Lager (Banks Breweries, Barbados) One of the Caribbean's best brews, this golden yellow lager offers crisp hops and a clean finish. Distinctive toasty, malt character.

Carib Lager Beer (Carib Brewery, Trinidad and Tobago) This great beach refresher is pale yellow color with a foamy head. Fruity and sweet malty corn aromas, it is sometimes referred to as the "Corona of the Caribbean."

Kalik Gold (Commonwealth Brewery LTD., New Providence, Bahamas) Clear straw color with gentle hoppy, herbal notes, this is an easy drinking, warm weather lager.

Medalla Light (Puerto Rico) This bright gold lager is substantial for a light beer. It's a local favorite.

Red Stripe (Jamaica) The Jamaican lager pours golden yellow in color with lots of carbonation. Light bodied, crisp, and smooth.

Carib Lager Beer

Piton (St. Lucia) Light and sparkly with subtle sweetness, this pale yellow lager is pleasant enough, but barely flavored.

Presidente (Domincan Republic) Slight citrus aroma, light body, and fizziness, plus a clean finish make for easy drinking. Perfect pairing for barbecued meats.

Wadadli (Antigua Brewery Ltd., Antigua and Barbuda) A crisp, light-bodied American-style lager. Toasty malt on the nose.

Banks Beer

(left) Red Stripe, (right) Presidente

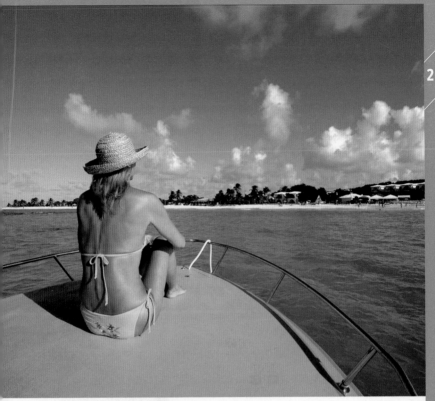

Anguilla

WORD OF MOUTH

"[W]e just prefer Anguilla because of the beaches, the people, and the food. Much more of an island vibe."

—MaryD

WELCOME TO ANGUILLA

TRANQUIL AND UPSCALE

This dry limestone isle is the most northerly of the Leeward Islands, lying between the Caribbean Sea and the Atlantic Ocean. The island is only 16 miles (26 km) long and 3 miles (5 km) wide at its widest point. A low-lying island, its highest spot is 213 feet above sea level. Since there are neither streams nor rivers—only saline ponds used for salt production—water is provided by cisterns that collect rainwater, or desalinization plants.

In tiny Anguilla, where fishermen have been heading out to sea for centuries in hand-made boats, the beaches are some of the Caribbean's best and least crowded. Heavy development has not spoiled the island's atmospheric corners, and independent restaurants still thrive. Resorts run the gamut from over-the-top palaces to quaint inns.

Restaurants ▼		Hotels & Rentals ▼	
Blanchard's **20**	Madeariman Reef **11**	Allamanda **3**	Frangipani Beach Club **1**
Blanchard's Beach Shack .. **19**	Mango's **16**	Anacaona **15**	Indigo Reef **13**
da'Vida **10**	Picante **17**	Anguilla Great House **7**	Paradise Cove **9**
Dolce Vita **3**	Roy's Bayside Grille **5**	Arawak Beach Inn **5**	Serenity Cottages **4**
English Rose **8**	SandBar **4**	Cap Juluca **10**	Sheriva Villa Hotel **11**
Firefly **15**	Smokey's **14**	Carimar Beach Club **17**	Shoal Bay Villas **2**
Geraud's Patisserie **6**	Straw Hat **1**	Covecastles Villa Resort . **12**	Turtle's Nest Beach Resort **16**
Hibernia **13**	Tasty's **7**	CuisinArt Golf Resort & Spa **8**	The Viceroy **14**
Jacala Beach Restaurant . **21**	Trattoria Tramonto **18**	Easy Corner Villas **6**	
KoalKeel **9**	Veya **2**		
	Zara's **12**		

TOP REASONS TO VISIT ANGUILLA

1 Beautiful Beaches: Miles of brilliant beach ensure you have a high-quality spot in which to lounge.

2 Great Restaurants: The dining scene offers both fine dining and delicious casual food.

3 Fun, Low-Key Nightlife: A funky late-night local music scene features reggae and string bands.

4 Upscale Accommodations: Excellent luxury resorts coddle you in comfort.

5 Hidden Bargains: You'll find a few relative bargains if you look hard enough.

ANGUILLA BEACHES

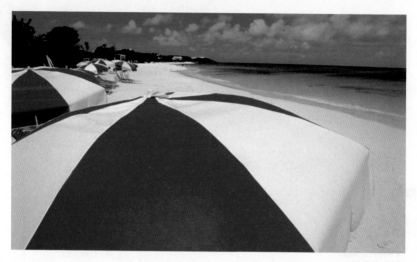

You can always tell a true beach fanatic: say "Anguilla" and watch for signs of ecstasy. They say there are 33 beaches on the island's 34 square miles; we say, "Who's counting? Pack the sunscreen!"

(Above) Shoal Bay (Bottom right) Cove Bay (Top right) Shoal Bay

Renowned for their beauty, Anguilla's 30-plus beaches are among the best in the Caribbean. You can find long, deserted stretches suitable for sunset walks, or beaches lined with lively bars and restaurants—all surrounded by crystal-clear warm waters in several shades of turquoise. The sea is calmest at 2½-mile-long Rendezvous Bay, where gentle breezes tempt sailors. But Shoal Bay (East) is the quintessential Caribbean beach. The white sand is so soft and abundant that it pools around your ankles. Cove Bay and Maundays Bay, both on the southeast coast, must also rank among the island's best beaches. Maundays is the location of the island's top resort, Cap Juluca, and smaller Cove Bay is just a walk away. In contrast to the French islands, topless sunbathing is not permitted.

DAZZLING WHITE

The dazzling white sand of Anguilla's famous beaches, as fine and soft as confectioners' sugar, is a result of calcareous marine algae called Halimeda, which thrive in the rich offshore sea-grass beds and reefs. Its coral-like skeleton is broken down by wave action and swept ashore by swift currents where it mixes with the eroded tertiary limestone of Anguilla's surface.

2

NORTHEAST COAST

Captain's Bay. On the north coast just before the eastern tip of the island, this quarter-mile stretch of perfect white sand is bounded on the left by a rocky shoreline where Atlantic waves crash. If you make the tough, four-wheel-drive-only trip along the dirt road that leads to the northeastern end of the island toward Junk's Hole, you'll be rewarded with peaceful isolation. The surf here slaps the sands with a vengeance, and the undertow is strong—so wading is the safest water sport.

Island Harbour. These mostly calm waters are surrounded by a slender beach. For centuries Anguillians have ventured from these sands in colorful handmade fishing boats. It's not much of a beach for swimming or lounging, but there are several restaurants (Hibernia, Arawak Café, Côtée Mer, and Smitty's), and this is the departure point for the three-minute boat ride to Scilly Cay, where a thatched beach bar serves seafood. Just hail the restaurant's free boat and plan to spend most of the day (the all-inclusive lunch starts at $40 and is worth the price—Wednesday, Friday, and Sunday only).

NORTHWEST COAST

Road Bay. The big pier here is where the cargo ships dock, but so do some pretty sweet yachts, sailboats, and fishing boats. The brown-sugar sand is home

to terrific restaurants that hop from day through dawn, including Dolce Vita, SandBar, Veya, Roy's Bayside Grille, Barrel Stay, the Pumphouse, and Elvis's quintessential beach bar. There are all kinds of boat charters available here. The snorkeling isn't very good, but the sunset vistas are glorious, especially with a rum punch in your hand.

Sandy Island. A popular day trip for Anguilla visitors, tiny Sandy Island shelters a pretty lagoon, nestled in coral reefs about 2 miles (3 km) from Road Bay. Most of the operators in Sandy Ground can bring you here.

★ Fodor's Choice **Shoal Bay.** Anchored by sea grape and coconut trees, the 2-mile (3-km) powdered-sugar strand at Shoal Bay (not to be confused with Shoal Bay West at the other end of the island) is universally considered one of the world's prettiest beaches. You can park free at any of the restaurants, including Elodia's, Uncle Ernie's, or Gwen's Reggae Grill, most of which either rent or provide chairs and umbrellas for patrons for about $20 a day for two. There is plenty of room to stretch out in relative privacy, or you can bar-hop, take a ride on Junior's Glass Bottom Boat, or arrange a wreck dive at PADI-certified Shoal Bay Scuba near Kú, where ZaZaa, the island's chic-est boutique, will satisfy fans of St. Barth shopping. The relatively broad beach has

Catamarans beached on beautiful Rendezvous Bay

shallow water that is usually gentle, making this a great family beach; a coral reef not far from the shore is a wonderful snorkeling spot. Sunsets over the water are spectacular.

SOUTHWEST COAST

★ Fodor's Choice **Cove Bay.** Follow the signs to Smokey's at the end of Cove Road, and you will find water that is brilliantly blue and sand that is as soft as sifted flour. It's just as spectacular as its neighbors Rendezvous Bay and Maundays Bay. You can walk here from Cap Juluca for a change of pace, or you can arrange a horseback ride along the beach. Weekend barbecues with terrific local bands at Smokey's are an Anguillian must.

★ Fodor's Choice **Maundays Bay.** The dazzling, mile-long platinum-white beach is especially great for swimming and long beach walks. It's no wonder that Cap Juluca, one of Anguilla's premier resorts, chose this as its location. Public parking is straight ahead at the end of the road near Cap Juluca's Pimms restaurant. Depending on the season

you can book a massage in one of the beachside tents.

Rendezvous Bay. Follow the signs to Anguilla Great House for public parking at this broad swath of pearl-white sand that is some 1½ miles (2½ km) long. The beach is lapped by calm, bluer-than-blue water and a postcard-worthy view of St. Martin. Don't miss the daylong party at the tree-house Dune Preserve, where Bankie Banx, Anguilla's most famous musician, presides.

Shoal Bay West. This glittering bay bordered by mangroves and sea grapes is a lovely place to spend the day. The mile-long beach is home to the dazzling Covecastles and Altamer villas. The tranquillity is sublime, with coral reefs for snorkeling not too far from shore. Punctuate your day with a meal at beachside Trattoria Tramonto. Reach the beach by taking the main road to the West End and bearing left at the fork, then continuing to the end. Note that similarly named Shoal Bay is a separate beach on a different part of the island.

2

By Elise Meyer

Peace, pampering, great food, and a wonderful local music scene are among the star attractions on Anguilla (pronounced ang-*gwill*-a). Beach lovers may become giddy when they first spot the island from the air; its blindingly white sand and lustrous blue-and-aquamarine waters are intoxicating. And if you like sophisticated cuisine served in casually elegant open-air settings, this may be your culinary Shangri-la.

The island's name, a reflection of its shape, is most likely a derivative of *anguille,* which is French for "eel." (French explorer Pierre Laudonnaire is credited with having given the island this name when he sailed past it in 1556.) In 1631 the Dutch built a fort here, but so far no one has been able to locate its site. English settlers from St. Kitts colonized the island in 1650, with plans to cultivate tobacco and, later, cotton and then sugar. But the thin soil and scarce water doomed these enterprises to fail. Except for a brief period of independence, when it broke from its association with St. Kitts and Nevis in the 1960s, Anguilla has remained a British colony ever since.

From the early 1800s various island federations were formed and disbanded, with Anguilla all the while simmering over its subordinate status and enforced union with St. Kitts. Anguillians twice petitioned for direct rule from Britain and twice were ignored. In 1967, when St. Kitts, Nevis, and Anguilla became an associated state, the mouse roared; citizens kicked out St. Kitts's policemen, held a self-rule referendum, and for two years conducted their own affairs. To what *Time* magazine called "a cascade of laughter around the world," a British "peacekeeping force" of 100 paratroopers from the Elite Red Devil unit parachuted onto the island, squelching Anguilla's designs for autonomy but helping a team of royal engineers stationed there to improve the port and build roads and schools. Today Anguilla elects a House of Assembly and its own leader to handle internal affairs, and a British governor is responsible for public service, the police, the judiciary, and external affairs.

LOGISTICS

Getting to Anguilla: There are no nonstop flights to Anguilla (AXA) from the United States, so you will almost always have to fly through San Juan, St. Maarten, or some other Caribbean island. You'll ordinarily be making the hop on a smaller plane. You can also take a ferry from St. Maarten.

Hassle Factor: Medium.

On the Ground: Some hotels provide transfers from the airport or ferry pier, especially the more expensive ones. For everyone else, if you don't rent a car, the taxi ride from the airport to your hotel will be less than $25 even to the West End (and considerably less if you're going to Sandy Ground).

Getting Around the Island: It's possible to base yourself in Sandy Ground, Rendezvous Bay, Meads Bay, or Shoal Bay without a car, but restaurants and resorts are quite spread out, so for the sake of convenience you may wish to rent a car for a few days or for your entire stay. If you do, prepare to drive on the left. Taxis are fairly expensive on Anguilla, another reason to consider renting a car.

The territory of Anguilla includes a few islets (or cays, pronounced "keys"), such as Scrub Island, Dog Island, Prickly Pear Cay, Sandy Island, and Sombrero Island. The 16,000 or so residents are predominantly of African descent, but there are also many of Irish background, whose ancestors came over from St. Kitts in the 1600s. Historically, because the limestone land was unfit for agriculture, attempts at enslavement never lasted long; consequently, Anguilla doesn't bear the scars of slavery found on so many other Caribbean islands. Instead, Anguillians became experts at making a living from the sea and are known for their boatbuilding and fishing skills. Tourism is the stable economy's growth industry, but the government carefully regulates expansion to protect the island's natural resources and beauty. New hotels are small, select, and casino-free; Anguilla emphasizes its high-quality service, serene surroundings, and friendly people.

PLANNING

WHEN TO GO

As in much of the Caribbean, high season runs from mid-December through mid-April, and some resorts in Anguilla still close from August through mid-December, though many remain open year-round. Many resorts require long minimum stays until after New Year's Day.

GETTING HERE AND AROUND

AIR TRAVEL

There are no nonstop flights to Anguilla from the United States. Trans-Anguilla Airways offers daily flights from Antigua, St. Thomas, and St. Kitts. Windward Islands Airways flies several times a day from St. Maarten. Anguilla Air Services is a reliable charter operation. LIAT

comes in from Antigua, Nevis, St. Kitts, St. Thomas, and Tortola. Cape Air has two daily flights from San Juan (three on peak travel days).

Airport Clayton J. Lloyd Airport ☎ *264/497–3510.*

Local Airline Contacts Anguilla Air Services ☎ *264/498–5922, 264/235–7122* ⊕ *www.anguillaairservices.com.* **Cape Air** ☎ *866/227–3247, 508/771–6944* ⊕ *www.capeair.net.* **LIAT** ☎ *264/497–5002* ⊕ *www.liatairline.com.* **TransAnguilla Airways** ☎ *264/497–8690* ⊕ *www.transanguilla.com.* **Windward Islands Airways** ☎ *264/497–2748* ⊕ *www.fly-winair.com.*

BOAT AND FERRY TRAVEL

Ferries run frequently between Anguilla and St. Martin. Boats leave from Blowing Point on Anguilla approximately every half hour from 7:30 am to 6:15 pm and from Marigot, St. Martin, every 45 minutes from 8 am to 7 pm. You pay a $20 departure tax before boarding ($5 for day-trippers—but be sure to make this clear at the window where you pay), in addition to the $15 one-way fare. On very windy days the 20-minute trip can be bouncy. Remember that the drive between the Marigot ferry terminal and the airport can take up to 45 minutes with traffic. Private transfers by speedboat are sometimes offered from a dock right at the airport, at a cost of about $75 per person (arranged through your Anguilla hotel). Private ferry companies, including Shauna, run six or more round-trips a day, coinciding with major flights, from Blowing Point direct to the airport in St. Maarten. On the St. Maarten side they will bring you right to the terminal in a van, or you can just walk across the parking lot. These trips are $35 one-way or $60 round-trip (cash only). Shauna also can arrange charters.

Contacts Anguilla Ferries ☎ *264/235–6205* ⊕ *www.anguillaferry.com.* **Link Ferries** ☎ *264/497–2231* ⊕ *www.link.ai.* **Shauna Ferries** ☎ *264/476–6534.*

CAR TRAVEL

Although most of the rental cars on-island have the driver's side on the left as in North America, Anguillian roads are like those in the United Kingdom—driving is on the left side of the road. It's easy to get the hang of, but the roads can be rough, so be cautious, and observe the 30 mph (48 kph) speed limit. Roundabouts are probably the biggest driving obstacle for most. As you approach, give way to the vehicle on your right; once you're in the rotary, you have the right of way.

Car Rentals: A temporary Anguilla driver's license is required to rent a car—you can get into real trouble if you're caught driving without one. You get it for $20 (good for three months) at any of the car-rental agencies at the time you pick up your car; you'll also need your valid driver's license from home. Rental rates start at about $45 to $55 per day, plus insurance.

Car-Rental Contacts Apex/Avis ✉ *Airport Rd.* ☎ *264/497–2642* ⊕ *www.avisanguilla.com.* **Bryans Car Rental** ✉ *Blowing Point* ☎ *264/497–6407.* **Triple K Car Rental/Hertz** ✉ *Airport Rd.* ☎ *264/497–2934.*

TAXI TRAVEL

Taxis are fairly expensive, so if you plan to explore the island's many beaches and restaurants, it may be more cost-effective to rent a car. Taxi rates are regulated by the government, and there are fixed fares from point to point, which are listed in brochures the drivers should have handy and are also published in the local guide *What We Do in Anguilla*. It's $24 from the airport or $22 from Blowing Point Ferry to West End hotels. Posted rates are for one or two people; each additional passenger adds $5 to the total, and there is a $1 charge for each piece of luggage beyond the allotted two. You can also hire a taxi for the hourly rate of $28. Surcharges of $4–$10 apply to trips after 6 pm. You'll always find taxis at the Blowing Point Ferry landing and at the airport. You'll need to call them to pick you up from hotels and restaurants, and arrange ahead with the driver who took you if you need a taxi late at night from one of the nightclubs or bars.

Taxi Contacts Airport Taxi Stand ☎ *264/235–3828.* **Blowing Point Ferry Taxi Stand** ☎ *264/497–6089.*

ESSENTIALS

Banks and Exchange Services Legal tender is the Eastern Caribbean (EC) dollar, but U.S. dollars are widely accepted. ATMs dispense both U.S. and EC dollars. All prices quoted in this chapter are in U.S. dollars.

Electricity 110 volts, just as in the United States; no adapter required for American electronics.

Emergencies As in the United States, dial 911 in any emergency.

Passport Requirements All visitors must carry a valid passport and have a return or ongoing ticket.

Phones Most hotels will arrange with a local provider for a cell phone to use during your stay (or you can rent one). A prepaid, local cell gives you the best rates. Some U.S. GSM phones will work in Anguilla, some not. To call Anguilla from the United States, dial 1 plus the area code 264, then the local seven-digit number. To call the United States and Canada, dial 1, the area code, and the seven-digit number.

Safety Anguilla is a quiet, relatively safe island, but crime has been on the rise, and there's no sense in tempting fate by leaving your valuables unattended in your hotel room, on the beach, or in your car. Avoid remote beaches, and lock your car, hotel room, and villa. Most hotel rooms are equipped with a safe for stashing your valuables.

Taxes The departure tax is $20 for adults and $10 for children, payable in cash, at the airport at Blowing Point Ferry Terminal. If you are staying in Anguilla but day-tripping to St. Martin, be sure to mention it, and the rate will be only $5. A 10% accommodations tax is added to hotel bills along with a $1-per-night marketing tax, plus whatever service charge the hotel adds.

Tipping Despite any service charge, it's usually expected that you will tip more—$5 per day for housekeeping, $20 for a helpful concierge, and $10 per day to beach attendants. Many restaurants include a service charge of 10% to 15% on the bill; if there's no surcharge, tip about 15%. Taxi drivers should receive 10% of the fare.

ACCOMMODATIONS

Anguilla is known for its luxurious resorts and villas, but there are also a few places that mere mortals can afford (and some that are downright bargains).

HOTEL AND RESTAURANT PRICES

Prices in the restaurant reviews are the average cost of a main course at dinner or, if dinner is not served, at lunch; taxes and service charges are generally included. Prices in the hotel reviews are the lowest cost of a standard double room in high season, excluding taxes, service charges, and meal plans (except at all-inclusives). Prices for rentals are the lowest per-night cost for a one-bedroom unit in high season.

VISITOR INFORMATION

Contacts Anguilla Tourist Office ⊠ *Coronation Ave., The Valley* ☎ *264/497–2759, 800/553–4939 from U.S.* ⊕ *www.anguilla-vacation.com.*

WEDDINGS

Weddings are common, but there's a huge $284 fee for a license.

EXPLORING ANGUILLA

Exploring on Anguilla is mostly about checking out the spectacular beaches and resorts. The island has only a few roads, but they have been improving significantly in recent years, and the lack of adequate signage is being addressed. Locals are happy to provide directions, but using the readily available tourist map is the best idea. Visit the Anguilla Tourist Board, centrally located on Coronation Avenue in The Valley.

The Anguilla Heritage Trail is a free, self-guided tour of 10 important historical sights that can be explored independently in any order. Wallblake House, in The Valley *(see* ➪ *Exploring Anguilla)*, is the main information center for the trail, or you can just look for the large boulders with descriptive plaques.

WHAT TO SEE

Bethel Methodist Church. Not far from Sandy Ground, this charming little church is an excellent example of skillful island stonework. It also has some colorful stained-glass windows. ⊠ *South Hill* ☎ *No phone.*

Heritage Museum Collection. Don't miss this remarkable opportunity to learn about Anguilla. Old photographs and local records and artifacts trace the island's history over four millennia, from the days of the Arawaks. The tiny museum (complete with gift shop) is painstakingly curated by Colville Petty. High points include the historical documents of the Anguilla Revolution and the albums of photographs chronicling island life, from devastating hurricanes to a visit from Queen Elizabeth in 1964. You can see examples of ancient pottery shards and stone tools along with fascinating photographs of the island in the early 20th century—many depicting the heaping and exporting of salt and the christening of schooners—and a complete set of beautiful postage stamps issued by Anguilla since 1967. ⊠ *East End at Pond Ground* ☎ *264/235-7440* ✉ *petty@anguillanet.com* 🖙 *$5* ⊙ *Mon.–Sat. 10–5.*

★ **Island Harbour.** Anguillians have been fishing for centuries in the brightly painted, simple, hand-crafted fishing boats that line the shore of the harbor. It's hard to believe, but skillful pilots take these little boats out to sea as far as 50 or 60 miles (80 or 100 km). Late afternoon is the best time to see the day's catch.■ TIP➔ Hail the free boat to Gorgeous Scilly Cay, a classic little restaurant offering sublime lobster and Eudoxie Wallace's knockout rum punches on Wednesday and Sunday. ⊠ *Island Harbor Rd.* ⊕ *www. scillycayanguilla.com.*

Old Factory. For many years the cotton grown on Anguilla and exported to England was ginned in this beautiful historic building, now home of the Anguilla Tourist Office. Some of the original ginning machinery is intact and on display. ⊠ *The Valley* ☎ *264/497–2759* ⊕ *www.old-factory-anguilla.ai* ▨ *Free* ☉ *Weekdays 10–noon and 1–4.*

Old Prison. The ruins of this historic jail on Anguilla's highest point—213 feet above sea level—offer outstanding views. ⊠ *Valley Rd. at Crocus Hill.*

Sandy Ground. Almost everyone who comes to Anguilla stops by this central beach, home to several popular open-air bars and restaurants, as well as boat-rental operations. You can also tour the Pyrat rum factory, also in Sandy Ground. Finally, this is where you catch the ferry for tiny Sandy Island, just 2 miles (3 km) offshore.

Wallblake House. The only surviving plantation house in Anguilla, Wallblake House was built in 1787 by Will Blake (Wallblake is probably a corruption of his name) and has recently been thoroughly and thoughtfully restored. The place is associated with many a tale involving murder, high living, and the French invasion in 1796. On the grounds are an ancient vaulted stone cistern and an outbuilding called the Bakery (which wasn't used for making bread at all but for baking turkeys and hams). Tours are usually offered three days a week, and you can only visit on a guided tour. It's also the information center for the Anguilla Heritage Tour. ⊠ *Wallblake Rd., The Valley* ☎ *264/497–6613* ⊕ *www. wallblake.ai* ▨ *Free* ☉ *Mon., Wed., and Fri. tours at 10 and 2.*

Warden's Place. This former sugar-plantation great house was built in the 1790s and is a fine example of island architecture. It now houses KoalKeel restaurant and a sumptuous bakery upstairs. But for many years it served as the residence of the island's chief administrator, who also doubled as the only medical practitioner. Across the street you can see the oldest dwelling on the island, originally built as slave housing. It's a stop on the Heritage Trail. ■ TIP➔ Go in the morning from 8 to 10 for breakfast, then tour the historic building. ⊠ *Coronation Ave., The Old Valley* ☎ *264/497–2930* ⊕ *www.koalkeel.com.*

WHERE TO EAT

Despite its small size, Anguilla has around 70 restaurants ranging from stylish temples of haute cuisine to classic, barefoot beachfront grills, roadside barbecue stands, food carts, and casual cafés. Many have breeze-swept terraces, where you can dine under the stars. Call ahead—in winter to make a reservation and in late summer and fall to confirm whether the place you've chosen is open. Anguillian restaurant meals are leisurely events, and service is often at a relaxed pace, so settle in and enjoy. Most restaurant owners are actively and conspicuously present, especially at dinner. It's a special treat to take the time to get to know them a bit when they stop by your table to make sure you are enjoying your meal.

What to Wear: During the day, casual clothes are widely accepted: shorts will be fine, but don't wear bathing suits and cover-ups unless you're at a beach bar. In the evening, shorts are okay at the extremely casual eateries. Elsewhere, women wear sundresses or nice casual slacks; men will be fine in short-sleeve shirts and casual pants. Some hotel restaurants are slightly more formal, but that just means long pants for men.

$$$$
AMERICAN
Fodor's Choice
★

✕ **Blanchard's.** This absolutely delightful restaurant, a mecca for foodies, is considered one of the best in the Caribbean. Proprietors Bob and Melinda Blanchard moved to Anguilla from Vermont in 1994 to fulfill their culinary dreams. A festive atmosphere pervades the handsome, airy white room, which is accented with floor-to-ceiling teal-blue shutters to let in the breezes, and colorful artwork by the Blanchards' son Jesse on the walls. A masterful combination of creative cuisine, an upscale atmosphere, attentive service, and an excellent wine cellar (including a selection of aged spirits) pleases the star-studded crowd. The nuanced contemporary menu is ever changing but always delightful; house classics like corn chowder, lobster and shrimp cakes, and a Caribbean sampler are crowd-pleasers, and vegetarians will find ample choices. For dessert, you'll remember concoctions like the key lime "pie-in-a-glass" or the justly famous "cracked coconut" long after your suntan has faded. A recent addition is a three-course prix-fixe menu that includes many of the signature dishes and is a bargain at $45. ⇨ *Blanchard's Beach Shack, on the beach next to the restaurant.* ⑤ *Average main: $49* ⊠ *Meads Bay* ☎ *264/497–6100* ⊕ *www.blanchardsrestaurant.com* ⚐ *Reservations essential* ⊗ *Closed Sun. Closed Mon. May–mid-Dec. No lunch.*

$
MODERN
AMERICAN
☾
★

✕ **Blanchards Beach Shack.** You'll find the perfect antidote to high restaurant prices right on the sands of Meads Bay Beach. Opened in late 2011 by, and located right beside, Blanchards, this chartreuse-and-turquoise cottage serves yummy lunches and dinners of lobster rolls, all-natural burgers, tacos, and terrific salads and sandwiches—you can dine at nearby picnic tables. Frozen drinks like mango coladas and icy mojitos please grown-ups, while kids dig into the fresh-made frozen yogurt concoctions. Organic produce, compostable paper goods, and happy smiles are always on offer. Lots of choices for kids and vegetarians, too. ■TIP➡ Diners are welcome to hang around on the beach. ⑤ *Average main: $20* ⊠ *Meads Bay* ☎ *264/498–6100.*

$$$ ✕ **da'Vida.** Sometimes you really can have it all. Right on exquisite
CARIBBEAN Crocus Bay, this beautifully designed resort-cum-restaurant-cum-club
☾ is a place where you could spend the whole day dining, drinking, and
lounging under umbrellas on the comfortable chairs. New in 2012 is
a beachside spa. Snorkeling equipment and kayaks are available for
rent, and there's even a boutique. You can picnic at the Beach Grill
(burgers, hot dogs, wraps, salads) or head inside the main building
for contemporary choices such as dumplings, soups, pastas, and piz-
zas. Lunch starts at 11, and you can get tapas and sunset drinks from
about 3. At dinner, the stylish wood interior (built by craftsmen from
St. Vincent) is accented by candlelight. On the menu are such dishes
as tasty seared snapper with gingered kale, coconut-crusted scallops,
and Angus steaks. Go for the music on weekend nights. Owners David
and Vida Lloyd, brother and sister, who also operate Lloyd's Guest
House, grew up right here, and they have taken pains to get it all just
right. ⑤ *Average main: $35* ⌧ *Crocus Bay* ☎ *264/498–5433* ⊕ *www.
davidaanguilla.com* ☾ *Closed Mon.*

$$$$ ✕ **Dolce Vita Italian Beach Restaurant & Bar.** Longtime visitors remember
ITALIAN proprietors Abbi and Christopher from previous stints at Caprice and
★ Luna Rosa. They now run their own restaurant, preparing serious Ital-
ian cuisine and providing warm and attentive service in a romantic
beachside pavillion in Sandy Ground. Fresh-made pasta stars in classic
lasagna, fettuccini bolognese, pappardelle with duck sauce, and a meat-
less eggplant parmigiana. A carniverous quartet can pre-order suckling
pig, or a sample first-quality chops and steaks. Italian wine fans will
discover new favorites from the cellar. What's for dessert? Limoncello
Cheese Cake! ⑤ *Average main: $32* ⌧ *Sandy Ground* ☎ *264/497–8668*
⊕ *www.dolcevitasandyground.com* ⌕ *Reservations essential* ☾ *Closed
Sun. No lunch Sat.*

$ ✕ **English Rose.** Lunchtime finds this neighborhood hangout packed with
CARIBBEAN locals: cops flirting with sassy waitresses, entrepreneurs brokering deals
with politicos, schoolgirls in lime-green outfits doing their homework.
The decor is not much to speak of, but this is a great place to eaves-
drop or people-watch while enjoying island-tinged specialties like beer-
battered shrimp, jerk-chicken Caesar salad, snapper creole, and buffalo
wings. There is karaoke on Friday. ⑤ *Average main: $12* ⌧ *Carter Rey
Blvd., The Valley* ☎ *264/497–5353.*

$$$ ✕ **Firefly Restaurant.** Set on a breezy poolside patio, Firefly—the res-
CARIBBEAN taurant at Anacaona Boutique Hotel—serves huge portions of tasty
☾ Caribbean fare by an Anguillian chef appropriately named "Fresh."
★ The pumpkin-coconut soup is a winner, as are preparations of local
snapper, mahimahi, and crayfish. Breakfast and Lunch are served also.
■ TIP→ For great value, and terrific fun, book a table at the Thursday night
buffet, with a lively performance by the folkloric theater company May-
oumba, or the Monday night three-course prix-fixe dinner with musical
entertainment by the Happy Hits. ⑤ *Average main: $26* ⌧ *Meads Bay*
☎ *264/497–6827* ⊕ *anacaonahotel.com.*

$ ✕ **Geraud's Patisserie.** A stunning array of absolutely delicious French
FRENCH pastries and breads—and universal favorites like cookies, brownies, and
muffins—are produced by Le Cordon Bleu dynamo Geraud Lavest in

this tiny, well-located shop. Come in the early morning for cappuccino and croissants, and pick up fixings for a wonderful lunch later (or choose from among the list of tempting daily lunch specials). The little shop carries a small selection of interesting condiments, teas, and gourmet goodies. During the high

season (December through May), there's a terrific Sunday brunch. Geraud also does a lively off-site catering business, from intimate villa and yacht dinners to weddings. $⑤ Average main: $13 ✉ South Hill Plaza ☎ 264/497–5559 ⊕ www.anguillacakesandcatering.com ⊘ Closed Mon. No dinner.

$$$$ ✕**Hibernia.** Some of the island's most creative dishes are served in this
ECLECTIC wood-beam cottage restaurant–art gallery overlooking the water at
Fodor's Choice the far eastern end of Anguilla. Unorthodox yet delectable culinary
★ pairings—inspired by chef-owners Raoul Rodriguez and Mary Pat's annual travels to the Far East (most recently Japan)— constantly bring new tastes and energy to the tables. The restaurant uses local organic products whenever possible. Long-line fish is served with a gratin of local pumpkin, shiitake mushrooms, and an essence of bitter oranges grown beside the front gate. Every visit here is an opportunity to share in Mary Pat and Raoul's passion for life, expressed through the vibrant combination of setting, art, food, unique tableware, beautiful gardens, and thoughtful hospitality. ■TIP➔ **Mary Pat stocks the tiny art gallery with amazing, and surprisingly reasonable, finds from her roaming around the globe.** $⑤ Average main: $41 ✉ Island Harbour ☎ 264/497–4290 ⊕ www.hiberniarestaurant.com ⊘ Closed mid-Aug.–mid-Oct. Call for seasonal hrs.

$$$ ✕**Jacala Beach Restaurant.** Right on beautiful Meads Bay, this restau-
FRENCH rant opened to raves in 2010. Alain the chef and Jacques the maître d'
★ (from Malliouhana) have joined forces, and the happy result is carefully prepared and nicely presented French food served with care in a lovely open-air restaurant, accompanied by good wines and a lot of personal attention. A delicious starter terrine of feta and grilled vegetables is infused with pesto. For an entrée, you must try hand-chopped steak tartare, or seared and marinated sushi-grade tuna on a bed of delightful mashed plantain. Lighter lunchtime options include a tart cucumber-yogurt soup garnished with piquant tomato sorbet. After lunch you can digest on the beach in one of the "Fatboy" loungers. In any case, save room for the chocolate *pot de crème.* $⑤ Average main: $25 ✉ Meads Bay ☎ 264/498–5888 ⊘ Closed Mon.–Tues. and Aug.–Sept.

$$$ ✕**KoalKeel.** Dinner at KoalKeel is a unique culinary and historic treat
CARIBBEAN not to be missed on Anguilla. Originally part of a sugar and cotton
Fodor's Choice plantation, the restaurant, with its beautiful dining verandah, is owned
★ and lovingly overseen by Lisa Gumbs, a descendant of the slaves once housed here. A tour of the history-rich buildings is a must. A 200-year-old rock oven is used in the bakery upstairs, and with a day's notice you can enjoy a slow-roasted whole chicken from that oven. New,

young chef Nick Dellinger concentrates on island produce and local fish. Try Island Pigeon-Pea soup, or spiny lobster salad with mango and grilled avocado. Be sure to save room for the incredible desserts. Wine lovers, take note of the exceptional 15,000-bottle wine cellar, in an underground cistern. Anguilla's savvy early risers show up here for the fresh French bread, croissants, and *pain au chocolat,* which are sold out by 9 am. The no-cell-phone rule means quiet conversations. ■TIP➜ At this writing there is a shuttle service between West End hotels and the restaurant, so you don't have to worry about drinking and driving. $ *Average main: $33* ⊠ *Coronation Ave., The Valley* 🕾 *264/497–2930* ⊕ *www.koalkeel.com* ⌕ *Reservations essential* ⊘ *Closed Mon.*

$$ ✕ **Madeariman Reef Bar and Restaurant.** This casual, feet-in-the-sand bis-
BRASSERIE tro right on busy, beautiful Shoal Bay is open for breakfast, lunch, and dinner; the soups, salads, and simple grills here are served in generous portions with a bit of French flair, and the pizza is cooked in a stone oven. Come for lunch and stay to lounge on the beach chaises ($20 for two includes umbrella) or barhop between here and Uncle Ernie's bar-becue next door. At night it feels like St. Barth. $ *Average main: $14* ⊠ *Shoal Bay East* 🕾 *264/497–5750.*

$$$$ ✕ **Mango's.** One meal at Mango's and you'll understand why it's a peren-
SEAFOOD nial favorite of repeat visitors to Anguilla. Sparkling-fresh fish specialties have starring roles on the menu here. Light and healthful choices include spicy grilled whole snapper, and Cruzan Rum barbecued chicken. Save room for dessert—the warm apple tart and the coconut cheesecake are worth the splurge. Come at lunch for sandwiches and burgers. There's an extensive wine list, and the Cuban cigar humidor is a luxurious touch. $ *Average main: $37* ⊠ *Barnes Bay* 🕾 *264/497–6479* ⊕ *www. mangosseasidegrill.com* ⌕ *Reservations essential* ⊘ *Closed Tues.*

$$ ✕ **Picante.** This casual, bright-red roadside Caribbean *taquería,* opened
MEXICAN by a young California couple, serves huge, tasty burritos with a choice
ℭ of fillings, fresh warm tortilla chips with first-rate guacamole, seafood enchiladas, and tequila-lime chicken grilled under a brick. Passion-fruit margaritas are a must, and the creamy Mexican chocolate pud-ding makes a great choice for dessert. Seating is at picnic tables; the friendly proprietors cheerfully supply pillows on request. Reservations are recommended. $ *Average main: $21* ⊠ *West End Rd., West End* 🕾 *264/498–1616* ⊕ *www.picante-restaurant-anguilla.com* ⊘ *Closed Tues. and Sept. and Oct. No lunch.*

$$$ ✕ **Roy's Bayside Grille.** Some of the best grilled lobster on the island is
CARIBBEAN served here, along with burgers, great fish-and-chips, and good home-
★ style cooking. On Friday there's a happy hour with a special menu. On Sunday you can get roast beef and Yorkshire pudding, and there's free Wi-Fi. $ *Average main: $25* ⊠ *Road Bay, Sandy Ground* 🕾 *264/497–2470* ⊕ *www.roysbaysidegrill.com* ⊘ *No lunch Mon.*

$ ✕ **SandBar.** Tasty, sharable small plates, great cocktails, a friendly vibe,
TAPAS and gorgeous sunsets add up to an Anguilla "must" on the beach at
★ Sandy Ground. Cool music combines with gentle prices, a hammock on the beach, and potent, inventive drinks—at Whisky's Rum Bar you can sample a flight of rums or mixed cocktails like the sea cooler, a mix of rum, cucumber juice, lime, mint, and sugar syrup. Inventive tapas

Straw Hat's outdoor patio on Forest Bay

are freshly made to order, with choices for any palate. The spicy fries are a favorite, as are the ginger beef wontons, salt-fish beignets with lemon-chive aioli, and a refreshing dish of watermelon, feta, and olives. Check them out on Facebook for specials. $ *Average main: $9* ✉ *Sandy Ground* ☎ *264/498–0171* ⊘ *Closed Sun. No lunch.*

$$ BARBECUE ☺ ★
✗ **Smokey's.** This quintessential Anguillian beach barbecue, part of the Gumbs family mini-empire of authentic and delicious eateries, is on pretty Cove Bay. On the beach, lounges with umbrellas welcome guests. Hot wings, honey-coated smoked ribs, curry goat, smoked chicken salad, and grilled lobsters are paired with local staple side dishes such as spiced-mayonnaise coleslaw, hand-cut sweet-potato strings, and crunchy onion rings. If your idea of the perfect summer lunch is a roadside lobster roll, be sure to try the version here, served on a home-baked roll with a hearty kick of hot sauce. The dinner menu includes lobster fritters, grilled tuna with lemon-caper butter, and rum chicken. On Saturday afternoon a popular local band enlivens the casual, laid-back atmosphere, and on Sunday the restaurant is party central for locals and visitors alike. $ *Average main: $25* ✉ *Cove Rd., Cove Bay* ☎ *264/497–6582* ⊕ *www.smokeysatthecove.com.*

$$$ ECLECTIC ☺ Fodor'sChoice ★
✗ **Straw Hat.** Since this Anguilla favorite moved to the beautiful sands of Meads Bay (at the Frangipani) its many fans now enjoy breakfast, lunch, and dinner on the tropical beachfront patio. Charming owners Peter and Anne Parles, the sophisticated and original food, and friendly service are the main reasons the restaurant has been in business since the late 1990s. The menu features appealing small plates like lobster spring rolls and clever "chips 'n fish," which diners can share or mix and match for the perfect meal. The curried goat here sets the bar for the

island. And "fish of the day" truly means fish caught that day. A terrific redesign in 2011 put big flat-screens with satellite TV in the bar—a fine place to catch the game or make some new friends. $ *Average main: $39* ⊠ *Frangipani Beach Club, Meads Bay* ☎ *264/497–8300* ⊕ *www. strawhat.com* ⌣ *Reservations essential* ⊙ *Closed Sept. and Oct.*

$$$ ✕ **Tasty's.** Once your eyes adjust to the quirky kiwi, lilac, and coral color
CARIBBEAN scheme, you'll find that breakfast, lunch, or dinner at Tasty's is, well, very tasty. It's open all day long, so if you come off a midafternoon plane starving, head directly here—it's right near the airport. Chef-owner Dale Carty trained at Malliouhana, and his careful, confident preparation bears the mark of French culinary training, but the menu is classic Caribbean. It's worth leaving the beach at lunch for the lobster salad here. A velvety pumpkin soup garnished with roasted coconut shards is superb, as are the seared jerk tuna and the garlic-infused marinated conch salad. Yummy desserts end meals on a high note. This is one of the few restaurants that do not allow smoking, so take your Cubans elsewhere for an after-dinner puff. The popular Sunday brunch buffet features island specialties like salt-fish cakes. $ *Average main: $26* ⊠ *Main Rd., South Hill Village, South Hill* ☎ *264/497–2737* ⊕ *www. tastysrestaurant.com/* ⌣ *Reservations essential.*

$$$ ✕ **Trattoria Tramonto and Oasis Beach Bar.** The island's only beachfront
ITALIAN Italian restaurant features a dual (or dueling) serenade of Andrea Bocelli
⟳ on the sound system and gently lapping waves a few feet away. Chef Valter Belli artfully adapts recipes from his home in Emilia-Romagna. Try the delicate lobster ravioli in truffle-cream sauce. For dessert, don't miss the tiramisu. Though you might wander in here for lunch after a swim, when casual dress is accepted, you'll still be treated to the same impressive menu. You can also choose from a luscious selection of champagne fruit drinks, a small but fairly priced Italian wine list, and homemade grappa. $ *Average main: $28* ⊠ *Shoal Bay West* ☎ *264/497–8819* ⊕ *www.trattoriatramonto.com* ⌣ *Reservations essential* ⊙ *Closed Mon. and Aug.–Oct.*

$$$$ ✕ **Veya.** On the suavely minimalist, draped, four-sided veranda, the
ECLECTIC stylishly appointed tables glow with flickering candlelight (in white-
Fodor'sChoice matte, sea urchin–shape votive holders made of porcelain). A lively
★ lounge where chic patrons mingle and sip mojitos to the purr of soft jazz anchors the room. Inventive, sophisticated, and downright delicious, Carrie Bogar's "Cuisine of the Sun" features thoughtful but ingenious preparations of first-rate provisions. Ample portions are sharable works of art—sample Moroccan-spiced shrimp "cigars" with roast tomato–apricot chutney or Vietnamese-spiced calamari. Jerk-spiced tuna is served with a rum-coffee glaze on a juicy slab of grilled pineapple with curls of plantain crisps, and crayfish in beurre blanc is beyond divine. Dessert is a must. Sublime warm chocolate cake with chili-roasted banana ice cream and caramelized bananas steals the show. Great music in the lounge invites after-dinner lingering. Downstairs is a café that serves breakfast and light lunches such as salads and panini, as well as delicious bakery goodies. It opens at 6:30 am for early risers. $ *Average main: $37* ⊠ *Sandy Ground* ☎ *264/498–8392* ⊕ *www.veya-axa.com* ⌣ *Reservations essential* ⊙ *Closed Sun., Aug., and weekends June–Oct.*

$$$
ECLECTIC

× Zara's. Chef Shamash Brooks presides at this cozy restaurant with beamed ceilings, terra-cotta floors, and colorful artwork. His kitchen turns out tasty fare that combines Caribbean and Italian flavors with panache (Rasta Pasta is a specialty). Standouts include a velvety pumpkin soup with coconut milk, crunchy calamari, lemon pasta scented with garlic, herbed rack of lamb served with a roasted applesauce, and spicy fish fillet steamed in banana leaf. ⑤ *Average main: $25* ⊠ *Allamanda Beach Club, Upper Shoal Bay* ☎ *264/497–3229* ⊘ *No lunch.*

WHERE TO STAY

Tourism on Anguilla is a fairly recent phenomenon—most development didn't begin until the early 1980s, so most hotels and resorts are of relatively recent vintage. The lack of native topography and, indeed, vegetation, and the blindingly white expanses of beach have inspired building designs of some interest; architecture buffs might have fun trying to name some of the most surprising examples. Inspiration largely comes from the Mediterranean: the Greek Islands, Morocco, and Spain, with some Miami-style art deco thrown into the mixture.

Anguilla accommodations basically fall into two categories: grand resorts and luxury resort-villas, or low-key, simple, locally owned inns and small beachfront complexes. The former can be surprisingly expensive, the latter surprisingly reasonable. In the middle are some condo-type options, with full kitchens and multiple bedrooms, which are great for families or for longer stays. Private villa rentals are becoming more common and are increasing in number and quality every season as development on the island accelerates.

A good phone chat or email exchange with the management of any property is a good idea, as units within the same complex can vary greatly in layout, accessibility, distance to the beach, and view. When calling to reserve a room, ask about special discount packages, especially in spring and summer. Most hotels include continental breakfast in the price, and many have meal-plan options. But keep in mind that Anguilla is home to dozens of excellent restaurants before you lock yourself into an expensive meal plan that you may not be able to change. All hotels charge a 10% tax, a $1 per room/per day tourism marketing levy, and—in most cases—an additional 10% service charge. A few properties include these charges in the published rates, so check carefully when you are evaluating prices.

For expanded reviews, facilities, and current deals, visit Fodors.com.

PRIVATE VILLAS AND CONDOS

The tourist office publishes an annual *Anguilla Travel Planner* with informative listings of available vacation apartment rentals.

2

Anguilla Luxury Collection. Anguilla Luxury Collection is operated by Sue and Robin Ricketts, longtime Anguilla real estate experts, who manage a collection of first-rate villas. They also manage a range of attractive properties in the Anguilla Affordable Collection linked through the same Web site. ☎ 264/497–6049 ⊕ *www.anguillaluxurycollection.com.*

Ani Villas. Two stunning cliffside villas for up to 24 guests, offer breathtaking views and total luxury to families or groups looking for total pampering. Included in the rental rate comes private boat transfers from St. Martin, rental car, a full service team: concierge, butler, chef, housekeepers, breakfasts, dinner chef service, and all beverages. Tennis pros, spa services, trainers and guides are all available on demand. There is room for 100 guests for a party or a wedding; and a dramatic and romantic promontory for the ceremony. A tennis court, bikes, fitness room, pool, cliffside hot-tubs, and playrooms mean that except for beach going, you never have to leave. Check for promotions that include unlimited golf at the Cuisinart Golf Course. ☎ 264/497–7888 ⊕ *www.anivillas.com.*

myCaribbean. myCaribbean is the largest local private villa-rental company. Gayle Gurvey and her staff manage and rent more than 100 local villas, and have been in business since 2000. ☎ 877/392–0828 ⊕ *www. mycaribbean.com.*

RECOMMENDED HOTELS AND RESORTS

$
RENTAL

Allamanda Beach Club. Youthful, active couples from around the globe happily fill this casual, three-story, white-stucco building hidden in a palm grove just off the beach, opting for location and price over luxury. **Pros:** front row for all Shoal Bay's action; young crowd; good restaurant. **Cons:** location requires a car; rooms are clean, but not at all fancy. **TripAdvisor:** "peaceful and serene," "very friendly," "simple and delightful." ⑤ *Rooms from: $170* ⊠ *The Valley* ☎ 264/497–5217 ⊕ *www.allamanda.ai* ↝ *20 units* ⊙ *No meals.*

$$$
HOTEL

Anacaona. Veteran Anguilla hoteliers Sue and Robin Ricketts run this low-key resort (its name is pronounced "an-nah-cah-*oh*-na") overlooking Meads Bay, having created an affordable yet chic hideaway imbued with the culture and traditions of the island. **Pros:** friendly clientele, sensitive to local culture; modern, clean, and good value; nice high-tech amenities. **Cons:** bit of a walk to beach; smallish rooms. **TripAdvisor:** "access to a perfect beach," "warm staff," "tranquility on Paradise Island." ⑤ *Rooms from: $250* ⊠ *Meads Bay* ☎ 264/497–6827, 877/647–4736 ⊕ *www.anacaonahotel.com* ↝ *27 rooms* ⊙ *Multiple meal plans.*

$$
HOTEL

Anguilla Great House Beach Resort. These traditional West Indian—style bungalows strung along one of Anguilla's longest beaches are old-school Caribbean, and the gentle prices and interconnected rooms appeal to families and groups of friends traveling together. **Pros:** real, old-school Caribbean; right on the gorgeous beach, young crowd; gentle prices. **Cons:** rooms are very simple, and bathrooms are the bare basics. **TripAdvisor:** "the best beach in the Caribbean," "a friendly place to stay," "relaxed and fun." ⑤ *Rooms from: $210* ⊠ *Rendezvous Bay* ☎ 264/497–6061, 800/583–9247 ⊕ *www.anguillagreathouse.com* ↝ *31 rooms* ⊙ *No meals.*

CuisinArt Resort and Spa, Rendezvous Bay

$$
B&B/INN
Arawak Beach Inn. These hexagonal two-story villas are a good choice for a funky, budget-friendly, low-key guesthouse experience. **Pros:** funky, casual crowd; friendly owners; gentle rates. **Cons:** not on the beach; isolated location makes a car a must. **TripAdvisor:** "delightful informality," "caters to all needs," "extremely friendly." ⑤ *Rooms from: $165* ✉ *The Valley, Island Harbour* ☎ *264/497–4888, 877/427–2925 reservations* ⊕ *www.arawakbeach.com* ➴ *17 rooms* ⦿ *Multiple meal plans.*

$$$$
RESORT
☾
Cap Juluca. Sybaritic and serene, this 179-acre resort wraps around breathtaking Maundays Bay. **Pros:** lots of space to stretch out on miles of talcum-soft sand; warm service; romantic atmosphere; all on-site water sports are included, even waterskiing. **Cons:** bathrooms need updating. **TripAdvisor:** "ultimate relaxation," "best beach," "dream place." ⑤ *Rooms from: $995* ✉ *Maundays Bay* ☎ *264/497–6779, 888/858–5822 in U.S.* ⊕ *www.capjuluca.com* ➴ *72 rooms, 7 patio suites, 6 pool villas* ⦿ *Multiple meal plans.*

$$$$
RENTAL
Carimar Beach Club. This horseshoe of bougainvillea-draped Mediterranean-style buildings on beautiful Meads Bay has the look of a Sun Belt condo. **Pros:** tennis courts; easy walk to restaurants and spa; great beach location; laundry facilities. **Cons:** no pool or restaurant; only bedrooms have a/c. **TripAdvisor:** "tranquil paradise," "phenomenal staff," "perfect apartment and beach." ⑤ *Rooms from: $425* ✉ *Meads Bay* ☎ *264/497–6881, 866/270–3764* ⊕ *www.carimar.com* ➴ *24 apartments* ⊘ *Closed Sept.–Oct. 15* ⦿ *No meals.*

$$$$
RENTAL
Covecastles Villa Resort. Though this secluded Myron Goldfinger–designed enclave resembles a series of giant concrete baby carriages from the outside, the airy curves and angles of the skylighted interiors

are comfortable, if a little dated, with the sort of oversize wicker furniture and raw-silk accessories that defined resort-chic in the late 1980s. **Pros:** secluded, large, private villas; private beach with reef for snorkeling; great service. **Cons:** beach is small and rocky; located at the far end of the island; redecoration is a bit overdue. **TripAdvisor:** "beautiful beach and privacy," "warm caring staff," "a little piece of heaven." $ *Rooms from: $895* ⊠ *Shoal Bay West* ☎ *264/497–6801, 800/223–1108* ⊕ *www.covecastles.com* ⇨ *16 apartments* ⦿| *No meals.*

$$$$
RESORT
☺
Fodor's Choice
★

⌂ **CuisinArt Golf Resort and Spa.** This family-friendly beachfront resort's design—gleaming white-stucco buildings, blue domes and trim, glass-block walls—blends art deco with a Greek Islands feel. **Pros:** family-friendly; great spa and sports; gorgeous beach and gardens. **Cons:** food service can be slow; pool area is noisy. **TripAdvisor:** "amazing views," "as good as it gets," "fantastic food." $ *Rooms from: $800* ⊠ *Rendezvous Bay* ☎ *264/498–2000, 800/943–3210* ⊕ *www.cuisinartresort.com* ⇨ *93 rooms, 2 penthouses, 6 villas* ⦿ *Closed Sept. and Oct.* ⦿| *Multiple meal plans.*

$$$
RESORT

⌂ **Frangipani Beach Club.** This flamingo-pink Mediterranean-style property perches on the beautiful champagne sands of Meads Bay. **Pros:** great beach; good location for restaurants and resort-hopping; first-rate on-site restaurant; helpful staff. **Cons:** some rooms have no view, so be sure to ask. **TripAdvisor:** "romantic and peaceful," "relaxing in paradise," "gorgeous property with warm hospitality." $ *Rooms from: $395* ⊠ *Meads Bay* ☎ *264/497–6442, 877/593–8988* ⊕ *www.frangipaniresort.com* ⇨ *18 rooms, 7 suites* ⦿ *Closed Sept. and Oct.* ⦿| *No meals.*

$$
RENTAL
☺
★

⌂ **Indigo Reef.** If you are looking for the antidote to the big resort developments on the island but still want attractive, modern, private villa accommodations close to the restaurants, resorts, and beautiful beaches of West End, this intimate enclave of eight small villas (with one to four bedrooms) nestled at the tip of the island could be just the thing. **Pros:** cozy, fresh, and well designed; great for groups traveling together; far from the madding crowd but still on the West End. **Cons:** the beach here is rocky and the water's rough; a/c only in bedrooms; must have car. **TripAdvisor:** "affordable paradise," "ideal spot in an amazing location," "beautiful and charming." $ *Rooms from: $285* ⊠ *Indigo Reef, West End* ☎ *264/497–6144* ⊕ *www.indigoreef.com* ⇨ *8 villas* ⦿| *No meals.*

$$$$
RENTAL
☺
★

⌂ **Sheriva Villa Hotel.** This intimate, luxury-villa hotel comprises three cavernous private villas containing a total of 20 guest rooms and seven private swimming pools overlooking a broad swath of turquoise sea. **Pros:** incredible staff to fulfill every wish; all the comforts of home and more; good value for large family groups. **Cons:** not on the beach; you risk being spoiled for life by the staff's attentions. **TripAdvisor:** "absolute perfection," "quick stopover in paradise," "caters to its higher end clientele." $ *Rooms from: $1,500* ⊠ *Maundays Bay Rd., West End* ☎ *264/498–9898* ⊕ *www.sheriva.com* ⇨ *20* ⦿| *Multiple meal plans.*

$$$
RENTAL
☺
★

⌂ **Paradise Cove.** This simple complex of reasonably priced one- and two-bedroom apartments compensates for its location away from the beach with two whirlpools, a large pool, and tranquil tropical gardens where you can pluck fresh guavas for breakfast. **Pros:** reasonable rates;

Viceroy Anguilla, Meads Bay.

great pool; lovely gardens. **Cons:** a bit far from the beach; decor is bland. **TripAdvisor:** "a tranquil paradise," "top notch customer service," "very comfortable." ⑤ *Rooms from: $320* ⊠ *The Cove* ☎ *264/497–6959, 264/497–6603* ⊕ *www.paradise.ai* ⤳ *12 studio suites, 17 1- and 2-bedroom apartments* ❢⊙❢ *No meals.*

$$ ⚄ **Serenity Cottages.** Despite the name of this property, it comprises not
RENTAL cottages but rather large, fully equipped, and relatively affordable one-
☾ and two-bedroom apartments (and studios created from lockouts) in a
★ small complex set in a lush garden at the farthest end of glorious Shoal Bay Beach. **Pros:** big apartments; quiet end of beach; snorkeling right outside the door; very reasonable rates for weeklong packages. **Cons:** no pool; more condo than hotel in terms of staff; location at the end of Shoal Bay pretty much requires a car and some extra time to drive to the West End. ⑤ *Rooms from: $325* ⊠ *Shoal Bay East* ☎ *264/497–3328* ⊕ *www.serenity.ai* ⤳ *2 1-bedroom suites, 8 2-bedroom apartments* ⊘ *Closed Sept.* ❢⊙❢ *No meals.*

$$$ ⚄ **Shoal Bay Villas.** Some recent redecorating, and the addition of air-
RENTAL conditioning in the rooms, has spiffed up this old-style property well
☾ located right on Shoal Bay's incredible 2-mile beach. **Pros:** friendly; casual; full kitchens; beachfront. **Cons:** not fancy; at this writing, construction is under way for a new building. **TripAdvisor:** "perfect beach," "great little hideaway," "a modest paradise." ⑤ *Rooms from: $370* ⊠ *Shoal Bay* ☎ *264/497–2051* ⊕ *sbvillas.ai* ⤳ *12 units* ❢⊙❢ *No meals.*

$$$ ⚄ **Turtle's Nest Beach Resort.** This collection of studios and one- to three-
RENTAL bedroom oceanfront condos is right on Meads Bay beach, with some of
☾ the island's best restaurants a sandy stroll away. **Pros:** beachfront; huge apartments; well-kept grounds and pool. **Cons:** no elevator. **TripAdvisor:**

"spacious condo," "breathtaking beautiful views," "beyond our expectations." ⑤ *Rooms from: $340* ⊠ *Meads Bay* ☎ *264/462–6378* ⊕ *www. turtlesnestbeachresort.com* ⟿ *29 units* ⫶◎⫶ *No meals.*

$$$$
RESORT
☾
Fodor's Choice
★

🏨 **The Viceroy.** On a promontory over 3,200 feet of the gorgeous pearly sand on Meads Bay, Kelly Wurstler's haute-hip showpiece will wow the chic international-sophisticate set, especially those lucky enough to stay in one of the spacious two- to five-bedroom villas, complete with private infinity pools and hot tubs, indoor-outdoor showers, electronics galore, and a gourmet professional kitchen stuffed with high-end equipment, not to mention a house manager to keep it all running smoothly. **Pros:** state-of-the-art luxury; cutting-edge contemporary design; flexible, spacious rooms. **Cons:** international rather than Caribbean in feel; very large resort; kind of a see-and-be-seen scene. **TripAdvisor:** "elegance and comfort," "indescribable experience," "stunning property." ⑤ *Rooms from: $795* ⊠ *Barnes Bay, West End* ☎ *264/497–7000, 866/270–7798 in U.S.* ⊕ *www.viceroyhotelsandresorts.com* ⟿ *163 suites, 3 villas* ⊘ *Closed Sept.* ⫶◎⫶ *Breakfast.*

NIGHTLIFE

In late February or early March, reggae star and impresario Bankie Banx stages Moonsplash, a three-day music festival that showcases local and imported talent around the nights of the full moon. At the end of July is the International Arts Festival, which hosts artists from around the world. BET (Black Entertainment Television) sponsors the Tranquility Jazz Festival in November, attracting major musicians such as Michel Camilo, James Moody, Bobby Watson, and Dee Dee Bridgewater.

Most hotels and many restaurants offer live entertainment in high season and on weekends, ranging from pianists and jazz combos to traditional steel and calypso bands. Check the local tourist magazines and newspaper for listings. Friday and Saturday, Sandy Ground is the hot spot; Wednesday and Sunday the action shifts to Shoal Bay East.

The nightlife scene here runs late into the night—the action doesn't really start until after 11 pm. If you do not rent a car, be aware that taxis are not readily available at night. If you plan to take a taxi back to your hotel or villa at the end of the night, be sure to make arrangements in advance with the driver who brings you or with your hotel concierge.

Dune Preserve. The funky Dune Preserve is the driftwood-fabricated home of Bankie Banx, Anguilla's famous reggae star. He performs here weekends and during the full moon. There's a dance floor and a beach bar, and sometimes you can find a sunset beach barbecue in progress. In high season there's a $15 cover charge. ⊠ *Rendezvous Bay* ☎ *264/497– 6219* ⊕ *www.bankiebanx.net.*

Fodor's Choice
★

Elvis' Beach Bar. This is the perfect locale (it's actually a boat) to hear great music and sip the best rum punch on earth. The bar is open every day but Tuesday, and there's live music on Wednesday through Sunday nights during the high season—as well as food until 1 am. Check to see if there's a full-moon LunaSea party. You won't be disappointed. ⊠ *Sandy Ground* ☎ *264/772–0637* ⊕ *www.elvisbeachbar.net.*

★ **Johnno's Beach Stop.** Things are lively at Johnno's, where there is live music and alfresco dancing every night and on Sunday afternoon, when just about everybody drops by. This is *the* classic Caribbean beach bar, attracting a funky eclectic mix, from locals to movie stars. It's open Tuesday–Sunday from 11 to 9. ⊠ *Sandy Ground* ☎ *264/497–2728.*

★ **Pumphouse.** At the Pumphouse, in the old rock-salt factory, you can find live music most nights—plus surprisingly good pub grub, and a mini-museum of artifacts and equipment from 19th-century salt factories. There's calypso-soca on Thursday; it's open from noon until 3 am daily, except Sunday. ⊠ *Sandy Ground* ☎ *264/497–5154* ⊕ *www. pumphouse-anguilla.com.*

SHOPPING

Anguilla is by no means a shopping destination. In fact, if your suitcase is lost, you will be hard-pressed to secure even the basics on-island. If you're a hard-core shopping enthusiast, a day trip to nearby St. Martin will satisfy. Well-heeled visitors sometimes organize boat or plane charters through their hotel concierge for daylong shopping excursions to St. Barth, and Anguilla Air Services started a reasonably priced daily round-trip to St. Barth in 2012. The island's tourist publication, *What We Do in Anguilla,* has shopping tips and is available free at the airport and in shops. Pyrat rums—golden elixirs blending up to nine aged and flavored spirits—are a local specialty available at the Anguilla Rums distillery and several local shops. For upscale designer sportswear, check out the small boutiques in hotels (some are branches of larger stores in Marigot on St. Martin). Outstanding local artists sell their work in galleries, which often arrange studio tours (you can also check with the Anguilla Tourist Office).

Anguilla Arts and Crafts Center. This gallery carries island crafts, including textiles and ceramics. Of particular interest are unique ceramics by Otavia Fleming, lovely spotted-glaze items with adorable lizards climbing on them. Look for special exhibits and performances—ranging from puppetry to folk dance—sponsored by the Anguilla National Creative Arts Alliance. ⊠ *Brooks Building, The Valley* ☎ *264/497–2200.*

Cheddie's Carving Studios. Cheddie's showcases Cheddie Richardson's fanciful wood carvings and coral and stone sculptures. ⊠ *West End Rd., The Cove* ☎ *264/497–6027* ⊕ *www.cheddieonline.com.*

Devonish Art Gallery. This gallery purveys the wood, stone, and clay creations of Courtney Devonish, an internationally known potter and sculptor, plus creations by his wife, Carolle, a bead artist. Also available are works by other Caribbean artists and regional antique maps. ⊠ *West End Rd., George Hill* ☎ *264/497–2949.*

★ **Hibernia Restaurant and Gallery.** Hibernia has striking pieces culled from the owners' travels, from contemporary Eastern European artworks to traditional Indo-Chinese crafts. ⊠ *Island Harbour* ☎ *264/497–4290.*

★ **Savannah Gallery.** Here you'll find works by local Anguillian artists as well as other Caribbean and Central American art, including oil paintings by Marge Morani. You'll also find works by artists of the renowned

Haitian St. Soleil school, as well as Guatemalan textiles, Mexican pottery, and brightly painted metalwork. ⊠ *Coronation St., Lower Valley* ☎ *264/497–2263* ⊕ *www.savannahgallery.com.*

★ **The Galleria at World Art and Antiques.** The peripatetic proprietors of World Arts, Nik and Christy Douglas, display a veritable United Nations of antiquities: exquisite Indonesian ikat hangings to Thai teak furnishings, Aboriginal didgeridoos to Dogon tribal masks, Yuan Dynasty jade pottery to Uzbeki rugs. There is also handcrafted jewelry and handbags. ⊠ *Cove Rd., West End* ☎ *264/497–5950, 264/497–2767.*

ZaZaa. Sue Ricketts, the first lady of Anguilla marketing, owns ZaZaa boutiques in South Hill on the Main Road, and at Anacaona Resort, on Meads Bay. Buy Anguillian crafts as well as wonderful ethnic jewelry and beachwear from around the globe, such as sexy Brazilian bikinis and chic St. Barth goodies. There are beach sundries and souvenirs as well. ⊠ *Lower South Hill, West End Rd, South Hill* ☎ *264/235–8878* ⊕ *www.anguillaluxurycollection.com.*

SPORTS AND ACTIVITIES

Anguilla's expanding sports options are enhanced by its beautiful first golf course, designed by Greg Norman to accentuate the natural terrain and maximize the stunning ocean views over Rendezvous Bay. Players say the par-72, Troon-managed course is reminiscent of Pebble Beach. Personal experience says bring a lot of golf balls! The Anguilla Tennis Academy, designed by noted architect Myron Goldfinger, operates in the Blowing Point area. The 1,000-seat stadium, equipped with pro shop and seven lighted courts, was created to attract major international matches and to provide a first-class playing option for tourists and locals.

BOATING AND SAILING

Anguilla is the perfect place to try all kinds of water sports. The major resorts offer complimentary Windsurfers, paddleboats, and water skis to their guests.

Sandy Island Enterprises. If your hotel lacks facilities, you can get in gear at Sandy Island Enterprises, which rents Sunfish and Windsurfers and arranges fishing charters. ⊠ *Sandy Ground* ☎ *264/476–6534* ⊕ *www. mysandyisland.com.*

DIVING

Sunken wrecks; a long barrier reef; terrain encompassing walls, canyons, and hulking boulders; varied marine life, including greenback turtles and nurse sharks; and exceptionally clear water—all of these make for excellent diving. Prickly Pear Cay is a favorite spot. **Stoney Bay Marine Park,** off the northeast end of Anguilla, showcases the late-18th-century *El Buen Consejo,* a 960-ton Spanish galleon that sank here in 1772. Other good dive sites include **Grouper Bowl,** with exceptional

A Day at the Boat Races

If you want a different kind of trip to Anguilla, try for a visit during Carnival, which starts on the first Monday in August and continues for about 10 days. Colorful parades, beauty pageants, music, delicious food, arts-and-crafts shows, fireworks, and nonstop partying are just the beginning. The music starts at sunrise jam sessions—as early as 4 am—and continues well into the night. The high point? The boat races. They are the national passion and the official national sport of Anguilla.

Anguillians from around the world return home to race old-fashioned, made-on-the-island wooden boats that have been in use on the island since the early 1800s. Similar to some of today's fastest sailboats, these are 15 to 28 feet in length and sport only a mainsail and jib on a single 25-foot mast. The sailboats have no deck, so heavy bags of sand, boulders, and sometimes even people are used as ballast. As the boats reach the finish line, the ballast—including some of the sailors—gets thrown into the water in a furious effort to win the race. Spectators line the beaches and follow the boats on foot, by car, and from even more boats. You'll have almost as much fun watching the fans as the races.

hard-coral formations; **Ram's Head,** with caves, chutes, and tunnels; and **Upper Flats,** where you are sure to see stingrays.

Anguillian Divers. This is a full-service dive operator with a PADI five-star training center. The five-dive packages are a good deal, and they offer open-water certifications, too. ⊠ *Meads Bay* ☎ *264/497–4750* ⊕ *www. anguilliandiver.com.*

Shoal Bay Scuba and Watersports. Single-tank dives start at $50 and two-tank dives at $90 at this shop in beautiful Shoal Bay. They run up to five different dives daily. Daily snorkeling trips at 1 pm are $25 per person. ⊠ *Shoal Bay East Beach, Shoal Bay* ☎ *264/497–4371* ⊕ *www. shoalbayscuba.com.*

GOLF

CuisinArt Golf Club. This 7,200-yard, $50 million wonder designed by superstar Greg Norman has 13 of its 18 holes directly on the water. The course features sweeping sea vistas and an ecologically responsible watering system of ponds and lagoons that snake through the grounds. Players thrill to the spectacular vistas of St. Maarten and blue sea at the tee box of the 390-yard starting hole. Pro Ryan Bowey runs teaching clinics and programs to suit every player, and experienced golfers love the state-of-the-art equipment. The greens fee for 18 holes during peak times is $225 (less if you are a CuisinArt guest). There is a gorgeous Italian restaurant for lunch. ■ TIP→ Appropriate dress is required, including long shorts or slacks and a collared shirt. ⊠ *Long Bay* ☎ *264/498–5602* ⊕ *www.cuisinartresort.com.*

GUIDED TOURS

A round-the-island tour by taxi takes about 2½ hours and costs $55 for one or two people, $5 for each additional passenger.

Anguilla Tourist Office. Contact the Anguilla Tourist Office to arrange the tour by Sir Emile Gumbs, the island's former chief minister, of the Sandy Ground area. This tour, which highlights historic and ecological sites, is on Tuesday at 10 am. The $20 fee benefits the Anguilla Archaeological Historical Society. Gumbs also organizes bird-watching expeditions that show you everything from frigate birds to turtledoves. ⊠ *Coronation Ave., The Valley* ☎ *264/497–2759, 800/553–4939* ⊕ *ivisitanguilla.com.*

Bennie's Travel & Tours. This is one of the island's more reliable tour operators. ⊠ *Blowing Point* ☎ *264/497–2788.*

Malliouhana Travel and Tours. Malliouhana Travel and Tours will create personalized package tours of the island. ⊠ *Albert Lake Dr., The Quarter* ☎ *264/497–2431* ⊕ *www.malliouhanatravel.com/.*

HORSEBACK RIDING

Seaside Stables. Seaside Stables, located in Cove Bay, offers rides and instruction, if a sunset gallop (or slow clomp) has always been your fantasy. Private rides at any time of the day are about $85, group rides in the morning or afternoon are $70; or try a full-moon ride for $90; prior riding experience is not required. Choose from English, Western, or Australian saddles. ⊠ *Paradise Dr., Cove Bay* ☎ *264/497–3667* ⊕ *www.seaside-stables-anguilla.com.*

SEA EXCURSIONS

A number of boating options are available for airport transfers, day trips to offshore cays or neighboring islands, night trips to St. Martin, or just whipping through the waves en route to a picnic spot.

Chocolat. This 35-foot catamaran available for private charter or scheduled excursions to nearby cays. Captain Rollins is a knowledgeable, affable guide. Rates for day sails with lunch (prepared by the captain's wife, Jacquie, of Ripples Restaurant) are about $80 per person. ⊠ *Sandy Ground* ☎ *264/497–3394.*

Funtime Charters. This charter and shuttle service operates five power-boats ranging in size from 32 to 38 feet. They will arrange private boat transport to the airport ($65 per person), day trips to St. Barth, or other boat excursions. ⊠ *The Cove* ☎ *264/497–6511, 866/334–0047* ⊕ *www.funtime-charters.com.*

Junior's Glass Bottom Boat. For an underwater peek without getting wet, catch a ride ($20 per person) on Junior's Glass Bottom Boat. Snorkeling trips and instruction are available, too. Just show up at Shoal Bay Beach and look for the boat or ask for Junior at the Dive Shop. ⊠ *Sandy Ground* ☎ *264/497–4456* ⊕ *www.junior.ai.*

No Fear Sea Tours. In addition to private airport transportation, day snorkeling trips, sunset cruises, and fishing trips on three 32-foot speedboats and a 19-foot ski boat, this charter service offers water-sports rentals (tubing, skiing, knee-boarding). ⊠ *The Cove* ☎ *264/235–6354* ⊕ *www. nofearseatours.com.*

Sandy Island Enterprises. Picnic, swimming, and diving excursions to Prickly Pear Cay, Sandy Island, and Scilly Cay are available through Sandy Island Enterprises. Fans of TV's *The Bachelor* might recall the Valentine's Day picnic date in 2011. You, too, can enjoy rum punch and lobster here. The Sandy Island sea shuttle leaves from the small pier in Sandy Ground daily November–July, and by reservation August–October. ⊠ *The Valley* ☎ *264/476–6534* ⊕ *mysandyisland.com.*

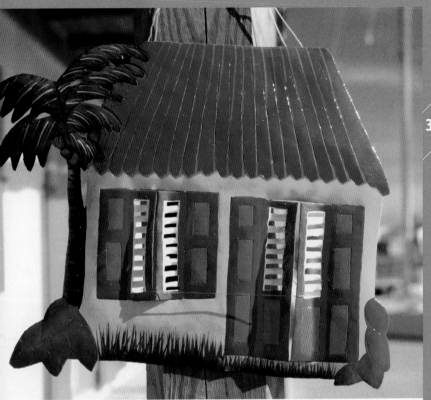

Antigua and Barbuda

WORD OF MOUTH

"Check out the historic Nelson's Dockyard. It's very unique. They have so much to see there, including the Copper and Lumber store, which they converted into a hotel and restaurant. It has that beautiful Georgian architecture with an arched courtyard where you just step back in time."

—Knowing

WELCOME TO ANTIGUA AND BARBUDA

KEY

- ⚓ Beaches
- 🚢 Cruise Ship Terminal
- 🔺 Dive Sites
- **1** Restaurants
- **1** Hotels

0 — 2 mi
0 — 2 km

Barbuda
see detail
map

Boon Pt.
Hodges Bay
Prickly Pear Island
Beggar's Pt.
Long Island

15 Cedar Grove
8
6 **7**

9 **16** – **19**

Dickenson Bay
Runaway Beach
10

Deepwater Harbour
11

Andes

St. John's
1 **2**

Five Islands
20
21

Potters

V.C. Bird International Airport

Parham

Parham
Rd.

Hawksbill's Beaches

Fullerton Pt.
Five Islands Harbour

Pearns Pt.
1

Jennings

Pares

Betty's Hope

Jolly Harbour
2
3
3 **4**

Bolans

Megaliths of Greencastle Hill

Boggy Peak

All Saints

Darkwood Beach

Johnson's Point
Johnson's Point

Urlings

Fig Tree Drive
Fig Tree Drive

Ft. George

🔺 Cades Reef

Old Road
5 **6** **4**

Carlisle Bay

Pigeon Point
Rendezvous Bay

Falmouth
Falmouth Bay

7 Nelson's Dockyard
English Harbo.

9 **10**
8
5
Shirley Heights

Excellent beaches—365 of them—might make you think that the island has never busied itself with anything more pressing than the pursuit of pleasure. But for much of the 18th and 19th centuries English Harbour sheltered Britain's Caribbean fleet. These days, pleasure yachts bob where galleons once anchored.

ANTIGUA AND BARBUDA BEACHES

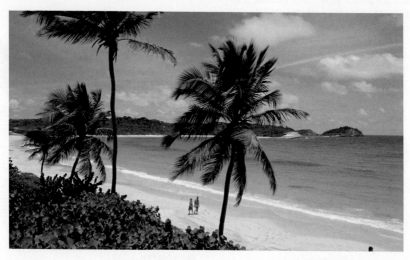

Antigua and Barbuda proudly offer 365 beaches, one for every day of the year. And you could probably spend a year beach-hopping their beautiful shores—some lined with bars and sports concessions and some virtually deserted.

(Above) Half Moon Bay
(Bottom right) Darkwood
Beach (Top right) Jet-skiing in
Dickenson Bay

Antigua's beaches are public, and many are lined with resorts that have water-sports outfitters and beach bars. The government does a fairly good job of cleaning up seaweed and garbage. Most restaurants and bars on beaches won't charge for beach-chair rentals if you buy lunch or drinks; otherwise the going rate is $3 to $5. Access to some of the finest stretches, such as those at the Five Islands Peninsula resorts, is restricted to hotel guests (though, often, if you're polite, the guards will let you through). Sunbathing topless is strictly illegal except on one small beach at Hawksbill by Rex Resorts. When cruise ships dock in St. John's, buses drop off loads of passengers on most of the west-coast beaches. Choose such a time to visit one of the more remote east-end beaches or take a day trip to Barbuda.

EASY, BREEZY

Most Antiguan beaches feature talcum-powdery sand right out of a brochure. Those on the windward side, such as Dutchman's Bay in the north, and Nonsuch, Long, and Half Moon bays to the east, receive brisk breezes, making them favorites of windsurfers and boarders. Blissfully undeveloped Barbuda seems like one big beach; indeed, sand exceeds lobster as its primary export.

3

ANTIGUA

Darkwood Beach. This ½-mile (1-km) beige ribbon on the southwest coast has stunning views of Montserrat. Although popular with locals and cruise-ship passengers on weekends, it's virtually deserted during the week. Waters are generally calm, but there's scant shade, no development other than Darkwood Beach Bar (and Admiral's Bar across the coastal road), and little to do other than bask in solitude. ⊠ *2 miles (3 km) south of Jolly Harbour and roughly ½ mile (1 km) southwest of Valley Church, off main coast road.*

Dickenson Bay. Along a lengthy stretch of powder-soft white sand and exceptionally calm water you can find small and large hotels, water sports, concessions, and beachfront restaurants. There's decent snorkeling at either point. ⊠ *2 miles (3 km) northeast of St. John's, along main coast road.*

Half Moon Bay. This ½-mile (1-km) ivory crescent is a prime snorkeling and windsurfing area. On the Atlantic side, the water can be rough, attracting hardcore surfers and wake-boarders. The northeastern end, where a protective reef offers spectacular snorkeling, is much calmer. A tiny bar has restrooms, snacks, and beach chairs. Half Moon is a real trek, but one of Antigua's showcase beaches. ⊠ *On southeast coast, 1½ miles (2½ km) from Freetown.*

Johnson's Point/Crabbe Hill. These connected, deserted beaches on the southwest coast look out toward Montserrat, Guadeloupe, and St. Kitts. Notable beach bar–restaurants include OJ's, Gibson's, and Turner's. The water is placid, but not good for snorkeling. ⊠ *3 miles (5 km) south of Jolly Harbour complex, on main west-coast road.*

Pigeon Point. Near Falmouth Harbour lie two fine white-sand beaches. The leeward side is calmer, the windward side is rockier, and there are sensational views and snorkeling around the point. Several restaurants and bars are nearby, though Bumpkin's (with its banana coladas) satisfies most needs. ⊠ *Off main south-coast road, southwest of Falmouth.*

BARBUDA

★ **Fodor's Choice** **Pink Beach.** You can walk miles of this strand without encountering another footprint. It has a champagne hue, with sand soft as silk; crushed coral often imparts a rosy glint, hence its unofficial name (the part in front of the former K Club has been renamed Princess Diana Beach). The water can be rough with a strong undertow in spots, though it's mainly protected by the reefs that make the island a diving mecca. Hire a taxi to take you here, since none of the roads are well marked. ⊠ *1 mile (2 km) from ferry and airstrip along unmarked roads.*

By Jordan
Simon

The wonder of Antigua, and especially its astonishingly undeveloped sister island, Barbuda, is that you can still play Robinson Crusoe here. Travel brochures trumpet the 365 sensuous beaches, "one for every day of the year," as locals love saying, though when the island was first developed for tourism the unofficial count was 52 ("one for every weekend"). Either way, even longtime residents haven't combed every stretch of sand.

The island's extensive archipelago of cays and islets is what attracted the original Amerindian settlers—the Ciboney—at least 4,000 years ago. The natural environment, which is rich in marine life, flora, and fauna, has been likened to a "natural supermarket." Antigua's superior anchorages and strategic location naturally caught the attention of the colonial powers. The Dutch, French, and English waged numerous bloody battles throughout the 17th century (eradicating the remaining Arawaks and Caribs in the process), with England finally prevailing in 1667. Antigua remained under English control until achieving full independence on November 1, 1981, along with Barbuda, 26 miles (42 km) to the north.

Boats and beaches go hand in hand with hotel development, and Antigua's tourist infrastructure has mushroomed since the 1950s. Though many of its grandes dames such as Curtain Bluff remain anchors, today all types of resorts line the sand, and the island offers something for everyone, from gamboling on the sand to gambling in casinos. Environmental activists have become increasingly vocal about preservation and limiting development, and not just because green travel rakes in the green. Antigua's allure is precisely that precarious balance and subliminal tension between its unspoiled, natural beauty and its sun-sand-surf megadevelopment. And the British heritage persists, from teatime (and tee times) to fiercely contested cricket matches.

PLANNING

WHEN TO GO

The high season runs from mid-December through April; after that time, you can find real bargains, as much as 40% off the regular rates, particularly if you book an air-hotel package. A fair number of the restaurants and properties close for part of the time between August and October.

GETTING HERE AND AROUND

AIR TRAVEL

Nonstop Flights are available from Atlanta (Delta, twice weekly in season), Charlotte (US Airways), Miami (American, Caribbean Airlines, Continental), New York–JFK (Caribbean), and Newark (Continental).

Airport Contact V. C. Bird International Airport ✉ *VNU* ☎ *268/462-4672, 268/462-0358.*

Airline Contacts American Airlines/American Eagle ☎ *268/462-0950* ⊕ *www.aa.com.* **Antigua Barbuda Montserrat Air** ☎ *268/562-8033, 268/562-7183* ⊕ *www.abm-air.com.* **Caribbean Airlines** ☎ *268/480-2900, 800/744-2225* ⊕ *www.caribbean-airlines.com.* **Continental Airlines** ☎ *268/462-5355* ⊕ *www.continental.com.* **Delta Airlines** ☎ *800/532-4777, 268/562-5951* ⊕ *www.delta.com.* **LIAT.** In addition to many nonstop flights from the United States, LIAT has daily flights to and from many other Caribbean islands. ☎ *268/480-5600* ⊕ *www.liatairline.com.* **US Airways** ☎ *268/480-5601* ⊕ *www. usairways.com.*

BOAT AND FERRY TRAVEL

Barbuda Express. Barbuda Express runs five days a week (generally Tuesday–Saturday, but call for the changing schedule) from Antigua's Heritage Quay Ferry Dock. Fare is EC$110 one-way, EC$220 round-trip (day tour costs US$159); children 12 and under receive discounts. ☎ *268/560-7989* ⊕ *www.antiguaferries.com.*

CAR TRAVEL

The main roads are mostly in good condition, with some bumpy dirt stretches at remote locations and a few hilly areas that flood easily and become impassable for a day. Driving is on the left. To rent a car, you need a valid license and a temporary permit ($20), available through the rental agent. Costs start at about $50 per day in season, with unlimited mileage, though multiday discounts are standard. Most agencies offer automatic or stick shift and right- and left-hand drive. Four-wheel-drive vehicles ($55 per day) will get you more places and are useful because so many roads are full of potholes.

Contacts Avis ☎ *268/462-2840* ⊕ *www.avisantigua.com.* **Budget** ☎ *268/462-3009.* **Dollar** ☎ *268/462-0362* ⊕ *www.dollarantigua.com.* **Hertz** ☎ *268/481-4440.* **Thrifty** ☎ *268/462-9532.*

TAXI TRAVEL

Some cabbies may take you from St. John's to English Harbour and wait for about a half hour while you look around, for about $50.

Contact St. John's taxi stand. You can always call a cab from the St. John's taxi stand. ☎ *268/462-5190, 268/460-5353 for 24-hr service.*

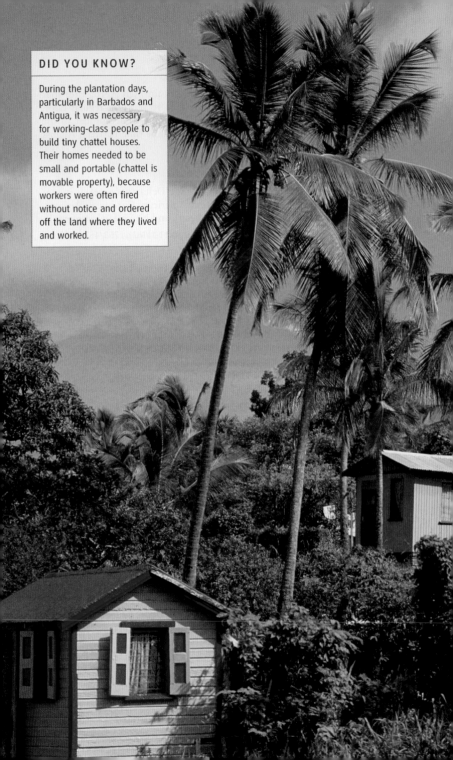

LOGISTICS

Getting to Antigua and Barbuda: Antigua is a Caribbean base, and several airlines fly there nonstop. There is ferry service to Barbuda several days a week, though it's geared for day-trippers. Antigua Barbuda Montserrat Air provides flights between the two islands. Good package deals are often available from resorts.

Hassle Factor: Low for Antigua, medium for Barbuda.

On the Ground: Taxis meet every flight, and drivers will offer to guide you around the island. Taxis are unmetered, but rates are posted at the airport. Drivers must carry a rate card with them. The fixed rate from the airport to St. John's is $12 (although drivers have been known to quote in Eastern Caribbean dollars), to Dickenson Bay $16, and to English Harbour $31.

If you are staying at an isolated resort or wish to sample the island's many fine restaurants, a car is a necessity, less so if you are staying at an all-inclusive with limited island excursions. It's possible to get by without a car if you are staying near St. John's or English Harbour, but taxi rates mount up quickly. A temporary driving permit is required on the island ($20), and you drive on the left.

ESSENTIALS

Banks and Exchange Services The local currency is the Eastern Caribbean dollar (EC$); at this writing US$1 is worth approximately EC$2.70. American dollars are readily accepted, although change is often in EC dollars. Exchanging currency really isn't necessary, especially if you are staying in an all-inclusive resort. Most hotels, restaurants, and duty-free shops take major credit cards. ATMs (dispensing EC$) are available at the island's banks and at the airport.

Electricity 110 volts, 50 cycles.

Emergency Services Ambulance ☎ *268/462–0251, 999.* **Fire** ☎ *268/462–0044, 911.* **Police assistance** ☎ *268/462–0125.*

Phones GSM tri-band mobile phones from the United States and United Kingdom usually work on Antigua; you can also rent one from LIME (formerly Cable & Wireless) and APUA (Antigua Public Utilities Authority). Basic rental costs range between EC$25 and EC$50 per day. You can use the LIME Phone Card (available in $5, $10, and $20 denominations in most hotels and post offices) for local and long-distance calls.

APUA ✉ *Cassada Gardens, St. John's* ☎ *268/480–7000* ⊕ *www.apua.ag.* **LIME** ✉ *Woods Centre, St. John's* ☎ *268/480–2628* ⊕ *www.time4lime.com* ✉ *Long St., St. John's* ☎ *268/480–4236* ✉ *Clare Hall, St. John's* ☎ *268/480–4000.*

Passport Requirements All visitors must carry a valid passport and must have a return or ongoing ticket.

Taxes and Service Charges The departure tax is $28, payable in cash only—either U.S. or EC currency. Hotels collect an 8½%–10½% government room tax; some restaurants will add a 7% tax. Hotels and restaurants also usually add a 10% service charge to your bill.

Tipping Restaurants, 5% beyond the regular service charge added to your bill; taxi drivers 10%; porters and bellmen about $1 per bag; maids $2 to $3 per night. Staff at all-inclusives aren't supposed to be tipped unless they've truly gone out of their way.

ACCOMMODATIONS

In Antigua you're almost certain to have an excellent beach regardless of where you stay. Dickenson Bay and Five Islands Peninsula suit beachcombers who want proximity to St. John's, and Jolly Harbour offers affordable options and activities galore. English Harbour and the southwest coast have the best inns and several excellent restaurants—although many close from August well into October; it's also the yachting crowd's hangout. Resorts elsewhere on the island are ideal for those seeking seclusion; some are so remote that all-inclusive packages or rental cars are mandatory. Barbuda has one posh resort, one fairly upscale hotel, and several guesthouses.

All-Inclusive Resorts: Most of the all-inclusives aim for a mainstream, package-tour kind of crowd—with varying degrees of success—though offerings such as Galley Bay and Curtain Bluff are more upscale.

Luxury Resorts: A fair number of luxury resorts cater to the well heeled in varying degrees of formality on both Antigua and Barbuda.

Small Inns: A few small inns, some historic, can be found around Antigua, mostly concentrated in or near English Harbour.

HOTEL AND RESTAURANT PRICES

Prices in the restaurant reviews are the average cost of a main course at dinner or, if dinner is not served, at lunch; taxes and service charges are generally included. Prices in the hotel reviews are the lowest cost of a standard double room in high season, excluding taxes, service charges, and meal plans (except at all-inclusives). Prices for rentals are the lowest per-night cost for a one-bedroom unit in high season.

VISITOR INFORMATION

Contacts Antigua & Barbuda Department of Tourism ⊠ *Government Complex, Queen Elizabeth Hwy., St. John's* ☎ *268/462-0480* ⊕ *www.antigua-barbuda.org.* **Antigua & Barbuda Tourist Offices** ☎ *212/541-4117 in New York City, 305/381-6762 in Miami, 888/268-4227* ⊕ *www.antigua-barbuda.org.* **Antigua Hotels & Tourist Association** ⊠ *Newgate St., St. John's* ☎ *268/462-0374* ⊕ *www.antiguahotels.org.* **Barbudaful.net** ⊕ *www.barbudaful.net.*

WEDDINGS

No minimum residency or blood test is required. A license application fee is $150. You must have valid passports as proof of citizenship and, in the case of previous marriages, the original divorce or annulment decree. A marriage certificate registration fee is $40.

Nelson's Dockyard at English Harbour

EXPLORING

ANTIGUA

Hotels provide free island maps, but you should get your bearings before heading out on the road. Street names aren't listed (except in St. John's), though *some* easy-to-spot signs lead the way to major restaurants and resorts. Locals generally give directions in terms of landmarks (turn left at the yellow house, or right at the big tree). Wear a swimsuit under your clothes—one of the sights to strike your fancy might be a secluded beach.

WHAT TO SEE

Betty's Hope. Just outside the village of Pares, a marked dirt road leads to Antigua's first sugar plantation, founded in 1650. You can tour the twin windmills, various ruins, still-functional crushing machinery, and the visitor center's exhibits (often closed) on the island's sugar era. The private trust overseeing the restoration has yet to realize its ambitious, environmentally aware plans to replant indigenous crops destroyed by the extensive sugarcane plantings. Indeed, the site is somewhat neglected, with goats grazing the grounds. ⊠ *Pares* ☎ *268/462–1469* ▧ *$2* ☉ *Tues.–Sat. 10–4.*

Devil's Bridge. This limestone arch formation, sculpted by the crashing breakers of the Atlantic at Indian Town, is a national park. Blowholes have been carved by the hissing, spitting surf. The park also encompasses some archaeological excavations of Carib artifacts.

Falmouth. This town sits on a lovely bay backed by former sugar plantations and sugar mills. The most important historic site here is St. Paul's Church, which was rebuilt on the site of a church once used by troops during the Horatio Nelson period.

Fig Tree Drive. This often muddy, rutted, steep road takes you through the rain forest, which is rich in mangoes, pineapples, and banana trees (*fig* is the Antiguan word for "banana"). The rain forest is the island's hilliest area—1,319-foot Boggy Peak (renamed Mt. Obama), to the west, is the highest point. At its crest, Elaine Francis sells seasonal local fruit juices—ginger, guava, sorrel, passion fruit—and homemade jams at a stall she dubs the Culture Shop. A few houses down (look for the orange windows) is the atelier of noted island artist Sallie Harker (shimmering seascapes and vividly hued fish incorporating gold leaf). You'll also pass several tranquil villages with charming churches and Antigua Rainforest Canopy Tours *(⇨ Zip-Lining under Sports and Activities later in this chapter)* here.

Ft. George. East of Liberta—one of the first settlements founded by freed slaves—on Monk's Hill, this fort was built from 1689 to 1720. Among the ruins are the sites for 32 cannons, water cisterns, the base of the old flagstaff, and some of the original buildings.

Harmony Hall. Northeast of Freetown (follow the signs), this art gallery–cum–restaurant is built on the foundation of a 17th-century sugar-plantation greathouse. No longer affiliated with the original Jamaican outpost, the Antigua facility is run by enterprising Italians who operate a fine restaurant and six chic, charming cottages (with a villa development planned). Its remote location is a headache, but you can allot the whole afternoon to enjoying lunch (dinner Wednesday through Saturday), soaking in the historic ambience and panoramic ocean views, browsing through the exhibits, combing the beach, and perhaps even snorkeling at nearby Green Island via the property's boat, *Luna*. ⊠ *Brown's Mill Bay, Brown's Mill* ☎ *268/460–4120* ⊕ *www.harmonyhallantigua.com* ⊗ *June–mid-Nov., daily 10–6, later Wed., Fri., and Sat.*

Megaliths of Greencastle Hill. It's an arduous climb to these eerie rock slabs in the south-central part of the island. Some say the megaliths were set up by early inhabitants for their worship of the sun and moon or as devices for measuring time astronomically; others believe they're nothing more than unusual geological formations. ⊕ *www. nationalparksantigua.com.*

Nelson's Dockyard. Antigua's most famous attraction is the world's only Georgian-era dockyard still in use, a treasure trove for history buffs and nautical nuts alike. In 1671 the governor of the Leeward Islands wrote to the Council for Foreign Plantations in London, pointing out the advantages of this landlocked harbor. By 1704 English Harbour was in regular use as a garrisoned station.

In 1784, 26-year-old Horatio Nelson sailed in on the HMS *Boreas* to serve as captain and second-in-command of the Leeward Island Station. Under him was the captain of the HMS *Pegasus*, Prince William Henry, duke of Clarence, who was later crowned King William IV.

The prince acted as best man when Nelson married Fannie Nisbet on Nevis in 1787.

When the Royal Navy abandoned the station at English Harbour in 1889, it fell into a state of decay, though adventuresome yachties still lived there in near-primitive conditions. The Society of the Friends of English Harbour began restoring it in 1951; it reopened with great fanfare as Nelson's Dockyard on November 14, 1961. Within the compound are crafts shops, restaurants, and two splendidly restored 18th-century hotels, the Admiral's Inn and the Copper & Lumber Store Hotel, worth peeking into. (The latter, occupying a supply store for Nelson's Caribbean fleet, is a particularly fine example of Georgian architecture and has an interior courtyard evoking Old England.) The Dockyard is a hub for oceangoing yachts and serves as headquarters for the annual Sailing Week Regatta in late April and early May. Water taxis will ferry you between points for EC$5. The Dockyard National Park also includes serene nature trails accessing beaches, rock pools, and crumbling plantation ruins and hilltop forts.

The **Dockyard Museum,** in the original Naval Officer's House, presents ship models, mock-ups of English Harbour, displays on the people who worked there and typical ships that docked, silver regatta trophies, maps, prints, antique navigational instruments, and Nelson's very own telescope and tea caddy. ⊠ *English Harbour* ☎ *268/481–5027 for Dockyard Museum, 268/481–5028 for National Parks Authority* ⊕ *www. nationalparksantigua.com* ⊠ *$2 suggested donation* ☉ *Daily 9–5.*

NEED A BREAK?

Admiral's Inn. The restaurant at the Admiral's Inn is a must for Anglophiles and mariners. Soak up the centuries at the inside bar, where 18th-century sailors reputedly carved their ships' names on the dark timbers. Most diners sit on the flagstone terrace under shady Australian gums to enjoy the views of the harbor complex and trendy exhibition kitchen; yachts seem close enough to eavesdrop. Specialties include pumpkin soup and fresh snapper with equally fresh limes. ⊠ *Nelson's Dockyard, English Harbour* ☎ *268/460–1027.*

Parham. This sleepy village is a splendid example of a traditional colonial settlement. St. Peter's Church, built in 1840 by English architect Thomas Weekes, is an octagonal Italianate building with unusual ribbed wooden ceiling, whose facade is richly decorated with stucco and keystone work, though it suffered considerable damage during an 1843 earthquake.

Shirley Heights. This bluff affords a spectacular view of English Harbour. The heights are named for Sir Thomas Shirley, the governor who fortified the harbor in 1787. At the top is Shirley Heights Lookout, a restaurant built into the remnants of the 18th-century fortifications. Most notable for its boisterous Sunday barbecues that continue into the night with live music and dancing, it serves dependable burgers, pumpkin soup, grilled meats, and rum punches.

Dows Hill Interpretation Centre. Not far from Shirley Heights is the Dows Hill Interpretation Centre, where observation platforms provide still more sensational vistas of the English Harbour area. A multimedia sound-and-light presentation on island history and culture, spotlighting lifelike figures and colorful tableaux accompanied by running commentary and music, provides a cheery, if bland, portrait of Antiguan life from Amerindian times to the present. ☎ *268/460–1379 for National Parks Authority* ⊕ *www.nationalparksantigua.com* ☒ *EC$15* ☉ *Daily 9–5*

St. John's. Antigua's capital, with some 45,000 inhabitants (approximately half the island's population), lies at sea level at the inland end of a sheltered northwestern bay. Although it has seen better days, a couple of notable historic sights and some good waterfront shopping areas make it worth a visit.

At the far south end of town, where Market Street forks into Valley and All Saints roads, haggling goes on every Friday and Saturday, when locals jam the **Public Market** to buy and sell fruits, vegetables, fish, and spices. Ask before you aim a camera; your subject may expect a tip. This is old-time Caribbean shopping, a jambalaya of sights, sounds, and smells.

Museum of Antigua and Barbuda. Signs at the Museum of Antigua and Barbuda say "Please touch," encouraging you to explore Antigua's past. Try your hand at the educational video games or squeeze a cassava through a *matapi* (grass sieve). Exhibits interpret the nation's history, from its geological birth to its political independence in 1981. There are fossil and coral remains from some 34 million years ago; models of a sugar plantation and a wattle-and-daub house; an Arawak canoe; and a wildly eclectic assortment of objects from cannonballs to 1920s telephone exchanges. The museum occupies the former courthouse, which dates from 1750. The superlative museum gift shop carries such unusual items as calabash purses, seed earrings, warri boards (warri being an African game brought over to the Caribbean), and lignum vitae pipes, as well as historic maps and local books (including engrossing, detailed monographs on varied subjects by the late Desmond Nicholson, a long-time resident). ☒ *Long and Market Sts., St. John's* ☎ *268/462–1469* ⊕ *www.antiguamuseum.org* ☒ *$3; children under 12 free* ☉ *Mon.–Fri. 8:30–4, Sat. 10–2, closed Sun.*

Anglican Cathedral of St. John the Divine. At the south gate of the Anglican Cathedral of St. John the Divine are figures of St. John the Baptist and St. John the Divine, said to have been taken from one of Napoléon's ships and brought to Antigua. The original church was built in 1681, replaced by a stone building in 1745, and destroyed by an earthquake in 1843. The present neo-baroque building dates from 1845; the parishioners had the interior completely encased in pitch pine, hoping to forestall future earthquake damage. Tombstones bear eerily eloquent testament to the colonial days. ☒ *Between Long and Newgate Sts., St. John's* ☎ *268/461–0082*

Heritage Quay. Shopaholics head directly for Heritage Quay, an ugly multimillion-dollar complex. The two-story buildings contain stores that sell duty-free goods, sportswear, down-island imports (paintings, T-shirts, straw baskets), and local crafts. There are also restaurants, a

Barbuda

GOAT ISLAND
RABBIT ISLAND
Goat Pt.
Hog Pt.
Billy Pt.
The Caves ◆
Two Foot Bay
Cedar-Tree Pt.
Codrington Lagoon
Bird Sanctuary ◆
○ Codrington
Low Bay
◆ Airstrip
Martello Tower ◆
◆ The River Landing
Palmetto Pt.
0   5 miles
0   5 km
The Castle ◆
Pink Beach ◆ Airstrip
Spanish Pt.

bandstand, and a casino. Cruise-ship passengers disembark here from the 500-foot-long pier. Expect heavy shilling. ⊠ *High and Thames Sts.*

Redcliffe Quay. Redcliffe Quay, at the water's edge just south of Heritage Quay, is the most appealing part of St. John's. Attractively restored (and superbly re-created) buildings in a riot of cotton-candy colors house shops, restaurants, and boutiques and are linked by courtyards and landscaped walkways. ⊠ *St. John's.*

BARBUDA

This flat, 62-square-mile (161-square-km) coral atoll—with 17 miles (27 km) of gleaming white-sand beaches (sand is the island's main export)—is 26 miles (42 km) north of Antigua. Most of Barbuda's 1,200 people live in Codrington. Nesting terns, turtles, and frigate birds outnumber residents at least 10 to 1. Goats, guinea fowl, deer, and wild boar roam the roads, all fair game for local kitchens. There are a few very basic efficiencies and guesthouses, but most visitors stay overnight at the deluxe Coco Point Lodge (two other glam properties have closed). Pink Beach lures beachcombers, a bird sanctuary attracts ornithologists, caves and sinkholes filled with rain forest or underground pools (containing rare, even unique crustacean species) attract spelunkers, and reefs and roughly 200 offshore wrecks draw divers and snorkelers. Barbuda's sole historic ruin is the 18th-century, cylindrical, 56-foot-tall **Martello Tower,** which was probably a lighthouse built by the Spaniards before English occupation. The **Frigate Bird Sanctuary,** a wide mangrove-filled lagoon, is home to an estimated 400 species of birds, including frigate birds with 8-foot wingspans. Your hotel can make arrangements.

It's reachable by boat, the *Barbuda Express*, although the 95-minute ride is extremely bumpy ("a chiropractor's nightmare—or fantasy," quipped one passenger).

WHERE TO EAT

Antigua's restaurants are almost a dying breed since the advent of all-inclusives. But several worthwhile hotel dining rooms and nightspots remain, especially in the English Harbour and Dickenson Bay areas. Virtually every chef incorporates local ingredients and elements of West Indian cuisine.

Most menus list prices in both EC and U.S. dollars; if not, ask which currency the menu is using. Always double-check whether credit cards are accepted and service is included. Dinner reservations are needed during high season.

What to Wear: Perhaps because of the island's British heritage, Antiguans tend to dress more formally for dinner than dwellers on many other Caribbean islands. Wraps and shorts (no beach attire) are de rigueur for lunch, except at local hangouts.

$$
PIZZA
✕ **Big Banana—Pizzas in Paradise.** This tiny, often crowded spot is tucked into one side of a restored 18th-century rum warehouse with broad plank floors, wood-beam ceiling, and stone archways. Cool, Benetton-style photos of locals and musicians jamming adorn the brick walls. Big Banana serves some of the island's best pizza—try the lobster or the seafood variety—as well as such tasty specials as conch salad, fresh fruit crushes, classic pastas, and sub sandwiches bursting at the seams. There's live entertainment some nights, and a large-screen TV for sports fans. Ⓢ *Average main: $16* ✉ *Redcliffe Quay, St. John's* ☎ *268/480–6985* ⊕ *www.bigbanana-antigua.com* ☾ *Closed Sun.*

$$$
ECLECTIC
★
✕ **Cecilia's High Point Café.** The eponymous owner, a vivacious, striking Swedish ex-model, floats (and once in a while flirts) about the tables in this cozy beachfront Creole cottage. An equally animated cross section of Antiguan life usually packs the coveted patio tables (it's a terrific spot to eavesdrop on island gossip). The day's selections, including wine specials, are written on a blackboard. Stellar standbys run from a fried eggplant napoleon layered with tomatoes and mozzarella to mushroom ravioli nestled in spinach with a gossamer creamy pesto, but the high points are the setting and Cecilia herself. As a bonus, Wi-Fi access is free. Ⓢ *Average main: $27* ✉ *Dutchman's Bay* ☎ *268/562–7070* ⊕ *www.highpointantigua.com* ⚹ *Reservations essential* ☾ *Closed Tues. and Wed. No dinner Thurs.–Sun.*

$$$$ ╳ **Coconut Grove.** Coconut palms grow through the roof of this open-
ECLECTIC air thatched restaurant, flickering candlelight illuminates colorful local
★ murals, waves lap the white sand, and the warm waitstaff provides just
the right level of service. Jean-François Bellanger's superbly presented
dishes fuse French culinary preparations with island ingredients. Top
choices include smoked salmon with watermelon-ginger jam, sundried
tomatoes, and tapenade; pan-seared snapper medallions served with
roasted sweet potato in a saffron white-wine curry; Caribbean bouillabaisse with coconut milk and pumpkin aioli; and chicken stuffed with
creole vegetables in mango-kiwi sauce. The kitchen can be uneven, the
wine list is unimaginative and overpriced (save for the occasional $31
specials), and the buzzing happy-hour bar crowd lingering well into dinnertime can detract from the otherwise romantic atmosphere. Nonetheless, Coconut Grove straddles the line between casual beachfront boîte
and elegant eatery with aplomb. ⑤ *Average main: $30* ⊠ *Siboney Beach
Club, Dickenson Bay* ☎ *268/462–1538* ⊕ *www.coconutgroveantigua.
net* ⌂ *Reservations essential.*

$$$$ ╳ **East.** Imposing Indonesian carved doors usher you into this bold and
ASIAN FUSION sexy Asian fusion spot. Flames flicker in the outdoor lily pond while
candles illuminate lacquered dark-wood tables with blood-red napery
and oversize fuchsia-color chairs. Exquisite pan-Pacific fare (with delicious detours to the Indian subcontinent) courts perfection through sim-
plicity and precision: prawn spring rolls with hoisin–sweet chili sauce;
superlative sashimi; entrées from Thai lobster curry to tandoori chicken,
to tilapia *katsudon* (lightly fried fillets served with onion *dashi* broth,
egg, and rice); and green tea crème brûlée. The small main courses man-
date tapas-style dining; the comprehensive wine list is pricey but offers
values from intriguing lesser-known regions. ⑤ *Average main: $31*
⊠ *Carlisle Bay, Old Road* ☎ *268/484–0000* ⌂ *Reservations essential.*

$$$$ ╳ **La Bussola.** Blend a genuinely *simpatico* welcome with lapping waves,
ITALIAN the murmur of jazz, and expert Italian fare and you have Omar Taglia-
★ venti and family's recipe for the perfect beachfront bistro. Bleached-
wood ceilings, billowing white curtains, old island photos of Antigua,
boating paraphernalia, and brightly painted plates enhance the relaxed,
romantic mood. The presentation is invariably pretty, and Omar has
a particularly facile touch with seafood; try the artichoke-shrimp pie
in satiny garlic sauce, lobster-asparagus risotto, shark tartare with
grapefruit nestling on a bed of arugula, mahimahi with olive "pâté"
in filo, or the "fishermen's" spaghetti. The carefully considered wine
list showcases lesser-known Italian regions. Your evening ends with a
complimentary grappa, Frangelico, or *limoncello* (lemon liqueur), representing northern, central, and southern Italy. La Bussola means "the
compass" in Italian, and it certainly takes the right gastronomic direction. ⑤ *Average main: $29* ⊠ *Runaway Bay* ☎ *268/562–1545* ⊕ *www.
labussolarestaurant.net* ⌂ *Reservations essential* ⊘ *Closed Tues.*

$$$$ ╳ **Le Bistro.** This Antiguan institution's peach, periwinkle, and pistachio
FRENCH accents subtly match the tile work, jade chairs, mint china, and painted
★ lighting fixtures. Trellises divide the large space into intimate sections.
Chef Patrick Gaducheau delights in blending classic regional fare with
indigenous ingredients, displaying an especially deft hand with delicate

sauces. The kitchen now runs smoothly after bouts of inconsistency. Opt for daily specials, such as smoked marlin carpaccio with pink peppercorns, cold carrot soup with mango chutney, fresh snapper with spinach and grapefruit in thyme-perfumed lime-butter sauce, lobster medallions in basil-accented old-rum sauce with roasted red peppers, and almost anything swaddled in puff pastry. The fine wine list hits all the right spots, geographically and varietally, without outrageous mark-ups. Co-owner Phillipa Esposito doubles as hostess and pastry chef; her passion-fruit mousse and chocolate confections are sublime. ⑤ *Average main: $34* ⊠ *Hodges Bay* ☎ *268/462–3881* ⊕ *www.antigualebistro.com* ⌂ *Reservations essential* ⊘ *Closed Mon. No lunch.*

$$$$ ✕ **Le Cap Horn.** As Piaf and Aznavour compete with croaking tree frogs
FRENCH   in a trellised, plant-filled room lighted by straw lamps, it's easy to imagine yourself in a tropical St-Tropez. From the small but select menu, begin with escargots in a lovely tomato, onion, and pepper sauce (sop it up with the marvelous home-baked bread) or the ultimate in hedonism (and expense), lobster–foie gras millefeuille; then segue into tiger shrimp swimming in gossamer vanilla-lobster sauce or duck breast wrapped with mango in rice sheet floating in rum-tamarind sauce. Gustavo Belaunde (he's Peruvian of Catalan extraction) elicits fresh, delicate, almost ethereal flavors from his ingredients; his versatility is displayed in the restaurant's other half, a pizzeria replete with wood-burning oven (with much lower prices and rowdier ambience). Finish with wife Hélène's divine desserts or a cognac and cigar. ⑤ *Average main: $43* ⊠ *English Harbour* ☎ *268/460–1194* ⊘ *Closed Aug., Sept., and Thurs. Closed Wed. in low season (May–July, Oct. and Nov.). No lunch.*

$$$ ✕ **Papa Zouk.** Who would have thought that two jovial globe-trotting
CARIBBEAN   German gents could create a classic Caribbean hangout? But the madras tablecloths, fishnets festooned with Christmas lights, painted bottles of homemade hot sauces, colorful island clientele, and lilting rhythms on the sound system justify the name (*zouk* is a sultry, musical stew of soul and calypso). Seafood is king, from Guyanese butterfish to Barbudan snapper, usually served either deep-fried or steamed with a choice of such sauces as guava-pepper teriyaki or tomato-basil-coriander. Tangy Caribbean bouillabaisse with garlicky Parmesan mayonnaise and fish 'n' rum (spike it with a vinegar hot sauce) are specialties, as are the knock-out rum punches. Finish dinner with a snifter of aged rum: the tiny bar holds 250 varieties from around the globe. Dine family style in front or more intimately in back. ⑤ *Average main: $23* ⊠ *Hilda Davis Dr., Gambles Terrace, St. John's* ☎ *268/464–7576, 268/464–6044* ⊟ *No credit cards* ⊘ *Closed May–Oct. and Sun. No lunch sometimes; call ahead for hrs.*

$$ ✕ **Russell's.** Convivial owner Russell Hodge had the brilliant idea of
CARIBBEAN   restoring a part of Ft. James, with its glorious views of the bay and headlands, and converting it into a semi-alfresco eatery. Potted plants, jazz on the sound system (live musicians Friday and Sunday), and red or black hurricane lamps lend a romantic aura to the beamed, stone-and-wood terrace. The limited menu—local specialties emphasizing seafood—includes fabulous chunky conch fritters and whelks in garlic butter. Sadly, Russell passed in March 2011, but his daughter Danielle

maintains the tradition. Russell's sister Faye co-owns Papa Zouk, and sister Valerie runs Shirley Heights Lookout; the Hodges might well be Antigua's first family of food. $ *Average main: $20* ⊠ *Fort James* ☎ *268/462–5479* ⊘ *No lunch Sun.*

$$
ECLECTIC
★
✕ **Sheer Rocks.** This sensuous eatery, a series of tiered wood decks carved into a sheer cliff side, showcases the setting sun from the staggered, thatched dining nooks, many separated by billowing white-gauze curtains. Large white beds surround plunge pools, making it equally sybaritic for daytime lounging. The menu encompasses a tapestry of creative tapas that can be served in larger portions. Chef Alex Grimley's philosophy emphasizes simplicity, detail, and only the best ingredients to create a symphonic counterpoint of flavors and textures—subtle to lusty, crispy to creamy. Witness seared scallops with crispy pork and pumpkin puree; caramelized red-onion tart with roasted beetroot, goat cheese, and fine herbs; or baked mahimahi with red-pepper pesto and aubergine cannelloni. Add a dash of sultry music, season with smashing views, complement with an admirable wine list (not to mention inventive cocktails), and you have the recipe for a tropical St-Tropez experience. $ *Average main: $19* ⊠ *CocoBay, Valley Church* ☎ *268/562–4510, 268/464–5283* ⊕ *www.sheer-rocks.com* ⌖ *Reservations essential* ⊘ *Closed Tues., Wed. (bar open for tapas). No dinner Sun. No lunch Mon., Wed., and Thurs.*

$$$
SEAFOOD
✕ **The Tides.** The look of this seaside eatery subtly suggests a yacht: decks on either side, steering wheels, oars hung as artwork, and petrified-driftwood mobiles, as well as antique Asian doors and lovely local ceramics for color. Although the kitchen isn't quite shipshape, it isn't shipwrecked, making visits to several gastronomic ports of call from the Mediterranean to the Pacific Rim. Start with Pepper Tiger prawns, flambéed in Cognac, or lobster gnocchi, then segue to herb-crusted salmon in fennel beurre blanc over saffron risotto or Black Angus sirloin with wild mushroom sauce or red wine reduction. More affordable, lunch emphasizes rotis and foccacia, alongside more ambitious offerings like the almost-by-the-book bouillabaisse. Management also runs several affordable beachfront cottages next door. $ *Average main: $34* ⊠ *St. George* ☎ *268/462–8433* ⊕ *www.thetidesantigua.com* ⊘ *Closed Aug., Mon., and Tues.*

WHERE TO STAY

Scattered along Antigua's beaches and hillsides are exclusive, elegant hideaways; romantic restored inns; and all-inclusive hot spots for couples. Check individual lodgings for restrictions (many have minimum stays during certain high-season periods). Look also for specials on the Web or from tour packagers, since hotels' quoted rack rates are often negotiable (up to 45% off in season). There are several new condo and villa developments; although not reviewed in this edition, Sugar Ridge opened in December 2009 in the Jolly Harbour area. (Despite its nice if smallish units, elegant setting, Aveda Spa, and fine upscale restaurant, it may suffer from the lack of beachfront.) At this writing, Tamarind Hills is one of several other major developments slated to open by 2014.

For expanded reviews, facilities, and current deals, visit Fodors.com.

$
B&B/INN
★
🖼 **Admiral's Inn.** This Georgian brick edifice, originally the shipwright's offices in what is now Nelson's Dockyard, has withstood acts of God and war since the early 18th century. **Pros:** historic ambience; central English Harbour location; fine value; charming restaurant setting. **Cons:** occasionally noisy when yachties take over the bar; recently remodeled bathrooms are still cramped; no beach. **TripAdvisor:** "great service," "a port in a storm," "lovely historic hotel." ⑤ *Rooms from: $160* ⊠ *English Harbour* ☎ *268/460–1027, 268/460–1153* ⊕ *www.admiralsantigua.com* ⤳ *14 rooms, 1 2-bedroom apartment* ⦿ *No meals.*

$$$$
HOTEL
★
🖼 **Blue Waters Hotel.** A well-heeled Brit crowd goes barefoot at this swank yet understated seaside retreat. **Pros:** pomp without pretension; exquisite setting; trendy minimalist decor. **Cons:** small beachfront; little steps along the hillside make it less accessible for the physically challenged; trendy minimalist decor; difficulty obtaining reservations at Vyvien's at peak times. **TripAdvisor:** "amazingly friendly," "spectacular setting," "lots of relaxation." ⑤ *Rooms from: $830* ⊠ *Boon Point, Soldier's Bay* ☎ *268/462–0290, 800/557–6536 reservations only* ⊕ *www. bluewaters.net* ⤳ *65 rooms, 32 suites, 3 villas, 4 penthouses* ☉ *Closed Sept.* ⦿ *Multiple meal plans.*

$$$$
RESORT
★
🖼 **Carlisle Bay.** This cosmopolitan, boutique sister property of London's trendy One Aldwych hotel daringly eschews everything faux colonial and Creole. **Pros:** luxury resort; attentive service; family-friendly. **Cons:** aggressively hip; lovely beach but often murky water; pricey restaurants; no elevators. **TripAdvisor:** "relaxing," "a true deluxe property," "fabulous family find." ⑤ *Rooms from: $920* ⊠ *Carlisle Bay, Old Road* ☎ *268/484–0000, 866/502–2855 reservations only* ⊕ *www.carlisle-bay. com* ⤳ *82 suites* ☉ *Closed late Aug.–early Oct.* ⦿ *Breakfast.*

$
HOTEL
★
🖼 **Catamaran Hotel.** The main building at the congenial, cozy, harbor-front "Cat Club" evokes a plantation greathouse with verandas, white columns, and hand-carved doors. **Pros:** intimacy; central location; friendly staff; children under 12 stay free. **Cons:** small beach (swimming not advised); smallish rooms; restaurant closed until further notice; surrounding area has limited dining and nightlife options during off-season (May–November). **TripAdvisor:** "a perfect week," "excellent service," "fantastic location." ⑤ *Rooms from: $170* ⊠ *Falmouth Harbour* ☎ *268/460–1036* ⊕ *www.catamaran-antigua.com* ⤳ *12 rooms, 2 suites* ⦿ *No meals.*

$$$
ALL-INCLUSIVE
🖼 **CocoBay.** This healing hideaway on a hillside aims to "eliminate all potential worries" by emphasizing simple natural beauty and West Indian warmth. **Pros:** emphasis on local nature and culture; beautiful views; nice main pool and bar area; generally pleasant helpful staff. **Cons:** mediocre food; stifling on breezeless days; difficult climb for those with mobility problems; smallish beaches; bar closes early; poor bedroom lighting. **TripAdvisor:** "paradise," "perfect relaxing getaway," "worth every penny." ⑤ *Rooms from: $380* ⊠ *Valley Church* ☎ *268/562–2400, 877/385–6516* ⊕ *www.cocobayresort.com* ⤳ *49 rooms, 4 2-bedroom houses* ⦿ *All-inclusive.*

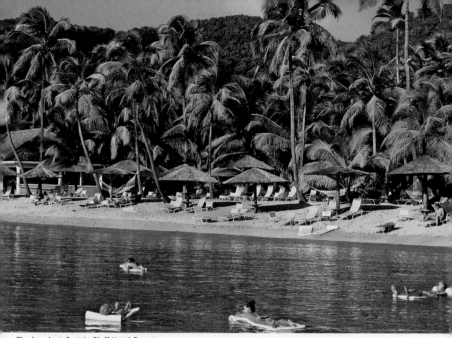

The beach at Curtain Bluff Hotel Resort.

$$$$ 🏨 **Curtain Bluff.** An incomparable beachfront setting, impeccable service, superb extras (free scuba diving and deep-sea fishing), effortless
ALL-INCLUSIVE   elegance: Curtain Bluff is that rare retreat that stays modern while exud-
Fodor's Choice   ing a magical timelessness. **Pros:** luxury lodging; sublime food; beauti-
★   ful beaches; incredible extras. **Cons:** some find clientele standoffish;
lodgings atop bluff not ideal for those with mobility problems; despite
offering value, pricey by most standards; limited menu selection. **Trip-
Advisor:** "the most relaxing vacation," "old school charm," "incredibly
kind staff." ⑤ *Rooms from: $1,095* ✉ *Morris Bay* ☎ *268/462–8400,
888/289–9898 for reservations* ⊕ *www.curtainbluff.com* ⇄ *18 rooms,
54 suites* ☉ *Closed early Aug.–Oct.* ⑩ *All-inclusive.*

$ 🏨 **Dickenson Bay Cottages.** Lush landscaping snakes around the two-
RENTAL   story buildings and pool at this small hillside complex, which offers
★   excellent value for families. **Pros:** relatively upscale comfort at down-
home prices; walking distance to Dickenson Bay dining and activities.
Cons: hike from beach; lacks cross-breeze in many units. **TripAdvisor:**
"quiet and convenient," "peaceful," "so relaxing." ⑤ *Rooms from:
$170* ✉ *Marble Hill* ☎ *268/462–4940* ⊕ *www.dickensonbaycottages.
com* ⇄ *11 units* ⑩ *No meals.*

$$$$ 🏨 **Galley Bay.** This posh all-inclusive channels the fictional Bali H'ai
ALL-INCLUSIVE   (with colonial architectural flourishes) on 40 impossibly lush acres. **Pros:**
★   luxury lodging; gorgeous beach and grounds, including croquet lawn;
impeccable maintenance; fine food by all-inclusive standards. **Cons:**
some lodgings are claustrophobic and lack a view; outdoor spa can
get hot; surf is often too strong for weaker swimmers; only suites have
tubs; no waitstaff service on the long beach. **TripAdvisor:** "excellent
secluded resort," "nice quiet place," "holiday bliss." ⑤ *Rooms from:*

$940 ⊠ *Five Islands* ☎ 268/462–0302, 866/237–1644, 800/858–4618 *reservations only* ⊕ *www.galleybayresort.com* ⇲ 98 *rooms* ⊙ *Closed mid-Aug.–early Sept.* ⦿| *All-inclusive.*

$$
ALL-INCLUSIVE
★

⊡ **Jolly Beach Resort.** If you're looking for basic sun-sand-surf fun, this active resort—Antigua's largest—fits the bill for few bills, luring a gregarious blend of honeymooners, families, and singles. **Pros:** inexpensive; great range of activities for the price; nice beach; good food for a cheaper all-inclusive; incredible online specials. **Cons:** many cramped, ugly rooms; overrun by tour groups; often impersonal service; lack of elevators and rambling layout make it difficult for the physically challenged. **TripAdvisor:** "beautiful," "amazing beach," "the most hospitable staff." ⑤ *Rooms from: $362* ⊠ *Jolly Harbour* ☎ 268/462–0061, 866/905–6559 ⊕ *www.jollybeachresort.com* ⇲ 461 *units, 2 2-bedroom cottages, 1 1-bedroom cottage* ⦿| *All-inclusive.*

$
RENTAL

⊡ **Jolly Harbour Villas.** These duplex, two-bedroom villas ring the marina of a sprawling, 500-acre compound offering every conceivable facility from restaurants and shops to a casino and golf course. **Pros:** nice beach; good value; plentiful recreational, dining, and nightlife choices nearby. **Cons:** mosquito problems; reports of hidden surcharges; inability to charge most restaurants and activities to your villa; some units have 220-volt outlets requiring adapters. **TripAdvisor:** "hidden gem," "beautiful beaches," "a dream." ⑤ *Rooms from: $166* ⊠ *Jolly Harbour* ☎ 268/462–6166 ⊕ *www.hbkvillas.com* ⇲ 150 *villas* ⦿| *No meals.*

$$$$
ALL-INCLUSIVE
☽
★

⊡ **Jumby Bay.** This refined resort proffers all the makings of a classic Caribbean private island hideaway, right from the stylish airport sedan pickup, private launch, dockside greeting, and registration at your leisure. **Pros:** isolated private island location; sterling cuisine; complimentary Caloi bicycles; inventive kids' activities; thoughtful extras upon request such as cooking classes and wireless baby monitors. **Cons:** isolated private island location; jet noise occasionally disturbs the main beach. **TripAdvisor:** "your own private island paradise," "terrific service," "close to perfection." ⑤ *Rooms from: $1495* ⊠ *Long Island* ☎ 268/462–6000, 888/767–3966 ⊕ *www.jumbybayresort.com* ⇲ 40 *suites, 14 villas* ⦿| *All-inclusive.*

$
B&B/INN

⊡ **Ocean Inn.** Views of English Harbour, affable management, and affordability distinguish this homey inn. **Pros:** fabulous views; affable staff; inexpensive. **Cons:** rickety paths down a steep hill linking cottages; worn rooms need updating; Wi-Fi dodgy; gym is very basic and public. **TripAdvisor:** "great view," "friendly staff," "wonderful oasis." ⑤ *Rooms from: $110* ⊠ *English Harbour* ☎ 268/463–7950 ⊕ *www. theoceaninn.com* ⇲ 6 *rooms, 4 with bath; 4 cottages* ⦿| *Breakfast.*

$$$$
RESORT

⊡ **St. James's Club.** Management has diligently smartened the public spaces and exquisite landscaping here, taking full advantage of the peerless location straddling 100 acres on Mamora Bay. **Pros:** splendid remote location; beautiful beaches and landscaping; complimentary Wi-Fi in public areas; long-overdue ongoing upgrades improving the property; plentiful activities; additional adult pools offer more privacy. **Cons:** remote location makes a car a necessity for non-all-inclusive guests; tour groups can overrun the resort; uneven food and service; sprawling hilly layout not ideal for physically challenged. **TripAdvisor:**

Other Lodgings to Consider on Antigua

We can't include every property deserving mention without creating an encyclopedia. Consider the following accommodations, many of which are popular with tour operators.

Antigua Yacht Club Marina & Resort. Antigua Yacht Club Marina & Resort is a handsome collection of 19 hotel rooms and 30 studio and one-bedroom condos (for rent when owners are off-island), climbing a hill with stunning marina views. Accommodations are stylish if spare, with island crafts and the occasional high-tech amenity; the adjacent marina is a center of nautical hubbub with several restaurants (Southern Cross serves estimable Italian fare), pubs, and shops. ⊠ *Falmouth Harbour* ☎ *268/562–3030, 888/790–5264* ⊕ *www.aycmarina.com.*

Coconut Beach Club. Coconut Beach Club sits on a beach overlooking the ruins of Ft. James. The food in the restaurants is creative; all 38 units feature smashing sea views, and the price is right—for now. ⊠ *Yepton Beach* ☎ *268/462–3239, 877/385–6517* ⊕ *www.coconutbeachclub.com.*

Grand Pineapple Beach Resort. Grand Pineapple Beach Resort is a Sandals-owned, Sandals-branded all-inclusive (formerly Allegro/Occidental) on a tranquil beach amid lush landscaping. It's in the midst of ongoing renovations, restoring its sheen. Buildings and 180 rooms feature almost edible pastel hues inside and out; the beachfront units and 500 block offer smashing east-coast views. ⊠ *Long Bay* ☎ *268/463–2006, 800/327–1991* ⊕ *www. grandpineapple.com.*

Hermitage Bay. Hermitage Bay is a deluxe enclave of 30 beachfront and hillside cottages on a secluded, hard-to-reach but pretty stretch of sand. Affecting a look and ambience that borrow from both Carlisle Bay and Curtain Bluff, the minimalist-chic lodgings include a garden shower and private plunge pool. The kitchen turns out admirable organic fare, much of it sourced from its gardens. ⊠ *Hermitage Bay* ☎ *268/562–5500, 855/562–8080 toll-free* ⊕ *www.hermitagebay. com.*

Rex Halcyon Cove Beach Resort. Rex Halcyon Cove Beach Resort is a large, impersonal but admirably outfitted resort (from dive shop to car rental) on one of Antigua's top beaches. Buildings are a bit institutional-looking, and you'll have to watch out for stampeding tour groups; however, you can usually find good package deals here. ⊠ *Dickenson Bay* ☎ *268/462–0256, 305/471–6170* ⊕ *www.rexresorts.com.*

3

"superb resort," "perfect place," "a little piece of heaven." ⑤ *Rooms from: $740* ⊠ *Mamora Bay* ☎ *268/460–5000, 800/858–4618 Reservations only, 866/237–2071* ⊕ *www.stjamesclubantigua.com* ⇌ *215 rooms, 72 villas (usually 36 in rental pool)* ⑩ *Multiple meal plans.*

$$$$
ALL-INCLUSIVE
⌖ **Sandals Grande Antigua Resort & Spa.** The sumptuous public spaces, lovely beach, glorious gardens, and plethora of facilities almost mask this once-sterling resort's impersonal atmosphere and often apathetic service. **Pros:** lovely beach; excellent spa; good dining options; huge online advance booking savings. **Cons:** sprawling layout; too bustling; uneven service. **TripAdvisor:** "impeccable," "such a beautiful place," "classy

and relaxing." $ *Rooms from: $654* ✉ *Dickenson Bay* ☎ *888/726–3257 reservations only, 268/484–0100* ⊕ *www.sandals.com* ⤳ *100 rooms, 257 suites, 16 rondavels* ⭘| *All-inclusive* ⌖ *3-night minimum.*

$ | **Siboney Beach Club.** This affordable beachfront oasis nestled in a tran-

HOTEL quil corner of Dickenson Bay delights with intimacy and warmth, and

Fodor's Choice knowledgeable Aussie owner Tony Johnson gladly acts as a de facto

★ tourist board. **Pros:** friendly service; superb location; great value; well maintained with rooms smartly refurbished regularly. **Cons:** no TV in bedrooms; patios lack screens, thus forcing a choice between swel- tering and swatting pests on rare still days; no elevator; inconsistent Wi-Fi signal. **TripAdvisor:** "nearly perfect," "small and good spirit," "great staff." $ *Rooms from: $190* ✉ *Dickenson Bay* ☎ *268/462–0806, 800/533–0234* ⊕ *www.siboneybeachclub.com* ⤳ *12 suites* ⭘| *No meals.*

$$$ | **Verandah Resort & Spa.** Though local activists disagree, this ecocen-

ALL-INCLUSIVE tric resort on Antigua's wild east coast emphasizes low-impact envi-

☾ ronmental responsibility without sacrificing upscale contemporary

★ conveniences. **Pros:** gorgeous remote location; sprawling but cleverly centralized; good kids' facilities with own pool. **Cons:** remote loca- tion makes a car a necessity to explore; smallish beaches; inconsistent food and service. **TripAdvisor:** "amazing service," "excellent family vacation," "perfect place to relax." $ *Rooms from: $590* ✉ *Long Bay* ☎ *268/562–6848, 800/858–4618, 866/237–1785 reservations only* ⊕ *www.verandahresortandspa.com* ⤳ *200 suites* ⭘| *All-inclusive.*

NIGHTLIFE

Most of Antigua's evening entertainment takes place at the resorts, which occasionally present calypso singers, steel bands, limbo danc- ers, and folkloric groups. Check with the tourist office for up-to-date information. In addition, a cluster of clubs and bars pulsate into the night in season around English and Falmouth Harbours.

BARS

Abracadabra. It's always a party at busy, bright trattoria Abracadabra. Late nights often turn into a disco with live music or DJs spinning reg- gae and 1980s dance music, and special events run from art exhibits to masquerades to fashion shows. There's even a fine late-night Italian snack menu and a fun, funky boutique. ✉ *Nelson's Dockyard, English Harbour* ☎ *268/460–2701.*

Carmichael's. Carmichael's is the fine-dining hilltop aerie at the Sugar Ridge residential complex. Nestle into a banquette or lounge in the infinity pool while sipping luscious libations that match the setting sun's colorful display. It's also a splendid spot for a postprandial cigar and port or single malt. You can always head downhill to sister nightspot, the bustling, buzzing **Sugar Club** (by the resort entrance) for live music (jazz to funk) and DJ disco evenings. ✉ *Tottenham Park, across from Jolly Harbour* ☎ *268/562–7700* ⊕ *www.sugarridgeantigua.com.*

Castaways. Castaways is a boisterous beach bar–bistro with a thatched roof, kids' playground, and colorful local murals that serves an

inexpensive menu of tapas and pub grub along with occasional entertainment. ⊠ *Jolly Harbour* ☎ *268/562–4445.*

★ **Indigo on the Beach.** Indigo on the Beach is a soigné yet relaxed spot any
time of day for creative tapas, salads, grills, and burgers, but the beautiful people turn out in force come evening to pose at the fiber-optically
lighted bar or on white lounges scattered with throw pillows. ⊠ *Carlisle
Bay, Old Road* ☎ *268/480–0000.*

Inn at English Harbour Bar. The Inn at English Harbour Bar, with its
green leather, wood beams, fieldstone walls, 19th-century maps, steer-
ing-wheel chandeliers, petit point upholstery, and maritime prints, is
uncommonly refined. ⊠ *English Harbour* ☎ *268/460–1014.*

Mad Mongoose. The Mad Mongoose is a wildly popular yachty (and
singles') joint, splashed in vivid Rasta colors, with tapas and martini
menus, live music Fridays (and most Tuesdays), a game room, and satellite TV. ⊠ *Falmouth Harbour* ☎ *268/463–7900.*

Mainbrace Pub. The Mainbrace Pub has a historic ambience, right down
to its warm brick walls and hardwood accents, and is known as a beer,
darts, and fish-and-chips kind of hangout for the boating set. ⊠ *Copper
& Lumber Store Hotel, English Harbour* ☎ *268/460–1058.*

★ **Shirley Heights Lookout.** Sunday-afternoon barbecues continue into the
night with reggae, soca, and steel-band music and dancing that sizzles
like the ribs on the grill. Residents and visitors gather for boisterous
fun, the latest gossip, and great sunsets. Most tourist groups vanish by
7 pm, when the real partying begins. There's another, less frenetic party
Thursday from 4 to 8 pm. Sips & Seconds, held every Friday evening,
provides a fine introduction to Antiguan cuisine and culture, accompanied by steel pan. ⊠ *Shirley Heights* ☎ *268/460–1785, 268/728–0636,
268/764–0389* ⊕ *www.shirleyheightslookout.com.*

★ **Trappa's.** Trappa's is a hipster hangout set in a bamboo-walled courtyard
hung with huge hibiscus paintings. It serves delectable, sizable tapas
(tuna sashimi, deep-fried Brie with black-currant jelly, Thai mango
chicken curry, beer-batter shrimp with garlic dip) for reasonable prices
(EC$24–EC$48) into the wee hours. Live music is often on the menu.
⊠ *Main Rd., English Harbour* ☎ *268/562–3534.*

CASINOS

There are three full casinos on Antigua, as well as several holes-in-the-
wall that have mostly one-arm bandits. Hours depend on the season,
so it's best to inquire upon your arrival.

Grand Bay Casino. Grand Bay Casino is delightfully garish, from gold
accents to Greco-Roman urns. More than 100 slots and video-poker
machines, table games, and Texas Hold 'Em tournaments compete
for guests' attention with live bands, DJs, and karaoke–trivia nights.
⊠ *Dickenson Bay* ☎ *268/481–7700.*

King's Casino. You can find abundant slots and gaming tables at the
somewhat dilapidated, unintentionally retro (icicle chandeliers, Nauga-
hyde seats, and 1970s soul crooners on the sound system) King's Casino.
The best time to go is Friday night, which jumps with energetic karaoke

competitions, live bands, and dancing. ⊠ *Heritage Quay, St. John's* ☎ *268/462–1727.*

DANCE CLUBS

The Coast. The Coast attracts a casually swanky, over-21 mix of locals and tourists for fine island food, rollicking live bands, fire-blowing bartenders, occasional fashion shows, theme nights like "Wednesday Wine and Jazz," and the latest in techno and house in a dockside setting. ⊠ *Heritage Quay, St. John's* ☎ *268/562–6278* ⊕ *www.coast.ag.*

Rush. Rush lures mostly young, lively locals in cool club gear for disco, Latin, and reggae-soca mixes; sea views from the romantic terrace; Leah's restaurant; and the Conors Billiards Lounge (which opens earlier, with happy hours and pub grub). The nightclub itself only opens Friday, but the eateries open nightly. ⊠ *Runaway Bay* ☎ *268/480–2030, 268/562–7874.*

SHOPPING

Antigua's duty-free shops are at Heritage Quay, one reason so many cruise ships call here. Bargains can be found on perfumes, liqueurs, and liquor (including English Harbour Antiguan rum), jewelry, china, and crystal. As for other local items, check out straw hats, baskets, batik, pottery, Susie's hot sauce, and hand-printed cotton clothing. Fine artists to look for include Gilly Gobinet, Heather Doram, Jan Farara, Jennifer Meranto, and Heike Petersen (delightful dolls and quilts). Several artists and craftspeople have banded together to form ⊕ *www.antiguanartists. com,* which lists their information, including whether they accept atelier visits by appointment.

SHOPPING AREAS

Fodor'sChoice
★

Redcliffe Quay, on the waterfront at the south edge of St. John's, is by far the most appealing shopping area. Several restaurants and more than 30 boutiques, many with one-of-a-kind wares, are set around landscaped courtyards shaded by colorful trees.

Heritage Quay, in St. John's, has 35 shops—including many that are duty-free—that cater to the cruise-ship crowd, which docks almost at its doorstep. Outlets here include Benetton, the Body Shop, Sunglass Hut, Dolce & Gabbana, and Oshkosh B'Gosh. There are also shops along **St. John's, St. Mary's, High,** and **Long streets.** The tangerine-and-lilac-hue four-story **Vendor's Mall** at the intersection of Redcliffe and Thames streets gathers the pushy, pesky vendors who once clogged the narrow streets. It's jammed with stalls; air-conditioned indoor shops sell some higher-price, if not higher-quality, merchandise. On the west coast the Mediterranean-style, arcaded **Jolly Harbour Marina** holds some interesting galleries and shops, as do the marinas and the main road snaking around English and Falmouth Harbours.

SPECIALTY STORES

ALCOHOL AND TOBACCO

Manuel Dias Liquor Store. Head to Manuel Dias Liquor Store for a wide selection of Caribbean rums and liqueurs. ⊠ *Long and Market Sts., St. John's* ☎ *268/462–0490.*

Quin Farara. You'll find terrific deals on both hard liquor and wines as well as cigars at Quin Farara. ⊠ *Long St. and Corn Alley, St. John's* ☎ *268/462–3869* ⊠ *Heritage Quay, St. John's* ☎ *268/462–1737* ⊠ *Jolly Harbour* ☎ *268/462–6245.*

ART

Fine Art Framing. Jennifer Meranto's incomparable hand-colored black-and-white photos of Caribbean scenes; Heather Doram's exquisite, intricately woven "collage" wall hangings; and ever-changing exhibits are on display at Fine Art Framing. ⊠ *Redcliffe Quay, St. John's* ☎ *268/562–1019.*

★ **Harmony Hall.** This is Antigua's top exhibition venue. A large space is used for one-person shows; other rooms display works in various mediums, from Aussie Aboriginal carvings to Antillean pottery. The sublime historic ambience, sweeping vistas, and fine Italian fare compensate for the remote location. ⊠ *Brown's Mill Bay, Brown's Mill* ☎ *268/460–4120.*

BOOKS AND MAGAZINES

Best of Books. This bookstore is an excellent, extensive source for everything from local cookbooks and nature guides to international newspapers. Check out the works of Jamaica Kincaid, whose writing about her native Antigua has won international acclaim. You'll also find an intriguing selection of crafts and artworks. ⊠ *Lower St. Mary's St., St. John's* ☎ *268/562–3198.*

CLOTHING

Exotic Antigua. This shop sells everything from antique Indonesian ikat throws to crepe de chine caftans to Tommy Bahama resort wear. ⊠ *Redcliffe Quay, St. John's* ☎ *268/562–1288.*

★ **Galley Boutique.** At Galley Boutique, Janey Easton personally seeks out exclusive creations from both international (Calvin Klein, Adrienne Vittadini) and local Caribbean designers, ranging from swimwear to evening garb. She also sells handicrafts and lovely hammocks. ⊠ *Nelson's Dockyard, English Harbour* ☎ *268/460–1525.*

Jacaranda. This shop sells batik, sarongs, and swimwear as well as Caribbean food, perfumes, soaps, and artwork. ⊠ *Redcliffe Quay, St. John's* ☎ *268/462–1888.*

New Gates. For duty-free threads, head to New Gates, an authorized dealer for such name brands as Ralph Lauren, Calvin Klein, and Tommy Hilfiger. ⊠ *Redcliffe Quay, St. John's* ☎ *268/562–1627.*

★ **Noreen Phillips.** Glitzy appliquéd and beaded evening wear—inspired by the colors of the sea and sunset—in sensuous fabrics ranging from chiffon and silk to Italian lace and Indian brocade are created at Noreen Phillips. ⊠ *Redcliffe Quay, St. John's* ☎ *268/462–3127.*

Sunseakers. At Sunseakers, you'll find every conceivable bathing suit and cover-up—from bikini thongs to sarongs—by top designers. ⊠ *Heritage Quay, St. John's* ☎ *268/462–3618.*

DUTY-FREE GOODS

Abbott's. You'll find luxury items from Breitling watches to Belleek china to Kosta Boda art glass in a luxurious, air-conditioned showroom at Abbott's. ⊠ *Heritage Quay, St. John's* ☎ *268/462–3107* ⊕ *www. abbottsjewellery.com.*

Lipstick. You'll find high-priced imported scents and cosmetics—from Clarins to Clinique and Gucci to Guerlain—at Lipstick. ⊠ *Heritage Quay, St. John's* ☎ *268/562–1130.*

Passions. This shop gives Abbott's a run for its (and your) considerable money on luxury brands like Chanel, Hermès, and Lalique. ⊠ *Heritage Quay, St. John's* ☎ *268/562–5295.*

HANDICRAFTS

★ **Cedars Pottery.** The airy studio of Michael and Imogen Hunt is Cedars Pottery. Michael produces a vivid line of domestic ware and Zen-simple teapots, vases, and water fountains featuring rich earth hues and sensuous lines. Imogen fashions ethereal paper-clay fish sculptures, and mask-shaped, intricately laced light fixtures and candelabras. ⊠ *St. Clare Estate, Buckleys* ☎ *268/460–5293* ⊕ *www.cedarspottery.com.*

Eureka. The offerings at Eureka span the globe, from Azerbaijani hand-blown glass to Zambian weavings and carvings. ⊠ *Thames St., St. John's* ☎ *268/560–3654.*

Isis. Island and international bric-a-brac, such as antique jewelry, hand-carved walking sticks, and glazed pottery, is available at Isis. ⊠ *Redcliffe Quay, St. John's* ☎ *268/462–4602.*

Pottery Shop. This shop sells the work of gifted potter Sarah Fuller, whose hand-painted tiles, wind chimes, and plates and cobalt-blue glazes are striking (as are her driftwood hangings mixed with clay and copper). You can also visit her studio–gallery on Dutchman's Bay. ⊠ *Redcliffe Quay, St. John's* ☎ *268/562–1264, 268/462–5503* ⊕ *www. sarahfullerpottery.com.*

★ **Rhythm of Blue Gallery.** Nancy Nicholson co-owns Rhythm of Blue Gallery; she's renowned for her exquisite glazed and matte-finish ceramics, featuring Caribbean-pure shades, as well as her black-and-white yachting photos. You'll also find exhibitions showcasing leading regional artists working in mediums from batik to copper. ⊠ *Dockyard Dr., English Harbour* ☎ *268/562–2230.*

★ **Things Local.** The wondrous wood carvings of Carl Henry—who fashions local mahogany into boats, fish, and warri boards (an African game brought over to the Caribbean)—are featured at Things Local. ⊠ *Nelson's Dockyard, English Harbour* ☎ *268/562–5386, 268/461–7595, 268/770–5780.*

JEWELRY

Colombian Emeralds. The largest retailer of Colombian emeralds in the world also carries a wide variety of other gems. ⊠ *Heritage Quay, St. John's* ☎ *268/462–3462.*

Diamonds International. You'll find a huge selection of loose diamonds as well as a variety of watches, rings, brooches, bracelets, and pendants at Diamonds International. Several resorts have branches. ⊠ *Heritage Quay, St. John's* ☎ *268/481–1880.*

★ **Goldsmitty.** Hans Smit is the Goldsmitty, an expert goldsmith who turns gold, black coral, and precious and semiprecious stones into one-of-a-kind works of art. ⊠ *Redcliffe Quay, St. John's* ☎ *268/462–4601* ⊕ *www.goldsmitty.com.*

SPORTS AND ACTIVITIES

Several all-inclusives offer day passes that permit use of all sporting facilities, from tennis courts to water-sports concessions, as well as free drinks and meals. The cost begins at $50 for singles (but can be as much as $200 for couples at Sandals), and hours generally run from 8 am to 6 pm, with extensions available until 2 am. Antigua has long been famed for its cricketers (such as Viv Richards and Richie Richardson); aficionados will find one of the Caribbean's finest cricket grounds right by the airport, with major test matches running January through June.

ADVENTURE TOURS

Antigua is developing its ecotourist opportunities, and several memorable offshore experiences involve more than just snorkeling. The archipelago of islets coupled with a full mangrove swamp off the northeast coast is unique in the Caribbean.

★ **Adventure Antigua.** The enthusiastic Eli Fuller, who is knowledgeable not only about the ecosystem and geography of Antigua but also about its history and politics (his grandfather was the American consul), runs Adventure Antigua. His thorough seven-hour excursion (Eli dubs it "re-creating my childhood explorations") includes stops at Guiana Island (for lunch and guided snorkeling; turtles, barracuda, and stingrays are common sightings), Pelican Island (more snorkeling), Bird Island (hiking to vantage points to admire the soaring ospreys and frigate and red-billed tropic birds), and Hell's Gate (a striking limestone rock formation where the more intrepid may hike and swim through sunken caves and tide pools painted with pink and maroon algae). The company also offers a fun, shorter "Xtreme amusement park ride" variation on a racing boat catering to adrenaline junkies who "feel the need for speed" that also visits Stingray City, as well as a more sedate Antigua Classic Yacht sail-and-snorkel experience that explains the rich West Indian history of boatbuilding. ☎ *268/727–3261, 268/726–6355* ⊕ *www. adventureantigua.com.*

★ **"Paddles" Kayak Eco Adventure.** "Paddles" Kayak Eco Adventure takes you on a 3½-hour tour of serene mangroves and inlets with informative narrative about the fragile ecosystem of the swamp and reefs and the rich diversity of flora and fauna. The tour ends with a hike to sunken caves and snorkeling in the North Sound Marine Park, capped by a rum punch at the fun Creole-style clubhouse. Experienced guides double as kayaking and snorkeling instructors, making this an excellent opportunity for novices. Conrad and Jennie's brainchild is one of Antigua's better bargains. ⊠ *Seaton's Village* ☎ *268/463–1944* ⊕ *www. antiguapaddles.com.*

☾ **Stingray City Antigua.** Stingray City Antigua is a carefully reproduced "natural" environment nicknamed by staffers the "retirement home," though the 30-plus stingrays, ranging from infants to seniors, are frisky. You can stroke, feed, even hold the striking gliders ("they're like puppy dogs," one guide swears), as well as snorkel in deeper, protected waters. The tour guides do a marvelous job of explaining the animals' habits, from feeding to breeding, and their predators (including man). ⊠ *Seaton's Village* ☎ *268/562–7297* ⊕ *www.stingraycityantigua.com.*

BOATING

Antigua's circular geographic configuration makes boating easy, and its many lovely harbors and coves provide splendid anchorages. Experienced boaters will particularly enjoy Antigua's east coast, which is far more rugged and has several islets; be sure to get a good nautical map, as there are numerous minireefs that can be treacherous. If you're just looking for a couple of hours of wave-hopping, stick to the Dickenson Bay or Jolly Harbour area.

Nicholson Yacht Charters. Nicholson Yacht Charters are real professionals, true pioneers in Caribbean sailing, with three generations spanning 60 years of experience. A long-established island family, they can offer you anything from a 20-foot ketch to a giant schooner. ⊠ *English Harbour* ☎ *268/460–1530, 305/433–5533* ⊕ *www.nicholson-charters.com.*

Ondeck. Ondeck runs skippered charters on the likes of Farr and Beneteau out of the Antigua Yacht Club Marina in Falmouth Harbour, terrific one- and two-day sailing workshops, and eco-adventure trips to Montserrat on a racing yacht. You can even participate in official regattas. Instructors and crew are all seasoned racers. ☎ *268/562–6696* ⊕ *www.ondeckoceanracing.com.*

Sunsail. Sunsail has an extensive modern fleet of dinghies and 32-foot day-sailers starting at $25 per half day, $50 for a full day (always call in advance, as the Nelson's Dockyard office is open sporadically). It also arranges bareboat yachting, often in conjunction with hotel stays. ☎ *268/460–2615, 888/350–3568* ⊕ *www.sunsail.com.*

DIVING

Antigua is an unsung diving destination, with plentiful undersea sights to explore, from coral canyons to sea caves. Barbuda alone features roughly 200 wrecks on its treacherous reefs. The most accessible wreck is the 1890s bark *Andes*, not far out in Deep Bay, off Five Islands Peninsula. Among the favorite sites are **Green Island, Cades Reef,** and **Bird Island** (a national park). Memorable sightings include turtles, stingrays, and barracuda darting amid basalt walls, hulking boulders, and stray 17th-century anchors and cannon. One advantage is accessibility in many spots for shore divers and snorkelers. Double-tank dives run about $90.

Dive Antigua. Certification courses and day and night dives are offered at Dive Antigua. Advantages include the central location, knowledgeable crew, satellite technology sounding the day's best dive sites, free drinks after dives, and exceptionally priced packages. Drawbacks include generally noisy groups and inconsistent maintenance (less safety than hygiene concerns). ⊠ *Rex Halcyon Cove Beach Resort, Dickenson Bay* ☎ *268/462–3483* ⊕ *www.diveantigua.com.*

Dockyard Divers. Owned by British ex-merchant seaman Captain A.G. "Tony" Fincham, Dockyard Divers is one of the island's most established outfits and offers diving and snorkeling trips, PADI courses, and dive packages with accommodations. They're geared to seasoned divers, but staff work patiently with novices. Tony is a wonderful source of information on the island; ask him about the "Fincham's Follies" musical extravaganza he produces for charity. ⊠ *Nelson's Dockyard, English Harbour* ☎ *268/460–1178* ⊕ *www.dockyard-divers.com.*

FISHING

Antigua's waters teem with game fish such as marlin, wahoo, and tuna. Most boat trips include equipment, lunch, and drinks. Figure at least $495 for a half day, $790 for a full day, for up to six people.

Obsession. The 45-foot Hatteras Sportfisherman *Obsession* has top-of-the-line equipment, including an international-standard fighting chair, outriggers, and handcrafted rods. ☎ *268/462–3174* ⊕ *www.charternet.com/charters/obsession/.*

Overdraft. *Overdraft* is a sleek, spacious, fiberglass 40-footer outfitted with the latest techno-gadgetry and operated by Frankie Hart, a professional fisherman who knows the waters intimately and regales clients with stories of his trade. He also rents the 26-foot *H2O*, a ProKat versatile enough to accommodate fly-fishing and deeper-water bay bait fishing. ☎ *268/464–4954, 268/463–3112* ⊕ *www.antiguafishing.com.*

GOLF

Though Antigua hardly qualifies as a duffer's delight, its two 18-hole courses offer varied layouts.

Cedar Valley Golf Club. Northeast of St. John's, Cedar Valley Golf Club has a driving range and par-70, 6,157-yard, 18-hole course. The not terribly well-maintained terrain offers some challenges with tight hilly fairways and numerous doglegs (Hole 7 is a perfect example). The 5th hole has exceptional ocean vistas from the top of the tee, and the par-5 9th offers the trickiest design with steep slopes and swales. Greens fees are $49 ($25 for 9 holes); carts are $42 ($22 for 9 holes). The Spinach Cafe offers free Wi-Fi. ⊠ *Friar's Hill* ☎ *268/462–0161* ⊕ *www.cedarvalleygolf.ag.*

Jolly Harbour Golf Course. Jolly Harbour Golf Course is a par-71, 6,001-yard (officially, but it's really 5,587 yards from the back tees), 18-hole course designed by Karl Litten. The flat Florida-style layout is lushly tropical, with seven lakes adding to the challenge. The 15th is the signature hole, with a sharp dogleg and long carry over two hazards.

Unfortunately, fairways are often dry and patchy, drainage is poor, and the pro shop and "19th hole" are barely adequate. Greens fees are $57.50 ($97.75 including motorized cart) or $34.50/$23 for 9 holes. Visitors can participate in regular tournaments and "meet-and-greet" events. ⊠ *Jolly Harbour* ☏ *268/462–7771.*

GUIDED TOURS

Almost all taxi drivers double as guides; an island tour with one costs about $25 an hour. Every major hotel has a cabbie on call and may be able to negotiate a discount, particularly off-season. Several operators specialize in off-road four-wheel-drive adventures that provide a taste of island history and topography.

D&J Tours. Day-trippers can experience Barbuda with D&J Tours; their excursion to the island includes round-trip transport with a beach picnic and full tour for $120. ☏ *268/773–9766, 268/726–9133.*

Island Safaris. Four-wheel off-road adventures by Island Safaris, which also runs other land- and water-based excursions, enables you to fully appreciate the island's natural beauty, history, folklore, and cultural heritage as you zoom about the southwest part of Antigua. Hiking is involved, though it's not strenuous. Lunch and snorkeling are also included. Active adventurers will particularly enjoy the combo Land Rover–kayak outback ecotour. Prices start at $99 per adult, $60–$75 children 7–12. ☏ *268/480–1225* ⊕ *www.tropicaladventures-antigua. com.*

Scenic Tours. Scenic Tours gives affordable half- and full-day island tours, geared toward cruise passengers, that focus on such highlights as Devil's Bridge, Shirley Heights, and English Harbour, as well as soft adventure hikes. ⊠ *Woods Mall, St. John's* ☏ *268/764–3060, 888/380–1234* ⊕ *www.scenictoursantigua.com.*

HORSEBACK RIDING

Comparatively dry Antigua is best for beach rides, though you won't find anything wildly romantic and deserted à la *Black Stallion*.

Spring Hill Riding Club. Spring Hill Riding Club specializes in equestrian lessons in show jumping and dressage but also offers $50 hour-long trail rides on the beach or through the bush past ruined forts (swimming is an additional $20); half-hour private lessons from a British Horse Society instructor are $25. ⊠ *Falmouth Harbour* ☏ *268/460–7787, 268/773–3139* ⊕ *www.springhillridingclub.com.*

SAILING AND SNORKELING

Not a sailor yourself? Consider signing up for one of the following boat tours. Each tour provides a great opportunity to enjoy the seafaring life while someone else captains the ship.

Miguel's Holiday Adventures. Miguel's Holiday Adventures leaves every Tuesday, Thursday, and Saturday morning at 10 am from the Hodges

Bay jetty for snorkeling, rum punches, and lunch at Prickly Pear Island, which offers both shallow- and deepwater snorkeling, as well as hiking. In this comfortable family operation, Miguel's wife, Josephine, prepares an authentic, lavish West Indian buffet including lobster, and Miguel and his son Terrence are caring instructors. ☎ *268/460–9978, 268/772–3213, 268/723–7418 mobile* ⊕ *www.pricklypearisland.com*.

Tropical Adventures. Barbuda day trips on the catamaran *Excellence* overflow with rum and high spirits, as do circumnavigations of Antigua. Tropical Adventures also operates ecokayaking tours and slightly more sedate, intimate catamaran cruises from sunset to snorkeling on the *Mystic*. ☎ *268/480–1225* ⊕ *www.tropicaladventures-antigua.com*.

Wadadli Cats. Wadadli Cats offers several cruises, including a circumnavigation of the island and snorkeling at Bird Island or Cades Reef, on its five sleek catamarans, including the handsome, fully outfitted *Spirit of Antigua*. Prices are fair ($95–$110), and advance direct bookers get a free T-shirt. ☎ *268/462–4792* ⊕ *www.wadadlicats.com*.

WINDSURFING AND KITEBOARDING

Most major hotels offer windsurfing equipment. The best areas are Nonsuch Bay and the east coast (notably Half Moon and Willoughby bays), which is slightly less protected and has a challenging juxtaposition of sudden calms and gusts.

KiteAntigua. KiteAntigua offers lessons in the Caribbean's hot new sport, kiteboarding, where a futuristic surfboard with harness is propelled only by an inflated kite; kite-board rentals (for the certified) are also available at $30 per hour, $50 half day, $70 full day. The varied multi-day lesson packages are expensive but thorough; a four-hour beginners course is $260. KiteAntigua closes from September through November, when winds aren't optimal. The center is on a stretch near the airport, but road trips to secret spots are arranged for experienced kitesurfers seeking that sometimes harrowing "high." ⊠ *Jabberwock Beach* ☎ *268/720–5483, 268/727–3983* ⊕ *www.kitesurfantigua.com*.

Windsurfing Antigua. Patrick Scales of Windsurfing Antigua has long been one of Antigua's, if not the Caribbean's, finest instructors; he now offers a mobile service in high season. He provides top-flight equipment for $25 per hour ($75 per day), two-hour beginner lessons for $80, and specialty tours to Half Moon Bay and other favorite spots for experienced surfers. ⊠ *Jabberwock Beach* ☎ *268/461–9463, 268/773–9463* ⊕ *www.windsurfantigua.net*.

ZIP LINING

Antigua Rainforest Canopy Tours. Play Tarzan and Jane at Antigua Rainforest Canopy Tours. You should be in fairly good condition for the ropes challenges, which require upper-body strength and stamina; there are height and weight restrictions. But anyone (vertigo or acrophobia sufferers, beware) can navigate the intentionally rickety "Indiana Jones–inspired" suspension bridges, then fly (in secure harnesses) over a rain-forest-filled valley from one towering turpentine tree to the next on lines with names like "Screamer" and "Leap of Faith." There are 21 stations, as well as a bar–café and interpretive signage. First-timers, fear not: the "rangers" are affable, amusing, and accomplished. Admission varies slightly, but is usually $85. It's open Monday–Saturday from 8 to 6, with two scheduled tours at 9 and 11 (other times by appointment). ⊠ *Fig Dr., Wallings* ☎ *268/562–6363* ⊕ *www.antiguarainforest.com.*

Aruba

WORD OF MOUTH

"I've been to Aruba 3 times. Each time we've had beautiful weather. It's a dry desertlike island due to the lack of rain. It's definitely hot. but I love the breeze that is always blowing. I guess there is humidity, but I've never really felt that. The shade is always a nice place to be."

—aruba1006

WELCOME TO ARUBA

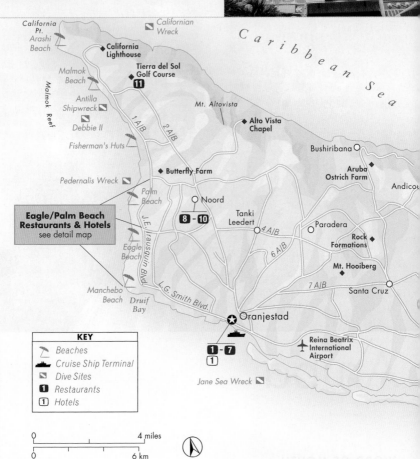

KEY

Beaches
Cruise Ship Terminal
Dive Sites
Restaurants
Hotels

California Pt.
Arashi Beach
Californian Wreck
California Lighthouse
Malmok Beach
Tierra del Sol Golf Course 11
Malmok Reef
Antilla Shipwreck
Debbie II
Fisherman's Huts
Mt. Altovista
Alto Vista Chapel
Bushiribana
Aruba Ostrich Farm
Andicou
Pedernalis Wreck
Butterfly Farm
Palm Beach
Noord
Tanki Leedert
4 A/B
Paradera
Rock Formations
6 A/B
Mt. Hooiberg
7 A/B
Santa Cruz

Eagle/Palm Beach Restaurants & Hotels
see detail map

8 - 10

J.E. Irausquin Blvd.
Eagle Beach
Manchebo Beach
Druif Bay
L.G. Smith Blvd.
Oranjestad
Reina Beatrix International Airport
Jane Sea Wreck

1 A/B
2 A/B

Caribbean Sea

0 ———— 4 miles
0 ———— 6 km

1 - 7
1

The pastel-color houses of Dutch settlers still grace the waterfront in the capital city of Oranjestad. Winds are fierce, even savage, on the north coast, where you'll find a landscape of cacti, rocky desert, and wind-bent divi-divi trees. On the west coast the steady breezes attract windsurfers to the shallow, richly colored waters.

THE A IN THE ABC ISLANDS

The A in the ABC Islands (followed by Bonaire and Curaçao), Aruba is small—only 19½ miles (31½ km) long and 6 miles (9½ km) across at its widest point. It became an independent entity within the Netherlands in 1986. The official language is Dutch, but almost every native speaks English and Spanish as well. The island's population is 108,000.

Restaurants ▼
Bucaneer **10**
Cuba's Cookin' **5**
El Gaucho
Argentine Grill **2**
Gasparito Restaurant
& Art Gallery **8**
Gostoso **4**
L. G. Smith's
Steak & Chop House **1**
Marandi **3**
Papiamento **9**
Pinchos Grill & Bar **6**
Qué Pasa? **7**
Ventanas del Mar **11**

Hotels ▼
Renaissance
Aruba Resort & Casino .. **1**

4

ARUBA

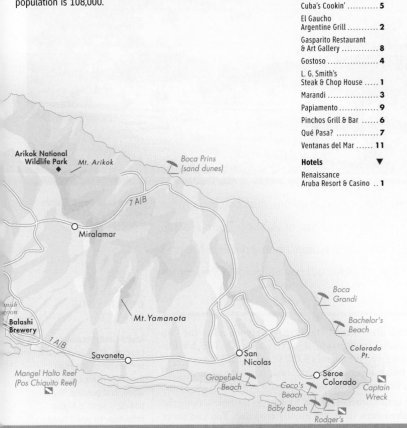

Arikok National Wildlife Park
Mt. Arikok
Boca Prins (sand dunes)
7 A|B
Miralamar
Boca Grandi
Bachelor's Beach
Mt. Yamanota
Balashi Brewery
1 A|B
Savaneta
San Nicolas
Colorado Pt.
Mangel Halto Reef (Pos Chiquito Reef)
Grapefield Beach
Coco's Beach
Seroe Colorado
Captain Wreck
Baby Beach
Rodger's

TOP REASONS TO VISIT ARUBA

1 The Nightlife: Some of the best in the Caribbean. The colorful Kukoo Kunuku party bus picks you up and pours you out at your hotel.

2 The Beaches: Powder-soft beaches and turquoise waters are legendary.

3 The Restaurants: Great restaurants offer a wide range of cuisine as good as any in the Caribbean.

4 The Casinos: Aruba's casinos will please both casual and serious gamblers.

5 The Welcome: A friendly population devoted to tourism guarantees welcoming smiles throughout the island.

ARUBA BEACHES

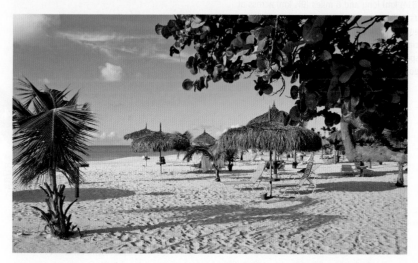

There are few destinations that can match the glorious beach vistas of Aruba. There's white sand, turquoise waters, and constant breezes that are a lovely cool counterpoint to the intense sunshine.

(Above) Eagle Beach (Bottom right) Baby Beach (Top right) Fisherman's Huts

There's also virtually no litter—everyone takes the "no tira sushi" (no littering) signs very seriously, which is fortunate given the island's $280 fine. Virtually every popular beach has a resort attached, but because nearly all beaches are public, there is never a problem with access.

The major beaches, which back up to the hotels along the southwestern strip, are usually crowded. You can make the hour-long hike from the Holiday Inn to the Tamarijn without ever leaving sand. Make sure you're well protected from the sun—scorching happens fast here. Luckily, there's at least one covered bar (and often an ice-cream stand) at virtually every hotel. On the island's northeastern side, stronger winds make the waters too choppy for swimming, but the vistas are great, and the terrain is wonderful for exploring.

BRING YOUR SHADES

Aruba's most popular beaches, from Druif Beach to the end of the High Rise Resort area, are wide, white, and pristine. The powdery sand is highly reflective, so you'll need your sunglasses. Beaches on the island's North Coast are much rockier, and swimming is not advisable. Baby Beach on the southwestern tip is a bit of a drive, but the wide stretch of icing-sugar sand makes it worthwhile.

Arashi Beach. This is a 1-km (½-mile) stretch of gleaming white sand. Although it was once rocky, nature—with a little help from humans—has turned it into an excellent place for sunbathing and swimming. Despite calm waters, the rocky reputation keeps most people away, making it relatively uncrowded. **Amenities:** parking. **Best for:** swimming; walking. ⊠ *West of Malmok Beach, on west end.*

☺**Baby Beach.** On the island's eastern tip (near the refinery), this semicircular beach borders a placid bay that's just about as shallow as a wading pool—perfect for tots, shore divers, and terrible swimmers. Thatched shaded areas are good places to cool off. Down the road is the island's rather unusual pet cemetery. Stop by the nearby snack truck for burgers, hot dogs, beer, and soda. The road to this beach (and several others) is through San Nicolas and along the road toward Seroe Colorado. Just before reaching the beach, keep an eye out for a strange 300-foot natural seawall made of coral and rock that was thrown up overnight when Hurricane Ivan swept by the island in 2004. **Amenities:** food and drink. **Best for:** snorkeling; swimming; walking. ⊠ *Near Seroe Colorado, on east end.*

Boca Grandi. This is a great spot for windsurfers, but swimming is not advisable. It's near Seagrape Grove and the

Aruba Golf Club, toward the island's eastern tip. **Amenities:** none. **Best for:** walking; windsurfing. ⊠ *Near Seagrape Grove, on east end.*

★Fodor's Choice **Eagle Beach.** On the southwestern coast, across the highway from what is quickly becoming known as Time-Share Lane, is one of the Caribbean's—if not the world's—best beaches. With all the resorts here, this mile-plus-long beach is always hopping. The white sand is literally dazzling, and sunglasses are essential. Many of the hotels have facilities on or near the beach, and refreshments are never far away. **Amenities:** food and drink; toilets. **Best for:** swimming; walking; sunset. ⊠ *J.E. Irausquin Blvd., north of Manchebo Beach.*

Fisherman's Huts (Hadicurari). Next to the Holiday Inn is a windsurfer's haven with good swimming conditions and a decent, slightly rocky, white sand beach. Take a picnic lunch (tables are available) and watch the elegant purple, aqua, and orange sails struggle in the wind. ⊠ *1 A/B, at Holiday Inn SunSpree Aruba.*

Grapefield Beach. To the southeast of San Nicolas, a sweep of blinding-white sand in the shadow of cliffs and boulders is marked by an anchor-shape memorial dedicated to seamen. Pick sea grapes from January to June. Swim at your own risk; the waves here can be rough. This is not a popular tourist

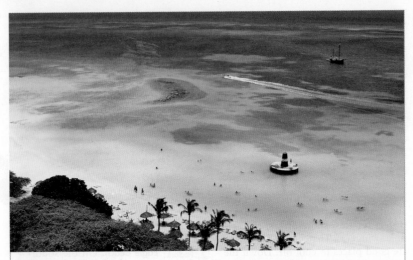

Looking down on Palm Beach

beach, so finding a quiet spot is almost guaranteed, but the downside of this is a complete lack of facilities or nearby refreshments. **Amenities:** none. **Best for:** solitude. ⊠ *Southwest of San Nicolas, on east end.*

Malmok Beach *(Boca Catalina).* On the northwestern shore, this small, nondescript beach borders shallow waters that stretch 300 yards from shore. There are no snack or refreshment stands here, but shade is available under the thatched umbrellas. It's the perfect place to learn to windsurf. Right off the coast here is a favorite haunt for divers and snorkelers—the wreck of the German ship *Antilla,* scuttled in 1940. ⊠ *At end of J.E. Irausquin Blvd., Malmokweg.*

Manchebo Beach *(Punta Brabo).* Impressively wide, the white-sand shoreline in front of the Manchebo Beach Resort is where officials turn a blind eye to the occasional topless sunbather. This beach merges with Druif Beach, and most locals use the name Manchebo to refer to both. **Amenities:** food and drink; toilets. **Best for:** swimming. ⊠ *J.E. Irausquin Blvd., at Manchebo Beach Resort.*

Palm Beach. This stretch runs from the Westin Aruba Resort, Spa & Casino to the Marriott's Aruba Ocean Club. It's the center of Aruban tourism, offering good swimming, sailing, and other water sports. In some spots you might find a variety of shells that are great to collect, but not as much fun to step on barefoot—bring sandals. **Amenities:** food and drink; toilets; water sports. **Best for:** swimming; walking. ⊠ *J.E. Irausquin Blvd., between Westin Aruba Resort, Spa & Casino and Marriott's Aruba Ocean Club.*

⟲ **Rodger's Beach.** Near Baby Beach on the island's eastern tip, this beautiful curving stretch of sand is only slightly marred by its proximity to the oil refinery at the bay's far side. Swimming conditions are excellent here. The snack bar at the water's edge has beach-equipment rentals and a shop. Drive around the refinery perimeter to get here. **Amenities:** food and drink; water sports. **Best for:** swimming. ⊠ *Next to Baby Beach, on east end.*

By Vernon
O'Reilly-
Ramesar

Cruise ships gleam in Oranjestad Harbour, and thousands of eager tourists scavenge through souvenir stalls looking for the perfect memento. The mile-long stretch of L.G. Smith Boulevard is lined with cafés, designer stores, and signs for the latest Vegas-style shows. The countryside is dotted with colorful *cunucu* (country-style houses) and small neighborhood shops. Suddenly, the rocky desert landscape is startlingly austere.

Aruba offers a lot of variety in a small package. Tourists flock here for the sunny climate, perfect waters, and excellent beaches—so much so that the area around beautiful Eagle Beach is an almost unbroken line of hotels, restaurants, and bars. Here on the south coast, the action is nonstop both day and night, whereas the fiercely rugged north coast is a desolate and rocky landscape that has so far resisted development.

As with Bonaire and Curaçao, the island was originally populated by the Caquetio, an Amerindian people related to the Arawak. After the Spanish conquered the island in 1499, Aruba was basically left alone, since it held little in the way of agricultural or mineral wealth. The Dutch took charge of the island in 1636, and things remained relatively quiet until gold was discovered in the 1800s.

Like the trademark *watapana* (divi-divi) trees that have been forced into bonsai-like angles by the constant trade winds, Aruba has always adjusted to changes in the economic climate. Mining dominated the economy until the early part of the 20th century, when the mines became unprofitable. Shortly thereafter, Aruba became home to a major oil-refining operation, which was the economic mainstay until the early 1990s, when its contribution to the local economy was eclipsed by tourism. Today, after being so resolutely dedicated to attracting visitors for so many years, Aruba's national culture and tourism industry are inextricably intertwined.

LOGISTICS

Getting to Aruba: Many airlines fly nonstop to Aruba from several cities in North America; connections will usually be at a U.S. airport. Smaller airlines connect the Dutch islands in the Caribbean, often using Aruba as a hub. Travelers to the United States clear U.S. Customs and Immigration before leaving Aruba.

Hassle Factor: Low.

On the Ground: A taxi from the airport to most hotels takes about 20 minutes. An hour-long island taxi tour costs about $45, with up to four people. Rides into town from Eagle Beach run about $10; from Palm Beach, about $11. If you want to explore the countryside at your leisure and try different beaches, then you should rent a car, but for just getting to and around town, taxis are preferable, and you can use tour companies to arrange your activities. If you rent a car, try to make reservations before arriving, and rent a four-wheel-drive vehicle if you plan to explore the island's natural sights. Some companies have minimum ages for renting a car.

With more than a million visitors a year, Aruba is not a destination that will appeal to those trying to avoid the beaten path—but you should visit Aruba if you're looking for a pleasant climate, excellent facilities, lots of nightlife, and no unpleasant surprises. The U.S. dollar is accepted everywhere, and English is spoken universally, which makes Aruba a popular spot for Americans who want an overseas trip to a place that doesn't feel foreign. In fact, Americans go through U.S. customs right at the airport in Aruba, so there are no formalities upon landing in the United States.

PLANNING

WHEN TO GO

Aruba's popularity means that hotels are usually booked solid during the high season, from mid-December through mid-April or early May, so early booking is essential. During other times of the year, rate reductions can be dramatic.

Aruba doesn't really have a rainy season and hardly ever sees a hurricane, so you take fewer chances by coming here in late summer and fall. However, if you travel at this time, remember that hurricanes and tropical storms are not unheard of—just rare.

February or March witnesses a spectacular **Carnival**, a riot of color whirling to the tunes of steel bands and culminating in the Grand Parade, where some of the floats rival the extravagance of those in the Big Easy's Mardi Gras.

GETTING HERE AND AROUND
AIR TRAVEL
Many airlines fly nonstop to Aruba from several cities in North America; connections will usually be at a U.S. airport.

Nonstop Flights There are nonstop flights from Atlanta (Delta), Boston (American, JetBlue, US Airways), Charlotte (US Airways), Chicago (United—weekly), Fort Lauderdale (Spirit—weekly), Houston (Continental), Miami (American), Newark (Continental), New York–JFK (American, Delta, JetBlue), New York–LGA (Continental—weekly), Philadelphia (US Airways—twice weekly), and Washington, D.C.–Dulles (United).

The island's **Reina Beatrix International Airport** (AUA) is equipped with thorough security, lots of flight displays, and state-of-the-art baggage-handling systems.

ARUBA DRIVING TIPS

International traffic signs and Dutch-style traffic signals (with an extra light for a turning lane) can be misleading if you're not used to them; use extreme caution, especially at intersections, until you grasp the rules of the road. Speed limits are rarely posted but are usually 50 mph (80 kph) in the countryside. Aside from the major highways, the island's winding roads are poorly marked. Gas prices average about $1.63 a liter (roughly $6.20 a gallon), which is reasonable by Caribbean standards.

4

Airline Contacts American Airlines ☎ 297/582-2700 on Aruba, 800/433-7300 ⊕ www.aa.com. **Continental Airlines** ☎ 297/588-0044 on Aruba, 800/523-3273 for U.S. and Mexico reservations, 800/231-0856 for international reservations ⊕ www.continental.com. **Delta Airlines** ☎ 297/588-0044 on Aruba, 800/221-1212 for U.S. reservations, 800/241-4141 for international reservations ⊕ www.delta.com. **Dutch Antilles Express** ☎ 599/717-0808 ⊕ www.flydae.com. **JetBlue** ☎ 800/538-2583 ⊕ www.jetblue.com. **KLM** ☎ 297/582-3546 on Aruba, 31/20-4-747-747 in Amsterdam ⊕ www.klm.com. **Spirit Airlines** ☎ 800/772-7117, 586/791-7300 ⊕ www.spiritair.com. **United Airlines** ☎ 297/588-6544 on Aruba, 800/538-2929 in North America ⊕ www.united.com. **US Airways** ☎ 297/587-7479 on Aruba, 800/428-4322 for U.S. and Canada reservations, 800/622-1015 for international reservations ⊕ www.usairways.com.

BUS TRAVEL

Buses run hourly trips between the beach hotels and Oranjestad. The one-way fare is $1.25 ($2.25 round-trip), and exact change is preferred (so be sure to keep some U.S. change handy if you plan to pay in U.S. currency). There are also minibuses that will pick you up at the same stops for the same price; just be sure to look for the "ATA approved" sign. Buses also run down the coast from Oranjestad to San Nicolas for the same fare.

Contacts Arubus ⊕ www.arubus.com.

CAR TRAVEL

If you want to explore the countryside and try different beaches, then you should rent a car. Try to make reservations before arriving, and rent a four-wheel drive if you plan to explore the island's natural sights. For just getting to and around town, taxis are preferable, and you can use tour companies to arrange your activities.

To rent a car you'll need a driver's license, and you must meet the minimum age requirements of the company (Budget, for example, requires drivers to be over 25; Avis, between 23 and 70; and Hertz, over 21). A deposit of $500 (or a signed credit-card slip) is required. Rates are between $47 and $75 a day (local agencies generally have lower rates).

Contacts Avis ⊠ *Kolibristraat 14, Oranjestad* ☎ *297/582-8787, 800/522-9696* ⊕ *www.avis.com* ⊠ *Airport* ☎ *297/582-5496.* **Budget** ⊠ *Kolibristraat 1, Oranjestad* ☎ *297/582-8600, 800/472-3325* ⊕ *www.budget.com.* **Dollar** ⊠ *Grendeaweg 15, Oranjestad* ☎ *297/582-2783* ⊕ *www.dollar.com* ⊠ *Airport* ☎ *297/582-5651.* **Economy** ⊠ *Kolibristraat 5, Oranjestad* ☎ *297/582-5176* ⊕ *www.economyaruba.com.* **Hertz** ⊠ *Sabana Blanco 35, near airport, Oranjestad* ☎ *297/582-1845* ⊕ *www.arubarentcar.com.* **National** ⊠ *Tanki Leendert 170, Noord* ☎ *297/587-1967, 800/227-7368* ⊕ *www.nationalcar.com* ⊠ *Airport* ☎ *297/582-5451.* **Thrifty** ⊠ *Balashi 65, Santa Cruz* ☎ *297/585-5300* ⊕ *www.thrifty.com* ⊠ *Airport* ☎ *297/583-5335.*

TAXI TRAVEL

There's a dispatch office at the airport; you can also flag down taxis on the street (look for license plates with a "TX" tag). Rates are fixed (i.e., there are no meters; the rates are set by the government and displayed on a chart), though you and the driver should agree on the fare before your ride begins. Add $2 to the fare after midnight and $3 on Sunday and holidays. An hour-long island tour costs about $45, with up to four people. Rides into town from Eagle Beach run about $10; from Palm Beach, about $11.

Contact Airport Taxi Dispatch ☎ *297/582-2116.*

ESSENTIALS

Banks and Exchange Services The local currency is the Aruban florin (AFl 1.79 to US$1). The florin is pegged to the U.S. dollar, and Arubans accept U.S. dollars readily, so you need acquire local currency only for pocket change. Note that the Netherlands Antilles florin used on Curaçao is not accepted on Aruba. ATMs are easy to find.

Electricity 110 volts, 50 cycles.

Emergency Services Ambulance, Fire, and Police ☎ *911.* **Dr. Horacio Oduber Hospital** ⊠ *L.G. Smith Blvd. 47, Manchebo Beach* ☎ *297/587-4300.*

Language Everyone on the island speaks English, but the official languages are Dutch and Papiamento. Most locals speak Papiamento—a rapid-fire mix of Spanish, Dutch, English, French, and Portuguese—in normal conversation. Here are a few helpful phrases: *bon dia* (good day), *bon nochi* (good night), *masha danki* (thank you very much).

Taxes The airport departure tax is a hefty $37 for departures to the United States and $33.50 to other international destinations (including Bonaire and Curaçao), but the fee is usually included in your ticket price. Hotels collect 9.5% in taxes (2% of which goes to marketing to tourists) on top of a typical 11% service charge, for a total of 20.5%. A 3% B.B.O. tax (turnover tax) is included in the price charged in most shops.

Tipping Restaurants generally include a 10% to 15% service charge. If service isn't included, a 10% tip is standard; if it is included, it's customary to add something extra at your discretion. Taxi drivers, 10% to 15%; porters and bellhops, about $2 per bag; housekeeping, about $2 a day.

ARUBA ACCOMMODATIONS

Almost all of the resorts are along the island's southwest coast, along L.G. Smith and J.E. Irausquin boulevards, with the larger high-rise properties being farther away from Oranjestad. A few budget places are in Oranjestad itself. Since most hotel beaches are equally fabulous, it's the resort, rather than its location, that's going to be a bigger factor in how you enjoy your vacation.

Boutique Resorts: You'll find a few small resorts that offer more personal service, though not always the same level of luxury as the larger places. But smaller resorts are better suited to the natural sense of Aruban hospitality you'll find all over the island.

Large Resorts: These all-encompassing vacation destinations offer myriad dining options, casinos, shops, water-sports centers, health clubs, and car-rental desks. The island has only a handful of all-inclusives, though these are gaining in popularity.

Time-shares: Large time-share properties are cropping up in greater numbers, luring visitors who prefer to prepare some of their own meals and have a bit more living space than in a typical resort hotel room.

HOTEL AND RESTAURANT PRICES

Prices in the restaurant reviews are the average cost of a main course at dinner or, if dinner is not served, at lunch; taxes and service charges are generally included. Prices in the hotel reviews are the lowest cost of a standard double room in high season, excluding taxes, service charges, and meal plans (except at all-inclusives). Prices for rentals are the lowest per-night cost for a one-bedroom unit in high season.

VISITOR INFORMATION

Aruba Tourism Authority ✉ *L.G. Smith Blvd. 172, Eagle Beach* ☎ *954/767–6477 in Fort Lauderdale, 201/330–0800 in Weehawken, NJ, 297/582–3777 in Aruba* ⊕ *www.aruba.com.*

WEDDINGS

You must be over 18 and submit the appropriate documents one month in advance. Couples are required to submit birth certificates with raised seals, through the mail or in person, to Aruba's Office of the Civil Registry. They also need an apostille—a document proving they are free to marry—from their country of residence. Most major hotels have wedding coordinators, and there are other independent wedding planners on the island.

Contacts Aruba Fairy Tales *297/993–0045* ⊕ *www.arubafairytales.com.* **Aruba Weddings for You** ✉ *Nune 92, Paradera* ☎ *297/583–7638* ⊕ *www. arubaweddingsforyou.com.*

EXPLORING ARUBA

Aruba's wildly sculpted landscape is replete with rocky deserts, cactus clusters, secluded coves, blue vistas, and the trademark divi-divi tree. To see the island's wild, untamed beauty, you can rent a car, take a sight-seeing tour, or hire a cab for $45 an hour (for up to four people). The main highways are well paved, but on the windward side (the north- and east-facing side) some roads are still a mixture of compacted dirt and stones. Although a car is fine, a four-wheel-drive vehicle will allow you to explore the unpaved interior.

Traffic is sparse, but signs leading to sights are often small and hand-lettered (this is slowly changing as the government puts up official road signs), so watch closely. Route 1A travels southbound along the western coast, and 1B is simply northbound along the same road. If you lose your way, just look to the divi-divi trees, which always lean southwest.

WHAT TO SEE

Alto Vista Chapel. Alone near the island's northwest corner sits this sce-nic little chapel. The wind whistles through the simple mustard-color walls, eerie boulders, and looming cacti. Along the side of the road back to civilization are miniature crosses with depictions of the stations of the cross and hand-lettered signs with "Pray for us Sinners" and other heartfelt evocations of faith. ✚ *To get here, follow the rough, winding dirt road that loops around the island's northern tip, or, from the hotel strip, take Palm Beach Road through three intersections and watch for the asphalt road to the left just past the Alto Vista Rum Shop.* ✉ *Oranjestad.*

Arikok National Park. Nearly 20% of Aruba is part of this national park, which sprawls across the eastern interior and the northeast coast. The park is the keystone of the government's long-term plan to preserve Aruba's resources and showcases the island's flora and fauna as well as ancient Arawak petroglyphs, the ruins of a gold-mining operation at Miralmar, and the remnants of Dutch peasant settlements at Masiduri. Arikok Center, at the park's main entrance, houses offices, restrooms, and food facilities. All visitors must stop here upon entering so that officials can manage the traffic flow and hand out information on park rules and features. Within the confines of the park are Mt. Arikok and the 620-foot Mt. Yamanota, Aruba's highest peak.

Anyone looking for geological exotica should head for the park's caves, found on the northeastern coast. Baranca Sunu, the so-called Tunnel of Love, has a heart-shape entrance and naturally sculpted rocks farther inside that look like the Madonna, Abraham Lincoln, and even a jaguar. Fontein Cave, which was used by indigenous peoples centuries ago, is marked with ancient drawings (rangers are on hand to offer explana-tions). Bats are known to make appearances—don't worry, they won't bother you. Although you don't need a flashlight because the paths are well lighted, it's best to wear sneakers. ☎ *297/585–1234.*

★ **Aruba Ostrich Farm.** Everything you ever wanted to know about the world's largest living birds can be found at this farm. A large *palapa* (palm-thatched roof) houses a gift shop and restaurant that draws large bus tours, and tours of the farm are available every half hour. This operation is virtually identical to the facility in Curaçao; it's owned by the same company. ✉ *Makividiri Rd., Paradera* ☎ *297/585–9630* ⊕ *www.arubaostrichfarm.com* 🏷 *$12* ⊘ *Daily 9–4.*

Balashi Brewery. The factory that manufactures the excellent local beer, Balashi, offers daily tours to the public that will take you through every stage of the brewing process. It makes for a fascinating hour, and the price of the tour includes a free drink at the end. Note that closed shoes are required for the tour. Those more interested in beer drinking than beer making might want to visit the factory Friday evening from 6 to 9 for happy hour, when there's live music. ✉ *Balashi 75, Balashi* ☎ *297/592–2544* ⊕ *www.balashi.com* 🏷 *$6.*

⊘ **Butterfly Farm.** Hundreds of butterflies from around the world flutter about this spectacular garden. Guided 30- to 45-minute tours (included in the price of admission) provide an entertaining look into the life cycle of these insects, from egg to caterpillar to chrysalis to butterfly. After your initial visit, you can return as often as you like for free during your vacation. ✉ *J.E. Irausquin Blvd., Palm Beach* ☎ *297/586–3656* ⊕ *www. thebutterflyfarm.com* 🏷 *$15* ⊘ *Daily 9–4:30; last tour at 4.*

California Lighthouse. The lighthouse, built by a French architect in 1910, stands at the island's far northern end. Although you can't go inside, you can climb the hill to the lighthouse base for some great views. It's surrounded by huge boulders and sand dunes; in this stark landscape you might feel as though you've just landed on the moon. ✉ *Oranjestad.*

Mt. Hooiberg. Named for its shape (*hooiberg* means "haystack" in Dutch), this 541-foot peak lies inland just past the airport. If you have the energy, you can climb the 562 steps to the top for an impressive view of Oranjestad (and Venezuela on clear days). ✉ *Oranjestad.*

Oranjestad. Aruba's charming capital is best explored on foot. L.G. Smith Boulevard, the palm-lined thoroughfare in the center of town, runs between pastel-painted buildings, old and new, of typical Dutch design. You'll find many malls with boutiques and shops here.

Archaeological Museum of Aruba. This small museum has two rooms chock-full of fascinating artifacts from the indigenous Arawak people, including farm and domestic utensils dating back hundreds of years. ✉ *J.E. Irausquin Blvd. 2A, Oranjestad* ☎ *297/582–8979* 🏷 *Free* ⊘ *Tues.–Sun. 10–5.*

Aruba Aloe. Learn all about aloe—its cultivation, processing, and production—at this farm and factory. Guided tours lasting about a half hour will show you how the gel—revered for its skin-soothing properties—is extracted from the aloe vera plant and used in a variety of products, including after-sun creams, soaps, and shampoos. Though not the most exciting tour on the island—and unlikely to keeps kids entertained—it might be a good option on a rainy day. You can purchase the finished goods in the gift shop. ✉ *Pitastraat 115, Oranjestad* ☎ *297/588–3222* 🏷 *Free* ⊘ *Weekdays 8:30–4, Sat. 9–noon.*

Ft. Zoutman. One of the island's oldest edifices, Aruba's historic fort was built in 1796 and played an important role in skirmishes between

4

British and Curaçao troops in 1803. The Willem III Tower, named for the Dutch monarch of that time, was added in 1868 to serve as a lighthouse. Over time the fort has been a government office building, a police station, and a prison; now its historical museum displays Aruban artifacts in an 18th-century house. ⊠ *Zoutmanstraat, Oranjestad* ☎ *297/582–6099* 🖅 *Free* ⊙ *Weekdays 8–noon and 1–4.*

Numismatic Museum. This museum displays more than 40,000 historic coins and paper money from around the world. A few pieces were salvaged from shipwrecks in the region. Some of the coins circulated during the Roman Empire, the Byzantine Empire, and the ancient Chinese dynasties; the oldest dates from the 3rd century BC. The museum had its start as the private collection of an Aruban who dug up some old coins in his garden. It's now run by his granddaughter. ⊠ *Weststraat, Oranjestad* ☎ *297/582–8831* 🖅 *$5* ⊙ *Weekdays 9–4, Saturday 8–noon.*

Rock Formations. The massive boulders at Ayo and Casibari are a mystery, as they don't match the island's geological makeup. You can climb to the top for fine views of the arid countryside. On the way you'll doubtless pass Aruba whiptail lizards—the males are cobalt blue, and the females are blue-gray with light-blue dots. The main path to Casibari has steps and handrails, and you must move through tunnels and along narrow steps and ledges to reach the top. At Ayo you can find ancient pictographs in a small cave (the entrance has iron bars to protect the drawings from vandalism). You may also encounter boulder climbers, who are increasingly drawn to Ayo's smooth surfaces. Access to Casibari is via Tanki Highway 4A; you can reach Ayo via Route 6A. Watch carefully for the turnoff signs near the center of the island on the way to the windward side.

San Nicolas. During the oil refinery heyday, Aruba's oldest village was a bustling port; now its primary purpose is tourism. The major institution in town is Charlie's Restaurant & Bar. Stop in for a drink and advice on what to see and do in this little town. Aruba's main red-light district is here and will be fairly apparent to even casual observers. ⊠ *San Nicolas.*

WHERE TO EAT

Arubans tend to eat their main meal at lunchtime, so feel free to follow suit and save money by trying the lunch menus at the better restaurants. Be sure to try such Aruban specialties as *pan bati* (a mildly sweet bread that resembles a pancake) and *keshi yena* (a baked concoction of Gouda or Edam cheese, spices, and meat or seafood in a rich brown sauce). On Sunday you may have a hard time finding a restaurant outside a hotel that's open for lunch, and many restaurants are closed for dinner on Sunday or Monday. Reservations are essential for dinner in high season.

The **Aruba Gastronomic Association** (AGA ⊕ *www.arubadining.com*) offers Dine-Around packages that involve more than 20 island restaurants. Here's how it works: you can buy tickets for three dinners ($117 per person), five dinners ($190), seven dinners ($262), or five breakfasts or lunches plus four dinners ($230). Dinners include an appetizer, an entrée, dessert, coffee or tea, and a service charge (except when a restaurant is a "VIP member," in which case $38 will be deducted from your final bill instead).

What to Wear. Even the finest restaurants require at most a jacket for men and a sundress for women. If you plan to eat in the open air, remember to bring along insect repellent—the mosquitoes sometimes get unruly.

$$$$ ✕ **Buccaneer.** Imagine you're in a sunken ship where sharks, barracu-
ECLECTIC das, and grouper swim past the portholes. That's what you can find at Buccaneer, a restaurant with its own fantastic 7,500-gallon saltwater aquarium. The chefs prepare acceptable but not especially noteworthy fare. Head to this stone building flanked by heavy black chains early (around 5:45 pm) to snag a booth beside the aquarium; then order the catch of the day. The restaurant participates in AGA's Dine-Around program. ⑤ *Average main: $31 ⊠ Gasparito 11 C, Noord ☎ 297/586–6172 ⊕ www.buccaneeraruba.com ☽ Closed Sun. No lunch.*

$$$ ✕ **Cuba's Cookin'.** Nightly entertainment, great authentic Cuban food,
CUBAN and a lively crowd are the draws here. The empanadas are excellent,
★ as is the chicken stuffed with plantains. Don't leave without trying the roast pork, which is pretty close to perfection. The signature dish is the *ropa vieja*, a sautéed flank steak served with a rich sauce (the name literally translates as "old clothes"). Service can be a bit spotty at times, depending on how busy it gets. There's often live music. ⑤ *Average main: $24 ⊠ Renaissance Marketplace, L.G. Smith Blvd. 82, Oranjestad ☎ 297/588–0627 ⊕ www.cubascookin.com.*

$$$$ ✕ **El Gaucho Argentine Grill.** Faux-leather-bound books, tulip-top lamps,
STEAKHOUSE wooden chairs, and tile floors decorate this Argentina-style steak house,
☾ which has been in business since 1977. The key here is meat served in mammoth portions (think 16-ounce steaks). A welcome feature is a children's playroom, which allows adults to dine while the kids are entertained with videos and games. Be warned, though: even with the kids out of sight, the noise level can still be a bit high in this busy restaurant. ⑤ *Average main: $45 ⊠ Wilhelminastraat 80, Oranjestad ☎ 297/582–3677 ⊕ www.elgaucho-aruba.com ☽ No lunch Sun.*

$$$ ✕ **Gasparito Restaurant & Art Gallery.** You can find this enchanting hide-
CARIBBEAN away in a *cunucu* (country) house in Noord, not far from the hotels.
★ Dine indoors, where works by local artists are showcased on softly lighted walls, or on the outdoor patio. Either way, the service is excellent. The Aruban specialties—pan bati, keshi yena—are feasts for the eye as well as the palate. The standout dish is the Gasparito chicken; the sauce recipe was passed down from the owner's ancestors and features seven special ingredients, including brandy, white wine, and pineapple juice. (The rest, they say, are secret.) Gasparito is an AGA Dine-Around member. ⑤ *Average main: $24 ⊠ Gasparito 3, Noord ☎ 297/586–7044 ⊕ www.gasparito.com ☽ Closed Sun. No lunch.*

$$ ✕ **Gostoso.** Locals adore the magical mixture of Portuguese, Aruban,
CARIBBEAN and international dishes on offer at this consistently excellent estab-
lishment. The decor walks a fine line between kitschy and cozy, but the atmosphere is relaxed and informal and outdoor seating is available. The *bacalhau* vinaigrette (dressed salted cod) is a delightful Portuguese appetizer and pairs nicely with most of the Aruban dishes on the menu. Meat lovers are sure to enjoy the Venezuelan mixed grill, which includes

a 14-ounce steak and chorizo accompanied by local sides like fried plantain. ⑤ *Average main: $24* ⊠ *Caya Ing Roland H. Lacle 12, Oranjestad* ☎ *297/588-0053* ⊕ *www.gostosoaruba.com* ⌂ *Reservations essential* ⊘ *Closed Mon.*

$$$$ ✕**Hostaria Da' Vittorio.** Part of the fun at this family-oriented spot is
ITALIAN   watching chef Vittorio Muscariello prepare authentic Italian regional specialties in the open kitchen. The staff helps you choose wines from the extensive list and recommends portions of hot and cold antipasti, risottos, and pastas. Those on a tight budget should stick to the pizza offerings. Service can be a bit dismissive during busy periods. As you leave, pick up some limoncello (lemon liqueur) or olive oil at the gourmet shop. Be aware that the decibel level of the crowd can be high. A 15% gratuity is automatically added to your bill. It's an AGA VIP member. ⑤ *Average main: $38* ⊠ *L.G. Smith Blvd. 380, Palm Beach* ☎ *297/586-3838* ⊕ *hostariavittorio.com.*

$$$ ✕**L.G. Smith's Steak & Chop House.** A study in teak, cream, and black,
STEAKHOUSE   this fine steak house offers some of the best beef on the island. Sub-
★   dued lighting and cascading water create a pleasant atmosphere, and the view over L.G. Smith Boulevard to the harbor makes for an exceptional dining experience. The menu features high-quality cuts of meat, all superbly prepared. The casino is steps away if you fancy some slots after dinner. ⑤ *Average main: $29* ⊠ *Renaissance Aruba Beach Resort & Casino, L.G. Smith Blvd. 82, Oranjestad* ☎ *297/523-6115* ⊕ *www. lgsmiths.com* ⊘ *No lunch.*

$$$$ ✕**Madame Janette's.** Named after a local chili pepper (and not a local
EUROPEAN   temptress), this restaurant seems haunted by the spirit of Auguste
Fodor's Choice   Escoffier. Large portions and cream sauces are well represented on the
★   menu, and hollandaise and cheese sauces abound. Presentation is an essential part of the dining experience here, and entrées rise majestically off their plates. The best part is that everything tastes as good as it looks, so those looking for a more traditional but exquisite meal will be very pleased. Try the lamb or beef rotisseries with one of the special sauces; if you're in the mood for something lighter, there are tasty salads. For an overwhelming finish, top off your meal with a sundae that billows over the edges of a massive champagne glass. Savor each course in the outdoor pebble garden, where tabletop candles cast a soft glow. Note that you may feel a bit hot in the outdoor area given the relative lack of breezes. ⑤ *Average main: $37* ⊠ *Cunucu Abao 37, Cunucu Abao* ☎ *297/587-0184* ⊕ *www.madamejanette.info* ⊘ *No lunch.*

$$$ ✕**Marandi.** This seaside restaurant, whose name means "on the water"
ECLECTIC   in Malaysian, is simultaneously cozy and chic. Tables are tucked under
Fodor's Choice   a giant thatched roof by the water's edge. The emphasis here is on fresh-
★   caught fish. A popular option is cactus, figs, and Aruban mushrooms with the catch of the day. ⑤ *Average main: $30* ⊠ *Bucutiweg 50, Oranjestad* ☎ *297/582-0157* ⊕ *www.marandi-aruba.com* ⌂ *Reservations essential* ⊘ *No lunch.*

$$$$ ✕**Papiamento.** The Ellis family converted its 175-year-old manor into a
ECLECTIC   bistro with an atmosphere that is elegant, intimate, and always romantic.
★   You can feast in the dining room, which is filled with antiques, or outdoors on the terrace by the pool (sitting on plastic patio chairs covered

CLOSE UP

Cunucu Houses

Pastel houses surrounded by cacti fences adorn Aruba's flat, rugged *cunucu* ("country" in Papiamento). The features of these traditional houses were developed in response to the environment. Early settlers discovered that slanting roofs allowed the heat to rise and that small windows helped to keep in the cool air. Among the earliest building materials was *caliche*, a durable calcium carbonate substance found in the island's southeastern hills. Many houses were also built using interlocking coral rocks that didn't require mortar (this technique is no longer used, thanks to concrete). Contemporary design combines some of the basic principles of the earlier homes with touches of modernization: windows, though still narrow, have been elongated; roofs are constructed of bright tiles; pretty patios have been added; and doorways and balconies present an ornamental face to the world beyond.

in fabric). The chefs mix continental and Caribbean cuisines to produce sumptuous seafood and meat dishes. Entrées cooked "on the stone" are as popular for the drama of the sizzling stone as for the incredible aromas that envelop you when they are presented. Service is unhurried, so don't come here if you're in a rush. ⑤ *Average main: $36 ⊠ Washington 61, Noord ☎ 297/586–4544 ⊕ www.papiamentorestaurant.com* ⌾ *Reservations essential* ⊗ *Closed Mon. No lunch.*

$$$$
FRENCH
✕**Papillon.** Despite being inspired by Henri Charrière's escape from Devil's Island, the food here couldn't be more removed from from bread and water. The owners use the famous story as a metaphor for a culinary journey to freedom as classic French cuisine is transformed with Caribbean flair. There are whimsical prison touches throughout the restaurant and especially in the washrooms. The menu includes classics like beef bourguignonne but isn't afraid to offer more adventurous dishes such as a standout crispy duck breast served with passion fruit and chocolate. Whatever you order, you'll find the presentation is always impeccable. ⑤ *Average main: $36 ⊠ J.E. Irausquin Blvd. 348A, The Village, Palm Beach ☎ 297/586–5400 ⊕ www.papillonaruba.com* ⌾ *Reservations essential.*

$$$$
CARIBBEAN
Fodor's Choice
★
✕**Passions.** Every night the Amsterdam Manor Beach Resort (⇨ *Where to Stay*) transforms the area of Eagle Beach in front of the hotel into a magical and romantic beach dining room. Tiki torches illuminate the white sand, and the linen-covered tables are within inches of the lapping water. Dine on imaginative dishes that are as beautiful as they are delicious. The huge tropical watermelon salad presented in a watermelon half is refreshing and whets the appetite with a slight chili heat. In this so-called "reef cuisine" the main courses lean toward seafood, though meat lovers also are indulged. After dinner, relax with your toes in the sand and enjoy the best show that nature has to offer over signature cocktails. ⑤ *Average main: $31 ⊠ J.E. Irausquin Blvd 252, Eagle Beach, Eagle Beach ☎ 297/527–1100 ⊕ www.passions-restaurant-aruba.com* ⌾ *Reservations essential.*

$$$$ ✕ **Pinchos Grill & Bar.** Built on a pier,
ECLECTIC   this casual spot with only 11 tables
Fodor's Choice   has one of the most romantic set-
★   tings on the island. At night the restaurant glimmers from a distance
as hundreds of lights reflect off the
water. Guests can watch as chef
Robby Peterson prepares delectable meals on the grill in his tiny
kitchen. His wife and co-owner,
Anabela, keeps diners comfortable
and happy. The fish-cakes appetizer
with a pineapple-mayonnaise dressing is a marriage made in heaven.
The bar area is great for enjoying
ocean breezes over an evening cocktail, and there is live entertainment
every weekend. Many visitors consider a visit to Pinchos an essential
part of the Aruba experience. $ *Av-
erage main: $32* ✉ *L.G. Smith Blvd. 7, Oranjestad* ☎ *287/583–2666*
✆ *Closed Mon. No lunch.*

$$$ ✕ **Qué Pasa?.** This funky eatery serves as something of an art gallery–res-
ECLECTIC   taurant, where diners can appreciate the colorful, eclectic works of local
★   artists while enjoying a meal or savoring a drink. The terra-cotta out-
door spaces are illuminated by strings of lights. Inside, jewel-color walls
serve as an eye-popping backdrop for numerous paintings. Despite the
name, there isn't a Mexican dish on the menu, which includes sashimi,
rack of lamb, and fish dishes (they are especially good). Everything is
done with Aruban flair, and the staff is helpful and friendly. Save room
for one of the delightfully comforting desserts, such as a banana split
or a brownie with ice cream. The bar area is fun, too. $ *Average main:
$25* ✉ *Wilhelminastraat 18, Oranjestad* ☎ *297/583–4888* ⊕ *www.
quepasaaruba.com* ✆ *No lunch.*

$$$$ ✕ **Ruinas del Mar.** Locally cut limestone walls, lush gardens, and falling
CARIBBEAN   water make this one of the most stylish restaurants on the island. Chef
Miguel Garcia creates memorable Spanish-influenced dishes that help
complete the romantic picture. If possible, try and get a seat near the
torch-lighted pond, so that you can admire the black swans while din-
ing. Those wishing to splurge even more can try the $90, five-course
tasting menu. The Sunday champagne brunch buffet is a wonder. A
15% service charge is added to your check. $ *Average main: $46*
✉ *Hyatt Regency Aruba Beach Resort & Casino, J.E. Irausquin Blvd.
85, Palm Beach* ☎ *297/586–1234* ✆ *No lunch. No dinner Sun.*

$$$ ✕ **Ventanas del Mar.** Floor-to-ceiling windows provide ample views
ECLECTIC   across the lovely Tierra del Sol golf course and beyond to rolling sand
dunes and the sea off the island's western tip. Dining on the intimate
terrace amid flickering candles inspires romance. Sandwiches, salads,
conch fritters, nachos, and quesadillas fill the midday menu; at night
the emphasis is on seafood and meat. Crispy whole red snapper in a

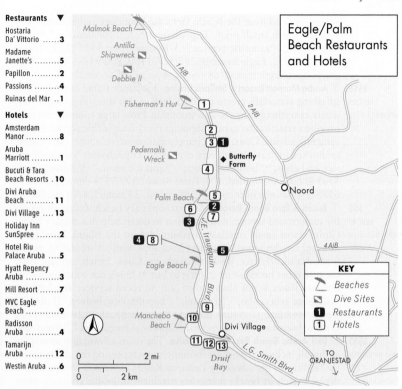

Restaurants ▼

Hostaria
Da' Vittorio **3**

Madame
Janette's **5**

Papillon **2**

Passions **4**

Ruinas del Mar ..**1**

Hotels ▼

Amsterdam
Manor **8**

Aruba
Marriott **1**

Bucuti & Tara
Beach Resorts . **10**

Divi Aruba
Beach **11**

Divi Village **13**

Holiday Inn
SunSpree **2**

Hotel Riu
Palace Aruba **5**

Hyatt Regency
Aruba **3**

Mill Resort **7**

MVC Eagle
Beach **9**

Radisson
Aruba **4**

Tamarijn
Aruba **12**

Westin Aruba **6**

sweet-and-sour sauce and crab-and-corn chowder are specialties. The restaurant is an AGA VIP member. $ *Average main: $31* ⊠ *Tierra del Sol Resort, Malmokweg* ☎ *297/586–7800* ⊕ *www.tierradelsol.com/restaurant* ⊘ *Closed Sun. Apr.–Nov.*

WHERE TO STAY

Hotels on the island are categorized as low-rise or high-rise and are grouped in two distinct areas along L.G. Smith and J.E. Irausquin boulevards north of Oranjestad. The low-rise properties are closer to the capital, the high-rises in a swath a little farther north. Hotel rates, with the exception of those at a few all-inclusives, generally do not include meals or even breakfast. The larger resorts are destinations unto themselves, with shopping, entertainment, and casinos.

For expanded reviews, facilities, and current deals, visit Fodors.com.

$$

HOTEL

Fodor's Choice

★

Amsterdam Manor Beach Resort. An intimate, family-run hotel with a genuinely friendly staff and an authentic Dutch-Caribbean atmosphere, this little place offers excellent value for the money. **Pros:** feels like a European village; very good family restaurant; friendly and helpful staff; minigrocery on-site; modern and airy rooms; public bus stop in front of hotel for easy access to downtown and the high-rise area. **Cons:**

across the road from the beach; lacks the boutiques and attractions of a larger hotel; small pool. **TripAdvisor:** "ideal for families," "great little resort," "fantastic service." $ *Rooms from: $305* ⊠ *J.E. Irausquin Blvd. 252, Eagle Beach* ☎ *297/527–1100, 800/932–6509* ⊕ *www. amsterdammanor.com* ➥ *68 rooms, 4 suites* ⍟ *No meals.*

$$$$
RESORT
Fodor'sChoice
★

🏨 **Aruba Marriott Resort & Stellaris Casino.** The gentle sound of the surf and splashing waterfalls create the backdrop of this sprawling compound, where everything seems to run smoothly. **Pros:** large rooms; variety of excellent restaurants; great shopping; every imaginable service is conveniently on-site. **Cons:** large, impersonal resort; reception can become gridlocked in peak season; very expensive. **TripAdvisor:** "customer service and class," "beautiful resort," "fantastic room." $ *Rooms from: $569* ⊠ *L.G. Smith Blvd. 101, Palm Beach* ☎ *297/586–9000, 800/223–6388* ⊕ *www.marriott.com* ➥ *388 rooms, 23 suites* ⍟ *No meals.*

$$$
RESORT
Fodor'sChoice
★

🏨 **Bucuti & Tara Beach Resorts.** An extraordinary beach setting, impeccably understated service, and attention to detail help this elegant Green Globe resort easily outclass anything else on the island. **Pros:** great atmosphere; impeccable service; luxurious without insulating guests from island life; free Wi-Fi throughout. **Cons:** beach can get busy, because other hotels share it; little to buy at hotel; eco concerns means that hot water is not always that hot; no room service. **TripAdvisor:** "complete relaxation," "tranquil," "breathtaking beauty." $ *Rooms from: $448* ⊠ *L.G. Smith Blvd. 55B, Eagle Beach* ☎ *297/583–1100* ⊕ *www.bucuti.com* ➥ *63 rooms, 38 suites, 3 bungalows* ⍟ *Breakfast.*

$$$$
ALL-INCLUSIVE
☻

🏨 **Divi Aruba Beach Resort All Inclusive.** The main advantages to staying at this all-inclusive resort are its many room types and the ability to use the facilities of the adjoining Tamarijn Resort (⇨ *below*). **Pros:** on wonderful stretch of beach; margarita machines in lobby; common areas feel light and airy; live nightly entertainment. **Cons:** poolside area can get pretty noisy; the gourmet restaurant isn't that good; Internet access isn't included in rates. **TripAdvisor:** "property is beautiful," "a bit of paradise," "best on the island." $ *Rooms from: $600* ⊠ *L.G. Smith Blvd. 93, Manchebo Beach* ☎ *297/582–3300, 800/554–2008* ⊕ *www. diviaruba.com* ➥ *203 rooms* ⍟ *All-inclusive* ☞ *5-night minimum.*

$
RESORT
★

🏨 **Divi Village Golf & Beach Resort.** Although it's just across the road from its sister Divi properties, this all-suites version is quieter and more refined. **Pros:** excellent golf course; spacious rooms; lushly landscaped grounds; great savings for being a mere 20 yards from the beach. **Cons:** bit of a hike from some rooms to the lobby; you must cross a busy road to get to the beach; it might be a bit too quiet for some. **TripAdvisor:** "excellent facilities," "fantastic Divi golf," "comfortable stay." $ *Rooms from: $225* ⊠ *J.E.Irausquin Blvd. 93, Oranjestad* ☎ *297/583–5000, 297/583–5000* ⊕ *www.divivillage.com* ➥ *250 suites* ⍟ *Multiple meal plans* ☞ *3-night minimum.*

$
RESORT
☻

🏨 **Holiday Inn SunSpree Aruba Beach Resort & Casino.** This popular, family-oriented package-tour resort has three seven-story buildings filled with spacious rooms lining a sugary, palm-dotted shore. **Pros:** affordable and predictable quality; great beachfront location; lots of activities for the kids. **Cons:** hallways feel a little institutional; lines at reception can make you feel you are back at the airport; restaurants are mediocre at

Amsterdam Manor Beach Resort

best and service can be a problem. **TripAdvisor:** "nice beach," "the best staff," "great experience." ⑤ *Rooms from: $189* ✉ *J.E. Irausquin Blvd. 230, Palm Beach* ☎ *297/586–3600, 800/465–4329* ⊕ *www. caribbeanhi.com/aruba* ⇰ *600 rooms, 7 suites* ⑩ *No meals.*

$$$$
ALL-INCLUSIVE

🏨 **Hotel Riu Palace Aruba.** This white wedding cake of a resort towers over Palm Beach with one 8-story and two 10-story towers. **Pros:** beautiful vistas; drink dispensers in all rooms; large and lively pool area. **Cons:** resort is large and impersonal; pool area is always crowded and very loud; unimpressive à la carte restaurants; interior decor is a bit jarring for an island destination. **TripAdvisor:** "great beach," "sunny and accommodating," "delicious food." ⑤ *Rooms from: $520* ✉ *J.E. Irausquin Blvd. 79, Palm Beach* ☎ *297/586–3900, 800/345–2782* ⊕ *www. riuaruba.com* ⇰ *450 rooms* ⑩ *All-inclusive.*

$$$$
RESORT
✧
Fodor's Choice
★

🏨 **Hyatt Regency Aruba Beach Resort & Casino.** This 12-acre resort is popular with families, but honeymooners head here, too, since the resort is big enough that there are still some quietly romantic corners. **Pros:** beautiful grounds; great for kids; excellent restaurants. **Cons:** small balconies for a luxury hotel; some rooms are quite a stretch from the beach. **TripAdvisor:** "beach getaway," "great vacation," "beautiful hotel." ⑤ *Rooms from: $645* ✉ *J.E. Irausquin Blvd. 85, Palm Beach* ☎ *297/586–1234, 800/554–9288* ⊕ *www.aruba.hyatt.com* ⇰ *342 rooms, 18 suites* ⑩ *No meals.*

$
RESORT
✧
★

🏨 **Mill Resort & Suites.** This lovely low-rise resort has genuinely friendly staff who are devoted to the needs of guests, and it's deservedly popular with travelers in the know. **Pros:** entire compound has an intimate feel; lively bar area; theme nights are fun; numerous activities to keep kids amused. **Cons:** not on the beach; pool area can be busy and noisy; rates are not quite the steal they used to be. **TripAdvisor:** "friendly hardworking staff," "cute hotel," "great pool." [$] *Rooms from: $267* ⊠ *J.E. Irausquin Blvd. 330, Palm Beach* ☎ *297/586–7700* ⊕ *www.millresort. com* ⇘ *64 studios, 128 suites* ⎮◯⎮ *Multiple meal plans.*

$

HOTEL

☺

★

‡‡ **MVC Eagle Beach.** This is a great bargain given the excellent location across from Eagle Beach. **Pros:** unbeatable price; popular restaurant with food at affordable prices; since the main language is Dutch, you feel that you're someplace other than South Florida here; very short walk to beach; friendly and helpful staff. **Cons:** Spartan accommodations; not for those who want to be away from kids. **TripAdvisor:** "lovely staff," "the best beach in Aruba," "perfect base for exploring." [$] *Rooms from: $145* ⊠ *J.E. Irausquin Blvd. 240, Eagle Beach* ☎ *297/587–0110* ⊕ *www.mvceaglebeach.com* ⇘ *16 rooms, 3 suites* ⎮◯⎮ *No meals.*

$$$$

RESORT

☺

★

‡‡ **Radisson Aruba Resort & Casino.** The lavish rooms at this 14-acre resort are appointed with colonial West Indian–style furniture, including four-poster beds, and their large balconies overlook the ocean or tropical gardens. **Pros:** rooms feel homey; fitness fans will love the top-notch facilities; one of the best spas on the island; free high-speed Internet in rooms. **Cons:** restaurants are good but not great; some rooms are on the small side and don't seem worth the cost; you never forget you are in a big hotel. **TripAdvisor:** "great island getaway," "best pool and beach," "beautiful hotel." [$] *Rooms from: $592* ⊠ *J.E. Irausquin Blvd. 81, Palm Beach* ☎ *297/586–6555* ⊕ *www.radisson.com* ⇘ *321 rooms, 34 suites* ⎮◯⎮ *No meals.*

$$$$

HOTEL

★

‡‡ **Renaissance Aruba Resort & Casino.** This downtown hotel consists of two distinct parts: the Renaissance Marina Hotel and the Renaissance Ocean Suites. **Pros:** in the heart of the downtown shopping district; lobby and shopping areas are always lively; pool area offers an unmatched view of the port; access to private island with beaches. **Cons:** rooms overlooking the atrium can be a bit claustrophobic; beach is off-site; hard to find a quiet spot; no hotel grounds; no balconies in downtown section. **TripAdvisor:** "friendly staff," "great for adults," "property is terrific." [$] *Rooms from: $492* ⊠ *L.G. Smith Blvd. 82, Oranjestad* ☎ *297/583–6000, 800/421–8188* ⊕ *www.renaissancearuba. com* ⇘ *287 rooms, 269 suites* ⎮◯⎮ *No meals.*

$$$$

ALL-INCLUSIVE

‡‡ **Tamarijn Aruba All-Inclusive Beach Resort.** An upscale alternative to its sister property, the Divi Aruba (⟿ *above*), this resort is pleasantly laid-back for an all-inclusive. **Pros:** stunning beach; access to the Divi Aruba All Inclusive next door; perfect for families. **Cons:** being right on the beach can mean noise during busy periods; the linear layout means some rooms are quite far from the lobby; Wi-Fi is an additional charge. **TripAdvisor:** "relaxing and refreshing," "amazing island," "perfect beach vacation." [$] *Rooms from: $575* ⊠ *J.E. Irausquin Blvd. 41, Punta Brabo* ☎ *297/525–5200, 800/554–2008* ⊕ *www.tamarijnaruba.com* ⇘ *236 rooms, 97 suites* ⎮◯⎮ *All-inclusive* ⌔ *5-night minimum.*

$$$$

RESORT

Fodor'sChoice

★

‡‡ **Westin Aruba Resort & Casino.** Although these tasteful rooms aren't as large as those at some other resorts, they are beautifully furnished, with plentiful wood accents. **Pros:** chic and airy rooms; magnificent beachfront and pool area; comprehensive spa facilities; great restaurants.

Cons: immediate area is congested and busy; resort feels vast (and it is). **TripAdvisor:** "friendly service," "beautiful beaches," "great family vacation." $ *Rooms from: $529* ✉ *J.E. Irausquin Blvd. 77, Palm Beach* ☎ *297/586–4466, 877/822–2222* ⊕ *www.westinaruba.com* ⇆ *481 rooms, 81 suites* ⦿ *No meals.*

NIGHTLIFE AND THE ARTS

NIGHTLIFE

Unlike many islands, Aruba's nightlife isn't confined to the touristy folkloric shows at hotels. Arubans like to party. They usually start celebrating late, and the action doesn't pick up until around midnight.

Kukoo Kunuku. To many repeat visitors, this wandering party bus is an integral part of the Aruba experience. Every night except Sunday you can find as many as 40 passengers traveling among three bars from sundown to around midnight. The $59 fee per passenger includes a so-so dinner, some drinks, and pickup at your hotel. The main point is the nonstop entertainment and the chance to make friends with a fun-loving crowd. ☎ *297/586–2010* ⊕ *www.kukookunuku.com.*

BARS

Bambu. This local joint offers typical Aruban food, cheap drinks, and a lively crowd on the terrace on weekends. ✉ *Babijn 53, Paradera* ☎ *No phone.*

Charlie's Bar. An Aruba institution since 1941, Charlie's is a bit far from most hotels, but certainly worth the trip. Expect a raucous (and, most likely, very drunk) crowd. The food here is quite good as well, all the better for padding your stomach before the margaritas, but go easy on the cocktails if you have to drive back. ✉ *Zeppenfeldstraat 56, San Nicolas* ☎ *297/584–5086.*

Iguana Joe's. The reptilian-themed decor is as colorful and creative as the specialty cocktails served here. ✉ *Royal Plaza Mall, L.G. Smith Blvd. 94, Oranjestad* ☎ *297/583–9373.*

Mambo Jambo. Sip one of several concoctions sold nowhere else on the island, then browse for memorabilia at a shop next door. Painted parrots flock on the ceiling in a space that's daubed in sunset colors. ✉ *Royal Plaza Mall, L.G. Smith Blvd. 94, Oranjestad* ☎ *297/583–3632.*

Palms Beach Bar. With front-row seats to view the green flash—that ray of light that supposedly flicks through the sky as the sun sinks into the ocean—the Palms Beach Bar is the perfect spot to enjoy the sunset. ✉ *Hyatt Regency Aruba Beach Resort & Casino, J.E. Irausquin Blvd. 85, Palm Beach* ☎ *297/586–1234.*

CASINOS

Aruban casinos offer something for both high and low rollers, as well as live, nightly entertainment in their lounges. Die-hard gamblers may want to look for the largest or the most active casinos, but many simply visit the casino closest to their hotel.

★ **Alhambra Casino.** Amid the Spanish-style arches and leaded glass, you can try your luck at blackjack, Caribbean stud poker, three-card poker, roulette, craps, or one of the 300 slot machines that accept American nickels, quarters, and dollars. A casual atmosphere and $5 tables further the welcoming feel. Head to one of the novelty touch-screen machines, each of which has a variety of games. There's also bingo every Saturday, Monday, and Thursday beginning at 1 pm. If you fill your card, you can collect the grand prize of a few hundred dollars—not bad for a $5 investment. Be sure to sign up for the Alhambra Advantage Card, which gives you a point for each dollar you spend—even if you lose at the tables, you can still go home with prizes. Of course, winners can spend their earnings immediately at the many on-site shops. The casino is owned by the Divi Divi resorts, and golf carts run to and from nearby hotels every 15 minutes or so. The slots here open daily at 10 am; gaming tables operate from 6 pm until 4 am. ⊠ *L.G. Smith Blvd. 47, Oranjestad* ☎ *297/583–5000* ⊕ *www.casinoalhambra.com.*

Casablanca Casino. The Westin Aruba's Resort & Casino's elegant casino has a Humphrey Bogart theme and a tropical color scheme. Spend some time at the blackjack, roulette, craps, stud poker, and baccarat tables, or the slot machines. Seek out the unique Feature Frenzy machines, which reportedly pay out $6,000 jackpots daily. If gambling isn't your style, visit the Casablanca Casino Bar for exotic cocktails and live jazz most nights at 9. Or you can take in the Aruba Carnival Tropical shows. The casino is open daily from noon to 4 am. ⊠ *Westin Aruba Resort, Spa & Casino, J.E. Irausquin Blvd. 77, Palm Beach* ☎ *297/586–4466.*

The Casino at the Radisson Aruba Resort. Although it measures 16,000 square feet, this casino takes a bit of seeking out. Descend the stairs at the corner of the resort's lobby, following the sounds of the piano player's tunes. The nightly action here includes Las Vegas–style blackjack, roulette, craps, and slot machines. Overhead, thousands of lights simulate shooting stars. A host of shops and restaurants let you chip away at your newfound wealth. The slots here open daily at noon, and the table action begins at 6 pm. Everything shuts down at 4 am. ⊠ *Radisson Aruba Resort & Casino, J.E. Irausquin Blvd. 81, Palm Beach* ☎ *297/586–4045.*

★ **Crystal Casino.** Adorned with Austrian crystal chandeliers and gold-leaf columns, the Renaissance Aruba's glittering casino evokes Monaco's grand establishments. The Salon Privé offers serious gamblers a private room for baccarat, roulette, and high-stakes blackjack. This casino is popular among cruise-ship passengers, who stroll over from the port to watch and play in slot tournaments and bet on sporting events. The Crystal Lounge, which overlooks the betting floor, offers live music along with cocktails. ⊠ *Renaissance Aruba Resort & Casino, L.G. Smith Blvd. 82, Oranjestad* ☎ *297/583–6000.*

Excelsior Casino. The Excelsior, the birthplace of Caribbean stud, also offers blackjack, craps, and roulette tables; plenty of slot machines; and a bar featuring live entertainment. There's also a poker room for Texas hold 'em, seven-card stud, and Caribbean stud. It's the only casino on Palm Beach with an ATM adjacent to the cashier. Afternoon bingo overtakes the main floor every weekday at 3:30 pm. The casino is open daily from 8 am to 4 am; slots begin spinning at 9 am, and tables open at 12:30 pm. ⊠ *Holiday Inn SunSpree Aruba Beach Resort & Casino, J.E. Irausquin Blvd. 230, Palm Beach* ☎ *297/586–7777, 297/586–3600* ⊕ *www.excelsiorcasino.com.*

★ **Hyatt Regency Casino.** Ablaze with neon, this hotel casino is an enormous complex with a Carnival-in-Rio theme. The most popular games here are slots, blackjack, craps, and baccarat. Slots and some other games are available at noon, the dice start rolling at 6 pm, and all other pursuits are open by 8 pm. From 9 pm to 2 am there's live music at the stage near the bar—you'll find it hard to steal away from the pulsating mix of Latin and American tunes. You can register for free dinners and brunches and hotel discounts at the hostess station. The casino is open until 4 am. ⊠ *Hyatt Regency Aruba Beach Resort & Casino, J.E. Irausquin Blvd. 85, Palm Beach* ☎ *297/586–1234* ⊕ *www.aruba.hyatt.com.*

Seaport Casino. The low-key gambling here is at a waterside location adjacent to the Renaissance conference center, Beach Tower, and Marketplace. More than 200 slot machines are in daily operation from 10 am to 4 am, and tables are open from 4 pm to 4 am. From here you can see the boats on the ocean and enjoy not only the games you'd find at other casinos but also shops, restaurants, bars, and movie theaters. Stop by on Tuesday, Thursday, or Sunday for the casino's popular bingo tournaments. ⊠ *L.G. Smith Blvd. 9, Oranjestad* ☎ *297/583–6000.*

★ **Stellaris Casino.** Mirrors on the ceilings reflect the glamorous chandeliers at this 24-hour facility. Take your pick between craps, roulette, Caribbean stud poker, minibaccarat, and superbuck (like blackjack with suits). Every night except Sunday there's a performance by musician Cesar Olarta that may boost your luck. Check in with the casino when you arrive at the hotel and you can get a membership card. If you play high enough stakes at the tables, you can win free meals and other prizes. If not, you can at least get a postcard in the mail offering a special rate on future stays. The hotel offers a 30% discount to those who play at least four hours each day. This is the largest casino on the island. ⊠ *Aruba Marriott Resort, L.G. Smith Blvd. 101, Palm Beach* ☎ *297/586–9000.*

DANCE AND MUSIC CLUBS

★ **Garufa Cigar & Cocktail Lounge.** Most nights there's jazz and other live entertainment at this cozy spot, which serves as a lounge for customers waiting for a table at the nearby Gaucho Argentine Grill (you're issued a beeper so you know when your table is ready). While you wait, have a drink, enjoy some appetizers, and take in the leopard-print carpet and funky bar stools. The ambience may very well draw you back for an after-dinner cognac. A powerful smoke-extractor system helps keep the air clear. ⊠ *Wilhelminastraat 63, Oranjestad* ☎ *297/582–7205.*

THE ARTS

ART GALLERIES

★ **Access.** This gallery, a major venue for Caribbean art, is also home to a thriving cultural scene that includes poetry readings, chamber music concerts, and screenings of feature films and documentaries. It's in the downtown shopping district. The owner, artist Landa Henriquez, is also a bolero singer. ⊠ *Caya G.F. Betico Croes 16–18, Oranjestad* ☎ *297/588–7837.*

Galeria Eterno. You can find local and international artists at work here, as well as concerts by classical guitarists, dance performances, visual-arts shows, and plays. ⊠ *Emanstraat 92, Oranjestad* ☎ *297/583–9607.*

Galeria Harmonia. The island's largest exhibition space has a permanent collection of works by local and international artists. ⊠ *Zeppenfeld-straat 10, San Nicolas* ☎ *297/584–2969.*

Gasparito Restaurant & Art Gallery. A permanent exhibition by Aruban artists is featured here. ⊠ *Gasparito 3, Noord* ☎ *297/586–7044.*

ISLAND CULTURE

★ **Bon Bini Festival.** This year-round folklore event (the name means "welcome" in Papiamento), is held every Tuesday from 6:30 pm to 8:30 pm at Ft. Zoutman in Oranjestad. In the inner courtyard you can check out the Antillean dancers in resplendent costumes, feel the rhythms of the steel drums, browse among the stands displaying local artwork, and sample local food and drink. Admission is usually around $3, but can be as high as $10, depending on what is on offer. ⊠ *Oranjestad.*

Carubbian Festival. Held most Thursdays from 6 to 10 pm, this family-friendly festival turns San Nicolas's Main Street into a party full of Aruban music, street food, culture, and booths selling handicrafts. Hotel packages to the festival, which include round-trip bus transportation, cost about $50.

SHOPPING

"Duty-free" *is* a magical term in the Caribbean—but it's not always accurate. The duty-free shopping zone in Aruba closed several years ago, so the only true duty-free shopping is in the departure area of the airport. (Passengers bound for the United States should be sure to shop before proceeding through U.S. customs in Aruba.) Downtown stores often advertise "duty-free prices," with markdowns of up to 25%, but that doesn't mean comparison shopping should go out the window. Major credit cards are welcome virtually everywhere, U.S. dollars are accepted almost as readily as the local currency, and traveler's checks can be cashed with proof of identity.

Aruba's souvenir and crafts stores are full of Dutch porcelains and figurines, as befits the island's heritage. Dutch cheese is a good buy, as are hand-embroidered linens and any products made from the native aloe vera plant—sunburn cream, face masks, or skin refreshers. Local arts and crafts run toward wood carvings and earthenware emblazoned with "Aruba: One Happy Island" and the like. Since there's no sales tax, the price you see on the tag is usually what you pay. (Large stores in town and at hotels include the value-added tax of 3%, but tiny shops and studios may add it separately.) Don't try to bargain. Arubans consider it rude to haggle, despite what you may hear to the contrary.

AREAS AND MALLS

Caya G.F. Betico Croes. Aruba's chief shopping street, Caya G.F. Betico Croes is lined with several shops advertising "duty-free prices" (again, these are not truly duty-free), boutiques, and jewelry stores noted for the aggressiveness of their vendors on cruise-ship days. .

Alhambra Casino Shopping Arcade. Souvenir shops, boutiques, and fast-food outlets fill the arcade, which is open until midnight. It's attached to the popular casino. ⊠ *L.G. Smith Blvd. 47, Manchebo Beach.*

Holland Aruba Mall. You'll find a collection of stylish shops and decent eateries here. ⊠ *Havenstraat 6, Oranjestad.*

Paseo Herencia. It's all about style at this shopping center, which is just minutes away from the high-rise hotel area. The great bell tower, the nightly dancing-waters shows, and the selection of restaurants pull in shoppers. Offerings include Cuban cigars, the fine leather goods of Mario Hernandez, Italian denim goods at Moda & Stile, perfumes, cosmetics, and lots of souvenir shops. ⊠ *L.G. Smith Blvd., Palm Beach* ☎ *297/586–6533.*

Port of Call Marketplace. Stores here sell fine jewelry, perfumes, low-priced liquor, batiks, crystal, leather goods, and fashionable clothing. ⊠ *L.G. Smith Blvd. 17, Oranjestad.*

Renaissance Mall. The upscale stores here, which include Guess, Lacoste, and Calvin Klein, have prices that are about the same or higher than in the U.S. The Crystal Casino and the Renaissance Hotel are both nearby. ⊠ *L.G. Smith Blvd. 82, Oranjestad.*

Renaissance Marketplace. Five minutes from the cruise-ship terminal, the Renaissance Marketplace, also known as Seaport Mall, has more than 120 stores selling merchandise to meet every taste and budget; the Seaport Casino is also here. ⊠ *L.G. Smith Blvd. 82, Oranjestad.*

Royal Plaza Mall. Across from the cruise-ship terminal, the Royal Plaza Mall has cafés, a post office (open weekdays 8 to 3:30), and such stores as Nautica, Benetton, Tommy Hilfiger, and Gandelman Jewelers. There's also a cybercafé for those who want to send email and get their caffeine all in one stop. ⊠ *L.G. Smith Blvd. 94, Oranjestad.*

SPECIALTY STORES

CLOTHING

★ **Wulfsen & Wulfsen.** One of the most highly regarded clothing stores in Aruba and the Netherlands Antilles, Wulfsen & Wulfsen carries elegant suits for men and linen cocktail dresses for women. It's also a great place to buy Bermuda shorts. ⊠ *Caya G.F. Betico Croes 52, Oranjestad* ☎ *297/582–3823.*

HANDICRAFTS

Artistic Boutique. This boutique is known for its Giuseppe Armani figurines from Italy, usually sold at a 20% discount; Aruban hand-embroidered linens; gold and silver jewelry; and porcelain and pottery from Spain. ⊠ *L.G. Smith Blvd. 90–92, Oranjestad* ☎ *297/588–2468* ✉ *Holiday Inn SunSpree Aruba Beach Resort & Casino, J.E. Irausquin Blvd. 230, Palm Beach* ☎ *297/583–3383.*

★ **The Mask.** Come here for intriguing souvenirs. Buds from the *mopa mopa* tree are boiled to form a resin, which is colored using vegetable dyes, then stretched by hand and mouth. Tiny pieces are cut and layered to form intricate designs—these are truly unusual gifts. ⊠ *Paseo Herencia, J.E. Irausquin Blvd. 382-A, Local C017, Oranjestad* ☎ *297/596–2900* ✉ *Royal Plaza Mall, L.G. Smith Blvd. 94, Oranjestad* ☎ *297/582–7862.*

JEWELRY

Boolchand's. Filling 6,000 square feet of space, Boolchand's sells jewelry and watches. It also stocks leather goods, cameras, and electronics. ⊠ *Renaissance Mall, L.G. Smith Blvd. 82, Oranjestad* ☎ *297/583–0147.*

Colombian Emeralds. If green fire is your passion, Colombian Emeralds has a dazzling array. There are also fine European watches. ⊠ *Renaissance Mall, L.G. Smith Blvd. 82, Oranjestad* ☎ *297/583–6238.*

Kenro Jewelers. With two stores in the same mall, this is one popular store. On offer are bracelets and necklaces from Ramon Leopard; jewelry by Arando, Micheletto, and Blumei; and various watches. There are also six other locations, including some in major hotels. ⊠ *Renaissance Mall, L.G. Smith Blvd. 82, Oranjestad* ☎ *297/583–4847, 297/583–3171.*

PERFUMES

Aruba Trading Company. For perfumes, cosmetics, men's and women's clothing, and leather goods (including Bally shoes), stop in at Aruba Trading Company, which has been in business since the 1930s. ⊠ *Caya G.F. Betico Croes 12, Oranjestad* ☎ *297/582–2602.*

J.L. Penha & Sons. A venerated name in Aruba, J.L. Penha sells high-end perfumes and cosmetics. It stocks such brands as Boucheron, Cartier, Dior, and Givenchy. ⊠ *Caya G.F. Betico Croes 11/13, Oranjestad* ☎ *297/582–4160, 297/582–4161.*

★ **Little Switzerland.** This Caribbean retail giant is the place to go for brand-name men's and women's fragrances, as well as china, crystal, and fine tableware. ⊠ *Caya G.F. Betico Croes 14, Oranjestad* ☎ *297/582–1192* ✉ *Royal Plaza Mall, L.G. Smith Blvd. 94, Oranjestad* ☎ *297/583–4057.*

Weitnauer. You can find specialty Lenox items as well as a wide range of fragrances here. ⊠ *Caya G.F. Betico Croes 29, Oranjestad* ☎ *297/582–2790.*

SPORTS AND ACTIVITIES

On Aruba you can participate in every conceivable water sport, as well as play tennis and golf or go on a fine hike through Arikok National Wildlife Park.

BIKING

Biking is a great way to get around the island; the climate is perfect, and the trade winds help to keep you cool.

Melchor Cycle Rental. ATVs and bikes. ⊠ *Bubali 106B, Noord* ☎ *297/587–1787.*

Rancho Notorious. Exciting mountain-biking tours are available here. The 2.5-hour tour to the Alto Vista Chapel and the California Lighthouse are $50 ($75 with bike rental). ⊠ *Boroncana, Noord* ☎ *297/586–0508* ⊕ *www.ranchonotorious.com.*

DAY SAILS

If you plan to take a cruise around the island, keep in mind that the trade winds can make the waters choppy and that catamaran rides are much smoother than those on single-hull boats. Sucking on a peppermint or ginger candy may soothe your queasy stomach; avoid boating with an empty or overly full stomach. Moonlight cruises cost about $40 per person. There are also a variety of snorkeling, dinner and dancing, and sunset party cruises to choose from, priced from $30 to $60 per person. Many of the smaller operators work out of their homes; they often offer to pick you up (and drop you off) at your hotel or meet you at a particular hotel pier.

★ **Octopus Sailing Charters.** The drinks flow freely on Octopus's trimaran. It holds about 20 people for a three-hour afternoon sail, which costs $35. ⊠ *Sali-a Cerca 1G, Oranjestad* ☎ *297/586–4281* ⊕ *www.octopusaruba.com.*

Red Sail Sports. Choose between four catamarans, including the 70-foot *Rumba.* The popular sunset sail includes drinks and a lively atmosphere for $59 per person; the dinner cruise package includes a three-course meal and open bar for $95. Red Sail Sports also has locations at the Hyatt and Occidental hotels. ⊠ *L.G. Smith Blvd. 17, Oranjestad* ☎ *297/583–1603, 877/733–7245 in U.S.* ⊕ *www.redsailaruba.com.*

Tranquilo Charters Aruba. Operated by Captain Hagedoorn, Tranquilo offers entertaining cruises, including a six-hour tour to the south side of the island for $75. Snorkeling equipment and free lessons are included in the package, and so is the very good "mom's Dutch pea soup" served with lunch (also included). ⊠ *Sibelius St. 25, Oranjestad* ☎ *297/586–1418* ⊕ *www.tranquiloaruba.com.*

DIVING AND SNORKELING

With visibility of up to 90 feet, the waters around Aruba are excellent for snorkeling and diving. Advanced and novice divers alike will find plenty to occupy their time, as many of the most popular sites—including some interesting shipwrecks—are found in shallow waters ranging from 30 to 60 feet. Coral reefs covered with sensuously waving sea fans and eerie giant sponge tubes attract a colorful menagerie of sea life, including gliding manta rays, curious sea turtles, shy octopuses, and grunts, groupers, and other fish. Marine preservation is a priority on Aruba, and regulations by the Conference on International Trade in Endangered Species make it unlawful to remove coral, conch, and other marine life from the water.

Expect snorkel gear to rent for about $20 per day and trips to cost around $45. Scuba rates are around $50 for a one-tank reef or wreck dive, $75 for a two-tank dive, and $55 for a night dive. Resort courses, which offer an introduction to scuba diving, average $65 to $80. If you want to go all the way, complete open-water certification costs around $450.

★ **De Palm Watersports.** This is one of the best choices for your undersea experience; the options go beyond basic diving. You can don a helmet and walk along the ocean floor near De Palm Island, home of huge blue parrot fish. You can even do snuba—which is like scuba diving but without the heavy air tanks—a four-hour snuba adventure costs $133. ⊠ *L.G. Smith Blvd. 142, Oranjestad* ☏ *297/582–4400, 800/766–6016* ⊕ *www.depalm.com.*

Dive Aruba. Resort courses, certification courses, and trips to interesting shipwrecks make Dive Aruba worth checking out. ⊠ *Wilhelminastraat 8, Oranjestad* ☏ *297/582–7337* ⊕ *www.divearuba.com.*

Native Divers Aruba. Underwater naturalist courses are taught by PADI-certified instructors here, and the company has legions of return customers. ⊠ *Koyari 1, Noord* ☏ *297/586–4763* ⊕ *www.nativedivers.com.*

☾ **Red Sail Sports.** Red Sail offers courses for children and others new to scuba diving. An introductory class costs about $95. ⊠ *J.E. Irausquin Blvd. 83, Oranjestad* ☏ *297/586–1603, 877/733–7245 in U.S.* ⊕ *www. aruba-redsail.com.*

FISHING

Deep-sea catches here include barracuda, kingfish, wahoo, bonito, and tuna. November to April is the catch-and-release season for sailfish and marlin. Many skippered charter boats are available for half- or full-day sails. Packages include tackle, bait, and refreshments. Prices range from $300 to $500 for a half-day charter and from $550 to $700 for a full day.

Pelican Tours & Watersports. In operation since 1984, this company will help you catch trophy-size fish. Scuba and snorkeling trips are also available, as are various boating cruises. ⊠ *Pelican Pier, near Holiday Inn and Playa Linda hotels, Palm Beach* ☏ *297/587–2302, 587–2307* ⊕ *www.pelican-aruba.com.*

A bouquet of colorful reefs can be explored in the waters of Aruba

Red Sail Sports. This company can arrange everything for your fishing trip. ⊠ *J.E. Irausquin Blvd. 83, Oranjestad* ☎ *297/586–1603, 877/733–7245 in U.S.* ⊕ *www.redsail.com.*

Teaser Charters. The expertise of the Teaser crew is matched by a commitment to sensible fishing practices, which include catch and release and avoiding ecologically sensitive areas. The company's two boats are fully equipped, and the crew seem to have an uncanny ability to locate the best fishing spots. Captain Kenny runs a thrilling expedition. ⊠ *St. Vincentweg 5, Oranjestad* ☎ *297/582–5088* ⊕ *www.teasercharters.com.*

GOLF

Aruba Golf Club. This 9-hole course has 20 sand traps, five water traps, roaming goats, and lots of cacti. There are also 11 greens covered with artificial turf, making 18-hole tournaments a possibility. The clubhouse has a bar and locker rooms. Greens fees are $12 for 9 holes, $16 for 18 holes. Golf carts are available. ⊠ *Golfweg 82, San Nicolas* ☎ *297/584–2006.*

The Links at Divi Aruba. This 9-hole course was designed by Karl Litten and Lorie Viola. The par-36, paspalum-grass course (best for seaside courses) takes you past beautiful lagoons. Amenities include a golf school with professional instruction, a swing-analysis station, a driving range, and a two-story golf clubhouse with a pro shop. Two restaurants are available: Windows on Aruba for fine dining and Mulligan's for a casual and quick lunch. Greens fees are $80 for 9 holes, $112 for 18 from December to April; guests of the Divi properties get a discount. ✉ *J.E. Irausquin Blvd. 93, Oranjestad* ☎ *297/581–4653.*

★ **Tierra del Sol.** This stunning course is on the northwest coast near the California Lighthouse. Designed by Robert Trent Jones Jr., this 18-hole championship course combines Aruba's native beauty—cacti and rock formations—with the lush greens of the world's best courses. The greens fees vary depending on the time of day (from December to March it is $159 in the morning, $129 for early afternoon, and $100 from 3 pm). The fee includes a golf cart equipped with a communications system that allows you to order drinks for your return to the clubhouse. Half-day golf clinics, a bargain at $45, are available Monday, Tuesday, and Thursday. The pro shop is one of the Caribbean's most elegant, with an extremely attentive staff. ✉ *Malmokweg* ☎ *297/586–0978.*

GUIDED TOURS

De Palm Tours. This operator has a near monopoly on Aruban sightseeing. The basic 3½-hour tour hits highlights of the island. Wear sneakers or hiking shoes, and bring a lightweight jacket or wrap, as the air-conditioned bus gets cold. You can make reservations through its general office or at hotel tour-desk branches. ✉ *L.G. Smith Blvd. 142, Oranjestad* ☎ *297/582–4400, 800/766–6016* ⊕ *www.depalm.com.*

HIKING

Hiking Aruba's arid and rugged countryside will give you the best opportunities to see the island's wildlife and flora. Arikok National Wildlife Park is an excellent place to glimpse the real Aruba, free of the trappings of tourism. The heat can be oppressive, so be sure to take it easy, wear a hat, and have a bottle of water handy.

☾ **Aruba Nature Sensitive Tours.** Eddy Croes, a former park ranger whose ★ passion for the area is seemingly unbounded, runs this outfitter with care. Groups are never larger than eight people, so you'll see as much detail as you can handle. Expect frequent stops, when Eddy asks for silence so that you can hear the sounds of the park. The hikes are done at an easy pace and are suitable for basically anyone. A moonlight walk is available for those looking to avoid the heat. ✉ *Pos Chiquito 13E, Savaneta* ☎ *297/585–1594* ⊕ *www.naturesensitivetours.com.*

HORSEBACK RIDING

Ranches offer short jaunts along the beach or longer rides along trails passing through countryside flanked by cacti, divi-divi trees, and aloe vera plants. Ask if you can stop off at Cura di Tortuga, a natural pool that's reputed to have restorative powers. Rides are also possible in Arikok National Wildlife Park. Rates run from $35 for an hour-long trip to $65 for a three-hour tour; private rides cost slightly more.

☾ **De Palm Tours.** The dependable outfitter arranges excursions on horseback. ✉ *L.G. Smith Blvd. 142, Oranjestad* ☎ *297/582–4400, 800/766–6016* ⊕ *www.depalm.com.*

Rancho Daimari. Rancho Daimari will lead your horse to water—either at Natural Bridge or Natural Pool—in the morning or afternoon for $75 per person. The "Junior Dudes" program is tailored to young riders. There are even ATV trips. ✉ *Palm Beach 33B, Noord* ☎ *297/586–6284* ⊕ *www.ranchodaimari.com.*

Rancho Notorious. The seven one- to three-hour tours here include one to the countryside for $45 and a snorkeling trip to the beach for $120. All skill levels are welcome. The company also organizes ATV and mountain-biking trips. ✉ *Boroncana, Noord* ☎ *297/586–0508* ⊕ *www. ranchonotorious.com.*

KAYAKING

Kayaking is a popular sport on Aruba, especially along the south coast, where the waters are calm. It's a great way to explore the coastline.

Aruba Watersport Center. Operating since 1960, Aruba Watersport offers both single and double kayaks. ✉ *L. G. Smith Blvd. 81B, Noord* ☎ *297/586–6613.*

De Palm Tours. Every day except Sunday, De Palm offers a four-hour guided kayaking tour that includes some snorkeling. The cost, including lunch, is $99. ✉ *L.G. Smith Blvd. 142, Oranjestad* ☎ *297/582–4400, 800/766–6016* ⊕ *www.depalm.com.*

SUBMARINE EXCURSIONS

Atlantis Submarines. Explore an underwater reef teeming with marine life without getting wet. Atlantis operates a 65-foot air-conditioned sub, *Atlantis VI,* which takes 48 passengers for a two-hour tour 95 to 150 feet below the surface along Barcadera Reef ($99 per person). The company also owns the *Seaworld Explorer,* a semisubmersible that allows you to sit and view Aruba's marine habitat from 5 feet below the surface ($44 per person). Make reservations a day in advance. ✉ *Renaissance Marina, L.G. Smith Blvd. 82, Oranjestad* ☎ *297/583–6090* ⊕ *www. depalmtours.com.*

WINDSURFING

★ The southwestern coast's tranquil waters make windsurfing conditions ideal for both beginners and intermediates, as the winds are steady but sudden gusts rare. Experts will find the Atlantic coast, especially around Grapefield and Boca Grandi beaches, more challenging; winds are fierce and often shift course without warning. Most operators also offer complete windsurfing vacation packages. Kitesurfing (sometimes called kiteboarding) is also popular in Aruba.

Aruba Active Vacations. Aruba Active Vacations is a major windsurfing center on the island. ✉ *L.G. Smith Blvd. 486, near Fisherman's Huts, Palm Beach* ☎ *297/586–3940* ⊕ *www.aruba-active-vacations.com.*

Pelican Adventures Tours & Watersports. Pelican usually has rental boards and sails on hand. ✉ *Pelican Pier, near Holiday Inn and Playa Linda hotels, Palm Beach* ☎ *297/586–3600* ⊕ *www.pelican-aruba.com.*

Sailboard Vacations. Complete windsurfing packages, including accommodations, can be arranged with Sailboard Vacations. Equipment can be rented for $60 a day. ⊠ *L.G. Smith Blvd. 462, Malmok Beach* ☎ *297/586–2527* ⊕ *www.sailboardvacations.com.*

Vela Aruba. This is the place to meet other windsurfers in town. It's a major kitesurfing center as well. ⊠ *L.G. Smith Blvd. 101, Palm Beach* ☎ *297/586–3735* ⊕ *www.velawindsurf.com.*

Barbados

WORD OF MOUTH

"Imagine an ideal day on a Caribbean island with beautiful beaches and as much sightseeing and activities as you desire. Add wonderful food! You're in Barbados."

—Knowing

"Barbados is paradise. Excellent beaches, friendly people, just wonderful...highly recommend it!"

—KatieR

WELCOME TO BARBADOS

Broad vistas, sweeping seascapes, craggy cliffs, and acre upon acre of sugarcane—that's Barbados. Beyond that, what draws visitors to the island is the Bajan hospitality, the welcoming hotels and resorts, the sophisticated dining, the never-ending things to see and do, the exciting nightspots, and, of course, the sunny beaches.

TOP REASONS TO VISIT BARBADOS

1 Great resorts: They run the gamut—from unpretentious to knock-your-socks-off.

2 Great Golf: Golfers can choose from some of the best championship courses in the Caribbean.

3 Restaurants Galore: Great food includes everything from street-party barbecue to the finest dining.

4 Wide Range of Activities: With a broad assortment of land and water sports, sightseeing options, and nightlife, there's always plenty to do.

5 Welcoming Locals: Bajans are friendly, welcoming, helpful, and hospitable. You'll like them; they'll like you.

KEY

- Beaches
- Cruise Ship Terminal
- Dive Sites
- **1** Restaurants
- **①** Hotels

BARBADOS BASICS

Barbados stands apart—both geographically and geologically—from its Caribbean neighbors; it's a full 100 miles (161 km) east of the Lesser Antilles chain. The top of a single submerged mountain of coral and limestone, the island is 21 miles (34 km) long, 14 miles (22½ km) wide, and relatively flat. The population is about 300,000, and the capital city is Bridgetown.

Cuckold Pt.

Gay's Cove

St. Nicholas Abbey
Cherry Tree Hill
arbados
ife Reserve
Morgan Lewis
Sugar Mill
Farley Hill
1

Belleplaine

Barclays Park Beach

Chalky Mount

ST. ANDREW

Mt. Hillaby

Bathsheba/ Cattlewash Beach

Soup Bowl

Bathsheba
11 **15** **16**

Flower Forest

ST. JOSEPH
12

Andromeda Botanic Gardens
10 **14**

Conset Bay

Welchman Hall Gully

Blackmans

Codrington Theological College

Harrison's Cave

ST. JOHN

THOMAS

Groves

Four Crossroads

Marley Vale

Ragged Pt.

Orchid World

Gun Hill

Gun Hill Signal Station

ST. GEORGE

ST. PHILIP

Bottom Bay

Warrens
2

Sunbury Plantation House & Museum

MICHAEL

3

Edgecumbe

Crane Beach

t Gay Rum
rs Centre

4

13

ol Cat Heritage Village

9

The Crane

Emancipation Statue

CHRIST CHURCH

Crane Bay

George Washington House

Barbados Museum
Rockley

COBBLER'S REEF

5

tings

Worthing

7

Casuarina Beach

9

Barbados Concorde Experience

St. Lawrence Gap

8

Oistins
8 **10**

Grantley Adams International Airport

3

4 **5**

Oistins Bay

Long Bay

6 **7** **6** **7**

Miami Beach

11

12

Silver Sands Beach

South Pt.

Sandy Beach

0   2 mi

0   2 km

BARBADOS BEACHES

Geologically, Barbados is a coral-and-limestone island (not volcanic) with few rivers and, as a result, has beautiful beaches, particularly along the island's southern and southeastern coastlines.

(Above) Bathsheba, Barbados
(Bottom right) Surfers at Soup
Bowl, Bathsheba (Top right)
Couple on beach in Barbados

The west coast has some lovely beaches as well, but they're more susceptible to erosion after major autumn storms, if any, have taken their toll. With long stretches of open beach, crashing ocean surf, rocky cliffs, and verdant hills, the Atlantic (windward) side of Barbados is where Bajans spend their own holidays, but these beaches aren't safe for swimming. The surf and currents are too strong, even for experienced swimmers. All Bajan beaches have fine white sand, and all are open to the public. Most have public access from the road, so nonguest bathers don't have to pass through hotel properties. When the surf is too high and swimming becomes dangerous, a red flag will be hoisted on the beach. A yellow flag—or a red flag at half-staff—means swim with caution. Topless sunbathing—on the beach or at the pool—is not allowed anywhere in Barbados by government regulation.

LOTS OF BEACHES

All along the south and west coasts you'll find excellent beaches with broad swaths of white sand. Both the unique pink coral sand at Crane Beach and the magnificent—and rather remote—Bottom Bay Beach lure romantics. Sand on the east-coast beaches is equally white, but the treacherous surf means you can only wade or stroll, not swim.

SOUTH COAST

A young, energetic crowd favors the south-coast beaches, which are broad and breezy, blessed with powdery white sand, and dotted with tall palms. The reef-protected areas with crystal-clear water are safe for swimming and snorkeling. The surf is medium to high, and the waves get bigger and the winds stronger (windsurfers take note) the farther southeast you go.

Accra Beach. This popular beach, also known as Rockley Beach, is next to the Accra Beach Hotel. Look forward to gentle surf and a lifeguard, plenty of nearby restaurants for refreshments, a children's playground, and beach stalls for renting chairs and equipment for snorkeling and other water sports. Parking is available at an on-site lot. ⊠ *Hwy. 7, Rockley, Christ Church.*

★ **Bottom Bay Beach.** Popular for fashion and travel-industry photo shoots, Bottom Bay is the quintessential Caribbean beach. Surrounded by a coral cliff, studded with a stand of palms, and with an endless ocean view, this dreamy enclave is near the southeastern tip of the island. The waves can be too strong for swimming, but it's *the* picture-perfect place for a picnic lunch. Park at the top of the cliff and follow the steps down to the beach. ⊠ *Dover, St. Philip.*

Word of Mouth "[C]heck out Bottom Bay. There are limestone cliffs with a small

field of palm trees and a natural-looking gorgeous beach. It's featured in most of the promotional commercials for Barbados, and for a reason." —Blamona

Pebbles Beach. On the southern side of Carlisle Bay, adjacent to the Hilton Barbados just south of Bridgetown, this broad half-circle of white sand is one of the island's best beaches—but it can become crowded on weekends and holidays. Park at Harbour Lights or at the Boatyard Bar and Bayshore Complex, both on Bay Street, where you can also rent umbrellas and beach chairs and buy refreshments. ⊠ *Aquatic Gap, Needham's Point, St. Michael.*

Word of Mouth "Carlisle bay is calm and has the most beautiful crystal clear aqua water." —nunnles

★ **Casuarina Beach.** Stretched in front of the Almond Casuarina Resort, this broad strand of powdery white sand is great for both sunbathing and strolling, with the surf from low to medium. Find public access and parking on Maxwell Coast Road, near the Bougainvillea Resort. ⊠ *Maxwell Coast Rd., Dover, Christ Church.*

★ **Fodor's Choice** **Crane Beach.** This exquisite crescent of pink sand on the southeast coast was named not for the elegant long-legged wading birds but for the crane used to haul and load cargo when this area was a busy port. Crane Beach usually has a steady breeze and

5

Miami Beach.

lightly rolling surf that is great for body-surfing. A lifeguard is on duty. Access down to the beach is either via 98 steps or the hotel's cliff-side, glass-walled elevator. ⊠ *Crane Bay, St. Philip.*

Word of Mouth "[Crane Beach] has pink sand like baby powder. The cliffs are a sight." —kmw1211

★ **Fodor's Choice** **Miami Beach.** Also called Enterprise Beach, this isolated spot on the coast road, just east of Oistins, is an underrated slice of pure white sand with cliffs on either side and crystal-clear water. You can find a palm-shaded parking area, snack carts, and chair rentals. Bring a picnic. ⊠ *Enterprise Beach Rd., Enterprise, Christ Church.*

Sandy Beach. This beach has shallow, calm waters and a picturesque lagoon, making it an ideal location for families with small kids. Park right on the main road. You can rent beach chairs and umbrellas, and plenty of places nearby sell food and drinks. ⊠ *Hwy. 7, Worthing, Christ Church.*

Silver Sands–Silver Rock Beach. Nestled between South Point, the southernmost

tip of the island, and Inch Marlow Point, Silver Sands–Silver Rock is a beautiful strand of white sand that always has a stiff breeze. That makes this beach the best in Barbados for intermediate and advanced windsurfers and, more recently, kiteboarders. ⊠ *Off Hwy. 7, Christ Church.*

EAST COAST

Be cautioned: swimming at east-coast beaches is treacherous, even for strong swimmers, and is *not* recommended. Waves are high, the bottom tends to be rocky, the currents are unpredictable, and the undertow is dangerously strong.

Barclays Park Beach. Serious swimming is unwise at this beach, which follows the coastline in St. Andrew, but you can take a dip, wade, and play in the tide pools. A lovely shaded area with picnic tables is directly across the road. ⊠ *Ermy Bourne Hwy., north of Bathsheba, St. Andrew.*

★ **Bathsheba/Cattlewash Beaches.** Although not safe for swimming, the miles of untouched, windswept sand along the East Coast Road in St. Joseph Parish are great for beachcombing and wading. As you approach Bathsheba

Soup Bowl, the southernmost stretch just below Tent Bay, the enormous mushroom-shape boulders and rolling surf are uniquely impressive. This is also where expert surfers from around the world converge each November for the Independence Classic Surfing Championship. ✉ *East Coast Rd., Bathsheba, St. Joseph.*

WEST COAST

Gentle Caribbean waves lap the west coast, and leafy mahogany trees shade its stunning coves and sandy beaches. The water is perfect for swimming and water sports. An almost unbroken chain of beaches runs between Bridgetown and Speightstown. Elegant homes and luxury hotels face much of the beachfront property in this area, dubbed Barbados's "Platinum Coast."

West-coast beaches are considerably smaller and narrower than those on the south coast. Also, prolonged stormy weather in September and October may cause sand erosion, temporarily making the beach even narrower. Even so, west-coast beaches are seldom crowded. Vendors stroll by, selling handmade baskets, hats, dolls, jewelry, even original watercolors; owners of private boats offer waterskiing, parasailing, and snorkeling excursions. There are no concession stands, but hotels and beachside restaurants welcome nonguests for terrace lunches (wear a cover-up), and you can buy picnic items at supermarkets in Holetown.

Brighton Beach. Calm as a lake, this is where you can find locals taking a quick dip on hot days. Just north of Bridgetown, Brighton Beach is also home to the Cockspur Beach Club. ✉ *Spring Garden Hwy., Brighton, St. Michael.*

★ **Fodor's Choice** **Mullins Beach.** This lovely beach just south of Speightstown is a perfect place to spend the day. The water is safe for swimming and

snorkeling, there's easy parking on the main road, and Mullins Restaurant serves snacks, meals, and drinks—and rents chairs and umbrellas. ✉ *Hwy. 1, Mullins Bay, St. Peter.*

Paynes Bay Beach. The stretch of beach just south of Sandy Lane is lined with luxury hotels. It's a very pretty area, with plenty of beach to go around and good snorkeling. Public access is available at several locations along Highway 1; parking is limited. ✉ *Hwy. 1, Paynes Bay, St. James.*

Word of Mouth "Paynes Bay Beach… almost always has pretty calm water and is one of the nicest beaches on the island. You can walk the beach far north to Sandy Lane Resort and south way past Tamarind." —xkenx

Mullins Beach.

By Jane E. Zarem

Barbados stands apart from its neighbors in the Lesser Antilles archipelago, the chain of islands that stretches in a graceful arc from the Virgin Islands to Trinidad. Barbados is isolated in the Atlantic Ocean, 100 miles (160 km) due east of St. Lucia, its nearest neighbor.

Geologically, most of the Lesser Antilles are the peaks of a volcanic mountain range, whereas Barbados is the top of a single, relatively flat protuberance of coral and limestone—the source of building blocks for many a plantation manor. Several of those historic "great houses," in fact, have been carefully restored. Some are open to visitors.

Bridgetown, both capital city and commercial center, is on the southwest coast of pear-shape Barbados. Most of the 280,000 Bajans (*Bay*-juns, which derives from the phonetic British pronunciation of Barbadian) live and work in and around Bridgetown, elsewhere in St. Michael Parish, or along the idyllic west coast or busy south coast. Others reside in tiny villages that dot the interior landscape. Broad sandy beaches, craggy cliffs, and numerous coves make up the coastline, and the interior is consumed by forested hills and gullies and acre upon acre of sugarcane.

Without question, Barbados is the "most British" island in the Caribbean. In contrast to the turbulent colonial past experienced by neighboring islands, which included repeated conflicts between France and Britain for dominance and control, British rule in Barbados carried on uninterrupted for 340 years—from the first established British settlement in 1627 until independence was granted in 1966. That's not to say, of course, that there weren't significant struggles in Barbados, as elsewhere in the Caribbean, between the British landowners and their African-born slaves and other indentured servants.

With that unfortunate period of slavery relegated to the history books, the British influence on Barbados remains strong today in local manners, attitudes, customs, and politics—tempered, of course, by the characteristically warm nature of the Bajan people. In keeping with British-born traditions, many Bajans worship at the Anglican church, afternoon tea is a ritual, cricket is the national pastime (a passion,

LOGISTICS

Getting to Barbados: Several airlines fly nonstop to Barbados, or you may have to connect in Miami or San Juan. Grantley Adams International Airport (BGI) is in Christ Church Parish on the south coast; the airport is about 15 minutes from hotels situated along the south coast, 45 minutes from the west coast, and 30 minutes from Bridgetown.

Hassle Factor: Low.

On the Ground: Ground transportation is available immediately outside the customs area. Airport taxis aren't metered, but fares are regulated ($38–$40 to Speightstown, $30–$35 to west-coast hotels, $16–$22 to south-coast hotels). Be sure, however, to establish the fare before getting into the taxi and confirm whether the price quoted is in U.S. or Barbadian dollars.

Getting Around the Island: If you are staying in an isolated area, you may want or need to rent a car; but bus service is good, especially between Bridgetown and stops along the west and south coasts. Taxis, of course, are always an option.

most admit), dressing for dinner is a firmly entrenched tradition, and patrons at some bars are as likely to order a Pimm's Cup or a shandy as a rum and Coke. And yet, Barbados is hardly stuffy—this is still the Caribbean, after all.

Tourist facilities are concentrated on the west coast in St. James and St. Peter parishes (appropriately dubbed the Platinum Coast) and on the south coast in Christ Church Parish. Traveling along the west coast to historic Holetown, the site of the first British settlement, and continuing north to the city of Speightstown, you can find posh beachfront resorts, luxurious private villas, and fine restaurants enveloped by lush gardens and tropical foliage. The trendier, more commercial south coast offers competitively priced hotels and beach resorts, and its St. Lawrence Gap area is jam-packed with shops, restaurants, and nightlife. The relatively wide-open spaces along the southeast coast are proving ripe for development, and some wonderful inns and hotels already take advantage of the intoxicatingly beautiful ocean vistas. For their own vacations, though, Bajans escape to the rugged east coast, where the Atlantic surf pounds the dramatic shoreline with unrelenting force.

All in all, Barbados is a sophisticated tropical island with a rich history, lodgings to suit every taste and pocketbook, and plenty to pique your interest both day and night—whether you're British or not!

PLANNING

WHEN TO GO

Barbados is busiest in the high season, which extends from December 15 through April 15. Off-season hotel rates can be half of those required during the busy period. During the high season, too, a few hotels may require you to buy a meal plan, which is usually not required in the low season. As noted in the listings, some hotels close in September and October, the slowest months of the off-season, for annual renovations. Some restaurants may close for brief periods within that time frame as well.

GETTING HERE AND AROUND

AIR TRAVEL

Nonstop Flights: You can fly nonstop to Barbados from Atlanta (Delta), Charlotte (US Airways), Dallas-Ft. Worth (American), Miami (American), New York–JFK (American and JetBlue), and Philadelphia (US Airways).

Other Flights: American Eagle flies nonstop from San Juan, so many American Airlines customers transfer there instead of in Miami. Caribbean Airlines offers connecting service from Fort Lauderdale, Miami, and New York via Port of Spain, Trinidad, but this adds at least two hours to your flight time even in the best of circumstances and may not be the best option for most Americans. Barbados is also well connected to other Caribbean islands via LIAT. Mustique Airways and SVG Air connect Barbados to St. Vincent and the Grenadines, and many passengers use Barbados as a transit hub, often spending the night each way. RedJet flies between Barbados and Guyana, Jamaica, and Trinidad.

Airline Contacts: Not all airlines flying into Barbados have local numbers. If your airline doesn't have a local contact number on the island, you will have to pay for the call.

Airport Grantley Adams International Airport. Grantley Adams International Airport is a stunning, modern facility located on the south coast of Barbados, with an efficient immigration, customs, and baggage system and extensive duty-free shopping in the departure area. The airport is about 15 minutes from hotels situated along the south or east coasts, 45 minutes from the west coast, and 30 minutes from Bridgetown. ⊠ *BGI, Christ Church* ☎ *246/428–7101.*

Airline Contacts American Airlines/American Eagle ☎ *246/428-4170* ⊕ *www.aa.com.* **Caribbean Airlines** ☎ *246/428-1650, 800/744-2225* ⊕ *www. caribbean-airlines.com.* **LIAT** ☎ *246/434-5428, 888/844-5428* ⊕ *www.liatairline. com.* **Mustique Airways** ☎ *246/428-1638* ⊕ *www.mustique.com.* **Redjet** ☎ *246/827-2727* ⊕ *www.flyredjet.com.* **SVG Air** ☎ *246/247-3712.*

BUS TRAVEL

Bus service is efficient and inexpensive. Blue buses with a yellow stripe are public, yellow buses with a blue stripe are private, and private "Zed-R" vans (so called for their ZR license plate designation) are white with a maroon stripe. All buses travel frequently along Highway 1 (St. James Road) and Highway 7 (South Coast Main Road), as well as inland routes. The fare is Bds\$1.50 (75¢) for any one destination; exact change in either local or U.S. currency is appreciated. Buses run about every 20 minutes. Small signs on roadside poles that say "To City" or "Out of City," meaning the direction relative to Bridgetown, mark the bus stops. Flag down the bus with your hand, even if you're standing at the stop. Bridgetown terminals are at Fairchild Street for buses to the south and east and at Lower Green for buses to Speightstown via the west coast.

CAR TRAVEL

Barbados has good roads, but traffic can be heavy, particularly around Bridgetown. Be sure to keep a map handy, as the road system in the countryside can be very confusing—although the friendly Bajans are always happy to help you find your way. Drive on the left, British-style. When someone flashes headlights at you at an intersection, it means "after you." Be especially careful negotiating roundabouts (traffic circles). The speed limit is 30 mph (50 kph) in the country, 20 mph (30 kph) in town. Bridgetown actually has rush hours: 7 to 9 and 4 to 6. Park only in approved parking areas; downtown parking costs Bds75¢ to Bds$1 per hour.

Car Rentals: Most car-rental agencies require renters to be between 21 and either 70 or 75 years of age. Dozens of agencies rent cars, jeeps, or minimokes (small, open-sided vehicles). Rates are about $60 per day for a minimoke to $85 or more per day for a four-wheel-drive vehicle (or $225 to $400 or more per week) in high season. Most firms also offer discounted three-day rates, and many require at least a two-day rental in high season.

Car-Rental Agencies Coconut Car Rentals ⊠ *Bayside, Bay St., Bridgetown, St. Michael* ☎ *246/437–0297* ⊕ *www.coconutcars.com.* **Courtesy Rent-A-Car** ⊠ *Grantley Adams International Airport, Christ Church* ☎ *246/431–4173, 246/431–4160* ⊕ *www.courtesyrentacar.com.* **Drive-a-Matic Car Rental** ⊠ *CWTS Complex* ☎ *246/422–3000, 800/581–8773* ⊕ *www.carhire.tv.*

TAXI TRAVEL

Taxis operate 24 hours a day. They aren't metered but charge according to fixed rates set by the government. They carry up to three passengers, and the fare may be shared. Sample one-way fares from Bridgetown are $20 to Holetown, $25 to Speightstown, $20 to St. Lawrence Gap, and $35 to Bathsheba. Drivers can also be hired for an hourly rate of about $35–$40 for up to three people.

ESSENTIALS

Banks and Exchange Services The Barbados dollar is pegged to the U.S. dollar at the rate of Bds$1.98 to $1. The U.S. dollar is widely accepted. Barbados National Bank has a branch at Grantley Adams International Airport open daily from 8 am until the last plane lands or departs. ATMs are available 24 hours a day throughout the island. All prices quoted in this chapter are in U.S. dollars.

Electricity The electric current throughout Barbados is 110 volts, 50 cycles, U.S. standard.

Emergency Services Ambulance ☎ *511.* **Divers' Alert Network** ☎ *246/684–8111, 246/684–2948.* **Fire** ☎ *311.* **Hyperbaric Chamber in Barbados** ☎ *246/436–5483 to treat decompression illness in divers.* **Police** ☎ *211 emergencies, 246/430–7100 nonemergencies.*

Passport Requirements All visitors must have a valid passport and a return or ongoing ticket to enter Barbados.

Phones The area code for Barbados is 246. Local calls from private phones are free; some hotels charge a small fee. For directory assistance, dial 411. U.S. visitors can dial 1-800 CALL USA (225–5872) to call home from any phone; it's less expensive than using a calling card, a credit card, or calling collect. Calls from pay phones cost Bds25¢ for five minutes. Prepaid phone cards, which can be used throughout Barbados and other Caribbean islands, are sold at shops, attractions, transportation centers, and other convenient outlets.

Most U.S. cell phones will work in Barbados, though roaming charges can be expensive. Renting a cell phone or buying a local SIM card for your own unlocked phone may be a less expensive alternative if you're planning an extended stay or expect to make a lot of local calls. A cell phone can be rented for as little as $5 a day (minimum one-week rental); prepaid cards in varying denominations and top-off services are available at several locations throughout the island.

Taxes and Service Charges A departure tax ($31.50) is automatically added into the price of your airfare. An 8.75% government tax is added to all hotel bills. A 10% service charge is often added to hotel bills and restaurant checks. A 17.5% V.A.T. is imposed on restaurant meals, admissions to attractions, and merchandise sales (other than those that are duty-free). Prices are often tax-inclusive; if not, the V.A.T. will be added to your bill.

Tipping If no service charge is added to your bill, tip waiters 10% to 15% and maids $2 per room per day. Tip bellhops and airport porters $1 per bag. Taxi drivers and tour guides appreciate a 10% tip.

ACCOMMODATIONS

Most people stay either in luxurious enclaves on the fashionable west coast—north of Bridgetown—or on the action-packed south coast with easy access to small, independent restaurants, bars, and nightclubs. A few inns on the remote southeast and east coasts offer ocean views and tranquillity, but those on the east coast don't have good swimming beaches nearby. Prices in Barbados are sometimes twice as high in season as during the quieter months. Most hotels include no meals in their rates; some include breakfast, many offer a meal plan, some require you to purchase the meal plan in the high season, and a few offer all-inclusive packages.

Resorts: Great resorts run the gamut—from unpretentious to knock-your-socks-off—in terms of size, intimacy, amenities, and price. Many are well suited to families.

Small Inns: A few small, cozy inns may be found in the east and southeast regions of the island.

Villas and Condos: Families and long-term visitors may choose from a wide variety of condos (everything from busy time-share resorts to more sedate vacation complexes). Villas and villa complexes can be luxurious, simple, or something in between.

HOTEL AND RESTAURANT PRICES

Prices in the restaurant reviews are the average cost of a main course at dinner or, if dinner is not served, at lunch; taxes and service charges are generally included. Prices in the hotel reviews are the lowest cost of a standard double room in high season, excluding taxes, service charges, and meal plans (except at all-inclusives). Prices for rentals are the lowest per-night cost for a one-bedroom unit in high season.

VISITOR INFORMATION

Contacts Barbados Tourism Authority ✉ *Harbour Rd., Bridgetown, St. Michael* ☎ *246/427–2623* ⊕ *www.visitbarbados.org* ✉ *Grantley Adams International Airport, Christ Church* ☎ *246/428–5570* ✉ *Cruise-ship terminal, Deep Water Harbour, Bridgetown, St. Michael* ☎ *246/426–1718.*

WEDDINGS

There are no minimum residency requirements to get married; however, you need to obtain a marriage license from the Ministry of Home Affairs (☎ *246/228–8950*). If either was divorced or widowed, appropriate paperwork must be presented to obtain the license.

EXPLORING BARBADOS

The terrain changes dramatically from any one of the island's 11 parishes to the next, and so does the pace. Bridgetown, the capital, is a somewhat sophisticated city. West-coast resorts and private estates ooze luxury, whereas the small villages and vast sugar plantations found throughout central Barbados reflect the island's history. The relentless Atlantic surf shaped the cliffs of the dramatic east coast, and the northeast is called Scotland because of its hilly landscape and broad vistas. Along the lively south coast, the daytime hustle and bustle produce a palpable energy that continues well into the night at countless restaurants, dance clubs, and nightspots.

BRIDGETOWN

This bustling capital city is a major duty-free port with a compact shopping area. The principal thoroughfare is Broad Street, which leads west from National Heroes Square.

WHAT TO SEE

The Careenage. In the early days, Bridgetown's natural harbor and gathering place is where schooners were turned on their sides (careened) to be scraped of barnacles and repainted. Today, the Careenage serves as a marina for pleasure yachts and excursion boats. A boardwalk skirts the north side of the Careenage; on the south side, a lovely esplanade has pathways and benches for pedestrians and a statue of Errol Barrow, the first prime minister of Barbados. The Chamberlain Bridge and the Charles Duncan O'Neal Bridge cross the Careenage. ✉ *Bridgetown, St. Michael.*

National Heroes Square. Across Broad Street from the Parliament Buildings and bordered by High and Trafalgar streets, this triangular plaza marks the center of town. Its monument to Lord Horatio Nelson (who was in Barbados only briefly in 1777 as a 19-year-old navy lieutenant) predates Nelson's Column in London's Trafalgar Square by 36 years. Also here are a war memorial and a fountain that commemorates the advent of running water on Barbados in 1865. ✉ *Broad St., across from Parliament, Bridgetown, St. Michael.*

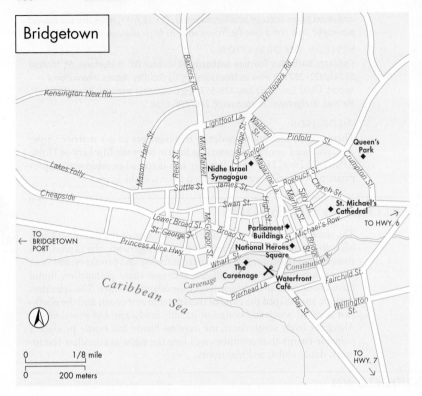

Bridgetown

Nidhe Israel Synagogue. Providing for the spiritual needs of one of the oldest Jewish congregations in the Western Hemisphere, this synagogue was formed by Jews who left Brazil in the 1620s and introduced sugarcane to Barbados. The adjoining cemetery has tombstones dating from the 1630s. The original house of worship, built in 1654, was destroyed in an 1831 hurricane, rebuilt in 1833, and restored with the assistance of the Barbados National Trust in 1987. Friday-night services are held during the winter months, but the building is open to the public year-round. Shorts are not acceptable during services but may be worn at other times. ⊠ *Synagogue La., Bridgetown, St. Michael* ☎ *246/436–6869* 💷 *Donation requested* ☉ *Weekdays 9–4.*

Parliament Buildings. Overlooking National Heroes Square in the center of town, these Victorian buildings were constructed around 1870 to house the British Commonwealth's third-oldest parliament. A series of stained-glass windows depicts British monarchs from James I to Victoria. The National Heroes Gallery & Museum is located in the West Wing. ⊠ *National Heroes Sq., Trafalgar St., Bridgetown, St. Michael* ☎ *246/427–2019* 💷 *Donations welcome* ☉ *Tours weekdays at 11 and 2, when parliament isn't in session.*

Queen's Park. Northeast of Bridgetown, Queen's Park contains one of the island's two immense baobab trees. Brought to Barbados from Guinea,

West Africa, around 1738, this tree has a girth of more than 60 feet. Queen's Park Art Gallery, managed by the National Culture Foundation, is the island's largest gallery; exhibits change monthly. Queen's Park House, built in 1783 and the historic home of the British troop commander, has been converted into a theater, with an exhibition room on the lower floor and a restaurant. Originally called King's House, the name was changed upon Queen Victoria's accession to the throne. ⊠ *Constitution Rd., Bridgetown, St. Michael* ☎ *246/427–2345 gallery* ☞ *Free* ⊙ *Daily 9–5.*

St. Michael's Cathedral. Although no one has proved it, George Washington is said to have worshipped here in 1751 during his only trip outside the United States. By then, the original structure was nearly a century old. Destroyed twice by hurricanes, it was rebuilt in 1784 and again in 1831. ⊠ *Spry St., east of National Heroes Sq., Bridgetown, St. Michael.*

SOUTH COAST

5

Christ Church Parish, which is far busier and more developed than the west coast, is chockablock with condos, high- and low-rise hotels, and beach parks. It is also the location of St. Lawrence Gap, with its many places to eat, drink, shop, and party. As you move southeast, the broad, flat terrain comprises acre upon acre of cane fields, interrupted only by an occasional oil rig and a few tiny villages. Along the byways are colorful chattel houses, which were the traditional homes of tenant farmers. Historically, these typically Barbadian, ever-expandable small buildings were built so they could be dismantled and moved, as required.

WHAT TO SEE

ⓒ **Barbados Concorde Experience.** Opened to the public in April 2007, the
★ Concorde Experience focuses on the British Airways Concorde G-BOAE (Alpha Echo, for short) that for many years flew between London and Barbados and has made its permanent home here. Besides boarding the sleek supersonic aircraft itself, you'll learn about how the technology was developed and how this plane differed from other jets. You may or may not have been able to fly the Concorde when it was still plying the Atlantic, but this is your chance to experience some unique modern history—up close and personal. ⊠ *Grantley Adams International Airport, adjacent to the terminal building, Christ Church* ☎ *246/420–7738* ⊕ *www.barbadosconcorde.com* ☞ *$20* ⊙ *Daily 9–5.*

ⓒ **Barbados Museum.** This intriguing museum, established in 1933 in the
Fodor'sChoice former British Military Prison (1815) in the historic St. Ann's Garri-
★ son area, has artifacts from Arawak days (around 400 BC) along with galleries that depict 19th-century military history and everyday social history. You can see cane-harvesting tools, wedding dresses, ancient (and frightening) dentistry instruments, and slave sale accounts kept in spidery copperplate handwriting. The museum's Harewood Gallery showcases the island's flora and fauna, its Cunard Gallery has a permanent collection of 20th-century Barbadian and Caribbean paintings and engravings, and its Connell Gallery features European decorative arts. Additional galleries include one with exhibits targeted to children. The Shilstone Memorial Library houses rare West Indian

documentation—archival documents, genealogical records, photos, books, and maps—dating back to the 17th century. The museum also has a gift shop and a café. ⊠ *St. Ann's Garrison, Hwy. 7, Garrison, St. Michael* ☎ *246/427–0201* ⊕ *www.barbmuse.org.bb* ☜ *$7.50* ⊙ *Mon.– Sat. 9–5, Sun. 2–6.*

Codrington Theological College. An impressive stand of royal palms lines the road leading to the coral-stone buildings and serene grounds of Codrington College, an Anglican theological seminary opened in 1745 on a cliff overlooking Conset Bay. The benefactor of the college was Christopher Codrington III (1668–1710), a former governor-general of the Leeward Islands whose antislavery views were unpopular in the plantocracy of the times. In an effort to "Christianize" the slaves and provide them with a general education, Codrington's will established that "300 negroes at least" would always be allowed to study at the institution; the planters who acted as trustees, however, were loath to teach the slaves how to read and write. You're welcome to tour the buildings, explore the grounds, and walk the nature trails. Keep in mind, though, that beachwear is not appropriate here. ⊠ *Sargeant St., Conset Bay, St. John* ☎ *246/423–1140* ⊕ *www.codrington.org* ☜ *Donations welcome* ⊙ *Daily 10–4.*

Emancipation Statue. This powerful statue of a slave—whose raised hands, with broken chains hanging from each wrist, evoke both contempt and victory—is commonly referred to as the Bussa Statue. Bussa was the man who, in 1816, led the first slave rebellion on Barbados. The work of Barbadian sculptor Karl Brodhagen, the statue was erected in 1985 to commemorate the emancipation of the slaves in 1834. ⊠ *St. Barnabas Roundabout, intersection of ABC Hwy. and Hwy. 5, Haggatt Hall, St. Michael.*

☾
★ **George Washington House.** George Washington slept here! This carefully restored and refurbished 18th-century plantation house in Bush Hill was the only place where the future first president of the United States actually slept outside North America. Teenage George and his older half-brother Lawrence, who was suffering from tuberculosis and seeking treatment on the island, rented this house overlooking Carlisle Bay for two months in 1751. Opened to the public in January 2007, the lower floor of the house and the kitchen have period furnishings; the upper floor is a museum with both permanent and temporary exhibits that display artifacts of 18th-century Barbadian life. The site includes an original 1719 windmill and bathhouse, along with a stable added to the property in the 1800s. Guided tours begin with an informative 15-minute film appropriately called *George Washington in Barbados.* ⊠ *Bush Hill, Garrison, St. Michael* ☎ *246/228–5461* ⊕ *www. georgewashingtonbarbados.org* ☜ *$10* ⊙ *Mon.–Sat. 9–4:30.*

Fodor'sChoice **Sunbury Plantation House and Museum.** Lovingly rebuilt after a 1995 fire
★ destroyed everything but the thick flint-and-stone walls, Sunbury offers an elegant glimpse of the 18th and 19th centuries on a Barbadian sugar estate. Period furniture, old prints, and a collection of horse-drawn carriages lend an air of authenticity. A buffet luncheon is served daily in the courtyard for $31 per person. A five-course candlelight dinner is

Sunbury Plantation House

served ($100 per person, reservations required) two nights a week at
the 200-year-old mahogany dining table in the Sunbury dining room.
⊠ *Off Hwy. 5, Six Cross Roads, St. Philip* ☎ *246/423–6270* ⊕ *www.
barbadosgreathouse.com* 🖾 *$7.50* ⊗ *Daily 9–4:30.*

Tyrol Cot Heritage Village. This coral-stone cottage just south of
Bridgetown was constructed in 1854 and is preserved as an example of
period architecture. In 1929 it became the home of Sir Grantley Adams,
the first premier of Barbados and the namesake of its international
airport. Part of the Barbados National Trust, the cottage is filled with
antiques and memorabilia that belonged to the late Sir Grantley and
Lady Adams. It's also the centerpiece of an outdoor "living museum,"
where artisans and craftsmen have their workshops in a cluster of traditional chattel houses. Workshops are open, crafts are for sale, and
refreshments are available at the "rum shop" primarily during the winter season and when cruise ships are in port. ⊠ *Rte. 2, Codrington Hill,
St. Michael* ☎ *246/424–2074* 🖾 *$5.75* ⊗ *Weekdays 9–5.*

CENTRAL BARBADOS

On the west coast, in St. James Parish, Holetown marks the center of the
Platinum Coast—so called for the vast number of luxurious resorts and
mansions that face the sea. Holetown is also where Captain John Pow-
ell and the crew of the British ship *Olive Blossom* landed on May 14,
1625, to claim the island for King James I (who had actually died of a
stroke seven weeks earlier). On the east coast, the crashing Atlantic surf
has eroded the shoreline, forming steep cliffs and exposing prehistoric
rocks that look like giant mushrooms. Bathsheba and Cattlewash are

favorite seacoast destinations for local folks on weekends and holidays. In the interior, narrow roads weave through tiny villages and along and between the ridges. The landscape is covered with tropical vegetation and is rife with fascinating caves and gullies.

WHAT TO SEE

Fodor's Choice
★
Andromeda Botanic Gardens. More than 600 beautiful and unusual plant specimens from around the world are cultivated in 6 acres of gardens nestled among streams, ponds, and rocky outcroppings overlooking the sea above the Bathsheba coastline. The gardens were created in 1954 with flowering plants collected by the late horticulturist Iris Bannochie. They're now administered by the Barbados National Trust. The Hibiscus Café serves snacks and drinks. ⊠ *Bathsheba, St. Joseph* ☎ *246/433–9384* ✑ *$10* ☉ *Daily 9–5.*

Chalky Mount. This tiny east-coast village is perched high in the clay-yielding hills that have supplied local potters for about 300 years. A number of working potteries are open daily to visitors. You can watch as artisans create bowls, vases, candleholders, and decorative objects—which are for sale. ⊠ *Chalky Mount, St. Andrew.*

☉ **Cockspur Beach Club.** Just north of Bridgetown, the fun-loving folks at West Indies Rum Distillery, makers of Cockspur and Malibu rums, invite visitors to enjoy a day at the beach, a variety of water-sports options, and a complimentary rum punch. Changing rooms with lockers and showers are available for beachgoers to use, along with beach umbrellas and chairs. Snorkeling equipment can be rented for the day ($5). The beachside grill serves lunch and drinks. This is a very popular outing for cruise-ship passengers. ⊠ *Brighton Beach, Black Rock, Brighton, St. Michael* ☎ *246/425–9393* ✑ *$10* ☉ *Daily 8:30–4:30.*

Fodor's Choice
★
Flower Forest. It's a treat to meander among fragrant flowering bushes, canna and ginger lilies, puffball trees, and more than 100 other species of tropical flora in a cool, tranquil forest of flowers and other plants. A ½-mile-long (1-km-long) path winds through the 53.6-acre grounds, a former sugar plantation; it takes about 30 to 45 minutes to follow the path, or you can wander freely for as long as you wish. Benches throughout the forest give you places to pause and reflect. There's also a snack bar, a gift shop, and a beautiful view of Mt. Hillaby, at 1,100 feet the highest point of land on Barbados. ⊠ *Hwy. 2, Richmond, St. Joseph* ☎ *246/433–8152* ⊕ *www.flowerforestbarbados.com* ✑ *$10* ☉ *Daily 9–5.*

☉ **Folkestone Marine Park and Visitor Centre.** The mission of family-oriented Folkestone Marine Park, a marine protected area just north of Holetown, is to provide high-quality recreational activities in a sustainable way that will educate and entertain Barbadians and visitors alike. Facilities include a playground, basketball court, picnic area, museum, and beach with lifeguards. The museum (two rooms with artifacts and photos of how the sea is used for various purposes) illuminates some of the island's marine life. For some firsthand viewing, there's an underwater snorkeling trail (equipment rental, $10 for the day) around Dottins Reef, just off the beach in the protected marine reserve area; nonswimmers can enjoy a glass-bottom boat tour. A barge sunk in shallow water is home to myriad fish, making it a popular dive site. The park is open around the clock, with full security; lifeguards are on duty at the beach from 9 to 5:30 every day. A canteen serves snacks and drinks. ⊠ *Hwy. 1, Church Point, Holetown, St. James* ☎ *246/425–2871* 🖃 *Free; 60 cents to view the exhibits* ⊘ *Park daily 24 hrs; museum weekdays 9:30–5.*

Gun Hill Signal Station. The 360-degree view from Gun Hill, 700 feet above sea level, gave this location strategic importance to the 18th-century British army. Using lanterns and semaphores, soldiers based here could communicate with their counterparts at the Garrison on the south coast and at Grenade Hill in the north. Time moved slowly in 1868, and Captain Henry Wilkinson whiled away his off-duty hours by carving a huge lion from a single rock—which is on the hillside just below the tower. Come for a short history lesson but mainly for the view; it's so gorgeous that military invalids were once sent here to convalesce. ⊠ *Gun Hill, St. George* ☎ *246/429–1358* 🖃 *$5* ⊘ *Weekdays 9–5.*

Fodor's Choice
★

Harrison's Cave. This limestone cavern, complete with stalactites, stalagmites, subterranean streams, and a 40-foot waterfall, is a rare find in the Caribbean—and one of Barbados's most popular attractions. Tours include a nine-minute video presentation and a 40-minute underground journey through the cavern via electric tram. The visitor center has interactive displays, life-size models and sculptures, a souvenir shop, restaurant facilities, and elevator access to the tram for people with disabilities. Tours fill up fast, so make a reservation. ⊠ *Hwy. 2, Welchman Hall, St. Thomas* ☎ *246/417–3700* ⊕ *www.harrisonscave.com* 🖃 *$30* ⊘ *Daily 8:30–4:30 (last tour 3:45).*

Fodor's Choice
★

Mount Gay Rum Visitors Centre. On this popular tour you learn the colorful story behind the world's oldest rum—made in Barbados since 1703. Although the distillery is in the far north, in St. Lucy Parish, tour guides explain the rum-making procedure. Equipment, both historic and modern, is on display, and rows and rows of barrels are stored in this location. The 45-minute tour runs hourly (last tour begins at 3:30 weekdays; 2:30 on Saturday) and concludes with a tasting and an opportunity to buy bottles of rum and gift items—and even have lunch or cocktails, depending on the time of day. ⊠ *Spring Garden Hwy., Brandons, St. Michael* ☎ *246/425–8757* ⊕ *www.mountgayrum.com* 🖃 *$7, $50 with lunch; $35 with cocktails* ⊘ *Weekdays 9–5.*

★

Orchid World. Follow meandering pathways through tropical gardens filled with thousands of colorful orchids. You'll see Vandaceous orchids attached to fences or wire frames, Schomburgkia and Oncidiums stuck on mahogany trees, Aranda and Spathoglottis orchids growing in a grotto, and Ascocendas suspended from netting in shady enclosures. You'll find seasonal orchids, scented orchids, multicolor Vanda orchids, and more. Benches are well placed to stop for a little rest, admire the flowers, or simply take in the expansive view of the surrounding cane fields and distant hills of Sweet Vale. Snacks, cold beverages, and other refreshments are served in the café. ⊠ *Hwy. 3B, Groves, St. George* ☎ *246/433–0306* 🖃 *$10* ⊘ *Daily 9–5.*

Welchman Hall Gully. This 1½-mile-long (2-km-long) natural gully is really a collapsed limestone cavern, once part of the same underground network as Harrison's Cave. The Barbados National Trust protects the peace and quiet here, making it a beautiful place to hike past acres of labeled flowers and stands of trees. You can see and hear some interesting birds—and, with luck, a native green monkey. The tour is self-guided (although a guide can be arranged with 24 hours' notice) and takes about 30 to 45 minutes; the last tour begins at 4 pm. ⊠ *Welchman Hall, St. Thomas* ☎ *246/438–6671* ⊕ *www.welchmanhallgullybarbados.com* ☞ *$12* ⊘ *Daily 9–4:30.*

NORTHERN BARBADOS

Speightstown, the north's commercial center and once a thriving port city, now relies on its appealing local shops and informal restaurants. Many of Speightstown's 19th-century buildings, with traditional overhanging balconies, have been restored. The island's northernmost reaches, St. Peter and St. Lucy parishes, have a varied topography and are lovely to explore. Between the tiny fishing towns along the northwestern coast and the sweeping views out over the Atlantic to the east are forest and farm, moor and mountain. Most guides include a loop through this area on a daylong island tour—it's a beautiful drive.

WHAT TO SEE

Ⓒ **Animal Flower Cave.** Small sea anemones, or sea worms (resembling flowers when they open their tiny tentacles), live in small pools in this sea cave at the island's very northern tip. The cave itself, discovered in 1780, has a coral floor that ranges from 126,000 to 500,000 years old, according to geological estimates. The view of breaking waves from inside the cave is magnificent. ⊠ *North Point, St. Lucy* ☎ *246/439–8797* ☞ *$7.50* ⊘ *Daily 9–4.*

Ⓒ
★ **Barbados Wildlife Reserve.** The reserve is the habitat of herons, innumerable land turtles, screeching peacocks, shy deer, elusive green monkeys, brilliantly colored parrots (in a large walk-in aviary), a snake, and a caiman. Except for the snake and the caiman, the animals run or fly freely—so step carefully and keep your hands to yourself. Late afternoon is your best chance to catch a glimpse of a green monkey. ⊠ *Farley Hill, St. Peter* ☎ *246/422–8826* ☞ *$12* ⊘ *Daily 10–5.*

Farley Hill. At this national park in northern St. Peter, across the road from the Barbados Wildlife Reserve, gardens and lawns, along with an avenue of towering royal palms and gigantic mahogany, whitewood, and casuarina trees, surround the imposing ruins of a plantation great house built by Sir Graham Briggs in 1861 to entertain royal visitors from England. Partially rebuilt for the filming of *Island in the Sun*, the classic 1957 film starring Harry Belafonte and Dorothy Dandridge, the structure was destroyed by fire in 1965. Behind the estate, there's a sweeping view of the region called Scotland for its rugged landscape. ⊠ *Farley Hill, St. Peter* ☞ *$2 per car, pedestrians free* ⊘ *Daily 8:30–6.*

Ⓒ **Morgan Lewis Sugar Mill.** Built in 1727, the mill was operational until 1945. Today it's the only remaining windmill in Barbados with its wheelhouse and sails intact. No longer used to grind sugarcane, except for occasional demonstrations, it was donated to the Barbados National Trust in 1962 and eventually restored to its original working

St. Nicholas Abbey.

specifications in 1998 by millwrights from the United Kingdom. The surrounding acres are now used for dairy farming. ⊠ *Southeast of Cherry Tree Hill, Morgan Lewis, St. Andrew* ☎ 246/422–7429 ▣ *$5* ⊙ *Weekdays 9–5.*

Fodor's Choice ★ **St. Nicholas Abbey.** The island's oldest great house (circa 1650) was named after the original British owner's hometown, St. Nicholas Parish near Bristol, and Bath Abbey nearby. Its stone-and-wood architecture makes it one of only three original Jacobean-style houses still standing in the Western Hemisphere. It has Dutch gables, finials of coral stone, and beautiful grounds that include an old sugar mill. The first floor, fully furnished with period furniture and portraits of family members, is open to the public. Fascinating home movies, shot by a previous owner's father, record Bajan life in the 1930s. Behind the great house is a rum distillery with a 19th-century steam press. Visitors can purchase artisanal plantation rum produced nearby (the Abbey's production will become fully aged about 2018) and enjoy light refreshments at the terrace café. ⊠ *Cherry Tree Hill, St. Peter* ☎ 246/422–5357 ⊕ *www. stnicholasabbey.com* ▣ *$17.50* ⊙ *Sun.–Fri. 10–3:30.*

WHERE TO EAT

First-class restaurants and hotel dining rooms serve quite sophisticated cuisine—often prepared by chefs with international experience and rivaling that served in the world's best restaurants. Most menus include seafood: dolphin—the fish, not the mammal, and also called dorado or mahimahi—kingfish, snapper, and flying fish prepared every way imaginable. Flying fish is so popular that it has officially become a national symbol. Shellfish also abounds, as do steak, pork, and local black-belly lamb.

Local specialty dishes include *buljol* (a cold salad of pickled codfish, tomatoes, onions, sweet peppers, and celery) and *conkies* (cornmeal, coconut, pumpkin, raisins, sweet potatoes, and spices, mixed together, wrapped in a banana leaf, and steamed). *Cou-cou*, often served with steamed flying fish, is a mixture of cornmeal and okra, usually topped with a spicy creole sauce made from tomatoes, onions, and sweet peppers. Bajan-style pepper pot is a hearty stew of oxtail, beef chunks, and "any other meat" in a rich, spicy gravy and simmered overnight.

BEST BETS FOR DINING

Fodor's Choice★

The Atlantis, Brown Sugar, Champers, The Cliff, Daphne's, Fish Pot, Pisces, The Tides

BEST VIEW
L'Azure at the Crane, Atlantis, Waterside

BEST FOR FAMILIES
Angry Annie's, Bellini's Trattoria

MOST ROMANTIC
The Mews, Lone Star

BEST FOR LOCAL BAJAN CUISINE
Cliffside at New Edgewater, Naniki, Waterfront Café

For lunch, restaurants often offer a traditional Bajan buffet of fried fish, baked chicken, salads, macaroni pie (macaroni and cheese), and a selection of steamed or stewed provisions (local roots and vegetables). Be cautious with the West Indian condiments—like the sun, they're hotter than you think. Typical Bajan drinks, besides Banks Beer and Mount Gay, Cockspur, or Malibu rum, are *falernum* (a liqueur concocted of rum, sugar, lime juice, and almond essence) and *mauby* (a nonalcoholic drink made by boiling bitter bark and spices, straining the mixture, and sweetening it). You're sure to enjoy the fresh fruit or rum punch.

What to Wear: The dress code for dinner in Barbados is conservative, casually elegant, and, on occasion, formal—a jacket and tie for gentlemen and a cocktail dress for ladies in the fanciest restaurants and hotel dining rooms, particularly during the winter holiday season. Jeans, shorts, and T-shirts (either sleeveless or with slogans) are always frowned upon at dinner. Beach attire is appropriate only at the beach.

BRIDGETOWN

$$$　✕ **Waterfront Café.** This friendly bistro alongside the Careenage is the
CARIBBEAN　perfect place to enjoy a drink, snack, or meal—and to people-watch. Locals and tourists alike gather for all-day alfresco dining on sandwiches, salads, fish, pasta, pepper-pot stew, and tasty Bajan snacks such as buljol, fish cakes, or plantation pork (plantains stuffed with spicy minced pork). The panfried flying-fish sandwich is especially popular. In the evening you can gaze through the arched windows while savoring nouvelle Caribbean cuisine, enjoying cool trade winds, and listening to live jazz. There's a special Caribbean buffet and steel-pan music on Tuesday night from 7 to 9. ⑤ *Average main: $25* ⊠ *The Careenage,*

Bridgetown, St. Michael ☎ *246/427–0093* ⊕ *www.waterfrontcafe.com. bb* ☉ *Closed Sun.*

SOUTH COAST

$$$
ITALIAN
☾

✕ **Bellini's Trattoria.** Classic northern Italian cuisine is the specialty at Bellini's, on the main floor of the Little Bay Hotel. The atmosphere here is smart-casual. Toast the evening with a Bellini cocktail (ice-cold sparkling wine with a splash of fruit nectar) and start your meal with bruschetta, an individual gourmet pizza, or perhaps a homemade pasta dish with fresh herbs and a rich sauce. Move on to the signature garlic shrimp entrée or the popular chicken parmigiana—then top it all off with chocolate mousse cake. On the other hand, the three-course daily special menu is the best deal. We recommend making your reservations early; request a table on the Mediterranean-style verandah to enjoy one of the most appealing dining settings on the south coast. ⑤ *Average main: $25* ⊠ *Little Bay Hotel, St. Lawrence Gap, Dover, Christ Church* ☎ *246/420–7587* ⊕ *www.bellinisbarbados.com* ⚑ *Reservations essential.*

$$$
CARIBBEAN
☾
Fodor'sChoice
★

✕ **Brown Sugar.** Set back from the road in a traditional Bajan home, the lattice-trimmed dining patios here are filled with ferns, flowers, and water features. Brown Sugar is a popular lunch spot for local business-people, who come for the nearly 30 delicious local and creole dishes spread out at the all-you-can-eat, four-course Bajan buffet. Here's your chance to try local specialties such as flying fish, cou-cou, buljol, *souse* (pickled pork, stewed for hours in broth), fish cakes, and pepper pot. In the evening, the à la carte menu has dishes such as fried flying fish, coconut shrimp, and plantain-crusted mahimahi; curried lamb, filet mignon, and broiled pepper chicken; and seafood or pesto pasta. Bring the kids—there's a special children's menu with fried chicken, fried flying-fish fingers, and pasta dishes. Save room for the warm pawpaw (papaya) pie or Bajan rum pudding with rum sauce. ⑤ *Average main: $26* ⊠ *Bay St., Aquatic Gap, St. Michael* ☎ *246/426–7684* ⊕ *www. brownsugarbarbados.com* ☉ *No lunch Sat.*

$$$$
ECLECTIC

✕ **Café Luna.** The sweeping view of pretty Miami (Enterprise) Beach from Café Luna, the alfresco dining deck on top of the Mediterranean-style Little Arches Hotel, is spectacular at lunchtime and magical in the moonlight. At lunch (for hotel guests only), sip on crisp white wine or a fruity cocktail while you await your freshly made salad, pasta, or sandwich. At dinner, co-owner and executive chef Mark de Gruchy prepares contemporary favorites from around the world, including fresh Scottish salmon grilled to perfection, oven-roasted New Zealand rack of lamb, fresh seafood bouillabaisse, and local chicken breast with mango chutney. Sushi is a specialty on Thursday and Friday nights; on Saturday night a champagne and lobster option enhances the regular menu. ⑤ *Average main: $33* ⊠ *Little Arches Hotel, Enterprise Beach Rd., Oistins, Christ Church* ☎ *246/420–4689* ⊕ *www.littlearches.com* ⚑ *Reservations essential.*

$$
MEXICAN
☾

✕ **Café Sol.** Have a hankerin' for good Tex-Mex food? Enjoy nachos, tacos, burritos, empanadas, fajitas, and tostadas in this Mexican bar and grill at the entrance to busy St. Lawrence Gap. Or choose a burger, honey-barbecue chicken, or flame-grilled steak from the gringo menu.

Helpings of rice and beans, a Corona, and plenty of jalapeño peppers, guacamole, and salsa give everything a Mexican feel. Some people come just for the margaritas—15 fruity varieties rimmed with Bajan sugar instead of salt. Café Sol has two happy hours every night. This place gets really busy, and reservations are only accepted for parties of four or more. ⑤ *Average main: $18* ⊠ *St. Lawrence Gap, Dover, Christ Church* ☎ *246/435–9531* ⊕ *www.cafesolbarbados.com* ⌖ *Reservations not accepted* ⊘ *No lunch.*

$$$$
ECLECTIC
Fodor'sChoice
★

✕ **Champers.** Chiryl Newman's snazzy seaside restaurant and popular watering hole is in an old Bajan home on a quiet lane just off the main south-coast road in Rockley. Luncheon guests—about 75% local businesspeople—enjoy repasts such as char-grilled beef salad, Champers fish pie, grilled barracuda, or chicken-and-mushroom fettuccine in a creamy chardonnay sauce. Dinner guests swoon over dishes such as the roasted rack of lamb with spring vegetables and mint-infused jus, the sautéed sea scallops with stir-fried vegetables and noodles with red Thai curry sauce, and the Parmesan-crusted barracuda with whole-grain mustard sauce. But this isn't nouvelle cuisine. The portions are hearty and the food is well seasoned with Caribbean flavors, "just the way the locals like it," says Newman. The cliff-top setting overlooking the eastern end of Accra Beach offers diners a panoramic view of the sea and a relaxing atmosphere for daytime dining. At night, particularly at the bar, there's a definite buzz in the air. Nearly all the artwork gracing the walls is by Barbadian artists and may be purchased through the on-site gallery. ⑤ *Average main: $35* ⊠ *Skeetes Hill, off Hwy. 7, Rockley, Christ Church* ☎ *246/434–3463* ⊕ *www.champersbarbados. com* ⌖ *Reservations essential.*

$$$$
SEAFOOD
☾

✕ **L'Azure at the Crane.** Perched on an oceanfront cliff, L'Azure is an informal breakfast and luncheon spot by day that becomes elegant after dark. Enjoy seafood chowder or a light salad or sandwich while absorbing the breathtaking panoramic view of Crane Beach and the sea beyond. At dinner, candlelight and a soft guitar enhance tamarind-glazed snapper or a fabulous Caribbean lobster seasoned with herbs, lime juice, and garlic butter and served in its shell; if you're not in the mood for seafood, try the crusted rack of lamb or herb-infused pork tenderloin. The dinner menu is prix fixe (two courses, $35; three courses and a glass of wine, $50). Sunday is really special, with a Gospel Brunch at 10 am and a Bajan Buffet at 12:30 pm. ⑤ *Average main: $38* ⊠ *The Crane, Crane Bay, St. Philip* ☎ *246/423–6220* ⊕ *www.thecrane.com* ⌖ *Reservations essential.*

$$$$
SEAFOOD
Fodor'sChoice
★

✕ **Pisces.** For seafood lovers, this is nirvana. Prepared in every way by chef-owner Larry Rogers—from charbroiled to gently sautéed—seafood specialties may include conch strips in tempura, rich fish chowder, pan-fried fillets of flying fish with a toasted-almond crust and a light mango-citrus sauce, and seared prawns in a fragrant curry sauce. Landlubbers in your party can select from the chicken, beef, and pasta dishes on the menu. Whatever you choose, the herbs that flavor it and the accompanying vegetables will have come from the chef's own garden. Save room for the homemade bread pudding, yogurt-lime cheesecake, or rum-raisin ice cream. Twinkling white lights reflect on the water as you dine. $ *Average main: $32* ⊠ *St. Lawrence Gap, Dover, Christ Church* ☎ *246/435–6564* ⊕ *www.piscesbarbados.com* ⌂ *Reservations essential* ⊘ No lunch.

$$$$

SEAFOOD

✕ **Waterside Restaurant.** You won't get much closer to dining on the water without being on a boat. Tables here are placed on a broad porch suspended over the beach and either gently rolling or crashing surf, depending on the weather. They're also spaced generously to allow for pleasant and private conversation. All the bustle of vibrant St. Lawrence Gap is left at the door. Once inside, the setting becomes sophisticated, tranquil, and definitely picturesque; the mood, quiet and intimate. And then there's the food. Chef Michael Hinds earned his stripes in world-class restaurants in New York, Miami, and London, as well as at Sandy Lane and Daphne's in Barbados. His truly elegant cuisine includes menu choices such as seared and crusted red snapper with tarragon emulsion, fire-roasted tiger prawns on bamboo and lemon-scented basmati rice with cashews, spice-rubbed loin of pork with sweet-potato gaufrettes, five-spice braised short rib with garlic mashed potatoes, molasses-glazed rack of lamb and minted couscous with sun-dried tomatoes, and more. For dessert, don't miss the spiced banana spring rolls with coconut ice cream and brandy caramel coulis. Hungry yet? $ *Average main: $32* ⊠ *St. Lawrence Gap, Dover, Christ Church* ☎ *203/418–9750* ⊕ *www.watersidebarbados.com* ⌂ *Reservations essential* ⊘ Closed Mon. No lunch.

EAST COAST

$$$

CARIBBEAN

Fodor's Choice

★

✕ **The Atlantis.** For decades, an alfresco lunch on the Atlantis deck overlooking the ocean has been a favorite of visitors touring the east coast and Bajans alike. Totally renovated and reopened in 2009 by the owners of Little Good Harbour and the Fishpot on the west coast, the revived restaurant effectively combines the atmosphere and good food that have always been the draw with an up-to-date, rather elegant dining room and a top-notch menu that focuses on local produce, seafood, and meats. The Bajan buffet lunch on Wednesday and Sunday is particularly popular; it's also well used for special occasions for local folks. At dinner, entreés include fresh fish, lobster (sometimes), roasted black-belly lamb or free-range chicken, fricassee of rabbit, and more. Or choose more traditional pepper pot, saltfish, or chicken stew with peas and rice, cou-cou, yam pie, or breadfruit mash, all of which are available at the Bajan buffet. Rotis and cutters (sandwiches) are always available, along with pasta specials, salads, soups, and fried flying fish. $ *Average main: $30* ⊠ *Tent Bay, St. Joseph* ☎ *246/433–9445* ⊕ *www. atlantishotelbarbados.com* ⌂ *Reservations essential* ⊘ No dinner Sun.

$$$

CARIBBEAN

☾

✕ **Cliffside at New Edgewater.** The outdoor deck of this restaurant in the New Edgewater hotel provides one of the prettiest, breeziest ocean views in all Barbados and, therefore, is a good stop for lunch when touring the east coast. From noon to 3 pm, choose the Bajan buffet or select from the menu. Either way, you might enjoy fried flying fish, roast or stewed chicken, local lamb chops, rice and peas, steamed root vegetables, sautéed plantains, and salad. Afternoon tea with scones, pastries, and sandwiches is served from 3:30 to 6 pm. Dinner is also served, but mostly to hotel guests and local residents, who are able to find their way home in the dark on the neighborhood's winding, often unmarked roads. $ *Average main: $25* ⊠ *New Edgewater Hotel, Bathsheba, St. Joseph* ☎ *246/433–9900* ⊕ *www.newedgewater.com* ⌂ *Reservations essential.*

$$ ✕ **Naniki Restaurant.** Rich wooden beams and stone tiles, clay pottery,
CARIBBEAN straw mats, colorful dinnerware, and fresh flowers from the adjacent anthurium farm set the style here. Huge picture windows and outdoor porch seating allow you to enjoy the exhilarating panoramic view of surrounding fields and hills and, when making the alfresco choice, a refreshing breeze along with your lunch of exquisitely prepared Caribbean standards. Seared flying fish, grilled dorado, stewed lambi (conch), curried chicken, and jerk chicken or pork are accompanied by cou-cou, peas and rice, or salad. For dinner (by special request only), start with conch fritters or Caribbean fish soup; then try roasted Bajan blackbelly lamb, grilled snapper, or shrimp garnished with tarragon. Sunday brunch is a Caribbean buffet often featuring great jazz music by some of the Caribbean's best musicians. Vegetarian dishes are always available. $ *Average main: $28* ⊠ *Lush Life Nature Resort, Suriname, St. Joseph* ☎ *246/433–1300* ⊕ *www.lushlife.bb* ⌂ *Reservations essential.*

WEST COAST

$$$$ ✕ **The Cliff.** Chef Paul Owens's mastery is the foundation of one of the
ECLECTIC finest dining experiences in the Caribbean, with prices to match. Steep
Fodor's Choice steps hug the cliff on which the restaurant sits to accommodate those
★ arriving by yacht, and every candlelit table has a sea view. Starter suggestions include smoked salmon ravioli with garlic sauce or grilled portobello mushroom on greens with truffle vinaigrette; for the main course, try char-grilled swordfish with Thai yellow curry sauce, roasted duck breast with wild mushroom fumée, seared tuna with saffron caper sauce and tomato coulis, or Cajun salmon with pesto cream sauce. Dessert falls into the sinful category, and service is impeccable. The prix-fixe menu will set you back $105 per person for a two-course meal (starter–main course or main course–dessert) or $125 per person for a three-course meal. Reserve days or even weeks in advance to snag a table at the front of the terrace for the best view. $ *Average main: $105* ⊠ *Hwy. 1, Derricks, St. James* ☎ *246/432–1922* ⊕ *www.thecliffbarbados.com* ⌂ *Reservations essential* ⊙ *Closed Sun. Apr. 15–Dec. 15. No lunch.*

$$$$ ✕ **Daphne's.** The beachfront restaurant of The House, Daphne's is the
ITALIAN chic Caribbean outpost of the famed London eatery Daphne's of Chel-
Fodor's Choice sea. Chef Marco Festini Cromer whips up contemporary Italian cui-
★ sine. Grilled mahimahi, for example, becomes "modern Italian" when combined with Marsala wine, *peperonata* (stewed peppers, tomatoes, onions, and garlic), and zucchini. Perfectly prepared *melanzane* (eggplant) and zucchini alla parmigiana is a delicious starter, and a half portion of risotto with porcini mushrooms, green beans, and Parma ham is fabulously rich. Pappardelle with braised duck, red wine, and oregano is a sublime pasta choice. The extensive wine list features both regional Italian and fine French selections. $ *Average main: $45* ⊠ *The House, Hwy. 1, Paynes Bay, St. James* ☎ *246/432–2731* ⊕ *www. daphnesbarbados.com* ⌂ *Reservations essential* ⊙ *No lunch. Closed Mon. June–Nov.*

$$$$
MEDITERRANEAN
Fodor's Choice
★

✕ **Fish Pot.** Just north of the little fishing village of Six Men's Bay, toward the northern end of the west coast of Barbados, this attractive seaside restaurant serves excellent Mediterranean cuisine and some of the island's freshest fish. Gaze seaward through windows framed with pale-green louvered shutters while lunching on a seafood crepe, a grilled panino, snow-crab salad, or perhaps pasta with seafood or roasted-pepper-and-chili tomato sauce; in the evening, the menu may include seafood bouillabaisse; seared, herb-crusted tuna on garlic-and-spinach polenta; sun-dried-tomato risotto tossed with vegetables; or cracker-crusted rack of lamb with thyme jus on roasted ratatouille. Bright and cheery by day and relaxed and cozy by night, the Fish Pot offers a tasty dining experience in a setting that's classier than its name might suggest. ⑤ *Average main: $35* ⊠ *Little Good Harbour Hotel, Shermans, St. Peter* ☎ *246/439–3000* ⊕ *www.littlegoodharbourbarbados.com* ⌂ *Reservations essential.*

$$
CARIBBEAN

✕ **Fisherman's Pub.** This is as local as local gets. Fisherman's Pub is an open-air, waterfront restaurant built on stilts just a stone's throw from the Speightstown fish market. For years, fishermen and other locals have come here daily for the inexpensive, authentic Creole buffet served at lunchtime. For $10 or less, you can soak up the atmosphere and fill your plate with fried flying fish, stewed chicken or pork, curried goat or lamb, macaroni pie, fried plantain, cou-cou, and crisp green salad. On Wednesday nights, fill your plate from the buffet and dance—or simply listen—to catchy steel pan or calypso music. (Whether dinner is served varies from season to season, so call ahead.) ⑤ *Average main: $20* ⊠ *Queen's St., Speightstown, St. Peter* ☎ *246/422–2703* ⌂ *Reservations not accepted.*

$$$$
EUROPEAN

✕ **Lone Star.** In the 1940s, this was the only commercial garage on the west coast; today, it's a snazzy restaurant in the tiny but chic Lone Star Hotel, where top chefs in the open-plan kitchen turn the finest local ingredients into gastronomic delights. The menu is extensive but pricey, even for lunch. All day, such tasty dishes as fish soup with rouille, Caesar or Thai chicken salad, tuna tartare, rotisserie chicken, and linguine with tomato-basil sauce and feta cheese are served in the oceanfront beach bar. At sunset, the casual daytime atmosphere turns trendy. You might start with tuna tartare with mango or Thai crab cakes with peppers and lemongrass dip, followed by crispy Peking duckling, grilled fish of the day, or lamb shank with basil mashed potatoes—or choose from dozens of other tasty land, sea, and vegetarian dishes. ⑤ *Average main: $32* ⊠ *Lone Star Hotel, Hwy. 1, Mount Standfast, St. James* ☎ *246/419–0599* ⊕ *www.thelonestar.com.*

$$$$
EUROPEAN

✕ **The Mews.** Dining at the Mews is like being invited to a friend's very chic home for dinner. This restaurant once was, in fact, a private home. The front room is now an inviting bar, and an interior courtyard is an intimate, open-air dining area. The second floor is a maze of small dining rooms and dining balconies, but you've come for the food, after all. The international cuisine is presented with contemporary flair. A plump chicken breast, for example, will be stuffed with cream cheese, smoked salmon, and herb pâté and served on a garlic-and-chive sauce. A braised lamb shank is presented on a bed of cabbage with a port-thyme

5

jus and creamed potatoes, and fillet of mahimahi is poached in a lemongrass, ginger, and cilantro broth. The warm molten chocolate cake is a must for dessert. Some call the atmosphere avant-garde; others call it quaint. Everyone calls the food delicious. But don't stop at dinner; by about 10 pm the bar begins to bustle. On weekends, the fun spills out into the street. ⑤ *Average main: $38* ✉ *2nd St., Holetown, St. James* ☎ 246/432–1122 ⌂ *Reservations essential* ⊘ *Closed Sun. No lunch.*

$$$$
EUROPEAN
Fodor'sChoice
★

✕ **The Tides.** Local residents and repeat visitors agree that the Tides is one of the island's best restaurants. Enter into a pretty courtyard and have a cocktail at the cozy bar or the coral-stone lounge in what was once a private mansion (or visit the on-site art gallery), then proceed to your seaside table. Perhaps the most intriguing feature of this stunning setting—besides the sound of waves crashing onto the shore just feet away—is the row of huge tree trunks growing right through the dining room. The food is equally dramatic. Chef Guy Beasley and his team give a contemporary twist to fresh seafood, fillet of beef, rack of lamb, and other top-of-the-line main courses by adding inspired sauces and delicate vegetables and garnishes. Save room for the sticky toffee pudding—definitely worth the calories. ⑤ *Average main: $40* ✉ *Balmore House, Hwy. 1, Holetown, St. James* ☎ 246/432–8356 ⊕ *www.tidesbarbados.com* ⌂ *Reservations essential* ⊘ *No lunch weekends.*

WHERE TO STAY

Most visitors stay on either the fashionable west coast, north of Bridgetown, or on the action-packed south coast. On the west coast, the beachfront resorts in St. Peter and St. James parishes are mostly luxurious, self-contained enclaves. Highway 1, a two-lane road with considerable traffic, runs past these resorts, which can make strolling to a nearby bar or restaurant a bit difficult. Along the south coast in Christ Church Parish, many hotels are clustered near the busy strip known as St. Lawrence Gap, convenient to dozens of small restaurants, bars, and nightclubs. On the much more remote east coast, a few small inns offer oceanfront views and get-away-from-it-all tranquillity.

In keeping with the smoke-free policy enforced throughout Barbados, smoking is restricted to open outdoor areas such as the beach. It is not permitted in hotels (neither rooms nor public areas) or in restaurants.

Prices in Barbados may be twice as high in season (December 15–April 15) compared with the quieter months. Most hotels include no meals in their rates, but some include breakfast, and many offer a meal plan. Some require you to purchase a meal plan in the high season, and a few offer all-inclusive packages.

Resorts run the gamut—from unpretentious to exceedingly formal—in terms of size, intimacy, amenities, and price. Families and long-term visitors may choose from a wide variety of villas and condos. A few small, cozy inns are found along the east and southeast coasts, as well as the northwest. They can be ultra-luxurious, fairly simple, or something in between.

Villa and condo complexes, which are continually cropping up along the south and west coasts of Barbados, may be the most economical option for families, other groups, or couples vacationing together. Non-owner vacationers rent individual units directly from the property managers, the same as reserving hotel accommodations. Units with fully equipped kitchens, two to six bedrooms, and as many baths run $200 to $2,500 per night in the off-season—double that in winter.

For expanded reviews, facilities, and current deals, visit Fodors.com.

PRIVATE VILLAS AND CONDOS

Local real-estate agencies will arrange vacation rentals of privately owned villas and condos along the west coast in St. James and St. Peter. All villas and condos are fully furnished and equipped, including appropriate staff depending on the size of the villa or unit—which can range from one to eight bedrooms; the staff usually works six days a week. Most villas have TVs, DVDs and/or VCRs, and CD players; all properties have telephones, and some have Internet access. International telephone calls are usually blocked; plan on using your own mobile phone or a phone card or calling card. Vehicles generally are not included in the rates, but rental cars can be arranged for and delivered to the villa upon request. Linens and basic supplies (such as bath soap, toilet tissue, and dishwashing detergent) are normally included.

Units with one to six bedrooms and as many baths run $200 to $2,500 per night in summer, and double that in winter. Rates include utilities and government taxes. The only additional cost is for groceries and staff gratuities. A security deposit is required upon booking and refunded seven days after departure less any damages or unpaid miscellaneous charges.

Apartments are available for vacation rentals in buildings or complexes that can have as few as three or four units or as many as 30 to 40 units—or even more. Prices range from $30 to $300 per night.

Villa Rental Contacts Altman Real Estate. ⊠ *Hwy. 1, Derricks, St. James* ☎ *246/432–0840, 866/360–5292 in the U.S.* ⊕ *www.aaaltman.com.* **Bajan Services.** ⊠ *Newton House, Battaleys, St. Peter* ☎ *246/422–2618, 866/978–5239 in the U.S.* ⊕ *www.bajanservices.com.* **Island Villas.** ⊠ *Trents Bldg., Holetown, St. James* ☎ *246/432–4627, 866/978–8499 in the U.S.* ⊕ *www.island-villas.com.*

Apartment Rental Contacts Barbados Tourism Authority. The Barbados Tourism Authority on Harbour Road in Bridgetown has a listing of apartments in

---

BEST BETS FOR LODGING

Fodors Choice★

Accra Beach Hotel, Almond Beach Club, Almond Beach Village, Atlantis Hotel, Coral Reef Club, Hilton Barbados, Little Arches Hotel, Peach and Quiet, Sandy Lane, The Sandpiper, Sweetfield Manor

BEST FOR HONEYMOONERS
Cobblers Cove, Fairmont Royal Pavilion, The House, Treasure Beach

BEST FOR FAMILIES
Almond Beach Village, Almond Casuarina, Bougainvillea, Royal Westmoreland, Tamarind, Turtle Beach

5

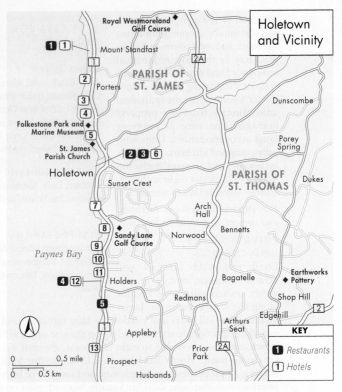

Holetown
and Vicinity

prime resort areas on both the south and west coasts, complete with facilities offered and current rates. ⊠ *Harbour Rd., Bridgetown, St. Michael* ☎ *246/427–2623* ⊕ *www.visitbarbados.org* ▭ *No credit cards.*

SOUTH COAST

$

HOTEL

Fodor'sChoice

★

🖼 **Accra Beach Hotel and Spa.** An excellent choice if you prefer a full-service resort in the middle of the busy south coast, the Accra is large, it's modern, it faces a great beach, and it's competitively priced. **Pros:** right on a great beach and, on the street side, near shopping, restaurants, and nightspots; terrific value; pleasant staff. **Cons:** standard rooms are fairly ordinary—at least opt for accommodations with a pool or ocean view. **TripAdvisor:** "staff is warm and friendly," "lovely beach," "great relaxing getaway." [$] *Rooms from: $218* ⊠ *Hwy. 7, Rockley, Christ Church* ☎ *246/435–8920, 888/712–2272 in the U.S.* ⊕ *www.accrabeachhotel. com* ↝ *188 rooms, 36 suites* ¶❍¶ *Multiple meal plans.*

$$$$

RESORT

ALL-INCLUSIVE

🕙

🖼 **Almond Casuarina Beach Resort.** One of three all-inclusive Almond properties in Barbados—and the only one on the south coast—Almond Casuarina Beach Resort offers guests countless opportunities for dining, socializing, and water and land sports. **Pros:** great beach and beautiful garden; every amenity you could imagine; wonderful for kids. **Cons:** lots of good restaurants to try in nearby St. Lawrence Gap, but you've paid for an all-inclusive. **TripAdvisor:** "excellent staff," "beautiful location," "world class beach." $ *Rooms from: $465* ⊠ *St. Lawrence Gap, at Maxwell Coast Rd., Dover, Christ Church* ☎ *246/428–3600* ⊕ *www. almondresorts.com* ⌁ *280 rooms* ⦿ *All-inclusive.*

$

RESORT

☾

▦ Bougainvillea Beach Resort. Attractive seaside townhouses, each with a separate entrance, wrap around the pool or face the beachfront; the suites are huge compared with hotel suites elsewhere in this price range, are decorated in appealing Caribbean pastels, and have full kitchens. **Pros:** great for families but also appeals to honeymooners; popular wedding venue; easy stroll to St. Lawrence Gap or to Oistins. **Cons:** rooms are on four levels with no elevator; sea can be rough for swimming. **TripAdvisor:** "excellent customer care," "superior accommodation," "brilliant scenery and beach." $ *Rooms from: $271* ⊠ *Maxwell Coast Rd., Maxwell, Christ Church* ☎ *246/418–0990, 800/495–1858 in the U.S.* ⊕ *www.bougainvillearesort.com* ⌁ *138 suites* ⦿ *Multiple meal plans.*

$

HOTEL

▦ Courtyard Bridgetown by Marriott. Comfortable, contemporary, convenient, and economical, this place is pleasant and the rooms are well appointed. **Pros:** Good value; especially suited to business travelers; modern, attractive accommodations. **Cons:** Walk to beach and restaurants; comparatively little "Caribbean" atmosphere; minimum onsite dining options. **TripAdvisor:** "comfortable and convenient," "very good service," "great for business or pleasure." $ *Rooms from: $199* ⊠ *The Garrison, Hastings, Christ Church* ☎ *246/625–0000* ⊕ *www. marriott.com* ⌁ *118* ⦿ *No meals.*

$

▦ The Crane. Hugging a seaside bluff on the southeast coast, the Crane is the island's oldest hotel in continuing operation; today, the original coral-stone hotel building (1887) is the centerpiece of a luxurious, 40-acre villa complex. **Pros:** enchanting view; lovely beach; fabulous suites; great restaurants. **Cons:** remote location; rental car recommended; not all villas have laundry facilities. **TripAdvisor:** "in a class of its own," "what a location," "great entertainment." $ *Rooms from: $264* ⊠ *Crane Bay, St. Philip* ☎ *246/423–6220* ⊕ *www.thecrane.com* ⌁ *4 rooms, 14 suites, 202 villas* ⦿ *Multiple meal plans.*

$

RESORT

☾

▦ Divi Southwinds Beach Resort. The all-suites Divi Southwinds is on 20 acres of lawn and gardens bisected by action-packed St. Lawrence Gap. **Pros:** beautiful beach; beach villas are the best value; close to shopping, restaurants, and nightspots. **Cons:** few water sports available and none included; some rooms aching for renovations; comparatively pricey for the value received. **TripAdvisor:** "very relaxing," "great location," "amazing staff." $ *Rooms from: $218* ⊠ *St. Lawrence Main Rd., Dover, Christ Church* ☎ *246/428–7181* ⊕ *www.divisouthwinds.com* ⌁ *121 1-bedroom suites, 12 2-bedroom suites* ⦿ *Multiple meal plans.*

$$

HOTEL

☾

Fodor's Choice

★

▦ Hilton Barbados. Beautifully situated on the sandy Needham's Point peninsula, all 350 rooms and suites in the high-rise Hilton Barbados have private balconies overlooking either the ocean or Carlisle Bay; 77 rooms are on executive floors, with a private lounge and concierge services. **Pros:** great location near town and on a beautiful beach; excellent accommodations; lots of services and amenities; frequent promotional deals provide real value. **Cons:** huge convention hotel; attracts groups; lacks "island" ambience. **TripAdvisor:** "beautiful location," "fantastic staff," "exceptional stay." $ *Rooms from: $299* ⊠ *Needham's Point,*

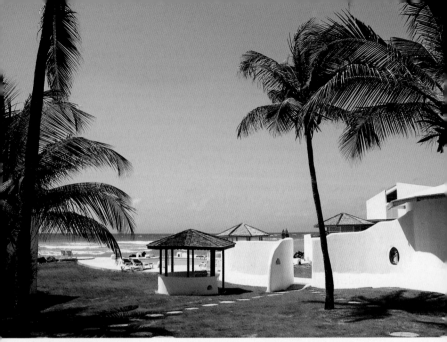

Peach and Quiet

St. Michael ☎ 246/426–0200 ⊕ www.hiltonbarbadoshotel.com ⇆ 317 rooms, 33 suites ⦿ Multiple meal plans.

$$
ALL-INCLUSIVE
🏨 **Island Inn Hotel.** Originally constructed in 1804 as a rum storage facility for the British regiment, this quaint, all-inclusive boutique hotel—less than a mile from Bridgetown and steps away from beautiful Pebbles Beach on Carlisle Bay—appeals to singles, couples, and families. **Pros:** friendly, accommodating atmosphere; smartly decorated rooms; excellent value. **Cons:** small pool; request a room near the pool, as rooms near the front (the restaurant and entertainment) can be noisy and don't have a patio. **TripAdvisor:** "lovely small friendly hotel," "beautiful little gem," "clean and modern." ⑤ Rooms from: $350 ⊠ Garrison Historic Area, Aquatic Gap, St. Michael ☎ 246/436–6393 ⊕ www.islandinnbarbados.com ⇆ 20 rooms, 4 suites ⦿ All-inclusive.

$$
HOTEL
★
🏨 **Little Arches Hotel.** Just east of the fishing village of Oistins, this classy boutique hotel has a distinctly Mediterranean ambience and a perfect vantage point overlooking the sea. **Pros:** stylish accommodations; good restaurant; across from fabulous Miami Beach; on-site car rental. **Cons:** fairly remote; rental car advised. **TripAdvisor:** "home away from home," "wonderful stay," "amazing boutique hotel." ⑤ Rooms from: $295 ⊠ Enterprise Beach Rd., Enterprise, Christ Church ☎ 246/420–4689 ⊕ www.littlearches.com ⇆ 8 rooms, 2 suites ⦿ Multiple meal plans.

$
HOTEL
Fodor's Choice
★
🏨 **Peach and Quiet.** Forgo the flashy accoutrements of a resort and, instead, claim one of the stylish suites in this small seaside inn just east of Oistins. **Pros:** the rates alone make this inn a great choice; peace and quiet; adults-only environment; engaging owners; stargazing and nature walks are special treats. **Cons:** inn is closed half the year; remote

location requires a rental car. **TripAdvisor:** "peace and quiet," "what a spectacular view," "perfect holiday." ⑤ *Rooms from: $119 ⊠ Inch Marlow Main Rd., Inch Marlow, Christ Church ☎ 246/428–5682 ⊕ www. peachandquiet.com ⇌ 22 suites ⊗ Closed May–Oct. ⑩ No meals.*

$$
HOTEL
🏨 **Silver Point Hotel.** This gated community of modern condos at Silver Sands–Silver Rock Beach is operated as a trendy boutique hotel that appeals to singles, couples, and families—but especially to windsurfers. **Pros:** stylish suites; perfect location for windsurfers; gated community. **Cons:** very remote; not within walking distance of anything except the beach; sea can be rough for swimming; rental car recommended. **TripAdvisor:** "friendly staff," "relaxing," "perfect retreat." ⑤ *Rooms from: $343 ⊠ Silver Sands, Christ Church ☎ 246/420–4416 ⊕ www. silverpointhotel.com ⇌ 60 suites ⑩ Multiple meal plans.*

$
B&B/INN
Fodor's Choice
★
🏨 **Sweetfield Manor.** George and Ann Clarke transformed a decrepit manse (circa 1900) perched on a ridge about a mile from Bridgetown—the former residence of the Dutch ambassador to Barbados—into the island's most delightful bed-and-breakfast inn. **Pros:** peaceful enclave primarily suitable for adults; inviting pool and gardens; gracious and friendly innkeepers; delicious gourmet breakfast; perfect wedding venue. **Cons:** long walk to beach; rental car advised; not the best choice for kids. **TripAdvisor:** "fantastic breakfasts," "paradise in Barbados," "fantastic in every way." ⑤ *Rooms from: $175 ⊠ Britton New Road, St. Michael ☎ 246/429–8356 ⊕ www.sweetfieldmanor.com ⇌ 6 rooms, 4 with bath, 1 suite ⑩ Breakfast.*

$$$
ALL-INCLUSIVE
☾
🏨 **Turtle Beach Resort.** Families flock to Turtle Beach because it offers large, bright suites and enough all-included activities for everyone to enjoy. **Pros:** perfect for family vacations; nice pools; roomy accommodations; lots of services and amenities. **Cons:** beach is fairly narrow and congested compared with other south-coast resorts; open vent between room and hallway can be noisy at night. **TripAdvisor:** "excellent service," "friendliest people on Earth," "first class." ⑤ *Rooms from: $729 ⊠ St. Lawrence Gap, Dover, Christ Church ☎ 246/428–7131 ⊕ www. turtlebeachresortbarbados.com ⇌ 164 suites ⑩ All-inclusive.*

EASTERN BARBADOS

$
B&B/INN
Fodor's Choice
★
🏨 **The Atlantis Hotel.** The legendary Atlantis Hotel, a fixture on the rugged east coast for more than a century and renowned for its spectacular oceanfront location, was completely renovated and reopened in 2009 by the owners of Little Good Harbour. **Pros:** historical and modern blend works wonderfully; spectacular oceanfront location; excellent restaurant. **Cons:** oceanfront rooms have fabulous views, but the smashing waves can be noisy at night; remote location, so rental car advised; no beach for swimming. **TripAdvisor:** "wildly romantic," "charming and great food," "everything was wonderful." ⑤ *Rooms from: $255 ⊠ Tent Bay, St. Joseph ☎ 246/433–9445 ⊕ www.atlantishotelbarbados. com ⇌ 5 rooms, 3 suites, 2 apartments ⊗ Closed Sept. ⑩ Breakfast.*

WEST COAST

$$$
ALL-INCLUSIVE
🏨 **Almond Beach Club and Spa.** Among several similar beachfront resorts south of Holetown, Almond Beach Club distinguishes itself as an adults-only environment with all-inclusive rates (only spa and salon services

Coral Reef Club luxury cottage.

are extra) and reciprocal guest privileges (including shuttle service) at its enormous sister resorts, Almond Beach Village farther north and Almond Casuarina on the south coast. **Pros:** adults only; intimate atmosphere; short walk to Holetown; next door to Sandy Lane Beach. **Cons:** beach erodes to almost nothing at certain times of the year—usually the result of fall storms; rooms could use updating. **TripAdvisor:** "every little thing taken care of," "great staff," "relaxing." *⑤ Rooms from: $450 ⊠ Hwy. 1, Vauxhall, St. James ☎ 246/432–7840 ⊕ www.almondresorts. com ⟿ 133 rooms, 28 suites ⫶⊙⫶ All-inclusive.*

$$$
ALL-INCLUSIVE
☾
★
▦ **Almond Beach Village.** Barbados's premier family resort is massive enough to be a popular conference venue and romantic enough to host intimate weddings. **Pros:** family resort with adult-only areas; lots to do and all included, including Bajan cooking lessons; sugar mill is a popular wedding venue. **Cons:** it's huge; more emphasis could be placed on service and room renovations. **TripAdvisor:** "welcoming staff," "rustic ocean front setting," "lovely." *⑤ Rooms from: $470 ⊠ Hwy. 1B, Heywoods, St. Peter ☎ 246/422–4900 ⊕ www.almondresorts.com ⟿ 373 rooms, 29 suites ⫶⊙⫶ All-inclusive.*

$$$$
HOTEL
▦ **Cobblers Cove Hotel.** "English Country" best describes the style of this lovely resort favored by British sophisticates. **Pros:** very classy establishment; lovely grounds; the penthouse suites are amazing; very quiet. **Cons:** too quiet for some; only bedrooms have a/c. **TripAdvisor:** "excellent small hotel," "deliciously relaxing," "wonderful atmosphere." *⑤ Rooms from: $870 ⊠ Road View, Speightstown, St. Peter ☎ 246/422–2291 ⊕ www.cobblerscove.com ⟿ 40 suites ⫶⊙⫶ Multiple meal plans.*

$$$$ ☷ **Colony Club Hotel.** As the signature hotel of five Elegant Hotel proper-
RESORT   ties on Barbados, the Colony Club is certainly elegant—but with a quiet,
★   friendly, understated style. **Pros:** clubby atmosphere; some rooms open
directly onto the lagoon pool. **Cons:** relatively pricey; beach comes and
goes, depending on storms. **TripAdvisor:** "relaxing and comfortable,"
"great location," "wonderful family vacation." ⑤ *Rooms from: $719*
⊠ *Hwy. 1, Porters, St. James* ☎ *246/422–2335* ⊕ *www.colonyclubhotel.*
com ⟿ *64 rooms, 32 junior suites* ❖❚ *Multiple meal plans.*

$$$$ ☷ **Coral Reef Club.** The upscale Coral Reef Club offers the epitome of
RESORT   elegance and style, along with a welcoming, informal atmosphere. **Pros:**
Fodor'sChoice   absolutely delightful; elegant yet informal; beautiful suites with huge
★   verandas; delicious dining; six computers with free Internet access available to guests. **Cons:** few room TVs (if that matters); narrow beach
sometimes disappears, depending on the seasonal weather; no kids
mid-January to mid-March. **TripAdvisor:** "a class act," "relaxed elegance," "lush resort." ⑤ *Rooms from: $805* ⊠ *Hwy. 1, Porters, St.*
James ☎ *246/422–2372* ⊕ *www.coralreefbarbados.com* ⟿ *29 rooms,*
57 suites, 2 villas ⊗ *Closed mid-May–mid-July, September.* ❖❚ *Multiple*
meal plans.

$$$$ ☷ **Fairmont Royal Pavilion.** Every guest room and suite in this luxurious
RESORT   adults-oriented resort (kids welcome April to October) has immediate
Fodor'sChoice   access to 11 acres of lush tropical gardens and an uninterrupted view
★   of the sea from its broad balcony or patio. **Pros:** beautiful resort; excellent service—everyone remembers your name; dining is excellent. **Cons:**
dining is expensive; in fact, everything here is expensive. **TripAdvisor:**
"fabulous setting," "quiet hideaway," "impeccable service." ⑤ *Rooms*
from: $975 ⊠ *Hwy. 1, Porters, St. James* ☎ *246/422–5555* ⊕ *www.*
fairmont.com ⟿ *48 rooms, 24 suites, 1 3-bedroom villa* ❖❚ *Multiple*
meal plans.

$$$$ ☷ **The House.** Privacy, luxury, and service are hallmarks of this intimate
RESORT   adult sanctuary next door to sister resort Tamarind. **Pros:** trendy and
★   stylish; striking public areas; privacy assured; pure relaxation. **Cons:**
suites due for updating; atmosphere can be a little stuffy, but you can
always head next door to Tamarind for a reality check. **TripAdvisor:**
"quite a gem," "relaxing and enjoyable," "expectations exceeded."
⑤ *Rooms from: $749* ⊠ *Hwy. 1, Paynes Bay, St. James* ☎ *246/432–*
5525, 888/996–9948 in the U.S. ⊕ *www.thehousebarbados.com* ⟿ *34*
suites ❖❚ *Breakfast.*

$$$ ☷ **Little Good Harbour.** This cluster of modern, spacious, self-catering cot-
RESORT   tages with one-, two-, and three-bedroom duplex suites overlooks a nar-
☾   row strip of beach in the far north of Barbados—just beyond the fishing
village of Six Men's Bay. **Pros:** laid-back atmosphere; good for families;
individualized experience. **Cons:** busy road; tiny beach; remote loca-
tion. **TripAdvisor:** "tranquil," "can't beat the views," "laid back chic."
⑤ *Rooms from: $399* ⊠ *Hwy. 1B, Shermans, St. Peter* ☎ *246/439–3000*
⊕ *www.littlegoodharbourbarbados.com* ⟿ *21 suites* ⊗ *Closed Sept.*
❖❚ *No meals.*

$$$ ☷ **Mango Bay.** In the heart of Holetown, this convenient boutique resort
ALL-INCLUSIVE   is within walking distance of shops, restaurants, nightspots, historic
sites, and the public bus to either Bridgetown or Speightstown. **Pros:**

nice rooms; great food; friendly staff; walk to Holetown shopping and entertainment. **Cons:** small pool; narrow beach; although heroic measures continue to be taken to address the problem, a natural drainage stream on the north side of the property can become odoriferous when it floods. **TripAdvisor:** "ideal place to wind down," "total relaxation," "small and beautiful." [$] *Rooms from: $400* ⊠ *2nd St., Holetown, St. James* ☎ *246/432–1384* ⊕ *www.mangobaybarbados.com* ⤴ *64 rooms, 10 suites, 2 penthouse suites* ⧖⧘*All-inclusive.*

$$$$
RENTAL

Port St. Charles. A luxury residential marina development near historic Speightstown on the northwest tip of Barbados, Port St. Charles is a perfect choice for boating enthusiasts who either arrive on their own yacht or plan to charter one during their stay. **Pros:** a boater's dream; well-appointed units with beautiful views; friendly and safe; great restaurant. **Cons:** not the best spot for little kids; minimum 14-night stay for some units in high season; noise is a problem for villas adjacent to the main road. **TripAdvisor:** "professional staff," "elegant and warm," "beautiful sunsets and fabulous accommodation." [$] *Rooms from: $507* ⊠ *Hwy. 1B, Heywoods, St. Peter* ☎ *246/419–1000* ⊕ *www. portstcharles.com* ⤴ *25 villas* ⧖⧘*No meals.*

$$$$
RESORT
Fodor's Choice
★

The Sandpiper. This little gem just north of Holetown is every bit as elegant as its sister hotel, Coral Reef Club, yet the atmosphere is more like a private hideaway. **Pros:** chic and sophisticated, the Tree Top Suites are fabulous; the bathrooms are amazing. **Cons:** beach is small—typical of west-coast beaches; hotel is small and many guests return year after year, so reservations can be hard to get. **TripAdvisor:** "wonderful hospitality," "lovely hotel for relaxing," "a perfect stay." [$] *Rooms from: $805* ⊠ *Hwy. 1, Holetown, St. James* ☎ *246/422–2251* ⊕ *www.sandpiperbarbados.com* ⤴ *22 rooms, 25 suites* ⊘ *Closed Sept.* ⧖⧘*Multiple meal plans.*

$$$$
HOTEL
☕
Fodor's Choice
★

Sandy Lane Hotel and Golf Club. Few places on Earth can compare to Sandy Lane's luxurious facilities and ultrapampering service—or to its astronomical prices. **Pros:** top of the line, cream of the crop—no debate about that; excellent dining; lovely beach; amazing spa; great golf courses. **Cons:** over the top for most mortals; very formal—you'll feel like dressing up just to walk through the lobby. **TripAdvisor:** "wonderful stay in paradise," "perfect visit," "relaxed luxury." [$] *Rooms from: $2,355* ⊠ *Hwy. 1, Paynes Bay, St. James* ☎ *246/444–2000* ⊕ *www. sandylane.com* ⤴ *96 rooms, 16 suites, 1 5-bedroom villa* ⧖⧘*Breakfast.*

$$
HOTEL

St. James Apartment Hotel. These apartments are perfectly situated right on Paynes Bay Beach, one of the best on the west coast. **Pros:** save money by cooking some meals yourself; great quarters for independent travelers and long stays; great beach and sundeck; convenient to shopping and restaurants. **Cons:** no pool; no organized activities. [$] *Rooms from: $280* ⊠ *Hwy. 1, Paynes Bay, St. James* ☎ *246/432–0489* ⊕ *www. the-stjames.com* ⤴ *11 apartments* ⧖⧘*No meals.*

$$$$
RESORT
☕
★

Tamarind. This sleek Mediterranean-style resort, completely renovated and modernized in 2010, sprawls along 750 feet of prime west-coast beachfront and is large enough to cater to sophisticated couples and active families while, at the same time, offering cozy privacy to honeymooners. **Pros:** very big resort, yet layout still affords privacy;

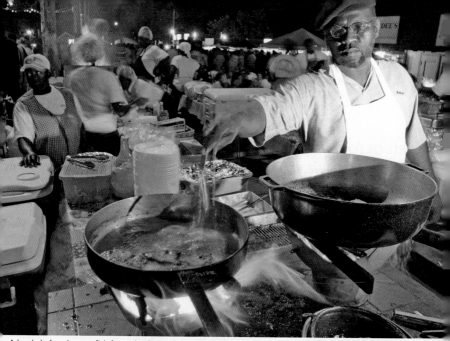

A local chef cooks up a fish fry at the Oistins fish market in Bridgetown.

central location right on Paynes Bay beach; lots of free water sports. **Cons:** even after the renovations, some rooms need a little TLC; uninspired buffet breakfast. **TripAdvisor:** "totally relaxing," "excellent location," "nice people." ⑤ *Rooms from: $535* ✉ *Hwy. 1, Paynes Bay, St. James* ☎ *246/432–1332* ⊕ *www.tamarindbarbados.com* ⇲ *57 rooms, 47 suites* ❍⃝ *Multiple meal plans.*

$$$$ 🏨 **Treasure Beach.** Quiet, upscale, and intimate, this boutique all-suites
HOTEL   hotel has a residential quality. **Pros:** cozy retreat; congenial crowd; swimming with the turtles just offshore. **Cons:** narrow beach; only bedrooms are air-conditioned; offshore turtles attract boatloads of tourists. **TripAdvisor:** "delightful staff," "absolutely lovely," "nice people." ⑤ *Rooms from: $575* ✉ *Hwy. 1, Paynes Bay, St. James* ☎ *246/432–1346, 800/355–6161 in the U.S.* ⊕ *www.treasurebeachhotel.com* ⇲ *35 suites* ◔ *Closed Sept.–mid-Oct.* ❍⃝ *Multiple meal plans.*

NIGHTLIFE

When the sun goes down, the people come out to "lime" (which may be anything from a chat to a full-blown "jump-up" or street party). Performances by world-renowned stars and regional groups are major events, and tickets can be hard to come by—but give it a try. Most resorts have nightly entertainment in season, and nightclubs often have live bands for listening and dancing. The busiest bars and dance clubs rage until 3 am. On Saturday nights some clubs—especially those with live music—charge a cover of about $15.

Barbados supports the rum industry with more than 1,600 "rum shops," simple bars where (mostly) men congregate to discuss the world or life in general, drink rum, and eat a cutter (sandwich). In more sophisticated establishments, you can find upscale rum cocktails made with the island's renowned Mount Gay and Cockspur brands—and no shortage of Barbados's own Banks Beer.

BRIDGETOWN

Boatyard. There's never a dull moment at The Boatyard, a popular pub with both a DJ and live bands. From happy hour until the wee hours, the patrons are mostly local and visiting professionals. ⊠ *Bay St., south of town, Carlisle Bay, Bridgetown, St. Michael* ☎ *246/436–2622* ⊕ *www.theboatyard.com.*

Harbour Lights. This open-air, beachfront club claims to be the "home of the party animal" and has dancing under the stars most nights to live reggae and soca music. ⊠ *Upper Bay St., Bridgetown, St. Michael* ☎ *246/436–7225* ⊕ *www.harbourlightsbarbados.com.*

Waterfront Café. There's live jazz in the evening at Waterfront Cafe, which also has a small dance floor. The location alongside the wharf is also a draw. ⊠ *The Careenage, Bridgetown, St. Michael* ☎ *246/427–0093.*

SOUTH COAST

Bubba's Sports Bar. On the south coast, Bubba's offers merrymakers and sports lovers live sports on three 10-foot video screens and a dozen TVs, along with a Bajan à la carte menu and drinks at the bar. ⊠ *Main Rd., Rockley, Christ Church* ☎ *246/435–6217* ⊕ *bubbassportsbar.net.*

McBride's Pub. McBride's is, as you night have guessed, a popular Irish pub with Irish beer on tap, pub grub from the kitchen, and Irish music, karaoke, reggae, rock, Latin, or techno music every night. Happy hour(s) run from 11 pm to 1 am every night. ⊠ *St. Lawrence Gap, Dover, Christ Church* ☎ *246/436–6352.*

Ⓒ **Oistins Fish Fry.** Oistins is the place to be on Friday evenings, when the
Fodor'sChoice   south-coast fishing village becomes a convivial outdoor street party.
★   Barbecued chicken and a variety of fish are served right from the grill, along with all the traditional sides (rice and peas, yams, fries, salad, etc.) and consumed at roadside picnic tables; servings are huge, and prices are inexpensive—about $10 per plate. Drinks, music, and dancing add to the fun. ⊠ *Oistins, Christ Church.*

Ⓒ **Plantation Restaurant and Garden Theater.** On Wednesday and Friday eve-
Fodor'sChoice   nings the Tropical Spectacular calypso cabaret presents *Bajan Roots*
★   *and Rhythms*, a delightful extravaganza representing West Indian culture that the whole family will enjoy. The show includes steel-band music, fire eating, limbo, and dancing to the reggae, soca, and pop music sounds of popular Barbadian singer John King and the Plantation House Band. The fun begins at 8 pm. A Barbadian buffet dinner, unlimited drinks, transportation, and the show cost $85; for the show and drinks only, it's $50. ⊠ *Plantation Complex, St. Lawrence Main Rd., Dover, Christ Church* ☎ *246/621–5048* ⊕ *www.plantationtheatre.com.*

★ **Reggae Lounge.** This is a popular nightspot in the Gap, where live bands or DJs play the latest Jamaican hits and old reggae favorites. ✉ *St. Lawrence Gap, Dover, Christ Church* ☎ *246/435–6462.*

WEST COAST

★ **Lexy Piano Bar.** Lexy's is a cool, trendy club named for owner Alex Santoriello, a transplanted Broadway singer and actor. A changing roster of singer-pianists play sing-along standards, classic rock, R&B, and Broadway tunes—and you can also enjoy a treat from the sushi bar. Most any night, you'll find Santoriello there. ✉ *2nd St., Holetown, St. James* ☎ *246/432–5399* ⊕ *www.lexypianobar.com* ☽ *Closed Mon.*

SHOPPING

WHAT TO BUY

One of the most long-lasting souvenirs to bring home from Barbados is a piece of authentic Caribbean art. The colorful flowers, quaint villages, mesmerizing seascapes, and fascinating cultural experiences and activities that are endemic to the region and familiar to visitors have been translated by local artists onto canvas and into photographs, sculpture, and other media. Gift shops and even some restaurants display local artwork for sale, but the broadest array of artwork will be found in a gallery. Typical crafts include pottery, shell and glass art, wood carvings, handmade dolls, watercolors, and other artwork (both originals and prints).

Although many of the private homes, great houses, and museums in Barbados are filled with priceless antiques, you'll find few for sale—mainly British antiques and some local pieces, particularly mahogany furniture. Look especially for planters' chairs and the classic Barbadian rocking chair, as well as old prints and paintings.

DUTY-FREE SHOPPING

Duty-free luxury goods—china, crystal, cameras, porcelain, leather items, electronics, jewelry, perfume, and clothing—are found in Bridgetown's Broad Street department stores and their branches, at the high-end Limegrove Lifestyle Centre in Holetown, at the Bridgetown Cruise Terminal shops (for passengers only), and in the departure-lounge shops at Grantley Adams International Airport. Prices are often 30% to 40% less than at home. To buy goods at duty-free prices, you must produce your passport, immigration form, or driver's license, along with departure information (such as flight number and date) at the time of purchase—or you can have your purchases delivered free to the airport or harbor for pickup. Duty-free alcohol, tobacco products, and some electronic equipment *must* be delivered to you at the airport or harbor.

5

Where de Rum Come From

For more than 300 years (from 1655 through "Black Tot Day, July 31, 1970"), a daily "tot" of rum (2 ounces) was duly administered to each sailor in the British Navy—as a health ration. At times, rum has also played a less appetizing—but equally important—role. When Admiral Horatio Nelson died in 1805 aboard ship during the Battle of Trafalgar, his body was preserved in a cask of his favorite rum until he could be properly buried.

Hardly a Caribbean island doesn't have its own locally made rum, but Barbados is truly "where de rum come from." Mount Gay, the world's oldest rum distillery, has continuously operated on Barbados since 1703, according to the original deed for the Mount Gay Estate, which itemized two stone windmills, a boiling house, seven copper pots, and a still house. The presence of rum-making equipment

on the plantation at the time suggests that the previous owners were actually producing rum in Barbados long before 1703.

Today, much of the island's interior is still planted with sugarcane—where the rum really does come from—and several great houses, on historic sugar plantations, have been restored with period furniture and are open to the public.

To really fathom rum, however, you need to delve a little deeper than the bottom of a glass of rum punch. Mount Gay offers an interesting 45-minute tour of its main plant, followed by a tasting. You can learn about the rum-making process from cane to cocktail, hear more rum-inspired anecdotes, and have an opportunity to buy bottles of its famous Eclipse or Extra Old rum at duty-free prices. Bottoms up!

BRIDGETOWN

Bridgetown's **Broad Street** is the primary downtown shopping area. **DaCosta Manning Mall,** in the historic Colonnade Building on Broad Street, has more than 25 shops that sell everything from Piaget watches to postcards; across the street, **Mall 34** has 22 shops where you can buy duty-free goods, souvenirs, and snacks. At the **cruise-ship terminal** shopping arcade, passengers can buy both duty-free goods and Barbadian-made crafts at more than 30 boutiques and a dozen vendor carts and stalls.

★ **Pelican Craft Centre.** Pelican is made up of a cluster of workshops halfway between the cruise-ship terminal and downtown Bridgetown, where craftspeople create and sell locally made leather goods, batik, basketry, carvings, jewelry, glass art, paintings, pottery, and other items. It's open weekdays 9 to 5 and Saturday 9 to 2; things here are most active when cruise ships are in port. ⊠ *Princess Alice Hwy., Bridgetown, St. Michael* ☎ *246/427–5350.*

SOUTH COAST

The St. Lawrence Gap, like Holetown, has a **Chattel House Village,** where you can buy locally made crafts and other souvenirs. In Rockley, Christ Church, **Quayside Shopping Center** houses a small group of boutiques, restaurants, and services.

Best of Barbados. Best of Barbados was the brainchild of architect Jimmy Walker as a place to showcase the works of his artist wife. Now with five locations, the shops offer products that range from Jill Walker's frameable prints, housewares, and textiles to arts and crafts in both "native" style and modern designs. Everything is made or designed on Barbados. ⊠ *Quayside Centre, Main Rd., Rockley, Christ Church* ☎ *246/435–6820* ⊕ *www.best-of-barbados.com.*

WEST COAST

Holetown has the upscale **Limegrove Lifestyle Centre,** a stylish shopping mall with high-end designer boutiques, as well as **Chattel House Village,** a cluster of shops selling local products, fashions, beachwear, and souvenirs. Also in Holetown, **Sunset Crest Mall** has two branches of the Cave Shepherd department store, a bank, a pharmacy, and several small shops; at **West Coast Mall** you can buy duty-free goods, island wear, and groceries.

Fodor's Choice **Earthworks Pottery.** Earthworks is a family-owned and -operated pottery ★ workshop, where you can purchase anything from a dish or knickknack to a complete dinner service or one-of-a-kind art piece. You can find the characteristically blue or green pottery—and, more recently, peach and brown hues—decorating hotel rooms and for sale in gift shops throughout the island; but the biggest selection (including some "seconds") is at Earthworks, where you also can watch the potters at work. ⊠ *Edgehill Heights, St. Thomas* ☎ *246/425–0223* ⊕ *www.earthworkspottery.com* ⊘ *Closed Sun.*

Gallery of Caribbean Art. This gallery is committed to promoting Caribbean art from Cuba to Curaçao, including a number of pieces by Barbadian artists. A branch gallery is at the Hilton Barbados hotel, Needham's Point. ⊠ *Northern Business Centre, Queen St., Speightstown, St. Peter* ☎ *246/419–0858* ⊕ *www.artgallerycaribbean.com* ⊘ *Closed Sun.*

On the Wall Art Gallery. This gallery, adjacent to Earthworks Pottery, has an array of original paintings by Barbadian artists, along with arts and crafts products. An additional gallery is in dedicated space at Champers restaurant on the south coast. ⊠ *Earthworks Pottery, Edgehill Heights, St. Thomas* ☎ *246/425–0223* ⊕ *www.onthewallartgallery. com* ⊘ *Closed Sun.*

SPORTS AND ACTIVITIES

Cricket, football (soccer), polo, and rugby are extremely popular sports in Barbados among participants and spectators alike, with local, regional, and international matches held throughout the year. Contact the Barbados Tourism Authority or check local newspapers for information about schedules and tickets.

DIVING AND SNORKELING

More than two dozen dive sites lie along the west coast between Maycocks Bay and Bridgetown and off the south coast as far as the St. Lawrence Gap. Certified divers can explore flat coral reefs and see dramatic sea fans, huge barrel sponges, and more than 50 varieties of fish. Nine sunken wrecks are dived regularly, and at least 10 more are accessible to experts. Underwater visibility is generally 80 to 90 feet. The calm waters along the west coast are also ideal for snorkeling. The marine reserve, a stretch of protected reef between Sandy Lane and the Colony Club, contains beautiful coral formations accessible from the beach.

On the west coast, **Bell Buoy** is a large, dome-shape reef where huge brown coral tree forests and schools of fish delight all categories of divers at depths ranging from 20 to 60 feet. At **Dottins Reef,** off Holetown, you can see schooling fish, barracudas, and turtles at depths of 40 to 60 feet. **Maycocks Bay,** on the northwest coast, is a particularly enticing site; large coral reefs are separated by corridors of white sand, and visibility is often 100 feet or more. The 165-foot freighter *Pamir* lies in 60 feet of water off Six Men's Bay; it's still intact, and you can peer through its portholes and view dozens of varieties of tropical fish. **Silver Bank** is a healthy coral reef with beautiful fish and sea fans; you may get a glimpse of the *Atlantis* submarine at 60 to 80 feet. Not to be missed is the *Stavronikita*, a scuttled Greek freighter at about 135 feet; hundreds of butterfly fish hang out around its mast, and the thin rays of sunlight filtering down through the water make fully exploring the huge ship a wonderfully eerie experience.

Farther south, **Carlisle Bay** is a natural harbor and marine park just below Bridgetown. Here you can retrieve empty bottles thrown overboard by generations of sailors and see cannons and cannonballs, anchors, and six unique shipwrecks (*Berwyn, Fox, CTrek, Eilon,* the barge *Cornwallis,* and *Bajan Queen*) lying in 25 to 60 feet of water, all close enough to visit on the same dive. The *Bajan Queen,* a cruise vessel that sank in 2002, is the island's newest wreck.

Dive shops provide a two-hour beginner's "resort" course ($85 to $100) followed by a shallow dive, or a weeklong certification course (about $425). Once you're certified, a one-tank dive runs about $60 to $75; a two-tank dive is $90 to $100. All equipment is supplied, and you can purchase multidive packages. Gear for snorkeling is available (free or for a small rental fee) from most hotels. Snorkelers can usually accompany dive trips for $25 for a one- or two-hour trip. Most dive shops have relationships with several hotels and offer special dive packages, with transportation, to hotel guests.

Dive Shop, Ltd. Near the Carlisle Bay marine park just south of Bridgetown, the Dive Shop, Ltd—the island's oldest dive shop—offers daily reef and wreck dives, plus beginner classes, certification courses, and underwater photography instruction. Underwater cameras are available for rent. Free transfers are provided between your hotel and the dive shop. ✉ *Amey's Alley, Upper Bay St., Bridgetown, St. Michael* ☎ *246/426–9947, 888/898–3483 in the U.S.* ⊕ *www.divebds.com.*

Hightide Watersports. On the west coast, Hightide Watersports offers three dive trips—one- and two-tank dives and night reef–wreck–drift dives—daily for up to eight divers, along with PADI instruction, equipment rental, and free transportation. ✉ *Coral Reef Club, Hwy. 1, Holetown, St. James* ☎ *246/432–0931, 800/970–0016, 800/513–5763* ⊕ *www.divehightide.com.*

Reefers & Wreckers Dive Shop. In Speightstown, the most northerly dive shop allows easy access to the unspoiled reefs in the north but also offers regular trips to the dive sites and wrecks along the west coast and in Carlisle Bay. ✉ *Queen St., Speightstown, St. Peter* ☎ *246/422–5420* ⊕ *www.scubadiving.bb.*

FISHING

Fishing is a year-round activity in Barbados, but its prime time is January through April, when game fish are in season. Whether you're a serious deep-sea fisher looking for marlin, sailfish, tuna, and other billfish or you prefer angling in calm coastal waters where wahoo, barracuda, and other small fish reside, you can choose from a variety of half- or full-day charter trips departing from the Careenage in Bridgetown. Expect to pay $175 per person for a shared half-day charter; for a private charter, expect to pay $500 to $600 per boat for a four-hour half-day or $950 to $1,000 for an eight-hour full-day charter. Spectators who don't fish are welcome for $50 per person.

Billfisher II. *Billfisher II*, a 40-foot Pacemaker, accommodates up to six passengers with three fishing chairs and five rods. Captain Winston ("The Colonel") White has been fishing these waters since 1975. His full-day charters include a full lunch and guaranteed fish (or a 25% refund); all trips include drinks and transportation to and from the boat. ✉ *Bridge House Wharf, The Careenage, Bridgetown, St. Michael* ☎ *246/431–0741.*

Blue Jay & Blue Marlin. *Blue Jay* is a spacious, fully equipped, 45-foot Sport Fisherman; *Blue Marlin* is a 36-foot Sport Fisherman. Each has a crew that knows the water's denizens—blue marlin, sailfish, barracuda, and kingfish. Most fishing is done by trolling. Drinks, snacks, bait, tackle, and transfers are provided. ✉ *Fishing Charters Barbados, Inc., 50 Ridge Ave., Durants, Christ Church* ☎ *246/234–1688* ⊕ *www.bluemarlinbarbados.com.*

Cannon II. *Cannon II*, a 42-foot Hatteras Sport Fisherman, has three chairs and five rods and accommodates six passengers; drinks and snacks are complimentary, and lunch is served on full-day charters. ✉ *Cannon Charters, Prior Park, St. James* ☎ *246/424–6107.*

GOLF

Barbadians love golf, and golfers love Barbados. In addition to the courses listed *below*, Almond Beach Village has a 9-hole, par-3 executive course open only to guests.

Barbados Golf Club. Barbados Golf Club, the first public golf course on Barbados, is an 18-hole championship course (6,805 yards, par 72) redesigned in 2000 by golf course architect Ron Kirby. Greens fees with a cart are $125 for 18 holes; $80 for 9 holes. Unlimited three-day and seven-day golf passes are available. Several hotels offer preferential tee-time reservations and reduced rates. Club and shoe rentals are available. ⊠ *Hwy. 7, Durants, Christ Church* ☎ *246/428–8463* ⊕ *www.barbadosgolfclub.com.*

Fodor'sChoice **Country Club at Sandy Lane.** At the prestigious Country Club at Sandy
★ Lane, golfers can play on the Old Nine or on either of two 18-hole championship courses: the Tom Fazio–designed Country Club Course or the spectacular Green Monkey Course, reserved for hotel guests and club members only. Golfers have complimentary use of the club's driving range. The Country Club Restaurant and Bar, which overlooks the 18th hole, is open to the public. Greens fees in high season are $155 for 9 holes ($135 for hotel guests) or $240 for 18 holes ($205 for hotel guests). Golf carts, caddies, or trolleys are available for hire, as are clubs and shoes. Carts are equipped with GPS, which alerts you to upcoming traps and hazards, provides tips on how to play the hole, and allows you to order refreshments! ⊠ *Sandy Lane, Hwy. 1, Paynes Bay, St. James* ☎ *246/444–2500* ⊕ *www.sandylane.com/golf.*

Rockley Golf and Country Club. Rockley Golf and Country Club, on the south coast, has a challenging 9-hole course (2,800 yards, par 35) that can be played as 18 from varying tee positions. Club and cart rentals are available. Greens fees are $61.50 for 18 holes and $51 for 9 holes. Weekly rates are available. ⊠ *Golf Club Rd., Rockley, Christ Church* ☎ *246/435–7873* ⊕ *www.rockleygolfclub.com.*

★ **Royal Westmoreland Golf Club.** The Royal Westmoreland Golf Club has a well-regarded Robert Trent Jones Jr.–designed, 18-hole championship course (6,870 yards, par 72) that meanders through the 500-acre property. This challenging course is primarily for villa renters, with a few midmorning tee times for visitors subject to availability. Greens fees for villa renters or guests at hotels with golf privileges at the club are $300 for tee times before 10 am or $250 after 10 am for 18 holes and $125 after 2 pm for 9 holes. Greens fees for visitors (10 am to 11 am tee times only) are $375. Greens fees include use of an electric cart (required); club rental is available. ⊠ *Royal Westmoreland Resort, Westmoreland, St. James* ☎ *246/419–0394* ⊕ *www.royal-westmoreland.com.*

GUIDED TOURS

Taxi drivers will give you a personalized tour of Barbados for about $35 to $40 per hour for up to three people. Or you can choose an overland mountain-bike journey, a 4x4 safari expedition, or a full-day bus excursion. The prices vary according to the mode of travel and the number and kind of attractions included. Ask guest services at your hotel to help you make arrangements.

Highland Adventure Centre. Highland Adventure Centre offers mountain-bike tours for $60 per person, including transportation, guides, and refreshments. The trip is an exhilarating 7½-mile (12-km) ride (15%

Continued on page 196

SPORT FISHING

Marlise Kast

With its abundance of marlin, sailfish, tuna, and Mahi Mahi, the Caribbean has enough catch to beckon any angler. Crystal-blue waters, white-sand beaches, and tropical weather make this the perfect place to set sail. From Barbados and the Bahamas to Puerto Rico and the Virgin Islands, there is plenty of opportunity to cast your line.

Fishing on sailing boat, Grenadines Islands.

FISH FINDER

Turks and
Caicos Islands

Little
Cayman
Cayman
Brac
Grand
Cayman

Jamaica

Haiti Hispaniol

G R E A T E R

Tuna
(up to 15 ft.)

20 FEET

Black Marlin
(up to 15 ft.)

15 FEET

Swordfish
(up to 15 ft.)

10 FEET

Sailfish
(up to 10 ft.)

Wahoo
(up to 8 ft.)

5 FEET

Barracuda
(up to 5.9 ft.)

Dorado
(up to 5 ft.)

Billfish*
Tuna
Dorado
Wahoo
Barracuda
Bonito

*Billfish include marlin,
sailfish, and swordfish

LEEWARD ISLANDS

Dominican
Republic

St. John   Tortola
St.   Virgin
Thomas   Gorda
                          Anguilla
            St. Maarten/   St. Barthélemy
            St. Martin   Barbuda
                  Saba
Puerto   St.   St. Eustatius
Rico   Croix   St. Kitts   Antigua
ANTILLES   Nevis
                 Montserrat
                 Guadeloupe   Marie
                              Galante
                 Dominica

                 Martinique
                                    WINDWARD ISLANDS
0   200 mi
                 St. Lucia
0   200 km   Barbados
                 St. Vincent
LESSER   ANTILLES   Bequia
                 The Grenadines
Aruba   Carriacou

Curaçao   Bonaire
                 Grenada
        Islas Los
        Roques   Tobago

                        Trinidad

So many islands, so little time. Among anglers' favorites are the **Virgin Islands**, known for bluefish, wahoo, swordfish, and shark. These deep-sea fishing waters host annual tournaments where eight world records for blue marlin have been set. Equally attractive to deep-sea fishermen are the **Cayman Islands**, home to tuna, wahoo, and marlin. Bottom dwellers, such as grouper and snapper are always an easy hook in this area.

For great bonefishing, head to nearby Little Cayman at Bloody Bay. Between January and June, the **Dominican Republic** is popular with sport fishermen in search of sailfish, bonito, marlin, and wahoo. Although the bonefish-laden **Bahamas** cater to fly-fishermen, **Barbados** is a paradise for both deep-sea anglers reeling in billfish, and for coastal catchers forging for wahoo, barracuda, and smaller fish. Luring fishermen from afar, **Puerto Rico's** coast has reeled in 30+ world records, making it the fishing capital of the Caribbean.

DEEP SEA VS. SHALLOW WATERS

Swordfish

Too deep or not too deep? That is the question!

From fly-fishing at the river mouth to sport fishing in the open waters, the Caribbean can satisfy any angler's longing to reel one in. It's a question of what type of experience you're looking for. How active vs. passive of an experience do you want?

If you're feeling strong head for the deep. Any quest for catch below 30 meters (98 ft) is considered deep-sea fishing. The massive sport fish that frequent the deeper waters are magnificent specimens, and it's a thrilling experience to wrestle one from the deep. Albacore, marlin, barracuda, and tuna are the common catch, and it requires a tremendous amount of patience, strength, and effort to properly hook and land these mighty creatures.

For a more tranquil way to enjoy the Caribbean waters, try shallow-water fishing over reefs and shipwrecks. Tarpon, permit, pompano, wahoo, and small barracuda are the primary catch. Casting your line inshore is both convenient and affordable because chartering a large boat is unnecessary.

TAKE THE BAIT

In the Caribbean, it is best to use natural bait such as ballyhoo, tuna strips, or flying fish. Because a variety of big game fish feed on ballyhoo, they are considered ideal enticers when trolling the open waters. Live bait will also help lure larger fish, which are attracted to the blood and movement on the line. Depending on the type of catch you are after, almost any baitfish can be used including squid, shrimp, conch, and sardines. Aiding in the hunt are digital fishfinders, commonly utilized by sport fishermen to detect schools of fish. Bait is the same for both inshore and deepsea fishing, and rarely are artificial lures used in the Caribbean.

A golden catch from shallow waters.

PRACTICAL INFORMATION

TYPE OF FISHING	COSTS	CHARACTERISTICS
OFFSHORE TRIPS	Start at $325 for a half-day, $625 for a full day.	Many packages include roundtrip transportation to and from your hotel, a boat crew, food, beverages, bait, gear, taxes and licenses. Tips are not included.
REEF FISHING	$300 to $600 per day; or cut the fee in half by opting for a 4-hour trip. A bonefishing guide is $250 for a half-day.	An experienced captain to steady the boat directly over the reefs is recommended. Most reefs are home to large schools of fish, but some areas are barren. Use a braided line, which is more abrasion resistant than monofiliament lines, to keep your line from snapping between the crevices.
DEEP-SEA FISHING	From $500 for a half-day to $1,500 for a full day.	The open waters are where you'll find the big catch. Most operators offer half-day and full-day charters with an experienced crew that knows where to find that trophy fish. Packages generally include your captain, crew, fishing tackle, bait, license and fees.

Private boat owners who plan on fishing for tuna, shark, swordfish and billfish in the Atlantic Ocean, (including the Gulf of Mexico and Caribbean Sea), must obtain an **Atlantic Highly Migratory Species** (HMS) permit for $16.00. Valid from the date of issue through December of that same year, permits can be ordered online through the **National Marine Fisheries Service** (⊕ www.hmspermits.noaa.gov).

MAN OVERBOARD: RULES/REGULATIONS

Although guidelines vary from island to island, it is safe to assume that a permit is required for fishing in the Caribbean. These licenses are usually included in sport fishing tours and packages, but it is best to inquire prior to booking. Because hundreds of fish can be hooked in a single day in the Caribbean waters, the catch-and-release method is vital for conservation. Throughout the entire region, spear fishing is illegal as is fishing within the boundaries of any marine park. It's advisable to utilize the services of licensed professionals.

Many of the Caribbean territories do not require a saltwater fishing license. One definite exception is the British Virgin Islands, where private charters must obtain permits for $45, valid up to one month. Fishing permits are available from the Department of Conservation and Fisheries ☎ 284/494–5681.

STAYING AFLOAT: SAFETY

Before setting sail, be sure to inform someone of your intended whereabouts as well as the time of your scheduled return. If you're fishing solo, double check all safety equipment including your means of communication, life jackets, and emergency supplies. Above all, inquire about local weather conditions and policies before booking your charter.

Deep-sea fishing boats.

uphill) through the heart of northern Barbados, ending up at Barclays Park on the east coast. ⊠ *Cane Field, St. Thomas* ☎ *246/438–8069.*

Island Safari. Island Safari will take you to all the popular spots via a 4x4 Land Rover—including some gullies, forests, and remote areas that are inaccessible by conventional cars and buses. The cost for half-day or full-day tours ranges from $50 to $92.50 per person, including snacks or lunch. ⊠ *CWTS Complex, Salters Rd., Lower Estate, St. George* ☎ *246/429–5337* ⊕ *www.islandsafari.bb.*

HIKING

Hilly but not mountainous, the northern interior and the east coast are ideal for hiking.

Arbib Heritage and Nature Trail. The Arbib Heritage and Nature Trail, maintained by the Barbados National Trust, is actually two trails— one offers a rigorous hike through gullies and plantations to old ruins and remote north-country areas; the other is a shorter, easier walk through Speightstown's side streets and past an ancient church and chattel houses. Three-hour guided hikes take place daily at 9:30 and 2:30 and cost $50 for one or two people; group rates are available. Book ahead, preferably four days in advance. Not recommended for children under 5. ⊠ *Speightstown, St. Peter* ☎ *246/426–2421* ⊕ *trust. funbarbados.com.*

Hike Barbados. A program of free walks sponsored by the Barbados National Trust, Hike Barbados treks take place year-round on Sunday from 6 am to about 9 am and from 3:30 pm to 6 pm; once a month a moonlight hike substitutes for the afternoon hike and begins at 5:30 pm (bring a flashlight). Experienced guides group you with others of similar levels of ability. Stop and Stare hikes go 5 to 6 miles (8 to 10 km); Here and There, 8 to 10 miles (13 to 16 km); and Grin and Bear, 12 to 14 miles (19 to 23 km). Wear loose clothes, sensible shoes, sunscreen, and a hat, and bring your camera and a bottle of water. Routes and locations change, but each hike is a loop, finishing in the same spot where it began. Check local newspapers, call the Trust, or check online for the full hike schedule or the scheduled meeting place on a particular Sunday. ⊠ *Wildey House, Wildey, St. Michael* ☎ *246/436–9033, 246/426–2421* ⊕ *www.trust.funbarbados.com.*

SEA EXCURSIONS

Mini-submarine voyages are enormously popular with families and those who enjoy watching fish but don't wish to snorkel or dive. Party boats depart from Bridgetown's Deep Water Harbour for sightseeing and snorkeling or romantic sunset cruises. Prices are $75 to $90 per person for daytime cruises and $60 to $85 for three-hour sunset cruises, depending on the type of refreshments and entertainment included; transportation to and from the dock is provided. For an excursion that may be less splashy in terms of a party atmosphere—but is definitely splashier in terms of the actual experience—turtle tours allow participants to feed and swim with a resident group of hawksbill and leatherback sea turtles.

☾ **Atlantis Submarine.** The 48-passenger *Atlantis* Submarine turns the Caribbean into a giant aquarium. The 45-minute underwater voyage aboard the 50-foot submarine ($104 per person, including transportation) takes you to wrecks and reefs as deep as 150 feet. Children love the adventure, but they must be at least 3 feet tall to go on board. ✉ *Shallow Draught, Bridgetown, St. Michael* ☎ *246/436–8929* ⊕ *barbados. atlantissubmarines.com.*

Cool Runnings. On the catamaran *Cool Runnings*, owner Captain Povey skippers a five-hour lunch cruise with stops to swim with the fishes, snorkel with sea turtles, and explore a shallow shipwreck. A four-hour sunset cruise includes swimming, snorkeling, and exploring underwater as the sun sinks below the horizon. Delicious meals with wine, along with an open bar, are part of all cruises. ✉ *Carlisle House, Carlisle Wharf, Hincks St., Bridgetown, St. Michael* ☎ *246/436–0911* ⊕ *www. coolrunningsbarbados.com.*

Jolly Roger 1. The whole family will get a kick out of a "pirate" ship sailing adventure on *Jolly Roger 1.* The four-hour day and sunset cruises along the island's west coast include a barbecue lunch or dinner, free-flowing drinks, lively music, swimming with turtles, and "pirate" activities such as walking the plank and rope swinging. ✉ *Shallow Draught, Bridgetown, St. Michael* ☎ *246/436–2885, 246/826–7245* ⊕ *www. barbadosblackpearl-jollyroger1.com.*

☾ **MV Harbour Master.** Five-hour daytime cruises along the west coast on the 100-foot MV *Harbour Master* party boat (four decks of fun) stop in Holetown and land at beaches along the way; evening cruises are shorter but add a buffet dinner and entertainment. Day or night you can view the briny deep from the ship's onboard 34-seat semisubmersible. ✉ *Shallow Draught, Bridgetown, St. Michael* ☎ *246/430–0900* ⊕ *www.tallshipscruises.com.*

Tiami. The 53-foot catamaran *Tiami* offers a luncheon cruise to a secluded bay or a romantic sunset and moonlight cruise with special catering and live music. ✉ *Shallow Draught, Bridgetown, St. Michael* ☎ *246/430–0900* ⊕ *www.tallshipscruises.com.*

SURFING

The best surfing is at Bathsheba Soup Bowl on the east coast, but the water here, on the windward (Atlantic Ocean) side of the island, is safe only for the most experienced surfers. Surfers also congregate at Surfer's Point, at the southern tip of Barbados near Inch Marlow, where the Atlantic Ocean meets the Caribbean Sea.

Dread or Dead Surf Shop. Dread or Dead Surf Shop promises to get beginners from "zero to standing up and surfing" in a single afternoon. The four-hour course—"or until you stand up or give up"—costs $75 per person and includes a board, wax, a rash guard (if necessary), a ride to and from the surf break, and an instructor; additional lessons cost $37.50. Intermediate or experienced surfers can get all the equipment and the instructor for a full day of surfing for $150. ⊠ *Hastings Main Rd., Hastings, Christ Church* ☎ *246/228–4785* ⊕ *www.dreadordead. com.*

Zed's Surfing Adventures. Zed's Surfing Adventures rents surfboards, offers lessons, and offers surf tours—which include equipment, a guide, and transportation to surf breaks appropriate for your experience. ⊠ *Surfer's Point, Inch Marlow, Christ Church* ☎ *246/428–7873* ⊕ *www.barbadossurfholidays.com.*

WINDSURFING AND KITEBOARDING

Barbados is on the World Cup Windsurfing Circuit and is one of the prime locations in the world for windsurfing—and, increasingly, for kiteboarding. Winds are strongest November through April at the island's southern tip, at Silver Sands–Silver Rock Beach, which is where the Barbados Windsurfing Championships are held in mid-January. Use of windsurfing boards and equipment, as well as instruction, is often among the amenities included at larger hotels and sometimes can be rented by nonguests. Kiteboarding is a more difficult sport that requires several hours of instruction to reach proficiency; Silver Sands is about the only location where you'll find kiteboarding equipment and instruction.

deAction Surf Shop. At his shop, directly on Silver Sands–Silver Rock Beach, Brian "Irie Man" Talma stocks a range of rental surfing equipment and offers beginner windsurfing, kiteboarding, and surfing lessons taught by a professional team of instructors. The conditions here are ideal, with waves off the outer reef and flat water in the inner lagoon. Kiteboarding, which isn't easy, generally involves six hours of instruction broken up into two or three sessions: from flying a small kite to getting the body dragged with a big kite to finally getting up on the board. All equipment is provided. ⊠ *Silver Sands–Silver Rock Beach, Silver Sands, Christ Church* ☎ *246/428–2027* ⊕ *www.briantalma.com.*

Bonaire

WORD OF MOUTH

"We just got back from a wonderful week in Bonaire—it was the first, but definitely not the last time there....There is little to do on the island if you don't dive or snorkel, so keep that in mind."

—xyz99

WELCOME TO BONAIRE

At the market in Kralendijk, hagglers vie for produce brought in by boat from lusher islands. But nature holds sway over human pursuits on this scrubby, cactus-covered landfall. Divers come to explore some of the best sites this side of Australia's Great Barrier Reef. Above the water are more than 15,000 flamingos—the biggest flock in the Western Hemisphere.

Boca Kokalishi

Washington

Mt. Brandaris

Playa Funchi

Main Park Enterance

Boca Slagbaai

Washington/ Slagbaai National Park

Gotomeer

Northern Scenic Route

Landhuis Karpata

Karpata

Rappel

TOP REASONS TO VISIT BONAIRE

1 The Diving: As locals say, you come here to dive, eat, dive, sleep, and dive.

2 The Snorkeling: You don't have to be a certified diver to appreciate Bonaire's reefs; snorkelers can see a lot of the beauty just below the surface of the water.

3 The Quiet: Visitors came to enjoy the tranquillity of the island long before they started exploring offshore.

4 The Dining: Dining is surprisingly good and varied for such a small island.

5 The Smiles: Bonaireans are genuinely friendly without a hint of the phoniness sometimes found on other tourist-dependent islands.

DIVER'S PARADISE

With just over 14,000 people, this little island (112 square miles [290 square km]) has a real, small-town atmosphere. Kralendijk, the capital, has just 3,000 inhabitants. The entire coastline—from the high-water tidemark to a depth of 200 feet—is protected as part of the Bonaire Marine Park, making it one of the best diving destinations in the Western Hemisphere.

Caribbean Sea

◆ Onima

○ Fontein

◆ Rincon

NORTH BONAIRE

1,000 Steps

Barcadera Cave

14

Small Wall 13

12 11

16

Bari Reef

15 10

Something Special

9

Klein Bonaire

13

14 ★ Kralendijk

Forest

Calabas Reef 2

1 1 - 9

Windsock Steep

10 3

5 4

Windsock Beach

6 7

Angel City

Alice in Wonderland

Flamingo Airport

Wanapa ○

Trans-World Radio Tower

Salt Flats

Slave Huts ◆

Flamingo Sanctuary

Pink Beach

Pekel Meer

Spelonk ○

Lagoen

Seroe Largu ◆

Antriol ○

Boven Bolivia

Punto Blanco

SOUTH BONAIRE

○ Nikiboko

J.A. Abraham Blvd.

Rooi Lamoenchi Kunuku

Mangrove Forest

Lac Bay Cai

Lac Bay Beach

11

12 Sorobon

8

Sorobon Beach

Willemstoren Lighthouse ◆

Lacre Pt.

Krava Gubernador N.

Depot

Southern Scenic Highway

KEY

⚓	Beaches
🚩	Dive Sites
1	Restaurants
1	Hotels

0 _____ 4 mi
0 _____ 4 km

BONAIRE BEACHES

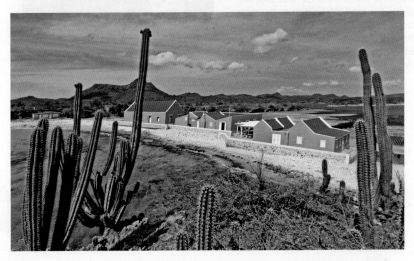

Although most of Bonaire's charms are underwater, there are a few excellent beaches. Even those beaches that are unsuitable for sunbathing can be worth a visit if only to view the intense turquoise waters that surround this little desert island.

(Above) Boca Slagbaai beach
(Bottom right) The coast of Klein Bonaire (Top right) Grab a chair at Sorobon Beach

Don't expect long stretches of glorious powdery sand. Bonaire's beaches are small, and though the water is blue (several shades of it, in fact), the sand isn't always white. Bonaire's National Parks Foundation requires all nondivers to pay a $10 annual Nature Fee to enter the water anywhere around the island (divers pay $25). The fee can be paid at most dive shops, and the receipt will also allow access to Washington–Slagbaai National Park.

SALT AND PEPPER

Sorobon Beach offers white powder. Many beaches have white sand but are also peppered with broken coral and rocks, which makes strolling difficult. At the rugged Washington–Slagbaai National Park you'll find the black sand of Boca Cocolishi, a testament to the island's past volcanic activity. Pink Beach near Kralendijk is popular with families but offers no facilities and no shade.

Boca Slagbaai. Inside Washington–Slagbaai Park is this beach of coral fossils and rocks with interesting offshore coral gardens that are good for snorkeling. Bring scuba boots or canvas sandals to walk into the water, because the beach is rough on bare feet. The gentle surf makes it an ideal place for swimming and picnicking. ⊠ *Off main park road, in Washington–Slagbaai National Park.*

Klein Bonaire. Just a water-taxi hop across from Kralendijk, this little island offers picture-perfect white-sand beaches. The area is protected, so absolutely no development has been allowed. Make sure to pack everything before heading to the island, including water and an umbrella to hide under, because there are no refreshment stands or changing facilities, and there's almost no shade to be found. Boats leave from the Town Pier, across from the City Café, and the round-trip water-taxi ride costs roughly $20 per person. .

Lac Bay Beach. Known for its festive music on Sunday nights, this open bay area with pink-tinted sand is equally dazzling by day. It's a bumpy drive (10 to 15 minutes on a dirt road) to get here, but you'll be glad when you arrive. It's a good spot for diving, snorkeling, and kayaking (as long as you bring your own), and there are public restrooms

and a restaurant for your convenience. ⊠ *Off Kaminda Sorobon, Lac Cai.*

Playa Funchi. This Washington–Slagbaai National Park beach is notable for the lagoon on one side, where flamingos nest, and the superb snorkeling on the other, where iridescent green parrot fish swim right up to shore. ⊠ *Off main park road, in Washington–Slagbaai National Park.*

Sorobon Beach. This is *the* windsurfing beach on Bonaire and one of the most beautiful beaches on the island, with a wide swath of soft white sand sloping gently into the intense blue waters of the sheltered cove. You can find a restaurant-bar next to the resort and windsurfing outfitters on the beach. The public beach area has restrooms and huts for shade. Take E.E.G. Boulevard south from Kralendijk to Kaya I.R. Randolf Statuuis Van Eps, and then follow this route straight on to Sorobon Beach. ⊠ *Kaya I.R. Randolf Statuuis Van Eps, Sorobon Beach.*

Windsock Beach (*aka Mangrove Beach*). Near the airport (just off E.E.G. Boulevard), this pretty little spot looks out toward the north side of the island and has about 200 yards of white sand along a rocky shoreline. It's a popular dive site, and swimming conditions are good. ⊠ *Off E.E.G. Blvd., near Flamingo Airport.*

6

By Vernon O'Reilly Ramesar

Bonaire is widely regarded as one of the best destinations in the Caribbean for shore diving, and with good reason. The dry climate and coral composition of the island mean that there's little soil runoff, allowing near-perfect visibility in the coastal waters. The islanders have exploited this advantage, and you can find local businesses that cater to virtually every diving need.

Even though tourism is the backbone of the economy here, authorities try to ensure that the booming hotel industry does not damage the environment upon which it is based. Thankfully, the fact that most visitors to Bonaire come for the natural beauty has prevented the kind of tourism that has turned neighboring islands such as Aruba into commercialized tourist magnets.

Islanders are serious about conserving Bonaire's natural beauty. All the coastal waters of the island were turned into a national park in 1979, and in 1999 Bonaire purchased the 1,500-acre privately owned outlying island of Klein Bonaire to prevent unwanted development. Anyone diving around the island must purchase a one-year permit, and park rangers patrol the waters, handing out hefty fines to people who violate park rules. Spearfishing, removing coral, and even walking on coral are just some of the restricted activities. Rather than restricting legitimate divers, these rules have resulted in a pristine marine environment that makes for a supremely satisfying dive experience. Damage to the reefs caused by rare passing hurricanes is usually quickly repaired by the healthy ecosystem. Small wonder that even the license plates in Bonaire declare it a diver's paradise.

Bonaire also offers a variety of experiences above the surface to those willing to explore its 112 square miles (290 square km). The southern salt flats give an interesting glimpse into the island's economic history. Washington–Slagbaai National Park, in the north, has the island's highest peak (784 feet) and is a haven for some of the thousands of flamin-

LOGISTICS

Getting to Bonaire: Most flights from the United States connect in San Juan or Aruba. If you want to connect through Aruba, you'll more likely than not have to book your flight directly with an island-based airline. Bonaire's Flamingo Airport (BON) is tiny but welcoming (the KLM 747 almost dwarfs the airport when it lands).

Hassle Factor: Medium to high.

On the Ground: Rental cars and taxis are available, but try to arrange for pickup through your hotel. A taxi will run between $11 and $15 (for up to four people) to most hotels; $26 to the Sorobon Beach Resort. Fares are 25% extra from 7 pm to midnight and 50% extra from midnight to 6 am. If you anticipate having to change your flight details while on Bonaire, be mindful that some airline counters may close at 5 pm. Many folks just use bicycles to get around, unless they are going more than a few miles.

gos that make Bonaire their home. The near-perfect climate also makes Bonaire the ideal destination for soaking in some sun.

Although many islanders claim that the name Bonaire comes from the French for "good air," this explanation is unlikely, particularly because the island was never colonized by the French. The island was first inhabited by an Amerindian people (related to the Arawaks) called the Caquetios. Alonso de Ojeda and Amerigo Vespucci landed here in 1499 and claimed it for Spain. It seems likely that they adopted the Amerindian name for the island, which probably sounded very much like Bonaire and meant "low country." Because the Spanish found little use for the island except as a penal colony, the original inhabitants were shipped off to work on the plantations of Hispaniola, and Bonaire remained largely undeveloped. When the Dutch seized the islands of Aruba, Bonaire, and Curaçao in 1633, they started building the salt industry in Bonaire, which fueled the economy then and remains an important industry today.

The majority of the 15,000 inhabitants live in and around the capital, Kralendijk. The word almost universally applied to this diminutive city with a downtown area that can be traversed in less than three minutes is cute. Part of the BES Islands, Bonaire, St. Eustatius, and Saba were made special municipalities of the Netherlands in late 2010. Before this change Bonaire was governed from neighboring Curaçao.

PLANNING

WHEN TO GO

High season in Bonaire mirrors that in much of the Caribbean: basically from mid-December through mid-April. In the off-season, rates will be reduced at least 25% and often more. Hurricanes and severe tropical storms are rare—though still possible—in Bonaire, which means the island has good weather almost year-round.

GETTING HERE AND AROUND

AIR TRAVEL

Canadians and Americans will usually have to change planes in Curaçao or Aruba. Dutch Antilles Express provides connecting service. KLM offers daily direct flights from Amsterdam. The only nonstops are from New York–Newark, New York–JFK, Houston, Miami, and Atlanta.

Airline Contacts Continental Airlines ☎ *800/231–0856.* **Delta** ☎ *800/221–1212.* **Dutch Antilles Express** ☎ *599/717–0808* ⊕ *www.flydae.com.* **Insel Air** ☎ *599/737–0444* ⊕ *www.fly-inselair.com.* **KLM** ☎ *599/717–5600.*

Airport Flamingo Airport. Continental Airlines offers once-weekly direct service to Flamingo Airport from Houston and Newark, Insel Air offers once-weekly service from Miami, and Delta offers once-weekly service from Atlanta. ⊠ *BON* ☎ *599/717–3800.*

BIKE AND MOPED TRAVEL

Scooters are a great way to get around the island. Rates are about $25 per day for a one-seater and up to $35 for a deluxe two-seater. A valid driver's license and cash deposit or credit card are required.

Contacts Bonaire Motorcycle Shop. Bonaire Motorcycle Shop rents Harley-Davidson motorcycles. ⊠ *Kaya Grandi 64, Kralendijk* ☎ *599/717–7790.* **Rento Fun Drive.** The folks at Rento Fun Drive will have you zipping about. ⊠ *Kaya Grandi 47, Kralendijk* ☎ *599/717–2408.*

CAR TRAVEL

Minimum and maximum age to rent a car are 21 and 70. There's a government tax of 5% per rental; no cash deposit is needed if you pay by credit card.

Gas prices are about double those of the United States. Main roads are well paved, but during the rainy season (October and November), mud—called Bonairean snow—can be difficult to navigate. Traffic is to the right, and there's not a single traffic light.

Contacts Avis ⊠ *Flamingo Airport, Kralendijk* ☎ *599/717–5795.* **Budget** ⊠ *Flamingo Airport, Kralendijk* ☎ *599/717–4700.* **Bonaire Rent a Car** ⊠ *Kaya International 1, Kralendijk* ☎ *599/786–6090.* **Hertz** ⊠ *Flamingo Airport, Kralendijk* ☎ *599/717–7221.* **Island Rentals** ⊠ *Plaza Resort, J.A. Abraham Blvd. 80, Kralendijk* ☎ *599/717–2100.*

TAXI TRAVEL

Taxis are unmetered; fixed rates are controlled by the government. From most hotels into town it costs between $11 and $15. Fares increase from 7 pm to midnight by 25% and from midnight to 6 am by 50%. Drivers will conduct half-day tours; they charge about $28 per hour for up to four passengers.

Contacts Airport Taxi Stand. Fare to your hotel with Airport Taxi Stand is $10 to $22 for up to four passengers. ☎ *599/717–8100.* **Taxi Central Dispatch** ☎ *599/717–8100.*

ESSENTIALS

Banks and Exchange Services In January 2011 the U.S. dollar became the official currency, replacing the NAf guilder. You can find ATMs at the airport, in Kralendijk, and at Hato branches of MCB, as well as at the Sand Dollar Condominium Resort and the Plaza Resort; at the Tourism Corporation Bonaire; and at Banco di Caribe on Kaya Grandi.

Electricity 120 AC/50 cycles. A transformer and occasionally a two-prong adapter are required. Some appliances may work slowly; hair dryers may overheat, and sensitive equipment may be damaged.

Emergency Services Ambulance ☎ *599/717–8900.* **Fire** ☎ *599/717–8000.* **Police emergencies** ☎ *599/717–8000.* **Scuba-diving emergencies** ☎ *599/717–8187.*

Language The official language is Dutch, but the everyday language is Papiamento, a mix of Spanish, Portuguese, Dutch, English, and French, as well as African tongues. You can light up your waiter's eyes if you can say *masha danki* (thank you very much) and *pasa un bon dia* (have a nice day). English is spoken by almost everyone on the island.

Passport Requirements U.S. citizens must carry valid passports. In addition, everyone must have a return or ongoing ticket, and you are advised to confirm reservations 48 hours before departure. The maximum stay is 90 days.

Phones The country code for Bonaire is 599; 717 is the exchange for every four-digit number on the island. Phone cards from home rarely work on Bonaire. You can try AT&T by dialing 001–800/872–2881 from public phones. To call Bonaire from the United States, dial 011–599/717 plus the local four-digit number.

Taxes The departure tax when going to Curaçao, St. Maarten, St. Eustatius, Saba, or Aruba is $9. For all other destinations it's $35. This tax is supposed to be included in the ticket price. Hotels charge a room tax of $6.50 per person, per night in addition to the V.A.T. (value-added tax). Many hotels add a 10% to 15% service charge to your bill. A V.A.T. of 6% is tacked on to dining and lodging costs. The V.A.T. may or may not be included in your quoted room rates, so be sure to ask. It's almost always included in restaurant prices.

ACCOMMODATIONS

Alongside the numerous lodges that offer only the basics (mostly catering to divers), you can now find some real resorts. Families can find self-catering accommodations, and many smaller inns will appeal to budget travelers. The best resorts are often on decent beaches, but these are mostly man-made. Almost all the island's resorts are clustered around Kralendijk.

HOTEL AND RESTAURANT PRICES

Prices in the restaurant reviews are the average cost of a main course at dinner or, if dinner is not served, at lunch; taxes and service charges are generally included. Prices in the hotel reviews are the lowest cost of a standard double room in high season, excluding taxes, service charges, and meal plans (except at all-inclusives). Prices for rentals are the lowest per-night cost for a one-bedroom unit in high season.

WEDDINGS

One person must apply for temporary residency. Official witnesses must also apply for residency, but most wedding coordinators can arrange for local witnesses. After the marriage, an apostille (official seal) must be placed on the marriage license and certificate. Blood tests are not required.

EXPLORING BONAIRE

Two routes, north and south from Kralendijk, the island's small capital, are possible on the 24-mile-long (39-km-long) island; either route will take from a few hours to a full day, depending on whether you stop to snorkel, swim, dive, or lounge. Those pressed for time will find that it's easy to explore the entire island in a day if stops are kept to a minimum.

KRALENDIJK

Bonaire's small, tidy capital city (population 3,000) is five minutes from the airport. The main drag, J.A. Abraham Boulevard, turns into **Kaya Grandi** in the center of town. Along it are most of the island's major stores, boutiques, and restaurants. Across Kaya Grandi, opposite the Littman jewelry store, is Kaya L.D. Gerharts, with several small supermarkets, a handful of snack shops, and some of the better restaurants. Walk down the narrow waterfront avenue called Kaya C.E.B. Hellmund, which leads straight to the **North and South piers.** In the center of town, the Harbourside Mall has chic boutiques. Along this route is **Ft. Oranje,** with its cannons. From December through April, cruise ships dock in the harbor once or twice a week. The diminutive ocher-and-white structure that looks like a tiny Greek temple is the **fish market;** local anglers no longer bring their catches here (they sell out of their homes these days), but you can find plenty of fresh produce brought over from Colombia and Venezuela. Pick up the brochure *Walking and Shopping in Kralendijk* from the tourist office to get a map and full listing of all the monuments and sights in the town.

SOUTH BONAIRE

The trail south from Kralendijk is chock-full of icons—both natural and man-made—that tell Bonaire's mini-saga. Rent a four-wheel-drive vehicle (a car will do, but during the rainy season of October through November the roads can become muddy) and head out along the Southern Scenic Route. The roads wind through dramatic desert terrain, full of organ-pipe cacti and spiny-trunk mangroves—huge stumps of saltwater trees that rise from the marshes like witches. Watch for long-haired goats, wild donkeys, and lizards of all sizes.

☾ ★ **Rooi Lamoenchi Kunuku.** Owner Ellen Herrera restored her family's homestead north of Lac Bay, in the Bonairean *kadushi* (cactus) wilderness, to educate tourists and residents about the history and tradition of authentic kunuku living and show unspoiled terrain in two daily tours. You must make an appointment in advance and expect to spend a couple of hours. ⊠ *Kaya Suiza 23, Playa Baribe* ☎ *599/717–8489* 💲 *$21* ☾ *By appointment only.*

Salt Flats. You can't miss the salt flats—voluptuous white drifts that look like mountains of snow. Harvested once a year, the "ponds" are owned by Cargill, Inc., which has reactivated the 19th-century salt industry with great success (one reason for that success is that the ocean on this part of the island is higher than the land—which makes irrigation a snap). Keep a lookout for the three 30-foot obelisks—white, blue, and red—that were used to guide the trade boats coming to pick up the salt. Look also in the distance across the pans to the abandoned solar salt-works that's now a designated **flamingo sanctuary.** With the naked eye you might be able to make out a pink-orange haze just on the horizon; with binoculars you will see a sea of bobbing pink bodies. The sanctuary is completely protected, and no entrance is allowed (flamingos are extremely sensitive to disturbances of any kind).

Slave Huts. The salt industry's gritty history is revealed in Rode Pan, the site of two groups of tiny slave huts. The white grouping is on the right side of the road, opposite the salt flats; the second grouping, called the red slave huts (though they appear yellow), stretches across the road toward the island's southern tip. During the 19th century, slaves working the salt pans by day crawled into these huts to rest. Each Friday afternoon they walked seven hours to Rincon to weekend with their families, returning each Sunday. Only very small people will be able to enter, but walk around and poke your head in for a look.

Willemstoren Lighthouse. Bonaire's first lighthouse was built in 1837 and is now automated (but closed to visitors). Take some time to explore the beach and notice how the waves, driven by the trade winds, play a crashing symphony against the rocks. Locals stop here to collect pieces of driftwood in spectacular shapes and to build fanciful pyramids from objects that have washed ashore.

NORTH BONAIRE

The Northern Scenic Route takes you into the heart of Bonaire's natural wonders—desert gardens of towering cacti (kadushi, used to prepare soup, and the thornier *yatu*, used to build cactus fencing), tiny coastal coves, and plenty of fantastic panoramas. The road also weaves between eroded pink-and-black limestone walls and eerie rock formations with fanciful names such as the Devil's Mouth and Iguana Head (you'll need a vivid imagination and sharp eye to recognize them). Brazil trees growing along the route were used by Indians to make dye (pressed from a red ring in the trunk). Inscriptions still visible in several island caves were made with this dye.

A snappy excursion with the requisite photo stops will take about 2½ hours, but if you pack your swimsuit and a hefty picnic basket (forget about finding fast food), you could spend the entire day exploring this northern sector. Head out from Kralendijk on Kaya Gobernador N. Debrot until it turns into the Northern Scenic Route. Once you pass the Radio Nederland towers, you cannot turn back to Kralendijk. The narrow road becomes one way until you get to Landhuis Karpata, and you have to follow the cross-island road to Rincon and return via the main road through the center of the island.

1,000 Steps. Directly across the road from the Radio Nederland towers on the main road north, you'll see a short yellow marker that points to the location of these limestone stairs carved right out of the cliff. If you trek down the stairs, you can discover a lovely coral beach and protected cove where you can snorkel and scuba dive. Actually, you'll count only 67 steps, but it feels like 1,000 when you walk back up carrying scuba gear.

Barcadera Cave. Once used to trap goats, this cave is one of the oldest in Bonaire; there's even a tunnel that looks intriguingly spooky. It's the first sight along the northern route; watch closely for a yellow marker on your left before you reach the towering Radio Nederland antennas. Pull off across from the entrance to the Bonaire Caribbean Club, and you can discover some stone steps that lead down into a cave full of stalactites and vegetation.

Gotomeer. This saltwater lagoon near the island's northern end is a popular flamingo hangout. Bonaire is one of the few places in the world where pink flamingos nest. The shy, spindly-leg creatures—affectionately called "pink clouds"—are magnificent birds to observe, and there are about 15,000 of them in Bonaire (more than the number of human residents). The best time to catch them at home is January to June, when they tend to their gray-plumed young. For the best view take the paved access road alongside the lagoon through the jungle of cacti to the parking and observation area on the rise overlooking the lagoon and Washington–Slagbaai National Park beyond.

Landhuis Karpata. This mustard-color building was the manor house of an aloe plantation in the 19th century. The site was named for the *karpata* (castor bean) plants that are abundant in the area—you can see them along the sides of the road as you approach. Notice the rounded outdoor oven where aloe was boiled down before the juice was exported. Although the government has built a shaded rest stop at Karpata, there's still no drink stand.

Mangazina di Rei. Built around the second-oldest stone structure on Bonaire, this cultural park a few miles before Rincon provides a fascinating insight into the island's history. The museum commands an excellent view of the surrounding countryside and contains artifacts tracing the often hard lives of the early settlers. There are numerous traditional structures built around the museum illustrating how living conditions have changed over the years. The park is usually filled with local school kids learning how to use traditional musical instruments and how to cook local foods. ⊠ *Kaya Rincon z/n, Rincon* ☎ *599/786–2101* ⊕ *www.mangazinadirei.org* ⊴ *$10 adults, $5 children under 12* ⊗ *Tues.–Sat. 10–5.*

Onima. Small signposts direct the way to the Indian inscriptions found on a 3-foot limestone ledge that juts out like a partially formed cave entrance. Look up to see the red-stained designs and symbols inscribed on the limestone, said to have been the handiwork of the Arawak Indians when they inhabited the island centuries ago. The pictographs date back at least to the 15th century, and nobody has a clue what they mean. To reach Onima, pass through Rincon on the road that heads back to Kralendijk, but take the left-hand turn before Fontein.

Rincon. The island's original Spanish settlement, Rincon is where slaves brought from Africa to work the plantations and salt fields lived. Superstition and voodoo lore still have a powerful impact here, more so than in Kralendijk, where the townspeople work hard at suppressing old ways. Rincon is now a well-kept cluster of pastel cottages and 19th-century buildings that constitute Bonaire's oldest village. Watch your driving here—goats and dogs often sit right in the middle of the main drag.

Seroe Largu. Just off the main road, this spot, at 394 feet, is one of the highest on the island. A paved but narrow and twisting road leads to a magnificent daytime view of Kralendijk's rooftops and the island of Klein Bonaire. A large cross and figure of Christ stand guard at the peak, with an inscription reading *ayera* (yesterday), *awe* (today), and *semper* (always).

Washington–Slagbaai National Park. Once a plantation producing divi-divi trees (the pods were used for tanning animal skins), aloe (used for medicinal lotions), charcoal, and goats, the park is now a model of conservation. It's easy to tour the 13,500-acre tropical desert terrain on the dirt roads. As befits a wilderness sanctuary, the well-marked, rugged routes force you to drive slowly enough to appreciate the animal life and the terrain. (Think twice about coming here if it has rained recently—the mud you may encounter will be more than inconvenient.) If you're planning to hike, bring a picnic lunch, camera, sunscreen, and plenty of water. There are two routes: the long one (22 miles [35½ km]) is marked by yellow arrows, the short one (15 miles [24 km]) by green arrows. Goats and donkeys may dart across the road, and if you keep your eyes peeled, you may catch sight of large iguanas camouflaged in the shrubbery.

Bird-watchers are really in their element here. Right inside the park's gate, flamingos roost on the salt pad known as **Salina Mathijs,** and exotic parakeets dot the foot of **Mt. Brandaris,** Bonaire's highest peak, at 784 feet. Some 130 species of birds fly in and out of the shrubbery in the park. Keep your eyes open and your binoculars at hand. Swimming, snorkeling, and scuba diving are permitted, but you're asked not to frighten the animals or remove anything from the grounds. Absolutely no hunting, fishing, or camping is allowed. A useful guide to the park is available at the entrance for about $6. To get here, take the secondary road north from the town of Rincon. The Nature Fee for swimming and snorkeling also grants you free admission to this park—simply present proof of payment and some form of photo ID. ☎ 599/717–8444 ⊕ *www.washingtonparkbonaire.org* ⊠ *Free with payment of scuba diving Nature Fee ($25) or $15 without* ☉ *Daily 8–5; you must enter before 3.*

WHERE TO EAT

Dining on Bonaire is far less expensive than on Aruba or Curaçao, and you can find everything from continental to Tex-Mex to Asian fare. Many restaurants serve only dinner—only a few establishments not affiliated with hotels are open for breakfast, so check ahead.

$$
EUROPEAN
★

×**Appetite.** This delightful establishment is an oasis of chic. The historic house offers cozy private rooms and a large courtyard, which always seems to be buzzing. The menu encourages diners to forget the main course and order a series of starters, but such items as stewed veal cheek with crispy sweetbreads are worth the splurge. The restaurant is just a few steps away from the Tourism Corporation Bonaire office. ⑤ *Average main: $25* ⊠ *Kaya Grandi 12, Kralendijk* ☎ *599/717–3595* ⊙ *Closed Sun.*

$$
FRENCH
Fodor'sChoice
★

×**Bistro de Paris.** Any restaurant that welcomes you with a free glass of Kir and a personal greeting from the owner should be taken very seriously. Patrice Rannou has transformed an unassuming house into a lovely bistro serving the best French food on the island. The low-key decor (complete with Perrier-bottle vases) belies the extraordinary food on offer. Lamb lovers will fall to pieces over the char-grilled chops served with haricots verts and asparagus. The dinner menu is very reasonably priced, but those on an extremely tight budget should at least explore the lunch offerings or even order sandwiches to take along on a day of exploring. Those with kids and a lot of patience may want to try the novelty of the grill stone, which lets diners cook their own meal at the table. Many patrons choose to dine on the outdoor patio. ⑤ *Average main: $21* ⊠ *Kaya Gobernador N. Debrot 46, Kralendijk* ☎ *599/717–7070* ⊙ *Closed Sun. No lunch Sat.*

$
ECLECTIC
★

×**Boudoir.** Despite the nighttime-bedroom connotation this excellent patio eatery at the Royal Palm Mall is open only for breakfast, lunch, and late-afternoon snacks. Besides having some of the best coffee on the island, Boudoir offers a range of soups, salads, sandwiches, and burgers that should please even the most discerning of diners. It's the perfect place to relax with an iced coffee and a smoked-salmon-and-capers sandwich after a day of exploring Kralendijk. ⑤ *Average main: $11* ⊠ *Kaya Grandi 26 F/G, Royal Palm Mall, Kralendijk* ☎ *599/717–4321.*

$$$
ITALIAN
★

×**Capriccio.** This splendid, family-run Italian eatery has plenty to boast about. The pastas are handmade daily, and fresh mozzarella is imported from Italy once a week. The wine cellar includes hundreds of labels and thousands of bottles. You can opt for casual à la carte dining on the terrace or a romantic meal in the tonier, air-conditioned dining room. If your appetite is hearty, go for the five-course prix-fixe menu. Otherwise, choose one of the 50 regular offerings. ⑤ *Average main: $24* ⊠ *Kaya Hellmund 5, Kralendijk* ☎ *599/717–7230* ⊕ *www.emporiocapriccio. com* ⊙ *Closed Tues. No lunch weekends.*

$$
ECLECTIC
Fodor'sChoice
★

×**City Café/City Restaurant.** This busy waterfront eatery is also one of the most reliable nightspots on the island, so it's always hopping day or night. Breakfast, lunch, and dinner are served daily at reasonable prices. Seafood is always featured, as are a variety of sandwiches and salads. The pita sandwich platters are a good lunchtime choice for the budget challenged. Weekends, there's always live entertainment and dancing. This is the place to people-watch on Bonaire, as it seems everyone ends up at City Café eventually. ⑤ *Average main: $19* ⊠ *Hotel Rochaline, Kaya Grandi 7, Kralendijk* ☎ *599/717–8286* ⊕ *www.citybonaire.com.*

$$$$
ECLECTIC

×**It Rains Fishes.** Those seeking upscale urban chic flock to this waterfront establishment where beautiful people serve beautiful food. The grilled seafood platter is superb, and the ambience is unbeatable. Despite its popularity and large size, by Bonaire standards, service is impeccable and efficient. The funky bar is a popular hangout until late in the night, and live entertainment is sometimes featured. $ *Average main: $32* ⊠ *Kaya Jan N.E. Craane 24, Kralendijk* ☎ *599/717–8780* ⊕ *www. itrainsfishesbonaire.com* ⌂ *Reservations essential* ☉ *Closed Sun.*

$$ ✕**Kontiki Beach Club.** The dining room is a harmonious blend of terra-
ECLECTIC cotta tile floors and rattan furnishings around a limestone half-moon bar. There's also a brick terrace for alfresco dining. Chef-owners Miriam and Martin are especially proud of their Dutch *kibbeling* (fish in a beer batter served with chili sauce). Those in the know order the Antillean fish soup, a delightful blend of fresh seafood and finely diced carrots and cucumber. The display of local art on the walls changes constantly. It's quite far from downtown, but the view of the lagoon and intimate ambience mean it is definitely worth the drive for breakfast, lunch, or dinner. $ *Average main: $20* ⊠ *Kaminda Sorobon 64, Lac Bay* ☎ *599/717–5369* ⊕ *www.kontikibonaire.com.*

$$ ✕**La Guernica.** This trendy eatery overlooking the boardwalk and the
ECLECTIC harbor is great for people-watching; there's outdoor seating as well as
Fodor'sChoice a couch-and-pillow-filled lounge area. The interior is done in hacienda
★ style, with terra-cotta tiles, clay decorations, and comfy lounge chairs. Though many come here for the excellent tapas, those with heartier appetites can choose from a variety of seafood and meat main courses, including an excellent beef tenderloin with a blue-cheese sauce. The lunch menu offers a range of sandwiches and salads. This is *the* place to sip a cocktail and be seen. $ *Average main: $25* ⊠ *Kaya Bonaire 4C, Kralendijk* ☎ *599/717–5022* ⊕ *www.laguernica.com.*

$$$$ ✕**Mona Lisa Bar & Restaurant.** Here you can find continental, Carib-
EUROPEAN bean, and Indonesian fare as well as throngs of regulars who would
Fodor'sChoice not dream of visiting Bonaire without a meal here. Popular bar dishes
★ include Wiener schnitzel and fresh fish with curry sauce. The intimate stucco-and-brick dining room, presided over by a copy of the famous painting of the lady with the mystic smile, is decorated with Dutch artwork, lace curtains, and whirring ceiling fans. The colorful bar adorned with baseball-style caps is a great place for late-night schmoozing and noshing on light snacks or the catch of the day, which is served until 10 pm. There is a four-course fixed-price dinner on offer most evenings. $ *Average main: $32* ⊠ *Kaya Grandi 15, Kralendijk* ☎ *599/717–8718* ⌂ *Reservations essential* ☉ *Closed Sun. No lunch.*

$$ ✕**Paradise Moon.** The menu at this Texan-owned waterfront eatery
MEXICAN favors Tex-Mex, but there are also Asian and continental choices. The food is reasonably priced by Bonaire standards, and portions are huge by any definition. Fans of throwing calorie caution to the wind will appreciate such Texan touches as deep-fried cheesecake and homemade apple pie floating in a sea of melted butter. $ *Average main: $19* ⊠ *Kaya Korsou 1, Kralendijk* ☎ *599/717–5025* ⊕ *www.paradisebonaire.com* ☉ *Closed Sat. No lunch.*

$$$$ ✕**Patagonia Argentinean Steakhouse.** Meat lovers pack this 60-seat water-
STEAKHOUSE front establishment. Though it caters largely to steak lovers with everything from top sirloin to prime rib, there's a respectable selection of

seafood and other meats, too. The quality of some of the lower-price steaks can be a bit erratic, however, and the occasional use of frozen vegetables is puzzling. Portions are huge, and the quality of the high-end cuts is consistently good. The restaurant's popularity can lead to lengthy wait times, but you can mosey over to the cozy bar area to pass some time. $ *Average main: $30* ⊠ *Harbour Village Marina, in lighthouse, Kralendijk* ☎ 599/717–7725 ⚓ *Reservations essential* ⊘ *Closed Mon. No lunch weekends.*

$$$ × **Richard's Waterfront Dining.** Animated, congenial Richard Beady owns
SEAFOOD this casually romantic waterfront restaurant. The daily menu is listed on
★ large blackboards, and the seafood is consistently excellent. Fish soup is usually offered and is sure to please, as is the grilled wahoo. Service can be erratic, depending on the level of staffing and the number of diners. $ *Average main: $29* ⊠ *J.A. Abraham Blvd. 60, Kralendijk* ☎ 599/717–5263 ⊕ *www.richardsofbonaire.com* ⊘ *Closed Mon. No lunch.*

$$$ × **Sunset Bar & Grill.** This casual restaurant at the Den Laman Condo-
EUROPEAN miniums offers a great variety of family-friendly options. The lunch
Fodor'sChoice and dinner menu includes a broad selection, ranging from seafood to
★ pastas, and there is always a nightly themed buffet option. Given the casual atmosphere, the quality of the food is excellent, and the presentation is eye-popping. The open-air oceanfront setting is unbeatable and especially great at sunset. $ *Average main: $27* ⊠ *Den Laman Condominiums, Kaya Gobernador N. Debrot 77, Kralendijk* ☎ 599/717–2698 ⊘ *Closed Wed.*

$ × **Wind & Surf Beach Hut Bar.** Part of Bonaire Windsurf Place—and
EUROPEAN located right on the beach—this fun eatery is one of the most casual dining experiences on the island. Tables and chairs are set directly in the sand under a straw-roof structure so that cooling winds sweep through the space. The food is simple but very good; the main offerings are sandwiches, salads, and burgers. The experience of dining with your toes in the sand is sure to leave lingering pleasant memories. The weekly barbecue on Wednesday nights with live entertainment is well worth the drive. $ *Average main: $12* ⊠ *Sorobon Beach* ☎ 599/717–2288 ⊟ *No credit cards.*

$$ × **Zeezicht Bar & Restaurant.** Zeezicht (pronounced zay-*zeekt* and mean-
ECLECTIC ing "sea view") serves three meals a day and is a Kralendijk institution.
★ At breakfast and lunch you get basic American fare with an Antillean touch, such as a fish omelet; dinner is more Caribbean and mostly seafood, served either on the terrace overlooking the harbor or in the nautically themed, homey, rough-hewn main room. Locals are dedicated to this hangout, especially for the ceviche, conch sandwiches, and the Zeezicht special soup with conch, fish, and shrimp. The location makes it a popular spot for sunset watchers. $ *Average main: $24* ⊠ *Kaya J.N.E. Craane 12, Kralendijk* ☎ 599/717–8434.

WHERE TO STAY

Although meal plans are available at most hotels, the island has many excellent—and often inexpensive—restaurants. If you're planning a dive vacation, look into the many attractive dive packages.

For expanded reviews, facilities, and current deals, visit Fodors.com.

RENTAL APARTMENTS

If you prefer do-it-yourself home-style comfort over the pampering and other services offered by a hotel, you can rent a fully furnished apartment.

RENTAL CONTACTS

Bonaire Hotel & Tourism Association. The Bonaire Hotel & Tourism Association has information on a variety of properties ranging from budget to upscale. ☎ *599/717-5134* ⊕ *www.bonhata.org* .

Sun Rentals. Sun Rentals offers quite a range of accommodations. You can choose among private ocean-view villas in luxurious areas like Sabadeco, furnished oceanfront apartments (with a pool) in town, or bungalows in Lagoenhill, an inland community. The Sun Oceanfront Apartments are an excellent budget choice for families. ☎ *599/717–6130* ⊕ *www.sunrentalsbonaire.com.*

RECOMMENDED HOTELS AND RESORTS

$$
HOTEL
Fodor'sChoice
★

Bellafonte Chateau de la Mer. Although it lacks the amenities of a large resort—including a pool—the intimacy and exclusivity of this elegant palazzo-style hotel near Kralendijk more than compensate. **Pros:** well-designed rooms; diving straight from hotel pier; upper rooms have excellent views; free Wi-Fi; groceries can be ordered online before arrival. **Cons:** no restaurant or bar; no elevator; no pool. **TripAdvisor:** "fantastic little hotel," "great location," "spectacular views." $ *Rooms from: $130* ✉ *E.E.G. Blvd. 10, Belnem* ☎ *599/717–3333* ⊕ *www.bellafontebonaire.com* ⇋ *6 studios, 8 1-bedroom suites, 8 2-bedroom suites, 2 penthouses* ⦿ *No meals.*

$
B&B/INN
★

Bruce Bowker's Carib Inn. The cozy rooms and owner–dive-instructor Bruce Bowker's personal touch have given his inn the highest return-visitor ratio on the island. **Pros:** intimate and friendly; excellent dive courses; Wi-Fi throughout. **Cons:** smaller size means fewer amenities such as shopping; nondivers will find little to entertain them. **TripAdvisor:** "very giving staff," "perfect for ocean lovers," "diver's paradise." $ *Rooms from: $109* ✉ *J.A. Abraham Blvd. 46, Kralendijk* ☎ *599/717–8819* ⊕ *www.caribinn.com* ⇋ *10 units* ⦿ *No meals.*

$$
RESORT
☾

Buddy Dive Resort. Well-equipped rooms, a nicely landscaped compound, and excellent dive packages keep guests coming back to this large resort. **Pros:** excellent dive shop; rooms are spacious; open-air restaurant has one of the best ocean views on the island. **Cons:** complex can feel like a maze; room amenities vary, depending on where they are on the property. **TripAdvisor:** "great base of operations for diving," "perfect low-key dive resort," "great place even for non-divers." $ *Rooms from: $134* ✉ *Kaya Gobernador N. Debrot 85, Kralendijk* ☎ *599/717–5080, 866/462–8339* ⊕ *www.buddydive.com* ⇋ *6 rooms, 72 apartments* ⦿ *No meals.*

$$
HOTEL
★

Captain Don's Habitat. Bonaire's first hotel catering to divers remains a favorite, with a PADI five-star dive center offering more than 20 specialty courses. **Pros:** variety of accommodation types; pizzeria with wood-burning oven; excellent diving facilities. **Cons:** little to entertain nondivers; Wi-Fi coverage is spotty; staff can sometimes seem aloof.

6

TripAdvisor: "very relaxing," "the best for serious divers," "excellent restaurant." ⑤ *Rooms from: $215* ⊠ *Kaya Gobernador N. Debrot 113, Kralendijk* ☎ *599/717–8290, 800/327–6709* ⊕ *www.habitatbonaire. com* ↻ *24 rooms, 12 junior suites, 5 villas, 19 cottages* ❑│*No meals.*

$ ▦ **Coco Palm Garden & Casa Oleander.** Friends and neighbors operate this
RENTAL series of cozy cottages and villas, each fully equipped and individually
ℭ decorated to the point where the hard part is choosing among them.
★ **Pros:** charming and quirky with no two rooms alike; friendly staff; quiet pool area. **Cons:** not close to downtown or shopping; limited on-site dining options; long walk from the villas to get to the common areas and office; charge for using the air-conditioner. **TripAdvisor:** "quiet stay," "utilitarian," "feels like home." ⑤ *Rooms from: $66* ⊠ *Kaya I.R. Randolf Statuuis van Eps 9, Belnem* ☎ *599/717–2108, 599/790–9080* ⊕ *www.cocopalmgarden.org* ↻ *19 rooms, 6 villas* ❑│*No meals.*

$ ▦ **Den Laman Condominiums.** Though the exterior of this property will
RENTAL not win any design awards, the location and beautifully finished interi-
★ ors are definitely first-class. **Pros:** excellent restaurant on-site; rooms are chicly appointed; convenient to downtown. **Cons:** no elevator means upper rooms can require a climb; common areas feel a little sterile; spotty Wi-Fi coverage. **TripAdvisor:** "great accommodations if you are diving," "great view," "wonderful apartments." ⑤ *Rooms from: $129* ⊠ *Kaya Gobernador N. Debrot 77, Kralendijk* ☎ *599/717–1700* ⊕ *www.denlaman.com* ↻ *16 condos* ❑│*No meals.*

$$ ▦ **Divi Flamingo Resort.** The brightly colored buildings of this resort are a
RESORT two-minute stroll from downtown, but the main draw is the combination
ℭ of a top-notch dive program and the only casino on Bonaire. **Pros:** beauti-
Fodor'sChoice fully landscaped grounds; steps from downtown and restaurants; on-site
★ casino. **Cons:** pool can get crowded; beach is quite small. **TripAdvisor:** "great dive operation," "relaxing," "a charming gem." ⑤ *Rooms from: $175* ⊠ *J.A. Abraham Blvd. 40, Kralendijk* ☎ *599/717–8285, 800/367–3484* ⊕ *www.diviflamingo.com* ↻ *129 rooms* ❑│*No meals.*

$$$$ ▦ **Harbour Village Beach Club.** This snazzy enclave of ocher-color build-
HOTEL ings is the benchmark for luxury accommodations on the island. **Pros:**
ℭ great for a secluded getaway; not awash with budget tourists; conve-
Fodor'sChoice nient to downtown. **Cons:** some rooms are quite far from the beach;
★ grounds can feel a bit deserted. **TripAdvisor:** "great snorkeling on the hotel beach," "fabulous place," "absolutely perfect." ⑤ *Rooms from: $590* ⊠ *Kaya Gobernador N. Debrot 71, Kralendijk* ☎ *599/717–7500, 800/424–0004* ⊕ *www.harbourvillage.com* ↻ *40 rooms, 14 1-bedroom suites, 6 2-bedroom suites* ❑│*No meals.*

$$ ▦ **Plaza Resort Bonaire.** No other property in Bonaire can match the range
RESORT of activities offered here, with everything from tennis to water sports, not to mention a gorgeous beach. **Pros:** every imaginable recreational activity is available; good shopping in hotel; beautiful grounds; most rooms are huge. **Cons:** size of the compound can make getting around a chore; not an easy walk to downtown; Wi-Fi reception is spotty except in lobby. **TripAdvisor:** "good place with the right room," "diving para-dise," "nice resort for the casual diver." ⑤ *Rooms from: $260* ⊠ *J.A. Abraham Blvd. 80, Kralendijk* ☎ *599/717–2500, 800/766–6016* ⊕ *www. plazaresortbonaire.com* ↻ *174 rooms, 48 villas* ❑│*No meals.*

Pool at the Harbour Village Beach Club.

$ **Roomer.** This excellent, economically priced family hotel has small
HOTEL   rooms, but they are individually decorated with tasteful splashes of color.
Pros: very family-oriented; excellent for budget travelers; kid-friendly
pool area; free Wi-Fi. **Cons:** not on the ocean; miles from downtown.
TripAdvisor: "great home cooked meals," "quiet and cozy," "pleasant surroundings." *⑤ Rooms from: $110 ⊠ E.E.G. Blvd. 97, Belnem*
☎ 599/717–7488 ⊕ www.roomerbonaire.com ⟿ 10 rooms ⟊No meals.

$$ **Sand Dollar Condominium Resort.** This condo complex has family-
RENTAL   friendly apartments ranging from studios to three-bedrooms, each of
which is individually owned and decorated for a comfortable, lived-
in feeling. **Pros:** all rooms have great ocean views; well equipped for
families; grocery and ATM on property. **Cons:** few rooms have phones;
no beach bar, landscaping can be a bit shabby; air conditioning in liv-
ing room costs an extra $10 per day. **TripAdvisor:** "peace and quiet,"
"friendly people," "pitch perfect condo." *⑤ Rooms from: $128 ⊠ Kaya*
Gobernador N. Debrot 79, Kralendijk ☎ 599/717–8738, 800/288–
4773 ⊕ www.sanddollarbonaire.com ⟿ 50 condos ⟊No meals.

$$ **Sorobon Beach Resort.** This basic, family-oriented property on Lac Bay
RESORT   is all about the beach. **Pros:** stunning beachfront; Wi-Fi throughout;
next to one of the island's most popular windsurfing centers. **Cons:**
miles from shopping and restaurants; no radios or TVs in rooms; rooms
are a bit sparse. **TripAdvisor:** "the ultimate boutique resort," "paradise on Earth," "a relaxing windsurfing vacation." *⑤ Rooms from:*
$225 ⊠ Sorobon Beach ☎ 599/717–8080 ⊕ www.sorobonbeachresort.
com ⟿ 28 1-bedroom chalets, 1 2-bedroom chalet, 1 3-bedroom house
⟊No meals.

$$
RENTAL
Fodor's Choice
★

☒ **Waterlands Village.** These individually owned, roomy cottages offer all the comforts of home and feature thoughtful touches such as canopy beds and the option of an private outdoor shower. **Pros:** great price for relatively upscale accommodations; lovely pool area. **Cons:** no ocean view; airport noise can be an issue from time to time; bit of a walk to downtown; hefty $95 cleaning charge per stay. **TripAdvisor:** "perfect getaway," "very pleasant resort," "beautiful spacious cottages." ⑤ *Rooms from: $125* ☒ *Kaya International, Kralendijk* ☎ *599/701–5540* ⊕ *www.bonairecomfortrentals.com* ⇆ *24 cottages (18 for rent)* ◎ *No meals.*

$
RENTAL
★

☒ **Yachtclub Apartments.** Across from Harbour Village, these apartments offer some of the best budget lodging on the island. **Pros:** reasonable price for excellent accommodations; expansive pool area is great for sunbathing; close to several good restaurants, and the on-site restaurant is excellent. **Cons:** no ocean view; hotel is on the main road to Kralendijk and can get a bit dusty; stays less than 7 days incur a 25% rate surcharge. ⑤ *Rooms from: $93* ☒ *Kaya Gobernador N. Debrot 52, Kralendijk* ☎ *599/717–7424* ⊕ *www.yachtclubapartmentsbonaire.com* ⇆ *13 apartments* ◎ *No meals* ⌇ *2-night minimum.*

NIGHTLIFE

Most divers are exhausted after they finish their third, fourth, or fifth dive of the day, which may explain why there are no full-time discos on Bonaire. Strange as it may sound, the most effective approach to finding the best hot spot is to stand downtown, listen for the loudest music, and then follow your ears. Most of the time nightlife consists of sitting on a quiet beach sipping a local Amstel Bright beer. Top island performers, including the Foyan Boys, migrate from one resort to another throughout the week. You can find information in the free magazines (published once a year) *Bonaire Affair* and *Bonaire Nights.* The twice-monthly *Bonaire Update Events and Activities* pamphlet is available at most restaurants.

Carnival, generally held in February, is the usual nonstop parade of steel bands, floats, and wild costumes, albeit on a much smaller scale than on some other islands. It culminates in the ceremonial burning in effigy of King Momo, representing the spirit of debauchery.

BARS

City Café. Downtown, City Café is a wacky hangout splashed in magenta, banana, and electric blue. Here you can find cocktails, snack food, live music on weekends, and karaoke on Wednesday nights. ☒ *Hotel Rochaline, Kaya Grandi 7, Kralendijk* ☎ *599/717–8286.*

Deco Stop Bar. The Thursday-night happy hour at Deco Stop Bar is popular. ☒ *Captain Don's Habitat, Kaya Gobernador N. Debrot 113, Kralendijk* ☎ *599/717–8286.*

Karel's. Perched on stilts above the sea, Karel's is *the* place for mingling—especially Friday and Saturday nights, when there's live island and pop music. ☒ *Kaya J.N.E. Craane 12, Kralendijk* ☎ *599/717–8434.*

La Guernica. With an ultrachic bar and a comfy couch-lined terrace facing the ocean, La Guernica is the place to be seen on weekend nights. ⊠ *Kaya Bonaire 4C, Kralendijk* ☎ *599/717–5022.*

CASINO

Divi Flamingo Resort. This is the only casino on the island; it operates until 4 am. ⊠ *J.A. Abraham Blvd., Kralendijk* ☎ *599/717–8285.*

DANCE CLUBS

★ **City Café.** City Café is the island's closest thing to a dance club. On weekend nights the restaurant moves the tables aside and it becomes an instant dance floor. ⊠ *Kaya Grandi 7, Kralendijk* ☎ *599/717–8286.*

Lac Cai. On Sunday afternoon at Lac Cai enjoy the festive **Sunday Party,** where locals celebrate the day with live music, dancing, and food from 3 to 11. Take a taxi, especially if you plan to imbibe a few rum punches. ⊠ *Lac Cai.*

SHOPPING

6

You can get to know all the shops in Kralendijk in an hour or so, but sometimes there's no better way to enjoy some time out of the sun and sea than to go shopping (particularly if your companion is a dive fanatic and you're not). Almost all the shops are on the Kaya Grandi and adjacent streets and in tiny malls. Harbourside Mall is a pleasant, open-air mall with several fine air-conditioned shops. The most distinctive local crafts are fanciful painted pieces of driftwood and hand-painted *kunuku,* or little wilderness houses. ■ TIP→ Buy as many flamingo T-shirts as you want, but don't take home items made of goatskin or tortoiseshell; they aren't allowed into the United States. Remember, too, that it's forbidden to take sea fans, coral, conch shells, and all other forms of marine life off the island.

SPECIALTY STORES

CLOTHING

Benetton. This Benetton outpost claims that its prices for men's, women's, and children's clothes are 30% lower than in New York. ⊠ *Kaya Grandi 29, Kralendijk* ☎ *599/717–5107.*

Best Buddies. You'll find a good selection of Indonesian batik shirts, pareus, and T-shirts at Best Buddies. ⊠ *Kaya Grandi 32, Kralendijk* ☎ *599/717–7570.*

Island Fashions. At Island Fashions you can buy swimsuits, sunglasses, T-shirts, and costume jewelry. ⊠ *Kaya Grandi 5, Kralendijk* ☎ *599/717–7071.*

DUTY-FREE GOODS

Flamingo Airport Duty Free. Perfumes and cigarettes are available at Flamingo Airport Duty Free. ⊠ *Flamingo Airport* ☎ *599/717–5563.*

Perfume Palace. This shop sells perfumes and makeup from Lancôme, Estée Lauder, Chanel, Ralph Lauren, and Clinique. ⊠ *Harbourside Mall, Kaya Grandi 31, Kralendijk* ☎ *599/717–5288.*

HANDICRAFTS

JanArt Gallery. On the outskirts of town, JanArt Gallery sells unique paintings, prints, and art supplies; artist Janice Huckaby also hosts art classes. ⊠ *Kaya Gloria 7, Kralendijk* ☎ *599/717–5246.*

Kas di Arte. The works of local and international artists—including such notables as Ronald Verhoeven—are featured at Kas di Arte. ⊠ *Kaya J.N.E. Craane 34, Kralendijk* ☎ *No phone* ☉ *Closed Sun.*

Maharaj Gifthouse. Hand-painted Delft blue china, local artwork, and stainless-steel and crystal items available at Maharaj Gifthouse make great presents. ⊠ *Kaya Grandi 11, Kralendijk* ☎ *599/717–4402.*

Yenny's Art. Whatever you do, make a point of visiting Yenny's Art. Roam around her house, which is a replica of a traditional Bonaire town complete with her handmade life-size dolls and the skeletons of all her dead pets. Lots of fun (and sometimes kitschy) souvenirs made out of driftwood, clay, and shells are all handmade by Jenny. ⊠ *Kaya Betico Croes 6, near post office, Kralendijk* ☎ *599/717–5004.*

JEWELRY

★ **Atlantis.** This shop carries a large range of precious and semiprecious gems; the tanzanite collection is especially beautiful. You will also find Sector, Raymond Weil, and Citizen watches, among others, all at great savings. Since gold jewelry is sold by weight here, it's an especially good buy. ⊠ *Kaya Grandi 32B, Kralendijk* ☎ *599/717–7730.*

Littman's. Owner Steven Littman handpicks many of the items available in this upscale jewelry and gift shop during his regular trips to Europe. Look for Rolex, Omega, Cartier, and Tag Heuer watches; fine gold jewelry; antique coins; nautical sculptures; resort clothing; and accessories. ⊠ *Kaya Grandi 33, Kralendijk* ☎ *599/717–8160* ⊠ *Harbourside Mall, Kaya Grandi 31, Kralendijk* ☎ *599/717–2130.*

SPORTS AND ACTIVITIES

BICYCLING

Bonaire is generally flat, so bicycles are an easy way to get around. Because of the heat it's essential to carry water if you're planning to cycle for any distance and especially if your plans involve exploring the deserted interior. There are more than 180 miles (290 km) of unpaved routes (as well as the many paved roads) on the island.

Cycle Bonaire. Cycle Bonaire rents mountain bikes and gear (trail maps, water bottles, helmets, locks, repair and first-aid kits) for $25 a day or $100 for six days; half-day and full-day guided excursions start at $65, not including bike rental. ⊠ *Kaya Gobernador N. Debrot 77A, Kralendijk* ☎ *599/717–2229.*

Tropical Travel. This tour operator offers bikes for $11 per day or $55 per week (a $300 deposit is required). ⊠ *Plaza Resort Bonaire, J.A. Abraham Blvd. 80, Kralendijk* ☏ *599/701–1232* ⊕ *www.tropicaltravelbonaire.com.*

DAY SAILS AND SNORKELING TRIPS

Regularly scheduled sunset sails and snorkeling trips are popular (prices range from $35 to $50 per person), as are private or group sails (expect to pay about $500 per day for a party of four).

Kantika de Amor Watertaxi. Kantika de Amor Watertaxi provides daily rides to Klein Bonaire and drift snorkel and evening cruises with complimentary cocktails. ⊠ *Kaya J.N.E. Craane 24, opposite the restaurant It Rains Fishes, Kralendijk* ☏ *599/796–7254.*

Mushi Mushi. The *Mushi Mushi* is a catamaran offering a variety of two- and three-hour cruises starting at $50 per person. It departs from the Bonaire Nautico Marina in downtown Kralendijk (opposite the restaurant It Rains Fishes). ☏ *599/790–5399.*

Tropical Travel. If you want to do some sailing on your own, Tropical Travel offers a variety of cruise packages, with prices available on request. ⊠ *Plaza Resort Bonaire, J.A. Abraham Blvd. 80, Kralendijk* ☏ *599/701–1232* ⊕ *www.tropicaltravelbonaire.com.*

Woodwind. The *Woodwind* is a 37-foot trimaran that offers regular sailing and snorkeling trips as well as charters. It leaves from the dock at Divi Flamingo and offers a sail-snorkel–sunset cruise for $50 per person. ☏ *599/786–7055* ⊕ *www.woodwindbonaire.com.*

DIVING AND SNORKELING

Bonaire has some of the best reef diving this side of Australia's Great Barrier Reef. It takes only 5 to 25 minutes to reach many sites, the current is usually mild, and although some reefs have sudden, steep drops, most begin just offshore and slope gently downward at a 45-degree angle. General visibility runs 60 to 100 feet, except during surges in October and November. You can see several varieties of coral: knobby-brain, giant-brain, elkhorn, staghorn, mountainous star, gorgonian, and black. You can also encounter schools of parrot fish, surgeonfish, angelfish, eel, snapper, and grouper. Beach diving is excellent just about everywhere on the leeward side, so night diving is popular. There are sites here suitable for every skill level; they're clearly marked by yellow stones on the roadside.

Bonaire, in conjunction with *Skin Diver* magazine, has also developed the **Guided Snorkeling Program.** The highly educational and entertaining program begins with a slide show on important topics, from a beginner's look at reef fish, coral, and sponges to advanced fish identification and night snorkeling. Guided snorkeling for all skill levels can be arranged through most resort dive shops. The best snorkeling spots are on the island's leeward side, where you have shore access to the reefs, and along the west side of Klein Bonaire, where the reef is better developed. All snorkelers and swimmers must pay a $10 Nature Fee,

6

A Bonaire diver shows off her photographic buoyancy control.

which allows access to the waters around the island and Washington–Slagbaai National Park for one calendar year. The fee can be paid at most dive shops.

Fodor's Choice
★

Bonaire Marine Park. In the well-policed Bonaire Marine Park, which encompasses the entire coastline around Bonaire and Klein Bonaire, divers take the rules seriously. Don't even *think* about (1) spearfishing; (2) dropping anchor; or (3) touching, stepping on, or collecting coral. In order to dive (as opposed to simply swimming and entering the water), you must pay a fee of $25 (used to maintain the park), for which you receive a colored plastic tag (to attach to an item of scuba gear) entitling you to one calendar year of unlimited diving. Checkout dives—dives you do first with a master before going out on your own—are required, and you can arrange them through any dive shop. All dive operations offer classes in free buoyancy control, advanced buoyancy control, and photographic buoyancy control. Tags are available at all scuba facilities and from the Marine Park Headquarters. ⊠ *Karpata* ☎ *599/717–8444* ⊕ *www.bmp.org.*

DIVE SITES

The *Guide to the Bonaire Marine Park* lists 86 dive sites (including 16 shore-dive-only and 35 boat-dive-only sites). Another fine reference book is the *Diving and Snorkeling Guide to Bonaire,* by Jerry Schnabel and Suzi Swygert. Guides associated with the various dive centers can give you more complete directions. It's difficult to recommend one site over another; to whet your appetite, here are a few of the popular sites.

★ **Angel City.** Take the trail down to the shore adjacent to the Radio Nederland tower station; dive in and swim south to Angel City, one of the

Bonaire Marine Park

The Bonaire Marine Park was founded in 1979 in an effort to protect the island's most precious natural resource. Covering an area of less than 700 acres, the park includes all the waters around the island from the high-water mark to the 60-meter depth. Legislation prevents collecting (or even walking on) coral, using spearguns, or removing marine life. It also means that boats may not drop anchor in most of the island's waters and that divers may not use gloves unless they're needed for ascending or descending a line.

Because the island has so zealously protected its marine environment, Bonaire offers an amazing diversity of underwater life. Turtles, rays, and fish of every imaginable color abound in the pristine waters of the park. The charge ($10 for swimmers and snorkelers, $25 for divers) for a swimming or diving tag allows unlimited use of the park for a year, and every cent goes toward the care and management of the Bonaire Marine Park. It's money well spent, islanders and most visitors will tell you.

shallowest and most popular sites in a two-reef complex that includes Alice in Wonderland. The boulder-size green-and-tan coral heads are home to black margates, Spanish hogfish, gray snappers, stingrays, and large purple tube sponges.

Bari Reef. Catch a glimpse of the elkhorn and fire coral, queen angelfish, and other wonders of Bari Reef, just off the Sand Dollar Condominium Resort's pier.

★ **Calabas Reef.** Off the coast of the Divi Flamingo Resort, this is the island's busiest dive site. It's replete with Christmas-tree worms, sponges, and fire coral adhering to a ship's hull. Fish life is frenzied, with the occasional octopus putting in an appearance.

Forest. You need to catch a boat to reach Forest, a dive site off the southwest coast of Klein Bonaire. Named for the abundant black-coral forests found in it, the site gets a lot of fish action, including a resident spotted eel that lives in a cave.

Rappel. This spectacular site is near the Karpata Ecological Center. The shore is a sheer cliff, and the lush coral growth is the habitat of some unusual varieties of marine life, including occasional orange sea horses, squid, spiny lobsters, and spotted trunkfish.

Small Wall. One of Bonaire's three complete vertical wall dives (and one of its most popular night-diving spots), Small Wall is in front of the Black Durgon Inn, near Barcadera Beach. Because the access to this site is on private property, this is usually a boat-diving site. The 60-foot wall is frequented by squid, turtles, tarpon, and barracuda, and has dense hard and soft coral formations; it also allows for excellent snorkeling.

Something Special. South of the marina entrance at Harbour Village Beach Club, this spot is famous for its garden eels. They wave about from the relatively shallow sand terrace looking like long grass in a breeze.

Town Pier. Known for shielding one of Bonaire's best night dives, the pier is right in town, across from the City Café. Divers need permission from the harbormaster and must be accompanied by a local guide.

Windsock Steep. This excellent shore-dive site (from 20 to 80 feet) is in front of the small beach opposite the airport runway. It's a popular place for snorkeling. The current is moderate, the elkhorn coral profuse; you may also see angelfish and rays.

DIVE OPERATORS

Many of the dive shops listed *below* offer PADI and NAUI certification courses and SSI, as well as underwater photography and videography courses. Some shops are also qualified to certify dive instructors. Full certification courses cost approximately $385; open-water refresher courses run about $240; a one-tank boat dive with unlimited shore diving costs about $40; a two-tank boat dive with unlimited shore diving is about $65. As for equipment, renting a mask, fin, and snorkel costs about $12 all together; for a BC (buoyancy compensator) and regulator, expect to pay about $20. Check out children's programs such as Aquakids and Ocean Classroom—or inquire about their equivalents.

Most dive shops on Bonaire offer a complete range of snorkel gear for rent and will provide beginner training; some dive operations also offer guided snorkeling and night snorkeling. The cost for a guided snorkel session is about $50 and includes slide presentations, transportation to the site, and a tour. Gear rental is approximately $10 per 24-hour period.

☺ **Bonaire Dive & Adventure.** For first-timers who want a stress-free introduction to the sport, Bonaire Dive & Adventure is probably the best choice. ⊠ *Sand Dollar Condominium Resort, Kaya Gobernador N. Debrot 77A, Kralendijk* ☎ *599/717–2229* ⊕ *www.bonairediveandadventure.com.*

Bonaire Scuba Center ⊠ *Black Durgon Inn, Kaya Gobernador N. Debrot 145, Kralendijk* ☎ *599/717–5736.*

Bruce Bowker's Carib Inn Dive Center ⊠ *J.A. Abraham Blvd. 46, Kralendijk* ☎ *599/717–8819* ⊕ *www.caribinn.com.*

☺ **Buddy Dive Resort** ⊠ *Kaya Gobernador N. Debrot 85, Kralendijk* ☎ *599/717–5080* ⊕ *www.buddydive.com.*

Captain Don's Habitat Dive Shop ⊠ *Kaya Gobernador N. Debrot 113, Kralendijk* ☎ *599/717–8290* ⊕ *www.habitatbonaire.com.*

Dive Friends Bonaire ⊠ *Kaya Grandi 6, Kralendijk* ☎ *599/717–3911* ⊕ *www.dive-friends-bonaire.com.*

★ **Divi Dive Bonaire** ⊠ *Divi Flamingo Resort & Casino, J.A. Abraham Blvd. 40, Kralendijk* ☎ *599/717–8285* ⊕ *www.diviflamingo.com.*

☺ ★ **Larry's Shore & Wild Side Diving.** Run by a former army combat diver, Larry's Shore & Wild Side Diving offers a variety of appealing options ranging from the leisurely to downright scary. This company has become an extremely popular choice, so try to book as early as possible. ☎ *599/790–9156* ⊕ *www.larryswildsidediving.com.*

☺ **Toucan Diving.** The Aquakids program—for children ages 5 to 12—is offered by Toucan Diving. ⊠ *Plaza Resort Bonaire, J.A. Abraham Blvd. 80, Kralendijk* ☎ *599/717–2500* ⊕ *www.toucandiving.com.*

Touch the Sea with Dee Scarr *599/717–8529* ⊕ *www.touchthesea.com.*

Wannadive ⊠ *Eden Beach Resort, Kaya Gobernador N. Debrot 73, on the beach* ☎ *599/717–8884* ⊕ *www.wannadivebonaire.com.*

FISHING

Multifish Charters. This operator rents 20-foot fishing boats; the cost is $95 for a half day, $180 for a full day. ☎ *599/786–1228* ⊕ *www. bonairefishing.net.*

Piscatur Charters. Piscatur Charters offers light-tackle angler reef fishing for jackfish, barracuda, and snapper. Rates are $475 for a half day. You can charter the 42-foot Sport Fisherman *Piscatur,* which carries up to six people, for $550 for a half day, $700 for a full day. ⊠ *Kaya H.J. Pop 3, Kralendijk* ☎ *599/717–8774* ⊕ *www.piscatur.com.*

GUIDED TOURS

Achie Tours. This tour operator offers several half- and full-day options. ⊠ *Kaya Nikiboko Noord 33, Kralendijk* ☎ *599/717–8630.*

Bonaire Tours & Vacations. Bonaire Tours & Vacations will chauffeur you around on two-hour tours of either the island's north or south sides. An all-day tour of Washington Park ($80), which includes lunch and a snorkel, is also offered. ⊠ *Kaya Gobernador N. Debrot 79, Kralendijk* ☎ *599/717–8778* ⊕ *www.bonairetours.com.*

Or simply ask any taxi driver for an island tour (be sure to negotiate the price up front).

HORSEBACK RIDING

☉ **Riding Academy Club.** You can take hour-long trail rides at the 166-acre Riding Academy Club for $120. A guide takes you through groves of cacti where iguanas, wild goats, donkeys, and flamingos reside; there is even an opportunity to swim with the horses. Reserve one of the gentle pintos or Paso Finos a day in advance, and try to go early in the morning, when it's cool. Tours are available by reservation only and are limited to two people. ⊠ *Near airport, east of Kralendijk* ☎ *599/560–7949, 599/786–2094.*

KAYAKING

Divers and snorkelers can use kayaks to reach otherwise inaccessible dive sites and simply tow the craft along during their dive. Nondivers can take advantage of the calm waters around the island to explore the coastline and the fascinating stands of mangrove around the Lac Bay area. The mangrove harbors myriad wildlife and acts as a hatchery for marine life. Almost all of the kayaks used are of the sit-on-top variety, which are able to negotiate shallow waters better.

Bonaire Dive & Adventure. This operator rents kayaks and also leads guided trips. ⊠ *Kaya Gobernador N. Debrot 79, Kralendijk* ☎ *599/717–2229,* ⊕ *www.bonairediveandadventure.com.*

Jibe City. At Jibe City, which is primarily a windsurfing outfit, kayaks are free if you are renting surf equipment. Otherwise, they go for $10 (single) and $15 (double) for the first two hours; $25 and $30, respectively, per half day. ⊠ *Sorobon Beach* ☎ *599/717–5233,* ⊕ *www.jibecity. com* ⊘ *Closed Sept.*

★ **Mangrove Info & Kayak Center.** Mangrove Info & Kayak Center offers guided kayak tours of the mangrove forest at 9 am and 11 am daily, for $27 an hour and $46 for two hours. The center houses a unique mangrove aquarium designed to study the Lac Bay mangroves' effect on the global ecosystem as well as a photo gallery showing underwater existence within the forest like never before. The tours are pleasant even for the exercise-challenged and usually provide a great way to work on your tan. The two-hour tour includes snorkeling and is a lot more fun. ⊠ *Kaminda Lac 141, on road to Lac Cai, Lac Bay* ☎ *599/780–5353* ⊕ *www.mangrovecenter.com.*

WINDSURFING

With near-constant breezes and calm waters, Bonaire is consistently ranked among the best places in the world for windsurfing. Lac Bay, a protected cove on the east coast, is ideal for windsurfing. The island's windsurfing companies are headquartered there on Sorobon Beach.

★ **Bonaire Windsurf Place.** The Bonaire Windsurf Place, commonly referred to as "the Place," rents the latest Hot Sails Maui, Starboard, and RRD equipment for $144 for a two-day rental. A one-hour group lesson costs $50; private lessons are $80 per hour (these rates do not include equipment, which adds at least $40 to the price). Groups are generally limited to four people. Owners Elvis, Roger, and Constantine are all former windsurfing champs. ⊠ *Sorobon Beach* ☎ *599/717–2288* ⊕ *www.bonairewindsurfplace.com.*

Jibe City. Jibe City offers lessons for $50 (includes board and sail for beginners only); board rentals start at $25 an hour, $50 for a half day. There are pickups at all the hotels at 9 am and 1 pm; ask your hotel to make arrangements. ⊠ *Sorobon Beach* ☎ *599/717–5233* ⊕ *www. jibecity.com.*

British Virgin Islands

WORD OF MOUTH

"We loved our time on Tortola. Go to Quito's at night, [Bomba's Surfside] Shack . . . if you can, head over to Jost van Dyke. Just make sure to check out the cruise ship schedules!"

—DavefromCA

WELCOME TO BRITISH VIRGIN ISLANDS

NATURE'S LITTLE SECRETS

Most of the 60-some islands, islets, and cays that make up the British Virgin Islands (BVI) are remarkably hilly and volcanic in origin, having exploded from the depths of the sea some 25 million years ago. The exception is Anegada, which is a flat coral-limestone atoll. Tortola (about 10 square miles/26 square km) is the largest member of the chain.

The British Virgin Islands are mostly quiet and casual, so don't expect to party until dawn, and definitely leave the tux at home. Luxury here means getting away from it all rather than getting the trendiest state-of-the-art amenities. And the jackpot is the chance to explore the many islets and cays by sailboat.

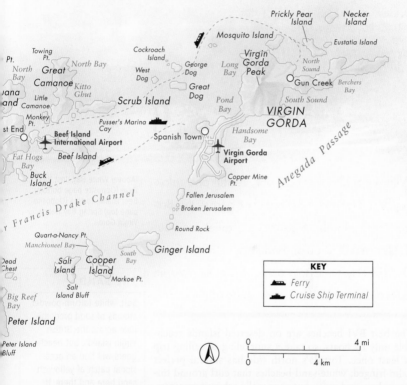

TOP REASONS TO VISIT BRITISH VIRGIN ISLANDS

1 The Perfect Place to Sail: With more than 60 islands in the chain, sailors can drop anchor at a different, perfect beach every day.

2 Low-Key Resorts: Laid-back (but luxurious) resorts offer a full-scale retreat from your everyday life.

3 Diving and Snorkeling: Both are great, and vibrant reefs are often just feet from the shore.

4 Jost Van Dyke: Your trip isn't complete until you've chilled at the casual beach bars here.

5 Few Crowds: There's no mass tourism; the farther you get from Tortola, the quieter things become.

BVI BEACHES

With a couple of exceptions, restful and relaxing best describe most beaches across the British Virgin Islands. If peace and quiet are your goals, avoid popular beaches such as Cane Garden Bay on Tortola and The Baths on Virgin Gorda on days when cruise ships are in port.

(Above) White Bay, Jost Van Dyke (Opposite page bottom) Beef Island, Tortola (Opposite page top) Spring Bay Beach, Virgin Gorda

THE SAND

Soft, white talcum-powder strands of sand predominate across the British Virgin Islands, but beachgoers will find an occasional patch of yellowish sand here and there. If you have to draw a line in the sand, Virgin Gorda has the best selection of beaches, but you'll find similar beaches out near the airport on Tortola.

The best BVI beaches are on deserted islands reachable only by boats, so take a snorkeling or sailing trip at least once. Tortola's north side has several perfect palm-fringed, white-sand beaches that curl around turquoise bays and coves, but none really achieves greatness. Nearly all are accessible by car (preferably a four-wheel-drive vehicle), albeit down bumpy roads that corkscrew precipitously. Some of these beaches are lined with bars and restaurants as well as water-sports equipment stalls; others have absolutely nothing.

Anybody going to Virgin Gorda must experience swimming or snorkeling among its unique boulder formations, which can be visited at several sites along Lee Road. The most popular is The Baths, but there are several other similar places nearby that are easily reached.

For complete information on these beaches, see individual beach sections within the chapter.

TORTOLA

Apple Bay, including nearby Little Apple Bay and Capoon's Bay, is your spot if you want to surf—although the white, sandy beach itself is narrow. If you're swimming and the waves are up, take care not to get dashed on the rocks. **Cane Garden Bay** is a silky stretch of sand with exceptionally calm, crystalline waters—except when storms at sea turn the water murky. Snorkeling is good along the edges. **Long Bay, Beef Island** has superlative scenery: the beach stretches seemingly forever, and you can catch a glimpse of Little Camanoe and Great Camanoe islands. If you walk around the bend to the right, you can see little Marina Cay and Scrub Island. Long Bay is also a good place to search for seashells. Swim out to wherever you see a dark patch for some nice snorkeling. **Long Bay West** is a stunning, mile-long stretch of white sand; have your camera ready to snap the breathtaking approach. The entire beach is open to the public. **Smuggler's Cove,** a beautiful, palm-fringed beach, is down a pothole-filled dirt road. You probably won't be alone on weekends, though, when the beach fills with snorkelers and sunbathers. There's a fine view of Jost Van Dyke from the shore.

VIRGIN GORDA

The Baths is a national park that features a stunning maze of huge granite boulders that extend into the sea. It's usually crowded midday with day-trippers. The snorkeling is good, and you're likely to see a wide variety of fish, but watch out for dinghies coming ashore from the numerous sailboats anchored offshore. **Nail Bay,** at the island's north tip, will reward you with a trio of beaches within the Nail Bay Resort complex that are ideal for snorkeling. Mountain Trunk Bay is perfect for beginners, and Nail Bay and Long Bay beaches have coral caverns just offshore. **Savannah Bay** is a wonderfully private beach close to Spanish Town. It may not always be completely deserted, but you can find a spot to yourself on this long stretch of soft, white sand. **Spring Bay Beach** is a national-park beach that gets much less traffic than the nearby Baths, and has the similarly large, imposing boulders that create interesting grottoes for swimming. The snorkeling is excellent, and the grounds include swings and picnic tables.

JOST VAN DYKE

Sandy Cay is a gleaming scimitar of white sand, with marvelous snorkeling. **White Bay** has a long stretch of white sand that is especially popular with boaters who come ashore for a libation at one of the beach bars.

7

Updated by
Lynda Lohr
and Susanna
Henighan
Potter

Once a collection of about 60 sleepy islands and cays, the British Virgin Islands—particularly the main island of Tortola—now see huge cruise ships crowding the dock outside Road Town. Shoppers clog the downtown area, and traffic occasionally comes to a standstill. Even the second-largest island, Virgin Gorda, gets its share of smaller ships anchored off the main village of Spanish Town. Despite this explosive growth in the territory's tourism industry, it's still easy to escape the hubbub. Hotels outside Road Town usually provide a quiet oasis, and those on the other islands can be downright serene.

Each island has a different flavor. Want access to lots of restaurants and shopping? Make Tortola your choice. The largest of the BVIs, it covers 10 square miles (26 square km) and sits only a mile from St. John in the United States Virgin Islands (USVI). If you want to kick back at a small hotel or posh resort, try Virgin Gorda. Sitting nearly at the end of the chain, the 8-square-miles (21-square-km) island offers stellar beaches and a laid-back atmosphere. If you really want to get away from it all, the outermost islands, including Anegada and Jost Van Dyke, will fill the bill. Some of the smallest—Norman, Peter, Cooper, and Necker—are home to just one resort or restaurant. Others remain uninhabited specks on the horizon.

Visitors have long visited the BVI, starting with Christopher Columbus in 1493. He called the islands Las Once Mil Virgines—the 11,000 Virgins—in honor of the 11,000 virgin companions of St. Ursula, martyred in the 4th century AD. Pirates and buccaneers followed, and then came the British, who farmed the islands until slavery was abolished in 1834. The BVI are still politically tied to Britain, so the queen appoints a royal governor, but residents elect a local Legislative Council. Offshore banking and tourism share top billing in the territory's economy, but the

LOGISTICS

Getting to the BVI: There are no nonstop flights to the BVI from the United States. Most travelers connect in San Juan or St. Thomas. You can fly to Tortola, Virgin Gorda, or Anegada, but only on a small plane. There are also ferries from St. Thomas, with regular service to Tortola and Virgin Gorda.

Hassle Factor: Medium to high.

On the Ground: Although taxi service is good, you may wish to rent a car on Tortola or Virgin Gorda to explore farther afield or try many different beaches (you may need to if you are staying at an isolated resort).

On Anegada it's possible to rent a car, but most people rely on taxis for transportation. Jost Van Dyke has a single road, and visitors travel on foot or by local taxi.

Getting Around the Islands: Most people take ferries to get from island to island, though flights are possible (some are regularly scheduled, or there are plenty of charter opportunities if you are traveling in a group). Once on the ground, you'll find that taxi rates aren't set in the BVI and have to be negotiated. Your hotel or villa manager can help with expected fares.

majority of the islands' jobs are tourism-related. Despite the growth, you can usually find a welcoming smile.

PLANNING

WHEN TO GO

High season doesn't really get into full swing until Christmas and ends sooner (usually by April 1) than on most Caribbean islands. In the off-season, rates can be a third less. Locals and yachties gather at Foxy's bar on Jost Van Dyke for the annual **St. Patrick's Day** celebration in March.

Glimpse the colorful spinnakers as sailing enthusiasts gather for the internationally known **BVI Spring Regatta and Sailing Festival,** which begins during the last week in March and continues until the first weekend in April. Tortola celebrates **Carnival** on and around August 1 to mark the anniversary of the end of slavery in 1834. A slew of activities culminating with a parade through the streets take place in Road Town. Hotels fill up fast, so make sure to reserve your room and rental car well in advance.

In August you can also try your hand at sportfishing, as anglers compete to land the largest catch at the **BVI Sportfishing Tournament.**

GETTING HERE AND AROUND

AIR TRAVEL

Several airlines have regularly scheduled service to either Tortola or Virgin Gorda. Although it may be cheaper to fly via Puerto Rico, the connections are better through St. Thomas. If you have seven or more people in your party, you can also charter a plane from St. Thomas or San Juan.

Airports Tortola (TOC), Virgin Gorda (VIJ), and Anegada (no code).

Airline Contacts Air Sunshine ☎ *800/327–8900, 800/435–8900 in Florida, 888/879–8900 in USVI, 284/495–8900 in BVI* ⊕ *www.airsunshine.com.* **American Airlines/American Eagle** ☎ *800/433–7300, 340/776–2560 in St. Thomas, 340/778–2000 in St. Croix, 284/340–1128 in Tortola* ⊕ *www.aa.com.* **Cape Air** ☎ *800/352–0714, 284/495–1440 in Tortola* ⊕ *www.flycapeair.com.* **Fly BVI** ☎ *284/495–1747* ⊕ *www.bviaircharters.com).* **LIAT** ☎ *888/844–5428, 866/549–5428 in USVI, 284/495–1596 in Tortola* ⊕ *www.liat.com.*

Airport Transfers Mahogany Rentals and Taxi Service ✉ *The Valley, Virgin Gorda* ☎ *284/495–5469* ⊕ *www.mahoganycarrentalsbvi.com.*

BOAT AND FERRY TRAVEL

Frequent daily ferries connect Tortola with St. Thomas (both Charlotte Amalie and Red Hook) and St. John. Ferries also link Tortola with Jost Van Dyke, Peter Island, and Virgin Gorda. Tortola has three ferry terminals—one at West End, one on Beef Island (at the airport), and one in Road Town. Schedules vary, and not all companies make daily trips. All Red Hook–bound ferries stop in Cruz Bay to clear customs and immigration.

Ferries also connect Virgin Gorda with St. Thomas (both Charlotte Amalie and Red Hook) and St. John, but not daily. All Red Hook–bound ferries stop in Cruz Bay to clear customs and immigration. Ferries to Virgin Gorda land in Spanish Town. Schedules vary by day, and not all companies make daily trips.

The BVI Tourist Board website ⊕ *www.bvitourism.com/inter-island-ferries* has links to all the ferry companies, and these sites are the best sources for ever-changing routes and schedules.

CAR TRAVEL

Driving in the BVI is on the left, British style, but your car will always have its steering wheel on the left, as in the United States. Your valid U.S. license will also do for driving in the BVI. The minimum age to rent a car is 25. Most agencies offer both four-wheel-drive vehicles and cars (often compacts). Both Tortola and Virgin Gorda have a number of car-rental agencies.

Tortola Car-Rental Contacts Avis ✉ *Opposite police station, Road Town* ☎ *284/494–3322* ⊕ *www.avis.com* ✉ *Towers, West End* ☎ *284/495–4973.* **D&D** ✉ *West End Rd., West End* ☎ *284/495–4765.* **Dollar** ✉ *Long Bay Beach Resort, Long Bay* ☎ *284/495–4252* ⊕ *www.dollar.com* ✉ *East End* ☎ *284/494–6093.* **Hertz** ✉ *West End* ☎ *284/495–4405* ⊕ *www.hertz.com* ✉ *Airport, Beef Island* ☎ *284/495–6600* ✉ *Road Town* ☎ *284/494–6228.* **Itgo Car Rental** ✉ *Wickham's Cay I, Road Town* ☎ *284/494–2639* ⊕ *www.itgobvi.com.* **National** ✉ *Airport, Beef Island* ☎ *284/495–2626* ⊕ *www.national.com* ✉ *Duffs Bottom, Road Town* ☎ *284/494–3197.*

Virgin Gorda Car-Rental Contacts L&S Jeep Rental ✉ *South Valley, Virgin Gorda* ☎ *284/495–5297* ⊕ *www.landsjeeprental.com.* **Mahogany Rentals & Taxi Service** ✉ *Spanish Town, Virgin Gorda* ☎ *284/495–5469* ⊕ *www.mahoganycarrentalsbvi.com.* **Speedy's Car Rentals** ✉ *The Valley, Virgin Gorda* ☎ *284/495–5240* ⊕ *www.speedysbvi.com.*

TAXI TRAVEL

Taxi rates aren't set in the BVI, so you should negotiate the fare with your driver before you start your trip. Fares are per destination, not per person here, so it's cheaper to travel in groups. The taxi number is always on the license plate.

Tortola Taxi Contacts BVI Taxi Association ☎ *284/494–3942.* **Waterfront Taxi Association** ☎ *284/494–6362.* **West End Taxi Association** ☎ *284/495–4934.*

Virgin Gorda Taxi Contacts Andy's Taxi and Jeep Rental ✉ *The Valley, Virgin Gorda* ☎ *284/495–5252.* **Mahogany Rentals and Taxi Service** ✉ *The Valley, Virgin Gorda* ☎ *284/495–5469* ⊕ *www.mahoganycrrentalsbvi.com.*

ESSENTIALS

Banks and Exchange Services The currency in the BVI is the U.S. dollar. ATMs are common in Road Town, Tortola, and around Virgin Gorda Yacht Harbour.

Electricity 110 volts, the same as in North America, so American appliances work just fine.

Emergency Services In an emergency, dial ☎ *999.*

Passport Requirements All travelers going to the British Virgin Islands need to have a valid passport, even if they are traveling by private yacht.

Phones The area code for the BVI is 284; when you make calls from North America, you need to dial only the area code and the number. To call anywhere in the BVI once you've arrived, dial all seven digits. A local call from a pay phone costs 25¢, but such phones are sometimes on the blink. An alternative is a Caribbean phone card, available in $5, $10, and $20 denominations. They're sold at most major hotels and many stores and can be used to call within the BVI, as well as all over the Caribbean, and to access **USADirect** (☎ *800/872–2881, 111 from a pay phone*) from special phone-card phones. For credit-card or collect long-distance calls to the United States, use a phone-card telephone or look for special USADirect phones, which are linked directly to an AT&T operator. USADirect and pay phones can be found at most hotels and in towns.

Taxes The departure tax is $5 per person by boat and $20 per person by plane. There are separate booths at the airport and ferry terminals to collect this tax, which must be paid in cash in U.S. currency. Most hotels add a service charge ranging from 5% to 18% to the bill. A few restaurants and some shops tack on an additional 10% charge if you use a credit card. There's no sales tax in the BVI. However, there's a 7% government tax on hotel rooms.

ACCOMMODATIONS

Pick your island carefully, because each is different, as are the logistics of getting there. **Tortola** gives you a wider choice of restaurants, shopping, and resorts. **Virgin Gorda** has fewer off-resort places to eat and shop, but the resorts themselves are often better, and the beaches are wonderful. **Anegada** is remote and better suited for divers. **Jost Van Dyke** has some classic Caribbean beach bars, along with fairly basic accommodations.

When you want to be pampered and pampered some more, consider a remote, **private-island resort** reached only by ferry, or even one of the appealing outer-island resorts that are still somewhat affordable for mere mortals.

If you want to enjoy everything the BVI have to offer, **charter a sailboat** so you can drop anchor where and when you want.

The largest resort in the British Virgin Islands has 120-some rooms, and most have considerably fewer. Luxury here is more about personal service than over-the-top amenities. The best places are certainly comfortable, but they aren't showy. You'll find **villas and condos** in abundance, and they are a good option for families.

HOTEL AND RESTAURANT PRICES

Prices in the restaurant reviews are the average cost of a main course at dinner or, if dinner is not served, at lunch; taxes and service charges are generally included. Prices in the hotel reviews are the lowest cost of a standard double room in high season, excluding taxes, service charges, and meal plans (except at all-inclusives). Prices for rentals are the lowest per-night cost for a one-bedroom unit in high season.

VISITOR INFORMATION

Contacts BVI Tourist Board ☎ *212/563–3117, 800/835–8530 in New York* ⊕ *www.bvitourism.com.*

WEDDINGS

You must apply in person for your license ($110) weekdays at the attorney general's office in Road Town, Tortola. You must wait three days to pick it up at the registrar's office in Road Town. If you plan to be married in a church, announcements (called *banns* locally) must be published for three consecutive Sundays in the church bulletin. Only the registrar or clergy can perform ceremonies. The registrar charges $35 at the office and $100 at another location. No blood test is required.

Contacts BVI Wedding Planners and Consultants ☎ *284/494–5306* ⊕ *www.bviweddings.com.*

TORTOLA

By Lynda Lohr   Once a sleepy backwater, Tortola is definitely busy these days, particularly when several cruise ships tie up at the Road Town dock. Passengers crowd the streets and shops, and open-air jitneys filled with cruise-ship passengers create bottlenecks on the island's byways. That said, most folks visit Tortola to relax on its deserted sands or linger over lunch at one of its many delightful restaurants. Beaches are never more than a few miles away, and the steep green hills that form Tortola's spine are fanned by gentle trade winds. The neighboring islands glimmer like emeralds in a sea of sapphire. It can be a world far removed from the hustle of modern life, but it simply doesn't compare to Virgin Gorda in terms of beautiful beaches—or even luxury resorts, for that matter.

Initially settled by Taíno Indians, Tortola saw a string of visitors over the years. Christopher Columbus sailed by in 1493 on his second voyage to the New World, and ships from Spain, Holland, and France made periodic visits about a century later. Sir Francis Drake arrived in 1595, leaving his name on the passage between Tortola and St. John. Pirates and buccaneers followed, with the British finally laying claim to the island in the late 1600s. In 1741 John Pickering became the first lieutenant governor of Tortola, and the seat of the British government moved from Virgin Gorda to Tortola. As the agrarian economy continued to grow, slaves were imported from Africa. The slave trade was abolished in 1807, but slaves in Tortola and the rest of the BVI did not gain their freedom until August 1, 1834, when the Emancipation Proclamation was read at Sunday Morning Well in Road Town. That date is celebrated every year with the island's annual Carnival.

Visitors have a choice of accommodations, but most fall into the small and smaller-still categories. Only Long Bay Resort on Tortola's North Shore qualifies as a resort, but even some of the smaller properties add an amenity or two. A couple of new hotel projects are in the works, so look for more growth in the island's hotel industry over the next decade.

EXPLORING TORTOLA

Tortola doesn't have many historic sights, but it does have lots of beautiful natural scenery. Although you could explore the island's 10 square miles (26 square km) in a few hours, opting for such a whirlwind tour would be a mistake. There's no need to live in the fast lane when you're surrounded by some of the Caribbean's most breathtaking panoramas. Also, the roads are extraordinarily steep and twisting, making driving demanding. The best strategy is to explore a bit of the island at a time. For example, you might try Road Town (the island's tiny metropolis) one morning and a drive to Cane Garden Bay and the little town of West End the next afternoon. Or consider a visit to East End, a *very* tiny town exactly where its name suggests. The North Shore is where all the best beaches are found. Sights are best seen when you stumble on them on your round-the-island drive.

ROAD TOWN AND ENVIRONS

The bustling capital of the BVI looks out over Road Harbour. It takes only an hour or so to stroll down Main Street and along the waterfront, checking out the traditional West Indian buildings painted in pastel colors and with corrugated-tin roofs, bright shutters, and delicate fretwork trim. For sightseeing brochures and the latest information on everything from taxi rates to ferry schedules, stop in at the BVI Tourist Board office. Or just choose a seat on one of the benches in Sir Olva Georges Square, on Waterfront Drive, and watch the people come and go from the ferry dock and customs office across the street.

Dolphin Discovery. Get up close and personal with dolphins as they swim in a spacious seaside pen. There are three different programs. In the Royal Swim, dolphins tow participants around the pen. The less expensive Adventure and Discovery programs allow you to touch the dolphins. ⊠ *Prospect Reef Resort, Road Town* ☎ *284/494–7675, 888/393–5158* ⊕ *www.dolphindiscovery.com* ⊴ *Royal Swim $149, Adventure $99, Discovery $79* ☉ *Royal Swim daily at 10, noon, 2, and 4. Adventure and Discovery daily at 11 and 1.*

The Chikuzen

J. R. O'Neal Botanic Gardens ♦

Treasure Isle Rd.

Waterfront Dr.

FREE BOTTOM

Wickhams Cay Rd

PORT PURCELL

1 Wickhams Cay 2

Long Bush Rd.

Waterfront

1

2

Wickhams Cay 1

Peter Island Ferry ♦

6

BLYDEN YARD

Main St.

5 ♦ Romasco Place

2 **3**

ROAD TOWN

♦ Sir Olva Georga's Plaza

4 ♦ Ferry Dock

Watling Rd.

♦ Customs House

Road Bay

Fort Charlotte Rd.

Old Government House Museum

Cedar Rd.

7 ♦

Careening Cove

Burnt Point

0   1/4 mi

0   1/4 km

Fort Burt ♦

MacNamara Rd.

ROAD REEF

Road Town

Rough Pt.

Shark Bay

Hell Hole

Brewers Bay Pinnacle

Brewers Bay

Brewers Bay

Dubois Pt.

Mt. Healthy National Park ♦

Todman Pk.

Skyworld

15

Cane Garden Bay Rd.

Ridge Rd.

Joe's Hill Rd.

Leonard's ○

Road Town see inset

13 **8**

14

Cane Garden Bay ○

A T L A N T I C   O C E A N

Windy Hill

Carrot Bay ○

Sage Mountain National Park ♦

Ridge Rd.

10 **5**

Apple Bay

Lower Belmont Bay

Long Bay West

12 **7**

Sage Mtn.

16

Dolphin Discovery

Great Thatch Island

Smuggler's Cove

11 **6**

Sea Cows Bay

Sea Cows Bay

Steele Pt.

Zion Hill Rd.

Freshwater Pond

3

Soper's Hole

9

○ West End

Little Thatch Island

8 ○

Soper's Hole

Frenchman's Cay

4 ♦ **Fort Recovery**

← TO ST. THOMAS

0   2 mi

0   2 km

The Indians

Tortola

TO ANEGADA →

Longman's Pt.

Muskmellon Bay

North Bay

Guana Island

White Bay

Monkey Pt.

Rogue's Pt.

Ridge Rd.

Buta Mt.

Mt. Belle-Vue

Baughers Bay

Ft. Shirley

Wickhams Cay

Road Harbour

Long Look

Parham Town

Long Swamp

12

Elizabeth Beach

Little Camanoe

East End

Long Bay, Beef Island

10

Beef Island International Airport

17 **9**

Buck Island

Paraquita Bay

Fat Hogs Bay

Bluff Bay

Beef Island

Wash Ballock Pt.

Great Camanoe

Lee Bay

Kitto Ghut

Scrub Island

Marina Cay

11

Trellis Bay

TO VIRGIN GORDA →

Sir Francis Drake Channel

13

KEY	
☂	Beaches
◩	Dive Sites
⛴	Ferry
🚢	Cruise Ship Terminal
1	Restaurants
1	Hotels
....	Trail

Blonde Rock
Painted Walls
RMS Rhone

Ft. Burt. The most intact historic ruin on Tortola was built by the Dutch in the early 17th century to safeguard Road Harbour. It sits on a hill at the western edge of Road Town and is now the site of a small hotel and restaurant. The foundations and magazine remain, and the structure offers a commanding view of the harbor. ⊠ *Waterfront Dr., Road Town* 🕾 *No phone* 🖃 *Free* 🕙 *Daily dawn–dusk.*

★ **J.R. O'Neal Botanic Gardens.** Take a walk through this 4-acre showcase of lush plant life. There are sections devoted to prickly cacti and succulents, hothouses for ferns and orchids, gardens of medicinal herbs, and plants and trees indigenous to the seashore. From the tourist office

DRIVING ON TORTOLA

Tortola's main roads are well paved, for the most part, but there are exceptionally steep hills and sharp curves. Road Town's traffic and parking can be horrific. Try to avoid driving along the Waterfront Drive at morning and afternoon rush hours. It's longer, but often quicker, to take a route through the hills above Road Town. Parking can be very difficult in Road Town, particularly during the busy winter season. There's parking along the waterfront and on the inland side on the eastern end of downtown.

in Road Town, cross Waterfront Drive and walk one block over to Main Street and turn right. Keep walking until you see the high school. The gardens are on your left. ⊠ *Botanic Station, Road Town* 🕾 *284/494–3650* ⊕ *www.bvinationalparkstrust.org* 🖃 *$3* 🕙 *Mon.–Sat. 8:30–4:30.*

Fodor'sChoice **Old Government House Museum.** The official government residence until ★ 1997, this gracious building now displays a nice collection of artifacts from Tortola's past. The rooms are filled with period furniture, hand-painted china, books signed by Queen Elizabeth II on her 1966 and 1977 visits, and numerous items reflecting Tortola's seafaring legacy. ⊠ *Waterfront Dr., Road Town* 🕾 *284/494–4091* 🖃 *$3* 🕙 *Weekdays 9–3.*

WEST END

Ft. Recovery. The unrestored ruins of a 17th-century Dutch fort sit amid a profusion of tropical greenery on the grounds of Fort Recovery Beachfront Villas and Suites. There's not much to see here, and there are no guided tours, but you're welcome to stop by and poke around. ⊠ *Waterfront Dr., Pockwood Pond* 🕾 *284/495–4467* 🖃 *Free.*

Soper's Hole. On this little island connected by a causeway to Tortola's western end, you can find a marina and a captivating complex of pastel West Indian–style buildings with shady balconies, shuttered windows, and gingerbread trim that house art galleries, boutiques, and restaurants. Pusser's Landing is a lively place to stop for a cold drink (many are made with Pusser's famous rum) and a sandwich and to watch the boats in the harbor. ⊠ *Soper's Hole.*

NORTH SHORE

Cane Garden Bay. Once a sleepy village, Cane Garden Bay has become one of Tortola's most important destinations. Stay at a small hotel or guesthouse here, or stop by for lunch, dinner, or drinks at a seaside restaurant. You can find a few small stores selling clothing and basics such as suntan lotion, and one of Tortola's most popular beaches is at

Old Government House Museum, Road Town

your feet. The roads in and out of this area are dauntingly steep, so use caution when driving. ⊠ *Tortola*.

MID-ISLAND

Mount Healthy National Park. The remains of an 18th-century sugar plantation can be seen here. The windmill structure has been restored, and you can see the ruins of a mill, a factory with boiling houses, storage areas, stables, a hospital, and many dwellings. It's a nice place to picnic. ⊠ *Ridge Rd., Todman Peak* ☎ *No phone* ⊕ *www.bvinationalparkstrust. org* ✉ *Free* ⊘ *Daily dawn–dusk*.

★ **Sage Mountain National Park.** At 1,716 feet, Sage Mountain is the highest peak in the BVI. From the parking area, a trail leads you in a loop not only to the peak itself (and extraordinary views) but also to a small rain forest that is sometimes shrouded in mist. Most of the forest was cut down over the centuries for timber, to create pastureland, or for growing sugarcane, cotton, and other crops. In 1964 this park was established to preserve what remained. Up here you can see mahogany trees, white cedars, mountain guavas, elephant-ear vines, mamey trees, and giant bullet woods, to say nothing of such birds as mountain doves and thrushes. Take a taxi from Road Town or drive up Joe's Hill Road and make a left onto Ridge Road toward Chalwell and Doty villages. The road dead-ends at the park. ⊠ *Ridge Rd., Sage Mountain* ☎ *284/852–3650* ⊕ *www.bvinationalparkstrust.org* ✉ *$3* ⊘ *Daily dawn–dusk*.

★ **Skyworld.** Drive up here and climb the observation tower for a stunning 360-degree view of numerous islands and cays. On a clear day you can even see St. Croix (40 miles [64 km] away) and Anegada (20 miles [32 km] away). ⊠ *Ridge Rd., Joe's Hill* ☎ *No phone* ✉ *Free*.

BEACHES

WEST END

Long Bay West. This beach is a stunning, mile-long stretch of white sand; have your camera ready to snap the breathtaking approach. Although Long Bay Resort sprawls along part of it, the entire beach is open to the public. The water isn't as calm here as at Cane Garden or Brewers Bay, but it's still swimmable. Rent water-sports equipment and enjoy the beachfront restaurant at the resort. Turn left at Zion Hill Road; then travel about half a mile. **Amenities:** food and drink; toilets; water sports. **Best for:** swimming. ⊠ *Long Bay Rd.*

Smuggler's Cove. A beautiful, palm-fringed beach, Smuggler's Cove is down a pothole-filled dirt road. After bouncing your way down, you'll feel as if you've found a hidden piece of the island. You probably won't be alone on weekends, though, when the beach fills with snorkelers and sunbathers. There's a fine view of Jost Van Dyke from the shore. The beach is popular with Long Bay Resort guests who want a change of scenery, but there are no amenities other than vendors selling food and drink during the winter season. Follow Long Bay Road past Long Bay Resort, keeping to the roads nearest the water until you reach the beach. It's about a mile past the resort. **Amenities:** food and drink (in winter season). **Best for:** snorkeling; swimming. ⊠ *Long Bay Rd.*

NORTH SHORE

Apple Bay. Along with nearby Little Apple Bay and Capoon's Bay, this is your spot if you want to surf—although the white, sandy beach itself is narrow. Sebastian's, a casual hotel, caters to those in search of the perfect wave. The legendary Bomba's Surfside Shack—a landmark festooned with all manner of flotsam and jetsam—serves drinks and casual food. Otherwise, there's nothing else in the way of amenities. Good waves are never a sure thing, but you're more apt to find them in January and February. If you're swimming and the waves are up, take care not to get dashed on the rocks. **Amenities:** food and drink; toilets. **Best for:** surfing; swimming. ⊠ *North Shore Rd. at Zion Hill Rd.*

Brewers Bay. This beach is easy to find, but the steep, twisting paved roads leading down the hill to it can be a bit daunting. An old sugar mill and ruins of a rum distillery are off the beach along the road. You can actually reach the beach from either Brewers Bay Road East or Brewers Bay Road West. **Amenities:** none. **Best for:** snorkeling, swimming. ⊠ *Brewers Bay Rd. E, off Cane Garden Bay Rd.*

Cane Garden Bay. A silky stretch of sand, Cane Garden Bay has exceptionally calm, crystalline waters—except when storms at sea turn the water murky. Snorkeling is good along the edges. Casual guesthouses, restaurants, bars, and shops are steps from the beach in the growing village of the same name. The beach is a laid-back, even somewhat funky place to put down your towel. It's the closest beach to Road Town—one steep uphill and downhill drive—and one of the BVI's best-known anchorages (unfortunately, it can be very crowded). Water-sports shops rent equipment. **Amenities:** food and drink; toilets; water sports. **Best for:** snorkeling; swimming. ⊠ *Cane Garden Bay Rd., off Ridge Rd.*

EAST END

Elizabeth Beach. Home to Lambert Beach Resort, Elizabeth Beach is a palm-lined, wide, and sandy beach with parking along its steep downhill access road. Other than at the hotel, which welcomes nonguests, there are no amenities aside from peace and quiet. Turn at the sign for Lambert Beach Resort. If you miss it, you wind up at Her Majesty's Prison. **Amenities:** food and drink; parking; toilets. **Best for:** solitude; swimming. ⊠ *Lambert Rd., off Ridge Rd., on eastern end of island.*

★ **Long Bay, Beef Island.** Long Bay on Beef Island has superlative scenery: the beach stretches seemingly forever, and you can catch a glimpse of Little Camanoe and Great Camanoe islands. If you walk around the bend to the right, you can see little Marina Cay and Scrub Island. Long Bay is also a good place to search for seashells. Swim out to wherever you see a dark patch for some nice snorkeling. There are no amenities, so come prepared with your own drinks and snacks. Turn left shortly after crossing the bridge to Beef Island. **Amenities:** none. **Best for:** snorkeling; swimming. ⊠ *Beef Island Rd., Beef Island.*

> **BVI FERRIES**
>
> BVI ferries can be confusing for newcomers. Ferries depart from three different places in Totola—Road Town, West End, and Beef Island—so make sure you get to the right place at the correct time. Sometimes boats bound for Jost Van Dyke, Virgin Gorda, Anegada, St. Thomas, and St. John depart minutes apart; other times the schedule is skimpy. Departures can be suddenly canceled, particularly in the summer season. To avoid being stranded, always call your ferry company on the morning of departure, and check with the locals catching a ferry if you're still not sure.

7

WHERE TO EAT

Local seafood is plentiful on Tortola, and although other fresh ingredients are scarce, the island's chefs are a creative lot who apply their skills to whatever the boat delivers. Contemporary American dishes with Caribbean influences are very popular, but you can find French and Italian fare as well. The more expensive restaurants have dress codes: long pants and collared shirts for men and elegant but casual resort wear for women. Prices are often a bit higher than they are back home, and the service can be a tad on the slow side, but enjoy the chance to linger over the view.

ROAD TOWN AND VICINITY

$$$

ECLECTIC

✕ **The Boat House.** A popular spot for local yachties, this open-air restaurant dishes up tasty food at very reasonable prices. Try the Caribbean lobster cake served with a curried tartar sauce as an appetizer. The offerings range from a grilled-vegetable and feta-cheese sandwich to chicken Parmesan served with a salad. The blueberry-pineapple cheesecake is divine. $ *Average main: $24* ⊠ *Manuel Reef Marina, Waterfront Dr., Sea Cow's Bay* ☎ *284/495–0007* ⊕ *www.theboathousebvi. com* ☉ *Closed Sun.*

$ ✕ **Capriccio di Mare.** Stop by this casual, authentic Italian outdoor café
ITALIAN for an espresso, a fresh pastry, a bowl of perfectly cooked penne, or a
Fodor'sChoice crispy tomato-and-mozzarella pizza. Drink specialties include a mango
★ Bellini, an adaptation of the famous cocktail served at Harry's Bar
in Venice. ⑤ *Average main: $12* ✉ *Waterfront Dr.* ☎ *284/494–5369*
⌣ *Reservations not accepted* ۞ *Closed Sun.*

$$$ ✕ **The Dove.** The food matches the romantic feeling at this Road Town
ECLECTIC restaurant. Start with jumbo prawns sautéed with a vanilla bean and
almonds before moving on to the mushroom-and-parmesan-crusted
rib-eye steak. Desserts are often new twists on old standards, as with
the soursop crème brûlée. ⑤ *Average main: $29* ✉ *Waterfront Dr.*
☎ *284/494–0313* ۞ *Closed Sun. and Mon. No lunch.*

$$ ✕ **Le Cabanon.** Birds and bougainvillea brighten the patio of this breezy
FRENCH French restaurant and bar, a popular gathering spot for locals and
visitors alike. French onion soup and smoked salmon salad are good
appetizer choices. From there, move on to the grilled tuna with wasabi
sauce, sole in a brown butter sauce, or beef tenderloin with green peppercorn sauce. Save room for such tasty desserts as chocolate cake and
crème brûlée, or opt for a platter of French cheeses. ⑤ *Average main:*
$14 ✉ *Waterfront Dr.* ☎ *284/494–8660* ۞ *Closed Sun.*

$$ ✕ **The Pub.** At this lively waterfront spot tables are arranged along a ter-
ECLECTIC race facing a small marina and the harbor in Road Town. Hamburgers,
salads, and sandwiches are typical lunch offerings. In the evening you
can also choose grilled fish, sautéed conch, sizzling steaks, or barbecued
ribs. There's live entertainment Thursday and Friday, and locals gather
here nightly for spirited games at the pool table. ⑤ *Average main: $18*
✉ *Waterfront Dr.* ☎ *284/494–2608* ⌣ *Reservations not accepted* ۞ *No*
lunch Sun.

$$ ✕ **Pusser's Road Town Pub.** Almost everyone who visits Tortola stops
ECLECTIC here at least once to have a bite to eat and to sample the famous Puss-
۞ er's Rum Painkiller (fruit juices and rum). The nonthreatening menu
includes cheesy pizza, shepherd's pie, fish-and-chips, and hamburgers.
Dine inside in air-conditioned comfort or outside on the verandah,
which looks out on the harbor. ⑤ *Average main: $20* ✉ *Waterfront Dr.*
☎ *284/494–3897* ⊕ *www.pussers.com.*

$$$$ ✕ **Village Cay Restaurant.** Docked sailboats stretch nearly as far as the
ECLECTIC eye can see at this busy Road Town restaurant. Its alfresco dining and
convivial atmosphere make it popular with both locals and visitors.
For lunch, try the grouper club sandwich with an ancho chili mayonnaise. Dinner offerings run to fish served a variety of ways, including
West Indian style with okra, onions, and peppers, as well as a seafood
jambalaya with lobster, crayfish, shrimp, mussels, crab, and fish in a
mango-passion-fruit sauce. ⑤ *Average main: $32* ✉ *Wickhams Cay I*
☎ *284/494–2771.*

$$$ ✕ **Virgin Queen.** The sailing and rugby crowds head here to play darts,
ECLECTIC drink beer, and eat Queen's Pizza—a crusty, cheesy pie topped with sau-
sage, onions, green peppers, and mushrooms. Also on the menu is excel-
lent West Indian and English fare: barbecued ribs with beans and rice,
bangers and mash, shepherd's pie, and grilled sirloin steak. ⑤ *Average*
main: $22 ✉ *Fleming St.* ☎ *284/494–2310* ۞ *Closed Sun. No lunch Sat.*

WEST END

$$$ ✕**Jolly Roger Restaurant.** This casual, open-air restaurant near the ferry
ECLECTIC terminal is as popular with locals as it is with visitors. The menu includes
burgers and rib-eye steaks as well as the island favorite, local lobster.
Try the savory fritters filled with tender local conch and herbs for a good
start to your dinner. End it with a slice of sweet key lime pie. ⑤ *Average
main: $22* ⊠ *West End* ☎ *284/495–4559* ⊕ *www.jollyrogerbvi.com.*

$$$ ✕**Pusser's Landing.** Yachters navigate their way to this waterfront restau-
AMERICAN rant. Downstairs, from late morning to well into the evening, you can
Ⓒ belly up to the outdoor mahogany bar or sit downstairs for sandwiches,
fish-and-chips, and pizzas. At dinnertime head upstairs for a harbor
view and a quiet alfresco meal of grilled steak or fresh fish. ⑤ *Average
main: $30* ⊠ *Soper's Hole* ☎ *284/495–4554* ⊕ *www.pussers.com.*

NORTH SHORE

$$$ ✕**1748 Restaurant.** Relax over dinner in this open-air eatery at Long Bay
INTERNATIONAL Beach Resort. Tables are well spaced, offering enough privacy for inti-
mate conversations. The menu changes daily, but several dishes show up
regularly. Start your meal with a seafood cocktail, creamy carrot soup,
or a mixed green salad. Entrées include grilled London broil served with
a rosemary mushroom sauce, roasted potatoes and vegetables, grilled
tuna steak in a spicy cilantro coconut sauce, and a pesto-marinated
grilled vegetable plate. There are always at least five desserts, and they
might include Belgian chocolate mousse, strawberry cheesecake, or
a fluffy lemon-and-coconut cake. ⑤ *Average main: $21* ⊠ *Long Bay
Beach Resort, Long Bay* ☎ *284/495–4252* ⊕ *www.longbay.com.*

$$$ ✕**Myett's Garden and Grille.** Partly because it's right on the beach, this
ECLECTIC bi-level restaurant and bar is hopping day and night. Chowder made
with fresh conch is the specialty here, and the menu includes vegetarian
dishes as well as grilled shrimp, steak, and tuna. There's live entertainment every night in winter. ⑤ *Average main: $24* ⊠ *Cane Garden Bay*
☎ *284/495–9649* ⊕ *www.myettent.com.*

$$$ ✕**The New Quito's Restaurant.** This rustic beachside bar and restaurant
CARIBBEAN is owned and operated by island native Quito Rymer, a multitalented
recording star who plays and sings solo on Tuesday and Thursday and
performs with his reggae band on Friday. The menu is Caribbean, with
an emphasis on fresh fish; try the conch fritters or the barbecue chicken.
⑤ *Average main: $24* ⊠ *Cane Garden Bay* ☎ *284/495–4837* ⊕ *www.
quitorymer.com.*

$$$ ✕**Sebastian's Beach Bar and Restaurant.** The waves practically lap at your
ECLECTIC feet at this beachfront restaurant on Tortola's North Shore. The menu
emphasizes seafood—especially lobster, conch, and local fish—but you
can also find dishes such as ginger chicken and filet mignon. It's a perfect
spot to stop for lunch on your around-the-island tour. Try the grilled
dolphinfish (mahimahi) sandwich, served on a soft roll with an oniony
tartar sauce. Finish off with a cup of Sebastian's coffee, spiked with
home-brewed rum. ⑤ *Average main: $23* ⊠ *North Coast Rd., Apple
Bay* ☎ *284/494–4212* ⊕ *www.sebastiansbvi.com.*

$$$ ✕**Sugar Mill Restaurant.** Candles gleam, and the background music is
ECLECTIC peaceful in this romantic restaurant inside a 17th-century sugar mill.
Fodor's Choice Well-prepared selections on the à la carte menu, which changes nightly,
★

include some pasta and vegetarian entrées. Lobster bisque with basil croutons and a creamy conch chowder are good starters. Favorite entrées include fresh fish with soba noodles, shiitake mushrooms, and a scallion broth; filet mignon topped with an herb-cream sauce; grilled shrimp and scallops with mango salsa; and pumpkin-and-black-bean lasagna. $ *Average main: $30* ⊠ *Sugar Mill Hotel, Apple Bay* ☎ *284/495–4355* ⊕ *www.sugarmillhotel.com* ⊘ *No lunch.*

EAST END

$$$ ✕ **CalaMaya.** Casual fare is what you can find at this waterfront res-
ECLECTIC taurant. You can always order a burger or Caesar salad; the chicken wrap with sweet-and-sour sauce is a tasty alternative. For dinner, try the mahimahi with sautéed vegetables and rice. $ *Average main: $30* ⊠ *Hodge's Creek Marina, Blackburn Hwy.* ☎ *284/495–2126.*

MID-ISLAND

$$ ✕ **Sky.** The top of a mountain is the location for this casually elegant
ASIAN dining room with a menu that features sushi and sashimi, as well as Indian dishes in an adjacent room. You'll find the usual tuna, sea bass, and shrimp on the sushi menu, but locals like the tropical-style sushi with smoked salmon and mango. If you like some heat, try the Hurricane. If you're renting a villa in the area, the takeout menu will save you some kitchen chores. $ *Average main: $15* ⊠ *Ridge Rd., Joe's Hill* ☎ *284/494–3567* ⊘ *No lunch.*

WHERE TO STAY

Luxury on Tortola is more about a certain state of mind—serenity, seclusion, gentility, and a bit of Britain in the Caribbean—than about state-of-the-art amenities and fabulous facilities. Some properties, especially the vacation villas, are catching up with current trends, but others seem stuck in the 1980s. But don't let a bit of rust on the screen door or a chip in the paint on the balcony railing mar your appreciation of the ambience. You will likely spend most of your time outside, so the location, size, or price of a hotel should be more of a factor to you than the decor.

Hotels in Road Town don't have beaches, but they do have pools and are within walking distance of restaurants, bars, and shops. Accommodations outside Road Town are relatively isolated, but most face the ocean. Tortola resorts are intimate—only a handful have more than 50 rooms. Guests are treated as more than just room numbers, and many return year after year. This can make booking a room at popular resorts difficult, even off-season, despite the fact that more than half the island's visitors stay aboard their own or chartered boats.

A few hotels lack air-conditioning, relying instead on ceiling fans to capture the almost constant trade winds. Nights are cool and breezy, even in midsummer, and never reach the temperatures or humidity levels that are common in much of the United States. Note that all accommodations listed here have air-conditioning unless we mention otherwise. Remember that some places may be closed during the peak of hurricane season—August through October—to give their owners a much-needed break.

For expanded reviews, facilities, and current deals, visit Fodors.com.

PRIVATE VILLAS

Renting a villa is growing in popularity. Vacationers like the privacy, the space to spread out, and the opportunity to cook meals. As is true everywhere, the most important thing is location. If you want to be close to the beach, opt for a villa on the North Shore. If you want to dine out in Road Town every night, a villa closer to town may be a better bet. Prices per week during the winter season run from around $2,000 for a one- or two-bedroom villa up to $10,000 for a five-room beachfront villa. Rates in summer are substantially less. Most, but not all, villas accept credit cards.

VILLA RENTAL CONTACTS

Areana Villas. Areana Villas represents top-of-the-line properties. Pastel-color villas with one to five bedrooms can accommodate up to 10 guests. Many have pools, whirlpool tubs, and tiled courtyards. *284/494–5864 ⊕ www.areanavillas.com.*

McLaughlin-Anderson Luxury Villas. The St. Thomas–based McLaughlin-Anderson Luxury Villas manages nearly two dozen properties around Tortola. Villas range from one to six bedrooms and come with full kitchens and stellar views. Most have pools. The company can hire a chef and stock your kitchen with groceries. *340/776–0635, 800/537–6246 ⊕ www.mclaughlinanderson.com.*

Smiths Gore. Although Smiths Gore has properties all over the island, many are in the Smuggler's Cove area. They range from two to five bedrooms: all have stellar views, lovely furnishings, and lush landscaping. *284/494–2446 ⊕ www.smithsgore.com.*

ROAD TOWN AND VICINITY

$ **Moorings-Mariner Inn.** If you enjoy the camaraderie of a busy marina,
HOTEL this inn on the edge of Road Town may appeal to you. **Pros:** good dining options; friendly guests; excellent spot to charter boats. **Cons:** busy location; long walk to Road Town; need car to get around. **TripAdvisor:** "peaceful," "the perfect place to relax," "marina paradise." [$] *Rooms from: $220 ⊠ Waterfront Dr. ☎ 284/494–2333, 800/535–7289 ⊕ www.bvimarinerinnhotel.com ⊲ 32 rooms, 7 suites ⊘ No meals.*

$ **Nanny Cay Hotel.** This quiet oasis is far enough from Road Town to
HOTEL give it a secluded feel but close enough to make shops and restaurants convenient. You're just steps from the hotel's restaurant, boat charters, and the chance to stroll the busy boatyard to gawk at the yachts under repair, but you still have to drive a good 20 minutes to get to the closest beach at Cane Garden Bay. **Pros:** nearby shops and restaurant; pleasant rooms; marina atmosphere. **Cons:** busy location; need car to get around. **TripAdvisor:** "helpful and courteous," "great room," "breakfast in paradise." [$] *Rooms from: $185 ⊠ Nanny Cay ☎ 284/494–2512 ⊕ www.nannycay.com ⊲ 38 rooms ⊘ No meals.*

$ **Village Cay Hotel and Marina.** If you want to be able to walk to restau-
HOTEL rants and shops, you simply can't beat Village Cay's prime location in the heart of Road Town. **Pros:** prime location; shops and restaurants

American or British?

Yes, the Union Jack flutters overhead in the tropical breeze, schools operate on the British system, place-names have British spellings, Queen Elizabeth II appoints the governor—and the queen's picture hangs on many walls. Indeed, residents celebrate the queen's birthday every June with a public ceremony. You can overhear that charming English accent from a good handful of expats when you're lunching at Road Town restaurants, and you can buy "biscuits"—what Americans call cookies—in the supermarkets.

But you can pay for your lunch and the biscuits with American money, because the U.S. dollar is legal tender here. The unusual circumstance is a matter of geography. The practice started in the mid-20th century, when BVI residents went to work in the nearby USVI. On trips home,

they brought their U.S. dollars with them. Soon they abandoned the barter system, and in 1959 the U.S. dollar became the official form of money. Interestingly, the government sells stamps (for use only in the BVI) that often carry pictures of Queen Elizabeth II and other royalty with the monetary value in U.S. dollars and cents.

The American influence continued to grow when Americans began to open businesses in the BVI because they preferred its quiet to the hustle and bustle of St. Thomas. Inevitably, cable and satellite TV's U.S.–based programming, along with Hollywood-made movies, further influenced life in the BVI. And most goods are shipped from St. Thomas in the USVI, meaning you can find more American products than British ones on the supermarket shelves.

nearby; nautical ambience. **Cons:** little parking; busy street; need car to get around. **TripAdvisor:** "charming host," "comfortable," "nicest place on the waterfront." ⑤ *Rooms from: $150* ⊠ *Wickham's Cay I* ☎ *284/494–2771* ⊕ *www.villagecayhotelandmarina.com* ⤵ *17 rooms, 5 suites* ⊙*No meals.*

WEST END

$$ ⚏ **Fort Recovery Beachfront Villas.** This is one of those small but spe-
RESORT cial properties that stand out because of their friendly service and the
☾ chance to get to know your fellow guests rather than the poshness of
★ the rooms and the upscale amenities. **Pros:** beautiful beach; spacious units; historic site. **Cons:** need car to get around; isolated location. **TripAdvisor:** "relaxing and great staff," "nice location," "perfect for an island getaway." ⑤ *Rooms from: $310* ⊠ *Waterfront Dr., Pockwood Pond* ☎ *284/495–4467, 800/367–8455* ⊕ *www.fortrecovery.com* ⤵ *29 suites, 1 villa* ⊙*Breakfast.*

NORTH SHORE

$ ⚏ **Long Bay Beach Resort.** If you want all the resort amenities, including
RESORT a beach, scads of water sports, tennis courts, and even a pitch-and-putt golf course, then this is your only choice for Tortola. **Pros:** resort atmosphere; good restaurants; many activities. **Cons:** need car to get around; sometimes curt staff; uphill hike to some rooms. **TripAdvisor:**

"convenient," "most beautiful beach," "great tropical getaway." ⑤ *Rooms from: $232* ⊠ *Long Bay* ☎ *284/495–4252, 800/858–4618* ⊕ *www.longbay.com* ⤴ *53 rooms, 37 suites, 26 villas* ♚ *No meals.*

$ | **Myett's.** Tucked away in a beachfront garden, this tiny hotel puts
HOTEL | you right in the middle of Cane Garden Bay's busy hustle and bustle. **Pros:** beautiful beach; good restaurant; shops nearby. **Cons:** busy location; need car to get around. **TripAdvisor:** "totally tropical accommodations," "my oasis," "best location." ⑤ *Rooms from: $195* ⊠ *Cane Garden Bay* ☎ *284/495–9649* ⊕ *www.myettent.com* ⤴ *6 rooms, 4 cottages, 1 villa* ♚ *No meals.*

$ | **Sebastian's on the Beach.** Sitting on the island's north coast, Sebastian's
RESORT | definitely has a beachy feel, and that's its primary charm. **Pros:** nice beach; good restaurants; beachfront rooms. **Cons:** on busy road; some rooms nicer than others; need car to get around. **TripAdvisor:** "nice beach and patio," "fun and plenty of sun," "great beachfront room." ⑤ *Rooms from: $185* ⊠ *Apple Bay* ☎ *284/495–4212, 800/336–4870* ⊕ *www.sebastiansbvi.com* ⤴ *26 rooms, 9 villas* ♚ *No meals.*

$$ | **Sugar Mill Hotel.** Though it's not a sprawling resort, the Sugar Mill
RESORT | Hotel has a Caribbean cachet that's hard to beat, and it's a favorite
Fodor's Choice | place to stay on Tortola. **Pros:** lovely rooms; excellent restaurant; nice
★ | views. **Cons:** on busy road; small beach; need car to get around. **TripAdvisor:** "gorgeous property," "perfect in every way," "outstanding care and service." ⑤ *Rooms from: $340* ⊠ *Apple Bay* ☎ *284/495–4355, 800/462–8834* ⊕ *www.sugarmillhotel.com* ⤴ *19 rooms, 2 suites, 1 villa, 1 cottage* ♚ *No meals.*

EAST END

$ | **Hodge's Creek Marina Hotel.** Sitting marina-side on the island's East
HOTEL | End, this hotel puts you in the middle of the nautical action. **Pros:** marina atmosphere; good restaurant; some shopping. **Cons:** bland rooms; need car to get around. ⑤ *Rooms from: $130* ⊠ *Hodge's Creek* ☎ *284/494–5000* ⊕ *www.pennhotels.com* ⤴ *24 rooms* ♚ *No meals.*

$ | **Lambert Beach Resort.** Although this isolated location on the north-
RESORT | east coast puts you far from Road Town, Lambert Bay is one of the island's loveliest stretches of sand and the main reason to recommend this resort. **Pros:** lovely beach; beautiful setting; good restaurant. **Cons:** bland rooms; isolated location; need car to get around. **TripAdvisor:** "romantic," "great beach," "beautiful but remote and somewhat inconvenient." ⑤ *Rooms from: $169* ⊠ *Lambert Bay, East End* ☎ *284/495–2877* ⊕ *www.lambertresort.com* ⤴ *38 rooms, 2 villas, 27 condos* ♚ *No meals.*

$$$$ | **Surfsong Villa Resort.** Nested in lush foliage right at the water's edge,
RESORT | this small resort on Beef Island provides a pleasant respite for vacation-
Fodor's Choice | ers who want a villa atmosphere with some hotel amenities. **Pros:** lovely
★ | rooms; beautiful beach; chef on call. **Cons:** need car to get around; no restaurants nearby. **TripAdvisor:** "tranquil slice of paradise," "idyllic retreat," "incredible food." ⑤ *Rooms from: $495* ⊠ *Beef Island* ☎ *284/495–1864* ⊕ *www.surfsong.net* ⤴ *1 suite, 7 villas* ♚ *No meals.*

7

Surfsong Village Resort

NIGHTLIFE AND THE ARTS

NIGHTLIFE

Like any other good sailing destination, Tortola has watering holes that are popular with salty and not-so-salty dogs. Many offer entertainment; check the weekly *Limin' Times* (⊕ *www.limin-times.com*) for schedules and up-to-date information. Bands change like the weather, and what's hot today can be old news tomorrow. The local beverage is the Painkiller, an innocent-tasting mixture of fruit juices and rums. It goes down smoothly but packs quite a punch, so give yourself time to recover before you order another.

Bomba's Surfside Shack. By day, you can see that Bomba's, which is covered with everything from crepe-paper leis to ancient license plates to spicy graffiti, looks like a pile of junk; by night it's one of Tortola's liveliest spots. There's a fish fry and a live band every Wednesday and Sunday. People flock here from all over on the full moon, when bands play all night long. ⊠ *Apple Bay* ☎ *284/495–4148.*

Jolly Roger. At the Jolly Roger, an ever-changing roster of local and down-island bands plays R & B, reggae, and rock every Friday and Saturday—and sometimes Sunday—starting at 8. ⊠ *West End* ☎ *284/495–4559* ⊕ *www.jollyrogerbvi.com.*

Fodor'sChoice ★ **Myett's.** Local bands play at this popular spot, which has live music during happy hour, and there's usually a lively dance crowd. ⊠ *Cane Garden Bay* ☎ *284/495–9649* ⊕ *www.myettent.com.*

Pub. At this popular watering hole there's a happy hour from 5 to 7 every day and live music on Thursday and Friday. ⊠ *Waterfront St., Road Town* ☎ *284/494–2608.*

Pusser's Road Town Pub. Courage is what people are seeking here—John Courage beer by the pint. Or try Pusser's famous mixed drink, called the Painkiller, and snack on the excellent pizza. ⊠ *Waterfront St., Road Town* ☎ *284/494–3897* ⊕ *www.pussers.com.*

The New Quito's Restaurant and Bar. BVI recording star Quito Rhymer sings island ballads and love songs at his rustic beachside bar–restaurant. Solo shows are on Tuesday and Thursday at 8:30; on Friday at 9:30 Quito performs with his band. ⊠ *Cane Garden Bay* ☎ *284/495–4837* ⊕ *www.quitorymer.com.*

Sebastian's. There's often live music at Sebastian's on Thursday and Sunday evenings, and you can dance under the stars. ⊠ *Apple Bay* ☎ *284/495–4212* ⊕ *www.sebastiansbvi.com.*

THE ARTS

Fodor's Choice
★
BVI Music Festival. Every May hordes of people head to Tortola for this popular three-day festival to listen to reggae, gospel, blues, and salsa music by musicians from around the Caribbean and the U.S. mainland. ⊠ *Cane Garden Bay* ⊕ *www.bvimusicfestival.com.*

Performing Arts Series. Musicians from around the world take to the stage during the island's Performing Arts Series, held from October to May each year. Past artists have included Britain's premier a cappella group, Black Voices; the Leipzig String Quartet; and pianist Richard Ormand. ⊠ *H. Lavity Stoutt Community College, Paraquita Bay* ☎ *284/494–4994* ⊕ *www.hlscc.edu.vg/arts.*

SHOPPING

The BVI aren't really a shopper's delight, but there are many shops showcasing original wares, such as jams, spices, resort wear, and often-excellent artwork.

SHOPPING AREAS

Many shops and boutiques are clustered along and just off Road Town's **Main Street.** You can shop in Road Town's **Wickham's Cay I** adjacent to the marina. The **Crafts Alive Market** on the Road Town waterfront is a collection of colorful West Indian–style buildings with shops that carry items made in the BVI. You might find pretty baskets or interesting pottery or perhaps a bottle of home-brewed hot sauce. A growing number of art and clothing stores are opening at **Soper's Hole** in West End.

SPECIALTY STORES

ART

Allamanda Gallery. Photography by the gallery's owner, Amanda Baker, is on display here. ⊠ *124 Main St., Road Town* ☎ *284/494–6680* ⊕ *www. virginportraits.com.*

Sunny Caribbee. This gallery has many paintings, prints, and watercolors by artists from around the Caribbean. ⊠ *Main St., Road Town* ☎ *284/494–2178* ⊕ *www.sunnycaribbee.com.*

Most of Tortola's shops are in Road Town.

CLOTHES AND TEXTILES

Arawak. This boutique carries batik sundresses, sportswear, and resort wear for men and women. There's also a selection of children's clothing. ⊠ *Dock, Nanny Cay* ☎ *284/494–3983.*

Latitude 18°. This store sells Maui Jim, Ray-Ban, and Oakley sunglasses; Freestyle watches; and a fine collection of beach towels, sandals, Crocs, sundresses, and sarongs. ⊠ *Main St., Road Town* ☎ *284/494–6196* ⊕ *www.latitude18.com.*

Pusser's Company Store. The Road Town Pusser's sells nautical memorabilia, ship models, and marine paintings. There's also an entire line of clothing for both men and women, handsome decorator bottles of Pusser's rum, and gift items bearing the Pusser's logo. ⊠ *Main St. at Waterfront Rd., Road Town* ☎ *284/494–2467* ⊕ *www.pussers.com.*

Zenaida's of West End. Vivian Jenik Helm travels through South America, Africa, and India in search of batiks, hand-painted and hand-blocked fabrics, and interesting weaves that can be made into pareus (women's wraps) or wall hangings. The shop also sells unusual bags, belts, sarongs, scarves, and ethnic jewelry. ⊠ *Soper's Hole Marina, West End* ☎ *284/495–4867.*

FOOD

Ample Hamper. Head here to stock your yacht or rental villa—or have the staff do it for you. It carries an outstanding collection of cheeses, wines, fresh fruits, and canned goods from the United Kingdom and the United States. ⊠ *Inner Harbour Marina, Road Town* ☎ *284/494–2494* ⊠ *Frenchman's Cay Marina, West End* ☎ *284/495–4684* ⊕ *www.amplehamper.com.*

Best of British. This boutique has lots of nifty British food you won't find elsewhere. Shop here for Marmite, Vegemite, shortbread, frozen meat pies, and delightful Christmas "crackers" filled with surprises. ⊠ *Wickham's Cay I, Road Town* ☎ *284/494–3462.*

RiteWay. This market carries a good (but not massive) selection of the usual supplies. RiteWay will stock villas and yachts. ⊠ *Waterfront Dr. at Pasea Estate, Road Town* ☎ *284/494–2263* ⊕ *www.rtwbvi.com* ⊠ *Fleming St., Road Town* ☎ *284/494–2263* ⊕ *www.rtwbvi.com.*

GIFTS

Fodor'sChoice **Bamboushay.** Some of the handcrafted Tortola-made pottery sold here
★ comes in shades that reflect the sea. ⊠ *Nanny Cay Marina, Nanny Cay* ☎ *284/494–0393* ⊕ *www.bamboushay.com.*

Sunny Caribbee. In a brightly painted West Indian house, this store packages its own herbs, teas, coffees, vinegars, hot sauces, soaps, skin and suntan lotions, and exotic concoctions—Arawak Love Potion and Island Hangover Cure, for example. ⊠ *Main St., Road Town* ☎ *284/494–2178* ⊕ *www.sunnycaribbee.com.*

JEWELRY

Colombian Emeralds International. This Caribbean chain caters to the cruise-ship crowd and is the source for duty-free emeralds and other gems in gold and silver settings. ⊠ *Wickham's Cay I, Road Town* ☎ *284/494–7477* ⊕ *www.colombianemeralds.com.*

Samarkand. The charming jewelry sold here includes gold-and-silver pendants, earrings, bracelets, and pins, many with island themes such as seashells, lizards, pelicans, and palm trees. There are also reproduction Spanish pieces of eight (old Spanish coins) similar to those found on sunken galleons. ⊠ *Main St., Road Town* ☎ *284/494–6415.*

STAMPS

BVI Post Office. The BVI's post office has a worldwide reputation for exquisite stamps in all sorts of designs. Although the stamps carry U.S. monetary designations, they can only be used for postage in the BVI. ⊠ *Blackburn Rd., Road Town* ☎ *284/494–3701.*

SPORTS AND ACTIVITIES

DIVING AND SNORKELING

Clear waters and numerous reefs afford some wonderful opportunities for underwater exploration. In some spots visibility reaches 100 feet, but colorful reefs teeming with fish are often just a few feet below the sea surface. The BVI's system of marine parks means the underwater life visible through your mask will stay protected.

There are several popular dive spots around the islands. **Alice in Wonderland** is a deep dive south of Ginger Island with a wall that slopes gently from 15 feet to 100 feet. It's an area overrun with huge mushroom-shape coral, hence its name. Crabs, lobsters, and shimmering fan corals make their homes in the tunnels, ledges, and overhangs of **Blonde Rock,** a pinnacle that goes from 15 feet below the surface to 60 feet deep. It's between Dead Chest and Salt Island. When the currents aren't too strong, **Brewers Bay Pinnacle** (20 to 90 feet down) teems with sea life. At the **Indians,** near Pelican Island, colorful coral decorates canyons and grottoes created by four large, jagged pinnacles that rise 50 feet from the ocean floor. The **Painted Walls** is a shallow dive site where coral and sponges create a kaleidoscope of colors on the walls of four long gullies. It's northeast of Dead Chest.

The *Chikuzen,* sunk northwest of Brewers Bay in 1981, is a 246-foot vessel in 75 feet of water; it's home to thousands of fish, colorful corals, and big rays. In 1867 the **RMS *Rhone*,** a 310-foot royal mail steamer, split in two when it sank in a devastating hurricane. It's so well preserved that it was used as an underwater prop in the 1977 movie *The Deep.* You can see the crow's nest and bowsprit, the cargo hold in the bow, and the engine and enormous propeller shaft in the stern. Its four parts are at various depths, from 30 to 80 feet. Get yourself some snorkeling gear and hop aboard a dive boat to this wreck near Salt Island (across the channel from Road Town). Every dive outfit in the BVI runs scuba and snorkel tours to this part of the BVI National Parks Trust; if you have time for only one trip, make it this one. Rates start at around $70 for a one-tank dive and $100 for a two-tank dive.

Your hotel probably has a dive company right on the premises. If not, the staff can recommend one nearby. Using your hotel's dive company makes a trip to the offshore dive and snorkel sites a breeze. Just stroll down to the dock and hop aboard. All dive companies are certified by PADI, the Professional Association of Diving Instructors, which ensures that your instructors are qualified to safely take vacationers diving. The boats are also inspected to make sure they're seaworthy. If you've never dived, try a short introductory dive, often called a resort course, which teaches you enough to get you under water. In the unlikely event you get a case of the bends, a condition that can happen when you rise to the surface too fast, your dive team will take you to the decompression chamber at Roy L. Schneider Regional Medical Center in nearby St. Thomas.

Blue Waters Divers. If you're chartering a sailboat, Blue Waters Divers' boat will meet yours at Peter, Salt, Norman, or Cooper Island for a rendezvous dive. The company teaches resort, open-water, rescue, and advanced diving courses, and also makes daily dive trips. Rates include all equipment as well as instruction. Reserve two days in advance. ⊠ *Nanny Cay* ☎ *284/494–2847* ⊕ *www.bluewaterdiversbvi.com* ⊠ *Soper's Hole, West End* ☎ *284/495–1200* ⊕ *www.bluewaterdiversbvi.com.*

FISHING

Most of the boats that take you deep-sea fishing for bluefish, wahoo, swordfish, and shark leave from nearby St. Thomas, but local anglers like to fish the shallower water for bonefish. A half day for two people runs about $480, a full day around $850. Wading trips are $325.

Caribbean Fly Fishing. ⊠ *Nanny Cay* ☎ *284/494–4797* ⊕ *www.caribflyfishing.com.*

HIKING

Sage Mountain National Park attracts hikers who enjoy the quiet trails that crisscross the island's loftiest peak. There are some lovely views and the chance to see rare species that grow only at higher elevations.

Continued on page 262

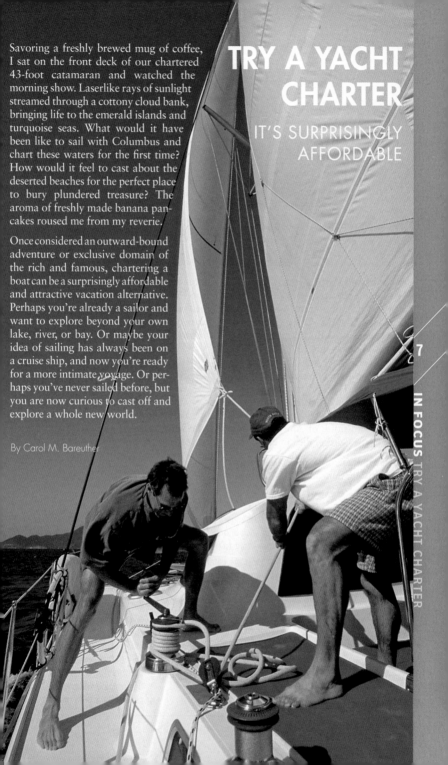

TRY A YACHT CHARTER

IT'S SURPRISINGLY AFFORDABLE

Savoring a freshly brewed mug of coffee, I sat on the front deck of our chartered 43-foot catamaran and watched the morning show. Laserlike rays of sunlight streamed through a cottony cloud bank, bringing life to the emerald islands and turquoise seas. What would it have been like to sail with Columbus and chart these waters for the first time? How would it feel to cast about the deserted beaches for the perfect place to bury plundered treasure? The aroma of freshly made banana pancakes roused me from my reverie.

Once considered an outward-bound adventure or exclusive domain of the rich and famous, chartering a boat can be a surprisingly affordable and attractive vacation alternative. Perhaps you're already a sailor and want to explore beyond your own lake, river, or bay. Or maybe your idea of sailing has always been on a cruise ship, and now you're ready for a more intimate voyage. Or perhaps you've never sailed before, but you are now curious to cast off and explore a whole new world.

By Carol M. Bareuther

CREWED CHARTER

On a crewed charter, you sit back and relax while the crew provides for your every want and need. Captains are licensed by the U.S. Coast Guard or the equivalent in the British maritime system. Cooks—preferring to be called chefs—have skills that go far beyond peanut butter and jelly sandwiches. There are four meals a day, and many chefs boast certificates from culinary schools ranging from the Culinary Institute of America in New York to the Cordon Bleu in Paris.

The advantage of a crewed yacht charter, with captain and cook, is that it takes every bit of stress out of the vacation. With a captain who knows the local waters, you get to see some of the coves and anchorages that are not necessarily in the guidebooks. Your meals are prepared, cabins cleaned, beds made up every day—and turned down at night, too. Plus, you can sail and take the helm as often as you like. But at the end of the day, the captain is the one who will take responsibility for anchoring safely for the night while the chef goes below and whips up a gourmet meal.

COSTS	PROS	CONS
$4,100–$6,450 for 2 people for 5 days	■ Passengers just have to lay back and relax (unless they want to help sail)	■ More expensive than a bareboat, especially if you get a catamaran
$5,200–$8,200 for 2 people for 7 days	■ Most are catamarans, offering more space than monohulls	■ Less privacy for your group than on a bareboat
$8,200–$13,200 for 6 people for 5 days	■ You have an experienced, local hand on board if something goes wrong	■ Captain makes ultimate decisions about the course
$9,700–$16,900 for 6 people for 7 days	■ Water toys and other extras are often included	■ Chance for personality conflicts: you have to get along with the captain and chef. This is where a charter yacht broker is helpful in determining what yachts and crews might be a good fit.
Prices are all-inclusive for a 50- to 55-foot yacht in high season except for 15%–20% gratuity.	■ Competively priced within an all-inclusive resort	

(top) Family sailing in the British Virgin Islands

BAREBOAT

If you'd like to bareboat, don't be intimidated. It's a myth that you must be a graduate of a sailing school in order to pilot your own charter boat. A bareboat company will ask you to fill out a resume. The company checks for prior boat-handling experience, the type of craft you've sailed (whether powerboat or sailboat), and in what type of waters. Real-life experience, meaning all those day and weekend trips close to home, count as valuable know-how. If you've done a bit of boating, you may be more qualified than you think to take out a bareboat.

Costs can be very similar for a bareboat and crewed charter, depending on the time of year and size of the boat. You'll pay the highest rates between Christmas and New Year's, when you may not be allowed to do a charter of less than a week. But there are more than 800 bareboats between the USVI and BVI, so regardless of your budget, you should be able to find something in your price range. Plus, you might save a bit by chartering an older boat from a smaller company instead of the most state-of-the-art yacht from a larger company.

7

IN FOCUS TRY A YACHT CHARTER

COSTS	PROS	CONS
$2,800–$4,800 for a small monohull (2–3 cabins)	■ The ultimate freedom to set the yacht's course	■ Must be able to pass a sailing test
$4,800–$8,400 for a large monohull (4–5 cabins)	■ A chance to test your sailing skills	■ Those unfamiliar with the region may not find the best anchorages
$5,200–$6,400 for a small catamaran (2 cabins)	■ Usually a broader range of boats and prices to choose from	■ You have to cook for and clean up after yourself
$6,800–$13,300 for a large catamaran (4 cabins)	■ More flexibility for meals (you can always go ashore if you don't feel like cooking)	■ You have to do your own provisioning and planning for meals
Prices exclude food, beverages, fuel, and other supplies. Most bareboat rates do not include water toys, taxes, insurance, and permits.	■ You can always hire a captain for a few days	■ If something goes wrong, there isn't an experienced hand onboard

Three women rigging the sails.

WHAT TO CONSIDER

Whether bareboat or a crewed yacht, there are a few points to ponder when selecting your boat.

HOW BIG IS YOUR GROUP?

As a general rule, count on one cabin for every two people. Most people also prefer to have one head (bathroom) per cabin. A multihull, also called a catamaran, offers more space and more equal-size cabins than a monohull sailboat.

WHAT TYPE OF BOAT?

If you want to do some good old traditional sailing, where you're heeling over with the seas at your rails, monohulls are a good option. On the other hand, multihulls are more stable, easier to board, and have a big salon for families. They're also ideal if some people get seasick or aren't as gung-ho for the more traditional sailing experience. If you'd like to cover more ground, choose a motor yacht.

DO YOU HAVE A SPECIAL INTEREST?

Some crewed charter boats specialize in certain types of charters. Among these are learn-to-sail excursions, honeymoon cruises, scuba-diving adventures, and family-friendly trips. Your broker can steer you to the boats that fit your specific needs.

WHAT KIND OF EQUIPMENT DO YOU WANT ONBOARD?

Most charter boats have satellite navigation systems and autopilots, as well as regulation safety gear, dinghies with motors, and even stereos and entertainment systems. But do you want a generator or battery-drive refrigeration system? How about a/c? Do you want a satellite phone? Do you want water toys like kayaks, boogie boards, and Windsurfers?

Now that you've decided on bareboat versus crewed charter and selected your craft, all you need to do is confirm the availability of the date with the company or broker and pay a nonrefundable deposit equal to 50% of the charter price.

TO SAIL OR NOT TO SAIL?

If you're not sure whether a charter yacht vacation is right for you, consider this: would you enjoy a floating hotel room where the scenery outside your window changed according to your desires? A "yes" may entice wary companions to try chartering. A single one-week trip will have them hooked.

Two catamaran sailboats seen from behind.

CATAMARANS
Multihulls are more stable, easier to board and have a big salon for families. Seasickness is less of an issue.

MOTOR YACHT
Best if you want to cover more ground, but costs a lot more than a sailboat.

MONOHULLS
Good for more traditional and active sailing, but the movement may not appeal to non-sailors.

CHOOSING A CHARTER

Information on charters is much easier to find now than even a decade ago. Web sites for bareboat companies show photos of different types of boats—both interiors and exteriors—as well as layout schematics, lists of equipment and amenities, and sample itineraries. Many sites will allow you to book a charter directly, while others give you the option of calling a toll-free number to speak with an agent first.

There are two types of Web sites for crewed charters. If you just want some information, the **Virgin Islands Charteryacht League** (⊕ www.vicl.org) and the **Charter Yacht Society of the British Virgin Islands** (⊕ www.bvicrewedyachts.com) both help you understand what to look for in a crewed charter, from the size of the boat to the amenities. You can't reserve on these sites, but they link to the sites of brokers, who are the sales force for the charter yacht industry. Most brokers, whether they're based in the Caribbean, the United States, or Europe, attend annual charter yacht shows in St. Thomas, Tortola, and Antigua. At these shows, brokers visit the boats and meet the crews. This is what gives brokers their depth of knowledge for "matchmaking," or linking you with a boat that will meet your personality and preferences.

The charter companies also maintain Web sites. About 30% of the crewed charter yachts based out of the U.S. and British Virgin Islands can be booked directly. This saves the commission an owner has to pay to the broker. But while "going direct" might seem advantageous, there is usually little difference in pricing, and if you use a broker, he or she can help troubleshoot if something goes wrong or find a replacement boat if the boat owner has to cancel.

Timing also matters. Companies may offer last-minute specials that are available only online. These special rates—usually for specific dates, destinations, and boats—are updated weekly or even daily.

PREPARING FOR YOUR CHARTER

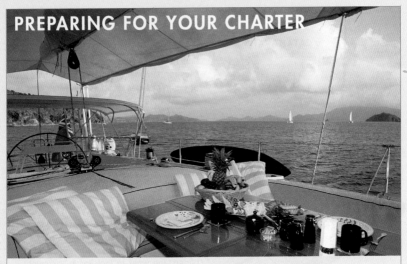

British Virgin Islands—anchorage in a tropical sea with breakfast on board.

PROVISIONING

Bareboaters must do their own provisioning. It's a good idea to arrange provisioning at least a week in advance.

Bobby's Market Place ⊠ *Wickham's Cay I, Road Town, Tortola* ☎ *284/494–2189* ⊕ *www.bobbysmarketplace.com*) offers packages from $18 to $28 per person per day. **Ample Hamper** (⊠ *Inner Harbour Marina, Road Town, Tortola* ☎ *284/494–2494* ⊠ *Frenchmans Cay Marina, West End, Tortola* ☎ *284/495–4684* ⊕ *www.amplehamper.com*) offers more than 1,200 items but no pre-arranged packages.

Provisioning packages from the charter company are usually a bit more expensive, at $30 to $35 per person per day, but they save you the hassle of planning the details. You can also shop on arrival. Both St. Thomas and Tortola have markets, though larger grocery stores may require a taxi ride. If you shop carefully, this route can still save you money. Just be sure to allow yourself a few hours after arrival to get everything done.

PLANNING

For a crewed charter, your broker will send a preference sheet for both food and your wishes for the trip. Perhaps you'd like lazy days of sleeping late, sunning, and swimming. Or you might prefer active days of sailing with stops for snorkeling and exploring ashore. If there's a special spot you'd like to visit, list it so your captain can plan the itinerary accordingly.

PACKING TIPS

Pack light for any type of charter. Bring soft-sided luggage (preferably a duffle bag) since space is limited and storage spots are usually odd shapes. Shorts, T-shirts, and swimsuits are sufficient. Bring something a bit nicer if you plan to dine ashore. Shoes are seldom required except ashore, but you might want beach shoes to protect your feet in the water. Most boats provide snorkel equipment, but always ask. Bring sunscreen, but a type that will not stain cockpit cushions and decks.

WHAT YOU'LL SEE IN THE USBVI

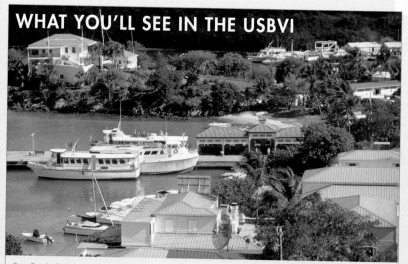

Cruz Bay in St. John

MAIN CHARTER BASES

The U.S. and British Virgin Islands boast more than 100 stepping-stone islands and cays within a 50-nautical-mi radius. This means easy line-of-sight navigation and island-hopping in protected waters, and it's rare that you'll spend more than a few hours moving between islands.

Tortola, in the British Virgin Islands, is the crewed charter and bareboat mecca of the Caribbean. This fact is plainly apparent from the forest of masts rising out from any marina.

The U.S. Virgin Islands fleet is based in **St. Thomas.** Direct flights from the mainland, luxurious accommodations, and duty-free shopping are drawing cards for departures from the U.S. Virgin Islands, whereas the British Virgins are closer to the prime cruising grounds.

POPULAR ANCHORAGES

On a typical weeklong charter you could set sail from Red Hook, St. Thomas, then cross Pillsbury Sound to St. John, which offers popular north-shore anchorages in Honeymoon, Trunk, or Francis bays.

But the best sailing and snorkeling always includes the British Virgin Islands (which require a valid passport or passport card). After clearing customs in West End, Tortola, many yachts hop along a series of smaller islands that run along the south side of the Sir Francis Drake Channel. But some yachts will also visit Guana Island, Great Camanoe, or Marina Cay off Tortola's more isolated east end.

The islands south of Tortola include **Norman Island,** the rumored site of Robert Lewis Stevenson's *Treasure Island*. The next island over is **Peter Island,** famous for it's posh resort and a popular anchorage for yachters. Farther east, off Salt Island, is the wreck of the **RMS** *Rhone*—the most magnificent dive site in the eastern Caribbean. Giant boulders form caves and grottos called The Baths at the southern end of **Virgin Gorda.**

A downwind run along Tortola's north shore ends at **Jost Van Dyke,** where that famous guitar-strumming calypsonian Foxy Callwood sings personalized ditties that make for a memorable finale.

SAILING

The BVI are among the world's most popular sailing destinations. They're clustered together and surrounded by calm waters, so it's fairly easy to sail from one anchorage to the next. Most of the Caribbean's biggest sailboat charter companies have operations in Tortola. If you know how to sail, you can charter a bareboat (perhaps for your entire vacation); if you're unschooled, you can hire a boat with a captain. Prices vary depending on the type and size of the boat you wish to charter. In season, a weekly charter runs from $1,500 to $35,000. Book early to make sure you get the boat that fits you best. Most of Tortola's marinas have hotels, which give you a convenient place to spend the nights before and after your charter.

If a day sail to some secluded anchorage is more your cup of tea, the BVI have numerous boats of various sizes and styles that leave from many points around Tortola. Prices start at around $80 per person for a full-day sail, including lunch and snorkeling equipment.

Aristocat Charters. This company's 48-foot catamaran sets sail daily to Jost Van Dyke, Norman Island, and other small islands. ☒ *West End* ☎ *284/499–1249* ⊕ *www.aristocatcharters.com.*

BVI Yacht Charters. The 31- to 52-foot sailboats for charter here come with or without a captain and crew, whichever you prefer. ☒ *Port Purcell, Road Town* ☎ *284/494-4289, 888/615-4006* ⊕ *www.bviyachtcharters.com.*

Catamaran Charters. The catamarans here come with or without a captain. ☒ *Village Cay Marina, Hodge's Creek, Road Town* ☎ *284/494-6661, 800/262-0308* ⊕ *www.catamarans.com.*

Moorings. One of the world's best bareboat operations, The Moorings has a large fleet of monohulls and catamarans. Hire a captain or sail the boat yourself. ☒ *Wickham's Cay II, Road Town* ☎ *284/494-2332, 800/535-7289* ⊕ *www.moorings.com.*

Regency Yacht Vacations. If you prefer a powerboat, call Regency Yacht Vacations. It handles both bareboat and captained sail and powerboat charters. ☒ *Wickham's Cay I, Road Town* ☎ *284/495–1970, 800/524–7676* ⊕ *www.regencyvacations.com.*

Sunsail. A full fleet of boats to charter with or without a captain is available here. ☒ *Wickham's Cay II, Road Town* ☎ *284/495-4740, 800/327-2276* ⊕ *www.sunsail.com.*

Voyage Charters. Voyage has a variety of sailboats for charter, with or without a captain and crew. ☒ *Soper's Hole Marina, West End* ☎ *284/494-0740, 888/869-2436* ⊕ *www.voyagecharters.com.*

White Squall II. This 80-foot schooner has regularly scheduled day sails to The Baths at Virgin Gorda, Cooper, the Indians, and the Caves at Norman Island. ☒ *Village Cay Marina, Road Town* ☎ *284/494-2564* ⊕ *www.whitesquall2.com.*

SURFING

Surfing is big on Tortola's north shore, particularly when the winter swells come into Josiah's and Apple bays. Rent surfboards starting at $65 for a full day.

HIHO. Lots of good surfboards are here, for rent as well as for sale. The staff will give you advice on the best spots to put in your board. ✉ *Trellis Bay, Road Town* ☎ *284/494–7694* ⊕ *www.go-hiho.com.*

WINDSURFING

Steady trade winds make windsurfing a breeze. Three of the best spots for sailboarding are Nanny Cay, Slaney Point, and Trellis Bay on Beef Island. Rates for sailboards start at about $25 an hour or $100 for a two-hour lesson.

Boardsailing BVI Watersports. This company rents equipment and offers private and group lessons. ✉ *Trellis Bay, Beef Island* ☎ *284/495–2447* ⊕ *www.windsurfing.vi.*

SIDE TRIPS FROM TORTOLA

There are several islands that make great side trips from Tortola, including lovely Marina Cay and tony Peter Island. Both have great accommodations, so you might want to spend the night.

The following reviews have been condensed for this book. Please go to Fodors.com for expanded reviews of each property.

MARINA CAY

Beautiful little Marina Cay is in Trellis Bay, not far from Beef Island. Sometimes you can see it and its large J-shape coral reefs—a most dramatic sight—from the air soon after takeoff from the airport on Beef Island. Covering 8 acres, this islet is considered small even by BVI standards. On it there's a restaurant, Pusser's Store, and a six-unit hotel. Ferry service is free from the dock on Beef Island.

WHERE TO STAY

For expanded reviews, facilities, and current deals, visit Fodors.com.

$ **Pusser's Marina Cay Hotel and Restaurant.** If getting away from it all is
HOTEL   your priority, this may be the place for you, because there's nothing to do on this beach-rimmed island other than swim, snorkel, and soak up the sun—there's not even a TV to distract you. **Pros:** lots of character; beautiful beaches; interesting guests. **Cons:** older property; ferry needed to get here. **TripAdvisor:** "nice location," "great view of the harbor," "beautiful seclusion." ⑤ *Rooms from: $175* ✉ *West side of Marina Cay* ☎ *284/494–2174* ⊕ *www.pussers.com/t-marina-cay.aspx* ⊸ *4 rooms, 2 2-bedroom villas* ⦿ *Breakfast.*

PETER ISLAND

Although Peter Island is home to the resort of the same name, it's also a popular anchorage for charter boaters and a destination for Tortola vacationers. The scheduled ferry trip from Peter Island's shore-side base outside Road Town runs $15 round-trip for nonguests. The island is lush, with forested hillsides sloping seaward to meet white sandy beaches. There are no roads other than those at the resort, and there's nothing to do but relax at the lovely beach set aside for day-trippers. You're welcome to dine at the resort's restaurants.

WHERE TO STAY

For expanded reviews, facilities, and current deals, visit Fodors.com.

$$$$
RESORT
🖼 **Peter Island Resort.** Total pampering and prices to match are the ticket at this luxury resort. **Pros:** lovely rooms; nice beach. **Cons:** need ferry to get here; pricey rates. **TripAdvisor:** "fabulous and relaxing," "ridiculously amazing," "lovely place and great staff." ⑤ *Rooms from: $740* ⊠ *Peter Island* ☎ *284/495–2000, 800/346–4451* ⊕ *www.peterisland. com* ⌁ *52 rooms, 3 villas* ⦿ *Multiple meal plans.*

VIRGIN GORDA FERRIES

The ferry service from the public dock in Spanish Town can be erratic. Call ahead to confirm the schedule, get there early to be sure it hasn't changed, and ask at the dock whether you're getting on the right boat. Thursday and Sunday service between Virgin Gorda and St. John is particularly prone to problems.

VIRGIN GORDA

By Lynda Lohr

Virgin Gorda, or "Fat Virgin," received its name from Christopher Columbus. The explorer envisioned the island as a pregnant woman in a languid recline, with Gorda Peak being her big belly and the boulders of The Baths her toes. Different in topography from Tortola, with its arid landscape covered with scrub brush and cactus, Virgin Gorda has a slower pace of life, too. Goats and cattle own the right-of-way, and the unpretentious friendliness of the people is winning.

EXPLORING VIRGIN GORDA

One of the most efficient ways to see Virgin Gorda is by sailboat. There are few roads, and most byways don't follow the scalloped shoreline. The main route sticks resolutely to the center of the island, linking The Baths on the southern tip with Gun Creek and Leverick Bay at North Sound. The craggy coast, cut through with grottoes and fringed by palms and boulders, has a primitive beauty. If you drive, you can hit all the sights in one day. The best plan is to explore the area near your hotel (either Spanish Town or North Sound) first, then take a day to drive to the other end. Stop to climb Gorda Peak, which is in the island's center. There are few signs, so come prepared with a map.

THE VALLEY

☺
Fodor's Choice
★

The Baths. At Virgin Gorda's most celebrated sight, giant boulders are scattered about the beach and in the water. Some are almost as large as houses and form remarkable grottoes. Climb between these rocks to swim in the many placid pools. Early morning and late afternoon are the best times to visit if you want to avoid crowds. If it's privacy you crave, follow the shore northward to quieter bays—Spring Bay, the Crawl, Little Trunk, and Valley Trunk—or head south to Devil's Bay. ⊠ *Off Tower Rd., The Baths* ☎ *284/852–3650* ⌁ *$3* ☽ *Daily dawn–dusk.*

Copper Mine Point. A tall stone shaft silhouetted against the sky and a small stone structure that overlooks the sea are part of what was once a copper mine, now in ruins. Established 400 years ago, it was worked first by the Spanish, then by the English, until the early 20th century. The route is not well marked, so turn inland near LSL Restaurant and

The Baths

look for the hard-to-see sign pointing the way. ✉ *Copper Mine Rd.* ☎ *No phone* ⊕ *www.bvinationalparkstrust.org* 💲 *Free.*

Spanish Town. Virgin Gorda's peaceful main settlement, on the island's southern wing, is so tiny that it barely qualifies as a town at all. Also known as the Valley, Spanish Town has a marina, some shops, and a couple of car-rental agencies. Just north of town is the ferry slip. At the Virgin Gorda Yacht Harbour you can stroll along the dock and do a little shopping. ✉ *Virgin Gorda.*

NORTHWEST SHORE

Coastal Islands. You can easily reach the quaintly named Fallen Jerusalem Island and the Dog Islands by a boat, which you can rent in either Tortola or Virgin Gorda. They're all part of the National Parks Trust of the Virgins Islands, and their seductive beaches and unparalleled snorkeling display the BVI at their beachcombing, hedonistic best. ✉ *Virgin Gorda* ☎ *No phone* ⊕ *www.bvinationalparkstrust.org* 💲 *Free.*

★ **Virgin Gorda Peak National Park.** There are two trails at this 265-acre park, which contains the island's highest point, at 1,359 feet. Small signs on North Sound Road mark both entrances; sometimes, however, the signs are missing, so keep your eyes open for a set of stairs that disappears into the trees. It's about a 15-minute hike from either entrance up to a small clearing, where you can climb a ladder to the platform of a wooden observation tower and a spectacular 360-degree view. ✉ *North Sound Rd., Gorda Peak* ☎ *No phone* 💲 *Free.*

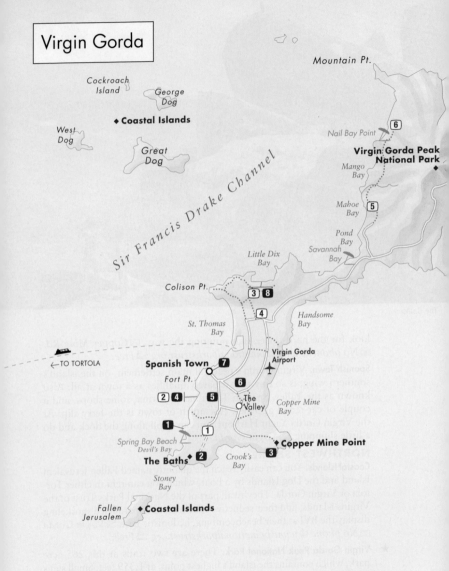

Virgin Gorda

Coastal Islands

Cockroach Island

George Dog

West Dog

Great Dog

Sir Francis Drake Channel

Mountain Pt.

Nail Bay Point — 6

Virgin Gorda Peak National Park ✦

Mango Bay

Mahoe Bay — 5

Pond Bay

Savannah Bay

Little Dix Bay

Colison Pt. — 3 8

4

Handsome Bay

St. Thomas Bay

← TO TORTOLA

Spanish Town — 7

Fort Pt.

2 4 — 5

6

The Valley

Copper Mine Bay

Virgin Gorda Airport

1

Spring Bay Beach

Devil's Bay

1

The Baths ✦ — 2

3

✦ **Copper Mine Point**

Crook's Bay

Stoney Bay

Fallen Jerusalem

✦ **Coastal Islands**

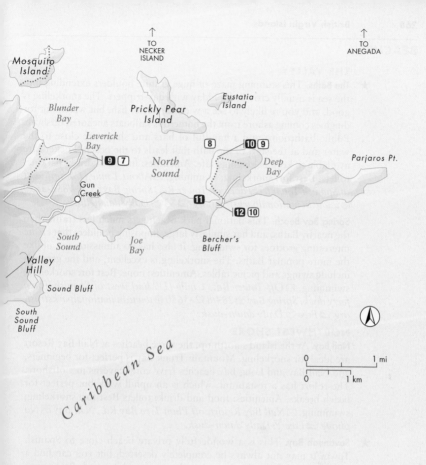

Mosquito Island

Blunder Bay

Leverick Bay

9 **7**

Gun Creek

North Sound

South Sound

Valley Hill

Joe Bay

Sound Bluff

South Sound Bluff

↑
TO
NECKER
ISLAND

Prickly Pear Island

Eustatia Island

8 **10** **9**

Deep Bay

Bercher's Bluff

11

12 **10**

↑
TO
ANEGADA

Parjaros Pt.

Caribbean Sea

0 _____ 1 mi

0 _____ 1 km

KEY
⚓ *Beaches*
🚢 *Ferry*
🚢 *Cruise Ship Terminal*
1 *Restaurants*
1 *Hotels*
······· *Trail*

BEACHES

THE VALLEY

★ **The Baths.** This stunning maze of huge granite boulders extending into the sea is usually crowded midday with day-trippers. The snorkeling is good, and you're likely to see a wide variety of fish, but watch out for dinghies coming ashore from the numerous sailboats anchored offshore. Public bathrooms and a handful of bars and shops are close to the water and at the start of the path that leads to the beach. Lockers are available to keep belongings safe. **Amenities:** food and drink; parking; toilets. **Best for:** snorkeling; swimming. ⊠ *About 1 mile [1½ km] west of Spanish Town ferry dock on Tower Rd., Spring Bay* ☎ *284/852-3650* ⊕ *www.bvinationalparkstrust.org* ⊠ *$3* ⊘ *Daily dawn–dusk.*

Spring Bay Beach. This national-park beach gets much less traffic than the nearby Baths, and has similarly large, imposing boulders that create interesting grottoes for swimming. It also has no admission fee, unlike the more popular Baths. The snorkeling is excellent, and the grounds include swings and picnic tables. **Amenities:** none. **Best for:** snorkeling; swimming. ⊠ *Off Tower Rd., 1 mile [1½ km] west of Spanish Town ferry dock, Spring Bay* ☎ *284/852–3650* ⊕ *www.bvinationalparkstrust. org* ⊠ *Free* ⊘ *Daily dawn–dusk.*

NORTHWEST SHORE

Nail Bay. At the island's north tip, the three beaches at Nail Bay Resort are ideal for snorkeling. Mountain Trunk Bay is perfect for beginners, and Nail Bay and Long Bay beaches have coral caverns just offshore. The resort has a restaurant, which is an uphill walk but perfect for beach breaks. **Amenities:** food and drink; toilets **Best for:** snorkeling; swimming. ⊠ *Nail Bay Resort, off Plum Tree Bay Rd., Nail Bay* ☎ *No phone* ⊠ *Free* ⊘ *Daily dawn–dusk.*

★ **Savannah Bay.** This is a wonderfully private beach close to Spanish Town. It may not always be completely deserted, but you can find a spot to yourself on this long stretch of soft, white sand. Bring your own mask, fins, and snorkel, as there are no facilities. The view from above is a photographer's delight. **Amenities:** none. **Best for:** solitude; snorkeling; swimming. ⊠ *Off N. Sound Rd., ¾ mile [1¼ km] east of Spanish Town ferry dock, Savannah Bay* ☎ *No phone* ⊠ *Free* ⊘ *Daily dawn–dusk.*

WHERE TO EAT

Most folks opt to have dinner somewhere at or near their hotel to avoid driving on Virgin Gorda's twisting roads at night. The Valley does have a handful of restaurants if you're sleeping close to town.

THE VALLEY

$$
ECLECTIC
✕ **Bath and Turtle.** You can sit back and relax at this informal tavern with a friendly staff—although the noise from the television can sometimes be a bit much. Well-stuffed sandwiches, homemade pizzas, pasta dishes, and daily specials such as conch soup round out the casual menu. Local musicians perform many Wednesday and Sunday nights.

⑤ *Average main: $18* ✉ *Virgin Gorda Yacht Harbour, Spanish Town* ☎ *284/495–5239* ⊕ *www.bathandturtle.com*.

$$$ ✕**Chez Bamboo.** This pleasant little hideaway isn't difficult to find; look
ECLECTIC for the building with the purple-and-green latticework. Candles in the dining room and on the patio help make this a mellow place where you can enjoy a bowl of lobster bisque, something from the tapas menu, or one of the specialties such as lobster curry. For dessert, try the chocolate cake or crème brûlée. Stop by Friday night for live music. ⑤ *Average main: $29* ✉ *Across from and a little north of Virgin Gorda Yacht Harbour, Spanish Town* ☎ *284/495–5752* ⊕ *www.chezbamboo.com* ✉ *No lunch*.

$$$ ✕**Fischer's Cove Restaurant.** Dine seaside at this alfresco restaurant that's
ECLECTIC open to the breezes. If pumpkin soup is on the menu, give it a try for a true taste of the Caribbean. Although you can get burgers and salads at lunch, local fish (whatever is available) and *fungi* (a cornmeal-based side dish) is a tasty alternative. For dinner, try the Caribbean lobster or grilled mahimahi with lemon and garlic. ⑤ *Average main: $29* ✉ *Lee Rd., The Valley* ☎ *284/495–5252* ⊕ *www.fischerscove.com*.

$$$$ ✕**Little Dix Bay Pavilion.** For an elegant evening, you can't do better
INTERNATIONAL than this—the candlelight in the open-air pavilion is enchanting, the always-changing menu sophisticated, the service attentive. Superbly prepared seafood, meat, and vegetarian entrées draw locals and visitors alike. Favorites include a Cajun pork loin with mango salsa and scallion potatoes, and mahimahi with warm chorizo and chickpea salad served with a zucchini and tomato chutney. The Monday evening buffet shines. ⑤ *Average main: $33* ✉ *Little Dix Bay Resort, Spanish Town* ☎ *284/495–5555* ⊕ *www.littledixbay.com* ⟟ *Reservations essential*.

$$$$ ✕**LSL Bake Shop & Restaurant.** Along the road to The Baths, this small
ECLECTIC restaurant with pedestrian decor is a local favorite. You can always find fresh fish on the menu, but folks with a taste for other dishes won't be disappointed. Try the pork tenderloin pesto with herb potatoes and a peppercorn sauce or the banana curry shrimp with a coconut milk sauce. ⑤ *Average main: $33* ✉ *Tower Rd., The Valley* ☎ *284/495–5151*.

$$$$ ✕**Mine Shaft Café.** Perched on a hilltop that offers a view of spectacular
ECLECTIC sunsets, this restaurant near Copper Mine Point serves simple, well-prepared food, including grilled fish, steaks, and baby back ribs. Tuesday night features an all-you-can-eat Caribbean-style barbecue. The monthly full-moon parties draw a big local crowd. ⑤ *Average main: $33* ✉ *Copper Mine Point, The Valley* ☎ *284/495–5260*.

$$$$ ✕**The Rock Café.** Good Italian cuisine and seafood is served among the
ITALIAN waterfalls and giant boulders that form the famous Baths. For dinner at this open-air eatery, feast on chicken and penne in a tomato-cream sauce, spaghetti with lobster sauce, or fresh red snapper in a butter-and-caper sauce. For dessert, don't miss the chocolate mousse. ⑤ *Average main: $33* ✉ *The Valley* ☎ *284/495–5482* ⊕ *www.bvidining.com* ✉ *No lunch*.

$$$$ ✕**Top of the Baths.** At the entrance to The Baths, this popular restaurant
ECLECTIC has tables on an outdoor terrace or in an open-air pavilion; all have
ⵙ stunning views of the Sir Francis Drake Channel. The restaurant starts serving at 8 am; for lunch, hamburgers, coconut chicken sandwiches, and fish-and-chips are among the offerings. For dessert, the key lime

pie is excellent. The Sunday barbecue, served from noon until 3 pm, is an island event. ⑤ *Average main: $35* ✉ *The Valley* ☎ *284/495–5497* ⊕ *www.topofthebaths.com* ⊗ *No dinner Mon.*

NORTH SOUND

$$$$
INTERNATIONAL

✕ **Biras Creek Restaurant.** This hilltop restaurant at the Biras Creek Hotel has eye-popping views of North Sound. The four-course prix-fixe menu changes daily and includes several choices per course. For starters, there may be an artichoke, green bean, and wild mushroom salad topped with balsamic vinaigrette, or cream of sweet potato soup accompanied by potato straws. Entrées may include pan-seared snapper over horseradish pearl pasta. The desserts, including a lemon ricotta cheesecake with a spicy passion-fruit sauce, are stupendous. Dinner ends with Biras Creek's signature offering of cheese and port. Most days, lunch is a barbecue on the beach. ⑤ *Average main: $100* ✉ *Biras Creek Hotel, North Sound* ☎ *284/494–3555, 800/223–1108* ⊕ *www.biras.com* ⌫ *Reservations essential.*

$$$
ECLECTIC
★

✕ **The Clubhouse.** The Bitter End Yacht Club's open-air waterfront restaurant is a favorite rendezvous for sailors and their guests, so it's busy day and night. You can find lavish buffets for breakfast, lunch, and dinner, as well as an à la carte menu. Dinner selections include grilled mahimahi or tuna, local lobster, and porterhouse steak, as well as vegetarian dishes. ⑤ *Average main: $22* ✉ *Bitter End Yacht Club, North Sound* ☎ *284/494–2745* ⊕ *www.beyc.com* ⌫ *Reservations essential.*

$$
ECLECTIC
☺

✕ **Fat Virgin's Café.** This casual beachfront eatery offers a straightforward menu of baby back ribs, chicken roti, vegetable pasta, grouper sandwiches, and fresh fish specials for lunch and dinner. You can also find a good selection of Caribbean beer. ⑤ *Average main: $19* ✉ *Biras Creek Resort, North Sound* ☎ *284/495–7052* ⊕ *www.fatvirgin.com.*

$$$$
ECLECTIC

✕ **Restaurant at Leverick Bay.** The laid-back menu at this beach restaurant draws cruise-ship passengers on tour as well as hotels guests and locals. The menu includes burgers, pizza, roti, chili, and fish-and-chips for lunch. At dinner the menu becomes more upscale, with dishes that feature wild salmon and Kobe beef. ⑤ *Average main: $39* ✉ *Leverick Bay Resort & Marina, Leverick Bay* ☎ *284/495–7154* ⊕ *www.therestaurantatleverickbay.com.*

WHERE TO STAY

Villas are scattered all over Virgin Gorda, but hotels are centered in and around The Valley, Nail Bay, and in the North Sound area. Except for Leverick Bay Resort, which is around the point from North Sound, all hotels in North Sound are reached only by ferry.

For expanded reviews, facilities, and current deals, visit Fodors.com.

PRIVATE VILLAS

Those craving seclusion would do well at a villa. Most have full kitchens and maid service. Prices per week in winter run from around $2,000 for a one- or two-bedroom villa up to $10,000 for a five-room beachfront villa. Rates in summer are substantially less. On Virgin Gorda a villa in the North Sound area means you can pretty much stay put at night unless you want to make the drive on its narrow roads. If you opt for a spot near The Baths, it's an easier drive to town.

VILLA RENTAL AGENTS

McLaughlin-Anderson Luxury Villas. The St. Thomas–based McLaughlin-Anderson Luxury Villas represents about 18 properties all over Virgin Gorda. Villas range in size from two bedrooms to six bedrooms, and come with full kitchens, pools, stellar views, and other amenities. The company can hire a chef and stock your kitchen with groceries. A seven-night minimum is required during the winter season. ⊠ *1000 Blackbeard's Hill, Suite 3, Charlotte Amalie, Virgin Gorda, U.S. Virgin Islands* ☎ *340/776–0635, 800/537–6246* ⊕ *www.mclaughlinanderson.com.*

Tropical Care Services. This management company's dozen properties stretch from The Baths to the Nail Bay area. Several budget properties are included among the pricier offerings. Most houses have private pools, and a few are right on the beach. A sister company at the same number, Tropical Nannies, provides babysitting services. *284/495–6493* ⊕ *www.tropicalcareservices.com.*

Virgin Gorda Villa Rentals. This company's 40 or so properties are all near Leverick Bay Resort and Mahoe Bay, so they are perfect for those who want to be close to activities. Many of the accommodations—from studios to six or more bedrooms—have private swimming pools and air-conditioning, at least in the bedrooms. All have full kitchens, are well maintained, and have spectacular views. *284/495–7421, 800/848–7081* ⊕ *www.virgingordabvi.com.*

THE VALLEY

$
RESORT
☾
Fischer's Cove Beach Hotel. The rooms are modest, the furniture is discount-store-style, and the walls are thin, but you can't beat the location right on the beach and within walking distance of Spanish Town's shops and restaurants. **Pros:** beachfront location; budget price; good restaurant. **Cons:** very basic units; thin walls; no a/c in some rooms. **TripAdvisor:** "gorgeous," "comfortable and clean," "gorgeous beach." ⑤ *Rooms from: $125* ⊠ *Lee Rd.* ☎ *284/495–5252* ⊕ *www.fischerscove.com* ⋧ *12 rooms, 8 cottages* ❍*No meals.*

$
RENTAL
★
Guavaberry Spring Bay Vacation Homes. Rambling back from the beach, these hexagonal one- and two-bedroom villas give you all the comforts of home—and that striking boulder-fringed beach is just

minutes away. **Pros:** short walk to The Baths (and excellent snorkeling); easy drive to town; great beaches nearby. **Cons:** few amenities; older property; basic decor. **TripAdvisor:** "simple but nice," "well run," "beautiful beach." ⑤ *Rooms from: $240* ✉ *Tower Rd.* ☎ *284/495–5227* ⊕ *www.guava berryspringbay.com* ⇔ *12 1-bedroom units, 6 2-bedroom units, 1 3-bedroom unit, 16 villas* ⊟ *No credit cards* ⦿ *No meals.*

$$$$
RESORT
☾
★

Rosewood Little Dix Bay. This laidback luxury resort offers a gorgeous crescent of sand, plenty of activities, and good restaurants. **Pros:** convenient location; lovely grounds; near many restaurants. **Cons:** expensive; very spread out; insular though not isolated. **TripAdvisor:** "the perfect beach vacation resort experience," "beautiful property," "special place." ⑤ *Rooms from: $665* ✉ *Box 70, off North Sound Rd., Little Dix Bay* ☎ *284/495–5555* ⊕ *www.littledixbay.com* ⇔ *73 rooms, 20 suites, 7 villas* ⦿ *No meals.*

$
RENTAL

Virgin Gorda Village. All the condos in this upscale complex a few minutes' drive from Spanish Town have at least partial ocean views. **Pros:** close to Spanish Town; lovely pool; recently built units. **Cons:** no beach; on a busy street; some noisy roosters nearby. **TripAdvisor:** "peaceful and relaxing," "nicely decorated condos," "amazingly chilled." ⑤ *Rooms from: $250* ✉ *North Sound Rd.* ☎ *284/495–5544* ⊕ *www.virgingordavillage.com* ⇔ *30 condos* ⦿ *No meals.*

NORTHWEST SHORE

$
RENTAL

Mango Bay Resort. Sitting seaside on Virgin Gorda's north coast, this collection of contemporary condos and villas will make you feel right at home. **Pros:** nice beach; lively location; good restaurant. **Cons:** construction in area; drab decor; some units have lackluster views. **TripAdvisor:** "perfect paradise," "wonderful setting," "great beach." ⑤ *Rooms from: $195* ✉ *Off Nail Bay Rd.* ☎ *284/495–5672* ⊕ *www.mangobayresort. com* ⇔ *17 condos, 5 villas* ⦿ *No meals.*

$
RESORT
★

Nail Bay Resort. On a hill above the coast, this beachfront resort offers a wide selection of rooms and suites. **Pros:** full kitchens; lovely beach; close to town. **Cons:** busy neighborhood; bit of a drive from main road; uphill walk from beach. **TripAdvisor:** "first-rate service," "beautiful beaches," "awe inspiring views." ⑤ *Rooms from: $240* ✉ *Off Nail Bay Rd.* ☎ *284/494–8000, 800/871–3551* ⊕ *www.nailbay.com* ⇔ *4 rooms, 4 suites, 9 villas* ⦿ *No meals.*

NORTH SOUND

$$$$
RESORT
★

Biras Creek Resort. Tucked out of the way on the island's North Sound, Biras Creek has a get-away-from-it-all feel that's a major draw for its well-heeled clientele. **Pros:** luxurious rooms; professional staff; good dining options; private, white-sand beach. **Cons:** very expensive;

isolated; difficult for people with mobility problems. **TripAdvisor:** "sophisticated escape," "unspoiled natural setting," "quiet retreat." $ *Rooms from: $970* ⊠ *North Sound* ☎ *284/494–3555, 877/883–0756* ⊕ *www.biras.com* ↩ *31 suites* ⦿ *All meals.*

$$$$
ALL-INCLUSIVE
☾
Fodor's Choice
★

☷ **Bitter End Yacht Club.** Sailing's the thing at this busy hotel and marina in the nautically inclined North Sound, and the use of everything from small sailboats to kayaks to windsurfers is included in the price. **Pros:** lots of water sports; good diving opportunities; friendly guests. **Cons:** expensive rates; isolated; lots of stairs. **TripAdvisor:** "heaven on earth for families," "sailor's delight," "great rooms." $ *Rooms from: $500* ⊠ *North Sound* ☎ *284/494–2746, 800/872–2392* ⊕ *www.beyc.com* ↩ *85 rooms* ⦿ *All-inclusive.*

$
RESORT

☷ **Leverick Bay Resort and Marina.** With its colorful buildings and bustling marina, Leverick Bay is a good choice for visitors who want easy access to water-sports activities. **Pros:** fun location; good restaurant; small grocery store. **Cons:** small beach; no laundry in units; 15-minute drive to town. **TripAdvisor:** "pure heaven," "good base," "a lovely family vacation." $ *Rooms from: $149* ⊠ *Off Leverick Bay Rd., Leverick Bay* ☎ *284/495–7421, 800/848–7081* ⊕ *www.leverickbay.com* ↩ *13 rooms, 4 apartments* ⦿ *No meals.*

$
RESORT

☷ **Saba Rock Resort.** Reachable only by a free ferry or by private yacht, this resort on its own tiny cay is perfect for folks who want to mix and mingle with the sailors who drop anchor for the night. **Pros:** party atmosphere; convenient transportation; good diving nearby. **Cons:** tiny beach; isolated location; on a very small island. **TripAdvisor:** "the most beautifully unique place," "restaurant was excellent," "great R&R." $ *Rooms from: $150* ⊠ *North Sound* ☎ *284/495–7711, 284/495– 9966* ⊕ *www.sabarock.com* ↩ *7 1-bedroom suites, 1 2-bedroom suite* ⦿ *Breakfast.*

NIGHTLIFE

Pick up a free copy of the *Limin' Times* (⊕ *www.limin-times.com*)— available at most resorts and restaurants—for the most current local entertainment schedule.

Bath and Turtle. During high season, the Bath and Turtle is one of the liveliest spots on Virgin Gorda, hosting island bands Wednesday from 8 pm until midnight. ⊠ *Virgin Gorda Yacht Harbour, Spanish Town* ☎ *284/495–5239* ⊕ *www.bathandturtle.com.*

Bitter End Yacht Club. Local bands play several nights a week at the Bitter End Yacht Club during the winter season. ⊠ *North Sound* ☎ *284/494– 2746* ⊕ *www.beyc.com.*

Chez Bamboo. This is the place for calypso and reggae on Friday night. ⊠ *Across from Virgin Gorda Yacht Harbour, Spanish Town* ☎ *284/495– 5752* ⊕ *www.chezbamboo.com.*

Mine Shaft Café. The cafe has music on Tuesday and Friday. ⊠ *Copper Mine Point, The Valley* ☎ *284/495–5260* ⊕ *www.mineshaftbvi.com.*

Restaurant at Leverick Bay. This resort's main restaurant hosts music on Tuesday and Friday in season. ⊠ *Leverick Bay Resort & Marina, Leverick Bay* ☎ *284/495–7154* ⊕ *www.therestaurantatleverickbay.com.*

Rock Café. There's live piano music nearly every night during the Rock Café's winter season. ⊠ *The Valley* ☎ *284/495–5177* ⊕ *www.bvidining. com.*

SHOPPING

Most boutiques are within hotel complexes or at Virgin Gorda Yacht Harbour. Two of the best are at Biras Creek and Little Dix Bay. Other properties—the Bitter End and Leverick Bay—have small but equally good boutiques.

Pusser's Company Store. On offer here: a trademark line of sportswear, rum products, and gift items. ⊠ *Leverick Bay* ☎ *284/495–7371* ⊕ *www. pussers.com.*

FOOD

Bitter End Emporium. This store at the Bitter End is the place for local fruits, cheeses, baked goods, and gourmet prepared food. ⊠ *Bitter End Yacht Harbor, North Sound* ☎ *284/494–2746* ⊕ *www.beyc.com.*

Buck's Food Market. This market is the closest the island offers to a full-service supermarket, with an in-store bakery and deli as well as fresh fish and produce departments. ⊠ *Virgin Gorda Yacht Harbour, Spanish Town* ☎ *284/495–5423* ⊕ *www.bucksmarketplace.com* ⊠ *Gun Creek, North Sound* ☎ *284/495–7368* ⊕ *www.bucksmarketplace.com.*

Chef's Pantry. This store has the fixings for an impromptu party in your villa or on your boat—fresh seafood, specialty meats, imported cheeses, fresh-baked breads and pastries, and an impressive wine and spirit selection. ⊠ *Leverick Bay* ☎ *284/495–7677.*

GIFTS

Reeftique. This store carries island crafts and jewelry, clothing, and nautical odds and ends with the Bitter End logo. ⊠ *Bitter End Yacht Harbor, North Sound* ☎ *284/494–2746* ⊕ *www.beyc.com.*

Thee Nautical Gallery. This boutique sells attractive handcrafted jewelry, paintings, and one-of-a-kind gift items, as well as books about the Caribbean. ⊠ *Leverick Bay* ☎ *284/495–7479.*

SPORTS AND ACTIVITIES

DIVING AND SNORKELING

Where you go snorkeling and what company you pick depends on where you're staying. Many hotels have on-site dive outfitters, but if they don't, one won't be far away. If your hotel does have a dive operation, just stroll down to the dock and hop aboard—no need to drive anywhere. The dive companies are all certified by PADI. Costs vary, but count on paying about $75 for a one-tank dive and $110 for a two-tank dive. All dive operators offer introductory courses as well as certification and advanced courses. Should you get an attack of the bends, which

You can learn to sail at the Bitter End Yacht Club.

can happen when you ascend too rapidly, the nearest decompression chamber is at Roy L. Schneider Regional Medical Center in St. Thomas.

There are some terrific snorkel and dive sites off Virgin Gorda, including areas around The Baths, the North Sound, and the Dogs. The Chimney at Great Dog Island has a coral archway and canyon covered with a wide variety of sponges. At Joe's Cave, an underwater cavern on West Dog Island, huge groupers, eagle rays, and other colorful fish accompany divers as they swim. At some sites you can see 100 feet down, but divers who don't want to go that deep and snorkelers will find plenty to look at just below the surface.

Bitter End Yacht Club. The BEYC schedules two snorkeling trips a day. ⊠ *North Sound* ☎ *284/494–2746* ⊕ *www.beyc.com.*

Dive BVI. In addition to day trips, Dive BVI also offers expert instruction and certification. ⊠ *Virgin Gorda Yacht Harbour, Spanish Town* ☎ *284/495–5513, 800/848–7078* ⊕ *www.divebvi.com* ⊠ *Leverick Bay Resort and Marina, Leverick Bay* ☎ *284/495–7328, 800/848–7078* ⊕ *www.divebvi.com.*

Sunchaser Scuba. Resort, advanced, and rescue courses are all available here. ⊠ *Bitter End Yacht Club, North Sound* ☎ *284/495–9638, 800/932–4286* ⊕ *www.sunchaserscuba.com.*

MINIATURE GOLF

Golf Virgin Gorda. The 9-hole mini-golf course Golf Virgin Gorda is delightfully nestled between huge granite boulders. ⊠ *Copper Mine Point, next to the Mine Shaft Café, The Valley* ☎ *284/495–5260.*

SAILING AND BOATING

The BVI waters are calm, and terrific places to learn to sail. You can also rent sea kayaks, waterskiing equipment, dinghies, and powerboats, or take a parasailing trip.

Bitter End Sailing School. Classroom, dockside, and on-the-water lessons are available for sailors of all levels. Private lessons are $75 per hour. ⊠ *Bitter End Yacht Club, North Sound* ☎ *284/494–2746* ⊕ *www.beyc. com.*

Double "D" Charters. If you just want to sit back, relax, and let the captain take the helm, choose a sailing or power yacht from Double "D" Charters. Rates are $75 for a half-day trip and $125 for a full-day island-hopping excursion. Private full-day cruises or sails for up to eight people run from $950. ⊠ *Virgin Gorda Yacht Harbour, Spanish Town* ☎ *284/499–2479* ⊕ *www.doubledbvi.com).*

Leverick Bay Watersports. If you want to rent a Sunfish or a dinghy, check out Leverick Bay Watersports. ⊠ *Leverick Bay, North Sound* ☎ *284/495–7376* ⊕ *www.watersportsbvi.com).*

WINDSURFING

Bitter End Yacht Club. The North Sound is a good place to learn to windsurf: it's protected, so you can't be easily blown out to sea. The Bitter End Yacht Club gives lessons and rents equipment for $40 to $60 per hour for nonguests. A half-day Windsurfer rental runs $75. ⊠ *North Sound* ☎ *284/494–2746* ⊕ *www.beyc.com.*

JOST VAN DYKE

Updated by Susanna Henighan Potter

Named after an early Dutch settler, Jost Van Dyke is a small island northwest of Tortola. It's also a place to truly get away from it all. Mountainous and lush, the 4-mile-long (6½-km-long) island—with fewer than 200 full-time residents—has one tiny resort, some rental houses and villas, a campground, a few shops, a handful of cars, and a single road. There are no banks or ATMs on the island, and many restaurants and shops accept only cash. It's a good idea to buy groceries on St. Thomas or Tortola before arriving if you're staying for a few days. Life definitely rolls along on "island time," especially during the off-season from August to November, when finding a restaurant open for dinner can be a challenge. Water conservation is encouraged, as the source is rainwater collected in basement-like cisterns. Many lodgings will ask you to follow the Caribbean golden rule: "In the land of sun and fun, we never flush for number one." Jost is one of the Caribbean's most popular anchorages, and there are a disproportionately large number of informal bars and restaurants, which have helped earn Jost its reputation as the "party island" of the BVI.

BEACHES

Sandy Cay. Just offshore, the little islet known as Sandy Cay is a gleaming sliver of white sand with marvelous snorkeling and an inland nature trail. You can hire any boatman on Jost Van Dyke to take you out; just

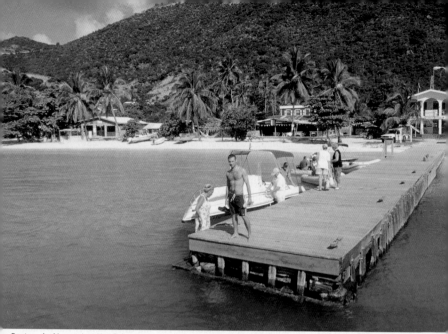

Boaters docking at Jost Van Dyke

be sure to agree on a price and a time to be picked up again. **Amenities:** none. **Good for:** snorkeling. ⊠ *Jost Van Dyke.*

☺ **White Bay.** On the south shore, west of Great Harbour, this long stretch
★ of picturesque white sand is especially popular with boaters who come ashore for a libation at one of the beach bars. **Amenities:** food and drink; toilets. **Good for:** swimming. ⊠ *Jost Van Dyke.*

WHERE TO EAT

Restaurants on Jost Van Dyke are informal (some serve meals family-style at long tables) and often charming. The island is a favorite charter-boat stop, and you're bound to hear people exchanging stories about the previous night's anchoring adventures. Most restaurants don't take reservations (but for those that do, they are usually required). In all cases, dress is casual.

$$$ ✕ **Abe's by the Sea.** Many sailors who cruise into this quiet bay come so
ECLECTIC they can dock right at this open-air eatery to enjoy the seafood, conch, lobster, and other fresh catches. Chicken and ribs round out the menu, and affable owners Abe Coakley and his wife, Eunicy, add a pinch and dash of hospitality that makes a meal into a memorable evening. Casual lunches are also served, and an adjoining market sells ice, canned goods, and other necessities. Dinner reservations are required by 5 pm. ⑤ *Average main: $30* ⊠ *Little Harbour* ☎ *284/495–9329* ⌂ *Reservations essential.*

$$$
SEAFOOD
★

✕ Ali Baba's. Lobster is the main attraction at this beach bar with a sandy floor, which is just some 20 feet from the sea. Grilled local fish, including swordfish, kingfish, and wahoo, are specialties and caught fresh daily. There's also a pig roast here on Monday night in season, and Friday night is roti night. Beware: Ali Baba's special rum punch is as potent as it is delicious. Reservations aren't mandatory for dinner, but you will probably find yourself waiting a long time without them. ⑤ *Average main: $29* ⊠ *Great Harbour* ☎ *284/495-9280.*

$$$
ECLECTIC

✕ Corsairs Beach Bar and Restaurant. On an island known for seafood, it's the pizza that draws raves at this friendly beach bar considered by some to be Jost's version of *Cheers.* If pizza doesn't appeal, then try the outstanding sushi, northern Italian pasta dishes, and fresh seafood, including a brilliant lobster stuffed with shrimp and scallops. Bring an appetite to breakfast, when the choices include hearty omelets and breakfast burritos. The bar is easily recognized by its signature pirate paraphernalia and a restored U.S. military M37 Dodge truck parked next to the steps-from-the-sea dining room. Live music, potent libations, and the only Jägermeister machine in the territory (it chills your shots to 28°F) keep things moving from happy hour into the night. Even if you're not hungry, this is a great hangout. ⑤ *Average main: $30* ⊠ *Great Harbour* ☎ *284/495-9294* ⊕ *www.corsairsbvi.com.*

$$$
ECLECTIC
★

✕ Foxy's Tamarind Bar and Restaurant. The big draw here is the owner, Foxy Callwood, a famed calypso singer who will serenade you with lewd and laugh-worthy songs as you fork into burgers, grilled chicken, barbecue ribs, and lobster. Check out the pennants, postcards, and weathered T-shirts that adorn every inch of the walls and ceiling of this large, two-story beach shack; they've been left by previous visitors. On Friday and Saturday nights in season Foxy hosts Caribbean-style barbecue with grilled fresh fish, chicken and ribs, peas and rice, salad, and more, followed by live music. Other nights choose from steak, fresh lobster, pork, or pasta; at lunch Foxy serves sandwiches and salads. Whether because of the sheer volume of diners or the experience of the management, Foxy's is one of the most reliable eating establishments on Jost. And it's also home to the only espresso on the island. You're unlikely to find Foxy performing at night, but he takes the mike many afternoons, making this a popular happy-hour pit stop. ⑤ *Average main: $29* ⊠ *Great Harbour* ☎ *284/495-9258* ⊕ *www.foxysbar.com.*

$$
ECLECTIC
★

✕ Harris' Place. All-you-can-eat lobster in a garlic butter sauce on Monday; freshly caught seafood on Thursday; pork, chicken, and ribs on Saturday: three good reasons to make your reservations early in the day at this quaint restaurant with the distinctive red roof and picnic tables underneath. Owner Cynthia Harris is as famous for her friendliness as she is for her food. Homemade key lime pie and expertly blended bushwackers are "to live for," as Cynthia would say, but diners also praise the fresh fish and lobster. Live music on Monday and Saturday evenings turns dinner into a party. Breakfast and lunch are served, too. ⑤ *Average main: $19* ⊠ *Little Harbour* ☎ *284/495-9302.*

$$
ECLECTIC
★

✕ One Love Bar and Grill. It's a toss-up whether Seddy Callwood's magic tricks or the finger-lickin' ribs and johnnycakes he serves are a greater draw. The Food Network's Alton Brown sought out this beachfront eatery and featured its stewed conch on a 2008 flavor-finding trip. Try that, the coconut shrimp, or a fresh fish sandwich, washed down with the house specialty, a Bushwhacker. Seddy, Foxy Callwood's son, built his bar himself and decorated it with the flotsam and jetsam he has collected over his years as a fisherman. $ *Average main: $20* ⊠ *White Bay* ☎ *284/495–9829* ⊕ *www.onelovebar.com.*

$$$$
ECLECTIC
✕ **Soggy Dollar Bar.** At night, candles illuminate this tiny beachfront, palm-lined dining room, making it one of the most romantic settings on the island. The cuisine is familiar yet sophisticated, with choices like sweet and sour glazed pork, pan-fried snapper, and coq au vin. Don't miss the Painkiller ice cream, inspired by the cocktail, invented here. For lunch, if you can find your way through the throngs ordering Painkillers at the bar, choose from flying-fish sandwiches, hamburgers, chicken roti, and conch fritters. Reservations aren't essential for dinner, but they're still a good idea. $ *Average main: $33* ⊠ *White Bay* ☎ *284/495–9888* ⊕ *www.soggydollar.com.*

$$$$
ECLECTIC
✕ **Sydney's Peace and Love.** Here you can find great local lobster and fish, as well as barbecue chicken and ribs with all the fixings, including peas and rice, corn, coleslaw, and potato salad. Book early for all-you-can-eat lobster on Monday and Thursday nights. Meals are served on an open-air terrace or in an air-conditioned dining room at the water's edge. The find here is a sensational (by BVI standards) jukebox. The cognoscenti sail here for dinner, since there's no beach—and therefor no annoying sand fleas. Breakfast and lunch are served, too, and guests help themselves at the honor bar. $ *Average main: $33* ⊠ *Little Harbour* ☎ *284/495–9271.*

WHERE TO STAY

For expanded reviews, facilities, and current deals, visit Fodors.com.

$$
HOTEL
🛏 **Sandcastle.** Sleep steps from beautiful White Bay beach at this tiny beachfront hideaway, an island favorite for more than 40 years. **Pros:** beachfront rooms; near restaurants and bars; comfy hammocks. **Cons:** some rooms lack air-conditioning; beach sometimes clogged with day-trippers; no children allowed. **TripAdvisor:** "best beach," "great place to just chill," "pure rest and relaxation." $ *Rooms from: $285* ⊠ *White Bay* ☎ *284/495–9888* ⊕ *www.soggydollar.com* ⤢ *2 rooms, 4 1-bedroom cottages* ⎮○⎮ *Multiple meal plans.*

$
RENTAL
☾
★
🛏 **White Bay Villas and Seaside Cottages.** Beautiful views and friendly staff keep guests coming back to these hilltop one- to three-bedroom villas and cottages. **Pros:** incredible views; full kitchens; friendly staff. **Cons:** 10- to 15-minute walk to White Bay and Great Harbour's restaurants and beaches; rental cars recommended. **TripAdvisor:** "return to paradise," "relaxing and beautiful," "a little piece of heaven." $ *Rooms from: $220* ⊠ *White Bay* ☎ *410/571–6692, 800/778–8066* ⊕ *www.jostvandyke.com* ⤢ *7 villas, 3 cottages* ⎮○⎮ *No meals.*

NIGHTLIFE

★ Jost Van Dyke is the most happening place to go barhopping in the BVI, so much so that it is an all-day enterprise for some. In fact, yachties will sail over just to have a few drinks. All the spots are easy to find, clustered in three general locations: Great Harbour, White Bay, and Little Harbour (⇨ see *Where to Eat, above*). On the Great Harbour side you can find Foxy's, Corsairs, and Ali Baba's; on the White Bay side are the One Love Bar and Grill and the Soggy Dollar Bar, where legend has it the famous Painkiller was first concocted; and in Little Harbour are Harris' Place, Sydney's Peace and Love, and Abe's By The Sea. If you can't make it to Jost Van Dyke, you can have a Painkiller at almost any bar in the BVI.

SPORTS AND ACTIVITIES

Abe and Eunicy Rentals. This company's two-door Suzukis ($65 a day), four-door Suzukis ($75 a day), and four-door Monteros ($80 a day) will help you explore by land. There's pickup and drop-off service from anywhere on the island. ⊠ *Little Harbour* ☎ *284/495–9329.*

JVD Scuba and BVI Eco-Tours. Check out the undersea world around the island with dive master Colin Aldridge. One of the most impressive dives in the area is off the north coast of Little Jost Van Dyke. Here you can find the Twin Towers: a pair of rock formations rising an impressive 90 feet. A one-tank dive costs $85, a two-tank dive $115, and a four-hour beginner course $120. Colin also offers day trips to Sandy Cay and Sandy Spit, excursions to The Baths on Virgin Gorda, and custom outings. ⊠ *Great Harbour* ☎ *284/495–0271* ⊕ *www.bvi-ecotours.com.*

Paradise Jeep Rentals. Paradise Jeep Rentals offers the ideal vehicles to tackle Jost Van Dyke's steep, winding roads. Even though Jost is a relatively small island, you really need to be in shape to walk from one bay to the next. This outfit rents two-door Suzukis for $60 per day and four-door Grand Vitaras and Sportages for $70. Discounts are availble for rentals of six or more days. It's next to the Fire Station in Great Harbour. Reservations are a must. ⊠ *Back St., Great Harbour* ☎ *284/495–9477.*

ANEGADA

Updated
by Susanna
Henighan
Potter

Anegada lies low on the horizon about 14 miles (22½ km) north of Virgin Gorda. Unlike the hilly volcanic islands in the chain, this is a flat coral-and-limestone atoll. Nine miles (14 km) long and 2 miles (3 km) wide, the island rises no more than 28 feet above sea level. In fact, by the time you're able to see it, you may have run your boat onto a reef. (More than 300 captains unfamiliar with the waters have done so since exploration days; note that bareboat charters don't allow their vessels to head here without a trained skipper.) Although the reefs are a sailor's nightmare, they (and the shipwrecks they've caused) are a scuba diver's dream. Snorkeling, especially in the waters around Loblolly Bay on the North Shore, is a transcendent experience. You can float in shallow, calm water just a few feet from shore and see one coral formation after another, each shimmering with a rainbow of colorful fish. Many local captains are happy to take visitors out fishing for bonefish. Such watery pleasures are complemented by ever-so-fine, ever-so-white sand (the northern and western shores have long stretches of the stuff) and the occasional beach bar (stop in for burgers, local lobster, or a frosty beer). The island's population of about 180 lives primarily in a small south-side village called the Settlement, which has two grocery stores, a bakery, and a general store. In 2009 Anegada got its first bank, but it's open only one day a week, and there's still no ATM. Many restaurants and shops take only cash.

WHERE TO EAT

There are between 6 and 10 restaurants open at any one time, depending on the season and on whim. Check when you're on the island. Fresh fish and lobster are the specialties of the island. The going rate for a lobster dinner is $50, and it's always the most expensive thing on any restaurant menu.

$$$$ ✕ **Anegada Reef Hotel Restaurant.** Seasoned yachters gather here nightly to
SEAFOOD share tales of the high seas; the open-air bar is the busiest on the island. Dinner is by candlelight under the stars and always includes famous Anegada lobster, steaks, and succulent baby back ribs—all prepared on the large grill by the little open-air bar. The ferry dock is right next door, so expect a crowd shortly after it arrives. Dinner reservations are required by 4 pm. Breakfast favorites include lobster omelets and rum-soaked French toast; at lunch the Reef serves salads and sandwiches. $ *Average main: $37* ⊠ *Setting Point* ☎ *284/495–8002* ⌣ *Reservations essential.*

$$$ ✕ **Big Bamboo.** This beachfront bar and restaurant tucked among sea
SEAFOOD grape trees at famous Loblolly Bay is the island's most popular destina-
★ tion for lunch. After you've polished off a plate of succulent Anegada lobster, barbecue chicken or fresh fish, you can spend the afternoon on the beach, where the snorkeling is excellent and the view close to perfection. Fruity drinks from the cabana bar and ice cream from the freezer will round out your day. Dinner is by request only. If your heart is set on lobster, it's a good idea to call in the morning or day before to put in your request. $ *Average main: $29* ⊠ *Loblolly Bay West* ☎ *284/495–2019.*

$$$$ ✕ **Cow Wreck Bar and Grill.** Named for the cow bones that once washed
SEAFOOD up on shore, this wiggle-your-toes-in-the-sand beachside eatery on the north shore is a fun place to watch the antics of surfers and kite-board-ers skidding across the bay. Tuck into conch ceviche or the popular hot wings for lunch. The homemade coconut pie is a winner. Pack your snorkel gear and explore the pristine reef just a few strokes from the shore before you eat, or browse the on-site gift shop. Dinner is served by request; reservations required by 4 pm. $ *Average main: $35* ⊠ *Loblolly Bay East* ☎ *284/495–8047* ⊕ *www.cowwreckbeach.com* ⌣ *Reservations essential.*

$$$$ ✕ **Neptune's Treasure.** The owners, the Soares family, have lived on the
SEAFOOD island for more than half a century, and the Soares men catch, cook,
↻ and serve the seafood at this homey bar and restaurant a short distance from Setting Point. The fresh lobster, swordfish, tuna, and mahimahi are all delicious. Homemade bread, a symphony of sides, and made-from-scratch desserts (including key lime pie and chocolate brownies) round

Anegada has miles of beautiful white-sand beaches.

out your meal. Dinner is by candlelight at the water's edge, often with classic jazz playing softly in the background. If you've tired of seafood, Neptune's has a nice variety of alternatives, including vegetarian pasta, pork loin, and orange chicken. The view is spectacular at sunset. Breakfast is also served. Dinner reservations are essential by 4 pm. ⑤ *Average main: $36* ⊠ *Benders Bay* ☎ *284/495-9439* ⊕ *www.neptunestreasure. com* ⌂ *Reservations essential* ⊘ *No lunch.*

$$$$
SEAFOOD

✕ **Pomato Point Restaurant.** This relaxed restaurant and bar sits on one of the best beaches on the island and enjoys Anegada's most dramatic sunset views. Entrées include lobster, stewed conch, and freshly caught seafood. It's open for lunch daily; call by 4 pm for dinner reservations. Be sure to take a look at owner Wilfred Creque's displays of island artifacts, including shards of Arawak pottery and 17th-century coins, cannonballs, and bottles. These are housed in a little one-room museum adjacent to the dining room. ⑤ *Average main: $38* ⊠ *Pomato Point* ☎ *284/495-9466* ⌂ *Reservations essential* ⊘ *Closed Sept.*

WHERE TO STAY

For expanded reviews, facilities, and current deals, visit Fodors.com.

$
HOTEL

▦ **Anegada Reef Hotel.** Head here if you want to bunk in comfortable lodging near Anegada's most popular anchorage. **Pros:** everything you need is nearby; nice sunsets. **Cons:** basic rooms; no beach; often a party atmosphere at the bar. **TripAdvisor:** "what a lovely spot," "brilliant place," "very friendly hosts." ⑤ *Rooms from: $175* ⊠ *Setting Point* ☎ *284/495-8002* ⊕ *www.anegadareef.com* ⇲ *20 rooms* ⑩ *Multiple meal plans.*

$ **Neptune's Treasure.** Basic waterfront rooms with simple furnishings
B&B/INN and lovely views of the ocean are the hallmark of this family-owned
guesthouse. **Pros:** waterfront property; run by a family full of tales of the island; nice sunset views. **Cons:** simple rooms; no kitchens; no beach. **TripAdvisor:** "nice comfortable rooms," "spectacular location," "lovely people." $ *Rooms from: $150* ✉ *Benders Bay* ☎ *284/495–9439* ⊕ *www.neptunestreasure.com* ⤳ *9 rooms, 2 cottages* ⦿ *No meals.*

SPORTS AND THE OUTDOORS

Anegada Reef Hotel. Call the Anegada Reef to arrange bonefishing and sportfishing outings with seasoned local guides. ✉ *Anegada* ☎ *284/495–8002* ⊕ *www.anegadareef.com.*

Danny Vanterpool. Danny offers half-, three-quarter-, and full-day bonefishing excursions around Anegada. The cost ranges from $350 to $550. ✉ *Anegada* ☎ *284/441–6334* ⤳ *bonesrus@dannysbonefishing.com.*

OTHER BRITISH VIRGIN ISLANDS

COOPER ISLAND

This small, hilly island on the south side of the Sir Francis Drake Channel, about 8 miles (13 km) from Road Town, Tortola, is popular with the charter-boat crowd. There are no paved roads (which doesn't really matter, as there aren't any cars), but you can find a beach restaurant, a casual hotel, a few houses (some are available for rent), and great snorkeling at the south end of Manchioneel Bay.

WHERE TO STAY

For expanded reviews, facilities, and current deals, visit Fodors.com.

$ **Cooper Island Beach Club.** Diving is the focus at this small resort, but
RESORT folks who want to simply swim, snorkel, or relax can also feel right
Fodor's Choice at home. **Pros:** lots of quiet; the Caribbean as it used to be. **Cons:**
★ small rooms; modest furnishings (and wattage); island accessible only by ferry. **TripAdvisor:** "sophisticated paradise," "perfect vacation getaway," "the quintessential Caribbean experience." $ *Rooms from: $250* ✉ *Manchioneel Bay* ☎ *284/495–9084, 800/542–4624* ⊕ *www. cooperislandbeachclub.com* ⤳ *10 rooms* ⦿ *Multiple meal plans.*

GUANA ISLAND

Guana Island sits off Tortola's northeast coast. Sailors often drop anchor at one of the island's bays for a day of snorkeling and sunning. The island is a designated wildlife sanctuary, and scientists often come here to study its flora and fauna. It's home to a back-to-nature resort that offers few activities other than relaxation. Unless you're a hotel guest or a sailor, there's no easy way to get here.

WHERE TO STAY

For expanded reviews, facilities, and current deals, visit Fodors.com.

$$$$
RESORT
Fodor's Choice
★

Guana Island Resort. Here's a good resort if you want to stroll the hillsides, snorkel around the reefs, swim at its seven beaches, and still enjoy some degree of comfort. **Pros:** secluded feel; lovely grounds. **Cons:** very expensive; need boat to get here. **TripAdvisor:** "a very social resort," "attentive and friendly," "a select setting with distinctive character." ⑤ *Rooms from: $1,250* ⊠ *Guana Island,* ☎ *284/494–2354, 800/544–8262* ⊕ *www.guana.com* ⤴ *15 rooms, 1 1-bedroom villa, 1 2-bedroom villa, 1 3-bedroom villa* ⦿| *All meals.*

NORMAN ISLAND

This uninhabited island is the supposed setting for Robert Louis Stevenson's *Treasure Island*. The famed caves at Treasure Point are popular with day-sailors and powerboaters. If you land ashore at the island's main anchorage in the Bight, you can find a small beach bar and behind it a trail that winds up the hillside and reaches a peak. From here there's a fantastic view of the Sir Francis Drake Channel to the north.

$$
ECLECTIC

✕ **Willy T.** The ship, a former Baltic trader and today a floating bar and restaurant anchored to the north of the Bight, serves lunch and dinner in a party-hearty atmosphere. Try the conch fritters for starters. For lunch and dinner, British-style fish-and-chips, West Indian roti sandwiches, and the baby back ribs are winners. ⑤ *Average main: $17* ⊠ *The Bight* ☎ *284/496–8603* ⊕ *www.williamthornton.com* ⧄ *Reservations essential.*

Cayman Islands

WORD OF MOUTH

"Sting Ray city is a must! Try to book through the Ritz-Carlton. The boats are nice, and they only take a small group, so you are not crammed together with 100 people . . . . The restaurants on the Island are fabulous. The Wharf is great as well and is perfect for a sunset dinner, and then you can feed the tarpons off the deck."

—Travelcrazy45

WELCOME TO CAYMAN ISLANDS

KEY	
🏖	Beaches
🔷	Dive Sites

Caribbean Sea

LITTLE CAYMAN

Jacksons Pt.

Bloody Bay Wall 🔷

Anchorage Bay

Gov. Gore B
Sanctuary

South Town

South Sound

West End Point

Edward Bodden Airfield

Ower
Island

Tarpoon 🔷
Alley

🔷 Eagle Ray Pass

Head of
Barkers

🔷 Stingray
City

MARINE PARK
Rum Point

DISTANCE ON MAP IS COMPRESSED

Water Cay

Cayman Kai

Old Man Bay

A4

*West
Bay*

A1

*North
Sound*

Booby
Cay

HUTLAND

Malportas
Pond

OLD
MAN
BAY

GRAND CAYMAN

PEASE
BAY

BREAKERS

A4

HALF
MOON
BAY

NORTH
SOUND
ESTATES

BELFORD
ESTATES

A3

Pease
Bay

A3

NEWLANDS

A2

Ironshore
Point

SAVANNAH

A2

Bodden
Bay

Southweat
Point

A5

Grand Cayman may be the world's largest offshore finance hub, but other offshore activities have put the Caymans on the map. Pristine waters, breathtaking coral formations, and plentiful and exotic marine creatures beckon divers from around the world. Other vacationers are drawn by the islands' mellow civility.

FUN ON AND OFF SHORE

Grand Cayman, which is 22 miles (36 km) long and 8 miles (13 km) wide, is the largest of the three low-lying islands that make up this British colony. Its sister islands (Little Cayman and Cayman Brac) are almost 90 miles (149 km) north and east. The Cayman Trough between the Cayman Islands and Jamaica is the deepest part of the Caribbean.

TOP REASONS TO VISIT CAYMAN ISLANDS

1 Diving: Underwater visibility is among the best in the Caribbean, and nearby reefs are healthy.

2 Safety and Comfort: With no panhandlers, little crime, and top-notch accommodations, it's an easy place to vacation.

3 Dining Scene: The cosmopolitan population extends to the varied dining scene, from Italian to Indian.

4 Fabulous Snorkeling: A snorkeling trip to Stingray City is an experience you'll always remember.

5 Beaches: Grand Cayman's Seven Mile Beach is one of the Caribbean's best sandy beaches.

8 CAYMAN ISLANDS

CAYMAN ISLANDS BEACHES

Limestone, coral, shells, water, and wind collaborated to fashion the Cayman Islands beaches. It's a classic example of the interaction between geology and marine biology.

(Above) A beach lounger at the Ritz-Carlton, Grand Cayman (Bottom right) Horseback riding at Barkers (Top right) Snorkelers at Stingray Sandbar

Most of the beaches in Cayman, especially on Grand and Little Cayman, resemble powdered ivory. A few, including those on Cayman Brac, are more dramatic, a mix of fine beige sand and rugged rocky "ironshore," which often signals the healthiest reefs and best snorkeling. The islands are limestone outcroppings, the thrusting summits of a submarine mountain range called the Cayman Ridge. Grand Cayman's beaches range from cramped, untrammeled coves to long stretches basking like a cat in the sun, lined with bustling bars and water-sports concessions. There are some sandy beaches on Cayman Brac, especially along the southwest coast, but these beaches are also lined with turtle grass. Little Cayman has some spectacular white-sand beaches. All beaches are public, though access can be restricted by resorts. Remember that the Cayman Islands is a conservative place: nudity is strictly forbidden and punishable by a hefty fine and/ or prison time.

CORAL SAND

On most limestone-coral-based islands around the world, the hue and texture of the sand are derived from various micro-skeletons, such as the coral-like *foraminifera* and the calcareous algae Halimeda (a genus embracing a dozen species), which flourish in offshore reefs and sea-grass beds. These form the powdery, pearly sand on Seven Mile Beach and Rum Point, as well as Point of Sand on Little Cayman.

GRAND CAYMAN

East End Beaches. Just drive along and look for any sandy beach, park your car, and enjoy a stroll. The vanilla-hue stretch at Colliers Bay, by the Reef and Morritts resorts, is a good clean one with superior snorkeling. ⊠ *Queen's Hwy., East End.*

Rum Point. This North Sound beach has hammocks slung in towering casuarina trees, picnic tables, the Wreck Bar and Grill for dining, a well-stocked shop for seaworthy sundries, and Red Sail Sports, which offers various water sports and boats to explore Stingray City. The barrier reef ensures safe snorkeling and soft sand. The bottom remains shallow for a long way from shore, but it's littered with small coral heads, so kids shouldn't wrestle in the water here. The Wreck is ablaze with color—yellow with navy-blue trim and lime-and-mango picnic tables—as if trying to upstage the snorkeling just offshore; an ultracasual hangout turns out outstanding pub grub from fish-and-chips to wings, as well as lethal mudslide cocktails. Showers are available. ⊠ *Rum Point, North Side.*

Seven Mile Beach. Grand Cayman's west coast is dominated by the famous Seven Mile Beach—actually a 6½-mile-long (10-km-long) expanse of powdery white sand overseeing lapis water stippled with a rainbow of parasails and kayaks. The

width of the beach varies with the season; toward the south end it narrows and disappears altogether south of the Marriott, leaving only rock and ironshore. It starts to broaden into its normal silky softness anywhere between Tarquyn Manor and the Reef Grill at Royal Palms. Free of litter and pesky peddlers, it's an unspoiled (though often crowded) environment. At the public beach toward the north end you can find chairs for rent ($10 for the day, including a beverage), a playground, water toys aplenty, two beach bars, restrooms, and showers. The best snorkeling is at either end, by the Marriott and Treasure Island or off the northern section called Cemetery Reef Beach. ⊠ *West Bay Rd., Seven Mile Beach.*

Smith's Cove. South of the Grand Old House, this tiny but popular protected swimming and snorkeling spot makes a wonderful beach wedding location. The bottom drops off quickly enough to allow you to swim and play close to shore. Although slightly rocky, there's little debris and few coral heads, plenty of shade, picnic tables, restrooms, and parking. Surfers will find some decent swells just to the south. Local scuttlebutt calls it a place for dalliances during work hours; it's also a romantic sunset spot. ⊠ *Off S. Church St., George Town.*

8

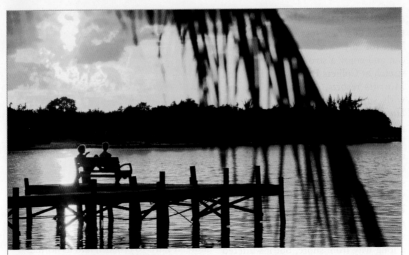

Looking ou at Owen Island, Little Cayman, at sunset.

South Sound Cemetery Beach. A narrow, sandy driveway takes you past the small cemetery to a perfect beach. The dock here is primarily used by dive boats during winter storms. You can walk in either direction; the sand is talcum-soft and clean, the water calm and clear (though local surfers take advantage of occasional small reef breaks; if wading, wear reef shoes, since the bottom is somewhat rocky and dotted with sea urchins). You'll definitely find fewer crowds. ☒ *S. Sound Rd., Prospect.*

CAYMAN BRAC

The island has several sandy beaches, mostly along the southwest coast. In addition to the hotel beaches, where everyone is welcome, there is a public beach with good access to the reef; it's well marked on tourist maps. The north-coast beaches, predominantly rocky ironshore, offer excellent snorkeling.

LITTLE CAYMAN

★ **Fodor's Choice** **Owen Island.** This private, forested island can be reached by rowboat, kayak, or an ambitious 200-yard swim. Anyone is welcome to come across and enjoy the deserted beaches and excellent snorkeling. Nudity is forbidden as "idle and disorderly" in the Cayman Islands, though that doesn't always stop skinny-dippers (who may not realize they can be seen quite easily from shore on the strands facing Little Cayman).

★ **Fodor's Choice** **Point of Sand.** Stretching more than a mile on the easternmost point of the island, this secluded beach is great for wading, shell collecting, and snorkeling. On a clear day you can see 7 miles (11 km) across to Cayman Brac. It serves as a green- and loggerhead turtle nesting site in spring, and a mosaic of coral gardens blooms just offshore. It's magical, especially at moonrise, when it earns its nickname, Lovers' Beach. There's a *palapa* (thatch-roof shelter) for shade but no facilities. The current can be strong, so watch the kids.

By Jordan Simon

This British Overseas Territory, which consists of Grand Cayman, smaller Cayman Brac, and Little Cayman, is one of the Caribbean's most popular destinations, particularly among Americans, who have become homeowners and constant visitors. The island's extensive array of banks also draws travelers. There are relatively few signs of the devastation caused by Hurricane Ivan in 2004, and Cayman Brac has almost completely recovered from Hurricane Paloma in November 2008.

8

Columbus is said to have sighted the islands in 1503 and dubbed them Las Tortugas after seeing so many turtles in the sea. The name was later changed to Cayman, referring to the caiman crocodiles that once roamed the islands. The Cayman Islands remained largely uninhabited until the late 1600s, when England seized them and Jamaica from Spain. Emigrants from England, Holland, Spain, and France arrived, as did refugees from the Spanish Inquisition and deserters from Oliver Cromwell's army in Jamaica; many brought slaves with them as well. The Cayman Islands' caves and coves were also perfect hideouts for the likes of Blackbeard, Sir Henry Morgan, and other pirates out to plunder Spanish galleons. Many ships fell afoul of the reefs surrounding the islands, often with the help of Caymanians, who lured vessels to shore with beacon fires.

Today's Cayman Islands are seasoned with suburban prosperity (particularly Grand Cayman, where residents joke that the national flower is the satellite dish) and stuffed with crowds (the hotels that line the famed Seven Mile Beach are often full, even in the slow summer season). Most of the 52,000 Cayman Islanders live on Grand Cayman, where the cost of living is at least 20% higher than in the United States, but you won't be hassled by panhandlers or fear walking around on a dark evening (the crime rate is very low). Add political and economic stability to the mix, and you have a fine island recipe indeed.

LOGISTICS

Getting to the Cayman Islands: There are plenty of nonstop flights to Grand Cayman (GCM) from the United States. Most people hop over to the Brac and Little Cayman (LYB) on a small plane from Grand Cayman; a weekly nonstop from the Brac to Miami may be reinstated. Flights land at Owen Roberts Airport (Grand Cayman), Gerrard Smith Airport (Cayman Brac), or Edward Bodden Airstrip (Little Cayman).

Hassle Factor: Low for Grand Cayman; medium for Little Cayman and Cayman Brac.

On the Ground: In Grand Cayman you must take a taxi or rent a car at the airport, since most hotels are not permitted to offer airport shuttles. Hotel pickup is more readily available on Cayman Brac and Little Cayman.

Getting Around the Islands: It's possible to get by without a car on Grand Cayman if you are staying in the Seven Mile Beach area, where you could walk, take a local bus, or ride a bike. If you want to explore the rest of the island—or if you are staying elsewhere—you'll need a car. Though less necessary on Cayman Brac or Little Cayman, cars are available on both islands.

PLANNING

WHEN TO GO

High season begins in mid-December and continues through early to mid-April. During the low season you can often get a substantial discount of as much as 40%.

GETTING HERE AND AROUND

AIR TRAVEL

You can fly nonstop to Grand Cayman from Atlanta (Delta), Boston (US Airways, once weekly), Charlotte (US Airways), Chicago (Cayman Airways, twice weekly), Detroit (Delta, once weekly), Fort Lauderdale (Cayman Airways), Houston (Continental, once weekly), Miami (American, Cayman Airways), Minneapolis (Delta, once weekly), New York–JFK (Cayman Airways), New York–Newark (Continental, once weekly), Philadelphia (US Airways, once weekly), Tampa (Cayman Airways), and Washington, D.C. (Cayman Airways, twice weekly, and United).

Almost all nonstop air service is to Grand Cayman, with connecting flights on Cayman Airways Express to Cayman Brac and Little Cayman on a small propeller plane; there's also interisland charter-only service on Island Air. There is a once-weekly nonstop on Cayman Airways between Miami and Cayman Brac.

Airports Owen Roberts Airport ⊠ *GCM, Grand Cayman* ☎ *345/943–7070.*
Gerrard Smith International Airport ⊠ *CYB, Cayman Brac* ☎ *345/948–1222.*
Edward Bodden Airstrip ⊠ *LYB, Little Cayman* ☎ *345/948–0021.*

Airline Contacts **American Airlines/American Eagle** ☎ *345/949–0666.* **Cayman Airways** ☎ *345/949–2311.* **Delta** ☎ *345/945–8430.* **Island Air** ☎ *345/949–5252* ⊕ *www.islandair.ky.* **US Airways** ☎ *345/949–7488.*

BUS TRAVEL

On Grand Cayman, bus service—consisting of minivans marked "Omni Bus"—is efficient, inexpensive, and plentiful, running roughly every 15 minutes in the Seven Mile Beach area and George Town with fares from CI$1.50 to CI$2.

CAR TRAVEL

Driving is easy on Grand Cayman, but there can be considerable traffic, especially during rush hour. One major road circumnavigates most of the island. Driving is on the left, British-style, and there are roundabouts. Speed limits are 30 mph (50 kph) in the country, 20 mph (30 kph) in town. There's much less traffic on Cayman Brac and even less on Little Cayman. Gas is expensive.

Car Rentals: You'll need a valid driver's license and a credit card to rent a car. Most agencies require renters to be between 21 and 70, though some require you to be 25. If you are over 75, you must have a certified doctor's note attesting to your ability. A local driver's permit, which costs $7.50, is obtained through the rental agencies. Rates can be expensive (from $40 to $95 per day), but usually include insurance.

Car-Rental Contacts (Grand Cayman) **Ace Hertz** ☎ *345/949–2280, 800/654–3131* ⊕ *www.acerentacarltd.com.* **Andy's Rent a Car** ☎ *345/949–8111* ⊕ *www.andys.ky.* **Avis** ☎ *345/949–2468* ⊕ *www.aviscayman.com.* **Budget** ☎ *345/949–5605, 800/527–0700* ⊕ *www.budgetcayman.com.* **Coconut Car Rentals** ☎ *345/949–4037, 345/949–7703, 800/941–4562* ⊕ *www.coconutcarrentals.com.* **Dollar** ☎ *345/949–4790* ⊕ *www.dollarlac.com.* **Economy** ☎ *345/949–9550* ⊕ *www.economycarrental.com.ky.* **Thrifty** ☎ *345/949–6640, 800/367–2277* ⊕ *www.thrifty.com.*

Car-Rental Contacts (Cayman Brac) **B&S Motor Ventures** ☎ *345/948–1646* ⊕ *www.bandsmv.com.* **CB Rent-a-Car** ☎ *345/948–2424, 345/948–2847* ⊕ *www.cbrentacar.com.* **Four D's Car Rental** ☎ *345/948–1599.*

Car-Rental Contacts (Little Cayman) **McLaughlin Rentals** ☎ *345/948–1000.*

TAXI TRAVEL

On Grand Cayman, taxis operate 24 hours a day; if you anticipate a late night, however, make pickup arrangements in advance. You generally cannot hail a taxi on the street except occasionally in George Town. Fares are not metered but set, and are not cheap, but basic fares include as many as three passengers. Taxis are scarcer on the Sister Islands; rates are also fixed and fairly prohibitive. Your hotel will provide recommended drivers.

ESSENTIALS

Banks and Exchange Services You should not need to change money in Grand Cayman, since U.S. dollars are readily accepted. ATMs generally offer the option of U.S. or Cayman dollars. The Cayman dollar is pegged to the U.S. dollar at the rate of CI$1.25 to $1. Be sure you know which currency is being quoted when making a purchase.

Electricity Electricity is reliable and is the same as in the United States (110 volts/60 cycles).

Emergency Services Ambulance ☎ *911.* **Cayman Hyperbaric** ✉ *Hospital Rd., George Town, Grand Cayman* ☎ *345/949–2989.* **Fire** ☎ *911.* **Police** ☎ *911.*

Passport Requirements All visitors must have a valid passport and a return or ongoing ticket to enter the Cayman Islands. A birth certificate and photo ID are *not* sufficient proof of citizenship.

Phones The area code for the Cayman Islands is 345. To make local calls (on or between any of the three islands), dial the seven-digit number. Many international cell phones work in the Cayman Islands, though roaming charges can be significant. Mobile phone rental is available from LIME and Digicel, the two major providers; you can stay connected for as little as CI$5 per day plus the cost of a calling card (denominations range from CI$10 to CI$100). International per-minute rates usually range from CI35¢ to CI60¢.

Taxes At the airport, each adult passenger leaving Grand Cayman must pay a departure tax of $25 (CI$20), payable in cash. It isn't usually added to airfare—check with your carrier. A 10% government tax is added to all hotel bills. A 10% service charge is often added to hotel bills and restaurant checks in lieu of a tip.

Tipping At large hotels a service charge is generally included; smaller establishments and some villas and condos leave tipping up to you. Although tipping is customary at restaurants, note that some automatically include 15% on the bill—so check the tab carefully. Taxi drivers expect a 10% to 15% tip.

ACCOMMODATIONS

Grand Cayman draws the bulk of Cayman Island visitors. It's expensive during the high season but offers the widest range of resorts, restaurants, and activities both in and out of the water. Most resorts are on or near Seven Mile Beach, but a few are north in the West Bay Area, near Rum Point, or on the quiet East End. Both Little Cayman and Cayman Brac are more geared toward serving the needs of divers, who make up the majority of visitors. Beaches on the Sister Islands, as they are called, don't measure up (literally) to Grand Cayman's Seven Mile Beach. The smaller islands are cheaper than Grand Cayman, but with the extra cost of transportation, the overall savings are minimized.

Grand Cayman: Grand Cayman has plenty of medium-size resorts as well as the Ritz-Carlton, a large seven-story resort on Seven Mile Beach. The island also has a wide range of condos and villas, many in resortlike compounds on or near Seven Mile Beach and the Cayman Kai area. There are even a few small guesthouses for budget-minded visitors.

The Sister Islands: Cayman Brac has mostly intimate resorts and family-run inns. Little Cayman has a mix of small resorts and condos, most appealing to divers.

HOTEL AND RESTAURANT PRICES

Prices in the restaurant reviews are the average cost of a main course at dinner or, if dinner is not served, at lunch; taxes and service charges are generally included. Prices in the hotel reviews are the lowest cost of a standard double room in high season, excluding taxes, service charges, and meal plans (except at all-inclusives). Prices for rentals are the lowest per-night cost for a one-bedroom unit in high season.

VISITOR INFORMATION

Contacts Cayman Islands Department of Tourism ☎ *305/599–9033 in Miami, 847/678–6446 in Chicago, 212/889–9009 in New York City, 713/461–1317 in Houston, 877/422–9626, 213/738–1968 in Los Angeles* ⊕ *www. caymanislands.ky.*

WEDDINGS

Getting married in the Cayman Islands is a breeze. Documentation can be prepared ahead of time or in one day while on the island. There's no on-island waiting period. Larger resorts have on-site wedding coordinators.

GRAND CAYMAN

Grand Cayman has long been known for two offshore activities: banking (the new piracy, as locals joke) and scuba diving. With 296 banks, the capital, George Town, is relatively modern and usually bustles with activity, but never more so than when two to seven cruise ships are docked in the harbor, an increasingly common occurrence. Accountants in business clothes join thousands of vacationers in their tropical togs, jostling for tables at lunch. When they're not mingling in the myriad shops or getting pampered and pummeled in spas, vacationers delve into sparkling waters to snorkel and dive; increasingly, couples come to be married, or at least to enjoy their honeymoon.

The effects of recent devastating hurricanes, such as Omar in October 2008 and Paloma in November 2008 are visible only in the mangrove swamps and interior savanna. There is a lot of new construction and plenty of traffic, so check with a local to plan driving time. It can take 45 minutes during rush hours to go 8 miles (13 km).

EXPLORING GRAND CAYMAN

The historic capital of George Town, on the southwest corner of Grand Cayman, is easy to explore on foot. If you're a shopper, you can spend days here; otherwise, an hour will suffice for a tour of the downtown area. To see the rest of the island, rent a car or scooter or take a guided tour. The portion of the island called West Bay is noted for its jumble of neighborhoods and a few attractions. When traffic is heavy, it's about a half hour to West Bay from George Town, but the opening of a new bypass road that runs parallel to West Bay Road has made the journey easier. The less-developed East End has natural attractions from blowholes to botanical gardens, as well as the remains of the island's original settlements. Plan at least 45 minutes for the drive out from George Town (more during rush hours). You need a day to explore the entire island—including a stop at a beach for a picnic or swim.

WHAT TO SEE

GEORGE TOWN

Begin exploring the capital by strolling along the waterfront Harbour Drive to **Elmslie Memorial United Church,** named after the first Presbyterian missionary to serve in Cayman. Its vaulted ceiling, wooden arches, and sedate nave reflect the religious nature of island residents. In front of the court building, in the center of town, names of influential Caymanians are inscribed on the **Wall of History,** which commemorates the islands' quincentennial in 2003. Across the street is the **Cayman Islands Legislative Assembly Building,** next door to the **1919 Peace Memorial Building**. In the middle of the financial district is the **General Post Office,** built in 1939. Let the kids pet the big blue iguana statues.

⏃ **Cayman Islands National Museum.** Built in 1833, the historically significant
Fodor's Choice clapboard home of the national museum has had several different incar-
★ nations over the years, serving as courthouse, jail, post office, and dance hall. It features an ongoing archaeological excavation of the Old Gaol and excellent 3-D bathymetric displays, murals, dioramas, and videos that illustrate local geology, flora and fauna, and island history. There are also temporary exhibits focusing on aspects of Caymanian culture, a local art collection, and interactive displays for kids. ⊠ *Harbour Dr.* 🕾 *345/949–8368* ⊕ *www.museum.ky* ☎ *$8* ☉ *Weekdays 9–5, Sat. 9–1.*

★ **National Gallery.** A worthy nonprofit organization, the museum was established in 1996 to display and promote the range of Caymanian artists and craftspeople, both established and grassroots. The gallery coordinates a wealth of first-rate outreach programs for everyone from infants to inmates. It usually mounts six major exhibitions a year, including three large-scale retrospectives or thematic shows and multimedia installations. The gallery has also developed an Artist Trail Map with the Department of Tourism and can facilitate studio tours. The gallery's large new quarters near Seven Mile Beach on Harquail Bypass opened in early 2012. ⊠ *Esterly Tibbetts Highway at Harquail Bypass, Seven Mile Beach* 🕾 *345/945–8111* ⊕ *www.nationalgallery.org. ky* ☎ *Free* ☉ *Weekdays 9–5, Sat. 11–2.*

NEED A BREAK?

Full of Beans Cafe. On the surprisingly large, eclectic, Asian-tinged menu using ultrafresh ingredients, standouts include homemade carrot cake, mango smoothies, a curried chicken-cucumber wrap, cranberry-Brie-pecan salad, and a rosemary-roasted portobello panino. Owner Cindy Butler fashions a feast for weary eyes as well, with rotating artworks and stylish mosaic mirrors contrasting with faux-brick walls and vintage hardwood tables. ⊠ *Pasadora Place, Smith Rd.* 🕾 *345/943–2326, 345/814–0157.*

National Trust. For a wonderful map of the historic and natural attractions, go to the office of the National Trust. The Trust sells books and guides to Cayman. The fabulous website has more than 50 information sheets on cultural and natural topics from iguanas to schoolhouses. Take advantage of the regularly scheduled activities, from boat tours through the forests of the Central Mangrove Wetlands to cooking classes with local chefs to morning walking tours of historic George Town. Stop here first before you tour the island. Be forewarned: though

Boatswain's Beach, Grand Cayman

the office is walkable from George Town, it's an often-hot 20-minute hike from downtown. ⊠ *Dart Park, 558 S. Church St.* ☎ *345/749–1121* ⊕ *nationaltrust.org.ky* ⊗ *Weekdays 9–5:30.*

Seven Fathoms Rum. Surprisingly, this growing company, established in 2008, is Cayman's first distillery. It's already garnered medals in prestigious international competitions for its artisanal small-batch rums. You can stop by for a tasting and self-guided tour, learning how they age the rum at 7 fathoms (42 feet) deep; supposedly the natural kinetic motion of the currents enables the rum to maximize contact with the oak, extracting its rich flavors and enhancing complexity. Based on the results, it's not just yo-ho-hokum. ⊠ *Waterfront, next to Hammerhead's* ☎ *345/925–5379, 345/926–8186* ⊕ *www.sevenfathomsrum.com.*

SEVEN MILE BEACH

Camana Bay Observation Tower. This 75-foot structure provides striking 360-degree panoramas of otherwise flat Grand Cayman, sweeping from George Town and Seven Mile Beach to the North Sound. The double-helix staircase is impressive in its own right. ⊠ *Extending between Seven Mile Beach and North Sound, 2 miles (3 km) north of George Town, Camana Bay* ☎ *345/640–3500* ⊕ *www.camanabay.com* ⊠ *Free* ⊗ *Sunrise–10 pm.*

WEST BAY

Fodor'sChoice

Boatswain's Beach. Cayman's premier attraction, the Turtle Farm, has been rebranded and transformed into a marine theme park. The expanded complex now has several souvenir shops and restaurants. Still, the turtles remain a central attraction, and you can tour ponds in the original research–breeding facility with thousands in various stages

Grand Cayman

Tarpoon Alley

Boatswain's Beach ◆

◆ **Hell**

Old Homestead ◆

West Bay

Butterfly Farm ◆

George Town ○

Southweat Point

A1

Conch Point

Palmetto Point Rd.

Conch Point Rd.

Capt. Reg Parson's Rd.

BARKERS

14

BIRCH TREE HILL

MOUNT PLEASANT

17

13

CORAL GABLES

NW Point

○ **West Bay**

Town Hall Rd.

North West Point Rd.

15

BATABANO

Head of Barkers

18 19

Little Salt Creek

Orange Canyon

Trinity Caves

Cemetery Reef

12

UPPERLAND

Salt Creek

A1

West Bay Rd.

Seven Mile Beach

Aquarium

Grand Cayman Yacht Club ◆

Governors Creek

GOVERNORS HARBOUR

The Links at Safehaven Golf Course

Welch Point

A1

11

Paradise Reef

West Bay

15 16

9

10

13 7

8 14

11 12

5

6

Brittania Golf Course

9

10

Galleria Plaza ◆

Galleria Loop

7 8

Cayman National Gallery

West Shore Center

6

North Sound

Marquee Plaza ◆

4

WHITEHALL ESTATES

West Bay Rd.

3

Camana Bay Observation Tower ◆

2

Eastern Av.

George Town ○

North Sound Rd.

1 - 4

Wreck of the Cali

A1

Owen Roberts International Airport ✈

Eden Rock

A2

Elgin Av.

Smith Rd.

A2

Crewe Rd.

Black Reef Skate Park ◆

1

A5

S. Church St.

Walkers Rd.

Smith's Cove

A5

South Sound

South Sound Rd.

Prospect Point

5

0 _____ 2 mi

0 _____ 2 km

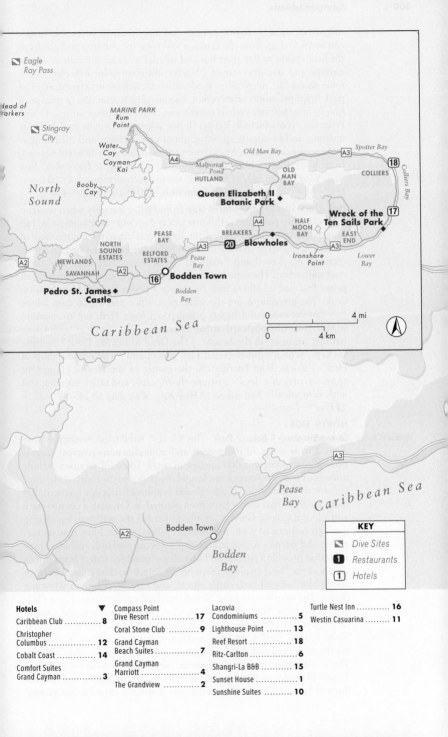

Eagle
Ray Pass

Head of
Barkers

Stingray
City

North
Sound

MARINE PARK
Rum
Point

Water
Cay
Cayman
Kai

Booby
Cay

Old Man Bay

Spotter Bay

Malportas
Pond
HUTLAND

OLD
MAN
BAY

COLLIERS

A4

A3

18

Colliers Bay

Queen Elizabeth II
Botanic Park

Wreck of the
Ten Sails Park

17

PEASE
BAY

NORTH
SOUND
ESTATES

NEWLANDS

SAVANNAH

A2

A2

BELFORD
ESTATES

16

BREAKERS

A4

20

HALF
MOON
BAY

Blowholes

Pease
Bay

A3

Bodden Town

Ironshore
Point

EAST
END

A3

Lower
Bay

Pedro St. James
Castle

Bodden
Bay

Caribbean Sea

0   4 mi

0   4 km

Pease
Bay

Caribbean Sea

A3

Bodden Town

A2

Bodden
Bay

of growth, some up to 600 pounds and more than 70 years old. Turtles can be picked up from the tanks, a real treat for children and adults as the little creatures flap their fins and splash the water. Four areas—three aquatic and one dry—cover 23 acres; different-color bracelets determine access (the steep full-pass admission includes snorkeling gear). The park helps promote conservation, encouraging interaction (a tidal pool houses invertebrates such as starfish and crabs) and observation. Animal Program events include Keeper Talks, where you might feed birds or iguanas, and biologists speaking about conservation and their importance to the ecosystem. Audio tours are available with different focuses, from butterflies to bush medicine. ⊠ *825 Northwest Point Rd., Box 812, West Bay* ☎ *345/949–3894* ⊕ *www.boatswainsbeach.ky* ☑ *Comprehensive ticket $45; Turtle Farm only, $30* ⊙ *Daily 8:30–4:30.*

Hell. Quite literally the tourist trap from Hell, especially when overrun by cruise-ship passengers, this attraction does offer free admission, fun photo ops, and sublime surrealism. Its name refers to the quarter-acre of menacing shards of charred brimstone thrusting up like vengeful spirits (actually blackened and "sculpted" by acid-secreting algae and fungi over millennia). The eerie lunarscape is now cordoned off, but you can prove you had a helluva time by taking a photo from the observation deck. The attractions are the small post office and a gift shop where you can get cards and letters postmarked from Hell, not to mention wonderfully silly postcards titled "When Hell Freezes Over" (depicting bathing beauties on the beach), "The Devil Made Me Do It" bumper stickers, Scotch bonnet–based Hell sauce, and "The coolest shop in Hell" T-shirts. Ivan Farrington, the owner of the Devil's Hang-Out store, cavorts in a devil's costume (horn, cape, and tails), regaling you with demonically bad jokes. ⊠ *Hell Rd., West Bay* ☎ *345/949–3358* ☑ *Free* ⊙ *Daily 9–6.*

NORTH SIDE

Fodor'sChoice **Queen Elizabeth II Botanic Park.** This 65-acre wilderness preserve show-
★ cases a wide range of indigenous and nonindigenous tropical vegetation, approximately 2,000 species in total. Splendid sections include numerous water features from limpid lily ponds to cascades; a Heritage Garden with a traditional cottage and "caboose" (outside kitchen) that includes crops that might have been planted on Cayman a century ago; and a Floral Colour Garden arranged by color, the walkway wandering through sections of pink, red, orange, yellow, white, blue, mauve, lavender, and purple. A 2-acre lake and adjacent wetlands includes three islets that provide a habitat and breeding ground for native birds just as showy as the floral displays: green herons, black-necked stilts, American coots, blue-winged teal, cattle egrets, and rare West Indian whistling ducks. The nearly mile-long Woodland Trail encompasses every Cayman ecosystem from wetland to cactus thicket, buttonwood swamp to lofty woodland with imposing mahogany trees. You'll encounter birds, lizards, turtles, agoutis, and more, but the park's star residents are the protected endemic blue iguanas, found only in Grand Cayman. The world's most endangered iguana, they're the focus of the National Trust's Blue Iguana Recovery Program, a captive breeding and reintroduction facility. This section of the park is usually closed to the general

public, though released "blue dragons" hang out in the vicinity. The Trust conducts 90-minute behind-the-scenes safaris Monday–Saturday at 11 am for $30. ✉ *367 Botanic Rd.* ☎ *345/947–9462* ⊕ *www.botanicpark.ky* 💲*$10* ⊘ *Apr.–Sept., daily 9–6:30; Oct.–Mar., daily 9–5:30; last admission 1 hr before closing.*

EAST END

Ⓒ **Blowholes.** When the easterly trade winds blow hard, crashing waves force water into caverns and send impressive geysers shooting up as much as 20 feet through the ironshore. The blowholes were partially filled during Hurricane Ivan in 2004, so the water must be rough to recapture their former elemental drama. ✉ *Frank Sound Rd., roughly 10 miles (16 km) east of Bodden Town, near East End.*

Bodden Town. In the island's original south-shore capital you can find an old cemetery on the shore side of the road. Graves with A-frame structures are said to contain the remains of pirates. There are also the ruins of a fort and a wall erected by slaves in the 19th century. The National Trust runs tours of the restored 1840s Mission House. A curio shop serves as the entrance to what's called the Pirate's Caves ($8), partially underground natural formations that are more hokey (decked out with fake treasure chests and mannequins in pirate garb, with an outdoor petting zoo) than spooky.

Mission House. The Mission House is a classic gabled two-story Caymanian home on wooden posts, with wattle-and-daub accents, dating to the 1840s and restored by the National Trust. The building earned its sobriquet thanks to early missionaries, teachers, and families who lived here while helping establish the Presbyterian ministry and school in Bodden Town. Shards of 19th-century glass and ceramics found onsite and period furnishings are on display. The posted opening hours are irregular, especially during the off-season. ✉ *63 Gun Square Rd., Bodden Town* ☎ *345/749–1132* ⊕ *www.nationaltrust.org.ky* 💲*CI$5* ⊘ *Wed.–Sat. 9–5:30*

Pirate's Caves. You enter the Pirate's Caves through a surprisingly good curio shop (the owner is noted for jewelry fashioned from doubloons). The caves themselves are pure yo-ho-hokum, tricked up with more faux "skeletons," swords jutting from limestone formations, and other rusted artifacts of dubious authenticity (such as fake treasure chests), lanterns, and conch shells, as well as an authentic fossilized bone or two. Beware the steep descent (with only rope handrails). Very informative sheets on history and the native plants are provided, as well as good interpretive signage within the grounds. ✉ *South Shore Rd., Bodden Town* ☎ *345/947–3122* 💲*$8* ⊘ *Daily 9–6.*

Cayman Islands Brewery. This brewery occupies the former Stingray facility; free tours are available on the hour (you must call first). Caybrew is a full-bodied yet light lager with a crisp hop finish. The guide will explain the iconic imagery of the bottle and label, and the nearly three-week process: seven days' fermentation, 10 days' lagering (storage), and one day in the bottling tank. The brewery's ecofriendly features are also championed: local farmers receive the spent grains used to produce the beer to serve as cattle feed at no charge, while waste liquid is

8

channeled into one of the Caribbean's most advanced water-treatment systems. Then enjoy your complimentary tasting with the knowledge that you're helping the local environment and economy. ⊠ *366 Shamrock Rd., Red Bay* ☎ *345/947–6699* ⊕ *www.cib.ky* ⌑ *Free* ☉ *Weekdays 9–5, Sat. 10–5.*

Fodor'sChoice **Pedro St. James Castle.** Built in 1780, the great house is Cayman's oldest
★ stone structure and the only remaining late-18th-century residence on the island. In its capacity as courthouse and jail, it was the birthplace of Caymanian democracy, where in December 1831 the first elected parliament was organized and in 1835 the Slavery Abolition Act signed. The structure still has original or historically accurate replicas of sweeping verandas, mahogany floors, rough-hewn wide-beam ceilings, outside louvers, stone and oxblood- or mustard-color lime-wash-painted walls, brass fixtures, and Georgian furnishings (from tea caddies to canopy beds to commodes). Paying obsessive attention to detail, the curators even fill glasses with faux wine. The mini-museum also includes a hodgepodge of displays from slave emancipation to old stamps. The buildings are surrounded by 8 acres of natural parks and woodlands. You can stroll through landscaping of native Caymanian flora and experience one of the most spectacular views on the island from atop the dramatic Great Pedro Bluff. First watch the impressive multimedia theater show, complete with smoking pots, misting rains, and two film screens where the story of Pedro's Castle is presented on the hour. The poignant Hurricane Ivan Memorial outside uses text, images, and symbols to represent important aspects of that horrific 2004 natural disaster. ⊠ *Pedro Castle Rd., Box 305, Savannah* ☎ *345/947–3329* ⊕ *www. pedrostjames.ky* ⌑ *$10* ☉ *Daily 9–5.*

Wreck of the Ten Sails Park. This lonely, lovely park on Grand Cayman's windswept eastern tip commemorates the island's most (in)famous shipwreck. On February 8, 1794, the *Cordelia,* heading a convoy of 58 square-rigged merchant vessels en route from Jamaica to England, foundered on one of the treacherous East End reefs. Its warning cannon fire was tragically misconstrued as a call to band more closely together due to imminent pirate attack, and nine more ships ran aground. The local sailors, who knew those rough seas, demonstrated great bravery in rescuing all 400-odd seamen. Popular legend claims (romantically but inaccurately) that King George III granted the islands an eternal tax exemption. Queen Elizabeth II dedicated the park's plaque in 1994. Interpretive signs document the historic details. The ironically peaceful headland provides magnificent views of the reef (including more recent shipwrecks); bird-watching is superb from here half a mile south along the coast to the Lighthouse Park, perched on a craggy bluff. ⊠ *Gun Bay, East End* ☎ *345/949–0121 (National Trust)* ⌑ *Free* ☉ *Daily.*

WHERE TO EAT

Despite its small size, comparative geographic isolation, and British colonial trappings, Grand Cayman offers a smorgasbord of gastronomic goodies. With more than 100 eateries, something should suit and sate every palate and pocketbook (factoring in the fast-food franchises sweeping the islandscape like tumbleweed, and stands dispensing local specialties). The term *melting pot* describes both the majority of menus and the multicultural population. The sheer range of dining options from Middle Eastern to Mexican reflects the island's cosmopolitan clientele. Imported ingredients make up their own United Nations, with chefs sourcing salmon from Norway, foie gras from Périgord, and lamb from New Zealand. Wine lists can be equally global in scope. And don't be surprised to find both Czech and Chilean staffers at a remote East End restaurant. As one restaurateur quipped, "Cayman is the ultimate culture-shock absorber."

Prices are about 25% more than those in a major U.S. city. Many restaurants add a 10% to 15% service charge to the bill; be sure to check before leaving a tip. Alcohol with your meal can send the tab skyrocketing. Buy liquor duty-free before you leave the airport and enjoy a cocktail or nightcap from the comfort of your room or balcony. Cayman customs limits you to two bottles per person. You should make reservations at all but the most casual places, particularly during the high season. Note that many bars offer fine fare (and many eateries have hip, hopping bar scenes).

What to Wear: Grand Cayman dining is casual (shorts are okay, but *not* beachwear and tank tops). Mosquitoes can be pesky when you are dining outdoors, especially at sunset, so plan ahead or ask for repellent. Winter can be chilly enough to warrant a light sweater.

GEORGE TOWN AND ENVIRONS

$$$
ECLECTIC
✕ **The Brasserie.** Actuaries, bankers, and CEOs frequent this contemporary throwback to a colonial country club for lunch and "attitude adjustment" happy hours for cocktails and complimentary canapés. Inviting fusion cuisine, emphasizing local ingredients whenever possible (the restaurant even has its own boat), includes terrific bar tapas like the "Mini Argentinian" (skirt steak, house-made chorizo, chimichurri sauce), or melted Brie with white truffle–and-mango marmalade. Dishes deftly balance flavors and textures without sensory overload: this is serious food with a sense of playfulness. Save room for desserts, from an artisanal cheese plate to an ice-cream-and-sorbet tasting menu to elaborate architectural confections. Lunch is more reasonably priced but equally creative; the adjacent Market excels at takeout, and the wine list is well considered. ⑤ *Average main: $31* ⊠ *171 Elgin Ave., Cricket Sq.* ☎ *345/945–1815* ⊕ *www.brasseriecayman.com* ⌒ *Reservations essential* ☉ *Closed weekends.*

BEST BETS FOR DINING

Fodor's Choice ★
Blue by Eric Ripert, Michael's Genuine, Ortanique

BEST VIEW
Cracked Conch, Reef Grill at Royal Palms

MOST ROMANTIC
Grand Old House

BEST FOR LOCAL CUISINE
Chicken! Chicken!, Cimboco, Over the Edge

HOT SPOTS
Agua, Guy Harvey's Island Grill, Ragazzi, Yoshi Sushi

8

$$
CARIBBEAN
✕ **Breezes by the Bay.** There isn't a bad seat in the house at this nonstop feel-good fiesta festooned with tiny paper lanterns, Christmas lights, ship murals, model boats, and Mardi Gras beads (you're "lei'd" upon entering). Wraparound balconies take in a dazzling panorama from South Sound to Seven Mile Beach. It's a joyous nonstop happy hour all day every day, especially at Countdown to Sunset. Signs promise "the good kind of hurricanes," referring to the 23-ounce signature "category 15" cocktails with fresh garnishes; rum aficionados will find 48 varieties (flights available). Equally fresh food at bargain prices, including homemade baked goods and ice creams, isn't an afterthought. Chunky, velvety conch chowder served in a bread bowl or near-definitive conch fritters are meals in themselves. Hefty sandwiches are slathered with yummy jerk mayo or garlicky aioli. Signature standouts include meltingly moist whole fish escoveitch, curry chicken, popcorn shrimp, jerk-glazed pork chops, and any pie from the new pizza station. ⑤ *Average main: $19* ✉ *Harbor Dr.* ☎ *345/943–8439* ⊕ *www.breezesbythebay.com.*

$$$$
EUROPEAN
✕ **Grand Old House.** Built in 1908 as the Petra Plantation House and transformed into the island's first upscale establishment decades ago, this grande dame is that rare restaurant that genuinely transports diners to a gracious era of bygone grandeur sans pretension. The interior rooms, awash in crystal and mahogany, recall its plantation-house origins. Classical and jazz pianists enhance the period ambience, but outside, hundreds of sparkling lights adorn the gazebos to compete with the starry sky. Rumors of a charming blond ghost trailing white chiffon complete the picture: this is a place to propose or let someone down easily. You'll find such expertly executed classics as butter-poached lobster with saffron risotto and fennel-parsnip puree or beef tenderloin with a choice of five sauces, but the increasingly innovative menu has adopted Asian and even Southwestern influences. Pistachio-and-herb-crusted chicken is spiced by apple mole, and grilled jumbo shrimp and bacon-wrapped smoked wahoo swim in ginger-plum sauce with roasted pumpkin and asparagus. The subtle yet complex flavor interactions, stellar service, and encyclopedic if stratospherically priced wine list ensure legendary landmark status. ⑤ *Average main: $51* ✉ *648 S. Church St.* ☎ *345/949–9333* ⊕ *www.grandoldhouse.com* ⌁ *Reservations essential* ☉ *Closed Sept. No lunch weekends.*

$$$
SEAFOOD
✕ **Guy Harvey's Island Grill.** This stylish, sporty, upstairs bistro celebrates the sea, from decor to cuisine. You half expect to find Hemingway regaling fellow barflies in the clubby interior with mahogany furnishings, ship's lanterns, porthole windows, whirring ceiling fans, fishing rods, and Harvey's action-packed marine art. The cool blues echo the sea and sky on display from the inviting balcony. Seafood is carefully chosen to exclude overexploited and threatened species. Seasonally changing dishes are peppered with Caribbean influences but pureed through the French chef's formal training. Hence, silken lobster bisque is served with puff pastry, scallops Rockefeller with spinach and béarnaise sauce, and the signature crab cakes with roasted-red-pepper aioli. You can select your fish baked, pan-sautéed, or grilled with any of eight sauces. Carnivores needn't despair, with rack of lamb in balsamic

glaze or an intensely flavored filet mignon Roquefort (frites optional). Many specialties are cheaper at lunch. Nightly specials for CI$9.99 and the four-course CI$30 dinner reel in savvy locals. $ *Average main: $35* ⊠ *Aquaworld Duty-Free Mall, 55 S. Church St.* ☎ *345/946–9000* ⊕ *www.guyharveysgrill.com.*

$$$$
SEAFOOD

× **Lobster Pot.** The nondescript building belies the lovely marine-motif decor and luscious seafood at the intimate, second-story restaurant overlooking the harbor. No surprise that fish seem to jump from the plate (or to it, as fishermen cruise up to the dock downstairs). Enjoy lobster prepared a half-dozen ways along with reasonably priced wine, which you can sample by the glass (particularly fine Austrian selections) in the cozy bar. The two musts are the Cayman Trio (lobster tail, grilled mahimahi, and garlic shrimp), and the Pot (lobster, giant prawns, and crab), but the kitchen can happily provide reduced-oil and -fat alternatives to most dishes. The balcony offers a breathtaking view of the sunset tarpon feeding. Lobster is market price and can be as much as $60; other entrées are less expensive. $ *Average main: $47* ⊠ *245 N. Church St.* ☎ *345/949–2736* ⊕ *www.lobsterpot.ky* ⊗ *No lunch weekends.*

SEVEN MILE BEACH

$$$$
SEAFOOD
Fodor's Choice
★

× **Blue by Eric Ripert.** *Top Chef* judge Eric Ripert consulted on every aspect of the first outpost bearing his name, from decor to dishware. His trademark ethereal seafood (executed by his handpicked brigade), flawless but not fawning service, swish setting, and soothing sophistication sans pretension make this one of the Caribbean's finest restaurants. Choose from a regular three-course or the chef's hedonistic tasting menu (with or without wine pairing). Many dishes are clever improvisational riffs on the mother restaurant (New York's celebrated Le Bernardin), using the island's natural bounty (the tribute to the great Bernardin tuna foie gras adds Cayman sea salt). The sensuous counterpoint of flavors, textures, even colors is unimpeachable, as in sautéed kingklip with avocado-coconut cream, sunflower sprouts, and lime sauce *vierge*; sautéed ocean yellowtail in bourbon-lime–guajillo-pepper broth with mango-jalapeño salad; or melt-in-your-mouth chocolate mousse with caramelized banana, mango-saffron sauce, and cocoa sorbet. The vast wine list offers big names but also showcases hot new regions and lesser-known varietals that offer quality and comparative value. $ *Average main: $111* ⊠ *Ritz-Carlton Grand Cayman, West Bay Rd., Seven Mile Beach* ☎ *345/943–9000* ◬ *Reservations essential* ⊗ *Closed Sun. and Mon. No lunch.*

$
CARIBBEAN
ᗧ

× **Chicken! Chicken!.** Chicken! Chicken! Devotees would probably award four exclamation points to the marvelously moist chicken, slow-roasted on a hardwood open-hearth rotisserie. Most customers grab takeout, but the decor is appealing for a fast-food joint; the clever interior replicates an old-time Cayman cottage. Bright smiles and home cooking completely from scratch enhance the authentic vibe. Hearty but (mostly) healthful heaping helpings of sides include scrumptious Cayman-style corn bread, honey-rum beans, jicama coleslaw, and spinach-pesto pasta. $ *Average main: $12* ⊠ *West Shore Centre, West Bay Rd., Seven Mile Beach* ☎ *345/945–2290* ⊕ *www.chicken2.com.*

8

$$ **✕Cimboco.** This animated celebration of all things fun, funky, and
ECLECTIC Caribbean is saturated in psychedelic colors: orange, lemon, and lav-
★ ender walls; cobalt glass fixtures; paintings of musicians in fevered
Fauvist hues; a mosaic of flames dancing up the exhibition kitchen's
huge wood-burning oven. History buffs may be interested to know
that the *Cimboco* was the first motorized sailing ship built in Cayman
(in 1927) and for 20 years the main connection—lifeline to the out-
side world; National Archive photographs and old newspapers invest
the space with still more character. Everything from breads (superla-
tive bruschetta and jalapeño corn bread) to ice creams is made from
scratch. Artisanal pizzas betray a (Wolfgang) Puck-ish sensibility with
such toppings as balsamic-roasted eggplant, pine nuts, pesto, and feta;
or curried chicken with pineapple and spinach. Signature items include
banana-leaf-roasted snapper, fire-roasted bacon-wrapped shrimp, and
mahimahi ceviche salad, but the daily specials are also inspired. The
popular breakfast and brunch are equally creative. Amazingly good
desserts start with a moist, intensely rich brownie. The small but well-
considered wine list features more than a dozen by the glass. $ *Average
main: $19* ⊠ *The Marquee, West Bay Rd. at Harquail Bypass, Seven
Mile Beach* ☎ *345/947–2782* ⊕ *www.cimboco.com.*

$$ **✕Eats Cafe.** This happy, hopping hangout is more eclectic and styl-
ECLECTIC ish than any diner, with dramatic decor (crimson booths and walls,
☻ flat-screen TVs lining the counter, pendant steel lamps, an exhibition
kitchen, gigantic flower paintings, and Andy Warhol reproductions)
and vast menu (Cajun to Chinese), including smashing breakfasts. The
15 burgers alone (Rasta Mon Jerkya to Cajun Peppercorn to I'm Sooo
Bleu, as well as fish and veggie versions) could satisfy almost any craving, but you could also get a Caesar salad or sushi, Philly cheese steak
or chicken chimichangas. It's noisy, busy, buzzing, and hip—but not
aggressively so. $ *Average main: $20* ⊠ *Falls Plaza, West Bay Rd.,
Seven Mile Beach* ☎ *345/943–3287* ⊕ *www.eats.ky.*

$$$$ **✕Luca.** Owners Paolo Polloni and Andi Marcher spared no expense in
ITALIAN realizing their vision of a smart (in every sense) beachfront trattoria that
wouldn't be out of place in L.A. Everything was painstakingly handpicked, from the wine "wall" dramatically displaying more than 3,000
bottles from around the globe to the Murano glass fixtures, blown-up
photographs in glossy, glassy frames, leather banquettes, and a curving
onyx-top bar. Chef Frederico Destro delights in unorthodox pairings,
all gorgeously presented. Spicy tuna tartare is served with satiny pepper
sauce and crunchy alfalfa sprouts. Hudson Valley foie gras knits spinach sauce with Anjou pear or caramelized pineapple. His homemade
pastas shine, particularly the pumpkin ravioli in drawn thyme butter
and fantastically fluffy spinach gnocchi tossed with shrimp and asparagus in pesto and poppy seeds. Entrées are invariably solid; the standout is whole Mediterranean striped bass baked in salt crust. His wit
and whimsy truly inform the desserts, which are more ambitious and
intellectual than successful (chocolate-aubergine mousse or chocolate
pappardelle in coriander sauce with pistachio ice cream), yet stimulate
the palate and conversation. $ *Average main: $37* ⊠ *Caribbean Club,*

871 West Bay Rd., Seven Mile Beach ☎ *345/623–4550* ⚐ *Reservations essential* ☾ *No lunch Sun.*

$$$$ ✕ **Michael's Genuine Food & Drink.** James Beard Award–winning chef
ECLECTIC   Michael Schwartz and handpicked executive chef Thomas Tennant
Fodor'sChoice   have successfully imported the slow-food philosophy of the ground-
★   breaking original Michael's Genuine in Miami, using seasonal, locally
sourced produce that travels short distances from the on-site garden
and carefully chosen Cayman farmers, fishermen, and ranchers. The
results live up to the Schwartz mantra of "fresh, simple, pure": honest, uncluttered food that sings with color and flavor right down to the
homemade sodas. Lunch offers a more traditional but lengthy selection, whereas dinner dishes are divided into small, medium, large, and
extra-large portions to encourage family-style sharing and exploration.
Sublime staples on the ever-changing menu include burrata (look for
such seasonal standouts as heirloom tomato or breadfruit) and sweet-
and-sour pork belly (juxtaposing crunchy kimchi with crisp yet unctu-
ously fatty meat). You can't go wrong with any wood-oven-roasted
dish, whether pizza, snapper (memorably accented by roasted fennel,
grilled lemon, and smoked Cayman sea salt), or *poulet rouge* chicken.
The well-considered wine list offers occasional bargains; the menu suggests creative pairings from the vast beer selection. Tennant has also
devised an inspired solution to the invasive lionfish population: look
for it as a menu special, and if you dive, ask about the Lionfish Safari.
⑤ *Average main: $34* ✉ *47 Forum La., Canella Court, Camana Bay*
☎ *345/640–6433* ⊕ *www.michaelsgenuine.com* ☾ *No lunch Sun.*

$$$$ ✕ **Ortanique.** The original Miami Ortanique—a royal marriage between
ECLECTIC   celebrity chef Cindy Hutson and Delius Shirley, son of Jamaican doy-
Fodor'sChoice   enne of cooking Norma Shirley—helped revolutionize Floribbean fusion
★   fare, and the vibrant food at their Cayman outpost lives up to the nickname "Cuisine of the Sun." Even the interior gleams in rich yellows and
oranges that subtly recall plantation living, though prize seating is on the
inviting patio, shaded by sea grape trees overlooking a small islet. Cuisine of the Sun emphasizes Caribbean and South American gastronomy
infused with Asian inspirations. Seemingly disparate, they share similar
landscapes and ingredients. Executive Chef Sara Mair, a semifinalist on
Top Chef, reinvents classics with an island twist: witness jerk-rubbed foie
gras, cooled by burnt-orange marmalade, or plump Mediterranean mussels in Red Stripe broth with shallots, Scotch bonnet peppers, tomatoes,
and Jamaican thyme. Or try the signature jerked double pork chop, its
fire tamed by guava-spiced rum glaze. Save room for such decadent desserts as a deceptively airy Cloud of Coconut Joy or rum-soaked banana
fritters. ⑤ *Average main: $40* ✉ *47 Forum La., The Crescent, Camana
Bay* ☎ *345/640–7710* ⊕ *www.ortaniquerestaurants.com.*

$$$ ✕ **Ragazzi.** The name means "good buddies," and this strip-mall jewel
ITALIAN   offers simpatico ambience indeed, always percolating with conversation
★   and good strong espresso. The airy space is convivial: blond woods,
periwinkle walls and columns, and handsome artworks of beach scenes,
sailboats, and palm trees (against a striking yellow sky) with the scenes
extended onto the frame. Chef Adriano Usini turns out magnificent,
meticulously prepared standards (the antipasto alone is worth a visit,

8

as are the homemade breadsticks and focaccia, and definitive carpaccio and insalata Caprese). The shellfish linguine (shrimp, scallops, and mussels in a light, silken tomato sauce, with cherry-tomato skins pulled back and crisped) and gnocchi in four-cheese sauce with brandy and pistachios will please any pasta perfectionist. Two dozen first-rate pizzas emerge from the wood-burning oven, and meat and seafood mains are beautifully done, never overcooked. The wine list is notable (400-odd choices) for a casual eatery, showcasing great range and affordability even on high-ticket, hard-to-find heavy hitters such as Biondi Santi Brunello, Jermann Pinot Grigio, and Giacosa Barbaresco; the affable, knowledgeable staff will gladly suggest pairings, including unusual finds. ⑤ *Average main: $29* ⊠ *Buckingham Sq., West Bay Rd., Seven Mile Beach* ☎ *345/945–3484* ⊕ *www.ragazzi.ky.*

$$$$ ✕ **Reef Grill at Royal Palms.** This class act appeals to a casually suave
ECLECTIC crowd, many of them regulars, who appreciate its consistent quality, attentive yet unobtrusive service, soothing seaside setting, top-notch entertainment, and surprisingly reasonable prices. The space is cannily divided into four areas, each with its own look and feel. Co-owner–chef George Dahlstrom gives his perfectly prepared, familiar dishes just enough twist to satisfy jaded palates: calamari is fried in arborio rice batter with lemon aioli; toasted, sesame-crusted, seared tuna kicks with kimchi; melt-in-your-mouth braised short ribs, one of the smaller "lite bites" (think mega-tapas), come with blue cheese-peppercorn poutine (fries covered with cheese curds and gravy); and sea scallops are pan-seared with a creamy roasted corn–smoked bacon mash. Dance the calories off to the estimable reggae, calypso, and soca sounds of Coco Red or really sweat it out during Chill Wednesdays, and then adjourn to the cozy lounge for an aged rum or single malt. It's equally enticing at lunch, when it exudes a soigné beach bar ambience. ⑤ *Average main: $28* ⊠ *537 West Bay Rd., Seven Mile Beach* ☎ *345/945–6358* ⊕ *www. reefgrill.com* ⊘ *No dinner Sun. May–Nov.*

$$ ✕ **Yoshi Sushi.** The superlative sushi's fresh—and the clientele sometimes
JAPANESE even fresher—at this modish, modern locals' lair. Scarlet cushions,
★ cherry pendant blown-glass lamps, leather-and-bamboo accents, and maroon walls help create a sensuous, even charged vibe in the main room. The backlighted bar sees its share of carefree customers trying to manipulate their chopsticks after a few kamikaze sake bomber missions (plunging hot cups of sake into frosty Kirin beer). Savvy diners literally leave themselves in Yoshi's hands (the rolls and nightly special sushi "pizzas" are particularly creative), and the raw-phobic can choose from fine cooked items, from beef tataki to tempura to teriyaki. The congenial staff recommends intriguing sake and beer pairings, though the wine list and martini selection are also admirable for an Asian eatery. ⑤ *Average main: $24* ⊠ *Falls Plaza, West Bay Rd., Seven Mile Beach* ☎ *345/943–9674* ⊕ *www.eats.ky* ◬ *Reservations essential.*

WEST BAY

$$$$ ✕ **Cracked Conch.** This longtime institution, rebuilt after Hurricane Ivan,
ECLECTIC effortlessly blends upscale and down-home. The interior gleams from the elaborate light-and-water sculpture at the gorgeous mosaic-and-mahogany entrance bar to the plush booths with subtly embedded

lighting. You can drink in the remarkable water views through large shutters, but for maximum impact, dine on the multitiered patio. Executive Chef Gilbert Cavallaro similarly revitalized the kitchen with dazzling juxtapositions of color, taste, and texture. Newfangled variations on old-fashioned cuisine include honey-jerk-glazed tuna with tomato sorbet, crispy calamari with cardamom-marinated carrots and chipotle sauce, and crab cakes with red-pepper reduction and passion-fruit demiglace. Sample stellar signature items include the definitive conch chowder or ceviche, silken short rib ravioli with truffles and Parmesan foam, and mahimahi poached *sous vide* over cannellini emulsion drizzled with truffle oil. Desserts delight, from a gossamer vanilla crème brûlée with pineapple-bergamot salsa to a miraculously moist guava-glazed bread-and-butter pudding. Locals flock to Sunday brunch or Monday's all-you-can-eat barbecue bash, or they just hang out at the dockside Macabuca tiki bar (fab sunsets, sunset-hued libations), which lives up to its mellow name, indigenous Taíno for "What does it matter?" [$] *Average main: $44* ⊠ *Northwest Point Rd., West Bay* ☎ *345/945–5217* ⊕ *www.crackedconch.com.ky.*

$$$ ✕**Morgans Harbour.** Energetic, effervescent Janie Schweiger patrols the
ECLECTIC   front while husband Richard rules the kitchen at this simpatico seaside spot with smashing North Sound views. Locals (and fishermen) literally cruise into the adjacent dock for refueling of all sorts. You can sit in one of the cozy buildings decorated with Depression-era chandeliers and vivid aquatic artworks ("It's the House of Doors," Janie quips. "Twenty-five ways in but of course we don't want you to leave") or admire the dexterous marine maneuverings from the interlocking decks. Richard's menu dances just as deftly from Asia to his Austrian home. Nifty, nimbly prepared nibbles include the wildly popular 10-ounce Brie-topped jerk burger and ceviche, but everything from chicken schnitzel to seafood risotto is expertly cooked to order, often with a creative twist. Lunch offers several of the restaurant's greatest hits at even more palatable prices. [$] *Average main: $28* ⊠ *Morgan's Harbour, West Bay* ☎ *345/946–7049* ⊕ *www.morgansharbour.net.*

EAST END

$$$$ ✕**The Lighthouse.** The nonworking, conical, white-stucco lighthouse
SEAFOOD   surrounded by fluttering flags serves as a beacon for hungry East End explorers. The interior replicates a yacht: polished hardwood floors, ship's lanterns, mosaic hurricane lamps, steering wheels, marine artworks, portholes, and waiters in crew's garb with chevrons. Most tables afford sweeping sea vistas, but prize romantic seating is on the little deck. Shipshape starters include Miss Nell's red conch chowder (she lives in the pink house behind the restaurant) or flash-fried calamari with sweet chili dip. Photo-shoot-worthy entrées (such as a platter of seafood floating on linguine alfredo) sing with color and flavor. Carnivores can devour osso bucco ravioli or porcini-dusted chicken breast with rosemary-Marsala sauce. Vegetarians will delight in the curries, tofu stir-fries, and pastas. Save room for desserts, including the tropical cheesecake. The comprehensive wine list extends to a superb postprandial selection of liqueurs, aged rums, ports, and grappas. The gift shop offers lovely jewelry and handmade ceramic lighthouses. [$] *Average*

main: $34 ⊠ Oceanside, Breakers, East End ☎ 345/947–2047 ⊕ www. lighthouse.ky.

$ ✕ **Vivine's Kitchen.** Cars practically block the road at this unprepossessing

CARIBBEAN hot spot for classic Caymanian food. You're literally eating in Vivine and Ray Watler's home; the prime seating is in the waterfront courtyard, where you will be serenaded by rustling sea grape leaves, crashing surf, and screeching gulls dive-bombing for their lunch. Daily changing menu items, all sourced locally to guarantee freshness, are scrawled on a blackboard: perhaps stewed turtle, curried goat, barbecued chicken, and snapper made to order, with cassava and sweet-potato cake sides. Burgers, dogs, and chicken-and-chips make a concession to more timid taste buds. Alcohol isn't served, but fresh tamarind, mango, and sorrel juices pack a flavorful punch. Vivine's generally closes early (and occasionally on Monday night), but stays open if there's demand—and any food left. ⑤ *Average main: $11 ⊠ Austin Dr., Gun Bay, East End* ☎ 345/947–7435 ▭ *No credit cards.*

WHERE TO STAY

Brace yourself for resort prices—there are few accommodations in the lower price ranges. You'll find no big all-inclusive resorts on Grand Cayman (though the Reef Resort offers an optional AI plan to its guests), and very few offer a meal plan other than breakfast. Parking is always free at island hotels and resorts. Although the island has several resorts (mostly along Seven Mile Beach), the majority of accommodations are vacation rentals, and these are scattered throughout the island. Some of the condo complexes even offer resort-style amenities.

They may be some distance from the beach and short on style and facilities, but the island's guesthouses offer rock-bottom prices, a friendly atmosphere, and your best shot at getting to know the locals. Rooms are clean and simple, and most have private baths.

For expanded reviews, facilities, and current deals, visit Fodors.com.

PRIVATE VILLAS AND CONDOMINIUMS

Most condo complexes are very similar, with telephones, satellite TV, air-conditioning, living and dining areas, patios, and parking. Differences are amenities, proximity to town and beach, and the views. As with resorts, rates are higher in winter, and there may be a three- or seven-night minimum. There are dozens of large private villas available on the beach, especially on the North Side near Cayman Kai. A growing trend: "green" condos. We no longer recommend individual private villas, especially since they frequently change agents. However, among the properties we've inspected worth looking for are Coral Reef, Venezia, Villa Habana, Great Escapes, Fishbones, and Pease Bay House. Several of the condo and villa rental companies have websites where you can see pictures of the privately owned units and villas they represent.

VILLA RENTAL AGENCIES

Blue Escapes. Blue Escapes is an up-and-coming international broker that also works with top-notch on-island realtors. ☎ 512/892–3301 ⊕ *www.blueescapes.com.*

BEST BETS FOR LODGING

Fodor's Choice ★
Caribbean Club, Lighthouse Point,
Reef Resort, Ritz-Carlton Grand
Cayman

BEST BEACHFRONT
Coral Stone Club, Lacovia Condo-
miniums, Reef Resort, Southern Cross
Club, Westin Casuarina

**BEST FOR AN ECOFRIENDLY
TRIP**
Cobalt Coast, Compass Point, Light-
house Point

BEST FOR FAMILIES
Ritz-Carlton Grand Cayman

BEST SERVICE
The Alexander, Reef Resort, Ritz-
Carlton Grand Cayman

BEST FOR ROMANCE
Caribbean Club, Cotton Tree, Shangri-
La B&B, Turtle Nest Inn

Cayman Island Vacations. Cayman Island Vacations was started by the affable couple Don and Linda Martin in 1989. Longtime Cayman homeowners, they represent more than 50 villas and condos (including their own). Extremely helpful with island suggestions, they can make arrangements for a rental car and extras. They arrange diving discounts, and Linda is one of Cayman's leading wedding coordinators. ☎ *813/854–1201, 888/208–8935* ⊕ *www.caymanvacation.com.*

Cayman Villas Cayman Villas represents villas and condos on Grand and Little Cayman. ⊠ *Grand Cayman* ☎ *800/235–5888, 345/945–4144* ⊕ *www.caymanvillas.com.*

Grand Cayman Villas. Grand Cayman Villas was started by Virginia resident Jim Leavitt, who carries listings for dozens of fine properties island-wide. ⊠ *Grand Cayman* ☎ *866/358–8455* ⊕ *www. grandcaymanvillas.net.*

Island Hideaways. Island Hideaways rents villas all over the Caribbean, including some in the Cayman Islands. ⊠ *Grand Cayman* ☎ *800/832–2302* ⊕ *www.islandhideaways.com.*

Wimco. Wimco, or the West Indies Management Company, is synonymous with quality throughout the world, especially the Caribbean. ⊠ *Grand Cayman* ☎ *866/850–6140* ⊕ *www.wimco.com.*

GEORGE TOWN AND ENVIRONS

$$$ 🏨 **Sunset House.** This amiable seaside dive-oriented resort is on the iron-
HOTEL shore south of George Town, close enough for a short trip to stores and restaurants yet far enough to feel secluded. **Pros:** great shore diving and dive shop; lively bar scene; fun international clientele; great package rates. **Cons:** often indifferent service; somewhat run-down; no real swimming beach; spotty Wi-Fi signal. **TripAdvisor:** "excellent dive hotel," "nothing fancy," "truly great sunsets." 💲 *Rooms from: $251* ⊠ *390 S. Church St.* ☎ *345/949–7111, 800/854–4767* ⊕ *www. sunsethouse.com* ⌧ *58 rooms, 2 suites* ⏹ *No meals.*

SEVEN MILE BEACH

$$$$ 🖼 **Caribbean Club.** Sleek but not slick, this gleaming boutique facility
RENTAL   includes a striking lobby filled with aquariums, a stunning infinity pool,
Fodor'sChoice   and the aggressively contemporary trattoria, Luca. **Pros:** luxurious,
★   high-tech facilities beyond the typical apartment complex; trendy Italian restaurant on-site; service on the beach. **Cons:** stratospheric prices;
though families are welcome, they may find it rather imposing; smaller
balconies on top floor (albeit amazing views). **TripAdvisor:** "heavenly,"
"fabulous top-story apartment," "first class." ⑤ *Rooms from: $1256*
✉ *871 West Bay Rd., Seven Mile Beach* ☎ *345/623–4500, 800/941–*
1126 ⊕ *www.caribclub.com* ⬦ *37 3-bedroom condos* ⦿| *No meals.*

$$$ 🖼 **Christopher Columbus.** This enduring favorite is quite a discovery for
RENTAL   families, sitting on the peaceful northern end of Seven Mile Beach.
☾   **Pros:** excellent snorkeling from a fine stretch of beach; great value; free
Wi-Fi. **Con:** car really needed; often overrun by families during holi-
day seasons and summer; top floors feature splendid vistas but difficult
access for physically challenged. **TripAdvisor:** "great condo," "pictures
don't do it justice," "exceptional." ⑤ *Rooms from: $365* ✉ *2013 West*
Bay Rd., Seven Mile Beach ☎ *345/945–4354, 866/311–5231* ⊕ *www.*
christophercolumbuscondos.com ⬦ *30 2- and 3-bedroom condos*
⦿| *No meals.*

$$ 🖼 **Comfort Suites Grand Cayman.** This no-frills, all-suites hotel has an
HOTEL   ideal location on West Bay Road, next door to the Marriott and near
numerous shops, restaurants, and bars. **Pros:** affordable; nice complimentary extras like continental breakfast and Wi-Fi; fun young-ish
crowd. **Cons:** rooms nearly a block from the beach; new condominium
blocks sea views; no balconies; bar closes early. **TripAdvisor:** "good for
first time visit to island," "comfortable stay," "great service." ⑤ *Rooms*
from: $208 ✉ *West Bay Rd.* ☎ *345/945–7300, 800/517–4000* ⊕ *www.*
caymancomfort.com ⬦ *108 suites* ⦿| *Breakfast.*

$$$$ 🖼 **Coral Stone Club.** This exclusive enclave shines in the shadow of the
RENTAL   Ritz-Carlton by offering understated barefoot luxury and huge three-
★   bedroom condos. **Pros:** largest ratio of beach and pool space to guests;
walking distance to several restaurants and shops; stellar service; excellent off-season deals. **Cons:** expensive in high season; Ritz-Carlton
guests sometimes wander over from their packed section of sand trying to poach beach space. **TripAdvisor:** "perfect facility," "best views
and accommodations," "amazing helpful staff." ⑤ *Rooms from: $775*
✉ *West Bay Rd., Seven Mile Beach* ☎ *345/945–5820, 888/927–2322*
⊕ *www.coralstoneclub.com* ⬦ *30 3-bedroom condos* ⦿| *No meals.*

$$$$ 🖼 **Grand Cayman Beach Suites.** The former Hyatt all-suites section, now
RESORT   locally run, offers a terrific beachfront location and trendy eateries.
Pros: fine beach; superior dining and water-sports facilities; free use of
gym (unusual on Grand Cayman); supermarkets and restaurants within
walking distance. **Cons:** most entrances face the street, making it noisy
on weekends; several units need refurbishment; music often blaring
around the pool. **TripAdvisor:** "a wonderful small resort," "tropical
heaven on earth," "great room." ⑤ *Rooms from: $695* ✉ *West Bay*
Rd., Seven Mile Beach ☎ *345/949–1234* ⊕ *www.grand-cayman-beach-*
suites.com and www.gcbs.ky ⬦ *53 suites* ⦿| *No meals.*

$$$
RESORT
★
🏨 **Grand Cayman Marriott Beach Resort.** The soaring, stylish, if impersonal marble lobby (with exquisite art glass, spectacular blown-up underwater photos, and fun elements such as red British-style telephone boxes) sets the tone for this bustling beachfront property. **Pros:** lively bars and restaurants; good snorkeling and water sports; convenient to both George Town and Seven Mile Beach; airport connectivity enables you to print your boarding pass. **Cons:** often overrun by tour groups and conventioneers; narrowest section of Seven Mile Beach; pool and bar often noisy late. **TripAdvisor:** "amazing staff," "property average," "excellent buffet breakfast." ⑤ *Rooms from: $349* ✉ *389 West Bay Rd., Seven Mile Beach* ☎ *345/949–0088, 800/223–6388* ⊕ *www.marriott.com* ⥲ *273 rooms, 22 suites* ⑩ *No meals.*

$$$$
RENTAL
☊
🏨 **The Grandview.** This older but well-groomed property lives up to its ostentatious billing: all 69 two- and three-bedroom units (though sadly only 15 are generally in the rental pool) look smack onto the Caribbean and the beach past splendidly maintained gardens (families play soccer on the expansive lawn). **Pros:** terrific snorkeling; restaurants and shops within walking distance; free Wi-Fi (when it's available); screened-in patios keep mosquitoes out. **Cons:** the long beach can be rocky; some units a tad worn though meticulously maintained; not all units have access to the free Wi-Fi signal. **TripAdvisor:** "could not have been better," "sun and relaxation," "tranquility personified." ⑤ *Rooms from: $475* ✉ *95 Snooze La., Seven Mile Beach* ☎ *345/945–4511, 866/977–6766* ⊕ *www.grandviewcondos.com* ⥲ *69 2- and 3-bedroom condos* ⑩ *No meals.*

$$$$
RENTAL
★
🏨 **Lacovia Condominiums.** The carefully manicured courtyard of this handsome arcaded Mediterranean Revival property could easily be mistaken for a peaceful park. **Pros:** central location; exquisite gardens; extensive beach. **Cons:** rear courtyard rooms can be noisy from traffic and partying from West Bay Road; pool fairly small (though most people prefer the beach). **TripAdvisor:** "comfortable well-equipped suites," "perfect for families," "simply amazing." ⑤ *Rooms from: $415* ✉ *697 West Bay Rd., Seven Mile Beach* ☎ *345/949–7599* ⊕ *www.lacovia.com* ⥲ *35 1-, 2-, and 3-bedroom condos* ⑩ *No meals.*

$$$$
RESORT
☊
Fodor's Choice
★
🏨 **Ritz-Carlton Grand Cayman.** Posh and pampering without pretension, the Ritz-Carlton offers unparalleled luxury and service infused with a welcome sense of place, including works by top local artists and craftspeople. **Pros:** exemplary service; exceptional facilities with many complimentary extras; marvelous local artworks including a corridor-length gallery with rotating exhibits. **Cons:** annoyingly high per-night resort fee; somewhat sprawling with a confusing layout; long walk to beach (over an interior bridge) from most rooms. **TripAdvisor:** "splendor and service," "phenomenal from start to finish," "fabulous resort has it all." ⑤ *Rooms from: $495* ✉ *West Bay Rd., Seven Mile Beach* ☎ *345/943–9000* ⊕ *www.ritzcarlton.com* ⥲ *329 rooms, 12 suites, 24 condos* ⑩ *Breakfast.*

$$
HOTEL
🏨 **Sunshine Suites Resort.** This friendly, all-suites hotel is an impeccably clean money saver. **Pros:** good value and deals; cheerful staff; rocking little restaurant; thoughtful free extras. **Cons:** poor views; not on the beach. **TripAdvisor:** "fantastic staff and great amenities,"

8

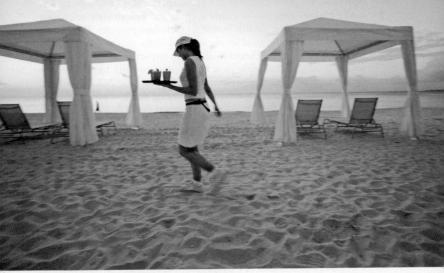

Shaded beach loungers at the Ritz-Carlton, Grand Cayman

"great location," "best bang for your buck." ⑤ *Rooms from: $202* ⊠ *1465 Esterley Tibbetts Hwy., off West Bay Rd., Seven Mile Beach* ☎ *345/949–3000, 877/786–1110* ⊕ *www.sunshinesuites.com* ⤳ *130 suites* ⏺ *Breakfast.*

$$$$
RESORT
☺

🏨 **Westin Casuarina Resort and Spa.** The Westin has something to offer everyone, from conventioneers to honeymooners to families, not to mention an excellent location. **Pros:** terrific children's programs; superb beach (the largest resort stretch at 800 feet). **Con:** occasionally bustling and impersonal when large groups book. **TripAdvisor:** "very Grand Cayman," "quite a nice place," "best Sunday brunch on the islands." ⑤ *Rooms from: $369* ⊠ *West Bay Rd., Seven Mile Beach* ☎ *345/945–3800, 800/937–8461* ⊕ *www.westincasuarina.net* ⤳ *339 rooms, 8 suites* ⏺ *No meals.*

WEST BAY

$$$
RESORT
★

🏨 **Cobalt Coast Resort and Suites.** This small ecofriendly hotel is perfect for divers who want a sparkling, spacious room or suite right on the ironshore far, far from the madding crowds and who don't want to pay high prices. **Pros:** superb dive outfit; friendly service and clientele; free Wi-Fi; environmentally aware. **Cons:** poky golden-sand beach; unattractive concrete pool area; remote location, so a car (included in some packages) is necessary. **TripAdvisor:** "clean comfortable rooms," "outstanding friendly dive resort," "great people." ⑤ *Rooms from: $290* ⊠ *18-A Sea Fan Dr., West Bay* ☎ *345/946–5656, 888/946–5656* ⊕ *www.cobaltcoast.com* ⤳ *7 rooms, 14 suites* ⏺ *Multiple meal plans.*

$$$$
RENTAL
★

Cotton Tree. The motto of this exclusive villa enclave in tranquil West Bay could easily be "If luxe could kill." **Pros:** peaceful and quiet setting; beautifully designed and outfitted accommodations; complimentary airport transfers; wonderful immersion in local culture. **Cons:** luxury comes with a price tag; remote location means a car is required; beach narrow and tangled with sea grape trees. **TripAdvisor:** "a dream vacation," "spectacular people and inn," "absolutely amazing." ⑤ *Rooms from: $890* ⊠ *375 Conch Point Rd., West Bay* ☎ *345/943–0700* ⊕ *www.caymancottontree.com* ⊅ *4 2-bedroom cottages* ⊘ *Closed Sept.* ⊙ *No meals.*

$$$$
RESORT
Fodor's Choice
★

Lighthouse Point. For travelers who want to "live lightly on the planet," leading scuba operator DiveTech's stunning new development takes the lead, from sustainable wood interiors and recycled concrete to an ecosensitive gray-water system, energy-saving appliances and lights, and Cayman's first wind turbine generator. **Pros:** ecofriendly; fantastic shore diving (and state-of-the-art dive shop); creative and often recycled upscale look. **Cons:** no real beach; car necessary; bit difficult for physically challenged to navigate. ⑤ *Rooms from: $450* ⊠ *571 N.W. Point Rd., West Bay* ☎ *345/949–1700* ⊕ *www.lighthouse-point-cayman.com* ⊅ *9 2-bedroom apartments* ⊙ *No meals.*

$$
B&B/INN
★

Shangri-La B&B. Accomplished pianist George Davidson and wife Eileen built this lavish lakeside retreat and truly make guests feel at home, along with dogs Roxie and Stella. **Pros:** use of kitchen; elegant decor. **Cons:** rental car necessary; not on the beach. **TripAdvisor:** "wonderful stay in paradise," "one-of-a-kind gem," "nice quiet place." ⑤ *Rooms from: $149* ⊠ *1 Sticky Toffee Lane, West Bay* ☎ *345/526–1170* ⊕ *www.shangrilabandb.com* ⊅ *6 rooms, 1 apartment* ⊙ *Breakfast.*

EAST END

$$$
RESORT
★

Compass Point Dive Resort. This tranquil, congenial little getaway run by the admirable Ocean Frontiers scuba operation would steer even nondivers in the right direction. **Pros:** top-notch dive operation; good value especially with packages; affable international staff and clientele. **Cons:** no restaurant or bar; isolated location requires a car. **TripAdvisor:** "a true diver's place," "keeps getting better," "a beautiful complex." ⑤ *Rooms from: $295* ⊠ *Austin Conolly Dr., East End* ☎ *345/947–7500, 800/348–6096, 345/947–0000* ⊕ *www.compasspoint.ky* ⊅ *17 1-bedroom, 9 2-bedroom, and 3 3-bedroom condos* ⊙ *No meals.*

$$$$
RESORT
Fodor's Choice
★

Reef Resort. This exceedingly well-run time-share property (don't worry: no aggressive hawking!) seductively straddles a 600-foot beach on the less hectic East End. **Pros:** romantically remote; glorious beach; enthusiastic staff (including a crackerjack wedding coordinator); great packages. **Cons:** remote; few dining options within easy driving distance; sprawling layout. **TripAdvisor:** "a Caribbean paradise," "beachfront perfection," "incredible staff." ⑤ *Rooms from: $351* ⊠ *Queen's Hwy., East End* ☎ *345/947–3100, 888/232–0541* ⊕ *www.thereef.com.ky and www.thereef.com* ⊅ *152 suites* ⊙ *Multiple meal plans.*

$$
RENTAL
★

Turtle Nest Inn and Condos. This affordable, intimate, Mediterranean-style seaside inn has roomy one-bedroom apartments and a pool overlooking a narrow beach with good snorkeling. **Pros:** wonderful snorkeling; thoughtful extras; caring staff; free Wi-Fi. **Cons:** car

8

necessary; occasional rocks and debris on beach; ground-floor room views slightly obscured by palms; road noise in back rooms. **TripAdvisor:** "great snorkeling," "three acres of paradise," "beautiful people." ⑤ *Rooms from: $149* ✉ *166 Bodden Town Rd., Bodden Town* ☎ *345/947–8665* ⊕ *www.turtlenestinn.net* ⤴ *8 apartments, 10 2-bedroom condos* ⦿ *No meals.*

NIGHTLIFE

Grand Cayman nightlife is surprisingly good for such a quiet-seeming island. Check the Friday edition of the *Caymanian Compass* for listings of music, movies, theater, and other entertainment. Bars are open during evening hours until 1 am, and clubs are generally open from 10 pm until 3 am, but none may serve liquor after midnight on Saturday and none can offer dancing on Sunday. Competition is fierce between Grand Cayman's many bars and restaurants. In addition to entertainment (fish feeding to fire-eating), even upscale joints host happy hours offering free hors d'oeuvres and/or drinks.

GEORGE TOWN AND ENVIRONS

BARS AND MUSIC CLUBS

★ **My Bar.** This bar is optimally perched on the water's edge, looking almost due west with a perfect vantage point for watching the sunset. The leviathan open-sided cabana is drenched in vivid Rasta colors and crowned by an intricate South Seas–style thatched roof (containing approximately 36,000 palm fronds). Christmas lights and the occasional customer dangle from the rafters year-round. Great grub and a mischievous mix of locals, expats, and tourists from all walks of life prove that ecocentric Cayman offers wild life alongside the wildlife. ✉ *Sunset House, S. Church St.* ☎ *345/949–7111* ⊕ *www.sunsethouse.com.*

Rackam's Waterfront Pub and Restaurant. A Cayman mosaic of fishermen to Who's-the-Hugo-Boss financiers savors sensational sunsets followed by exuberantly pirouetting tarpon feeding at the open-air, marine-theme happenin' bar built on a jetty jutting into the harbor (boaters, even snorkelers cruise right up the ladder for drinks while anglers leave their catch on ice) that has complimentary snacks on Friday and serves pub fare at fair prices until midnight. ✉ *93 N. Church St.* ☎ *345/945–3860* ⊕ *www.rackamswaterfront.ky.*

SEVEN MILE BEACH

BARS AND MUSIC CLUBS

★ **Aqua Beach Bar.** This place feels like a country bar gone (coco)nuts: palm trees burst through thatching; art naïf portraits of musicians explode in neon reds, yellows, blues, and greens; private tiki huts provide intimacy; and neon beer signs illuminate the wood paneling. Fairly good Tex-Mex fare is dished out late. There's a variety of live bands, open-mike nights, and theme nights, such as Thursday acoustic jams. Also, there are plenty of daily drink-and-eat specials such as Sunday's NASCAR Bud buckets. ✉ *426 West Bay Rd., Seven Mile Beach* ☎ *345/949–8498.*

★ **The Attic.** The Attic is a chic sports bar with three billiard tables, classic arcade games (Space Invaders, Donkey Kong), air hockey, and large-screen TVs (you can nab a private booth with its own flat-panel job). Events encompass daily happy hours, trivia nights, and the Caribbean's reputedly largest Bloody Mary bar on Sunday. Along with downstairs sister hot spot "O" Bar, it's ground zero for the Wednesday Night Drinking Club. For a $25 initiation fee (you get a T-shirt and personalized leather wristband, toga optional) and $10 weekly activity fee, you'll be shuttled by bus to several different bars, with free shots and drinks specials all night. ⊠ *Queen's Court, 2nd fl., West Bay Rd., Seven Mile Beach* ☎ *345/949–7665* ⊕ *www.attic.ky.*

★ **Calico Jack's.** For a casual drink, visit this friendly outdoor beach bar at the north end of the public beach with a DJ on Saturday and open-mike night on Tuesday, bands many Friday nights, and riotous parties during the full moon when even Ritz-Carlton guests let their hair and inhibitions down. ⊠ *West Bay Rd., Seven Mile Beach* ☎ *345/945–7850.*

Coconut Joe's. You can sit at the bar or swing under a century-old poinciana tree and watch the traffic go by. There are murals of apes everywhere, from gorillas doing shots to a baboon in basketball uniform (in keeping with management's facetious suggestion that you attract your server's attention by pounding your chest while screeching and scratching yourself). It's particularly popular with the younger tourism- and hospitality-industry crowds (ply them with beers for some hair- and eyebrow-raising backstage stories). Friday really swings with DJs and free happy-hour munchies. ⊠ *Across from Comfort Suites, West Bay Rd., Seven Mile Beach* ☎ *345/943–5637.*

Legendz. A sports bar with a clubby, retro feel (Marilyn Monroe and Frank Sinatra photos channel the glamour days), it's the usual testosterone test drive with plentiful scoring of both types. Good luck wrestling a spot at the bar for Pay-Per-View and major live sporting events (though 10 TVs, including two 6-by-8 foot, high-resolution screens broadcast to every corner). It doubles as an entertainment venue, booking local bands, stand-up comics, and leading island DJs. ⊠ *Falls Centre, West Bay Rd., Seven Mile Beach* ☎ *No phone.*

Lone Star Bar and Grill. The bar and restaurant proudly calls itself Cayman's top dive (and indeed, locals from dive masters to dentists get down and occasionally dirty over kick-ass margaritas). The noisy bar glorifies sports, Texas, T&A, and the boob tube, from murals of Cowboys cheerleaders to an amazing sports memorabilia collection (including items signed by both Bushes), and 14 big-screen TVs tuned to different events. ⊠ *686 West Bay Rd., Seven Mile Beach* ☎ *345/945–5175* ⊕ *www.lonestarcayman.com.*

Stingers Resort and Pool Bar. Stingers Resort and Pool Bar offers tasty food in an appealing setting (check out the stupendous "stinger" mosaic), with cover-free live music and dancing Thursday and Friday. Wednesday and Saturday nights there's a very affordable all-you-can-eat Caribbean luau. The band Heat, a local institution, sizzles with energetic, emotionally delivered calypso, reggae, soca, salsa, and oldies; then the limbo dancers and fire-eaters keep the temperature rising. If you recoil from audience participation, stay far away. More exhibitionistic "spring break" sorts might find their photo adorning the "Wall of Shame," but the worst blackmail is persuading you to buy another blue-green Stingers punch. ⊠ *Comfort Suites, West Bay Rd., Seven Mile Beach* ☎ *345/945–3000.*

The Wharf. You can dance near the water to mellow music on Saturday evenings; when there's a wedding reception in the pavilion, the crashing surf and candles twinkling as if competing with the stars bathe the proceedings in an almost Gatsby-esque glow. For something less sedate, Roger and Sarah conduct sizzling salsa dancing and lessons on Tuesdays after dinner, while most Fridays morph into a wild 1970s disco night. The stunning seaside setting on tiered decks compensates for often undistinguished food and service. The Ports of Call bar is a splendid place for sunset fanciers, and tarpon feeding off the deck is a nightly 9 pm spectacle. ⊠ *West Bay Rd.* ☎ *345/949–2231.*

CIGAR AND WINE LOUNGES

★ **Silver Palm Lounge.** The Silver Palm drips with cash and cachet. One section faithfully replicates a classic English country library (perfect for civilized, proper afternoon tea or a pre- or postdinner champagne or single malt). Then there's the sexy, überhip, black-clad Taikun lounge, with hardwood wainscoting, carved bamboo, marble floors, lacquer tables, and model (in both senses) waitstaff. Also on tap: fab cocktails, including specialty martinis (the Silver Palm cosmopolitan is a winner—Ketel One citron, triple sec, a squeeze of fresh lime juice, and a splash of cranberry topped off with Moët champagne); pages of wines by the glass; an impressive list of cigars, cognacs, and aged rums; and marvelous sushi and creative tapas. Everyone's chic-by-jowl after 10 pm, especially on funked-out DJ Fridays, when Arab sheiks mingle with American CEOs, and tonsorially challenged agent-types wear trophy wives (and mistresses) on their arms like Rolexes: it puts the sin in scintillating. ⊠ *Ritz-Carlton, West Bay Rd., Seven Mile Beach* ☎ *345/943–9000.*

DANCE CLUBS

★ **"O" Bar.** "O" Bar is a trendy black-and-crimson, industrial-style dance club with mixed music and juggling, flame-throwing bartenders—practically local celebs—flipping cocktails with cojones every night. It's as close to a stand-and-pose milieu as you'll find on Cayman, with the occasional fashion fascist parading in Prada. An upper-level private loft is available by reservation. ⊠ *Queen's Court, West Bay Rd., Seven Mile Beach* ☎ *345/943–6227* ⊕ *www.obar.ky.*

EAST END

BARS AND MUSIC CLUBS

Rusty Pelican. This spot draws an eclectic group of dive masters, expats, honeymooners, and mingling singles. The knockout, colorful cocktails pack quite a punch, making the sunset last for hours. The bar dialogue is entertainment enough, but don't miss local legend, country-calypsonian Barefoot Man, when he plays "upstairs" at Pelican's Reef—he's to Cayman what Jimmy Buffett is to Key West. ⊠ *Reef Resort, Colliers, East End* ☎ *345/947–3100* ⊕ *www.thereef.com.ky.*

SHOPPING

On Grand Cayman the good news is that there's no sales tax *and* there's plenty of duty-free merchandise. Locally made items to watch for include woven mats, baskets, jewelry made of a marblelike stone called Caymanite (from the cliffs of Cayman Brac), and authentic sunken treasure, though the latter is never cheap. In addition, there are several noteworthy local artists, some of whose atelier–homes double as galleries, such as Al Ebanks, Horacio Esteban, and Luelan Bodden. Unique items include Cayman sea salt and luxury bath salts (solar harvested in an ecologically sensitive manner), and Tortuga rum and rum cakes. Seven Fathoms is the first working distillery actually in Cayman itself, its award-winning rums aged underwater (hence the name). Cigar lovers take note: some shops carry famed Cuban brands, but you must enjoy them on the island; bringing them back to the United States is illegal.

Although you can find black-coral products in Grand Cayman, they're controversial. Most of the coral sold here comes from Belize and Honduras; Cayman Islands marine law prohibits the removal of live coral from its own sea (although most of it has been taken illegally). Black coral grows at a very slow rate (3 inches every 10 years) and is an endangered species. Consider buying other products instead.

GEORGE TOWN AND ENVIRONS
ART GALLERIES

★ **Al Ebanks Studio Gallery.** This gallery shows the eponymous artist's versatile, always provocative work in various media. Since you're walking into his home as well as atelier, everything is on display. Clever movable panels maximize space "like Art Murphy beds." His work, while inspired by his home, could never be labeled traditional Caribbean art, exhibiting vigorous movement through abstract swirls of color and textural contrasts. Though non-representational (save for his equally intriguing sculpture and ceramics), the focal subject from carnivals to iguanas is always subtly apparent. Ask him about the Native Sons art movement he co-founded. ⊠ *186B Shedden Rd.* ☎ *345/927–5365, 345/949–0693.*

★ **Cathy Church's Underwater Photo Centre and Gallery.** Come see a collection of the acclaimed underwater shutterbug's spectacular color and limited-edition black-and-white underwater photos. Have Cathy autograph her latest coffee-table book and regale you with anecdotes of her globe-trotting adventures. The store also carries the latest marine camera equipment, and she'll schedule private underwater photography instruction as well on her own dive boat outfitted with special graphics-oriented computers to critique your work. She also does wedding photography, both above and underwater. ⊠ *S. Church St.* ☎ *345/949–7415* ⊕ *www.cathychurch.com.*

★ **Guy Harvey's Gallery and Shoppe.** This is where world-renowned marine biologist, conservationist, and artist Guy Harvey showcases his aquatic-inspired action-packed art in nearly every conceivable medium, branded tableware, and sportswear (even logo soccer balls and Zippos). The soaring, two-story 4,000-square-foot space is almost more theme park than store, with monitors playing his sportfishing videos, wood floors

8

inlaid with tile duplicating rippling water, dangling catboats "attacked" by lifelike shark models, and life-size murals honoring such classics as Hemingway's *Old Man and the Sea*. Original paintings, sculpture, and drawings are expensive, but there's something (tile art, prints, lithographs, and photos) in most price ranges. ⊠ *49 S. Church St.* ☎ *345/943–4891.*

FOODSTUFFS

There are seven modern, U.S.-style supermarkets for groceries (three of them have full-service pharmacies) on Grand Cayman. The biggest difference you'll find between these and supermarkets on the mainland is in the prices, which are about 25% to 30% more than at home.

Foster's Food Fair-IGA. The island's biggest supermarket chain has five stores. The Airport Centre and Strand stores have full-service pharmacies. These stores are open from Monday through Saturday, 7 am to 11 pm. ⊠ *Airport Centre, 63 Dorcy Dr.* ☎ *345/949–5155* ⊕ *www.fosters-iga.com.*

Tortuga Rum Company. This company bakes, then vacuum-seals, more than 10,000 of its world-famous rum cakes daily, adhering to the original "secret" century-old recipe. There are eight flavors, from banana to Blue Mountain coffee. The 12-year-old rum, blended from private stock though actually distilled in Guyana, is a connoisseur's delight for after-dinner sipping. You can buy a fresh rum cake at the airport on the way home at the same prices as at the factory store. ⊠ *N. Sound Rd., Industrial Park* ☎ *345/949–7701* ⊕ *www.tortugarumcakes.com.*

JEWELRY

★ **Bernard Passman.** The black-coral creations of Bernard Passman have won the approval of the British royal family, who chose him to create a wedding present for Prince Charles and Princess Diana. His fabulous flatware and fanciful candelabras would stand out in the Addams Family manse. He even creates three-dimensional bas-relief scenes with cavorting dolphins, as well as mermaids with glittering gold gilt tails and golfers (each movement of the swing depicted by a dozen clubs in 18K gold). ⊠ *Cardinal Ave.* ☎ *345/949–0123.*

SEVEN MILE BEACH
JEWELRY

★ **Mitzi's Fine Jewelry.** Mitzi's is a treasure trove of salvaged 18th-century coins, silver, Caymanite pieces, and black coral; the store also carries Italian porcelain and the Carrera y Carrera line of jewelry and sculptures. Self-taught, vivacious proprietor Mitzi Callan, who specializes in handmade pieces, is usually on hand to help. ⊠ *5 Bay Harbour Centre, West Bay Rd., Seven Mile Beach* ☎ *345/945–5014.*

★ **24K-Mon Jewelers.** This store sells works of art from many jewelers, including Wyland, Merry-Lee Rae, and Stephen Douglas, as well as designs courtesy of owner-goldsmith Gale Tibbetts and her friends, incorporating everything from Swarovski crystals to Spanish doubloons. Most pieces are inspired by the sea. The adjacent gallery is one of the few commercial outlets for local artists such as Miguel Powery. ⊠ *Buckingham Sq., Seven Mile Beach* ☎ *345/949–1499* ⊕ *www.24k-monjewelers.com.*

CAYMAN DIVE DEVELOPMENTS

The Cayman Islands government acquired the 251-foot, decommissioned U.S. Navy ship *USS Kittiwake*. Sunk in January 2011, it has already become an exciting new dive attraction, while providing necessary relief for some of the most frequently visited dive sites. The top of the bridge is just 15 feet down, making it accessible to snorkelers. There's a single-use entry fee of $10 ($5 for snorkelers).

The **Cayman Dive 365** (⊕ *www. divecayman.ky/dive365*) initiative is part of a commitment to protect reefs from environmental overuse. New dive sites will be introduced while certain existing sites are "retired" to be rested and refreshed. Visitors are encouraged to sponsor and name a new dive site from the list of selected coordinates.

SPORTS AND ACTIVITIES

BIRD-WATCHING

Silver Thatch Tours. Silver Thatch Tours is run by Geddes Hislop, who knows his birds and his island (though he's Trinidadian by birth). He specializes in customizable five-hour natural and historic heritage tours that culminate at the Queen Elizabeth II Botanic Park's nature trail and lake or other prime birding spots. The cost is $50 per hour for one to four people. Serious birders leave at the crack of dawn, but you can choose the time and leave at the crack of noon instead. The cost includes guide service, pickup and return transport, and refreshments such as local drinks (a great excuse for discourse on herbal medicinal folklore); tours must be arranged in advance. ⊠ *Grand Cayman* ☎ *345/925–7401* ✎ *silvert@hotmail.com.*

DIVING

One of the world's leading dive destinations, Grand Cayman's dramatic underwater topography features plunging walls, soaring skyscraper pinnacles, grottoes, arches, swim-throughs adorned with vibrant sponges, coral-encrusted caverns, and canyons patrolled by Lilliputian grunts to gargantuan groupers, hammerheads to hawksbill turtles.

There are more than 200 pristine dive sites, many less than half a mile from land and easily accessible, including wreck, wall, and shore options. Add exceptional visibility from 80 to 150 feet and calm, current-free water at a constant bathlike 80°F. Cayman is serious about conservation, with Marine Park, Replenishment, and Environmental Park Zones and stringently enforced laws to protect the fragile, endangered marine environment (fines of up to $500,000 and a year in prison are the price for damaging living coral, which can take years to regrow). Most boats use biodegradable cleansers and environmentally friendly drinking cups; moorings at popular sites prevent coral and sponge damage caused by continual anchoring, and diving with gloves is prohibited to reduce the temptation to touch.

Pristine clear water, breathtaking coral formations, and plentiful marine life mark the **North Wall**—a world-renowned dive area along the North

8

Side of Grand Cayman. **Trinity Caves,** in West Bay, is a deep dive with numerous canyons starting at about 60 feet and sloping to the wall at 130 feet. The South Side is the deepest, its wall starting 80 feet deep before plummeting, though its shallows offer a lovely labyrinth of caverns and tunnels in such sites as Japanese Gardens. The less-visited, virgin East End is less varied geographically beyond the magnificent Ironshore Caves and Babylon Hanging Gardens ("trees" of black coral plunging 100 feet) but teems with "Swiss-cheese" swim-throughs and exotic life in such renowned gathering spots as the Maze.

Other good shore-entry snorkeling spots include **West Bay Cemetery,** north of Seven Mile Beach, and the reef-protected shallows of the island's **north and south coasts.** Ask for directions to the shallow wreck of the *Cali* in the George Town harbor area; there are several places to enter the water, including a ladder at Rackam's Pub. Among the wreckage you'll recognize the winch and, of course, lots of friendly fish.

★ **Devil's Grotto.** Its neighbor, Devil's Grotto, resembles an abstract painting of anemones, tangs, parrotfish, and bright purple Pederson cleaner shrimp (nicknamed the dentists of the reef, as they gorge on whatever they scrape off fish teeth and gills). Extensive coral heads and fingers teem with blue wrasse, horse-eyed jacks, butterfly fish, Indigo hamlets, and more. The cathedral-like caves are phenomenal, but tunnel entries here aren't clearly marked, so you're best off with a dive master.

★ **Eden Rock.** If someone tells you that the silverside minnows are in at Eden Rock, drop everything and dive here (on South Church Street in George Town across from Harbour Place Mall by Paradise Restaurant). The schools swarm around you as you glide through the grottoes, forming quivering curtains of liquid silver as shafts of sunlight pierce the sandy bottom. The grottoes themselves are safe—not complex caves—and the entries and exits are clearly visible at all times. Snorkelers can enjoy the outside of the grottoes as the reef rises and falls from 10 to 30 feet deep. Avoid carrying fish food unless you know how not to get bitten by eager yellowtail snappers.

Fodor's Choice ★ **Stingray City.** Most dive operators offer scuba trips to Stingray City in the North Sound. Widely considered the best 12-foot dive in the world, it's a must-see for adventurous souls. Here dozens of stingrays congregate—tame enough to suction squid from your outstretched palm. You can stand in 3 feet of water at **Stingray Sandbar** as the gentle stingrays glide around your legs looking for a handout. Don't worry—these stingrays are so acclimated to tourist encounters that they pose no danger; the experience is often a highlight of a Grand Cayman trip.

Turtle Reef. Turtle Reef, at the Cracked Conch restaurant in West Bay, begins 20 feet out and gradually descends to a 60-foot mini-wall pulsing with sea life and corals of every variety. From there it's just another 15 feet to the dramatic main wall. Ladders provide easy entrance to a shallow cover perfect for pre-dive checks, and since the area isn't buoyed for boats, it's quite pristine.

CLOSE UP

Learn to Dive

Diving is an exciting experience that does not have to be strenuous or stressful. Almost anyone can enjoy scuba, and it's easy to test the waters via a three-hour resort course costing $120 to $150, including one or two dives. After a quick rundown of dos and don'ts, you stand in the shallow end of a pool, learning how to use the mask and fins and breathe underwater with a regulator. The instructor then explains some basic safety skills, and before you know it, you're in the drink. The instructor hovers as you float above the reef, watching fish react to you. Don't worry—there are no dangerous fish in Cayman, and they don't bite (as long as you're not "chumming," or handling fish food). You can see corals and sponges, maybe even a turtle or ray. It's an amazing world that you can enter with very little effort.

The resort course permits only shallow, instructor-guided dives in Cayman's calm, clear waters. The next step is full open-water certification (generally three or four days, including several dives, for around $450, less as part of a hotel package). This earns you a C-card, your passport to the underwater world anywhere you travel. From there, addicts will discover dozens of specialty courses. The leading teaching organizations, both with their adherents, are PADI (Professional Association of Dive Instructors) and NAUI (National Association of Underwater Instructors), affectionately nicknamed "Pay and Dive Immediately" and "Not Another Underwater Idiot" (those are the polite versions in scuba's colorful slang). Worry not: Cayman's instructors are among the world's best. And the water conditions just might spoil you.

8

DIVE OPERATORS

As one of the Caribbean's top diving destinations, Grand Cayman is blessed with many top-notch dive operations offering diving, instruction, and equipment for sale and rent. A single-tank boat dive averages $75, a two-tank dive about $100. Snorkel-equipment rental is about $15 a day. Divers are required to be certified and possess a C-card. If you're getting certified, to save time during your limited vacation, you can start the book and pool work at home and finish the open-water portion in warm, clear Cayman waters. Certifying agencies offer this referral service all around the world.

Ambassador Divers. Ambassador Divers is an on-call, guided scuba-diving operation offering dive trips to parties of two to eight persons. Co-owner Jason Washington's favorite spots include the excellent dive sites on the West Side and South and North Wall. Ambassador offers three boats, a 28-foot custom Parker (maximum six divers), another 28-foot completely custom overhauled boat, and a 26-footer primarily for snorkeling. They are available around the clock, and interested divers can be picked up from their hotels or condos. The price for a two-tank boat dive is $105 ($90 for two or more days). ⊠ *Comfort Suites, West Bay Rd., Seven Mile Beach* ☎ *345/743–5513, 345/949–4530* ⊕ *www. ambassadordivers.com.*

Diving at one of the Cayman Islands' famous coral reefs

Cayman Aggressor IV. *Cayman Aggressor IV*, a 110-foot live-aboard dive boat refitted in 2007, offers one-week cruises for divers who want to get serious bottom time, as many as five dives daily. Nine staterooms with en suite bathrooms sleep 18. The fresh food is basic but bountiful (three meals, two in-between snacks), and the crew offers a great mix of diving, especially when weather allows the crossing to Little Cayman. Digital photography and video courses are also offered (there's an E-6 film-processing lab aboard) as well as Nitrox certification. The price is $2,495 to $2,895 double occupancy for the week. ⊠ *Grand Cayman* ☎ *345/949–5551, 800/348–2628* ⊕ *www.aggressor.com.*

Ⓒ **DiveTech.** DiveTech has opportunities for shore diving at its two north-
Fodor'sChoice coast locations, which provide loads of interesting creatures, a mini-
★ wall, and the North Wall. With quick access to West Bay, the boats are quite comfortable. Technical training (a specialty of owner Nancy Easterbrook) is unparalleled, and the company offers good, personable service as well as the latest gadgetry such as underwater DPV scooters. They even mix their own gases, and there are multiple dive instructors for different specialties, with everything from extended cross-training Ranger packages to Dive and Art workshop weeks, popular photog-raphy–video seminars with Courtney Platt, deep diving, less disruptive free diving, search and recovery, stingray interaction, reef awareness, and underwater naturalist. Snorkel and diving programs are available year-round for children ages eight and up, SASY (supplied-air snorkel-ing, which keeps the unit on a personal flotation device) for five and up. Excellent multiday discounts are a bonus. ⊠ *Cobalt Coast Resort & Suites, 18-A Sea Fan Dr., West Bay* ☎ *345/946–5658, 888/946–5656*

⊕ *www.divetech.com* ⊠ *Lighthouse Point, near Boatswain's Beach, 571 N.W. Point Rd., West Bay* ☎ *345/949–1700.*

Don Foster's Dive Cayman Islands. Don Foster's Dive Cayman Islands has a pool with a shower as well as snorkeling along the ironshore at Casuarina Point, easily accessed starting at 20 feet, extending to depths of 55 feet. There's an underwater photo center, and there are night dives and Stingray City trips with divers and snorkelers in the same boat (perfect for families). Specialties include Nitrox courses and Underwater Naturalist guided dives. Rates are competitive, and there's free shuttle pickup–drop-off along Seven Mile Beach. If you go out with Don, he might recount stories of his wild times as a drummer in the islands, but all the crews are personable and efficient. The drawback is larger boats and groups. ⊠ *218 S. Church St.* ☎ *345/949–5679, 345/945–5132* ⊕ *www.donfosters.com.*

★ **Indigo Divers.** Indigo Divers is a full-service PADI teaching facility specializing in exclusive guided dives from its 28-foot Sea Ray Bow Rider or 32-foot Donzi Express Cruiser. Comfort and safety are paramount, and the attention to detail is superior. Luxury transfers in a Chevy Avalanche are included, and the boat is stocked with goodies like fresh fruit and homemade cookies. Captain Chris Alpers has impeccable credentials: a licensed U.S. Coast Guard captain, PADI master scuba diver trainer, and Cayman Islands Marine Park officer. Katie Alpers specializes in wreck, DPV, dry suit, boat, and deep diving, but her primary role is resident videographer, and she edits superlative DVDs of your adventures, complete with music and titles. They guarantee a maximum of six divers. The individual attention is a bit pricier, but the larger your group, the more you save. ⊠ *Seven Mile Beach* ☎ *345/946–7279, 345/525–3932* ⊕ *www.indigodivers.com.*

Fodor's Choice
★ **Ocean Frontiers.** Ocean Frontiers is an excellent ecocentric operation, offering friendly small-group diving and a technical training facility, exploring the less trammeled, trafficked East End. The company provides valet service, personalized attention, a complimentary courtesy shuttle, and an emphasis on green initiatives and specialized diving, including unguided computer, Technical, Nitrox Instructor, and cave diving for advanced participants. But even beginners and rusty divers (there's a wonderful Skills Review and Tune-Up course) won't feel over their heads. Special touches include hot chocolate and homemade muffins on night dives; the owner, Steve, is an ordained minister and will conduct weddings in full face masks. ⊠ *Compass Point, 346 Austin Connelly Dr., East End* ☎ *345/947–7500, 800/348–6096, 345/947–0000* ⊕ *www.oceanfrontiers.com.*

↻ **Red Sail Sports.** Red Sail Sports offers daily trips from most of the major hotels. Dives are often run as guided tours, a perfect option for beginners. If you're experienced and your air lasts a long time, consult the boat captain to see if he requires that you come up with the group (determined by the first person who runs low on air). There is a full range of kids' dive options for ages 5 to 15, including SASY and Bubblemakers. The company also operates Stingray City tours, dinner and sunset sails, and just about every major water sport from Wave Runners to windsurfing. ⊠ *Grand Cayman* ☎ *345/949–8745, 345/623–5965, 877/506–6368* ⊕ *www.redsailcayman.com.*

Sunset Divers. Sunset Divers, a full-service PADI teaching facility at the George Town hostelry catering to the scuba set, has great shore diving and six dive boats to hit all sides of the island. Divers can be independent on their boats as long as they abide by the maximum time and depth standards. Instruction and packages are comparatively inexpensive. Though the company is not directly affiliated with acclaimed underwater shutterbug Cathy Church (whose shop is also at the hotel), she'll often work with the instructors on special courses. ⊠ *Sunset House, 390 S. Church St.* ☎ *345/949–7111, 800/854–4767* ⊕ *www. sunsethouse.com.*

FISHING

If you enjoy action fishing, Cayman waters have plenty to offer. Experienced, knowledgeable local captains charter boats with top-of-the-line equipment, bait, ice, and often lunch included in the price (usually $550 to $750 per half day, $900 to $1,500 for a full day). Options include deep-sea, reef, bone, tarpon, light-tackle, and fly-fishing. June and July are good all-around months for fishing for blue marlin, yellow- and blackfin tuna, dolphinfish, and bonefish. Bonefish have a second season in the winter months, along with wahoo and skipjack tuna.

Black Princess Charters. Black Princess Charters, owned by Captain Chuckie Ebanks, is fully equipped for deep-sea and reef fishing as well as snorkel trips on his fully equipped and supplied eponymous 40-foot Sea Ray. His rates are comparatively reasonable, and he can arrange clean, inexpensive local accommodations. ⊠ *Grand Cayman* ☎ *345/916–6319, 345/949–0400* ⊕ *www.fishgrandcayman.com.*

★ **R&M Fly Shop and Charters.** Captain Ronald Ebanks of R&M Fly Shop and Charters is arguably the island's most knowledgeable fly-fishing guide, with more than 10 years' experience in Cayman and Scotland. He also runs light-tackle trips on a 24-foot Robalo. Everyone from beginners—even children—to experienced casters will enjoy and learn from the trip (whether wading or poling from a boat); free transfers are included. Captain Ronald even ties his own flies (he'll show you how). ⊠ *Grand Cayman* ☎ *345/947–3146, 345/946–0214* ⊕ *www. flyfishgrandcayman.com.*

★ **Sea Star Charters.** Sea Star Charters, aka Clinton's Watersports, is run by Clinton Ebanks, a fine and very friendly Caymanian who will do whatever it takes to make sure that you have a wonderful time on his two 27- and 28-foot cabin cruisers (and from the 35-foot trimaran used primarily for snorkeling cruises), enjoying light-tackle, bone-, and bottom-fishing. He's a good choice for beginners and offers a nice cultural experience as well as sailing charters and snorkeling with complimentary transportation and equipment. Only cash and traveler's checks are accepted. ⊠ *Grand Cayman* ☎ *345/949–1016, 345/916–5234.*

GOLF

Britannia. The Britannia golf course, next to the Grand Cayman Beach Suites, was designed by Jack Nicklaus. The course is really three in one—a 9-hole, par-70 regulation course; an 18-hole, par-57 executive course; and a Cayman course played with a Cayman ball that travels about half the distance of a regulation ball. Signature tough holes include 3 and 10; beware tricky winds on 7 through 11. Greens fees are $100 for 9 holes, $150 for 18 ($75/$100 during the off-season), including the cart. Amenities include a full pro shop and the Britannia Golf Grille (with particularly good breakfasts and local fare). ⊠ *West Bay Rd., Seven Mile Beach* ☎ *345/745–4653* ⊕ *www.britannia-golf.com.*

North Sound Club. Formerly the Links at Safehaven, the par-71, 6,605-yard, 18-hole North Sound Club is infamous among duffers for its strong gusts, giving the ball unexpected loft or backspin. Roy Case factored the wind into his design, which incorporates lots of looming water and sand traps; the handsome setting features many mature mahogany and silver thatch trees where iguana skulk. Wear shorts at least 14 inches long (15 inches for women); no T-shirts are allowed, only collared shirts. Greens fees change seasonally; in winter it's $175 ($105 for 9 holes) including cart. There are twilight and walking discounts (though carts are recommended), a fine pro shop, and an open-air bar with large-screen TVs. ⊠ *Off West Bay Rd., Seven Mile Beach* ☎ *345/947–4653* ⊕ *www.northsoundclub.com.*

GUIDED TOURS

Taxi drivers will give you a personalized tour of Grand Cayman for about $25 per hour for up to three people. Or you can choose a fascinating helicopter ride, a horseback or mountain-bike journey, a 4x4 safari expedition, or a full-day bus excursion. Ask your hotel to help you make arrangements.

Costs and itineraries for island tours are about the same regardless of the tour operator. Half-day tours average $40 to $50 a person and generally include a visit to Hell and the Turtle Farm at Boatswain's Beach aquatic park in West Bay, as well as shopping downtown. Full-day tours ($60 to $90 per person) add lunch, a visit to Bodden Town (the first settlement), and the East End, where you stop at the Queen Elizabeth II Botanic Park, blowholes (if the waves are high) on the ironshore, and the site of the wreck of the *Ten Sails* (not the wreck itself—just the site). The pirate graves in Bodden Town were destroyed during Hurricane Ivan in 2008, and the blowholes were partially filled. As you can tell, land tours here are low-key. Children under 12 often receive discounts.

A.A. Transportation Services. A.A. Transportation Services offers taxis and tour buses—ask for Burton Ebanks. ⊠ *Grand Cayman* ☎ *345/949–6598, 345/926–8294, 345/949–7222.*

Cayman Safari. Cayman Safari hits the usual sights but emphasizes interaction with locals, so you learn about craft traditions, folklore, and herbal medicines; careening along in Land Rovers is incidental fun. ⊠ *Grand Cayman* ☎ *345/925–3001, 866/211–4677* ⊕ *www. caymansafari.com.*

Majestic Tours. Majestic Tours caters mostly to cruise-ship and incentive groups but also offers similar options to individuals and can customize tours; it's particularly good for West Bay, including Boatswain's Beach and Hell. ⊠ *Grand Cayman* ☎ *345/949–7773* ⊕ *www. majestic-tours.com.*

McCurley Tours. McCurley Tours is owned by B.A. McCurley, a free-spirited, freewheeling Midwesterner who's lived in Cayman since the mid-1980s and knows everything and everyone on the East End. Not only is she encyclopedic and flexible, but she also offers car rentals and transfers for travelers staying on the North Side or East End; don't be surprised if she tells you what to order at lunch, especially if it's off the menu. ⊠ *Grand Cayman* ☎ *345/947–9626, 345/916–0925.*

Tropicana Tours. Tropicana Tours offers several excellent Cayman highlights itineraries on its larger buses, including Stingray City stops, as well as reef runner adventures across the North Sound through the mangrove swamps. ⊠ *Grand Cayman* ☎ *345/949–0944 ⊕ www.tropicana-tours.com.*

HIKING

★ **Mastic Trail.** The National Trust's internationally significant Mastic Trail, used in the 1800s as the only direct path to and from the North Side, is a rugged 2-mi (3-km) slash through 776 dense acres of woodlands, black mangrove swamps, savanna, agricultural remnants, and ancient rock formations. It embraces more than 700 species, including Cayman's largest remaining contiguous ancient forest (one of the heavily deforested Caribbean's last examples). A comfortable walk depends on weather—winter is better because it's drier, though flowering plants such as the banana orchid set the trail ablaze in summer. Call the National Trust to determine suitability and to book a guide for $30; tours are run daily from 9 to 5 by appointment only, regularly on Wednesday at 9 am (sometimes earlier in summer). Or walk on the wild side with a $5 guidebook that provides information on the ecosystems you traverse, the endemic wildlife you might encounter, seasonal changes, poisonous plants to avoid, and folkloric uses of various flora. The trip takes about three hours. ⊠ *Frank Sound Rd., entrance by fire station at botanic park, Breakers, East End* ☎ *345/749–1121, 345/749–1124 for guide reservations ⊕ www.nationaltrust.org.ky.*

HORSEBACK RIDING

Coral Stone Stables. Coral Stone Stables offers 90-minute leisurely horseback rides along the white-sand beaches at Bodden Town and inland trails at Savannah; complimentary photos are included. Your guide is Nolan Stewart, whose ranch contains 20 horses, chickens, and "randy" roosters. Nolan offers a nonstop narrative on flora, fauna, and history. He's an entertaining, endless font of local information, some of it unprintable. Rides are $80; swim rides cost $120. ⊠ *Grand Cayman* ☎ *345/916–4799 ⊕ www.csstables.com.*

☾ **Pampered Ponies.** Pampered Ponies offers what is called "the ultimate tanning machine": horses walking, trotting, and cantering along the beaches. You can do either private tours or a variety of guided trips, including sunset, moonlight, and swim rides along the uninhabited beach from Conch Point to Morgan's Harbour on the north tip beyond West Bay. ⊠ *Grand Cayman* ☎ *345/945–2262, 345/916–2540 ⊕ www.ponies.ky.*

KAYAKING

★ **Cayman Kayaks.** Cayman Kayaks explores Grand Cayman's protected
☾ mangrove wetlands, providing an absorbing discussion of the indigenous animals (including a mesmerizing stop at a gently pulsing, non-
stinging Cassiopeia jellyfish pond) and plants, the effects of hurricanes,
and conservation efforts. Even beginners will find the tours easy (the
guides dub it low-impact aerobics), and the sit-on-top tandem kayaks are quite stable and comfortable. The Bio Bay tour involves more
strenuous paddling, but the underwater light show is magical as millions of bio-luminescent microorganisms called dinoflagellates glow like
fireflies when disturbed. It runs only on moonless nights for full effect
and books well in advance. All tours depart from Kaibo Beach Bar in
Cayman Kai; costs run from $39 to $59 (some tours offer kids' and
group discounts). ✉ *Grand Cayman* ☎ *345/746–3249, 345/926–4467*
⊕ *www.caymankayaks.com.*

SEA EXCURSIONS

The most impressive sights in the Cayman Islands are on and underwater, and several submarines, semisubmersibles, glass-bottom boats,
and Jules Verne–like contraptions allow you to see these wonders without getting your feet wet. Sunset sails, dinner cruises, and other theme
(dance, booze, pirate) cruises are available from $30 to $70 per person.

☾ **Atlantis Submarines.** This submarine takes 48 passengers safely and com-
★ fortably along the Cayman Wall down to 100 feet. You peep through
panoramic portholes as good-natured guides keep up a humorous but
informative patter. A guide dons scuba gear to feed fish, who form a
whirling frenzy of color rivaling anything by Picasso. At night, the
10,000-watt lights show the kaleidoscopic underwater colors and nocturnal stealth predators more brilliantly than during the day. Try to
sit toward the front so you can watch the pilot's nimble maneuverings
and the depth gauge. If that literally in-depth tour seems daunting, get
up close and personal on the *Seaworld Observatory* semisubmersible
(glorified glass-bottom boat), which just cruises the harbor (including
glimpses of the *Cali* and *Balboa* shipwrecks). The cost is $89–$99 (children $49–$59) for the submarine, $39 for the semisubmersible. There
are frequent online booking discounts. ✉ *30 S. Church St.* ☎ *345/949–*
7700, 800/887–8571 ⊕ *www.caymanislandssubmarines.com.*

☾ **Deep See Cayman.** Scientists often call our oceans just as mysterious as
Fodor's Choice deep space, and Deep See Cayman provides spellbinding proof. Its per-
★ sonable owner was pilot for Paul Allen's *Octopus,* one of the world's
largest yachts; helped film David Attenborough's compelling *The Blue
Planet;* and currently works with Scripps on underwater research with
his little toy, an ROV underwater robot that plumbs the Cayman
Trench's depths down to 2,400 feet while you comfortably watch the
real-time high-definition images it transmits aboard a luxury yacht, the
Deep Seeker. Some wrecks have gradually sunk to those depths, but the
real prize is otherworldly oddly-shaped creatures straight out of sci-fi.
The two-hour excursions depart from the West Bay dock several times
daily (including a night tour), with an 8-person maximum, costing a
reasonable $74 ($5 discount for advance online booking). Gary will
even let kids particularly adept with joysticks from video game mastery

navigate the Little Tyche (an appropriate name, given the eager would-be pilots). ☎ 345/926–3343 ⊕ www.deepseecayman.com.

🕓 **Jolly Roger.** The *Jolly Roger* is a two-thirds-size replica of Christopher Columbus's 15th-century Spanish galleon *Niña*; the company also owns the *Anne Bonny,* a wooden Norwegian brig built in 1934 that holds more than 100 passengers. On the afternoon snorkel cruise, play Captain Jack Sparrow while experiencing swashbuckling pirate antics, including a trial, sword fight, and walking the plank; the kids can fire the cannon, help hoist the main sail, and scrub the decks (it's guaranteed that they will love it even if they loathe doing chores at home). The evening options (sunset and dinner sails) are more standard booze cruises, less appropriate for the kiddies. Food is more appropriate to the brig, and it's more yo-ho-hokum than remotely authentic, but it's fun. Prices range from $40 to $60. ⊠ *Grand Cayman* ☎ 345/945–7245 ⊕ www.jollyrogercayman.com.

🕓 **Sea Trek.** Sea Trek offers helmet diving, permitting you to walk and breathe 26 feet underwater—without getting your hair wet—for an hour. No training or even swimming ability is required, and you can wear glasses. Guides give a thorough safety briefing, and a sophisticated system of compressors and cylinders provides triple the amount of air necessary for normal breathing while a safety diver program ensures four distinct levels of backup. The result at near-zero gravity resembles an exhilarating moonwalk. The minimum age is eight. The cost is $89 to $99 per person (the latter for an "Ultimate Stingray City" excursion). ⊠ *Grand Cayman* ☎ 345/949–0008 ⊕ www.seatrekcayman.com.

SNORKELING

Stingray Sandbar is the most popular snorkeling destination by far, and dozens of boats head that way several times a day. It's a not-to-be-missed experience that you will remember for years to come. The area is always less crowded if you can go on a day when there aren't too many cruise ships in port.

SNORKELING OPERATORS

Bayside Watersports. Bayside Watersports offers half-day snorkeling trips, North Sound beach lunch excursions, Stingray City and dinner cruises, and full-day deep-sea fishing. The company operates several popular boats out of West Bay's Morgan's Harbour. Full-day trips include lunch and conch diving in season (November–April). ⊠ *Grand Cayman* ☎ 345/949–3200 ⊕ www.baysidewatersports.com.

🕓 **Fantasea Tours.** Captain Dexter Ebanks runs Fantasea Tours on his 38-foot trimaran, *Don't Even Ask.* He doesn't pack you in like sardines (20 people max) and is particularly helpful with first-timers. Like many of the captains, he has his own pet names for the rays (ask him to find Lucy, whom he "adopted") and rattles off fascinating factoids during an entertaining, non-stop narration. It's a laid-back trip, with Bob Marley and Norah Jones on the sound system, and fresh fruit and rum punch on tap. ☎ 345/916–0754 ⊕ www.dexters-fantaseatours.com.

🕓 **Red Sail Sports.** Red Sail Sports offers Stingray City, sunset, and evening sails (including dinner in winter) on its luxurious 65-foot catamarans, the *Spirits of Cayman, Poseidon, Calypso,* and *Ppalu.* It often carries

A group of stingrays patrols the grassy shallows of Grand Cayman.

large groups; although the service may not be personal, it will be efficient. In addition to the large cats, a glass-bottom boat takes passengers to Stingray City/Sandbar and nearby coral reefs. The cost ranges from $40 to $80. ⊠ *Grand Cayman* ☎ *345/949–8745, 345/623–5965, 877/506–6368* ⊕ *www.redsailcayman.com.*

CAYMAN BRAC

Cayman Brac is named for its most distinctive feature, a rugged limestone bluff ("brac" in Gaelic) that runs up the center of the 12-mile (19-km) island, pocked with caves and culminating in a sheer 140-foot cliff at its eastern end. The Brac, 89 miles (143 km) northeast of Grand Cayman, is accessible via Cayman Airways. It's a splendidly serene destination for eco-enthusiasts, offering world-class birding, scuba diving, bonefishing in the shallows or light-tackle and deep-sea angling, hiking, spelunking, and rock climbing. With only 1,800 residents—they call themselves Brackers—the island has the feel and easy pace of a small town. Brackers are known for their friendly attitude toward visitors, so it's easy to strike up a conversation. Locals wave at passing and might invite you home for a traditional rundown (a thick, sultry fish stew) and storytelling, usually about the sea, the turtle schooners, and the great hurricane of 1932 (when the caves offered shelter to islanders).

Brackers are as calm and peaceful as their island is rugged, having been violently sculpted by sea and wind, most recently by Hurricane Paloma, which leveled the island in November 2008 (locals quip that all 18 churches sustained significant damage—but no bars).

EXPLORING CAYMAN BRAC

★ **Cayman Brac Museum.** Here you'll find a diverse, well-displayed collection of historic Bracker implements from scary dental pliers to pistols to pottery. A meticulously crafted scale model of the Caymanian catboat *Alsons* has pride of place. The front room faithfully reconstructs the Customs, Treasury, bank, and post office as they would have looked decades ago. Permanent exhibits include those on the 1932 hurricane, turtling, shipbuilding, and typical old-time home life, including a child's bedroom; the back room hosts rotating exhibits such as one on herbal folk medicine. ⊠ *Old Government Administration Bldg., Stake Bay* ☎ *345/948–2622, 345/244–4446* 🖼 *Free* ⊙ *Weekdays 9–4, Sat. 9–noon.*

★ **Parrot Preserve.** The likeliest place to spot the endangered Cayman Brac parrot—and other indigenous and migratory birds—is along this National Trust hiking trail off Major Donald Drive, aka Lighthouse Road. Prime time is early morning or late afternoon; most of the day they're camouflaged by trees, earning them the moniker "stealth parrot." The loop trail incorporates part of a path the Brackers used in olden days to cross the bluff to reach their provision grounds on the south shore or to gather coconuts, once a major export crop. It passes through several types of terrain: old farmland under grass and native trees from mango to mahogany unusually mixed with orchids and cacti. Wear sturdy shoes, as the terrain is rocky, uneven, and occasionally rough. The 6-mile (10-km) gravel road continues to the lighthouse at the bluff's eastern end, where there's an astonishing view from atop the cliff to the open ocean—the best place to watch the sunrise. ⊠ *Lighthouse Rd., ½ mile (1 km) south of town, Tibbetts Turn* ☎ *345/948–0319* 🖼 *Free* ⊙ *Daily sunrise–sunset.*

WHERE TO STAY

Cayman Brac has a handful of hotels and resorts, as well as a decent bed-and-breakfast and several apartments. Several private villas on Cayman Brac can also be rented, most of them basic but well maintained, ranging from one to four bedrooms. Most resorts offer optional meal plans, but there are several restaurants, some of which provide free transport from your hotel. Most restaurants serve island fare (local seafood, chicken, and curries). On Friday and Saturday nights the spicy scent of jerk chicken fills the air; several roadside stands sell takeout dinners. This is a nature and outdoor island; if the weather is bad, there are no indoor activities, so bring a good book just in case.

For expanded reviews, facilities, and current deals, visit Fodors.com.

$$ 🖼 **Alexander Hotel.** This chic boutique business hotel elevates Brac lodg-
HOTEL ing to a new level, though with no on-site activities to offer vacationers
★ who make up the larger proportion of Brac travelers, its ultimate target audience is unclear. **Pros:** high-tech amenities; stylish yet affordable; next door to small shopping mall for sundries and food; delightful alfresco bar. **Cons:** two-minute walk to a pebbly beach; small pool; inadequate bedside and bathroom lighting; no on-site activities; Wi-Fi

Cayman Brac and Little Cayman

KEY
- Beaches
- Dive Sites
- [1] Hotel/s

LITTLE CAYMAN

Little Cayman Research Center

Gov. Gore Bird Sanctuary

Little Cayman Museum

Bloody Bay Wall

West End Pt.

Anchorage Bay

South Town

Edward Bodden Airfield

Jacksons Pt.

Lower Spot Bay

Owen Island

Crawl Bay

Charles Bight

Point of Sand

East Pt.

C a r i b b e a n   S e a

CAYMAN BRAC

Gerrard-Smith Airport

West End Pt.

West End

Frenchman's Fort

Stake Bay Pt.

Deadman's Pt.

Cayman Brac Museum

Parrot Preserve

Cedar Pt.

Tiara Beach

Brac Reef Beach

Tibbetts Turn

Spot Bay

North East Pt.

Booby Pt.

North East Pt.

Pollard Bay

Cat Head Bay

Tom Jennett's Bay

Sea Feather Bay

North East Bay

M.V. Capt. Keith Tibbetts

0   2 km
0   2 mi

Alexander Hotel **9**	Little Cayman Beach Resort **3**
Brac Caribbean and Carib Sands **8**	Paradise Villas **2**
Brac Reef Beach Resort **7**	Pirates Point Resort **1**
Cayman Breakers **11**	Southern Cross Club **5**
The Club **4**	Walton's Mango Manor ... **10**
Conch Club **6**	

8

spotty in some rooms. **TripAdvisor:** "friendly bar staff," "most relaxed I have been," "quiet getaway." $ *Rooms from: $156* ⊠ *Cayman Brac* ☎ *345/948–8222, 800/381–5094* ⊕ *www.alexanderbrac.com* ⇴ *29 rooms, 2 2-bedroom suites* ⽥ *No meals.*

$$
RESORT
❄ **Brac Caribbean and Carib Sands.** These neighboring, beachfront, sister complexes, almost completely rebuilt (and expanded) after Paloma, offer condos with one to four bedrooms, all individually owned and decorated beyond a "starter" design. **Pros:** lively restaurant-bar; excellent value for families, especially with weekly discounts. **Cons:** pretty but narrow, often unmaintained beach; limited staff; Wi-Fi dodgy. **TripAdvisor:** "a very nice condo," "the absolutely most perfect vacation," "relaxing stay." $ *Rooms from: $148* ⊠ *Bert Marson Dr.* ☎ *345/948–2265, 866/843–2722* ⊕ *www.866thebrac.com* ⇴ *65 condos* ⽥ *No meals.*

$$
RESORT
★
❄ **Brac Reef Beach Resort.** Popular with divers, this well-run ecofriendly resort, entirely rebuilt from the ground up, features a beautiful sandy beach shaded by sea grape trees slung with hammocks. **Pros:** lovely beach; great dive outfit; friendly staff and clientele; free Wi-Fi; good online packages. **Cons:** noise from planes; view often obscured from ground-floor units; mandatory airport transfer of $20 per person. **TripAdvisor:** "the most relaxing vacation," "great diving," "cozy and comfortable." $ *Rooms from: $157* ⊠ *West End* ☎ *345/948–1323, 727/323–8727 for reservations in Florida, 800/594–0843* ⊕ *www. bracreef.com* ⇴ *40 rooms* ⽥ *Multiple meal plans.*

$
RENTAL
★
❄ **Cayman Breakers.** This attractive, pink-brick, colonnaded condo development sitting between the bluff and the southeast coastal ironshore caters to climbers, who scale the bluff's sheer face, as well as divers, who appreciate the good shore diving right off the property. **Pros:** spectacular views; thoughtful extras like complimentary bikes, jigsaw puzzles, and climbing-route guides; very attentive managers who live on-site. **Cons:** nearest grocery is a 15-minute drive; gorgeous beach is rocky and has rough surf; some units slightly musty and faded. **TripAdvisor:** "quiet," "great accommodations," "decent condo." $ *Rooms from: $150* ⊠ *Cayman Brac* ☎ *345/948–1463* ⊕ *www.caybreakers. com* ⇴ *26 2-bedroom condos* ⽥ *No meals.*

$
B&B/INN
★
❄ **Walton's Mango Manor.** This beautifully restored traditional West Indian home has five rooms (all with bath), accented with lovely antique furnishings, nautical gadgets, maps, model catboats, and bric-a-brac from the Waltons' world travels. **Pros:** true Caymanian hospitality; beautiful grounds; excellent snorkeling; free Wi-Fi access. **Cons:** poky beach across the street; car required. **TripAdvisor:** "one of a kind," "tremendous hospitality," "a great place to chill." $ *Rooms from: $120* ⊠ *Stake Bay* ☎ *345/948–0518, 321/226–0440 from U.S., 888/866–5809* ⊕ *www.waltonsmangomanor.com* ⇴ *5 rooms, 1 2-bedroom cottage* ⽥ *Breakfast.*

CLOSE UP

Sculpting Cayman

A sculptor named Foots dreamed since childhood of creating his own version of Plato's lost city of Atlantis. He fulfilled that dream by creating and then sinking huge concrete sculptures in 45 feet of water off the north shore of Cayman Brac. The result is an astounding dive site and artificial reef with more than 100 sculptures covering several acres. The story starts at the Archway of Atlantis (each of the two bases weighs 21,000 pounds). The Elders' Way, lined with 5-foot temple columns, leads to the Inner Circle of Light, where there is a sundial large enough to sit in. Each Elder is modeled after an actual person who has contributed to the Cayman Islands. Foots is doing this almost entirely on his own and has made an incredible donation to the divers of the Brac. The technical marvel encompasses nearly 300,000 pounds.

SPORTS AND THE OUTDOORS

DIVING AND SNORKELING

Cayman Brac's waters are celebrated for their rich diversity of sea life, from hammerhead and reef sharks to stingrays to sea horses. Divers and snorkelers alike will find towering coral heads, impressive walls, and fascinating wrecks. The snorkeling off the **north coast** is spectacular, particularly at West End, where coral formations close to shore attract all kinds of critters. The walls feature remarkable topography with natural gullies, caves, and fissures blanketed with Technicolor sponges, black coral, gorgonians, and sea fans. Some of the famed sites are the West Chute, Cemetery Wall, Airport Wall, and Garden Eel Wall. The South Wall is a wonderland of sheer drop-offs carved with a maze of vertical swim-throughs, tunnels, arches, and grottoes that divers nickname Cayman's Grand Canyon. Notable sites include Anchor Wall, Rock Monster Chimney, and the Wilderness. Many fish have colonized the 330-foot MV *Capt. Keith Tibbetts,* a Russian frigate—now broken in two—that was deliberately scuttled within swimming distance of the northwest shore. An artist named Foots has created an amazing underwater Atlantis off Radar Reef. The island's two dive operators offer scuba and snorkel training and PADI certification.

★ **Reef Divers.** Pluses here include five boats, valet service, and enthusiastic, experienced staff. Certified divers can purchase à la carte dive packages even if they aren't guests of the hotel. ⊠ *Brac Reef Beach Resort, West End* ☎ *345/948–1642, 345/948–1323* ⊕ *www.bracreef.com.*

HIKING

Brac Tourism Office. Free printed guides to the Brac's many heritage and nature trails can be obtained from the Brac Tourism Office; you can also get the guides at the airport or at your hotel. Traditional routes across the bluff have been cleared and marked; trailheads are identified with signs along the road. It's safe to hike on your own, though some trails are fairly hard going (wear light hiking boots) and others could

8

be better maintained. ⊠ *West End Community Park, west of airport* ☎ *345/948–1649.*

Christopher Columbus Gardens. For those who prefer less-strenuous walking, Christopher Columbus Gardens has easy trails and boardwalks. The park showcases the unique natural flora and features of the bluff, including two cave mouths. This is a peaceful spot dotted with gazebos and wooden bridges that traverses several ecosystems from cacti to mahogany trees. ⊠ *Ashton Reid Dr. [Bluff Rd.], just north of Ashton Rutty Centre.*

Sister Islands District Administration. The administration arranges free, government-sponsored, guided nature and cultural tours with trained local guides. Options include the Parrot Reserve, nature trails, wetlands, Lighthouse/Bluff View, caving, birding, and heritage sites. You just supply the wheels and spirit of adventure. ⊠ *Cayman Brac* ☎ *345/948–2222.*

SPELUNKING

If you plan to explore Cayman Brac's caves, wear good sneakers or hiking shoes, as some paths are steep and rocky and some cave entrances are reachable only by ladders. **Peter's Cave** offers a stunning aerial view of the northeastern community of Spot Bay. **Great Cave**, at the island's southeast end, has numerous chambers and photogenic ocean views. In **Bat Cave** you may see bats hanging from the ceiling (try not to disturb them). **Rebecca's Cave** houses the grave site of a 17-month-old child who died during the horrific hurricane of 1932.

★ **NIM Things.** Artist and raconteur Tenson Scott fashions exquisite jewelry from Caymanite (he climbs down from the lighthouse without ropes to chisel the stone), triton shells, sea eggs, and more unusual materials—hence the name, which stands for Native Island Made. His wife, Starry, creates delicate works from sea urchins, hardening the shell with epoxy: cute turtles, bud vases, and planters decorated with minuscule shells. ⊠ *Northeast Bay Rd., Spot Bay* ☎ *345/948–0582, 345/939–5306.*

LITTLE CAYMAN

The smallest, most tranquil of the three Cayman Islands, Little Cayman has a full-time population of only 170, most of whom work in the tourism industry. This 12-square-mile (31-square-km) island is still unspoiled and has only a sand-sealed airstrip, no official terminal building, and few vehicles. The speed limit remains 25 mph (40 kph), as no one is in a hurry to go anywhere. In fact, the island's iguanas use roads more regularly than residents; signs created by local artists read "Iguanas Have the Right of Way." With little commercial development, the island beckons ecotourists who seek wildlife encounters, not urban wildlife. It's probably best known for its spectacular diving on world-renowned Bloody Bay Wall and adjacent Jackson Marine Park. The ravishing reefs and plummeting walls encircling the island teem with more than 500 different species of fish and more than 150 kinds of coral. Fly-, lake-, and deep-sea fishing are also popular, as well as snorkeling, kayaking, cycling, and hiking. And the island's certainly for the birds. The National Trust Booby Pond Nature Reserve is a designated wetland of international importance, which protects around 20,000 red-footed boobies, the Western Hemisphere's largest colony. It's just one of many superlative spots to witness avian aerial acrobatics. Pristine wetlands, secluded beaches, unspoiled tropical wilderness, mangrove swamps, lagoons, bejeweled coral reefs: Little Cayman practically redefines escape. Yet aficionados appreciate that the low-key lifestyle doesn't mean sacrificing the high-tech amenities, and some of the resorts cater to a quietly wealthy yet unpretentious crowd.

EXPLORING LITTLE CAYMAN

Little Cayman Museum. The museum displays relics and artifacts, including a new wing devoted to maritime memorabilia, that provide a good overview of this tiny island's history and heritage. ⊠ *Across from Booby Pond Nature Reserve, Blossom Village* ☎ *No phone at museum, 345/948–1033 for Little Cayman Beach Resort* ☑ *Free* ⊙ *Thurs. and Fri. 3–5, by appointment only.*

Fodor'sChoice ★ **Little Cayman National Trust.** This traditional Caymanian cottage overlooks the Booby Pond Nature Reserve; telescopes on the breezy second-floor deck permit close-up views of their markings and nests, as well as the other feathered friends. Inside you'll find shell collections, panels and dioramas discussing endemic reptiles, models "in flight," and diagrams on the growth and life span of red-footed boobies, frigate birds, egrets, and other island "residents." The shop sells exquisite jewelry made from Caymanite and spider-crab shells, extraordinary duck decoys and driftwood carvings, and great books on history, ornithology, and geology. Mike Vallee holds an iguana information session and tour every Friday at 4 pm. ⊠ *Blossom Village* ☎ *No phone* ⊕ *www. nationaltrust.org.ky* ⊙ *Mon.–Sat. 9–noon and 2–6.*

★ **Little Cayman Research Center.** Near the Jackson Point Bloody Bay Marine Park reserve, this vital research center supports visiting students and researchers, with a long list of projects studying the biodiversity, human impact, reef health, and ocean ecosystem of Little Cayman. Tours explain the center's mission and ecosensitive design (including Peter's Potty, an off-the-grid bathroom facility using compostable toilets that recycle fertilizer into gray water for the gardens); sometimes you'll get a peek at the upstairs functional wet labs and dormitories. To make it layperson-friendlier, scientists occasionally give talks and presentations. The Dive with a Researcher program (where you actually help survey and assess environmental impact and ecosystem health, depending on that week's focus) is hugely popular. ⊠ *North Side* ☎ *345/948–1094* ⊕ *www.reefresearch.org* ⊙ *By appointment only.*

Fodor'sChoice ★ **Owen Island.** This private, forested island can be reached by rowboat, kayak, or an ambitious 200-yard swim. Anyone is welcome to come across and enjoy the deserted beaches and excellent snorkeling. Nudity is forbidden as "idle and disorderly" in the Cayman Islands, though that doesn't always stop skinny-dippers (who may not realize they can be seen quite easily from shore on the strands facing Little Cayman). ⊠ *Little Cayman.*

Fodor's Choice **Point of Sand.** Stretching over a mile on the easternmost point of the
★ island, this secluded beach is great for wading, shell collecting, and
snorkeling. On a clear day you can see 7 miles (11 km) across to Cayman Brac. It serves as a green- and loggerhead turtle nesting site in
spring, and a marvelous mosaic of coral gardens blooms just offshore.
It's magical, especially at moonrise, when it earns its nickname, Lovers'
Beach. There's a palapa for shade but no facilities. The current can be
strong, so watch the kids carefully. ⊠ *Little Cayman.*

WHERE TO STAY

Accommodations are mostly in small lodges, many of which offer meal
and dive packages. The meal packages are a good idea; the chefs in most
places create wonderful dishes with often limited resources.

For expanded reviews, facilities, and current deals, visit Fodors.com.

$$$ ⚇ **The Club.** These ultramodern, luxurious, three-bedroom condos are
RENTAL Little Cayman's newest and nicest units, though only five are usually
included in the rental pool. **Pros:** luxurious digs; lovely beach; hot tub.
Cons: housekeeping not included; rear guest bedrooms dark and some-
what cramped; handsome but heavy old-fashioned decor. ⑤ *Rooms
from: $311* ⊠ *South Hole Sound, Blossom Village* ☎ *345/948–1033,
727/323–8727, 800/327–3835* ⊕ *www.theclubatlittlecayman.com* ⇆ *8
condos* ⦿*No meals.*

$$$ ⚇ **Conch Club.** The handsome oceanfront development grafts Caribbean-
RENTAL style gingerbread onto New England maritime architecture with gables
☾ and dormers. **Pros:** splendid views; gorgeous beach; complimentary
airport transfers; beachfront hot tub; complimentary bicycles and kayaks. **Cons:** long walk to nearby restaurants; dated decor; housekeeping
surcharge. **TripAdvisor:** "tranquility extraordinaire," "fantastic beachfront condo," "absolute perfection." ⑤ *Rooms from: $350* ⊠ *Blossom
Village* ☎ *345/948–1026, 345/925–2875* ⊕ *www.conchclubcondos.com*
⇆ *18 2-bedroom condos, 2 3-bedroom condos* ⦿*No meals.*

$$$ ⚇ **Little Cayman Beach Resort.** This two-story hotel, the island's larg-
RESORT est, offers the most options for fun-seekers and modern facilities yet
☾ a boutique vibe. **Pros:** extensive facilities; fun crowd; state-of-the-art
★ technology; glorious LED-lighted pool. **Cons:** less intimate feel than
other island resorts; tiny patios; fee to rent bikes. **TripAdvisor:** "best
ever dive trip," "a place to unwind," "lovely place." ⑤ *Rooms from:
$395* ⊠ *Blossom Village* ☎ *345/948–1033, 800/327–3835* ⊕ *www.
littlecayman.com* ⇆ *40 rooms* ⦿*Multiple meal plans.*

$$ ⚇ **Paradise Villas.** The cozy, sunny, one-bedroom units have beachfront
RENTAL terraces and hammocks and are simply but immaculately appointed
with rattan furnishings, marine artwork, painted driftwood, and bright
abstract fabrics. **Pros:** good value; friendly staff; frequent online-only
deals in addition to good dive packages. **Cons:** noisy some weekend
nights in season; poky beach; now a (minimal) charge for bike use;
dive shop no longer on-site (though the contracted operation runs
smoothly). **TripAdvisor:** "a Caribbean gem," "great family vacation,"
"beautiful location and friendly staff." ⑤ *Rooms from: $195* ⊠ *South*

Hole Sound ☎ *345/948–0001, 877/322–9626* ⊕ *www.paradisevillas. com* ⇋ *12 1-bedroom villas* ⊘ *Closed mid-Sept.–late Oct.* ⦿ *No meals.*

$$$$
RESORT
Fodor'sChoice
★

⌂ **Pirates Point Resort.** The large repeat clientele attests that everything from the comfortable rooms to the fine cuisine lives up to the billing at this hideaway nestled between sea grape and casuarina pines on a sparkling sweep of palapa-dotted sand. **Pros:** fabulous food; fantastic beach; dynamic dive program; fun-loving staff and owner. **Cons:** everyone respects honeymooners' privacy, but this isn't a resort for antisocial types; tasteful rooms are fairly spare; occasional Internet problems. **TripAdvisor:** "best dive resort," "island paradise," "genuine Caymanian food." ⑤ *Rooms from: $484* ⊠ *Pirates Point* ☎ *345/948–1010* ⊕ *www.piratespointresort.com* ⇋ *11 rooms* ⊘ *Closed Sept.–mid-Oct.* ⦿ *Multiple meal plans.*

$$$$
RESORT
Fodor'sChoice
★

⌂ **Southern Cross Club.** Little Cayman's first resort was cofounded in the 1950s as a private fishing club by the CEO of Sears-Roebuck and CFO of General Motors, and its focus is still on fishing and diving. **Pros:** barefoot luxury; complimentary use of kayaks and snorkel gear; splendiferous beach; international staff regales you with globe-trotting exploits. **Cons:** not child-friendly (though families can rent a separate cottage); Wi-Fi promised but still not available in some rooms, with spotty signal otherwise. **TripAdvisor:** "Gilligan's Island does exist," "barefoot elegance," "truly breathtaking." ⑤ *Rooms from: $617* ⊠ *South Hole Sound* ☎ *345/948–1099, 800/899–2582* ⊕ *www.southerncrossclub. com* ⇋ *11 rooms, 3 suites, 1 2-bedroom cottage* ⊘ *Closed mid-Sept.– mid-Oct.* ⦿ *All meals.*

SPORTS AND ACTIVITIES

8

BIRD-WATCHING

★ **Booby Pond Nature Reserve.** The reserve is home to 20,000 red-footed boobies (the largest colony in the Western Hemisphere) and Cayman's only breeding colony of magnificent frigate (or man-of-war) birds; other sightings include the near-threatened West Indian whistling duck and vitelline warbler. The RAMSAR Convention, an international treaty for wetland conservation, designated the reserve a wetland of global significance. Near the airport, the sanctuary is open to the public, and has a gift shop and reading library. ⊠ *Little Cayman.*

DIVING AND SNORKELING

Expect to pay around $95 for a two-tank boat dive and $25–$30 for a snorkeling trip. The island is small and susceptible to wind, so itineraries can change like a sudden gust.

Fodor'sChoice
★

Bloody Bay Wall. This beach, named for having been the site of a spectacular 17th-century sea battle, has been declared one of the world's top three dive sites by no less than the *maîtres* Jacques and Philippe Cousteau and forms part of a protected marine reserve. It plunges dramatically from 18 to 6,000 feet, with a series of staggeringly beautiful drop-offs and remarkable visibility. Even snorkelers who are strong swimmers can access the edge from shore, gliding among shimmering silver curtains of minnows, jacks, bonefish, and more. The critters are amazingly friendly, including Jerry the Grouper, whom dive masters joke is a representative for the Cayman Islands Department of Tourism. ⊠ *Little Cayman*.

Pirate's Point Dive Resort. This popular resort has fully outfitted 42-foot Newtons with dive masters who excel at finding odd and rare creatures, and encourage computer diving so you can stay down longer. ⊠ *Little Cayman* ☎ *345/948–1010* ⊕ *www.piratespointresort.com*.

Reef Divers. Little Cayman Beach Resort's oufitter also offers a full-service photo and video center; their custom boats' state-of-the-art outfitting includes AEDs (defibrillators). ⊠ *Little Cayman* ☎ *345/948–1033* ⊕ *www.littlecayman.com*.

Southern Cross Club. The Southern Cross Club limits each of its boats to 12 divers and has its own dock. It's particularly good with specialty courses and mandates computer diving. ⊠ *Little Cayman* ☎ *345/948– 1099, 800/899–2582* ⊕ *www.southerncrossclub.com*.

FISHING

Bloody Bay is equally celebrated for fishing and diving, and the flats and shallows including South Hole Sound Lagoon across from Owen Island, Tarpon Lake, and the Charles Bight Rosetta Flats offer phenomenal light-tackle and fly-fishing action: surprisingly large tarpon, small bonefish, and permit (a large fish related to pompano) weighing up to 35 pounds. Superior deep-sea fishing is available right offshore for game fish such as blue marlin, dolphin, wahoo, tuna, and barracuda.

Southern Cross Club. The Southern Cross Club offers light-tackle and deep-sea fishing trips. ⊠ *Little Cayman* ☎ *345/948–1099, 800/899– 2582* ⊕ *www.southerncrossclub.com*.

Curaçao

WORD OF MOUTH

"Curacao is an interesting island. I love it—been there twice....I think that Piscadera Bay is probably the best area to stay because you are close to Willemstad but away from the bustle of the town. Another interesting consideration is Kura Hurlanda, which I would recommend as it is right in the town and is one of the most interesting hotels I have ever stayed at. "

—Carib_Ian

WELCOME TO CURAÇAO

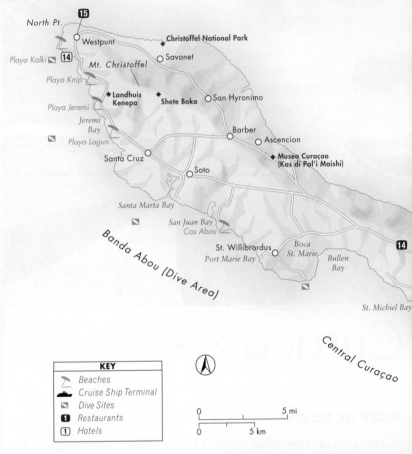

North Pt.

15

Westpunt

14

Playa Kalki

Playa Knip

Mt. Christoffel

◆ Landhuis Kenepa

Playa Jeremi

Jeremi Bay

Playa Lagun

Santa Cruz

◆ Christoffel National Park

○ Savonet

◆ Shete Boka

○ San Hyronimo

○ Soto

Barber

○ Ascencion

◆ Museo Curaçao (Kas di Pal'i Maishi)

Santa Marta Bay

San Juan Bay

Cas Abou

St. Willibrordus ○

Port Marie Bay

Boca St. Marie

Bullen Bay

14

Banda Abou (Dive Area)

St. Michiel Bay

Central Curaçao

KEY	
⊁	*Beaches*
⚓	*Cruise Ship Terminal*
◩	*Dive Sites*
1	*Restaurants*
①	*Hotels*

0   5 mi

0   5 km

Willemstad's fancifully hued, strikingly gabled town houses glimmer across Santa Anna Bay, and vendors at the Floating Market sell tropical fruit from their schooners. Curaçao's diverse population mixes Latin, European, and African ancestries. Religious tolerance is a hallmark here. All people are welcome in Curaçao, and even tourists feel the warmth.

AN ISLAND REBORN
AND REDISCOVERED

The largest and most populous of the Netherlands Antilles is 38 miles (61 km) long and no more than 7½ miles (12 km) wide. Its capital, Willemstad, has been restored and revived over the past few years and is a recognized UNESCO World Heritage Site. The colorful waterfront town houses are unique to the island.

CURAÇAO

9

TOP REASONS TO VISIT CURAÇAO

1 Below the Belt: Because it sits below the hurricane belt, the weather in Curaçao is almost always alluring, even during the off-season.

2 Carnival: Curaçao's biggest party draws an increasingly large crowd.

3 Culture: The island's cultural diversity is reflected in the good food from many different cultures.

4 History You Can See: Striking architecture and fascinating historic sights give you something to see when you're not shopping or sunning on the charming beaches.

CURAÇAO BEACHES

Beautiful beaches are not hard to find on Curaçao. The island boasts more than three dozen beaches, with many of the best ones on the western side. The more popular beaches offer a wide range of facilities and excellent restaurants.

(Above) Snorkeling Playa Knip
(Bottom right) Windsurfers on Seaquarium Beach (Top right) Cas Abao Beach

Beaches in Curaçao range from small inlets shielded by craggy cliffs to longer expanses of sparkling sand. Beaches along the southeast coast tend to be rocky in the shallow water (wear reef shoes—some resorts lend them out for free); the west side has more stretches of smooth sand at the shoreline. Exploring the beaches away from the hotels is a perfect way to soak up the island's character. Whether you're seeking a lovers' hideaway, a special snorkeling adventure, or a great spot to wow the kids, you're not likely to be disappointed. There are snack bars and restrooms on many of the larger beaches, but it's at the smaller ones with no facilities where you might find utter tranquillity, especially during the week. Most spots with entry fees offer lounge chairs for rent at an additional cost, typically $2 to $3 per chair.

THE SCOOP

The most popular beaches on the west and south sides of the island have beautiful, powdery white sand. Those seeking solitude and inspiration can find beaches of all sizes on the north and east coasts. The rugged and windswept nature of these coasts means that the white sand will usually be liberally sprinkled with pebbles, which can make sunbathing uncomfortable and walking difficult.

EAST END

Seaquarium Beach. This 1,600-foot stretch of sandy beach is divided into separate sections, each uniquely defined by a seaside resort or restaurant as its central draw. By day, no matter where you choose to enter the palm-shaded beach, you can find lounge chairs in the sand, thatched shelters, and restrooms. The sections at Mambo and Kontiki beaches also have showers. The island's largest water-sports center (Ocean Encounters at Lions Dive) caters to nearby hotel guests and walk-ins. Mambo Beach is always a hot spot and quite a scene on weekends, especially during the much-touted Sunday-night fiesta that's become a fixture of the island's nightlife. The ubiquitous beach mattress is also the preferred method of seating for the Tuesday-night movies at Mambo Beach (check the *K-Pasa* guide for listings—typically B-films or old classics—and reserve your spot with a shirt or a towel). At Kontiki Beach you can find a spa, a hair braider, and a restaurant that serves refreshing piña colada ice cream. Unless you're a guest of a resort on the beach, the entrance fee to any section is $3 until 5 pm, then free. After 11 pm, you must be 18 or older to access the beach. ✉ *About 1 mile (1½ km) east of downtown Willemstad, Bapor Kibra z/n.*

WEST END

🕙 **Cas Abao.** This white-sand gem has the brightest blue water in Curaçao, a treat for swimmers, snorkelers, and sunbathers alike. You can take respite in the hut-shaded snack bar. The restrooms and showers are immaculate. The only drawback is the weekend crowds, especially Sunday, when local families descend in droves; come on a weekday for more privacy. You can rent beach chairs, paddleboats, and snorkeling and diving gear. The entry fee is $3, and the beach is open from 8 to 6. Turn off Westpunt Highway at the junction onto Weg Naar Santa Cruz; follow until the turnoff for Cas Abao, and then drive along the winding country road for about 10 minutes to the beach. ✉ *West of St. Willibrordus, about 3 miles (5 km) off Weg Naar Santa Cruz*

Playa Jeremi. No snack bar, no dive shop, no facilities, no fee—in fact, there's nothing but sheer natural beauty. Though the beach is sandy, there are rocky patches, so barefoot visitors should exercise care. The parking area is offset from the beach, and vehicle break-ins are common. Quite a bit of development is planned for this beach, so have a look before it's too late. ✉ *Off Weg Naar Santa Cruz, west of Lagun*

Playa Kalki. Noted for its spectacular snorkeling, this beach is at the western tip of the island. Sunbathers may find the narrow and rocky beach less than

Looking down at the splendid cove of Playa Lagun

ideal. The Ocean Encounters dive shop is here. ⊠ *Near Jaanchi's, Westpunt*

Playa Knip. Two protected coves offer crystal-clear turquoise waters. Big (Groot) Knip is an expanse of alluring white sand, perfect for swimming and snorkeling. You can rent beach chairs and hang out under the *palapas* (thatch-roof shelters) or cool off with ice cream at the snack bar. There are restrooms here but no showers. It's particularly crowded on Sunday and school holidays. Just up the road, also in a protected cove, Little (Kleine) Knip is a charmer, too, with picnic tables and palapas. Steer clear of the poisonous manchineel trees. There's no fee for these beaches. ⊠ *Just east of Westpunt, Banda Abou*

Playa Lagun. This northwestern cove is caught between gray cliffs, which dramatically frame the Caribbean blue. Cognoscenti know this as one of the best places to snorkel—even for kids—because of the calm, shallow water. It's also a haven for fishing boats and canoes. There's a small dive shop on the beach, a snack bar (open weekends), and

restrooms, but there's no fee. ⊠ *West of Santa Cruz, Banda Abou*

Playa Porto Mari. Calm, clear water and a long stretch of white sand are the hallmarks of this beach. Without the commercial bustle of Seaquarium Beach, it's one of the best for all-around fun, and it therefore draws throngs of local families and tourists on the weekends. A decent bar and restaurant, well-kept showers, changing facilities, and restrooms are all on-site; a nature trail is nearby. The double coral reef—explore one, swim past it, explore another—is a special feature that makes this spot popular with snorkelers and divers. The entrance fee (including one free beverage) is $2 on weekdays, $3 on Sunday and holidays. From Willemstad, drive west on Westpunt Highway for 4 miles (7 km); turn left onto Willibrordus Road at the Porto Mari billboard, and then drive 3 miles (5 km) until you see a large church; follow signs on the winding dirt road to the beach. ⊠ *Off Willibrordus Rd.*

Updated
by Vernon
O'Reilly
Ramesar

The sun smiles down on Curaçao, which sits on the outer fringe of the so-called hurricane belt. Gentle trade winds help keep temperatures generally in the 80s. Water sports— including outstanding reef diving—attract enthusiasts from all over the world. Curaçao claims 38 beaches—some long stretches of silky sand, most smaller coves suitable for picture postcards. In the countryside, the dollhouse look of planta- tion houses, or *landhuizen* (literally, "land houses"), makes a cheerful contrast to stark cacti and austere shrubbery.

The sprawling city of Willemstad is the island's capital. Its historic downtown and the natural harbor (*Schottegat*) around which it's built are included on UNESCO's World Heritage List, a coveted distinction reserved for the likes of the Palace of Versailles and the Taj Mahal. The "face" of Willemstad delights like a kaleidoscope—rows of sprightly painted town houses with gabled roofs sit perched alongside the steely-blue Santa Anna Bay. Local lore has it that in the 1800s the governor claimed he suffered from migraines and blamed the glare from the sun's reflection off the then-white structures. To alleviate the problem, he ordered the facades painted in colors.

Curaçao was discovered by Alonzo de Ojeda (a lieutenant of Colum- bus) in 1499. The first Spanish settlers arrived in 1527. In 1634 the Dutch came via the Netherlands West Indies Company. Eight years later Peter Stuyvesant began his rule as governor (in 1647, Stuyvesant became governor of New Amsterdam, which later became New York). Twelve Jewish families arrived in Curaçao from Amsterdam in 1651, and by 1732 a synagogue had been built; the present structure is the oldest synagogue in continuous use in the Western Hemisphere. Over the years the city built fortresses to defend against French and British invasions—the standing ramparts now house restaurants and hotels. The Dutch claim to Curaçao was recognized in 1815 by the Treaty of Paris. From 1954 through 2006, Curaçao was the seat of government

LOGISTICS

Getting to Curaçao: If you want to connect through Aruba, more likely than not you'll have to book your flight on a tiny island-hopper directly with the island-based airline Insel Air. Hato International Airport (CUR) has car-rental facilities, duty-free shops, and restaurants.

Hassle Factor: Medium to high.

On the Ground: It takes about 20 minutes to get to the hotels

in Willemstad by taxi. Taxis have meters, but drivers still use set fares when picking passengers up at the airport. Verify which method your driver will use before setting off; fixed rates apply for up to four passengers in a single vehicle. Fares from the airport to Willemstad and the nearby beach hotels run about $18 to $22, and those to hotels at the island's western end about $40 to $47.

of the Netherlands Antilles, a group of islands under the umbrella of the Kingdom of the Netherlands. In October 2010, after discussions with the Netherlands, Curaçao's island council granted the territory autonomy (the same status Aruba attained in 1986).

Tourism is on a fast track to surpassing harbor-related activities as the island's primary source of income, with a corresponding surge in hotel development in recent years. The government has committed funds to an expansion plan to accommodate future growth. The opening of a massive pier has boosted the number of cruise-ship passengers to record highs. In addition, the government and private sources have invested substantially in the restoration of the island's graceful colonial buildings.

Today Curaçao's population derives from nearly 60 nationalities—an exuberant mix of Latin, European, and African roots speaking a Babel of tongues—resulting in superb restaurants and a flourishing cultural scene. Although Dutch is the official language, Papiamento is the vernacular of all the Netherlands Antilles and the preferred choice for communication among the locals. English and Spanish are also widely spoken. The island, like its Dutch settlers, is known for its religious tolerance, and tourists are warmly welcomed.

PLANNING

WHEN TO GO

High season in Curaçao mirrors that in much of the Caribbean: basically from mid-December through mid-April. In the off-season, rates will be reduced at least 25% and often more. Hurricanes and severe tropical storms are rare—though still possible—in Curaçao, which means the island has good weather almost year-round.

GETTING HERE AND AROUND
AIR TRAVEL

Most travelers will make a connection in San Juan, Montego Bay, or Aruba. To connect through Aruba, you'll likely have to book your flight on a tiny island-hopper directly with the island-based airline.

Nonstop Flights Atlanta (Delta, seasonal), Miami (American), and New York–Newark (Continental). American Airlines also offers service from San Juan.

Airport Hato International Airport. Hato International Airport has car-rental facilities, duty-free shops, and restaurants. ⊠ *CUR* ☎ *5999/839–1000.*

Airline Contacts American Airlines ☎ *5999/736–7799.* **Continental Airlines** ☎ *800/231–0856, 5999/839–1196.* **Dutch Antilles Express.** Dutch Antilles Express offers connecting service from Aruba, Caracas, Santo Domingo, and St. Maarten. ☎ *5999/461–3009* ⊕ *www.flydae.com.*

CAR TRAVEL

Many of the larger hotels have free shuttles into Willemstad, or you can take a quick, cheap taxi ride; hotels in Willemstad usually provide a free beach shuttle, so it's possible to get by without a car. If you're planning to do country driving or rough it through Christoffel National Park, a four-wheel-drive vehicle is best. All you need is a valid driver's license. Driving in Curaçao is on the right-hand side of the road; right turns on red are prohibited. Seat belts are required, and motorcyclists must wear helmets. Children under age four must be in child safety seats.

Car Rental: You can rent a car from any of the major car agencies at the airport or have one delivered free to your hotel. Rates are about $40–$47 a day for a compact car to $55–$65 for a four-door sedan or four-wheel-drive vehicle; add 5% tax and optional daily insurance.

Contacts Avis ☎ *5999/461–1255, 800/331–1084.* **Budget** ☎ *5999/868–3466, 800/472–3325.* **Hertz** ☎ *5999/888–0088.* **National Car Rental** ☎ *5999/869–4433.* **Thrifty** ☎ *5999/461–3089.*

TAXI TRAVEL

Fares from the airport to Willemstad and the nearby beach hotels run about $18 to $22, and those to hotels at the island's western end about $40 to $47 (be sure to agree on the rate before setting off). The government-approved rates, which do not include waiting time, can be found in a brochure called "Taxi Tariff Guide," available at the airport, hotels, cruise-ship terminals, and the tourist board. Rates are for up to four passengers. There's a 25% surcharge after 11 pm.

Contact Central Dispatch. Taxis are readily available at hotels and at taxi stands at the airport, in Punda, and in Otrobanda; in other cases, call Central Dispatch. ☎ *5999/869-0752.*

ESSENTIALS

Addresses In street addresses that do not specify a house number, the *z/n* is a Dutch abbreviation for *zonder nummer* (no number).

Banks and Exchange Services U.S. dollars are accepted nearly everywhere. Currency in Curaçao is the florin (also called the guilder) and is indicated by *fl* or *NAf* on price tags. The official rate of exchange at this writing was NAf 1.77 to US$1. The currency is expected to be changed to the Caribbean guilder in 2013.

Electricity 110–130 volts/50 cycles.

Emergency Services Ambulance ☎ *912.* **On-call doctors** ☎ *1111.* **Police and fire** ☎ *911.* **Tourist Emergencies** ☎ *917.*

Passport Requirements A valid passport is required. All visitors must be able to show an ongoing or return ticket as well as have proof of sufficient funds to support their stay on the island.

Phones To call Curaçao direct from the United States, dial 011–5999 plus the number in Curaçao.

International roaming for most GSM mobile phones is available in Curaçao. Local companies are UTS (United Telecommunication Services) and Digicel. You can also rent a mobile phone or buy a prepaid SIM card for your own phone.

Taxes and Service Charges The departure tax is $32.50 (including flights to Aruba), and the departure tax to other former members of the Netherlands Antilles islands is $8. This must be paid in cash, in either florins or U.S. dollars. Hotels add a 12% service charge to the bill and collect a 7% government room tax; restaurants typically add 10% to 15%. Most goods and services purchased on the island will also have a 5% OB tax (a goods-and-services tax) added to the purchase price.

Tipping Service is usually included, but if you find the staff exemplary, you can add another 5% to 10% to the bill. Porters and bellhops, about $1 a bag; housekeeping, $2 to $3 per day; taxi, about 10%.

ACCOMMODATIONS

Resort development is concentrated around the capital, Willemstad, so most resorts are within easy reach of town, by shuttle or on foot. As the island becomes more developed, visitors have more options, and there are a few resorts farther removed as well, but it's the amenities that should drive your decision more than location. Choose the type of lodging that best appeals to your interests and style. Those spending a bit more time gravitate to villas and bungalows.

Resorts: Most of Curaçao's larger hotels are midsize resorts of 200 to 300 rooms, and many of them are within easy striking distance of town. The island offers a full range of resorts from the intimate and luxurious to historic properties—few other destinations offer a downtown hotel with a saltwater infinity pool complete with palm-lined beach.

Dive Resorts: Most of the resorts catering to divers are smaller operations of fewer than 100 rooms (often much smaller). Although some of these are in and around Willemstad, there are also a few on the secluded west end of the island, and that's where shore diving is best.

Villas and Bungalows: Though they are marketed primarily to European travelers who have more time to spend on the island, self-catering accommodations are an option for anyone who has at least a week to spend in Curaçao.

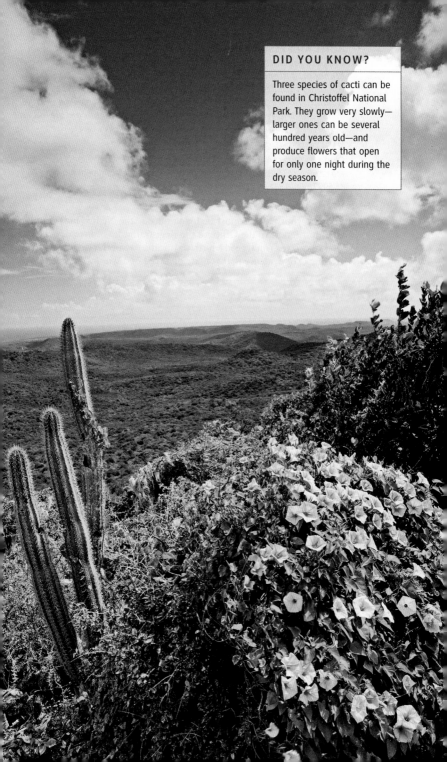

HOTEL AND RESTAURANT PRICES

Prices in the restaurant reviews are the average cost of a main course at dinner or, if dinner is not served, at lunch; taxes and service charges are generally included. Prices in the hotel reviews are the lowest cost of a standard double room in high season, excluding taxes, service charges, and meal plans (except at all-inclusives). Prices for rentals are the lowest per-night cost for a one-bedroom unit in high season.

VISITOR INFORMATION

Contacts Curaçao Tourist Board ✉ *Pietermaai 19, Punda, Willemstad* ☎ *5999/434–8200* ⊕ *www.curacao.com* ✉ *Hato International Airport* ☎ *5999/868–1341.*

WEDDINGS

You and your partner must be living outside the Netherlands Antilles; you must report to the Office of the Registrar at least three days before your marriage. You'll need a birth certificate, passport, evidence that you are single, or evidence that you are divorced or a widow or widower.

EXPLORING CURAÇAO

WILLEMSTAD

What does the capital of Curaçao have in common with New York City? Broadway, for one thing. Here it's called Breedestraat, but the origin is the same. Dutch settlers came here in the 1630s, about the same time they sailed through the Verazzano Narrows to Manhattan, bringing with them original red-tile roofs, first used on the trade ships as ballast and later incorporated into the architecture of Willemstad.

The city is cut in two by Santa Anna Bay. On one side is the Punda—crammed with shops, restaurants, monuments, and markets—and on the other is Otrobanda (literally, the "other side"), with lots of narrow, winding streets full of private homes notable for their picturesque gables and Dutch-influenced designs. In recent years the ongoing regeneration of Otrobanda has been apparent, marked by a surge in development of new hotels, restaurants, and shops; the rebirth, concentrated near the waterfront, was spearheaded by the creation of the elaborate Kura Hulanda complex.

There are three ways to cross the bay: by car over the Juliana Bridge; by foot over the Queen Emma pontoon bridge; or by free ferry, which runs when the pontoon bridge is swung open for passing ships. All the major hotels outside town offer free shuttle service to town once or twice daily. Shuttles coming from the Otrobanda side leave you at Riffort. From here it's a short walk north to the foot of the pontoon bridge. Shuttles coming from the Punda side leave you near the main entrance to Ft. Amsterdam.

WHAT TO SEE

Curaçao Museum. Housed in an 1853 plantation house, this small museum is filled with artifacts, paintings, and antiques that trace the island's history. This is also a venue for visiting art exhibitions.

✉ *V. Leeuwenhoekstraat z/n, Otrobanda* ☎ *5999/462–3873* 🎫 *Free*
🕐 *Weekdays 8:30–4:30, Sun. 10–4.*

★ **Floating Market.** Each morning dozens of Venezuelan schooners laden
with tropical fruits and vegetables arrive at this bustling market on
the Punda side of the city. Mangoes, papayas, and exotic vegetables
vie for space with freshly caught fish and herbs and spices. The buying is best at 6:30 am—too early for many people on vacation—but
there's plenty of action throughout the afternoon. Any produce bought
here should be thoroughly washed or peeled before being eaten. ✉ *Sha
Caprileskade, Punda.*

**NEED A
BREAK?**

Old Vienna Ice Café. For a cooling break from your explorations, Old
Vienna Ice Café serves scrumptious homemade ice cream. Indulge your
sweet tooth with such flavors as green apple, mango, and rum plum.
There's also a full menu of light bites and outdoor seating along the harbor.
✉ *Handelskade 6 C, Punda* ☎ *5999/736–1086.*

Ft. Amsterdam. Step through the archway of this fort and enter another
century. The entire structure dates from the 1700s, when it was the
center of the city and the island's most important fortification. Now it
houses the governor's residence, a church (which has a small museum),
and government offices. Outside the entrance, a series of majestic

A daring, mast-eye view of the Handelskade in Punda

gnarled *wayaka* trees are fancifully carved with human forms—the work of local artist Mac Alberto. ⊠ *Foot of Queen Emma Bridge, Punda* ☎ 5999/461–1139 ✉ *Fort free, church museum $2* ⊙ *Weekdays 9:30–1, Sun. service at 10.*

Fodor's Choice ★ **Kura Hulanda Museum.** This fascinating anthropological museum reveals the island's diverse roots. Housed in a restored 18th-century village, the museum is built around a former mercantile square (Kura Hulanda means "Holland courtyard"), where the Dutch once sold slaves. An exhibit on the transatlantic slave trade includes a gut-wrenching replica of a slave-ship hold. Other sections feature relics from West African empires, examples of pre-Columbian gold, and Antillean art. The complex is the brainchild of Dutch philanthropist Jacob Gelt Dekker, and the museum grew from his personal collection of artifacts. ⊠ *Klipstraat 9, Otrobanda* ☎ 5999/434–7765 ⊕ *www.kurahulanda.com* ✉ *$9* ⊙ *Thurs.–Sat. 10–5.*

Maritime Museum. The museum—designed to resemble the interior of a ship—gives you a sense of Curaçao's maritime history, using model ships, historic maps, nautical charts, navigational equipment, and audiovisual displays. Topics explored in the exhibits include the development of Willemstad as a trading city, Curaçao's role as a contraband hub, the remains of *De Alphen* (a Dutch marine freighter that exploded and sank in St. Anna Bay in 1778 and was excavated in 1984), the slave trade, the development of steam navigation, and the role of the Dutch navy on the island. The museum also offers a two-hour guided tour (Wednesday and Saturday, 2 pm) on its "water bus" through Curaçao's harbor—a route familiar to traders, smugglers, and pirates. The museum is wheelchair accessible. ⊠ *Van der Brandhofstraat 7, Scharloo* ☎ *5999/465–2327* ⊕ *www.curacaomaritime.com* ⚌ *Museum $6, museum and harbor tour $15* ☉ *Tues.–Sat. 9–4.*

★ **Mikvé Israel-Emanuel Synagogue.** The temple, the oldest in continuous use in the Western Hemisphere, is one of Curaçao's most important sights and draws thousands of visitors a year. The synagogue was dedicated in 1732 by the Jewish community, which had already grown from the original 12 families who came from Amsterdam in 1651. They were later joined by Jews from Portugal and Spain fleeing persecution from the Inquisition. White sand covers the synagogue floor for two symbolic reasons: a remembrance of the 40 years Jews spent wandering the desert, and a re-creation of the sand used by secret Jews, or *conversos*, to muffle sounds from their houses of worship during the Inquisition. English and Hebrew services are held Friday at 6:30 pm and Saturday at 10 am. Men who attend should wear a jacket and tie. Yarmulkes are provided to men for services and tours.

Jewish Cultural Museum. The Jewish Cultural Museum, in back of the synagogue, displays antiques—including a set of circumcision instruments—and artifacts from around the world. Many of the objects are used in the synagogue, making it a "living" museum. ☎ *5999/461–1633* ⊠ *Hanchi Snoa 29, Punda* ☎ *5999/461–1067* ⊕ *www.snoa.com* ⚌ *$6; donations also accepted* ☉ *Weekdays 9–4:30.*

Old Market (*Marche Bieuw*). Local cooks prepare hearty Antillean lunches in coal pots at this covered market behind the post office. Enjoy such Curaçaoan specialties as *funchi* (polenta), goat stew, fried fish, or stewed okra. Prices range from $5 to $14. ⊠ *De Ruyterkade, Punda.*

Plaza Piar. This plaza is dedicated to Manuel Piar, a native Curaçaoan who fought for the independence of Venezuela under the liberator Simón Bolívar. On one side of the plaza is the Waterfort, built in the late 1820s to help defend the old city. The original cannons are still positioned in the battlements. The foundation, however, now forms the walls of the Howard Johnson Plaza Hotel Curaçao & Casino.

Queen Emma Bridge. Affectionately called the Swinging Old Lady by the locals, this bridge connects the two sides of Willemstad—Punda and Otrobanda—across the Santa Anna Bay. The bridge swings open at least 30 times a day to allow passage of ships to and from the sea. The original bridge, built in 1888, was the brainchild of the American consul Leonard Burlington Smith, who made a mint off the tolls he charged for using it: 2¢ per person for those wearing shoes, free to those crossing barefoot. Today it's free to everyone. The bridge was dismantled and completely repaired and restored in 2005.

Queen Juliana Bridge. This 1,625-foot-long bridge stands 200 feet above the water, and it's the highest bridge in the Caribbean. It's the crossing for motor traffic between Punda and Otrobanda and affords breathtaking views (and photo ops) of the city, day and night.

Scharloo. The Wilhelmina Drawbridge connects Punda with the once-flourishing district of Scharloo, where the early Jewish merchants built stately homes. The architecture along Scharlooweg (much of it from the 17th century) is magnificent, and, happily, many of the colonial mansions that had become dilapidated have been meticulously renovated. The area closest to Kleine Werf is a red-light district and fairly run-down, but the rest is well worth a visit.

ELSEWHERE ON CURAÇAO

The Weg Maar Santa Cruz through the village of Soto winds to the island's northwest tip through landscape that Georgia O'Keeffe might have painted: towering cacti, flamboyant dried shrubbery, and aluminum-roof houses. Throughout this *cunucu,* or countryside, you can see fishermen hauling nets, women pounding cornmeal, and an occasional donkey blocking traffic. Land houses—large plantation houses from centuries past—dot the countryside. To explore the island's eastern side from Willemstad, take the coastal road called Martin Luther King Boulevard about 2 miles (3 km) to Bapor Kibra. This is where you can find the Sea Aquarium and the Dolphin Academy. Farther east are a nature park at Caracas Bay and the upscale Spanish Water neighborhood and marina. To the far northeast is Groot St. Joris, home of Curaçao's aloe plantation and one of the largest ostrich-breeding farms outside Africa.

WHAT TO SEE

★ **Christoffel National Park.** The 1,239-foot Mt. Christoffel, Curaçao's highest peak, is at the center of this 4,450-acre garden and wildlife preserve. The exhilarating climb up—a challenge to anyone who hasn't grown up scaling the Alps—takes about two hours for a reasonably fit person. On a clear day the panoramic view from the peak stretches to the mountain ranges of Venezuela.

Throughout the park are eight hiking trails and a 20-mi (32-km) network of driving trails (use heavy-treaded tires if you wish to explore the unpaved stretches). All these routes traverse hilly fields full of prickly pear cacti, divi-divi trees, bushy-haired palms, and exotic flowers. Guided nature walks, horseback rides, and jeep tours can be arranged through the main park office. If you're going without a guide, first study the *Excursion Guide to Christoffel Park,* sold at the visitor center. It outlines the various routes and identifies the indigenous flora and fauna. Start out early, as by 10 am the park starts to feel like a sauna.

Watch for goats and small animals that might cross your path, and consider yourself lucky if you see any of the elusive white-tailed deer. Every day at 4 pm, guides lead 15-minute expeditions to track the protected herd. Birds are abundant, and experts lead the way twice daily. White-tailed hawks may be seen along the green hiking route, white orchids along the yellow hiking route. There are also ancient Indian drawings and caves where you might hear the rustling of bat wings or spot scuttling, nonpoisonous scorpions.

Horseback tours are conducted from Rancho Alfin, which is in the park. Reservations are required. Additionally, most island sports outfitters offer some kind of activity in the park, such as kayaking, specialized hiking tours, and drive-through tours *(⇨ Sports and Activities, below).* ⊠ *Savonet* ☎ *5999/864–0363 for information and tour reservations, 5999/462–6262 for jeep tours, 5999/864–0535 for horse-*

Plantation house in Christoffel National Park with Mt. Christoffel in the distance

back tours ☐ *$10* ☉ *Mon.–Sat. 8–4, Sun. 6–3; last admission 90 min before closing.*

Curaçao Aloe Plantation & Factory. Drop in for a fascinating tour that takes you through the various stages of production of aloe vera, renowned for its healing powers. You'll get a look at everything from the fields to the final products. At the gift shop you can buy CurAloe products, including homemade goodies like soap, pure aloe gel, and pure aloe juice, as well as sunscreen and other skin-care products. The plantation is on the way to the Ostrich Farm and run by the same owner. Tours begin throughout the day. ⊠ *Weg Naar Groot St. Joris z/n, Groot St. Joris* ☎ *5999/767–5577* ⊕ *www.aloecuracao.com* ☐ *$7* ☉ *Mon.–Sat. 9–4; last tour at 3.*

☺ **Curaçao Sea Aquarium.** You don't have to get your feet wet to see the
★ island's underwater treasures. The aquarium has about 40 saltwater tanks filled with more than 400 varieties of marine life. A restaurant, a snack bar, two photo centers, and souvenir shops are on-site.

  Dolphin Academy. At the Dolphin Academy you can watch a fanciful dolphin show (included with Sea Aquarium admission). For up-close interactions, you may choose from several special programs (extra charges apply and reservations are essential) to encounter the dolphins in shallow water, or to swim, snorkel, or dive with them. ☎ *5999/465–8900* ⊕ *www.dolphin-academy.com* ⊠ *Seaquarium Beach, Bapor Kibra z/n* ☎ *5999/461–6666* ⊕ *www.curacao-sea-aquarium.com* ☐ *Aquarium $19; Dolphin Academy $89–$169* ☉ *Aquarium daily 8:30–5:30, Dolphin Academy daily 8:30–4:30.*

★ **Den Paradera.** Dazzle your senses at this organic herb garden, where guides will explain the origins of traditional folk medicines used to treat everything from stomach ulcers to diabetes. Owner Dinah Veeris is a renowned expert and author in the field. The kitchen is a factory of sorts where three busy people turn homegrown plants like cactus, aloe vera, and calabash into homemade body- and skin-care products like shampoos, ointments, and oils—all for sale at the gift shop. Reservations are essential for guided tours. ⊠ *Seru Grandi Kavel 105A, Banda Riba* ☎ *5999/767-5608* ⊡ *$7 with guided tour* ☉ *Mon.–Sat. 9–6.*

★ **Hato Caves.** Stalactites and stalagmites form striking shapes in these 200,000-year-old caves. Hidden lighting adds to the dramatic effect. Indians who used the caves for shelter left petroglyphs about 1,500 years ago. More recently, slaves who escaped from nearby plantations used the caves as a hideaway. Hour-long guided tours wind down to the pools in various chambers. Keep in mind that there are 49 steps to climb up to the entrance and the occasional bat might not be to everyone's taste. To reach the caves, head northwest toward the airport, take a right onto Gosieweg, follow the loop right onto Schottegatweg, take another right onto Jan Norduynweg and a final right onto Rooseveltweg, and follow signs. ⊠ *Rooseveltweg z/n, Hato* ☎ *5999/868-0379* ⊡ *$8* ☉ *Daily 10–4.*

Landhuis Kenepa. With the island's largest slave population, this plantation was the site of a revolt in 1795 that spurred the abolition of slavery on the island. The renovated plantation house near the island's western tip is filled with period furnishings and clothing. ⊠ *Weg Naar Santa Cruz, Knip* ☎ *5999/864-0244* ⊡ *$2* ☉ *Weekdays 9–4, weekends 10–4.*

Museo Curaçao (*Kas di Pal'i Maishi*). The thatch-roof cottage is filled with antique furniture, farm implements, and clothing typical of 19th-century colonial life. Out back is a small farm and vegetable garden. Look closely at the fence—it's made of living cacti. There's also a snack bar. A festival featuring live music and local crafts takes place here on the first Sunday of each month. ⊠ *Dokterstuin 27, on road to Westpunt from Willemstad, Westpunt* ☎ *5999/864-2742* ⊡ *$2* ☉ *Tues.–Fri. 9–4, weekends 9–5.*

☾ ★ **Ostrich Farm.** If you (and the kids) are ready to stick your neck out for an adventure, visit one of the largest ostrich farms outside Africa. Every hour, guided tours show the creatures' complete development from egg to mature bird. Kids enjoy the chance to hold an egg, stroke a day-old chick, and sit atop an ostrich for an unusual photo op. At the **Restaurant Zambezi** you can sample local ostrich specialties and other African dishes (reservations are recommended; closed Monday; no dinner Tuesday). The gift shop sells handicrafts made in southern Africa, including leather goods and wood carvings, as well as products made by local artisans. ⊠ *Groot St. Joris* ☎ *5999/747-2777* ⊕ *www.ostrichfarm.net* ⊡ *$15* ☉ *Tues.–Sun. 9–5.*

Senior Curaçao Liqueur Distillery. The famed Curaçao liqueur, made from the peels of the bitter Laraha orange, is produced at this mansion, which dates to the 1800s. Don't expect a massive factory—it's just a small showroom in an open-air foyer. There are no guides, but delightful old hand-painted posters explain the distillation process, and you can watch workers filling the bottles by hand. Assorted flavors are available to sample for free. If you're interested in buying—the orange-flavor chocolate liqueur is delicious over ice cream—you can choose from a complete selection in enticing packaging, including miniature Dutch ceramic houses. ⊠ *Landhuis Chobolobo, Salina* ☎ *5999/461–3526* 🖃 *Free* ⊘ *Weekdays 8–noon and 1–5.*

★ **Shete Boka.** The name of this park means "Seven Inlets" in Papiamento. Indeed, the sea has carved out seven magnificent grottoes, the largest of which is Boka Tabla, where you can watch and listen to the waves crashing against the rocks beneath a limestone overhang. Boka Pistol is also spectacular, with thunderous waves smashing into the rocks and jetting up into towering plumes of spray, often leaving rainbows lingering in the mist. Several of the surrounding caverns serve as turtle nesting places; you might also see flocks of parakeets emerge in formation, hawks soar and dip, and gulls dive-bomb for their lunch. ⊠ *Westpunt Hwy., just past village center, Soto* 🖃 *$1.50* ⊘ *Daily 9–5.*

WHERE TO EAT

Dine beneath the boughs of magnificent old trees, on the terraces of restored mansions and plantation houses, or on the ramparts of 18th-century forts. Curaçaoans partake of generally outstanding fare, with representation from a remarkable smattering of ethnicities. Outdoor or open-air sheltered dining is commonplace; note that most restaurants offer a smoking section or permit smoking throughout. Fine dining tends to be pricey, mostly because of the high cost of importing products to the island. For cheap eats with a local flair, drop by the Old Market for lunch, or stop at one of the snack bars or snack trucks you can find all over the island (have some guilders handy—many of them won't have change for dollars).

What to Wear. Dress in restaurants is almost always casual (though beachwear isn't acceptable). Some of the resort dining rooms and more elegant restaurants require that men wear jackets, especially in high season; ask when you make reservations.

$ ✕ **Angelica's Kitchen.** For an immersive, hands-on experience with the
CARIBBEAN cuisine of the island, you might want to try this unusual Otrobanda establishment. Self-taught cook Angelica Schoop puts guests in an apron and walks them through the process of creating their own meal in her fully equipped kitchen. Dishes may include anything from plantain soup to funchi. After the cooking is done, guests head to the back porch and enjoy the fruits of their labor. The minimum group size is 10 people, so gather up a few friends and prepare for four hours of culinary fun. Less adventurous folks can just cross the road and enjoy fine pastries and champagne at Angelica's Delights or join her on a culinary walking tour of the city. ⑤ *Average main: $95* ⊠ *Hoogstraat 49, Otrobanda* ☎ *5999/562–3699* ⊕ *www.angelicas-kitchen.com* ⚄ *Reservations essential* ☞ *Price is for group of 10.*

$
CAFÉ
✕ **Awa di Playa.** Formerly a fisherman's hangout, this ramshackle shed-like structure located on an ocean inlet gives way to an equally ramshackle interior and some of the best local lunches anywhere on the island. There's no menu—the waiter will tell you what's available, and you can watch it being cooked in the tiny kitchen. The presentation isn't fancy, and the occasional fly makes an appearance, but the food is honest and delicious. $ *Average main: $8* ⊠ *Behind Hook's Hut and Hilton, Piscadera Bay, Willemstad* ☎ *5999/462–6939* ▭ *No credit cards* ◷ *No dinner.*

$$$$
EUROPEAN
Fodor's Choice
★
✕ **Bistro Le Clochard.** Built into a 19th-century fort, this romantic gem anchors the entrance to the 21st-century Riffort Village complex, the waterside terrace offering an enchanting view of the floating bridge and harbor. Switzerland and France are the key influences on the sublime preparations. The signature dish is La Potence—a spike-covered metal ball resembling a medieval weapon. It's brought to your table blazing hot and covered with bits of sizzling tenderloin and sausage, served with various dipping sauces. Though more gimmicky fun than fine dining, it makes for a popular photo opportunity. The cheese fondue definitely keeps diners coming back. Game lovers can have their fill from the seasonal menu. No matter what, leave room for the sumptuous Toblerone chocolate mousse. $ *Average main: $55* ⊠ *Harborside Terr., Riffort Village, Otrobanda, Willemstad* ☎ *5999/462–5666* ⊕ *www.bistroleclochard.com* ⌲ *Reservations essential.*

$$
EUROPEAN
★
✕ **Blues.** Jutting out onto a pier over the ocean, this jazzy spot is an alluring place for dinner. The small menu is surprisingly comprehensive, with a special emphasis on seafood. The fish, mussel, and shrimp ceviche is a popular and refreshing appetizer. For meat lovers, the Spare Ribs New Orleans Style holds a spot at the top of the charts. Live music on Thursday and Saturday evenings includes seductive vocalists and top-notch musicians. If you'd rather be removed from the scene, you can arrange for a cozy dinner on the beach; whether it's a table for two or for a larger group, you'll be nestled in the sand on colorful oversize pillows. There's also a terrific prix-fixe tapas buffet on Friday. $ *Average main: $20* ⊠ *Avila Hotel, Penstraat 130, Punda, Willemstad* ☎ *5999/461–4377* ⊕ *www.avilahotel.com* ◷ *Closed Mon. No lunch.*

$$$
EUROPEAN
★
✕ **Fort Nassau Restaurant.** On a hill above Willemstad, this elegant restaurant is built into an 18th-century fort with a 360-degree view. For the best perspective, sit beside the huge bay windows in the air-conditioned interior; the terrace has a pleasant breeze and is generally more popular with diners, but the view is not quite optimal. Among the highlights of the diverse menu is the medley of Caribbean seafood with mahimahi, shrimp, and grilled octopus. Scrumptious desserts will leave you feeling sated. $ *Average main: $26* ⊠ *Schottegatweg 82, near Juliana Bridge, Otrobanda, Willemstad* ☎ *5999/461–3450, 5999/461–3086* ⊕ *www.fortnassau.com* ⌲ *Reservations essential* ◷ *No lunch weekends.*

$$
ECLECTIC
★
✕ **Gouverneur de Rouville Restaurant & Café.** Dine on the verandah of a restored 19th-century Dutch mansion overlooking the Santa Anna Bay and the resplendent Punda skyline. Though often busy and popular with tourists, the ambience makes it worth a visit. Intriguing soup options include Cuban banana soup and Curaçao-style fish soup. *Keshi yena*

(seasoned meat wrapped in cheese and then baked) and spareribs are among the savory entrées. After dinner, you can stick around for live music at the bar, which stays open until 1 am. The restaurant is also popular for lunch and attracts crowds when cruise ships dock. Reserve ahead if you would like a balcony table. ⑤ *Average main: $24* ⌧ *De Rouvilleweg 9, Otrobanda, Willemstad* ☎ *5999/462–5999* ⊕ *www. de-gouverneur.com.*

$$
CARIBBEAN

✕**Jaanchies Restaurant.** Over the years this has become something of a road marker on Curaçao's beaten tourist path, with prices to match. You'll be greeted by the owner, Jaanchi himself, a self-described "walking, talking menu," who will recite your choices of dishes for lunch. Jaanchi's iguana soup, touted in folklore as an aphrodisiac, is famous on the island. It's quite a sight when so-called sugar-thief birds flock to feeders outside the restaurant when the owner periodically fills them with sugar. Although predominantly a lunch spot, the restaurant will accommodate groups of four or more for dinner by prior arrangement. ⑤ *Average main: $25* ⌧ *Westpunt 15, Westpunt* ☎ *5999/864–0126.*

$$$
ASIAN
★

✕**Jaipur.** The subtle lighting and sound of the nearby waterfall seem to make the food even more sublime at this outdoor Pan-Asian restaurant—with distinct Indian and Thai influences—that's part of the expansive Kura Hulanda complex. The samosas filled with ground lamb make a great starter, and the tandoori mixed platter—with chicken, shrimp, and lamb kebabs—is a treat. The Thursday-night Asian buffet is a feast for the senses. ⑤ *Average main: $28* ⌧ *Langestraat 8, Otrobanda, Willemstad* ☎ *5999/461–3482* ☯ *Closed Sun.–Mon. No lunch.*

$$
SEAFOOD
☾

✕**La Bahia Seafood & Steakhouse.** As you dine on a sheltered terrace with a remarkable view of the harbor front, you're so close to the passing ships that it seems you can almost touch them. The menu runs the gamut from burgers and pastas to keshi yena and other local specialties. Even if the food doesn't appeal, this is a great spot to relax with a cup of coffee or a cocktail after a day of exploring. It is a short walk from the Queen Emma Bridge. ⑤ *Average main: $20* ⌧ *Otrobanda Hotel & Casino, Breedestraat, Otrobanda, Willemstad* ☎ *5999/462–7400* ⊕ *www.otrobandahotel.com.*

$$$$
STEAKHOUSE

✕**L'aldea Steakhouse.** A long drive from downtown hotels along sometimes bumpy roads leads to this Brazilian steak house with a decidedly Mayan theme. Clashing motifs are quickly forgotten as you enter the lush interior filled with stone carvings and greenery. The price of dinner includes the largest salad bar on the island and a nonstop procession of servers at your table, carving a delectable selection of grilled meats until told to stop. Each table has three buttons—to hail the waiter, manager, and request the check. It isn't cheap, but the service and fare are top-notch. ⑤ *Average main: $49* ⌧ *Sta. Catharina #66, Willemstad* ☎ *5999/767–6777* ⊕ *www.laldeacur.com/restaurant.html* ⌸ *Reservations essential* ☯ *Closed Mon. No lunch weekdays.*

$$$
CARIBBEAN
★

✕**Landhuis Daniel.** Many of the tasty meals served here have their roots in the restaurant's garden. Fruits, vegetables, and herbs are organically grown at this landmark plantation house—dating from 1711—and used unsparingly in the menu, which changes according to seasonal crop yield. The chef draws on creole, French, and Mediterranean influences

9

for his creations. One option is the prix-fixe "surprise menu"—just tell your waiter your preference for meat, fish, or vegetarian, and any dislikes. There's also a small inn here. ⑤ *Average main: $28* ☒ *Weg Naar, Westpunt* ☏ *5999/864–8400* ⊕ *www.landhuisdaniel.com.*

$$$ ✕ **Rodeo House of Ribs.** A haven for meat lovers, this family-owned res-
STEAKHOUSE taurant has been in business since 1980. The staff (dressed in cowboy
ⓒ outfits, of course) keeps the place lively. For kicks, ride the mechanical bull in the backyard: you could win a free meal if you stay on for more than two minutes. There's live music on Saturday nights. ⑤ *Average main: $27* ☒ *Fokkerweg 3, Saliña* ☏ *5999/465–9465* ⊙ *Closed Mon. No lunch.*

$$ ✕ **Scampi's.** Part of the Waterfort dining complex, this family-friendly
SEAFOOD eatery offers great basic food right next door to the decidedly more upscale eateries that share its waterfront location. The food is simple but well made, and better yet, very affordable. There is a good selection of fresh seafood and steaks at surprisingly reasonable prices, and kids can choose from their own menu. ⑤ *Average main: $22* ☒ *Waterfortstraat 41–42, Punda* ☏ *5999/465–0769.*

$$$$ ✕ **Shor.** Despite its setting in the swanky Hyatt Regency, this airy sea-
AMERICAN food grill overlooking the ocean is surprisingly relaxed. Appetizers range from a simple but exquisite gravlax salmon salad to a huge serving of bubbling crab dip served with bread that can easily feed two. The main grill courses require a bit of pleasing deliberation, as both meat and seafood offerings are fully customizable, with choices of seasoning, sauce, and side. Although the restaurant is quite a drive if you're not staying at the Hyatt, the ambience and excellent food are worth it. ⑤ *Average main: $33* ☒ *Hyatt Regency Curaçao, Santa Barbara Plantation, Nieuwpoort* ☏ *5999/840–1234* ⊕ *www.curacao.hyatt.com.*

$$$ ✕ **Tempo Doeloe.** The hillside location, Balinese decor, and authentic
INDONESIAN Indonesian cuisine draw both visitors and locals to this sprawling establishment. Although dishes may be ordered individually, the excess of either the full rijstaffel or more manageable—though without seafood—small rijstaffel is an experience not easily forgotten. Call ahead to request a table with a view. ⑤ *Average main: $30* ☒ *La Vista Resort, Piscaderaweg, Willemstad* ☏ *5999/461–2881* ⊕ *www.tempodoeloe.net* ⚐ *Reservations essential.*

WHERE TO STAY

You'll generally find that hotels at all price levels provide friendly, prompt, detail-oriented service; however, the finer points of service are in some cases still in nascent stages. Many of the large-scale resorts east and west of Willemstad proper have lovely beaches and provide a free shuttle to the city, 5 to 10 minutes away, but you'll find utmost seclusion at hotels on the island's southwestern end, a 30- to 45-minute drive from town. Most hotels in town provide beach shuttles.

For expanded reviews, facilities, and current deals, visit Fodors.com.

VILLAS AND RENTALS

Villa and bungalow rentals are especially popular with divers and European visitors and are generally good options for large groups or longer stays. The Curaçao Tourist Board (⊕ *www.curacao.com*) has a complete list of rental apartments, villas, and bungalows on its website.

Livingstone Jan Thiel Resort. The 128 villas at Livingstone Jan Thiel Resort surround a swimming pool in a low-rise complex that offers a mini-market on-site, free access to the beach across the street, Wi-Fi in the open-air lobby, and a playground and special programs for kids. Festive decor includes a large painted mural at the entrance and beaded shades on tabletop candleholders at the poolside restaurant. Reasonable rates even in high season make this an appealing choice for those looking for self-catering facilities. ⊠ *Jan Thiel* ☎ *5999/747–0332* ⊕ *www.janthielresort.com* ↪ *128 villas.*

Papagayo Beach Resort. The bungalows at Papagayo Beach Resort give you a unique option: on a whim you can open up a full wall so that your wraparound wooden terrace becomes part of your living space. Suddenly you're as close as it gets to living outdoors. These well-designed and nicely furnished homes include two bedrooms, a full kitchen with dishwasher, and bathroom (showers only). The restaurant menu changes seasonally; the pool bar is a cozy place to meet your neighbors. There's no beachfront, but you get free access to the beach across the street. Special programs and entertainment for kids are offered during school vacation periods. ⊠ *Jan Thiel* ☎ *5999/747–4333* ⊕ *www.papagayo-beach.com* ↪ *75 bungalows.*

RECOMMENDED HOTELS AND RESORTS

$$
RESORT
Fodor's Choice
★

Avila Hotel. The right blend of old-world touches, modern amenities, alluring beachfront, and attentive staff makes this resort the place of choice for the visiting Dutch royalty (well, all guests actually). The well-run hotel on a delightful beach has blossomed around the 18th-century mansion at its center. **Pros:** wide variety of room types and decor; old-world charm; excellent restaurants; choice of upscale shops on-site. **Cons:** bit of a walk to the city; because it caters to a largely European clientele, most rooms only have 220 outlets. **TripAdvisor:** "elegant comfort on the ocean," "incredible experience," "a perfect break in the sun." ⑤ *Rooms from: $310* ⊠ *Penstraat 130, Willemstad* ☎ *5999/461–4377, 800/747–8162* ⊕ *www.avilahotel.com* ↪ *154 rooms, 11 suites* �ⓄⅠ *No meals.*

$$$
RESORT
Fodor's Choice
★

Baoase. No other resort on Curaçao can match this Balinese-inspired gem for understated elegance and attention to detail. **Pros:** beautiful landscaping; complete privacy and quiet. **Cons:** lacks some of the distractions of a larger resort; a bit far from downtown shopping. **TripAdvisor:** "perfect luxurious stay," "beautiful Balinese property," "outstanding experience." ⑤ *Rooms from: $375* ⊠ *Winterswijkstraat 2, Willemstad* ☎ *5999/461–1799* ⊕ *www.baoase.com* ↪ *9 villas, 3 1-bedroom suites* ⓄⅠ *No meals.*

$
RENTAL

Blue Bay Village. This property is a 10-minute drive from Willemstad but offers a quiet setting, beautiful villas, thoughtfully decorated rooms, and the perfect location for golf lovers. **Pros:** spacious units; ideal location for golfers; far from the madding crowd; on-site restaurant is quite

9

good for basic family meals. **Cons:** a bit isolated, so a car is absolutely necessary; no nightlife in the area. **TripAdvisor:** "beautiful beach but far away," "wonderful resort," "very nice surroundings." ⑤ *Rooms from: $184* ✉ *Landhuis Blauw z/n, Willemstad* ☎ *5999/888–8800* 📨 *48 apartments, 36 3-bedroom villas* ⑩ *No meals.*

$$
ALL-INCLUSIVE
♻

🏨 **Breezes Curaçao Resort, Spa & Casino.** You might enjoy the conviviality at the island's only all-inclusive, but unless you venture off the lushly landscaped grounds you won't get much taste of the real Curaçao; on the other hand, you won't have much reason to leave. **Pros:** ample distractions for the whole family; beautiful landscaping; great price for families. **Cons:** some rooms are in need of refurbishing; free drinks mean the pool area is always crowded. **TripAdvisor:** "relaxing," "amazing beach and weather," "fun and relaxing." ⑤ *Rooms from: $300* ✉ *Martin Luther King Blvd. 78, Willemstad* ☎ *5999/736–7888, 800/467–8737* ⊕ *www.breezes.com* 📨 *285 rooms, 54 suites* ⑩ *All-inclusive* ♻ *3-night minimum.*

$$
RESORT
♻
Fodor's Choice
★

🏨 **Curaçao Marriott Beach Resort & Emerald Casino.** The cream of the crop of Curaçao's resorts beckons you to live it up from the moment you arrive. **Pros:** no need to leave the compound for anything but sightseeing; excellent beach location; first-class fitness center; five-star PADI dive shop. **Cons:** feels big and impersonal; pool area can get very busy. **TripAdvisor:** "great beach," "friendly hotel that does not overwhelm," "beautiful resort." ⑤ *Rooms from: $249* ✉ *John F. Kennedy Blvd., Willemstad* ☎ *5999/736–8800* ⊕ *www.curacaomarriott.com* 📨 *237 rooms, 10 suites* ⑩ *Multiple meal plans.*

$
HOTEL

🏨 **Floris Suite Hotel.** Dutch interior designer Jan des Bouvrie has used warm mahogany shades offset by cool, sleek stainless-steel adornments in the suites of this modernist hotel, all of which have a balcony or porch and a full kitchen. **Pros:** great for a quiet escape; beautifully designed rooms and public spaces. **Cons:** decor lacks romantic feel; bit of a hike to decent shopping and restaurants. **TripAdvisor:** "very relaxing and comfortable stay," "spacious suites," "pure relaxation in style." ⑤ *Rooms from: $145* ✉ *Piscaderaweg, Piscadera Bay, Willemstad* ☎ *5999/462–6111* ⊕ *www.florissuitehotel.com* 📨 *72 suites* ⑩ *No meals.*

$$
RESORT
♻
★

🏨 **Hilton Curaçao.** Two beautiful beaches of pillowy white sand beyond the open-air lobby make this resort a jewel in its price range. **Pros:** gorgeous beachfront; close to great shopping and off-site restaurants; friendly staff. **Cons:** hallways are a bit bland; rooms could be in a Hilton anywhere on the planet. **TripAdvisor:** "very good services," "spacious grounds," "stunning views." ⑤ *Rooms from: $229* ✉ *Piscaderaweg, Willemstad* ☎ *5999/462–5000* ⊕ *www.hiltoncaribbean.com/curacao* 📨 *196 rooms, 12 suites* ⑩ *No meals.*

$$
HOTEL
Fodor's Choice
★

🏨 **Hotel Kura Hulanda Spa & Casino.** Guest rooms here are tucked in restored 18th-century houses built along pebble-stone alleyways that diverge from a central courtyard. The pools and gardens are exquisite, especially at night, when lighting casts a romantic glow. **Pros:** unique historic feel; top-notch restaurants; incredible museum in compound; downtown shopping just steps away; free Internet access in rooms. **Cons:** no beach nearby; getting around the compound can be like negotiating a maze. **TripAdvisor:** "a wonderfully unique and special resort," "best of the best," "a hotel with character." $ *Rooms from: $320* ✉ *Langestraat 8, Otrobanda, Willemstad* ☎ *5999/434–7700* ⊕ *www.kurahulanda.com* ⤴ *82 rooms, 12 suites* ⦿ *No meals.*

$

HOTEL

Howard Johnson Plaza Hotel & Casino. Everything the city has to offer is at your doorstep at this colorful hotel on the main square of Otrobanda, an especially coveted location during the holidays and Carnival. **Pros:** in the heart of downtown with easy access to Punda; excellent price for a downtown location; some rooms have great views of Punda and Queen Emma Bridge. **Cons:** no beach; downtown noise can sometimes be a problem. **TripAdvisor:** "staff friendly," "good value," "fabulous view." $ *Rooms from: $129* ✉ *Brionplein, Otrobanda, Willemstad* ☎ *5999/462–7800* ⊕ *www.hojo-curacao.com* ⤴ *70 rooms* ⦿ *No meals.*

$$$

RESORT

☾

Hyatt Regency Curaçao. Miles away from any other property, Curaçao's new luxury resort is ideal for a self-contained getaway. **Pros:** Camp Arawak kids program that runs from 9 am to 9 pm is a boon for parents; gorgeous location miles away from the hustle and bustle of downtown; elegant public areas; impeccable service throughout the property. **Cons:** long drive or expensive taxi ride away from everything; feels a bit sterile even by large resort standards. **TripAdvisor:** "modern resort," "wonderful staff but very remote," "great food." $ *Rooms from: $239* ✉ *Santa Barbara Plantation, Nieuwpoort* ☎ *5999/840–1234* ⊕ *www. curacao.hyatt.com* ⤴ *335 rooms, 15 suites* ⦿ *Breakfast.*

$

B&B/INN

☾

Lagun Blou Dive & Beach Resort. Travelers on a budget will love this family-owned and -run hotel that combines a great view with an intimate setting. **Pros:** relaxed atmosphere; family-run; intimate setting; bargain for families. **Cons:** far from shopping and restaurants; lacks the amenities of a big resort; rooms cleaned once each week. **TripAdvisor:** "excellent location," "quiet and relaxed," "fabulous views." $ *Rooms from: $120* ✉ *Seaquarium Beach, Bapor Kibra z/n* ☎ *5999/864–0557* ⊕ *www.lagunblou.nl* ⤴ *13 rooms, 8 bungalows* ⦿ *No meals.*

$

RESORT

☾

Lions Dive & Beach Resort. Divers are lured by the first-rate program here, but this low-key resort has a lot to offer nondivers as well. **Pros:** ideal for diving; beautiful private beach and access to Seaquarium Beach; family-friendly, Olympic-length pool. **Cons:** beach can get busy; kids everywhere. **TripAdvisor:** "beautiful resort," "nice laid-back property," "excellent beach retreat." $ *Rooms from: $201* ✉ *Seaquarium Beach, Bapor Kibra z/n* ☎ *5999/434–8888* ⊕ *www.lionsdive.com* ⤴ *102 rooms, 10 suites, 1 penthouse* ⦿ *No meals.*

$$

RESORT

Fodor's Choice

★

Lodge Kura Hulanda & Beach Club. On the island's remote western tip, this sprawling resort with tranquil gardens will make you feel far removed from the daily grind. **Pros:** perfect for a complete escape; unparalleled ocean views; beautifully appointed rooms; free Wi-Fi. **Cons:** a bit quiet for some tastes; miles away from everything; although there's a shuttle, a rental car is necessary if you want to explore the island. **TripAdvisor:** "well run place," "nature lover's Eden," "fantastic ocean views." $ *Rooms from: $265* ✉ *Playa Kalki 1, Westpunt* ☎ *5999/839–3600* ⊕ *www.kurahulanda.com* ⤴ *42 rooms, 32 suites, 3 3-bedroom villas* ⦿ *Multiple meal plans.*

9

$$$
RESORT
Fodor's Choice
★

Renaissance Curaçao Resort & Casino. The four gabled buildings of this new downtown resort are painted in colors that seem to mirror those of Punda across the harbor and fit in perfectly with the historic surroundings. **Pros:** coolest (and only) pool-beach in town; every amenity imaginable; walking distance to all the attractions of both Otrobanda and Punda; exceptionally helpful staff. **Cons:** Rif Fort area is a major tourist draw and can get busy; room and common area color scheme is not exactly calming. **TripAdvisor:** "pleasant stay," "hot spot area," "beautiful resort." $ *Rooms from: $386* ⊠ *Pater Euwensweg, Otrobanda, Willemstad* ☎ *5999/435–5000* ⊕ *www.renaissancecuracao.com* ➔ *223 rooms, 14 suites* ⦿| *No meals.*

NIGHTLIFE

Friday is a big night out, with rollicking happy hours and live music at many bars and hotels. And although it might sound surprising, Sunday-night revelry into the wee hours is an island tradition. Pick up a copy of the weekly free entertainment listings, *K-Pasa,* available at most restaurants and hotels.

Fodor's Choice
★

Carnival. Outrageous costumes, blowout parades, pulsating Tumba rhythms, miniprocessions known as jump-ups, and frenetic energy characterize Carnival. The season lasts longer here than on many other islands: the revelries begin at New Year's and continue until midnight the day before Ash Wednesday. One highlight is the Tumba Festival (dates vary), a four-day musical event featuring fierce competition between local musicians for the honor of having their piece selected as the official road march during parades. For the Grand Parade, space is rented along the route and people mark their territory by building wooden stands, some lavishly decorated and furnished. .

BARS

De Gouverneur. Wednesday-night jam sessions are hot at De Gouverneur. ⊠ *De Rouvilleweg 9, Otrobanda, Willemstad* ☎ *5999/462–5999.*

Grand Café de Heeren. Grand Café de Heeren is a great spot to grab a locally brewed Amstel Bright and meet a happy blend of tourists and transplanted Dutch locals. ⊠ *Zuikertuintjeweg, Bloempot* ☎ *5999/736–0491.*

Hook's Hut. By day Hook's Hut is a beach hangout for locals and tourists stationed at the nearby hotels. The daily happy hour from 5 to 6 kicks off a lively nighttime scene. The outdoor pool table is in terrible shape, but it's one of the few bar tables around. ⊠ *Next to Hilton Curaçao, Piscadera Bay* ☎ *5999/462–6575.*

Waterfort Arches. The seaside outdoor deck at the Waterfort Arches comprises a connecting strip of several bars and restaurants that have live entertainment on various nights of the week. ⊠ *Waterfortstraat Boog 1, Punda, Willemstad* ☎ *5999/465–0769.*

Wet & Wild Beach Club. There's never a dull moment at Wet & Wild Beach Club, where the name speaks for itself every weekend. Friday happy hour features free barbecue; on Saturday a DJ or live band jams until it's too late to care about the time. On Sunday things get charged, starting with happy hour at 6; the fiesta goes on past midnight. ⊠ *Seaquarium Beach, Bapor Kibra z/n* ☎ *5999/561–2477.*

CASINOS

Casino gambling is becoming ever more popular on Curaçao, and hotels are refurbishing their casinos or adding new ones to keep up. Still, the sass and sparkle of the Vegas-style casinos is virtually nonexistent on the island. Although you might hear some hoots and hollers from a craps table, some clanking of coins from the slot machines, and the perpetual din of money changing hands, don't expect bells and whistles, glitzy decor, or cocktail waitresses in thematic costumes.

The following hotels have casinos that are open daily: Breezes Curaçao, the Curaçao Marriott Beach Resort & Emerald Casino, the Hilton Curaçao, the Hotel Kura Hulanda Spa & Casino, the Holiday Beach Hotel & Casino, Howard Johnson Plaza Hotel & Casino, and the Otrobanda Hotel & Casino. Even the biggest of these rooms offer only a few card games, and some are limited to slot machines. As for ambience, only the casino at the Marriott—which features pleasant live entertainment some nights—even approaches the class of a Bond-like establishment. A few Texas Hold 'Em tables are available here, but games start up only when enough players express interest. The Veneto Casino at the Holiday Beach Resort is the largest on the island, and the only one with sports betting—you can watch the live action on TV. Unfortunately, the casino is dreary. Around the island, slot machines open earlier than table games, between 10 am and 1 pm. Most of the rooms have penny and nickel slots in addition to the higher-priced machines. Tables generally open at 3 pm or 4 pm. Casinos close about 1 am or 2 am weekdays; some stay open until 4 am on weekend nights.

DANCE AND MUSIC CLUBS

★ **Blues.** Live jazz electrifies the pier at Blues on Thursday—*the* night to go—and Saturday. ⊠ *Avila Hotel, Penstraat 130, Punda, Willemstad* ☎ *5999/461–4377.*

Emerald Lounge Seafood Beat. The dance floor at the Emerald Lounge comes alive on weekends, and is especially steamy on Friday salsa nights. ⊠ *Curaçao Marriott Beach Resort, Piscadera Bay* ☎ *5999/736–8800.*

Mambo Beach. Mambo Beach, an open-air bar and restaurant, draws a hip, young crowd that dances the night away under the stars. On Sunday, come in time for happy hour and warm up for the nightlong party with some beach volleyball. ⊠ *Seaquarium Beach, Bapor Kibra z/n* ☎ *5999/461–8999.*

Club Facade. Locals flock here on Thursday and Friday nights to dance the night away to local music on three floors. ⊠ *Lindberghweg 32–34, Willemstad* ☎ *5999/461–4640.*

9

SHOPPING

From Dutch classics like embroidered linens, Delft earthenware, cheeses, and clogs to local artwork and handicrafts, shopping in Curaçao can turn up some fun finds. But don't expect major bargains on watches, jewelry, or electronics; Willemstad is not a duty-free port (the few establishments that claim to be "duty-free" are simply absorbing the cost of some or all of the tax rather than passing it on to consumers); however, if you come prepared with some comparison prices, you might still dig up some good deals.

SHOPPING AREAS

Willemstad's **Punda** is a treat for pedestrians, with most shops concentrated within a bustling area of about six blocks, giving you plenty of opportunity for people-watching to boot. Closed to traffic, Heerenstraat and Gomezplein are pedestrian malls covered with pink inlaid bricks. Other major shopping streets are Breedestraat and Madurostraat. Here you can find jewelry, cosmetics, perfumes, luggage, and linens—and no shortage of trinkets and souvenirs. Savvy shoppers don't skip town without a stop across the bay to **Otrobanda**, where the Riffort Village Shopping Mall houses a variety of retailers. It's worth noting that many of the bargain-price designer labels found in smaller clothing shops are just knockoffs from Latin America. The Renaissance Mall right next to Riffort has retailers such as Guess and Tiffany & Co. next to local shops offering a range of jewelry and fashion.

There are also some retail shops in the Kura Hulanda complex.

SPECIALTY STORES

ART GALLERIES

Gallery Alma Blou. Works by top local artists are displayed at Gallery Alma Blou; you can find shimmering landscapes, dazzling photographs, ceramics, even African-inspired Carnival masks. ⊠ *Frater Radulphusweg 4, Otrobanda* ☎ *5999/462–8896.*

Hortence Brouwn Gallery. Sculpted human forms (sometimes abstract) in bronze, concrete, marble, and limestone are sold at the Hortence Brouwn Gallery. ⊠ *Kaya Tapa Konchi 12, Brievengat* ☎ *5999/737–2193.*

Nena Sanchez Gallery. At the Nena Sanchez Gallery you can find this local artist's cheerful paintings in characteristically bright yellows, reds, greens, pinks, and blues. Her work depicting marine life and island scenes is available in various forms, including posters, mouse pads, and picture frames. ⊠ *Bloempot Shopping Mall, Schottegatweg Oost 17, Bloempot* ☎ *5999/738–2377.*

CIGARS

Cigar Emporium. A sweet aroma permeates Cigar Emporium, where you can find the largest selection of Cuban cigars on the island, including H. Upmann, Romeo y Julieta, and Montecristo. Visit the climate-controlled cedar cigar room. However, remember that Cuban cigars cannot be taken back to the United States legally. ⊠ *Gomezplein, Punda, Willemstad* ☎ *5999/465–3955.*

CLOTHING

Bamali. This shop sells funky, fabulous women's apparel, including Indonesian batik clothing; charming jewelry made of beads, shells, gemstones, and silver; handbags of leather and other fabrics; and lots of other unique accessories. Custom-made clothing is available here, too. ⊠ *Breedestraat, Punda, Willemstad* ☎ *5999/461–2258.*

Bikini Shop. Get suited up for the beach at the Bikini Shop, where you can find women's bathing suits (Vix, Becca, La Goufe) and accessories like cover-ups, flip-flops, and sunglasses. ⊠ *Seaquarium Beach, Bapor Kibra z/n* ☎ *5999/461–7343.*

Casa Janina. You can find a large selection of Calvin Klein apparel at Casa Janina, which also carries Levi's jeans. ⊠ *Madurostraat 13, Punda, Willemstad* ☎ *5999/461–1371.*

Tommy Hilfiger. This label's Curaçao outpost carries the full designer line for men, women, and children. ⊠ *Heerenstraat 3, Punda, Willemstad* ☎ *5999/461–2266.*

Wulfsen & Wulfsen. You can find a large selection of smart men's and women's wear at Wulfsen & Wulfsen, from European and American designers like Gant, Kenneth Cole, and Passport. ⊠ *Wilhelminaplein 1, Punda, Willemstad* ☎ *5999/461–6768.*

FOOD

Centrum Supermarket. This is one of the better markets in terms of variety and quality. A bakery is on the premises, too. ⊠ *Weg Naar Bullenbaai z/n, Piscadera* ☎ *5999/869–6222.*

Plaza's Gourmet & Fresh Mart. Located in the upscale Zuikertuin Mall, Plaza's Gourmet & Fresh Mart is a relatively small market selling a variety of gourmet items in addition to the basics. ⊠ *Zuikertuintjeweg, Santa Rosa* ☎ *5999/737–0188.*

GIFTS

Boolchand's. Head here for electronics, jewelry, Swarovski crystal, Swiss watches, cameras, and more, sold behind a façade of red-and-white checkered tiles. ⊠ *Heerenstraat 4B, Punda, Willemstad* ☎ *5999/461–6233.*

Julius L. Penha & Sons. Near the Pontoon Bridge, Julius L. Penha & Sons sells French perfumes and cosmetics, clothing, and accessories in a baroque-style building dating from 1708. ⊠ *Heerenstraat 1, Punda, Willemstad* ☎ *5999/461–2266.*

Little Switzerland. You can find jewelry, watches, crystal, china, and leather goods at significant savings at Little Switzerland. ⊠ *Breedestraat 44, Punda, Willemstad* ☎ *5999/461–2111.*

HANDICRAFTS

Caribbean Handcraft Inc. It's worth visiting this shop just for the spectacular hilltop view; an elaborate assortment of locally handcrafted souvenirs is available here. ⊠ *Kaya Kakina 8, Jan Thiel* ☎ *5999/767–1171.*

Landhuis Groot Santa Martha. Artisans with disabilities make the ceramic vases, dolls, leather goods, and other products sold at Landhuis Groot Santa Martha. There's a $3 entrance fee, and it's closed weekends. ⊠ *Santa Martha Bay* ☏ *5999/864–1323, 5999/864–2969.*

JEWELRY

Clarisa. This shop specializes in cultured pearls and also carries European gold jewelry and watches. ⊠ *Gomezplein 10, Punda, Willemstad* ☏ *5999/461–2006.*

Different Design. Gorgeous custom-made pendants and rings of precious gems and gold are on display at Different Design. ⊠ *Gomezplein 7, Punda, Willemstad* ☏ *5999/465–2944.*

Freeport Jewelers. A fine selection of watches and jewelry (lines include Movado, David Yurman, and Maurice Lacroix) is available at Freeport Jewelers. ⊠ *Renaissance Mall #208, Otrobanda, Willemstad* ☏ *5999/461–2857.*

Gandelman. Watches by Cartier and Rolex, leather goods by Prima Classe, and Baccarat and Daum crystal are all available at Gandelman. ⊠ *Breedestraat 35, Punda, Willemstad* ☏ *5999/461–1854.*

Pieters Jewelers. This jewelry store carries watches, including Seiko, Tissot, and Swatch, as well as gold jewelry, gemstones, and glassware. ⊠ *Promenade Shopping Center, Piscadera Bay, Willemstad* ☏ *5999/736–5833.*

LINENS

New Amsterdam. Hand-embroidered tablecloths, napkins, and pillowcases, as well as blue Delft, are available at New Amsterdam. ⊠ *Gomezplein 14, Punda, Willemstad* ☏ *5999/461–2437* ⊠ *Breedestraat 29, Punda, Willemstad* ☏ *5999/461–3239.*

PERFUMES AND COSMETICS

Yellow House. This shop offers a vast selection of perfumes at low prices. ⊠ *Breedestraat 23, Punda, Willemstad* ☏ *5999/461–3222.*

SPORTS AND ACTIVITIES

☾ **Caracas Bay Peninsula.** For the full gamut of activities in one spot, nature buffs (especially bird-watchers), families, and adventure seekers may want to visit Caracas Bay Peninsula. Things to do here include hiking, mountain biking, canoeing, kayaking, windsurfing, jet skiing, and snorkeling. There's a fully equipped dive shop, a restaurant, and a bar on premises. Admission to the scenic area is $5; activities cost extra. ☏ *5999/747–0777.*

ATVS AND SCOOTERS

Eric's ATV Adventures. Hit the road in rugged style behind the wheel of an all-terrain vehicle with Eric's ATV Adventures. All you need for a guided tour of the countryside is a regular driver's license. If you're 10 or older, you can ride as a passenger in the backseat. Helmets and goggles are provided. ✉ *Babor Kibra z/n, Seaquarium Beach, Willemstad* ☎ *5999/524–7418.*

Curaçao Buggy Adventures. Strap on a helmet for an adventurous, guided excursion around the island's most popular sites with Curaçao Buggy Adventures. Visit caves and forts, stop for a swim or snorkel; you can even design your own tour if you're a group of four or more people. Three-hour beach buggy trips are $140 per couple, and the fee includes safety equipment, insurance, gas, a guide, and pickup at your hotel. There is also a five-hour buggy tour for $275 per couple, which includes lunch. Experience isn't required, but cyclists will have an easier time maneuvering a scooter. You'll get some instruction and the chance to race around a practice course before you go. Children under 16 may ride as passengers. Wear sneakers, sunglasses, and sunscreen; bring a swimsuit, insect repellent, and a camera—and you're off! ✉ *Breezes Curaçao, Martin Luther King Blvd. 8, Willemstad* ☎ *5999/523–8618* ⊕ *www.curacaobuggyadventures.com.*

BIKING

Wanna Bike Curaçao. So you wanna bike Curaçao? Wanna Bike Curaçao has the fix: kick into gear and head out for a guided mountain-bike tour through the Caracas Bay Peninsula and the salt ponds at the Jan Thiel Lagoon. Although you should be fit to take on the challenge, mountain-bike experience is not required. Tour prices vary, depending on skill level and duration, and cover the bike, helmet, water, refreshments, park entrance fee, and guide—but don't forget to bring a camera. ✉ *Jan Thiel Beach z/n, Jan Thiel, Willemstad* ☎ *5999/527–3720* ⊕ *www.wannabike.com.*

DIVING AND SNORKELING

The **Curaçao Underwater Marine Park** includes almost a third of the island's southern diving waters. Scuba divers and snorkelers can enjoy more than 12½ miles (20 km) of protected reefs and shores, with normal visibility from 60 to 150 feet. With water temperatures ranging from 75°F to 82°F (24°C to 28°C), wet suits are generally unnecessary. No coral collecting, spearfishing, or littering is allowed. An exciting wreck to explore is the SS *Oranje Nassau,* which ran aground in 1906. The other two main diving areas are Banda Abou, along the southwest coast between Westpunt and St. Marie, and along central Curaçao, which stretches between Bullen Bay to the Breezes Curaçao resort. The north coast—where conditions are dangerously rough—is not recommended for diving.

Introductory scuba resort courses run about $75 for one dive and $140 for two dives. Open-water certification courses run about $425 for the five-dive version. Virtually every operator charges $40 to $55 for a single-tank dive and $70 to $85 for a two-tank dive. One day of unlimited shore diving runs about $22 to $25. Snorkeling gear commonly rents for $10 to $16 per day.

9

Diveversity Blue Bay. This outfitter offers a full range of dive services and equipment rental, and is a fully certified PADI diving school. ✉ *Blue Bay Golf & Dive Resort, Piscadera* ☎ *5999/888–6479.*

🕑 **Ocean Encounters.** Ocean Encounters is the largest dive operator on the
★ island. Its operations cover the popular east-coast dive sites, including the *Superior Producer* wreck, where barracudas hang out, and a tugboat wreck. West-end hot spots—including the renowned Mushroom Forest and Watamula dive sites—are accessible from the company's outlet at Westpunt. Ocean Encounters offers a vast menu of scheduled shore and boat dives and packages, as well as certified PADI instruction. In July the dive center sponsors a kids' sea camp in conjunction with the Sea Aquarium. ✉ *Lions Dive & Beach Resort, Seaquarium Beach, Bapor Kibra z/n* ☎ *5999/461–8131* ⊕ *www.oceanencounters.com.*

FISHING

Let's Fish. Let's Fish, a 50-foot, fully rigged fishing boat, can accommodate groups of up to 11 people on half-day or full-day fishing trips to Klein Curaçao or Banda Abou in search of dolphinfish, marlin, wahoo, and more. ✉ *Caracasbaaiweg 407N, Caracas Bay* ☎ *5999/561–1812, 5999/747–4489* ⊕ *www.letsfish.net.*

Pro Marine Yacht Services. With seven fishing vessels among the 14 yachts (and their captains) under his purview, Captain J.R. Van Hutten, nicknamed Captain Jaro, of Pro Marine Yacht Services, is *the* man to see about deep-sea fishing excursions and other fishing trips or parties. Some deals offer free pickup at your hotel. Most boats keep your catch, so check in advance if you want it. You can book the 54-foot yacht *War Eagle,* captained by Jaro himself, and head out in search of marlin, barracuda, mahimahi, and wahoo. ✉ *Warawaraweg 7, Van Engelen* ☎ *5999/560–2081.*

GOLF

Blue Bay Curaçao Golf & Beach Resort. In the mood to hit the greens? Try the links at Blue Bay Curaçao Golf & Beach Resort. This 18-hole, par-72 course beckons experts and novices alike. Facilities include a golf shop, locker rooms, and a snack bar. Greens fees range from $90 to $110 in high season, and you can rent carts, clubs, and shoes. If you'd like to drive your game to a new level, take a lesson from the house pro ($50 for a half hour). ✉ *Landhuis Blauw, Blue Bay z/n* ☎ *5999/868–1755* ⊕ *golf.bluebay-curacao.com.*

Old Quarry Golf Course. The Old Quarry Golf Course belies its name, as it's actually a lush, 18-hole, par-72 course designed by Pete Dye with some incredible vistas. There are a full range of facilities, and with the Hyatt Regency nearby, drinks and fine dining are mere steps away. Greens fees range from $55 to $175 in high season, and you can rent carts, clubs, and shoes. ✉ *Santa Barbara Plantation, Porta Blancu, Nieuwpoort z/n* ☎ *5999/840–6886* ⊕ *www.santabarbaraplantation.com.*

GUIDED TOURS

Most tour operators have pickups at the major hotels, but if your hotel is outside the standard zone, there may be an additional charge of around $5. Tours are available in several languages, including English.

Atlantis Adventures. The so-called Trolley Train visits historic sites in Willemstad on a 1½-hour guided tour. This tour begins at Ft. Amsterdam, and there's no hotel pickup. ⊠ *Hilton Curaçao, J.F. Kennedy Blvd., Box 2133, Piscadera Bay* ☎ *5999/461–0011* ⊕ *www.atlantissubmarines. com/curacao.*

Dutch Dream Adventures. Dutch Dream Adventures targets the action seeker with guided canoe and kayak safaris, mountain-bike excursions through Christoffel National Park for groups of 10 or more, or custom-designed tours to suit your group's interests. ☎ *5999/461–9393* ⊕ *www. dutchdreamcuracao.com.*

Explore Curaçao. Although it's aimed primarily at incentive and convention travelers, Explore Curaçao can arrange any activities on the island, from airport transfers to island adventure tours. ⊠ *E-Commerce Park Unit B-07, E-Zone Vredenberg, Willemstad* ☎ *5999/433–8814* ⊕ *www. explore-international.com.*

Peter Trips. Peter Trips offers full-day island tours departing from the hotels Tuesday, Wednesday, Friday, and Sunday at 9 am, with visits to many points of interest, including Ft. Amsterdam, Spanish Water, Scharloo, and Ft. Nassau. The cost is $50, and lunch is included. East-side half-day tours and a beach trip are offered Monday for $25 and $45, respectively. ☎ *5999/561–5368, 5999/465–2703* ⊕ *www.petertrips.com.*

Taber Tours. Among the favorites at Taber Tours is the Christoffel National Park–Cas Abou Beach combo: start the day with a guided hike up Mt. Christoffel followed by a tour of the park, and wind up at the beach to relax or snorkel. ⊠ *Kaya Schilling 170, Willemstad* ☎ *5999/868–7012* ⊕ *www.tabertours.com.*

Yellow Tourism Solutions. Yellow Tourism Solutions offers a full range of half- and full-day tours, whether you want to check out town, beaches, or historical sites, or head out with a group for horseback riding, diving, or snorkeling. The company's Yellow Jeep Safari takes you to Christoffel National Park aboard a bright yellow Land Rover, driven by a guide who will take you off the beaten (and paved) path, deep into the park's natural terrain. ⊠ *Curaçao Marriott Beach Resort, Piscadera Bay* ☎ *5999/562–4895* ⊕ *www.tourism-curacao.com.*

WALKING TOURS

When making reservations for any tour, mention that you speak English.

Anko van der Woude. Walking tours of historic Otrobanda, focusing on the unique architecture of this old section of town, are led by architect Anko van der Woude upon request. ☎ *5999/461–3554.*

Eveline van Arkel. The Talk of the Town tour with Eveline van Arkel will take you through historical Punda to visit sites including Ft. Amsterdam, the restored Fort Church, the Queen Emma pontoon bridge, and the Mikvé Israel-Emanuel Synagogue (call for reservations; English tours are on Tuesday at 9:30 am). ⊠ *Punda, Willemstad* ☎ *5999/747–4349, 5999/562–1861.*

Gigi. Gigi leads expert tours of Punda focusing on Jewish heritage, including an insider's look at the synagogue. ⊠ *Punda, Willemstad* ☎ *5999/697–0290.*

SEA EXCURSIONS

Many sailboats and motorboats offer sunset cruises and daylong snorkeling and picnic trips to Klein Curaçao, the uninhabited island between Curaçao and Bonaire, and other destinations. Prices are around $50 to $90 for a half-day trip (including food and drinks).

Jonalisa. The half-day lunch and snorkel trip on the *Jonalisa*, a 54-foot catamaran, features sailing, snorkeling, and swimming. It includes an open bar and barbecue lunch. ☎ *5999/560–1887* ⊕ *www.bountyadventures.com.*

Insulinde. One option aboard the 120-foot Dutch sailing ketch *Insulinde* is a snorkeling-and–scenic tour combo, capped off by a return cruise into the sunset, for $55. ☎ *5999/560–1340* ⊕ *www.insulinde.com.*

Mermaid. The *Mermaid* is a 66-foot motor yacht that carries up to 60 people to Klein Curaçao three times a week. A buffet lunch, beer, and soft drinks are provided at the boat's exclusive beach house, which has picnic tables, shade huts, and facilities. ☎ *5999/560–1530* ⊕ *www.mermaidboattrips.com.*

Miss Ann. The 76-foot *Miss Ann* motorboat offers snorkeling or diving, moonlight, and party trips for up to 100 people. ☎ *5999/767–1579* ⊕ *www.missannboattrips.com.*

Seaworld Explorer. For a unique vantage point, soak up the local marine life on a 1½-hour-long tour of the coral reefs aboard the glass-bottom, semisubmersible *Seaworld Explorer.* ☎ *5999/461–0011* ⊕ *www.atlantissubmarines.com/curacao/explorer.*

WATER SPORTS

Caribbean Sea Sports. Caribbean Sea Sports runs a tight ship when it comes to all sorts of water sports, including kayaking, windsurfing, banana boats, tube rides, diving, and snorkeling. ⊠ *Curaçao Marriott Beach Resort, Piscadera Bay* ☎ *5999/462–2620* ⊕ *www.caribseasports.com.*

Let's Go Watersports. Captain "Goodlife" at Let's Go Watersports will help you plan kayaking and other boat outings so you can live it up on the water and snorkel in some special spots. He also grills up a tasty lunch at the dock. ⊠ *Santa Cruz Beach 1, Santa Cruz* ☎ *5999/520–1147, 5999/864–0438.*

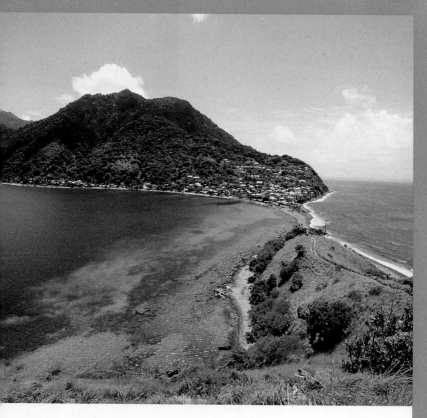

Dominica

WORD OF MOUTH

"There are some fantastic snorkeling sites in Dominica. Best of which I can remember is called Champagne Beach. The reef at Champagne Beach lies under a sulphur spring which drops bubbles up the surface. This place is seriously amazing and is worth a visit."

—caribbeanexpert

WELCOME TO DOMINICA

Dominica Passage

Capucin Pt.

Morne Aux Diables National Park

Toucari Beach and Reef

Morne Aux Diables

Vieille Case

Hodges

Pointe Baptiste

Northeast Coast

Cabrits National Park

Douglas Bay

Hampstead Beach

L'Anse Tortue

Woodford Hill Bay

Cabrits Drop-off

Purple Beach

Indian Rd.

21

Portsmouth

20

Calibishie

Fort Shirley

Bense

Melville Hall Airport

Marigot

Londonderry Bay

Prince Rupert Bay

Picard Beach

Indian River

Indian R.

Picard R.

23 22

Syndicate Rd.

Pt. Ronde

Morne Diablotin

19

Dublanc

Morne Diablotin National Park

Colihaut

Carib Indian Territory

Nose Reef

18

Brain Coral Garden

Castle Bruce

Salisbury Falls

17 16

Salisbury

Mero

Layou River

Castaways

Emerald Pool

Petit Soufrière Bay

Rodney's Rock

Macoucherie River

Rosalie

Bout Sable

Mahaut

Pont Casse

Pringles Bay

10

Morne Trois Pitons National Park

Cochrane

Laudat

12

Pt. Gire

Canefield Airport

14

15

Trafalgar

10 9

La Pla

13

Woodbridge Bay

Wotten Waven Rd.

8 11

Petite Savanne/Delices Rd.

6 7

1 7

Roseau

1 2 3

4

Roseau

5 8

9

Pointe Michel

Champagne

Grand Bay

Soufrière Bay

Soufrière

Soufrière Marine Park

Scotts Head Village

Scotts Head

Martinique Passage

Caribbean Sea

0 ———— 4 miles
0 ———— 6 km

Dominica is far removed from the concerns of the rest of the world. Pleasures are simple rather than sybaritic, made all the more enjoyable by the traditional polite ways of the islanders. It's a land of mountains, fresh-flowing rivers, greenery, and waterfalls.

THE NATURE ISLAND

The island is 29 miles (47 km) long and 16 miles (26 km) wide, with approximately 72,900 citizens. Because it was a British colony (achieving independence in 1978), you may wonder about the prevalence of French names. Although the English first claimed Dominica in 1627, the French controlled it from 1632 until 1759, when it passed back into English hands.

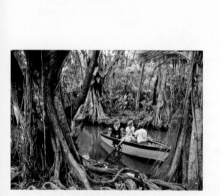

Restaurants ▼		Hotels ▼	
Cocorico	**7**	Anchorage Hotel	**3**
Cornerhouse Café	**5**	Beau Rive	**18**
Crystal Terrace	**8**	Calibishie Lodges	**21**
Garage Bar and Grill	**3**	Castle Comfort Lodge	**4**
Guiyave	**6**	Cocoa Cottage	**11**
Miranda's Corner	**10**	Crescent Moon	**12**
Pearl's Cuisine	**2**	Evergreen Hotel	**5**
Port of Call	**1**	Fort Young Hotel	**1**
Rainforest Restaurant	**9**	Garraway Hotel	**2**
Waterfront Restaurant	**4**	Hummingbird Inn	**14**
		Itassi	**7**
		Jungle Bay	**13**
		Papillote	**10**
		Picard Beach Cottages	**22**
		Rainforest Shangri-La Resort	**15**
		Red Rock Haven	**20**
		Roseau Valley Hotel	**6**
		Secret Bay	**23**
		Silks Hotel	**19**
		Sunset Bay Club	**17**
		Tamarind Tree	**16**
		Tia's Bamboo Cottages	**8**
		Zandoli Inn	**9**

DOMINICA

10

KEY	
	Beaches
	Cruise Ship Terminal
	Dive Sites
1	*Restaurants*
1	*Hotels*

TOP REASONS TO VISIT DOMINICA

1 Fewer Crowds: Dominica is a delightful respite from the more crowded, commercial islands.

2 Unspoiled Nature: The island's natural environment is the major draw.

3 Great Dives: Diving pristine reefs full of colorful sea life or in bubbly, volcanic water is amazing.

4 Natural Spas: Dominica has an abundance of natural sulfur pools, some of which have become makeshift spas.

DOMINICA BEACHES

Most of Dominica's beaches are in the north and east; they are windswept, dramatic, and uncrowded, lending themselves more to relaxing than swimming. That is because many have undercurrents.

(Above) Pointe Baptiste (Bottom right) Champagne Beach (Top right) Hampstead Beach

However, slightly farther north there are beautiful secluded beaches and coves. Although northeast-coast beaches offer excellent shallow swimming, their wind-tossed beauty can be dangerous; there are sometimes strong currents with the whipped-cream waves. From these beaches you can see the islands of Marie-Galante and Les Saintes and parts of Guadeloupe. On the south-west coast, beaches are fewer and made mostly of black sand and rounded volcanic rocks. Swimming off these rocky shores has its pleasures, too: the water is usually as flat as a lake, deep and blue, and especially good for snorkeling. In general, the west coast is more for scuba diving and snorkeling than for beachgoing.

VOLCANIC SAND

As a volcanic island, Dominica offers many powder-fine black-sand beaches. On the far north you'll find white- or brown-sand beaches with coves often speckled with volcanic sand. The beaches of the southwest coast are mostly black sand and volcanic rock.

🌀 **Champagne.** On the west coast, just south of the village of Pointe Michel, this stony beach is hailed as one of the best spots for swimming, snorkeling, and diving but not for sunning. It gets its name from volcanic vents that constantly puff steam into the sea, which makes you feel as if you are swimming in warm champagne. A boardwalk leads to the beach from Soufrière/Scotts Head Marine Reserve. ⊠ *1 mile (1½ km) south of Pointe Michel, Soufrière.*

🌀 **Hampstead Beach.** This isolated gold-with-speckled-black-sand shoreline on the northeast coast actually encompasses three bays. It is divided into two beaches. The Red River meets the sea at Hampstead Beach I. In *Pirates of the Caribbean: Dead Man's Chest,* Johnny Depp is chased by natives here. The palm tree–lined Hampstead Beach II is on the sheltered and calm Batibou Bay. Come here to relax, suntan, and swim. A 4x4 is the preferred mode of transportation to get here or be prepared hike in from the road. Both beaches ooze with charm and are worth the effort. There are no facilities, so it is BYOBC (bring your own beach chair). ⊠ *Off Indian Rd., west of Calibishie.*

L'Anse Tortue. On the northeast coast, this isolated, golden-sand beach with dabs of black is also known as Turtle Bay. It is a favorite for egg-laying turtles and for those who want seclusion

without having to drive all the way out to Hampstead Beach. It sits on a cove just past Woodford Hill, an easy, although sometimes steep, walk down from the road. There is no sign marking the trail or the beach, but it starts just across the road from a brown-building snack shop sporting Fanta signs. ⊠ *East of Calibishie.*

Mero Beach. The silver-gray stretch of beach on the west coast is just outside the village of Mero. It's the closest beach to Roseau, so the entire community comes to party here on Sunday. It's good for sunbathing and swimming. ⊠ *Near Roseau, Mero.*

🌀 **Pointe Baptiste.** Extravagantly shaped red-sandstone boulders surround this beautiful golden-sand beach. Access is a 15-minute walk, entering through private property (Pointe Baptiste Guest House or Red Rock Haven), so the beach is quiet and unpopulated. Relax, take a dip, climb the incredible rock formations, or grab a snack at the Escape Beach Bar & Grill. ⊠ *Calibishie.*

Scotts Head. At the southernmost tip of the island, a small landmass is connected to the mainland by a narrow stretch of stony beach. It's a fantastic spot for snorkeling. Lunch at one of the village restaurants, where you'll always find fresh-caught red snapper and mahimahi. ⊠ *Near Soufrière, Scotts Head Village.*

10

THE ORIGINAL CARIBBEANS

Blame Christopher Columbus: his logs give accounts of the "gentle, laughing" Arawak and the "ferocious, cannibalistic" Carib, both type-casts that pigeonholed the Caribbean's two indigenous peoples and persist to this day. Historians have had to wade through a lot of colonial romanticism to get at the truth.

Archaeologists have determined that the first Amerindian migration to the islands took place around 1000 BC from northern South America. "War and Peace" could describe the divergence between the agrarian Arawak and the more militant Carib. The Arawak—the umbrella term encompassed many smaller groups, most notably the Taíno people on the larger islands—were easily subjugated by Spanish explorers; the Carib, less so, but eventually they succumbed, too. Warfare and disease—the indigenous peoples had never encountered smallpox until the Europeans' arrival—caused populations of both groups to dwindle to a few thousand by the end of the 18th century.

TODAY'S INDIGENOUS PEOPLES

Common wisdom holds that the Arawak are extinct and the Carib subsist today only in Dominica's Carib Territory. Neither is exactly true. A few thousand Arawak people survive, but in northern South America. Most Puerto Ricans and Arubans can also claim Arawak ancestry. The enclave in Dominica, established in 1903, has its own governing body for a population of 3,000, but smaller Carib communities live in Trinidad and St. Vincent. Descendants of Carib intermarriage with African slaves—the so-called "Black Caribs"—live on as Central America's Garífuna people.

Language. Carib warfare resulted in the capture of many Arawak women. As a result, early Spanish arrivals were puzzled by what appeared to be gender-specific languages, with men speaking the Carib Kalinago language, and women, one of several Arawakan tongues. Historians debate the notion of a persistent gender-communication divide between what the British would later call Island Carib and Island Arawak. The languages gave several of the islands their names: Bequia ("cloud"), Canouan ("turtle"), Carriacou ("reef"), Saba ("rock"), and Tobago ("tobacco"). The English words barbecue, hurricane, and potato have their roots in indigenous Caribbean languages, too.

Religion. The Carib adopted many of the tenets of Arawak religion, essentially a system of animism and ancestor worship. Shamans held the keys to unlocking contact with the spirit world, thus occupying esteemed roles in their communities. Tobacco played a prominent role in worship ceremonies. (*Tabaco* is yet another Amerindian word that found its way into English.) Petroglyphs, rock carvings dedicated to objects of indigenous veneration, can be seen today in Puerto Rico, St. Kitts, St. John, and Grenada.

Innovations. With the construction of their *canoas*—source of the word canoe—indigenous Caribbean peoples

were able to establish interisland transport. (The Arawak used their vessels for trade; the Carib, for warfare.) And the next time you laze in a hammock, acknowledge the Arawak. *Hamacas* were a regular fixture in their homes.

Women. Carib and Arawak women participated in surprisingly egalitarian societies. Women were eligible to be a community's *cacique* (chief) and frequently served on its ruling council. Society did, however, ascribe gender roles: men went off to war while women tended agriculture and took care of domestic chores.

Food. Fishing was a major source of nourishment for the Carib and Arawak. Perhaps no food is more identified with Caribbean indigenous peoples than the cassava or yuca, a starchy tuber and a major source of carbohydrates, with one major god even being the patron of this important crop.

Cannibalism? What of the charges of cannibalism among the Carib people? Columbus wrote that he saw the practice, but most historians side with today's Carib descendants who insist it never went on. They suggest that Spanish explorers had religious and economic motives for perpetuating the myth of cannibalism. Conversion to Christianity and even slavery would have to be better than such "barbarism" in their eyes.
—Jeffrey Van Fleet

Wedged between the two French islands of Guadeloupe and Martinique, Dominica (pronounced dom-in-ee-ka) is as close to the Garden of Eden as you're likely to get. Wild orchids, anthurium lilies, ferns, heliconia, and myriad fruit trees sprout profusely. Much of the interior is still covered by luxuriant rain forest and remains inaccessible by road.

With this bountiful natural abundance, there's also a lot of active watching—flying birds and butterflies, turtles hatching, plus jumping dolphins and breaching whales. Even when you're not looking, something is sure to capture your gaze. The sensory overload isn't just visual. Your soul may be soothed by the refreshing smell of clean river water and cleaner air, your taste buds will be tantalized by the freshest fruits and vegetables, and your skin will be caressed by the purest natural soaps.

A natural fortress, the island protected the Caribs (the region's original inhabitants) against European colonization. The rugged northeast is still reserved as home to the last survivors of the Caribs, along with their traditions and mythology.

Dominica—with a population of approximately 72,900—did eventually become a British colony. It attained independence in November 1978 and has a seat in the United Nations as the central Caribbean's only natural World Heritage Site. Its official language is English, although most locals communicate with each other in Creole; roads are driven on the left; family and place-names are a mélange of English, Carib, and French; and the economy is still heavily dependent on agriculture.

With fewer than 76,500 overnight visitors annually, Dominica is a little-known destination with no major hotel chains, but the island's forestry service has preserved more national forests, marine reserves, and parks, per capita, than almost anywhere on Earth.

Dominica is an ideal place to be active—hike, bike, trek, kayak, dive, snorkel, or sail in marine reserves. Explore the rain forests, waterfalls, and geothermal springs, or search for whales and dolphins. Discover Dominica's vibrant Carib culture. To experience Dominica is really to know Earth as it was created.

LOGISTICS

Getting to Dominica: There are no nonstops from the United States, so you'll have to transfer in the British Virgin Islands, Antigua, Barbados, Martinique, San Juan, or St. Lucia. There is also a ferry (90 minutes) from Guadeloupe or Martinique.

Hassle Factor: High.

On the Ground: Taxis and minibuses are available at the airports and in Roseau as well as at most hotels and guesthouses. Rates are fixed by the government (if you share a taxi with other passengers going in the same direction, you can negotiate a special price; a trip from Melville Hall Airport to Roseau can cost as little as $26 per person). Taxi drivers also offer tours anywhere on the island beginning at $25 to $30 an hour for up to four people; a four- to five-hour island tour costs approximately $150. It's best to get a recommendation from your hotel. You can recognize a taxi or minibus by the H, HA, and HB plates; simply flag them down or make your way to the nearest bus stop.

PLANNING

WHEN TO GO

Dominicans boast that they have the most spontaneous carnival in the region, Mas Domnik. It's fun to join a band, get all costumed and painted, and revel in the streets during Carnival Monday and Tuesday. Celebrations usually heat up the last 10 days or so before Ash Wednesday. Independence Day on November 3 celebrates not only Dominica's independence from Great Britain, but also the Creole culture. On the last weekend in October or first weekend of November, the awesome, three-day Annual World Creole Music Festival draws performers and Creole music enthusiasts from around the globe.

The high season is December to April, when many Americans and Europeans come. May 1 to November 1 is hurricane season.

GETTING HERE AND AROUND

10

AIR TRAVEL

There are no nonstops from the United States.

Aiport Contacts Canefield Airport. Canefield Airport is served by only a few small Caribbean-based airlines. ⊠ *DCF, Canefield* ☎ *767/449–1199.* **Melville Hall Airport.** Melville Hall Airport, where most flights arrive, is 75 minutes from Roseau. ⊠ *DOM, Marigot* ☎ *767/445–7100.*

Airline Contacts American/American Eagle ☎ *767/446–0628, 800/433–7300* ⊕ *www.aa.com.* **Conviasa** ☎ *767/448–2181* ⊕ *www.conviasa.aero.* **LIAT** ☎ *767/445–7242 for baggage inquiries, 767/445–8143* ⊕ *www.liatairline.com.*

BOAT AND FERRY TRAVEL

There is a ferry (90 minutes) from Guadeloupe or Martinique.

Express des Isles. Express des Isles has regularly scheduled interisland jet catamaran ferry service connecting Dominica to Guadeloupe, Martinique, and St. Lucia. Generally, the ferry arrives and departs at the Roseau Ferry Terminal on Monday, Wednesday, Friday, Saturday, and

Sunday from Guadeloupe; it continues south to Martinique, as well as St. Lucia, on specific days. The round-trip crossing costs €74.80 to Martinique, takes approximately 90 minutes, and offers superb views of the other islands. ☏ 767/448–2181 ⊕ *www.express-des-iles.com.*

CAR TRAVEL

Unless you are staying in Roseau or doing extensive guided tours, a car may be a necessity. Cabs can be very expensive. Daily car-rental rates begin at about $50 to $60 per day (weekly and long-term rates can be negotiated). A refundable $800 to $1,800 deposit or credit card confirmation is required at the time of pickup. You'll need to buy a visitor's driving permit for $12 at one of the airports or at the Traffic Division office on High Street in Roseau or at vehicle-rental offices. Gasoline stations are all over the island; at this writing, gas costs about $5.50 per gallon. Driving in Dominica is on the left side, though you can rent vehicles with a steering wheel on either the left or the right.

Contacts **Best Deal Rent-A-Car** ✉ *15 Hanover St., Roseau* ☏ *767/449–9204.* **Courtesy Car Rental** ✉ *10 Winston Lane, Goodwill* ☏ *767/448–7763* ⊕ *www. dominicacarrentals.com.*

TAXIS

Contacts **Dominica Taxi Association.** Dominica Taxi Association has fixed rates from the airport. From Melville Hall to Canefield/Roseau/ Newtown/Portsmouth/Picard, rates are $26. Other destinations run from $15–$40. ☏ *767/449–9173.* **Nature Island Taxi Association.** Nature Island Taxi Association has fixed rates from Melville Hall Airport to different parts of the island. ☏ *767/440–4439.*

ESSENTIALS

Banks and Exchange Services The official currency is the Eastern Caribbean dollar (XCD). The exchange rate hovers around XCD $2.70 to the US$1. U.S. dollars and major credit cards are widely accepted. You can find ATMs in all the banks in Roseau and airports as well as some in larger villages such as Portsmouth. They dispense EC dollars only and accept international bank cards.

Electricity 220–240 volts, AC/50 cycles. North American appliances require an adapter and transformer; however, many establishments provide these and often have dual-voltage fittings.

Emergencies Ambulance, police, and fire ☏ *999.*

Passport Requirements Valid passport plus a return or onward ticket.

Phones To call Dominica from the United States, dial the area code (767) and the local access code (44), followed by the five-digit local number. On the island, dial only the seven-digit number that follows the area code.

Taxes and Service Charges The departure-embarkation tax is EC$55 or about $21.85, payable in cash only at the airport at the time of departure from the island. Hotels collect a 15% government hotel occupancy tax and restaurants a 15% government V.A.T. (value-added tax).

Tipping Most hotels and restaurants add a 10% service charge to your bill. A 5% tip for exceptionally good service on top of the service charge is always welcome; otherwise just tip accordingly.

ACCOMMODATIONS

There are few upscale options in Dominica and absolutely no large resorts. Most accommodations are in small lodges and guesthouses.

HOTEL AND RESTAURANT PRICES

Prices in the restaurant reviews are the average cost of a main course at dinner or, if dinner is not served, at lunch; taxes and service charges are generally included. Prices in the hotel reviews are the lowest cost of a standard double room in high season, excluding taxes, service charges, and meal plans (except at all-inclusives). Prices for rentals are the lowest per-night cost for a one-bedroom unit in high season.

VISITOR INFORMATION

Contact **Discover Dominica Authority** (*Dominica Tourist Office*). ☎ 767/448–2045, 866/522–4057 *in U.S.* ⊕ *www.discoverdominica.com.*

WEDDINGS

Two days' minimum residency. A valid passport, original birth certificate, and divorce decree or death certificate for the former spouse (if applicable) is required. The parties must sign a statutory declaration on marital status, which must be obtained and sworn in Dominica in the presence of a local lawyer. At least two witnesses must be present at the ceremony.

EXPLORING DOMINICA

Despite the small size of this island, it can take a couple of hours to travel between the popular destinations. Many sights are isolated and difficult to find; you may be better off taking an organized excursion. If you do go it alone, drive carefully; roads can be narrow and winding. Plan at least eight hours to see the highlights. To fully experience the island, set aside about five days so you can enjoy the water and take some hikes.

WHAT TO SEE

� **Cabrits National Park.** Along with Brimstone Hill in St. Kitts, Shirley Heights in Antigua, and Ft. Charlotte in St. Vincent, the Cabrits National Park's Ft. Shirley ruins are among the most significant historic sites in the Caribbean. Just north of the town of Portsmouth, this 1,300-acre park includes a marine park and herbaceous swamps, which are home to several species of rare birds and plants. At the heart of the park is the Ft. Shirley military complex. Built by the British between 1770 and 1815, it once comprised 50 major structures, including storehouses that were also quarters for 700 men. With the help of the Royal Navy (which sends sailors ashore to work on the site each time a ship is in port) and local volunteers, historian Dr. Lennox Honychurch restored the fort and its surroundings, incorporating a small museum that highlights the natural and historic aspects of the park and an open canteen-style restaurant. ⊠ *Portsmouth* ☎ *No phone* ✉ *$5* ⊙ *Museum open daily 9–4.*

� **Carib Indian Territory.** In 1903, after centuries of conflict, the Caribbean's
★ first settlers, the Kalinago (more popularly known as the Caribs), were

granted approximately 3,700 acres of land on the island's northeast coast. Here a hardened lava formation, **L'Escalier Tête Chien** (Snake's Staircase), runs down into the Atlantic. The name is derived from a snake whose head resembles that of a dog. The ocean alongside Carib Territory is particularly fierce. The shore is full of countless coves and inlets. According to Carib legend, every night the nearby Londonderry Islets transform into grand canoes to take the spirits of the dead out to sea.

A chief administers the Carib Territory on which about 3,000 natives reside. The reservation's Catholic church in Salybia has a canoe as its altar, which was designed by Dr. Lennox Honychurch, a local historian, author, and artist.

The Kalinago resemble native South Americans and are mostly farmers and fishermen. Others are entrepreneurs who have opened restaurants, guesthouses, and little shops that offer exquisite baskets and hand-crafted items. Craftspeople have retained their knowledge of basket weaving, wood carving, and canoe building through generations. They fashion long, elegant canoes from the trunk of a single *gommier* tree.

Kalinago Barana Autê. You might catch canoe builders at work at Kalinago Barana Autê, the Carib Territory's place to learn about Kalinago customs, history, and culture. A guided, 45-minute tour explores the village, stopping along the way to see some traditional dances and to learn about plants, dugout canoes, basket weaving, and cassava bread making. The path offers wonderful viewpoints of the Atlantic and a chance to glimpse Isukulati Falls. ⊠ *Crayfish River, Carib Territory* ☎ *767/445–7979* ⊕ *www.kalinagobaranaaute.com* ✉ *Basic package is about $10* ⊗ *Daily 9–5.*

☾ **Emerald Pool.** Quite possibly the most visited nature attraction on the island, this emerald-green pool fed by a 50-foot waterfall is an easy trip to make. To reach this spot in the vast Morne Trois Pitons National Park, you follow a trail that starts at the side of the road near the reception center (it's an easy 20-minute walk). Along the way, there are lookout points with views of the windward (Atlantic) coast and the forested interior. If you don't want a crowd, check whether there are cruise ships in port before going out, as this spot is popular with cruise-ship tour groups.

☾ **Indian River.** The mouth of the Indian River, which flows into the ocean at Portsmouth, was once a Carib Indian settlement. A rowboat ride down this river, which was featured in *Pirates of the Caribbean: Dead Man's Chest,* is both relaxing and educational. The river is lined with trees whose buttress roots spread up to 20 feet. Clear, brackish water is a playground for young barracudas and crayfish. Except for singing yellow warblers, flitting hummingbirds, or wing-flapping egrets, there is an eerie silence. To arrange such a trip, stop by the visitor center in Portsmouth and ask for one of the "Indian River boys," of the Portsmouth Indian River Tour Guides Association. Most boat trips take you up as far as Rahjah's Jungle Bar. You can usually do an optional guided walking tour of the swamplands and the remnants of one of Dominica's oldest plantations. Tours last one to three hours, for roughly $20 per person, but the actual price depends on your guide.

Morne Aux Diables. This peak soars 2,826 feet above sea level and slopes down to Toucari and Douglas bays and long stretches of dark-sand beach on the north side of the island. To reach it, take the road along the Caribbean coast. It twists by coconut, cocoa, and banana groves, past fern-festooned embankments, over rivers, and into villages where brightly painted shanties are almost as colorful as all the flora and fauna.

Morne Diablotin National Park. Here Dominica's highest mountain, Morne Diablotin, soars 4,747 feet. The peak takes its name from a bird known in English as the black-capped petrel. Now extinct on the island, it was prized by hunters in the 18th century. Dominica is still a major birding destination with many exotic—and endangered—species such as the green-and-purple Sisserou parrot (*Amazona imperialis*) and the Jaco, or red-neck, parrot (*Amazona arausiaca*). Before this national park was established, its Syndicate Nature Trail was aided by some 6,000 schoolchildren—each donated 25¢ to protect the area's habitat. The west-coast road (at the bend near Dublanc) runs through three types of forest and leads to the park. The trail offers a casual walk; just bring a sweater and binoculars. But the five- to eight-hour hike up Morne Diablotin is no walk in the park. You will need a guide, sturdy hiking shoes, warm clothing, and a backpack with refreshments and a change of clothes (including socks). All should be wrapped in plastic to keep them dry.

Bertrand Jno Baptiste. A good guide for Morne Diablotin is local ornithology expert Bertrand Jno Baptiste. ☎ 767/245–4768.

★ **Morne Trois Pitons National Park.** A UNESCO World Heritage Site, this 17,000-acre swath of lush, mountainous land in the south-central interior (covering 9% of Dominica) is the island's crown jewel. Named after one of the highest (4,600 feet) mountains on the island, it contains the island's famous "boiling lake," majestic waterfalls, and cool mountain lakes. There are four types of vegetation zones here. Ferns grow 30 feet tall, wild orchids sprout from trees, sunlight leaks through green canopies, and a gentle mist rises over the jungle floor. A system of trails has been developed in the park, and the Division of Forestry and Wildlife works hard to maintain them—with no help from the excessive rainfall and the profusion of vegetation that seems to grow right before your eyes. Access to the park is possible from most points, though the easiest approaches are via the small mountaintop villages of Laudat (pronounced lau-*dah*) and Cochrane.

About 5 miles (8 km) out of Roseau, the Wotten Waven Road branches off toward Sulphur Springs, where you can see the belching, sputtering, and gurgling releases of volcanic hot springs. At the base of Morne Micotrin you can find two crater lakes: the first, at 2,500 feet above sea level, is **Freshwater Lake.** According to a local legend, it's haunted by a vindictive mermaid and a monstrous serpent. Farther on is **Boeri Lake,** fringed with greenery and with purple hyacinths floating on its surface.

10

Emerald Pool is one of Dominica's most popular natural attractions.

On your way to Boiling Lake you pass through the **Valley of Desolation,** a sight that definitely lives up to its name. Harsh sulfuric fumes have destroyed virtually all the vegetation in what must once have been a lush forested area. Small hot and cold streams with water of various colors—black, purple, red, orange—web the valley. Stay on the trail to avoid breaking through the crust that covers the hot lava. During this hike you'll pass rivers where you can refresh yourself with a dip (a particular treat is a soak in a hot-water stream on the way back). At the beginning of the Valley of Desolation trail is the **TiTou Gorge,** where you can swim in the pool or relax in the hot-water springs along one side. If you're a strong swimmer, you can head up the gorge to a cave (it's about a five-minute swim) that has a magnificent waterfall; a crack in the cave about 50 feet above permits a stream of sunlight to penetrate the cavern.

Also in the national park are some of the island's most spectacular waterfalls. The 45-minute hike to **Sari Sari Falls,** accessible through the east-coast village of La Plaine, can be hair-raising. But the sight of water cascading some 150 feet into a large pool is awesome. So large are these falls that you feel the spray from hundreds of yards away. Just beyond the village of Trafalgar and up a short hill is the reception facility, where you can purchase passes to the national park and find guides to take you on a rain-forest trek to the twin **Trafalgar Falls;** the 125-foot-high waterfall is called the Father, and the wider, 95-foot-high one, the Mother. If you like a little challenge, let your guide take you to the riverbed and the cool pools at the base of the falls (check whether there's a cruise ship in port before setting out; this sight is popular with the tour operators). You need a guide for the arduous 75-minute hike to **Middleham Falls.** It's best if you start at Laudat (the turnoff for the trailhead is just before the village); the trip is much longer from Cochrane Village. The trail takes you to another spectacular waterfall, where water cascades 100 feet over boulders and vegetation and then into an ice-cold pool (a swim here is absolutely exhilarating). Guides for these hikes are available at the trailheads; still, it's best to arrange a tour before even setting out.

Boiling Lake. The undisputed highlight of the park is the Boiling Lake. Reputedly one of the world's largest such lakes, it's a cauldron of gurgling gray-blue water, 70 yards wide and of unknown depth, with water temperatures from 180°F to 197°F. Although generally believed to be a volcanic crater, the lake is actually a flooded fumarole—a crack through which gases escape from the molten lava below. As many visitors discovered in late 2004, the "lake" can sometimes dry up, though it fills again within a few months and, shortly after that, once more starts to boil. It has returned to its pre-2004 levels. The two- to four-hour (one way) hike up to the lake is challenging (on a very rainy day, be prepared to slip and slide the whole way up and back). You'll need attire appropriate for a strenuous hike, and a guide is a must. Most guided trips start early (no later than 8:30 am) for this all-day, 7-mile (11-km) round-trip trek.

Northeast Coast. Steep cliffs, dramatic reefs, and rivers that swirl down through forests of mangroves and fields of coconut define this section of Dominica. The road along the Atlantic, with its red cliffs, whipped-cream waves, and windswept trees, crosses the Hatton Garden River before entering the village of Marigot. In the northeastern region there are numerous estates—old family holdings planted with fruit trees. Beyond Marigot and the Melville Hall Airport is the beautiful Londonderry Estate. The beach here is inspiring, with driftwood strewn about its velvety black sands, which part halfway where the Londonderry River spills into the Atlantic (swimming isn't advised because of strong currents, but a river bath here is a memorable treat). Farther along the coast, beyond the village of Wesley (which has a gas station and a shop that sells wonderful bread) and past Eden Estate, there are still more beautiful beaches and coves. The swimming is excellent at Woodford Hill Bay, Hodges Beach, Hampstead Estate, Batibou Bay, and L'Anse Tortue (Turtle Bay), where you might glimpse a turtle plodding on the beach to lay her eggs. At the charming community of Calibishie you'll find beach bars and restaurants, as well as laid-back villas and guesthouses. At Bense, a village in the interior just past Calibishie, you can take a connector road to Chaudiere, a beautiful swimming spot in a valley; the only crowd you're likely to encounter is a group of young villagers frolicking in the 15-foot-deep pool and diving off the 25-foot-high rocks.

Portsmouth. In 1782 Portsmouth was the site of the Battle of Les Saintes, a naval engagement between the French and the English. The English won the battle but lost the much tougher fight against malaria-carrying mosquitoes that bred in the nearby swamps. Once intended to be the capital of Dominica, thanks to its superb harbor on Prince Rupert Bay,

10

it saw as many as 400 ships in port at one time in its heyday, but on account of those swamps, Roseau, not Portsmouth, is the capital today. Maritime traditions are continued here by the yachting set, and a 2-mile (3-km) stretch of sandy beach fringed with coconut trees runs to the Picard Estate area. ⊠ *Portsmouth.*

Roseau. Although it's one of the smallest capitals in the Caribbean, Roseau has the highest concentration of inhabitants of any town in the eastern Caribbean. Caribbean vernacular architecture and a bustling marketplace transport visitors back in time. Although you can walk the entire town in about an hour, you'll get a much better feel for the place on a leisurely stroll.

For some years now, the Society for Historical Architectural Preservation and Enhancement (SHAPE) has organized programs and projects to preserve the city's architectural heritage. Several interesting buildings have already been restored. **Lilac House,** on Kennedy Avenue, has three types of gingerbread fretwork, latticed verandah railings, and heavy hurricane shutters. The **J.W. Edwards Building,** at the corner of Old and King George V streets, has a stone base and a wooden second-floor gallery. The **Old Market Plaza** is the center of Roseau's historic district, which was laid out by the French on a radial plan rather than a grid, so streets such as Hanover, King George V, and Old radiate from this area. South of the marketplace is the Fort Young Hotel, built as a British fort in the 18th century; the nearby statehouse, public library, and Anglican cathedral are also worth a visit. New developments at the bay front on Dame M.E. Charles Boulevard have brightened up the waterfront.

Botanical Gardens. The 40-acre Botanical Gardens, founded in 1891 as an annex of London's Kew Gardens, is a great place to relax, stroll, or watch a cricket match. In addition to the extensive collection of tropical plants and trees, there's also a parrot aviary. At the Forestry Division office, which is also on the garden grounds, you can find numerous publications on the island's flora, fauna, and national parks. The forestry officers are particularly knowledgeable on these subjects and can also recommend good hiking guides. ⊠ *Valley Rd.* ☎ *767/266–3811, 767/266–3812* ⊕ *www.da-academy.org/dagardens. html* ☜ *Free* ⊙ *Daily 6 am–7 pm.*

Dominica Museum. The old post office now houses the Dominica Museum. This labor of love by local writer and historian Dr. Lennox Honychurch contains furnishings, documents, prints, and maps that date back hundreds of years; you can also find an entire Carib hut as well as Carib canoes, baskets, and other artifacts. ⊠ *Dame M.E. Charles Blvd., opposite cruise-ship berth* ☎ *767/448–2401* ☜ *$3* ⊙ *Weekdays 9–4, Sat. 9–2; closed Sun. except when a cruise ship is in port* ⊠ *Southwest side of the island, Roseau.*

Soufrière. Tourism is quietly mingling with the laid-back lifestyle of the residents of this gently sunbaked village in the southwest, near one of the island's two marine reserves. Although it was first settled by French lumbermen in the 17th century, it's mainly fishermen you'll find here today. In the village sits one of the island's prettiest churches, a historic 18th-century Catholic church built of volcanic stone; the ruins of the

L. Rose Lime Oil factory; Sulphur Springs, with its hot mineral baths to the east; and some of the best diving and snorkeling on the island is within the **Soufrière/Scotts Head Marine Reserve.** To the west is Bois Cotlette (a historic plantation house) and to the south the Scotts Head Peninsula—at the island's southern tip—which separates the Caribbean from the Atlantic. So if there isn't enough treasure here to satisfy you, there's always the rain forest waiting to be challenged. ⊠ *Southern tip of the island, Soufrière.*

WHERE TO EAT

You can expect an abundance of vegetables, fruits, and root crops to appear on menus around the island. Dominica's economy, after all, is based on agriculture. Sweet ripe plantains, *kushkush* (cornmeal), yams, breadfruit, dasheen (also called taro), fresh fish, and chicken prepared at least a dozen different ways are all staples. The local drink is a spiced rum steeped with herbs such as anisette (called nanny) and *pweve* (lemongrass). Dominican cuisine is also famous for its use of local game, such as the *manicou* (a small opossum) and the agouti (a large indigenous rodent), but you'll have to be an intrepid diner to go that route. At the time of this writing, the government had banned mountain chicken (a euphemism for a large frog called *crapaud*) because of problems with disease.

What to Wear: Most Dominicans dress nicely but practically when eating out—for dinner it's shirts and trousers for men and modest dresses for women. During the day, nice shorts are acceptable at most places; beach attire is frowned upon unless you're eating on the beach.

$ ✕ **Cocorico.** It's hard to miss the umbrella-shaded chairs and tables at
ECLECTIC this Parisian-style café on a prominent bay-front corner in Roseau.
☕ Breakfast crepes, croissants, baguette sandwiches, and piping-hot café
★ au lait are available beginning at 8:30 am. Throughout the day you can relax indoors or out and enjoy any of the extensive menu selections with the perfect glass of wine, and you can even surf the Internet on its computers. In the cellar downstairs the Cocorico wine store has a reasonably priced selection from more than eight countries plus a wide assortment of pâtés and cheeses, crepes, sausages, cigars, French bread, and chocolates. ⑤ *Average main: $10* ⊠ *Bay Front at Kennedy Ave., Roseau* ☎ *767/449–8686* ⊕ *www.natureisle.com/cocorico/* ☉ *Closed Sun. unless ship is in port, then 10–4.*

$ ✕ **Cornerhouse Café.** This Internet café offers an eclectic menu to sustain
AMERICAN you while surfing: bagels with an assortment of toppings, delicious soups, vegetarian dishes, Mexican, fish, sandwiches, salads, cakes, and coffee. Computers are rented by the half hour (US$3); relax on soft chairs and flip through books and magazines while you wait. ⑤ *Average main: $8* ⊠ *Old and King George V Sts., Roseau* ☎ *767/449–9000* ⊕ *www.avirtualdominica.com/cornerhouse/home.htm* ▭ *No credit cards* ☉ *Mon–Sat 8:30–4.*

$$$$ ✕ **Crystal Terrace Restaurant & Bar.** You can find classic local food with
CARIBBEAN a very elegant twist at this restaurant in the Evergreen Hotel. Selections range from starters like fresh soup or salad dressed with local

10

produce to authentic creole and international main courses and, when in season, tasty crab backs. Breakfast, lunch, and dinner daily. On Friday evenings there is entertainment as well as a special menu. $ *Average main: $32* ✉ *Evergreen Hotel, Castle Comfort* ☎ *767/448–3288* ⊕ *www.evergreenhoteldominica.com/.*

$$$ ✕ **Garage Bar & Grill.** This former garage has become the only true grill ECLECTIC on the island. It boasts "cool drinks, great food." The menu includes prime steaks, pasta, and seafood as well as creole food and jerk chicken. The former digs are not forgotten, evidenced by the bar stools that are anchored by old tires, and a selection of vittles like the 4x4 (ribs) and 6 Cylinders (spicy chicken wings). In early evening it is a very happening place with the locals. Breakfast, lunch, and dinner are served. $ *Average main: $17* ✉ *15 Hanover St. at Kennedy Ave., Roseau* ☎ *767/448–5433.*

$$ ✕ **Guiyave.** This popular restaurant in a quaint Caribbean town house CARIBBEAN also has a shop downstairs serving a scrumptious selection of sweet and savory pastries, tarts, and cakes. These yummy morsels can also be ordered upstairs, along with breakfast and a Caribbean buffet for lunch. Choose to dine either in the airy dining room or on the sunny, narrow balcony perched above Roseau's colorful streets—the perfect spot to indulge in one of the fresh-squeezed tropical juices. $ *Average main: $16* ✉ *15 Cork St., Roseau* ☎ *767/448–2930* ☉ *Closed Sun. No dinner.*

$ ✕ **Miranda's Corner.** Just past Springfield on the way to Pont Casse, you'll CARIBBEAN begin to see hills full of flowers. At a big bend, a sign on a tree reads "Miranda's Corner," referring to a bar, rum shop, and diner all in one. Here Miranda Alfred is at home, serving everyone from Italian tourists to banana farmers. Many of her ingredients are grown in her adjacent garden. The specialties are numerous, including *titiree* (when it's fresh and in season) and tropical juices. All are prepared with a potion of passion and a fistful of flavor. Miranda's is open for breakfast, lunch, and dinner and is a great pit stop if you are in the area; call ahead to make sure it's open. $ *Average main: $11* ✉ *Mount Joy, Springfield* ☎ *767/449–2509.*

$ ✕ **Pearl's Cuisine.** In a Creole town house in central Roseau, chef Pearl, CARIBBEAN with her robust and infectious character, prepares some of the island's best local cuisine, such as callaloo soup, fresh fish, and rabbit. Her menu changes daily, but she offers such local delicacies as *sousse* (pickled pigs' feet), blood pudding, and rotis. When sitting down, ask for a table on the open-air gallery that overlooks Roseau and prepare for an abundant portion, but make sure you leave space for dessert. If you're on the go, enjoy a quick meal from the daily, varied menu in the ground-floor snack bar. You're spoiled for choice when it comes to the fresh fruit juices. $ *Average main: $12* ✉ *50 King George V St., Roseau* ☎ *767/448–8707* ☉ *Closed Sun. No dinner.*

$$ ✕ **Port of Call Restaurant & Bar.** This haunt of middle-aged barristers and CARIBBEAN laid-back locals is ideally located, just around the corner from the bay front in downtown Roseau. This breezy restaurant with a soothing gray-and-white color scheme occupies a traditional stone building and is open for breakfast, lunch, and dinner. The layout is such that you can have your privacy and a relaxing meal. Management here is always ready to meet your needs for home-style local shrimp, chicken, or fish,

à la carte dishes such as a hamburger and fries, or your favorite libation. $ *Average main: $16* ☒ *3 Kennedy Ave., Roseau* ☎ *767/448–2910* ☉ *Closed Sun.*

$$$
CARIBBEAN

✕ **Rainforest Restaurant at Papillote.** Savor a lethal rum punch while lounging in a hot mineral bath in the Papillote Wilderness Retreat gardens. Then try the bracing callaloo soup, dasheen puffs, fish "rain forest" (marinated with papaya and wrapped in banana leaves), or the succulent freshwater prawns. This handsome Caribbean restaurant has quite possibly one of the best views in the region. Dine at an altitude cool enough to demand a throw blanket and inspire after-dinner conversation. $ *Average main: $23* ☒ *Papillote Wilderness Retreat, Trafalgar Falls Rd., Trafalgar* ☎ *767/448–2287* ⊕ *www.papillote.dm* ☍ *Reservations essential* ☉ *Closed Sept. and Oct.*

$$$
ECLECTIC
☺
Fodor'sChoice
★

✕ **Waterfront Restaurant.** At the southern end of Roseau's bay front, this elegant and romantic restaurant overlooks the Caribbean coastline. You can dine outdoors on the wraparound verandah while listening to the sounds of the sea or indoors in the air-conditioned formal dining room. The restaurant's menu incorporates spa-vegetarian choices alongside the traditional international and local dishes. Tropical desserts include cheesecake and guava tart. The menu dips into a wide range of cuisines, from creole specialties like callaloo soup to beef, lamb, duck, and even skewered shrimp with a Thai sauce. No matter what your choice, it will be served by a friendly and efficient waitstaff. The bar's happy-hour steel band adds a nice touch. Waterfront Restaurant is closed in September and early October, but meals are served in the Marquis Restaurant, which has a regular Monday-night buffet. $ *Average main: $22* ☒ *Fort Young Hotel, Victoria St., Roseau* ☎ *767/448–5000* ⊕ *www.fortyounghotel.com* ☍ *Reservations essential.*

WHERE TO STAY

Many properties offer packages with dives, hikes, tours, and meal plans included, along with all the usual amenities. Some advertise winter rates with a discount for either summer or longer stays.

For expanded reviews, facilities, and current deals, visit Fodors.com.

10

$
HOTEL
☺

▣ **Anchorage Hotel.** Adventure seekers of every age come to this lodge for diving, whale-watching, or other tours led by the in-house tour company. **Pros:** a fine range of water activities; wheelchair accessible; upstairs rooms have balconies; small meeting room. **Cons:** no-frills accommodations. **TripAdvisor:** "basic," "kind and accommodating staff," "service above and beyond." $ *Rooms from: $95* ☒ *Castle Comfort* ☎ *767/448–2638* ⊕ *www.anchoragehotel.dm* ⇘ *32 rooms* ⊠ *No meals.*

$
B&B/INN
★

▣ **Beau Rive.** Owner Mark Steele puts Zen-like elegance and creative soul into every detail of this secluded boutique hotel. **Pros:** lovely rooms; very good food; all rooms have fans and awesome ocean views. **Cons:** ocean is too rough for swimming; no TVs, room phones, or a/c (though the latter is not needed). **TripAdvisor:** "five-star service," "the epitome of elegance," "great meals." $ *Rooms from: $180* ☒ *Between Castle Bruce and Sineku* ☎☎ *767/445–8992* ⊕ *www.beaurive.com* ⇘ *10*

rooms ♥ *Closed Aug. and Sept.*
|O| *Breakfast* ⌖ *2-night minimum.*

$ 🏨 **Calibishie Lodges.** Close to one of
HOTEL Dominica's most picturesque sea-
♺ side villages, six self-contained one-
Fodor's Choice bedroom units emerge from behind
★ terraced lemongrass. **Pros:** plenty
of charm; people-pleasing owners;
meal plans available; 20 minutes
from Melville airport. **Cons:** at
least an hour's drive from Roseau;
no a/c. **TripAdvisor:** "good central
location," "a slice of paradise,"
"cultural immersion." ⑤ *Rooms
from: $125* ✉ *Calibishie Main
Rd., Calibishie* 🕾 *767/445–8537*
⊕ *www.calibishie-lodges.com* ⇆ *6
apartments* |O| *Breakfast.*

$ 🏨 **Castle Comfort Lodge.** The boats anchored just off the pier, the telltale
HOTEL dive log, and the guests with mask imprints on their foreheads give it all
away—this is the best dive lodge in Dominica. **Pros:** a favorite retreat for
divers; good location. **Cons:** rooms are very basic. **TripAdvisor:** "a great
dive operation," "hidden jewel," "lovely people." ⑤ *Rooms from: $120*
✉ *Castle Comfort* 🕾 *767/448–2188, 767/448–2062, 646/502–6800 in
U.S.* ⊕ *www.castlecomfortdivelodge.com* ⇆ *14 rooms* ♥ *Closed Sept.*
|O| *Breakfast.*

$ 🏨 **Cocoa Cottage.** This ecosensitive, hand-constructed wood-and-stone
B&B/INN lodge has a cozy tree-house feel, and, though very basic, is comfortable. **Pros:** immersive tropical mountain experience; artistic vibe. **Cons:**
a bit far removed; somewhat difficult to find. **TripAdvisor:** "delicious
dinners," "artistic and inspiring," "stylish and comfortable." ⑤ *Rooms
from: $125* ✉ *Trafalgar* 🕾 *767/448–0412* ⊕ *www.cocoacottages.com*
⇆ *6 rooms* |O| *Breakfast.*

$ 🏨 **Crescent Moon Cabins.** In a hidden valley where waterfalls and a
HOTEL river run rampant, this small, family-run, forest resort is so deep in
♺ the bush, you might genuinely believe you're camping—except you
★ have the benefit of basic yet ecofriendly facilities with balconies
and hammocks. **Pros:** one-of-a-kind property; excellent food. **Cons:**
facilities are about two steps above camping; road here is difficult to
navigate. **TripAdvisor:** "the perfect getaway," "warm atmosphere,"
"awesome views." ⑤ *Rooms from: $154* ✉ *Sylvania* 🕾 *767/449–3449*
⊕ *www.crescentmooncabins.com* ⇆ *4 cabins* ♥ *Closed Aug. and Sept.*
|O| *Breakfast* ⌖ *2-night minimum.*

$ 🏨 **Evergreen Hotel.** This family-run, modern, oceanfront inn is a non-
HOTEL diver's oasis in diver-friendly Castle Comfort. **Pros:** friendly staff;
♺ pleasant surroundings; breakfast included. **Cons:** though it is just 1
mile (1½ km) from Roseau, it's a good idea to take a cab at night as
the road is not well lit. **TripAdvisor:** "great location," "friendly little
hotel," "welcome amenities." ⑤ *Rooms from: $137* ✉ *Castle Comfort*

Fort Young Hotel

☎ 767/448–3288 ⊕ *www.evergreenhoteldominica.com* ⌑ *16 rooms, 1 cottage* ⦿ *Breakfast.*

$
RESORT
☺
Fodor's Choice
★

🖼 **Fort Young Hotel.** Sitting on the edge of a cliff just to the south of Roseau, this hotel has ample-size rooms and balconies with either a limited or full ocean view. **Pros:** cosmopolitan vibe; friendly staff. **Cons:** can get crowded during the Friday-night happy hour. **TripAdvisor:** "excellent experience," "beautiful place," "great service." ⑤ *Rooms from: $85* ⊠ *Victoria St., Dutchman's Bay, Roseau* ☎ *767/448–5000* ⊕ *www. fortyounghotel.com* ⌑ *70 rooms, 3 suites* ⦿ *No meals.*

$
HOTEL
☺

🖼 **Garraway Hotel.** A bay-front, city-style hotel on the western edge of Roseau offers lovely vistas from the higher floors such as of the town's quaint architecture, the ocean, or the imposing mountains. **Pros:** spacious rooms; well located in the heart of Roseau; free Ethernet. **Cons:** rooms are a bit sparse; lower-level rooms do not have good views. **TripAdvisor:** "friendly," "good location," "safe and comfortable." ⑤ *Rooms from: $100* ⊠ *Place Heritage, 1 Dame Eugenia Charles Blvd., Roseau* ☎ *767/449–8800* ⊕ *www.garrawayhotel.com* ⌑ *20 rooms, 10 suites* ⦿ *No meals.*

10

$
B&B/INN

🖼 **Hummingbird Inn.** The ocean vistas, lushly fragrant garden, and naturally sensuous atmosphere at this hillside retreat provide a romantic setting for honeymooners and, needless to say, hummingbirds. **Pros:** gorgeous view; if you are into lizards, this is a sanctuary for the rare *iguana delicatissima.* **Cons:** very basic rooms; a charge for in-room TV; road to the property has a very steep turn and is challenging after it rains; no a/c. **TripAdvisor:** "authentic," "sweet spot," "beautiful place." ⑤ *Rooms from: $75* ⊠ *Rock-A-Way, Canefield* ☎☎ *767/449–1042* ⊕ *www.thehummingbirdinn.com* ⌑ *9 rooms, 1 suite* ⦿ *Breakfast.*

A Place to Get Soaked

Wotten Waven is no thriving metropolis. In fact, the hamlet at the north end of the Roseau Valley is minuscule. But don't miss it. Hidden in its bush are sulfur-enriched, burping waters, fumaroles, and cascades. A few local entrepreneurs have made it a spa destination. Now, if you're thinking big-time pampering, think again. It is strictly BYOT (bring your own towel). There are four outdoor "spas." Each is unique. **Rainforest Shangri-La Resort**, with its steam and hot springs, is hand-hewed and ecofriendly. **Tia's Bamboo Cottages** are perched on a hill. The springs are at the bottom by the river. Don't want to dip? Well, the owner's teen

daughters at **Ti Kwen Glo Cho** will take you on a tour down a flower-border path to lush gardens, a small menagerie of native wildlife, and a waterfall. Ti Kwen Glo Cho's state-of-the-art spa consists of four old-fashioned claw-foot bathtubs. Mineral water is jerry-rigged into them via a series of bamboo poles. **Screw's Sulphur Spa** is the most posh. It offers mud packs and wraps plus six pools, each a different temperature and a different depth. Screw, and that is his name, doesn't let you leave without giving you fresh juice or fruit. Dominica's spas are a far reach from the Golden Door, but then again, that is their charm.

$ **Itassi Cottages.** You forget how close these three cottages are to Roseau
RENTAL as you swing on your hammock overlooking the ocean. **Pros:** very
☾ friendly atmosphere; great bang for your buck; weekly and monthly
rates available. **Cons:** 20-minute drive to closest beach (Mero). ⑤ *Rooms
from: $60* ⊠ *Morne Bruce* ☎ *767/449–8700* ⊕ *www.avirtualdominica.
com/itassi* ⇆ *3 cottages* ⊙I *No meals.*

$ **Jungle Bay Resort & Spa.** Sweeping views of the untamed Atlantic sur-
RESORT round this resort, which sits on 55 acres of the only developed section
★ of the island's southeast. **Pros:** perfect for active vacationers; lovely
rooms; outdoor showers; basic plan includes breakfast; tours of the
island offered. **Cons:** facility is remote; water is too rough for swimming; no a/c; long trek to many of the rooms; not wheelchair accessible. **TripAdvisor:** "amazing service," "excellent staff," "amazing hiking
and nature." ⑤ *Rooms from: $188* ⊠ *Point Mulatre* ☎ *767/446–1789*
⊕ *www.junglebaydominica.com* ⇆ *35 cottages* ⊙ *Closed Sept.* ⊙I *Multiple meal plans.*

$ **Papillote Wilderness Retreat.** This family-friendly, recently updated and
B&B/INN welcoming destination in the middle of a tropical forest has a mind-bog-
☾ gling collection of rare and indigenous plants on its botanic trail. **Pros:**
lovely grounds; adjacent to Morne Trois Pitons National Park and close
to Trafalgar Falls; only 10 minutes by car from Roseau. **Cons:** Though
bus service to/from Roseau is available, a rental car is a much better
option. **TripAdvisor:** "total relaxation," "a really special place," "gorgeous gardens." ⑤ *Rooms from: $115* ⊠ *Trafalgar Falls Rd., Trafalgar*
☎ *767/448–2287* ⊕ *www.papillote.dm* ⇆ *3 rooms, 4 suites* ⊙ *Closed
Sept. and Oct.* ⊙I *Multiple meal plans.*

$ 🏠 **Picard Beach Cottages.** Eighteen cottages, on the grounds of an old
B&B/INN   6-acre coconut plantation and its lovely landscaped gardens, are just
⟳   steps away from Dominica's longest grayish-sand beach. **Pros:** has some
spa facilities; nice beach; free Wi-Fi. **Cons:** property is not well lighted
and can be difficult to navigate at night without a flashlight; this part
of the island can get pretty buggy. **TripAdvisor:** "great island living,"
"amazing morning view," "comfortable cottages." Ⓢ *Rooms from:*
$120 ✉ *Prince Rupert Bay* ☎ *767/445–5131* ⊕ *picardbeachcottages.*
dm ⤵ *18 1-bedroom cottages* ⦿❘ *No meals.*

$ 🏠 **Rainforest Shangri-La Resort.** Fitness and nature take the spotlight at
HOTEL   this pristine retreat set 1,000 feet above sea level. **Pros:** fitness and
wellness focus; yoga; Tai Chi. **Cons:** rooms are a bit sparse; in-room
food is discouraged; not wheelchair accessible. **TripAdvisor:** "friendly
staff," "paradise for nature lovers," "very relaxing and great food."
Ⓢ *Rooms from: $47* ✉ *Wotten Waven, Wotten Waven* ☎ *767/440–5093*
⤵ *3 rooms, 3 bungalows* ⦿❘ *No meals.*

$$ 🏠 **Red Rock Haven.** Perched above the secluded Pointe Baptiste Beach and
HOTEL   tucked away amid lush landscape are posh accommodations accented
⟳   with wood, stone, bamboo, a laddered loft for the kids, and elegant
bathrooms. **Pros:** modern and lovely accommodations. **Cons:** steep
paths, so difficult for people with mobility problems; car rental nec-
essary. **TripAdvisor:** "sheer delight," "magical oasis," "a unique and
special place." Ⓢ *Rooms from: $150* ✉ *Calibishie* ☎ *767/445–7997*
⊕ *www.redrockhaven.com* ⤵ *3 1-bedroom suites, 1 2-bedroom villa*
⦿❘ *Breakfast.*

$ 🏠 **Roseau Valley Hotel.** With tile floors and cheerful decor, this little hotel
HOTEL   is quite inviting. **Pros:** reasonable and pleasant. **Cons:** a 2-mile (3-km)
⟳   walk to Roseau (but there is local bus service). **TripAdvisor:** "home
away from home," "great food," "cozy retreat." Ⓢ *Rooms from: $60*
✉ *2 miles (3 km) east of Roseau, Roseau* ☎ *767/449–8176* ⤵ *10 rooms*
⦿❘ *Breakfast.*

$$ 🏠 **Secret Bay.** Private and luxurious, this small indoor/outdoor property
B&B/INN   (two villas and two bungalows) perched above the water offers stunning
panoramas and outdoor showers, plus lots of privacy and amenities—
even a chef to prepare your meals. **Cons:** no children under 12; pricey
for Dominica; no restaurant. **TripAdvisor:** "pure romanticism," "brilliant accommodation," "unbelievable paradise." Ⓢ *Rooms from: $252*
✉ *Tibay Beach, northwest part of island, Portsmouth* ☎ *767/445–4444*
⊕ *secretbay.dm* ⤵ *4 rooms* ⦿❘ *Some meals.*

$ 🏠 **Silks Hotel.** French taste transformed this 17th-century mansion and
HOTEL   former rum distillery into one of the most posh hotels on the island.
★   **Pros:** one of the most luxurious lodgings on the island; close to the air-
port; air-conditioned. **Cons:** more than an hour's drive from Roseau.
TripAdvisor: "romantic," "great place to relax," "a perfect hideaway."
Ⓢ *Rooms from: $165* ✉ *Hatton Garden, Marigot* ☎ *767/445–8846*
⊕ *www.silkshotel.com* ⤵ *5 rooms* ⊙ *Closed Sept.–Oct. 15* ⦿❘ *Breakfast.*

$ 🏠 **Sunset Bay Club.** Sunset is a simple but comfortable beachfront
HOTEL   hotel on a stretch of Dominica's spectacular west coast. **Pros:** gar-
⟳   dens and views are beautiful; great food; kid friendly. **Cons:** rooms
are basic. **TripAdvisor:** "a terrific escape," "great diving," "beautiful

10

small resort." $ *Rooms from: $132* ✉ *Batalie Beach, Coulibistrie* ☎ *767/446–6522* ⊕ *www.sunsetbayclub.com* ⌂ *12 rooms, 1 suite* ⦿| *Multiple meal plans.*

$
B&B/INN
☺

⊡ **Tamarind Tree Hotel & Restaurant.** The warmth and friendliness of owners Annette and Stefan Loerner-Peyer are this small inn's most valuable asset. **Pros:** extremely friendly owners; good food; very child friendly; one of the owners is a certified tour guide. **Cons:** no-frills rooms. **TripAdvisor:** "wonderful getaway," "peaceful place with personal attention," "charming rooms." $ *Rooms from: $113* ✉ *Salisbury* ☎ *767/446–7395, 767/449–7007* ⊕ *www.tamarindtreedominica.com* ⌂ *12 rooms* ⊘ *Closed Sept.* ⦿| *Breakfast.*

$
HOTEL

⊡ **Tia's Bamboo Cottages.** Tia himself built these charming but rustic cabins, which sit on the side of a hill, amid a picturesque, natural setting. **Pros:** proximity to river and natural springs; extremely helpful staff. **Cons:** cottages are very sparse. **TripAdvisor:** "romantic and rustic," "tropical paradise setting," "a rural retreat." $ *Rooms from: $80* ✉ *Wotton Waven, in Roseau Valley* ☎ *767/225–4823* ⌂ *3 cottages* ▭ *No credit cards* ⊘ *Closed June* ⦿| *No meals.*

$
HOTEL
★

⊡ **Zandoli Inn.** Overlooking a 111-foot cliff on the southeast Atlantic coast, this small inn has a stunning view—water and mountains. **Pros:** drop-dead vistas; full-service bar and restaurant. **Cons:** steep walk to the beach, which is not the best place to take a plunge. **TripAdvisor:** "outstanding food," "breathtaking spot," "great views." $ *Rooms from: $145* ✉ *Roche Cassée, Stowe* ☎ *767/446–3161* ⊕ *www.zandoli.com* ⌂ *5 rooms* ⦿| *No meals.*

NIGHTLIFE AND THE ARTS

The friendly, intimate atmosphere and colorful patrons at the numerous bars and hangouts will keep you entertained for hours. If you're looking for jazz, calypso, reggae, steel band, soca (a variation of calypso), cadence-zouk, or jing ping—a type of folk music featuring the accordion, the *quage* (a kind of washboard instrument), drums, and a "boom boom" (a percussion instrument)—you're guaranteed to find it. Wednesday through Saturday nights are really lively, and during Carnival, Independence, and summer celebrations, things can be intense. Indeed, Dominica's Carnival, the pre-Lenten festival, is the most spontaneous in the Caribbean. Other big cultural events include Emancipation celebrations hosted by the National Cultural Council each August.

Fodor'sChoice
★

World Creole Music Festival. The annual World Creole Music Festival in late October or early November also packs in the action, with three days and nights of pulsating rhythm and music. Creole music enthusiasts come from all over the world to listen to the likes of Kassav, Aswad, and Tabou Combo. Throughout the year, however, most larger hotels have some form of live evening entertainment. ⊕ *www.wcmfdominica.com.*

NIGHTLIFE

Once Friday afternoon rolls around, you can sense the mood change. Local bars crank up the music, and each village and community has its own particular nightly entertainment. If by this point in your trip you have made friends with some locals, they will be only too happy to take you to the current hot spot.

Balas Bar & Courtyard. Every Friday night from 6 to 8 Balas Bar & Courtyard has a very happening rum-punch happy hour with a live band and drink specials. ⊠ *Fort Young Hotel, Victoria St., Roseau* ☎ *767/448–5000.*

Garage Bar & Grill. Garage Bar & Grill is lively, very popular with locals, and stays open until the last person leaves the bar. ⊠ *15 Hanover St., Roseau* ☎ *767/448–5433.*

Melvina's Champagne Bar & Restaurant. Melvina's Champagne Bar & Restaurant is a popular hangout for locals and tourists, especially on Friday and Saturday nights. ⊠ *Champagne Hwy., Pointe Michel* ☎ *767/235–6072.*

Symes Zee's. Symes Zee's draws a crowd on Thursday night from 9 until the wee hours of the morning, when there's a jazz-blues-reggae band. There's no cover, and the food, drinks, and cigars are reasonably priced. ⊠ *34 King George V St., Roseau* ☎ *767/448–2494.*

SHOPPING

Dominicans produce distinctive handicrafts, with various communities specializing in their specific products. The crafts of the Carib Indians include traditional baskets made of dyed *larouma* reeds and water-proofed with tightly woven *balizier* leaves. These are sold in the Carib Indian Territory and Kalinago Barana Autê as well as in Roseau's shops. Vertivert straw rugs, screw-pine tableware, *fwije* (the trunk of the forest tree fern), and wood carvings are just some examples. Also notable are local herbs, spices, condiments, and herb teas. Café Dominique, the local equivalent of Jamaican Blue Mountain coffee, is an excellent buy, as are the Dominican rums Macoucherie and Soca. Proof that the old ways live on in Dominica can be found in the number of herbal remedies available. One stimulating memento of your visit is rum steeped with *bois bandé* (scientific name *Richeria grandis*), a tree whose bark is reputed to have aphrodisiacal properties. It's sold at shops, vendors' stalls, and supermarkets. The charismatic roadside vendors can be found all over the island bearing trays laden with local and imported souvenirs, T-shirts, and trinkets. Duty-free shopping is also available in specific stores around Roseau.

Dominican farmers island-wide bring their best crops to the Roseau Market, at the end of Dame Eugenia Boulevard and Lange Lane, every Friday and Saturday from 6 am to 1 pm. It may well be the largest farmers' market in the Caribbean. They start setting up on Friday night, and often customers begin their shopping then. Vendors are usually out on roadsides when there are cruise ships in port.

10

One of the easiest places to pick up a souvenir is the Old Market Plaza, just behind the Dominica Museum, in Roseau. Slaves were once sold here, but today handcrafted jewelry, T-shirts, spices, souvenirs, batik, and trays, plus lacquered and woven bamboo boxes, are available from a group of vendors in open-air booths set up on the cobblestones. They are usually busiest when there's a cruise ship berthed across the street. On these days you can also find a vast number of vendors along the bay front.

SPECIALTY STORES

ART

Most artists work from their home studios, and it often takes the right contact to find them. You can usually see the work of the island's artists at the Old Mill Cultural Center (⇨ *Nightlife and the Arts, above*).

Indigo. The tree-house studio and café at Indigo sells works by in-house artists Clem and Marie Frederick and also serves fresh sugarcane juice or bush teas. ⊠ *Bournes* ☎ *767/445–3486* ⊕ *www.indigo.wetpaint.com.*

CLOTHING

There's such a wide selection when it comes to clothing stores in Roseau that it really is best to walk around and explore for yourself. However, for classic Caribbean and international designer clothing, there are several reliable boutiques to try.

Ego Boutique. Ego Boutique carries an extensive selection of designer clothing and exquisite crafts and home accessories from around the world. ⊠ *9 Hillsborough St., Roseau* ☎ *767/448–2336.*

GIFTS AND SOUVENIRS

As cruise-ship visits have increased in frequency, duty-free shops are cropping up, including some name-brand stores, mostly within Roseau's bay front.

Baroon International. Baroon International sells unusual jewelry from Asia, the United States, and other Caribbean islands. It also features pieces that are assembled in the store, as well as personal accessories, souvenirs, and special gifts. ⊠ *Kennedy Ave. at Old St., Roseau* ☎ *767/449–2888.*

Jeweller's International. Jeweller's International carries perfumes, crystals, liquor, and other gift items such as gold and silver jewelry and baubles with emeralds, diamonds, and other gems. ⊠ *Fort Young Hotel, Victoria St., Roseau* ☎ *767/440–3319.*

Land. For high-quality leather goods and other personal accessories, try Land at the Duty-Free Emporium next to the Royal Bank. ⊠ *Bay Front, Roseau* ☎ *767/448–3394.*

Pirates. Pirates is the place for booze, Cuban cigars, cheese, watches, and souvenirs. ⊠ *6 Long Lane, Roseau* ☎ *767/449–3394* ⊘ *Weekdays 8:30–5, Sat. 8:30–2.*

Whitchurch Duty-Free. Whitchurch Duty-Free has a large assortment of items, including perfumes, leather goods, and designer sunglasses. ⊠ *Fort Young Hotel, Victoria St., Roseau* ☎ *767/448–7177, 767/448–2181.*

HANDICRAFTS

Kalinago Barana Autê. Kalinago Barana Autê sells handicrafts including carvings, pottery, and lovely handwoven baskets, which you can watch the women weave. ⊠ *Salybia, Carib Territory* ☎ *767/445–7979* ⊕ *www. kalinagobaranaaute.com* ⊙ *Daily 9–5.*

Papillote Wilderness Retreat. Papillote Wilderness Retreat has an intimate gift shop with local handcrafted goods and particularly outstanding wood carvings by Louis Desire. ⊠ *Trafalgar* ☎ *767/448–2287.*

SPORTS AND ACTIVITIES

ADVENTURE PARKS

Rainforest Adventures Dominica. Rainforest Adventures Dominica gives you a bird's-eye view of a pristine forest aboard an open, eight-person gondola. For 90 minutes to two hours, you slowly skim the treetop canopy while a guide provides scientific information about the flora and fauna. At the top there is an optional walking tour that is worth the steps. The cost is $64. A zip line has recently been added (tram & zip US$99 or trail and zip US$50). Transportation and lunch are extra. This is a popular attraction for cruise-ship passengers, so try to reserve ahead. ⊠ *Laudat* ☎ *767/448–8775, 767/440–3266, 866/759–8726 in U.S.* ⊕ *www.rfat.com.*

Wacky Rollers. Wacky Rollers will make you feel as if you are training for the marines as you swing on a Tarzan-style rope and grab onto a vertical rope ladder, rappel across zip lines, and traverse suspended log bridges, a net bridge, and four monkey bridges (rope loops). It costs $65 for the adult course and should take from 1½ to 3½ hours to conquer the 28 "games." There is also an abbreviated kids' course for $25 (kids 10 and under). Wacky Rollers also organizes adventure tours around the island plus kayak and tubing trips. Although the office is in Roseau, the park itself is in Hillsborough Estate, about 20 to 25 minutes north of Roseau. ⊠ *Front St., Roseau* ☎ *767/440–4386* ⊕ *www.wackyrollers.com.*

10

BIKING

Cyclists find Dominica's rugged terrain to be an exhilarating challenge, and there are routes suitable for all levels of bikers.

Nature Island Dive. Nature Island Dive has a fleet of bikes in good condition. You can rent a mountain bike for $30, but if you prefer a knowledgeable guide to lead you through specific areas, the cost ranges from $65 for a half day to $96 for a full day, which includes lunch, snacks, and drinks. ⊠ *Soufrière* ☎ *767/449–8181.*

DIVING AND SNORKELING

Fodor's Choice ★ Not only is Dominica considered one of the top 10 dive destinations in the world by *Skin Diver* and *Rodale's Scuba Diving* magazines, but it has won many other awards for its underwater sites. They are truly memorable. The west coast of the island has awesome sites, but the best are those in the southwest—within and around **Soufrière/Scotts Head Marine Reserve.** This bay is a submerged volcanic crater. The Dominica Watersports Association has worked along with the Fisheries Division for years to establish this reserve and has set stringent regulations to prevent the degradation of the ecosystem. Within ½ mile (¾ km) of the shore there are vertical drops from 800 feet to more than 1,500 feet, with visibility frequently extending to 100 feet. Shoals of boga fish, Creole wrasse, and blue cromis are common, and you might even see a spotted moray eel or a honeycomb cowfish. Crinoids (rare elsewhere) are also abundant here, as are giant barrel sponges. There is a $2 fee per person to dive, snorkel, or kayak in the reserve. Other noteworthy dive sites include **Salisbury Falls, Nose Reef, Brain Coral Garden,** and—even farther north—**Cabrits Drop-Off** and **Toucari Reef.** The conditions for underwater photography, particularly macrophotography, are unparalleled. Rates start at about $55 for a single-tank dive and about $90 for a two-tank dive or from about $75 for a resort course with one open-water dive. All scuba-diving operators also offer snorkeling. Equipment rents for $10 to $25 a day; trips with gear range from $15 to $35. A 10% tax is not included.

Anchorage Dive & Whale Watch Center. The Anchorage Dive & Whale Watch Center has two dive boats that can take you out day or night. It also offers PADI instruction (all skill levels), snorkeling and whale-watching trips, and shore diving. It has many of the same trips as Dive Dominica. ⊠ *Anchorage Hotel, Castle Comfort* 📞 *767/448–2638* ⊕ *www.anchoragehotel.dm.*

Cabrits Dive Center. Cabrits Dive Center is the only PADI five-star dive center in Dominica. Nitrox courses are also available for $250. Since Cabrits is the sole operator on the northwest coast, its dive boats have the pristine reefs almost to themselves, unlike other operations, whose underwater territories may overlap. ⊠ *Picard Estate, Portsmouth* 📞 *767/445–3010* ⊕ *www.cabritsdive.com.*

Dive Dominica. Dive Dominica, one of the island's dive pioneers, conducts NAUI, PADI, and SSI courses as well as Nitrox certification courses. With four boats, it offers diving, snorkeling, and whale-watching trips and packages including accommodation at the Castle Comfort Lodge. Its trips are similar to Anchorage's. ⊠ *Castle Comfort Lodge, Castle Comfort* 📞 *767/448–2188, 646/502–6800 in U.S.* ⊕ *www.divedominica.com.*

Fort Young Dive Centre. Fort Young Dive Centre conducts snorkeling, diving, and whale-watching trips that depart from the hotel's private dock. ⊠ *Fort Young Hotel, Victoria St., Roseau* 📞 *767/448–5000* ⊕ *www.fortyounghotel.com/activities/diving/#diving.*

Irie Safari. Irie Safari takes snorkelers to Champagne and the nearby tall grasses where turtles like to hang out. ⊠ *Soufrière/Scotts Head Marine Reserve, Soufrière* 📞 *767/440–5085.*

Nature Island Dive. Nature Island Dive is run by an enthusiastic crew who offer diving, snorkeling, kayaking, and mountain biking as well

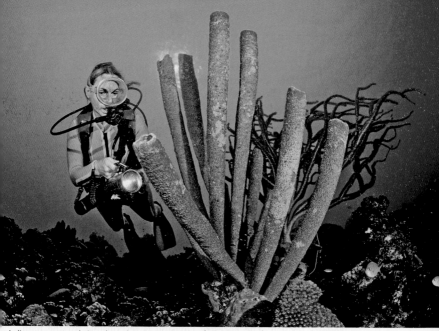
A diver pauses to admire a lavender stovepipe sponge (aplysina archeri).

as resort and full PADI courses. Some of the island's best dive sites are right outside its door. ⊠ *Soufrière* ☎ *767/449–8181.*

FISHING

Anchorage Hotel. Contact the Anchorage Hotel for information about fishing excursions. Fees are $550 for a half-day trip and $1,050 for a full day. ⊠ *Castle Comfort* ☎ *767/448–2638, 888/790 US reservations, 0-800/7297 UK reservations.*

GUIDED TOURS

Because Dominica is such a nature-centered destination, there's no shortage of certified guides, as well as numerous tour and taxi companies. Ask the staff at your hotel for a recommendation. Generally tours start off in the Roseau area, but most operators will arrange convenient pickups. Prices range between $35 and $75 per person, depending on the duration, amenities provided, and number of people on the excursion.

Dominica Tours. Dominica Tours is one of the island's largest tour companies, offering a range of hikes and bird-watching trips. ☎ *767/448–2638* ⊕ *www.experience-dominica.com.*

Ken's Hinterland Adventure Tours & Taxi Service. Ken's Hinterland Adventure Tours & Taxi Service offers a range of island tours and guided hikes, including some oriented specifically for families with children. ⊠ *Fort Young Hotel, Victoria St., Roseau* ☎ *767/448–4850, 767/448–1660, 866/880–0508 US* ⊕ *www.khattstours.com.*

HIKING

★ Dominica's majestic mountains, clear rivers, and lush vegetation conspire to create adventurous hiking trails. The island is crisscrossed by ancient footpaths of the Arawak and Carib Indians and of the Nègres Maroons, escaped slaves who established camps in the mountains. Existing trails range from easygoing to arduous. To make the most of your excursion, you'll need sturdy hiking boots, insect repellent, a change of clothes (kept dry), and a guide. Hikes and tours run $25 to $80 per person, depending on destinations and duration. A poncho or light raincoat is recommended. Some of the natural attractions within the island's national parks require visitors to purchase a site pass. These are sold for varying numbers of visits. A single-entry site pass costs $5, and a week pass $12.

Bertrand Jno Baptiste. Local bird and forestry expert Bertrand Jno Baptiste leads hikes up Morne Diablotin and along the Syndicate Nature Trail; if he's not available, ask him to recommend another guide. ☎ 767/245–4768.

Discover Dominica Authority. Hiking guides can be arranged through the Discover Dominica Authority. ✉ *Kennedy Ave., 1st Floor Financial Centre, Roseau* ☎ *767/448–2045* ⊕ *www.discoverdominica.com.*

Forestry Division. The Forestry Division is responsible for the management of forests and wildlife and has numerous publications on Dominica as well as a wealth of information on reputable guides. ✉ *Dominica Botanical Gardens, between Bath Rd. and Valley Rd., Roseau* ☎ *767/266–3811, 767/266–3812.*

WHALE-WATCHING

Ⓒ
Fodor'sChoice
★

Dominica records the highest species counts of resident cetaceans in the southern Caribbean region, so it's not surprising that tour companies claim 90% sighting success for their excursions. Humpback whales, false killer whales, minke, and orcas are all occasionally seen, as are several species of dolphin. But the resident sperm whales (they calve in Dominica's 3,000-foot-deep waters) are truly the stars of the show. During your 3½-hour expedition, which costs about $55 plus tax, you may be asked to assist in recording sightings, data that can be shared with local and international organizations. Although there are resident whale and dolphin populations, more species can be observed from November through February. Turtle-watching trips are also popular.

Anchorage Dive & Whale Watch Center. The Anchorage Dive & Whale Watch Center offers whale-watching trips. ✉ *Anchorage Hotel, Castle Comfort* ☎ *767/448–2638* ⊕ *www.anchoragehotel.dm.*

Dive Dominica. Dive Dominica is a major whale-watching operator. ✉ *Castle Comfort Lodge, Castle Comfort* ☎ *767/448–2188* ⊕ *www.divedominica.com.*

Dominican Republic

WORD OF MOUTH

"The Punta Cana area lends itself more to those looking for the type of vacation where the resort has everything and one never has to go outside the gates. Note the nearest city, Higuey, is about a 40-minute drive away. Beyond the resorts is mostly empty country-side. You can literally walk for miles along the beach. . . ."

—Steelersfan

WELCOME TO DOMINICAN REPUBLIC

Ocean World Adventure Park **8**

Cofresí Beach
15 - **18**   *Playa Dorada*   **14** **10**

Luperón Beach   **19**   **7**   **13**   *Playa Cabarete*

Montecristi

Puerto Plata   Sosúa   Cabarete   **1** - **6**   *Cabo Francés Viejo*

Museo de Ambar Dominicano   **8** - **12**   **Laguna Grí-Grí**

Guayubín

Mt. Isabel de Torres   Gregorie Luperón International Airport   Cabrera   *Playa Grande*

H A I T I

9   Santiago   Moca   *Bahía Escocesa*   *Las Terrenas*   **7**

Pico Duarte   La Vega Vieja   San Francisco de Macorís   *Playa Cosón*

Jarabacoa   Nagua   *Los Haitises National Park*   Taíno Par   *Bahía Samaná*

← TO HAITI   **HISPANIOLA**   Sabana de la Mar

San Juan   Monte Plata

Lago Enriquillo   Neiba   **Las Américas International Airport**

Duvergé   Azua   San Cristóbal   Santo Domingo   *Boca Chica*   *Jua Do*

Bahía de Ocoa   Bani   **Santo Domingo** see detail map

Barahona   *Playa Bahoruco*   Pto. Palenque

C a r i b b e a n   S e a

Oviedo

Cabo Beata

Like the merengue seen on all the dance floors in Santo Domingo, the Dominican Republic is charismatic yet sensuous, energetic yet elegant. The charm of the people adds special warmth: a gracious wave of greeting here, a hand-rolled cigar tapped with a flourish there. Dazzling smiles just about everywhere will quickly beguile you.

LA ISLA ESPAÑOLA

The Dominican Republic covers the eastern two-thirds of the island of Hispaniola (Haiti covers the other third). At 18,765 square miles (48,730 square km), it's the second-largest Caribbean country (only Cuba is larger), and with more than 8.8 million people, the second-most-populous country, too. It was explored by Columbus on his 1492 voyage to the New World.

Restaurants ▼
B.Y.O.W. Restaurant **10**
Cabahá **6**
Castle Club **5**
EZE **2**
Emerald Beach Club **1**
Hemingway's Cafe **7**
Il Pasticcio **9**
Lucia **8**
Miró **3**
Natura Restaurant at
Natura Cabana **4**

Hotels ▼
Balcones del Atlantico ..**7**
Barcelo Puerto Plata ..**18**
Blue Bay
Villas Doradas **16**
Casa Colonial **15**
Casa de Campo **1**
Dreams La Romana **2**
Gran Ventana Beach
Resort **17**
Hotel Casa Valeria **14**

Hotel El Magnifico **12**
Iberostar
Costa Dorada **19**
Iberostar
Hacienda Dominicus **3**
Natura Cabana **9**
Ocean Point **8**
Peninsula House **6**
Sea Horse Ranch **13**
Velero Beach Resort ...**11**
Villa Serena **5**
Villa Taìna **10**
Viva Wyndham
Dominicus Palace **4**

KEY
⤢ Beaches
◺ Dive Sites
1 Restaurants
① Hotels

TOP REASONS TO VISIT DOMINICAN REPUBLIC

1 Great Beaches. There are some 1,000 miles of excellent beaches, some of which are pearl-white.

2 Great Value. You'll find the best-value all-inclusive resorts in the Caribbean here.

3 Myriad Water Sports. Every imaginable activity—world-class golf, horseback riding, white-water rafting, surfing, diving, windsurfing, and more—is available here.

4 Friendly People. The genuine hospitality of the people and their love of norteamericanos.

5 Happening Nightlife. The Dominicans love to party, dance, drink, and have a good time at happening bars and clubs.

DOMINICAN REPUBLIC BEACHES

Its beaches are what put the D.R. on the touristic sonar. The east coast beaches (near Punta Cana, Juanillo, Bávaro), which are washed by the Caribbean, rival any in the Antilles—possibly the world. The government partnered with the hospitality industry and beautified many beaches not as naturally endowed. Think cosmetic surgery. Think hundreds of millions of dollars.

The Dominican Republic has more than 1,000 miles (1,600 km) of beaches, including the Caribbean's longest stretch of white sand: Punta Cana–Bávaro. Many beaches are accessible to the public (in theory, all beaches in this country, from the high-water mark down, are open to everyone) and may tempt you to stop for a swim. That's part of the uninhibited joy of this country. Do be careful, though: some have dangerously strong currents, which may be the reason why they are undeveloped.

(Above) Kitesurfing the waters of Punta Cana (Bottom right) Kiteboarding the waves of Cabrete (Top right) Looking down on Cabrete Beach

WHAT'S YOUR PREFERENCE?

Is white sand a must? Then you are talking the Punta Cana region. If you can go nearly white, say, a light taupe, then it's the southeast coast. Bayahibe, with its half-crescent beaches, is a charmer. Juan Dolio's Villas de Mar beach has been reborn with tons of white sand trucked in. The amber sands of Playa Dorada and Cabarete have also been enhanced with truckloads of white sand.

Playa Bahoruco. This isolated, gorgeous stretch of virgin beach goes on for miles in either direction, with rugged cliffs dropping to golden sand and warm, blue water. It's a wild, undeveloped Caribbean beach, but many sections are pebbly, so you need surf shoes for swimming. In nearby San Rafael are beach shacks where you can buy meals of fresh fish, even whole sea bass in coconut sauce. ⊠ *Carretera La Costa, Km 17, 8 miles (13 km) south of Barahona.*

Playa Boca Chica. You can walk far out into the gin-clear waters protected by coral reefs. Unfortunately, some areas are cluttered with plastic furniture, pizza stands, and cottages. If you're staying in the capital, this is the closest good beach. Grab lunch at one of the larger beachfront restaurants such as El Pelicano or nearby, the trendy waterfront restaurants Boca Marina or Neptuno's Club. ⊠ *Autopista Las Americas, 21 miles (34 km) east of Santo Domingo, Boca Chica.*

Playa Cabarete. Follow the coastal road east from Playa Dorada to find this beach, which has strong waves and ideal, steady winds (from 15 to 20 knots), making it an integral part of the international windsurfing circuit. Segments are strips of golden sand punctuated only by palm trees. In the most commercial area, restaurants and bars are back-to-back, spilling onto the sand.

The informal scene is young and fun, with expats and tourists from every imaginable country. ⊠ *Sosúa–Cabarete road, Cabarete.*

Playa Dorada. On the north's Amber Coast, this is one of the D.R.'s most established resort areas. Each hotel has its own slice of the beach, which is soft beige sand, with lots of reefs for snorkeling. Gran Ventana Beach Resort, which is on a point, marks the end of the major hotel development. The Atlantic waters are great for windsurfing, waterskiing, and fishing. ⊠ *Off Autopista Luperon, 10 mins east of Puerto Plata, Playa Dorada.*

Playa Grande. On the North Coast, between the towns of Río San Juan and Cabrera, is this long stretch of powdery sand. The public entrance is about a mile after Playa Grande Golf Course, at Km 9. Here the beach is on a lovely cove, with towering cliffs on both sides. A few beach shacks fry up fresh fish and keep the beer on ice. An outcropping separates this beach from Playa Precioso. During the week you'll have little company, but on Sunday afternoons the locals are here in full force. ⊠ *Carretera Río San Juan–Cabrera, Km 11.*

Playa Sosúa. Sosúa Bay is a gorgeous, natural harbor with coral reefs and dive sites, about a 20-minute drive from Puerto Plata. Swimming is delightful, except after a heavy rain when litter

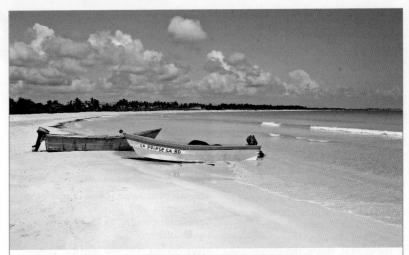

A beach on Isla Saona island, a national park just off the tip of the southeastern coast

floats in. From the beach you can see mountains in the background, the cliffs that surround the bay, and seemingly miles of coastline. Snorkeling from the beach is good, but the best spots are farther offshore, closer to the reefs. (Don't bother going to Three Rocks.) Unfortunately, the backdrop is a string of tents where hawkers push souvenirs, snacks, drinks, and water-sports equipment rentals. Lounge chairs can usually be had for RD$75. ⊠ *Carretera Puerto Plata–Sosúa, Sosúa.*

Punta Cana Beaches. The area encompasses Cabeza de Torres and Playa Bávaro, and continues all the way around the peninsula to Playa de Uvero Alto. Each hotel has its own strip of sand with rows of chaise longues, and you can call in advance for a day pass. The stretch between Club Med and the PuntaCana Resort & Club (Playa Punta Cana) is one of the most beautiful. Playa El Cortecito is more how life used to be, with fishermen bringing in their catch. The public beach at Macao is no longer a good option, having been taken over by four-wheeler excursions. A rough road leads to more-deserted stretches in the Uvero Alto area, but outside of the resorts there are few services. ⊠ *Off Autopista Las Americas, east of Higüey, Punta Cana.*

Samaná Beaches. On the north coast of the Samaná Peninsula, tall palms list toward the sea, and the beaches are extensive and postcard perfect, with crystalline waters and soft, golden sand. There's plenty of color—vivid blues, greens, and yellows—as well as colorful characters. To the west is Playa El Cosón, opposite Cayo Ballena, a great whale-watching spot (from January to April). Samaná has some of the country's best beaches and drop-dead scenery, the rough roads notwithstanding. ⊠ *Carretera Las Terrenas, Las Terrenas.*

A beach on Isla Saona island, a national park just off the tip of the southeastern coast

By Eileen Robinson Smith

Dominicans will extend a gracious welcome, saying, "This is your home!" and indeed are happy to share their beautiful island bathed by the Atlantic Ocean to the north and the Caribbean Sea to the south. Among its most precious assets are 1,000 miles (1,600 km) of gorgeous beaches studded with coconut palms and sands ranging from pearl-white to golden brown to volcanic black. The Caribbean sun kisses this exotic land, which averages 82°F year-round. It's a fertile country blessed with resources, particularly cocoa, coffee, rum, tobacco, and sugarcane.

A land of contrasts, the Dominican Republic has mountain landscapes, brown rivers with white-water rapids, rain forests full of wild orchids, and fences of multicolor bougainvillea. Indigenous species from crocodiles to the green cockatoo, symbol of the island, live in these habitats. Bird-watchers, take note: there are 29 endemic species flying around here.

The contrasts don't stop with nature. You can see signs of wealth, for the upper strata of society lives well indeed. In the capital, the movers and shakers ride in chauffeur-driven silver Mercedes. On the country roads you'll be amazed that four people with sacks of groceries and a stalk of bananas can fit on a smoky old *motoconcho* (motorbike-taxi). This is a land of *mestizos* who are a centuries-old mix of native Indians, Spanish colonists, and African slaves, plus every other nationality that has settled here, from Italian to Arabic.

Accommodations offer a remarkable range—surfers' camps, exclusive boutique hotels, and amazing megaresorts that have brought the all-inclusive hotel to the next level of luxury. Trendy restaurants, art galleries, boutique hotels, and late-night clubs help make Santo Domingo a superb urban vacation destination. Regrettably, most Dominican towns and cities are neither quaint nor particularly pretty, and poverty still prevails. However, the standard of living has really come up along

LOGISTICS

Getting to the Dominican Republic: The D.R. has six major international airports. Plan your air travel carefully so you don't end up flying into Punta Cana when you are staying at Casa de Campo, a two-hour-plus drive. Travel between the island's many developed tourism zones can be arduous and expensive, with few domestic flights available.

Hassle Factor: Low for popular destinations. High for off-the-beaten-path places.

Getting Around the Island: Most travelers to the Dominican Republic take guided tours or participate in organized excursions. Independent travel is easier if you rent a car, but car rentals are expensive and signage is bad (and some working knowledge of Spanish is strongly advisable). For longer distances, buses are the best alternative, but locally, taxis are widely available in all major resort areas.

On the Ground: Most travelers book packages that include airport transfers. Otherwise, you'll have to take a local taxi, which can be quite expensive.

with the growth of North American tourism. Food prices are higher than they have been, which means prices at all-inclusive resorts are up; however, a vacation in the D.R. can still be a relative bargain. Even the new, small boutique hotels are still well priced for the Caribbean.

The vibrant lifestyle of this sun-drenched Latin-Caribbean country, where Spanish is the national language and where the people are hospitable and good-natured, makes the Dominican Republic a different cultural experience. If you pick up the rhythm of life here, as freewheeling as the island's trademark merengue, this can be a beguiling tourist destination.

PLANNING

WHEN TO GO

The D.R. is busy year-round. During the somewhat quieter summer season, Europeans keep rates high from mid-June through August. However, in late spring (after Easter until early June) and early fall (September to October—peak rainy season, with hurricanes a threat) you can get good deals.

Unlike on many islands, where rain showers are usually passing things, the rains in the D.R. can linger, especially from June through November.

GETTING HERE AND AROUND

AIR TRAVEL

You can fly nonstop to the Dominican Republic from Atlanta (Delta, AirTran), Boston (jetBlue), Charlotte (US Airways), Fort Lauderdale (Spirit), Miami (American), New York–JFK (American, JetBlue), New York–Newark (JetBlue, United), and Philadelphia (US Airways), but not all airlines fly to all destinations in the D.R., and many flights connect in San Juan or some airport in the United States. Many visitors fly

11

nonstop on charter flights direct from the U.S. East Coast and Midwest, particularly into Punta Cana; these charters are part of a package and can be booked only through a travel agent.

Airport Transfers: If you book a package through a travel agent, your airport transfer fee will almost certainly be included. If you book independently, you will have to take a taxi, rent a car, or hire a private driver-guide.

Airports **Cibao International Airport** (STI) in Santiago; **President Juan Bosch International Airport** (AZS) in Catey, Samaná; **Gregorio Luperon International Airport** (POP) in Puerto Plata; **La Isabella International Dr. Joaquin Balaguer** (DHG) in Higüero; **La Romana/Casa de Campo International Airport** (LRM) in La Romana; **Las Américas International Airport** (SDQ) in Santo Domingo; and **Punta Cana International Airport** (PUJ) in Punta Cana.

Airline Contacts **Air Antilles Express** ☎ *809/621–8888.* **Air Caraïbes** ☎ *809/621–8888, 0590/82–47–00 in Guadeloupe.* **Airtran Airways** ☎ *809/959–3014 in the D.R., 800/247–8726 in the U.S.* ⊕ *www.airtranairways. com.* **American Airlines/American Eagle** ☎ *809/959–2420 in Punta Cana, 800/433–7300.* **Delta** ☎ *809/200–9191 in D.R., 800/221–1212 in U.S..* **JetBlue** ☎ *809/273–2771 in D.R. (tickets), 809/947–2297 in D.R. (Santo Domingo), 800/538–2583 in U.S.* ⊕ *www.jetblue.com.* **LIAT** ☎ *809/621–8888.* **Spirit** ☎ *800/772–7117 in U.S.* ⊕ *www.spirit.com.* **United** ☎ *809/262–1060 in the D.R., 800/538–2929 in the U.S.* ⊕ *www.united.com.* **US Airways** ☎ *800/622– 1015 in D.R..*

Domestic and Charter Airlines **Aerodomca** ✉ *La Isabela International Dr. Joaquin Balaguer, Higuero* ☎ *809/738–3014 DomShuttle.* **Air Century** ✉ *La Isabela International Dr. Joaquin Balaguer, Higuero* ☎ *305/677–9641, 809/224–3399 for charters, 809/738–3014 for DominicanShuttle* ⊕ *www. aircentury.com.* **DominicanShuttles.com** ✉ *Near Las Américas Airport (SDQ), Villa Panamericana, JOZ 1 A-La Caleta, Las Américas* ☎ *809/738–3014, 809/481–0707* ⊕ *www.DominicanShuttles.com.* **Helidosa Helicopters** ✉ *Punta Cana* ☎ *809/552–6069* ⊕ *www.helidosa.com* ✉ *Playa Dorada, Puerto Plata* ☎ *809/320–2009.*

BUS TRAVEL

Privately owned buses are the cheapest way to get around the country (for example, one-way bus fare from Santo Domingo to Puerto Plata is about $8, and the trip takes 3½ hours). The companies make regular runs to Santiago, Puerto Plata, Punta Cana, and other destinations from Santo Domingo. Frequent service from Santo Domingo to the town of La Romana is provided by Express Bus, leaving every hour on the hour from 5 am to 9 pm. However, there's no office and no phone, though a ticket taker will take your $4 just before departure. Travel time is about 1¾ hours. Once in town, you can take a taxi from the bus stop to your resort. Espreso Baváro buses depart from Plaza Los Girasoles at Avenida Máximo Gómez at Juan Sánchez Ruiz; the buses are not the best, but cost only $5. If you're going to one of the Punta Cana resorts, you get off at the stop before the last and take a cab waiting at the taxi stand.

Bus Contacts Caribe Tours ☎ *809/221–4422* ⊕ *www.caribetours.com.do.* **Espreso Baváro** ☎ *809/682–9670.* **Express Bus** ☎ *809/556–4192, 809/550–4585.* **Metro Buses** ☎ *809/582–9111 in Santiago, 809/566–7126 in Santo Domingo, 809/586–6062 in Puerto Plata.*

CAR TRAVEL

Driving in the D.R. can be a harrowing and expensive experience; we don't recommend that the typical vacationer rent a car. It's best if you don't drive outside the major cities at night. If you must, use extreme caution, especially on narrow, unlighted mountain roads.

Car-Rental Contacts The major agencies can be found in most of the island's airports. **Avis** ☎ *800/331–1084* ⊕ *www.avis.com* ✉ *Las Américas Airport, San Domingo* ☎ *809/549–0468* ✉ *Gregorio Luperón International Airport, Puerto Plata* ☎ *809/586–0214* ✉ *Francisco Castillo Marquez, corner of Duarte, La Romana* ☎ *809/550–0600.* **Budget** ☎ *800/472–3325* ⊕ *www.budget.com* ✉ *Las Américas Airport, Santo Domingo* ☎ *809/549–0351* ✉ *Gregorio Luperón International Airport, Puerto Plata* ☎ *809/466–2028.* **Europcar** ✉ *Las Américas Airport, Santo Domingo* ☎ *809/549–0942* ⊕ *www.europcar.com* ✉ *Gregorio Luperón International Airport, Puerto Plata* ☎ *809/586–0215* ✉ *Punta Cana International Airport, Bavaro, Punta Cana* ☎ *809/959–0177.* **Hertz** ☎ *800/654–3001* ⊕ *www.hertz.com* ✉ *Las Américas Airport, Santo Domingo* ☎ *809/549–0454* ✉ *Puerto Plata* ☎ *809/586–0200.* **National** ☎ *809/549–8333, 809/523–3333.*

Local Car-rental Agencies MC Auto Rental Car ✉ *Las Américas Airport* ☎ *809/549–8911* ⊕ *www.mccarrental.com.*

TAXI TRAVEL

Wherever you are, hotel taxis are generally the best option. Carry small bills; drivers rarely have change. Recommendable radio-taxi companies in Santo Domingo are Tecni-Taxi (which also operates in Puerto Plata) and Apolo. You can use taxis to travel to out-of-town destinations at quoted rates. Check with your hotel or the dispatcher at the airport. From the Zona Colonial in Santo Domingo to Playa Dorada with Tecni-Taxi is $160. If you book through your hotel concierge, it can be more.

Contacts Apolo Taxi ☎ *809/537–0000, 809/537–1245 for a limo which must be booked far in advance.* **Taxi-Cabarete** ☎ *809/571–0767 in Cabarete.* **Taxi-Queen** ☎ *809/570–0000 in Santiago.* **Taxi-Sosúa** ☎ *809/571–3097 in Sosúa.* **Tecni-Taxi** ☎ *809/567–2010 in Santo Domingo, 809/566–7272 in Santo Domingo, 809/320–7621 in Puerto Plata.*

ESSENTIALS

Banks and Exchange Services Currency is the Dominican peso (written RD$). At this writing, the exchange rate is approximately RD$36 to US$1. You will not need to change money unless you plan to travel independently around the D.R. Banco Popular has many locations throughout the country, with ATMs that accept international cards.

Electricity 110–120 volts/60 cycles, the same as in the United States.

Emergency Services In Santo Domingo and major destinations, 911 is the general emergency number; you'll normally find an operator who can speak some English. If you need to speak to the police, contact

11

Politur, a police force that has been created and specially trained to aid tourists. Most officers speak some English, are polite, and are not as accustomed to thinking about getting money on the side—although it happens.

Health Never drink tap water in the D.R. (look for a hotel or restaurant that has earned an *H* for food-service hygiene or that has a Crystal America certification). Don't buy from the street vendors. Use mosquito repellant to protect yourself from mosquito-borne illnesses; long sleeves and long pants also help.

National Centers for Disease Control & Prevention (*CDC*). ☎ 877/394–8747 *international travelers' health line* ⊕ *www.cdc.gov/travel.*

Language Spanish is spoken in the D.R. Most staff at major tourist attractions and front-desk personnel in most major hotels speak English. Outside the popular tourist establishments, English is spoken less frequently.

Passport Requirements All U.S. citizens must carry a valid passport. Additionally, all visitors must have a valid tourist card, which costs $10 (purchased on arrival in cash with U.S. currency only).

Phones To call the D.R. from the United States, dial 1–809, and the local number. From the D.R. you also need dial only 1–809, then the number. To make a local call, you must dial 809 plus the seven-digit number (dial 1–809 if you are calling a cell phone). Directory assistance is 1411.

Safety Violent crime is rare. Nevertheless, poverty is everywhere in the D.R., and petty theft, pickpocketing, and purse snatching are an increasing concern, particularly in Santo Domingo. Pay attention, especially when leaving a bank or casino. Take hotel-recommended taxis at night.

Taxes The departure tax of $20 is almost always included in the price of your airline ticket. The government tax (IBIS) is a whopping 16% and is added to almost everything—bills at restaurants, hotels, sports activities, rental cars, and even many items at the supermarkets.

Tipping A 10% service charge is included in all hotel and restaurant bills. In restaurants, the bill will say *propino incluido* or simply *servis*. Even then it's still expected that you will tip an extra 5% to 10% if the service was good. Hotel maids typically get $1–$2 per day; taxi drivers, 10%; skycaps and hotel porters, $1 per bag.

ACCOMMODATIONS

A hotel in **Santo Domingo** allows you to enjoy the capital's great restaurants, nightlife, and historical sights, but most travelers visit the busy, overwhelming city as a day trip.

Boca Chica and **Juan Dolio** offer some of the island's cheapest—but most mediocre—all-inclusives, along with crowded beaches.

La Romana has Casa de Campo as well as a few resorts on other, better beaches, like on Bayahibe Bay; the region is within reasonable striking distance of Santo Domingo for those needing a taste of history to go with their *plátanos* (plantains).

The isolated, though beautiful, **Barahona** region offers a respite from development and overcrowding but is more than a three-hour drive from Santo Domingo.

Punta Cana reigns supreme for its many reasonably priced and now luxurious all-inclusives; it's better for those looking for a resort-based vacation than for the adventurous.

Samaná is somewhat isolated, less developed, and more bohemian. It is easier to reach now, with more flights arriving into the new El Catey International Airport, 25 miles (40 km) west of Samaná, and the new two-lane toll highway from Santo Domingo, with drive time just about two hours.

Playa Dorada, the D.R.'s original resort area, is still a complex of decent all-inclusives with a well-rated golf course, but more independent-minded travelers (and all windsurfers) may prefer **Sosúa** and **Cabarete,** where you'll still find a few charming independent inns and small resorts.

HOTEL AND RESTAURANT PRICES

Prices in the restaurant reviews are the average cost of a main course at dinner or, if dinner is not served, at lunch; taxes and service charges are generally included. Prices in the hotel reviews are the lowest cost of a standard double room in high season, excluding taxes, service charges, and meal plans (except at all-inclusives). Prices for rentals are the lowest per-night cost for a one-bedroom unit in high season.

VISITOR INFORMATION

Contacts **Dominican Republic One**. Dominican Republic One is a "trusted site" of the Secretariat de Turismo. It's written by bilingual staffers at the ministry and delivers the official word on the latest news, travel, and airline information. ⊕ *www.dr1.com.* **Dominican Republic Tourist Office.** ☎ *212/588–1012 in New York City, 888/374–6361 in New York City, 888/358–9594 in Miami* ⊕ *www. godominicanrepublic.com.*

WEDDINGS

There are no residency requirements. Blood tests are not mandatory. Original birth certificates and passports are required. Divorce certificates and proof that the bride and groom are single must be stamped by the Dominican Consulate. Documents must be submitted two weeks before the wedding and translated into Spanish.

EXPLORING THE DOMINICAN REPUBLIC

SANTO DOMINGO

Parque Independencia separates the old city from modern Santo Domingo, a sprawling, noisy city with a population of close to 2 million. The 12 cobblestone blocks of Santo Domingo's Zona Colonial contain most of the major sights in town. It's one of the most appealing historic districts in the Caribbean and is best explored on foot. The Zone ends at the seafront, called the Malecón.

11

Spanish civilization in the New World began in Santo Domingo's
12-block **Zona Colonial**. As you stroll its narrow streets, it's easy to
imagine this old city as it was when the likes of Columbus, Cortés, and
Ponce de León walked the cobblestones, pirates sailed in and out, and
colonists started settling. Tourist brochures claim that "history comes
alive here"—a surprisingly truthful statement. Almost every Thursday
to Sunday night at 8:30 a typical "folkloric show" is staged at Parque
Colón and Plaza de España. During the Christmas holidays there is
an artisans' fair and live-music concerts take place. A fun horse-and-
carriage ride throughout the Zona costs $25 for an hour, with any
commentary in Spanish. The steeds are no thoroughbreds, but they
clip right along. You can also negotiate to use them as a taxi, say, to
go down to the Malecón. The drivers usually hang out in front of the
Hostal Nicolas de Ovando. You can get a free walking-tour map and
brochures in English at the Secretaria de Estado de Turismo office at
Parque Colón (Columbus Park), where you may be approached by
freelance, English-speaking guides who will want to make it all come
alive for you. They'll work enthusiastically for $25 an hour for four
people. Simply put, the Zona is not as safe as it once was—particularly
at night and during festivals. Don't carry a lot of cash or your passport
(leave them in the hotel safe).

WHAT TO SEE

Alcazar de Colón. The castle of Don Diego Colón, built in 1517, has 40-inch-thick coral-limestone walls. The Renaissance-style structure, with its balustrade and double row of arches, has strong Moorish, Gothic, and Isabelline influences. The 22 rooms are furnished in a style to which the viceroy of the island would have been accustomed—right down to the dishes and the viceregal shaving mug. Costumed "docents" appear on Saturday morning. ⊠ *Plaza de España, off Calle Emiliano Tejera, Zona Colonial* ☎ *809/682–4750* ☜ *RD$100* ☉ *Mon.–Sat. 9–5, Sun. 9–4. Closed if no cruise ship in port.*

★ **Calle Las Damas.** "Ladies Street" was named after the elegant ladies of the court: in the Spanish tradition, they promenaded in the evening. Here you can see a sundial dating from 1753 and the Casa de los Jesuitas, which houses a fine research library for colonial history as well as the **Institute for Hispanic Culture**; admission is free, and it's open weekdays from 8 to 4:30. If you follow the street going toward the Malecón, you will pass a picturesque alley, fronted by a wrought-iron gate, where there are perfectly maintained colonial structures owned by the Catholic Church.

Casa de Tostado. The house, built in the early 16th century, was the residence of writer Don Francisco Tostado. Note its unique twin Gothic windows. It houses the Museo de la Familia Dominicana (Museum of the Dominican Family), which has exhibits on well-heeled 19th-century Dominican society. The house, garden, and antiquities have all been restored. ⊠ *Calle Padre Bellini 22, near Calle Arzobispo Meriño, Zona Colonial* ☎ *809/689–5000* ☜ *RD$60* ☉ *Mon.–Sat. 9–4.*

Casa del Cordón. This structure, built in 1503, is the western hemisphere's oldest surviving stone house. Columbus's son, Diego Colón, viceroy of the colony, and his wife lived here until the Alcazar was finished. It was in this house, too, that Sir Francis Drake was paid a ransom to prevent him from totally destroying the city. ⊠ *Calle Emiliano Tejera, at Calle Isabel la Católica, within Banco Popular, Zona Colonial* ☎ *809/544–8915* ☜ *Free* ☉ *Weekdays 9–4.*

★ **El Museo de las Casas Reales.** This is a remarkable museum that will help you comprehend the discovery of the New World by Christopher Columbus and the entire 16th-century epic. Housing Taíno finds, colonial artifacts, coins salvaged from wrecks of Spanish galleons, authentic colonial furnishings, as well as a collection of weapons, the museum also has one of the handsomest colonial edifices in the Zone. Built in the Renaissance style, it was the seat of Spanish government, housing the governor's office and the royal court. It has beautiful windows, for example, done in the Plateresque style. A frequent wedding venue, it also functions as an art gallery, with rotating shows. When candlelit at night, it's truly magical. ⊠ *Calle Las Damas, Zona Colonial* ☎ *809/688–8298* ☜ *RD$75* ☉ *Tues.–Sun. 9–5.*

Iglesia Santa Bárbara. This combination church and fortress, the only one of its kind in Santo Domingo, was completed in 1562. ⊠ *Av. Mella, between Calle Isabel la Católica and Calle Arzobispo Meriño, Zona*

The architecture in the town of Altos de Chavón re-creates a 16th-century Mediterranean village.

Colonial ☎ 809/682–3307 ⌨ *Free* ⊙ *Mon.–Sat. 6:00 am–6:45 pm; Sun. masses begin at 8 am; last mass at 6 pm.*

Monasterio de San Francisco. Constructed between 1512 and 1544, the St. Francis Monastery contained the church, convent, and hospital of the Franciscan order. Sir Francis Drake's demolition squad significantly damaged the building in 1586, and in 1673 an earthquake nearly finished the job, but when it's floodlit at night, the eerie ruins are dramatic indeed. The Spanish government has donated money to turn this into a beautiful cultural center, but we are still waiting. In the meantime, there's music many nights at 7 pm (often live), and it becomes an old-fashioned block party. Zone residents mingle with expats and tourists, who snap pictures of the octogenarians dancing the merengue and the bachata. Others who come are content to just sit in white plastic chairs, swaying and clapping. It's nice. ⊠ *Calle Hostos at Calle Emiliano, Zona Colonial* ☎ 809/687–4722.

Pantheon Nacional. The National Pantheon (circa 1714) was once a Jesuit monastery and later a theater. The real curiosity here is the military guard, who stays as still as the statues, despite the schoolchildren who try to make him flinch. ⊠ *Calle Las Damas, near Calle de Las Mercedes, Zona Colonial* ☎ 809/689–6010 ⌨ *Free* ⊙ *Mon.–Sat. 8 am to 9 pm.*

Parque Colón. The huge statue of Christopher Columbus in the park named after him dates from 1897, and is the work of sculptor Ernesto Gilbert. Like all the parks in the Zona Colonial, this one is quite a social gathering place. ⊠ *El Conde at Arzobispo Meriño, Zona Colonial.*

THE SOUTHWEST

Barahona. The drive west from Santo Domingo zigs and zags through small towns, passing coco and banana plantations until you get on the Carretera Azua, a fine highway with mountain views and fences of bougainvillea hiding fields of peppers and flowers. The city of Barahona is 120 miles (193 km) southwest of Santo Domingo, and about 3½ hours by car. It is the least cosmopolitan of the country's midsize cities, yet it is a college town. There is a Malecón (seafront promenade), which comes alive on weekends, where you can find popular seafood restaurants. It is west of the city, in the country, where simple pleasures and hostelries can be found. You can swim in the cascades of icy mountain rivers that flow down to beaches like San Rafael, just past Bahoruco, or submerge in hot thermal springs surrounded by dense foliage, *llanai* vines, and fruit trees. The Barahona region can be a tropical Garden of Eden.

Think of a trip to the Dominican Republic's southwestern provinces as an exotic safari. The variety of flamingos, crocodiles, iguanas, and many other kinds of animals is truly amazing. If you come to this wild part of the island, you can experience nature the way you were meant to, whether on solitary walks into the mountains or on daylong ecotours.

SOUTHEAST COAST

Las Américas Highway (built by the dictator Rafael Trujillo so his son could race his sports cars) runs east along the coast from Santo Domingo to La Romana—a two-hour drive. Midway are the well-established beach resorts such as Juan Dolio, and Sammy Sosa's hometown, San Pedro de Macorís. East of La Romana are Punta Cana and Bávaro, glorious beaches on the sunrise side of the island. Along the way is Higüey, an undistinguished city notable only for its giant concrete cathedral and shrine (someone had a vision of the Virgin Mary here), which resembles a pinched McDonald's arch.

★ **Altos de Chavón.** This re-creation of a 16th-century Mediterranean village sits on a bluff overlooking the Río Chavón, about 3 miles (5 km) east of the main facilities of Casa de Campo. There are cobblestone streets lined with lanterns, wrought-iron balconies, wooden shutters, courtyards swathed with bougainvillea, and **Iglesia St. Stanislaus**, the romantic setting for many a Casa de Campo wedding. More than a museum piece, this village is a place where artists live, work, and play. Dominican and international painters, sculptors, and artisans come here to teach sculpture, pottery, silk-screen printing, weaving, dance, and music at the school, which is affiliated with New York's Parsons School of Design. The artists work in their studios and crafts shops selling their finished wares.

FLAT TIRE

Blowout? A *gomero* can make a flat tire round! There are many such fellows, because the rough roads are rubber-eaters. You will see their signs on the highways and if stranded in a town, just ask: *¿Donde esta un gomero?*

The village also has an amber museum, an archaeological museum, five restaurants, and a number of unique shops.

Amphitheater. A 5,000-seat amphitheater features *Kandela*, a spectacular musical extravaganza showcasing the island's sensuous Afro-Caribbean dance moves, music, and culture. Concerts and celebrity performances by such singers as Julio Iglesias, his son Enrique, Sting, and the Pet Shop Boys share the amphitheater's schedule of events. Show dates vary to coincide with cruise-ship arrivals; the price is $35 for adults, $15 for children up to 12 years old. Many people make dinner reservations at **La Piazzetta** (Altos de Chavón ☎ 809/523–3333), the high-end Italian restaurant in Altos that belongs to Casa de Campo, prior to curtain call, as it is close to the amphitheater. It is known for its antipasto selections, homemade pasta, and authentic regional dishes; strolling musicians enliven its rustic ambience of ceramic tiles and cobblestone terrace. ⊠ *La Romana* ☎ *809/523–2424 for Kandela tickets* ⊕ *www.kandela.com.do* ⊠ *La Romana.*

Isla Saona. Off the east coast of Hispaniola lies this island, inhabited by sea turtles, pigeons, and other wildlife, but also not nearly as pristine as it should be for a national park (it's part of Parque Nacional Del Este). Indians once used caves here. The beaches are beautiful, and legend has it that Columbus once strayed here. Getting here, on catamarans and other excursion boats, is half the fun, but it can be a crowd scene. Vendors are allowed to sell to visitors, and there are a number of beach shacks serving lunch and drinks. Most boats traveling here leave out of the beach at Bayahibe Village. ⊠ *Bayahibe.*

San Pedro de Macorís. The national sport and the national drink are both well represented in this city, an hour or so east of Santo Domingo. Some of the country's best baseball games are played in Tetelo Vargas Stadium. Many Dominican baseball stars have their roots here, including George Bell, Tony Fernandez, Jose Río, and Sammy Sosa. The Macorís Rum distillery is on the eastern edge of the city. From 1913 through the 1920s this was a very important town—a cultural center—and mansions from that era are being restored by the Office of Cultural Patrimony, as are some remaining vestiges of 16th-century architecture and the town's cathedral, which has a pretense to Gothic architecture, even gargoyles. There is a nice promenade (the Malecón) along the port, and by night the beer and rum kiosks come alive. The Dominicans, Europeans, and now North Americans, who take self-catering apartments or condos in Juan Dolio, frequent San Pedro since it has the closest *supermercados* (Jumbo, Iberia—which also has a big pharmacy) and other small businesses.

SAMANÁ PENINSULA

Samaná is a dramatically beautiful peninsula, like an island unto itself, of coconut trees stretching into the sea. It's something of a microcosm of the Dominican Republic: here you'll see poverty and fancy resorts, good and bad (and really bad) roads, verdant mountainsides, tropical forests, tiny villages lined with street-side fruit vendors, secluded beaches, and the radiant warmth of the Dominican people.

A visit here is really about two things: exploring the preserved natural wonders and relaxing at a small beachfront hotel. The latter is most readily accomplished in **Las Terrenas,** the only true tourist center, where you can find picturesque restaurants, accommodations of all types, and great beaches. Reach it by taking a winding road through the mountains from the town of Sánchez. At Las Terrenas you can enjoy peaceful *playas,* take advantage of the vibrant nightlife (including a casino), and make all your plans for expeditions on the peninsula. The other pleasures are solitary—quiet beaches, the massive national park Los Haitises, and water sports and hiking. A relatively new toll road connects Santo Domingo to the peninsula; it's about a 2½-hour drive. Small El Catey International Airport is near Las Terrenas but receives primarily charter flights.

Fodor's Choice
★

Los Haitises National Park. One of the highlights of a trip to the Dominican Republic—and probably the most extraordinary part of a visit to the Samaná Peninsula—is a chance to explore Los Haitises National Park. Los Haitises (pronounced High-*tee*-sis), which is across Samaná Bay from the peninsula, is famous for its karst limestone formations, caves, and grottoes filled with pictographs and petroglyphs left by indigenous Taíno Indians who inhabited this area before Columbus's arrival.

The park is accessible only by boat, and a professionally guided tour is highly recommended—especially so you can kayak along the shoreline (there's no place to rent a kayak without a guide). Another option is to hire a fisherman to take you over on a small boat, but then you'll miss the guidance that an experienced operator can provide.

A good tour will let you visit the many caverns. Your flashlight will illuminate Taíno and pre-Taíno petroglyphs. You'll also find out how the forest slowly consumes the caves. But the best experience is being able to kayak here. Unlike mangrove kayaking trips in, say, the Florida Everglades, the mangroves here are dramatically flanked by the karst formations. It's a continual sensory delight. The islands rise dramatically and have wild growths of plant life and birds swooping around. You'll feel tiny, like a human speck surrounded by geological grandeur. ✉ *Samaná Bay* ☎ *no phone* 🎫 *Admission included with guided tour (recommended)* ☉ *Daily dawn–dusk.*

Taíno Park. This unique park attempts to tell the story of a lost civilization. The Taíno Indians, the indigenous people of this island, were the inhabitants here some 1,500 years ago…that is, until Christopher Columbus discovered it. And then came the inevitable clash between the Spanish colonials and these peaceful natives. The major exhibits comprise 25 animated scenes with life-size figures depicting the life of the Taínos and their conflict with the Spanish conquistadors. Their costumes came from the best movie-company makers in Europe. The museum has an archaeological exhibition of more than 200 pieces—bone, clay, stone, and wood. The tour is fully roofed, so you can visit the park even if it's raining. Plan on at least one hour with a personal audio guide (available in five languages). ✉ *Los Róbalos, Samaná* ☎ *809/729-1514* 🎫 *$15* ☉ *9–6, last entrance at 4:30.*

NORTH COAST

11

The Autopista Duarte ultimately leads (via a three- to four-hour drive) from Santo Domingo to the North Coast, sometimes called the Amber Coast because of its large, rich amber deposits. The coastal area around Puerto Plata, notably Playa Dorada, is a region of well-established, all-inclusive resorts and developments; the North Coast has more than 70 miles (110 km) of beaches, with condominiums and villas going up fast. The farther east you go from Puerto Plata and Sosúa, the prettier and less spoiled the scenery becomes. The autopista runs past Cabarete, a village that's a popular windsurfing haunt, and Playa Grande, which has a miraculously unspoiled white-sand beach.

PUERTO PLATA

Although it has been sleeping for decades, this was a dynamic city in its heyday, and it is coming back. You can get a feeling for this past in the magnificent Victorian gazebo in the central **Parque Independencia.** Recently painted a crisp white, the park looks postcard pretty, with gleaming new statuary. On Puerto Plata's own Malecón, which has had a multimillion-dollar refurbishment, the **Fortaleza de San Felipe** protected the city from many a pirate attack and was later used as a political prison. Nearby, a new amphitheater is in the planning stages. The nearby **lighthouse** has been restored. Big changes are in store in this town, which is just realizing what it needs to do to become a tourist destination. The Office of Cultural Patrimony, which has done an admirable job of pulling the Zona Colonial from the darkness, is at work. Simultaneously, a group of private business owners and investors have developed a long-term plan for beautifying this city, which has hundreds of classic wooden gingerbread buildings. Mansions, including Casa Olivores and the Tapounet family home, are being restored; a Victorian mansion on Calle Jose del Carmen is now a gallery and coffee shop. Architect Sara Garcia is redesigning the family home of Independence hero Gregory Luperon to create a museum for national heroes.

Mt. Isabel de Torres. Southwest of Puerto Plata, this mountain soars 2,600 feet above sea level and is notable for its huge statue of Christ. Up there also are botanical gardens that, despite efforts, still are not memorable. You can choose to hire a knowledgeable English-speaking guide for $5 a person. A cable car takes you to the top for a spectacular view. The cars usually wait until filled to capacity before going up—which makes them cozy; and should the electricity happen to go off, there is no backup generator. You should visit in the morning, preferably by 9 am; by afternoon the cloud cover rolls in, and you can see practically nothing. ■ TIP➔ The vendors are particularly tenacious here. ⊠ *Off Autopista Duarte, follow signs, Puerto Plata* ☎ *809/970–0438* 🖂 *Cable car RD$350* ☾ *Mon.–Sun. 9–6.*

Museo de Ambar Dominicano (*Dominican Amber Museum*). In a lovely old galleried mansion, this museum displays and sells the Dominican Republic's national stone: semiprecious, translucent amber. Amber is essentially prehistoric hardened tree sap, and Dominican amber is considered the best in the world. Many pieces are fascinating for what they have trapped inside, and the museum contains a piece with a lizard reported to be 50 million years old, give or take a few millennia. The museum's English text is informative. Shops on the museum's first floor sell amber, souvenirs, and ceramics. ⊠ *Calle Duarte 61, Puerto Plata* ☎ *809/261–3610* ⌦ *RD$50* ☉ *Mon.–Fri. 9–5, Sat 9–noon.*

Ocean World Adventure Park. This multimillion-dollar aquatic park in Cofresí has marine and wildlife interactive programs, including dolphin and sea lion shows and encounters, a double-dolphin swim, a tropical reef aquarium, stingrays, shark tanks, a rain forest, and a Tiger Grotto inhabited by Bengal tigers. You don't have to come on a tour, but you must make advance reservations if you want to participate in one of the swims or encounters. For example, if you are brave enough for the shark encounter, you will feed them and touch them in the shark lagoon; the stingray encounter is included as well. If you're staying in the Puerto Plata or Cabarete area, ask at your hotel for tour schedules; if you are at nearby Lifestyle resorts, transfers are free. ⊠ *Calle Principal 3, Cofresí, Puerto Plata* ☎ *809/291–1000* ⊕ *www.oceanworldadventurepark.com* ⌦ *$55, extra for additional activities/encounters* ☉ *Daily 9–5.*

SOSÚA

This small community was settled during World War II by 600 Austrian and German Jews. After the war many of them returned to Europe or went to the United States, and most who remained married Dominicans. Only a few Jewish families reside in the community today, and there's only the original one-room wooden synagogue. A small park has been built on the waterfront to commemorate the Jewish colony.

Sosúa is called Puerto Plata's little sister, and consists of two communities—El Batey, the modern hotel development, and Los Charamicos, the old quarter—separated by a cove and one of the island's prettiest beaches. The sand is soft and white, the water crystal-clear and calm. The walkway above the beach is packed with tents filled with souvenirs, pizzas, and even clothing for sale. The town had developed a reputation for prostitution, but much is being done to eliminate that and to clean up the more garish elements. Upscale condos and hotels are springing up, and the up-and-coming Dominican families are coming back to the big houses on the bay.

Museo Judío Sosúa. Sosúa is not a destination known for its sights. However, this museum stands as an exception, chronicling the immigration and settlement of the Jewish refugees in the 1940s. This is a fascinating place, and depending on the docent, you may hear that the Jewish settlers experienced a certain amount of prejudice here when they arrived. The adjacent small wooden synagogue is the wedding spot for many Jewish couples from abroad. Be sure to call ahead to arrange your visit. ⊠ *Calle Dr. Rosen at David Stern, Sosúa* ☎ *809/571–2633* ⌦ *RD$75.*

CIBAO VALLEY

The heavily trafficked four-lane highway north from Santo Domingo, known as the Autopista Duarte, cuts through the banana plantations, rice and tobacco fields, and royal poinciana trees of the Cibao Valley.

Hand-rolling cigars in the Cibao Valley

Along the road are stands where a few pesos buy pineapples, mangoes, avocados, *chicharrones* (fried pork rinds), and fresh-fruit drinks.

SANTIAGO

The second city of the D.R., where many past presidents were born, sits about 90 miles (145 km) northwest of Santo Domingo and is about an hour's drive from Puerto Plata and 90 minutes from Cabarete via the scenic mountain road. An original route from centuries past, the four-lane highway between Santiago and Puerto Plata is dotted with sugar mills. The Office of Cultural Patrimony is overseeing their restoration. Although an industrial center, Santiago has a surprisingly charming, provincial feel; the women of Santiago are considered among the country's most beautiful. High on a plateau is an impressive monument honoring the restoration of the republic. Traditional yet progressive, Santiago is still relatively new to the tourist scene but already has several thriving restaurants and new hotels. It's definitely worth setting aside some time to explore the city. Colonial-style buildings—with wrought-iron details and tiled porticoes—date from as far back as the 1500s. Others are from the Victorian era, with the requisite gingerbread latticework and fanciful colors, and recent construction is nouveau Victorian. Santiago is the cigar-making center; the Fuente factory is here, though its cigars can be bought on the island only in special designated cigar stores and clubs. (If you see them for sale on the streets, they are counterfeit.)

Fodor's Choice
★

Centro León. Without question, this is a world-class cultural center for the Dominican arts. A postmodern building with an interior space full of light from a crystal dome, the center includes several attractions, including a multimedia biodiversity show, a museum dedicated to the history of the Dominican Republic, a simulated local market, a dramatic showcase of Dominican art and sculpture, galleries for special exhibits, a sculpture garden, an aviary, classrooms, and a replica of the León family's first cigar factory, where a dozen cigar rollers turn out handmade cigars. There's even a first-rate cafeteria and a museum shop where you can buy high-quality, artsy souvenirs and jewelry. Check the website for activities and night events. It can be a fine way to meet Santiagoans who have a high level of fluency in English. ⊠ *Av. 27 de Febrero 146, Villa Progresso, Santiago* ☏ *809/582–2315* ⊕ *www.centroleon.org.do* ⊡ *RD$100, guides in English RD$250* ⊙ *Exhibitions Tues.–Sun. 10–7.*

THE CIBAO VALLEY

Jarabacoa. Nature lovers should consider a trip to Jarabacoa, in the mountainous region known rather wistfully as the Dominican Alps. There's little to do in the town itself but eat and rest up for excursions on foot, horseback, or by motorbike taxi to the surrounding waterfalls and forests—quite incongruous in such a tropical country. Other activities include adventure tours, particularly white-water rafting or canoe trips, jeep safaris, and paragliding. Accommodations in the area are rustic but homey.

La Vega Vieja. Founded in 1495 by Columbus, La Vega is the site of one of the oldest settlements in the New World. You may find the tour of the ruins of the original settlement, Old La Vega, rewarding. About 3 miles (5 km) north of La Vega is Santo Cerro (Holy Mount), site of a miraculous apparition of the Virgin and therefore many local pilgrimages. The Convent of La Merced is here, and the views of the Cibao Valley are breathtaking. The town's remarkable Concepción de la Vega Church was constructed in 1992 to commemorate the 500th anniversary of the discovery of America. The unusual modern Gothic style—all curvaceous concrete columns, arches, and buttresses—is striking.

La Vega is also celebrated for its Carnival, featuring haunting devil masks. These papier-mâché creations are intricate, fanciful gargoyles painted in surreal colors; spiked horns and real cows' teeth lend an eerie authenticity. Several artisans work in dark, cramped studios throughout the area; their skills have been passed down for generations.

WHERE TO EAT

The island's culinary repertoire includes Spanish, Italian, Middle Eastern, Indian, Japanese, and *nueva cocina Dominicana* (contemporary Dominican cuisine). If seafood is on the menu, it's bound to be fresh. The dining scene in Santo Domingo is the best in the country and probably offers as fine a selection of restaurants as you will find anywhere in the Caribbean. Keep in mind that the touristy restaurants, such as those in the Zona Colonial, with mediocre fare and just-okay service, are becoming more and more costly, whereas the few fine-dining options here have lowered some of their prices—for example, La Residence now offers a daily chef's menu with three courses for about $22. Or you can order two generous appetizers for, say, $15. You will have caring service and be sequestered in luxe surroundings away from the tourist hustle. Know that *capitaleños* (residents of Santo Domingo) dress for dinner and dine late. The crowds pick up after 9:30 pm.

What to Wear: In resort areas, shorts and bathing suits under beach wraps are usually (but not always) acceptable at breakfast and lunch. For dinner, long pants, skirts, and collared shirts are the norm. Restaurants tend to be more formal in Santo Domingo, both at lunch and at dinner, with trousers required for men and dresses suggested for women. Ties aren't required anywhere, but jackets are (even at the midday meal) in some of the finer establishments.

SANTO DOMINGO

ZONA COLONIAL

$$ ✕ **Caffe Bellini.** This café has always had a panache far and above its
ITALIAN   counterparts, for the Italian owners also have the adjacent furniture
★   design center. The modern wicker-weave barrel chairs and the contemporary art and light fixtures are conspicuously hip. The democratic pricing usually offers pasta dishes, such as the trio of raviolis (spinach, beet, and pumpkin) for about $10. (Pricing is the same at lunch and dinner.) Also know that an amuse bouche, perhaps a tomato bruschetta, can usually suffice for an appetizer. The addition of grilled portabellas to a classic arugula-and-shaved-Parmesan salad is brilliant. Main courses of meat or seafood are accompanied by pasta or grilled vegetables and potato. You can enjoy Italian liquors here such as grappa; dessert might be dark-chocolate mousse and fresh mango sorbet. Service is laudable, the manager, Franco, both professional and charming—and the music like nothing you will hear on the street! $ *Average main: $14* ✉ *Plazaoleta Park, Arzobispo Meriño, corner of Padre Bellini, Zona Colonial, Santo Domingo* ☎ *809/686–0424, 809/686–3387* ⊗ *Closed Sun. Closed Mon. 3–6.*

$$$ ✕ **La Residence.** This fine-dining enclave has always had the setting—
FRENCH   Spanish-colonial architecture, with
Fodor's Choice   pillars and archways overlooking a
★   courtyard—but an esoteric lunch-dinner menu with high prices that did not always deliver offset it. Now it has a French Certified Master Chef, Denis Schetrit (there are only 300 such designated chefs), who serves classically grounded yet innovative cuisine. He also cleverly utilizes local produce and offers many moderately priced choices. An amuse bouche arrives before your meal, and there is an excellent bread service. The three-course daily *menu de chef* is less than $28, including tax. It could be brochettes of spit-roasted duck, chicken au

ON THE MENU

Among the best Dominican specialties are *queso frito* (fried cheese), *sancocho* (a thick stew of meats, served with rice and avocado slices), *arroz con pollo* (rice with beans and chicken), *pescado al coco* (fish in coconut sauce), *platanos* (plantains), and *tostones* (fried green plantains). Presidente is the best local beer. Brugal rum is popular with the Dominicans, but Barceló *añejo* (aged) rum is as smooth as cognac, and Barceló Imperial is so special that it's sold only around Christmastime.

poivre, or vegetable risotto. You could start with a salad of pan-fried young squid and leave room for a luscious French pastry. Veer from the daily specials menu, and prices can go higher, but they remain fair; even the grilled Angus fillet and braised oxtail with foie-gras sauce and wild mushrooms is reasonable. Often, musicians romantically serenade diners. $ *Average main: $21 ⊠ Hostal Nicolas de Ovando, Calle Las Damas, Zona Colonial ☏ 809/685–9955.*

PUNTA CANA

$$$
SEAFOOD
Fodor'sChoice
★

✕ **Blue Marlin.** The setting here is reminiscent of a fantasy island in the South Pacific, with dining beneath a palapa (an open-sided structure with a thatched palm roof) on a pier that sits over the Caribbean's gentle waters at the Sanctuary Cap Cana (⇨ *Where to Stay*). The Blue Marlin's own small fleet of fishing boats harvests the waters daily for fresh catch, which are among the most popular menu items. Fish specialties come from the island and around the world—Mexico, Peru, and Spain—with many dishes from the Pacific Rim. Appetizer examples include Caribbean lobster cakes and Asian calamari rolls with sweet-and-spicy chili sauce and cilantro. Symbols on the menu indicate if an item is healthful, vegetarian, or vegan. Lobster and other high-ticket seafood items do come with a supplement if you have the A-I plan. The executive chef, a French Canadian, elevates lunch offerings with innovations such as wasabi or spicy chipotle mayonnaise. (Nonhotel guests are welcome at this and all of the Sanctuary's fine restaurants, but they must make reservations to pass through the security gates.) $ *Average main: $24 ⊠ Sanctuary Cap Cana, Cap Cana, Playa Juanillo ☏ 809/562–9191 ⌂ Reservations essential.*

$$$
SEAFOOD
Fodor'sChoice
★

✕ **Jellyfish.** With round edges evoking the shape of its namesake, and double decks reminiscent of a yacht, this open-air restaurant on the sand puts the accent on maritime, and gets it right in both food as well as form. Main dining-room tables are on light wooden platforms, sheltered by thatched roofing but not fully enclosed. When weather demands it, sheer white linens are secured to the wooden railings to protect against sun, wind, or rain without obstructing the exquisite beachfront views. Other tables are under palapas right on the beach. At night, soft lighting creates a romantic effect, and lounge music enhances the ambience. Fresh seafood caught by local fishermen is the focus of the menu, but chicken and beef dishes are also available, as is a special children's menu. Lobster lovers can look forward to sinking their claws into the oven-baked *langosta de la casa* (house lobster tail, about 2½ lb.). For a more diverse shellfish meal, try the seafood grill for two, which includes crawfish, lobster, shrimp, conch, and octopus, with a grilled vegetable antipasto to start. If you spend a minimum of $100, Jellyfish includes free transportation back to your hotel (though not a free ride to the restaurant). Some resorts, like Paradisus Palma Real and the Barceló Bávaro complex, are within walking distance. The space is often closed for private parties and weddings (some 100 days a year now), so reservations are essential (and mandatory if you want complementary transportation). $ *Average main: $30 ⊠ On the beach, between*

Meliá Caribe Tropical and IFA Villas, Playa Bávaro ☎ *809/840–7684 restaurant, 809/868–3040 office* ⚓ *Reservations essential.*

$$
SEAFOOD
Fodor'sChoice
★

✕ **Playa Blanca.** On a white-sand beach shaded by coco palms, the dining area sheltered by a large palapa, understated coolness at this restaurant comes in shades of white on white: in the gauzy fabric, the geometric tableware, the contemporary Euro-chairs, and the servers' uniforms. Service is efficient, friendly, and fun; a DJ makes it a party on alternate Thursdays, Sundays, and holidays. Hedonistic detail emerges in the Balinese sun beds in the sand, and background chill-out music with a quickened pace completes the mood. Start with a perfectly executed cocktail—like a lime or mango daiquiri. Food is savvy and simple—fresh fish is still a staple; opt for fried or grilled. Each winter season of this young restaurant's life, though, the offerings have become more creative. More daring choices include a dip of mashed eggplant, Parmesan, and prosciutto; shrimp and crab tempura wrapped in rice paper with a mango-passion-fruit-coriander sauce; and spicy Dominican goat. The prices are an excellent value for the product: braised conch, as a main, is just $10, and there are pasta, risotto, and ravioli dishes in the early teens. You usually have to pay for the sides, but $3 for some yucca mashed with blue cheese—why not? The best dessert is the chocolate fondant filled with molten *dulce de leche,* with a scoop of vanilla ice cream. ⑤ *Average main: $20* ⊠ *Puntacana Resort & Club, Playa Blanca* ☎ *809/959–2714.*

NORTH COAST

The Cabarete area in particular—where all-inclusive resorts don't yet totally dominate the scene—has some fun, original restaurants, but these are often small places, so it's important that you make reservations in advance. Expat residents complain that the prices in this town have moved past the good-value-for-money mark. Also, more and more restaurants are insisting on cash only, be it pesos, dollars, or euros. Costa Dorada and Playa Dorada each have a lovely fine-dining option, *listed below.*

PUERTO PLATA

$$$
EUROPEAN
Fodor'sChoice
★

✕ **Lucía.** Lucía's menu is comprehensive and contemporary. The setting is as artistic as a gallery—befitting its location within Casa Colonial, a refined boutique hotel. Picture orchids galore, crisp white linens, and attentive waiters in white guayabera shirts. Guests love the one-of-a-kind appetizers, like the Tris-Viche, a ceviche of Chilean sea bass, tuna, and lobster. A main course headliner is the Duck Connection—a grilled breast, crispy leg confit, and foie gras served with rum-mango sauce and mashed pumpkin. Carnivores with more basic tastes can order an Angus fillet. The molten chocolate volcano with vanilla ice cream is the dessert you want. When the digestif cart is rolled over, be daring with a Brunello grappa or the local Brugal Unico rum, and look out to the orchids clinging to the trees and the tropical mangrove garden. It's the good life at Lucía. ⑤ *Average main: $25* ⊠ *Casa Colonial, Playa Dorada* ☎ *809/320–3232.*

SOSÚA

$ **× B.Y.O.W. Restaurant.** This restaurant's name stands for "Bring Your
EUROPEAN Own Wine." This new concept was established at the former Casa Valeria, and the evolved menu and exceptional prices have made this Sosúa's
in place. A palm tree snakes its way through the thatched roof that rises
above the salmon-colored adobe walls. From the expanded kitchen such
classics as escargots Provençales emerge, as well as inimitable pastas
such as a carbonara with a splash of Amaretto. Guests brag about the
filet mignon au poivre with caramelized onions and mashed potatoes.
Chill with the soothing CDs as you move on to crêpes with bitter orange
and Grand Marnier confit. Breakfast is also very popular here, notably
the yogurt parfaits and frittatas. Brand new is the afternoon teatime
menu: coffee or tea with scones and clotted cream or, say, house-made
tiramisu or chocolate mousse. $ *Average main: $12* ⊠ *Calle Dr. Rosen
28, El Batey, Sosúa* ☎ *809/463–3710* ⊘ *No lunch or dinner Wed.*

CABARETE

$ **× Cabahá.** The hip decor of this diminutive café a few steps from the
CAFÉ beach illustrates the same good taste as the music, top-shelf liquor,
fresh-fruit drinks, and healthful fare. The fresh mango juice with
añejo rum and triple sec may be the best cocktail you'll have in the
Dominican Republic—unless you try the special-recipe mojitos with
crushed ice. Breakfast can be anything from fresh smoothies to muesli,
omelets, crêpes, and fresh bagels. Organic salads and sandwiches, such
as smoked salmon and cream cheese on dark bread, are on the lunch
menu. *Picaderas* (tapas) and fish ceviche are on offer for dinner. New
American owners have kept many of the original items on the menu
(such as the hummus with a drizzle of house-made pepper oil), redeco-
rated, expanded the cocktail menu, and added more innovative sandwiches and high-quality wines (mainly French and Italian) available by
the glass and the bottle. Everything is low-calorie and healthful, which
leaves room for decadent desserts such as chocolate cake, which pairs
well with one of their specialty coffees. $ *Average main: $10* ⊠ *Paseo
Don Chiche 14, across from Fred's, Cabarete* ☎ *809/571–9222* ⊕ *www.
cabaha.com* ▭ *No credit cards* ⊘ *Closed Tues.*

$ **× EZE Bar & Restaurant.** This little place, at the far end of the beach,
ECLECTIC doesn't look like much, but it has an intensely loyal following, from wal-
let-watching windsurfers to wealthy *capitaleño* (from Santo Domingo)
families. Menu names, which reflect the jargon of the surfers who frequent the place, include Bluebird's Salad (chicken tenders over mixed
greens with a sweet chili salsa), the EZE Club Dude (curried grilled
chicken), and the Rocker (grilled, marinated beef with onions, peppers,
tomato, and tzitiki on a soft pita). You can get an energy kick from
yogurt-and-mango smoothies. Fresh-squeezed juices have morphed into
some of the most interesting, frosty, tropical cocktails. The blenders
also churn out healthful, organic vegetable drinks. Conversely, if you
need a bacon-cheeseburger fix, this is the place. EZE is an extremely
family- and dog-friendly place; there's an extensive children's menu and
lots of kids' beach toys and furniture. $ *Average main: $10* ⊠ *Cabarete Beach, in front of Carib Wind Center, Cabarete* ☎ *809/571–0586*
▭ *No credit cards.*

$$ ╳ **Miró Gallery & Restaurant.** The menu here continues to reflect the inter-
ECLECTIC   ests of the owner, Lydia Wazana, who is prominent in the local art scene.
★   From season to season, Lydia adds new ideas that she brings back from
her travels (even from nearby Santo Domingo), such as the mofongo
de platano maduro with queso frito. Another new menu addition is
a green gazpacho—a cool, delicious mixture of raw spinach, lettuce,
and cucumber. Innovative Italian favorites such as risotto of scallops
with mint still grace the menu; the chef's Caribbean creation of risotto
with sweet plantain, avocado, and shrimp may be the sweetest risotto
you've ever had. The *zarzuela* (seafood stew), lobster with bisque sauce,
Thai curry shrimp, and seared sesame tuna are all huge client favor-
ites. Despite the fact that it's smack on the beach, grilled local and
imported beef, as well as the churrasco burger, sell out rapidly. Sushi
continues to be prepared with high-quality ingredients, and Lydia is
very aware of celiac, gluten-free, vegetarian, and kosher needs. Lunch
is now served on weekends. Take a table on the sand and listen to the
gentle jazz. Miró sponsors sceney music events, too. Ⓢ *Average main:
$18* ⊠ *Cabarete Beach, Cabarete* ☎ *809/853–6848* ☉ *Closed Oct. 15–
Nov. 15. No weekdays.*

$$ ╳ **Natura Restaurant at Natura Cabana.** If you're staying at this beach-
SEAFOOD   front ecolodge, you'll likely take most of your meals here. If not, it's
★   definitely worth a trip, not only for the freshest of seafood, but for the
soothing ambience. Come early for a passion-fruit martini and stroll
the private beach as the sunset colors the sky. Seafood is at the heart
of the menu here, and appropriately so, because diners listen to the
sounds of the waves crashing on coral rock as they fork the catch of
the day. The menu changes with the seasons while holding tight to some
perennial favorites. Start with a tartare, a ceviche (*mixto* is the best),
or a carpaccio like the octopus or beef. It all tastes so fresh because it
is. (The vegetables and herbs are farmed at Natura's organic garden.)
The filet mignon with blue-cheese sauce and the grilled lobster with
garlic spaghetti are recommendable mains. For dessert, enjoy a classic
such as tiramisu. The wines are French, Spanish, and Chilean (go for
the *reservas*). Tables are set with geometric plates and oversize wine
glasses. Service is warm, caring, and efficient, the international music
atmospheric. Ⓢ *Average main: $19* ⊠ *Natura Cabana, Perla Marina,
Cabarete* ☎ *809/858–5822, 809/571–1507* ⚑ *Reservations essential.*

SANTIAGO

The D.R.'s second city, Santiago, has always been a lovely, provincial
place; the draw nowadays is the wonderful art gallery and museum,
Centro León. Most people come from the Puerto Plata area as day-
trippers, but a few spend the night, especially if they fly in directly from
New York. From Sosúa and Cabarete it's about a 1½-hour drive on the
scenic highway that passes through mountain villages; from Puerto Plata
it's about 1 hour, from Santo Domingo 2½ hours. Those who come for
the day can at least enjoy lunch in one of Santiago's great restaurants.

$ ╳ **Il Pasticcio.** Everyone from college students to cigar kings, presidents
ITALIAN   to politicos, and movie producers to stars packs this eccentrically
★

decorated culinary landmark, which opened in 1995. Tourists take photos of the bathrooms, with their ornate mirrors and Romanesque plaster sinks. Chef-owner Paolo, a true *paisano*, makes this bungalow a personality palace. If he is not on the premises, you can bet that either the yellow or pink Vespa is missing from the dining area, as he drives them to market. A living art gallery, this is where the artists, poets, and intelligentsia hang. His mouthwatering creations are authentic and fresh. Ask about the *menu degustacion* (tasting menu, $17). Or try the great antipasto selections; commence with the Pasticcio salad, which might have smoked salmon, mozzarella, anchovies, capers, and baby arugula. Even the bread service comes with three sauces: one is like pesto, there's a pomodoro, and the best is a creamy anchovy sauce. They can all be had on pasta, too. And if it's too dim to read the menu, just look up—it's also written on the ceiling. Finish with a shot of limoncello and cheesecake or handmade gelato with strawberries marinated in wine. The value here is remarkable. ⑤ *Average main: $14* ⊠ *Calle 3, No. 5, at Av. Del Llano, Cerros de Gurabo* ☎ *809/582–6061* ⊘ *Closed Mon. and 3:30–7 pm.*

WHERE TO STAY

The Dominican Republic has the largest hotel inventory (at this writing some 70,000 rooms, with even more under construction) in the Caribbean and draws large numbers of stateside visitors. Surfers can still find digs for $25 a night in Cabarete, and the new generation of luxurious all-inclusives in Punta Cana and Uvero Alto is simply incredible.

Santo Domingo properties generally base their tariffs on the European Plan (no meals)—though many include breakfast—and maintain the same room rates year-round. Beach resorts have high winter rates, with prices reduced for the shoulder seasons of late spring and early fall (summer has become another strong season). All-inclusives dominate in Punta Cana. Cabarete was a stronghold of the small inn, but it does have all-inclusives. Villa rentals are gaining in popularity all over the island, particularly in Cabarete and the Cabrera area.

During your stay your patience may be tested at times, particularly at all-inclusives. Even in the touristic zones, the D.R. still has vestiges of a third-world country. The nodding in and out of the electricity is one annoyance, and sometimes the *plantas* (generators) either don't kick in or wheeze and hiss from age. Service lapses and the language barrier can also be frustrating. But when an employee sincerely says, "How can I serve you, missus?" followed by, "It's a pleasure to help you. Have a happy day!" you're pleasantly reminded of the genuine hospitality of the locals. You gotta love it!

For expanded reviews, facilities, and current deals, visit Fodors.com.

SANTO DOMINGO

The seaside capital of the country is in the middle of the island's south coast. In Santo Domingo, most of the better hotels are on or near the Malecón, with several small, desirable properties in the trendy Zona

Colonial, allowing you to feel part of that magical environment. The capital is where you'll find some of the most sophisticated hotels and restaurants, not to mention nightlife. However, such an urban vacation is best coupled with a beach stay elsewhere on the island.

ZONA COLONIAL

$

B&B/INN

Coco Boutique Hotel. Behind the pale, Caribbean turquoise façade you'll find a very untypical bed-and-breakfast, not to mention earth tones with white—almost everywhere: the reception and lounge, the stark, wooden staircase, the grillwork on the French doors; it's breathtaking, actually, with the zebra-skin rug and dark green plants offering contrast. **Pros:** amazingly quiet for the Zona Colonial; opposite the picturesque Plaza Pellerano Castro; rooftop terrace with Balinese sun beds from which you can wave to the cruise ships. **Cons:** bathrooms are small; heels on the wooden staircase are noisy. **TripAdvisor:** "chic place," "serene and extraordinary service," "lovely place in great location." ⑤ *Rooms from: $105* ⊠ *Arzobispo Porte 7, corner of Las Damas, Zona Colonial* ☎ *809/685–8467* ⊕ *www.cocoboutiquehotel.com* ⌁ *5 rooms* ⑩ *Breakfast.*

$$

HOTEL

Fodor's Choice

★

Hostal Nicolas de Ovando. This branch of the M Gallery, a chain of historic boutique hotels, was sculpted from the residence of the first governor of the Americas, and it just might be the best thing to happen in the Zone since Diego Columbus's palace was finished in 1517. **Pros:** lavish breakfast buffet; beautifully restored historic section. **Cons:** breakfast is no longer included; pricey; rooms could be larger. **TripAdvisor:** "a real jewel," "very nice retreat with lots of character," "great food." ⑤ *Rooms from: $220* ⊠ *Calle Las Damas, Zona Colonial* ☎ *809/685–9955, 800/763–4835* ⊕ *www.mgallery.com* ⌁ *100 rooms, 4 suites.*

$

B&B/INN

★

Hotel La Atarazana. A white wrought-iron gate opens to a small foyer with a large mirror and a vase of long-stem tropical flowers at this artistically renovated town house. **Pros:** superior service; excellent, safe location near Plaza de España but not on a touristy block; impressive rooftop terrace has views and both sunny and shaded sitting areas. **Cons:** no luxurious creature comforts beyond cable TV, Wi-Fi, and now a/c in all rooms; the multilingual owners aside, employees are not fluent in English; rooms are not large by American standards. **TripAdvisor:** "wonderful staff," "small place with tons of charm," "yummy breakfast." ⑤ *Rooms from: $100* ⊠ *Vicente Celestino Duarte 19, next door to police station, Zona Colonial* ☎ *809/688–3693* ⊕ *www.hotel-atarazana.com* ⌁ *6 rooms* ⑩ *Breakfast.*

BEST BETS FOR LODGING

BEST FOR ROMANCE
Peninsula House, Excellence Punta Cana

BEST POOL
Casa Colonial Beach and Spa, Dreams Punta Cana Resort & Spa

BEST SERVICE
Hilton Santo Domingo, Tortuga Bay Villas

BEST FOR KIDS
Club Med Punta Cana, Casa de Campo

GAZCUE

$$
HOTEL
★

☷ **Hilton Santo Domingo.** This has become *the* address on the Malecón for businesspeople, convention attendees, and leisure travelers. **Pros:** Sunday brunch is one of the city's top tickets; luxe bedding; totally soundproof rooms; the executive-level lounge. **Cons:** little about the property is authentically Dominican; Vista Bar in lobby is closed on weekends. **TripAdvisor:** "a place to rest," "nice view of the sea," "the perfect gift." ⑤ *Rooms from: $189* ✉ *Av. George Washington 500, Gazcue* ☎ *809/685-0000* ⊕ *hiltoncaribbean.com/santodomingo* ⇄ *228 rooms, 32 suites* ☉ *No meals.*

$$
HOTEL

☷ **Renaissance Jaragua Hotel & Casino.** This sprawling pink oasis is perennially popular, particularly with Americans, for its beautiful grounds and huge free-form pool. **Pros:** hotel is busy and lively; hotel will match any discount Internet rate; BP and optional all-inclusive plan (rare in Santo Domingo) available. **Cons:** can be a bit too busy at times; nothing understated about the decor, which borders on glitzy; some rooms are still waiting for their renovation. **TripAdvisor:** "great pool," "excellent friendly staff," "perfect combo of business and relaxation." ⑤ *Rooms from: $155* ✉ *Av. George Washington 367, Gazcue* ☎ *809/221-2222* ⊕ *www.marriott.com* ⇄ *292 rooms, 8 suites* ☉ *No meals.*

SOUTHEAST COAST

La Romana is on the southeast coast, about a two-hour drive from Santo Domingo and the same distance southwest of Punta Cana. An international airport here has nonstop service from the United States. Casa de Campo's Marina Chavón, with its Mediterranean design and impressive yacht club and villa complex, is as fine a marina facility as can be found anywhere. The shops and restaurants are a big draw for all tourists to the area, as is Altos de Chavón, the re-created 16th-century Mediterranean town on the grounds of Casa de Campo. The resorts in nearby Bayahibe Bay, which has an idyllic, horseshoe-shape beach and a real fishing village, have always been popular with capitaleños and Europeans. But North Americans are also checking in here and leaving satisfied. Often, when guests want to party down, they buy an inexpensive night pass to the Viva Wyndhams, allowing them entry to the resort's discos along with dinner and drinks. The actual town of La Romana is not pretty or quaint, although it has a lovely central park and a couple of recommendable restaurants, and is a real slice of Dominican life. ■ **TIP**➔ One way to sample the wares at Casa de Campo if you can't afford to stay there is to buy the resort's day pass ($75 for adults, $45 for children 4–12 years). It will give you a place in the sun at Minitas Beach, towels, nonmotorized water sports, lunch at the Beach Club by Le Cirque, and entrance to Altos de Chavon.

PRIVATE VILLA RENTALS

Villas in the DR. Villas in the DR is a small, personalized business that rents, manages, and sells Casa de Campo properties. Altogether the company manages 40 different villas: most are comfortable and stylish, but moderately priced compared with some of the resort's luxury offerings. The company will also do your grocery shopping for $35 (maids will make breakfast and lunch, if requested). Since these are direct-from-owner rentals, not all units are always available. A $20-per-day resort fee ($10-per-day for children over 10) allows private-rental guests to tap into Casa's grand facilities. Check-in is at the villa owners' club at Casa reception; cash, wire transfers, money orders, and checks are accepted for payment. It is possible to rent a four-person golf cart. ■TIP→ Newly expanded rental options include villas in Punta Cana, Palmar Villa de Ocoa, and Villa Pajon in the mountains. ⊠ *La Romana* ☎ *809/299–0722 cell* ⊕ *www.VillasinDR.com.*

HOTELS AND RESORTS

$$$$
ALL-INCLUSIVE
☾
Fodor's Choice
★

Casa de Campo. The country's most illustrious resort, which set the benchmark for luxury travel in the Caribbean decades ago, has entered a new era with the dramatic renovation of its public spaces, rooms, and suites. **Pros:** excellent golf and tennis; the Beach Club by Le Cirque and La Casita in the marina are on the meal plan. **Cons:** not the largest beach; expensive food if not on an inclusive plan; a bit too sprawling although *gratis* golf carts minimize this. **TripAdvisor:** "the most complete resort," "amazing vacation for the whole family," "Caribbean golfer's paradise." ⑤ *Rooms from: $835* ☎ *809/523–3333, 305/856–5405, 800/877–3643* ⊕ *www.casadecampo.com.do* ⤴ *173 rooms, 12 suites, 50 villas* ⑩ *All-inclusive.*

$$$
ALL-INCLUSIVE
☾
Fodor's Choice
★

Dreams La Romana Resort & Spa. One of the better Dominican all-inclusives, this resort sits on an exceptional palm-fringed ribbon of white sand protected by a coral reef that offers great snorkeling from the beach. **Pros:** caring and efficient staff; top-shelf liquors available at the lobby bar for no extra charge; free Wi-Fi in lobby and in-room at the club level. **Cons:** large and busy property usually feels overly full; two hours from the major airports; efficient staff is sometimes overwhelmed. **TripAdvisor:** "beautiful beach," "dreams were made of this hotel," "excellent staff." ⑤ *Rooms from: $420* ⊠ *Bayahibe Bay, Bayahibe* ☎ *809/221–8880* ⊕ *www.dreamsresorts.com/drelr* ⤴ *774 rooms, 37 suites* ⑩ *All-inclusive.*

$$$
ALL-INCLUSIVE
☾
★

Iberostar Hacienda Dominicus. The resort's idyllic beach with its lighthouse bar is that perfect Caribbean postcard. **Pros:** international liquors available at the lobby lounge; shops with tropical fashions and artisan jewelry; Captain Nemo's underwater-themed disco. **Cons:** room decor is a bit outdated; always packed; reservations at à la carte restaurants not always available, and must be made very early in the morning. **TripAdvisor:** "majestic," "relax," "beautiful resort." ⑤ *Rooms from: $338* ⊠ *Playa Bayahibe, Bayahibe* ☎ *809/688–3600, 888/923–2722* ⊕ *www.iberostar.com* ⤴ *460 rooms, 38 junior suites* ⑩ *All-inclusive.*

$
ALL-INCLUSIVE
☾

Viva Wyndham Dominicus Palace. Older Americans may prefer this classier sister to the nearby Viva Wyndham Dominicus Beach resort. **Pros:** absolutely fabulous blue-flag beach; professional dive center; lots of stylish Europeans. **Cons:** always busy; no interior transportation even though resort grounds are sprawling; reservations needed for à la carte restaurants. **TripAdvisor:** "a fabulous choice," "a week of relaxation," "lots of activities." ⑤ *Rooms from: $220* ⊠ *Playa Bayahibe, Bayahibe* ☎ *809/686–5658* ⊕ *www.vivaresorts.com* ⤴ *330 rooms* ⑩ *All-inclusive.*

PUNTA CANA

The easternmost coast of the island has 35 miles (56 km) of incredible beach punctuated by coco palms; add to that a host of all-inclusive resorts, an atmospheric thatch-roof airport, and many more direct flights than any other D.R. resort area, and it's easy to see why this region—despite having almost 50,000 hotel rooms (more than on most other Caribbean islands)—can regularly sell out. It has become the Cancún of the D.R. You can usually get a room during hurricane season (late August–October), but booking far in advance for the better properties is advisable. Most hotels in the region are clustered around Punta Cana and Bávaro, where more than 90% of the existing properties are all-inclusive. But development continues to press outward—northward to the more remote locations of Macao and Uvero Alto, and southward to the nearby Juanillo—and several of the newer offerings are ultra-luxury resorts, not all-inclusives.

The region commonly referred to as Punta Cana actually encompasses the beaches and villages of Juanillo, Punta Cana, Bávaro, Cabeza de Toro, El Cortecito, Arena Gorda, Macao, and Uvero Alto, which hug an unbroken stretch of the eastern coastline; however, Uvero Alto, the farthest developed resort area to the north, lies an hour from the Punta Cana airport.

HOTELS AND RESORTS

$$$
ALL-INCLUSIVE
☺
★
⛱ Barceló Bávaro Beach Resort. Barceló deserves loud applause for the incredible face-lift that has totally transformed this property from an aging, middle-of-the-road has-been to a glamorous complex worthy of gushing praise. **Pros:** the whole place has been reinvented; enormous range of entertainment and activity options; no other kids club is this contemporary. **Cons:** pool gets crowded and noisy; high-volume resort draws large conventions; tacky go-go girls in the disco. **TripAdvisor:** "great relaxing place," "exceeded our expectation," "gorgeous tropical setting." ⑤ *Rooms from: $387* ⊠ *Carretera Bávaro, Bávaro* ☎ *809/686–5797* ⊕ *www.barcelo.com* ⇌ *1,990 rooms, 941 junior suites, 55 suites* ⧓ *All-inclusive.*

$$$$
ALL-INCLUSIVE
★
⛱ Club Med Punta Cana. Whimsy and camaraderie are characteristic of this family-friendly resort—Punta Cana's original all-inclusive—newly redesigned and situated on 75 tropical acres, with a coastline of white-sandy shores. **Pros:** Tiara, the luxury space within the resort; animated, global staff; themed weeks for music, dance, and sports; special events such as Wine & Food Festival. **Cons:** limited dining options; Wi-Fi is expensive and only in public spaces; in-room Internet cables (free) in Tiara suites only. **TripAdvisor:** "beautiful," "amazing in every way," "stay in paradise." ⑤ *Rooms from: $564* ⊠ *Plaua Punta Cana* ☎ *809/686–5500, 800/258–2633* ⊕ *www.clubmed.com* ⇌ *521 rooms, 32 family suites* ⧓ *All-inclusive.*

$$$
ALL-INCLUSIVE
☺
⛱ Dreams Palm Beach. This fine Dreams—a luxurious brand that's also family- and American-friendly—is perched on a gorgeous stretch of beach with white-sugar sand. **Pros:** bartenders at the swim-up bar are friendly and make delicious Caribbean cocktails; no wristbands to identify guests. **Cons:** singles may feel left out with all the families;

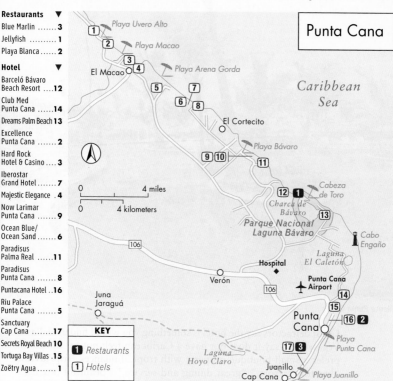

Restaurants ▼

Blue Marlin **3**

Jellyfish **1**

Playa Blanca **2**

Hotel ▼

Barceló Bávaro
Beach Resort **12**

Club Med
Punta Cana **14**

Dreams Palm Beach **13**

Excellence
Punta Cana **2**

Hard Rock
Hotel & Casino **3**

Iberostar
Grand Hotel **7**

Majestic Elegance . **4**

Now Larimar
Punta Cana **9**

Ocean Blue/
Ocean Sand **6**

Paradisus
Palma Real **11**

Paradisus
Punta Cana **8**

Puntacana Hotel ..**16**

Riu Palace
Punta Cana **5**

Sanctuary
Cap Cana **17**

Secrets Royal Beach **10**

Tortuga Bay Villas .**15**

Zoëtry Agua **1**

Punta Cana

*Caribbean
Sea*

KEY

1 *Restaurants*

1 *Hotels*

resort runs at high occupancy year-round. **TripAdvisor:** "best enter-tainment in all of Dominican Republic," "beautiful resort," "sit back and relax." ⑤ *Rooms from: $428* ⊠ *Cabeza de Toro, Bávaro* ☎ *809/552–6000, 866/237–3267* ⊕ *www.dreamsresorts.com* ⇆ *325 rooms* ⊙| *All-inclusive.*

$$$$

ALL-INCLUSIVE

Fodor's Choice

★

☷ **Excellence Punta Cana.** A sumptuous lovers' lair, this adults-only all-inclusive is particularly appealing to honeymooners, wedding parties, and couples celebrating anniversaries. **Pros:** gorgeous setting for wed-dings; new high-end 4,500-square-foot fitness center; à la carte restau-rant open late for breakfast; most all guest comments are *excellente.* **Cons:** far from shopping, other restaurants, and nightlife; isolating for singles; certain furnishings and decor are becoming dated. **TripAdvisor:** "beautiful beach and facilities," "staff makes this place great," "relax-ing vacation." ⑤ *Rooms from: $528* ⊠ *Playa Uvero Alto* ☎ *809/685–9880* ⊕ *www.excellence-resorts.com* ⇆ *452 suites* ⊙| *All-inclusive.*

$$$$

ALL-INCLUSIVE

Fodor's Choice

★

☷ **Hard Rock Hotel & Casino Punta Cana.** Hard Rock's first all-inclusive property is set on the spectacular Macao beach, pairing its famous brand with the latest hospitality trend in Punta Cana: delivering supe-rior luxury in an all-inclusive. **Pros:** the fun quotient; its pervasive, good-mood spirit; the quality and variety of the cuisine and waitstaff.

Excellence Punta Cana

Cons: detractors say the hotel is something you would find in Dallas or Vegas; some say it does not have a Caribbean feel; not for those who prefer a small boutique property with tropical nuances. **TripAdvisor:** "beautiful resort," "great dining and service," "beautiful beaches." ⑤ *Rooms from: $508* ⊠ *Blvd. Turístico del Este 74, Km 28, Playa Macao* ☎ *809/687–0000* ⊕ *www.hardrockhotels.com* ⤵ *1,787 rooms* ⑩ *All-inclusive.*

$$$$
ALL-INCLUSIVE
Fodor's Choice
★

▦ **Iberostar Grand Hotel.** Iberostar's adults-only Bávaro resort—an architectural gem—is a knockout from the moment you walk into the glamorous lobby. **Pros:** competent and caring Spanish managers; impressive selection of designer restaurants with contemporary cuisine; idyllic beach weddings and honeymoons with grand oceanfront suites, Jacuzzis for two, couples-oriented spa services. **Cons:** sometimes the decor outshines the food; although the staff's level of English is quite good, it should be better. **TripAdvisor:** "stunning hotel and service," "one-of-a-kind experience," "unique and fantastic." ⑤ *Rooms from: $650* ⊠ *Playa Bávaro* ☎ *809/221–6500, 888/923–2722* ⊕ *iberostar.com* ⤵ *260 suites, 13 grand suites, 1 presidential* ⑩ *All-inclusive.*

$$$
ALL-INCLUSIVE
★

▦ **Majestic Elegance.** Interestingly, the younger of Punta Cana's two Majestic resorts (the other is the Majestic Colonial) is actually priced lower than its sister unless you upgrade to the adults-only "Elegance Club," which is in high demand and now has 92 new rooms built in 2011. **Pros:** staff welcoming despite intense workload; premium liquors at all bars and à la carte restaurants; most consider it a good value. **Cons:** guests not in the VIP Club feel second-class; animation boys often exhibit risqué humor; beach doesn't have sufficient number of chaise longues. **TripAdvisor:** "fantastic staff," "friendly people on a beautiful beach," "majestic elegance." 💲*Rooms from: $390* ✉ *Arena Gorda, Bávaro* ☎ *809/221–9898* ⊕ *www.majestic-resorts.com* ⤳ *537 junior suites, 59 suites* 🍽 *All-inclusive.*

$$$
ALL-INCLUSIVE
☺
★

⚏ **Now Larimar Punta Cana.** This relatively new, moderately priced branch of the AmResorts family—which welcomes children—has style. **Pros:** whole complex is a welcome newcomer; most guests are very pro-Now; large housekeeping and entertainment team. **Cons:** some complaints about maintenance and repairs; shortage of pool chaises even at Preferred Club; food is sometimes mediocre. **TripAdvisor:** "great staff," "beautiful beach," "relaxing in paradise." 💲*Rooms from: $449* ✉ *Ave. Alemania s/n, El Cortecito, Bávaro* ☎ *809/221–4646* ⊕ *www. NowResorts.com* 🍽 *All-inclusive.*

$$
ALL-INCLUSIVE
☺

⚏ **Ocean Blue/Ocean Sand Golf & Beach Resort.** Designed like a small town, with restaurants, shops, and nightlife concentrated near a central public square, this huge resort still has many positive attributes considering its moderate price range—but it used to be better. **Pros:** noteworthy breakfast at the buffet; Mike's Coffee Shop; bowling alley; teen center. **Cons:** expensive charges for in-room Wi-Fi; beat-up interiors for many rooms; not for savvy, picky, and/or sophisticated travelers. **TripAdvisor:** "great facilities," "good service," "beautiful beach." 💲*Rooms from: $325* ✉ *Playa Arena Gorda, Bávaro* ☎ *809/476–2326* ⊕ *www.oceanhotels.net* ⤳ *708 junior suites* 🍽 *All-inclusive.*

$$$$
ALL-INCLUSIVE
☺
Fodor's Choice
★

⚏ **Paradisus Palma Real Resort.** A member of the Leading Hotels of the World, this luxury all-inclusive is a visual showstopper. **Pros:** enticing and professional spa; weaknesses are being corrected; adjacent Palma Real Shopping Center. **Cons:** restaurants and nightlife are far from some rooms; most rooms at The Reserve do not have sea views or have just partial sea views; few oceanfront rooms even at the Royal Level. **TripAdvisor:** "beautiful resort," "best meal of my life," "really great people." 💲*Rooms from: $520* ✉ *Bávaro* ☎ *809/688–5000,* ⊕ *www. paradisuspalmareal.com* ⤳ *554 suites* 🍽 *All-inclusive.*

$$$
ALL-INCLUSIVE
☺
★

⚏ **Paradisus Punta Cana.** Big-league improvements have been made in recent years at this seasoned tropical getaway (and there are more in the offing, as it has struggled to keep pace with the newer competition). **Pros:** some impressive architecture and decor; management has service down pat; The Reserve provides ultra-luxury, family-style. **Cons:** not for solo travelers; older rooms show signs of wear and are not so large; in The Reserve, kids can make the dining room noisy. **TripAdvisor:** "a hidden gem," "relaxing," "excellent experience." 💲*Rooms from: $430* ✉ *Bávaro* ☎ *809/687–9923* ⊕ *www.paradisuspuntacana. solmelia.com* ⤳ *509 suites, 80 Royal Service suites, 174 Reserve suites* 🍽 *All-inclusive.*

$
RESORT
☺
★

⚏ **Puntacana Hotel.** A plethora of amenities—not to mention meticulously kept grounds and world-class golf—await you at this charismatic resort, which spearheaded the area's tourism industry and has since kept pace with the times. **Pros:** expansive and beautiful grounds; spectacular golf and spa; one of the area's most gorgeous beaches. **Cons:** some of the color schemes in the last redecoration are not wonderful; limited nightlife on-site; solo travelers can feel left out; animation staff can be annoying. **TripAdvisor:** "peaceful paradise," "beautiful beach,"

All-Inclusive: The Concept

All-inclusive resorts are the most common type of accommodations you'll find in Punta Cana. Here's a primer for anyone unfamiliar with this style of lodging.

Meals: At least one buffet restaurant serves breakfast, lunch, and dinner. Often, at least one, and usually more, à la carte specialty restaurant is included (e.g., Mexican, Italian, Japanese, Asian Fusion, and Dominican). A few restaurants such as premium steak houses might carry an extra charge. Snack bars will get you through the interim periods.

Beverages: Soft drinks, bottled water, alcoholic beverages (generally non-premium brands, whether domestic or international), and domestic beer are included, as well as a stocked minibar in all guest rooms. Some resorts even have liquor dispensers in the rooms.

Room Service: Policies vary. Where available, it may cost extra, have limited hours, or be an option only on upgraded packages.

Kids' Clubs: Most resorts have special kids' programs, and they are typically geared to ages 4–12; a few hotels stand out with offerings in an extended (or more limited) range. Babysitters cost extra.

Activities: Nonmotorized water sports are generally included. Some resorts include one diving lesson in the pool. Diving and motorized sports are extra. There's always a slew of arranged activities going on—usually by the pool or in a games area. These might include dance lessons, Spanish lessons, stretching, yoga, water aerobics, volleyball, or pool tournaments. Some places have extras like bowling, rock climbing, or a trapeze.

Animation Teams: These are the folks who enthusiastically run the activities and try to generate a buzz among guests.

Tips: Though usually included, additional tipping for good service is not uncommon and is highly appreciated. Carrying extra $1 bills comes in handy.

Gyms and Spas: Use of the gym is included; personal trainers cost extra. Most resorts have a spa. Sometimes use of steam rooms, saunas, and hot tubs is included. Massages and other treatments cost extra.

Nightlife: Some resorts are renowned for a show that stands out; generally, nonresort guests can attend by purchasing a night pass. Entertainment usually rotates on a 7-day or 14-day cycle. Discos are standard; a few of the better ones are open to nonguests.

Casino: Many resorts have casinos with slot machines; some offer roulette and a few card tables with blackjack and assorted poker games. Texas Hold 'Em tables are not in abundance.

Excursions: Off-site excursions are not included.

Medical Care: Care is available 24 hours at on-site clinics. Charges for doctor services and medications are not included. International health insurance is accepted, but you must have the appropriate coverage.

Bracelets: When you arrive, most resorts will band you with a bracelet that identifies you as a guest and indicates your package level.

Secrets Sanctuary Cap Cana Resort and Spa

"activities for all." 💲 *Rooms from: $130* ✉ *PuntaCana Resort & Club, Playa Punta Cana* ☎ *809/959–2262, 888/442–2262* ⊕ *www.puntacana. com* ⤳ *175 rooms, 16 junior suites, 11 suites, 38 casitas* ⎮◉⎮ *Breakfast.*

$$
ALL-INCLUSIVE

🏨 **Riu Palace Punta Cana.** On a moonlit night this megaresort decorated with Arabian-style domes looks like a fairy-tale palace. **Pros:** 24-hour room service; grand hotel elements; buffeteria has outdoor seating; nightly entertainment in the Spanish-style plaza. **Cons:** not good for solo and/or young travelers; only ATM is at the main security gate; food is middle-of-the-road. **TripAdvisor:** "wonderful staff," "clean," "a trip to paradise." 💲 *Rooms from: $331* ✉ *Playa Arena Gorda, Bávaro* ☎ *809/687–4242* 🖷 *809/687–7878* ⊕ *www.riu.com* ⤳ *584 junior suites, 28 suites* ⎮◉⎮ *All-inclusive.*

$$$$
RESORT
Fodor'sChoice
★

🏨 **Sanctuary Cap Cana.** This stellar resort, the keystone of Cap Cana, has again been relaunched and now welcomes families, with The Fortress wing reserved for adults only; both all-inclusive and EP plans are offered. **Pros:** gorgeous beach; award-wining golf; a wonderful spirit and fun-quotient. **Cons:** the standard rooms (junior suites) are long but narrow; casino not operational presently, but there's free transportation to another; continuing development all around Cap Cana, including Las Iguanas golf course. **TripAdvisor:** "amazing staff," "beyond expectations," "a relaxing getaway." 💲 *Rooms from: $558* ✉ *Playa Juanillo, Cap Cana, Juanillo* ☎ *809/562–9191,* ⊕ *www.grandresortsatcapcana. com* ⤳ *115 junior suites, 27 suites, 33 villas* ⎮◉⎮ *Multiple meal plans.*

$$$$
ALL-INCLUSIVE
★

🏨 **Secrets Royal Beach.** The lobby at this sceney, adults-only resort is like a modern art gallery, with suspended fish sculptures immediately attracting the eye. **Pros:** idyllic for weddings and honeymoons; nightly entertainment at the main plaza; exceptional 17,000-square-foot Spa by

Pevonia. **Cons:** beach vendors and excursion salespeople can be annoying; some clients think food is not as stellar as the environment. **TripAdvisor:** "excellent service," "the best place for relaxing," "romantic like the best honeymoon." ⑤ *Rooms from: $597* ✉ *Avenida Alemania s/n, El Cortecito, Bávaro* ☎ *809/221–4646* ⊕ *www.SecretsResorts.com* ⤵ *372 suites* ⏐◯⏐ *All-inclusive.*

$$$$ ⌂ **Tortuga Bay Villas.** Shuttered French windows that open to grand vistas
RENTAL   of the sea and a cotton-white private beach are hallmarks of this luxury-
Fodor's Choice   villa enclave within the grounds of PuntaCana Resort & Club. **Pros:**
★   exceptional, personal service; sprawling grounds with virgin beaches; outstanding golf; VIP check-in at airport. **Cons:** little nightlife; Bamboo restaurant is pricey; too isolated for singles unless you roll on over to Playa Blanca. **TripAdvisor:** "ultimate relaxation," "great rooms," "best service." ⑤ *Rooms from: $1,050* ✉ *PuntaCana Resort & Club* ☎ *809/959–8229, 888/442–2262* ⊕ *www.puntacana.com* ⤵ *17 junior suites, 13 two-bedroom villas* ⏐◯⏐ *Breakfast.*

$$$$ ⌂ **Zoëtry Agua Resort & Spa.** No sea-stone is left unturned when it
ALL-INCLUSIVE   comes to ensuring satisfaction for guests at this serene, oceanfront
Fodor's Choice   resort, where rustic natural beauty and high architectural style blend
★   seamlessly. **Pros:** unsurpassed luxurious details; quality of the cuisine; gourmet coffee shop/bakery. **Cons:** mosquitoes; limited nightlife; not everyone takes to the more remote Uvero Alto location; one-way from the airport (45 minutes) is $80. **TripAdvisor:** "amazing property," "close to perfect," "great staff." ⑤ *Rooms from: $1,300* ✉ *Playa Uvero Alto* ☎ *809/468–0000* ⊕ *www.zoetryresorts.com* ⤵ *53 suites, 5 2- or 3-bedroom villas* ⏐◯⏐ *All-inclusive.*

SAMANÁ

Samaná is the name of both the peninsula that curves around the eponymous bay and of the largest town. Las Terrenas is at least a 2½-hour drive from Cabarete. Conveniently, El Catey Airport (AZS) is served regularly by American Eagle from San Juan; otherwise, Takeoff Destination Service offers regular flights from several D.R. airports. The nearest major international airport is Puerto Plata's International Gregorio Luperon, more than a three-hour-drive away *(⇨ By Air under Transportation in Dominican Republic Essentials).*

LAS TERRENAS

$$$$ ⌂ **Balcones del Atlantico- A Rockresort.** Long awaited, this Rockresort is a
RENTAL   condo hotel on a large tract of virgin land; its spacious accommodations
☺   are beyond stellar, with exceptional interior design, dreamy bedding,
★   and private Jacuzzis on terraces that are basically outdoor rooms. **Pros:** intelligent and caring concierge staff; everything is new, clean, and fresh. **Cons:** not smack on the beach, with marginal views; some amenities, such as tennis courts, are still under construction; accommodations around the glorious pool are subject to noise. **TripAdvisor:** "lovely condo," "beautiful property," "simple luxury in the real Caribbean." ⑤ *Rooms from: $450* ✉ *Across from Porto on Playa Las Terrenas, Las Terrenas* ☎ *809/240–5011* ⊕ *www.balcones.com.do* ⤵ *32 villas, 2 townhouses.*

$$$$ ⊞ **Peninsula House.** The gorgeous Victorian-style plantation house with
B&B/INN wraparound verandas overlooks miles of coconut palms down to the
Fodor'sChoice ocean. **Pros:** quiet and remote; luxurious; impeccable guest attention.
★ **Cons:** pricey; you may worry that you'll break something; fun-quo-
tient is absent; it's hard to escape. **TripAdvisor:** "barefoot elegance
and luxury," "sheer perfection," "wonderful service." ⑤ *Rooms from:
$540 ⊠ Camino Cosón, Las Terrenas ☎ 809/972–7447, 809/817–1152
⊕ www.thepeninsulahouse.com ⟿ 6 rooms* �‖❘*Breakfast.*

SANTA BÁBARA DE SAMANÁ

$$ ⊞ **The Bannister Hotel at Puerto Bahia Marina & Residences.** This new marina
HOTEL complex smack on the Bay of Samaná has changed the face of tour-
★ ism in this area of the peninsula; it has become the social center for
the upscale residents, another high-end enclave for wealthy capitale-
ños, a safe harbor for visiting yachtsmen and Caribbean charter boats,
and a deluxe-yet-reasonably-priced full-service hotel for international
visitors.**Pros:** wonderful ambience; natural beauty everywhere. **Cons:**
the one-bedroom hotel accommodations could be more spacious; too far
from town to walk. ⑤ *Rooms from: $220 ⊠ Carretera Sanchez Km. 5,
Puerto Bahia, Santa Bárbara de Samaná ☎ 809/503–6363 ⊕ www.
puertobahiasamana.com ⟿ 1 studio, 25 1-bedroom suites, 4 2-bed-
room suites.*

NORTH COAST

The northern coast of the island, with mountains on one side, is also
called the Amber Coast because of the large quantities of amber found
in the area. The sands on its 75 miles (121 km) of beach are also golden.
Major resort areas are Playa Dorada, Cabarete, and Sosúa. Plan to fly
into Puerto Plata's Gregorio Luperon International Airport.

PUERTO PLATA

$ ⊞ **Blue Bay Villas Doradas.** The stunning grand entrance (a Sara Gar-
ALL-INCLUSIVE cia design) at this adults-only resort with its slender white pillars uses
white fabric to shelter the lobby from tropical rainfalls. **Pros:** great
spa; handsome beach club and stellar beachfront; yoga and golf classes
included. **Cons:** standard and standard-plus rooms are not luxurious;
rooms near the stage can be noisy until 11 pm. **TripAdvisor:** "great
staff and food," "fantastic homely hotel," "lovely." ⑤ *Rooms from:
$170 ⊠ Playa Dorada, Puerto Plata ☎ 809/320–3000, 809/320–1600
for reservations ⊕ www.bluebayresorts.com ⟿ 245 rooms, 4 suites*
❘❖❘*All-inclusive.*

$$$ ⊞ **Casa Colonial Beach & Spa.** Done in the clean, sophisticated, contem-
HOTEL porary style of a boutique hotel, Casa Colonial is a surprise among
Fodor'sChoice the chockablock all-inclusives of Playa Dorada. **Pros:** architectural
★ gem offering the full luxury, boutique experience; glorious spa; exceptional gourmet room (Lucia). **Cons:** can feel empty during the low
season; large suites could use a splash of color; service is attentive
sometimes a bit off. **TripAdvisor:** "understated elegance," "beautiful
and relaxing with impeccable service," "luxurious getaway." ⑤ *Rooms
from: $350 ⊠ Playa Dorada, Puerto Plata ☎ 809/320–3232 ⊕ www.
casacolonialhotel.com ⟿ 50 suites* ❘❖❘*No meals.*

$ ⬚ **Cofresi Palm Beach & Spa Resort.** As golden and orange as the tropical
RESORT sunset view from the balcony, the contemporary decor here is offset by
☺ stonework. **Pros:** so much variety: several pools, many bars and restaurants, and a theater; 24-hour food and beverage. **Cons:** new buildings have generic stucco facades; too sprawling and hilly for anyone
with bad knees; most rooms don't have even a side view of the ocean;
high-volume tourism. ⑤ *Rooms from: $225 ⊠ 1 Paradise Dr., Cofresi,
Puerto Plata ☎ 809/970–7777 ⊕ www.cofresipalmresort.com ⬧ 468.*

$$ ⬚ **Gran Ventana Beach Resort.** This all-inclusive is filled primarily with
ALL-INCLUSIVE English-speaking clientele who like its sophisticated lobby, the latest
☺ renovations, the colorfully painted facades, and easy beach access.
Pros: consistently good food and service for this price point; plenty of
activities for the whole family; particulary efficient and caring front-
desk staff. **Cons:** feels busy year-round; some aspects of the rooms and
restaurants are still dated. **TripAdvisor:** "nice smaller resort," "great
food," "fabulous destination." ⑤ *Rooms from: $240 ⊠ Playa Dorada,
Puerto Plata ☎ 809/320–2111 ⊕ www.vhhr.com ⬧ 499 rooms, 2 suites,
1 penthouse ⏐◎⏐ All-inclusive.*

$$ ⬚ **Iberostar Costa Dorada.** This resort will dazzle you with its sprawling
ALL-INCLUSIVE lobby, its hardwood benches and sculptures, and its curvaceous pool
★ with a central Jacuzzi encircled by Roman pillars. **Pros:** good management makes for a happy staff and a fun resort; gorgeous spot along
the beach; top-shelf liquor in the lobby bar; Wi-Fi now available in the
rooms and public areas. **Cons:** popularity translates to high occupancy
year-round; you must pay for Wi-Fi; pool can be very noisy; house
wine is subpar. **TripAdvisor:** "relaxing stay," "beautiful," "it gets better
and better." ⑤ *Rooms from: $260 ⊠ Playa Costa Dorada, Carretera
Luperón, Km 4, Marapica ☎ 809/320–1000, 888/923–2722 ⊕ www.
iberostar.com ⬧ 498 rooms, 18 junior suites ⏐◎⏐ All-inclusive.*

$$ ⬚ **Presidential Lifestyle Suites.** Presidential Lifestyle Suites is a new name
ALL-INCLUSIVE and an apt description of the stucco buildings of this hilltop enclave.
★ **Pros:** the sexy, *moderne* suites; pool with the beds and cascading water-
fall; variety and quality of lounges and restaurants; VIP beach club;
caring employees and management try hard to please. **Cons:** a fast
shuttle from the beach; popular, so can feel overly crowded; restaurants
can jam up. ⑤ *Rooms from: $345 ⊠ Cofresí ☎ 809/970–7777 ⊕ www.
lhvcresorts.com ⬧ 60 2-bedroom suites ⏐◎⏐ All-inclusive.*

SOSÚA

$ ⬚ **Hotel Casa Valeria.** Evoking Mexico, this salmon-colored adobe, hous-
HOTEL ing a hotel and a restaurant, is a standout in this quiet neighborhood.
Pros: nicely renovated; rooms have cable TV; restaurant has evolved to
a higher level. **Cons:** service is attentive, but there are no resort services
or amenities; no ocean views. **TripAdvisor:** "nice and homey," "laid
back and relaxed," "perfect comfort." ⑤ *Rooms from: $55 ⊠ Calle Dr.
Rosen 28, El Batey, Sosúa ☎ 809/571–3536 ⊕ www.hotelcasavaleria.
com ⬧ 9 rooms ⏐◎⏐ No meals.*

$$$$ ⬚ **Sea Horse Ranch.** This enclave of 118 private homes, each with large
RESORT front and back yard and private pool, opened in 1993 as an elite bas-
★ tion set within a vast country club–like setting. **Pros:** one of the most
organized, well-managed groups of villas in the country; potent security

makes your vacation worry-free; location close to Puerto Plata and the airport; all villas have free, unlimited Wi-Fi. **Cons:** guests usually feel the need to rent a car or hire a driver; small beaches; if your laptop has to be configured for the Wi-Fi, you will need to pay for a tech. $ *Rooms from: $700* ⊠ *Cabarete, Sosúa* ☎ *809/571–3880, 800/635–0991* ⊕ *www.sea-horse-ranch.com* ⮐ *75 villas* ⎺⎺⎺ *No meals.*

CABARETE

$ ⎙ **Hotel El Magnifico.** You will find a healthy dose of unexpected luxury at
HOTEL this stellar, boutique condo-hotel. **Pros:** never feels crowded; the interior decor is très chic; the spaces are large and contemporary; children under 15 stay free. **Cons:** steep spiral staircases and no elevators; no restaurant or bar; no in-room phones and no way to communicate with reception unless you have a cell phone or rent one here. **TripAdvisor:** "tranquil paradise," "could not ask for a better hotel," "an oasis of beauty." $ *Rooms from: $100* ⊠ *Calle del Cementario, Cabarete* ☎ *809/571–0868* ⊕ *www.hotelmagnifico.com* ⮐ *7 rooms, 10 1-bedrooms, 6 2-bedrooms, 1 3-bedroom, 6 2-bedroom penthouses* ⎺⎺⎺ *No meals.*

$ ⎙ **Natura Cabana.** If your idea of perfection is thatched-roof cabanas
HOTEL and a quiet, private beach among the trees, then this is your oceanfront
★ ecolodge. **Pros:** natural, peaceful beachfront stay; good food; caring owner; spa; tree house for kids. **Cons:** car is almost a requirement; outside of downtown Cabarete (a one-hour walk by the beach); no TVs, phones, or air-conditioning, but sea breezes. **TripAdvisor:** "relaxing atmosphere," "chill and be still," "rooms are really beautiful." $ *Rooms from: $180* ⊠ *Playa Perla Marina, Cabarete* ☎☎ *809/571–1507* ⊕ *www.naturacabana.com* ⮐ *10 bungalows* ⎺⎺⎺ *Breakfast.*

$ ⎙ **Velero Beach Resort.** Laze in the hammock or swing on the palm that
HOTEL bends over the beach while you watch the kitesurfers work to become airborne, and you'll appreciate Velero's location, just a few minutes' walk east of the noise of town yet also just minutes from the happening bars and restaurants. **Pros:** blenders, microwaves, and DVDs in the junior suites and above; draped Balinese sun beds at the pool are wonderful. **Cons:** no elevators—it's a climb up the spiral staircases; standard rooms are not spacious. **TripAdvisor:** "very convenient location," "beautiful," "relaxed and nice." $ *Rooms from: $132* ⊠ *Calle la Punta 1, Cabarete* ☎ *809/571–9727* ⊕ *www.velerobeach.com* ⮐ *22 2-bedroom suites, 7 penthouses* ⎺⎺⎺ *No meals.*

NIGHTLIFE

Santo Domingo's nightlife is vast and ever changing. Check with the concierges and hip capitaleños. At this writing, there is still a curfew for clubs and bars; they must close at midnight during the week, and 2 am on Friday and Saturday nights. There are some exceptions to the latter, primarily those clubs and casinos in hotels. Sadly, the curfew has put some clubs out of business, but it has cut down on the crime and late-night noise, particularly in the Zona. Some clubs are now pushing the envelope and staying open until 3, but they do get in trouble with the authorities when caught, and you probably don't want to be there then.

Dominican Republic Jazz Festival

It's shades of Havana in the 1950s, of New York's Harlem in the 1920s, with bearded jazz musicians in berets playing among *cubanos* with white Panama hats and guayabera shirts. It's a fusion of African percussion and drums—bongos and congos, backed up by marimbas and maracas, sexy songbirds and their piano men. It's rotund tuba players and sweat-stained black shirts as trumpet and sax players blow it out.

In November, the town of Cabarete is transformed into a music venue when the biggest names in Latin jazz hit the North Coast, including such legends as Chuck Mangione, Sade, Carlos Santana, Mongo Santa Maria, Chucho Valdés, and Arturo Sandoval. And on one night, the festivities move to Santiago's Centro León.

As hot as salsa, the pulsating tropical sounds draw thousands of aficionados, from poor students to black-tie patrons of the arts, who come for the music, the energy, the art exhibits, the educational workshops, the sun, and the sea. This is one five-star event that is democratic—most tickets cost about $15, and beach concerts are free.

Sizzling hot nights inevitably climax in impromptu jam sessions at such venues as Miró Restaurant in Cabarete. In short, the D.R. Jazz Fest is one of the best parties of the year.

Resorts book up early, especially those that are hotbeds of jazz activity. Check out the festival's website for more information: ⊕ *www.drjazzfestival.com*.

Dancing is as much a part of the culture here as eating and drinking. As in other Latin countries, after dinner it's not a question of *whether* people will go dancing but *where* they'll go. Move with the rhythm of the merengue and the pulsing beat of salsa (adopted from neighboring Puerto Rico). Among the young, the word is that there's no better place to party in the Caribbean than Santo Domingo. Almost every resort in Puerto Plata and Punta Cana has live entertainment, dancing, or both.

The action can heat up—and the island does have casinos—but gambling in the Dominican Republic is more a sideline than a raison d'être. Most casinos are in the larger hotels of Santo Domingo, with a couple in Playa Dorada and elsewhere on the North Coast, plus many more in Punta Cana. All offer slot machines, blackjack, craps, and roulette and are generally open daily from 3 pm to 4 am, the exception being those in Santo Domingo, which, for now, must close at midnight (2 am on Friday and Saturday). You must be 18 to enter, and jackets are required at the chic casinos in the capital.

SANTO DOMINGO

BARS AND CLUBS

Guácara Taina. This is the only *discoteca* inside a cave once inhabited by Taíno Indians…and bats. (Santo Domingo has a network of natural caves within the city limits.) As you descend, you see hundreds of heads

Continued on page 452

PIRATES
IN THE
CARIBBEAN

Susan MacCallum Whitcomb & Julie Collazo Schwietert

Peg legs, parrots, and an easy-to-imitate "ahoy matey" lexicon: these are requisite elements in any pirate tale, but so are avarice and episodes of unspeakable violence. The combination is clearly compelling. Our fascination with pirates knows no bounds.

The true history of piracy has largely been obscured by competing pop-culture images. On one hand, there is the archetypal opportunist—fearsome, filthy, and foul-mouthed. On the other is the lovable scallywag epitomized by Captain Jack Sparrow in Disney's *Pirates of the Caribbean* franchise. Actual pirates, however, usually fell somewhere between these two extremes.

They could be uneducated men with limited life choices or crewmen from legitimate commercial and exploratory vessels left unemployed in the wake of changing political agendas. In either case, the piratical career path offered tempting benefits. Making a fast doubloon was only the beginning. Piracy also promised adventure plus egalitarian camaraderie—a kind of social equality unlikely to be found elsewhere during that class-conscious period.

Life aboard ship was governed by majority, as opposed to autocratic, rule. Pirates moreover, adhered to the Pirate's Code (a sort of "honor among thieves" arrangement). On the ships, at least, the common good took precedence.

✗ MARKS THE SPOT

Movie *Pirates of the Caribbean*.

Anegada

St. Thomas Tortola Virgin Gorda

Isla de Culebra

British Virgin Islands

Puerto Rico

St. John

Isla de Vieques

U.S. Virgin Islands

St. Croix

Tortola

St. Thomas *St. John*

The Caribbean offered easy pickings for pirates because Spanish imperialists had already done the heavy lifting, extracting gems and precious metals from their South American colonies. Pirates from competing powers (namely England and France) could simply grab the spoils as Spanish ships island-hopped homeward.

Jamaica
Calico Jack Rackham, his lover Anne Bonny, and Mary Read were ultimately captured in **Bloody Bay** near Negril. Reportedly the male crew members were too busy drinking rum to mount a proper defense.

Dominican Republic
The centuries-old Spanish architecture in Santo Domingo's **Zona Colonial** is so well-preserved you can almost picture the area populated with tankard-toting buccaneers and corset-clad wenches.

Puerto Rico
Massive fortifications, like **Castillo San Felipe del Morro** in Old San Juan, show just how far the Spanish were prepared to go to protect their assets from seagoing attackers, whether authorized or otherwise.

British Virgin Islands
Sir Francis Drake Channel, Jost Van Dyke, and Great Thatch Island were named for pirates or privateers. Ditto for **Norman Island**, which reputedly inspired the setting for R.L. Stevenson's *Treasure Island*.

St. Thomas
A strategic location, protected anchorages, plus easy-to-hide-in inlets made the U.S. Virgin Islands an ideal habitat for plunderers. High points like **Drake's Seat** and Blackbeard's Castle were used to survey the terrain.

Anguilla
Underwater heritage preserves let divers explore vessels that sailed during piracy's Golden Age. **Stoney Ground Marine Park** contains a Spanish galleon wrecked in 1772, plus cannons, anchors, and other artifacts.

Santo Domingo, Dominican Republic

Stoney Ground Marine Park

Pirate ship arrives for Pirates Week, the Cayman Islands.

Peppered Pickled Pirate Party, Nevis.

Castillo de San Felipe del Morro, Puerto Rico.

Anguilla

Maarten
Martin

St. Barthélemy

Saba

St. Eustatius   St. Kitts

Nevis

Barbuda

Antigua

Montserrat

Guadeloupe

Marie
Galante

Dominica

Martinique

St. Lucia

St. Vincent

PIRATES OF THE CARIBBEAN

Dominica
Convoys of booty-filled Spanish ships often stopped at this lush island. Pirates followed—and so did Hollywood. Key scenes for the second and third *Pirates of the Caribbean* movies were shot here.

St. Vincent
Sequences for the first three *Pirates of the Caribbean* installments were filmed on location here. The meticulously detailed cluster of buildings built to represent Port Royal can be seen at **Wallilabou Bay**.

PIRATE PARTIES

Cayman Islands
In mid-November, islanders celebrate their piratical past with an 11-day festival featuring treasure hunts, mock trials, and other themed events. The highlight is an invasion of **George Town** staged by *faux* pirates.

Nevis
Taking a page from the Cayman Islands book, Nevis introduced the weeklong **Peppered Pickled Pirate Party**. Held twice during the last week of October and November, It celebrates William Kidd and Black Bart with an "invasion," regattas, cooking and cocktail competitions, treasure hunts, and more

St. Barthélémy
Logically enough, Frenchman Daniel Montbars used this French island as his home base. Legend has it some of his treasure remains hidden in the beachfront caves around **Anse du Gouverneur**.

St. Lucia
Now a peaceful national park, **Pigeon Island** (on St. Lucia's northern tip) was once the hideout of François Le Clerc. This peg-legged pirate orchestrated attacks from his hilly vantage point in the late 16th century.

TIMELINE

1523 First Spanish
treasure ships seized

1577 Francis Drake begins
circumnavigating the globe

1604 James I re
Letters of M

1500

1550

1

1492 onward exploitation of
New World resources

1585–16C
Anglo-Spanish Wa

FAMOUS PIRATES

Years after they wreaked havoc on the high seas, history still remembers some of the most notorious pirates of the Caribbean.

SIR FRANCIS DRAKE

Drake was a busy fellow. The first Englishman to circumnavigate the globe, he popularized tobacco, led slave-trading expeditions, helped destroy the Spanish Armada, and still had time to terrorize treasure-laden ships with Queen Elizabeth's blessing. Drake led his country's fleet in epic encounters throughout the Caribbean.

HENRY MORGAN

Captain Morgan led a colorful life before lending his name to a ubiquitous brand of rum. Leaving Wales for the West Indies as a young man, he successfully segued from debauched buccaneer to semi-respectable privateer and, after dodging piracy charges in England, ended up

Captin Morgan

Edward "Blackbeard" Teach

as the Lieutenant Governor of Jamaica.

BLACKBEARD

Born Edward Teach, Blackbeard was notable for his business savvy (which included making profit-sharing deals with politicos) as well as his fiendish looks. His signature beard was braided and often laced with lit fuses to terrify enemies. Alas, in 1718 Blackbeard's head was severed in a dramatic showdown with Lt. Robert Maynard of the Royal Navy. It

was mounted on Maynard's ship as a warning to others.

WILLIAM KIDD

Life was a roller-coaster ride for the legendary Captain Kidd. Kidd was a retired privateer living in New York when he accepted a commission to hunt pirates and then became one himself with the encouragement of a mutinous crew. He was executed in London in 1701, but hopefuls still hunt for the treasure he supposedly left buried.

PIRATES, PRIVATEERS, AND BUCCANEERS

The "pirate" label is generally applied to sailors engaging in any type of maritime marauding. Yet there are variations on the theme.

Privateers such as Sir Francis Drake were licensed looters, their escapades were authorized by a royal Letter of Marque, which issued private commissions for strategic naval operations. Privateers were sanctioned to attack only specific enemy ships, with the goodies gained benefitting their government. Since this rogue diplomacy was intended to challenge Spain's

dominance in the Americas, many privateers felt they were protecting national interests. Hence, they were pirates... but patriotic.

Buccaneers, conversely, were a motley crew. The word, originally reserved for pirates from Hispaniola (the island shared by Haiti and the Dominican Republic), eventually included anyone from

Sir Francis Drake

1655 Jamaica established as privateer base	1674 Henry Morgan knighted	
1650	**1700**	**1750**

11

1618–1648
Thirty Years War

1689–1697
King William's War

1701–1714
War of Spanish Succession

IN FOCUS PIRATES IN THE CARIBBEAN

William Kidd

Calico Jack Rackman

Anne Bonny

BLACK BART ROBERTS

Though not the most famous pirate, he is often considered the most successful. He racked up impressive credits, plundering some 400 ships between 1719 and 1722. A snappy dresser who was fashionably attired even in battle, he was also a strict disciplinarian. Roberts quashed onboard gambling and banned music on Sunday.

DANIEL MONTBARS

Montbars proved Brits didn't hold a monopoly on bad behavior. French lineage aside, he differed from his 17th-century peers in that he was affluent and educated. His manners needed polishing, though. Violent outbursts (disemboweling Spaniards was a favorite sport) earned Montbars the nickname "The Exterminator."

CALICO JACK RACKHAM

An Englishman who ascended from mate to captain, Rackham, secured his legend by adding women to his crew. Workwise, his favorite tactic was attacking small vessels close to shore. Such boldness led to an inglorious end. Rackham was hung then tarred, feathered, and displayed in a cage in Port Royal, Jamaica.

ANNE BONNY AND MARY READ

Thought to be unlucky, female pirates were rare. Yet the comely Bonny and cross-dressing Read were respected by their shipmates... and feared by their victims. Captured together in 1720, they were sentenced to death. Both, however, escaped the noose by claiming to be pregnant.

the "Boys Gone Wild" school. Coming from diverse ethnic backgrounds, many buccaneers were fugitive slaves, escaped criminals, or other social outcasts who became plunderers by choice or force. Operating solely in their own interests and typically lacking a strategy or social order, they were the bottom feeders.

Political shifts could turn privateers into pirates (James I's decision to revoke Letters of Marque was a case in point). Desperation or moral degeneration could just as easily turn pirates into buccaneers.

PIRATE FLAGS

Flashy flags were to pirates what coats of arms were to royal families: visible signs of group identity. Each crew flew its own, depending on what attributes the captain wanted to emphasize or the degree of menace he wanted to convey.

The most recognizable is the "Jolly Roger": an iconic white-on-black skull cradled by crossbones.

bobbing and bodies gyrating among the stalactites: it's a unique sight. Banquettes and seating are carved into the limestone walls ornamented with Taíno pictographs. There are multiple bars and dual dance floors, but it's only open on Friday and Saturday nights and for special events (like those sponsored by liquor distributors). These are often open to the public, or whoever wants to pay the cover, which can be $20. Lights and videos flash, and apparently it's not subject to curfew. To find out what's going on, talk to your concierge. ⊠ *Av. Mirador del Sur 655, Bella Vista* ☎ *809/533–0671.*

Marrakesh Café & Bar. A sophisticated after-work crowd gathers here for American and international music and style straight out of *Casablanca*. Complimentary tapas come to the table, and you can get top-shelf liquors. Drinks are generous. Marrakesh is open from 4 to midnight, and there is sometimes live music between 6 and 9. ⊠ *Hotel Santo Domingo, Av. Abraham Lincoln at Av. Independencia, Gazcue* ☎ *809/221–1511.*

Trio Cafe. The cool, older crowd comes here to graze, drink, and dance, even though there's no real dance floor. The sound system is impressive, and wide-screen TVs show music videos while the DJ cranks. Patrons just stand around and groove, and chances are they will make new friends—as might you. A perennial fave, it is more and more being adopted by the young. ⊠ *Av. Abraham Lincoln Norte 12A, at Plaza Castilla Ensanche, Naco* ☎.

★ **Wine Tasting Room at El Catador.** This avant-garde wine bar and wine store was created by the major wine distributor El Catador. Cushy leather armchairs and hardwood floors help create a clubby atmosphere; there's also a small selection of cheese and prosciutto to graze upon. You will want to buy one of the 500 bottles of wine from around the winemaking world. It's open until 11 pm on weekdays, but only until 6 on Saturday. If you opt to buy a bottle, you have to do it by 10:15 (or 5:15) so as to finish up by closing time. ⊠ *Calle Jose Brea Péna 43, Avaristo Morales, Piantini* ☎ *809/540–1644.*

SOUTHEAST COAST

BARS AND CLUBS

Victory Club. This piano bar in a faux lighthouse at the very end of the marina's boardwalk is like a vacation fantasy. Drinks are expensive, but at least you don't have to pay just to sit down in the Italian designer chairs and black-leather couches. In the lounge there's contemporary art on the walls, not to mention a muted plasma TV and great views of the sea and moored yachts. The bar, which is shaped like a boat with a starry backdrop, has all the fashionable drinks and wine choices—mostly Italian—and top-shelf champagnes. Light Italian fare is also served. The club is open only on weekends. ⊠ *Casa de Campo, Paseo del Mar 10, Casa de Campo Marina, La Romana* ☎ *809/523–2264.*

PUNTA CANA

BARS AND CLUBS

Fodor's Choice
★

Imagine. Imagine you were dancing the night away in a natural cave, with earth-rocking acoustics. You can bounce back and forth between two separate, but equally hot dance floors, one featuring house/club jams, the other merengue/salsa/world beats. At Punta Cana's thriving hot spot, locals and tourists alike pack the various salas adorned with stalactites and stalagmites. Come late and stay early: things start getting steamy well after midnight, when many club crawlers descend via shuttle (round-trip) from the local resorts. (The free bus is great, but know that it stops at every resort in the area.) Special rates are offered for a weekly, multiple-entrance pass, with one night including an open bar. One massive chamber is reserved for concerts and private events. ✉ *Carretera Cocoloco–Riu, Coco Loco/Friusa, Bávaro* ☎ *809/466–1049* ⊕ *www.imaginepuntacana.com* ✉ *$40 (includes cover, transportation, and 2 drinks)* ⏱ *11 pm–after 4 am.*

Pacha. A favorite among locals and still one of the best resort-based dance spots, Pacha plays more merengue and bachata than most of the other clubs. Drinks here are cheaper, too. For a beer, expect to pay about 80 pesos (about $2.50); the price can be double in some of the other clubs. Cover charges apply when live bands perform; otherwise it's free to enter, and non-resort guests are welcome. ✉ *Av. Estados Unidos, at Riu complex, Bávaro* ☎ *809/221–7575.*

NORTH COAST

BARS AND CLUBS

Club 59. Club 59 is atop the infamous Merengue Bar, a red-light landmark. If you want to dance where the girls are, or at least gyrate to the Afro beat from your bar stool, then climb the stairs to 59. It has a long bar and is attractive, almost tasteful. There is usually no cover, but drinks cost more here than in other bars. Early on, around 10 pm, you'll see about 10 scantily dressed Dominican and Haitian *chicas* to each guy. As the night progresses, the men—mainly older white guys—come in ever greater numbers. ✉ *Pedro Clisante, corner of Calle Dr. Rosen, El Batey, Sosúa* ☎ *No phone.*

Hemingway's Cafe. This has long been the rockin' spot for the young and young at heart who love to party. There's rock or reggae by DJs or live bands, but only big-name merengue bands require a cover charge. On Saturday night there might be a Latin fiesta, and generally on Thursday the mike is taken over by karaoke singers. The kitchen, which doesn't close until 2 am, serves American-style fun food that includes good burgers, with fajitas a specialty. ✉ *Playa Dorada Plaza, Puerto Plata* ☎ *809/320–2230.*

★ **LAX.** LAX is a perennially popular open-air bar that really comes alive by night. You can sit in the sand in lounge chairs or jump into the action under the palapa, where a DJ will be spinning madly or a live band will be playing. There's good grazing chow, too, and special theme nights like Thai (it's not bad, either). Carefully made mojitos and other drinks (two-for-one specials from 5 to 7) mean you must be patient: getting one can take time when the bar backs up. It's next to a small hotel, so it must close early, around 1 am. ✉ *Cabarete Beach, Cabarete* ☎ *809/883–2684.*

The Nu Vudu. This expat hangout was formerly Beechers, the Voddo Lounge, Ruby's Lounge, and Deja Voodoo. Despite the constant name changes, it's still one of Sosúa's most upscale bars. English owners Mike and Jane believe that anything is an excuse for a party—and they have a slew of them: Latin nights, karaoke, nights when everyone is to wear white....A DJ pushes the buttons on weekends, and sometimes local blues and jazz musicians perform. There's no cover, and if you start drinking early, you will enjoy discounted prices. ✉ *Pedro Clisante, corner of Calle Arzeno, last building in Sosúa Bay complex, Sosúa* ☎ *No phone.*

Onno's Bar. Onno's Bar, right next to LAX, remains a serious party place. It is usually wall-to-wall and back-to-back as the young and fit pack the dance floor and groove to techno sounds while other multinational youth sit at the tables in the sand. It's easier to get served at the beach bar than the main one, and as you chill, people will pass by, introduce themselves, chat, and then move on. It's fun and friendly, although on Friday and Saturday nights in high season, when it stays open until 3 am, the scene can be rowdy. (In fact, some local expats say that the crowd it is now attracting is less than wonderful.) ✉ *Cabarete Beach, Cabarete* ☎ *809/571–0461.*

SHOPPING

Cigars continue to be the hottest commodity coming out of the D.R. Many exquisite hand-wrapped smokes come from the island's rich Cibao Valley, and Fuente Cigars—handmade in Santiago—are highly prized. Only reputable cigar shops sell the real thing, and many you will see sold on the street are fakes. You can also buy and enjoy Cuban cigars here, but they can't be brought back to the United States legally. Dominican rum and coffee are also good buys. Mamajuana, an herbal liqueur, is said to be the Dominican answer to Viagra. The D.R. is the homeland of designer Oscar de la Renta, and you may want to stop at the chic shops that carry his creations. La Vega is famous for its *diablos cajuelos* (devil masks), which are worn during Carnival. Look also for the delicate, faceless ceramic figurines that symbolize Dominican culture.

Though locally crafted products are often of a high caliber (and very affordable), expect to pay hundreds of dollars for designer jewelry made of amber and larimar. Larimar—a semiprecious stone the color of the Caribbean Sea—is found on the D.R.'s south coast. Prices vary according to the stone's hue and category, AAA being the highest. Amber has been mined extensively between Puerto Plata and Santiago. A fossilization of resin from a prehistoric pine tree, it often encases ancient animal and plant life, from leaves to spiders to tiny lizards. Beware of fakes, which are especially prevalent in street stalls. A reputable dealer can show you how to tell the difference between real larimar and amber and imitations.

Bargaining is both a game and a social activity in the D.R., especially with street vendors and at the stalls in El Mercado Modelo. Vendors are disappointed and perplexed if you don't haggle. They're also tenacious, so unless you really plan to buy, don't even stop to look.

SANTO DOMINGO

SHOPPING AREAS AND MALLS

Acropolis Mall, between Avenida Winston Churchill and Calle Rafael Augusto Sanchez, has become a favorite shopping arena for the young and/or hip capitaleños. Stores like Zara and Mango (both from Spain) have today's look without breaking your budget.

One of the main shopping streets in the Zona is **Calle El Conde,** a pedestrian thoroughfare. With the advent of so many restorations, the dull and dusty stores with dated merchandise are giving way to some hip, new shops. However, many of the offerings, including local designer shops, are still of a caliber and cost that the Dominicans can afford. Some of the best shops are on **Calle Duarte,** north of the Zona Colonial, between Calle Mella and Avenida de Las Américas. **El Mercado Modelo,** a covered market, borders Calle Mella in the Zona Colonial; vendors here sell a dizzying selection of Dominican crafts.

The **Malecón Center,** the latest complex, adjacent to the classy Hilton Santo Domingo, will eventually house 170 shops, boutiques, and services plus several movie theaters. In the tower above are luxury apartments and Sammy Sosa, in one of the penthouses.

Piantini is a swanky residential neighborhood that has an increasing number of fashionable shops and clothing boutiques. Its borders run from Avenida Winston Churchill to Avenida Lope de Vega and from Calle Jose Amado Soler to Avenida 27 de Febrero.

SOUTHEAST COAST

SHOPPING AREAS AND MALLS

Altos de Chavón. Altos de Chavón is a re-creation of a 16th-century Mediterranean village on the grounds of the Casa de Campo resort, where you can find art galleries, boutiques, and souvenir shops grouped around a cobbled square. At the Altos de Chavón Art Studios you can find ceramics, weaving, and screen prints made by local artists. Extra special is Casa Montecristo, a chic cigar lounge, which also offers a tour with cigar history and trivia. The mini-market sells sundries and some food items. ⊠ *Casa de Campo.*

The Casa de Campo Marina. Casa de Campo's top-ranked marina is home to shops and international boutiques, galleries, and jewelers scattered amid restaurants, an ice-cream parlor, bars, banks, beauty salons, and a yacht club. It's a great place to spend some time shopping, sightseeing, and staring at the extravagant yachts. The chic shopping scene at the marina includes Bleu Marine, Fiori Coleccion (leather), Mediterraneo (women's fashions from designers like Gucci and Versace), Everett Designs (high-end larimar and amber jewelry, even authentic Spanish coins). Art Arena sells local artisan jewelry and gifts. Dominican designer Jenny Polanco sells clothes, purses, and jewelry in the Bibi Leon boutique, which is known for its tropical-themed home accessories. There's also a marvelous Italian antiques shop, Nuovo Rinascimento, and the Club de Cigarro (Fumo). By the way, the supermercado Nacional at the marina has not only groceries but sundries, postcards, and snacks. ⊠ *Casa de Campo Marina, Calle Barlovento*.

PUNTA CANA

SHOPPING AREAS AND MALLS

Fodor'sChoice
★
Galerias at PuntaCana Village. The Galerias at PuntaCana Village lie within a still-blossoming shopping, dining, and residential complex built on the road to the Punta Cana International Airport. Originally the village was built to house employees of PuntaCana Resort & Club, but now the shops and restaurants are also a tourist draw. The village is comprised of a church, an international school, and a commercial area where you can find restaurants, shops, a supermarket, commercial banks, and doctors' offices. Free transportation is provided to guests at PuntaCana Resort & Club and Tortuga Bay. ⊠ *PuntaCana Resort & Club*.

Fodor'sChoice
★
Palma Real Shopping Village. A standout among the region's shopping centers, Palma Real Shopping Village is a swanky, partially enclosed mall (similar to something you would see in southern California). Fountains and tropical plants infuse life into the bright and airy interiors beneath the blue-tile roof. Music pipes through the stone-floor plaza in the center, where seating is available and security is tight. Upscale retail shops, which sell beachwear, clothing, skin-care products, and jewelry, line the walls. Several restaurants give visitors welcome dining alternatives beyond the gates of their resorts. There are two banks, ATMs, and a money exchange outlet. Stores are open 10–10, but the restaurants stay open later. It has the best pharmacy in the area. Shuttle buses run to and from many of the hotels, with pickups every two hours.

Palacio del Cine. Punta Cana's first movie theater, Palacio del Cine, opened here in 2009, and has three screens showing current films in English with Spanish subtitles. ☎ *809/552–8860* ⊠ *Bávaro* ☎ *809/552–8725* ⊕ *www.palmarealshoppingvillage.com*.

Plaza Bávaro Shopping Center. The sprawling Plaza Bávaro Shopping Center has dozens of shops spanning two sides of the main street that cuts through its center. It is a Dominican hodgepodge—like a neighborhood without any zoning restrictions. On the side closest to the beach you can find clothing stores, jewelry, cigars, and crafts, as well as three money-exchange spots, a DHL shipping station, and a pharmacy, all laid out in a square; in the middle is a bar where you can take a break from the bustle. Across the street, most of the booths sell artwork and handicrafts, and if your hair is long enough, you'll likely be approached by women offering to braid it on the spot. ⊠ *Bávaro* ☎ *No phone*.

Plaza Higüeyana. On the outskirts of Higüey, as you head into town along Carretera Higüey–La Otra Banda, you can find this artisans' market that draws busloads of tourists on the right-hand side of the road. Here you can browse through racks and shelves full of souvenirs, such as the herbal mamajuana liqueur, rum, cigars, T-shirts, amber and larimar jewelry, crafts, and ceramics. ⊠ *Carretera Higüey–La Otra Banda, at east end of Higüey, Higüey* ☎ *no phone.*

Plaza Uvero Alto. You won't find brand-name shops at Plaza Uvero Alto, which is a convenient shopping center for the hotels in the remote Uvero Alto area, with a bank and outdoor ATM, money exchange, Internet access, a small pharmacy, gift shops, and two minimarkets (one in the front, the other in the back row of booths). Here you can get sundries like suntan lotion and deodorant at prices much cheaper than in the hotels. Behind the first row of enclosed stores, visit the colorful kiosks full of handicrafts, paintings, ceramics, and other gift items. Most shopkeepers here, although very friendly, don't speak much English, so be prepared to practice your Spanish

For beautifully designed jewelry with larimar and amber as well as other locally made novelties, visit **Tesoro Caribeño** (No. 5, front row of stores), where the owner speaks fluent English. There's also a branch of the Politur (tourist police) in the plaza. ⊠ *Carretera Uvero Alto, Uvero Alto.*

NORTH COAST

SHOPPING AREAS AND MALLS

Calle Beller. In Puerto Plata you can find enough interesting stores to both quell your shopping urge and pick up a few funky gifts, like *mamajuana,* the Dominican herbal liqueur. A popular shopping street for costume jewelry and souvenirs is Calle Beller. ⊠ *Puerto Plata.*

Discount Plaza. The local equivalent of Wal-Mart (though on a smaller scale) carries bathing suits, flip-flops, baseball caps, and the like. You can choose from a pretty good selection of toiletries if you have forgotten anything, as well as rum. There are also cheap Dominican souvenirs. You can also exchange money and buy phone cards here (as well as make long-distance calls in private booths). ⊠ *Playa Dorada Plaza, Calle Duarte at Av. 30 de Marzo, Puerto Plata* ☎ *809/320–6645.*

SPORTS AND ACTIVITIES

Although there's hardly a shortage of activities here, the resorts have virtually cornered the market on sports, including every conceivable water sport. In some cases, facilities may be available only to guests of the resorts.

BIKING AND HIKING

Pedaling is easy on pancake-flat beaches, but there are also some steep hills in the D.R. Several resorts rent bikes to guests and nonguests alike.

NORTH COAST

Iguana Mama. Iguana Mama's offerings include mountain-bike tours that will take you along the coastal flats or test your mettle on steep climbs in the mountains. Downhill bike rides—which include a taxi up to the foothills, breakfast, and lunch—cost $99 for a full-day trip, $70 for a half-day trip without lunch. Advanced rides, on and off road, are $55 to $95.

Other half- and full-day trips—which range in price from $89 to $195—include hiking, swimming, climbing up and jumping off various waterfalls, rapelling, and natural waterslides. Guided day hikes cost $35 to $75; a three-day hike to the Caribbean's tallest peak, Pico Duarte in Jarabacoa, is $450. This well-established, safety-oriented company also offers horseback riding on the beach of Cabarete and in the countryside (from $45 for two hours), white-water rafting, ecotours, and lots of other adventure sports. ⊠ *Calle Principal 74, Cabarete, Dominican Republic* ☎ *809/571–0908, 809/571–0228* ⊕ *www. iguanamama.com.*

BOATING

Sailing conditions are ideal, with constant trade winds. Favorite excursions include day trips to Catalina and Saona islands—both in the La Romana area—and sunset cruises on the Caribbean. Prices for crewed sailboats of 26 feet and longer, with a capacity of 4 to 12 people, are fixed according to size and duration, from a low of $200 a day to the norm of $700 a day. Examples of other prices, taken from the new fleet at Cap Cana Marina, are as follows: Sportfishermen from 47 to 51 feet accommodating up to eight people (crewed with all equipment, snacks, and beverages with sandwiches on all day trips), $1,800 for four hours, $2,500 for eight hours; a 62-foot custom, luxury power-sail catamaran, $1,650 for two hours (everything included for Cap Cana guests); a 56-foot Sea Ray Sedan Bridge motor yacht, $2,000 for two hours, $2,500 for four hours, $3,500 for eight hours (everything included); and a luxury 90-foot custom motor yacht, ideal for an incentive group, $3,500 for two hours, $5,000 for four hours, $8,500 for eight hours.

SOUTHEAST COAST

Casa de Campo Marina. Casa de Campo Marina has much going on, from sailing to motor yachting and socializing at the Casa de Campo Yacht Club. A first for the marina was hosting the Rolex FARR 40 World's Championship 2010, held in April. One of the world's most important annual sailing events, this was the first time it came to the Caribbean. ⊠ *Casa de Campo, Calle Barlovento 3, La Romana* ☎ *809/523–3333, 809/523–3333.*

NORTH COAST

★ **Carib Wind Center.** Carib Wind Center is a renowned windsurfing center (known for decades as Carib BIC Center) that also rents Lasers, 17-foot catamarans, bodyboards, and sea kayaks. It has an Olympic Laser training center with a former racing instructor. Experts—even champions—come to train here. ⊠ *Cabarete* ☎ *809/571–0640* ⊕ *www. caribwind.com.*

Ocean World Marina. This state-of-the art marina is strategically positioned between the heavily traveled Florida-Bahamas region and the Puerto Rico–eastern Caribbean region. It has filled a large 300-mile (480-km) void on the North Coast where no full-service marina previously existed. The 35-acre complex has 120 slips that accommodate sailboats of up to 200 feet. It is a port of entry with its own immigration and customs office, concierge, laundry and shower facilities, duty-free shop, food and liquor store, car-rental service (even hourly rentals), and marina store with fishing supplies, as well as an entertainment clubhouse, nightclub, and casino. ⊠ *3 miles (5 km) west of Puerto Plata, Cofresí* ☎ *809/970–3373, 809/291–1111* ⊕ *www. oceanworldmarina.com.*

DIVING

Ancient sunken galleons, undersea gardens, and offshore reefs are among the lures here. Most divers head to the north shore. In the waters off Sosúa alone you can find a dozen dive sites (for all levels of ability) with such catchy names as Three Rocks (a deep, 163-foot dive), Airport Wall (98 feet), and Pyramids (50 feet). Some 10 dive schools are represented on Sosúa Beach; resorts have dive shops on-site or can arrange trips for you.

SAMANÁ

In 1979 three atolls disappeared after a seaquake off Las Terrenas, providing an opportunity for truly memorable dives. Also just offshore from Las Terrenas are the Islas Las Ballenas (the Whale Islands), a cluster of four little islands with good snorkeling. A coral reef is off Playa Jackson, a beach accessible only by boat.

Las Terrenas Divers. This PADI and SSI dive center will teach novices as well as take experienced divers night-, canyon-, cave-, wreck-, and deepwater diving. A dive is approximately $40; daily diving equipment rentals are $12. Learn-to-dive programs begin at $100. ⊠ *Hotel Bahía Las Ballenas, Playa Punta Bonita, Las Terrenas* ☎ *809/889–2422* ⊕ *www.lt-divers.com.*

NORTH COAST

Northern Coast Aquasports. A five-star, Gold Palm PADI dive center, Northern Coast Aquasports is also the only National Geographic diver certification site in the Dominican Republic. Professionalism is apparent in the initial classroom and pool practice, as well as in the selection of legendary dive sites around beautiful Sosúa Bay, where you can explore the reefs, walls, wrecks, and swim-throughs, from 25 to 130 feet. Successful completion of a three-day course and $399 earns you a PADI Open Water Certification card. Classrooms have air-conditioning and DVDs. ⊠ *Sosúa* ☎ *809/571–1028* ⊕ *www. northerncoastdiving.com.*

FISHING

Big-game fishing is big in Punta Cana, with blue and white marlin, wahoo, sailfish, and dorado among the most common catches in these waters. Several fishing tournaments are held every summer. The PuntaCana Resort & Club has hosted the ESPN Xtreme Billfishing Tournament every year since 2003. Blue-marlin tournaments are held at the La Mona Channel in Cabeza de Toro. Several tour operators offer organized deep-sea fishing excursions.

LA ROMANA

Casa de Campo Marina. Casa de Campo Marina is the best charter option in the La Romana area. Yachts (22 to 60 footers) are available for deep-sea fishing charters for half or full days. Prices go from $708 to $1,591. They can come equipped with rods, bait, dinghies, drinks, and experienced guides. Going out for the big billfish that swim the depths of the Caribbean is a major adrenaline rush.

Boat excursions for river fishing are available as well. A three-hour excursion takes you down the Chavón River and past the lush vegetation of the bordering tropical forest, and you can go light-tackle angling for championship-size snook (a freshwater fish) as you do so. The price of $110 (minimum two people) includes boat, river guide, tackle, bait, water, and sodas. ⊠ *Casa de Campo, Calle Barlovento 3, La Romana* ☎ *809/523–3333 3165, 809/523–3333 3166.*

PUNTA CANA

PuntaCana Marina. At PuntaCana Marina, on the southern end of the resort, there are many, many nautical options available for rent, from banana boats and waterskiing craft to sport fishing and diving charters. ⊠ *PuntaCana Resort & Club, Punta Cana* ☎ *809/959–2262* ⊕ *www. puntacana.com.*

GOLF

This island has earned a reputation as a golf destination, and deservedly so. The D.R. has some of the best courses in the Caribbean, designed by top golf architects; among these leading designers are Pete Dye, P.B. Dye, Jack Nicklaus, Robert Trent Jones, Gary Player, Tom Fazio, Nick Faldo, Tom Watson, and Severiano Ballesteros. The Dominican Republic was voted Golf Destination of the Year by the International Association of Golf Tour Operators (IAGTO) during its IAGTO Awards 2009 celebrations in Spain. IAGTO operators control more than 80% of golf holiday packages sold worldwide. Criteria for choosing the winner included customer satisfaction, quality of courses and accommodations, value for money, support from suppliers and tourist boards, and professional conduct. Most courses charge higher rates during the winter high season; some, but not all, reduce their rates between April and October, so be sure to ask. Also, some have cheaper rates in the afternoon (mornings are cooler). And guests of certain hotels get better prices.

LA ROMANA

Fodor'sChoice **Casa de Campo.** The famed 18-hole Teeth of the Dog course at Casa
★ de Campo, with seven holes on the sea, is ranked as the number-one
course in the Caribbean and is among the top courses in the world
(coming in 47th in the Top 100 Courses of the World rankings released
in late 2011). Greens fees in high season for nonhotel guests are $325
per round per golfer; $185 per round per player for guests. The Teeth
of the Dog also requires a caddy for each round, an additional $25
(plus tip). Pete Dye has designed this and two other globally acclaimed
courses here. Dye Fore, now with a total of 27 holes, is close to Altos
de Chavón, hugging a cliff that looks over the sea, a river, Dominican mountains, and the marina (in high season: $250 for nonguests,
$185 for guests). The Links—at this writing scheduled to reopen April
2012—is an 18-hole inland course (in high season: $175 for nonguests;
$155 for hotel guests). Resort guests must reserve tee times for all
courses at least one day in advance; nonguests should make reservations
earlier. Jim McLean recently opened a golf school at Casa de Campo;
an instructor is on site year-round. Half- and full-day lessons are available to individuals and groups; one-hour private lessons for adults are
priced at $150. ✉ *La Romana* ☎ *809/523–3333, 809/523–8115 golf
director* ⊕ *www.casadecampo.com.do.*

PUNTA CANA

Barceló Bávaro Golf. Barceló Bávaro Golf is an 18-hole, par-72 course
integrated within the Barceló Bávaro Beach Golf & Casino Resort complex, which is open to its own guests and those of other hotels. The
course, with numerous water obstacles, was designed by Juan Manuel
Gordillo, and was the first in the Bávaro area. Complete renovations
were executed by designer P. B. Dye in 2010. The best rates are available for guests of the more upscale Barceló hotels, such as the Barceló
Palace Deluxe. In high season they pay $50 for 18 holes (includes the
cart); after March 15th the cost drops to $40. The price for those not
staying at a Barceló is $125, which includes greens fees and golf cart.
✉ *Bávaro* ☎ *809/686–5797* ⊕ *www.barcelobavarogolf.net.*

Catalonia Caribe Golf Club. Challenging and reasonably priced, Catalonia
Caribe Golf Club is an 18-hole, par-72 course spread out on greens surrounded by five lakes and an abundance of shady palms. It is a short
course, and Alberto Sola, the architect, designed it so that it would be
challenging for both experienced and novice golfers. The rate structure
is a bit complex. ✉ *Catalonia Bávaro Resort, Cabeza de Toro, Bávaro*
☎ *809/321–7058* ⊕ *www.cataloniabavaro.com.*

Cocotal Golf Course. Named for the coconut plantation on which it was
built, Cocotal Golf Course, designed by Spaniard José "Pepe" Gancedo,
has 18 championship holes and 9 regular holes. It's a challenging par-
72 course dotted with palm trees and lakes within the residential community, Palma Real. There's also a driving range, clubhouse, pro shop,
and golf academy. ✉ *Bávaro* ☎ *809/687–4653, 809/221–1290* ⊕ *www.
cocotalgolf.com.*

★ **La Cana Golf Club.** La Cana Golf Club is comprised of 27 holes of championship golf designed by P. B. Dye, with spectacular ocean views—La

Cana, Arreclife, and Hacienda. La Cana Golf Course is a breathtaking, 18-hole championship course—four holes play right along the water. The latest, the Hacienda Course, opened in Jan. 2012. It is a handsome, inland course punctuated with many lakes amidst an unspoiled tropical landscape, a challenging addition to the existing, spectacular courses. For resort guests, 18 holes are $135.00 in season and $105.00 off season. External guests are $175.00 in season and $140.00 off season. Multiple round/ twilight packages are available as well. Caddies are optional. Lessons and golf schools are offered by PGA Professional staff. Reserve two weeks in advance from November through April. ⊠ *PuntaCana Resort & Club, Punta Cana* ☎ *809/959–4653* ⊕ *www. puntacana.com.*

Fodor'sChoice
★
Punta Espada Golf Course. Punta Espada Golf Course is a par-72 Jack Nicklaus signature golf course with striking bluffs, lush foliage, and winding waterways. There's a Caribbean view from all the holes, and eight of them play right along the sea. It's the first of three Jack Nicklaus signature courses planned at Cap Cana, and for years was the site of an annual, internationally televised PGA Champions Tour event. This exceptional golf club has concierge services, a restaurant, the Hole 19 bar, a pro shop, a members' trophy gallery, a library, lockers, an equipment repair shop, and a meeting room. Rates are discounted for guests in any of Cap Cana's accommodations and are $225 ($135 after 2 pm); greens fees are $375 for external guests ($230 after 2 pm); prices include golf cart, caddy, tees, water, and practice on the driving range. The course is closed Tuesdays for maintenance. In high season, it is best to make reservations two weeks in advance for tee times. ⊠ *Cap Cana, Carretera Juanillo, Playa Juanillo* ☎ *809/469– 7767* ⊕ *www.capcana.com.*

NORTH COAST

Playa Grande Golf Course. Playa Grande Golf Course, between Río San Juan and Cabrera on the North Coast, is sometimes described as the Pebble Beach of the Caribbean, with 10 holes along 60-ft cliffs overlooking the Atlantic Ocean. It carries the signature of Robert Trent Jones Sr. (At this writing a much-delayed plan to privatize the area into a golf-themed residential complex still hadn't come to pass.) Greens fees to play the 18-hole, par-72 course are $120 ($65 for 9 holes); all fees include the cost of a mandatory cart. Caddies, also mandatory, are an additional $30 for 18 holes, $22 for 9. Dress code dictates no tank tops, bikinis, or cutoffs. There's a pro shop as well as an open-air bar and restaurant offering a few dishes, including fish and burgers. ■ TIP→ Know that in the winter this course is heavily booked; call as far in advance as possible to find a time slot. ⊠ *Carretera Río San Juan–Cabrera, Km 9, Cabrera* ☎ *809/582–0860* ⊕ *www.playagrande.com.*

Playa Dorada Golf Club. *Golf Digest* has named Playa Dorada Golf Club one of the top 100 courses outside the United States. It's open to guests of all the hotels in the area. Greens fees for 9 holes are $47, 18 holes $79; caddies are mandatory for foursomes and will cost about $15 for 18 holes, $8 for 9 (plus tip); carts are optional, at $24 and $18, for 18 or 9 holes, respectively. The attractive clubhouse has lockers, a pro shop, a bar, and a restaurant. Reservations during high season should be made as far in advance as possible. Guests at certain hotels in the Playa Dorada complex get discounts. ⊠ *Playa Dorada, next door to Victoria Resort, Puerto Plata* ☎ *809/320–3472* ⊕ *www. playadoradagolf.com.*

GUIDED TOURS

Visitors to the Dominican Republic will have a plethora of excursions to choose from, but many options are not wonderful and are overpriced. Wait until you arrive before booking anything. As for group excursions, "interview" fellow guests to find out if their tour was worth the money and effort. Often the full-day excursions are too long and leave too early. Best are half-day trips—particularly boat excursions. Horseback riding can sound appealing, as the trails usually include some stretches of beach, but do not envision superior horseflesh, tack, instruction, or even guides who can speak English. And whatever, just enjoy! Clients traveling on a tour-company package tend to book excursions with the same company, or through the company affiliated with their resort.

SANTO DOMINGO

Private tours are a good option in Santo Domingo, but you will have to pay approximately $125 a day for a guide—more if the tour guide works with a driver. Your hotel concierge can best arrange these for you, and he or she will know the best English-speaking guides. Be sure you hire a guide who is licensed by the government.

LA ROMANA

Tropical Tours. The primary tour operator on the Southeast Coast is Tropical Tours (with headquarters at Casa de Campo in La Romana), whose prices are even less than some non-pros and some cruise-ship excursions. Their vans are new or nearly new and well maintained. Also, most of their staff speaks English as well as other languages. They can take you on a tour of Santo Domingo, to caves, on outback safaris, zip lining, or even out to a ballgame. The company also operates boat tours to the islands and provides transfers to the three area airports. ⊠ *Casa de Campo, La Romana* ☎ *809/556–5801, 809/523–2028* ⊕ *tropicaltoursromana.com.do.*

PUNTA CANA

Amstar DMC–Apple Vacations. Amstar is well managed and reliable, and is associated with Apple Vacations. ⊠ *Carretera Bávaro, Bávaro* ☎ *809/221–6626* ⊕ *www.amstardominicana.com or www. applevacations.com.*

★ **Go Golf Tours (GGT.** Go Golf has services tailored to clients seeking to make golf part of their getaway—whether it's the primary focus or just a one-time outing; the company will help arrange tee times, golf instruction, and transport to courses. ⊠ *Cocotal Golf & Country Club, Bávaro* ☎ *809/687–4653, 855/374–4653 toll free in U.S., 809/200–9556 toll free in D.R.* ⊕ *www.tee-off-times.info or golfreservationcenter.com.*

NORTH COAST

Most North Coast travelers arrange their activities and tours through the company that sold their travel package. Most such companies do a decent job, but there are also a few independent tour operators in the region.

Alf's Tours. In Sosúa, multilingual Alf's Tours has been a mainstay for years. ⊠ *Calle Pedro Clisante 12, across from North Coast Dive Center, El Batey, Sosúa* 🕾 *809/571–9904* ⊕ *www.alftour.com.*

Tours, Trips, Treks & Travel. Tours, Trips, Treks & Travel, founded by a veteran Iguana Mama trip leader who adheres to the tenet of experiential learning, specializes in educational, adventure, and other programs for groups; the company does cultural tours that employ local experts. ⊠ *Cabarete* 🕾 *809/867–8884* ⊕ *www.4Tdomrep.com.*

HORSEBACK RIDING

SOUTHEAST COAST

Equestrian Center at Casa de Campo. The 250-acre Equestrian Center at Casa de Campo has something for both Western and English riders—a dude ranch, a rodeo arena (where Casa's trademark "Donkey Polo" is played), guided trail rides, and jumping and riding lessons. Guided rides run about $56 an hour, $88 for two hours; lessons cost $65 an hour, and jumping lessons are $88 an hour or $55 a half-hour. There are early morning and sunset trail rides, too. Handsome, old-fashioned carriages are available for hire as well. Unlimited horseback riding is included if you are a hotel guest staying on the inclusive supplement. ⊠ *La Romana* 🕾 *809/523–3333* ⊕ *www.casadecampo.com.do.*

PUNTA CANA

Rancho Punta Cana. Rancho Punta Cana is across from the main entrance of the resort. A one-hour trail ride winds along the beach, the golf course, and through tropical forests. The two-hour jungle trail ride has a stopover at a lagoon fed by a natural spring, so wear your swimsuit under your long pants. You can also do a three-hour full-moon excursion or take riding lessons. The stock is comprised of Paso Finos. ⊠ *PuntaCana Resort & Club, Punta Cana* 🕾 *809/959–2714* ⊕ *www. puntacana.com.*

SAMANÁ PENINSULA

Rancho Cedric. This operator offers 80-minute rides on Playa Bonita for $27 and two-hour rides on Playa Cosón or Las Terrenas for $45. This is a simple, local operation; little English is spoken, and Western saddles are used. But it has a friendly atmosphere and is close to town. ⊠ *Playa Las Terrenas, behind Hotel Las Cayenas, Las Terrenas* 🕾 *809/847–4849.*

NORTH COAST

Sea Horse Ranch Equestrian Center. This equestrian center is a professional, well-staffed operation. The competition ring is built to international regulations, and there is a large schooling ring. Lessons, including dressage instruction, start at $35 an hour, and endurance rides are $30 for 90 minutes, $50 for three hours, including drinks and snacks—but make reservations. The most popular ride includes stretches of beach and a bridle path across a neighboring farm's pasture that's full of wild-flowers and butterflies. Feel free to tie your horse to a palm tree and jump into the waves. ⊠ *Sea Horse Ranch, Cabarete* ☎ *809/571–3880, 809/571–4462.*

WHALE-WATCHING

SAMANÁ PENINSULA

Humpback whales come to Samaná Bay to mate and give birth each year for a relatively limited period, from approximately January 15 through March 30. Samaná Bay is considered one of the top 10 destinations in the world to watch humpbacks. If you're here during the brief season, this can be the experience of a lifetime. You can listen to the male humpback's solitary courting song and witness incredible displays as the whales flip their tails and breach (humpbacks are the most active species of whales in the Atlantic).

Whale Samaná. Whale Samaná is owned by Kim Beddall, a Canadian who is incredibly knowledgeable about whales and Samaná at large, having lived here for decades. Her operation is far and away the region's best, most professional, and environmentally sensitive. On board a 55-foot motor vessel, a marine mammal specialist narrates and answers questions in several languages. Kim herself conducts almost all the English-speaking trips. The $50 price does not include the RD$100 Marine Mammal Sanctuary entrance fee (price is subject to change). Kim also welcomes cruise passengers, but requires advance reservations. Normal departure times are 9 am for the morning trip and 1:30 pm for the afternoon trip, but she is flexible whenever possible for cruisers. Kim also conducts trips to Los Haitises National Park on Tuesday, Thursday, and Saturday on the *Mistral*, a 45-foot catamaran. These tours, which cost $55 per person, include a terrific lunch and the $3 park entrance fee and last four to five hours. The boat has a dozen kayaks in which teams of two can explore the shore-line. ⊠ *Across street from town dock, beside park, Calle Sra. Morellia Kelly, Samaná* ☎ *809/538–2042* ✎ *kim.beddall@whalesamana.com* ⊕ *www.whaleSamana.com.*

WIND- AND KITESURFING

Fodor'sChoice
★

Between June and October, Cabarete Beach has what many consider to be optimal windsurfing conditions: wind speeds at 20 to 25 knots (they come from the side shore) and 3- to 10-foot Atlantic waves. The Professional Boardsurfers Association has included Cabarete in its international windsurfing slalom competition. The novice is also welcome to learn and train on wider boards with light sails.

Carib Wind Center. Windsurfing equipment and instruction are offered here, and lessons are generally $30 to $35 an hour; boards rent for $20 an hour. A gem of a club, this family-owned business has many repeat clients and is open year-round. In the complex is its beach bar, EZE, as well as a retail shop. It has all the paraphernalia for surfing and a good variety of sunglasses, including Maui Jim's, and some of the best bikinis, cute miniskirts, and dresses in town. ✉ *Cabarete* ☎ *809/571–0640* ⊕ *www.caribwind.com.*

Club Nathalie Simon. If you come to this sports club, don't ask to see Nathalie! (Yes, it's named after the French windboarder, but she is otherwise occupied. When Alain and Caroline Ponti bought the land here, they bought the franchise.) There are now six CNS outposts around the world. CNS is primarily a windboarding and kiteboarding school that also offers a wide range of on- and off-water activities, including standup paddling, surfing, kayaking, and horseback riding. Located directly at the entrance of both the windboard and kiteboard zones of Cabarete Bay, it also has on-site storage for equipment. ✉ *On Cabarete Beach, next to The Palms condo, Cabarete.*

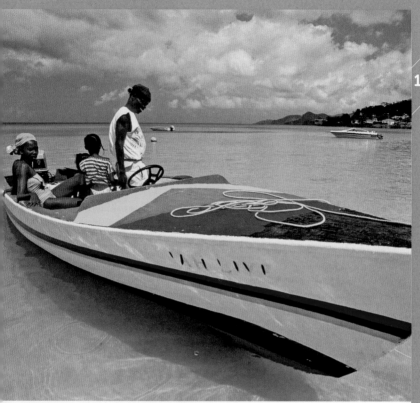

Grenada

WITH CARRIACOU

WORD OF MOUTH

"Grenada is a stunning, breathtaking island that will steal your heart for a lifetime . . . at least that is what has happened to me. It has everything that you are looking for, and you will still likely find things you never imagined. You can't go wrong with Grenada. I have not."

—caribheart

WELCOME TO GRENADA

THE SPICE ISLAND

A relatively small island, Grenada is 21 mi (34 km) long and 12 mi (19 km) wide; much of the interior is a lush rain forest. It's a major producer of nutmeg, cinnamon, mace, cocoa, and other spices and flavorings. Carriacou—23 mi (37 km) north of Grenada—is just 13 square mi (34 square km). Tiny Petite Martinique is 2 mi (3 km) farther north.

21 Sauter Bay
David Bay
Carib's Leap
Sauteurs
Morne Fendu
St. Mark Bay
Victoria
14
Gouyave Nutmeg ◆ Processing Coop
Gouyave
Mt. ▲ St. Catherine
◆ Dougaldston Spice Estate
Gouyave Bay
Concord Falls ◆
▲ Mt. Granby
Black Bay Pt.
▲ Mt. Qua Qua
Flamingo Bay
Grand Étang National Park and Forest Reserve
Halifax Harbour
Mar
Annandale Falls ◆
Molinère Reef
Molinère Pt.
Grand Mal Bay
Constantine
▲ Mt. Lebanon
▲ Mt. Sinai
Pomm Ros
St. George's
De La Grenade ◆ Industries
◆ Laura Herb and Spice Garden
St. David
Bianca C
St. George's Harbour
1 2
3 - 6
1 - 7
Boss Reef
Belmont
Westerhall Estate
La Sagesse Beach
Grand Anse Beach
8 9
18
13 20
Magazine Beach
Morne Rouge Bay
Morne Rouge Beach
Grand Anse
La Sagesse Bay
12 19
St. George's U.
14 L'Anse aux Epines
Westerhall Bay
Pink Gin Beach
Pt. Salines
8 13
11 17
7 10 - 12
Maurice Bishop International Airport
Prickly Bay
9 10
15 16

0 ————— 5 mi
0 ————— 5 km

These days, local people on the Isle of Spice busy themselves cultivating nutmeg, cloves, and other spices. Vestiges of Grenada's briefly turbulent past have all but disappeared. Renowned for its natural beauty, its fragrant air, and its friendly people, Grenada has lovely beaches and plenty of outdoor and cultural activities.

12

GRENADA

KEY

🏖 Beaches
⚓ Cruise Ship Terminal
◸ Dive Sites
1 Restaurants
① Hotels

TOP REASONS TO VISIT GRENADA

1 Old and New: Grenada successfully blends an "original" Caribbean atmosphere with all the comforts and amenities you expect today.

2 The Aroma: The scent of spices fills the air, perfumes the soap, improves the drinks, and even flavors the ice cream.

3 Nature Abounds: Spot monkeys in the mountains, watch birds in the rain forest, join fish in the sea, and build sand castles on the beach.

4 Local Hospitality: Grenadians go out of their way to make you feel welcome.

5 A Great Getaway: With no megaresorts, you really can get away from it all.

GRENADA AND CARRIACOU BEACHES

Grenada's best beaches are found along the island's southwestern coastline, which is also where you'll find most of the tourist facilities. Carriacou has lovely beaches that are an easy walk for day-trippers who arrive by ferry, but the deserted islands just offshore are the most memorable.

(Above) Grande Anse Beach (Bottom right) La Sagesse Beach (Top right) Sandy Island.

Grenada has some 80 miles (130 km) of coastline, 65 bays, and 45 beaches—many in little coves. The best beaches are just south of St. George's, facing the Caribbean, where most resorts are also clustered. Nude or topless bathing is against the law if you are in view of others.

On Carriacou, you'll find beaches within walking distance of the ferry jetty in Hillsborough—miles of soft, white sand that slopes gently down to the warm (average 83°F), calm sea. Carriacou's best beach experience, though, is a day spent swimming, snorkeling, and picnicking on one of the otherwise uninhabited islands just offshore.

BLACK AND WHITE

Grenada has primarily white-sand beaches; a few in the north have black sand. Grand Anse Beach has 2 miles (3 km) of white sand. Morne Rouge, nearby, is a perfect semi-circle of white sand.

On Carriacou, Paradise Beach has lovely white sand. Sandy Island and White Island require a water taxi from Hillsborough, but the powdery sand and crystal-clear water make the effort worth it.

12

GRENADA

Bathway Beach. This broad strip of sand on Grenada's far northern shore has a natural reef that protects swimmers from the rough Atlantic surf. There are changing rooms at the Levera National Park headquarters. ⊠ *Levera National Park, Levera St. Patrick.*

⭐ **Fodor's Choice** | **Grand Anse Beach.** Grenada's loveliest and most popular beach: a gleaming 2-mile (3-km) semicircle of white sand lapped by clear, gentle surf. Sea grape trees and coconut palms provide shady escapes. Brilliant rainbows frequently spill into the sea from the high green mountains that frame St. George's Harbour to the north. The Grand Anse Craft & Spice Market and a water taxi dock are at the midpoint of the beach. Public entrance is through Camerhogne Park, where there are restrooms and changing facilities. ⊠ *3 miles (5 km) south of St. George's, Grand Anse, St. George.*

La Sagesse Beach. Along the southeast coast at La Sagesse Nature Centre, this strip of powdery white sand surrounded by tropical vegetation provides a lovely, quiet refuge. Plan a full day of swimming, sunning, and nature walks, with lunch at La Sagesse's country inn adjacent to the beach. ⊠ *La Sagesse Nature Center, La Sagesse, St. David.*

Magazine Beach. Near the international airport in Point Salines, Magazine Beach

is a magnificent strip of pure white sand that stretches from the Aquarium Restaurant at its southern end to the Grenadian by Rex Resort. Never crowded, it's excellent for swimming and sunbathing. Cool drinks, light refreshments, or a full lunch are available at the Aquarium Restaurant. Access is next to the restaurant or the hotel. ⊠ *Point Salines, St. George.*

Morne Rouge Beach. One mile (1½ km) south of Grand Anse Bay, this ½-mile-long (¾-km-long) sheltered crescent with gentle surf is excellent for swimming. Light meals and snacks are available at adjacent hotels. ⊠ *Morne Rouge, St. George.*

CARRIACOU

Paradise Beach. This long, narrow stretch of beach in L'Esterre, between Hillsborough and Tyrrel Bay, has calm, clear water; there's also a casual restaurant and souvenir shop. ⊠ *L'Esterre, Petite Martinique.*

Sandy Island. This is a truly deserted island off Hillsborough—just a ring of white sand with a few young palm trees—except when people come by boat to snorkel and swim. Arrange transportation from the jetty at Hillsborough or the restaurant at Paradise Beach for $25 to $30 (EC$70) round-trip. Bring snorkeling gear and a picnic. ⊠ *Hillsborough Bay, Hillsborough, Petite Martinique.*

By Jane E. Zarem

Independent since 1974, this lush, green isle has developed a healthy tourism sector and a modern infrastructure, including welcoming hotels and resorts, good roads, up-to-date technology, and reliable utilities.

The nation of Grenada actually consists of three islands: Grenada, the largest, with a population of about 102,000; Carriacou (*car*-ree-a-coo), north of Grenada, with a population of just over 6,000; and Petite Martinique, with a population of about 500. Carriacou and Petite Martinique are popular for day trips, fishing adventures, or diving and snorkeling excursions, but most of the tourist activity is on the island of Grenada itself. People interested in a really quiet, get-away-from-it-all vacation will, however, appreciate the simple pleasures of Carriacou during an extended stay.

The island of Grenada has 45 beaches and countless secluded coves. Crisscrossed by nature trails and laced with spice plantations, its mountainous interior is made up mostly of a rain-forest preserve. St. George's, the capital, is one of the most picturesque cities in the Caribbean; Grand Anse is one of the region's finest beaches.

Although Christopher Columbus never set foot on Grenada, he did sight it in 1498, naming it Concepción. Spanish sailors following in his wake renamed it Granada, after the city in the hills of their homeland. Adapted to Grenade by French colonists, the transformation of the name to Grenada was completed by the British in the 18th century.

Throughout the 17th century, Grenada was the scene of many bloody battles between the indigenous Carib Indians and the French. Rather than surrender to the Europeans after losing their last battle in 1651, the Caribs committed mass suicide by leaping off a cliff that's now called Carib's Leap or Leapers Hill. The French were later overwhelmed by the British in 1762, the beginning of a seesaw of power between the two nations. By the Treaty of Versailles in 1783, Grenada was granted to the British. Almost immediately, thousands of African slaves were brought in to work the sugar plantations (although slavery in Grenada actually began with the French colonization in 1650). It was finally abolished in 1834.

LOGISTICS

Getting to Grenada and Carriacou:
Nonstop flights to Grenada are available several times per week from New York or Miami. Otherwise, connect through San Juan, Montego Bay, Barbados, or another nearby island on a regional airline. Fairly frequent air service on small planes and a daily ferry (a 90-minute ride each way) connect Grenada and Carriacou.

Hassle Factor: Low to medium for Grenada, medium-high for Carriacou.

On the Ground: Maurice Bishop International Airport, at Point Salines on the southwestern tip of Grenada, is a modern facility suitable for the largest jets—it's no more than a 10-minute drive from most hotels and resorts. On Carriacou, five minutes south of Hillsborough, Lauriston Airport is a lighted landing strip suitable for small planes, with a small building for ticket sales and shelter. On Grenada, taxis are always available for transportation between the airport and hotels. Fares to St. George's are $25; to the hotels of Grand Anse and L'Anse aux Épines, $15. Rides taken between 6 pm and 6 am incur a $4 surcharge.

At Carriacou's airport, taxis meet every plane; the fare to Hillsborough is $8; to Bogles, $12; to Tyrrel Bay or Windward, $16.

Forts that the French began to construct to protect St. George's Harbour during their colonization of Grenada were later completed and used by the British during theirs. Today Ft. George and Ft. Frederick are two of the most visited sites in St. George's. Besides their historical interest, the two locations have magnificent views of the harbor, the capital city itself, and the distant mountains and countryside. Not a single shot was fired from either fort for more than two centuries. In 1983, however, Prime Minister Maurice Bishop and seven others were murdered at Ft. George during a coup. That event triggered the request from Grenada's governor-general and the heads of state of neighboring islands for U.S. troops to intervene, which they did on October 25, 1983.

From that time forward, Grenada's popularity as a vacation destination has increased with each decade, as travelers continue to seek friendly, exotic islands to visit. Nearly all hotels, resorts, and restaurants in Grenada are family owned and run (mostly by Grenadians); their guests often become good friends. All Grenadians, in fact, have a well-deserved reputation for their friendliness, hospitality, and entrepreneurial spirit. You can be sure you'll be "enjoyin' it" when you visit Grenada.

PLANNING

WHEN TO GO

The high season stretches from December 15 to April 15. In the off-season, prices at Grenada resorts may be discounted by up to 40%. In September and early October some hotels close for annual maintenance and renovations. There are fewer seasonal rate changes on Carriacou, where the small hotels and guesthouses are all relatively inexpensive anyway.

GETTING HERE AND AROUND

AIR TRAVEL

Nonstop flights are available from New York and Miami.

Airline contacts American Airlines/American Eagle. American flies nonstop to Grenada from Miami and from other major cities by connecting with American Eagle in San Juan. ☎ *473/444–2121, 800/744–0006.*

Caribbean Airlines. Caribbean provides twice-weekly direct service from New York via Port-of-Spain, Trinidad. ☎ *800/744–2225.*

Delta Air Lines. Delta provides weekly nonstop service from New York. ☎ *800/241–4141.*

LIAT. LIAT offers frequent scheduled service linking Grenada with more than two dozen neighboring islands. ☎ *888/844–5428.*

SVG Air. SVG flies between Grenada and Carriacou, with some flights continuing on to Union Island to connect with flights to St. Vincent or Barbados. ☎ *473/444–3549, 800/744–7285, 473/443–8519 in Carriacou.*

Airport contacts Maurice Bishop International Airport. Maurice Bishop is a modern facility suitable for the largest jets. Best of all, it's no more than a 10-minute drive from most hotels and resorts, on the southwestern tip of Grenada. ⊠ *Point Salines, St. George* ☎ *473/444–4101.*

Lauriston Airport. Lauriston has a lighted landing strip suitable for small planes, with a small building for ticket sales and shelter. It's on Carriacou, five minutes south of Hillsborough. ⊠ *Carriacou* ☎ *473/443–6306.*

Transfers On Grenada, taxis are always available for transportation between the airport and hotels. Fares to St. George's are $25; to the hotels of Grand Anse and L'Anse aux Épines, $15. Rides taken between 6 pm and 6 am incur a $4 surcharge.

CAR TRAVEL

On Grenada, having a car or jeep is a convenience if you're staying at a resort in a location other than Grand Anse, which has frequent minibus service. If you don't have a car of your own, the round-trip taxi rides can get expensive if you plan to leave the resort frequently for shopping, meals, or visiting other beaches. Driving is also a reasonable option if you want to explore the island on your own. Most of Grenada's 650 miles (1,050 km) of paved roads are kept in fairly good condition—although they are steep, curving, and narrow beyond the Grand Anse area. Driving is on the left, British-style. Gas stations are in St. George's, Grand Anse, Grenville, Gouyave, and Sauteurs.

Renting a Car: To rent a car on Grenada, you need a valid driver's license and a local permit (available at the Central Police Station on the Carenage in the capital city of St. George's and at most car-rental firms), which costs $12 (EC$30). You can rent a car on Carriacou, but it's easier to take taxis.

Some rental agencies impose a minimum age of 21. Rental cars (including four-wheel-drive vehicles) cost $55 to $75 a day or $285 to $375 a week with unlimited mileage. In high season there may be a three-day minimum rental. Rental agencies offer free pickup and drop-off at either the airport or your hotel. A temporary driving permit, available through the rental agency, costs $12.

Contacts on Grenada David's Car Rentals ☎ *473/444–3399* ⊕ *www. davidscars.com.* **Indigo Car Rentals** ☎ *473/439–3300* ⊕ *www. indigocarsgrenada.com.* **McIntyre Bros. Ltd.** ☎ *473/444–3944* ⊕ *www. caribbeanhorizons.com.* **Y & R Car Rentals** ☎ *473/444–4448* ⊕ *www.y-r.com.*

Contact on Carriacou Barba's Auto Rentals ☎ *473/443–7454, 473/407–8167.*

FERRY TRAVEL

Osprey Express. The high-speed ferry *Osprey Express* makes two round-trip voyages daily from Grenada to Carriacou and on to Petite Martinique. The fare for the 90-minute trip from Grenada to Carriacou is $31 each way. For the 15-minute trip from Carriacou to Petite Martinique, the fare is $24 round-trip. The boat leaves Grenada from the Carenage in St. George's. ☎ *473/440–8126* ⊕ *www.ospreylines.com.*

TAXIS

On Grenada, taxis are plentiful, and rates are set. The trip between Grand Anse and St. George's is $20. A $4 surcharge is added for rides taken between 6 pm and 6 am. Taxis can be hired at an hourly rate of $30 as well.

In Carriacou the taxi fare from the jetty in Hillsborough to Belair is $6; to Prospect, $8; and to Tyrrel Bay or Windward, $10.

ALTERNATIVE TRANSPORTATION

The best way to travel between Grenada and Carriacou is by air or high-speed ferry, but if you're looking for adventure and economy rather than comfort and speed—and aren't prone to motion sickness—then cargo schooners from Grenada to Carriacou and Petite Martinique are another option. Mail boats *Alexia II, Alexia III,* and *Adelaide B* depart from the Carenage in St. George's early Tuesday, Wednesday, Friday, and Saturday mornings for the four-hour voyage to Carriacou; the return trip to Grenada departs from Carriacou on Monday, Wednesday, Thursday, and Sunday mornings. The fare between Grenada and Carriacou on these schooners is $10 each way. The *Adelaide B* continues on from Carriacou to Petite Martinique (a 1½-hour trip); the fare is about $5 each way. Reservations aren't necessary, but get to the wharf at daybreak to be sure you don't miss the boat.

Water taxis are available along the Esplanade, near the port area. For about $8 (EC$20) a motorboat will transport you on an exciting cruise between St. George's and the jetty at Grand Anse Beach. Water taxis are privately owned, unregulated, and don't follow any particular schedule—so make arrangements for a pickup time if you expect a return trip.

ESSENTIALS

Banks and Exchange Services Grenada uses the Eastern Caribbean dollar (EC$). The official exchange rate is fixed at EC$2.67 to US$1; for convenience, taxis, shops, and hotels sometimes use a lower rate (EC$2.50). You can exchange money at banks and hotels, but U.S. paper currency (no coins) and major credit cards are widely accepted.

Electricity Current on Grenada is 220 volts/50 cycles. U.S. standard appliances (110 volts) require a transformer and adapter plug. For dual-voltage computers and other devices, you'll still need an adapter plug; some hotels will lend adapters.

Language English is the official language in Grenada.

Passport Requirements To enter Grenada, visitors must produce a valid passport; a return or onward ticket is also required.

Phones The area code is 473. Prepaid phone cards, which can be used in special card phones throughout the Caribbean for local or international calls, are sold in denominations of EC$20 ($7.50), EC$30 ($12), EC$50 ($20), and EC$75 ($28) at shops, attractions, transportation centers, and other convenient outlets. For international calls using a major credit card, dial 111; to place a collect call or use a calling card, dial 800/225–5872 from any telephone.

Taxes and Service Charges The departure tax of $20 (EC$50) for adults and $10 (EC$25) for children ages 5–11 is incorporated into the price paid for airfare, eliminating the need to pay at the airport when departing the country. Grenada has a 10% V.A.T. (value-added tax) on hotel bills and a 15% V.A.T. on restaurant bills and retail sales. In addition, a 10% service charge is often added to hotel and restaurant bills.

Tipping If there is no service charge, then tip 10%; if a service charge has been included, additional tipping is optional. Bellhops, $1 per bag; housekeeping, $1 or $2 per night; taxi drivers and tour guides, 10% of the fare or fee.

ACCOMMODATIONS

Grenada's tourist accommodations are, for the most part, in the southwest part of the island—primarily on or near Grand Anse Beach or overlooking small bays along the island's southern coast. Carriacou is a small island, and several of its guesthouses are in or around Hillsborough.

Guesthouses: Small guesthouses predominate on Carriacou, where no property has more than 25 rooms.

Luxury Resorts: Grenada has a handful of luxurious inns and resorts. Spice Island Beach Resort is, arguably, the best resort on the island and one of the finest boutique resorts in the Caribbean.

Modest Resorts and Apartment Complexes: Most resorts and hotels on Grenada are small, and many are modest, but that is part of their charm.

HOTEL AND RESTAURANT PRICES

Prices in the restaurant reviews are the average cost of a main course at dinner or, if dinner is not served, at lunch; taxes and service charges are generally included. Prices in the hotel reviews are the lowest cost of a standard double room in high season, excluding taxes, service charges, and meal plans (except at all-inclusives). Prices for rentals are the lowest per-night cost for a one-bedroom unit in high season.

12

VISITOR INFORMATION

Contacts Grenada Board of Tourism ☎ 561/588–8176 in Lake Worth, FL, 800/927–9554 ⊕ www.grenadagrenadines.com. **Grenada Hotel & Tourism Association** ☎ 473/444–1353 ⊕ www.gogrenada.gd. **Grenada Board of Tourism** ✉ Burns Point, south end of the Carenage, St. George's ☎ 473/440–2001, 473/440–2279 ✉ Maurice Bishop International Airport, Point Salines, St. George ☎ 473/444–4140 ✉ Main St., Hillsborough, Carriacou ☎ 473/443–7948.

WEDDINGS

Three days' residency is required to get a marriage license; no blood test is necessary.

EXPLORING GRENADA AND CARRIACOU

GRENADA

Grenada is divided into six parishes, including one named St. George that includes the communities of Grand Anse, Morne Rouge, True Blue, L'Anse aux Épines, and the capital city of St. George's. Note that removing bark from trees, taking wildlife from the forest, and taking coral from the sea are all against the law.

WHAT TO SEE

Annandale Falls. This is a lovely, cool spot for swimming and picnicking. A mountain stream cascades 40 feet into a pool surrounded by exotic vines. A paved path leads to the bottom of the falls, and a trail leads to the top. ✉ *Main interior road, 15 mins northeast of St. George's, Annandale, St. George* ☎ 473/440–2452 ☜ *$1* ☼ *Daily 9–5.*

Carib's Leap. At Sauteurs (the French word for "leapers"), on the island's northernmost tip, Carib's Leap (or Leapers Hill) is the 100-foot vertical cliff from which the last of the indigenous Carib Indians flung themselves into the sea in 1651. After losing several bloody battles with European colonists, they chose to kill themselves rather than surrender to the French. A commemorative display recounts the event. ✉ *Sauteurs, St. Patrick.*

★ **Concord Falls.** About 8 miles (13 km) north of St. George's, a turnoff from the West Coast Road leads to Concord Falls—actually three separate waterfalls. The first is at the end of the road; when the currents aren't too strong, you can take a dip under the cascade. Reaching the two other waterfalls requires an hour's hike into the forest reserve. The third and most spectacular waterfall, at Fountainbleu, thunders 65 feet over huge boulders and creates a small pool. It's smart to hire a guide for that trek. The path is clear, but slippery boulders toward the end can be treacherous without assistance. ✉ *Off West Coast Rd., Concord, St. John* ☜ *Changing room $2* ☼ *Daily 9–5.*

De La Grenade Industries. In the suburb of St. Paul's, five minutes east of St. George's, De La Grenade produces syrups, jams, jellies, and a liqueur from nutmeg and other homegrown fruits and spices (it's based on a 19th-century secret formula). You're welcome to watch the manufacturing process and stroll around the adjacent herb and spice gardens.

⊠ *Morne Délice, St. Paul's, St. George* ☎ *473/440–3241* ⊕ *www. delagrenade.com* ⊠ *$1* ⊙ *Weekdays 8–5, Sat. 9–12:30.*

Dougaldston Spice Estate. Just south of Gouyave, this historic plantation, now primarily a museum, still grows and processes spices the old-fashioned way. You can see cocoa, nutmeg, mace, cloves, and other spices laid out on giant racks to dry in the sun. A worker will be glad to explain the process (and will appreciate a small donation). You can buy spices for about $4 a bag. ⊠ *Gouyave, St. John* ☎ *No phone* ⊠ *Free* ⊙ *Weekdays 9–4.*

Gouyave Nutmeg Processing Cooperative. Touring the nutmeg-processing
★ co-op, in the center of the west-coast fishing village of Gouyave (pronounced *gwahv*), is a fragrant, fascinating way to spend half an hour. You can learn all about nutmeg and its uses, see the nutmegs laid out in bins, and watch the workers sort them by hand and pack them into burlap bags for shipping worldwide. The three-story plant turned out 3 million pounds of Grenada's most famous export each year before Hurricane Ivan's devastating effect on the crop in 2004, when most of the nutmeg trees were destroyed. Locals estimate that it will still be several more years before the nutmeg industry returns to pre-hurricane levels. ⊠ *Gouyave, St. John* ☎ *473/444–8337* ⊠ *$1* ⊙ *Weekdays 10–1 and 2–4.*

Grand Anse. A residential and commercial area about 5 miles (8 km) south of downtown St. George's, Grand Anse is named for the world-renowned beach it surrounds. Grenada's tourist facilities—resorts, restaurants, some shopping, and most nightlife—are concentrated in this general area. **Grand Anse Beach** is a 2-mile (3-km) crescent of sand, shaded by coconut palms and sea grape trees, with gentle turquoise surf. A public entrance is at Camerhogne Park, just a few steps from the main road. Water taxis carry passengers between the Esplanade in St. George's and a jetty on the beach. **St. George's University,** which for years held classes at its enviable beachfront location in Grand Anse, has a sprawling campus in True Blue, a nearby residential community. ⊠ *Grand Anse, St. George.*

Grand Étang National Park & Forest Reserve. Deep in the mountainous inte-
★ rior of Grenada is a bird sanctuary and forest reserve with miles of hiking trails, lookouts, and fishing streams. **Grand Étang Lake** is a 36-acre expanse of cobalt-blue water that fills the crater of an extinct volcano 1,740 feet above sea level. Although legend has it the lake is bottomless, maximum soundings are recorded at 18 feet. The informative **Grand Étang Forest Center** has displays on the local wildlife and vegetation. A forest manager is on hand to answer questions. A small snack bar and souvenir stands are nearby. ⊠ *Main interior road, between Grenville and St. George's, St. Andrew* ☎ *473/440–6160* ⊠ *$1* ⊙ *Daily 8:30–4.*

Grenville Cooperative Nutmeg Association. Like its counterpart in Gouyave, this nutmeg-processing plant is open to the public for guided tours. You can see and learn about the entire process of receiving, drying, sorting, and packing nutmeg. ⊠ *Grenville, St. Andrew* ☎ *473/442–7241* ⊠ *$1* ⊙ *Weekdays 10–1 and 2–4.*

12

☾ **Laura Herb & Spice Garden.** The 6½-acre gardens are part of an old plantation in the village of Laura, in St. David Parish, just 6 miles (10 km) east of Grand Anse. On the 20-minute tour you will learn all about spices and herbs grown in Grenada—including cocoa, clove, nutmeg, pimiento, cinnamon, turmeric, and tonka beans (sometimes used in vanilla substitutes)—and how they're used for flavoring and for medicinal purposes. ⊠ *Laura* ☎ *473/443–2604* ☎ *$2* ☉ *Weekdays 8–4.*

Levera National Park & Bird Sanctuary. This portion of Grenada's protected parkland encompasses 450 acres at the northeastern tip of the island, where the Caribbean Sea meets the Atlantic Ocean. A natural reef protects swimmers from the rough Atlantic surf at Bathway Beach. Thick mangroves provide food and protection for nesting seabirds and seldom-seen parrots. The first islets of the Grenadines are visible from the beach. ⊠ *Levera, St. Patrick* ☎ *Free* ☉ *Daily dawn–dusk.*

Pearls Airport. Just north of Grenville, on the east coast, is the island's original airport, which was replaced in 1984 by Point Salines International Airport (now Maurice Bishop International Airport). Deteriorating Cuban and Soviet planes sit at the end of the old runway, abandoned after the 1983 intervention, when Cuban "advisers" helping to construct the airport at Point Salines were summarily removed from the island. There's a good view north to the Grenadines and a small beach nearby. ⊠ *Pearls, St. Andrew.*

River Antoine Rum Distillery. At this rustic operation (pronounced River An-*twyne*), kept open primarily as a museum, a limited quantity of Rivers rum is produced by the same methods used since the distillery opened in 1785. The process begins with the crushing of sugarcane from adjacent fields. The result is a potent overproof rum, sold only in Grenada, that will knock your socks off. (A less strong version is also available.) ⊠ *River Antoine Estate, St. Patrick* ☎ *473/442–7109* ☎ *$2* ☉ *Guided tours daily 9–4.*

St. George's. Grenada's capital is a bustling West Indian city, much of which remains unchanged from colonial days. Narrow streets lined with shops wind up, down, and across steep hills. Brick warehouses cling to the waterfront, and pastel-painted homes rise from the waterfront and disappear into steep green hills.

Picturesque **St. George's Harbour,** a submerged volcanic crater, is, arguably, the prettiest harbor in the Caribbean. Schooners, ferries, and tour boats tie up along the seawall or at the small dinghy dock. The **Carenage** (pronounced car-a-*nahzh*), which surrounds horseshoe-shape St. George's Harbour, is the capital's center. Warehouses, shops, and restaurants line the waterfront. The *Christ of the Deep* statue that sits on the pedestrian plaza at the center of the Carenage was presented to Grenada by Costa Cruise Line in remembrance of its ship, *Bianca C,* which burned and sank in the harbor in 1961 and is now a favorite dive site.

An engineering feat for its time, the 340-foot-long **Sendall Tunnel** was built in 1895 and named for an early governor. It separates the harbor side of St. George's from the Esplanade on the bay side of town, where you can find the markets (produce, meat, and fish), the Cruise Ship Terminal, the Esplanade Mall, and the public bus station.

Grenada National Museum. The Grenada National Museum, a block from the Carenage, is built on the foundation of a French army barracks and prison that was originally built in 1704. The small museum has exhibitions of news items, photos, and proclamations relating to the 1983 intervention, along with the childhood bathtub of Empress Joséphine (who was born on Martinique), and other memorabilia. ⊠ *Young and Monckton Sts., St. George's* ☎ *473/440–3725* ☜ *$1* ☉ *Weekdays 9–4:30, Sat. 10–1.*

Ft. George. Ft. George is high on the hill at the entrance to St. George's Harbour. It's Grenada's oldest fort—built by the French in 1705 to protect the harbor. No shots were ever fired here until October 1983, when Prime Minister Maurice Bishop and some of his followers were assassinated in the courtyard. The fort now houses police headquarters but is open to the public daily. The 360-degree view of the capital city, St. George's Harbour, and the open sea is spectacular. ⊠ *Church St., St. George's* ☜ *$2.*

Market Square. Don't miss St. George's Market Square, a block from the Cruise Ship Terminal. It's open every weekday morning but really comes alive on Saturday from 8 to noon. Vendors sell baskets, spices, brooms, clothing, knickknacks, coconut water, and heaps of fresh produce. Historically, Market Square is where parades begin and political rallies take place. ⊠ *Granby St., St. George's, St. George.*

St. George's Methodist Church. Built in 1820, this is the oldest church in the city. It was severely damaged by Hurricane Ivan in 2004 but has since been completely refurbished. ⊠ *Green St., near Herbert Blaize St., St. George's, St. George.*

St. George's Roman Catholic Church. The Gothic tower of St. George's Roman Catholic Church, the city's most visible landmark, dates from 1818. The damage that Hurricane Ivan inflicted on the building in 2004 has been repaired. ⊠ *Church St., St. George's, St. George.*

Ft. Frederick. Overlooking the city of St. George's and the inland side of the harbor, historic Ft. Frederick provides a panoramic view of about one-fourth of Grenada. The fort was started by the French and completed in 1791 by the British; it was also the headquarters of the People's Revolutionary Government before and during the 1983 coup. Today you can get a bird's-eye view of much of Grenada from here. ⊠ *Richmond Hill, St. George.*

Westerhall Estate. Back in the late 1800s, cocoa, sugarcane, coconuts (their oil was used for soap), and limes (their oil was used for perfumes) were produced on the 951-acre Westerhall Estate, which was called Bacaye then. More recently, Westerhall has concentrated its efforts on making rum. The Westerhall Estate tour includes an explanation of the ruins and sugar-processing machinery on the grounds, along with a small museum comprising the eclectic collection of the late Grenadian journalist Dr. Alistair Hughes (1919–2005). Particularly interesting items on display in the museum include old rum bottles and labels, Carib artifacts, a number of vintage sewing machines, a World War I Maxim machine gun, and a 1915 Willys Overland automobile.

✉ *Westerhall, St. David* ☎ *473/443–5477* ⊕ *www.westerhallrums.com*
🎫 *$4* ⊘ *Mon., Wed., and Fri. 9–3.*

CARRIACOU

12

Carriacou, the land of many reefs, is a hilly island with neither lakes nor rivers, so its drinking water comes from rainwater caught in cisterns and purified with bleach. It gets quite arid during the dry season (January through May). Nevertheless, pigeon peas, corn, and fruit are grown here, and the climate seems to suit the mahogany trees used for furniture making and the white cedar that's critical to the island's famed boatbuilding industry.

Hillsborough is Carriacou's main town. Just offshore, Sandy Island is one of the nicest beaches around (although recent storms and the gradually rising sea have taken their toll on this tiny spit of land). Almost anyone with a boat can give you a ride out to Sandy Island for a small fee (about $10 round-trip), and you can leave your cares on the dock. Rolling hills cut a wide swath through the middle of Carriacou, from Gun Point in the north to Tyrrel Bay in the south.

Despite its tiny size, Carriacou has several distinct cultures. Hillsborough is decidedly English; the southern region, around L'Esterre, reflects French roots; and the northern town of Windward has Scottish ties. African culture, though, is the overarching influence.

WHAT TO SEE

Belair. For a great bird's-eye view of Hillsborough and Carriacou's entire west coast, drive to Belair, 700 feet above sea level, in the north-central part of the island. On the way, you'll pass by the photogenic ruins of an old sugar mill and the Princess Royal Hospital. ✉ *Belair, Carriacou.*

Carriacou Museum. Housed in a building that once held a cotton gin, and just one block from the waterfront, the museum has exhibitions of Amerindian, European, and African artifacts, a collection of watercolors by native folk artist Canute Caliste, and a small gift shop with local items. ✉ *Paterson St., Hillsborough, Carriacou* ☎ *473/443–8288* 🎫 *$2* ⊘ *Weekdays 9:30–4, Sat. 10–4.*

Tyrrel Bay. Tyrrel Bay is a large protected harbor in southwest Carriacou. The bay is almost always full of sailboats, powerboats, and working boats—coming, going, or bobbing at their moorings. A few shops and snack bars face the waterfront. ✉ *Tyrrel Bay, Carriacou.*

☾ **Windward.** The small town of Windward, on the northeast coast, is a boatbuilding community. At certain times of year, primarily during school vacations, you may encounter a work in progress along the roadside, where Grenada's Ministry of Culture has set up a training ground for interested youngsters to learn skills from seasoned boatbuilders. Originally constructed for interisland commerce, the boats are now built primarily for fishing and pleasure sailing. ✉ *Windward, Carriacou.*

The lookout from Belair, with Hillsborough and Carriacou's west coast below

PETITE MARTINIQUE

Petite Martinique. Petite Martinique, 10 minutes north of Carriacou by boat, is tiny and residential, with a guesthouse or two but no tourist facilities or attractions—just peace and quiet. Meander along the beachfront and watch the boatbuilders at work. If by chance there's a boat launching, sailboat race, wedding, holiday, or cultural festival taking place while you're there, you're in for a treat. The music is infectious, the food bountiful, and the spirit lively. ⊠ *Petite Martinique.*

WHERE TO EAT

Grenada's crops include many kinds of citrus, mangoes, papaya (called paw paw here), callaloo (similar to spinach), dasheen (taro, a root vegetable), christophenes (a gourd also known as mirliton or chayote), yams (white, green, yellow, and orange), and breadfruit. And all restaurants prepare dishes with local produce and season them with the many spices grown here. Be sure to try the local flavors of ice cream: soursop, guava, rum raisin, coconut (the best), or nutmeg.

Soups—especially pumpkin and callaloo—are divine and often start a meal. Pepper pot is a savory stew of pork, oxtail, vegetables, and spices. *Oildown,* the national dish, is salted meat, breadfruit, onions, carrots, celery, dasheen, and dumplings all boiled in coconut milk until the liquid is absorbed and the savory mixture becomes "oily." A roti—curried chicken, beef, or vegetables wrapped in pastry and baked—is similar to a turnover and more popular in Grenada than a sandwich.

Fresh seafood of all kinds, including lobster, is plentiful. Conch, known here as *lambi*, often appears curried or in a stew. Crab back, though, is not seafood—it's land crab. Most Grenadian restaurants serve seafood and at least some local dishes.

Rum punches are ubiquitous and always topped with grated nutmeg. Clarke's Court and Westerhall are local rums. Carib, the local beer, is refreshing, light, and quite good. If you prefer a nonalcoholic drink, opt for fruit punch—a delicious mixture of freshly blended tropical fruit.

What to Wear: Dining in Grenada is casual. At dinner, collared shirts and long pants are appropriate for men (even the fanciest restaurants don't require jacket and tie), and sundresses or dress pants are fine for women. Beachwear and other revealing attire should be reserved for the beach.

GRENADA

$$
SEAFOOD
Fodor'sChoice
★

×**Aquarium Restaurant.** As the name suggests, fresh seafood is the specialty here. Many guests spend the day at the adjacent Magazine Beach (you can rent kayaks or snorkeling gear) and then break for a cool drink or satisfying lunch—a salad, sandwich or burger, fresh fish, or pasta—served on the waterfront deck. Lush plants and palms surround the dining room, and a waterfall adds romance in the evening. The dinner menu always includes fresh fish, grilled lobster, and specialties such as callaloo cannelloni. On Sunday there's a beach barbecue. Also, the Aquarium is convenient to the airport, so if you plan carefully, it's perfect for a preflight meal. ⑤ *Average main: $12* ✉ *LaSource Rd., Point Salines, St. George* ☎ *473/444–1410* ⊕ *www.aquarium-grenada.com* ⚎ *Reservations essential* ☉ *Closed Mon.*

$$
ECLECTIC
★

×**Beach House.** At this colorful restaurant, reachable via a short walk down the beach from Laluna resort or from the airport road, the gleaming white sand and sea views are the perfect backdrop for a salad or pasta lunch on the deck or a snack at the bar. At dinner, excellent entrées—rack of lamb, blackened fish, or prime rib—and superb wines give new meaning to the term beach party. A kids' menu is available, too. ⑤ *Average main: $20* ✉ *Airport Rd., on the beach, Point Salines, St. George* ☎ *473/444–4455* ⚎ *Reservations essential* ☉ *Closed Sun. No lunch June–July.*

$$
CARIBBEAN
☾
★

×**Belmont Estate.** Luncheon is served! If you're visiting the northern reaches of Grenada, plan to stop at Belmont Estate, a 400-year-old working nutmeg and cocoa plantation. Settle into the breezy open-air dining room, which overlooks enormous trays of nutmeg, cocoa, and mace drying in the sunshine. A waiter will offer some refreshing local juice and a choice of callaloo or pumpkin soup. Then head to the buffet and help yourself to salad, rice, stewed chicken, beef curry, stewed fish, and vegetables. Dessert may be homemade ice cream, ginger cake, or another delicious confection. Afterward, feel free to take a tour of the museum, cocoa fermentary, sugarcane garden, and old cemetery. Farm animals (and a couple of monkeys) roam the property, and there's often folk music and dancing on the lawn. ⑤ *Average main: $18* ✉ *Belmont, St. Patrick* ☎ *473/442–9524* ⊕ *www.belmontestate. net* ☉ *Closed Sat. No dinner.*

$$ ✕ **Coconut Beach Restaurant.** Take local seafood, add butter, wine, and
CARIBBEAN   Grenadian spices, and you have excellent French-creole cuisine.
Throw in a beautiful location at the northern end of Grand Anse
Beach, and this West Indian cottage becomes a perfect alfresco spot
for either lunch or dinner by moonlight. Lobster is a specialty, whether
it's lobster thermidor or perhaps wrapped in a crepe, dipped in gar-
lic butter, or added to pasta. Homemade coconut pie is a winner
for dessert. Dine "wet or fine," at a table on the beach or inside.
On Wednesday and Sunday nights in season, dinner is a beach bar-
becue with live music. $ *Average main: $20* ⊠ *Grand Anse Main
Rd., on the beach, Grand Anse, St. George* ☎ *473/444–4644* ⊕ *www.
coconutbeachgrenada.com* ⊙ *Closed Tues.*

$$$$ ✕ **La Belle Creole.** The marriage of contemporary and West Indian cui-
CARIBBEAN   sines and a splendid view of distant St. George's are the delights of this
★   romantic hillside restaurant at the Blue Horizons Garden Resort. The
always-changing five-course prix fixe and à la carte menus are based on
original recipes from the owner's mother, a pioneer in incorporating local
products into "foreign" dishes. Try, for instance, Grenadian caviar (roe of
the white sea urchin), lobster-egg flan, callaloo quiche, creole fish, baked
chicken roulade, or ginger pork chops—with homemade mango cheese-
cake for dessert. The inspired cuisine, romantic setting, and gracious
service are impressive. $ *Average main: $35* ⊠ *Blue Horizons Garden
Resort, Morne Rouge Rd., Grand Anse, St. George* ☎ *473/444–4316*
⊕ *www.grenadabluehorizons.com* ⌷ *Reservations essential.*

$$ ✕ **La Boulangerie.** This combination French bakery and Italian pizzeria,
CAFÉ   convenient to the hotels at Grand Anse, is a great place for an inexpen-
☺   sive breakfast or light meal—to eat in, take out, or have delivered. You'll
find freshly baked croissants and Danish pastry, focaccia and baguette
sandwiches, homemade pizza and pasta, fresh-squeezed juice or house
wine, coffee and espresso, and homemade gelato. $ *Average main: $14*
⊠ *Le Marquis Complex, Grand Anse, St. George* ☎ *473/444–1131.*

$$ ✕ **La Sagesse Nature Centre.** The perfect spot to soothe a frazzled soul,
SEAFOOD   La Sagesse's open-air seafood restaurant is on a secluded cove in a
nature preserve about 30 minutes from Grand Anse. Combine your
lunch or dinner with a nature walk or a day at the beach. Linger over
sandwiches, salads, or lobster for lunch. Lambi (conch), smoked marlin,
tuna steak, and a daily vegetarian entrée may be joined on the dinner
menu by specials such as chicken française. Transportation is available.
$ *Average main: $15* ⊠ *La Sagesse, St. David* ☎ *473/444–6458* ⊕ *www.
lasagesse.com* ⌷ *Reservations essential.*

$$ ✕ **The Nutmeg.** West Indian specialties, fresh seafood, great hamburgers,
CARIBBEAN   and a waterfront view make The Nutmeg a favorite with locals and
visitors alike. It's upstairs on the Carenage (above the Sea Change bookstore), with large, open windows from which you can view the harbor
activity as you eat. Try the callaloo soup, curried lambi, fresh seafood,
or a steak—or just stop by for a roti and a rum punch. $ *Average main:
$18* ⊠ *The Carenage, St. George's, St. George* ☎ *473/435–9525.*

$$ ✕ **Oasis at Jenny's Place.** Steps from the sand at the north end of Grand
SEAFOOD   Anse Beach, the open-air restaurant at this bed–and–breakfast special-
★   izes in pan-seared catch of the day—perhaps served with a tamarind

sauce—and other enticing dishes created by celebrated chef Roxanne Russell (of Bogles Round House in Carriacou). Sunday lunch features a lobster special. For a light waterside lunch anytime, try the fresh Greek salad, a slice of nutmeg cheesecake, and a glass of wine. ⑤ *Average main: $22* ✉ *Jenny's Place, Grand Anse Main Rd., Grand Anse, St. George* ☎ *473/439–5186* ⊕ *www.jennysplacegrenada.com* ⚓ *Reservations essential.*

$$$ ╳ **The Red Crab.** West Indian basics such as curried lambi and garlic
SEAFOOD shrimp—and old-fashioned international favorites such as lobster Newburg, Coquilles St. Jacques, and Wiener schnitzel—keep the regulars coming back to this family-run restaurant that has served lunch and dinner to locals and expats alike for decades. Seafood, particularly lobster, and steak (imported from the United States) are staples of the menu; hot garlic bread comes with every order. Eat inside or outside on the front patio, and enjoy live music Monday and Friday evenings in season. ⑤ *Average main: $22* ✉ *L'Anse aux Épines Rd., near Calabash Hotel, L'Anse aux Épines, St. George* ☎ *473/444–4424* ⚓ *Reservations essential* ⊘ *Closed Sun.*

$$$ ╳ **Rhodes' Restaurant.** This open-air hotel restaurant, named for the
ECLECTIC acclaimed British chef Gary Rhodes, is surrounded by palms, flower-
★ ing plants, and twinkling lights. Past menus have featured citrus-cured salmon with a lime, fennel, and paw paw (papaya) salad as a starter, followed by grilled swordfish steak with Caribbean paella risotto or fillet of beef on a roast potato cake with whole-grain-mustard cream. The passion-fruit panna cotta, light as a soufflé, is nothing short of divine. ⑤ *Average main: $30* ✉ *Calabash Hotel, L'Anse aux Épines, St. George* ☎ *473/444–4334* ⊕ *www.calabashhotel.com* ⚓ *Reservations essential* ⊘ *No lunch.*

$ ╳ **Tropicana.** The chef–owner here hails from Trinidad and specializes in
CARIBBEAN both Chinese and West Indian cuisine. Local businesspeople seem to be the best customers for the extensive menu of Chinese food, the tantalizing aroma of barbecued chicken notwithstanding. Eat in or take out—it's open from 7:30 am to midnight. Tropicana is at the Lagoon Road traffic circle, overlooking the marina. ⑤ *Average main: $12* ✉ *Lagoon Rd., St. George's* ☎ *473/440–1586* ⊕ *www.tropicanainn.com.*

$$$ ╳ **Västra Banken at Le Phare Bleu.** Fine dining is served aboard this historic
ECLECTIC lightship, brought to Grenada in 2006 and the centerpiece of Le Phare
★ Bleu Marina Hotel. The chef uses local ingredients to create contemporary cuisine served in a setting that's both nautical and romantic. Try the seafood ravioli or the callaloo and crab soufflé appetizer, followed by roasted rack of lamb or seared swordfish. The warm home-baked breads are wonderful, but the chocolate-plate dessert takes the cake. ⑤ *Average main: $28* ✉ *Le Phare Bleu Marina Hotel, Petite Calivigny Bay, Calvigny, St. George* ☎ *473/443–3443* ⊕ *www.lepharebleu.com* ⚓ *Reservations essential* ⊘ *No lunch. Closed Sun.*

$$$ ╳ **Water's Edge.** At this resort restaurant overlooking pristine St. David's
ECLECTIC Harbour, the dining experience is as exquisite as the view is mesmerizing. (The napkins are even folded into the shape of binoculars.) Tables are set on the covered verandah or on the garden patio. Chef Marc Banthrope's extensive menu includes fish and lobster from the surrounding

waters, fresh produce from nearby farms and the resort's own gardens, and imported meats—all delicately flavored with local herbs and spices. $ *Average main: $25* ⊠ *Bel Air Plantation, Corinth, St. David* ☎ *473/443–2822* ⚏ *Reservations essential.*

CARRIACOU

$$$
CARIBBEAN
Fodor'sChoice
★

✕ **Bogles Round House.** Surrounded by gardens and a handful of cottages for rent, this small round structure was built with a concrete-filled tree trunk as its central support and a long bench that was once the jawbone of a whale. The food is less peculiar: chef Roxanne Russell is celebrated for her elegant style of Caribbean cuisine. Her three-course, prix-fixe menu, which changes according to market availability, may include such starters as fish cakes and cream of callaloo soup and such entrées as rack of lamb au jus and grilled lobster with garlic butter—there's always a vegetarian dish, too. Pasta and pizza are available for kids upon request. Desserts, including the ice cream, are all homemade. $ *Average main: $30* ⊠ *Sparrow Bay, Bogles, Carriacou* ☎ *473/443–7841* ⊕ *www. boglesroundhouse.com* ⚏ *Reservations essential* ⊘ *Closed Wed.*

$
CARIBBEAN

✕ **Laurena II.** As you approach this popular restaurant and bar, just a few giant steps from the ferry wharf, the unmistakable scent of authentic Jamaican jerk chicken and pork greets you. That's the specialty (and personal favorite) of chef Purgeon Reece, who hails from Negril, although his menu also includes other local and regional dishes such as curried goat, baked chicken, or grilled fish with rice and peas. Daily specials are posted on a street-side blackboard. This "jerk center" is definitely a casual spot, the best bet for a delicious lunch, and a good place to catch the local vibe. $ *Average main: $11* ⊠ *Main St., Hillsborough, Carriacou* ☎ *473/443–8333* ⊘ *Closed Mon.*

$$$$
ECLECTIC

✕ **Lyme and Dine.** Claudia and Werner "Max" Nagel, who also operate Carriacou Silver Diving, serve breakfast and a three-course dinner at their cottage on Main Street in a lovely, informal garden setting. The prix-fixe menu changes daily, depending on what's fresh at the market, and runs the gamut from grilled or smoked fish or lambi fritters to roast pork, schnitzels, or even Italian cuisine—all accompanied by an excellent selection of wines. Call ahead to find out what's being served that day. $ *Average main: $40* ⊠ *Main St., Hillsborough, Carriacou* ☎ *473/444– 7979* ⊕ *www.lymeanddine.com* ⚏ *Reservations essential* ⊘ *No lunch.*

$
CARIBBEAN

✕ **Sandisland Café.** An unassuming local restaurant, the "dining room" is simply the tiny back porch of a Main Street building, with a couple of picnic tables overlooking Hillsborough Bay. Just steps north of the ferry landing, you can sample local food for lunch—try a roti or have a lambi, fish, or chicken lunch that includes rice and peas, salad, plantains, and other local vegetables beautifully arranged on the plate. Wash it down with a soda, beer, or fresh-squeezed local juice. Early risers enjoy the saltfish breakfast, but there's no dinner served. It's closed after 3 pm. $ *Average main: $8* ⊠ *Main St., Hillsborough, Carriacou* ☎ *473/443–6189* ▭ *No credit cards* ⊘ *No dinner.*

WHERE TO STAY

Hotels and resorts in Grenada tend to be small and intimate, with friendly management and attentive staff. All guest rooms are equipped with air-conditioning, an in-room TV, and telephone unless indicated otherwise. During the off-season (April 15 to December 15), prices may be discounted up to 40%.

For expanded reviews, facilities, and current deals, visit Fodors.com.

PRIVATE VILLAS AND CONDOS

Grenada was one of the last islands to offer private villas, but many properties are here now. Bacolet Bay Resort & Spa is an extensive villa development under way in St. David, on the (so far) remote southern coast of Grenada. Port Louis is a brand-new marina—the first phase of a $500 million project that, when the village is complete in the next few years, will transform the lagoon and St. George's Harbour areas in the capital city. In all these developments, individually owned villas will be made available to non-owner guests through management companies.

Villas and private homes are available for rent for a week or longer. The minimum staff includes a maid and a laundress, but a cook, house-keeper, gardener, and others can be arranged.

In Grenada, many rental properties are in and around L'Anse aux Épines, a beautiful residential peninsula that juts into the sea. In-season rates range from $1,000 a week for a small, two-bedroom home with no pool or air-conditioning to $8,000 a week for a five-bedroom house full of amenities, including a pool and beach access. In Carriacou, in-season rates range from $80 a day for a small cottage or in-town apartment suitable for two people to $350 a day for a two-bedroom villa with panoramic views and a swimming pool.

RENTAL CONTACTS

Altman Real Estate (Grenada). ⊠ *Le Marquis Shopping Complex, Grand Anse, St. George* ☏ *473/435–2081* ⊕ *www.realestategrenada.com.*

Down Island Villa Rentals. ⊠ *Craigston, Carriacou* ☏ *473/443–8182* ⊕ *www.islandvillas.com.*

Spice Isle Villas. ⊠ *Grand Anse, St. George* ☏ *473/439–2486* ⊕ *www. spiceislevillas.com.*

BEST BETS FOR LODGING

BEST FOR ROMANCE
La Source, Laluna, Petite Anse Hotel, Spice Island Beach Resort

BEST BEACHFRONT
Coyaba Beach Resort, Grenada Grand Beach Resort, Kalinago, La Sagesse Nature Centre, Laluna, Spice Island Beach Resort

12

GRENADA

$ **Allamanda Beach Resort.** Right on Grand Anse Beach, this small
HOTEL   hotel has some rooms with whirlpool baths; many rooms also have
☾   connecting doors, making it a good choice for families. **Pros:** location, location, location; great value. **Cons:** rooms are modest; don't

expect luxury at this price. **TripAdvisor:** "great location," "a gem in Georgetown," "friendly staff." ⑤ *Rooms from: $125* ✉ *Grand Anse, St. George* ☎ *473/444–0095* ⊕ *www.allamandaresort.com* ➘ *50 rooms* †⊖†*Multiple meal plans.*

$$ **Bel Air Plantation.** On an 18-acre peninsula on Grenada's southeastern
RESORT   coast, Bel Air's colorful gingerbread cottages dot a verdant hillside on
★   St. David's Harbour. **Pros:** beautifully decorated cottages; private; great pool; excellent restaurant. **Cons:** be prepared to walk up and down the hillside; far from town—far from anything, in fact. **TripAdvisor:** "peaceful and comfortable retreat," "very relaxing and welcoming," "stunning." ⑤ *Rooms from: $250* ✉ *St. David's Point, Corinth, St. David* ☎ *473/444–6305* ⊕ *www.belairplantation.com* ➘ *11 cottages* †⊖†*No meals.*

$ **Blue Horizons Garden Resort.** A short walk of 300 yards from Grand
RESORT   Anse Beach, "Blue" is especially popular among divers, nature lovers,
☺   and family vacationers. **Pros:** big rooms; excellent value; good dive
★   and hiking packages. **Cons:** not directly on the beach. **TripAdvisor:** "great location," "very pleasant," "tranquil and calm." ⑤ *Rooms from: $210* ✉ *Morne Rouge Rd., Grand Anse, St. George* ☎ *473/444–4316, 473/444–4592* ⊕ *www.grenadabluehorizons.com* ➘ *26 suites, 6 studios* †⊖†*Multiple meal plans.*

$$$$ **Calabash Hotel.** The elegant suites here are in 10 two-story cottages
RESORT   distributed in a horseshoe around 8 acres of lawn and gardens that hug
★   the beach on Prickly Bay (L'Anse aux Épines). **Pros:** excellent service; love those treats; breakfast on the verandah. **Cons:** pricey; taxi or rental car required to get around. **TripAdvisor:** "very comfortable," "perfect," "pure heaven." ⑤ *Rooms from: $710* ✉ *L'Anse aux Épines Rd., L'Anse aux Épines, St. George* ☎ *473/444–4334* ⊕ *www.calabashhotel.com* ➘ *30 suites* ⊙ *Closed Aug. 15–Oct. 15* †⊖†*Multiple meal plans.*

$$ **Coyaba Beach Resort.** Coyaba, which means "heaven" in the Arawak
RESORT   language, is one of a handful of hotels directly on beautiful Grand Anse Beach. **Pros:** excellent beachfront location; spacious grounds; swim-up pool bar. **Cons:** rooms are attractive but not extraordinary. **TripAdvisor:** "beautiful setting," "great hospitality," "wonderful hotel." ⑤ *Rooms from: $360* ✉ *Grand Anse, St. George 473/444–4129* ⊕ *www.coyaba. com* ➘ *80 rooms* †⊖†*Multiple meal plans.*

$ **Flamboyant Hotel & Villas.** The rooms at this venerable, Grenadian-
HOTEL   owned hotel, which is built on a hillside, have private verandas with
☺   panoramic views of Grand Anse Bay. **Pros:** great views; nightlife at the Owl bar. **Cons:** rooms are decidedly unflamboyant; lots of stairs. **TripAdvisor:** "fabulous views," "wonderful relaxing holiday," "agreeable." ⑤ *Rooms from: $250* ✉ *Morne Rouge Rd., Grand Anse, St. George 473/444–4247* ⊕ *www.flamboyant.com* ➘ *38 rooms, 27 suites, 2 cottages* †⊖†*Multiple meal plans.*

$ **Gem Holiday Beach Resort.** Owner Miriam Bedeau and her family oper-
HOTEL   ate this no-frills hotel on pretty Morne Rouge Beach. **Pros:** inexpensive; friendly, family-run hotel on a beautiful beach; excellent restaurant; popular bar, nightclub on-site. **Cons:** air-conditioning only in bedrooms. **TripAdvisor:** "beautiful beach," "comfortable place to stay," "very welcoming." ⑤ *Rooms from: $126* ✉ *Morne Rouge Rd., Morne Rouge,*

St. George ☎ 473/444–2288 ⊕ *www.gembeachresort.com* ⇔ *15 1-bed-room apartments, 5 2-bedroom apartments* ⋈ *No meals.*

$ 🏨 **Grenada Grand Beach Resort.** On 20 landscaped acres along a broad
RESORT   stretch of beautiful Grand Anse Beach, this resort offers comfortable
☉   rooms and extensive amenities. **Pros:** huge hotel full of amenities; fabulous pools; beautiful beachfront location. **Cons:** rooms are comfortable but not extraordinary; can be crowded due to meetings held here.
TripAdvisor: "so comfortable," "nice pool and location," "beautiful
facility." ⑤ *Rooms from: $193* ⋈ *Grand Anse, St. George* ☎ *473/444–
4371* ⊕ *www.grenadagrand.com* ⇔ *238 rooms, 2 suites* ⋈ *Breakfast.*

$ 🏨 **Grenadian by Rex Resorts.** This massive, Palladian-style beachfront
RESORT   resort on Tamarind Bay is particularly popular with Europeans. **Pros:**
☉   large play area for kids; excellent beach; minutes from the airport. **Cons:**
rooms are unremarkable; quite a hike from room to beach to lobby;
meals are comparatively expensive. **TripAdvisor:** "nice people," "relaxing time," "great staff." ⑤ *Rooms from: $248* ⋈ *Tamarind Bay, Point
Salines, St. George* ☎ *473/444–3333* ⊕ *www.rexresorts.com* ⇔ *202
rooms, 10 suites* ⋈ *Multiple meal plans.*

$ 🏨 **Kalinago Beach Resort.** This contemporary beachfront hotel is near
HOTEL   Grand Anse and adjacent to Gem Holiday Resort, which has the same
☉   owner. **Pros:** modern rooms; great beach; personalized attention. **Cons:**
walk to Grand Anse requires negotiating a steep hill; a rental car is a
good idea. **TripAdvisor:** "lovely beach and great service," "quiet gem,"
"perfect all the way." ⑤ *Rooms from: $210* ⋈ *Morne Rouge Rd., Morne
Rouge, St. George* ☎ *473/444–5254* ⊕ *www.kalinagobeachresort.com*
⇔ *29 rooms* ⋈ *Multiple meal plans.*

$$$$ 🏨 **Laluna.** You may think you've landed on an island in the South Pacific
RESORT   when you reach this upscale enclave, which is hidden away on a pristine
Fodor'sChoice   beach near Grenada's Quarantine Point. **Pros:** nifty cottages; great restau-
★   rant; fabulous beach; attentive staff. **Cons:** the long, bumpy, dirt access
road; very expensive; total seclusion could seem confining. **TripAdvisor:**
"total heaven," "tranquility," "unbelievably romantic." ⑤ *Rooms from:
$495* ⋈ *Morne Rouge, St. George* ☎ *473/439–0001, 866/452–5862*
⊕ *www.laluna.com* ⇔ *16 cottages* ⋈ *Multiple meal plans.*

$ 🏨 **La Sagesse.** Secluded on La Sagesse Bay—10 miles (16 km) east of the
B&B/INN   airport (about a 30-minute drive)—the grounds here include a country
inn, restaurant, and beach bar, along with a salt-pond bird sanctu-
ary, thick mangroves, nature trails, and ½ mile (¾ km) of palm tree–
shaded beach. **Pros:** charming; beautiful beach; excellent restaurant.
Cons: remote; you'll need a car to get anywhere else; no Internet access.
TripAdvisor: "treated like friends," "barefoot paradise," "spectacu-
lar." ⑤ *Rooms from: $185* ⋈ *La Sagesse Nature Center, La Sagesse,
St. David* ☎ *473/444–6458* ⊕ *www.lasagesse.com* ⇔ *9 rooms, 3 suites*
⋈ *No meals.*

$$$$ 🏨 **La Source.** Just about everything you could possibly want on an
ALL-INCLUSIVE   adults-only luxury vacation is included in the rates at this sparkling
★   property. **Pros:** loads of activities and daily spa treatments included
in the rates; congenial adult atmosphere. **Cons:** newshounds must get
their TV fix in the lounge; not a good choice for anyone with walking
difficulties; extremely expensive. **TripAdvisor:** "great fun and quality,"

"quite simply paradise," "relaxing and memorable." $ *Rooms from: $800 ⊠ Pink Gin Beach, Point Salines, St. George* ☎ *473/444–2556* ⊕ *www.theamazingholiday.com* ⟋ *91 rooms, 9 suites* ⅼ⊙ⅼ *All-inclusive.*

$$
RENTAL
☾
☷ **Le Phare Bleu Marina & Holiday Resort.** The spacious, self-catering accommodations at the family-friendly Le Phare Bleu (The Blue Light-house) are perfectly situated for those who arrive by boat or who like to be around boats. **Pros:** boater's delight; casual seaside atmosphere; family-friendly; minimart on-site. **Cons:** somewhat isolated; rental car advised. **TripAdvisor:** "very beautiful and tasteful," "a relaxing hide-away," "piece of paradise." $ *Rooms from: $285 ⊠ Petite Calivigny Bay, Calvigny, St. George* ☎ *473/443–3443* ⊕ *www.lepharebleu.com* ⟋ *9 cottages, 4 apartments, 1 villa* ⅼ⊙ⅼ *Breakfast.*

$$$$
RENTAL
Fodor'sChoice
★
☷ **Maca Bana Villas.** Clustered on a 2-acre hillside overlooking mile-long Magazine Beach, each of Maca Bana's seven villas offers a breathtaking view—of the white sand below, out to sea, up the coastline to pretty St. George's Harbour, and beyond to the cloud-capped mountains. **Pros:** roomy villas with huge kitchens; enormous decks with amazing views; excellent restaurant; fabulous beach. **Cons:** steep hill down to the restaurant and beach; expensive; tiny pool. **TripAdvisor:** "luxuri-ous and gorgeous," "beautiful villas," "great views." $ *Rooms from: $515 ⊠ Magazine Beach, on the hill above The Aquarium restaurant, Point Salines, St. George* ☎ *473/439–5355* ⊕ *www.macabana.com* ⟋ *2 1-bedroom villas, 5 2-bedroom villas* ⅼ⊙ⅼ *No meals.*

$$$$
RESORT
☾
☷ **Mount Cinnamon.** Beautifully situated on a hillside that rises above Grand Anse Beach, Mount Cinnamon comprises spacious, self-con-tained villas with one, two, or three bedrooms, full kitchens, Bose enter-tainment systems, cable TV, and such convenient extras as washers and dryers. **Pros:** excellent location on Grand Anse Beach; good choice for families. **Cons:** villas are on a steep hill, but golf-cart transport to res-taurant or beach is available. **TripAdvisor:** "wonderful place to relax," "great views," "a beachside dream." $ *Rooms from: $630 ⊠ Morne Rouge Rd., Grand Anse, St. George* ☎ *473/439–0000, 866/720–2616* ⊕ *www.mountcinnamongrenadahotel.com* ⟋ *21 units* ⅼ⊙ⅼ *Breakfast.*

$
RENTAL
☾
☷ **Petit Bacaye Cottage Hotel.** Hidden along the coast in St. David's, about a half-hour drive east of Grand Anse and the hustle and bustle of St. George's, Petit Bacaye is a tiny oasis of serenity. **Pros:** idyllically pri-vate, quiet spot; airport shuttle service; perfect for a wedding or hon-eymoon. **Cons:** remote (you'll need a car); access driveway is steep and scary for drivers; no Internet access. **TripAdvisor:** "stunning land-scaped gardens," "glorious retreat," "perfect accommodation for seclu-sion." $ *Rooms from: $132 ⊠ Westerhall* ☎ *473/443–2902* ⊕ *www. petitbacaye.com* ⟋ *5 cottages* ☉ *Closed Aug. and Sept.* ⅼ⊙ⅼ *No meals* ⟋ *7-day min stay.*

$$
HOTEL
★
☷ **Petite Anse Hotel.** Philip and Annie Clift built their delightful beach-front hotel at the northern tip of Grenada, surrounded by beautiful gardens on one side and an unobstructed view of the southern Grena-dines on the other. **Pros:** romantic setting; secluded palm-studded beach; fabulous views of the Grenadines. **Cons:** remote; rental car advised. **TripAdvisor:** "paradise with a cooked breakfast," "great views and location," "off the beaten path." $ *Rooms from: $270 ⊠ Sauteurs, St.*

Patrick ☎ 473/442–5252 ⊕ *www.petiteanse.com* ☞ *2 rooms, 9 cottages* ⦿⦿ *Multiple meal plans.*

$$$$
RESORT
☺
Fodor'sChoice
★

☷ **Spice Island Beach Resort.** Presenting the most luxurious resort experience in Grenada: exquisite rooms in dozens of gleaming white buildings that extend along 1,600 feet of Grand Anse Beach; the service is personalized and always impeccable. **Pros:** elegant and luxurious, yet family-friendly and casual; perfect beachfront location; excellent service; no-smoking resort. **Cons:** all this luxury doesn't come cheap; the nightly dinners, included in rates, are elegant but may be limiting during long stays or for families with kids; all this pampering may make it hard to get go home. **TripAdvisor:** "idyllic," "beautiful and stunningly exceptional," "relaxing and top-notch service." ⑤ *Rooms from: $800* ⊠ *Grand Anse, St. George 473/444–4258* ⊕ *www. spiceislandbeachresort.com* ☞ *64 suites* ⦿⦿ *Multiple meal plans.*

$
RESORT
☺

☷ **True Blue Bay Resort & Villas.** The lawns and gardens at this family-run resort, a former indigo plantation, slope down to True Blue Bay. **Pros:** nice accommodations at reasonable prices; complimentary shuttle to Grand Anse Beach. **Cons:** no beach for swimming; rental car recommended. **TripAdvisor:** "great for relaxation," "warm and friendly," "beautiful views and wonderful people." ⑤ *Rooms from: $242* ⊠ *Old Mill Ave., True Blue Bay, True Blue, St. George* ☎ *473/443–8783, 866/325–8322* ⊕ *www.truebluebay.com* ☞ *33 rooms, 5 villa suites* ⦿⦿ *Multiple meal plans.*

$
B&B/INN

☷ **Twelve Degrees North.** Named for its latitude, this small, secluded inn on 3 acres of hillside has one- and two-bedroom self-contained suites, all of which face the sea—and face west, providing beautiful sunset views from the balcony or patio. **Pros:** private getaway; personalized service; excellent snorkeling off the dock. **Cons:** beach not suitable for swimming because of reef; showers only; no Internet of any kind. **TripAdvisor:** "paradise in the tropics," "very peaceful and clean," "sea, sun, and calm." ⑤ *Rooms from: $225* ⊠ *L'Anse aux Épines, St. George* ☎ *473/444–4580* ⊕ *www.twelvedegreesnorth.com* ☞ *8 suites* ⦿⦿ *No meals.*

CARRIACOU

$
HOTEL

☷ **Ade's Dream Guest House.** By the jetty in Hillsborough, Ade's (pronounced add-ees) is a convenient—and popular—place to rest your weary head after a day snorkeling at Sandy Island or scuba diving at some of Grenada's best dive spots. **Pros:** steps from the jetty; convenient for an overnight on Carriacou; very affordable. **Cons:** basic accommodations; noise may be an issue in street-facing rooms. **TripAdvisor:** "nice place on a beautiful island," "no frills but good," "everything you need." ⑤ *Rooms from: $32* ⊠ *Main St., Hillsborough, Carriacou* ☎ *473/443–7317* ⊕ *www.adesdream.com* ☞ *23 rooms* ⦿⦿ *No meals.*

$
RESORT
☺

☷ **Bayaleau Point Cottages.** Four colorful gingerbread cottages were lovingly built, one by one, by owner Dave Goldhill, an expat American who has lived on Carriacou for more than 30 years; he opened Bayaleau (bee-*ah*-loo) in 1992. **Pros:** ideal for small groups or families (up to 16 people); swinging in your hammock is an "active" sport; beautiful Grenadines view. **Cons:** way off the beaten path; rental car advised. **TripAdvisor:** "simply beautiful," "great cottages," "charming and informal."

$ *Rooms from: $90* ⊠ *Bayaleau, Windward, Carriacou* 🕿 *473/443–7984* ⊕ *www.carriacoucottages.com* 📞 *4 cottages* ¶⊙¶ *No meals.*

$
RESORT
★

Bogles Round House. Pick your flavor: Lime, Mango, or Plum—Lime cottage is the largest of the three, with room for three or four people; Mango and Plum sleep two comfortably and a third person, if needed. **Pros:** the price; the restaurant; the ambience. **Cons:** no a/c; no communication with the outside world (although that may be a pro for some). **TripAdvisor:** "peace and quiet," "remote pretty location," "great dining experience." $ *Rooms from: $97* ⊠ *Sparrow Bay, Bogles, Carriacou* 🕿 *473/443–7841* ⊕ *www.boglesroundhouse.com* 📞 *3 cottages* ⊘ *Closed May* ¶⊙¶ *Breakfast.*

$
HOTEL

Carriacou Grand View Hotel. The view is lovely, particularly at sunset, from this perch high above Hillsborough Harbour. **Pros:** truly a grand view; friendly atmosphere; popular restaurant; late-night piano bar. **Cons:** accommodations are basic; it's a hot walk uphill from the town and beach. **TripAdvisor:** "intimate hotel with a view," "relaxing," "friendly." $ *Rooms from: $65* ⊠ *Beausejour, Carriacou* 🕿🕿 *473/443–6348* ⊕ *www.carriacougrandview.com* 📞 *7 rooms, 7 suites* ¶⊙¶ *No meals.*

$
B&B/INN

Green Roof Inn. You're guaranteed beautiful views of Hillsborough Bay and the offshore cays at this small inn, which makes the perfect location for a scuba-diving, snorkeling, or beachcombing vacation. **Pros:** great water view; homey; close to town. **Cons:** rooms are small; showers only. **TripAdvisor:** "charming," "incredible hospitality and service," "good food." $ *Rooms from: $70* ⊠ *Hillsborough Bay, Hillsborough, Carriacou* 🕿🕿 *473/443–6399* ⊕ *www.greenroofinn.com* 📞 *5 rooms, 1 cottage* ¶⊙¶ *Breakfast.*

$
HOTEL
☾

Hotel Laurena. Large by Carriacou standards, the family-owned, family-operated Hotel Laurena is within walking distance of downtown Hillsborough, the ferry wharf, shops, and some beaches. **Pros:** convenient to town; large rooms; some are wheelchair accessible. **Cons:** not particularly attractive views; no pool; walk to beach. **TripAdvisor:** "great food and service," "most beautiful hotel on the island," "a touch of paradise." $ *Rooms from: $85* ⊠ *Hillsborough, Carriacou* 🕿 *473/443–8759* ⊕ *www.hotellaurena.com* 📞 *20 rooms, 6 apartments* ¶⊙¶ *Breakfast.*

NIGHTLIFE

Grenada's nightlife is centered on the resort hotels and a handful of nightspots. During the winter season some resorts have a steel band or other local entertainment several nights a week.

BARS

Banana's Sports Bar. The students at nearby St. George's University like this casual restaurant and nightspot. There's happy hour every evening from 5 to 7 pm. Latin dance classes begin at 6:30 pm on Tuesday and Thursday nights. On Saturday night there's live entertainment beginning at 8 pm. Sunday and Monday are reserved for sports, with major events shown on big-screen TVs. ⊠ *True Blue Rd., True Blue, St. George* 🕿 *473/444–4662.*

DANCE CLUBS

Fantazia 2001. On weekends you can hear disco, soca, reggae, and international pop music from 9:30 pm until the wee hours at this spot. There's a cover charge that ranges from EC$10 to EC$20, depending on the entertainment. ✉ *Morne Rouge Beach, adjacent to Gem Holiday Beach Resort, Morne Rouge, St. George* ☎ *473/444–2288.*

Karma. Inside this club's 10,000 square feet are a stage and a dozen plasma TV screens. The club features karaoke on Wednesday night, "student night" on Thursday, video DJ entertainment on Friday, and special parties and headliner concerts on certain Saturday nights. The nightclub entrance fee is EC$25; admission for special events runs EC$50 and up. ✉ *The Carenage, St. George's* ☎ *473/409–2582* ⊕ *www.karmavip.com.*

The Owl. This club features crab racing on Monday night, karaoke on Thursday night, calypso on Friday night, and two happy hours (4–7 and 11–midnight) every night. It's open until 3 am every night. ✉ *Flamboyant Hotel, Morne Rouge Rd., Grand Anse, St. George* ☎ *473/444–4247.*

THEME NIGHTS

☾ ★ **Gouyave Fish Friday.** Every Friday from 4 pm until 1 am, the town of Gouyave, about 45 minutes north of St. George's, celebrates its deep-sea fishing heritage. Street vendors sell freshly caught fish, lobster, and other seafood cooked on open fires, as well as your favorite beverages. Local music and cultural performances make it an entertaining family event. ✉ *St. Francis and St. Dominic Sts., Gouyave, St. John* ☎ *473/444–8430, 473/444–9490* ⊕ *www.gogouyave.com.*

SHOPPING

Grenada's best souvenirs or gifts for friends back home are spice baskets filled with cinnamon, nutmeg, mace, bay leaves, cloves, turmeric, and ginger. You can buy them for as little as $5 to $10 in practically every shop, at the open-air produce market at **Market Square** in St. George's, at the vendor stalls along the Esplanade near the port, and at the Vendor's Craft & Spice Market on Grand Anse Beach. Vendors also sell handmade fabric dolls, coral jewelry, seashells, and hats and baskets handwoven from green palm fronds.

Here's some local terminology you should know. If someone asks if you'd like a "sweetie," you're being offered a candy. When you buy spices, you may be offered "saffron" and "vanilla." The "saffron" is really turmeric, a ground yellow root rather than the (much more expensive) fragile pistils of crocus flowers; the "vanilla" is extracted from locally grown tonka beans rather than from actual (also much more expensive) vanilla beans. No one is trying to pull the wool over your eyes; these are common local terms. That said, the U.S. Food and Drug Administration warns that "vanilla" extracts made from tonka beans can have toxic effects and may pose a significant health risk for individuals taking certain medications.

SHOPPING AREAS AND MALLS

In St. George's, on the north side of the harbor, **Young Street** is a main shopping thoroughfare; it rises steeply uphill from the Carenage, and then descends just as steeply to the market area. On Melville Street, near the Cruise Ship Terminal and Market Square, the **Esplanade Mall** has shops that offer duty-free jewelry, electronics, liquor, and gift items, as well as local crafts. On Lagoon Road in Belmont, just south of St. George's Harbor, the **Grenada Craft Center** houses several shops with handmade art and craft items; some items are made in workshops on-site.

In Grand Anse, a short walk from the resorts, the **Excel Plaza** has shops and services to interest locals and tourists alike, including a full-service health club and a three-screen movie theater. **Grand Anse Shopping Centre** has a supermarket and liquor store, a clothing store, a fast-food restaurant, a pharmacy, an art gallery, and several small gift shops. **Le Marquis Complex** has restaurants, shops, an art gallery, and tourist services. **Spiceland Mall** has a modern supermarket with a liquor section, clothing and shoe boutiques for men and women, housewares stores, a wineshop, gift shops, a food court, a bank, and a video-game arcade.

SPECIALTY STORES

DUTY-FREE GOODS

Duty-free shops at the airport sell liquor at impressive discounts of up to 50%, as well as perfumes, crafts, and Grenadian syrups, jams, and hot sauces. You can shop duty-free at some shops in town, but you must show your passport and outbound ticket to benefit from the duty-free prices.

Gittens. The three Gittens shops, spin-offs of a single pharmacy that opened in the 1940s, carry perfume and cosmetics. ⊠ *Halifax St., St. George's, St. George* ☎ *473/440–2165* ⊠ *Grand Anse Main Rd., Grand Anse, St. George* ☎ *473/444–4954* ⊠ *Maurice Bishop International Airport, Point Salines, St. George* ☎ *473/444–2549.*

FOODS

De La Grenade Industries. Nutmeg and guava jams and jellies, nutmeg syrup, nutmeg liqueur (from a 200-year-old family recipe), and a dozen other kinds of delicious jellies, marmalades, and condiments are all available from this famous local manufacturer. You can buy De La Grenade products at the processing plant and in food stores and gift shops throughout Grenada. ⊠ *Morne Délice, St. Paul's, St. George* ☎ *473/440–3241* ⊕ *www.delagrenade.com.*

Grenada Chocolate Company. Employees at this small factory, founded in 1999, use antique machinery to roast cocoa beans from the nearby Belmont Estate and then mix and temper the chocolate. Then the rich, dark chocolate is molded and wrapped by hand into high-quality, organic chocolate bars (cocoa powder is also available). The 82% chocolate bar was awarded the silver medal in 2011 by the London Academy of Chocolate. The candy bars sell in supermarkets and gift shops for about $5 each. ⊠ *Hermitage, St. Patrick* ☎ *473/442–0050* ⊕ *www. grenadachocolate.com.*

★ **Market Square.** This bustling produce market is open mornings; Saturday is the best—and busiest—time to stock up on fresh fruit to enjoy during your stay. It's also a particularly good place to buy island-grown spices, perhaps the best such market in the entire Caribbean. Vendors also sell crafts, leather goods, and decorative objects. ✉ *Foot of Young St., St. George's.*

12

Marketing & National Importing Board. At this local market you can get fresh fruits and vegetables, spices, hot sauces, and local syrups and jams at lower prices than in most gift shops. ✉ *Young St., St. George's, St. George* ☎ *473/440–1791.*

GIFTS

Arawak Islands. The spice-scented soaps, body oils, perfumes, insect repellents, balms, beeswax candles, and incense are all made by hand at this plant, where you can view the manufacturing process; the company's products, including gift baskets, are sold in most gift shops. ✉ *Frequente Industrial Park, Airport Rd., Point Salines, St. George* ☎ *473/444–3577* ⊕ *www.arawak-islands.com.*

Food Fair. The local supermarket chain is a great spot for spices, hot sauce, candy, snacks, and other edible gifts. Prices of locally produced goods are very reasonable; familiar brands imported from the United States may cost twice as much as back home. ✉ *The Carenage, St. George's* ☎ *473/440–2488* ✉ *Grand Anse Shopping Center, Grand Anse Main Rd., Grand Anse, St. George* ☎ *473/444–4573* ✉ *St. George's.*

Imagine. The main draws here are straw work, ceramics, island fashions, and batik fabrics. ✉ *Grand Anse Shopping Centre, Grand Anse Main Rd., Grand Anse, St. George* ☎ *473/444–4028.*

HANDICRAFTS

★ **Art Fabrik.** At Art Fabrik, you'll find batik fabric created by hand by as many as 45 home workers. It's sold either by the yard or as dresses, shirts, shorts, hats, and scarves. An area of the boutique is dedicated to demonstrating the batik process. ✉ *Young St., St. George's, St. George* ☎ *473/440–0568* ⊕ *www.artfabrikgrenada.com.*

Tikal. Regional artwork, jewelry, batik items, and fashions are the specialties at Tikal. ✉ *Young St., St. George's* ☎ *473/440–2310.*

Vendor's Craft & Spice Market at Grand Anse. Managed by the Grenada Board of Tourism, this market has 82 booths for vendors who sell arts, crafts, spices, music tapes, clothing, produce, and refreshments. It's open daily from 7 to 7. ✉ *Grand Anse Beach, Grand Anse, St. George* ☎ *473/444–3780.*

★ **Veronica's Vision.** A former nutmeg receiving station is now a shop for colorful silk-screened lengths of fabric, along with handmade totes, bags, women's dresses, men's shirts and ties, T-shirts, scarves, belts, cushions, and more. The fabrics and other products are all designed and created by artist Jessie-Ann Jessamy—the colors and themes celebrate the isle of spice—and hand-printed in her next-door workshop, on the main road at the turn-off to Concord Falls. ✉ *Main Rd., Concord Jct., Concord, St. John* ☎ *473/437–8154* ⊕ *www.grenadaspicecloth.com.*

SPORTS AND ACTIVITIES

BOATING AND SAILING

★ As the "Gateway to the Grenadines," Grenada attracts boatloads of seasoned sailors to its waters. Large marinas are at Port Louis along the Lagoon in St. George's, at Prickly Bay and True Blue on Grenada's south coast, at Petite Calivigny Bay and St. David's in southeast Grenada, and at Tyrrel Bay in Carriacou. You can charter a yacht, with or without crew, for weeklong sailing vacations through the Grenadines. Scenic day sails along Grenada's coast cost about $145 per person (with a minimum of four passengers), including lunch or snacks and open bar; a charter will cost $400 to $1,000 per day (with a five-day minimum), depending on the boat, for up to six people.

Carib Cats. Departing from Grand Anse Beach, Carib Cats' 60-foot sailing catamaran can be chartered for a full-day sail along the southwest coast, a half-day snorkel cruise to Molinère Bay, or a two-hour sunset cruise along the west coast. ⊠ *Grand Anse Beach, St. George* ☎ *473/444–3222.*

Footloose Yacht Charters. Operating from the Lagoon in St. George's, Footloose Yacht Charters has both a catamaran spacious enough for three couples and a 71-foot ocean ketch available for day trips around Grenada or longer charters to the Grenadines. ⊠ *Lagoon Rd., St. George's, St. George* ☎ *473/405–9531* ⊕ *www.grenadasailing.com.*

Horizon Yacht Charters. Bareboat or crewed charters, as well as day sails or five-day trips to the Grenadines, can be arranged through Horizon. ⊠ *True Blue Bay Marina, True Blue, St. George* ☎ *473/439–1000* ⊕ *www.horizonyachtcharters.com.*

Moorings. The diverse itinerary options from Moorings include one-way charters to the company's bases in either Canouan or St. Lucia. The company, based at Port Louis Marina in St. George's and offers bareboat or crewed charters on its custom-built 35-foot to 51-foot catamarans and monohulls. ⊠ *Port Louis Marina, Lagoon Rd., St. George's* ☎ *800/535–7289* ⊕ *www.moorings.com.*

DIVING AND SNORKELING

You can see hundreds of varieties of fish and some 40 species of coral at more than a dozen sites off Grenada's southwest coast—only 15 to 20 minutes by boat—and another couple of dozen sites around Carriacou's reefs and neighboring islets. Depths vary from 20 to 120 feet, and visibility varies from 30 to 100 feet.

OFF GRENADA

For a spectacular dive, visit the ruins of *Bianca C*, a 600-foot cruise ship that caught fire in 1961, sank to 100 feet, and is now a coral-encrusted habitat for giant turtles, spotted eagle rays, barracuda, and jacks. **Boss Reef** extends 5 miles (8 km) from St. George's Harbour to Point Salines, with a depth ranging from 20 to 90 feet. **Flamingo Bay** has a wall that drops to 90 feet. It teems with fish, sponges, sea horses, sea fans, and

12

coral. **Molinère Reef** slopes from about 20 feet below the surface to a wall that drops to 65 feet. Molinère is also the location of the Underwater Sculpture Park, a rather odd artificial reef consisting of more than 55 life-size figures that were sculpted by artist and scuba instructor Jason Taylor and placed on the sea bottom. An underwater bench gives divers a good view of the art gallery. Its most recent addition is a 2011 replica of Christ of the Deep, the statue that's on the promenade along the Carenage in St. George's. Molinère is a good dive for beginners; advanced divers can continue farther out to view the wreck of the *Buccaneer,* a 42-foot sloop.

OFF CARRIACOU

There's an active underwater volcano known as **Kick-em Jenny**, with plentiful coral and marine life in the vicinity and, usually, visibility up to 100 feet, though you can't dive down the 500 feet required to reach the actual volcano. **Sandy Island,** in Hillsborough Bay, is especially good for night diving and has fish that feed off its extensive reefs 70 feet below. For experienced divers, **Twin Sisters of Isle de Rhonde** is one of the most spectacular dives in the Grenadines, with walls and drop-offs of up to 185 feet and an underwater cave.

Most dive operators will take snorkelers along on dive trips or offer special snorkeling adventures. The best snorkeling in Grenada is at Molinère Point, north of St. George's; in Carriacou, Sandy Island is magnificent and just a few hundred yards offshore. Snorkeling trips cost about $35 per person.

The PADI-certified dive operators offer scuba and snorkeling trips to reefs and wrecks, including night dives and special excursions to the *Bianca C.* They also offer resort courses for beginning divers and certification instruction for more experienced divers. It costs about $60 for a one-tank dive, $105 for a two-tank dive, $65 for trips to the *Bianca C,* $145 to dive Isle de Rhonde, and $65 to $70 for night dives. Discounted 5- and 10-dive packages are usually offered. Resort courses cost about $100, and open-water certification runs from $265 to $460.

GRENADA DIVE OPERATORS

Aquanauts Grenada. Every morning Aquanauts Grenada heads out on two-tank dive trips, accommodating no more than eight divers, to both the Caribbean and Atlantic sides of Grenada. Also available: guided snorkel trips; beach snorkeling; and special activities, courses, and equipment for children. ⊠ *Spice Island Beach Resort, Grand Anse Beach, Grand Anse, St. George* ☎ *473/444–1126, 850/303–0330 in U.S.* ⊕ *www.aquanautsgrenada.com* ⊠ *True Blue Bay Resort, True Blue, St. George* ☎ *473/439–2500* ⊕ *www.aquanautsgrenada.com.*

Dive Grenada. Specializing in diving the *Bianca C* ruins and family snorkeling trips, Dive Grenada heads out twice daily (at 10 am and 2 pm). ⊠ *Flamboyant Hotel, Morne Rouge Rd., Morne Rouge, St. George* ☎ *473/444–1092* ⊕ *www.divegrenada.com.*

EcoDive. This company offers two dive trips daily, both drift and wreck dives, as well as weekly trips to dive Isle de Rhonde. EcoDive also runs Grenada's marine-conservation and education center, which conducts coral-reef monitoring. ⊠ *Coyaba Beach Resort, Grand Anse Beach, Grand Anse, St. George* ☎ *473/444–7777* ⊕ *www.ecodiveandtrek.com.*

ScubaTech Grenada. With two full-time diving instructors, ScubaTech Grenada offers the complete range of PADI programs—from "discover scuba," which allows novices to learn the basics and dive for the length of their vacation, to "dive master," the highest level a diver can achieve. Daily dive trips are also available. ⊠ *Calabash Hotel, Prickly Bay Beach, L'Anse aux Épines, St. George* ☎ *473/439–4346* ⊕ *www. scubatech-grenada.com.*

CARRIACOU DIVE OPERATORS

Arawak Divers. This company has its own jetty at Tyrrel Bay; it takes small groups on daily dive trips and night dives, offers courses in German and English, and provides pickup service from yachts. ⊠ *Tyrrel Bay, Carriacou* ☎ *473/443–6906* ⊕ *www.arawak.de.*

Carriacou Silver Diving. Able to fit up to 12 divers on one of its dive boats and up to six on another, Carriacou Silver Diving operates two guided single-tank dives daily as well as individually scheduled excursions. ⊠ *Main St., Hillsborough, Carriacou* ☎ *473/443–7882* ⊕ *www. scubamax.com.*

Lumbadive. The folks who operate Lumbadive aim to share their enthusiasm for safe, exciting scuba-diving adventures with both new and experienced divers. Lumbadive offers open-water diving courses that range from "discover" to "dive master." ⊠ *Tyrrel Bay, Carriacou* ☎ *473/443–8566* ⊕ *www.lumbadive.com.*

FISHING

Deep-sea fishing around Grenada is excellent, with the list of good catches including marlin, sailfish, yellowfin tuna, and dorado (also known as mahimahi or dolphin—the fish, not the mammal). You can arrange sportfishing trips that accommodate up to five people starting at $475 for a half day and $700 for a full day.

True Blue Sportfishing. British-born Captain Gary Clifford, who has been fishing since the age of six, has run True Blue Sportfishing since 1998. He offers big-game charters on the 31-foot *Yes Aye*. It has an enclosed cabin, a fighting chair, and professional tackle. Refreshments and courtesy transport are included. ⊠ *True Blue Bay Marina, True Blue, St. George* ☎ *473/444–2048* ⊕ *www.yesaye.com.*

GOLF

Grenada Golf & Country Club. Determined golfers might want to try the 9-hole course at the Grenada Golf & Country Club, about halfway between St. George's and Grand Anse. Greens fees are $16 (EC$40) or $24 (EC$60) to play the course twice, and club rental is available; your hotel can make arrangements for you. Popular with local businessmen, this course is convenient to most hotels and is the only public course on the island. The club has changing rooms as well as a bar and restaurant. ⊠ *Golf Course Hill, Belmont, St. George* ☎ *473/444–4128.*

Take an exciting safari-style tour of Grenada on an Adventure Jeep Tour.

GUIDED TOURS

Guided tours offer the sights of St. George's, Grand Étang National Park & Forest Reserve, spice plantations and nutmeg-processing centers, rain-forest hikes and treks to waterfalls, snorkeling trips to local islands, and day trips to Carriacou. A full-day sightseeing tour costs $70 to $75 per person, including lunch; a half-day tour, $45 to $55; a guided hike to Concord or Mt. Qua Qua, $55 to $60 per person. Grenada taxi drivers will conduct island sightseeing tours for $150 per day or $25 to $35 per hour for up to four people. Carriacou minibus drivers will take up to four people on a 2½-hour island tour for $60, and $20 per hour thereafter.

Adventure Jeep Tour. On Adventure Jeep Tour you ride in the back of a Land Rover, safari fashion, along scenic coastal roads, trek in the rain forest, have lunch at a plantation, take a swim, and skirt the capital. The company also combines a jeep tour with river tubing ($80 per person) and offers guided bike tours ($15 an hour). ☒ *St. George's, St. George* ☎ *473/444–5337* ⊕ *www.adventuregrenada.com.*

Caribbean Horizons. Personalized half- or full-day tours of historic and natural island sites, market and garden tours, and sailing excursions to Carriacou are all available from this company. ☒ *True Blue, St. George* ☎ *473/444–1555* ⊕ *www.caribbeanhorizons.com.*

Henry's Safari Tours. Denis Henry of Henry's Safari Tours knows Grenada like the back of his hand. He leads adventurous hikes and four-wheel-drive-vehicle nature safaris, or you can design your own tour. ☒ *Woburn, St. George* ☎ *473/444–5313* ⊕ *www.henrysafari.com.*

Mandoo Tours. From Mandoo you can arrange half- and full-day tours following northern, southern, or eastern routes, as well as hikes to Concord Falls and the mountains. ⊠ *St. George's, St. George* 🖼️ *473/440–1428* ⊕ *www.grenadatours.com.*

Sunsation Tours. You can go to all the usual sites or "as far off the beaten track as you want to go" on Sunsation Tours' customized and private island tours. These include garden tours, challenging hikes, and day sails on catamarans. ⊠ *Grand Anse, St. George* 🖼️ *473/444–1594* ⊕ *www. grenadasunsation.com.*

HIKING

Fodor'sChoice ★ **Grand Étang National Park & Forest Reserve.** Mountain trails wind through Grand Étang National Park & Forest Reserve; if you're lucky, you may spot a Mona monkey or some exotic birds on your hike. There are trails for all levels—from a self-guided nature trail around Grand Étang Lake to a demanding one through the bush to the peak of Mt. Qua Qua (2,373 feet) or a real trek up Mt. St. Catherine (2,757 feet). Long pants and hiking shoes are recommended. The cost is $25 per person for a four-hour guided hike up Mt. Qua Qua, $20 each for two or more, or $15 each for three or more; the Mt. St. Catherine hike starts at $35 per person. ⊠ *Grand Étang, St. Andrew* 🖼️ *473/440–6160.*

EcoTrek. This company takes small groups on day trips to the heart of the rain forest, where you'll find hidden waterfalls and hot-spring pools. A half-day hike to Seven Sisters Waterfall ($55 per person) is suitable for the reasonably fit; full-day adventures to other destinations are more strenuous. ⊠ *Port Louis Marina, St. George's, St. George* 🖼️ *473/232–7777* ⊕ *www.ecodiveandtrek.com.*

Henry's Safari Tours. The personalized hiking excursions here include trips through rich agricultural land and rain forest to Upper Concord Falls, to the summit of Mt. Qua Qua, and to other fascinating spots. ⊠ *Woburn, St. George* 🖼️ *473/444–5313* ⊕ *www.henrysafari.com.*

Telfor Bedeau, Hiking Guide. Over the years Telfor Bedeau has walked up, down, or across nearly every mountain, trail, and pathway on the island. He first began hiking at age 23. That was in 1962. In 2005 he hit the incredible milestone of having hiked 10,000 miles (16,000 km) throughout Grenada. Even in his seventies, his experience and knowledge make him an excellent guide, whether it's an easy walk with novices or the most strenuous hike with experts. ⊠ *Soubise, St. Andrew* 🖼️ *473/442–6200.*

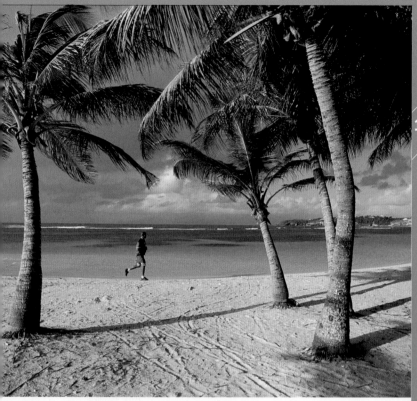

Guadeloupe

WORD OF MOUTH

"We stayed near Pigeon on Basse Terre. It's on the western half of the island and is mountainous. The east side is flat and has the more sandy beaches. We enjoyed the west side because of all the possibilities for activities. Tons of hiking, snorkeling, diving, canyoning etc."

—wug

WELCOME TO GUADELOUPE

Guadeloupe Passage

La Poin la Gran Vigie

Plage de la Chapelle à Anse Bertrand

Anse Bertrand

D122

N8

Campê

N6

Port Louis

Les Mangles

Beauport

N6 N6

Anse du Vieux Fort

Pte. Allègre

Petit-Canal

11 12

La Grande-Anse

10

Ilet à Fajou

Anse du Canal

GRAN

13

Ste-Rose

Vieux-Bourg

Morne-à-l'Eau

N2

Deshaies

Grand Cul-de-Sac Marin

Jabrun du Sud

Jabr du N

N2

Abymes

Lamentin

N1

✈ **Airport**

Pointe-Noire

B A S S E

Destrelan

N1

Pointe-à-Pitre

1

Fort Fleur d'Epée

1

Anse Caraïbe

Cascade aux Ecrevisses

N1

Bas-du-Fort

2

Ilet de Pigeon

Mahaut

La Traversée

D23

Vernou

Petit-Bourg

Aquarium de Car **la Guadeloupe**

Pigeon Island 🝐

Les Mamelles

Pigeon

Parc National de la Guadeloupe

Malendure

7

Goyave

Bouillante

T E R R E

Marigot

La Soufrière

Ste-Marie

N1

Vieux-Habitants

Le Musée Volcanologique

Capesterre-Belle-Eau

C a r i b b e a n   S e a

Matouba

Chutes du Carbet

Anse Chapelle

Plage de Rocroy

St-Claude

St-Sauveur

D11

Gourbeyre

N1

Bananier

Basse-Terre ★

D6

Trois-Rivières

D6

14

Anse Turlet

Vieux Fort

KEY

Symbol	Meaning
⟍	*Beaches*
⛴	*Cruise Ship Terminal*
⟍	*Dive Sites*
1	*Restaurants*
1	*Hotels*
🚢	*Ferry*

8 - 10

15 - 19

Iles des Saintes (Les Saintes)

Pompierres

Terre-de-Haut

Anse Crawen

Terre-de-Bas

La Coche

Grand Ilet

A heady blend of Afro-Caribbean customs, French style, and tropical delights, butterfly-shape Guadeloupe is actually two islands divided by a narrow channel: smaller, flatter, and drier Grande-Terre (Large Land) and wetter and more mountainous Basse-Terre (Low Land). Sheltered by palms, the beaches are beguiling, and the waterfront sidewalk cafés are a bit like the Riviera.

THE BUTTERFLY ISLAND

Guadeloupe, annexed by France in 1674, is not really a single island but rather an archipelago. The largest parts of the chain are Basse-Terre and Grande-Terre, which together are shaped somewhat like a large butterfly. The "out" islands are the Iles des Saintes, La Désirade, and Marie-Galante.

Restaurants	▼	Caraib Bay Hotel	13
Caraïbes Café	**1**	Club Med La Caravelle	**5**
Chez Henri	**13**	Hôtel Amaudo	**7**
Couleurs du Monde	**8**	Hotel Eden Palm	**6**
Iguane Café	**5**	Kawann Beach Hotel	**20**
Gran Kaz	**10**	Langley Hotel	**12**
L'Auberge Les Petits Saints	**9**	L'Auberge Les Petits Saints	**15**
La Toubana	**4**	La Cocoteraie	**9**
Le Rocher de Malendure	**7**	La Créole Beach	**2**
Les Portes	**6**	La Toubana Hôtel	**4**
Le Touloulou	**12**	Le Jardin de Malanga	**14**
Oualiri Breeze	**11**	Le Neem	**3**
Restaurant de la Vielle Tour	**3**	Lô Bleu Hôtel	**17**
Sun7Beach	**14**	Paradis Saintois	**16**
Zawag	**2**	Residence Anse Caraibe	**18**
Hotels	▼	Tainos Cottages	**11**
Aquarelle's Villas	**10**	Villa Dao	**19**
Auberge de la Vieille Tour	**1**		
Bwa Chik Hotel	**8**		

TOP REASONS TO VISIT GUADELOUPE

1 Creole Flavors: Guadeloupe's restaurants and hotel dining rooms highlight the island's fine creole cuisine.

2 Small Inns: Also called *relais,* and *gites* (apartments) these intimate accommodations give you a genuine island experience.

3 Adventure Sports: Parc National has plenty of activities to keep the adrenaline pumping.

4 La Désirade: Remote and affordable, this friendly island provides an escape-from-it-all experience.

GUADELOUPE BEACHES

Guadeloupe is an archipelago of five paradises surrounded by both the Caribbean and the Atlantic. Its beaches run the spectrum from white to black and everything in between.

(Above) La Grande Anse, overlooking Les Saintes' islands (Bottom right) Club Med Beach at Plage Caravalle (Top right) La Grande Anse

There are idyllic beaches, long stretches of unspoiled beach shaded by coconut palms, with soft warm sand. Admittedly, hotel beaches are generally narrow, although well maintained. Some hotels allow nonguests who patronize their restaurants to use their beach facilities. The popular public beaches tend to be cluttered with campers-turned-cafés and cars parked in impromptu lots on the sand. Sunday is the big day, but these same (free) beaches are often quiet during the week.

On the southern coast of Grande-Terre, from Ste-Anne to Pointe des Châteaux, you can find stretches of soft white sand and some sparsely visited stretches. The Atlantic waters on the northeast coast are too rough for swimming. Along the western shore of Basse-Terre signposts indicate small beaches. The sand starts turning gray in Malendure; it becomes volcanic black farther south. There's only one official nude beach, Pointe Tarare, but topless bathing is common.

SAND IN A BOTTLE

Guadeloupe's sand profile is literally encapsulated in one of its popular souvenirs—an airtight glass cylinder displaying variegated strata of sand. St-François is the lightest, followed by the blond of Ste-Anne. Next down is the golden sand of Gosier and Moule. Malendure presents dark-gray, volcanic sand that farther along the coast is black. North of Basse-Terre, Deshaies has both black and nearly white sand.

GRANDE-TERRE

L'Autre Bord. The waves on this Atlantic beach give the long expanse of sand a wild look. The beach, which is protected by an extensive coral reef, is a magnet for surfers and windsurfers. You can stroll on the seaside promenade fringed by flamboyant trees. ⊠ *Grande-Terre.*

Plage Caravelle. Just southwest of Ste-Anne is one of Grande-Terre's longest and prettiest stretches of sand, the occasional dilapidated shack notwithstanding. Protected by reefs, it's a fine snorkeling spot. Club Med occupies one end of this beach, and nonguests can enjoy its beach and water sports, as well as lunch and drinks, by buying a day pass. You can also have lunch on the terrace of La Toubana Hotel & Spa, then descend the stairs to the beach or enjoy lunch at its beach restaurant, wildly popular on Sunday. ⊠ *Rte. N4, southwest of Ste-Anne, Ste-Anne.*

Plage de la Chapelle à Anse-Bertrand. If you want a delightful day trip to the northern tip of Grande-Terre, aim for this spot, one of the loveliest white-sand beaches, whose gentle midafternoon waves are popular with families. When the tide rolls in, it's equally popular with surfers. Several little terrace restaurants at the far end of the beach sate your appetite, but you might want to bring your own shade, because none rent chaise longues. ⊠ *4 miles (6½ km) south of La Pointe de la Grand Vigie.*

Pointe Tarare. This secluded strip just before the tip of Pointe des Châteaux is the island's only nude beach. Small bar–cafés are in the parking area, but it's still best to bring some water, snacks, and beach chairs, as there's no place to rent them. What you do have is one of the coast's most dramatic landscapes; looming above are rugged cliffs topped by a huge crucifix. When approaching St-François Marina, go in the direction of Pointe des Châteaux at the roundabout and drive for about 10 minutes. ⊠ *Rte. N4, southeast of St-François.*

BASSE-TERRE

Plage de la Grande-Anse. One of Guadeloupe's widest beaches has soft beige sand sheltered by palms. To the west it's a round verdant mountain. It has a large parking area and some food stands, but no other facilities. The beach can be overrun on Sunday, not to mention littered. Right after the parking lot, you can see signage for the creole restaurant Le Karacoli; if you have lunch there (it's not inexpensive), you can *sieste* on the chaise longues. ⊠ *Rte. N6, north of Deshaies, Deshaies.*

Plage de Malendure. Across from Pigeon Island and the Jacques Cousteau Underwater Park, this long, gray, volcanic beach on the Caribbean's calm waters has restrooms, a few beach shacks offering cold drinks and snacks, and a huge parking lot. There might be some litter,

Les Pompierres

but the beach is cleaned regularly. Don't come here for solitude, as the beach is a launch point for many dive boats. The snorkeling here is good. Le Rocher de Malendure, a fine seafood restaurant, is perched on a cliff over the bay. ⊠ *Rte. N6, Bouillante.*

ILES DES SAINTES

Anse Crawen. This ½-mile (¾-km) stretch of white sand is secluded and was known for nude sunbathing, but don't plan on shedding your suit, because it's forbidden. Topless is still okay. To reach it, go past the resort Bois Joli and continue straight until you see the beach. ⊠ *Terre-de-Haut.*

Pompierres. This beach is particularly popular with families with small children, as there's a gradual slope, no drop-off, and a long stretch of shallow water. The calm water makes for good snorkeling. To get here, go to the seamen's church near the main plaza, and head in the direction of Marigot. Continue until you see Le Salako Snack Bar and some scurrying chickens, and—*voilà!*—you'll spy a palm-fringed, half-moon stretch of tawny sand. The curve of the beach is called the Bridge of Stone and you

can walk it—carefully—taking a dip in the crater that fills with water from the Atlantic. Morning sun is best; return to Salako for some grilled fresh fish and a cold one. ⊠ *Terre-de-Haut.*

LA DÉSIRADE

Le Soufleur Plage. To reach one of La Désirade's longest and best beaches from the ferry dock, face town and follow the main road to the right. It's about 15 minutes by car or motor scooter (about €20 a day). White sand, calm waters, and snacks and cold drinks from the beach restaurant await, but there are no chaises, so BYO beach towel. ⊠ *Dpmt. Rd. 207.*

MARIE-GALANTE

Anse de Vieux Fort. This gorgeous beach stretches alongside crystal-clear waters that border a large body of freshwater that is ideal for canoeing. It's a surprising contrast to the nearby mangrove swamp you can discover on the hiking trails. The beaches are wide because of the erosion of the sand dunes. It's known as a beach for lovers because of the solitude. Bring your own everything, because this is virgin territory. ⊠ *Rte. D205, just past Pointe Fleur d'Épée.*

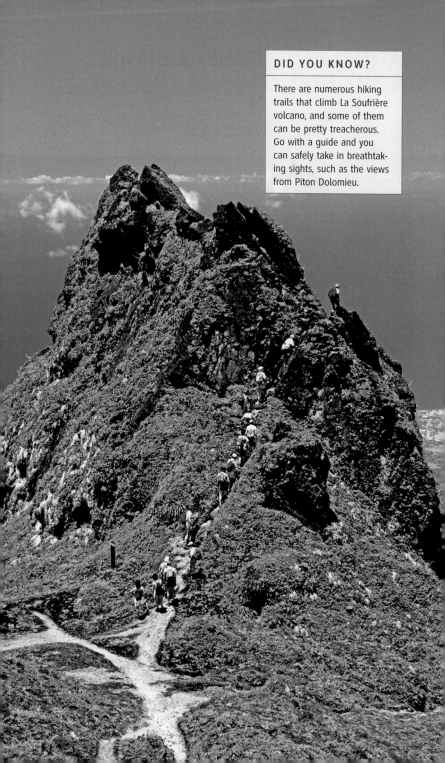

DID YOU KNOW?

There are numerous hiking trails that climb La Soufrière volcano, and some of them can be pretty treacherous. Go with a guide and you can safely take in breathtaking sights, such as the views from Piton Dolomieu.

EATING AND DRINKING WELL IN THE FRENCH WEST INDIES

Creole cuisine, a sultry mélange of African, European, Arawak, even Asian traditions, reflects the islands' turbulent territorial tugs-of-war.

(Above) Lobster Barbecue
(Bottom right) 'Ti Punch (Top right) Accras—Salt Cod Fritters

Deceptively simple yet robustly flavored, authentic "Kweyol" cuisine demands patience: continual macerating and marinating, then seasoning as the food simmers. Many dishes developed in response to economic necessities, recycling leftovers and incorporating ingredients such as starches (both hardy and impervious to spoilage). The indigenous Arawaks provided tubers such as tannia and yucca; lemongrass and capsicum for seasoning; arrowroot for thickening; and *roucou* (annatto, a yellowish-reddish seed) for coloring. The Africans imported plantains, pigeon peas, potatoes, and peppers. The French and British introduced tomatoes, onions, and less perishable salt cod. East Indian indentured servants brought cumin, cardamom, and coriander, notably used in *colombo*, a meat (try *cabri*, goat), poultry, or seafood dish that detonates the palate. Wash it down with fresh local juices from pulpy papaya to puckering passion fruit or the fine rums. Bon appétit!

'TI PUNCH

The primary ingredient in this aperitif is 100-proof rum. It's occasionally fruit-infused, muddled with fresh lime and simple cane syrup. Novices might want to request the lighter (weight) *ti-bete*. Another concoction worth sampling is the classic *planteur* (rum with fruit juices and spices); finish dinner with a *rhum vieux* (aged, cognac-quality rum) or *shrubb*, an orange- and spice-tinged rum-based liqueur. An excellent rhum vieux is Reimonenq's Ste. Rose.

Blaff. This typical method of preparation is usually used for firm, flaky, white fish such as mahimahi or grouper. The fish is poached in a seasoned broth, often a classic court-bouillon (a quick stock perfumed with fresh herbs). The broth is then doctored with lime, onion, garlic, cilantro, chilies, and other ingredients to create the incendiary "condiment" *sauce chien* (whose etymology is obscure, but may indeed have been named "dog's sauce" because it would render even canines edible).

Cod. France contributed many basic ingredients over time to economize, notably dried salt cod, which required no refrigeration and became a staple in creole cooking. *Accras de morue*, fluffy cod fritters, grace every menu. Other popular traditional dishes include *chiquetaille*, shredded cod usually served with a spicy vinaigrette, and *ferocé* (saltfish mixed with avocado and peppers, deep-fried in manioc flour). *Tinnain morue*, grilled cod and bananas believed to energize, still jump-starts many locals' days.

Crayfish. This spiky freshwater crustacean, both wild and, increasingly, farmed, is usually served whole with a variety of sauces. It goes by many names in the French West Indies, including the more Gallic *écrevisse*, patois *z'habitant* or *crebiche*, and *ouassou* (generally larger). A favorite preparation is stewed

13

with *dombrés* (manioc dumplings served pancake-style); you may also see it *étouffée* (stewed with vegetables, served over rice), underscoring the similarity to Cajun cuisine (alongside such dishes as *boudin*, blood sausage).

Poulet Boucané. "Buccaneer's chicken" is smoked slowly over burnt sugarcane (a centuries-old warning signal that pirates were coming) in a closed, chimney-topped barbecue. *Boucanage* is also a French preservation technique, "drying" seasoned meats and poultry on a wood fire (in this case using sugarcane husks). Roughly similar to Jamaica's jerk, it mingles smokiness, sweetness, and spiciness; the marinade typically is a variant of the combustible sauce chien, though milder versions might combine vinegar, lime, garlic, and clove.

Tripe. Another old-fashioned method of economizing was the use of internal organs, offal, which eventually became appropriated by haute cuisine. Tripe (small intestines) is particularly popular. The classic dish is *bébélé*, a stew of tripe, green bananas, tubers (usually breaded as croquettes or *domblés*), and gourds such as *giraumon* (similar to pumpkin).

—Jordan Simon

By Eileen Robinson Smith

Sail the waters around the Isles of Guadeloupe and you'll observe nuances in the ocean's color palette as you glide through the gin-clear sea. Things look better from the bow of a sailboat, from the storybook islands of Les Saintes to towns not as postcard pretty. This Caribbean coastline is dramatic with white and golden beaches, rocky promontories, and rugged cliffs that span the horizon.

Although Guadeloupe is thought of as one island, it is several, each with its own personality. "The mainland" consists of the two largest islands in the Guadeloupe archipelago: Basse-Terre and Grande-Terre, which look something like a butterfly. The outer islands—Les Saintes, Marie-Galante, and La Désirade—are finally being acknowledged as wonderfully unique, unspoiled travel destinations. Tourism officials are now wisely marketing their country as a plural, Les Iles de Guadeloupe. See which one is your place in the sun. *Vive les vacances!*

It's no wonder that in 1493 Christopher Columbus welcomed the sight of this emerald paradise, where fresh, sweet water flows in cascades. And it's understandable why France annexed it in 1674 and why the British schemed to wrench it from them. In 1749 Guadeloupe mirrored what was happening in the motherland. It, too, was an island divided between royalists and revolutionaries.

Surprisingly, the resident British sided with the royalists, so Victor Hugues was sent to banish the Brits. While here, he sent to the guillotine more than 300 loyal-to-the-royal planters and freed the slaves, thus all but destroying the plantocracy. An old saying of the French Caribbean refers to *les grands seigneurs de la Martinique et les bonnes gens de la Guadeloupe* (the lords of Martinique and the bourgeoisie of Guadeloupe), and that still rings true. You'll find more aristocratic descendants of the original French planters on Martinique (known as *békés*) and also more "expensive" people both living and vacationing there. That mass beheading is one of the prime reasons. Ironically, Napoléon—who ultimately ousted the royals—also ousted Hugues

LOGISTICS

Getting to Guadeloupe: You can connect through San Juan or another Caribbean island. Some travelers prefer the regularly scheduled ferry service from Dominica, St. Lucia, and Martinique, but the extra travel time certainly increases the hassle factor. The smaller islands—though charming and rewarding destinations—are harder to reach; even with regular ferries and air service, you will almost always need to spend some time on Guadeloupe both coming and going. Aéroport International Pôle Caraïbes, 3 miles (5 km) from Pointe-à-Pitre (PTP), is a fairly modern airport by Caribbean standards.

Hassle Factor: Medium for Guadeloupe to high for the smaller islands.

On the Ground: Cabs meet flights at the airport if you decide not to rent a car. The metered fare is about €25 to Pointe-à-Pitre, €30 to Gosier, and €70 or more to St-François. Fares go up 40% on Sunday and holidays and from 7 pm to 7 am. You can take a public bus from the airport to downtown Pointe-à-Pitre, but that's not an advisable alternative if you have a lot of luggage. And there are no recommendable hotels in the city.

13

and reestablished slavery. It wasn't until 1848 that an Alsatian, Victor Schoelcher, abolished it for good.

Guadeloupe became one of France's *départements d'outremer* in 1946, meaning that it's a dependent of France. It was designated a region in 1983, making it a part of France, albeit a distant part. This brought many benefits to the islanders, from their fine highway systems to the French social services and educational system, as well as a high standard of living. Certain tensions still exist, though the anticolonial resentment harbored by the older generations is dying out. Guadeloupe's young people realize the importance of tourism to the island's future, and you'll find them welcoming, smiling, and practicing the English and tourism skills they learn in school. Some *français* is indispensable, though you may receive a bewildering response in Creole.

Guadeloupe is a little bit of France, but far from the Metropole. Instead, the culture of this tropical paradise is more Afro-influenced. Savor the earthier pleasures here, exemplified by the wonderful potpourri of whole spices whose heady aromas flood the outdoor markets.

PLANNING

WHEN TO GO

The tourism industry thrives during the high season, which lasts from mid-November through May, and then the island is quiet the rest of the year. Prices decline 25% to 40% in the off-season.

GETTING HERE AND AROUND

AIR TRAVEL

The only non-stops available are from Orlando on Air France, seasonally.

Airline Contacts Air Antilles Express. Air Antilles Express has service to Martinique, St. Martin, St. Barth, and Santo Domingo, Dominican Republic. ☎ 0890/64-86-48 ⊕ www.airantilles.com.

Air Caraïbes. Air Caraïbes connects the island to St. Maarten, Martinique, the Dominican Republic, and Havana, Cuba. ■ TIP➡ This airline offers substantial discounts for seniors on some routes. ☎ 0820/83-58-35 ⊕ www.aircaraibes.com.

Air France. Air France flies between Miami and Guadeloupe in the winter season. ☎ 0590/21-13-03, 0820/82-08-20 ⊕ www.airfance.com.

American Airlines. You can also connect in San Juan with American Airlines. ☎ 0811/30-73-00 ⊕ www.aa.com.

American Eagle. American Eagle services Guadeloupe from San Juan. ☎ 0590/21-13-66 ⊕ www.aa.com.

LIAT. LIAT services several Caribbean islands, including Barbados and St. Lucia. LIAT code-shares with Air Caraïbes. ☎ 0590/21-13-93 ⊕ www.liatairline.com.

Airports and Transfers Aéroport International Pôle Caraïbes (PTP). Aéroport International Pôle Caraïbes (PTP), usually called the Pointe-à-Pitre Airport, is one of the largest and most modern in the Caribbean. Excellent signage makes it very manageable. It has shops, restaurants, and car-rental agencies. There is a tourism information booth in the terminal with bilingual staffers, an ATM, and a currency exchange. Ask your resort if airport transfers can be arranged, as they are almost always cheaper than taking a taxi. ☎ 0590/21-14-72, 0590/21-14-00.

Taxi fare to Pointe-à-Pitre is about €25, to Gosier resorts about €30, to Ste-Anne €60, and to St-François more than €70. Cabs meet flights at the airport if you decide not to rent a car.

CAR TRAVEL

Renting a Car: If you're based in Gosier or at a large resort, you'll probably need a car only for a day or two of sightseeing. That may be enough, since roundabouts, mountain roads, standard shifts, and fast, aggressive drivers are stressful. Your valid driver's license will suffice for up to 20 days. You can get a rental car from the airport or your hotel. Count on spending between €48 and €70 a day for a small car with standard shift; automatics are considerably more expensive and must be reserved in advance. Some companies, including Europcar, charge a €20 drop-off fee for the airport, even if you pick the car up there. Allow at least 30 to 60 minutes to drop off your car at the end of your stay. The chances of your getting lost on the way to the airport and to where you need to leave the car are such that you should probably allow a full hour. Conscientiously follow every sign that has a picture of a plane. You must return the car to the old (former) airport and wait for a shuttle to bring you back to the new airport. An alternative is to return it in Gosier and put that €20 toward a stress-free taxi ride.

Return your vehicle with the same amount of gas or you'll be charged an exorbitant rate.

Car Rental Contacts Avis ☎ *0590/21–13–54*. **Budget** ☎ *0590/21–13–49*. **Europcar**. Europcar, like most companies, charges a €20 drop-off fee for the airport, even if you pick the car up there. Europcar employees speak English and are professional; convertibles go for €113 per day. ☎ *0590/21–13–52*. **Hertz**. Hertz has some automatics and convertibles. ☎ *0590/21–13–46*. **Jumbo Car** ☎ *0590/91–91–66*. **Rent A Car** ☎ *0590/91–11–68*. **Sixt** ☎ *0590/21–13–44*.

Driving Tips: Guadeloupeans are fast and often impatient drivers, and they tailgate.

Driving around Grande-Terre is relatively easy. Basse-Terre requires more skill to navigate the hairpin bends in the mountains and around the eastern shore; at night the roads are unlighted and treacherous.

Roundabouts (*rond-pointes*) are everywhere. You should use your turn signal to indicate your direction, even if no one else does, and proceed cautiously. Avoid morning and evening rush hours, which start and end early, especially around Pointe-à-Pitre. If you're lost, don't stop to ask people standing on the side of the road; they are waiting for a lift and will jump in. Try to find a gas station. Chances are the attendants speak more Creole than French. Inside, the manager or other customers will speak French and maybe some English. *"Je suis perdue!"* (I am lost!) is a good phrase to know.

FERRY TRAVEL

Ferry schedules and fares often change, so phone ahead to confirm. You normally travel to the outlying islands in the archipelago in the morning, returning in the afternoon. Both Comatrile and Express des Isles operate ferries between Terre-de-Haut and Marie-Galante.

A new ferry, **jeans for freedom** (⊠ *Place du Marche, St-Pierre, Martinique* ☎ *97250; 0825/ 01–01–25* ⊕ *www.jeansforfreedom.com*) is plying the waters between Pointe-à-Pitre, Guadeloupe, and Ste. Pierre, Martinique; it also makes a brief stop in Dominica. Slightly undercutting the competition, the price is €70. It also connects Fort-de-France to St. Lucia (€70). In Guadeloupe, service is also available between Pointe-à-Pitre and Marie-Galante or Les Saintes for €25.

Contacts Brudey Frères Transport Maritime. Brudey Frères Transport Maritime travels between Terre-de-Haut, Les Saintes, and Trois-Rivières on Basse-Terre with some service from Pointe-à-Pitre. ☎ *0590/90–04–48 in Pointe-à-Pitre, 0590/92–69–74 in Trois-Rivières, 0590/92–69–74 in St-François, 0590/97–77–82 in Marie-Galante.*

Comatrile. Comatrile travels from St-François on Grande-Terre to La Désirade and to Marie-Galante and Les Saintes. ☎ *0690/50–05–09 [port], 0590/22–26–31.*

C.T.M. DEHER. C.T.M. DEHER plies the waters between Trois-Rivieres and Terre-de-Haut, Les Saintes. ☎ *0590/92–06–39, 0590/99–50–68* ⊕ *www.ctmdeher.com.*

Express des Isles. Express des Isles runs ferries to Marie Galante, Les Saintes, from Pointe-à-Pitre. Longer trips to other islands like Dominica and Martinique cost about €60 to €69 and take between three and four hours.■ TIP→ Be prepared for bad weather and choppy seas, which are especially likely on longer runs when the boats are in open water. ☎ *0825/35–90–00, 0590/91–98–53* ⊕ *www.express-des-iles.com.*

TAXI TRAVEL

Taxis are metered and fairly pricey. Fares jump by 40% between 7 pm and 7 am and on Sunday and holidays.

Contacts Radio Cabs. If your French is in order, call Radio Cabs (or ask your hotel receptionist to call them for you). ☎ *0590/82–00–00, 0590/20–74–74.*

ESSENTIALS

Banks and Exchange Services Few places accept U.S. dollars, so plan on exchanging for euros. You must exchange cash at your hotel or a *bureau de change*. One favorite company is Change Caraïbe, with branches near the tourist office and market in Pointe-à-Pitre. It's easier to use your ATM card to get euros. Make sure you have a four-digit PIN. ATMs, particularly those in smaller towns, don't always accept foreign bank cards. Visa and MasterCard are most often accepted, followed by American Express. There are just two ATMs on the main island, one at the ferry dock and the other next to the mayor's (Maire) office. Come with a cash reserve, for it's not unusual for the machines to run out of euros or to malfunction during electrical blackouts.

Electricity 220 volts/50 cycles. North American electronics and laptops require an adapter and a converter.

Emergency Services Ambulance ☎ *15.* **Fire** ☎ *18.* **Police emergencies** ☎ *17.* **SAMU.** SAMU is a medical service to see a doctor fast. ☎ *0590/89–11–00.*

Etiquette Guadeloupeans are deeply religious and traditional, particularly the older generations. Revealing shorts or swimwear away from the beach may be considered indecorous by some, and you should ask before taking a picture of any islander. The children, however, will probably flash you one of their happy smiles. Observe the courtesy of saying *bonjour* or *bonsoir* when you enter or leave a place or before asking someone a question or directions.

Language The official language is French, though most of the islanders also speak Creole, a lyrical patois that you won't be able to understand. Often, their French has a heavy Creole accent. Most of the staff in hotels knows some English as do some taxi drivers, but communicating is decidedly more difficult in the countryside. Arm yourself with a phrase book, a dictionary, patience, and a sense of humor.

Passport Requirements You must have a valid passport as well as a return or ongoing ticket to enter Guadeloupe.

Phones To make on-island calls, dial 0590 (0690 if it is a cellular phone) and then the six-digit phone number. To call Guadeloupe from the United States, dial 00–590–590, then the local number. For cell phone numbers, dial 00–590–690, then the local nufmber. If you're on one of the other islands in the French West Indies, dial 0590 and then the local number.

Taxes and Service Charges The *taxe de séjour* (room tax), which varies by hotel, is usually €1 but never exceeds €1.80 per person per day. Most hotel prices include a 10% to 15% service charge in their rates; if not, it'll be added to your bill. A 15% service charge is included in all restaurant prices, as are taxes.

Tipping Restaurants are required to include a 15% service charge in the menu price. No additional gratuity is necessary (although it's appreciated if service is particularly good). Tip skycaps and porters about €1 a bag, cabdrivers 10% of the fare (if they work for a cab company rather than having their own taxi), and housekeeping €1 per night.

ACCOMMODATIONS

Guadeloupe is actually an archipelago of large and small islands. Grande-Terre has the big package hotels that are concentrated primarily in four or five communities on the south coast, whereas wilder Basse-Terre has more locally owned hotels. More distant and much quieter are the Iles des Saintes, Marie-Galante, and La Désirade, in that order. On each of these smaller islands tourism is only a part of the economy and development is light, and any of them will give you a sense of what the Caribbean used to be.

Relais and Gites: These small inns offer a more personal—and authentic—kind of Caribbean experience.

Resorts: You can certainly opt for a big, splashy resort with all the amenities. Many of the island's large chain hotels cater to French package groups, yet an increasing number of them are being renovated to the degree that they will appeal more to the expectations of Americans.

Villas: Private villas are another option—particularly for families—but the language barrier is often a deterrent to Americans. Best to go through one of the rental agencies recommended here.

HOTEL AND RESTAURANT PRICES

Prices in the restaurant reviews are the average cost of a main course at dinner or, if dinner is not served, at lunch; taxes and service charges are generally included. Prices in the hotel reviews are the lowest cost of a standard double room in high season, excluding taxes, service charges, and meal plans (except at all-inclusives). Prices for rentals are the lowest per-night cost for a one-bedroom unit in high season.

VISITOR INFORMATION

Contacts Comité du Tourisme des Iles de Guadeloupe ⊠ *5 sq. de la Banque, Pointe-à-Pitre* ☎ *0590/82–09–30* ⊕ *www.lesilesdeguadeloupe.com.* **French Government Tourist Office** ☎ *310/271–6665 in Los Angeles* ⊕ *www. us.franceguide.com.* **Office du Tourisme de Marie-Galante** ⊠ *Rue du Port, BP 15, Grand-Bourg, Marie-Galante* ☎ *0590/97–56–51.* **Office du Tourisme de Terre de Haut** ⊠ *39 rue de la Grande Anse, Terre-de-Haut, Iles des Saintes* ☎ *0590/99–58–60.*

WEDDINGS

A long residency requirement makes weddings prohibitive.

EXPLORING GUADELOUPE

To see each "wing" of the butterfly, you'll need to budget at least one day. They are connected by a bridge, and Grande-Terre has pretty villages along its south coast and the spectacular Pointe des Châteaux. You can see the main sights in Pointe-à-Pitre in a half day. Touring the rugged, mountainous Basse-Terre is a challenge. If time is a problem, head straight to the west coast; you could easily spend a day traveling its length, stopping for sightseeing, lunch, and a swim. You can make day trips to the islands, but an overnight or more works best. Leave your heavy luggage in the baggage room of your "mainland" hotel.

GRANDE-TERRE

♻ **Aquarium de la Guadeloupe.** Unique in the Antilles, this aquarium in the marina near Pointe-à-Pitre is a good place to spend an hour. The well-planned facility has an assortment of tropical fish, crabs, lobsters, moray eels, coffer fish, and some live coral. It's also a fascinating turtle rescue center, and the shark tank is spectacular. ✉ *Pl. Créole off rte. N4, Pointe-à-Pitre, Grande-Terre* ☎ *0590/90–92–38* ⊕ *www. aquariumdelaguadeloupe.com* ✇ *€10.50* ☽ *Daily 9–7.*

Ft. Fleur d'Épée. The main attraction in Bas-du-Fort is this 18th-century fortress, which hunkers down on a hillside behind a deep moat. It was the scene of hard-fought battles between the French and the English in 1794. You can explore its well-preserved dungeons and battlements and take in a sweeping view of Iles des Saintes and Marie-Galante. ✉ *Bas-du-Fort, Grande-Terre* ☎ *0590/90–94–61* ✇ *Free* ☽ *Mon.–Sun. 9–5.*

■ TIP→ You may find that you adore the tropical ice-cream flavors such as mangue (mango) and coco (coconut). You may not realize that cacahuète translates to "peanut" and is addictive!

Gosier. Taking its name from the brown pelicans that nest on the islet of Gosier and along the south coast of Grande-Terre, Gosier was still a tiny village in the 1950s, a simple stopping place between Pointe-à-Pitre and Ste-Anne. However, it grew rapidly in the 1960s, when the beauty of the southern coastline began to bring tourists in ever-increasing numbers. Today Gosier is one of Guadeloupe's premier tourist areas while at the same time serving as a chic suburb of Pointe-à-Pitre. People sit at sidewalk cafés reading *Le Monde* as others flip-flop their way to the beach. The town has several hotels, nightclubs, and shops, a casino, and a long stretch of sand. ✉ *Grande-Terre.*

Le Moule. On the Atlantic coast, and once the capital city of Guadeloupe, this port city of 24,000 has had more than its share of troubles: it was bombarded by the British in 1794 and 1809 and by a hurricane in 1928. An important tourist center in past decades, it's experiencing a comeback. A large East Indian population, which originally came to cut cane, lives here. Canopies of flamboyant trees hang over the narrow streets, where colorful vegetable and fish markets do a brisk business. The town hall, with graceful balustrades, and a small 19th-century neoclassical church are on the main square. Le Moule's beach, protected by a reef, is perfect for windsurfing. ✉ *Le Moule, Grande-Terre.*

Morne-à-l'Eau. This agricultural town of about 16,000 people has an amphitheater-shape cemetery, with black-and-white-checkerboard tombs, elaborate epitaphs, and multicolor (plastic) flowers. On All Saints' Day (November 1), it's the scene of a moving (and photogenic) candlelight service. ⊠ *Grande-Terre.*

Musée du Costumes et Traditions. This museum is a labor of love by its creators, and seeing the dress of black, white, and *métisseé* (brown) societies is a fascinating way to visualize the island's tumultuous history. Items that you will remember: madras headdresses; baptism outfits; embroidered maternity dresses; colonial pith helmets and other various chapeaux as well as the doll collection. Make sure to go out back and visit the replica of a Guadeloupean *case* circa 1920. The museum is petite and privately owned; the founding owner is a retired English teacher, and she can act as your guide. Call before you go for directions and to make certain that a school group is not there. ⊠ *1 Perinette, Gosier, Grande-Terre* ☎ *0590/83–21–70, 0690/41–51–90* ☜ *€9* ⊗ *Tues.–Sun. 9–1, 3–5.*

Pointe-à-Pitre. Although not the capital, this is the island's largest city, a commercial and industrial hub in the southwest of Grande-Terre. The Isles of Guadeloupe have 450,000 inhabitants, 99.6% of whom live in the cities. Pointe-à-Pitre is bustling, noisy, and hot—a place of honking horns and traffic jams and cars on sidewalks for want of a parking place. By day its pulse is fast, but at night, when its streets are almost deserted, you don't want to be there.

The heart of the old city is Place de la Victoire; surrounded by wooden buildings with balconies and shutters (including the tourism office) and by sidewalk cafés, it was named in honor of Victor Hugues's 1794 victory over the British. During the French Revolution Hugues ordered the guillotine set up here so that the public could witness the bloody end of 300 recalcitrant royalists.

Even more colorful is the bustling marketplace, between rues St-John Perse, Frébault, Schoelcher, and Peynier. It's a cacophonous place, where housewives bargain for spices, herbs (and herbal remedies), and a bright assortment of papayas, breadfruits, christophenes, and tomatoes.

Cathédrale de St-Pierre et St-Paul. For fans of French ecclesiastical architecture, there's the imposing Cathédrale de St-Pierre et St-Paul, built in 1807. Although battered by hurricanes, it has fine stained-glass windows and Creole-style balconies and is reinforced with pillars and ribs that look like leftovers from the Eiffel Tower. ⊠ *Rue Alexandre Isaac at rue de l'Eglise, Grande-Terre.*

Musée St-John Perse. Anyone with an interest in French literature and culture (not your average sightseer) won't want to miss the Musée St-John Perse, which is dedicated to Guadeloupe's most famous son and one of the giants of world literature, Alexis Léger, better known as St-John Perse, winner of the Nobel Prize for literature in 1960. Some of his finest poems are inspired by the history and landscape—particularly the sea—of his beloved Guadeloupe. The museum contains a collection of his poetry and some of his personal belongings. Before you go, look for his birthplace at 54 rue Achille René-Boisneuf. ⊠ *rue Achille*

René-Boisneuf, Pointe-à-Pitre, Grande-Terre ☎ *0590/90–01–92* ⌨ *€3* ⊙ *Mon–Fri. 9–5, Sat. 8:30–12:30.*

Musée Schoelcher. Musée Schoelcher celebrates Victor Schoelcher, a high-minded abolitionist from Alsace who fought against slavery in the French West Indies in the 19th century. The museum contains many of his personal effects, and exhibits trace his life and work. ⊠ *24 rue Peynier, Grande-Terre* ☎ *0590/82–08–04* ⌨ *€3* ⊙ *Weekdays 9–5* ⊠ *Pointe-à-Pitre, Grande-Terre.*

Pointe des Châteaux. The island's easternmost point offers a breathtaking view of the Atlantic crashing against huge rocks, carving them into shapes resembling pyramids. There are spectacular views of Guadeloupe's southern and eastern coasts and the island of La Désirade. In high season, the dramatic scene is marred by a parking lot filled with tour buses and makeshift bars and snack stands, but if you are spending hours at the beach, you will need the sustenance. On weekends locals come in numbers to walk their dogs, surf, or look for romance. But change is afoot, and the *sauvage* beach is slated to become gentrified. The landmark crucifix (circa 1954), a symbol of protection for those at sea as well as a navigational site, has been restored. ⊠ *St-François, Grande-Terre.*

▌**NEED A BREAK?** If you don't want to take time for a two-hour French lunch, watch for gas stations such as **Shell Boutique, Total Boutique,** and **Esso Tigermart,** which sell food. The VITO station on the left going into St-François has good pizza for €8, roast chicken, and panini, as well as tables and chairs. A Total "fillin' station" might have barbecue ribs, chicken, and turkey.

Port Louis. This fishing village of about 7,000 people is best known for Le Soufleur Plage. It was once one of the island's prettiest, but it has become a little shabby. Although the beach is crowded on weekends, it's blissfully quiet during the week. The sand is fringed by flamboyant trees, and there are also spectacular views of Basse-Terre. ⊠ *Grande-Terre.*

Ste-Anne. In the 18th century this town, 8 miles (13 km) east of Gosier, was a sugar-exporting center. Sand has replaced sugar as the town's most valuable asset. La Caravelle and the other beaches are among the best in Guadeloupe. On a more spiritual note, Ste-Anne has a lovely cemetery with stark-white tombs. ⊠ *Grande-Terre.*

★ **St-François.** This was once a simple little village, primarily involved with fishing and harvesting tomatoes. The fish and tomatoes are still here, as are the old Creole houses and the lively market with recommendable food stalls in the centre ville, but increasingly, the St-François marina district is overtaking Gosier as Guadeloupe's most fashionable tourist resort area. La Cocoteraie, one of the island's ritziest hotels, is just off l'avenue de l'Europe, which runs between the marina and the rolling fairways and water obstacles of the 18-hole Robert Trent Jones–designed municipal golf course. On the marina side, a string of shops, hotels, bars, and restaurants caters to tourists. The Bwa Chik Hotel & Golf, an eco-chic study in recyclable materials, is here; it's a favorite of golfers. Other attractions include an array of beaches and the St. François casino. ⊠ *Grande-Terre.*

NEED A BREAK? Match, a *supermarche* on l'avenue de l'Europe/St-François Marina, has esoteric cheeses and baked goods such as pie-size tropical-fruit tarts. Other supermarkets to look for throughout the island that have good deli or bakery departments are those in the Leader Price and Carrefour chains.

BASSE-TERRE

13

Basse-Terre (which translates as "low land") is by far the highest and wildest of the two wings of the Guadeloupe butterfly, with the peak of the Soufrière volcano topping off at nearly 4,811 feet. Basse-Terre, where you can find the island's national park, is an ecotourist's treasure, with lush, equatorial plant life and adventurous opportunities for hikers and mountain bikers on the old *traces*, routes that porters once took across the mountains. You can still find numerous fishing villages and banana plantations stretching as far as the eye can see. The northwest coast, between Bouillante and Grande-Anse, is magnificent; the road twists and turns up steep hills smothered in vegetation and then drops down and skirts deep-blue bays and colorful seaside towns. Constantly changing light, towering clouds, and frequent rainbows only add to the beauty.

Basse-Terre. Because Pointe-à-Pitre is so much bigger, few people suspect that this little town of 15,000 is the capital and administrative center of Guadeloupe. But if you have any doubts, walk up the hill to the state-of-the-art Théâtre Nationale, where some of France's finest theater and opera companies perform. Paid for by the French government, it's a sign that Basse-Terre is reinventing itself. Founded in 1640, it has endured not only foreign attacks and hurricanes but sputtering threats from La Soufrière as well. The last major eruption was in the 16th century, though the volcano seemed active enough to warrant evacuating more than 70,000 people in 1975.

Jardin Botanique. The Jardin Botanique, or Botanical Garden, is an exquisitely tasteful 10-acre park populated with parrots and flamingos. A circuitous walking trail takes you by ponds with floating lily pads, cactus gardens, and every kind of tropical flower and plant, including orchids galore. A panoramic restaurant with surprisingly good meals and a snack bar are housed in terraced gingerbread buildings, one overlooking a waterfall, the other the mountains. The garden has a children's park and nature-oriented playthings in the shop. A local juice and a snack is offered to visitors. ⊠ *Deshaies, Basse-Terre* ☎ *0590/28–43–02* ⛱ *€15* ⊙ *Daily 9–5* ⊠ *Basse-Terre, Basse-Terre.*

Bouillante. The name means "boiling," and so it's no surprise that hot springs were discovered here. However, the biggest attraction is scuba diving on nearby Pigeon Island, which is accessed by boat from Plage de Malendure. There's a small information kiosk on the beach at Plage de Malendure that can help you with diving and snorkeling arrangements. ⊠ *Bouillante, Basse-Terre.*

Cascade aux Ecrevisses. Within the Parc National de la Guadeloupe, Crayfish Falls is one of the island's loveliest (and most popular) spots. There's a marked trail (walk carefully—the rocks can be slippery) leading to this splendid waterfall, which dashes down into the Corossol River—a good place for a dip. Come early, though; otherwise you definitely won't have it to yourself. ⊠ *St-Claude, Basse-Terre* ⊕ *www. guadeloupe-parcnational.com.*

Chutes du Carbet. You can reach three of the Carbet Falls (one drops from 65 feet, the second from 360 feet, the third from 410 feet) via a long, steep path from the village of Habituée. On the way up you pass the Grand Étang (Great Pond), a volcanic lake surrounded by interesting plant life. For horror fans there's also the curiously named Étang Zombi, a pond believed to house evil spirits. If there have been heavy rains, *don't even think about it.* ⊠ *St-Claude, Basse-Terre.*

Ilet de Pigeon. This tiny, rocky island a few hundred yards off the coast is the site of the Jacques Cousteau Underwater Park, the island's best scuba and snorkeling site. Although the reefs here are good, they don't rank among the top Caribbean dive spots. Several companies conduct diving trips to the reserve, and it's on the itinerary of some sailing and snorkeling trips *(⇨ Diving section in Sports and Activities).* ⊠ *Bouillante, Basse-Terre.*

Fodor'sChoice
★
La Bonifierie/Ti café. When it comes to the island's coffee and chocolate experiences, this place takes the gold. Within the attractive complex with fieldstone and wooden colonial houses, there's a display case for the truffles, chocolate candies, and confections. They are created from 100% local products, from cacao to tropical fruits. The French *chocolatiere* produces what may be *the* best chocolate, from the dark to the white, south of Paris. Call ahead and ask to be part of a group that is taught how to make candy bars and then enjoys a Franco-Caribbean buffet with tastings of island rum. The sophisticated courtyard café has a contemporary menu. The beef, like the coffee, is grown on the plantation and triggers a chemical reaction for the chocolate desserts. ⊠ *Rte. de Morin, St-Claude, Basse-Terre* ☎ *0590/80–06–05* ⊑ *Free* ⊙ *Tues.–Sun. 9–3:30.*

Les Mamelles. Two mountains—Mamelle de Petit-Bourg, at 2,350 feet, and Mamelle de Pigeon, at 2,500 feet—rise in the Parc National de la Guadeloupe. *Mamelle* means "breast," and when you see the mountains, you can understand why they are so named. Trails ranging from easy to arduous lace up into the surrounding mountains. There's a glorious view from the lookout point 1,969 feet up Mamelle de Pigeon. If you're a climber, plan to spend several hours exploring this area. Hark! If there have been heavy rainfalls, cancel your plans. ⊠ *St-Claude, Basse-Terre* ⊕ *www.guadeloupe-parcnational.com.*

★ **Parc National de la Guadeloupe.** This 74,100-acre park has been recognized by UNESCO as a Biosphere Reserve. Before going, pick up a *Guide to the National Park* from the tourist office; it rates the hiking trails according to difficulty, and most are quite difficult indeed. Most mountain trails are in the southern half. The park is bisected by the route de la Traversée, a 16-mile (26-km) paved road lined with masses of tree ferns, shrubs, flowers, tall trees, and green plantains. It's the ideal point of entry. Wear rubber-soled shoes and take along a swimsuit, a sweater, and perhaps food for a picnic. Try to get an early start to stay ahead of the hordes of cruise-ship passengers making a day of it. Check on the weather; if Basse-Terre has had a lot of rain, give it up. In the past, after intense rainfall, rockslides have closed the road for months. ⊠ *Administrative Headquarters, rte. de la Traversée, St-Claude, Basse-Terre* ☎ *0590/80–86–00* ⊕ *www.guadeloupe-parcnational.com* ☞ *Free* ⊗ *Weekdays 8–5:30.*

Pointe-Noire. Pointe-Noire is a good jumping-off point from which to explore Basse-Terre's little-visited northwest coast. A road skirts magnificent cliffs and tiny coves, dances in and out of thick stands of mahogany and gommier trees, and weaves through unspoiled fishing villages with boats and ramshackle houses as brightly colored as a child's finger painting. This town has two small museums devoted to local products.

La Maison du Bois. La Maison du Bois offers a glimpse into the traditional use of wood on the island. Superbly crafted musical instruments and furnishings are for sale. There are even dance demonstrations and a restaurant. It's open Tuesday to Sunday from 9:30 to 5:30 and charges €2 admission. ⊠ *Pointe Noire, Basse-Terre* ☎ *0590/98–16–09* ⊠ *Pointe Noire, Basse-Terre.*

Ste-Rose. In addition to a sulfur bath, there are two good beaches (Amandiers and Clugny) and several interesting small museums in Ste-Rose. The rum distillery, Domaine de Severin, is perhaps the biggest draw for tourists.

Domaine de Séverin. Domaine de Séverin, free and open daily from 8:30 to 5, is a historic rum distillery with a working waterwheel. A simple open-air dining room has a good menu. A petite train traverses the plantation from 9:30 to 10:45 and again from 3:30 to 5:30 from Sunday to Friday; this scenic tour costs €11. A gift shop sells rum, spices, and hot sauces. ⊠ *Ste-Rose, Basse-Terre* ☎ *0590/28–91–86* ⊕ *www.severinrhum.com* ⊠ *Ste-Rose, Basse-Terre.*

★ **Vieux-Habitants.** This was the island's first colony, established in 1635. Beaches, a restored coffee plantation, and the oldest church on the island (1666) make this village worth a stop.

Musée du Café/Café Chaulet. From the riverfront Musée du Café/Café Chaulet, dedicated to the art of coffee making, the tantalizing aroma of freshly ground beans reaches the highway. Plaques and photos tell of the island's coffee history. The shop sells excellent coffee and rum punches and jewelry made from natural materials. The "resident" chocolatier, a young French woman, hand-makes bonbons and festive holiday candies. You will even see the coffee cars—emblazoned Volkswagon Beetles. Admission is €6. It's open daily 9 to 5. ⊠ *Vieux-Habitants, Basse-Terre* ☎ *0590/98–54–96* ⊠ *Basse-Terre.*

ILES DES SAINTES

The eight-island archipelago of Iles des Saintes, often referred to as Les Saintes, dots the waters off the southern coast of Guadeloupe. The islands are Terre-de-Haut, Terre-de-Bas, Ilet à Cabrit, Grand Ilet, La Redonde, La Coche, Le Pâté, and Les Augustins. Columbus discovered them on November 4, 1493, and christened them Los Santos (Les Saintes in French) for All Saints' Day.

Only Terre-de-Haut and Terre-de-Bas are inhabited, with a combined population of little more than 3,000. Many of the Saintois are fair-haired, blue-eyed descendants of Breton and Norman sailors. Unless they are in the tourism industry, they tend to be taciturn and standoffish. Fishing still is their main source of income, and they take pride in their work. The shores are lined with their boats and *filets bleus* (blue nets dotted with orange buoys).

★ **Terre-de-Haut.** With 5 square miles (13 square km) and a population of about 1,500, Terre-de-Haut is the largest and most developed of Les Saintes. Its "big city" is Bourg, with one main street lined with bistros, cafés, and shops. Clutching the hillside are trim white houses with bright red or blue doors, balconies, and gingerbread frills.

Terre-de-Haut's ragged coastline is scalloped with lovely coves and beaches, including the semi-nude beach at Anse Crawen. The beautiful bay, complete with a "sugarloaf" mountain, has been called a mini Rio. There are precious few vehicles or taxis on island, so you'll often find yourself walking, despite the hilly terrain. Or you can add to the din and rent a motorbike. Take your time on these rutted roads, as around any bend there might be a herd of goats chomping on a fallen palm frond. Two traffic lights have brought a small amount of order to the motorbike hordes. When aggressively soliciting you, the scooter agencies will not tell you that it is prohibited to scoot in town from 9 to noon and from 2 to 4.

This island makes a great day trip, but you can really get a feel for Les Saintes if you stay overnight. It's not unlike St. Barth, but for a fraction of the price. Note: most shops and restaurants close for two hours in the afternoon.

■TIP➜ A wonderful introduction to the island as well as a travel keepsake, is the coffee-table book Carnet de Route-Les Saintes on sale in shops for €20.

Fort Napoléon. This museum is noted for its exhaustive exhibit of the greatest sea battles ever fought. You can also visit the well-preserved barracks and prison cells, or admire the botanical gardens, which specialize in cacti. ■TIP➜ This is a hill climb, and if you decide to walk, allow 30 minutes from the village, wear comfortable footwear, and bring water. You will be rewarded with outstanding views of the bay and neighboring islands. ✉ *Grand Bourg, Iles des Saintes* ☎ *0590/37–99–59* 🎫 *€4* ⊙ *Daily 9–noon* ✉ *Terre-de-Haut, Iles des Saintes.*

NEED A BREAK?
To reward yourself for making the trek to the fort, have a waffle cone at Tropico Gelato, on rue Jean Calot. This artisanal shop has such tempting tropical flavors as cinnamon and mango, as well as mint, apricot, and a dozen more. Its sidewalk café is the "waiting room" for the ferry, where you can also take a small quiche or panino to go.

OTHER ISLANDS

La Désirade. *Desirable* is the operative word here. This small, safe, somewhat remote island is an absolute find for those who prefer a road less traveled, who want their beaches long and white, and who don't mind that accommodations are simple if the price is right. The Désirade populace (all 1,700 of them) welcome tourism, and these dear hearts have a warm, old-fashioned sense of community.

According to legend, the "desired land" was so named by the crew of Christopher Columbus, whose tongues were dry for want of fresh water when they spied the island; alas, it was the season for drought. The 8-square-mile (21-square-km) island, 5 miles (8 km) east of St-François, is a chalky plateau, with an arid climate, perennial sunshine, cacti, and iguanas. You may even see two male iguanas locked in a prehistoric-looking battle. Rent a four-wheel-drive to climb the zigzag road that leads to the Grande Montagne. Make a photo stop at the diminutive white chapel, which offers a panorama of the sea below. Afraid that you might zig instead of zag down the precipice? Then take a fun, informative van tour that you join near the tourist office at the harbor. The ruins of the original settlement—a leper colony—are on the tour.

Only one road runs around the perimeter of the island, and if you're interested in visiting one of the many gorgeous beaches shaded by coco palms and sea grape trees, you can do that on a scooter. Driving is safer here than most anywhere. ⊠ *La Désirade.*

NEED A BREAK?

Chez Nounoune. La Désirade has a few cute and casual spots to grab a bite to eat. The goats and their kids that you pass on your island tour may end up in a curry at Chez Nounoune. ⊠ *La Providence, La Désirade* ☎ *0590/20-03-59.*

La Payotte. If you're on the beach, you might want to stop by La Payotte for the fresh catch, conch, or lobster, or the French owner's famous chicken with a sauce of *noix de cajou* (cashews). Mind you, avoid it when there is a tour group on the island. Also, there are six rooms in an attractive Creole house for rent (€50–€90). ⊠ *Plage de Beauséjour, La Désirade* ☎ *0590/20-01-29.*

★ **Marie-Galante.** This island resonates with history. Columbus sighted this 60-square-mile (155-square-km) island on November 3, 1493, named it after his flagship, the *Maria Galanda,* and sailed on. It's dotted with ruined 19th-century sugar mills, and sugar is still its major product. Honey and 59% rum are its other favored harvests. You should make it a point to see one of the distilleries. With its rolling hills of green cane still worked by oxen and men with broad-brim straw hats, it's like traveling back in time to when all of Guadeloupe was still a giant farm.

Although it's only an hour by high-speed ferry from Pointe-à-Pitre, the country folk here are still sweet and shy, and crime is a rarity. You can see swarms of yellow butterflies, and maybe a marriage carriage festooned with flowers, pulled by two white oxen. A daughter of the sea, Marie-Galante has some of the archipelago's most gorgeous, uncrowded beaches. Take time to explore the dramatic coast. You can find soaring cliffs—such as the Gueule Grand Gouffre (Mouth of the Giant Chasm) and Les Galeries (where the sea has sculpted a natural arcade)—and enormous sun-dappled grottos, such as Le Trou à Diable, whose underground river can be explored with a guide. Port Louis, the island's "second city," is the new hip spot. The ferry dock is

COMPETITIONS DES BOEUFS TIRANTS

The annual ox-pulling competitions on Marie-Galante go on for two weeks in November. Oxen were used for the sugar mills and still power the agriculture. Where else will you see this in your lifetime?

in Port Louis, and it's also on the charts for yachts and regattas. After sunset, the no-see-ums and mosquitoes can be a real irritation, so always be armed with repellent.

Château Murat. The Château Murat is a restored 18th-century sugar plantation and rum distillery housing exhibits on the history of rum making and sugarcane production and an admirable *ecomusée*, whose displays celebrate local crafts and customs. Just a mile from town, it's open daily from 9:15 to 5; admission is free. ⊠ *Rte. de Capesterre, Grand-Bourg, Marie-Galante* ☎ *0590/97–94–41*

Rhumeries Agricoles de Bellevue–"Rum Domaine de Bellevue". If time allows just one distillery, choose the modern, nonpolluting Domaine de Bellevue. Free tastings are just one inviting element here. There are award-winning, pure rums (50%–59%); excellent tropical liqueurs (punches); coffee-table books; and local organic products. Down from the windmill is a fascinating ecoboutique with everything made from natural materials such as calabash gourds. ⊠ *Section Bellvue, Capesterre, Marie-Galante* ☎ *0590/97–47–11* ⊡ *Free* ⊙ *9:30–1.*

Le Moulin de Bézard. Le Moulin de Bézard is reputedly the only rebuilt windmill in the Caribbean. Two gift shops and a café are housed in reproductions of slave quarters with wattle walls. ⊠ *Chemin de Nesmond, off D 202(follow the signs), Marie-Galante* ⊡ *€4* ⊙ *daily 10–2..*

Distillerie Poisson "Rhum du Père Labat." The Poisson Distillery produces rum (nearly 200,000 liters a year) that is considered some of the finest in the Caribbean, and its atelier turns out lovely pottery. Tasting is possible. Drivers be aware—the samples of the libations here are quite strong. ⊠ *Section Poisson, Grand-Bourg, Marie-Galante* ☎ *0590/97–03–79* ⊡ *Free* ⊙ *Mon.–Sat., 7 am–noon* ⊠ *Marie-Galante.*

WHERE TO EAT

Creole cooking is the result of a fusion of influences: African, European, Indian, and Caribbean. It's colorful, spicy, and made up primarily of local seafood and vegetables (including squashlike christophenes), root vegetables, and plantains, always with a healthy dose of pepper sauce. Favorite appetizers include *accras* (salted codfish fritters), *boudin* (highly seasoned blood sausage), and *crabes farcis* (stuffed land crabs). *Langouste* (lobster), *lambi* (conch), *chatrou* (octopus), and *ouassous*

Looking out over Marie-Galante

(crayfish) are considered delicacies. *Souchy* (Tahitian-style ceviche), raw fish that is "cooked" when marinated in lime juice or similar marinades, is best at seafront restaurants. *Moules et frites* (mussels in broth served with fries) can be found at cafés in Gosier and Bas du Fort Marina. Also in the marina is Rôtisseur des Isles, with aromatic roasted meats, a salad bar, and classic French desserts. Many of the most contemporary gastronomic restaurants are in Jarry, a commercial area near Pointe-à-Pitre. All restaurants and bars are smoke-free, as decreed by French law.

Diverse culinary options range from pizza and crepes to Indian cuisine. For a quick and inexpensive meal, visit a *boulangerie,* where you can buy luscious French pastries and simple baguette sandwiches. Look for the recommendable chain Délifrance, too. Good news: menu prices seem high but include tax and service (which is split among the entire staff). If service is to your liking, be generous and leave some extra euros, and they will think of Americans as "the good guys." In most restaurants in Guadeloupe (as throughout the Caribbean), lobster is the most expensive item on the menu. It can easily top €40 and often comes as part of a prix-fixe menu; *price ranges for the restaurants listed in this chapter do not include lobster for this reason.*

What to Wear: Dining is casual at lunch, but beach attire is a no-no except at the more laid-back marina and beach eateries. Dinner is slightly more formal. Long pants, collared shirts, and skirts or dresses are appreciated, although not required. Guadeloupean ladies like to "dress," particularly on weekends, so don't arrive in flip-flops—they'll be in heels.

STILL WATERS

Guadeloupe has some of the best-tasting mountain water in the Caribbean isles, but you'll rarely see anyone drinking it out of the tap (*robinet*). Some say that is because the city pipes are rusty, others that they can taste the chlorine. At restaurants, the server will usually ask if you want a bottle of water, and if so, what kind: *plat?* (pronounced plah, meaning "still"). Say *"Oui, Capes"* to request the main island brand.

You'll pay €3 to €4 for a big bottle (1½ liter), half the price of Evian. In your hotel minibar, a small bottle may cost that much. Stop at a gas station, minimart, or supermarche and buy the big ones for anywhere from €0.70 to €1.50. Or join the new movement to help save the environment by not using plastic bottles, and at restaurants ask for *une carafe d'eau du robinet*. Is it safe? Guadeloupe sells water to all the big ships.

GRANDE-TERRE

$$ ╳ **Caraïbes Café.** This sidewalk café straight out of Paris is the "in" place
CAFÉ for lunch and also a spot for a quick breakfast, a fresh juice cocktail—try *corossel* (a tropical fruit) and mango juices, a cappuccino, *un coupe* (a sundae), or a *pastis* while you people-watch and listen to French crooners. The *formule* (fixed-price menu) is always the best deal. Service is fast and friendly and can even be in English. ⑤ *Average main: €15* ⊠ *Pl. de la Victoire, Pointe-à-Pitre, Grande-Terre* ☎ *0590/82–92–23* ⊘ *Closed Sun. No dinner.*

$$$ ╳ **Iguane Café.** Iguanas are indeed the theme here, and you can spy them
CAFÉ in unexpected places—juxtaposed with antique cherubs and driftwood
Fodor's Choice mirrors. The salon seating for cocktails has a residential feel, with bas-
★ ket-weave rattan furniture and hot-pink accent pillows. Unquestionably original cuisine with Asian, Indian, and African influences is chef Sylvain Serouart's trademark. The menu is always evolving, yet some innovations don't always taste quite as good as they look. There is always a wonderful foie gras appetizer—a favorite is seared and flamed with vintage rum, served with a compote of papaya and tamarind. If it's available, move on to the melange of shellfish—scallops, shrimp, squid, clams, and mussels in a curry cream infused with chervil. Desserts are little marvels, such as the perfect dark-chocolate ganache (even better when it's part of a trio). A three-course lobster menu is €51, and a lavish menu degustation costs €79. And, yes, Iguane is a bit pricey. ⑤ *Average main: €30* ⊠ *Rte. de La Pointe des Châteaux, ½ mile (¾ km) from airport, St-François, Grande-Terre* ☎ *0590/88–61–37* ⊕ *www.iguane-cafe.com* ⊘ *Closed Tue. No lunch Mon.–Sat.*

$$$$ ╳ **La Toubana Restaurant** (*Le Gran Bleu*). Fresh lobsters, which swim
FRENCH in the canals that beautify the deck, draw many diners. The new chef prepares an impressive foie gras duo—a sauté and a torchon—paired with onion and fig compotes. The French cuisine gets a delicious Caribbean infusion, as in the fillet of *daurade* (fish) with vanilla sauce or the passion-fruit tart with meringue. The inside dining room, although open-air, has deep leather chairs, and, on occasion, a piano player and live music by pop-rock vocalists; local music is the norm on Thursday

night. You can listen whether you just "take a pop" (drink) or have dinner. Lunch patrons dine on the terrace near the infinity pool. With feet dangling in the water and an exotic cocktail in hand, you can watch the sea churn below. $ *Average main: €35* ⊠ *La Toubana Hotel & Spa, B. P. 63-Fonds Thezan, Ste-Anne, Grande-Terre* ☎ *0590/88–25–57.*

$$$ ✕ **Restaurant de la Vieille Tour.** A historic sugar mill is the backdrop for the artistic creations here, which preserve great French cuisine incorporating more recent culinary trends and local produce. The lunch menu is a mix of classic restaurant food and light fare. A "formula" is offered: a main course, a starter or dessert, a glass of wine, and coffee for €42. A créole menu is offered on Thursday and Sunday; other evenings feature a gastronomic menu. Roasted veal rib with chanterelles and seared sea scallops topped with passion-fruit butter are elegantly delicious. Desserts are dazzling, with lots of towers, sauces, and glacés. On Friday and Saturday night and Sunday morning a piano man plays. $ *Average main: €26* ⊠ *Auberge de la Vieille Tour, Rte. 1, Montauban 97, Gosier, Grande-Terre* ☎ *0590/84–23–23* ⚠ *Reservations essential.*

FRENCH
★

13

$$$ ✕ **Les Portes des Indes.** Dining here is truly a departure: the open-air pergola, the blue gates, the pungent aromas, and the bust of Ganesha. Within the paisley-covered menu you can find authentic creole dishes alongside such innovations as boneless chicken with crème fraîche, almonds, and raisins. Children may fill up on the addictive Indian cheese bread and be too stuffed for *kulfi,* Indian ice cream topped with ginger confit. The welcome here is always warm and the service dignified. Consistently good, its perennial popularity means that on weekends you really should make reservations. $ *Average main: €30* ⊠ *Desvarieux, St-François, Grande-Terre* ☎ *0590/21–30–87* ☉ *Closed mid-Sept.–mid-Oct. and Mon. No lunch Tues.–Sat. No dinner Sun.*

INDIAN
★

$$ ✕ **Zawag.** At this secret hideaway you'll see the churning sea below and hear the waves crashing against the coral rock upon which it sits. The interior architecture is all hardwood with matching furniture and white linen napkins. Primarily a grill, the simplicity is reflected in the food offerings. Kids are particularly fascinated when the lobster net is dipped into the tank and the thrashing begins. The fish of the night is fresh from the waters below, often accompanied by creole or tropical-fruit sauces. Creole dishes and sides are being gently contemporized by the French chef and offered as nightly specials. Depending on the season, Zawag is sometimes closed on Sunday. $ *Average main: €18* ⊠ *La Créole Beach Hotel & Spa, Pointe de la Verdure, Gosier, Grande-Terre* ☎ *0590/90–46–66* ⚠ *Reservations essential* ☉ *No lunch.*

SEAFOOD

BASSE-TERRE

$$$ ✕ **Le Rocher de Malendure.** Guests first climb the worn yellow stairs for the panoramic sea views, but return again and again for the food. If you arrive before noon, when the divers pull in, you might snag one of the primo tables in a gazebo that literally hangs over the Caribbean. Begin with a perfectly executed mojito. With fish just off the boat, don't hesitate to try the sushi *antillaise* or grilled crayfish and lobster from the pool. $ *Average main: €25* ⊠ *Bord de Mer, Malendure de*

FRENCH
★

Pigeon, Bouillante, Basse-Terre ☎ *0590/98–70–84* ⊘ *Closed Wed. and Sept.–early Oct.*

ILES DES SAINTES

$$
CAFÉ

✕ **Couleurs du Monde.** New arrivals from the ferries and those waiting to depart are immediately attracted to this second-floor, waterfront café–cum–art gallery. Under the green canopy, it's shades of Greenwich Village, with books and newspapers, teas and coffees, wine, and icy rum cocktails. Contemporary art, primarily from Didier Spindler, lines the walls, there for the buying, and some fab glassware adorns the tables. Global fare is featured, and now there is just a prix-fixe menu for €25 (€11 for children). Sushi, smoked-fish plates, and smoked duck salad often appear. The catch of the day with an exotic sauce is a wise choice. After sunset there are aperitifs, and although reservations are requested for dinner, the friendly, accommodating staff will take walk-ins. Finish off with the house-made Punch du Monde. Ⓢ *Average main: €25* ✉ *Main dock, Terre-de-Haut, Iles des Saintes* ☎ *0590/92–70–98* ⊘ *Closed Tues., Wed., and Sept.*

$$
ECLECTIC

✕ **L'Auberge les Petits Saints aux Anarcadiers Restaurant.** Owners Mireille and Pierre strive to create a cuisine that uses local products to flavor recipes from different parts of the world—especially French, Mediterranean, and creole dishes. The menu is more elaborate now, thanks to the new chef's recipes, which are still very much anchored in the island's offerings. The owners insist on top-grade prime rib and superior-quality duck for the confit with pineapple sauce. The fresh grilled lobster here is famous and is priced per gram. The chef is remarkably inventive with lambi (conch) and the local vegetables. Contemporary dinnerware brought from France complements the updated menu and presentation. And as is fashionable in France, you can order a sampling of appetizers that includes the island's smoked fish and tartares. Fresh fish is always a good choice, especially with curry sauce. Mireille has put a lot of effort into the wine menu, and now there is a full range of aged rums. For the finale, there is a generous selection of dazzling, house-made desserts. Service is on the veranda, where the night sounds of the tropics vie with jazz and sexy French *musique*. A separate children's menu is offered as well. Ⓢ *Average main: €20* ✉ *L'Auberge les Petits Saints aux Anarcadiers, La Savane, Terre-de-Haut, Iles des Saintes* ☎ *0590/99–50–99* ⚇ *Reservations essential* ⊘ *Closed Mon. and Sept. No lunch.*

$$$
CONTEMPORARY

✕ **Gran Kaz.** This small, convivial waterfront restaurant has a lot to recommend—it's artsy, with contemporary originals, hanging plants, hip music, and a talented chef-owner, Philippe Dade. Brochettes are the popular items, due to their dramatic presentation. Metal skewers of beef, lamb, and shrimp or ouassous are hooked to what looks like a hangmen's scaffold, and are accompanied by two sauces—chien and passion fruit—plus authentic *pomme frites. Le choucroute de la mer* has fish, scallops, and mussels in a bath of white wine. The pouffed marvel—a mango soufflé with raspberry coulis—must be ordered in advance. Ⓢ *Average main: €22* ✉ *Lô Bleu Hôtel, Fond de Curé, Terre-de-Haut, Iles des Saintes* ☎ *0590/92–40–00, 0590/99–57–63* ⊘ *Closed Mon. and Wed.*

MARIE-GALANTE

It's not gastronomic, but L'Ornata has the bay-front location if you're catching the ferry and don't want to chance missing it. Grab a cold one or a rich, tropical sundae. It serves three squares a day (cheap) and will have breakfast when you disembark.

$$ ✕**Chez Henri.** This hip place on the water, flanked by the town pier, is
CARIBBEAN named for its passionate chef–owner, Henri Vergerolle. An island character, he spent much of his life in France and returned to create this restaurant–cum–cultural center. Begin with a rum and fresh-squeezed juice. Smoked fish can be a component of a salad or an appetizer; interestingly, the creole omelet is an app, too. It's quite an original, with breadfruit and sweet potatoes. Another innovation is the fish of the day with a Caribe sauce. Kick back and listen to African blues (sometimes live) and view the latest art or sculpture exhibits. $ *Average main: €17* ✉ *8 rue des Caraibes, St. Louis, Marie Galante, Marie-Galante* ☎ *0590/97–04–57* ⊕ *www.chezhenri.net* ☾ *Closed Mon. No lunch Tues.–Thurs. during low season (Sept.–early Oct.).*

$$ ✕**Le Touloulou.** On the curve of Plage de Petite-Anse, this ultracasual
SEAFOOD eatery has tables in the sand. *Merci* to Hurricane Dean, a major renovation has it born again. Chef José Viator serves the freshest seafood; his standout dish just might be fricassee of conch or octopus with breadfruit. Set menus start at €20-something, and a simple, fresh lobster prix-fixe is just €30. For lunch, the best value is the *formule rapid*. Both the chicken and ouassous (jumbo crayfish) in coconut sauce are exceptional. And on Saturday and Sunday the creole brunch (from 11 to 4) is particularly celebratory. Pergola's, the circular bar, has the best in rum cocktails to sip while contemplating the sun's descent. At night the anteroom is a dance club, with salsa lessons on Friday and a disco beat on Saturday. $ *Average main: €18* ✉ *Plage de Petite-Anse, Capesterre, Marie-Galante* ☎ *0590/97–32–63* ⊕ *www.letouloulou.com* ☾ *Closed Mon. and mid-Sept.–mid-Oct. No dinner Sun.*

$$ ✕**Sun7Beach Bar Restaurant & Bungalows.** Sit with your feet in the sand
SEAFOOD and an icy Desperados Red (beer) in your hand and watch the sunsets turn the sky pink. Drinks and their prices are *veddy* potable here. Segue into dinner at this whimsical, colorful beach bar–restaurant that also has two simple bungalows (€40). Chef Gilbert, a Marie-Galantais, has fresh lobsters for €28; lambi (conch), flavorful local dishes, and three-course prix fixes range from €20 to €25. And the bilingual French manageress, Claire, will even let you take a kayak out while it is still light out. $ *Average main: €15* ✉ *Section Murat, Grand-Bourg, Marie-Galante* ☎ *0590/97–87–58, 0690/53–70–46* ☾ *No lunch. Closed Tues.*

LA DÉSIRADE

$ ✕**Oualiri Breeze Restaurant.** With tables smack in the sand, on the cov-
CARIBBEAN ered terrace, and under a conical tent, this beachfront eatery lays out a
☾ bountiful creole buffet on Friday nights and for Sunday brunch. Both are accompanied by live entertainment. You can always grab a continental breakfast, lunch, or dinner, and customize your own €15.50 prix fixe. Seafood is the obvious specialty, particularly creole fricassees of

lambi and chatrou. Sidle up to the fieldstone bar for a perfect planter's punch, and between courses, jump into the sea. Children have their own menus and love that this is also a *glacier* (ice-cream shop) with a litany of flavors; drizzle your scoops with cajou syrup. P.S.: You can check your email here. Also, the affable, English-speaking owner, Theodore Compper, will pick you up at the dock or airport. **$** *Average main: €15* ⊠ *Plage Beausejour, Beau Sejour, Le Désirade, La Désirade* ☎ *0590/20–20–08, 0690/71–24–76* ⊕ *www.im-caraibes.com/oualiri.*

WHERE TO STAY

Most of the island's resort hotels are on Grande-Terre: Gosier, St-François, and Bas-du-Fort are generally considered major resort areas, as is Ste-Anne. With each passing year, the hotels here improve. The Swedish-owned Langley Hotel Fort Royal has breathed new life into the north of Basse-Terre, the closest area of that island to Pointe-à-Pitre and Grande-Terre.

Often, hotel rates include a generous buffet breakfast; ask whether this is included in your rate quote. Many smaller properties do not accept American Express. As dictated by French law, all public spaces in hotels are no-smoking, but hotel rooms are considered private, and properties can choose to offer smoking rooms.

For expanded reviews, facilities, and current deals, visit Fodors.com.

PRIVATE VILLAS AND RENTALS
RENTAL CONTACTS
French Caribbean International. French Caribbean International handles hotel arrangements and private villa rentals, from charming cottages in Basse-Terre ($130 to $350 a night) to deluxe sea-view villas in Grande-Terre ($2,600 to $7,000 per week), all with pools. With three decades of experience in the French Caribbean, including Les Saintes and Marie-Galante, the company has a global reputation for honesty, exceptional service, and professionalism. ☎ *800/322–22–23, 805/967–9850 in U.S.* ⊕ *www.frenchcaribbean.com.*

Nouvelles Antilles. The progressive Nouvelles Antilles, based in St-François, acts as an agent for some 30 villas around the islands, mostly luxurious. In addition, the first online travel agency dedicated to the French West Indies can book your villa or hotel accommodations, flight, rental car, and sports activities, and create a well-priced package. It deals with all the Guadeloupe isles, Martinique, St. Barth, and St. Martin, too, and can customize a multi-destination package for groups up to 15. ⊠ *St-François, Grande-Terre* ☎ *0590/85–00–00* ⊕ *www.nouvellesantilles.com.*

BASSE-TERRE
$$ 📷 **Aquarelle's Villas.** In a securely gated community on Basse-Terre's north
RENTAL coast, these 15 homes have private pools on their sundecks, and five have direct sea views. **Pros:** villas are spacious; the beach has a raw, dramatic beauty. **Cons:** beach has no chaise longues; it is a fair walk to the swimmable end. **$** *Rooms from: €326* ⊠ *1 Domaine de Nogent, Ste-Rose* ☎ *0590/68–65–23* 📠 *0590/68–38–23* ⊕ *www.aquarelles-villas.com* ⊃ *15 2- to 5-bedroom homes* ⊗ *Closed Sept. 16–Nov. 1* ⧲ *No meals.*

$ 　　　⊞ **Le Neem.** These three attractive gites, or suites, have spicy names—
RENTAL　Vanille, Safron, and Canela (cinnamon), and that is the order of preference. **Pros:** fine beach just across the street; gites are newly built (2009);
owning couple are caring, and wife, Ancette, speaks *Anglais*. **Cons:** no
space between suites; no views; no hotel amenities. ⑤ *Rooms from:*
€100 ⊠ Rte. de la Pointe des Chateaux, Grande-Terre ⊕ www.leneem.
fr ⌁ 3 suites ¦⊙¦ Breakfast.

ILES DES SAINTES

$ 　　　⊞ **Residence Anse Caraibe.** This large residence, perched on a hill five
RENTAL　minutes from town, houses six apartments, from a studio to a three-
bedroom flat. **Pros:** English-speaking, French manager (Catherine Vogli-
macci), who can even arrange transportation on the mainland; two
apartments open onto spacious, private terraces that look to the bay;
all can be rented by the night (three-night minimum in high season,
two in low season) or week(s). **Cons:** no phones; steep hill; no cushy,
creature comforts. ⑤ *Rooms from: €50 ⊠ Emmanuel Laurent St., Terre*
de Haut ⊕ www.grandbaie.com ⌁ 4 studio apartments, 1 2-bedroom
apartment, 1 3-bedroom apartment ¦⊙¦ No meals.

$$ 　　⊞ **Villa Dao.** Ideally located smack on the bay and a five-minute walk
RENTAL　from the center of the town, this premium, four-bedroom house has a
high-tech kitchen, and each of the master bedrooms (two with water
views) are artfully decorated with reds and greens and fanciful objets
d'art. **Pros:** Living room can be totally opened to the sea or secured by
a push-button wall; a luxurious, hip cottage is ideal for teenagers or
children and their nannies. **Cons:** manager does not speak English but
translates and answers emails in English; doesn't have the full services
and amenities of a boutique hotel; no telephones (but Wi-Fi). ⑤ *Rooms*
from: €320 ⊠ 88–90 rue Benoit Cassin, Terre-de-Haut, Iles des Saintes
⊕ www.ker-iguane.com ⌁ 4 bedrooms, 4 baths ¦⊙¦ No meals.

RECOMMENDED HOTELS AND RESORTS

GRANDE-TERRE

$$$ 　⊞ **Auberge de la Vieille Tour.** An island classic fashioned around a his-
HOTEL　toric sugar mill, this hotel consistently renews itself. **Pros:** most rooms
Fodor'sChoice　have great views; breakfast (included) is a highlight; restaurant is one
★　of the island's best. **Cons:** expensive; exteriors of some sections are
unattractive 1960s style; it's a hill climb back from the pool and the
beach. **TripAdvisor:** "heaven on Earth," "pleasantly surprised," "clean
and comfortable." ⑤ *Rooms from: €450 ⊠ Rte. de Montauban, Gosier,*
Grande-Terre ☎ 0590/84–23–23 ⊕ www.mgallery.com ⌁ 70 rooms, 32
deluxe rooms, 1 suite ¦⊙¦ Breakfast.

$ 　　　⊞ **Bwa Chik Hotel & Golf.** This eco-chic, boutique hotel at the marina is
HOTEL　the buzz in St. François. **Pros:** ideal location; car unnecessary; welcoming staff; live jazz nights. **Cons:** no restaurant; pool was not renovated.
TripAdvisor: "Bwa chic," "impeccable," "great location." ⑤ *Rooms*
from: €146 ⊠ Ave. de l'Europe, St-François, Grande-Terre ☎ 0590/88–
60–60 ⊕ www.bwachik.com ⌁ 43 rooms, 11 duplexes.

13

$$$
ALL-INCLUSIVE
☼
★

🏨 **Club Med La Caravelle.** Facing one of the island's best white-sand beaches, La Caravelle, one of the oldest resorts in the Caribbean, is noted for its water sports. **Pros:** Internet café; exceptional boutique; good service. **Cons:** Club Med experience is not to everyone's taste; older standard rooms are small; kid-friendly atmosphere not for everyone. **TripAdvisor:** "sublime," "fab staff," "very French." ⑤ *Rooms from:* €392 ⊠ *Quartier Caravelle, Ste-Anne, Grande-Terre* ☎ *0590/85–49–50, 800/258–2633* ⊕ *www.clubmed.us* ⟲ *297 rooms, 37 suites* ⊙ *Sept.–early Nov.* ⊚ *All-inclusive.*

$
RESORT

🏨 **Hotel Eden Palm.** Set away from the tourist zones, this resort is brimming with sophisticated French style. **Pros:** known for its entertainment; front desk staff is efficient and genuinely caring; lovely Balinese poolside beds. **Cons:** you can't see the beach; beds take up a lot of the guest-room space. ⑤ *Rooms from:* €195 ⊠ *Lieu dit Le Helleux, Ste-Anne, Grande-Terre* ☎ *0590/88–48–48* ⊕ *www.edenpalm.com* ⟲ *57 rooms, 2 suites* ⊚ *Breakfast.*

$
B&B/INN

🏨 **Hotel Amaudo.** This *hotel de charme* is a small *madam-et-monsieur* operation, the mom 'n' pop being the sophisticated French managers. **Pros:** a moderate price tag for unobstructed sea views; safe (mechanized security gate). **Cons:** you need a car, as it is not in the tourist zone of St-François; no bar, restaurant or activities; could be too quiet and peaceful. **TripAdvisor:** "great view and service," "nice people," "wonderful management." ⑤ *Rooms from:* €130 ⊠ *Anse à la Barque, St-François, Grande-Terre* ☎ *0590/88–87–00* ⊕ *www.amaudo.fr* ⟲ *10 rooms* ⊚ *Breakfast.*

$$
HOTEL

🏨 **La Cocoteraie.** This boutique hotel, with its lobby of basket-weave rattan furnishings, decorative masks, and walls of burnt orange is a study in refinement. **Pros:** by a calm lagoon; sophisticated clientele; great, international crowd and light fare at the Indigo Bar. **Cons:** generic, white-plastic furniture on terraces; aqua tiles segue abruptly to red tiles. **TripAdvisor:** "the absolute best for accommodations," "Caribbean bliss meets French panache," "relaxing." ⑤ *Rooms from:* €230 ⊠ *Av. de l'Europe, St-François, Grande-Terre* ☎ *0590/88–79–81* ⊕ *www.lacocoteraie.com* ⟲ *50 suites* ⊙ *Closed late Aug.–mid Oct.* ⊚ *Breakfast.*

$$
RESORT
★

🏨 **La Créole Beach Hotel & Spa.** This 10-acre complex has a contemporary, colorful lobby, cosmopolitan bar, and the oversize rooms and ocean-view suites at Les Palms resemble those on a teak-appointed yacht. **Pros:** excellent management and long-term staff; exceptionally good buffets (upgraded by the French chef); lovely tropical gardens. **Cons:** guest rooms vary in quality; some rooms quite a hike from lobby; beach is nice but small. **TripAdvisor:** "perfect location," "nice beach and swimming pool," "great food." ⑤ *Rooms from:* €230 ⊠ *Pointe de la Verdure, Gosier, Grande-Terre* ☎ *0590/90–46–46* ⊕ *www.deshotelsetdesiles.com* ⟲ *353 rooms, 15 junior suites, 6 suites, 13 apartments* ⊚ *No meals.*

$$
RESORT
Fodor'sChoice
★

🏨 **La Toubana Hôtel & Spa.** Few hotels on Guadeloupe command such a panoramic view of the sea—spanning four islands, no less. **Pros:** a special place with sophisticated style; glass-enclosed cocktail lounge-library has remarkable views; restaurant continues to evolve and to earn praise; meal plans are available. **Cons:** the little beach is down the

La Toubana Hotel & Spa

hill by a paved path that's very steep; bedrooms are small by American standards. **TripAdvisor:** "charming," "small and beautiful," "hidden treasure." ⑤ *Rooms from: €304 ⊠ Ste-Anne, Grande-Terre ☎ 0590/88–25-57 ⊕ www.toubana.com ⇨ 32 bungalows, 1 suite* �‖*Breakfast.*

BASSE-TERRE

$

B&B/INN

☺

⊞ Caraib Bay Hotel. This complex of colorful duplex bungalows may not initially impress, but its admirable customer-satisfaction award backed up by the buzz on the street makes you want to book in. **Pros:** homey feel with multilingual library; moderate prices; innovative bar and flavorful creole specialties by night. **Cons:** good, long beach, but it's down and across the highway; not luxe. **TripAdvisor:** "pure paradise," "wonderful ambience," "charming and friendly." ⑤ *Rooms from: €156 ⊠ Allée du Cour, Ziotte, Deshaies, Basse-Terre ☎ 0590/28–41-71 ⊕ www.caraib-bay-hotel.com ⇨ 56 rooms, 3 villas* �‖*Breakfast.*

$

RESORT

☺

⊞ Langley Hotel Fort Royal. The island's Swedish connection is a major redo of a 1970s seafront high-rise with the addition of conical bungalows (14 beachfront). **Pros:** nearly all is nearly new; nonguests can sample the fun by paying €10 for a beach chaise or enjoying the sail and surf club; free Internet. **Cons:** not all hotel rooms have a sea view; beach is narrow; bungalows are petite. **TripAdvisor:** "friendly staff," "romantic location," "great beach and excellent service." ⑤ *Rooms from: €155 ⊠ Petit Bas Vent, Deshaies, Basse-Terre ☎ 0590/68–76-70 ⊕ www.fortroyal.eu ⇨ 126 rooms, 7 suites, 82 bungalows ⊗ Sept.–Oct.* �‖*Breakfast.*

Le Jardin de Malanga

$
B&B/INN
Fodor's Choice
★

 Le Jardin de Malanga. At this former coffee plantation, trees laden with fruit are like the temptations of the Garden of Eden. **Pros:** a romantic hideaway with history and character; superior cuisine (half-board is recommendable); signage and website directions greatly improved. **Cons:** still not easy to find and best navigated by day; no TV; the nearest beach is 20 minutes away by car. **TripAdvisor:** "lovely atmosphere," "authenticity and nature," "friendly welcoming staff." ⑤ *Rooms from: €265 ⌗ #60, Route de L'Hermitage, Hermitage, Trois-Rivières, Basse-Terre ☎ 0590/92–67–57 ⊕ www.deshotelsetdesiles.com ➽ 9 rooms, 1 suite* ⑩ *Breakfast.*

$$
B&B/INN

Tainos Cottages. Now *this* is a story: a globe-trotting Frenchman designed seven teakwood cottages resembling Guadeloupean *cases* from the 1920s, had them constructed in Indonesia, and imported the cottages to a site overlooking Plage de Grande-Anse. **Pros:** summer rates drop by half; get a discount by booking online; great long beach with no other commercial development. **Cons:** insects, particularly mosquitoes, are a drawback (but they use American mosquito traps that kill them outside the room); most rooms are open-air. **TripAdvisor:** "great place to unwind," "romantic," "exotic and relaxing." ⑤ *Rooms from: €300 ⌗ Plage de Grande-Anse, Deshaies, Basse-Terre ☎ 0590/28–44–42 ⊕ www.tainoscottages.com ➽ 7 bungalows ⊙ Closed mid-Aug.–mid-Oct.* ⑩ *Breakfast.*

ILES DES SAINTES

$
B&B/INN
★

L'Auberge les Petits Saints aux Anarcadiers. Fashionably eccentric, fun couples, hip families, and serious Caribbeanophiles gravitate to this charismatic inn. **Pros:** cool vibe, reminiscent of the island guesthouses of the 1970s; village just down the hill; free Wi-Fi. **Cons:** do not expect luxury, though improvements continue. **TripAdvisor:** "very tranquil," "where time stops," "great hosts." Ⓢ *Rooms from: €150* ⊠ *La Savane, Terre-de-Haut, Iles des Saintes* ☎ *0590/99–50–99* ⊕ *www.petitssaints. com* ⌨ *3 bungalows, 3 suites, 2 studios, 2 rooms* ☉ *Closed Sept.* �"⊙" *Breakfast.*

$ 🏨 **Lô Bleu Hôtel.** This cheerful hotel is painted sunset orange with marine-
HOTEL blue trim; dramatic nightlights illuminate the beach area, which is furnished with chaises and cushy Fatboys. **Pros:** smack on the bay; large front rooms with sea view and balconies; hip music; family-friendly with baby monitors and some bunk beds. **Cons:** no beautiful grounds; no resort amenities; the "front desk" does not always speak English. **TripAdvisor:** "very relaxing," "comfortable with a beautiful view," "tranquil." Ⓢ *Rooms from: €136* ⊠ *Fond de Curé, Terre-de-Haut, Iles des Saintes* ☎ *0590/92–40–00, 0690/63–80–36* ⊕ *www.lobleuhotel. com* ⌨ *10 rooms* �"⊙" *Breakfast.*

$ 🏨 **Paradis Saintois.** You'll feel like the king of the hill as you rock yourself
RENTAL to sleep in your hammock while gazing down on the Caribbean below. **Pros:** good fun quotient (even petanque); super managers; radio/CD/ mp3 players in all units; TVs in apartments and some studios. **Cons:** no phones or TVs in some rooms; a hike up the hill from town (15 minutes). Ⓢ *Rooms from: €70* ⊠ *211 Rte. des Pres Cassin, B. P. I., Terre-de-Haut, Iles des Saintes* ☎ *0590/99–56–16* ⊕ *www.ParadisSaintois. com* ⌨ *5 apartments, 3 studios, 1 room* ⛛ *No meals* ⌖ *3-night min.*

MARIE-GALANTE

Accommodations here run the gamut from inexpensive, locally owned beachfront bungalows to complexes with international owners.

$ 🏨 **Kawann Beach Hotel.** Marie Galante's only full-service hotel (formerly
HOTEL La Cohoba) reopened with a battery of sustainable-tourism features, and it's attracting ecoconscious travelers. **Pros:** professional French manager; ecoshop Atelier Nature; lovely pool with center island. **Cons:** simple accommodations still need new soft furnishings and décor, which are promised by summer 2012; cannot see beach from the rooms or pool. Ⓢ *Rooms from: €136* ⊠ *Folle Anse near St. Louis, Marie-Galante* ☎ *0590/97–50–50* ⌨ *100 suites* ☉ *Closed Sept.* ⛛ *Breakfast.*

NIGHTLIFE

Guadeloupeans maintain that the beguine began here, and for sure, the beguine and mazurkas were heavily influenced by the European quadrille and orchestrated melodies. Their merging is the origin of West Indian music, and it gave birth to zouk (music with an African-influenced Caribbean rhythm) at the beginning of the 1980s. Still the rage here, it has spread not only to France but to other European countries. Many resorts have dinner dancing or offer regularly scheduled entertainment by steel bands and folkloric groups.

Centre des Arts. The island's performing arts scene is centered on the Centre des Arts, where each season is more exciting than the last. Here you'll find exceptional jazz and blues concerts, musical comedies, and even art exhibitions. Hip-hop artists, break-dancers, and classical musicians have all performed here. Prices are democratic. Ask for the special deals. ⊠ *Pl. des Martyrs de la Liberté, Pointe-à-Pitre, Grande-Terre* ☎ *0590/82–79–78.*

BARS AND NIGHTCLUBS

Club Med. Club Med sells night passes (6 pm–2 am) that include all cocktails, dinner with wine, and a show in the theater, followed by admission to the disco. Passes cost €65; go on Friday (€75) for the gala dinner and the most creative show. It's a super option for single women, who will feel comfortable and safe at the disco, where there are plenty of fun staffers (G.O.s) willing to be dance partners. ⊠ *Quartier Caravelle, Ste-Anne, Grande-Terre* ☎ *0590/85–49–50* ☉ *Closed Sept.–early Nov.*

La Créole Beach Hotel & Spa. Something is always happening at the Créole Beach Hotel. The entertainment is often bands playing beguine and zouk, or a piano man, all of which are very danceable. The group of native dancers and the tom-tom drummers is exciting. ⊠ *Pointe de la Verdure, Gosier, Grande-Terre* ☎ *0590/90–46–46.*

★ **Le Bar at Auberge de la Vieille Tour.** Nightly entertainment (in high season) at Auberge de la Vieille Tour ranges from the talented piano man to jazz combos (Friday and Saturday only in low season). The atmospheric piano bar with its planter's chairs and whirring fan blades is as memorable as Rick's Café in *Casablanca.* Accras and munchies generally arrive with your cocktails. New is a selection of tapas and an extensive menu of rums that gives their histories and even offers flights. ⊠ *Rte. de Montauban, Gosier, Grande-Terre* ☎ *0590/84–23–23.*

Eden Palm Theater. The jazzed-up Eden Palm Theater presents a Cuban-influenced Caribbean musical review on Saturday nights. The spectacle—like nothing else on the island—has plumage, imaginative costumes, a super sound system, special effects, a bevy of dancers, even trapeze artists. The cost is €60 for an aperitif, dinner, wine, and a show. The multicourse dinner is Franco-Caribbean cuisine, and the new chef is innovative. The fast-moving, grand spectacle is celebratory; holidays like New Year's Eve are major happenings here (and are priced higher). ⊠ *Hotel Eden Palm, Lieu-dit le Helleux, Ste-Anne, Grande-Terre* ☎ *0590/88–48–48.*

Hemingway Restaurant & Lounge. Hemingway Restaurant & Lounge is the buzzword that is becoming synonymous with live music, dancing, and nightlife. It is another indicator that northern Basse-Terre is on a roll. A typical lineup is as follows: Friday night, "jazz fever"; Saturday, a tropical show with emcee and orchestra; Sunday, a buffet lunch and stellar live music with dancing on the dock overlooking the bay. Bring a swimsuit and snorkel. ⊠ *Chemin de la Batterie, Domaine Pointe Batterie, Deshaies, Basse-Terre* ☎ *0590/28–57–17* ⊕ *www.hemingway-restaurant.com.*

Zoo Rock Café. Hot spot Zoo Rock Café is a bar, a *rhumerie* (rum distillery), a restaurant, and a café where live music concerts happen. Theme nights are a house party, be it Havana night or Halloween; the crowd is young and mostly French from the Metropole. Open nightly, this place has a real sense of humor. ⊠ *La Marina Gosier, Gosier* ☎ *0590/90–77–77* ⊕ *www.zoorockcafe.com.*

CASINOS

Both of the island's casinos are on Grande-Terre and have American-style roulette, blackjack, and stud poker. The legal age for gambling is 18, and French law dictates that everyone show a passport, or for locals, a driver's license. Jacket and tie aren't required, but "proper attire" means no shorts, T-shirts, jeans, flip-flops, or sneakers.

Casino de Gosier. Casino de Gosier has a bar and a cinema; a well-priced buffet restaurant is open for lunch and dinner (closed Sunday and Monday). The higher-stakes gambling is behind a closed door—you'll have to change €100 into chips to be part of that action. However, the blackjack limit is €5 and roulette just €2. It's open daily from 9 pm; slot machines open at 10 am and shut down at 3 am. It is showing signs of age, but locals love it and jam the parking lot on weekends. The bar can really crank up on Saturday nights or holidays, with sexy island girls in brief silver lamé costumes dispensing free champagne. Local bands can add to the energy. ⊠ *#43 Pointe de la Vedure, Gosier, Grande-Terre* ☎ *0590/84–79–68.*

Casino de St-François. Casino de St-François, although petite, has a contemporary élan that makes you want to dress up and come on out. There's a dramatic water installation, leather furniture, and a small, appealing restaurant, Le Joker (à la carte, or €25 prix fixe with wine), with a piano bar and a stage for performers, which also doubles as a disco on Friday and Saturday. The lighting, installed by Martinique's MPA architectural firm, can project one or multiple colors, depending on the desired mood. It is truly a handsome showplace, and there are some 85 slots, as well as American roulette and gaming tables (stud poker, blackjack, etc.), English-speaking management (sometimes), and a parking lot. A calendar of events includes such celebrations as Oktoberfest and dance lessons. Make reservations well in advance for New Year's Eve. ⊠ *In front of golf course, near Centre Commercial, St-François, Grande-Terre* ☎ *0590/88–41–31.*

DISCOS

Night owls should note that carousing here isn't cheap. On the weekend and when there's live music, most discos charge a cover of at least €10, which might go up to as much as €20. Your cover usually includes a drink, and other drinks cost about €12 each.

Le Cheyenne. Le Cheyenne continues to draw the crowds. Look for the sculpture of a Cheyenne chief over the grand entrance. It's open every night and on weekends; there's a cover charge when the basement disco is open. With two separate sections, one caters to the young crowd—heavy on the techno—and the other is for the ageless. It has an attractive restaurant named Bora Bora that serves from 8 pm until midnight, until 2 am on *le weekend*. It offers seafood, pizza, sandwiches, and salads. The Ed Hardy by Christian Audigier Boutique is open every night. Models—gals and guys—walk the runway wearing sexy swimwear and beach togs for the stellar fashion shows. The crowds are lov-

ing it! ⊠ *Rte. de Montauban, Gosier, Grande-Terre* ☎ *0590/90–01–01*
⊕ *www.lecheyenne.com.*

SHOPPING

The island has a lot of desirable French products, from designer fashions for women and men and sensual lingerie to French china and liqueurs. As for local handicrafts, you can find attractive wood carvings, madras table linens, island dolls dressed in madras, woven straw baskets and hats, and *salakos*—fishermen's hats made of split bamboo, some covered in madras—which make great wall decorations. Of course, the favorite Guadeloupean souvenir is rum. Look for *rhum vieux*, the top of the line. For foodies, the market ladies sell aromatic fresh spices, crisscrossed with cinnamon sticks, in little baskets lined with madras.

AREAS AND MALLS

Bas-du-Fort. Bas-du-Fort's two shopping areas are the Cora Shopping Center and the marina, where there are 20 or so shops and quite a few restaurants. ⊠ *Pointe-à-Pitre, Grande-Terre.*

Destrelland. Grande-Terre's largest shopping mall, Destrelland, has more than 70 stores and is just minutes from the airport, which is a shopping destination in its own right. ⊠ *Abymes, Grande-Terre.*

Pointe-à-Pitre. In Pointe-à-Pitre you can enjoy browsing in the street stalls around the harbor quay and at the two markets (the best is the Marché de Frébault). The town's main shopping streets are rue Schoelcher, rue de Nozières, and the lively rue Frébault. At the St-John Perse Cruise Terminal there's an attractive mall with about two dozen shops. ⊠ *Pointe-à-Pitre, Grande-Terre.*

St-François. In St-François there are more than a dozen shops surrounding the marina, some selling French lingerie, swimsuits, and fashions. A supermarket has particularly good prices on French wines and cheeses, and if you pick up a fresh baguette, you'll have a picnic. (Then you can go get lost at a secluded beach.) ⊠ *St-François, Grande-Terre.*

SPECIALTY STORES

ART

Pascal Foy. Artist Pascal Foy produces stunning homages to traditional Creole architecture: paintings of houses that incorporate collage make marvelous wall hangings. As his fame has grown, his media attention has expanded, so prices have risen. You are more likely to find his mother manning the shop nowadays. ⊠ *Rte. à Pompierres, Terre-de-Haut, Iles des Saintes* ☎ *0590/99–52–29.*

CLOTHING

Côté Plage. In addition to T-shirts and other ideal island necessities, Côté Plage sells bikinis, sundresses, and straw beach totes. There's also a line of simple jewelry—turtles, geckos, and sea horses—made of sand and

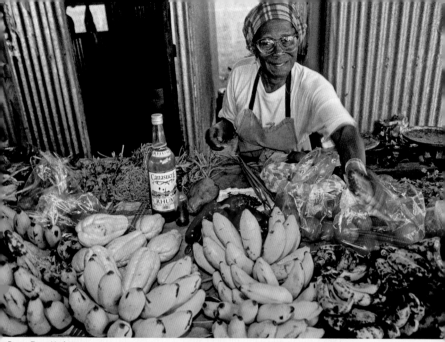

Basse-Terre Market

resin. It is located directly across from the produce market. ✉ *Pl. du Marché, Pointe-à-Pitre, Grande-Terre* ☎ *No phone.*

Dody. Across from the market, Dody is the place to go if you want white eyelet (blouses, skirts, dresses, even bustiers). The shop has a high-quality designer line, but you will pay €100 to €300 for a single piece. There's lots of madras, too, which is especially cute in children's clothing. ✉ *31 rue Frébault, Pointe-à-Pitre, Grande-Terre* ☎ *0590/82–18–59.*

Le Gall. Le Gall handles a line of fashionable resort wear for women and children, designed by French painter Jean Claude Le Gall, that has hand-painted figures like turtles and dolphins on high-quality cotton knits. There are several other branches of this French favorite across the island, at the Bas-du-Fort Marina and even on Les Saintes. A gift from this store is considered prestigious in the Motherland. ✉ *La Marina–La Coursive, St-François, Grande-Terre* ☎ *0590/88–69–40 No phone.*

COSMETICS AND PERFUME

Au Bonheur des Dames. In addition to its own perfumes, Au Bonheur des Dames sells several different lines of cosmetics and skin-care products. ✉ *49 rue Frébault, Pointe-à-Pitre, Grande-Terre* ☎ *0590/82–00–30.*

L'Artisan Parfumeur. You'll find top French and American brands as well as tropical scents at L'Artisan Parfumeur. ✉ *Centre St-John Perse, Pointe-à-Pitre, Grande-Terre* ☎ *0590/83–80–25.*

L'Atelier du Savon. L'Atelier du Savon makes all of its soaps from vegetable products, with scents including marine spice and mandarin orange. Beautifully packaged gift baskets include bath salts and aromatic oils. You never know when the sign: "Closed today, we are making soap," will go up. ⊠ *Impasse du Mouillage, near the pharmacy on rue Jean Calot, Terre-de-Haut, Iles des Saintes* ☎ *0590/99–56–24.*

Phoenicia. When you walk into Phoenicia and breathe in, the scents will trigger a sensual response. The shop's three locations mainly sell French perfumes. ⊠ *Bas-du-Fort, Grande-Terre* ☎ *0590/90–85–56* ⊠ *8 rue Frébault, Pointe-à-Pitre, Grande-Terre* ☎ *0590/83–50–36* ⊠ *121 bis rue Frébault, Pointe-à-Pitre, Grande-Terre* ☎ *0590/82–25–75.*

Vendôme. Guadeloupe's exclusive purveyor of Stendhal and Germaine Monteil cosmetics is Vendôme. ⊠ *8–10 rue Frébault, Pointe-à-Pitre, Grande-Terre* ☎ *0590/83–42–84.*

HANDICRAFTS

Centre Artisanat. The Centre Artisanat offers a wide selection of local crafts, including art composed of shells, wood, and stone. One of the outlets sells authentic Panama hats. It is located under a tent across from the waterfront as you first drive into the village. ⊠ *Ste-Anne, Grande-Terre* ☎ *No phone.*

★ **Madras Bijoux.** Madras Bijoux specializes in replicas of authentic Creole jewelry; it also creates custom designs and does repairs. ⊠ *115 rue Nozières, Pointe-à-Pitre, Grande-Terre* ☎ *0590/82–88–03.*

Maogany. At Maogany, the shop resembles a yacht. Artist and designer Yves Cohen, an island pioneer since 1976, has left the island for Brazil. The new owners Annie and Chakib continue to carry his batiks and clothing in luminescent seashell- and blue shades, which he continues to supply—long distance. Hand-loomed silk fabrics are embellished with gold thread; others are translucent, such as his sensual women's collection. Ladies love *pareos* (wraparound fabric for skirts) the colors of the sea, from pale green to deep turquoise, as well as the new jewelry collection. For men, there are authentic Panama hats and buccaneer shirts. Stylin' additions are the several lines of women's clothing by French designers. The shop is closed on Monday in the low season. ⊠ *26 Rue Jean Calot, Terre-de-Haut, Iles des Saintes* ☎ *0590/99–55–69, 0690/50–48–44* ⊕ *www.maogany.fr.*

LIQUOR AND TOBACCO

The airport duty-free stores have a good selection of rum and tobacco.

Délice Shop. Délice Shop is the spot for island rum and edibles from France—from cheese to chocolate. ⊠ *45 rue Achille René-Boisneuf, Pointe-à-Pitre, Grande-Terre* ☎ *0590/82–98–24.*

SPORTS AND ACTIVITIES

BIKING

The French are mad about *le cyclisme.* If you rent a bicycle, expect to be asked to leave a deposit, but the amount seems to vary; normally you can use a credit card to secure your rental. On Terre-de-Haut, there are a number of shops to the immediate left and right of the ferry dock; the farther from the dock they are, the lower the rates. And you can usually negotiate the price down—a little.

Eli Sport. On Grande-Terre, Eli Sport can set you up with a *vélo tout terrain,* or all-terrain bike. There are no children's bikes, however. The price is right at €10 a day, but reserve as far in advance as possible—or you may find yourself walking instead. ✉ *Rond Point de Grand-Camp, Grand Camp, Grande-Terre* ☎ *0590/90–37–50.*

BOATING AND SAILING

Generally speaking, most of the towns and cities of Guadeloupe are not beautiful; however, the craggy coastline and the waters of variegated blues and greens are gorgeous. If you plan to sail these waters, you should be aware that the winds and currents tend to be strong. There are excellent, well-equipped marinas in Pointe-à-Pitre, Bas-du-Fort, Deshaies, St-François, and Gourbeyre. You can rent a yacht (bareboat or crewed) from several companies. To make a bareboat charter, companies will evaluate your navigational and seamanship skills. If you do not pass, you must hire a skipper or be left on dry land.

Antilles Sail. Antilles Sail is a charter operation specializing in large, commodious catamarans from 40 to 62 feet, which can accommodate eight guests. For those who don't qualify to captain their own ship, or for those who want to just relax and be pampered, a skipper and crew can be hired. Provisioning and meal service can be arranged and VIP, dive, and other packages are available. The fleet also contains monohulls from 35 to 55 feet, which are used mainly for bareboating. Antilles Sail can actually arrange flights, lands stays, and your complete vacation package. ✉ *Bas-du-Fort Marina, Bas-du-Fort, Grande-Terre* ☎ *0590/90–16–81* ⊕ *www.antilles-sail.com.*

Sunsail. The giant yacht-rental company Sunsail has a base on Guadeloupe. Although it's primarily a bareboat operation, you can hire skippers by the week if you have limited experience, or you can get expert instruction in sailing techniques and the local waters. Windsurfers, kayaks, and kite boards can be rented, too, but these must be reserved in advance. Visit their website for special offers; online bookings are discounted 20%. ✉ *Bas-du-Fort Marina, Pointe-à-Pitre, Grande-Terre* ☎ *0590/90–92–02, 1–888/350–3568 Toll-free in U.S., 207/253–5400 in U.S.* ⊕ *www.sunsail.com.*

DIVING

The main diving area at the **Cousteau Underwater Park,** just off Basse-Terre near Pigeon Island, offers routine dives to 60 feet. The numerous glass-bottom boats and other craft make the site feel like a marine parking lot; however, the underwater sights are spectacular. Guides and instructors are certified under the French CMAS (some also have PADI, but none have NAUI). Most operators offer two-hour dives three times per day for about €45 to €50 per dive; three-dive packages are €120 to €145. Hotels and dive operators usually rent snorkeling gear.

Plaisir Plongee Karokera (PPK). Plaisir Plongee Karokera (PPK) has a good reputation and is well established among those who dive off Pigeon Island. One dive boat departs three times daily and charges €30 a dive. A second dive boat goes to Les Saintes, with two dives, one at a wreck, the other at a reef. The €85 price includes lunch. English-speaking dive masters are PADI certified. Show your Fodor's guide and ask for a discount. ⊠ *Plage de Malendure, Bouillante, Basse-Terre* ☎ *0590/98–82–43.*

☾ **Les Heures Saines.** Les Heures Saines is the premier operator for dives in the Cousteau Underwater Park. Trips to Les Saintes offer one or two dives for average and advanced divers, with plenty of time for lunch and sightseeing. Wreck, night, and Nitrox diving are also available. The instructors, many of them English speakers, are excellent with children. The company also offers winter whale- and dolphin-watching trips with marine biologists as guides. These tours, aboard a 60-foot catamaran, cost €55 (less for children). ⊠ *Le Rocher de Malendure, Plage de Malendure, Bouillante, Basse-Terre* ☎ *0590/98–86–63* ⊕ *www.heures-saines.gp.*

☾ **Pisquettes Club de Plongée Des Saintes.** With more than 10 years of experience, dive master Cedric Phalipon of Pisquettes Club de Plongée Des Saintes knows all the best sites. He gives excellent lessons, in English. Equipment is replaced frequently and is of a high caliber. Small tanks are available for kids, who are taken buddy diving. There are two PADI instructors, and an open-water, advanced PADI certificate is offered. Sec Pate is a famous underwater mountain, off the island's coast, in open seas. Les Saintes is known for its underwater hills, caves, canyons, and wall dives. Divers can see sponges of varied colors and gorgeous underwater trees that sway. ⊠ *Le Mouillage, Terre-de-Haut, Iles des Saintes* ☎ *0590/99–88–80* ⊕ *www.pisquettes.com.*

FISHING

Not far offshore from Pigeon-Bouillante, in Basse-Terre, is a bounty of big-game fish such as bonito, dolphinfish, captain fish, barracuda, kingfish, and tuna. You can also thrill to the challenge of the big billfish such as marlin and swordfish. Anglers have been known to come back with as many as three blue marlins in a single day. For Ernest Hemingway wannabes, this is it. To reap this harvest, you'll need to charter one of the high-tech sportfishing machines with flying bridges, competent skippers, and mates. The price is $430 to $600 a day, with lunch and drinks included. The boats can accommodate up to six passengers.

Centre de Peche Sportive. With a pair of state-of-the-art boats with covered fly bridges, Centre de Peche Sportive is known for success in showing anglers where to pull in the big billfish. The per-day rate is €500, and you do get your money's worth; the boat often doesn't come back until sunset, after a fine lunch and cold bevs. You can also go night fishing for swordfish, and the crew will cut the bills and fins off your catch. The company is affiliated with the restaurant Le Rocher de Malendure, which has two simple oceanfront bungalows on the cliffs—a real value for the money. ⊠ *Malendure de Pigeon, Bouillante, Basse-Terre* ☎ *0590/98–70–84.*

Michel. Michel is a reliable big-fishing charter outfit that can usually pick anglers up at their hotel and allows them to charge his fee to their hotel bills. Rates are €130 euro for each fisherman; €70 euro if someone is just coming along for the ride. The mates will be happy to take your picture with your catch of the day. ⊠ *Les Galbas, Ste-Anne, Basse-Terre* ☎ *0690/55–21–35.*

GUIDED TOURS

Le Haras de Saint-François. With Le Haras de Saint-François you can take a four-wheeler quad off road and onto the beach for two hours with a fun guide for €60. ⊠ *Chemin de la Princesse, St-François, Grande-Terre* ☎ *0690/39–90–00.*

Marius Voyages. Marius Voyages offers excursions to the southern and northern coasts of Basse-Terre; the latter includes a visit to the botanical gardens and a glass-bottom boat ride to Pigeon Island. Excursions are by land, sea, and air—everything from catamaran cruises to helicopter tours. Also, the group provides transport to the ferries for Marie-Galante and Les Saintes; you can even get to Martinique or Dominica for a couple of nights. Best of all, the company offers airport transfers to hotels in Ste-Anne and St-François at prices that beat taxi prices and can eliminate the need for a rental car. ⊠ *Main St., Ste-Anne, Grande-Terre* ☎ *0590/88–19–80.*

GOLF

Golf Municipal St-François. Golf Municipal St-François, across from La Cocoteraie hotel, is an 18-hole, par-71, Robert Trent Jones–designed course (1973). The long-awaited renovation of all 18 holes, from fairways to greens and bunkers, at a cost of €4.5 million, officially debuted in December 2010. A new clubhouse is slated for 2012. The course has an English-speaking pro, a clubhouse, a pro shop, and electric carts for rent. The greens fees are €28 for 9 holes, €43 for 18 holes. Carts rent for €26 for 9 holes, €37 for 18; chariots (pull carts) rent for €4 for 9 holes, €6 for 18 holes. There are no caddies. Clubs can be rented for about €27. The course is open daily from 7:30 am to 6 pm. It's best to reserve tee times a day or two in advance. La Cocoteraie and Bwa Chik Hotel & Golf guests enjoy a 20% discount.

Bwa Chik Hotel & Golf. Directly across from the golf course, the former Golf Marine Hotel has been transformed into a boutique hotel, renamed Bwa Chik Hotel & Golf, with surprisingly moderate rates. Recycled wood is used in the rooms and public spaces, which are decorated with contemporary wood sculpture. It's focus is on golfers, boaters, and sophisticated travelers. ☎ *0590/88–60–60* ⊕ *www.deshotelsetdesiles.com* ⊠ *St-François, Grande-Terre* ☎ *0590/88–41–87.*

HIKING

Fodor'sChoice
★
With hundreds of trails and countless rivers and waterfalls, the **Parc National de la Guadeloupe** on Basse-Terre is the main draw for hikers. Some of the trails should be attempted only with an experienced guide. All tend to be muddy, so wear a good pair of boots. Know that even the young and fit can find these outings arduous; the unfit may find

them painful. Start off slowly, with a shorter hike, and then go for the gusto. All water sports—even canoeing and kayaking—are forbidden in the center of the park. Scientists are studying the impact of these activities on the park's ecosystem. It retains its prestigious award for ongoing sustainable tourism development, given by the EUROPARC Federation, through 2012.

Les Heures Saines. A professional operation that has distinguished itself at sea, Les Heures Saines has come ashore to offer freshwater canyoning in a river outside the national park as well as hikes to La Randonnée and the volcano. There are three different canyoning circuits, including one called the Trail of the Three Waterfalls that lasts six to seven hours. On the bivouac trip you spend 24 reality-show-like hours in the forest. For many of these excursions, you have to wait for a group to be assembled. Book as far in advance as you can. Rates range from €45 to €115, and €28 to €50 for ages 8 to 14. ⊠ *Le Rocher de Malendure, Plage de Malendure, Bouillante, Basse-Terre* ☎ *0590/98–86–63* ⊕ *www. heures-saines.gp.*

Vert Intense. Vert Intense organizes fascinating hikes in the national park and to the volcano. You move from steaming hot springs to an icy waterfall in the same hike. Guides are patient and safety-conscious, and can bring you to heights that you never thought you could reach, including the top of Le Soufrière. The volcano hike costs only €30 but must be booked four days in advance. A mixed-adventure package spanning three days costs €225. The two-day bivouac and other adventures can be extreme sport, so before you decide to play Indiana Jones, know what is expected. The French-speaking guides, who also know some English and Spanish, can take you to other tropical forests and rivers, where the sport of canyoning can still be practiced. If you are just one or two people, the company can team you up with a group. ⊠ *Rte. de la Soufrière, Mourne Houel, Basse-Terre* ☎ *0590/99–34–73, 0690/55–40–47* ⊕ *www.vert-intense.com.*

HORSEBACK RIDING

Le Haras de Saint-François. A 50-horse stable, Le Haras de Saint-François has English lessons and Western trail rides for two hours (€50) or three hours (€60). The latter will take you to the beach, where you can go bareback into the sea. ⊠ *Chemin de la Princesse, St-François, Grande-Terre* ☎ *0690/39–90–00.*

KAYAKING AND OTHER WATER SPORTS

Centre Nautique. Centre Nautique, on the beach, rents sea kayaks for €10 an hour and Hobie Cats for €40 an hour, and can arrange fishing, catamaran, kayaking, diving, and motorboat excursions. It runs water taxis to the Islet du Gosier (€10) and to the outdoor market in Pointe-à-Pitre for €15. There are PADI instructors for the dive segment of the operation, and certifications are possible. Jet Ski rentals include a guide, and range from a half hour for €65 to €230 for five hours including lunch. Non-guests are welcome but must call in advance.

⊠ *La Créole Beach Hotel & Spa, Pointe de la Verdure, Gosier, Grande-Terre* ☎ *0590/90–46–59.*

Jouez dans l'eau. Jouez dans l'eau (water games) is great for underwater exploration without ever getting your hair wet. Rent a transparent kayak, which allows paddlers to see the myriad colors of one of the world's most beautiful bays. This creative company is still relatively new to the island, and you can expect good, informative, 90-minute tours with an audio guide for commentary on coral reefs and sea life. The English version is coming soon. The cost is €20 per person, with special family and group rates available. To find Jouez dans l'eau, take a left from the main dock and look for their sign on the right. ⊠ *Terre-de-Haut, Iles des Saintes* ☎ *0690/65–79–81* ⊕ *www.clearbluecaraibes.fr.*

SEA EXCURSIONS

🕙 **Evasion Tropicale.** Evasion Tropicale operates daylong whale-watching cruises. With the help of the onboard sonar, humpback whales are easy to find from December through March. Trips on the 51-foot motor sailer cost €60 per person, but every passenger must also buy an annual membership in the Association for Study and Census of Turtles, Marine and Mammals of the Caribbean for €25. ⊠ *Rue des paletuviers, Pigeon-Bouillante, Basse-Terre* ☎ *0590/92–74–24, 0690/57–19–44* ⊕ *www.evasiontropicale.org.*

Paradoxe. Attracting an upscale clientele, *Paradoxe* is a top-of-the-line catamaran that sails to Marie-Galante (anchoring at the idyllic beach, Anse Canot) for €95. It only sails to Les Saintes if the whole boat is booked by a group. (The off-season price can be significantly discounted.) It's not your typical booze cruise. Bottles of rum aboard? Sure, but passengers are more likely to be in it for the marine experience and the stopover on nature preserve Petit Terre. The music is soothing and the lunch tasty, with cheesy bread, fresh fish, barbecue chicken, ribs, and vegetarian dishes. ⊠ *St-François Marina, St-François, Grande-Terre* ☎ *0590/88–41–73.*

⚠ CAUTION: Rendezvous before departure, for these sails can be as early as 7:15. No skipper can completely guarantee calm waters. Free-flowing rum can take its toll, and it will also rain at some point. And the Cats usually don't return until 5:30. Keep that all in mind, especially if you have children.

WIND- AND KITESURFING

Most beachfront hotels can help you arrange lessons and rentals.

LCS. LCS, in business since the early 1980s, specializes in lessons for adults and children six and older. Instructors are certified by the French National Federation of Sailing. The company organizes offshore competitions and also runs a retail surf shop. The action takes place on remarkable Caravelle Beach. ⊠ *Ste-Anne Lagoon, Ste-Anne, Grande-Terre* ☎ *0590/88–15–17* ⊕ *www.lookasurf.com.*

UCPA Hotel Club. Windsurfing buffs congregate at the UCPA Hotel Club, where for moderate weekly rates (beginning at €805 or €115 a day) they sleep in hostel-style quarters, eat three meals a day, and do a lot of windsurfing. Lessons and boards (also available to nonguests) are included in the package, as are bikes to pedal to the lagoon. A sister club on Terre-de-Haut has a water-sports center in the middle of town, though the hotel itself is out on isolated Baie de Marigot. There is a lot of action at *le centre* UCPA, where island visitors can rent windsurfing equipment for €25, take a lesson for €30, or take a kitesurfing lesson for €60 (€20 if part of a group). Kayaks and dive tanks are available, too. ⊠ *Terre-de-Haut, Iles des Saintes* ☏ *0590/99–56–34 in-town sport center; hotel reservations, 0590/99–54–94* ⊕ *www.ucpa.com.*

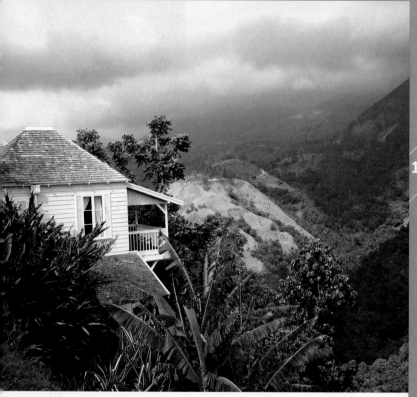

Jamaica

WORD OF MOUTH

"Believe me, I tell all our friends how beautiful Jamaica is. I really can't say enough about the beaches, the good times we've had, and the easy flight!"

—Knowing

WELCOME TO JAMAICA

KEY

- ⚓ Beaches
- 🚢 Cruise Ship Terminal
- 🔱 Dive Sites
- **1** Restaurants
- **1** Hotels

Map labels: Run, Montego Bay see detail map, Mahoe Bay, Greenwood Great House, Discovery Bay, Puert, Seco Beac, Cornwall Beach, Rose Hall, Falmouth, Duncans, Doctor's Cave Beach, Walter Fletcher Beach, Donald Sangster International Airport, Green Grotto Caves, Pedro Pt., Airport Reef, Martha Brae River, Clark's Town, Bro, Negril see detail map, Lucea, Montego Bay, Cockpit Country, Good Hope Great House, Alexan, Sandy Bay, Green Island, Montpelier, Albert Town, Glasgow, Savanna-la-Mar, Blue Hole, Christiana, Long Bay Negril Beach, Negril, Appleton Estate, Balaclava, Bluefields Beach, Bluefields, Middle Quarters, Black River, Mandeville, Southwest Pt., Y. S. Falls, Santa Cruz, Black River, Crane Beach, Treasure Beach, Lovers' Leap, Alligator Pond, Treasure Beach, Great Pedro Bluff, Old Woma Pt.

0 — 10 miles
0 — 15 km

Chances are you will never fully understand Jamaica in all its delightful complexity, but you will probably have a good time trying. You can party in Negril, shop in Montego Bay, or simply relax at one of the island's many all-inclusive resorts, but you'll also discover culture and delicious island cuisine.

OUT OF MANY, ONE PEOPLE

The third-largest island in the Caribbean (after Cuba and Hispaniola), Jamaica is 146 miles (242 km) long and is slightly smaller than the state of Connecticut. It has a population of 2.7 million. With about 800,000 people, the capital, Kingston, is the largest English-speaking city south of Miami (in the Western Hemisphere, at least). The highest point is Blue Mountain Peak at 7,402 feet.

14

JAMAICA

TOP REASONS TO VISIT JAMAICA

1 All-Inclusive Resorts: The all-inclusive resort was invented here.

2 Great Golf: Golfers will be delighted by the many wonderful courses.

3 Fun for the Kids: Every conceivable activity, great beaches, and many child-friendly resorts appeal to families.

4 Negril Beach: It's simply one of the Caribbean's best.

5 Unique Culture: Jamaica has rich cultural traditions—particularly local music, art, and cuisine.

JAMAICA BEACHES

As the Caribbean's third-largest island, Jamaica has no shortage of beaches, ranging from the North Coast's tourist-filled stretches of sand lined by exclusive resorts to the nearly deserted beaches of the South Coast, where beach action often means a fisherman cleaning his catch.

(Above) The beach at Sandals Whitehouse, on the South Shore (Bottom right) Doctor's Cave Beach, Montego Bay (Top right) Dunn's River Falls, Ocho Rios

North- and west-coast beaches tend to be busy, well supplied with amenities, and blessed with large expanses of sand. Both Negril (and its lovely Seven Mile Beach) and Montego Bay (which has both Doctor's Cave and Half Moon Bay) are renowned for their beaches, and both have many resorts directly on the beach to choose from. Beaches on the South Coast are generally less crowded but are smaller, with fewer services. The best South Coast beaches are in the Treasure Beach area near Calabash Bay. Kingston-area beaches are generally congested; ask your hotel concierge before heading out to any of them. Some of the best beaches are private, owned by the resorts and accessible only to resort guests or travelers who have purchased a day pass to gain access to the facilities.

BEST BEACHES?

Most of Jamaica's beaches are coral based, creating a medium-coarse, light-color sand. In general, the best Jamaican beach sand is on the north and west sides of the island. The softest and most beautiful beaches are in Negril, on the island's west coast, and in the Montego Bay area. Those on the South Coast are narrower and wilder, with coarser, darker sand.

Whereas hotel beaches are generally private and restricted to guests of the property, other beaches are public and are open to all kinds of vendors, who have a reputation of being rather aggressive. At resort areas, even if the beach area is considered private, the area below the high-water mark is always public, so vendors will roam longer beaches looking for business. In most cases, a simple "no thanks" will do.

14

MONTEGO BAY

★ **Doctor's Cave Beach.** Montego Bay's tourist scene has its roots right on the Hip Strip, the bustling entertainment district along Gloucester Avenue. Here a sea cave's waters were said to be curative and drew many travelers to bathe in them. Though the cave was destroyed by a hurricane generations ago, the beach is always busy and has a perpetual spring-break feel. It's the best beach in Jamaica outside one of the more developed resorts, thanks to its plantation-style clubhouse with changing rooms, showers, gift shops, a bar, a grill, and even a cybercafé. There's a $5 fee for admission; beach chairs and umbrellas are also for rent. Its location within the Montego Bay Marine Park—which contains protected corals and marine life—makes it a good spot for snorkeling. More active travelers can opt for parasailing, glass-bottom boat rides, or jet skiing. ⊠ *Gloucester Ave., Montego Bay* ☎ *876/952–2566.*

Walter Fletcher Beach. Though not as pretty as Doctor's Cave Beach, or as tidy, Walter Fletcher Beach is home to Aquasol Theme Park, which offers a large beach (with lifeguards and security), water trampolines, Jet Skis, Wave Runners, glass-bottom boats, snorkeling, tennis, go-kart racing, a disco at night, a bar, and a grill. The park is open daily from 10 to 10; admission is $5, with à la carte pricing for most activities. Near the center of town, the beach has protection from the surf on a windy day. This means you can find unusually fine swimming here; the calm waters make it a good bet for children. ⊠ *Gloucester Ave., Montego Bay* ☎ *876/979–9447.*

RUNAWAY BAY

Puerto Seco Beach. This public beach looks out on Discovery Bay, the location where, according to tradition, Christopher Columbus first came ashore on this island. The explorer sailed in search of freshwater but found none, naming the stretch of sand Puerto Seco, or "dry port." Today the beach is anything but dry; concession stands sell Red Stripe beer and local food, including jerk and patties, to a primarily local beach crowd. ⊠ *Discovery Bay, 5 miles (8 km) west of Runaway Bay.*

The Blue Lagoon, Port Antonio

OCHO RIOS

Dunn's River Falls Beach. You'll find a crowd (especially if there's a cruise ship in town) at the small beach at the foot of the falls. Although tiny—especially considering the crowds that pack the falls—it's got a great view, as well as a beach bar and grill. Look up from the sands for a spectacular view of the cascading water, whose roar drowns out the sea as you approach. ⊠ *Rte. A1 between St. Ann's Bay and Ocho Rios.*

James Bond Beach. Another alternative near Ocho Rios—if you don't mind the drive—is in the community of Oracabessa. This beach, on the estate of James Bond's creator, the late Ian Fleming, is owned by former Island Records producer Chris Blackwell, so it's no surprise that it often rocks with live music performances on the bandstand. Guests of the Goldeneye resort enjoy it for free; visitors must pay $5 per person. The beach is open daily except Monday from 9:30 to 6. ⊠ *Oracabessa* ☎ *876/726–1630.*

Turtle Beach. One of the busiest beaches in Ocho Rios is usually lively, and has a mix of both residents and visitors. It's next to the Sunset Jamaica Grande and looks out over the cruise port. ⊠ *Main St.*

PORT ANTONIO

Blue Lagoon. Though the beach is small, the large lagoon has to be seen to be believed. The cool, spring-fed waters cry out to swimmers and are a real contrast to the warmer sea waters. Floating docks encourage you to sun a little, or you can lie out on the small beach. Just how deep is the Blue Lagoon? You might hear it's bottomless (Jacques Cousteau verified that it is not), but the lagoon has been measured at a depth of 180 feet. At present, tour operators offer admission as part of their Port Antonio tours, and freelance operators at the gates sometimes offer entry, but for current (and official) conditions, call the Jamaica Tourist Board. ⊠ *9 miles (15 km) east of Port Antonio, 1 mile (2 km) east of San San Beach.*

Boston Beach. Considered the birthplace of Jamaica's famous jerk-style cooking, it's the beach where some locals visit just to buy dinner. You can get peppery jerk pork at any of the shacks spewing scented smoke along the beach. While you're there, you'll also find a small beach perfect for an after-lunch dip, although these waters are occasionally rough and much more popular for surfing. ✉ *11 miles (18 km) east of Port Antonio.*

★ **Frenchman's Cove.** This beautiful, somewhat secluded beach is petite perfection. Protected by two outcroppings that form the cove, the inlet's calm waters are a favorite with families. A small stream trickles into the cove. You'll find a bar and restaurant serving fried chicken right on the beach. If this stretch of sand looks a little familiar, it just might be because you've seen it in the movies; it has starred in *Club Paradise, Treasure Island* (the Charlton Heston version), and *The Mighty Quinn.* If you are not a guest of Frenchman's Cove, admission is $4.50 ($2.50 for children). ✉ *Rte. A4, 5 miles (8 km) east of Port Antonio.*

San San Beach. This small beach ($5 admission fee) has beautiful blue water. Just offshore, Monkey Island is a good place to snorkel (and, sometimes, surf). ✉ *5 miles (8 km) east of Port Antonio.*

THE SOUTH COAST

If you're looking for something off the main tourist routes, head for Jamaica's largely undeveloped South Coast. Because the population in this region is sparse, these isolated beaches are some of the island's safest, with hasslers practically nonexistent. You should, however, use common sense; never leave valuables unattended on the beach.

Treasure Beach. The most atmospheric beach in the southwest is in the community of Treasure Beach, which comprises four long stretches of sand as well as many small coves. Though it isn't as pretty as those to the west or north—it has more rocks and darker sand—the idea that you might be discovering a bit of the "real" Jamaica more than makes up for the small negatives. Both locals and visitors use the beaches here, though you're just as likely to find it completely deserted save for a friendly beach dog. ✉ *Treasure Beach township.*

NEGRIL

★ **Fodor's Choice**

Negril Beach. Stretching for 7 miles (11 km), the long, white-sand beach in Negril is arguably Jamaica's finest. It starts with the white sands of Bloody Bay north of town and continues along Long Bay all the way to the cliffs on the southern edge of town. Some stretches remain undeveloped, but these are increasingly few. Along the main stretch of beach, the sand is public to the high-water mark, so a nonstop line of visitors and vendors parades from end to end. The walk is sprinkled with many good beach bars and open-air restaurants, some of which charge a small fee to use their beach facilities. Bloody Bay is lined with large all-inclusive resorts, and these sections are mostly private. Jamaica's best-known nude beach, at Hedonism II, is always among the busiest; only resort guests or day-pass holders may sun here. ✉ *Norman Manley Blvd.*

Word of Mouth "Negril, hands down [is our favorite beach in Jamaica]. Friendly. Clear water. White sand beaches. miles of that. (sigh) wish I was there now." —lynzdee

14

Negril Beach

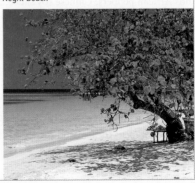

EATING AND DRINKING WELL IN JAMAICA

"We love to marinate our food longer even when using the same ingredients. Our food is also a bit hotter yet aromatic and pungent." — Jacqui Sinclair, Jamaican chef and food writer.

(Above) Lobster at Evita's Italian Restaurant (Bottom right) A bounty of native Jamaican fruits (Top right) Fresh seafood, a part of many memorable Jamaican meals

Jamaica's national motto, "Out of Many, One Country," serves equally well to describe its multicultural, melting-pot cuisine: a savvy, savory fusion of African, Asian, Arawak-Taíno, and European influences, ingredients, techniques, and traditions. Even the humble patty blends African peppers, Chinese soy sauce, and Cornish pasties. Sizzling Scotch bonnet peppers are indigenous, as are pimento—from which allspice is produced (Jamaica produces 80% of the world's supply), and the liberally used native ginger is stronger in Jamaica than elsewhere. Aspiring Anthony Bourdains should try beachfront or roadside vans, kiosks, and shacks dishing out darkly bubbling grub from cow foot to curried goat that might unnerve *Survivor* contestants. They offer authentic fare such as succulent slow-cooked jerk with heaping helpings of rice 'n' peas (beans) and provisions (tubers such as yam and cassava). —Jordan Simon

THE JERK TRAIL

In May 2009, citing the international popularity of jerk cuisine, Jamaica's Ministry of Tourism introduced the Culinary Jerk Trail, spanning the island from Negril through Mo'Bay and Ocho Rios to Kingston and Port Antonio. The attraction features 10 of the hottest jerk spots where diners can interact with chefs and learn the origins behind jerk cooking. For more information, go to ⊕ *www.visitjamaica. com/jerk.*

JERK

Arguably Jamaica's most famous export after reggae, jerk supposedly originated with the Maroons, freed descendants of slaves who settled the island's most remote, inhospitable areas. Meat (usually chicken or pork) is marinated for hours in a fiery blend of peppers, pimento, scallion, and thyme, then cooked over an outdoor pit lined with pimento wood. Low, slow heating retains the natural juices while infusing the meat with the flavor of the wood and spices and ensures that the meat lasts in the tropical heat.

SALTFISH AND ACKEE

The British brought salt cod with them as a cheap, long-lasting foodstuff for sailors and slaves alike. Ackee, a red tree fruit introduced to Jamaica from western Africa via Britain, is actually poisonous in its natural state. Once the pear-shape fruit's tough, toxic, ruddy membrane is removed, however, the boiled, yellowish, pulpy arils surprisingly resemble scrambled eggs in taste and texture.

EXOTICA

Goat figures in incendiary curries, as well as "mannish water," a lusty soup—believed to be an aphrodisiac, traditionally served on wedding nights—including the head and brains slow-cooked with various seasonings and tubers. Oxtail is a culinary constant from Italy to Indonesia. Jamaicans serve it stewed, braised, or in soup; inventive chefs might toss it with pasta in rum-cream sauce.

SEAFOOD ESCOVEITCH

Freshly caught fish—including snapper, tuna, wahoo, grouper, and marlin—is often served as *escoveitch* aka *escoveech* (stewed or sautéed, sometimes in coconut milk, with peppers, onions, chayote, carrots, Scotch bonnet peppers, and tomatoes). Despite the linguistic and gastronomic similarity to ceviche and *escabeche*, escoveitch is rarely served cold, though it is usually marinated in vinegar and lime juice before it is cooked.

PROVISIONS

Farmers traditionally cultivated carb-rich crops that could furnish energy for islanders' hardscrabble heavy labor without requiring refrigeration. Pumpkins, coconuts, plantains, breadfruit, sweet potatoes, cassava, yams, and other "provisions" (root and gourd vegetables as well as some fruits) became staples, sometimes replacing expensive imported ingredients (chayote was used in mock-apple crumble). Most homeowners still have kitchen gardens; Olympic champion Usain Bolt credits yams from his native Trelawny Parish for his speed. Today even sophisticated chefs creatively return to their "grow what you eat" locavore roots.

14

Updated by
Catherine
MacGillivray

Jamaicans define enthusiasm. Whether the topic is ackee or dominoes, politics or Carnival, the spirit of this island comes out in every interaction. Although the island is well known for its tropical beauty, reggae music, and cuisine, you may find that your interactions with local residents are what you truly remember.

The island is rich in beauty, but a quick look around reveals widespread poverty and a land where the disparity between the lives of the resort guests and the resort employees is often staggering. Where vacationers opt to make their Jamaican home away from home depends on factors ranging from the length of their vacation to personal interests. With its direct air connections to many cities in the United States, Montego Bay (or Mo'Bay) is favored by Americans taking short trips; many properties are just minutes from the airport. Other parts of the island can be reached from Montego Bay in 60 to 90 minutes; more far-flung areas may be more accessible through the island's other major airport in the capital, Kingston.

Some of the island's earliest residents were the Arawak Indians, who arrived from South America around 650 AD and named the island Xaymaca, or "land of wood and water." Centuries later, the Arawaks welcomed Christopher Columbus on his second voyage to the New World. Later, when the Spanish arrived, the peaceful inhabitants were executed or taken as slaves.

The Spanish maintained control of the island until 1655, when the English arrived. Soon, slavery increased as sugar became a booming industry. In 1834 slavery was abolished, but the sugar as well as banana industries continued. Jamaica's plantation owners looked for another source of labor. From 1838 to 1917, more than 30,000 Indians immigrated here, followed by about 5,000 Asians as well as immigrants from the Middle East, primarily from what is now Lebanon.

In the early 1900s the boats that took the banana crop off the island began returning with travelers. By 1960 the tourism industry had

LOGISTICS

Getting to Jamaica: Donald Sangster International Airport (MBJ), in Montego Bay, is the most efficient point of entry for travelers destined for Mo'Bay, Ocho Rios, Runaway Bay, the South Coast, and Negril. Norman Manley International Airport (KIN), in Kingston, is the best arrival point for travelers headed to the capital or to Port Antonio.

Hassle Factor: Low–high, depending on your distance from Mo'Bay.

On the Ground: Most all-inclusive resorts include transfers. If transfers are not included for your trip, you can get shared-van service from the airport in Montego Bay to your final destination. You can rent a car at either airport.

Getting Around the Island: Most travelers to Jamaica take guided tours on trips outside their resorts. The average traveler will not want to rent a car. Rentals are possible but are difficult to arrange on arrival and expensive, so make a reservation before your trip. In most places a taxi may suffice for occasional trips around town, but your resort may have a free shuttle, so ask. In isolated areas (Port Antonio, for instance), a taxi isn't practical.

14

become Jamaica's most important form of income. In 1962, Jamaica became an independent nation.

Although 95% of the population traces its bloodlines to Africa, Jamaica is a stockpot of cultures, including those of other Caribbean islands, Great Britain, the Middle East, India, China, Germany, Portugal, and South America. The third-largest island in the Caribbean (after Cuba and Hispaniola), Jamaica enjoys a considerable self-sufficiency based on tourism, agriculture, and mining.

PLANNING

WHEN TO GO

High season in Jamaica runs roughly from mid-December through mid-April. From May through mid-December, you can save from 20% to as much as 40% on rates, more if you use value-oriented travel packagers. There are several annual events in Jamaica that draw huge numbers of visitors.

GETTING HERE AND AROUND

AIR TRAVEL

You can fly to Jamaica from Atlanta (AirTran, Delta), Boston (Jet-Blue, US Airways), Charlotte (US Airways), Chicago (American), Dallas (American), Detroit (US Airways), Fort Lauderdale (Air Jamaica, Spirit), Houston (Continental), Las Vegas (American), Los Angeles (American), Miami (American), New York–JFK (Air Jamaica, American, JetBlue), New York–Newark (Continental), Orlando (JetBlue), Philadelphia (Air Jamaica, US Airways), Phoenix (US Airways), San Diego (American), or Tampa (American). Most flights come into Montego Bay, but some nonstops go to Kingston.

All international flights arrive in Montego Bay or Kingston. Jamaica's minor domestic airports accommodate only charters at this writing. If you need to continue to a smaller airport on Jamaica from your international flight, there are also a couple of options for domestic charters.

International Airports Donald Sangster International Airport (*MBJ*). ⊠ *Montego Bay* ☎ *876/952-3124* ⊕ *www.mbjairport.com.* **Norman Manley International Airport** (*KIN*). ⊠ *Kingston* ☎ *876/924-8452* ⊕ *www.nmia.aero.*

Domestic Airports Ian Fleming International Airport ⊠ *8 miles [14 km] east of Ocho Rios, Oracabessa* ☎ *876/975-3101.* **Negril Aerodrome** ⊠ *Negril* ☎ *876/957-5016.*

International Airline Contacts Air Jamaica ☎ *888/359-2475, 876/952-4300 in Montego Bay.* **Air Tran** ☎ *800/247-8726.* **American Airlines** ☎ *800/744-0006.* **Cayman Airways** ☎ *876/924-8650 in Kingston, 876/924-8809 in Montego Bay.* **Delta Airlines** ☎ *800/221-1212, 876/940-1834 in Montego Bay.* **JetBlue** ☎ *800/963-3014.* **United Airlines** ☎ *876/979-5845, 800/864-8331.* **US Airways** ☎ *876/940-0171.*

Domestic Airline Contacts Island Hoppers ☎ *876/974-1285* ⊕ *www. jamaicahelicopterservices.com.* **Tim Air.** Tim Air offers charter service between Montego Bay's Sangster International Airport and airports in Port Antonio, Ocho Rios, Runaway Bay, Kingston, and Negril. ☎ *876/952-2516 in Montego Bay* ⊕ *www.timair.com.*

BUS TRAVEL

Bus Contacts Knutsford Express. Knutsford Express, an air-conditioned bus, offers scheduled service between Montego Bay, Ocho Rios, and Kingston. For about $25, the bus company offers service from Montego Bay to Kingston three times daily. Service is also available from Montego Bay to Ocho Rios and Ocho Rios to Kingston for about $15. Pickups and drop-offs are not at the airports, however; service leaves from central locations. ☎ *876/971-1822* ⊕ *www. knutsfordexpress.com.* **Southcoast Express** ☎ *876/957-3751, 876/452-4748* ⊕ *www.southcoast-express.com.*

CAR TRAVEL

Driving in Jamaica can be an extremely frustrating chore. You must constantly be on guard—for enormous potholes, people and animals darting out into the street, and aggressive drivers. Local drivers are quick to pass other cars—and sometimes two cars will pass simultaneously. Gas stations are open daily but accept cash only. Gas costs roughly double the price found in the United States. Driving in Jamaica is on the left, British-style.

Car Rentals To rent a car, you must be at least 23 years old, have a valid driver's license (from any country), and have a valid credit card. You may be required to post a security deposit of several hundred dollars before taking possession of your car; ask about it when you make the reservation. Rates average $70 to $120 a day after the addition of the compulsory insurance, which you must usually purchase even if your credit card offers it.

Car-Rental Contacts Avis Rent a Car ☎ *876/952-0762* ⊕ *www.avis.com. jm.* **Budget** ☎ *876/952-3838* ⊕ *www.budgetjamaica.com.* **Fiesta Car Rentals**

☏ *876/926–0133* ⊕ *www.fiestacarrentals.com.* **Hertz** ☏ *876/979–0438* ⊕ *www. hertz.com.* **Island Car Rentals** ☏ *876/924–8075 in Kingston, 876/952–7225 in Montego Bay* ⊕ *www.islandcarrentals.com.*

TAXI TRAVEL

Some but not all of Jamaica's taxis are metered. If you accept a driver's offer of his services as a tour guide, be sure to agree on a price before the vehicle is put into gear. (Note that a one-day tour should run about $150 to $180, in U.S. dollars, depending on distance traveled.) All licensed taxis display red Public Passenger Vehicle (PPV) plates. You hotel concierge can call a taxi for you, or you can flag one down on the street. Rates are per car, not per passenger, and 25% is added to the metered rate between midnight and 5 am. Licensed minivans are also available and bear the red PPV plates. JUTA is the largest taxi franchise, with offices in all resort areas.

Taxi Contacts JCAL Tours ☏ *876/952–7574, 876/952–8277* ⊕ *www.jcaltours. com.* **JUTA Montego Bay** ☏ *876/952–0813* ⊕ *www.jutatoursltd.com.*

ESSENTIALS

Banks and Exchange Services The official currency is the Jamaican dollar, but few Americans bother to exchange money, since U.S. dollars are widely accepted. Some ATMs in Jamaica don't accept American ATM cards, and others will accept American ATM cards and dispense U.S. dollars. Major credit cards are widely accepted, although cash is required at gas stations, in markets, and in many small stores.

Electricity As in North America, the current in Jamaica is 110 volts but only 50 cycles, with outlets that take two flat prongs. Some hotels provide 220-volt plugs as well as special shaver outlets.

Emergency Services Ambulance and Fire Emergencies ☏ *110.* **Police Emergencies & Air Rescue** ☏ *119.* **Scuba-Diving Emergencies** ✉ *St. Ann's Bay Hospital, St. Ann's Bay* ☏ *876/972–2272.*

Passport Requirements All visitors must have a valid passport. A birth certificate and photo ID are not sufficient proof of citizenship.

Phones Cellular service is expanding throughout Jamaica, especially in Kingston and in the resort areas. GSM cell phones equipped with tri-band or world-roaming service will find coverage throughout much of the coastal region. Cellular service averages about $1.50 to $2 per minute on the island. Rates for local calls start at about 14¢ per minute, and incoming calls are free. Outgoing international calls to the United States start at about 30¢ per minute. Prepaid SIM cards cost about J$500. Providers Digicel and Lime also offer pre-paid international calling to the U.S. and Canada. Cellular-phone rentals are also available starting at about $20 per week.

Most hotels offer direct-dial telephone services with a substantial service change; local businesses provide fax services for a fee. Pay phones and calling cards are available.

To dial Jamaica from the United States, just dial 1 + area code 876. Some U.S. phone companies provide only limited credit-card calls from

Jamaica because they've been victims of fraud. The best option is to purchase Jamaican phone cards, sold in most stores across the island.

Safety Crime in Jamaica is, unfortunately, a persistent problem, so don't let the beauty of the island cause you to abandon the caution you would practice in any unfamiliar place. Many of the headlines are grabbed by murders in Kingston, often gang-related; violent crimes are, for the most part, largely a problem for residents who live in the city. Visitors should be extremely cautious about visiting many of the neighborhoods in Kingston that are outside the business district of New Kingston.

Property crime is an islandwide problem. Use your in-room safe and be sure to lock all doors—including balconies—when you leave your room or villa. Traveler's checks are a good idea in Jamaica, being safer than cash (just keep a record of the check numbers in a secure place so they can be replaced if necessary). Never leave your car unlocked, and never leave valuables inside it, even when it is locked. Ignore efforts, however persistent, to sell you ganja (marijuana), which is illegal across the island.

Taxes Almost all airline ticket prices include the J$100 departure tax; otherwise, it must be paid in cash. A General Consumption Tax (G.C.T.) of 17.5% is included in the cost of most goods and services; there is no longer a separate hotel-occupancy tax.

Tipping Most hotels and restaurants add a 10% service charge to your bill. When a service charge isn't included, a 10% to 20% tip is expected. Tips of 10% to 20% are customary for taxi drivers as well. However, many all-inclusives have a strict no-tipping policy.

ACCOMMODATIONS

Montego Bay has the largest concentration of resorts on the island; **Negril** is a more relaxed haven on the west coast. Both offer a mix of large and small resorts, plus good nightlife. **Runaway Bay** and **Ocho Rios** are more than an hour east of Mo'Bay. **Port Antonio**, a sleepy, laid-back haven, has a few resorts and a quiet atmosphere and is usually accessed by a short flight or long drive from Kingston. The **South Coast** has a few small resorts, uncrowded beaches, and only one large resort. Few vacationers choose to stay in the capital, **Kingston**, but the surrounding area also includes the **Blue Mountains**, home of the luxe Strawberry Hill resort.

All-Inclusive Resorts: Jamaica was the birthplace of the Caribbean all-inclusive resort, which is still the most popular vacation option here. Several of these are open only to couples.

Small Hotels: Particularly in Negril, you'll find smaller, more unique hotels and inns that aren't part of the big chains; they range in price from budget to luxury. The Island Outpost company operates several upscale boutique resorts all over Jamaica.

Villas: Jamaica is home to an increasing number of villas aimed at travelers looking for a home-away-from-home experience. Discovery Bay, near Runaway Bay, is a top location for many high-end villas. Many have a one-week minimum stay.

HOTEL AND RESTAURANT PRICES

Prices in the restaurant reviews are the average cost of a main course at dinner or, if dinner is not served, at lunch; taxes and service charges are generally included. Prices in the hotel reviews are the lowest cost of a standard double room in high season, excluding taxes, service charges, and meal plans (except at all-inclusives). Prices for rentals are the lowest per-night cost for a one-bedroom unit in high season.

VISITOR INFORMATION

Contacts **Jamaica Tourist Board** ☎ *305/665–0557 in Miami, 876/929–9200 in Kingston, 876/952–4425 in Montego Bay ⊕ www.visitjamaica.com.*

WEDDINGS

A 24-hour waiting period is required; many resorts offer free weddings.

14

EXPLORING JAMAICA

Touring Jamaica can be both thrilling and frustrating. Rugged (albeit beautiful) terrain and winding (often potholed) roads make for slow going. *Always* check conditions before you set off to explore the island by car, but especially in the rainy season from June through October, when roads can easily be washed out. Primary roads that loop around and across the island are two-lane routes but are not particularly well marked. Numbered addresses are seldom used outside major townships, locals drive aggressively, and people and animals seem to have a knack for appearing on the street out of nowhere. That said, Jamaica's scenery shouldn't be missed. To be safe and avoid frustration, stick to guided tours and licensed taxis.

If you're staying in Kingston or Port Antonio, set aside at least one day for the capital's highlights and another for a guided excursion to the Blue Mountains. You can find at least three days' worth of activity right along Mo'Bay's boundaries; you should also consider a day trip to Negril or Ocho Rios. If you're based in Ocho Rios, be sure to visit Dunn's River Falls; you may also want to stop by Firefly or Bob Marley's birthplace, Nine Mile. If Negril is your hub, take in the South Coast, including Y.S. Falls and the Black River.

MONTEGO BAY

Today many explorations of Mo'Bay are conducted from a reclining chair—frothy drink in hand—on Doctor's Cave Beach. As home of the north-shore airport, Montego Bay is the first taste most visitors have of the island. It's the second-largest city in Jamaica and has a busy cruise pier west of town. Travelers from around the world come and go in this bustling community year-round. The name Montego is derived from *manteca* ("lard" in Spanish). The Spanish first named this Bahía de Manteca, or Lard Bay. Why? The Spanish once shipped hogs from this port city. Jamaican tourism began here in 1924, when the first resort opened at Doctor's Cave Beach so that health seekers could "take the waters." If you can pull yourself away from the water's edge, you'll find some interesting colonial sights in the surrounding area.

WHAT TO SEE

★ **Greenwood Great House.** Unlike Rose Hall, Greenwood has no spooky legend to titillate, but it's much better than Rose Hall at evoking life on a sugar plantation. The Barrett family, from whom the English poet Elizabeth Barrett Browning descended, once owned all the land from Rose Hall to Falmouth; on their vast holdings they built this and several other great houses. (The poet's father, Edward Moulton Barrett, "the Tyrant of Wimpole Street," was born at nearby Cinnamon Hill, later the estate of country singer Johnny Cash.) Highlights of Greenwood include oil paintings of the Barretts, china made for the family by Wedgwood, a library filled with rare books from as early as 1697, fine antique furniture, and a collection of exotic musical instruments. There's a pub on-site as well. It's 15 miles (24 km) east of Montego Bay. ⊠ *Greenwood* ☎ *876/953–1077* ⊕ *www.greenwoodgreathouse.com* ✉ *$20* ☉ *Daily 9–6 (last tour at 5).*

WORD OF MOUTH

"The people of Jamaica were such warm people, and I got the feeling that they did want visitors to love Jamaica in the same way that they did. That was genuine and not because they wanted to sell me something or because they wanted a tip. It was a warmth that added to the beauty of the island."

—writealiving

Martha Brae River. This gentle waterway about 25 miles (40 km) southeast of Montego Bay takes its name from an Arawak woman who killed herself because she refused to reveal the whereabouts of a local gold mine. According to legend, she agreed to take her Spanish inquisitors there and, on reaching the river, used magic to change its course, drowning herself and the greedy Spaniards with her. Her *duppy* (ghost) is said to guard the mine's entrance. Rafting on this river is a very popular activity. ⊠ *Montego Bay.*

★ **Rocklands Bird Sanctuary.** A great place to spot birds is the sanctuary, which is south of Montego Bay. The station was the home of the late Lisa Salmon, one of Jamaica's first amateur ornithologists. Here you can sit quietly and feed birds—including the doctor bird (also known as the streamer-tail hummingbird), recognizable by its long tail—from your hand. A visit costs $15. ⊠ *Anchovy* ☎ *876/952–2009.*

Fodor's Choice
★ **Rose Hall.** In the 1700s it may well have been the greatest of great houses in the West Indies. Today it's popular less for its architecture than for the legend surrounding its second mistress, Annie Palmer. As the story goes, Annie was born in 1802 in England to an English mother and Irish father. When she was 10, her family moved to Haiti, and soon her parents died of yellow fever. Annie was adopted by a Haitian voodoo priestess and soon became skilled in the practice of voodoo. Annie moved to Jamaica, married, and built Rose Hall, an enormous plantation spanning 6,600 acres with more than 2,000 slaves. You can take a spooky nighttime tour of the property, and there's a pub on-site. ⊠ *North Coast Hwy., St. James* ✛ *15 miles (24 km) east of Montego Bay* ☎ *876/953–2323* ⊕ *www.rosehall.com* ✉ *$20* ☉ *Daily 9:15–5:15 and 6:30–9:15.*

COCKPIT COUNTRY

Fifteen miles (24 km) inland from Mo'Bay is one of the most untouched areas in the West Indies: a terrain of pitfalls and potholes carved by nature in limestone. For nearly a century after 1655 it was known as the Land of Look Behind, because British soldiers nervously rode their horses through here on the lookout for the guerrilla freedom fighters known as Maroons. Former slaves who refused to surrender to the invading English, the Maroons eventually won their independence. Today their descendants live in this area, untaxed and virtually ungoverned by outside authorities. Most visitors to the area stop in Accompong, a small community in St. Elizabeth Parish. You can stroll through town, take in the historic structures, and learn more about the Maroons—considered Jamaica's greatest herbalists.

14

RUNAWAY BAY

Green Grotto Caves. A good choice for rainy days, these caves offer 45-minute guided tours that include a look at a subterranean lake. The cave has a long history as a hiding place for everyone from fearsome pirates to runaway slaves to the Spanish governor (he was on the run from the British at the time). It's a good destination if you want to see one of Jamaica's caves without going too far off the beaten path. You'll feel like a spelunker, since you must wear a hard hat throughout the tour. ⊠ *North Coast Hwy., 2 miles (3 km) east of Discovery Bay, Runaway Bay* ☎ *876/973–2841* ⊕ *www.greengrottocavesja.com* ⊠ *$20* ⊙ *Daily 9–4.*

OCHO RIOS

Although Ocho Rios isn't near eight rivers as its name would seem to indicate, it does have a seemingly endless series of cascades that sparkle from limestone rocks along the coast. (The name Ocho Rios came about because the English misunderstood the Spanish *las chorreras*— "the waterfalls.") The town itself isn't very attractive and can be traffic-clogged, but the area has several worthwhile attractions, including the very popular and touristic Dunn's River Falls. A few steps from the main road in Ocho Rios are some of the most charming inns and oceanfront restaurants in the Caribbean. Lying on the sand of what seems to be your very own cove or swinging gently in a hammock while sipping a tropical drink, you'll soon forget the traffic that's just a stroll away. The original "defenders" stationed at the Old Fort, built in 1777, spent much of their time sacking and plundering as far afield as St. Augustine, Florida, and sharing their booty with the local plantation owners who financed their missions. Discovery Bay, 15 miles (24 km) west, is where Columbus landed and where there's a small museum with such artifacts as ships' bells and cannons and iron pots used for boiling sugarcane. Don't miss a drive through Fern Gully, a natural canopy of vegetation filtered by sunlight. (Jamaica has the world's largest number of fern species, more than 570.) To reach the stretch of road called Fern Gully, take the A3 highway south of Ocho Rios.

WHAT TO SEE

★ **Bob Marley Mausoleum.** Travelers with an interest in Bob Marley won't want to miss Nine Mile, the community where the reggae legend was born and is buried. Today his former home is a shrine to his music and values. Tucked behind a tall fence, the site is marked with green and gold flags. Tours are led by Rastafarians, who take visitors through the house and point out the single bed that Marley wrote about in "Is This Love". Visitors also step inside the mausoleum where the singer is interred with his guitar. The site includes a restaurant and gift shop. Visitors from Ocho Rios can arrange transport by taxi, but the round-trip fare is about $175; a less expensive option is the Chukka Bob Marley Jeep Safari ($74, 4½ hours, ages 18 and older), a guided tour with Chukka Caribbean. We strongly recommend a guided tour here since the hustlers that meet you outside the Bob Marley Centre are some of the most aggressive in Jamaica. ⊠ *Nine Mile, St. Ann* ☎ *876/843–0498* ⊕ *www.bobmarleymovement.com* ☞ *$19* ⊙ *Daily 9–5.*

★ **Coyaba Gardens and Mahoe Waterfalls.** Jamaica's national motto is "Out of Many, One People," and here you can see exhibits on the many cultural influences that have contributed to the creation of the one. The museum covers the island's history from the time of the Arawak Indians up to the present day. A guided 45-minute tour through the lush 3-acre garden, which is 1½ miles (2½ km) south of Ocho Rios, introduces you to the flora and fauna of the island. The complex includes a crafts and gift shop and a snack bar. ⊠ *Shaw Park Estate, Shaw Park Ridge Rd., Ocho Rios* ☎ *876/974–6235* ⊕ *www.coyabagardens.com* ☞ *$10* ⊙ *Daily 9–5.*

★ **Chukka Caribbean Adventures at Cranbrook Flower Forest.** Chukka Caribbean took over this attraction in 2011, where you can enjoy the north-coast rivers and flowers without the crowds. The botanical reserve is filled with blooming orchids, ginger, and ferns and is the private creation of Ivan Linton, who has pampered the plants of this former plantation since the early 1980s. Linton still proudly points out the birds-of-paradise, croton, ginger, heliconia, and begonias as if they were his dear children. The grounds are perfect for a picnic followed by a hike alongside shady Laughlin's Great River. The path climbs high into the hills to a waterfall paradise. Other attraactions include horseback riding, wading, and volleyball. The complex has a snack shop and restrooms. ⊠ *5 miles (8 km) east of Runaway Bay, 1 mile (2 km) off North Coast Hwy., Ocho Rios* ☎ *876/610–6509* ⊕ *www.chukkacaribbean.com* ☞ *$10, $15 for guided tour, and $30 for the hike to the riverhead* ⊙ *Daily 9–5.*

Fodor's Choice
★ **Dunn's River Falls.** One of Jamaica's most popular attractions is an eye-catching sight: 600 feet of cold, clear mountain water splashing over a series of stone steps to the warm Caribbean. The best way to enjoy the falls is to climb the slippery steps: don a swimsuit, take the hand of the person ahead of you, and trust that the chain of hands and bodies leads to an experienced guide. The leaders of the climbs are personable fellows who reel off bits of local lore while telling you where to step; you can hire a guide's service for a tip of a few dollars. After the climb, you exit through a crowded market, another reminder that this is one of Jamaica's top tourist attractions. If you can, try to schedule a visit on a

Climbing Dunn's River Falls, Ocho Rios

day when no cruise ships are in port. ■ TIP→ **Always climb with a licensed guide at Dunn's River Falls. Freelance guides might be a little cheaper, but the experienced guides can tell you just where to plant each footstep—helping you prevent a fall.** ⊠ *Off Rte. A1, between St. Ann's Bay and Ocho Rios, Ocho Rios* ☎ *876/974-4767* ⊕ *www.dunnsriverfallsja.com* 🎫 *$20* ⊙ *Daily 8:30-4 (last entry 3 pm).*

★ **Firefly.** About 20 miles (32 km) east of Ocho Rios near Port Maria, Firefly was once Sir Noël Coward's vacation home and is now a national monument managed by Chris Blackwell's Island company. Although the setting is Eden-like, the house is surprisingly spartan, considering that the playwright often entertained jet-setters and royalty. He wrote *High Spirits, Quadrille,* and other plays here, and his simple grave is on the grounds next to a small stage where his works are occasionally performed. Recordings of Coward singing about "mad dogs and Englishmen" echo over the lawns. Tours include a walk through the house and grounds where Coward is buried. The view from the house's hilltop perch is one of the best on the North Coast, making Firefly well worth the price of admission. A tour must be arranged in advance by phone. ⊠ *Port Maria* ☎ *876/622-9007, 876/726-1630* 🎫 *$10* ⊙ *By arrangement.*

Mystic Mountain. This is Ocho Rios' newest attraction, covering 100 acres of mountainside rain forest near Dunn's River Falls. Visitors board the Rainforest Sky Explorer, a chairlift that soars through and over the pristine rain forest to the apex of Mystic Mountain. On top, there is a restaurant with spectacular views of Ocho Rios, arts-and-crafts shops, and the attraction's signature tours, the Rainforest Bobsled Jamaica ride and the Rainforest Zipline Canopy ride. Custom-designed bobsleds, inspired by Jamaica's Olympic bobsled team, run downhill on steel rails with speed controlled by the driver, using simple push-pull levers. Couples can run their bobsleds in tandem. The zip-line tours streak through lush rain forest under the care of an expert guide who points out items of interest. The entire facility was built using environmentally friendly techniques and materials so as to leave the native rain forest undisturbed. ⊠ *North Coast Hwy., Ocho Rios* ☎ *876/974–3990* ⊕ *www.rainforestbobsledjamaica.com* ✉ *$47–$137* ⊙ *9–5 (adventures from 10–3:30).*

PORT ANTONIO

The first Port Antonio tourists arrived in the early 20th century seeking a respite from New York winters. In time, the area became fashionable among a fast-moving crowd that included everyone from Rudyard Kipling to Bette Davis; today celebs such as Tom Cruise, Eddie Murphy, Brooke Shields, and Denzel Washington dodge the limelight with a getaway in this quiet haven. Although the action has moved elsewhere, the area can still weave a spell. Robin Moore wrote *The French Connection* here, and Broadway's tall and talented Tommy Tune found inspiration for the musical *Nine* while being pampered at Trident. Today Port Antonio is one of Jamaica's quietest getaways, primarily preferred by long-staying Europeans. Even with the recent improvement of the North Coast Highway from Ocho Rios to Port Antonio, tourism remains slow here, and several attractions have shuttered their doors because of low tourism numbers. Port Antonio has also long been a center for some of the Caribbean's finest deep-sea fishing. Dolphin (the delectable fish, not the lovable mammal) is the likely catch here, along with tuna, kingfish, and wahoo. In October the weeklong Blue Marlin Tournament attracts anglers from around the world. By the time they've all had their fill of beer, it's the fish stories—rather than the fish—that carry the day.

WHAT TO SEE

Blue Lagoon. One of Port Antonio's best-known attractions is the Blue Lagoon, whose azure waters have to be seen to be believed. The colors of the spring-fed lagoon are a real contrast to the warmer waters of the ocean. Catch some rays on the floating docks, or relax on the small beach. Just how deep is the Blue Lagoon? You might hear it's bottomless, but the lagoon has been measured at a depth of 180 feet. Guests of nearby properties may have access to the lagoon, while those staying farther away can hire an operator for rafting trips. ⊠ *9 miles (13 km) east of Port Antonio, 1 mile (1½ km) east of San San Beach, Port Antonio.*

★ **Boston Beach.** A short drive east of Port Antonio is Boston Beach, a don't-miss destination for lovers of jerk pork. The recipe may have originated with the Arawak, the island's original inhabitants, but modern jerk was perfected by the Maroons. Eating almost nothing but wild hog preserved over smoking coals enabled these former slaves to survive years of fierce guerrilla warfare with the English. Jerk resurfaced in the 1930s, and the spicy barbecue drew diners from around the island.

Today a handful of small jerk stands, collectively known as the Boston Jerk Centre, offer fiery flavors cooled by some *festival* bread (similar to a southern hush puppy) and a cold Red Stripe. ⊠ *Rte. A4, east of Port Antonio, Port Antonio.*

Coronation Bakery. Need a Break? Coronation Bakery has served up freshly made baked goods for more than seven decades. Grab some hard-dough bread (originally brought to Jamaica by the Chinese), an unleavened bun called *bulla,* or even spicy patties. ⊠ *18 West St., Port Antonio* ☎ *876/993–2710.*

Folly Lighthouse. Since 1888, this red-and-white-stripe masonry lighthouse has stood watch at the tip of Folly Point. Administered by the Jamaica National Heritage Trust, the lighthouse is an often-photographed site near Port Antonio's East Harbour. ⊠ *Folly Point, Port Antonio.*

Rio Grande. Jamaica's river-rafting operations began here, on an 8-mi-long (13-km-long), swift, green waterway from Berrydale to Rafter's Rest. (Beyond that, the Rio Grande flows into the Caribbean Sea at St. Margaret's Bay.) The trip of about three hours is made on bamboo rafts pushed along by a guide who is likely to be quite a character. You can pack a picnic lunch to enjoy on the raft or on the riverbank; wherever you lunch, a Red Stripe vendor is likely to appear. A restaurant, a bar, and several souvenir shops can be found at Rafter's Rest. ⊠ *Rte. A4, 5 miles (8 km) west of Port Antonio, Port Antonio.*

★ **Somerset Falls.** On the Daniels River, these falls are in a veritable botanical garden. A concrete walk to the falls takes you past the ruins of a Spanish aqueduct and Genesis Falls before reaching Hidden Falls. At Hidden Falls you board a boat and travel beneath the tumbling water; more daring travelers can swim in a whirlpool or jump off the falls into a pool of water. A bar and restaurant specializing in local seafood is a great place to catch your breath. ⊠ *Rte. A4, 13 miles (21 km) west of Port Antonio, Port Antonio* ☎ *876/913–0046* ⊕ *www. somersetfallsjamaica.com* ▧ *$12* ◷ *Daily 9–5.*

KINGSTON

Few travelers—particularly Americans—take the time to visit Kingston, although organized day trips make the city accessible from Ocho Rios and Montego Bay. That's understandable, as Kingston is a tough city to love. It's big and, all too often, bad, with gang-controlled neighborhoods that are known to erupt into violence.

However, if you've seen other parts of the island and yearn to know more about the heart and soul of Jamaica, Kingston is worth a visit. This government and business center is also a cultural capital, home to numerous dance troupes, theaters, and museums. It's also home to the University of the West Indies, one of the Caribbean's largest universities. In many ways, Kingston reflects the true Jamaica—a wonderful cultural mix—more than the sunny havens of the North Coast. As one Jamaican put it, "You don't really know Jamaica until you know Kingston."

North of New Kingston, the city gives way to steep hills and magnificent homes. East of here, the views are even grander as the road winds into the Blue Mountains, one of the island's least developed yet most beautiful regions.

WHAT TO SEE

★ **Bob Marley Museum.** At the height of his career, Bob Marley purchased a house on Kingston's Hope Road and added a recording studio—painted Rastafarian red, yellow, and green, of course. It now houses this museum, the capital's best-known tourist site. The guided tour takes you through rooms wallpapered with magazine and newspaper articles that chronicle his rise to stardom. There's a 20-minute biographical film on Marley's career and a reference library if you want to learn more. A striking mural by Jah Bobby, *The Journey of Superstar Bob Marley*, depicts the hero's life from its beginnings, in a womb shaped like a coconut, to enshrinement in the hearts of the Jamaican people. ⊠ *56 Hope Rd., Kingston* ☎ *876/927–9152* ⊕ *www.bobmarley-foundation. com* ⊠ *$20* ☉ *Mon.–Sat. 9:30 am–4 pm.*

Devon House. Built in 1881 as the mansion of the island's first black millionaire, then bought and restored by the government in the 1960s, Devon House is filled with period furnishings, such as Venetian-crystal chandeliers and period reproductions. You can visit the two-story mansion (built with a South American gold miner's fortune) only on a guided tour. On the grounds you can find some of the island's best crafts shops, as well as one of the few mahogany trees to have survived Kingston's ambitious but not always careful development. ⊠ *26 Hope Rd., Kingston* ☎ *876/929–6602* ⊠ *House tour $9* ☉ *Mon–Fri 9:30–4.*

★ **National Gallery.** The artists represented at the National Gallery may not be household names, but their paintings are sensitive and moving. You can find works by such Jamaican masters as painter John Dunkley and sculptor Edna Manley. Among other highlights from the 1920s through 1980s are works by the artist Kapo, a self-taught painter who specialized in religious images. The gallery's exhibition program introduces visitors to the work of contemporary Jamaican artists through events such as The National Biennial and the National Visual Arts Competition and Exhibition, which are staged annually each July and August, respectively. Guided tours are offered for J$3000 for groups of up to 25 people and must be booked in advance of your visit. ⊠ *12 Ocean Blvd., near waterfront, Kingston* ☎ *876/922–1561* ⊕ *www.natgalja.org. jm* ⊠ *J$400* ☉ *Tues.–Thurs. 10–4:30, Fri. 10–4, Sat. 10–3.*

Port Royal. Just south of Kingston, Port Royal was called "the wickedest city in Christendom" until an earthquake tumbled much of it into the sea in 1692. The spirits of Henry Morgan and other buccaneers add energy to what remains. The proudest possession of St. Peter's Church, rebuilt in 1726 to replace Christ's Church, is a silver communion set said to have been donated by Morgan himself (who probably obtained it during a raid on Panama).

A ferry from the square in downtown Kingston goes to Port Royal at least twice a day, but most visitors arrive by road, continuing past the airport to this small community. If you drive out to Port Royal from

Kingston, you pass several other sights, including remains of old forts virtually overgrown with vegetation, an old naval cemetery (which has some intriguing headstones), and a monument commemorating Jamaica's first coconut tree, planted in 1863 (there's no tree there now, just plenty of cactus and scrub brush). You can no longer down rum in Port Royal's legendary 40 taverns, but a few small bars remain in operation.

Fort Charles. You can explore the remnants of Fort Charles, once the city's largest garrison. Built in 1662, this is the oldest surviving structure from the British occupation. On the grounds you can find an old artillery storehouse, called Giddy House, which gained its name after being tilted by the earthquake of 1907. Locals say its slant makes you dizzy. The Fort Charles Maritime Museum is housed in what was once the headquarters for the British Royal Navy. Admiral Horatio Nelson served as a naval lieutenant here in 1779. The museum features a re-creation of Nelson's private quarters, as well as other artifacts from the era, including models of various sailing vessels. Fort Charles is located just past Norman Manley International Airport. ⊠ *Fort Charles, Port Royal* ☎ *876/967–8438* 🖃 *$10* ⊙ *9–4:45*.

14

BLUE MOUNTAINS

★ **Blue Mountains.** Best known as the source of Blue Mountain coffee, these mountains rising out of the lush jungle north of Kingston are a favorite destination with adventure travelers, as well as hikers, birders, and anyone looking to see what lies beyond the beach. You can find guided tours to the mountains from the Ocho Rios and Port Antonio areas, as well as from Kingston. Unless you're traveling with a local, don't try to go on your own; the roads wind and dip without warning, and hand-lettered signs blow away, leaving you without a clue as to which way to go. It's best to hire a taxi (look for red PPV license plates to identify a licensed cab) or book a guided tour.

Mavis Bank Coffee Factory. The site of the coffee plant is in the small town of Mavis Bank, northeast of Kingston, on the main road to Blue Mountain peak. An hour-long guided tour of Mavis Bank Coffee Factory takes you through the processing of coffee, from planting to distribution and includes a sample cup of the drink. Inquire about tours when you arrive at the main office. ⊠ *Gordon Town Rd., Mavis Bank* ☎ *876/977–8005, 876/977–8528* ⊕ *www.jablumcoffee.com* 🖃 *$5* ⊙ *Weekdays 9–2*

SOUTH COAST

★ **Appleton Estate.** Before the rise of tourism as Jamaica's main industry, the island was highly prized for its sugarcane production. Vast fortunes were made here during colonial times, and many of the island's historic great houses remain as reminders of that time. Much of the sugarcane was processed into molasses, the main ingredient in the production of rum. Appleton Estate, still one of the Caribbean's premier rum distillers, offers guided tours illustrating the history of rum making in the region. After a lively discussion of the days when sugarcane was crushed by donkey power, the tours move on to a behind-the-scenes look at the modern facility. After the tour, samples flow freely, and every visitor receives a complimentary bottle of rum. There's a good restaurant here serving genuine Jamaican dishes. ⊠ *Hwy. B6, Siloah* ☎ *876/963–9215* ⊕ *www.appletonrumtour.com* 💰 *$25* ⊗ *Mon.–Sat. 9–3:30.*

High Mountain Coffee Factory. Grown on nearby plantations, coffee beans are brought here for processing. Call ahead for tours, or just stop by the gift shop for a sample taste. In addition to coffee, the gift shop features other High Mountain products like spices, condiments, and scented candles. ⊠ *Winston Jones Hwy., Williamsfield* ☎ *876/963–4211* ⊕ *www.jamaicastandardproducts.com* 💰 *J$200* ⊗ *Mon.–Thurs. 8–5, Fri. 8–4:30.*

★ **Y.S. Falls.** A quiet alternative to Dunn's River Falls in Ocho Rios, the falls are part of a cattle and thoroughbred horse farm and are reached via motorized jitney. If you aren't staying on the South Coast, companies in Negril offer excursions. The last tour of the day begins at 3:30. ⊠ *North of A2, just past town of Middle Quarters* ☎ *876/997–6360* ⊕ *www.ysfalls.com* 💰 *$16* ⊗ *Tues.–Sun. 9:30–4:30.*

EN ROUTE Although the constant roar of speeding trucks keeps the site from being idyllic, **Bamboo Avenue,** the section of Route A1 between Middle Quarters and Lacovia, is an often-photographed stretch of highway that's completely canopied with tall bamboo. Roadside vendors sell chilled coconuts, cracking them with machetes to reveal the jelly inside.

NEGRIL

In the 18th century, English ships assembled here in convoys for dangerous ocean crossings. The infamous pirate Calico Jack and his crew were captured right here while they guzzled rum. All but two of them were hanged on the spot; Mary Read and Anne Bonney were pregnant at the time, so their executions were delayed.

On the winding coast road 55 miles (89 km) southwest of Mo'Bay, Negril was once Jamaica's best-kept secret, but it has shed some of its bohemian, ramshackle atmosphere for the attractions and activities traditionally associated with Mo'Bay. One thing that hasn't changed about this west-coast center (whose only true claim to fame is a 7-mile [11-km] beach) is a casual approach to life. As you wander from lunch in the sun to shopping in the sun to sports in the sun, you'll find that swimsuits and cover-ups are common attire.

Negril stretches along the coast south from horseshoe-shape Bloody Bay (named when it was a whale-processing center) along the calm waters of Long Bay to the lighthouse. Nearby, divers spiral downward off 50-foot-high cliffs into the deep green depths as the sun turns into a ball of fire and sets the clouds ablaze with color. Sunset is also the time when Norman Manley Boulevard, which intersects West End Road, comes to life with busy beachside restaurants and reggae stage shows.

WHAT TO SEE

The Blue Hole. Located about 20 minutes from Negril near the community of Little Bay, the Blue Hole is a mineral spring and swimming pool. You can jump 22 feet off the cliff into the hole or climb down a ladder to swim and bathe in the icy water. Mud around the water's edge is said to be good for your skin, and the water itself is reputed to have therapeutic properties. For those who cannot jump or climb down into the hole, water has been pumped up into a swimming pool on the surface. A bar, a grill, cabanas, and a volleyball court add to the attractions. Take a charter from Negril, or call to organize a pickup. ⊠ *Brighton, Negril* ☎ *876/860–8805.*

☺ **Kool Runnings Adventure Park.** Billing itself as the place where "Jamaica
★ Comes to Play," this park makes a good beach alternative on days when the sea is rough or for travelers not staying at beachfront properties. Fun at the park includes 10 waterslides and a ¼-mile lazy-river float ride, as well as a go-kart track and kayaking. The park's adventure zone now features outdoor laser combat games and "Jamboo" rafting which allows the family to take to the water on floating bamboo. There is also bungee jumping and a "kool kanoe" adventure to tempt all ages. A wave pool was scheduled to open in early 2012, and a paint ball adventure was also due to be added to the list of attractions. Admission prices vary according to age and the adventure. ⊠ *Norman Manley Blvd., Negril* ☎ *876/957–5400* ⊕ *www.koolrunnings.com* 🏷 *$28* ☉ *Daily 11–5.*

14

WHERE TO EAT

It would be a shame to travel to the heart of this complex culture without having at least one typical island meal. Probably the most famous Jamaican dish is jerk pork—the ultimate island barbecue. The pork (purists cook a whole pig) is covered with a paste of Scotch bonnet peppers, pimento berries (also known as allspice), and other herbs, and cooked slowly over a coal fire. Many aficionados believe the best jerk comes from Boston Beach, near Port Antonio. Jerk chicken and fish are also seen on many menus. The ever-so-traditional rice and peas, also known as "coat of arms," is similar to the *moros y cristianos* of Spanish-speaking islands: white rice cooked with red kidney beans, coconut milk, scallions, and seasonings.

The island's most famous soup—the fiery pepper pot—is a spicy mixture of salt pork, salt beef, okra, and the island green known as callaloo. Patties (spicy meat pies) elevate street food to new heights. Although patties actually originated in Haiti, Jamaicans excel at making them. Curried goat is another island standout: young goat is cooked with spices and is more tender and has a gentler flavor than the lamb for which it was substituted by immigrants from India. Salted fish was once the best that islanders could do between catches. Out of necessity, a breakfast staple (and the national dish of Jamaica) was invented. It joins seasonings with saltfish and ackee, a red fruit that grows on trees throughout the island. When cooked in this dish, ackee reminds most people of scrambled eggs.

There are fine restaurants in all the resort areas, many in the resorts themselves, though the Kingston area has the widest selection. Many restaurants outside the hotels in Mo'Bay and Ocho Rios will provide complimentary transportation.

What to Wear: Dinner dress is usually casual chic (or just plain casual at many local hangouts, especially in Negril). There are a few exceptions in Kingston and at the top resorts; some require semiformal wear (no shorts; collared shirts for men) in the evening during high season. People tend to dress up for dinner; men might be more comfortable in nice slacks, women in a sundress.

BEST BETS FOR DINING

Fodor's Choice ★
Boston Jerk Centre, Evita's Italian Restaurant, Pork Pit, Redbones Blues Café, Scotchies Too, Strawberry Hill, Three Palms Restaurant

BEST LOCAL FOOD
Boston Jerk Centre, Pork Pit, Scotchies, Scotchies Too

BEST FOR A SPECIAL OCCASION
Strawberry Hill, Three Palms Restaurant

MONTEGO BAY

$$
ECLECTIC
✕ **Jamaican Bobsled Café.** The trials and triumphs of Jamaica's Olympic bobsled team, inspiration for the 1993 film *Cool Runnings*, are celebrated at this Hip Strip eatery. Offerings like the barbecue burger, the barbecue chicken pizza, and island spice curry goat make up the family-friendly menu. A percentage of the café's profits go toward supporting the team. ⑤ *Average main: $16* ⊠ *69 Gloucester Ave., Montego Bay* ☎ *876/940–7009.*

$$$$
SEAFOOD
✕ **Marguerites Seafood By the Sea.** At this romantic seaside restaurant, lobster, shrimp, and fish are the specialities, as is the Caesar salad, prepared table-side. ⑤ *Average main: $34* ⊠ *Gloucester Ave., Montego Bay* ☎ *876/952–4777* ⌕ *Reservations essential* ☾ *No lunch.*

$$
CARIBBEAN
✕ **The Native.** Shaded by a large poinciana tree and overlooking Gloucester Avenue, this open-air stone terrace serves Jamaican and international dishes. To go native, start with smoked marlin, move on to the *boonoonoonoos* platter (a sampler of local dishes), and round out with Blue Mountain coffee tiramisu. Candlelit tables make this a romantic choice for dinner on weekends. ⑤ *Average main: $15* ⊠ *29 Gloucester Ave., Montego Bay* ☎ *876/979–2769.*

$$$
SEAFOOD
✕ **Pier 1.** After tropical drinks at the deck bar, you'll be ready to dig into the international variations on fresh seafood; the best are the grilled lobster and any preparation of island snapper. Occasional party cruises leave from the marina here, and on Friday night the restaurant is mobbed by locals who come to dance. ⑤ *Average main: $22* ⊠ *Off Howard Cooke Blvd., Montego Bay* ☎ *876/952–2452.*

$
JAMAICAN
Fodor's Choice
★
✕ **Pork Pit.** A favorite with many Mo'Bay locals, this no-frills eatery serves Jamaican specialties including some fiery jerk—note that it's spiced to local tastes, not watered down for tourist palates. Many get their food to go, but you can also find picnic tables just outside. ⑤ *Average main: $10* ⊠ *27 Gloucester Ave., Montego Bay* ☎ *876/940–3008.*

CLOSE UP

Barbecue, Jamaica-Style

Modern jerk originated in the 1930s along Boston Beach, east of Port Antonio. Here the first wayside stands sprang up on the side of the road, offering fiery jerk served in a casual atmosphere. Today jerk stands are everywhere on the island, but many aficionados still return to Boston Beach for the "real thing," which is sold by the pound.

The practice of jerking meat was first recorded in 1698 by a French priest, who wrote of a jerk pit made with four forked sticks with crosspieces covered with a grill made of sticks. On the grill was placed a whole pig, stuffed with lime juice, salt, pimento,

and spices that helped preserve the meat in the hot climate.

Today jerk is still cooked in a pit that contains a fire made from pimento wood. The meat, which is primarily pork but can also be chicken, goat, or fish, is marinated with jerk sauce. Every cook has his own favorite recipe, but most include allspice (pimento berries), cloves, garlic, onion, ginger, cinnamon, thyme, and peppers. Commercial jerk sauces are also available. Once the jerk is cooked to perfection, it's served up with side dishes such as breadfruit, rice and peas, and a bread called festival.

14

$$
CARIBBEAN

✕ **Rum Jungle Restaurant.** Decorated like an indoor jungle, this expansive restaurant in the Coral Cliff entertainment center is casual and fun. The cuisine features Caribbean dishes ranging from escoveitch fish to jerk chicken, while the large bar pours from a selection of Caribbean and worldwide rums. Sunday brunch is popular. $ *Average main: $20* ✉ *Coral Cliff, 165 Gloucester Ave., Montego Bay* ☎ *876/952–4130.*

$
JAMAICAN

✕ **Scotchies.** Many call this open-air jerk eatery the best in Jamaica, but the new Scotchies Too in Ocho Rios certainly makes it a tough decision. Like its sister restaurant, Scotchies serves up genuine jerk—chicken, pork, fish, sausage, and more—with fiery sauce and delectable side dishes including festival (similar to a Southern hush puppy) and rice and peas. This restaurant is a favorite with Montego Bay residents; on a typical day you're likely to see a slap-the-table game of dominoes. $ *Average main: $10* ✉ *North Coast Hwy., across from Holiday Inn SunSpree, 10 miles (16 km) east of Montego Bay, Montego Bay* ☎ *876/953–3301.*

$$$$
ECLECTIC

✕ **Sugar Mill.** Caribbean international cuisine is served with flair at this terrace restaurant on the Half Moon golf course. The menu offers Caribbean fare with an Asian twist, and favorites include curried lamb with roti, lion fish, and flame-grilled Solomon's Boston jerk brochette. A well-stocked wine cellar rounds out the experience. $ *Average main: $35* ✉ *Half Moon, North Coast Rd., 7 miles (11 km) east of Montego Bay, Montego Bay* ☎ *876/953–2211* ⌕ *Reservations essential.*

$$$$
CARIBBEAN
Fodor's Choice
★

✕ **Three Palms Restaurant.** This fine-dining enclave serves Caribbean fusion cuisine. Within Cinnamon Hill Course Clubhouse, the restaurant includes both indoor and alfresco dining options. Dishes range from herb-crusted snapper to seafood rundown, a take on a traditional Jamaican seafood dish made with coconut milk and lemongrass.

$ *Average main: $36* ⊠ *Rose Hall Resort & Spa, North Coast Hwy., St. James* ✛ *15 miles (24 km) east of Montego Bay* ☎ 876/953-2650 ⊕ *www.RoseHallResort.com* ⚠ *Reservations essential* ⊘ *No lunch.*

OCHO RIOS

$$$
ECLECTIC
✕ **Almond Tree.** A longtime favorite in Ocho Rios, this restaurant is named for the massive tree growing through the roof. For many diners, the evening starts with a drink at the terrace bar overlooking the sea. Dinner, which can be enjoyed on the terrace or in the dining room, begins with pumpkin or pepper pot soup before moving on to such entrées as fresh fish, veal piccata, and fondue. The service can be somewhat slow, so for many diners this is the evening's activity. $ *Average main: $23* ⊠ *Hibiscus Lodge Hotel, 87 Main St., Ocho Rios* ☎ 876/974-2813.

$$
ECLECTIC
Fodor'sChoice
★
✕ **Evita's Italian Restaurant.** Evita's commands a wonderful view of Ocho Rios and the sea from its outdoor verandah dining area. Just about every celebrity who has visited Ocho Rios has dined at this hilltop restaurant, and Evita has the pictures to prove it. Guests feel like stars themselves, with attentive waitstaff helping to guide them through a list of about 30 kinds of pasta, ranging from lasagna Rastafari (vegetarian) and fiery jerk spaghetti to *Ravioli Eccellenza* (jumbo cheese ravioli tossed in baby-shrimp tomato-Alfredo sauce and laced with Sambuca). Kids under 12 eat for half price, and light eaters will appreciate half portions. $ *Average main: $20* ⊠ *Mantalent Inn, Eden Bower Rd., Ocho Rios* ☎ 876/974-2333.

$
JAMAICAN
✕ **Roadster.** A simple, rustic eatery across the road from Jamaica Inn, Roadster is a great place for good Jamaican food at unbeatable prices. You can eat under a tree or inside the basic restaurant, which is run by longtime German resident Marion Rose and her Jamaican husband. The menu has local favorites such as fried chicken and oxtail. Go early or call ahead with your order, because there's a limited amount of these treats each day. $ *Average main: J$400* ⊠ *Hibiscus Dr., Ocho Rios* ☎ 876/974-2910 ▬ *No credit cards.*

$$$$
CARIBBEAN
Fodor'sChoice
★
✕ **Scotchies Too.** The Ocho Rios branch of the longtime Montego Bay favorite has been lauded by international chefs for its excellent jerk. The open-air eatery offers plates of jerk chicken, sausage, fish, pork, and ribs, all accompanied by festival, bammy, and some fire-breathing hot sauce. Be sure to step over to the kitchen to watch the preparation of the jerk over the pits. $ *Average main: J$475* ⊠ *Drax Hall, North Coast Hwy., Ocho Rios* ☎ 876/794-9457.

$$$
ITALIAN
Fodor'sChoice
★
✕ **Toscanini.** At Harmony Hall, this longtime favorite offers seating in the dining room and on the garden verandah. The menu features classic Italian dishes and Jamaican fusion cuisine, all made with fresh, local produce. Look out for marinated marlin, caught in local waters, and the tuna, which customers will come specially from Kingston to enjoy. Huge juicy South Coast prawns also draw in customers. Desserts such as tiramisu, chocolate profiteroles, and a wicked affogato round off the meal beautifully. If you are staying in Ocho Rios, call for the complimentary shuttle. $ *Average main: $23* ⊠ *Harmony Hall, North Coast Hwy., Ocho Rios* ☎ 876/975-4785.

Fresh shrimp offered at a colorful roadside stand.

PORT ANTONIO

$$$$ ✕ **Mille Fleurs.** At this restaurant you can sit on a terrace surrounded by
JAMAICAN tropical vegetation and enjoy the sunset. The menu changes daily but
★ always includes dishes prepared with local ingredients such as ackee-
fruit soufflé or plantain fritters with black-bean dip. Lobster medallion
in a creamy passion sauce is a favorite; for something more unique, try
the jerk rabbit. Innovative vegetarian options, such as ratatouille with
feta and herb crumble, are always on the menu, and each week features
"Meatless Mondays." ⑤ *Average main: $36* ⊠ *Hotel Mockingbird Hill,
Point Ann, Port Antonio* ☎ *876/993–7267* ⌲ *Reservations essential.*

KINGSTON

$$$$ ✕ **Redbones Blues Café.** In a colonial-era residence, this restaurant lets
JAMAICAN you choose between tables in two dining rooms, outdoors on the ter-
Fodor's Choice race, or in the courtyard. Aspects of the menu were created by the late
★ Norma Shirley (the renowned chef of Norma's fame), so look for interesting dishes such as callaloo strudel (a savory phyllo-dough pastry)
and smoked marlin salad. Though it's open for lunch on weekdays as
well as dinner, the café really comes alive in the evenings, when meals
are accompanied by live music. Thursday nights feature jazz and blues,
and Fridays feature a variety of other music genres. Saturdays alter-
nate between Latin-theme nights and movies on the lawn. ⑤ *Average
main: $31* ⊠ *1 Argyle Rd., Kingston* ☎ *876/978–8262, 876/978–6091*
☽ *Closed Sun. No lunch Sat.*

BLUE MOUNTAINS

$$$$

JAMAICAN

Fodor'sChoice

★

✕ Strawberry Hill. A favorite with Kingstonians for its elegant Sunday brunch, Strawberry Hill is well worth the drive from the city. The open-air terrace has a spectacular view of Kingston and the countryside. The restaurant is open for lunch and dinner, offering a table d'hote menu with constantly changing dishes, depending on what fresh produce is available locally and seasonally. Entrées include rack of lamb served with herb potatoes and minted peas, and jerked cornish hen. $ *Average main: $33* ⊠ *Strawberry Hill, New Castle Rd., Irishtown* ☎ *876/944–8400* ⌂ *Reservations essential.*

SOUTH COAST

$$

JAMAICAN

★

✕ Billy's Grassy Park. A true side-of-the-road stop on the South Coast Highway, Billy's Grassy Park serves fiery Jamaican food, including scorching peppered shrimp caught just behind the kitchen. Dining's mostly a grab-and-go affair, although stands next door provide local desserts like fresh coconut jelly to cool the burn. $ *Average main: $22* ⊠ *A2, about 30 mins. east of Whitehouse, Middlequarters* ☎ *876/366–4182* ▭ *No credit cards.*

$$

ECLECTIC

★

✕ Jack Sprat Seafood and Pizza Restaurant. It's no surprise that this restaurant shares its home resort's bohemian style (it's the beachside dining spot at Jakes). From the casual outdoor tables to the late-night dancehall rhythm, it's a place to come and hang loose. Jerk crab joins favorites like pizzas and jerk chicken on the menu, all followed by house-made ice cream. $ *Average main: $18* ⊠ *Jakes, Calabash Bay, Treasure Beach* ☎ *876/965–3000.*

$$

JAMAICAN

★

✕ Little Ochie. This casual beachside eatery is a favorite with locals and travelers, favored for its genuine Jamaican dishes like fish tea, escoveitch fish, peppered shrimp, jerk chicken, seapuss (octopus), and more. Most of the seafood is brought in by fishermen just yards away. For those staying in Treasure Beach, a favorite way to reach Little Ochie is by boat. $ *Average main: $17* ⊠ *About 7 miles (11 km) south of A2, Alligator Pond* ☎ *876/382–3375* ⊕ *www.littleochie.com.*

NEGRIL

$$

SEAFOOD

✕ Cosmo's Seafood Restaurant and Bar. Owner Cosmo Brown has made this seaside open-air bistro a pleasant place to spend the afternoon—and maybe stay on for dinner. Fish is the main attraction, and the conch soup—a house specialty—is a meal in itself. You can also find lobster (grilled or curried), fish-and-chips, and the catch of the morning. Customers often drop cover-ups to take a dip before coffee and dessert and return to lounge in chairs scattered under almond and sea-grape trees (there's an entrance fee of $5 for the beach). $ *Average main: $17* ⊠ *Norman Manley Blvd., Negril* ☎ *876/957–4330, 876/957–4784.*

$$

ECLECTIC

★

✕ The Hungry Lion. The Hungry Lion has been a longtime favorite in the West End and features many vegetarian dishes. This atmospheric restaurant with stylish decor also serves seafood and chicken dishes. Highlights include vegetarian shepherd's pie, jerk chicken kebabs, and steamed coconut snapper. The restaurant is open for dinner only. $ *Average main: $17* ⊠ *West End Rd., Negril* ☎ *876/957–4486* ⏱ *4 pm–10 pm.*

$$$
CARIBBEAN
Fodor'sChoice
★

✗ **Ivan's Restaurant & Bar.** A combination of upscale Caribbean cuisine, stunning cliffside dining, and romantic ambience make this one of the best places to eat on Negril's West End. Arrive just before dusk and watch the spectacular sunset while enjoying a cocktail by the simple thatched bar and eatery, which is decorated with lots of unique, funky art pieces. Dinner opens with a delicious complimentary conch soup. Beautifully presented appetizers include options like the Calypso Trio—three of Ivan's most requested "treats" all in one—chicken, sweet pepper, tomato, and pineapple skewer; jerk shrimp; and a Caribbean crab cake with Ivan dip. Don't miss entrées like grilled lobster with garlic butter and mashed potatoes or the seafood linguine, which has a mixture of shrimp, lobster, and snapper in a creamy white-wine sauce. Try the flambeed banana or pineapple for dessert—the waitress will set overproof rum on fire for you to blow out after two minutes and pour over ice cream. You can dress up or dine in casual wear. $ *Average main: $25* ⊠ *Catcha Falling Star, West End Rd., Negril* ☎ *(876)/957–0390.*

$$
INTERNATIONAL
★

✗ **LTU Pub.** This thatched bar and eatery is one of the prettiest on the whole of the West End. Located right on the cliffs, the views are dazzling during the day and at sunset, with steps down to the water to swim. At night, you can dine under the stars. Expats and long-term visitors hang out here to enjoy the laid-back vibe that put Negril on the map. Appetizer highlights include chicken-and-cheese quesadillas and coconut shrimp. Entrees feature beef tenderloin in red-wine sauce, chicken Lola, and snapper stuffed with callaloo. There are lots of pasta choices too. All dinner orders come with a delicious complimentary pumpkin soup. $ *Average main: $15* ⊠ *West End Rd., Negril* ☎ *876/957–0382.*

$$
CARIBBEAN
Fodor'sChoice
★

✗ **The Rockhouse Restaurant.** With its seaside perch, the Rockhouse restaurant would already offer a memorable dining experience—but an incredible menu makes your meal that much more special. Serving what has been deemed "new Jamaican cuisine," Rockhouse offers Jamaican fare prepared with a light touch. Top entrées include blackened mahimahi with mango chutney, Old Time Synting (a mixture of seafood in a rundown sauce), and a Jamaican stir-fry with callaloo, chayote, carrot, cabbage, rice, and peas. A rich selection of international wines accompanies the menu, and the restaurant prides itself on its attentive waitstaff. $ *Average main: $17* ⊠ *Rockhouse, West End Rd., Negril* ☎ *876/957–4373* ⊕ *www.rockhousehotel.com.*

$
JAMAICAN
★

✗ **Shark's Restaurant.** This nicely decorated, thatched roadside eatery opposite Tensing Pen is one of the best places in Negril to sample local cooking in a friendly and laid-back atmosphere. Juliet, who owns and runs the restaurant, also cooks. There are just three tables, but all her food is delicious, including chicken fricassee, curried goat, and grilled lobster with lashings of garlic butter. $ *Average main: $8* ⊠ *West End Rd., Negril* ☎ *876/428–8411.*

WHERE TO STAY

Jamaica was the birthplace of the Caribbean all-inclusive resort, a concept that started in Ocho Rios and has spread throughout the island, now comprising the lion's share of hotel rooms. Package prices usually include airport transfers, accommodations, three meals a day, snacks, all bar drinks (often including premium liquors) and soft drinks, a full menu of sports options (including scuba diving and golf at high-end establishments), nightly entertainment, and all gratuities and taxes. At most all-inclusive resorts, the only surcharges are for such luxuries as spa and beauty treatments, telephone calls, tours, vow-renewal ceremonies, and weddings (though even weddings are often included at high-end establishments).

The all-inclusive market is especially strong with couples and honeymooners. To maintain a romantic atmosphere (no Marco Polo games by the pool), some resorts have minimum age requirements ranging from 12 to 18. Other properties court families with tempting supervised kids' programs, family-friendly entertainment, and in-room amenities especially for young travelers.

For expanded reviews, facilities, and current deals, visit Fodors.com.

PRIVATE VILLA RENTALS

Ocho Rios is filled with private villas, especially in the Discovery Bay area. In Jamaica, most luxury villas come with a full staff, including a housekeeper, a cook, a butler, a gardener, and often a security guard. Many can arrange for a driver, either for airport transfers, for daily touring, or for a prearranged number of days for sightseeing.

The island's villas were once mostly smaller homes, but recent years have seen an increased demand for larger, more luxurious properties. Numerous villas have five or more bedrooms spread around different parts of the building—or in different buildings altogether—for extra privacy.

Most villas come fully stocked with linens. You can often arrange for the kitchen to be stocked with groceries upon your arrival. Air-conditioning, even in the most luxurious villas, is typically limited to the bedrooms.

A four-night minimum stay is average for many villas although this can vary by season and property. Gratuities, usually split among the staff, typically range from 10% to 15%. Several private companies specialize in villa rentals, match-

---

BEST BETS FOR LODGING

Fodor's Choice ★
Breezes Grand Negril, Breezes Runaway Bay, the Caves, Half Moon, Hotel Mockingbird Hill, Jake's, Jamaica Inn, Rockhouse, Sandals Royal Caribbean, Sandals Royal Plantation Ocho Rios, Sandals Whitehouse, Strawberry Hill

BEST FAMILY RESORTS
Beaches Boscobel, Franklyn D Resort, Holiday Inn SunSpree, Hilton Rose Hall Resort and Spa, Sunset Beach Resort

BEST FOR ROMANCE
Catch a Falling Star, The Caves

ing up vacationers with accommodations of the right size and price range.

Villa-Rental Agents Jamaica Association of Villas and Apartments. Since 1967, the Jamaica Association of Villas and Apartments has handled villas, cottages, apartments, and condos across the island. ✉ *2706 W. Agatite, 2nd fl., Chicago, Illinois, USA* ☎ *800/845–5276, 876/974–2508, 773/463–6688* ⊕ *www. villasinjamaica.com.* **Jamaica Villas by Linda Smith.** Jamaica Villas by Linda Smith offers more than 80 fully staffed villas on the island. ✉ *8029 Riverside Dr., Maryland, USA* ☎ *301/3013* ⊕ *www.jamaicavillas.com.*

MONTEGO BAY

14

Mo'Bay has miles of hotels, villas, apartments, and duty-free shops. Although without much cultural stimulus, it presents a comfortable island backdrop for the many conventions it hosts. And it has the added advantage of being the closest resort area to the island's main airport.

$$$$
RESORT

🖼 **Coyaba Beach Resort and Club.** Privately owned and operated, this intimate property offers a relaxing, welcoming ambience. **Pros:** quiet atmosphere of an inn; excellent restaurants; good-size private beach. **Cons:** located directly on North Coast Highway; fairly small pool: climb to third-floor rooms can be difficult without elevator. **TripAdvisor:** "immaculate grounds," "excellent place to relax," "beautiful views." ⑤ *Rooms from: $360* ✉ *Little River* ☎ *876/953–9150* ⊕ *www. coyabaresortjamaica.com* ⇆ *50 rooms* ⑩ *Breakfast.*

$
HOTEL

🖼 **El Greco.** For visitors who don't have to be on the beach, El Greco is a budget-friendly option. **Pros:** good value; near many dining and night-life options; kitchens in rooms. **Cons:** not on the beach; bland room decor. **TripAdvisor:** "bring your own pillow," "good budget hotel," "great location." ⑤ *Rooms from: $135* ✉ *11 Queens Dr., Montego Bay* ☎ *876/940–6116* ⊕ *www.elgrecojamaica.com* ⇆ *93 suites* ⑩ *Breakfast.*

$$$
RESORT
☾
Fodor's Choice
★

🖼 **Half Moon, A Rockresort.** With its many room categories, massive villas (with three to seven bedrooms), shopping village, hospital, school, dolphin swims, golf course, and equestrian center, Half Moon almost seems more like a town than a mere resort. **Pros:** huge beach; many room categories, including villas; numerous on-site activities. **Cons:** some accommodations are a long walk from public areas; some activities are not within walking distance; some accommodations are more recently renovated than others. **TripAdvisor:** "unique and amazing," "gorgeous," "beautiful gracious beachfront property." ⑤ *Rooms from: $135* ✉ *North Coast Hwy., 7 miles (11 km) east of Montego Bay, Montego Bay* ☎ *876/953–2211* ⊕ *halfmoon.rockresorts.com* ⇆ *45 rooms, 158 suites, 33 villas* ⑩ *No meals.*

$$$
ALL-INCLUSIVE
☾

🖼 **Hilton Rose Hall Resort and Spa.** Popular with romance-minded couples, conference groups, as well as with families, this self-contained resort 4 miles (6 km) east of the airport is on the grounds of the 400-acre Rose Hall Plantation. **Pros:** executive chef Michael Dannecker's excellent cuisine; family-friendly dining and pool area; easy access to golf. **Cons:** beach is not as good as others in the area; kid-filled pool can be noisy; some activities located across highway. **TripAdvisor:** "so peaceful," "paradise at an affordable price," "great first impression of Jamaica."

Montego Bay

KEY

⌇ Beaches

1 Restaurants

①　Hotels

Caribbean Sea

Sir Donald Sangster International Airport

Cornwall Beach

Doctor's Cave Beach

Walter Fletcher Beach

Montego Bay

River Bay

Montego Bay Freeport

Bogue Is.

0 ——— 1 mi

0 ——— 1 km

$ Rooms from: $135 ⊠ North Coast Hwy., St. James ✛ 15 miles (24 km) east of Montego Bay ☎ 876/953–2650 ⊕ www.RoseHallResort. com ⤳ 488 rooms, 14 suites ❐ All-inclusive.

$

ALL-INCLUSIVE

⌕

Holiday Inn SunSpree Resort Montego Bay. Family fun is tops here, although many couples and singles are also drawn to the moderate prices and good location, 6 miles (10 km) east of the airport. **Pros:** good family atmosphere; easy access to shopping area; complimentary self-serve laundry. **Cons:** numerous children mean some areas can be noisy; only nonmotorized water sports included in rates; hotel located directly beside North Coast Highway. **TripAdvisor:** "lovely staff," "Caribbean gem," "good food." $ Rooms from: $135 ⊠ North Coast Hwy., 10 miles (16 km) east of Montego Bay, ☎ 876/953–2485 ⊕ www. caribbeanhi.com ⤳ 524 rooms, 27 suites ❐ All-inclusive.

14

$$$$

ALL-INCLUSIVE

Iberostar Rose Hall Grand Hotel. The most upscale of the three adjacent Iberostar resorts, this property differentiates itself with its adults-only policy. **Pros:** larger suites than those found at the other Iberostar properties; one complimentary round of golf at Cinnamon Hill per stay; guests can dine at the other two Iberostar resorts in the complex. **Cons:** some sports such as golf and scuba not included in all-inclusive rates; extremely large hotel complex. **TripAdvisor:** "beautiful resort," "great staff," "honeymooners paradise." $ Rooms from: $487 ⊠ North Coast Hwy., 8 miles (13 km) east of Montego Bay city center, Montego Bay ☎ 876/680–0000 ⊕ www.iberostar.com ⤳ 295 suites ❐ All-inclusive.

$$$$

RESORT

Ritz-Carlton Golf & Spa Resort, Rose Hall. A favorite with conference groups, golfers, and anyone demanding the highbrow service for which the chain is known, this expansive resort lies across the road from the historic Rose Hall estate. **Pros:** excellent meeting and business travel facilities; great golf; good children's program. **Cons:** generic decor gives no sense of Jamaican atmosphere; small beach; somewhat formal for a family-friendly resort. **TripAdvisor:** "nice if you want quiet," "enforced relaxation," "wonderful views." $ Rooms from: $359 ⊠ 1 Ritz Carlton Dr., 15 miles (24 km) east of Montego Bay, St. James ☎ 876/953–2800 ⊕ www.ritzcarlton.com ⤳ 427 rooms ❐ No meals.

$$$$

RESORT

Round Hill Hotel and Villas. A favorite of celebrities thanks to its private and elegant villas, this peaceful resort 8 miles (13 km) west of Mo'Bay also offers 36 traditional hotel rooms in the Pineapple House. **Pros:** personal service; stylish accommodations; quiet atmosphere. **Cons:** somewhat remote location; costly; some villas do not have pools. **TripAdvisor:** "beautiful resort," "we really relaxed," "charm and class with a view." $ Rooms from: $649 ⊠ North Coast Hwy., 8 miles (13 km) west of Montego Bay ☎ 876/956–7050 ⊕ www.roundhill.com ⤳ 36 rooms, 27 villas ❐ No meals.

$$$$

ALL-INCLUSIVE

Fodor's Choice

★

Sandals Royal Caribbean Resort and Private Island. Four miles (6 km) east of the airport, this elegant resort—the most upscale of the three Sandals properties in Mo'Bay—consists of Jamaican-style buildings arranged in a semicircle around attractive gardens. **Pros:** numerous room categories; offshore dining; complimentary airport shuttle and shuttle to other Sandals resorts in Montego Bay. **Cons:** some guests might feel the resort is too quiet; smaller beach than Sandals Montego Bay; couples-only policy means some guests can't stay here. **TripAdvisor:** "relaxing,"

Sandals Royal Caribbean Resort & Private Island, Montego Bay.

"amazing food and service," "wonderful people." ⑤ *Rooms from: $584* ⊠ *North Coast Hwy., 6 miles (9 km) east of Montego Bay city center, Montego Bay* ☎ *876/953–2231* ⊕ *www.sandals.com* ⇘ *176 rooms, 14 suites* ⦿ *All-inclusive* ⌕ *2-night minimum.*

$$$$
ALL-INCLUSIVE
⟳

⊡ Sunset Beach Resort, Spa and Waterpark. Often packed with charter groups, this expansive resort is a good value if you don't mind mass tourism. **Pros:** excellent beaches; good restaurants; numerous on-site activities. **Cons:** can be crowded; high-rise setup means lines for the elevator; somewhat remote location if you want to explore Montego Bay. **TripAdvisor:** "great food," "great atmosphere," "lovely hotel." ⑤ *Rooms from: $590* ⊠ *5 miles (8 km) west of Montego Bay on Rte. A1, Freeport* ☎ *876/979–8800* ⊕ *www.sunsetbeachresortsjamaica.com* ⇘ *430 rooms, 15 suites* ⦿ *All-inclusive.*

$$$$
ALL-INCLUSIVE

⊡ Tryall Club. The sumptuous villas—each with a private pool—and pampering staff lend a home-away-from-home atmosphere to this golfers' haven west of Mo'Bay. **Pros:** excellent golf; villa experience with the conveniences of a resort; good family program. **Cons:** nonmembers must become temporary members of Tryall Club for a fee of $20 per day per person; shared public facilities; somewhat formal atmosphere. **TripAdvisor:** "great food and great golf," "unbelievable villa and service," "totally relaxing." ⑤ *Rooms from: $550* ⊠ *North Coast Hwy., 15 miles (24 km) west of Montego Bay, Sandy Bay* ☎ *876/956–5660* ⊕ *www.tryallclub.com* ⇘ *86 villas* ⦿ *No meals.*

RUNAWAY BAY

The smallest of the resort areas, Runaway Bay, 50 miles (80 km) east of Montego Bay and about 12 miles (19 km) west of Ocho Rios, has a handful of modern hotels, a few all-inclusive resorts, and an 18-hole golf course.

$$$$
ALL-INCLUSIVE

Breezes Runaway Bay. This moderately priced SuperClubs resort, which underwent an extensive renovation and expansion in 2007, emphasizes an active, sports-oriented vacation—including golf (at the resort's own course), four tennis courts, and an array of water sports. **Pros:** extensive sports and water-sports options; complimentary airport shuttle; low-rise room blocks mean easy beach access. **Cons:** some public areas can feel crowded; small spa; some restaurants are too small to accommodate demand; older rooms are dowdy. **TripAdvisor:** "great vacation," "laughed for a week," "nice beach." $ Rooms from: $365 ⊠ North Coast Hwy., Runaway Bay ☎ 876/973–6099 ⊕ www.superclubs.com ⌸ 266 rooms, 20 suites ⦿ All-inclusive ⌁ 3-night minimum.

$$$$
ALL-INCLUSIVE
☺

FDR, Franklyn D Resort. A favorite for families with very young children, this relaxed resort goes a step beyond the usual supervised kids' programs, assigning you a professional caregiver who will assist you throughout your stay. **Pros:** good supervised kids' programs; nanny program especially good for young families; spacious accommodations. **Cons:** not appealing to travelers without children; small pool area; rooms need updating. **TripAdvisor:** "overall awesome," "relaxed," "perfect family resort." $ Rooms from: $780 ⊠ Main Rd., Runaway Bay ☎ 876/973–4124 ⊕ www.fdrholidays.com ⌸ 78 suites ⦿ All-inclusive.

OCHO RIOS

Ocho Rios lies on the North Coast, halfway between Port Antonio and Mo'Bay. Rivers, waterfalls, fern-shaded roads, and tropical lushness fill this fertile region. It's a favorite with honeymooners as well as Jamaicans who like to escape crowded Kingston for the weekend. The area's resorts, hotels, and villas are all a short drive from the frenetic, traffic-clogged downtown, which has a crafts market, boutiques, duty-free shops, restaurants, and several scenic attractions. The community lies 67 miles (111 km) east of Montego Bay, a drive that takes just under two hours thanks to an improved highway.

$$$$
ALL-INCLUSIVE
☺

Beaches Boscobel Resort and Golf Club. Although this resort is for anyone—including singles and couples—it's best suited for families, whose children enjoy supervised activities in one of five kids' clubs divided by age, from infants to teens. **Pros:** excellent children's program; numerous dining options; good options for adults, including spa. **Cons:** long drive from the airport; beach is a long walk (or an elevator ride) from the rooms; resort is distant from Ocho Rios attractions. **TripAdvisor:** "great location in the sun," "perfect for a family getaway," "amazing staff." $ Rooms from: $595 ⊠ North Coast Hwy., St. Ann's Bay ☎ 876/975–7777 ⊕ www.beaches.com ⌸ 123 rooms, 100 suites ⦿ All-inclusive.

14

NUDE BEACHES

It is perhaps ironic that Jamaica, one of the most conservative, religious islands in the Caribbean, has many opportunities for naturists to let it all hang out.

TAKING IT OFF

Breezes Rio Bueno gives you an opportunity to go nude, with an entire section of the resort set aside for nudists. In most places in Jamaica, letting it all hang out comes at a premium of up to 20% above the regular rates. Other clothing-optional beaches are found at Hedonism II, SuperFun Beach Resort (formerly Hedonism III),

Breezes Grand Resort and Spa Negril, Couples Negril, Couples Tower Isle, Couples Sans Souci, and Sunset Beach Resort and Spa.

KEEPING IT ON

If you'd rather enjoy the beach in your swimsuit, remember that most of Jamaica's resorts cater to the traditional beachgoer (and all public beaches require swimsuits by law). "Clothing-optional" means you're free to keep your swimsuit (or as much of it) on as you like. Only beaches deemed "nude" actually have a dress code that requires a birthday suit.

$$
B&B/INN
Fodor'sChoice
★

The Blue House. This stylish, boutique bed-and-breakfast is a nice alternative to the all-inclusive hotels on the North Coast. **Pros:** homey; great for single travelers; pool on the property. **Cons:** not on the beach; far from amenities. **TripAdvisor:** "what a treasure," "a feast for the senses," "gentle on my mind." ⑤ *Rooms from: $220* ⊠ *Marcliff, White River Estate, Ocho Rios* ☎ *876/994–1367* ⊕ *www.thebluehousejamaica.com* ⟿ *5* ⭢⬤⭠ *Breakfast.*

$$$
ALL-INCLUSIVE

ClubHotel Riu Ocho Rios. This sprawling resort, built in two U-shape wings each overlooking a pool, is presently the largest in Jamaica. **Pros:** numerous dining options; large rooms; expansive beach. **Cons:** long walk to beach; some public areas feel cramped; all-inclusive package is limited. **TripAdvisor:** "perfect for relaxation," "beautiful resort," "quiet." ⑤ *Rooms from: $334* ⊠ *North Coast Hwy., Mammee Bay* ☎ *876/972–2200* ⊕ *www.riu.com* ⟿ *478 rooms, 386 suites* ⭢⬤⭠ *All-inclusive.*

$$$
ALL-INCLUSIVE

Couples Sans Souci Resort and Spa. This classy all-inclusive encourages its guests to check their cares at the entrance and indulge in some soul-nurturing pampering. **Pros:** excellent spa; free weddings and expansive all-inclusive package; complimentary round-trip airport shuttle from Montego Bay airport. **Cons:** some rooms are very isolated and a long walk from public areas; beaches are not as good as others in area. **TripAdvisor:** "a great escape," "welcoming hospitality," "perfect service." ⑤ *Rooms from: $334* ⊠ *North Coast Hwy., 2 miles (3 km) east of Ocho Rios, Ocho Rios* ☎ *876/994–1206* ⊕ *www.couples.com* ⟿ *150 suites* ⭢⬤⭠ *All-inclusive.*

$$$
ALL-INCLUSIVE

Couples Tower Isle. This all-inclusive resort has beautiful contemporary decor. **Pros:** some free weddings; excellent beach facilities; reciprocal arrangement with Couples Sans Souci on Monday, Wednesday, and Friday. **Cons:** long distance from Montego Bay airport. **TripAdvisor:** "beautiful relaxing resort," "the best ever," "more than you could ask for." $ *Rooms from: $329* ✉ *Tower Isle, Rte. A1, 5 miles (8 km) east of Ocho Rios, St. Mary* ☎ *876/975–4271* ⊕ *www.couples.com* ⤶ *200 rooms, 17 suites* ⦿ *All-inclusive.*

$$
RENTAL
★

🏠 **Glory be.** When owner Karen Schleifer's aunt Marion Simmons first set eyes on this property, she exclaimed, "Glory be," and so the house, frequented by the fashionable art and literary crowd of the 1950s and 1960s, became known. Nowadays, Glory be is just as charming and has two cottages for rent. The Studio sleeps four comfortably (but is great for a romantic getaway for two), and Sunspots is small and compact with a covered outdoor terrace for dining. Both cottages have fabulous sea views and step access to the sea for swimming. **Pros:** private; pool; great location on the cliffs; close to Reggae Beach. **Cons:** no private beach on property; 4 miles from Ocho Rios town center. $ *Rooms from: $165* ✉ *Tower Isle, Ocho Rios* ☎ *876/975–4213* ⤶ *2 cottages* ⦿ *No meals.*

$$$$
RENTAL
Fodor's Choice
★

🏠 **Goldeneye.** Whether you're a James Bond buff or just a fan of luxury getaways, this exclusive address 20 minutes east of Ocho Rios holds special appeal. **Pros:** unique and spacious accommodations; plenty of privacy. **Cons:** remote location; limited dining options; may be too quiet for some. **TripAdvisor:** "license to chill," "laid back luxury," "relaxing and top notch service." $ *Rooms from: $840* ✉ *N. Coast Hwy., Oracabessa* ☎ *876/622–9007* ⊕ *www.goldeneye.com* ⤶ *1 house, 19 villas/cottages* ⦿ *Breakfast.*

$$$
RESORT
Fodor's Choice
★

🏠 **Hermosa Cove Villa Resort & Suites.** Exuding privacy and luxury, Hermosa Cove is ideal if you want seclusion and style, because each unit has its own pool, gazebo dining area, and outside shower, and is screened by lush tropical vegetation. **Pros:** stylish and comfortable suites and villas; close to Ocho Rios town center. **Cons:** small beach; limited menu at on-site restaurant. **TripAdvisor:** "perfect escape," "fantastic romantic place," "relaxing environment." $ *Rooms from: $350* ✉ *Hermosa Cove, Hermosa St., Ocho Rios* ☎ *876/974–3699* ⊕ *www.hermosacove. com* ⤶ *15 rooms* ⦿ *No meals.*

$$$$
RESORT
Fodor's Choice
★

🏠 **Jamaica Inn.** Start a conversation about elegant Jamaican resorts, and this quietly sophisticated hotel will surely be mentioned. **Pros:** elegant accommodations; exceptional service; good spa. **Cons:** some travelers may feel it's too quiet; too traditional and stiff for some visitors; no in-room TV. **TripAdvisor:** "old-world charm on an idyllic beach," "charming and relaxing," "excellent staff." $ *Rooms from: $503* ✉ *North Coast Hwy., 2 miles (3 km) east of Ocho Rios, Ocho Rios* ☎ *876/974–2514* ⊕ *www.jamaicainn.com* ⤶ *52 suites.*

$$$$
ALL-INCLUSIVE

🏠 **The Jewel Dunn's River Beach Resort & Spa.** The Jewel, an adults-only all-inclusive resort on a small stretch of beach, is a place where you can make friends, and there is enough entertainment to make it fun but not overwhelming. **Pros:** small for an all-inclusive; 9-hole golf course. **Cons:** small beach; must drive into Ocho Rios for shopping, excursions, and other attractions. **TripAdvisor:** "great relaxing vacation," "impeccable," "what a memory." $ *Rooms from: $539* ✉ *Mammee Bay, Ocho Rios* ☎ *876/972–7400* ⊕ *www.jeweldunnsriverresort.com* ⤶ *250 rooms* ⦿ *All-inclusive.*

14

Other Sandals Resorts on Jamaica

The Sandals company has the most hotels of any company in Jamaica. Sandals resorts are open only to couples and are all-inclusive in their pricing. *In addition to our favorites, which are reviewed in full in this chapter, the following resorts are also available.*

Sandals Grande Riviera Beach & Villa Golf Resort. is the largest resort in the Sandals chain. It includes the "Manor" side with great house and villas and the "Riviera" side with easy beach access. Villas, some fairly far from the public areas, have private pools; some villas have as many as four individual guest suites, each with its own kitchen and living area, that share a single pool. ⊠ North

Coast Hwy., Ocho Rios, Ocho Rios ☎ 876/974–5691 ⊕ www.sandals.com ⤳ 285 rooms, 244 villas.

Sandals Montego Bay. is minutes from the airport on the largest stretch of beach in Mo'Bay. The "Almond" block of rooms and extensive beach are the resort's best features. ⊠ N. Kent Ave., 1½ miles (2½ km) east of Montego Bay city center, Montego Bay ☎ 876/952–5510 ⊕ www.sandals.com ⤳ 250 rooms.

Sandals Negril Beach Resort and Spa. is at the top of Seven Mile Beach; in 2012 a new restaurant, La Bella Napoli, was added. ⊠ Norman Manley Blvd., Negril ☎ 876/957–5216 ⊕ www.sandals.com ⤳ 137 rooms, 86 suites.

$$$$
RESORT
Fodor's Choice
★

Sandals Royal Plantation Ocho Rios. In October 2010, Royal Plantation (which has been owned by Sandals since February 2000 but operated as a separate resort) joined the Sandals family of resorts, albeit without the all-inclusive trappings of its sisters. **Pros:** accommodations are expansive and stylish; good dining; room service offered. **Cons:** guest rooms and beach are on different levels; small pool; small beach. **TripAdvisor:** "paradise and pampering," "gorgeous heavenly tropical paradise," "a quiet relaxing getaway." ⑤ *Rooms from: $578* ⊠ *Main St., Ocho Rios* ☎ *876/974–5601* ⊕ *www.sandals.com* ⤳ *74 suites, 1 villa* �'⊙' *No meals* ⚑ *2-night minimum.*

PORT ANTONIO

There's a genuine alternative to the hectic tourist scene in Jamaica's bustling resorts Montego Bay and Ocho Rios: Port Antonio. This quiet community is on Jamaica's east end, 133 miles (220 km) east of Montego Bay, and is favored by those looking to get away from it all. Don't look for mixology classes or limbo dances here; this end of Jamaica is quiet and relaxed. The fun is usually found outdoors, followed by a fine evening meal. The area's must-do activities include rafting Jamaica's own Rio Grande, taking an eco-hike, and having lunch or a drink at the Jamaica Palace.

$
HOTEL

Demontevin Lodge Hotel. On Titchfield Hill, Demontevin Lodge is a fine example of elegant 19th-century Victorian architecture with decor and furnishings reminiscent of yesteryear. **Pros:** offers the opportunity to sample "old Jamaica"; central location **Cons:** limited amenities;

far from the beach; some rooms are shared bathroom. **TripAdvisor:** "Victorian charmer," "great service," "welcoming and truly unique." ⑤ *Rooms from: $90* ✉ *21 Fort George St., Port Antonio* ☏ *876/993–2604* ⊕ *www.demontevinslodgehotel.com* ➥ *13 rooms* ⬦ *No meals.*

$$$ ⬚ **Goblin Hill Villas at San San.** This lush, 12-acre estate atop a hill over-
RENTAL looking San San Bay is best suited for travelers looking for a home-away-from-home atmosphere, not a bustling resort. **Pros:** good for guests who would like a villa experience but with the facilities of a hotel; nice bay views from villa terraces and balconies; spacious accommodations. **Cons:** long walk to beach; shared lawn and public areas with other villas at complex. **TripAdvisor:** "wonderful and friendly," "a great place to relax," "pleasant surprise." ⑤ *Rooms from: $325* ✉ *Rte. A4, 3 miles (5 km) east of Port Antonio, San San* ☏ *876/925–8108* ⊕ *www.goblinhill.com* ➥ *28 villas* ⬦ *No meals.*

$$$ ⬚ **Hotel Mocking Bird Hill.** With only 10 rooms, some overlooking the sea
HOTEL and all with views of lush hillsides, Mocking Bird Hill is much more
Fodor'sChoice like a cozy bed-and-breakfast than a hotel. **Pros:** numerous ecotour-
★ ism options; environmentally conscious; excellent dining. **Cons:** limited on-site dining; somewhat remote location. **TripAdvisor:** "wonderful oasis of calm," "welcoming atmosphere," "great place for birding and relaxation." ⑤ *Rooms from: $325* ✉ *North Coast Hwy., Pt. Ann, Port Antonio* ☏ *876/993–7267* ➥ *10 rooms* ⬦ *No meals.*

KINGSTON

Visited by few vacationers but a frequent destination for business travelers and visitors with a deep interest in Jamaica heritage and culture, the sprawling city of Kingston is home to some of the island's finest business hotels. Skirting the city are the Blue Mountains, a completely different world from the urban frenzy of the capital city.

$$ ⬚ **Courtleigh Hotel and Suites.** In the heart of New Kingston (25 min-
HOTEL utes from Norman Manley International Airport), this hotel is in the city's premier financial district. **Pros:** large rooms; lively nightlife; good business facilities. **Cons:** limited dining options; noisy location; most rooms lack balconies. **TripAdvisor:** "service at its best," "very cozy," "great food and friendly staff." ⑤ *Rooms from: $205* ✉ *85 Knutsford Blvd., Kingston* ☏ *876/929–9000* ⊕ *www.courtleigh.com* ➥ *88 rooms, 41 suites* ⬦ *Breakfast.*

$$ ⬚ **Terra Nova All-Suite Hotel.** Although it's in New Kingston, this graceful
HOTEL hotel, a former colonial mansion, is definitely Old Jamaica. **Pros:** elegant atmosphere; great outdoor dining; near shopping and dining. **Cons:** fills up quickly on weekends; small rooms; dated decor. **TripAdvisor:** "great old-world charm and service," "great food," "superior service." ⑤ *Rooms from: $175* ✉ *17 Waterloo Rd., Kingston* ☏ *876/926–2211* ⊕ *www.terranovajamaica.com* ➥ *46* ⬦ *Breakfast.*

14

BLUE MOUNTAINS

$$$$
HOTEL
Fodor's Choice
★

Strawberry Hill. A 45-minute drive from Kingston—but worlds apart in terms of atmosphere—this exclusive resort was developed by Chris Blackwell, former head of Island Records (the late Bob Marley's label). **Pros:** stylish accommodations with great mountain views; cool retreat from the heat. **Cons:** remote location a distance from the beaches; limited on-site dining options; too quiet for some guests. **TripAdvisor:** "magic surroundings," "breathtaking location," "perfect colonial villas." ⑤ *Rooms from: $355 ⊠ New Castle Rd., Irishtown, , St. Andrew* ☎ *876/944–8400 ⊕ www.islandoutpost.com ➾ 12 cottages ⎮⊙⎮ Multiple meal plans.*

SOUTH COAST

In the 1970s Negril was Jamaica's most relaxed place to hang out. Today that distinction is held by the South Coast, a long stretch of coastline ranging from Whitehouse to Treasure Beach. Here local residents wave to cars, and travelers spend their days exploring local communities and their nights in local restaurants. The best way to reach the South Coast is from Montego Bay, driving overland, a journey of 90 minutes to two hours, depending on the destination.

$
HOTEL
Fodor's Choice
★

Jakes. The laid-back, neighborly feel of the South Coast is epitomized by Jake's, a relaxed place that's fun, funky, and friendly. **Pros:** unique accommodations; infused with South Coast friendliness; personalized service. **Cons:** some rooms can be cramped when housebound during rainy periods; no a/c in some rooms. **TripAdvisor:** "unplugged and unwound," "tranquility at its best," "personalized attention." ⑤ *Rooms from: $115 ⊠ Calabash Bay, Treasure Beach ☎ 876/965–3000 ⊕ www. jakeshotel.com ➾ 31 cottages, 4 villas ⎮⊙⎮ No meals.*

$$$$
ALL-INCLUSIVE

Sandals Whitehouse European Village and Spa. The newest Sandals resort in Jamaica and the first major resort on the South Coast, this property is one of the most upscale properties in the chain. **Pros:** great beach with no vendors; numerous dining options and an extensive all-inclusive package that includes airport shuttle; stylish accommodations in all room classes. **Cons:** some travelers won't like Disney-ish re-creation of European styles; Whitehouse area can be bug-ridden and hot. **TripAdvisor:** "visit to paradise," "beautiful," "a little slice of heaven." ⑤ *Rooms from: $540 ⊠ Whitehouse ☎ 876/640–3000 ⊕ www.sandals. com ➾ 360 ⎮⊙⎮ All-inclusive.*

$
HOTEL
★

Sunset Resort and Villas. Next door to Jake's, this resort lacks the style of its attention-getting neighbor, but it still offers a friendly getaway that's lovingly owner-managed. **Pros:** friendly staff; rooms are comfortably large; good location on Calabash Bay. **Cons:** decor is dated and fussy; limited dining choices. **TripAdvisor:** "welcome home," "beautiful views," "very accommodating." ⑤ *Rooms from: $115 ⊠ Calabash Bay, Treasure Beach ☎ 876/965–0143 ⊕ www.sunsetresort.com ➾ 14 rooms ⎮⊙⎮ No meals.*

NEGRIL

Some 50 miles (80 km) west of Mo'Bay, Negril was once a hippie hangout, favored for its inexpensive mom-and-pop hotels and laid-back atmosphere. Today there's still a bohemian flair, but the town's one of the fastest-growing tourism communities in Jamaica, with several large all-inclusives along Bloody Bay, northeast of town. The main strip of Negril Beach and the cliffs are still favored by vacationers who like to get out and explore.

$$$$
ALL-INCLUSIVE
Fodor'sChoice
★

Breezes Grand Resort and Spa Negril. Fancy touches at this resort are balanced by an expansive clothing-optional beach (including its own hot tub, bar, and grill), giving you one of Jamaica's best resorts, where it's fun to dress for dinner but equally good to strip down for a day of fun in the sun. **Pros:** excellent beaches; super-inclusive package, including complimentary room service for select rooms; elegant setting. **Cons:** some rooms need updating; central public area lacks view; clothing-optional pool is small. **TripAdvisor:** "water sport heaven," "island exodus," "beach is perfect." ⑤ *Rooms from: $580* ✉ *Norman Manley Blvd., Negril* ☎ *876/957–5010* ⊕ *www.superclubs.com* ⌁ *210 suites* ⫿⊘⫿ *All-inclusive.*

$$
HOTEL
Fodor'sChoice
★

Catcha Falling Star. Surely one of the prettiest properties on the West End cliffs, Catcha Falling Star is, as it proclaims, a place "to rekindle the romance." **Pros:** rooms for different budgets, starting at $95; romantic; every room is individual. **Cons:** no beach; the cheapest gatehouse cottage may get noise from the street. **TripAdvisor:** "fun and sun in paradise," "lovely gardens," "magical boutique hotel with great staff." ⑤ *Rooms from: $217* ✉ *West End Rd., Negril* ☎ *875/957–0390* ⌁ *15 rooms* ⫿⊘⫿ *No meals.*

$$$$
ALL-INCLUSIVE
Fodor'sChoice
★

The Caves. This 10-acre resort packs a lot of punch in its cliff-side location, drawing the Hollywood set as well as travelers looking for boutique-style pampering. **Pros:** stylish and unique accommodations; personal service including nightly turndown service; quiet atmosphere. **Cons:** limited on-site dining options; may be too quiet for some travelers; no beach (on cliffs). **TripAdvisor:** "thoroughly romantic," "unforgettable," "relaxation at its best." ⑤ *Rooms from: $608* ✉ *One Love Dr., Negril* ☎ *876/618–1081* ⊕ *www.islandoutpost.com/the_caves* ⌁ *12 cottages* ⫿⊘⫿ *All-inclusive.*

$$
B&B/INN

Charela Inn. Directly on Negril Beach, this quiet hotel is understated but elegant in a simple way and has a widely praised French-Jamaican restaurant. **Pros:** great dining; good beach location; good value for families. **Cons:** some guest rooms are small; facilities are not luxurious. **TripAdvisor:** "most beautiful beach," "they are always there for you," "truly enjoyable getaway." ⑤ *Rooms from: $217* ✉ *Norman Manley Blvd., Negril* ☎ *876/957–4648* ⊕ *www.charela.com* ⌁ *47 rooms* ⌖ *5-night minimum.*

$$
B&B/INN

Country Country. Owned by Kevin and Joanne Robertson, who also own Montego Bay's Coyaba, this small hotel carries the same home-away-from-home feel of its North Coast cousin but with a distinct Negril charm. **Pros:** charming guest rooms; oversize accommodations; good location on Negril Beach. **Cons:** may be too small for some travelers; some rooms can be noisy at night because of nearby

14

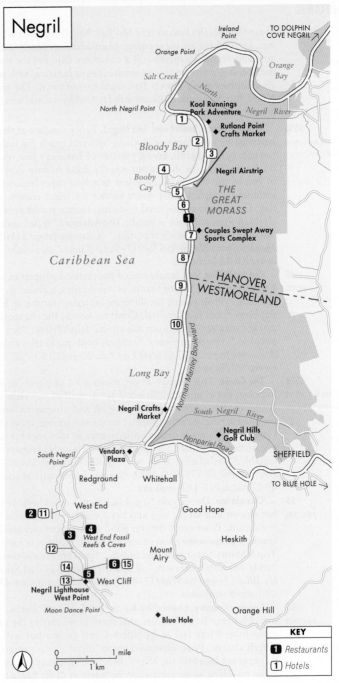

Negril

TO DOLPHIN
COVE NEGRIL

Ireland
Point

Orange Point

Orange
Bay

Salt Creek

North

Negril River

North Negril Point

Kool Runnings
Park Adventure

Rutland Point
Crafts Market

Bloody Bay

Negril Airstrip

Booby
Cay

THE
GREAT
MORASS

Couples Swept Away
Sports Complex

Caribbean Sea

HANOVER
WESTMORELAND

Norman Manley Boulevard

Long Bay

Negril Crafts
Market

South Negril River

Negril Hills
Golf Club

Nonpariel Road

SHEFFIELD

South Negril
Point

Vendors
Plaza

Redground

Whitehall

TO BLUE HOLE

West End

Good Hope

West End Fossil
Reefs & Caves

Mount
Airy

Heskith

West Cliff

Negril Lighthouse
West Point

Moon Dance Point

Orange Hill

Blue Hole

KEY

1 *Restaurants*
1 *Hotels*

0   1 mile
0   1 km

Margaritaville; limited on-site dining options. **TripAdvisor:** "wonderful place," "beautiful peaceful oasis," "home as it should be." ⑤ *Rooms from: $195* ✉ *Norman Manley Blvd., Negril* ☎ *876/957–4273* ⊕ *www.countrynegril.com* ↩ *19 rooms* ⦿ *Breakfast.*

$$$
ALL-INCLUSIVE
⬚ **Couples Negril.** This couples-only resort emphasizes romance and relaxation and is a more laid-back alternative to the nearby Sandals Negril. **Pros:** free weddings for guests staying six nights or more; complimentary airport shuttle; good stretch of beach. **Cons:** it's a long walk along the beach to the heart of the action if you want to sample life outside the all-inclusive **TripAdvisor:** "kick back and enjoy," "best romantic beach vacation," "breathtaking." ⑤ *Rooms from: $340* ✉ *Norman Manley Blvd., Negril* ☎ *876/957–5960* ⊕ *www.couples.com* ↩ *234 rooms, 18 suites* ⦿ *All-inclusive.*

$$$$
ALL-INCLUSIVE
⬚ **Couples Swept Away Negril.** Sports-minded couples are welcomed to this all-suites resort known for its expansive menu of sports offerings, top-notch facilities (the best in Jamaica and among the best in the Caribbean), and emphasis on healthy cuisine. **Pros:** excellent fitness and sports facilities; complimentary round-trip airport shuttle; great spa. **Cons:** healthful emphasis not for everyone; some facilities located across the road from resort. **TripAdvisor:** "relaxing," "excellent staff and exceptional service," "paradise on Earth." ⑤ *Rooms from: $365* ✉ *Norman Manley Blvd., Negril* ☎ *876/957–4061* ⊕ *www.couples.com* ↩ *312 suites* ⦿ *All-inclusive* ☞ *3-night minimum.*

$$$$
ALL-INCLUSIVE
⬚ **Grand Pineapple Beach Negril.** This low-rise resort (once Negril Gardens) epitomizes the relaxed and funky style for which Negril has long been known. **Pros:** a nice pool on the garden side with snacks available; good value; lovely beach; helpful staff. **Cons:** some rooms don't have balconies; nearby bars can be noisy; limit of three to a room. **TripAdvisor:** "authentic Jamaica in a resort," "wonderful hotel and staff," "gorgeous beach." ⑤ *Rooms from: $417* ✉ *Norman Manley Blvd., Negril* ☎ *876/957–4408* ⊕ *www.grandpineapple.com* ↩ *65 rooms* ⦿ *All-inclusive.*

$$$$
ALL-INCLUSIVE
⬚ **Hedonism II.** Promising a perpetual spring break for adults who are drawn to the legendary party atmosphere, this resort gets a lot of repeat business. **Pros:** good beaches; more economical than some adult all-inclusives; numerous activities. **Cons:** spring-break atmosphere not for everyone; nude beach and pool frequently overcrowded; rooms remain fairly basic. **TripAdvisor:** "good times," "a week off the grid," "a big fat party." ⑤ *Rooms from: $410* ✉ *Norman Manley Blvd., Rutland Point, Negril* ☎ *876/957–5200* ⊕ *www.superclubs.com* ↩ *280 rooms* ⦿ *All-inclusive* ☞ *3-night minimum.*

WORD OF MOUTH

"In my opinion the best Couples resort is Swept Away in Negril. I have stayed in Negril, Ocho, and Montego Bay, and by far Negril is the best. It has the best beaches and also faces west for beautiful sunsets. If you stay at Couples Swept Away, if you want a TV in your room, make sure to get a 'verandah room' in the new section." —chesney

14

$$ ⬚ **Rockhouse Hotel.** With a spectacular cliff-side location like that of
HOTEL the Caves—but with some viable options for avoiding the high price
Fodor's Choice tag—the small and trendy Rockhouse delivers both resort comforts and
★ funky style. **Pros:** excellent dining; unique accommodations; beautiful
pool area. **Cons:** no beach; may be too quiet for some visitors; tradi-
tional rooms are not nearly as nice as the villas. **TripAdvisor:** "divine,"
"gorgeous resort," "master the art of relaxation." ⑤ *Rooms from: $160*
⊠ *West End Rd., Negril* ☎ *876/957–4373* ⊕ *www.rockhousehotel.com*
⇩ *14 rooms, 20 villas* ⦿| *No meals.*

$$$$ ⬚ **The Spa Retreat.** This boutique resort on the cliffs features seven octag-
HOTEL onal stone and thatch cottages and eight rooftop and garden rooms, all
★ with sea views. **Pros:** large groups and wedding parties can rent whole
property; shuttle to beach; restaurant on-site. **Cons:** no beach; sea can
occasionally be too rough for swimming **TripAdvisor:** "perfect expe-
rience," "what a beautiful place," "outstanding cuisine." ⑤ *Rooms
from: $399* ⊠ *West End Rd., Negril* ☎ *876/957–4329, 855/843–7725*
⊕ *www.thespajamaica.com* ⇩ *15 rooms.*

$$$$ ⬚ **Sunset at the Palms Resort and Spa, Negril.** A sister property of the Sun-
ALL-INCLUSIVE set Resorts in Montego Bay and Ocho Rios—but far different in scale
and atmosphere—this relaxed all-inclusive is a favorite with ecotourists
thanks to its emphasis on environmentally sustainable tourism. **Pros:**
environmentally conscious hotel; beautiful grounds; unique accommo-
dations. **Cons:** beach is across street; eco-emphasis not for everyone;
not within walking distance of many Negril Beach attractions and res-
taurants. **TripAdvisor:** "perfect place to relax," "best family holiday
ever," "super special sunset." ⑤ *Rooms from: $590* ⊠ *Norman Man-
ley Blvd., Negril* ☎ *876/957–5350* ⊕ *www.sunsetatthepalms.com* ⇩ *85
rooms* ⦿| *All-inclusive.*

$ ⬚ **Tensing Pen.** Named for the inn's first dog (who was named for a
B&B/INN famed Sherpa), this hip and casual getaway is a top choice for travel-
Fodor's Choice ers who like to get out and explore. **Pros:** unique accommodations;
★ great snorkeling; spa; spacious rooms. **Cons:** not on beach; barking
dogs and other noise; rooms without a/c can get buggy. **TripAdvi-
sor:** "best of Jamaica," "paradise found," "amazing views and prop-
erty." ⑤ *Rooms from: $140* ⊠ *West End Rd., Negril* ☎ *876/957–0387*
⊕ *www.tensingpen.com* ⇩ *17 cottages* ⦿| *Breakfast.*

NIGHTLIFE

Nightlife includes both on-property shows at the all-inclusive resorts
and nightclubs ranging from indoor clubs to beach bashes. For starters,
there's reggae, popularized by the late Bob Marley and the Wailers and
performed today by son Ziggy Marley, Jimmy Tosh (the late Peter Tosh's
son), Gregory Isaacs, Jimmy Cliff, and many others. If your experience
of Caribbean music has been limited to steel drums and Harry Bela-
fonte, then the political, racial, and religious messages of reggae may set
you on your ear; listen closely and you just might hear the heartbeat of
the people. Dancehall is another island favorite, as is soca.

For the most part, the liveliest late-night happenings throughout
Jamaica are in the major resort hotels, with the widest variety of spots

probably in Montego Bay. Some of the all-inclusives offer a dinner-and-disco pass from about $50 to $100; to buy a pass, call ahead the afternoon before to check availability and be sure to bring a photo ID with you. Pick up a copy of the *Daily Gleaner*, the *Jamaica Observer*, or the *Star* (available at newsstands throughout the island) for listings of who's playing when and where. In Negril, trucks with loudspeakers travel through the streets in the afternoon announcing the hot spot for the evening.

MONTEGO BAY

ANNUAL EVENTS

Fodor'sChoice **Jamaica Jazz and Blues Festival.** In January, Montego Bay is packed with
★ music fans for this event held at the Rose Hall Aqueduct. ☎ 876/953–8282 ⊕ *jamaicajazzandblues.com*.

Fodor'sChoice **Red Stripe Reggae Sumfest.** Those who know and love reggae should visit
★ Montego Bay between mid-July and August for this weeklong concert—at the Bob Marley Performing Arts Center in the Freeport area—which attracts such big-name performers as Third World and Ziggy Marley and the Melody Makers. Tickets are sold for each night's performances or by multi-event passes. ☎ 876/953–2933 ⊕ *www.reggaesumfest.com*.

BARS AND CLUBS

Blue Beat. This sophisticated club moves to a jazz groove every night. Live shows are held regularly and other nights feature a DJ. It is a popular spot for a nightcap. ⊠ *Gloucester Ave., Montego Bay* ☎ 876/952–4777.

★ **Margaritaville Caribbean Bar and Grill.** With its location right on what's deemed Montego Bay's Hip Strip, the colorful bar and restaurant boasts a spring-break crowd during the season and a fun-loving atmosphere any night of the year; there is also a location at the Montego Bay airport, not to mention popular locations in both Negril and Ocho Rios. ⊠ *Gloucester Ave., Montego Bay* ☎ 876/952–4777.

The Twisted Kilt Lounge. The Hip Strip is home to Jamaica's first Irish pub. Especially popular with sports lovers for its big-screen TVs, this waterfront nightspot also serves fish-and-chips and pub grub. ⊠ *Gloucester Ave., Montego Bay* ☎ 876/952–9488.

OCHO RIOS

ANNUAL EVENTS

Jamaica Ocho Rios International Jazz Festival. In Ocho Rios, the biggest event of the year is held each June. The festival, which started in 1991 as a one-day concert, now spans 14 days and draws many top names. ☎ 876/927–3544 ⊕ *www.ochoriosjazz.com*.

BARS AND CLUBS

Margaritaville Caribbean Bar and Grill. One of the most popular nonresort nightspots in Ocho Rios is this chain, which is right on the beach. It's also a popular stop for cruise-ship visitors. ⊠ *Island Village, Turtle River Rd., Ocho Rios* ☎ 876/675–8800.

NEGRIL

BARS AND CLUBS

★ **Alfred's Ocean Palace.** You can find some of Negril's best live music at this bar, which stages reggae band performances right on the beach on Sunday, Tuesday, and Friday nights. ☒ *Norman Manley Blvd., Negril* ☎ *876/957–4669.*

★ **Hedonism II.** The sexy, always-packed disco at is the wildest dance spot on the island; Tuesday (pajama night) and Thursday (toga night) are tops. For nonguests, night passes are $89 and include meals, drinks, and use of the facilities from 6 pm to 2 am; bring a photo ID to obtain a pass, but you should call ahead for a reservation. ☒ *Norman Manley Blvd., Negril* ☎ *876/957–5200.*

The Jungle. The Jungle nightclub is the hottest nightspot in Negril, with two raised bars and a circular dance floor. ☒ *Norman Manley Blvd., Negril* ☎ *876/957–4005.*

Margaritaville Caribbean Bar and Grill. You'll find a branch of the popular burger-and-nightspot chain in Negril. ☒ *Norman Manley Blvd., Negril* ☎ *876/957–4467.*

Rick's Café. Sunset brings the crowds to Rick's Café to watch live reggae band performances. ☒ *West End Rd., Negril* ☎ *876/957–0380.*

SHOPPING

Shopping is not really one of Jamaica's high points, though you will certainly be able to find things to buy. Good choices include Jamaican crafts, which range from artwork to batik fabrics to baskets. Wood carvings are one of the top purchases; the finest carvings are made from the Jamaican national tree, lignum vitae, or tree of life, a dense wood that requires a talented carver to transform the hard, blond wood into dolphins, heads, or fish. Bargaining is expected with crafts vendors. Naturally, Jamaican rum is another top souvenir—there's no shortage of opportunities to buy it at gift shops and liquor stores—as is Tia Maria, the Jamaican-made coffee liqueur. Coffee (both Blue Mountain and the less expensive High Mountain) is sold at every gift shop on the island as well. The cheapest prices are found at the local grocery stores, where you can buy coffee beans or ground coffee.

There are several good cigar shops in Negril. Fine handmade cigars are available at the Montego Bay airport or at one of the island's many cigar stores. You can also buy Cuban cigars almost everywhere, though they can't be brought back legally into the United States.

As a rule, only rum distilleries, such as Appleton's and Sangster's, have better deals than the airport stores. Best of all, if you buy your rum at the airport stores, you don't have to tote all those heavy, breakable bottles to your hotel and then to the airport. (Note that if you purchase rum—or other liquids, such as duty-free perfumes—outside the airport, you'll need to place them in your checked luggage when returning home. If you purchase liquids inside the secured area of the airport, you may board with them, but, after clearing U.S. Customs on landing, you will need to place them in your checked bag if continuing on another flight.)

You can find Jamaican and even some Haitian paintings in galleries around the island. There are many other locally made goods available in the crafts markets in Montego Bay, Negril, and Ocho Rios. Reggae CDs that are locally recorded may be found nowhere else but Jamaica. Finally, liquor and tobacco products can be good buys.

MONTEGO BAY

AREAS AND MALLS

★ **Half Moon Shopping Village.** Half Moon Shopping Village, east of Half Moon resort, has bright yellow buildings filled with the finest and most expensive wares money can buy, but the park benches and outdoor pub here make the outdoor mall a fun stop for window-shoppers as well. ☒ *Half Moon Resort, North Coast Hwy., 7 miles (11 km) east of Montego Bay, Montego Bay* ☎ *876/953–2211.*

The Shoppes at Rose Hall. This upscale shopping center was designed to resemble an old-fashioned Main Street. The center, five minutes from the Hilton Rose Hall Resort & Spa, includes jewelry, cosmetics, and designer-apparel shops. Some hotels offer free shuttle service to this open-air mall. ☒ *Rose Hall, North Coast Hwy., 15 miles (24 km) east of Montego Bay, St. James.*

Holiday Shopping Centre. Less serious shopping takes place at the Holiday Shopping Centre directly across the street from the Holiday Inn SunSpree Resort. The casual shopping area has jewelry, clothing, and crafts stores. ☒ *Holiday Inn SunSpree Resort, North Coast Hwy., 10 miles (16 km) east of Montego Bay, Montego Bay.*

OCHO RIOS

AREAS AND MALLS

Ocho Rios has several malls that draw day-trippers from the cruise ships. The best are **Soni's Plaza** and the **Taj Mahal,** two malls on the main street with stores selling jewelry, cigars, and clothing. Another popular mall on the main street is **Ocean Village.** On the North Coast Highway slightly east of Ochos Rios are **Pineapple Place** and **Coconut Grove.**

Ocho Rios Crafts Market. The largest craft market is the Ocho Rios Crafts Market, with stalls selling everything from straw hats to wooden figurines to T-shirts. Vendors can be aggressive, and haggling is expected for all purchases. Your best chance of getting a good price is to come on a day when there's no cruise ship in port. ☒ *Main St., Ocho Rios* ☎ *No phone.*

Pineapple Craft Market. The Pineapple Craft Market is a small, casual market east of Ocho Rios that's operated at the site for two decades. Look for everything from carved figurines to coffee-bean necklaces. ☒ *North Coast Hwy., Ocho Rios* ☎ *No phone.*

14

NEGRIL

AREAS AND MALLS

For more serious shopping, head to **Time Square,** known for its luxury goods ranging from jewelry to cigars to watches. The gated shopping area has air-conditioned stores with high-dollar items.

★ **Time Square.** The mall is known for its luxury goods ranging from cigars to jewelry. ✉ *Norman Manley Blvd., Negril* ☎ *876/957–9263.*

MARKETS

★ **Rutland Point.** With its laid-back atmosphere, it's no surprise that most Negril shopping involves straw hats, woven baskets, and T-shirts, all plentiful at the Rutland Point, a crafts market on the northern edge of town. The atmosphere is more laid-back than at similar establishments in Montego Bay and Ocho Rios. ✉ *Norman Manley Blvd., Negril* ☎ *No phone.*

KINGSTON

Unlike the communities on the island's North Coast, Kingston isn't known for its duty-free stores. Shopping here is mostly limited to shops for residents. The city's Constant Spring Road and King Street are home to a growing roster of shopping malls offering fashions, housewares, and more.

SPORTS AND ACTIVITIES

The tourist board licenses all recreational activity operators and outfitters, which should assure you of fair business practices as long as you deal with companies that display its decals.

BIRD-WATCHING

Jamaica is a major bird-watching destination, thanks to its various natural habitats. The island is home to more than 200 species, some seen only seasonally or in particular parts of the island. Many bird-watchers flock here for the chance to see the vervain hummingbird (the world's second-smallest bird, larger only than Cuba's bee hummingbird) or the Jamaican tody (which nests underground).

MONTEGO BAY

Rocklands Bird Sanctuary and Feeding Station, which is in Anchovy south of Montego Bay, is a great place to go if you want an easy bird-watching experience *(see* ⇨ *Exploring Montego Bay, above).*

Jamaica Explorations. Among several guided tours for birders is a special hummingbird tour. ✉ *Hotel Mockingbird Hill, Port Antonio* ☎ *876/993–7267* ⊕ *www.jamaicaexplorations.com.*

Continued on page 602

REGGAE
Julie Schwietert Collazo
& Eric Wechter

There's an undeniable, universal appeal to reggae music. Its feel-good beat and impassioned lyrics resonate with listeners across the globe, but experiencing reggae in the country of its birth is the best way to enjoy the music.

Widely considered to be Jamaica's seminal music form, reggae was born out of other genres, including ska and rocksteady, and is relatively young compared to other Jamaican musical styles. In fact, the history of Jamaican music is as long as the history of the island itself. Reggae's origins are firmly rooted in traditions of African music, and its lyrics are inspired by Jamaicans' fervid resistance to colonialism and imperialism. Reggae can be distinguished from earlier music forms by its comparatively faster beat, its experimental tendencies, and a more prominent role for the guitar. Reggae is also more "ragged"—both in sound and in concept. That is it's both more earthy and down to earth, or folkloric. Lyrically, reggae is rife with social themes, primarily those that explore the plight of the working classes.

BUILDING A BEAT

Sly Dunbar, touring with Peter Tosh, 1979

Robbie Shakespeare, on tour with Peter Tosh, 1978

Pioneering reggae musicians, such as drummer **Sly Dunbar** and bassist **Robbie Shakespeare,** shaped the genre by distilling what they viewed as the best elements of ska and rocksteady. Reggae is not complex in terms of chord structure or rhythmic variation. There may be only one to three chords in a typical reggae song, and the danceable feel is propelled most commonly by a rhythm—or "riddim"—called the "drop beat" or "one drop." The bass drum emphasizes the third beat in a four-beat cycle, creating an anchor, or a pull, that the guitar and bass play on top of. For a more propulsive feel, the drummer may equally emphasize all four beats in each measure. Layered on top of this repetitive, solid foundation are socially conscious lyrics, which often preach resistance to the establishment or beseech listeners to love one another.

REGGAE AND RASTA

Reggae is a musical genre of, by, and for the people, and the influence of Rastafarianism has expanded its folk appeal. Rasta became pervasive in Jamaica in the 1950s, when resistance to colonialism peaked. Rasta, combining spiritual, political, and social concerns, had its origins in the crowning of **Haile Selassie I** as the emperor of Ethiopia in 1930. Selassie, the only black man to head an independent African nation at the time, became a vital figure and symbol of freedom for Africans in the diaspora. Greatly inspired by Selassie, Jamaicans integrated his empowering messages into many aspects of their culture. Musically, the Rasta influence is felt in reggae in two ways. The lyrics often advocate the idea of returning to Africa, and minor chords and a simple "riddim" structure characterize the songs. In the words of music historian Lloyd Bradley, Rastas were the "underclass of the underclass," and by 1959 more than one in every 25 Jamaicans identified with Rastafarianism. One of them was Bob Marley.

Haile Selassie I of Ethiopia

BOB MARLEY

Bob Marley is reggae's oracle, a visionary who introduced the world to the music of Jamaica and the struggles of its people. A stirring performer with a preternatural talent for connecting with audiences, Marley revealed the oppression of his countrymen and their indomitable spirit through his songs of hope, freedom, and redemption. His legacy extends far beyond reggae, influencing generations of artists across multiple genres.

Born in February 1945, Robert Nesta Marley left his home in rural St. Ann's Parish, Jamaica, at 14 to pursue a music career in Kingston. In 1963 Marley joined with singers Peter Tosh and Bunny Livingston to form the group the Wailers, and they began recording singles with a renowned local producer. After a series of stops and starts and a strengthened devotion to the teachings of the Rastafari faith, Bob Marley and the Wailers released *Catch a Fire* in 1973. It was their first release outside of Jamaica, and nearly instantly it became an international success. Mar-

ley's global popularity and acclaim grew with albums like *Burnin'* and *Natty Dread*. As Marley's stardom increased abroad, his influence at home became transcendent. Regarded by many of his countrymen as a prophet, Marley, whose songs of freedom and revolution reverberated throughout Jamaica, was perceived as threat in some corridors. In December 1976, he was wounded in an assassination attempt. Marley left Jamaica for more than a year and in 1977 released his biggest record thus far, *Exodus,* which included the hits "Jammin" and "One Love/People Get Ready." By 1980, Marley was poised to reach even greater heights with an extensive U.S. tour, but while jogging in New York he suddenly collapsed. Cancer had silently invaded his brain and lungs. He died in May, 1981, at age 36. Marley's spirit and music endure in the hearts and minds of fans worldwide. His greatest hits collection, *Legend,* is the top-selling reggae album of all time.

Bob Marley at Reggae Sunsplash

COMMUNING WITH THE SPIRIT

Bob Marley Museum, Kingston

Whether you're a serious enthusiast or have just a passing curiosity, Jamaica offers visitors plenty of opportunities to experience the music and culture of reggae.

Zion Bus Line Tour to Nine Mile. Marley fans won't want to miss this bus pilgrimage to the reggae icon's birthplace and final resting place. With the sounds of familiar reggae tunes thumping through the bus speakers, the guided tour takes you through the mountains to the small town of Nine Mile. The half-day tour includes a visit to Marley's house, a stop at Mount Zion (a rock where Marley meditated) and the opportunity to view Marley's mausoleum. The tour leaves from Ocho Rios. On the return trip from Nine Mile, the group stops at the Jerk Center for an authentic Jamaican lunch.

Reggae Sumfest in Montego Bay. This week-long reggae festival is held each July. In addition to featuring musical line-ups of the most popular reggae, dance hall, R&B, and hip hop acts, the Sumfest offers traditional Jamaican food and local crafts. Recent festivals have featured local favorite Tarrus Riley, as well as international performers, like LL Cool J and Mary J. Blige.

DID YOU KNOW?

The first appearance of the word *reggae* is widely attributed to the 1968 single by the Maytals called "Do the Reggay."

Burning Spear

Jimmy Cliff

The Congos

At **Reggae Yard & Island Life** (☎ 876/675–8795) in Ocho Rios you'll find an extensive selection of reggae CDs as well as other types of Caribbean music.

Bob Marley Museum in Kingston (☎ 876/927–9152). If the Zion Bus Tour only whets your appetite for Marley, visit the Bob Marley Museum for a glimpse at another chapter of his life. Housed inside the former headquarters of Marley's label, Tuff Gong Records, it is also the site of the failed attempt on Marley's life that inspired his song, "Ambush."

And, of course, your Jamaican reggae experience would not be complete without catching some live bands. Local acts play at **Bourbon Beach** (☎ 876/957–4405) in Negril on Monday, Thursday, and Saturday nights. Also in Negril is **Rick's Cafe** (☎ 876/957–0380), which features an in-house reggae band nightly.

REGGAE LINGO

Dancehall. A modern style that introduces elements of electronic dance music and improvised singing or rapping by DJs to raw reggae tracks.

Dub. A form of reggae characterized by the use of remixes of previously recorded material.

One-drop rhythm. The definitive beat of reggae characterized by a steady "drop" of the bass drum on the strong beat in each measure.

Ragamuffin (ragga). Similar to dancehall, ragga combines electronic dance music, hip-hop, and R&B with reggae for a more contemporary, club feel.

Riddim. The rhythmic foundation for nearly all reggae styles, characterized by a repetitive, driving drum and bass feel.

Rocksteady. A style of reggae that followed ska, rocksteady is marked by a slower tempo.

Ska. Precursor to reggae that combines traditional Caribbean rhythms, jazz, and calypso

RECOMMENDED LISTENING

Bob Marley
Uprising, Legend, Exodus, Burnin', Catch a Fire

Peter Tosh
Legalize It

Toots and the Maytals
Funky Kingston

Jimmy Cliff
The Harder They Come

Burning Spear
Marcus Garvey

Alton Ellis
Alton Ellis Sings Rock and Soul

The Congos
The Heart of the Congos

DIVING AND SNORKELING

Jamaica isn't a major dive destination, but you can find a few rich underwater regions, especially off the North Coast. Mo'Bay, known for its wall dives, has **Airport Reef** at its southwestern edge. The site is known for its coral caves, tunnels, and canyons. The first marine park in Jamaica, the **Montego Bay Marine Park,** was established to protect the natural resources of the bay; a quick look at the area and it's easy to see the treasures that lie beneath the surface. The North Coast is on the edge of the Cayman Trench, so it boasts a wide array of marine life.

Thanks to a marine area protected since 1966, the Ocho Rios region is also a popular diving destination. Through the years, the protected area grew into the **Ocho Rios Marine Park,** stretching from Mammee Bay and Drax Hall to the west to Frankfort Point on the east. Top dive sites in the area include **Jack's Hall,** a 40-foot dive dotted with all types of coral; **Top of the Mountain,** a 60-foot dive near Dunn's River Falls with many coral heads and gorgonians; and the **Wreck of the _Katryn_,** a 50-foot dive to a deliberately sunk 140-foot former minesweeper.

With its murkier waters, the southern side of the island isn't as popular for diving, especially near Kingston. **Port Royal,** which is near the airport, is filled with sunken ships that are home to many different varieties of tropical fish, although a special permit is required to dive some sites here. Prices range from $45 to $80 for a one-tank dive. All the large resorts have dive shops, and the all-inclusive places sometimes include scuba diving in their rates. To dive, you need to show a certification card, though it's possible to get a small taste of scuba diving and do a shallow dive—usually from shore—after taking a one-day resort diving course, which almost every resort with a dive shop offers. A couple of places stand out.

MONTEGO BAY

Jamaica Scuba Divers. Here are serious scuba facilities for dedicated divers. This PADI and NAUI operation also offers nitrox diving and instruction as well as instruction in underwater photography, night diving, and open-water diving. There's a pickup service for the Negril, Montego Bay, Runaway Bay, Discovery Bay, and Ocho Rios areas with cost depending on location. ✉ _Franklyn D. Resort, Runaway Bay_ ☎ _876/381–1113_ ⊕ _www.scuba-jamaica.com._

FALMOUTH

Scuba Jamaica. This company offers serious scuba facilities for dedicated divers. The PADI and NAUI operation also offers Nitrox diving and instruction as well as instruction in underwater photography, night diving, and open-water diving. There's a pickup service for the Montego Bay, Runaway Bay, Discovery Bay, and Ocho Rios areas. Along with the Falmouth location, Scuba Jamaica is also found at the Franklyn D. Resort in Runaway Bay and at Travellers Resort in Negril. ✉ _N- Resort, North Coast Hwy., Falmouth_ ☎ _876/617–2500, 876/973–4591 in Runaway Bay, 876/957–3039 in Negril_ ⊕ _www.scuba-jamaica.com._

NEGRIL

Negril Scuba Center. This dive shop has two locations in Negril, with operations at Negril Escape Resort and Spa as well as Boardwalk Village. ⊠ *Negril Escape Resort and Spa, West End Rd., Negril* ☎ *876/957–0392, 876/877–7517, 876/383–9533* ⊕ *www.negrilscubacenter.com.*

Wild Thing Water Sports. Cruises from this shop in the middle of Negril Beach include snorkeling with full use of equipment and instruction for those new to the sport. ⊠ *Norman Manley Blvd., Negril* ☎ *876/957–9930* ⊕ *www.wildthingwatersportsnegril.com.*

FISHING

Port Antonio makes deep-sea-fishing headlines with its annual Blue Marlin Tournament in October, and Mo'Bay and Ocho Rios have devotees who exchange tales (tall and otherwise) about sailfish, yellowfin tuna, wahoo, dolphinfish, and bonito. Licenses aren't required, and you can arrange to charter a boat at your hotel. A chartered boat (with captain, crew, and equipment) costs about $500 to $900 for a half day or $900 to $1,500 for a full-day excursion, depending on the size of the boat.

FALMOUTH

Glistening Waters Marina. This marina offers charter trips from the Falmouth area, including deep-sea fishing charters. The marina also has nighttime boat tours for a look at the lagoon, whose iridescence is caused by microscopic dinoflagellates that become luminescent when they move. ⊠ *North Coast Hwy., Falmouth* ☎ *876/954–3229* ⊕ *www. glisteningwaters.com.*

No Problem Sport Fishing. Charter fishing excursions are available aboard the *E-Zee*. Half- and full-day excursions take anglers in search of big catch. Plan on about $550 for a half-day charter and $1,100 for a full day on the seas; fees includes drinks and equipment. ⊠ *The Yacht Club, Montego Bay* ☎ *876/381-3229* ⊕ *www.montego-bay-jamaica. com/ajal/noproblem.*

GOLF

Golfers appreciate both the beauty and the challenges offered by Jamaica's courses. Caddies are almost always mandatory throughout the island, and rates are $15 to $45 per round of golf. Cart rentals are available at most courses; costs are $20 to $40. Some of the best courses in the country are found near Mo'Bay. Many resorts have their own courses (including several of the Sandals and SuperClubs resorts) and allow both guests and nonguests to play; there is generally a charge for nonguests at these courses.

MONTEGO BAY

★ **Golf at Half Moon.** This Robert Trent Jones–designed 18-hole course is the home of the Red Stripe Pro Am. Greens fees are $105 for guests, $150 for nonguests, with twilight packages ranging from $75 to $90. In 2005 the course received an upgrade from Jones protégé Roger Rulewich and draws international attention. The course is also home of the Half Moon Golf Academy, which offers one-day sessions, multi-day retreats, and hour-long private sessions. ⊠ *Half Moon Resort, North Coast Hwy., 7 miles (11 km) east of Montego Bay, Montego Bay* ☎ *876/953–2560* ⊕ *halfmoon.rockresorts.com/activities/golf.asp*.

Hilton Rose Hall Resort and Spa. This course 4 miles (6 km) east of the airport hosts several invitational tournaments. Greens fees run $149 7–10 am, $119 10 am–1:30 pm, and $99 for a twilight round at the 18-hole championship **Cinnamon Hill Ocean Course**. The course was designed by Robert von Hagge and Rick Baril and is adjacent to historic Cinnamon Hill estate. Rates include greens fees, cart, caddie, and tax, and apply to both guests and nonguests. ⊠ *North Coast Hwy., St. James* ✛ *15 miles (24 km) east of Montego Bay* ☎ *876/953–2650*.

★ **Ritz-Carlton Golf and Spa Resort, Rose Hall.** One of the nicest courses in Montego Bay, if not Jamaica, is the **White Witch** course at the Ritz-Carlton. The greens fees at this 18-hole championship course are $175 for resort guests, $185 for nonguests, and $109 for a twilight round. Designed by Robert von Hagge and Rick Baril, it is close to the grounds of historic Rose Hall Great House. ⊠ *1 Ritz Carlton Dr., Rose Hall, St. James* ☎ *876/684–0174* ⊕ *www.whitewitchgolf.com*.

Fodor'sChoice **Tryall Club Golf Course.** Probably the best-known golf course in Jamaica ★ is the course at this resort 15 miles (24 km) west of Montego Bay. The 18-hole championship course is on the site of a 19th-century sugar plantation. The famous 7th hole tees off between the stone pillars of a historic aqueduct; the adjacent waterwheel has been the subject of many photos. The course was designed by Ralph Plummer and is an official Professional Golf Association tour–approved course, having hosted events such as the Johnnie Walker World Championship. Greens fees for Tryall guests are $105 for 18 holes, and $75 for nine holes or $150 and $115, respectively, for non-guests. ⊠ *North Coast Hwy., Sandy Bay* ☎ *876/956–5681* ⊕ *www.tryallclub.com*.

RUNAWAY BAY AND VICINITY

SuperClubs Golf Club at Runaway Bay. This 18-hole course in Runaway Bay has hosted many championship events (greens fees are $80 for non guests; guests play for free) and is also home to an extensive golf academy. ⊠ *North Coast Hwy., Runaway Bay* ☎ *876/973–7319*.

OCHO RIOS

Sandals Golf and Country Club. The golf course in Ocho Rios is 700 feet above sea level (greens fees are $100 for 18 holes or $70 for 9 holes for non guests; free for guests). ⊠ *5 miles (8 km) southeast of Ocho Rios, turn south at White River and continue 4 miles (6 km), Ocho Rios* ☎ *876/975–0119*.

NEGRIL

Negril Hills Golf Club. Great golf, rolling hills, and a rolling "liquor-mobile" go hand in hand at the 18-hole golf course, the only one in Negril (it's east of town). Greens fees are $28.75 for 9 holes or $57.50 for 18 holes. ⊠ *Sheffield Rd., Negril* ☎ *876/957–4638* ⊕ *www. negrilhillsgolfclub.com*.

GUIDED TOURS

Because most vacationers don't rent cars for both safety and cost reasons, guided tours are a popular option if you want to take a break from the beach and explore. Check with your hotel concierge for information on half- and full-day tours that offer pickup at your resort. Jamaica's size and slow roads mean that you can't expect to see the entire island on any one trip; even a full-day tour will concentrate on just one part of the island. Most of the tours are similar in both content and price. If you're in Montego Bay, tours often include one of the plantation houses in the area. Several Negril-based companies offer tours to Y.S. Falls on the South Coast. Tours from Ocho Rios might include any of the area's top attractions, including Dunn's River Falls or Kingston. In almost all cases, you'll arrange your tour through the tour desk of your resort. However, a few of these tours are quite unique, including the following.

14

MONTEGO BAY

Montego Bay offers a wide array of guided tours, and most of the large resorts have tour desks where you can book a number of excursions and activities. Guided plantation and countryside visits are also popular. Almost all tour operators will pick you up if you are staying in one of the large resorts.

Island Routes Caribbean Adventure Tours. Run by Sandals, Island Routes provides luxury tours of Jamaica to both guests and nonguests of Sandals resorts. The company offers group and private guided tours with certified partners to a host of attractions. Guests have a choice of booking via the website or on-island at one of the Island Routes tour desks at participating resorts. ⊠ *Montego Bay* 🕾 *877/684–8672, 1-888/429–5478, 1-888/768–8370 (USA & Canada)* ⊕ *www.islandroutestours.com.*

OCHO RIOS

Zion Bus Tour. This tour will appeal to reggae buffs visiting Ocho Rios who want to visit Bob Marley's boyhood home. Travelers ride a country-style bus painted in bright colors to the island's interior and the village of Nine Mile. The tour includes a look at the simple home where Marley was born and is now buried. The tour ($84 including a lunch stop at a local jerk stand) lasts for five hours and is limited to guests age 18 and above. ⊠ *Chukka Caribbean Adventures, Llandovery, St. Ann's Bay* 🕾 *876/972–2506* ⊕ *www.chukkacaribbean.com.*

SOUTH COAST

Countrystyle Peace Village. This company allows visitors to the South Coast, Mandeville, and Kingston to experience more of the real Jamaica. Tours offers unique, personalized tours of island communities. You're linked with community residents based on your interests; tours can include anything from bird-watching in Mandeville to nightlife in Kingston. ⊠ *62 Ward Ave., Mandeville* 🕾 *876/962–7758, 876/488–7207* ⊕ *www.countrystylecommunitytourism.com.*

HORSEBACK RIDING

RUNAWAY BAY

Braco Stables. In the Braco area near Trelawny, between Montego Bay and Ocho Rios, this stable offers guided rides, including a bareback romp in the sea. Two estate rides are offered a day for $70, and riders are matched to horses based on riding ability. The trip also includes an optional barbecue lunch. Experienced riders can also opt for a mountain ride ($84) for a more rugged two-hour tour. ⊠ *Duncans* ☎ *876/954–0185* ⊕ *www.bracostables.com.*

OCHO RIOS

With its combination of hills and beaches, Ocho Rios is a natural for horseback excursions. Most are guided tours taken at a slow pace and perfect for those with no previous equestrian experience. Many travelers opt to pack long pants for horseback rides, especially those away from the beach.

Annandale Plantation. The 600-acre plantation is high above Ocho Rios and today serves as a working farm, although in its glory days it hosted dignitaries such as the Queen Mother. The great house is open for the tours. Horseback rides start at Drax Hall and include trails to the beach and, upon request, to the great house. ⊠ *4 miles (6 km) southwest of Ocho Rios, near town of Epworth* ☎ *876/974–2323* ⊕ *tourwise.org.*

Fodor'sChoice   **Chukka Caribbean Adventures.** Ocho Rios has excellent horseback riding,
★   but the best of the operations is Chukka Caribbean's Ocho Rios stable. You don't have to be an experienced rider to enjoy its tours; horses are well trained and Chukka provides attentive guides to assist all riders along the way. The company's 2½-hour beach ride ($74, $52 for children) is a highlight of many trips to Jamaica. ⊠ *Llandovery, St. Ann's Bay* ☎ *876/972–2506* ⊕ *www.chukkacaribbean.com.*

Hooves. This stable offers several guided tours, including a popular 2½-hour beach ride ($85 from Ocho Rios, $89 from Runaway Bay) suitable for adults and children taller than three feet. The trip begins with a visit to the Seville Great House Museum before making its way to the beach for a ride. Hooves is home to many rescue horses that have been rehabilitated. ⊠ *Windsor Rd., St. Ann's Bay* ☎ *876/972–0905* ⊕ *www.hoovesjamaica.com.*

Prospect Plantation. The plantation offers a horseback rides for ages eight and older. The price ($58) includes use of helmets; advance reservations are required. For the adventurous, Prospect Plantation also offers guided camel rides. ⊠ *Rte. A1, about 3 miles (5 km) east of Ocho Rios* ☎ *876/974–5335* ⊕ *www.prospectplantationtours.com.*

MOUNTAIN BIKING

Jamaica's hilly terrain creates a challenge for mountain bikers, though there are easier rides, especially near the beaches and on the western end of the island. Heavy, unpredictable traffic on the North Coast Highway makes it off-limits for bikers, but smaller country roads and winding trails weave a network through the countryside.

Rafting on the Rio Grande, near Port Antonio

OCHO RIOS

Blue Mountain Bicycle Tours. This company takes travelers on guided rides in the spectacular Blue Mountains. The all-day excursion starts high and glides downhill, so all levels of riders can enjoy the tour. The trip ends with a dip in a waterfall; the package price includes transportation from Ocho Rios or Kingston, lunch, and all equipment. ✉ *121 Main St., Ocho Rios* ☎ *876/974–7075* ⊕ *www.bmtoursja.com.*

RIVER BOATING AND RAFTING

Jamaica's many rivers mean a multitude of freshwater experiences, from mild to wild. Jamaica's first tourist activity off the beaches was relaxing rafting trips aboard bamboo rafts poled by local boatmen. Recently, soft-adventure enthusiasts have also been able to opt for white-water action as well with guided tours through several operators.

Fodor's Choice ★ Bamboo rafting in Jamaica originated on the **Río Grande,** a river in the Port Antonio area. Jamaicans had long used the bamboo rafts to transport bananas downriver; decades ago actor and Port Antonio resident Errol Flynn saw the rafts and thought they'd make a good tourist attraction, and local entrepreneurs quickly rose to the occasion. Today the slow rides are a favorite with romantic travelers and anyone looking to get off the beach for a few hours. The popularity of the Río Grande's trips spawned similar trips down the **Martha Brae River,** about 25 miles (40 km) from Mo'Bay. Near Ocho Rios, the **Great River** has lazy river rafting as well as energetic kayaking.

MONTEGO BAY

Jamaica Tours Limited. This big tour company conducts raft trips down the River Lethe, approximately 12 miles (19 km) southwest of Mo'Bay (a 50-minute trip); the four-hour excursion can include lunch if requested and takes you through unspoiled hill country. Bookings can be made through hotel tour desks. Price depends on the number of people on the trip. ✉ *Providence Dr., Montego Bay* ☎ *876/953–3700* ⊕ *www. jamaicatoursltd.com.*

Rio Grande Tours. Guided raft trips down the Rio Grande cost $72 per raft. (On top of the fee, raftsmen expect a tip of about $5 to $10.) The last raft trips depart about 3 pm, a good time to observe locals fishing and washing clothes along the riverbanks. ✉ *St. Margaret's Bay* ☎ *876/993–5778.*

River Raft Ltd. This company leads trips down the Martha Brae River, about 25 miles (40 km) from most hotels in Mo'Bay. The cost is $60 per person for the 1½-hour river run. ✉ *Martha Brae* ☎ *876/940–6398* ⊕ *www.jamaicarafting.com.*

OCHO RIOS

Caliche Rainforest Adventure Park. If you're looking for a rugged adventure, then consider a white-water rafting trip at this attraction. Two tours, both offered in inflatable rafts, traverse the waters of the Great River. The Grade II Rainforest Rafting Tour ($80) glides along with stops for a swim; ages four and up can participate. The Canyon White Water Rafting tour ($90–$100) traverses rapids up to Grade IV; travelers must be at least 12. In most cases you will be picked up at your hotel in Montego Bay, Ocho Rios, or Port Antonio, and the tour price includes the transfer cost. ✉ *Great River, Montego Bay* ☎ *876/940–6558* ⊕ *www.whitewaterraftingmontegobay.com.*

Chukka Caribbean Adventures. The big activity outfitter offers the Chukka River Tubing Safari on the White River, an easy trip that doesn't require any previous tubing experience. This tour allows you to travel in your very own tube through gentle rapids. This tour lasts for three hours and costs $64 for adults and $45 for children. ✉ *Llandovery, St. Ann's Bay* ☎ *876/972–2506* ⊕ *www.chukkacaribbean.com.*

SOUTH COAST

South Coast Safaris Ltd. This company takes visitors on slow boat cruises ($17.50) up the river to see the birds and other animals, including crocodiles. ✉ *1 Crane St., Black River* ☎ *876/965–2513.*

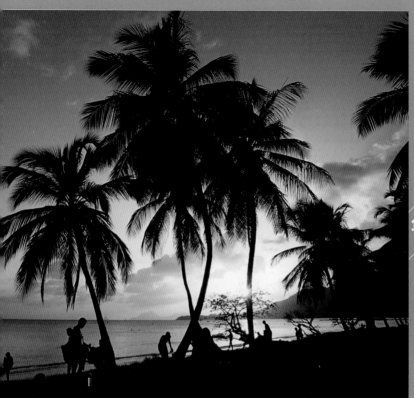

Martinique

WORD OF MOUTH

"Martinique is beautiful, historically interesting, has the French flair, easy to get around because, being a department of France, has very good, well-marked roads."

—xkenx

WELCOME TO MARTINIQUE

PARIS IN THE TROPICS

The largest of the Windward Islands, Martinique is 425 square miles (1,101 square km). The southern part of the island is all rolling hills and sugarcane fields; it's also where you'll find the best beaches and most development. In the north are craggy cliffs, lush vegetation, and one of the Caribbean's largest volcanoes, Mont Pelée.

Martinique Passage
Grand-Rivière   Macouba
Anse-Ceron
Ajoupa-Bou
Mont Pelée
Le Prêcheur
Le Morne Rouge
N2
8   St-Pierre
Rade de St-Pierre
Musée Gauguin ◆
Neisson Distillery ◆
5   Carbet   **4**   Morne Vert
Aqualand
N2
Caribbean Sea
Bellefontaine
Case-Pilo

0   5 mi
0   5 km

KEY	
⌁	*Beaches*
1	*Restaurants*
1	*Hotels*

Joie de vivre is the credo in this French enclave, which is often characterized as a Caribbean suburb of Paris. Exotic fruit grows on the volcanoes' forested flanks amid a profusion of wild orchids and hibiscus. The sheer lushness of it all inspired the tropical paintings of onetime resident Paul Gauguin.

TOP REASONS TO VISIT MARTINIQUE

1 The Romance: A magical sensuality infuses everything; it will awaken dormant desires and fuel existing fires.

2 Beautiful Beaches: A full roster of beautiful beaches will let you enjoy sun and sand.

3 The French Connection: Excellent French food, not to mention French music and fashion, makes the island a paradise for Francophiles.

4 Range of Accommodations: Hospitable, stylish small hotels abound; big resorts, too. Or play expat in a private, luxe villa.

5 Inviting Waters: The sea, Caribbean; the ocean, Atlantic—experience the water in a kayak or on a sailboat. Even a ferry works.

MARTINIQUE BEACHES

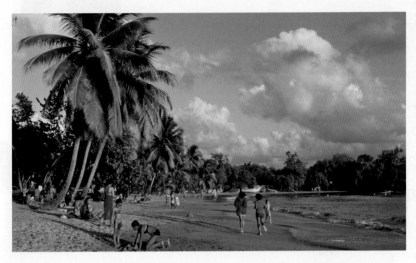

Take to the beach in Martinique. A Caribbean vacation can be a rough ride on Atlantic surf or a swim in calm Caribbean waters as tranquil as a blue lagoon. Experience the white sandbars known as Josephine's Baths, where Napoléon's Joséphine would bathe.

(Above) Anse Corps de Garde (Bottom right) Les Salines (Top right) Diamant Beach

All of Martinique's beaches are open to the public, but hotels charge a fee for nonguests to use changing rooms and other facilities. There are no official nudist beaches, but topless bathing is prevalent, as is the case on most French islands. Unless you're an expert swimmer, steer clear of the Atlantic waters, except in the area of Cap Chevalier (Cape Knight) and the Presqu'île du Caravelle (Caravelle Peninsula). The white-sand beaches are south of Fort-de-France; to the north, the beaches are silvery-black volcanic sand. Some of the most pleasant strips of sand are around Ste-Anne, Ste-Luce, and Havre du Robert. And one wonders how, some 15 minutes from Le François harbor, the white sandbars that form Josephine's Baths were created in the middle of the sea.

SHIFTY SANDS

Martinique's sand often belies its environment. The long tawny stretches of beach in Carbet and the neighboring town of St-Pierre, where the infamous volcano Mont Pelée is located, are *not* volcanic black sand. The famous black-sand beach of Diamant is nowhere near Mont Pelée. It is, however, across from Diamond Rock, a volcanic outcropping.

Anse Corps de Garde. On the southern Caribbean coast, this is one of the island's best long stretches of white sand. The public beach has picnic tables, restrooms, sea grape trees, and crowds, particularly on weekends, when you can find plenty of wandering food vendors. The water is calm, with just enough wave action to remind you it's the sea. From Fort-de-France, exit to the right before you get to the town of Ste-Luce. You first see signs for the Karibea Hotels and then one for Corps de Garde, which is on the right. At the stop sign take a left. ⊠ *Ste-Luce.*

Anse-Mitan. This is not the French Riviera, though there are often yachts moored offshore. This long stretch of beach can be particularly fun on Sunday. Small, family-owned seaside restaurants are half-hidden among palm trees and are footsteps from the lapping waves. Nearly all offer grilled lobster and some form of music, perhaps a zouk band. Inexpensive waterfront hotels line the clean, golden beach, which has excellent snorkeling just offshore. Chaise longues are available for rent from hotels for about €7. When you get to Pointe du Bout, take a left at the yellow office of Budget Rent-A-Car, then the next left up a hill, and park near the little white church. ⊠ *Pointe du Bout Les Trois-Ilets.*

Anse Tartane. This patch of sand is on the wild side of the Presqu'île du Caravelle. It's what the French call a *sauvage* (virgin) beach, and the only people you are likely to see are brave surfers who ride the high waves or some local families. Bliss, the surf school here, has taught many kids the ropes. Résidence Oceane looks down on all of this action but doesn't have a restaurant. Turn right before you get to La Trinité, and follow the route de Château past the Caravelle hotel. Instead of following the signs to Résidence Oceane, veer left and go downhill when you see the ocean. The road runs right beside the beach. There are several bays and *pointes* here, but if you keep heading to the right, you can reach the surf school. ⊠ *Tartane, La Trinité.*

Diamant Beach. The island's longest beach has a splendid view of Diamond Rock, but the Atlantic waters are rough, with lots of wave action. Often the beach is deserted, especially midweek, which is more reason to swim with prudence. Happily, it's a great place for picnicking and beachcombing; there are shade trees aplenty, and parking is abundant and free. The hospitable, family-run Diamant les Bains hotel is a good lunch spot; if you eat lunch there, the management may let you wash off in the pool overlooking the beach. From Les Trois-Ilets, go in the direction of Rivière Salée, taking the secondary road to the

15

Les Salines

east, toward Le Diamant. A coastal route, it leads to the beach. ⊠ *Le Diamant, Le Diamant.*

Les Salines. A short drive south of Ste-Anne brings you to a mile-long (1.5-km-long) cove lined with soft white sand and coconut palms. The beach is awash with families and children during holidays and on weekends but quiet during the week. The far end—away from the makeshift souvenir shops—is most appealing. The calm waters are safe for swimming, even for the kids. You can't rent chaise longues, but there are showers. Food vendors roam the sand. From Le Marin, take the coastal road toward Ste-Anne. You will see signs for Les Salines. If you see the sign for Pointe du Marin, you have gone too far. ⊠ *Ste-Anne.*

☾ **Pointe du Bout.** The beaches here are small, man-made, and lined with resorts, including the Hotel Bakoua. Each little strip is associated with its resident hotel, and security guards and closed gates make access difficult. However, if you take a left across from the main pedestrian entrance to the marina—after the taxi stand—then go left again, you will reach the beach for Hotel Bakoua, which has especially nice facilities and several options for lunch and drinks. If things are quiet—particularly during the week—one of the beach boys may rent you a chaise; otherwise, just plop your beach towel down, face forward, and enjoy the delightful view of the Fort-de-France skyline. The water is dead calm and quite shallow, but it eventually drops off if you swim out a bit. ⊠ *Pointe du Bout Les Trois-Ilets.*

Pointe du Marin. Stretching north from Ste-Anne, this is a good windsurfing and waterskiing spot. It's also a popular family beach, with restaurants, campsites, and clean facilities available for a small fee. Club Med is on the northern edge, and you can purchase a day pass. From Le Marin, take the coastal road to Ste-Anne. Make a right before town, toward Domaine de Belfond. You can see signs for Pointe du Marin. ⊠ *St. Anne.*

By Eileen Robinson Smith

Numerous scattered ruins and other historical monuments reflect the richness of Martinique's sugarcane plantocracy, *rhum,* and the legacy of slavery. Called the Rum Capital of the World, it is widely considered the best gourmet island in the Caribbean. It stirs the passions with its distinctive brand of culinary offerings. If you believe in magic, Martinique has it, along with a sensuality that fosters romance. It has become known as the island of *revenants,* those who always return. *Et pourquoi non?*

15

Martinique is simply one of the most enchanting destinations in the Western Hemisphere. Francophiles adore this French island, for its gastronomy, rum, its *musique* and élan, and the availability of the finest French products, from Chanel fashions to Limoges china. It is endowed with physical beauty, as varied as white-sand beaches and tropical rain forests. The volcano Mont Pelée looms over the harbor town of St-Pierre, known as the Pompeii of the Caribbean. The recent additions to the island's tourism product include dynamic changes in its largest city, Fort-de-France, enhanced attractions, and new restaurants and clubs. Martinicans will be glad you came, and you will be greeted with warm smiles and politesse.

Christopher Columbus first sighted this gorgeous island in 1502, when it was inhabited by the fierce Caraïbes, who had terrorized the peace-loving Arawaks. The Arawaks called their home Madinina (the Isle of Flowers), and for good reason. Exotic wild orchids, frangipani, anthurium, jade vines, flamingo flowers, and hundreds of vivid varieties of hibiscus still thrive here.

The island reflects its rich cultural history. In colonial days Martinique was the administrative, social, and cultural center of the French Antilles, a rich, aristocratic island famous for its beautiful women. The island even gave birth to an empress, Napoléon's Joséphine. It saw the full flowering of a plantocracy, with servants and soirees, wine cellars and snobbery.

Martinique is the largest stronghold of the *békés*—the descendants of the original French planters—and they are still the privileged class on any of the French-Caribbean islands. Numbering around 4,000, many control Martinique's most profitable businesses, from banana plantations and rum distilleries to car dealerships. The island's economy depends on *les bananes* (bananas), *l'ananas* (pineapples), cane sugar, rum, and fishing. The elite dress in designer outfits straight off the Paris runways. In general, the islanders have style. In the airport waiting room you can almost always tell the Martiniquaises by their fashionable clothes.

Of the island's 400,000 inhabitants, 100,000 live in Fort-de-France and its environs. It has 34 separate municipalities. Though the actual number of French residents from the Metropole (France) does not exceed 15% of the total population, Martinique is a part of France, an overseas *département* to be exact, and French is the official language, though the vast majority of the residents also speak Creole.

Thousands are employed in government jobs offering more paid holidays than most Americans can imagine. Martinicans enjoy their time off, celebrating everything from *le fin de la semaine* (the weekend) to Indian feast days, sailboat races, and Carnival. Their joie de vivre is infectious. Once you experience it, you'll be back.

PLANNING

WHEN TO GO

High season runs from mid-November through May, and the island can be quiet the rest of the year, with some hotels closing down for months, particularly in September and October. Those places that remain open offer significant discounts. Check ⊕ *www.martnique.org* for the latest deals.

GETTING HERE AND AROUND

AIR TRAVEL

There are no nonstop flights from the United States; most travelers connect in San Juan (American Eagle or Air France).

Airline Contacts American Eagle. Many travelers fly American Airlines and connect in San Juan to daily flights on American Eagle. ☎ *0590/21–13–66 in Guadeloupe, 800/433–7300 in the US* ⊕ *www.aa.com.*

Air Antilles Express. Air Antilles Express flies to Martinique from Guadeloupe, St. Maarten, St. Barth, and Santo Domingo. ☎ *0890/64–86–48, 0596/42–16–71, 0596/42–16–72* ⊕ *www.airantilles.com.*

Air Caraïbes. Air Caraïbes flies to Martinique from Guadeloupe, St. Maarten, St. Barth, and Santo Domingo. (This airline offers substantial discounts for seniors.) ☎ *0820/83–58–35, 0590/82–47–47* ⊕ *www. aircaraibes.com.*

Air France. Air France has service to and from Miami, with stops in neighboring islands, five times a week in the winter season ☎ *0820/82–08–20, 0892/68–29–72, 0596/55–34–72* ⊕ *www.airfrance.com.*

LOGISTICS

Getting to Martinique: Many travelers fly American Airlines and connect in San Juan to the daily flight out on American Eagle. Air Antilles Express flies from Guadeloupe, St. Maarten, and St. Barth. Air Caraïbes flies from Guadeloupe, St. Maarten, St. Barth, and Santo Domingo. (This airline offers substantial discounts for seniors.) Air France is another connection option; during the peak tourist season (winter), it has service from Miami five times a week, with stops in neighboring islands. LIAT connects Martinique with the English-speaking "down islands" such as St. Lucia. Other airlines, including Air Antilles Express, also offer service to Martinique from nearby islands (some of which are also connected to Martinique by ferries).

Hassle Factor: Medium to high.

On the Ground: Taxis in Martinique are expensive, so airport-transfer costs must become a part of your vacation budget. From the airport to Fort-de-France, you'll pay at least €20 (€30 at night or on Sunday); from the airport to Pointe du Bout, it's about €40 (€60 at night or on Sunday); fares to Francois or Tartane are approximately €50 (€70 at night or on Sunday). If you arrive at night or on Sunday, depending on where your hotel is, it may be cheaper (although not safer) to rent a car from the airport and keep it for 24 hours than to take a taxi to your hotel.

LIAT. LIAT connects Martinique with the English-speaking "down islands," like St. Lucia. It code-shares with Air Caraïbes (which offers substantial senior discounts). ■ TIP→ Daily flights from Saint-Lucia (UVF)—which has direct service from New York, Miami, Atlanta and Toronto—offer new opportunities for U.S. and Canadian visitors to Martinique to reach the island with fewer stopovers. ☎ *0596/42–16–11* ⊕ *www.liatairline.com.*

Airport Martinique Aimé Césaire Airport. Martinique Aimé Césaire Airport, in the commercial area of Lamentin, is relatively small and easy to maneuver; some staff members speak English. The airport is 15-min from Fort-de-France via taxi; it's 40 min from Les Trois-Ilets Peninsula. A public bus to Fort-de-France costs €1 (the bus stop is across the street from the terminal). ⊠ *FDF, Lamentin* ☎ *0596/42–16–00.*

CAR TRAVEL

The main highways, about 175 miles (280 km) of well-paved and well-marked roads, are excellent, but only in a few areas are they lighted at night. Many hotels are on roads that are barely passable, so get wherever you're going by nightfall or you could lose your way. Then tell a stranger, *"Je suis perdu!"* ("I am lost!"). It elicits sympathy. If they say, *"Suivez-moi!"*—that's "Follow me!"—stay glued to their bumper. Finally, drive defensively; although Martinicans are polite and lovely people, they drive with aggressive abandon.

Martinique, especially Fort-de-France and environs, is plagued with heavy traffic; if you must drive into Fort-de-France, do it on a weekend. Absolutely avoid the Lamentin Airport area and Fort-de-France during weekday rush hours, roughly 7 to 10 am and 4 to 7:30 pm, and on Sunday night. Even the smaller towns such as La Trinité have rush hours. Watch, too, for *dos d'ânes* (literally, donkey backs), speed bumps that are hard to spot—particularly at night. Gas is costly, some $6 per gallon. Be aware that the French gendarmes set up roadblocks, often on Sunday, to stop speeders and drunk drivers, and just to check papers.

Renting a Car: It's worth the hassle to rent a car—if only for a day or two—so that you can explore more of this beautiful island. Just be prepared for a manual shift, steep mountainous roads, and heavy traffic. Prices are expensive, about €70 per day or €330 per week (unlimited mileage) for a manual shift, perhaps more for an automatic, which is rare. You may save money by waiting to book your car rental on the island for a reduced weekly rate from a local agency. With the latter, though, know that some make up their own rules, and they will not be in your favor. There's an extra charge (about $20) if you drop the car off at the airport, having rented it somewhere else on the island. A valid U.S. driver's license and International Driver's Permit are needed to rent a car for up to 20 days. Tip: Often, the airline you fly in with will have a discount coupon for a rental car, right on the ticket, or in their in-flight magazine. Also, local publications often have ads with discounts that can be as much as 40% off. (You can often find these at the Tourism Information counter in the airport.)

Contacts **Avis** ☎ 0596/42–11–00 ⊕ www.avis-antilles.fr. **Budget** ☎ 0596/42–04–04 ⊕ www.Budget-Antilles.com. **Europcar.** Europcar will deliver the car to you and pick it up later, and its rates are usually among the lowest. The down side is that employees don't usually speak English. ☎ 0596/70–65–34 ⊕ www.eurocar.mg. **Hertz** ☎ 0596/42–16–90, 0810/32–31–13 ⊕ www.hertzantilles.com. **JumboCar.** Of the many agencies, JumboCar is the most likely to cut a deal (but few of its staffers speak English). ☎ 0596/42–22–22, 0820/22–02–30 ⊕ www.jumbocar.com.

FERRY TRAVEL

Weather permitting, *vedettes* (ferries) operate daily between Quai d'Esnambuc in Fort-de-France and the marinas in Pointe du Bout, Anse-Mitan, and Anse-à-l'Ane and are the best way to go into the capital. Any of these trips takes about 20 minutes. Ferries depart every 30 minutes on weekdays; less often in the low season. Round-trip tickets cost €6.50.

Contacts **Compagnie Maritime West Indies.** Compagnie Maritime West Indies provides rapid sea shuttle service from neighboring St. Lucia. Boats usually depart daily at 8 am and 10 am from Castries, St. Lucia. Fares are approximately €89 for adults and €69 for children. A number of airlines fly into St. Lucia, so making arrangements to land there and take Compagnie can be a good way to get to Martinique (especially if you are staying at Club Med or another resort in the south). ☎ 0696/21–77–76.

Jeans for Freedom. A new ferry is plying the waters between Pointe-à-Pitre, Guadeloupe, and St-Pierre, Martinique; it also makes a brief stop in Dominica. Slightly undercutting the competition, the price is €70. It also connects Fort-de-France to St. Lucia (€70). In Guadeloupe, service is also available between Pointe-à-Pitre and Marie-Galante or

Les Saintes for €25. ✉ *Place du Marche* ☎ *0825/01–01–25* ⊕ *www. jeansforfreedom.com.*

L'Express des Îles. *L'Express des Îles* connects Martinique with Dominica, St. Lucia, Guadeloupe, and Guadeloupe's "out-islands," Les Saintes and Marie-Galante. Each trip is €75 (one-way). The crossings generally take between three and four hours; if it is raining and the waters are choppy, it can be a rough passage. French films (sometimes R-rated) on flat screens help pass the time. Most of these services are daily, with extra departures on weekends, and ferries can sometimes be crowded. Boats depart from the nearly-new Terminal Inter Îles–Quai Ouest in Fort-de-France. The terminal is significantly better than the old one, with to-go options that offer much better fare than the snack bars on the boats. There are also discounted fares for babies, youths, seniors, and families. The bad news is that the ferry uses the same type of luggage scales as the airport, and overweight charges are now enforced. If traveling from Martinique to Dominica, Guadeloupe, or St. Lucia, a passenger is allowed three pieces of luggage that weigh no more than 25 kg (55 lb.) each; if traveling from Guadeloupe to its out-islands, you're allowed one less bag. In either direction, you're also allowed to carry on one piece of baggage that weighs 10 kg (22 lb.) or less. Be aware that this ferry company also follows airline rules for what you're allowed to pack inside checked and carry-on baggage; check the website for more information. ☎ *0825/35–90–00, 0596/63–12–11* ⊕ *www. express-des-iles.com.*

TAXI TRAVEL

Taxis, which are metered, are expensive, though you can try bargaining by offering to pay a flat rate to your destination.

Contacts Andre Lahoussaye Taxi & Guide Service. Andre Lahoussaye speaks English and has proven to be an excellent guide. He takes reservations via email. ✉ *andre.lahoussaye@orange.fr.*

J. Peloponese Taxis. J. Peloponese Taxis provides luxury service in new Mercedes-Benz cars. ☎ *0696/25–61–02.*

M. Martial Mercedes Taxis. Drivers of M. Martial Mercedes Taxis speak English, Spanish, and German as well as French. ☎ *0596/64–20–24, 0696/45–69–07 mobile.*

Taxi de Place. At Taxi de Place you will find some English-speaking drivers, lots of courtesy, and new SUVs. ☎ *0696/31–91–05.*

ESSENTIALS

Banks and Exchange Services The euro is the official currency in Martinique. U.S. dollars are accepted in some hotels but generally at an unfavorable rate. You can usually get the best rate by withdrawing euros from ATMs, which you'll find at the airport and at branches of the Crédit Agricole bank. Most hotels and restaurants accept major credit cards, but some establishments accept neither credit cards nor traveler's checks, particularly once you get away from Fort-de-France and Pointe du Bout. Many establishments don't accept American Express in any case. There is a change office at the beginning of Ernest Deproge Street next to the Banque Francaise. Change Caraïbes is at 14 rue Victor Hugo and Le Bord de Mer. They will still exchange both dollars and traveler's checks and usually offer fair rates.

Electricity 220-volt outlets. North American appliances require a converter and an adapter.

Emergency Services Ambulance ☎ *15, 0596/71–15–75.* **Fire** ☎ *18.* **Police** ☎ *17.*

Passport Requirements All visitors must have a valid passport and a return or ongoing ticket. A birth certificate and picture ID are *not* sufficient.

Phones To call Martinique from the United States, dial 011–596–596 plus the local six-digit number (yes, you must dial 596 *twice*). To call the United States from Martinique, dial 001, then the area code, then the local number.

Taxes and Service Charges A resort tax varies from city to city. Each has its own tax, with most between €0.76 and €1.25 per person per day; the maximum is €2.25. Rates quoted by hotels usually include a 10% service charge.

Tipping All restaurants include a 15% service charge in their menu prices. You can always add to this if you feel that service was particularly good.

ACCOMMODATIONS

Martinique's accommodations range from tiny inns called *relais créoles*, boutique hotels, and private villas, to splashy tourist resorts and restored plantation houses. Several hotels are clustered in Point du Bout on Les Trois-Ilets Peninsula, which is connected to Fort-de-France by ferry. Other clusters are in Ste-Luce, and Le François has become known for its boutique properties. Hotels and relais can be found all over the island. Since Martinique is the largest of the Windward Islands, this can mean a substantial drive to your hotel after a long flight or ferry trip. You may want to stay closer to the airport on your first night. Should you need to make a last-minute hotel reservation, head for the Tourism Information counter in the airport arrival hall (*0596/42–18–05*); it is open between 8 am and 9 pm every day except Sunday, when it's open from 2 pm to 9 pm.

Large Resorts: There are only a few deluxe properties on the island. Those that lack megastar ratings offer an equally appealing mixture of charisma, hospitality, and French style. Larger hotels often have the busy, slightly frenetic feel that the French seem to like.

Relais Créoles: Small, individually owned inns are still available on Martinique, though they may be far removed from the resort clusters.

Villas: Groups and large families can save money by renting a villa, but the language barrier can be problematic, and often you will need a car.

HOTEL AND RESTAURANT PRICES

Prices in the restaurant reviews are the average cost of a main course at dinner or, if dinner is not served, at lunch; taxes and service charges are generally included. Prices in the hotel reviews are the lowest cost of a standard double room in high season, excluding taxes, service charges, and meal plans (except at all-inclusives). Prices for rentals are the lowest per-night cost for a one-bedroom unit in high season.

VISITOR INFORMATION

Contacts Martinique Promotion Bureau ✉ *825 3rd Ave., 29th fl., New York, New York, USA* ☎ *212/838–6887 in New York* ⊕ *www.martinique.org.* **Comité Martiniquais du Tourisme** ✉ *Immeuble Beaupre, Pointe de Jaham, Schoelcher, Fort-de-France* ☎ *0596/61–61–77* ⊕ *www.martiniquetourisme.com.* **Office du Tourisme de Fort-de-France** ✉ *76 rue Lazare Carnot, Fort-de-France* ☎ *0596/60–27–73* ⊕ *www.tourismefdf.com.*

WEDDINGS

Martinique has a long residency requirement, so it's not really feasible to plan a wedding on the island. It is, however, a most romantic honeymoon destination.

EXPLORING MARTINIQUE

15

The northern part of the island will appeal to nature lovers, hikers, and mountain climbers. The drive from Fort-de-France to St-Pierre is particularly impressive, as is the one across the island, via Morne Rouge, from the Caribbean to the Atlantic. This is Martinique's wild side—a place of waterfalls, rain forest, and mountains. The highlight is Mont Pelée. The south is the more developed half of the island, where the resorts and restaurants are located, as well as the beaches.

SOUTH OF FORT-DE-FRANCE

Diamond Rock. This volcanic mound is 1 mile (1.5 km) offshore from the small, friendly village of Le Diamant and is one of the island's best diving spots. In 1804, during the squabbles over possession of the island between the French and the English, the latter commandeered the rock, armed it with cannons, and proceeded to use it as a strategic battery. The British held the rock for nearly a year and a half, attacking any French ships that came along. The French got wind that the British were getting cabin fever on their isolated island and arranged for barrels of rum to float up on the rock. The French easily overpowered the inebriated sailors, ending one of the most curious engagements in naval history.

Forêt de Montravail. A few miles north of Ste-Luce, this tropical rain forest is ideal for a short hike. Look for the interesting group of Carib rock drawings.

Lamentin. There's nothing pretty about Lamentin; the international airport is its most notable landmark. The rest of the town is a sprawling industrial and commercial zone. But many people come here for shopping in the big, fancy shopping mall, with a Carrefour supermarket as its anchor. La Galleria, a second megamall of roughly 100 shops and boutiques, offers everything from pâté de foie gras and Camembert to CDs and sunglasses.

Le François. With some 16,000 inhabitants, this is the main city on the Atlantic coast. Many of the old wooden buildings remain and are

MARTINIQUE TRANSPORTATION TIPS

Taxi: Taxis in Martinique are expensive, and you will pay more after dark. From the airport to Fort-de-France you'll pay at least €20 during the day, €40 at night; from the airport to Pointe du Bout, it's about €40 (€60 at night); to Francois or Tartane, the fare is approximately €50 (€70 at night). A 40% surcharge is levied between 7 pm and 6 am and on Sunday. If you arrive at night, depending on where your hotel is, it may be cheaper (although not safer) to rent a car from the airport and keep it for 24 hours than to take a taxi to your hotel.

Car Rental: Be prepared for a manual shift, steep mountainous roads, and heavy traffic. Prices are about €70 per day or €330 per week (unlimited mileage), substantially more for an automatic, which is rare. Usually, you won't find them unless you book in advance.

Alternative Transportation: Locals take *collectifs* (white vans holding up to 10 passengers) that cost just a few euros and depart from Pointe Simon, on the waterfront in Fort-de-France, to all parts of the island. Don't be shy; the difference can be €3 versus, say, €60 for a taxi to reach the same destination. Drivers don't usually speak English and there's no a/c.

Bus Mozaik. A private bus company, Bus Mozaik, with fares from €1.20 and a/c, has stops within the city, and services Lamentin, the Fort-de-France suburbs like Schoelcher, and as far into the interior of the island as St. Joseph. Buses leave from Pointe Simon, on the waterfront, where the public buses congregate. ⊕ *www.aquelleheure.fr/bus.htm*.

The tourist offices can help with maps and information.

juxtaposed with concrete structures. The classic West Indian cemetery, with its black-and-white tiles, is still here, and a marina is at the end of town. Two of Martinique's best hotels are in this area, as well as some of the most upscale residences. Le François is also noted for its snorkeling. Offshore are the privately owned Ilets de l'Impératrice. The islands received that name because, according to legend, this is where Empress Joséphine came to bathe in the shallow basins known as *les fonds blanc* because of their white-sand bottoms. Group boat tours leave from the harbor and include lunch and drinks. Prices vary (⇨ *Sports and Activities*). You can also haggle with a fisherman to take you out for a while on his boat. There's a fine bay 6 miles (10 km) farther along the coast where you can swim and go kayaking. The town itself is rather lackluster but authentic, and you'll find a number of different shops and supermarkets, owned by truly lovely, helpful residents.

Habitation Clément. Get a glimpse into Martinique's colonial past, into the elegance and privilege of plantation society. Visitors are now given a multilingual audio headset, which explains highlights of the self-guided tour, such as the animal mill. Signage further educates guests on everything from the rum-making process to the tropical flora and fauna of the botanical garden. The Palm Grove, with an avenue of palms and park benches, is delightful. It was all built with the wealth generated by its rum distillery, and its 18th-century splendor has been lovingly

Diamond Rock

preserved. The plantation's Creole house illustrates the adaption to life in the tropics up through the 20th century. Fascinating ancient maps, an early French typewriter, a crank-up telephone, and decades-old photos of the Clements and Hayots (béké families), are juxtaposed with some of the most avant-garde Afro-Caribbean art from Martinique and neighboring Caribbean islands. Enjoy the free tastings at the bar of the retail shop. Consider the Canne Bleu, Grappe Blanche, or one of the aged rums, some bottled as early as 1952. ■TIP➔ Sure children get a discount, but so do parents with children! Also, allow 1 1/2–2 hours to see everything. The ticket office closes at 5. ⊠ *Domaine de l'Acajou* ☎ *0596/54–62–07* ⊕ *www.habitation-clement.fr* ⊠ *€9* ⊘ *Daily 9–5.*

NEED A BREAK? Should you need a fast French lunch break in Le François, try **Le Grand Trianon Boulangerie Patisserie** near the new Carrefour Supermarket. Crisp baguettes and luscious pastries with ice cream are sold, and prix-fixe lunches with sandwiches or salads are offered.

Le Marin. The yachting capital of Martinique is also known for its colorful August carnival and its Jesuit church, circa 1766. From Le Marin a narrow road leads to picturesque Cap Chevalier, about 1 mile (1.5 km) from town. Most of the buildings are white and very European. The marina is lively, and there are waterfront restaurants and clubs.

Le Vauclin. The return of the fishermen at noon is the big event in this important fishing port on the Atlantic. There's also the 18th-century Chapel of the Holy Virgin. Nearby is the highest point in the south, Mont Vauclin (1,654 feet). A hike to the top rewards you with one of the best views on the island.

Les Trois-Ilets. Named after the three rocky islands nearby, this lovely little village (population 3,000) has unusual brick-and-wood buildings roofed with antique tiles. It's known for its pottery, straw, and wood-work but above all as the birthplace of Napoléon's empress, Joséphine. In the square, where there's also a market and a fine *mairie* (town hall), you can visit the simple church where she was baptized Marie-Joseph Tascher de la Pagerie. The Martinicans have always been enormously proud of Joséphine, even though her husband reintroduced slavery on the island and most historians consider her to have been rather shallow.

Musée de la Pagerie. A stone building that held the kitchen of the estate where Joséphine grew up houses the Musée de la Pagerie. It contains an assortment of memorabilia pertaining to her life and rather unfortunate loves, including a marriage certificate and a love letter written straight from the heart by Napoléon in 1796. The main house blew down in the hurricane of 1766, when she was 3, and the family lived for years above the sugarcane factory—a hot, odoriferous, and fly-ridden existence. At 16 she was wed (an arranged marriage because her father was a gambling man in need of money) to Alexandre de Beau-harnais. After he was assassinated during the Revolution, she married Napoléon. ■TIP→ Museum hours sometimes change, so be sure to call in advance. ☎ 0596/68-33-06 ⌨ €5 ⏰ Mon.–Fri. 9–1, 2–5:30; weekends 9:30–12:30, 3–5.

La Savane des Esclaves (*The Savanna of the Slaves*). Down a dirt road, in the countryside outside the tourist zone, a Martinican has called up the past with La Savane des Esclaves, a re-created slave village (circa 1800). This labor of love was created by Gilbert Larose, who has a fascination with the lives of his ancestors. The Antan Lontan Village is an in-depth look at a major element in Martinique's history and culture, with food tastings and artisan demonstrations. On Saturdays from 9 am to noon there are often more elaborate tastings, demonstrations, and traditional dance lessons ✉ Quartier La Ferme ☎ 0596/68-33-91 ⊕ www.lasavanedesesclaves.fr ⌨ €6 ⏰ Daily 9–noon and 2–5:30.

NEED A BREAK?

Just steps down the hill from the church in Les Trois-Ilets, a simple patis-serie, recognized by its awning, brews fresh coffee and bakes wonders such as éclairs with chocolate custard interiors. Sit at a table or take it to go.

Pointe du Bout. This tourist area has a marina and several resort hotels, among them the deluxe Hotel Bakoua (formerly a Sofitel and now a member of MGallery, a collection of unique, historic hotels). The ferry to Fort-de-France leaves from here. A cluster of boutiques, ice-cream parlors, and rental-car agencies forms the hub from which restaurants and hotels of varying caliber radiate, but it's a pretty quiet place in the low season. The beach at Anse-Mitan, which is a little west of Pointe du Bout proper, is one of the best on the island. There are also several small restaurants and inexpensive guesthouses here.

Ste-Anne. A lovely white-sand beach and a Catholic church are the highlights of this town on the island's southern tip. A bevy of small, inexpensive cafés offer seafood and creole dishes, pizza parlors, pro-duce markets, and barbecue joints—it's fun and lively. To the south of

Ste-Anne is Pointe des Salines, the southernmost tip of the island and site of one of Martinique's best beaches.

Ste-Luce. This quaint fishing village has a sleepy main street with tourist shops and markets, and you can see some cool types taking a Pernod. Many young, single people live in this town. From the sidewalk cafés there are panoramic sea views of St. Lucia. Nearby are excellent beaches and several resorts, notably three from the Karibea Hotel chain. To the east is Pointe Figuier, an excellent spot for scuba diving.

FORT-DE-FRANCE

With its historic fort and superb location beneath the towering Pitons du Carbet on the Baie des Flamands, Martinique's capital—home to about one-quarter of the island's 400,000 inhabitants—should be a grand place. It hasn't been for decades, but it's now coming up fast. An ambitious redevelopment project, still under way, hopes to make it one of the most attractive cities in the Caribbean. The plan includes the renovation of the park La Savane, the construction of a spectacular waterfront promenade (completed), and coming soon, the Pointe Simon Business and Tourist Center, which will have a 100-room hotel and luxury apartment building. The striking new 215,000-square-foot Cour Perrinon Mall houses a Carrefour supermarket, a bookstore, perfume shops, designer boutiques, a French bakery, and a café-brasserie. Across from the newly renovated theater, renamed for the island's famed poet Aimé Césaire, the mall is bordered by rue Perrinon. There is a small office of Tourism de Fort-de-France at 76 rue Lazare Carnot. It has some brochures in English and helpful, English-speaking staffers. They can organize English-language tours with advance notice. Walking tours are scheduled for Wednesday and Friday at 9 am. They take in a number of historic sites in about an hour and 45 minutes and cost €12. Another Point d'Information Touristique is near the cathedral, at the junction of rues Antoine Siger and Victor Schoelcher.

The new Stewards Urbains, easily recognized by their red caps and uniforms, are able to answer most visitor questions and give directions. These young gals and *garçons* are multilingual and knowledgeable. When a large cruise ship is in port, they are out in force, positioned in heavily trafficked tourist zones and at the front entrance of Lafayette's department store.

The most pleasant districts of Fort-de-France—Didier, Bellevue, and Schoelcher—are up on the hillside, and you need a car (or a taxi) to reach them. But if you try to drive here, you may find yourself trapped in gridlock in the warren of narrow streets downtown. Parking is difficult, and it's best to try for one of the garages or—as a second choice—outdoor public parking areas. Come armed with some euro coins for this purpose. A taxi or ferry from Pointe du Bout may be a better alternative. Even if your hotel isn't there, you can drive to the marina and park nearby.

There are some fine shops with Parisian wares (at Parisian prices) in which to buy French lingerie, St. Laurent or Cacharel, and sexy stiletto

15

heels. Near the harbor is a lively indoor marketplace (grand marché), where produce and spices are sold.

A playground on the Malecon, which now has a half-mile wooden boardwalk, has swings, trampolines, benches, and even *pétanque* grounds. The urban beach between the Malecon and the fort, La Française, has been also cleaned up; white sand was brought in.

An inviting oasis of nature and serenity amid the hustle and bustle of Fort-de-France, the newly redeveloped La Savane is a prime spot for walks, picnics, and meeting up with friends. Freshly squeezed juices, cocktails, sandwiches, pizzas, panini, pasta, cassava cakes, deliciously flavored homemade ice creams, creole, Indonesian, and vegetarian food, sushi crepes, and locally made candies are all available from vendors here; street merchants sell everything from jewelry to human hairpieces. A tourism kiosk on the historic Place de La Savane is open from 9 to 4:30 Tuesday through Saturday, 9 to 4 on Saturday (☎ 0596/74–41–44).

Cruise-ship traffic has greatly increased here. There were more than 100 port calls between early November 2011 and late April 2012. This translates to more than 125,000 passengers. Club Med, Holland America, Royal Caribbean, Costa Cruises, Windstar Cruises, and Silversea are just a few of the cruise lines that now stop here.

Bibliothèque Schoelcher. This wildly elaborate Romanesque public library was named after Victor Schoelcher, who led the fight to free the slaves in the French West Indies in the 19th century. The eye-popping structure was built for the 1889 Paris Exposition, after which it was dismantled, shipped to Martinique, and reassembled piece by ornate piece. ⊠ *At rue de la Liberté, which runs along west side of La Savane* ☎ 0596/70–26–67 ⌂ *Free* ☉ *Mon.–Thurs. 8:30–5:30, Fri.–Sat. 8:30–noon.*

La Savane. The heart of Fort-de-France, La Savane is a 12½-acre park filled with trees, fountains, and benches. It was a popular gathering place and the scene of promenades, parades, and impromptu soccer matches; and it has now been beautifully renovated to its former glory. A massive revitalization was completed in late 2010, and it is a focal point of the city again, with entertainment, shopping, and a pedestrian mall. Attractive wooden stands have been constructed along the edge of the park that house a tourism information office, public restrooms, arts and crafts vendors, a crepe stand, an ice-cream stand, and numerous other eateries. *(⇨ see Fort-de-France above).* Diagonally across from La Savane, you can catch the ferries for the 20-minute run across the bay to Pointe du Bout and the beaches at Anse-Mitan and Anse-à-l'Ane. It's relatively cheap as well as stress-free—much safer, more pleasant, and faster than by car.

The most imposing historic site in Fort-de-France is **Ft. St-Louis**, which runs along the east side of La Savane. It is no longer open to the public, as it is now functioning as a military installation.

★ **Le Musée Régional d'Histoire et d'Ethnographie.** This museum is a learning experience that is best undertaken at the beginning of your vacation, so you can better understand the history, background, and people of the island. Housed in an elaborate former residence (circa 1888) with balconies and fretwork, it has everything from displays of the garish

Anglers sitting on a dock in Fort de France harbor

gold jewelry that prostitutes wore after emancipation to reconstructed rooms of a home of proper, middle-class Martinicans. There's even a display of Creole headdresses with details of how they were tied to indicate if a woman was single, married, or otherwise occupied. ✉ *10 bd. Général de Gaulle* ☎ *0596/72–81–87* ✉ *€3* ☉ *Mon. and Wed.–Fri. 8:30–5, Tues. 2–5, Sat. 8:30–noon.*

◾TIP→ Admission to all regional museums is free the last Saturday of the month.

Parc Floral Aimé Cesaire. Parc Floral Aimé Cesaire (formerly The Galerie de Biologie et de Géologie) is in the northeastern corner of the city center. The park contains the island's official cultural center, where there are free evening concerts during the International Festival or on memorial days. ✉ *Pl. José-Marti, Sermac* ☎ *0596/71–66–25* ✉ *Free* ☉ *Daily dawn–10 pm.*

Rue Victor Schoelcher. Stores sell Paris fashions and French perfume, china, crystal, and liqueurs, as well as local handicrafts along this street running through the center of the capital's primary shopping district, a six-block area bounded by rue de la République, rue de la Liberté, rue Victor Severe, and rue Victor Hugo.

Schoelcher. Pronounced shell-*share*, this upscale suburb of Fort-de-France is home to the University of the French West Indies and Guyana, as well as Martinique's largest convention center, Palais de Congres de Madiana. Schoelcher was named after abolitionist Victor Schoelcher, who is credited with ending slavery on the island.

St-Louis Cathedral. The Romanesque cathedral with its lovely stained-glass windows was built in 1878, the sixth church on this site (the others were destroyed by fires, hurricanes, and earthquakes). ✉ *Rue Victor Schoelcher* ⊙ *Dawn to dusk*.

NORTH OF FORT-DE-FRANCE

Ajoupa-Bouillon. This flower-filled 17th-century village amid pineapple fields is the jumping-off point for several sights. The Saut Babin, a 40-foot waterfall, is a half-hour walk from Ajoupa-Bouillon. The Gorges de la Falaise is a river gorge where you can swim. ✉ *Ajoupa-Bouillon*.

Aqualand. This U.S.-style water park is a great place for families to have a wet, happy day. The large wave pool is well tended; little ones love it, as they do the pirate's galleon in their own watery playground. Older kids may prefer to get their thrill from the slides, including the hairpin turns of the Giant Slalom, the Colorado slide, and the Black Hole, which winds around in total darkness. In the best French tradition, the fast-food options are top-notch, including crepes, salads, and even beer. Phone first during the low season; it shuts down for months, but is normally open from April to September (and on weekends during French school holidays). ✉ *Rte. des Pitons, Carbet* ☎ *0596/78–40–00* ⊕ *www.aqualand-martinique.fr* ✆ *€21* ⊙ *Apr.–Sept., daily 10–6*.

Balata. This quiet little town has two sights worth visiting. Built in 1923 to commemorate those Martinicans who fought and died in World War I, **Balata Church** is an exact replica of Paris's Sacré-Coeur Basilica. The gardens, **Jardin de Balata,** are lovely.

Jardin de Balata (*Balata Gardens*). The Jardin de Balata has thousands of varieties of tropical flowers and plants. There are shaded benches from which to take in the mountain views and a plantation-style house furnished with period furniture. An aerial path gives visitors an astounding, bird's-eye view of the gardens and surrounding hills, from wooden walkways suspended 50 feet in the air. There is no restaurant, though beverages are available for purchase. You can order anthuriums and other tropical flowers to be delivered to the airport from the habitation's mesmerizing flower boutique. Just 15 minutes from Fort-de-France, in the direction of St-Pierre, this worthy site explains why Martinique is called the Island of Flowers. ■ TIP→ The gardens close at 6, but the ticket office will not admit anyone after 4:30 ✉ *Km. #10 Rte. de Balata, Balata* ☎ *0596/64–48–73* ⊕ *www.jardindebalata.fr* ✆ *€12.50* ⊙ *Daily 9–6* ✉ *Balata*.

Basse-Pointe. On the route to this village on the Atlantic coast at the island's northern end you pass many banana and pineapple plantations. Just south of Basse-Pointe is a **Hindu temple** built by descendants of the East Indians who settled in this area in the 19th century. The view of Mont Pelée from the temple is amazing.

Bellefontaine. This colorful fishing village has pastel houses on the hillsides and beautifully painted *gommiers* (fishing boats) bobbing in the water. Look for the restaurant built in the shape of a boat.

CLOSE UP

Making Nice in Martinique

Martinique is a polite society. Doors will open to you and you will win the favor of the Martinicans if you demonstrate proper French manners. Preface questions, particularly if asking directions, with *Bonjour* or *Bonsoir*, followed by *Excusez-moi*. Even friends greet each other with a *bonjour* rather than the equivalent of *hi* or *hello*. When finished, say, *"Merci beaucoup. Bonne journée"* ("Thank you very much. Have a good day") or *"Bonne nuit"* ("Good night"). Bone up on your French, and bring your phrase book with you, please (*s' il vous plait*, or when written, *s.v.p.*).

INTRODUCTIONS

You will likely be introduced as Madame Smith rather than *mademoiselle*, even if you are single, if you are over 30. When introduced say, *"Enchanté"* ("Enchanted"). Nice, no?

Do not call someone by their first name, especially someone who is older, until they tell you to. When they call you by your Christian name, you have carte blanche. U.S. southerners will have no difficulty remembering to say, *"Merci, madame"* (not *ma'am*) and *"No merci, monsieur."* When and if you are speaking French, use the formal *vous* for *you*, not the familiar *tu*.

The French islanders will kiss each other on both cheeks if they know the other person and often if they do not. If they realize that you are not French, they will most likely extend their hand for a handshake. And yes, the older gentlemen still kiss a lady's hand, although it will likely be a mock kiss, not touching skin.

15

Dubuc Castle. At the eastern tip of the Presqu'île du Caravelle are the ruins of this castle, once the home of the Dubuc de Rivery family, who owned the peninsula in the 18th century. According to legend, young Aimée Dubuc de Rivery was captured by Barbary pirates, sold to the Ottoman Empire, became a favorite of the sultan, and gave birth to Mahmud II.

You can park your car right after the turnoff for Résidence Oceane and walk the dirt road to the ruins. The castle still has a skeleton of stone walls, but it is mostly rubble; hikers go for the dramatic ocean views, raw nature, and birdlife. ⊠ *Tartane, La Trinité*.

Le Morne Rouge. This town sits on the southern slopes of the volcano that destroyed it in 1902. Today it's a popular resort spot and offers hikers some fantastic mountain scenery. From Le Morne Rouge you can start the climb up the 4,600-foot **Mont Pelée.** But don't try scaling this volcano without a guide unless you want to get buried alive under pumice stones. Instead, drive up to L'Auberge de la Montagne Pelée, which has had a name change and a total renovation of accommodations. (Ask for a room with a view!) From the parking lot it's 1 mile (1.5 km) up a well-marked trail to the summit. Bring a hooded sweatshirt, because there's often a mist that makes the air damp and chilly. From the summit follow the route de la Trace (Route N3), which winds south of Le Morne Rouge to St-Pierre. It's steep and winding, but that didn't stop the *porteuses* of old: balancing a tray, these women would carry

Le Morne Rouge

up to 100 pounds of provisions on their heads for the 15-hour trek to the Atlantic coast.

Le Prêcheur. This quaint village, the last on the northern Caribbean coast, is surrounded by volcanic hot springs. It was the childhood home of Françoise d'Aubigné, who later became the Marquise de Maintenon and the second wife of Louis XIV. At her request, the Sun King donated a handsome bronze bell, which still hangs outside the church. The Tomb of the Carib Indians commemorates a sadder event. It's a formation of limestone cliffs, from which the last of the Caraïbes are said to have flung themselves to avoid capture by the marquise's forebears.

Macouba. Named after the Carib word for "fish," this village was a prosperous tobacco town in the 17th century. Today its cliff-top location affords magnificent views of the sea, the mountains, and—on clear days—the neighboring island of Dominica. (Do not confuse it with Cap Macabou, which is near Le Vauclin.)

Route to Grand' Rivière. Macouba is the starting point for a spectacular drive, the 6-mi (10-km) Route to Grand' Rivière on the northernmost point. This is Martinique at its greenest: groves of giant bamboo, cliffs hung with curtains of vines, and human-size tree ferns that seem to grow as you watch them. Literally at the end of the road is Grand' Rivière, a colorful, sprawling fishing village at the foot of high cliffs. The Syndicat d'Initiative Riverain, the local tourism office in Macouba, can arrange hiking and boating excursions. ☎ 0596/55–72–74 ☎ 0596/55–72–74.

Neisson Distillery. The Mercedes of Martinique rum brewers is a small, family-run operation whose rum is produced from pure sugarcane juice rather than molasses. It's open for tours and tastings, and the shop sells *rhum extra-vieux* (vintage rum) that truly rivals cognac. Neisson is one of the distilleries that consistently brings home the gold (and the silver) from rum competitions in France. ✉ *Carbet* ☎ *0596/78–07–90* ⊕ *www. neisson.com* ✆ *Free* ☉ *Daily 9–4.*

Presqu'île du Caravelle. Much of the Caravelle Peninsula, which juts 8 miles (13 km) into the Atlantic Ocean, is under the protection of the Regional Nature Reserve and offers places for trekking, swimming, and sailing. This is also the site of Anse-Spoutourne, an open-air sports and leisure center operated by the reserve. The town of Tartane has a popular surfing beach with brisk Atlantic breezes. ✉ *Tartane.*

Ste-Marie. The winding, hilly route to this town of some 20,000 offers breathtaking views of the rugged Atlantic coastline. Ste-Marie is the commercial capital of the island's north. Look for a picturesque mid-19th-century church here. Most come to the area to visit the Musée du Rhum of the St. James Distillery, but the north is also filled with natural beauty.

Musée du Rhum. The Musée du Rhum, operated by the St. James Rum Distillery, is housed in a graceful, galleried Creole house. Guided tours can take in the plantation and the displays of the tools of the trade, the art gallery, and include a visit and tasting at the distillery. You can opt to take a little red train tour for €5. ■ **TIP→** Zee Petite Train now only runs Tuesday and Thursday mornings and Saturday afternoons.

This venue is known for its "happenings," from beauty contests to the largest, la Fete du Rhum, in December. It can be a somewhat wild scene when a dozen or more tour buses pull in, though. The museum and distillery are closed during the cane harvest, and weekend hours sometimes change; it's a good idea to call ahead. ☎ *0596/69–30–02* ✆ *Free* ☉ *Daily 9–5.*

Le Musée de la Banane. After navigating the narrow road, you probably won't find more cordial hostesses than those here at Le Musée de la Banane. Excellent graphics and beautiful prints tell the story of the banana (Martinique's primary export) as it makes its way from the fields to your table. This plantation has a vintage Creole cottage that serves as a well-stocked retail shop, and there's a bar and lunch counter with lots of edibles made from bananas, some free for the tasting. ✉ *Habitation Limbé* ☎ *0596/69–45–52* ⊕ *www.lemuseedelabanane.com* ✆ *€7* ☉ *Mon.–Sat. 9–5, Sun. 9–1.*

DID YOU KNOW? One man survived the volcano's eruption. His name was Cyparis, and he was a prisoner in an underground cell in the town's jail, locked up for public drunkenness. Later, he went on the road with the Barnum & Bailey Circus as a sideshow attraction.

St-Pierre. The rise and fall of St-Pierre is one of the most remarkable stories in the Caribbean. Martinique's modern history began here in 1635. By the turn of the 20th century St-Pierre was a flourishing city of 30,000, known as the Paris of the West Indies. As many as 30 ships at a time stood at anchor. By 1902 it was the most modern town in the Caribbean, with electricity, phones, and a tram. On May 8, 1902, two thunderous explosions rent the air. As the nearby volcano erupted,

Mont Pelée split in half, belching forth a cloud of burning ash, poisonous gas, and lava that raced down the mountain at 250 mph. At 3,600°F, it instantly vaporized everything in its path; 30,000 people were killed in two minutes.

The **Cyparis Express,** a small tourist train, will take you around to the main sights with running narrative (in French) for a half hour on Saturday, an hour on weekdays, for €10 (€5 for children).

An Office du Tourisme is on the *moderne* seafront promenade. Stroll the main streets and check the blackboards at the sidewalk cafés before deciding where to lunch. At night some places have live music. Like stage sets for a dramatic opera, there are the ruins of the island's first church (built in 1640), the imposing theater, and the toppled statues. This city, situated on its naturally beautiful harbor and with its narrow, winding streets, has the feel of a European seaside hill town. With every footstep you touch a page of history. Although many of the historic buildings need work, stark modernism has not invaded this burg. There is now a recommendable small hotel on the Bay as well as new ferry service between the town and Guadeloupe. As much potential as it has, this is one place in Martinique where real estate is cheap—for obvious reasons.

Musée Vulcanologique Frank Perret. For those interested in the eruption of 1902, the Musée Vulcanologique Frank Perret is a must. Established in 1933 by Frank Perret, a noted American volcanologist, who came down to study the volcano. The museum houses photographs of the old town, documents, and a number of relics—some gruesome—excavated from the ruins, including molten glass, melted iron, and contorted clocks stopped at 8 am. An English-speaking guide is often available. ⊠ *Rue Victor Hugo* ☎ *0596/78–15–16* ⊡ *€3* ⊙ *Daily 9–5.*

Le Centre de Découverte des Sciences de la Terre. If you want to know more about volcanoes, earthquakes, and hurricanes, check out Le Centre de Découverte des Sciences de la Terre. Housed in a sleek building that looks like a dramatic white box, this earth-science museum has high-tech exhibits and interesting films. Watch the documentary on the volcanoes in the Antilles, highlighting the eruption of the nearby Mont Pelée. This site has fascinating summer programs on Wednesday on dance, cuisine, and ecotourism. ■TIP➔ **The Depaz Distillery is nearby, and it's easy to visit both on the same day.** ⊠ *Habitation Perinelle* ☎ *0596/52–82–42* ⊡ *€5* ⊙ *Sept–May Tues.–Sun. 9–4:30; July–Aug. Tues.–Sun. 9–5:30.*

Depaz Distillery. An excursion to Depaz Distillery is one of the island's nicest treats. Established in 1651, it has sat at the foot of the volcano for four centuries. After a devastating eruption in 1902, the fields of blue cane were replanted, and in time, the rum making began all over again. A self-guided tour includes the workers' gingerbread cottages, and sometimes there will be an exhibit of art and sculpture made from wooden casks and parts of distillery machinery. The tasting room sells its rums, including golden and aged rum, and distinctive liqueurs made from orange, ginger, and basil, among other flavors, that can add creativity to your cooking. Unfortunately, the plantation's great house, or

The town of St-Pierre is beneath the 4,600-foot Mont Pelée.

château, which had opened for public tours for the first time, is once again closed. Apparently more renovations were needed, and there is no projected date for completion. A recommendable restaurant, **Le Moulin a Canne,** has both creole specialties and some French classics on the menu, plus—you guessed it—Depaz rum to wash it down. The restaurant is now a separate entity from the distillery and is open only for lunch (0596/69–80–44). ■**TIP→ Shutters are drawn at the tasting room and the staff leaves at exactly 5 pm, so plan to be there by at least 4.** ⊠ *Mont Pelée Plantation* 🕿 *0596/78–13–14* ⊕ *www.depazrhum.com* 🎟 *Distillery: free* 🕐 *Weekdays 10–5, Sat. 9–4.*

🔄 **Pointe du Bout.** The beaches here are small, man-made, and lined with resorts, including the Hotel Bakoua. Each little strip is associated with its resident hotel, and security guards and closed gates make access difficult. However, if you take a left across from the main pedestrian entrance to the marina—after the taxi stand—then go left again, you will reach the beach for Hotel Bakoua, which has especially nice facilities and several options for lunch and drinks. If things are quiet—particularly during the week—one of the beach boys may rent you a chaise; otherwise, just plop your beach towel down, face forward, and enjoy the delightful view of the Fort-de-France skyline. The water is dead calm and quite shallow, but it eventually drops off if you swim out a bit. ⊠ *Pointe du Bout, Les Trois-Ilets.*

WHERE TO EAT

Martinique cuisine is a fusion of African and French and is certainly more international and sophisticated than that of its immediate island neighbors. The influx of young chefs, who favor a contemporary, less caloric approach, has brought exciting innovations to the table. This haute-nouvelle creole cuisine emphasizes local products, predominantly starchy tubers such as plantains, white yams, yucca, and island sweet potatoes, as well as vegetables such as breadfruit, christophene, and taro leaves. Many creole dishes have been Francofied, transformed into mousselines, terrines, and gratins topped with creamy sauces. And then there's the bountiful harvest of the sea—*lambi* (conch), *langouste* (clawless local lobsters), and dozens of species of fish predominate, but you can also find *crevisses* (freshwater crayfish, which are as luscious as jumbo prawns).

Some local creole specialties are *accras* (cod or vegetable fritters), which are the signature appetizer of Martinique, *crabes farcis* (stuffed land crab), and *feroce* (avocado stuffed with saltfish and farina). You can fire up fish and any other dish with a hit of hot *chien* (dog) sauce. Not to worry—it's made from onions, shallots, hot peppers, oil, and vinegar. To cool your jets, have a 'ti punch—four parts white rum and one part sugarcane syrup.

Supermarkets often have snack bars that serve sandwiches, as do the bakeries and larger gas stations such as Esso and Total. Supermarkets, such as Carrefour, have good deli sections and sell French wines for significantly less than at home. Another French chain, Le Baguet Shop, has locations in most tourist areas. Travelers on a budget will find creperies and pizzerias, even an African pizza place in Le François. And there may be times when you just want to drive in to Mickey D's—however, brace yourself for the price hike.

In Fort-de-France's city market, ladies serve up creole prix-fixe meals that can include accras, fricassee of octopus and conch, chicken in coconut milk, or grilled whole fish. As for euro sticker shock, the consolation is that although menu prices may seem steep, they include tax and service. Prix-fixe menus, sometimes with wine, can help keep costs in line.

What to Wear. For dinner, casual resort wear is appropriate. Generally, men do not wear jackets and ties, as they did in decades past, but they do wear collared shirts. Women typically wear light cotton sundresses, short or long. At dinnertime, beach attire is too casual for most restaurants. Know that both the French ladies and the Martiniquais often "dress." They have an admirable French style, and almost always wear high heels.

Nice shorts are okay for lunch, depending on the venue, but jeans and shorts aren't acceptable at dinner. Keep in mind that in Martinique lunch is usually a wonderful three-course, two-hour affair.

SOUTH OF FORT-DE-FRANCE

$$$
FRENCH FUSION

✕ **Fleur de Sel.** Everything comes together here—the cuisine, *le musique*, the location, and the service. Situated in a 19th-century *maison bourgeoise*, Fleur de Sel has a new owner who has kicked things up a notch. The talented new chef, Damien Pelé, is from Tours in the Loire region of France and has spent five years working in the best spots in Martinique. Pre-island, he cheffed in five-star hotels and prestigious restaurants all over Europe and the Caribbean. He has teamed up with Jennifer Jasmine, who wears three hats—chef, server, and sommelier—and has created an intelligent wine list. The interesting clientele is a mix of locals and tourists (even some kids—children's plates are €10.) The ambience is relaxed, the service personalized, and the cuisine sophisticated and evolved. A luscious starter is the foie gras *péyi* (with bananas sautéed in aged rum); follow with sweetbreads, or a brochette of shrimp with a coulis of pumpkin and bergamot. A gourmet coffee with an upside-down lemon pie with four different textures, or a panna cotta à la rose, is a blissful ending. ⑤ *Average main: €22* ✉ *27 ave. de l'Impératrice Josephine, Les Trois-Ilets* ☎ *0596/68–42–11* ⊘ *No lunch. Closed Sun.*

$$$
FRENCH
★

✕ **Le Bélem.** To really experience this place, start with a cocktail in the superchic bar lined with old black-and-white photographs of the island; a simple 'ti punch gets an elaborate presentation. Le Bélem is the special-occasion restaurant for the well-heeled who enjoy innovative cuisine served in a contemporary setting. Alas, it is not inexpensive, but the complimentary amuse-bouche (single, bite-size hors d'oeuvres) may save you an appetizer, although the lobster ravioli is luscious. *Terrine de foie gras,* with apples caramelized in vanilla butter enhanced by a reduction of port and balsamic vinegar, is heaven on a plate. The menu changes seasonally and features such creations as linguine with truffles, scallops, cream, and a shellfish reduction dramatically presented by a bevy of servers. Lunch at Campeche, the beach restaurant, although less glamorous, is still decidedly a treat, and provides a more affordable alternative. It opens for dinner in high season. Hotel guests take breakfast at Le Bélem, and during high season the main restaurant is open seven nights a week. ⑤ *Average main: €27* ✉ *Cap Est Lagoon Resort & Spa, Quartier Cap Est, Le François* ☎ *0596/54–80–80* ⌲ *Reservations essential* ⊘ *No lunch. Closed some nights in low season.*

$$$
FRENCH FUSION
Fodor's Choice
★

✕ **Le Plein Soleil Restaurant.** Perennially popular with the chic set, Le Plein Soleil has a smashing contemporary, Creole look. But it's the inventive, beautifully executed menu that cements its well-deserved reputation. The young Martinican chef, Nathanael Ducteil, continues to draw applause for his use of the latest techniques from France coupled with remarkable twists on local products. Take a long and leisurely lunch (€35) on the terrace, which has a hilltop sea view; by night the mood is romantic, the service fine, the music heady. Soups are like a mixed-media collage. A velouté can be the canvas for a *raviole* of foie gras or pineapple, a slice of duck breast, or even a skewer of fish. The evening's three-course table d'hôte (€45) could have a lobster medallion flambéed with vintage rum or a thick tuna steak roasted with lemon confit and stacked on mushroom risotto. A memorable finale is the original basil custard topped with a red berry coulis. At dinner, guests can now choose

15

A How-To for Dining in Martinique

Dining in Martinique is a delightful culinary experience, but as with driving here, it is best to get some directions before you head out.

First of all, as in France, *entrées* are appetizers; the main courses will usually be labeled as follows: *poissons* (fish); *viandes* (meat); or *principal plats* (literally, main courses). You will notice that the appetizers are almost as expensive as the mains—and if the appetizer is foie gras, you'll pay just as much as for a main course, but it is oh so worth it.

Entrecôte is a sirloin steak, usually cut too thin. A filet mignon is a rarity, but you will see *filet mignon du*

porc, which is pork tenderloin. *Ecrivesses* (known also as *ouassous* or *z'habitants*) are incredible freshwater crayfish. Don't be alarmed when they are served with their heads on. Similarly, if a fish dish does not specify fillet, you will be looking into its eyes while carving flesh from its bones.

Every respectable restaurant has an admirable wine *carte*, and the offerings will be almost completely French, with few half bottles. Wines by the glass are often swill and best avoided.

Finally, don't ever embarrass yourself by asking for a doggie bag: you will be considered gauche!

from five different appetizers, main courses, and desserts. $ *Average main:* €45 ⊠ *Hôtel Le Plein Soleil, Villa Lagon Sarc, Pointe Thalèmont, Le François* ☎ 0596/38–07–77 ⌂ *Reservations essential* ⊗ *No dinner Sun. No lunch Mon., Tues., and Thurs.*

FORT-DE-FRANCE AND POINTS NORTH

$$
SEAFOOD
✕**Chez Les Pecheurs.** This is the kind of beach restaurant you search for but seldom find. It began when owner Palmont still made his living by fishing. Now Palmont's pink-and-blue boat is the best one bobbin'. People come for the fisherman's platter, the catch of the day (which could be tuna or a white fish) with a special red sauce, ripe tomatoes, and perfect red beans and rice. Fresh "crayfish on the barbie" can usually be had Thursday through Saturday. Bottles of Neisson rum are plunked in front of a table of, say, French doctors taking a time-out from their medical conference. On Friday night and Sunday afternoon, local bands play; they get everyone up and dancing in the sand. $ *Average main:* €20 ⊠ *Le Bord de Mer, Carbet* ☎ 0596/76–98–39, 0696/23–95–59 ⊗ *No dinner Sun.*

$$$
FRENCH
★
✕**La Table de Mamy Nounou.** If you looked at the business card for this dining room, you'd expect a creole menu served by an elderly island lady. Not! It's owned by a French family. The elegant Madame Mahler will greet you; her husband, Jean-Paul, presides as chef, and her son, Bastian, eloquently describes the menu in the King's English. Sip an aperitif while listening to the mesmerizing music and admiring the view from the lounge decorated with African art and fascinating finds from their travels. The chef is continually outdoing himself as the à la carte menu becomes more inventive and definitely au courant, with additions

like the foie gras crème brûlée and rock lobster pot de crème, capped with guacamole and cinnamon broth. An amuse-bouche arrives before outstanding appetizers. A member of Euro-toques, a group of European chefs who are dedicated to wholesome food, chef Jean-Paul wisely keeps on the menu perennial favorites such as the crawfish (*z'habitants*) in a sauce flamed with vintage rum; octopus (*chatrou*) with red wine sauce; and fish, shrimp, and scallops with a cinnamon-cider sauce. Finish with the *moelleux au chocolat* (a rich chocolate pudding) with caramel sauce, or sample a trio of desserts, which might include gingerbread ice cream. Lunch is served outdoors on the terrace and has a similar menu but is less expensive (and less elaborate), and includes some salads. $ *Average main: €25* ✉ *Anse L'Etang, Tartane, La Trinité* ☎ *0596/58–07–32* ⊘ *Closed Tues. and June and Sept.*

$$$$

CARIBBEAN

✗ **Le Brédas.** This culinary experience necessitates a trip into the interior, down winding roads where the dense foliage is jungle-like. It's best navigated, at least the first time, by day; come for lunch on a Sunday, and return for a memorable dinner Thursday through Saturday. Martinican chef Jean-Charles Brédas is well-known, having worked the better restaurants in Martinique and Manhattan. Recently he was awarded Maître Cuisinier and Maître Restaurateur de France; he also received a silver medal for tourism. His lovely wife, Marie-Julie, is a gracious hostess. The tasteful décor includes taupe linen runners on long tables speckled with colored-glass bits; the ceramic plates are the creations of an esteemed local potter, Victor Anicet. The foie gras is perfectly executed, especially when it's served with green bananas caramelized with rum and pineapple. (This appetizer, his signature dish, is a whopping €33.) One laudable main *plat* is the robust and tender beef marinated in cocoa, orange, and cardamom. The terrace dining room of this century-old house is covered by a peaked white awning. Chef Bredas' mission is to preserve the ancient *saveurs* (flavors), giving traditional island dishes and French classics a contemporary twist. A special-occasion restaurant, its holiday meals are celebratory, down to the roast suckling pigs. Note: if there is not a sufficient number of reservations for dinner, then they will not serve, but will call all those who reserved to cancel. $ *Average main: €34* ✉ *Entrée Presqu'île, St. Joseph* ☎ *0596/57–65–52* ⌲ *Reservations essential* ⊘ *Closed Mon–Wed. No lunch Sat. No dinner Sun.*

$$$

SEAFOOD

✗ **Le Petitbonum.** Billed as an artisan restaurant, it's a marriage of French island funkiness and Miami's South Beach. It's a one-of-a-kind in Martinique (if you don't count its sister restaurant in Fort-de-France). So is charismatic owner Guy Ferdinand, a tall Martinican with curly, blond-streaked hair who has made this a destination restaurant in the north coast's tiny town of Carbet. Smack on the beach, it's an ideal stopover if you're visiting nearby St-Pierre. Remember to wear your swimsuit. Kick off your shoes and order a perfect mojito. You can lounge on coral rubber chaises, shaded by umbrellas, and be sprayed intermittently with a gentle, cool mist. (Guy first experienced this in South Beach.) The appetizers—escargots, foie gras with a pear-and-banana chutney—are decadently rich for a feet-in-the-sand restaurant. For mains there is fresh tuna with a soy-sesame sauce; the signature dish is jumbo crayfish in a vanilla cream sauce flambeed with rhum vieux. Desserts such as the

15

pineapple crumble, tiramisu, or chocolate cake are special. Guy will quote you a special price if you want a three-course prix-fixe. Local bands play on Saturday night, and DJs spin for the Sunday afternoon beach party. $ *Average main: €25* ⌧ *Le Coin, Le Bord de Mer, Carbet* ☎ *0596/78–04–34*.

$$
CAFÉ
★

✕ **Mille & Une Brindilles.** At this trendy salon you can order anything from a glass of wine to an aromatic pot of tea in flavors like vanilla or mango. You'll find a litany of tapenades, olive cakes, and flans on the prix-fixe menu. Fred, the bubbly Parisian who is both chef and proprietress, is the queen of terrines, and she makes a delicious tart (like Roquefort and pear) or pâté out of any vegetable or fish. The Saturday brunch (€22) is a very social occasion. The best-ever desserts, such as the Amadéus—as appealing as the classical music that plays—and *moelleux au chocolat*, are what you would want served at your last meal on Earth. Look for the sign on the left side, for the place is easy to miss. $ *Average main: €18* ⌧ *27 rte. de Didier, Didier, Fort-de-France* ☎ *0596/71–75–61* ▭ *No credit cards* ⊙ *Closed Sun. and Wed. No dinner.*

$
ECLECTIC

✕ **Soup Bar du Centre Ville.** A sign reading "No Opium Smoking" is just one of the details that make this artsy eatery so much fun. This is one place that the island's colorful characters will tell you about if they think you're hip. Wild-looking art decorates one wall; on the other is a surfboard, signed by its American owner, who added "Thanks for the Soup." The list of soups is extensive, and includes local specialties such as soupe *z'habitant* (crawfish), a flavorful puree of green vegetables with pigs' tails added for flavor. Because a German owns the place, you can also get goulash and cold cream-of-cucumber soup. No matter what you order, the price is right: a huge bowl with some rolls ranges from €7 to €10. A few main courses are offered as well, topping out at €15; man-sized salads are €11-€20. This place is also a venue for art exhibits and live music. And yes, there is German beer and a petite sidewalk patio. The doors open at 6 pm, and they shut at 1:00 am. $ *Average main: €12* ⌧ *120 rue La Martine, Fort-de-France* ☎ *0596/60–48–96* ⊙ *Closed Sun. No lunch.*

WHERE TO STAY

Larger hotels usually include a big buffet breakfast of eggs, fresh fruit, cheese, yogurt, croissants, baguettes, jam, and café au lait. Smaller *relais* (inns) often have open-air, terrace kitchenettes. At almost all properties, you can request smoking or no-smoking rooms; the new French law banning smoking in public places went into effect in January 2008. Alas, hotel rooms are considered private. Most hotels do not have elevators and many are built on hillsides, so if you have issues with stairs or with climbing paths, be sure to ask about that.

For expanded reviews, facilities, and current deals, visit Fodors.com.

PRIVATE VILLAS AND CONDOS

If you're staying a week or longer, you can often save money by renting a villa or apartment with a kitchen where you can prepare your own meals. The more upscale rentals come with French-speaking maids and cooks. Don't forget to add the cost of a car rental to your vacation budget.

RENTAL CONTACTS

French Caribbean International. French Caribbean International, an English-speaking reservation service operated for decades by Gerard Hill, can help you with both villa rentals and hotel rooms. ✉ *Santa Barbara, California, USA* ☎ *800/322–2223, 805/967–9850 U.S. office* ⊕ *www.frenchcaribbean.com.*

Nouvelles Antilles. Nouvelles Antilles, a progressive operation based in St-François, Guadeloupe, acts as an agent for some 30 villas around the islands, mostly luxurious. In addition, the first online travel agency dedicated to the French West Indies can book your flight, rental car, and sports activities, and create a well-priced package. It deals with all the Guadeloupe isles, St. Barth, and St. Maarten, in addition to Martinique, and can customize a multidestination package for groups up to 15. ✉ *St-François, Guadeloupe* ☎ *0590/85–00–00* ⊕ *www.nouvellesantilles.com.*

15

SOUTH OF FORT-DE-FRANCE

$$$$
RESORT
Fodor's Choice
★

🖫 **Cap Est Lagoon Resort & Spa.** A member of the Relais and Châteaux group, Martinique's most exclusive resort has brought back celebrities and the wealthy international set. **Pros:** large central pool; island's most contemporary bar–lounge but with a Martinican feel; property has been well maintained. **Cons:** not a whole lot to do; somewhat isolated; beach is not expansive. **TripAdvisor:** "beautiful place," "quality and service," "what a great place to unwind." ⑤ *Rooms from: €600* ✉ *Quartier Cap Est, Le François* ☎ *0596/54–80–80, 800/735–2478* ⊕ *www.capest.com* ➳ *50 suites* ⊘ *Closed Aug. 31–Oct. 10* ⑩ *Breakfast.*

$
ALL-INCLUSIVE
★

🖫 **Club Med Buccaneer's Creek.** One of the French chain's most upscale villages, this flagship is part of Club Med's strategy of meeting the more refined needs of global travelers. **Pros:** still seems nearly new; Club Med energy is contagious; even waterskiing is included. **Cons:** annual membership is $60 for each adult; some first-timers just don't fancy the Club Med style. **TripAdvisor:** "great food," "fantastic club," "all-inclusive paradise." ⑤ *Rooms from: €250* ✉ *Pointe Marin, Ste-Anne* ☎ *0596/76–72–72* ⊕ *www.clubmed.us* ➳ *250 rooms, 44 suites* ⑩ *All-inclusive.*

$$
RESORT
★

🖫 **Hotel Bakoua.** Wrought-iron gates open to arguably one of Martinique's best resorts, what French guests call a "human hotel," where you can cocoon. **Pros:** the Bakoua exudes vintage Caribbean charisma; it's a classy classic; car not a must. **Cons:** constructed in stages, so some rooms show age whereas others are fresh; facades are not all pretty. **TripAdvisor:** "paradise found," "really beautiful," "very relaxing." ⑤ *Rooms from: €300* ✉ *Pointe du Bout, Les Trois-Ilets* ☎ *0596/66–02–02* ⊕ *www.mgallery.com* ➳ *133 rooms, 6 suites* ⑩ *Breakfast.*

$
RESORT
☺

🖫 **Hotel Cap Macabou.** Constructed in 2009 of handsome native hardwoods and designed in a Creole style, a large number of these 40 rooms and four suites have terraces with panoramas of the Atlantic Ocean. **Pros:** key staff speak English; all is clean and nearly new; known for its entertainment. **Cons:** it's a hard five minutes down a dirt road; not

FRENCH PLUMBING

If you aren't familiar with handheld showers and intricate levers, you can easily flood the bathroom and scald yourself. The French are not big on shower curtains either. So when the bellman gives you the walk-through, ask him to explain the plumbing. For example, toilets have two depressors; one is for a quick flush, the other a strong and serious flush and you'd better step aside. You can try for too long to figure out how to get the stopper in a bathtub to hold the water. Step into the tub and stomp down on that silver stopper. That should do it. It's as difficult to drain it. Leave it for the maid and tip heavily? Bidets are common. In self-catering villas, if there is a washing machine or a dishwasher, make sure you have a lesson before touching those dials or you'll be sorry. In some *toilettes* (public restrooms) there are new sanitary sinks where you depress a lever on the left, or a foot pedal. If you are looking to get some water and don't see any handles near the faucet, look down.

a good swimming beach; not much happens in Le Vauclin. $ *Rooms from: €111* ⊠ *Petit Macabou, Le Vauclin* ☎ *0596/74–24–24* ⊕ *www. capmacabou.com* ↝ *40 rooms, 4 suites* ⎪ *No meals.*

$

RESORT

☺

🖩 Karibea Sainte Luce Resort. This complex of three once-independent hotels, which share facilities, is on a nice stretch of beach and offers rooms at the right price. **Pros:** larger loggia rooms in Amandiers are best for Americans yet cost just 7% more; can walk the beach to town or take shuttle for €4 round-trip; you can use amenities at all three hotels. **Cons:** best with a rental car; no chaises on beach; getting down-at-the-heels. $ *Rooms from: €175* ⊠ *Quartier Désert, Ste-Luce* ☎ *0596/62–12–00, 0596/62–11–91 for reservations* ⊕ *www.karibea.com* ↝ *116 rooms (Amandiers), 108 junior suites (Amyris), 75 apartments (Caribia)* ⎪ *Breakfast.*

$

HOTEL

★

🖩 La Suite Villa. This hilltop boutique property gives Les Trois-Ilets a new, art-infused glamour quotient. **Pros:** inimitable, whimsical style with a profusion of Caribbean colors; entertaining and artistic owners; the upbeat social scene. **Cons:** great house has three floors and no elevator; no beach. **TripAdvisor:** "solitude and silence," "old-world charm," "the best of French style and food." $ *Rooms from: €240* ⊠ *Rte. du Fort d'Alet, Les Trois-Ilets* ☎ *0596/63–57–30* ⊕ *www.la-suite-villa.com* ↝ *6 suites, 9 villas (6 2-bedrooms, 3 3-bedrooms)* ⎪ *Breakfast.*

$

HOTEL

Fodor's Choice

★

🖩 Hotel Plein Soleil. Long one of our favorites, this heavenly hideaway has been featured so frequently in French, international, and American media that it has become a celebrity hotel. **Pros:** stimulating client mix; owner Jean Christophe is on-site and accessible; sophisticated and artistic ambience is unique in Martinique. **Cons:** rough road (particularly in rainy season); somewhat remote hilltop location; smallest rooms have small bathrooms. **TripAdvisor:** "stylish retreat with a great restaurant," "beautiful boutique hotel," "heavenly." $ *Rooms from: €195* ⊠ *Villa Lagon Sarc, Pointe Thalèmont, Le François* ☎ *0596/38–07–77* ⊕ *www. hotelpleinsoleil.fr* ↝ *16 bungalows* ☉ *Closed Sept.–Oct. 9* ⎪ *Breakfast.*

FORT-DE-FRANCE AND POINTS NORTH

$
B&B/INN
Engoulevent. This small B&B in a suburban home (about 10 minutes from Fort-de-France) has deluxe suites with contemporary decor, as well as up-to-date amenities like Wi-Fi. **Pros:** rooms are stellar; unique on the island; free in-room Wi-Fi. **Cons:** not all the benefits of a hotel; best with a car. *$ Rooms from: €165 ⊠ 22 rte. de l'Union Didier, Fort-de-France ☎ 0596/64–96–00 ⮧ 5 suites ⦿ Breakfast.*

$
HOTEL
Hotel La Caravelle. The energetic Mahler family transformed this simple hotel with a renovation and their artwork from Africa, where patriarch Jean-Paul worked for several decades as a manager of five-star hotels. **Pros:** caring service; interesting international family; gourmet cuisine. **Cons:** no pool; still a simple French hotel. **TripAdvisor:** "wonderful hotel and restaurant," "French Caribbean paradise," "great accommodations." *$ Rooms from: €84 ⊠ Anse L'Etang, Tartane, La Trinité ☎ 0596/58–07–32 ⊕ www.hotel-la-caravelle-martinique.com ⮧ 14 studios, 1 apartment ⦿ No meals.*

$
HOTEL
Hotel Villa St. Pierre. A simple, modern decor typifies this modest bayfront property that is somewhere between a hôtel de charme and a French business hotel. **Pros:** caring managers Maryse and Andre; downtown location. **Cons:** little English spoken; not luxurious. **TripAdvisor:** "intimate charm and discreet luxury," "lovely spot," "a little gem." *$ Rooms from: €140 ⊠ 108 rue Bouillé, St-Pierre ☎ 0596/78–68–45 ⊕ www.hotel-villastpierre.fr ⮧ 9 rooms ⊙ Closed Sept. ⦿ Breakfast.*

$
HOTEL
La Valmenière Hôtel. This high-rise, perched on a hillside overlooking Fort-de-France, is the closest to the airport (5 miles [8 km]) and is ideal for first- or last-night stays. **Pros:** always alive and active; excellent restaurant; suites have balconies. **Cons:** primarily a business hotel; rooms are large but simplistic; lacks panache. **TripAdvisor:** "convenient for the airport," "excellent restaurant," "for a brief stay." *$ Rooms from: €225 ⊠ Av. des Arawaks, Fort-de-France ☎ 0596/75–75–75 ⊕ www.karibea.com ⮧ 116 rooms, 4 suites ⦿ No meals.*

$
HOTEL
Le Domaine Saint Aubin. This former estate is perched on a verdant hilltop with a breathtaking view overlooking the Atlantic. **Pros:** you can daydream yourself into a more gracious era; hip owners are scintillating company; wheelchair-accessible rooms (and the pool has a chair-lift). **Cons:** somewhat remote location requires a car; original rooms are not stylish; breakfast is an additional €14. **TripAdvisor:** "a magical place to unwind," "very romantic and stylish," "unique location in peaceful surroundings." *$ Rooms from: €189 ⊠ Petite Rivière Salée, off rte. 1, La Trinité ☎ 0596/69–34–77, 0696/40–99–59 ⊕ www.ledomainesaintaubin.com ⮧ 30 rooms, 6 2-bedroom apartments.*

$$
HOTEL
Squash Hôtel. This well-run business hotel is ideally located if you need to sleep close to the airport (15 minutes away) or want to explore Fort-de-France (10 minutes). **Pros:** key staffers speak English; close to city but with suburban quiet; always good Franco-Caribbean cuisine and usually a *menu du jour*. **Cons:** not a handsome facade; few resort amenities. *$ Rooms from: €280 ⊠ 3 bd. de la Marne, Fort-de-France ☎ 0596/72–80–80 ⊕ www.karibea.com ⮧ 105 rooms, 2 suites, 1 business suite ⦿ Breakfast.*

15

NIGHTLIFE AND THE ARTS

There are lively discos and nightclubs in Martinique, but a good deal of the fun is to be had by befriending Martinicans, French residents, and other expats and hoping they will invite you clubbing or to their private parties. As for casinos, French law requires everyone to show a passport or license; the legal gambling age is 18.

CASINOS

Casino Batelière Plaza. On the outskirts of Fort-de-France, the classy Casino Batelière Plaza is built in a striking nouveau-plantation-house style. It has slot machines, video poker, and table games like Texas Hold 'Em and let-it-ride craps. Slots open at 10 am, but table games don't start until after 8 pm. There's always a bar open, and you can catch live entertainment on weekends from 8 to midnight. Closing time is 4 am on Friday and Saturday, 3 am the rest of the week. It's open Sunday night, when most places are shut tight, except the buffet restaurant (€15), which is open only Tuesday–Saturday. ■ TIP➜ You may see billboards that say: CASINO or even GEANTE CASINO, with directionals. Do not follow them if you are looking for a gambling casino. CASINO is the name of a supermarket chain. GEANTE means a megasupermarket. ⊠ *Schoelcher* ☎ *0596/61–73–23.*

Casino Trois-Ilets. The interior of this relatively new casino in a major tourist zone. Casino Trois-Ilets was designed with a French Quarter ambience and houses 70 slot machines, blackjack, U.S. roulette, and craps (Friday and Saturday). The casino is open daily 11 am to 3 am; the moderately priced fine-dining restaurant is open for lunch and dinner daily—including Sunday night, when many dining establishments are closed. On weekends a DJ spins Caribbean, Creole, and international beats, and there is a dance floor. Although it was highly anticipated, this casino does not have a strong spirit or fun quotient. Consequently, its appeal is more for locals looking for that "magic." ■ TIP➜ You must be 18 or older and have an ID to enter (bring you passport). ⊠ *Rte. de Pointe du Bout, near rte. de Trois-Ilets, Trois-Ilets* ☎ *0596/66–00–30.*

DANCE CLUBS

Your hotel or the tourist office can put you in touch with the current "in" places. It's also wise to check on opening and closing times and cover charges. Several free tourist publications that can be found at hotels tell of the latest happenings at the clubs. For the most part, the discos draw a mixed crowd—Martinicans and tourists—and although a younger crowd is the norm, people of all ages go dancing here.

Coconuts Club. The Coconuts Club houses a restaurant, bar–lounge, and disco. The motto here is "Life is a party!" ⊠ *Quartier Laugier, Riviére-Salée.*

Crazy Nights. This club remains popular because it's all about having one crazy time. With upward of 1,000 partying people, your chances of enjoying yourself are good. Live concerts are frequent, but dancing

Traditional Madras costumes in Martinique

and hip-swinging are the priorities. Islanders are drawn to this club, and some young 'n' fun tourists follow suit. ⊠ *Ste-Luce*.

Top Night Club. The former Le Top 50 is now Top Night Club. This popular nightspot is one of the few clubs in the area where tourists, surfers, and locals all come together to party. ⊠ *Zone Artisanale, La Trinité* ☎ *0596/58–61–43.*

FOLKLORIC PERFORMANCES

Most leading hotels offer nightly entertainment in season, including the marvelous **Grands Ballets de Martinique,** one of the finest folkloric dance troupes in the Caribbean. Consisting of a bevy of musicians and dancers dressed in traditional costume, the ballet revives the Martinique of yesteryear through dance rhythms such as the beguine and the mazurka. They appear on Wednesday at the Hotel Carayou & Spa in Les Trois-Ilets in a dinner performance coupled with an authentic creole buffet.

At the Amyris Hotel, the **Ballet Exotica,** comprising male and female dancers in Creole costumes, perform the island's traditional dances on Friday night. It costs €28 and includes a buffet dinner. Nonhotel guests should make reservations in advance, as seating is limited. In addition, many restaurants offer live entertainment, usually on weekends.

MUSIC CLUBS

Jazz musicians, like their music, tend to be informal and independent. They rarely hold regular gigs. Zouk mixes Caribbean rhythm and an Occidental tempo with Creole lyrics. Jacob Devarieux is the leading exponent of this style, and he occasionally performs on the island. Otherwise, you're likely to hear one of his followers.

Calebasse Café. Calebasse Café pleases a diverse—though mostly older—crowd. Jazz is the norm, and there's often a talented local singer. Funky and hip, the interior is a bit rough but civilized. On Saturday night, if you don't make a reservation you will not have a seat. The food here isn't wonderful, but if you have the conch tart and the grilled lobster, you'll leave satisfied and avoid the cover charge. There's sometimes a beach party; it's closed Monday. ⊠ *19 bd. Allègre, Le Marin* ☎ *0596/74–91–93.*

Club Med Buccaneer's Creek. At Club Med Buccaneer's Creek you can buy a night pass that, at €93, might seem expensive; it is, but it includes an impressive buffet dinner and a show in the theater. Friday costs more, €118. It's the best night, called the gala, with the elaborate food and the best show, which might be a Brazilian spectacle. Entertainment changes based on a two-week cycle; for example, Sunday there might be Celtic dancers. Following the show, it's on to dancing at the disco until 2 if you can hang. Single women feel comfortable here, and they find willing and very able dance partners, especially the G.O.s. The pass system allows you to decide whether it is your next vacation. Or plan on spending one overnight here; for a couple, the price difference is not that great. ⊠ *Pointe du Marin, Ste-Anne* ☎ *0596/76–83–36.*

Hotel Bakoua. Hotel Bakoua has nightly entertainment, from talented piano men to vocalists and jazz combos; the quality of the entertainment is known island-wide. The stage has moved to the alfresco Chateaubriand restaurant where drinks are served at your table. If you miss the bar, you can go to Le Gommier and order a tropical cocktail there first. There's a litany of island rums, from white to amber and rhum vieux. ⊠ *Pointe du Bout, Les Trois-Ilets* ☎ *0596/66–02–02.*

Hotel Cap Macabou. Hotel Cap Macabou in Vauclin has "dancing dinners" and theme nights on most Fridays and Saturdays. On Sunday there's usually a midday buffet with dancing to a band—you can even bring your bathing suit. Call to see if there's a salsa soiree with Latin music and a buffet on the first and third Friday of each month. ⊠ *Petit Macabou, Le Vauclin* ☎ *0596/74–24–24* ⊕ *www.capmacabou.com.*

La Marine. La Marine is an animated bar and restaurant with live entertainment, mainly on Saturday nights. ⊠ *Marina Pointe du Bout, Les Trois-Ilets* ☎ *0596/66–02–32.*

La Villa Créole. This restaurant's Martinican owner, Guy Bruere-Dawson, has been singing and strumming the guitar since the 1980s—in five languages, everything from François Cabrel to Elton John, some Italian and Creole ballads, even original ditties. Other singers perform, too, on Friday and Saturday nights. To see the show, you must order dinner; lobster is traditionally the best option. There's also a small dance floor, and a few tables are outside the open-air restaurant. If patrons aren't using them for dinner, you can just drink and more or less hear the music. ⊠ *Anse Mitan* ☎ *0596/66–05–53.*

SHOPPING

French fragrances; designer clothes, scarves, and sunglasses; fine china and crystal; leather goods; wine (amazingly inexpensive at supermarkets); and liquor are all good buys in duty-free Fort-de-France. Purchases are further sweetened by the 20% discount on luxury items when paid for with certain credit cards. Among the items produced on the island, look for *bijoux creole* (local jewelry, such as hoop earrings and heavy bead necklaces); white, dark, and aged rum; and handcrafted straw goods, pottery, and tapestries.

AREAS AND MALLS

The area around the cathedral in Fort-de-France has a number of small shops that carry luxury goods. Of particular note are the shops on rue Victor Hugo, rue Moreau de Jones, rue Antoine Siger, and rue Lamartine. The **Galleries Lafayette** department store on rue Schoelcher in downtown Fort-de-France sells everything from perfume to pâté. On the outskirts of Fort-de-France, the **Centre Commercial de Cluny, Centre Commercial de Dillon, Centre Commercial de Bellevue,** and **Centre Commercial la Rond Point** are among the major shopping malls.

You can find more than 100 thriving businesses—from shops and department stores to restaurants, pizzerias, fast-food outlets, a superb supermarket, and the Galleria Hotel—at **La Galleria** in Lamentin. In Pointe du Bout there are a number of appealing tourist shops and boutiques, both in and around **Village Créole**, which alone has 26, plus seven restaurants–bars. There is often live entertainment here at night.

SPECIALTY STORES

CHINA AND CRYSTAL

Roger Albert. Head here for designer crystal. ⊠ *7 rue Victor Hugo, Fort-de-France* ☎ *0596/71–71–71.*

CLOTHING

La Petite Boutique. La Petite Boutique offers a unique children's collection, including jewelry, madras dollies, and teeny underwear. ⊠ *Village Créole, Pointe du Bout, Les Trois-Ilets* ☎ *0596/38–00–65.*

Coté Plage Sarl. Stop in here for French sailor jerseys in creative colors, youthful straw purses in bold hues, fun teenage jewelry, and ladies' bathing suits. ⊠ *Village Créole, Pointe du Bout, Les Trois-Ilets* ☎ *0596/66–13–00.*

Lynx Optique. Lynx Optique has the latest designer sunglasses from Chanel, Gucci, Dior, Cartier, and Versace. (French designer brands are less expensive here.) And if you need a pair of prescription lenses, they can take care of that, too. ⊠ *20 rue Lamartine, Fort-de-France* ☎ *0596/71–38–48.*

Mounia. Owned by a former Yves St. Laurent model, Mounia carries the top French designers for women and men. It will have you opening your wallet wide. Hope for a *solde* (sale). ⊠ *Rue Perrinon, near old House of Justice, Fort-de-France* ☎ *0596/73–77–27.*

15

HANDICRAFTS

Antan Lontan. The work of Antan Lontan has to be seen. Sculptures, busts, statuettes, and artistic lamps portray Creole women and the story of the Martiniquaise culture. ☒ *Centre Commercial, La Veranda, Rue du Professeur Raymond Garcin, Fort-de-France* ☎ *0696/92–15–50.*

Art et Nature. Art et Nature carries Joel Gilbert's unique wood paintings, daubed with 20 to 30 shades of earth and sand. ☒ *Ste-Luce* ☎ *0596/62–59–19.*

Artisanat & Poterie des Trois-Ilets. Artisanat & Poterie des Trois-Ilets allows you to watch the creation of Arawak- and Carib-style pots, vases, and jars. ☒ *Les Trois-Ilets* ☎ *0596/68–03–44.*

Atelier Céramique. On display at Atelier Céramique are the ceramics, paintings, and miscellaneous souvenirs of owners and talented artists David and Jeannine England, members of the island's small British expat community. ☒ *Le Diamant* ☎ *0596/76–42–65.*

★ **Bois Nature.** This place is all about mood and mystique. Gift items at Bois Nature begin with scented soap, massage oil, aromatherapy sprays, and perfumes. Then there are wind chimes, mosquito netting, and sun hats made of coconut fiber. The big stuff includes natural wood-frame mirrors and furniture à la Louis XV. ☒ *La Semair, Le Robert* ☎ *0596/65–77–65.*

Domaine Château Gaillard. A large two-story shopping complex, Domaine Château Gaillard sells both handicrafts and tropical floral compositions at its nursery. You can also find pottery, jewelry, toys, paintings, and gifts. Coffee and chocolate are for sale, and there is a small museum chronicling both island products. Antique creole hats and madras items are on display, too. A petite train for the kids is there for the touring. A boutique with Wi-Fi helps keep you connected. There is even a heliport, and **Héli Blue** (☎ *0596/66–10–80* ⊕ *www.heliblue.com*) gives great 'copter tours of the island. Alas, the pleasant restaurant is no more. ☒ *Rte. des Trois-Ilets, Les Trois-Ilets* ☎ *0596/68–15–68.*

Galerie de Sophen. Across from the Village Créole, Galerie de Sophen is a combination of Sophie and Henry, both in name and content. This art gallery showcases the work (originals and limited prints) of a French couple who live aboard their sailboat and paint the beauty of the sea and the island, from exotic birds to banana trucks. ☒ *Pointe du Bout, Les Trois-Ilets* ☎ *0596/66–13–64.*

Galerie Jecy. At Galerie Jecy, owner Stephanie designs fanciful, colorful metalwork that is artistic enough to be called sculpture; her island themes include starfish, octopus, geckos, and impressive billfish. She also sells more portable souvenirs such as colorful wooden napkin rings, fruit plates, and trivets. Have a look while you wait for the ferry. ☒ *Pointe du Bout Marina, Les Trois-Ilets* ☎ *0596/66–04–98.*

JEWELRY

Thomas de Rogatis. At Thomas de Rogatis, authentic bijoux Creole jewelry, popularized after the abolition of slavery and seen in many museums, is for sale. This is the number one jewelry store in Martinique. ☒ *22 rue Antoine Siger, Fort-de-France* ☎ *0596/70–29–11.*

PERFUME

Roger Albert. This shop stocks popular scents by Dior, Chanel, Guerlain, and the like. Walk in, have a wiff, and think *Amour!* ⊠ *7 rue Victor Hugo, Fort-de-France* ☎ *0596/71–71–71.*

SALON

Hair du Temps. So you want to look French, oui? Yes, buy French designer resort wear, but the secret is a cool, sexy French haircut. Both ladies and men vie for appointments at Hair du Temps. Haircut prices do not include a blow-dry—that's extra, as are hairspray and mousse—€6 extra for whichever you choose. ⊠ *Arcade La Pagerie, Point du Bout, Les Trois-Ilets* ☎ *0596/66–02–51.*

SPORTS AND ACTIVITIES

BICYCLING

15

V.T. Tilt. Mountain biking is popular in mainland France, and now it has reached Martinique. You can rent a VTT (Vélo Tout Terrain), a bike specially designed with 18 speeds to handle all terrains, for €15 with helmet, delivery, and pickup from your hotel, although it requires a €150 credit card deposit. V.T. Tilt has an English-speaking owner who loves to put together groups for fun tours, either half day or full day, which include lunch. They can be beach, river, or mountain rides; tours of plantations or horse ranches; and historic, adventure, or nature experiences. Just know that the French pedal hard. ⊠ *Les Trois-Ilets* ☎ *0596/66–01–01.*

BOATING AND SAILING

You can rent Hobie Cats, Sunfish, and Sailfish by the hour from most hotel beach shacks. As for larger craft, bareboat charters can be had for $1,900 to $7,000 a week, depending on the season and the size of the craft. The Windward Islands are a joy for experienced sailors, but the channels between islands are often windy and have high waves. You must have a sailing license or be able to prove your nautical prowess, though you can always hire a skipper and crew. Before setting out, you can get itinerary suggestions; the safe ports in Martinique are many. If you charter for a week, you can go south to St. Lucia or Grenada or north to Dominica, Guadeloupe, and Les Saintes. One-way sailing to St. Martin or Antigua is a popular choice.

⚠ Don't even consider striking out on the rough Atlantic side of the island unless you're an experienced sailor. The Caribbean side is much calmer—more like a vast lagoon.

Punch Croisières. Punch Croisières is a local, French-owned charter company with a fleet of 17 sailboats, 14 of which are catamarans from 40 to 47 feet; they go out bareboat or crewed, and you can take a boat to a neighboring island. Rentals from one week to 11 months are available. ⊠ *Bd. Allègre, Port de Plaisance, Le Marin* ☎ *0596/74–89–18* ⊕ *www. punch-croisieres.com.*

Windward Island Cruising Company. Windward Island Cruising Company has sailboats from 30 to 70 feet, catamarans and motor yachts, for bareboat or crewed charters. If crewed, there is a choice of full- or half-board. This is a world-wide operation with 40 locations around the globe. ⊠ *Le Marin* ☎ *0596/74–31–14* ⊕ *www.sailing-adventure.com.*

■TIP→ **Located on the west coast, Anse-d'Arlets is a delightful fishing village with a historic church and wooden gingerbread houses.** It is yacht-friendly and has several sheltered coves; charter boats usually anchor on Grand Anse or Petite Anse. Ti Sable is a waterfront restaurant that has a fun scene. Sunday brunch is a big event, with a good and moderately priced buffet.

CANOPY TOURS

Canopy tours—also known as tree-topping tours—are relatively new to Martinique. Even younger kids can join in the fun on some courses. However, if your body parts—particularly knees and elbows—are not as supple as they once were, or if you're afraid of heights, stay back at the hotel pool. The "tour" consists of a series of wooden ladders and bridges suspended from the trees, connected with zip lines. Participants are secured in harnesses and ropes that are hitched to them like dog leashes. You connect to a cable and then fly and bellow like Tarzan until you get to the other side. Advance reservations are usually required.

Mangofil. Mangofil is a professionally run operation overseen by Frenchmen who managed a similar (zip-line) park in France. All of the platforms, ladders, and stations were installed by members of a special union in France that specializes in such work. Safety is key here, but there's also a lot of fun. The cost is €25 per person for adults, €15–20 for children, depending on height. It's open Wednesday–Sunday 9–4 and every day during French school holidays. ■TIP→ **If a Big Mango (adult) comes with a little Parcabout (kid), it is €25 + €5. They also rent quads (4x4s).** ⊠ *Rte. de Trois-Ilets, near Le Potterie, Les Trois-Ilets* ☎ *0596/68–08–08.*

CANYONING

Bureau de la Randonnée et du Canyoning. Bureau de la Randonnée et du Canyoning employs professionals with diplomas in *volcanisme* (volcanoes), *randonnée* (hiking), and canyoning, which is the sport of traversing rivers and streams using your body as a toboggan. For this adrenaline rush, you must be fit and able to hike in the forest for hours. These tropical adventures can take you to the Presqu'île du Caravelle, through canals, to Mont Pelée, even to the borders of the craters. Price depends on the destination and the duration. ⊠ *Joliment, Morne Vert* ☎ *0596/55–04–79, 0696/24–32–25* ⊕ *www.bureau-rando-martinique.com.*

Kayaking is a popular resort activity on Martinique.

DAY SAILS

Kata Mambo. The catamaran *Kata Mambo* offers a variety of options for half-day (€42) or full-day (€76, €84 for lobster lunch) sails to St-Pierre and visits to Depaz Distillery. For €76, you also get a 4x4 adventure through sugarcane and banana plantations. The full-day trip includes unlimited rum libations and a good multicourse lunch (half lobsters are €10 extra) with wine. The boat pulls into its slip at the marina at 5 pm. This is a fun day, and although there's no guarantee, chances are you'll have dolphin encounters. The fact that it's been in the biz since the early 1990s attests to its professionalism. ⊠ *Pointe du Bout Marina, Les Trois-Ilets* ☎ *0696/81–90–08, 0596/66–11–83.*

La Belle Kréole. La Belle Kréole runs one of the most popular excursion boats to les fonds blanc, also known as Empress Joséphine's baths. You can experience the unique Martinican custom of "baptism by rum" (tilt your head back while standing in waist-deep water, and one of the crew pours rum into your mouth). The price of the day trip depends on what you choose to eat and includes lunch, which is taken on the remote Isle de Thierry. There's Planter's Punch and dancing to Martinican CDs. Yes, it is touristy—a booze cruise with lots of loud music and animation. There is also a two-hour excursion to the baths. ⊠ *Baie du Simon, Le François* ☎ *0596/54–96–46, 0696/29–93–13* ⊕ *www. baignoiredejosephine.com.*

Les Ballades du Delphis. Les Ballades du Delphis is a catamaran experience that is delightfully civilized rather than a hyped-up booze cruise. It takes in the famous fond blancs or Joséphine's baths and the Baie du Robert and I'let Chancel to see the sea iguanas and ruins. And yes, you will be served Planter's Punch, accras, and a healthful lunch—quite a full day for €75. Nocturnal cruises are "by the light of the silvery moon." These romantic cruises (maximum 12 persons) are slated for three nights before the full moon and three nights after. For an idyllic travel memory, guests are serenaded by a violinist as they sup' on lobster and sip champagne. ⊠ *La Marina du François, Le François* ☎ *0696/90–90–36* ⊕ *www.catadelphis.com.*

DIVING AND SNORKELING

Martinique's underwater world is decorated with multicolor coral, crustaceans, turtles, and sea horses. Expect to pay €40 to €45 for a single dive; a package of three dives is around €110.

Okeanos Club. This dive operator has a morning trip close to shore; in the afternoon the boats go farther into open water. Lessons (including those for kids 8 to 12) with a PADI-certified instructor can be conducted in English. It's always a fun experience. The dive shop looks out to Diamant Rock, which has wonderful underwater caves and is one of the preferred dives on the island. Okeanos Club goes to 12 different sites; they gear the trips to the level of the clients, from rank beginners to certified divers. ⊠ *Village Pierre & Vacances, Ste-Luce* ☎ *0596/62–52–36* ⊕ *www.okeanos-club.com.*

Planète Bleue. Planète Bleue has a big up-to-date dive boat, hand-painted with tropical fish and waves, so it's impossible to miss. The English-speaking international crew is proud to have been in business since the early 1990s. The company hits 20 sites, including the Citadel and Salomon's Pool. A boat goes out mornings and afternoons. Thursday is a full day on the north coast, with breakfast, lunch, and all drinks included. Half-day dives include gear and a 'ti punch. Sunday is a day of rest, except for the first one in the month, when it's off to Diamant Rock. ⊠ *Pointe du Bout Marina, Les Trois-Ilets* ☎ *0596/58–61–43.*

FISHING

Deep-sea fishing expeditions in these waters hunt down tuna, barracuda, dolphinfish, kingfish, and bonito, and the big ones—white and blue marlins. You can hire boats from the bigger marinas, particularly in Pointe du Bout, Le Marin, and Le François; most hotels arrange these Hemingway-esque trysts, but will often charge a premium. If you call several days in advance, companies can also put you together with other anglers to keep costs down.

Centre de Peche. The *Centre de Peche*, a fully loaded Davis 47-foot fishing boat, is a sportfisherman's dream. It goes out with a minimum of five anglers for €195 per person for a half day, or €390 per person for a full day, including lunch. Nonanglers can come for the ride for €95 and €190, respectively. Captain Yves speaks English fluently and is a fun guy. ⊠ *Port de Plaisance, bd. Allègre, Le Marin* ☎ *0596/76–24–20, 0696/28–80–58* ⊕ *www.sailfish-marlin.com.*

GOLF

Golf de l'Impératrice Josephine. The 18-hole Le Golf de l'Impératrice Josephine has been renamed in honor of Empress Joséphine Napoléon, whose birthplace, La Pagerie, adjoins this 150-acre track of rolling hills. However, the course is 100% American in design. It is a par-71 Robert Trent Jones course with an English-speaking pro, pro shop, bar, and restaurant. The club offers special greens fees to cruise-ship passengers. Normal greens fees are €23 for 9 holes (after 3 pm) and €43 for 18; a cart costs another €25 for 9, €40 for 18. Inquire about weekly rates. For those who don't mind walking while admiring the Caribbean view between the palm trees, club trolleys are €6. There are no caddies. ⊠ *Les Trois-Ilets* 🕾 *0596/52–04–13.*

GUIDED TOURS

Your hotel front desk can help arrange a personalized island tour with an English-speaking driver. It's also possible to hire a taxi for the day or half day; there are set rates for certain itineraries, and if you share the ride with others, the per-person price will be whittled down.

The Office du Tourisme de Fort-de-France orchestrates tours, from walking tours of the city to bus excursions. They can arrange for English-speaking guides, too.

HIKING

Parc Naturel Régional de la Martinique. Two-thirds of Martinique is designated as protected land. Trails, all 31 of them, are well marked and maintained. At the beginning of each, a notice is posted advising on the level of difficulty, the duration of a hike, and any interesting facts. The Parc Naturel Régional de la Martinique organizes inexpensive guided excursions year-round. If there have been heavy rains, though, give it up. The tangle of ferns, bamboo trees, and vines is dramatic, but during rainy season the wet, muddy trails will temper your enthusiasm. ⊠ *9 bd. Général de Gaulle, Fort-de-France* 🕾 *0596/64–42–59 Secretary, 0596/64–45–64 Communication Department.*

HORSEBACK RIDING

☼ Horseback-riding excursions can traverse scenic beaches, palm-shaded forests, sugarcane fields, and a variety of other tropical landscapes. Trained guides often include running commentaries on the history, flora, and fauna of the island.

Ranch de Caps. Some guides are English-speaking at Ranch de Caps, where you can take a half-day ride (Western saddle) on the wild southern beaches and across the countryside for €45. These beautiful, deserted beaches are not accessible to cars. Guides will allow those who are capable to gallop. Rides go out in the morning (8:30 to noon) and afternoon (1:30 to 5) every day but Monday. If you can manage a full day in the saddle, it costs €75 and includes lunch. Seasoned riders may even want to attempt the two-day trip (€160).

A real treat is the full-moon ride, but it needs to accrue a group of 10. Most of the 20 mounts are Anglo-Arabs. Riders are encouraged to help cool and wash their horses at day's end. Reserve in advance. Riders of all levels are welcomed. ⊠ *Cap Macré, Le Marin* ☎ *0596/74–70–65, 0696/23–18–18* ⊕ *www.ranchdescaps.com.*

Ranch Jack. Ranch Jack has trail rides (English-style) across some beautiful country for €36 for two hours; half-day excursions for €54 (€62 with transfers from nearby hotels) go through the fields and forests to the beach. Short rides can range from €16 to €25. The lessons for kids are recommendable. ⊠ *Morne habitué, Trois-Ilets* ☎ *0596/68–37–69, 0696/92–26–58* ✉ *ranch.jack@wanadoo.fr.*

KAYAKING

Ecofriendly travelers will love skimming the shallow bay while paddling to bird and iguana reserves. Rent colorful fiberglass kayaks to explore the crystalline Havre du Robert, with its shallow pools (called fonds blanc), petite beaches, and islets such as Iguana Island.

Les Kayaks du Robert. You'll receive one of the island's warmest welcomes at Les Kayaks du Robert. After a memorable half-day paddle through shallow lagoons and mangrove swamps chasing colorful fish, you can enjoy a complimentary juice or Planter's Punch, all for €15 per person; a full day is €23. There are no longer guided group trips. ⊠ *Pointe Savane, Le Robert* ☎ *0596/65–33–89.*

WINDSURFING

Bliss, École de Surf de Martinique. This surf school has really grown up. In addition to surfing lessons for adults, adolescents, and kids, they rent equipment and offer instruction for body boards and stand-up paddling. They can also combine surfing lessons with oceanfront yoga classes. The multilingual team operates a surf camp and will arrange accommodations in clean, spartan digs. Group lessons are €29 per hour, and private lessons are €40 per hour. ⊠ *Anse Bonneville, near Résidence Oceane, Tartane, La Trinité* ☎ *0596/58–00–96* ⊕ *surf-martinique.com.*

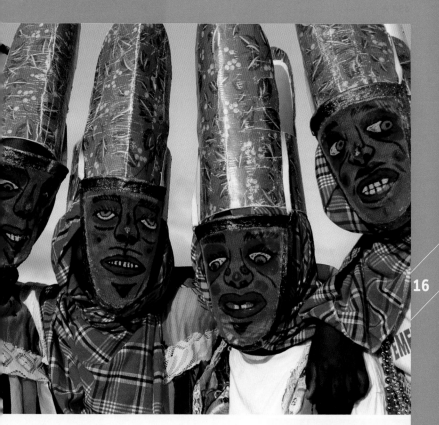

Montserrat

WORD OF MOUTH

"Montserrat is certainly for those who don't need a lot of entertainment and yet there is more than enough if you just know where to look. It makes the journey so much more interesting. and so much more to share."

—Lindawojcik

WELCOME TO MONTSERRAT

Although the Soufrière Hills volcano continues to rumble, the island is otherwise as peaceful as the Caribbean gets—almost a throwback to another time, with the occasional modern convenience (and convenience store) thrown in. Montserrat draws ecotourists, divers, and those who simply want to experience the Caribbean as it once was.

Restaurants ▼		Hotels ▼	
Gourmet Gardens	5	Erindell Villa	4
Olveston House	3	Gingerbread Hill	2
Royal Palm Club	2	Grand View Bed & Breakfast	5
Tina's	1	Olveston House	3
Ziggy's	4	Tropical Mansion	1

KEY	
⌇	Beaches
◹	Dive Sites
❶	Restaurants
①	Hotels

TOP REASONS TO VISIT MONTSERRAT

1 Geology: Volcano lovers will experience a landscape that's been pretty much left alone for more than a decade.

2 Diving: The diving is one of the Caribbean's unsung secrets, as the underwater terrain has also remained largely undisturbed.

3 Peace and Quiet: You'll find tranquillity in abundance; if you want to lie back and relax, this is the place for you.

4 Peace of Mind: There's virtually no crime, and you won't find a friendlier place in the Caribbean.

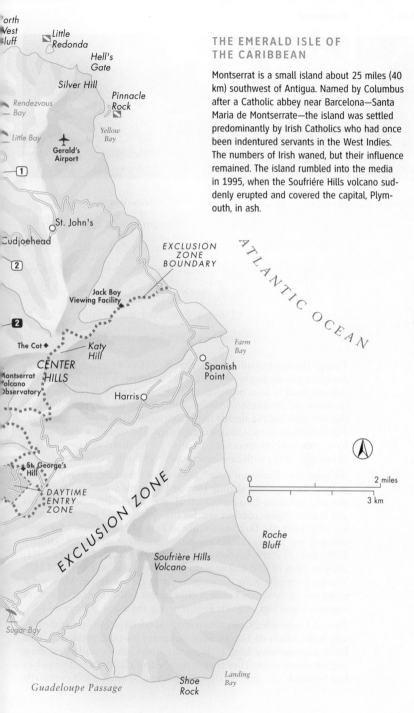

THE EMERALD ISLE OF THE CARIBBEAN

Montserrat is a small island about 25 miles (40 km) southwest of Antigua. Named by Columbus after a Catholic abbey near Barcelona—Santa Maria de Montserrate—the island was settled predominantly by Irish Catholics who had once been indentured servants in the West Indies. The numbers of Irish waned, but their influence remained. The island rumbled into the media in 1995, when the Soufriére Hills volcano suddenly erupted and covered the capital, Plymouth, in ash.

North West Bluff

Little Redonda

Hell's Gate

Silver Hill

Rendezvous Bay

Pinnacle Rock

Little Bay

Yellow Bay

Gerald's Airport

1

St. John's

Cudjoehead

2

ATLANTIC OCEAN

EXCLUSION ZONE BOUNDARY

Jack Boy Viewing Facility

2

The Cot

Katy Hill

Farm Bay

CENTER HILLS

Spanish Point

Montserrat Volcano Observatory

Harris

St. George's Hill

DAYTIME ENTRY ZONE

0   2 miles
0   3 km

EXCLUSION ZONE

Roche Bluff

Soufrière Hills Volcano

Sugar Bay

Guadeloupe Passage

Shoe Rock

Landing Bay

By Jordan
Simon

Aficionados have always regarded Montserrat as an idyllic, fairy-tale island. But in 1995, Grimm turned grim when the Soufrière Hills volcano erupted, literally throwing the island into the fire. The frilly Victorian gingerbreads of the capital, Plymouth, were buried, much of the tourism infrastructure was wiped out, and more than half the original 11,000 residents departed and have not been able to return.

Though the volcano still belches (plumes of ash are visible from as far as Antigua), plucky locals joke that new beachfront is being created. The volcano itself is an ecotourism spot, drawing travelers curious to see the awesome devastation. Ironically, other fringe benefits exist. Volcanic deposits enriched the already fertile soil; locals claim their fruit and vegetable crops have increased and improved. The slightly warmer waters have attracted even more varied marine life for divers and snorkelers to appreciate, along with new underwater rock formations.

Although an "Exclusion Zone" covers half the island, the rest is safe; in fact, the zone was slightly retracted after the volcano's lava dome partially collapsed during a pyroclastic flow in July 2003. Seismologists and vulcanologists conduct regular risk analyses and simulation studies; as a result, the Daytime Exclusion Zone shrank after a May 2006 collapse, and then expanded again after activity in early 2008, January 2009, and fall 2009. Borders retracted slightly in early 2010 and 2011, opening parts of Old Towne and Isles Bay to as far as Richmond Hill. Visitors expecting mass devastation are in for a surprise; Montserrat ranks among the region's most pristine, serene destinations, its luxuriant vegetation and jagged green hills justifying the moniker Emerald Isle.

Though Christopher Columbus named the island in 1493 (after the hillside Santa Maria de Montserrate monastery outside Barcelona), most locals are descended from 17th-century Irish Catholic settlers escaping English persecution. They routed the resident Caribs (who themselves had "evicted" the indigenous Saladoids and Arawaks) and eventually

LOGISTICS

Getting to Montserrat: There are no nonstop flights to Montserrat from North America. You can transfer on Antigua for a FlyMontserrat flight or the new ABM service. You can also take a ferry from Antigua.

Hassle Factor: Medium to high.

Getting Around the Island: The fixed taxi fare from the airport ranges from $10 (for Tropical Mansion) to $26 (to the Olveston/Salem area villas). Though you can take taxis, you'll best appreciate Montserrat's quiet beauty if you rent a car and do some exploring on your own.

Rates start at around $35 a day, but gas is expensive, so be sure to budget for that.

One main road runs from the north, down each side of the island, with little unnamed side roads streaming inland. Most addresses don't have street names or house numbers. Driving is on the left; the well-paved main road zigs, zags, climbs, and plummets precipitously, and many equally winding side roads are pocked with potholes. There are no traffic lights, but there are a few zebra pedestrian crossings; beware wandering pigs and goats.

16

imported slaves to work the plantations. The Gaelic influence lingers in place and family names, folklore, jigs, and even a wispy brogue.

The island's captivating beauty, low profile, and difficult access made it a hip destination in the 1970s and '80s. Sir George Martin (The Beatles' manager) founded Air Studios in 1979, luring icons such as Eric Clapton, Sir Paul McCartney, and Stevie Wonder to record. Destroyed by Hurricane Hugo in 1989, it was never rebuilt. But locals and expats alike still like a good band. The combined Carnival and Christmas festivities go on for nearly a month, when the island is awash with color, from calypso competitions to parades and pageants.

Other than the volcano, the steamiest activities are the fiercely contested domino games outside rum shops. That may soon change. The government speaks optimistically of building a new golf course, developing spa facilities to offer volcanic mud baths, even running tours—pending safety assessments—of Plymouth as a haunting Caribbean answer to Pompeii. An airport was constructed, partly in the hope of recapturing the villa crowd that once frequented the island. But these developments—as well as debates over the new capital and threatened lawsuits against the British government for restricting access and utility service to homesites—will simmer for quite some time. One thing won't change: the people, whether native-born or expat, are among the warmest anywhere. Chat them up, and don't be surprised if you're invited to a family dinner or beach picnic.

PLANNING

WHEN TO GO

The year's big event is **St. Patrick's Day,** which ushers in a week of festivities, highlighted by musical concerts and masquerades à la Carnival. **Tourism Week,** usually late September or early October, encourages village competitions in music, dance, crafts, and food.

Late October's **Police, Fire, Search, and Rescue Services Community Week** also explodes with sound and color, as jump-ups, concerts, and barbecues lure hundreds of revelers. Mid-December into the New Year sees **Christmas festival celebrations,** from Calypso competitions to pageants and parades.

GETTING HERE AND AROUND

AIR TRAVEL

There are nonstop flights to Antigua, where you can transfer to a Fly-Montserrat flight (most departures are scheduled to coincide with the international flight schedule) into the John A. Osborne Airport (MNI) in Geralds. ABM Air, a sister carrier of well-known SVG Air, offers flights from Antigua.

Airline Contacts ABM Air. A fairly new service and subsidiary of SVG Air, ABM flies twice daily between Antigua and Montserrat. ☎ 268 ⊕ www.abm-air.com.

FlyMontserrat. FlyMontserrat offers twice-daily flights from Antigua on nine-seat Britten Norman Islanders, and charter service to and from other destinations. ☎ 664/491–3434 ⊕ www.flymontserrat.com.

Winair. Winair has discontinued service from Antigua. ☎ 664/491–6988, 664/491–6030, 888/255–6889 in U.S. ⊕ www.fly-winair.com.

CAR TRAVEL

Temporary driver's licenses are available for $20 at the police headquarters in Brades, which is open 24 hours weekdays. You can rent jeeps and cars for roughly $30–$50 per day. Even if you rent a car, you're best off hiring a local guide, who will know where the best views are—and which parts of the island are off-limits because of volcanic activity. Respect the signs and closed gates that indicate the Exclusion Zone boundaries; though the Daytime Entry Zone is usually open 24/7, you should avoid it at night.

Car Rental Contacts Jefferson Car Rental ⊠ Palm Loop ☎ 664/491–2126. **Montserrat Enterprises** ⊠ Old Towne ☎ 664/491–2431. **Neville Bradshaw Agencies** ⊠ Olveston ☎ 664/491–5270.

FERRY TRAVEL

There's year-round ferry service between Little Bay and Antigua's Deep Water Harbour in St. John's, though the schedule changes constantly and has halted abruptly in the past. The two-hour-long trip takes place Wednesday–Saturday on the 127-passenger *Caribe Queen.* The fare is EC$150 each way. Call Ferry Agent Roosevelt Jemmotte (☎ 664/496–9912) on Montserrat and Jennifer Burke (☎ 268/788–9786) on Antigua for more info.

Carib World Travel ⊠ Antigua ☎ 268/480–2999 ⊕ caribworldtravel.com.

TAXI TRAVEL

Taxis don't have meters. Rates are fixed, and drivers can often serve as a useful guide. Many have set rates for this service.

ESSENTIALS

Banks and Exchange Services Local currency is the Eastern Caribbean dollar (EC$). US$1 is worth approximately EC$2.70. American dollars are readily accepted, although you usually receive change in EC$. If you decide to change money, you will get a slightly better exchange rate if you change your money in a bank than at your hotel (the exchange is sometimes rounded down to EC$2.50 in simpler transactions). Major credit cards are widely accepted. ATMs (dispensing EC$) are available at the Royal Bank of Canada and the Bank of Montserrat.

Electricity 220 volts, 50 to 60 cycles, but most lodgings also use 110 volts, permitting use of small North American appliances such as electric shavers. Outlets may be either two- or three-pronged, so bring an adapter.

Emergency Services Ambulance ☎ *411, 664/491–2802.* **Fire** ☎ *911.* **Glendon Hospital** ✉ *St. John's* ☎ *664/491–2552, 664/491–7404.* **Police** ☎ *999.*

Passport Requirements All visitors need a valid passport. All visitors must present a return or ongoing ticket.

Phones To place a local call, simply dial the local seven-digit number. To call Montserrat from the United States, dial 1 + 664 + the local seven-digit number. To call the United States and Canada, dial 1 + the area code + the seven-digit number. LIME phone cards are available at most hotels and post offices if you want to make an international call. LIME provides the island's cell-phone service.

Taxes and Service Charges The departure–airport-security tax is $21—cash only. Day-trippers from Antigua spending less than 24 hours on Montserrat pay only an EC$10 "security charge" and no departure tax on Antigua. Hotels collect a 10% government room tax, guesthouses and villas 7%. Hotels and restaurants also usually add a 10% service charge to your bill.

Tipping In restaurants, it's customary to leave 5% beyond the regular service charge added to your bill if you're pleased with the service. Taxi drivers expect a 10% tip; porters and bellmen, about $1 per bag; maids are not often tipped, but if you do, leave $2 to $3 per night.

ACCOMMODATIONS

With a few small guesthouses, villas, and one small hotel, Montserrat has no large-scale development. The island's best hotel, Vue Point, is likely permanently closed at this writing because of continued volcanic activity.

HOTEL AND RESTAURANT PRICES

Prices in the restaurant reviews are the average cost of a main course at dinner or, if dinner is not served, at lunch; taxes and service charges are generally included. Prices in the hotel reviews are the lowest cost of a standard double room in high season, excluding taxes, service charges, and meal plans (except at all-inclusives). Prices for rentals are the lowest per-night cost for a one-bedroom unit in high season.

VISITOR INFORMATION

Contact Montserrat Tourist Board. The Montserrat Tourist Board keeps track of accommodations, restaurants, activities, car-rental agencies, and tours available on the island and will prove to be an invaluable resource if you decide to plan a trip to Montserrat. ⊠ *7 Farara Pl., Bldgs. B & C, Brades* ☏ *664/491–2230* ⊕ *www.visitmontserrat.com* ⊠ *Montserrat Government Office, 180 King's Cross Rd., London, U.K.* ☏ *0207/031–0317.*

WEDDINGS

Getting married on Montserrat is relatively easy. No blood test required. For adults 18 years and over, the minimum residency is three days. Apply for a special or Governor's marriage license at the Department of Administration either via mail or in person between 8 am and 4 pm weekdays. Bring valid passports as proof of citizenship and, in the case of previous marriages, the original divorce or annulment decree; widows or widowers should present the original marriage and death certificates. Given the lack of on-island wedding planners and difficulty in transportation, most visitors choose to get married on Antigua and then take a honeymoon trip to Montserrat, and that's a good idea, because it will certainly allow you to spend some quiet time together.

Contact Department of Administration. You can reach the Department of Administration either via mail or in person between 8 am and 4 pm weekdays. ☏ *664/491–2365.*

EXPLORING MONTSERRAT

Though the more fertile—and historic—southern half of Montserrat was destroyed by the volcano, emerald hills still reward explorers. Hiking and biking are the best ways to experience this island's unspoiled rain forest, glistening black-sand beaches, and lookouts over the devastation.

The Cot. A fairly strenuous Centre Hills trail leads to one of Montserrat's few remaining historic sites—the ruins of the once-influential Sturges family's summer cottage—as well as a banana plantation. Its Duck Pond Hill perch, farther up the trail, dramatically overlooks the coastline, Garibaldi Hill, Old Towne, abandoned villages, and Plymouth. .

Jack Boy Viewing Facility. This vantage point—replete with telescope, barbecue grill and tables for picnickers, landscaped grounds, and washrooms—provides bird's-eye views of the old W.H. Bramble airport and eastern villages damaged by pyroclastic flows. ⊠ *Jack Boy Hill.*

★ **Montserrat National Trust.** The MNT's Natural History Centre aims to conserve and enhance the island's natural beauty and cultural heritage. The center has permanent and rotating exhibits on Arawak canoe building, colonial sugar and lime production (the term limey was first applied here to English sailors trying to avoid scurvy), indigenous marine life, West Indian cricket, the annual Calabash Festival, and the history of Sir George Martin's Air Studios, which once lured top musicians from Dire Straits to Stevie Wonder and Paul McCartney. Eventually one archival exhibit will screen videos of Montserrat's oral history related by its oldest inhabitants. The lovingly tended botanical gardens in back make for a pleasant stroll. It may occupy new headquarters in Little Bay by 2013; funding has been slow. ☒ *Main Road, Olveston* ☎ *664/491–3086* ⊕ *www.visitmontserrat.com/National_Trust* ☜ *$2 suggested donation* ⊙ *Weekdays 10–4.*

Montserrat Volcano Observatory. The island's must-see sight occupies capacious, strikingly postmodern quarters with stunning vistas of the Soufrière Hills volcano—a lunarscape encircled by brilliant green—and Plymouth in the distance. Unfortunately, the MVO staff no longer offers tours that explain monitoring techniques on sophisticated computerized equipment in riveting detail. But you can see graphic photos, artifacts like rock and ash, and diagrams that describe the various pyroclastic surge deposits. The Interpretation Center screens a high-impact film with IMAX footage, and interactive kiosks include working seismometers (kids can jump up and down to manufacture vibrations), and other real-time monitoring instruments. ☒ *Flemings* ☎ *664/491–5647* ⊕ *www.mvo.ms* ☜ *Observatory free, tours $4* ⊙ *Weekdays 8:30–4:30. Self-guided tours Mon.–Thurs. 10:15–4.*

NEED A BREAK?

D&D Bar and Grocery. D&D Bar and Grocery is an unprepossessing shack, just downhill off the first right turn from the MVO. Owner Dawn Davis mastered mixology while working at Nisbet Plantation on Nevis, and she proudly offers more than 30 libations at her Lilliputian bar (and accepts challenges). She also bakes sublime bread and serves delectable, cheap local fare—souse, fishwater (fish soup), macaroni pie, baked chicken—on weekdays, and just heavenly fried chicken for Saturday lunch. ☒ *Flemings* ☎ *664/491–9730.*

16

Plymouth. Montserrat's former capital has been off-limits to general tourists because of volcanic activity since the May 2006 dome collapse. Before that, the adventuresome could stroll its streets, albeit at their own risk; check with the police department to see if the situation has changed again. Once one of the Caribbean's loveliest towns, facing the vividly hued sea, it now resembles a dust-covered lunarscape, with elegant Georgian buildings buried beneath several feet of ash, mud, and rubble (though rain is slowly washing layers away). Entry is officially possible only with a police escort (lest you fall through a rickety roof), but can be arranged with the police headquarters in Brades only when approved by the Volcano Observatory. A hazard allowance of EC$150 is charged per individual or group. ☒ *Plymouth* ☎ *664/491–2230 for Montserrat Tourist Board* ☜ *Police escort EC$150* ⊙ *Daily during daylight hrs with police escort.*

Runaway Ghaut. Montserrat's *ghauts* (pronounced guts) are deep ravines that carry rainwater down from the mountains to the sea. This natural spring, a short, well-marked walk into the hilly bush outside Woodlands, was the site of bloody colonial skirmishes between the British and French. The legend is more interesting than the trail: "Those that drink its water clear they spellbound are, and the Montserrat call they must obey." If you don't want to hike or picnic, a drink from the roadside faucet should ensure that you return to Montserrat in your lifetime. ⊠ *Main Road, just south of Woodlands.*

St. George's Hill. The only access to this incredible vantage point over the devastation is across the Belham Valley, through a once-beautiful golf course now totally covered by volcanic mudflow. The area is sometimes reinstated in the Daytime Entry Zone when decreased volcanic activity permits. If it's accessible on your visit, be aware that routes aren't signposted on the rough road, which is often impassable after heavy rains, so it's best to hire an experienced guide. You'll drive through Cork Hill and Weekes, villages for the most part spookily intact (there's no way to provide utilities, though some enterprising souls are slowly installing solar power and water cisterns). Close to the summit, the equally eerie, abandoned, stark-white wind-generator project and the giant satellite dishes of the Gem and Antilles radio stations resemble abstract-art installations awaiting completion by Christo. At the top, Ft. St. George contains sparse ruins, including a few cannons, but the overwhelming sight is the panorama of destruction, an unrelenting swath of gray offset by vivid emerald fields and the turquoise Caribbean. ⊠ *St. George's Hill* ⊙ *Daylight hrs when open.*

BEACHES

Montserrat's beaches are public and, with one exception, composed of soft, light- to dark-gray volcanic sand.

Little Bay. Boats chug in and out of the port at the northern end of this otherwise comely crescent with calm waters. Several beach bars—Green Monkey, Pont's (fine cheap local lunch Tuesday–Sunday), Soca Cabana, Seaside and Sylvia's—provide cool shade and cooler drinks. Carlton's Fish Net Bar specializes in barbecued stuffed trunkfish (a shellfish delicacy). You may see locals casting lines for their own dinner. ⊠ *Approximately 1½ miles (2½ km) north of Brades off main road; look for turnoffs to Little Bay.*

★ **Rendezvous Bay.** The island's sole white-sand beach is a perfect cove tucked under a forested cliff whose calm, unspoiled waters are ideal for swimming and offer remarkable snorkeling. It's accessible only via the sea or a steep trail that runs over the bluff to adjacent Little Bay (you can also negotiate boat rides from the fishermen who congregate there). There are no facilities or shade, but its very remoteness and pristine reef teeming with marine life lend it exceptional charm. ⊠ *Rendezvous Bay.*

Woodlands. The only drawback to this secluded strand is the occasionally rough surf (children should be closely monitored). The breezy but covered picnic area on the cliff is one of the best vantage points to watch migratory humpback whales in spring and nesting green and hawksbill turtles in early fall. From here you can hike north, then down across a wooden bridge to even less trammeled Bunkum Bay, which has a friendly guesthouse and beach bar. ⊠ *At turnoff just outside Woodlands Village.*

WHERE TO EAT

Restaurants are casual affairs indeed, ranging from glorified rum shops to hotel dining rooms. Most serve classic Caribbean fare, including such specialties as goat water (a thick stew of goat meat, tubers, and vegetables that seems to have been bubbling for days), salt fish cake (codfish fritters), home-brewed ginger beer, and freshly made juices from soursop, mango, blackberry (different from the North American species), guava, tamarind, papaya, and gooseberry.

What to Wear: Dress is informal even at dinner, though skimpy attire is frowned upon by the comparatively conservative islanders. Long pants are preferred, albeit not required, for men in the evening.

$$
ECLECTIC

✕ **Gourmet Gardens.** This tranquil, secluded spot—a classic gingerbread chattel-house replica echoing the adjacent historic buildings of the former Olveston estate—fulfills more than half the name's promise. There are few more delightful experiences than relaxing on Mariet's verandah amid a virtual botanical garden or beneath the huge, shady tamarind tree. Lunches are excellent value, but Sunday brunch is the winner (scrumptious eggs Benedict). "Gourmet" is a slight exaggeration, but the all-homemade global menu more than satisfies most palates and wallets. Specialties include stroganoff, chicken cordon bleu, Wiener schnitzel, shrimp stir-fry, and any dessert (try the chocolate mousse or cheesecake). ⑤ *Average main: $16* ☒ *Olveston* ☎ *664/491–7859* ⌂ *Reservations essential* ▭ *No credit cards.*

$$
ECLECTIC

✕ **Olveston House.** Five different rums power the knockout Olveston Rum Punch, but it's also the animated chatter of island locals, expats, and international guests that generates its own potent buzz. Picture windows overlook the handsome veranda and gardens at this popular eatery. Chef Margaret Wilson creatively uses whatever ingredients are available. You might tuck into fresh wahoo in orange-ginger sauce, scrumptious garlic shrimp, lasagna, pork tenderloin glazed with homemade preserves, or flaky, flavorful chicken-and-mushroom, pork, and steak-and-kidney pies that elevate traditional English pub grub to an art form. And the sublime sticky toffee pudding, mango-ginger crumble, and pear tart justify Margaret's declaration, "I'd rather make desserts than clean the house," though daughter Sarah's lush, luscious cheesecakes (mango, chocolate hazelnut) are also winners. The sailing etchings, period cabinets with mismatched china, and serenading tree frogs create the ambience of dining at someone's country estate, Caribbean-style. Wednesday barbecue, Friday Pub Night, and Sunday classic English brunch are casual and cheap, with no reservations required. ⑤ *Average main: $18* ☒ *Olveston* ☎ *664/491–5210, 664/495–5210* ⊕ *www.olvestonhouse.com* ⌂ *Reservations essential* ☾ *Closed Jan., Mon., and dinner Sun.*

$$$
ECLECTIC
★

✕ **Royal Palm Club.** This gem feels like an update on a colonial Maugham tale, down to the eccentric expats, rumors of royal visits, and wildly eclectic yet elegant decor. Though it technically operates as a "private membership club," anyone can call for reservations. The gingerbread-trim house, swallowed up in elaborate gardens, reputedly hosted Queen Elizabeth II and Princess Margaret during their 1962 trip. The interior

16

features a marvelous mosaic bar (casual wine-and-pasta or pizza dinners are served here and at the downstairs poolside bar), stone walls, hardwood floors, stained glass, Turkish throw rugs, Indonesian kites, and 17th-century French sideboards. The enclosed patio, doubling as the main dining room, enchants with sweeping Caribbean views and fluttering butterflies. There are special evenings, such as the all-you-can-eat Italian and Chinese buffets and Tuesday film screenings. Four-course set-dinner menu choices might include garlic shrimp over linguine in a light Parmesan-cream sauce or slow-roasted pork tenderloin in orange-marmalade sauce. The peripatetic co-owners include the delightful Trevor Stephenson, who will regale you with his "lifestyles of the poor and infamous" anecdotes. $ *Average main: $26* ⊠ *Woodlands* ☎ *664/491–2671* ⊕ *www.montserratroyalpalmclubinn.com* ⚑ *Reservations essential* ▭ *No credit cards* ⊘ *Closed Mon. No lunch Tues.– Sat.; no dinner Sun.*

$$
CARIBBEAN

✕**Tina's.** This pretty, coral-and-white wooden building is garlanded year-round with Christmas lights, a harbinger of the good vibes within. It's the best place to eavesdrop on island gossip, as government functionaries file in for lunch (at least when day-trippers don't take over). Dine either in a trim room or on a breezy veranda (admittedly sans view). Occasionally you'll find old-time dishes like souse, but the menu is generally more upscale: specialties include velvety pumpkin soup, proper escargots, and tender lobster in sultry creole sauce or (even better) tangy garlic sauce; entrées are served with heaping helpings of salads and sides. Fine desserts (moist carrot cake, cheesecake, and wonderfully textured coconut pie) end the meal, and surprisingly good take-out pizza is available. $ *Average main: $18* ⊠ *Brades* ☎ *664/491–3538* ▭ *No credit cards* ⊘ *Closed Sun.*

$$$
ECLECTIC

✕**Ziggy's.** Vivacious owners John and Marcia Punter literally hacked Montserrat's most elegant eatery from the rain forest. They poured a concrete floor and dressed it with a billowing, white, rectangular tent, pergolas, palm fronds, potted plants, hardwood chairs, jade hurricane shutters, bronze sculpted candlesticks, and colorful Moroccan-inspired table settings: the ultimate in shack chic. The menu (posted on a blackboard) changes daily, but always offers one red meat, one white meat, and one seafood entrée. Generally well-executed dishes lean more toward bistro fare (emphasizing beef entrecote or goat cheese soufflé over such island staples as chicken and fish, though specials like oxtail ravioli happily marry both culinary traditions); the signature butterfly shrimp usually precede entrées. A decent wine list enhances the meal; save room for the Chocolate Sludge. Though the schedule is erratic (reconfirm reservations), the location hard to find, and the service too relaxed, the ambience is appealingly serene and upscale. $ *Average main: $28* ⊠ *Mahogany La., Woodlands* ☎ *664/491–8282* ⊕ *www. ziggysrestaurant.com* ⚑ *Reservations essential* ⊘ *No lunch.*

WHERE TO STAY

Currently, the island primarily offers villas (housekeepers and cooks can be arranged) or guesthouses, the latter often incorporating meals in the rate by request (ask if the 7% tax and 10% service charge are included), and there is one small hotel. Note that inns rarely have air-conditioning, relying instead on hillside breezes.

For expanded reviews, facilities, and current deals, visit Fodors.com.

PRIVATE VILLA RENTALS

In the prevolcano (and pre–Hurricane Hugo) days, when an international roster of celebrity musicians (Elton to Eric, the Rolling Stones to Sting) recorded at Sir George Martin's Air Studios, Montserrat was a favored spot for many rich and famous Britons (and the occasional American) to vacation. Today you can luxuriate in one of the handsome villas they called home when visiting and do so for comparatively affordable rates.

Tradewinds Real Estate. The leading villa rental company in Montserrat is Tradewinds Real Estate. Many of its 20-plus deluxe properties, ranging from one to four bedrooms, have plunge pools, amazing water vistas, and ultramodern conveniences from DVD players and Internet access to gourmet kitchens. Recommended properties with beach access and/or strategic hillside locations include Mango Falls, Woodlands Estate (a restored arrowroot factory), Cythera, Mango Pointe (owned by the former drummer of The Turtles), and Villa Pimenta. Caring owner Susan Edgecombe really tries to match guest to villa, remaining available throughout your stay to make any additional arrangements and offer touring and activity suggestions; she'll keep you updated back home with her informative newsletter. Rates run from $700 to $2,800 per week in high season. ⊠ *Main Rd., Olveston* ☎ *664/491–2004* ⊕ *www.tradewindsmontserrat.com.*

Montserrat Enterprises. Another recommended option, in business since 1962, is Montserrat Enterprises. Its inventory is generally smaller, but most of its properties offer splendid views and amenities. ⊠ *Bishop's View Rd., Old Towne* ☎ *664/491–2431* ⊕ *www.montserratenterprises.com.*

RECOMMENDED HOTELS AND INNS

$

B&B/INN

★

Erindell Villa Guesthouse. This tranquil rain-forest retreat is a photo album in the making, overflowing with character and characters. **Pros:** engaging owners; beautiful landscaping; fun makeshift entertainment; abundant freebies. **Cons:** hike to beach; occasionally raucous fun makeshift entertainment; occasional ash dustings. **TripAdvisor:** "excellent accommodations," "super people," "what a wonderful place." ⑤ *Rooms from: $75* ⊠ *Gros Michel Dr., Woodlands* ☎ *664/491–3655* ⊕ *www.erindellvilla.com* ⇱ *2 rooms* ═ *No credit cards* ⦿| *Breakfast.*

$

HOTEL

★

Gingerbread Hill. This secluded mountainside retreat offers remarkable value, splendid views, utter tranquillity, and exquisite grounds, where in-season you can pluck your breakfast straight from the mango, banana, citrus, papaya, and coconut trees. **Pros:** environmentally conscious; superb value; fascinating owners; delightful menagerie, including birds; constant refurbishment; access to washer/dryer. **Cons:** car necessary; no

16

beachfront; perhaps too "granola" for some. **TripAdvisor:** "run by a very nice family," "breathtaking sunsets," "serenity and peace." ⑤ *Rooms from: $45* ✉ *St. Peter's* ☎ *664/491–5812, 813/774–5270* ⊕ *www. volcano-island.com* ⟳ *2 rooms, 2 villas, 1 cottage* ⑩ *No meals.*

$

B&B/INN

⊡ **Grand View Bed & Breakfast.** This welcoming inn's basement holds a radio station, but contented guests send the most powerful signal thanks to energetic dynamo Theresa Silcott, who prides herself on being Montserrat's top hostess. **Pros:** splendid sweeping views; delightful gardens; congenial hostess; excellent local food (ask about medicinal folklore) by reservation. **Cons:** no pool or beachfront; very basic if clean rooms. ⑤ *Rooms from: $40* ✉ *Baker Hill* ☎ *664/491–2284* ⊕ *www. mnigrandview.com* ⟳ *2 suites, 5 rooms* ▤ *No credit cards* ⑩ *Breakfast.*

$

HOTEL

★

⊡ **Olveston House.** This 1950s villa, rented to island hotelier Carol Osborne by Beatles producer Sir George Martin, brims with history (including the owner's fabled Air Studios where Sting, Elton John, Eric Clapton, and Paul McCartney recorded). **Pros:** incredible value; gorgeous pool; glorious views of the glowing Soufrière; invigorating blend of locals, expats, and guests at the bar and dining room. **Cons:** no beach; occasional dusting of ash; Wi-Fi spotty. **TripAdvisor:** "the only place to stay in Montserrat," "Beatles connection," "charming house and staff." ⑤ *Rooms from: $119* ✉ *Olveston* ☎ *664/491–5210, 664/495–5210* ⊕ *www.olvestonhouse.com* ⟳ *6 rooms* ⊘ *Closed Jan.* ⑩ *Breakfast.*

$$

HOTEL

⊡ **Tropical Mansion Suites.** Despite the grandiose name, this is little more than a motel with neocolonial architectural pretensions and clean, spacious rooms. **Pros:** currently the island's only full-service lodging; centrally located. **Cons:** far from beaches; extra charge for air-conditioning; mediocre and comparatively pricey food. **TripAdvisor:** "excellent staff and property," "great accommodations," "awesome vacation spot." ⑤ *Rooms from: $129* ✉ *Main Rd., Sweeney's* ☎ *664/491–8767* ⊕ *www. tropicalmansion.com* ⟳ *17 rooms, 1 suite* ⑩ *Breakfast.*

NIGHTLIFE AND THE ARTS

Although Montserrat is better known for another kind of wildlife, Friday-night revelers lime in roadside rum shops scattered around the island, often spilling out on the street as part of the informal evening culture. There's no closing time, and many bars serve yummy, authentic local food. Little Bay is being developed as the island capital (the government will remain in Brades); in season the Hot Spot is a collection of a dozen watering holes between the "town" and Cultural Center; Festival City is another gathering of bars.

Club Paradise. Club Paradise is a surprisingly hip, retro-'70s nightspot, right down to the fog machine, strobe lights, and disco balls. The beat is decidedly au courant, with DJs spinning the latest soca to techno, as well as golden oldies. There's a splendid breezy patio and an intriguing mural of local scenes that curls around the bar. ✉ *Hilltop, Fogarty Hill* ☎ *664/496–4152, 664/496–1842* ▤ *EC$10* ⊘ *Open Fri.–Sun.*

Harriet Pease. In season, artist Harriet Pease runs a rollicking "Rumshop Tour" of three to four truly local watering holes where you can lime, drink, and play spirited dominoes. ☎ *664/491–7156.*

Garry Moore's Wide Awake Bar. Garry Moore's Wide Awake Bar is a perennial favorite that doesn't close as long as customers are thirsty. Don't be afraid to wake Garry to pay your tab: he often naps at the bar (when he isn't complaining—mostly humorously—about a plumber's hard life and long hours). ⊠ *Salem* ☎ *664/491–7156.*

Howe's Rum Shop. Howe's Rum Shop is the best spot for shooting pool and the breeze; get here early for luscious fried and barbecued chicken, liberally daubed with mouth- and eye-watering homemade sauces and seasonings. ⊠ *St. John's* ☎ *664/491–3008.*

Soca Cabana. Soca Cabana offers live Caribbean beats, as the name implies. But expat owner Tom Walker is passionate about the island's musical heritage, including the halcyon days of Air Studios. He salvaged the "Bar of the Stars" from Sir George Martin's celebrated recording space. It's a delightful liming spot, with the bamboo bar and white-washed patio accented in mint and turquoise overlooking the beach. Seemingly half the island descends on the hot spot Sunday for meals, music, and merriment. Karaoke Saturdays also reel partiers in. ⊠ *Little Bay* ☎ *664/492–1677* ⊕ *www.socacabana.com* ⊠ *Admission varies* ⊙ *Open for lunch daily; live music and dinner Wed., Fri., and Sat. nights; dinner Sun.*

Treasure Spot. Lydia, the owner of the newly refurbished Treasure Spot, often books the island's up-and-coming musicians (usually One Man Band but also Pops Morris, Hero, and Basil—reggae and soca artists beginning to develop a reputation outside Montserrat) to play weekends. ⊠ *Cudjoe Head* ☎ *664/493–2003.*

Montserrat Cultural Centre. Eight years in development, the impressive, colonnaded Montserrat Cultural Centre and its 500-seat, state-of-the-art Sir George Martin Auditorium present craft demonstrations, folkloric and fashion shows, pageants, movies (with popcorn and hot dogs), and the occasional dance and theatrical performance. During intermission, check out the Wall of Fame (bronzed handprints of musicians who recorded or performed on Montserrat, such as Sir Paul McCartney, Sir Elton John, and Mark Knopfler). Check with the tourist board or local newspaper listings for the current schedule. ⊠ *Little Bay* ☎ *664/491–4242, 664/491–4700* ⊕ *themontserratculturalcentre.com.*

SHOPPING

Montserrat offers a variety of local crafts and does a brisk trade in vulcanology mementos (many shops sell not only postcards and striking photographs but also small bottles of gray ash capped by colorful, homemade cloth).

David Lea. David Lea has chronicled Montserrat's volcanic movements in a fascinating eight-part video–DVD series, *The Price of Paradise*, each entry a compelling glimpse into the geological and social devastation—and regeneration. These, as well as rollicking local-music CDs by his son and other musicians, are available at his studio. ⊠ *Gingerbread Hill, St. Peter's* ☎ *664/491–5812* ⊕ *www.volcano-island.com.*

16

Last Chance Souvenir Shop. Last Chance Souvenir Shop is a terrific last-minute stop for high-quality local arts and crafts, such as photos, ceramics, painted gourds, and treats such as Volcano Rum. They also sell low-priced souvenirs. ⊠ *John A. Osborne Airport, Gerald's* ☎ *664/491–2752.*

Luv's Cotton Store. Luv's Cotton Store is the best source for sportswear made from sea island cotton, celebrated for its softness and high quality. ⊠ *Salem* ☎ *664/491–3906.*

Montserrat Philatelic Bureau. Also occupying the National Trust building, the Montserrat Philatelic Bureau sells a wealth of unusual stamps, including handsome first-day covers. ⊠ *Salem* ☎ *664/491–2042, 664/491–2996.*

Oriole Gift Shop. Oriole Gift Shop, run by the Montserrat National Trust, is an excellent source for books on Montserrat (look for the *Montserrat Cookbook* and works by the island's former acting governor, Sir Howard Fergus), as well as trail maps, handicrafts (wonderful dolls, hand-painted boxes, and calabash purses) and locally made food products. ⊠ *Salem* ☎ *664/491–3086.*

Woolcock's Craft & Photo Gallery. Woolcock's Craft & Photo Gallery promotes the work of local artists such as Donaldson Romeo and sells spectacular photos of the volcano as well as of indigenous birds and other wildlife. ⊠ *BBC Bldg., Brades* ☎ *664/491–2025.*

SPORTS AND ACTIVITIES

BIKING

Mountain biking is making a comeback, with a wide network of trails through the lush Centre Hills. Bikes are also a wonderful way to explore the island and enjoy the lovely coastal vistas along the main road.

Gingerbread Hill. Ecocentric expats David and Clover Lea rent state-of-the-art equipment from Cygnal and Mongoose ($15 to $20 per day) out of Gingerbread Hill. ⊠ *St. Peter's* ☎ *664/491–5812.*

DIVING

More than 30 practically pristine dive sites surround Montserrat. The even more bountiful marine life has had time to recover from the predations of human activities, and the pyroclastic flows formed boulders, pinnacles, ledges, and walls that anchor new coral reefs. **Carr's Bay** is a favorite for shore dives, with arrow crabs, basket stars, turtles, and shimmering blue tang darting about hulking boulders and a small, colorful cave; night dives are particularly memorable, as millions of bioluminescent microorganisms glow when disturbed. The shallow reefs surrounding **Woodlands Bay** feature varied underwater topography, including a small, colorful cave and thousands of banded coral shrimp, copper sweepers, sergeant majors, four-eyed butterfly fish, jackknife, attenuated trumpetfish, and turtles. **Rendezvous Bay** may be the finest spot for both snorkeling and diving, thanks to a sheltered reef and lack of ash or silt. You come face-to-face with spotted morays, porcupine fish, snake eels, octopuses, and more. You can even hang out with thousands of (harmless) fruit bats in partly submerged caves. Other top dive sites include **Lime Kiln Bay** and **Bunkum Bay,** as well as the spectacular submarine rock formations around **Little Redonda** and the **Pinnacles** off the rougher, more challenging northeastern shores.

Green Monkey Dive Shop. The Green Monkey Dive Shop offers PADI certification, snorkeling trips, and a variety of dives. Scuba Master Troy Depperman customizes trips for clients' interests and skill levels. The most intriguing regular option is Dive Redonda, a tour of the island "Kingdom of Redonda" 15 mi (24 km) northwest of Montserrat. The 45-minute boat ride offers scintillating views of the coast and Soufrière Hills volcano. Once there, underwater attractions include leviathan southern stingrays, morays, turtles, nurse sharks, and barracudas cruising around 6-foot barrel sponges and darting in and out of the caves and coral-encrusted barge at the "World's End" on the island's northernmost point. It also runs nature hikes, coastal kayak tours (and rentals), and ecotours. ⊠ *Little Bay* ☎ *664/491–2628, 664/491–2960, 664/496–3483* ⊕ *www.divemontserrat.com.*

☾ **Scuba Montserrat.** Andrew Myers and Emmy Aston of Scuba Montserrat provide experienced PADI certification; lengthy shore, boat, and kayak dives; snorkeling excursions (including a stop at a very cool bat cave); specialty courses from drift diving to digital underwater photography; and down the road the possibility of helping regenerate volcano-damaged sites. They're particularly family focused, stocking underwater Frisbees, torpedoes, and specialized children's gear. ⊠ *Little Bay* ☎ *664/496–7807* ⊕ *www.scubamontserrat.com.*

FISHING

Danny Sweeney. Deep-sea fishing (wahoo, bonito, shark, marlin, and yellowfin tuna) is superb, since the waters aren't disturbed by leviathan cruise ships. Affable Danny Sweeney has won several regional tournaments, including Montserrat's Open Fishing Competition. Half-day charters (up to four people) are $300. Though schools of game fish amazingly cavort just 2 to 3 miles (3 to 5 km) offshore, Danny's depth sounder picks up action in deeper waters. An extra bonus on the open sea is the gripping views of the volcanic devastation. ⊠ *Olveston* ☎ *664/491–5645.*

GUIDED TOURS

Avalon Tours. Joe "Fergus" Phillip, who operates Avalon Tours, often emails updates on Montserrat to visitors. ⊠ *Manjack* ☎ *664/491–3432, 664/492–1565* ✎ *joephillip@live.com.*

Furlonge Taxi & Tours. Reuben Furlonge of Furlonge Taxi & Tours is another hardy helpful local (and a "goat water specialist"; you may be stopped along the way by locals inquiring if he's made a batch). All the staff here are friendly, knowledgeable, and reliable taxi and tour drivers. ⊠ *Gerald's* ☎ *664/491–4376, 664/492–2790.*

16

HIKING

Montserrat's lush, untrammeled rain forest teeming with exotic flora, fauna, and birdlife is best experienced on foot. The tourist office provides lists of hiking trails, from easy to arduous. The most dramatic routes are gradually being upgraded as part of the Montserrat Tourism Development Project; in addition to improving their definition, the government will also be building viewing platforms and providing interpretative information at strategic points. Still, if you're not experienced or fit, go with a guide; always wear sturdy shoes and bring water. Most marked trails run through the biologically diverse, scenic Centre Hills region, offering stirring lookouts over the volcano's barren flanks, surrounding greenery, and ash-covered villages in the Exclusion Zone. The rain forest is home to many regionally endemic wildlife species (tree frogs, dwarf geckos, anoles, mountain chicken—actually a type of frog—and the half-snake-half-lizard galliwasp), as well as most of the 34 resident birds, from red-billed tropic birds to the rare national bird, the Montserrat oriole, with its distinctive orange-and-black plumage. The Silver Hills in the north are vastly different, with dry and deciduous forests and open plains blanketing a defunct, heavily faulted and eroded volcano; views here might provide a glimpse of how southern Montserrat will look millions of years from now.

Scriber's Adventure Tours. Scriber's Adventure Tours is run by James "Scriber" Daley ("a describer since I was little"), an employee of the Agricultural Department legendary for his uncanny birdcalls. He leads nature hikes through the rain forest for $20 to $40; he'll hire additional guides if there are more than 10 people per group, ensuring personal attention. Scriber also explains indigenous flora, from 42 fern species (kids love when he "tattoos" them with silver fern leaves) to others prized for medicinal properties (you might collect the makings of bush tea for back pain or menstrual cramps). He also conducts a memorable, if brief, evening mountain-chicken tour, distributing flashlights to find the foot-long frogs. ☎ 664/491–2546, 664/491–3412, 664/492–2943.

Puerto Rico

WORD OF MOUTH

"My husband and I just returned from celebrating our belated 10-year anniversary in Puerto Rico. We did not know what to expect but wanted somewhere with consistently nice weather and a direct flight from Washington, D.C. We absolutely loved it—the weather was perfect and it was a great mix of beach and urban for us."

—MILLERSU

WELCOME TO PUERTO RICO

KEY

- 🏖 Beaches
- ⛴ Ferry
- 🔢 Restaurants
- 🏨 Hotels
- 🌴 Rain Forrest

Restaurants ▼		
Archipiélago	10	
Cabuqui	11	
Calizo	1	
Conuco	7	
El Ancla	9	
El Bohío	16	
El Quenepo	8	
Juanita Bananas	4	
Mamacita's	3
Mix on the Beach	6
Pasión por el Fógon	2
Pool Bar Sushi	12
Restaurant Aaron	14
Rincón Tropical	13
Tamboo	15
Zaco's Tacos	5

Mother Spain is always a presence here—on a sun-dappled cobblestone street, in the shade of a colonial cathedral or fort. Yet multifaceted Puerto Rico pulses with New World energy. The rhythms of the streets are of Afro-Latin salsa and Bomba. And the U.S. flag flaps in the salty breezes wherever you go.

SPANISH AMERICAN

Puerto Rico is 110 mi (177 km) long and 35 mi (56 km) wide. With a population of almost 4 million, it's among the biggest Caribbean islands. The first Spanish governor was Juan Ponce de León in 1508; he founded Old San Juan in 1521. The United States won the island in the Spanish-American war in 1898 and made it a commonwealth in 1952.

Hotels ▼	Hacienda Tamarindo **6**	Mary Lee's by the Sea . **13**
Bravo Beach **10**	Hilton Ponce **11**	Rincón Beach Resort .. **15**
Casa Grande **23**	Horned Dorset Primavera **19**	Río Mar Beach Resort & Spa **1**
Casa Isleña **18**	Hotel Meliá **12**	St. Regis Bahia **3**
Club Seaborne **5**	Inn on the Blue Horizon **7**	Tres Sirenas **20**
Copamarina Beach Resort **14**	Lazy Parrot **17**	Villa del Mar Hau **22**
El Conquistador **4**	LemonTree **16**	Villa Montaña **21**
Gran Mélia Puerto Rico **2**	Malecón House **8**	W Retreat & Spa **9**

TOP REASONS TO VISIT PUERTO RICO

1 The Nightlife: Happening clubs and discos make San Juan one of the Caribbean's nightlife capitals, rivaling even Miami.

2 The Food: Great restaurants run the gamut from elegant places in San Juan to simple spots serving delicious *comida criolla*.

3 The Beaches: Both developed and wild, beaches here suit the needs of surfers, sunbathers, and families.

4 The Nature: Nature abounds, from the underground Río Camuy to El Yunque, the only Caribbean national forest.

PUERTO RICO BEACHES

With 365 different beaches in Puerto Rico, choosing where to spread out your towel might seem like a daunting task. The decision is easier now that four have been designated with a Blue Flag.

(Above) Playa Luquillo (Bottom right) Playa Luquillo (Top right) Playa Flamenco

Playa Flamenco, on the island of Culebra, made the cut. After all, it's rated one of the world's best beaches. More surprisingly, two of the beaches are in San Juan: Balneario Escambrón, in Puerta de Tierra, and Balneario Carolina, in Isla Verde. The fourth is Luquillo's Balneario Monserrate (Playa Luquillo). This means that three of Puerto Rico's finest beaches are within an hour's drive of the capital. In total the government maintains 13 *balnearios* (public beaches). They're gated and equipped with dressing rooms, lifeguards, parking, and, in some cases, picnic tables, playgrounds, and camping facilities.

BLUE FLAG

Chosen by the Foundation for Environmental Education, a nonprofit agency, Blue Flag beaches have to meet 27 criteria, focusing on water quality, the presence of a trained staff, and the availability of facilities such as water fountains and restrooms.

PUERTO RICO BEACHES

SAN JUAN

The city's beaches can get crowded, especially on weekends. There's free access to all of them, but parking can be an issue in the peak sun hours—arriving early or in the late afternoon is a safer bet.

Balneario de Carolina. When people talk of a "beautiful Isla Verde beach," this is the one they're talking about. A government-maintained beach, this *balneario* east of Isla Verde is so close to the airport that the leaves rustle when planes take off. The long stretch of sand, which runs parallel to Avenida Los Gobernadores, is shaded by palms and almond trees. There's plenty of room to spread out and lots of amenities: lifeguards, restrooms, changing facilities, picnic tables, and barbecue grills. ⊠ *Carolina* ⛱ *Parking $3* ⊙ *Daily 8–5.*

Balneario de Escambrón. In Puerta de Tierra, this government-run beach is just off Avenida Muñoz Rivera. The patch of honey-color sand is shaded by coconut palms and has surf that's generally gentle. Favored by families, it has lifeguards, bathhouses, bathrooms, and restaurants. ⊠ *Puerta de Tierra* ⛱ *Parking $4.28* ⊙ *Daily 6 am–7 pm.*

EASTERN PUERTO RICO

A long stretch of powdery sand near the Reserva Natural Las Cabezas de San

Juan, **Balneario Seven Seas** may turn out to be the best surprise of your trip. Facilities include picnic tables, changing areas, restrooms, and showers. Many restaurants are just outside the gates. Its calm, clear waters are perfect for swimming. ⊠ *Rte. 987, Las Croabas.*

★ **Fodor's Choice** Just off Route 3, gentle **Playa Luquillo** (or Balneario La Monserrate) is a magnet for families. It's well equipped with restrooms, showers, lifeguards, guarded parking, food stands, picnic areas, and even cocktail kiosks. Lounge chairs and umbrellas are available to rent. Its most distinctive facility is the Mar Sin Barreras (Sea Without Barriers), a low-sloped ramp leading into the water that allows wheelchair users to take a dip. The beach is open daily. Admission is $2 per car, $3 for minivans. ⊠ *Off Rte. 3.*

VIEQUES AND CULEBRA

Playa Caracas. Located on former U.S. Navy land on the eastern end of Vieques, this tiny yet beautiful beach is reached via a well-maintained dirt road. The water is crystal clear, and its location in Bahía Corcho means that it is sheltered from waves. ⊠ *Off Rte. 997, east of Playa Media Luna.*

★ **Fodor's Choice** **Playa Flamenco.** Consistently ranked one of the most beautiful in the world. Snow-white sands, turquoise waters, and lush hills that rise on all sides make it feel miles

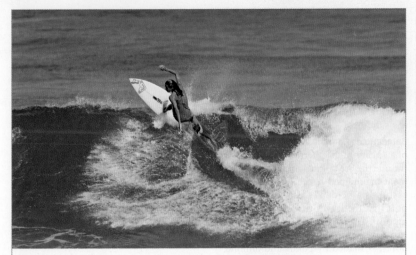

For some of the Caribbean's best waves, surfers head to western Puerto Rico.

away from civilization. During the week it's pleasantly uncrowded; on weekends it fills up fast with day-trippers from the mainland. It's the only beach on Culebra with amenities such as camping, restrooms, showers, and kiosks selling simple fare. ⊠ Rte. 251, west of airport ☎ 787/742–0700 *Daily dawn–dusk*.

Playa Sun Bay. The 1-mile-long (1½-km-long) white sands skirt a crescent-shaped bay. You'll find food kiosks, picnic tables, and changing facilities. It gets packed on holidays and weekends. On weekdays, when the crowds are thin, you might see wild horses grazing among the palm trees. Parking is $3, but often no one is at the gate to take your money. ⊠ *Rte. 997, east of Esperanza* ☎ 787/741–8198.

SOUTHERN PUERTO RICO

Caja de Muertos *(Coffin Island).* This island a few miles off the coast has the best beaches in the Ponce area and is, perhaps, the second-best spot in southern Puerto Rico for snorkeling, after La Parguera. Ask one of the many boatmen at La Guancha to take you out for about $30 round-trip. ⊠ *Boats leave from La Guancha, at end of Rte. 14, Ponce.*

WESTERN PUERTO RICO

Balneario de Rincón. Swimmers can enjoy the tranquil waters at this beach. The beautiful facility has a playground, changing areas, restrooms, and a clubhouse. It's within walking distance of the center of town. Parking is $2. ⊠ *Rte. 115.*

Playa Crashboat. Here you'll find the colorful fishing boats that are portrayed on postcards all over the island. The sand is soft and sugary, and the water's smooth as glass. Named after rescue boats used when Ramey Air Force Base was in operation, there are picnic huts, showers, parking, and restrooms. There's a food stand run by locals where the catch of the day is served with cold beer. ⊠ *End of Rte. 458, off Rte. 107.*

EATING AND DRINKING WELL IN PUERTO RICO

More chefs and restaurateurs are developing menus in the line of a Nuevo Latino cuisine. However, even the most modern chefs here include traditional ingredients as they update old favorites.

Standard meats like chicken, pork, and lamb are given an added zest by sauces made from such tropical fruits as tamarind, mango, or guava. Puerto Rican cooking uses a lot of local vegetables: plantains are cooked a hundred different ways, and yams and other root vegetables are served baked, fried, stuffed, boiled, and mashed. Rice and beans are accompaniments to almost every dish. *Sofrito*—a garlic, onion, sweet pepper, cilantro, oregano, and tomato puree—is used as a base for practically everything. *Arroz con pollo* (chicken with rice), pernil (roasted pork shoulder), *sancocho* (beef or chicken and tuber soup), and *encebollado* (steak and onions) are all typical plates. Also look for fritters served along highways and beaches. You may find *empanadillas* (stuffed fried turnovers), *sorullitos* (cheese-stuffed corn sticks), and *bacalaítos* (codfish fritters).

BLACK GOLD

Cultivated at high altitudes in cool, moist air and mineral-rich soil, the island's coffee beans (called cherries) are black and aromatic. The dominant bean is the *arabica*, known as the richest and most flavorful among the coffee varieties. A lengthy ripening process acts as a sort of "prebrew," imbuing the bean with a rich flavor and a slightly sweet aftertaste. Look for local brands: Yauco Selecto, Rioja, Yaucono, Café Rico, Crema, Adjuntas, Coqui, and Alto Grande Super Premium. Alto Grande, guaranteed to have been grown at high altitudes, has gained the most fame off the island.

Cocina Criolla: *Cocina criolla*—literally, creole cooking—is an aggregate of Caribbean cuisines, sharing basic ingredients common to Cuban, Dominican, and even Brazilian culinary traditions. Conventional wisdom says that the secret of the cocina criolla depends on the use of sofrito, achiote (the inedible fruit of a small Caribbean shrub whose seeds are sometimes ground as a spice or simmered in oil to release their color), lard, and the *caldero* (cooking pot).

Indigenous Fruits and Vegetables: Tropical fruits often wind up at the table in the form of delicious juices. A local favorite is pineapple juice from crops grown in the north of the island. Coconut, mango, papaya, lime, and tamarind are other local favorites. Puerto Rico is home to terrific lesser-known fruits; these include the *caimito* (also called a star apple), *quenepa* (a Spanish lime with a yellow sweet-tart pulp surrounded by a tight, thin skin), and *zapote* (a plum-size fruit that tastes like peach, avocado, and vanilla). The Plaza del Mercado in Santurce is a good place to look for the unusual.

Local Seafood: The freshest seafood is to be found on the northern and western coasts, where seaside shacks and kiosks serve up red snapper, conch, crab, and spiny lobster in traditional recipes. Fried fish is also popular, served with *mojo isleño*, a sauce made with olives,

onions, pimientos, capers, tomatoes, and vinegar.

Plantains and Mofongo: *Plátanos,* or plantains, are related to bananas but are larger and starchier. They are served mostly as side dishes and may be eaten green or ripe. They can be fried, baked, boiled, or roasted and served either whole or in slices. Of all the delicious plantain preparations, one of the tastiest is also the simplest—*mofongo*. Green plantains are mashed with a wooden *pilón*, mixed with garlic, pork fat, and other flavorings and fried in a pan. Served plain, it's often a side dish. But when it's stuffed with chicken, beef, or some other meat, *mofongo* becomes one of Puerto Rico's signature entrées.

Rice: Rice is omnipresent, and most often it's served with *habichuelas* (beans). Rice stuck to the pot, known as *pegao*, is the most highly prized, full of all the ingredients that have sunk to the bottom.

Rum: Although rum was first exported in 1897, it took a bit longer for it to become the massive industry it is today. The Bacardí family set up shop near San Juan in 1959. The company's product, lighter-bodied than those produced by most other distilleries, gained favor around the world. Today Puerto Rico produces more than 35 million gallons of rum a year. You might say it's the national drink.

17

Updated
by Heather
Rodino,
Marlise Kast,
Marie Elena
Martinez

Sunrise and sunset are both worth waiting for when you're in Puerto Rico. The pinks and yellows that hang in the early-morning sky are just as compelling as the sinewy reds and purples that blend into the twilight. It's easy to compare them, as Puerto Rico is small enough to have breakfast in Fajardo, looking eastward over the boats headed to Vieques and Culebra, and lobster dinner in Rincón as the sun is sinking into the inky-blue water.

Known as the Island of Enchantment, Puerto Rico conjures a powerful spell. Here traffic actually leads you to a "Road to Paradise," whether you're looking for a pleasurable, sunny escape from the confines of urbanity or a rich supply of stimulation to quench your cultural and entertainment thirst. On the island you have the best of both worlds, natural and urban thrills alike, and although city life is frenetic enough to make you forget you're surrounded by azure waters and warm sand, traveling a few miles inland or down the coast can easily make you forget you're surrounded by development.

Puerto Rico was populated primarily by Taíno Indians when Columbus landed in 1493. In 1508 Ponce de León established a settlement and became the first governor; in 1521 he founded what is known as Old San Juan. For centuries, while Africans worked on the coastal sugarcane fields, the French, Dutch, and English tried unsuccessfully to wrest the island from Spain. In 1898, as a result of the Spanish-American War, Spain ceded the island to the United States. In 1917 Puerto Ricans became U.S. citizens, and in 1952 Puerto Rico became a semiautonomous commonwealth.

Since the 1950s, Puerto Rico has developed exponentially, as witnessed in the urban sprawl, burgeoning traffic, and growing population (estimated at nearly 4 million); yet *en la isla* (on the island) a strong Latin sense of community and family prevails. Puertorriqueños are fiercely proud of their unique blend of heritages.

Music is another source of Puerto Rican pride. Like wildflowers, *velloneras* (jukeboxes) pop up almost everywhere, and when one is playing, somebody will be either singing or dancing along—or both. Cars often vibrate with *reggaetón,* a hard, monotonous beat with lyrics that express social malaise. Salsa, a fusion of West African percussion, jazz, and other Latin beats, is the trademark dance. Although it may look difficult to master, it's all achieved by just loosening your hips. You may choose to let your inhibitions go by doing some clubbing *a la vida loca* made famous by pop star Ricky Martin. Nightlife options are on par with any cosmopolitan city—and then some.

By day you can drink in the culture of the old world; one of the richest visual experiences in Puerto Rico is Old San Juan. Originally built as a fortress by the Spaniards in the early 1500s, the Old City has myriad attractions that include restored 16th-century buildings and 200-year-old houses with balustraded balconies of filigreed wrought iron that overlook narrow cobblestone streets. Spanish traditions are also apparent in the countryside festivals celebrated in honor of small-town patron saints. For quiet relaxation or experiences off the beaten track, visit coffee plantations, colonial towns, or outlying islets where nightlife is virtually nonexistent.

And you don't come to a Caribbean island without taking in some of the glorious sunshine and natural wonders. In the coastal areas the sun mildly toasts your body, and you're immediately healed by soft waves and cool breezes. In the misty mountains, you can wonder at the flickering night flies and the star-studded sky while the *coquís* (tiny local frogs) sing their legendary sweet lullaby. On a moonless night, watch the warm ocean turn into luminescent aqua-blue speckles on your skin. Then there are the island's many acres of golf courses, numerous tennis courts, rain forests, and dozens of beaches that offer every imaginable water sport.

PLANNING

WHEN TO GO

San Juan in particular is very expensive—many would say overpriced—during the busy tourist season from mid-December through mid-April; during the off-season, you can get good deals all over the island, with discounts of up to 40% off high-season rates.

GETTING HERE AND AROUND
AIR TRAVEL

San Juan's busy Aeropuerto Internacional Luis Muñoz Marín receives flights from all major American carriers, and there are dozens of daily flights to Puerto Rico from the United States. Nonstop options include: AirTran from Atlanta, Baltimore, Orlando, and Tampa; American Airlines from Chicago, Dallas, Hartford, Miami, Newark, New York–JFK, and Philadelphia; Delta from Atlanta, New York–LGA and JFK; JetBlue from Boston, Fort Lauderdale, Orlando, Tampa, and New York–JFK; Spirit Air from Fort Lauderdale and Orlando; United from Chicago, Houston, Newark, and Washington, D.C.–Dulles; US Airways from Baltimore, Charlotte, and Philadelphia.

LOGISTICS

Getting to Puerto Rico: There are dozens of daily flights to Puerto Rico from the U.S. San Juan's international airport is a major regional hub, so many travelers headed elsewhere in the Caribbean make connections here. Fares to San Juan are among the most reasonably priced to the region. The island also has airports in Aguadilla (BQN), Fajardo (FAJ), Ponce (PSE), and Mayagüez (MAZ), and on the islands of Vieques (VQS) and Culebra (CPX). Culebra and Vieques can also be reached by ferry.

Hassle Factor: Low.

On the Ground: Before arriving, check with your hotel about transfers: some hotels and resorts provide transport from the airport—free or for a fee—to their guests; some larger resorts run regular shuttles. Otherwise, your best bets are *taxis turísticos* (tourist taxis). Uniformed officials at the airport can help you make arrangements. They will give you a slip with your exact fare to hand to the driver. Rates are based on your destination. There's a $1 charge for each bag handled by the driver.

It's a major regional hub; many travelers make connections here. Fares to San Juan are among the most reasonably priced to the region. International carriers include Air Canada from Toronto, Air France from Paris, British Airways from London, Iberia from Madrid, and Condor from Germany. Air Flamenco and Vieques Air Link offer daily flights from SJU and Isla Grande Airport (SIG) in San Juan to Vieques and Culebra. Cape Air flies between SJU and Vieques.

Airline Contacts American Airlines ☎ 800/433–7300 ⊕ www.aa.com. **AirTran** ☎ 800/247–8726 ⊕ www.airtran.com. **Delta Airlines** ☎ 800/221–1212 *for U.S. reservations, 800/241–4141 for international reservations* ⊕ *www. delta.com.* **JetBlue** ☎ 800/538–2583 ⊕ www.jetblue.com. **Spirit Airlines** ☎ 800/772–7117 ⊕ www.spirit.com. **United Airlines** ☎ 800/864–8331 *for U.S. reservations, 800/538–2929 for international reservations* ⊕ www.united.com. **US Airways** ☎ 800/428–4322 *for U.S. and Canada reservations, 800/622–1015 for international reservations* ⊕ www.usairways.com.

Regional Airlines Air Flamenco ☎ 787/724–1818, 877/535–2636 ⊕ www. airflamenco.net. **Cape Air** ☎ 866/227–3247 ⊕ www.capeair.com. **Seaborne Airlines** ☎ 888/359–8687, 787/294–6161 ⊕ www.seaborneairlines.com. **Vieques Air Link** ☎ 787/741–8331, 888/901–9247 ⊕ www.viequesairlink.com.

Airports From either airport you can catch flights to Culebra, Vieques, and other destinations on Puerto Rico and throughout the Caribbean.

Aeropuerto Internacional Luis Muñoz Marín (*SJU*). Puerto Rico's main aiport serves as the gateway to the Caribbean, with flights from AirTran, American Airlines, Delta, JetBlue, Spirit Air, United, and US Airways. ☎ 787/791–3840.

Aeropuerto Fernando L. Ribas Dominicci (*SIG*). Sometimes known as Isla Grande, the Aeropuerto Fernando L. Ribas Dominicci is in Miramar, near the Convention Center. ☎ 787/729–8711.

BOAT AND FERRY TRAVEL

Ferry service is from the ferry terminal in Fajardo, about a 90-minute drive from San Juan. There are a limited number of seats on the ferries, so get to the terminal in plenty of time.

Contact **Autoridad de Transporte Marítimo.** The Maritime Transport Authority runs passenger ferries from Fajardo to Culebra and Vieques. ☎ 800/981–2005 ⊕ www.atm.gobierno.pr.

CAR TRAVEL

In San Juan it's more trouble than it's worth to rent a car. Elsewhere a car is probably a necessity. A valid driver's license from your country of origin can be used in Puerto Rico for three months. Rates start as low as $30 a day. Several well-marked multilane highways link population centers. Driving distances are posted in kilometers, whereas speed limits are posted in miles per hour. Road signs are in Spanish.

International Agencies Avis ✉ Aguadilla Airport, Borrinquen Aguadilla, Aguadilla ☎ 800/230–4898, 787/890–3311 ⊕ www.avis.com. **Hertz** ☎ 800/654–3131. **National** ☎ 888/222–9058. **Thrifty** ☎ 800/847–4389.

Local Agencies Charlie Car Rental ☎ 787/728–2418 ⊕ www.charliecars.com. **Vias** ☎ 787/791–4120.

TAXI TRAVEL

The Puerto Rico Tourism Company has instituted a well-organized taxi program. White taxis with the "taxi turistico" logo run from the airport or the cruise-ship piers to Isla Verde, Condado/Ocean Park, and Old San Juan, with fixed "zone" rates ranging from $10 to $20. If you take a cab going somewhere outside the fixed zones, insist on setting the meter. City tours start at $36 per hour. In other towns you can flag down cabs on the street, but it's easier to have your hotel call one for you. ■TIP➔ **Make sure the driver is clear on whether he or she will charge a flat rate or use a meter to determine the fare. In most places, the cabs are metered.**

Contacts Major Taxi ☎ 787/723–2460, 787/723–1300. **Metro Taxi** ☎ 787/725–2870, 787/945–5555 ⊕ www.metrotaxipr.com.

ESSENTIALS

Banks and Money The U.S. dollar is the official currency. Major credit cards are widely accepted, ATMs are readily available and reliable in the cities and less frequently in rural areas. Look to local banks such as Banco Popular and First Bank.

Electricity 110 volts/60 cycles.

Emergencies Dial 911.

For non-emergencies, you'll find that the Tourist Zone Police are particularly helpful to visitors

Tourist Zone Police ☎ 787/726–7020 for Condado, 787/728–2981 for Isla Verde.

Language Puerto Rico is officially bilingual, but Spanish dominates, particularly outside the tourist areas of San Juan. Although English is widely spoken, you'll probably want to take a Spanish phrase book along on your travels about the island.

Passport Requirements U.S. citizens don't need passports. You will not pass through immigration, but there is an agriculture inspection before you check in for your flight home.

Phones Most U.S. mobile phone users will not pay roaming charges in Puerto Rico; confirm with your company. Area codes are 787 and 939. Toll-free numbers (prefix 800, 888, or 877) are widely used, and many can be accessed from North America (and vice versa). To make a local call in Puerto Rico you must dial 1, the area code, and the seven-digit number. For international calls, dial 011, the country code, the city code, and the number. Dial 00 for an international long-distance operator. Phone cards are widely available (most drugstores carry them).

Safety San Juan, like any other big city, has its share of petty crime, so guard your wallet or purse on the city streets. Don't leave anything unattended on the beach. Leave your valuables in the hotel safe, and stick to the fenced-in beach areas of your hotel. Always lock your car and stash valuables and luggage out of sight. Avoid deserted beaches at night.

Taxes Accommodations incur a tax: for hotels with casinos it's 11%, for other hotels it's 9%, and for government-approved paradores it's 7%. Ask your hotel before booking. The tax, in addition to the standard 5% to 12% service charge or resort fee applied by most hotels, can add a hefty 20% or more to your bill. There's a 7% (6% state plus 1% municipal) sales tax in Puerto Rico.

Tipping Tips are expected, and appreciated, by restaurant waitstaff (15% to 20% if a service charge isn't included), hotel porters ($1 per bag), maids ($1 to $2 a day), and taxi drivers (15% to 18%).

ACCOMMODATIONS

If you want easy access to shopping, dining, and nightlife, then you should stay in San Juan, which also has decent—though by no means the island's best—beaches. Most of the other large, deluxe resorts are along the northeast coast. There are also a few resorts along the southern coast. Rincón, in the west, has a concentration of resorts and great surfing. Other small inns and hotels are around the island in the interior, including a few around El Yunque. Look to Vieques and Culebra if you want to find excellent beaches and little development. Many larger resorts in Puerto Rico charge resort fees, which are uncommon elsewhere in the Caribbean.

Big Hotels: San Juan's beaches are lined with large-scale hotels that include happening restaurants and splashy casinos. Most are spread out along Condado and Isla Verde beaches.

Paradores: Small inns (many offering home-style comida criolla cooking) are spread out around the island, though they are rarely on the beach.

Upscale Beach Resorts: All over the island—but particularly along the north coast—large tourist resorts offer all the amenities along with a hefty dose of isolation. Just be prepared for expensive food and few nearby off-resort dining opportunities.

HOTEL AND RESTAURANT PRICES

Prices in the restaurant reviews are the average cost of a main course at dinner or, if dinner is not served, at lunch; taxes and service charges are generally included. Prices in the hotel reviews are the lowest cost of a standard double room in high season, excluding taxes, service charges, and meal plans (except at all-inclusives). Prices for rentals are the lowest per-night cost for a one-bedroom unit in high season.

VISITOR INFORMATION

Contact **Puerto Rico Tourism Company** ✉ *500 Ochoa Bldg., Calle Tanca, across from Pier 1, Old San Juan, San Juan* ☎ *787/721–2400* ✉ *Rafael Hernández Airport, Hwy. 2, Km 148.7, Aguadilla* ☎ *787/890–3315* ⊕ *www. seepuertorico.com.*

WEDDINGS

There are no special residency requirements, but U.S. citizens must produce a birth certificate, as well as a driver's license or other state-issued photo identification. Both you and your intended must appear together at the office to purchase a marriage license. A judge or any member of the clergy may then perform your ceremony. The fee is usually between $150 and $350. Most large hotels on the island have marriage coordinators who can explain the necessary paperwork and help you complete it on time for your marriage ceremony.

Contact **Demographic Registry Office** ☎ *787/767–9120.*

17

EXPLORING PUERTO RICO

OLD SAN JUAN

Old San Juan, the original city founded in 1521, contains carefully preserved examples of 16th- and 17th-century Spanish colonial architecture. More than 400 buildings have been beautifully restored. Graceful wrought-iron balconies with lush hanging plants extend over narrow streets paved with *adoquines* (blue-gray stones originally used as ballast on Spanish ships). The Old City is partially enclosed by walls that date from 1633 and once completely surrounded it. Designated a U.S. National Historic Zone in 1950, Old San Juan is chockablock with shops, open-air cafés, homes, tree-shaded squares, monuments, and people. You can get an overview on a morning's stroll (bear in mind that this "stroll" includes some steep climbs). However, if you plan to immerse yourself in history or to shop, you'll need a couple of days.

TOP ATTRACTIONS

☺ **Castillo San Cristóbal.** This huge stone fortress, built between 1634 and
Fodor's Choice 1790, guarded the city from land attacks from the east. The largest
★ Spanish fortification in the New World, San Cristóbal was known in the 17th and 18th centuries as the Gibraltar of the West Indies. Five freestanding structures divided by dry moats are connected by tunnels. You're free to explore the gun turrets (with cannon in situ), officers' quarters, re-created 18th-century barracks, and gloomy passageways. Along with El Morro, San Cristóbal is a National Historic

Old San Juan

KEY

🚢 Cruise Ship Terminal

1️⃣ Exploring

1️⃣ Restaurants & Hotels

⛴ Ferry

ℹ️ Tourist Information

Site administered by the U.S. Park Service; it's a World Heritage Site as well. Rangers conduct tours in Spanish and English. ⊠ *Calle Norzagaray at Av. Muñoz Rivera, Old San Juan* ☎ *787/729–6777* ⊕ *www. nps.gov/saju* ⊠ *$3; $5 includes admission to El Morro* ☉ *Daily 9–6.*

Ⓒ **Castillo San Felipe del Morro** (*El Morro*). At the northwestern tip of the

Fodor'sChoice Old City is El Morro ("the promontory"), a fortress built by the Span-

★ iards between 1539 and 1786. Rising 140 feet above the sea, the massive six-level fortress was built to protect the harbor entrance. It is a labyrinth of cannon batteries, ramps, barracks, turrets, towers, and tunnels. Built to protect the port, El Morro has a commanding view of the harbor. You're free to wander throughout. The cannon emplacement walls and the dank secret passageways are a wonder of engineering. The fort's small but enlightening museum displays ancient Spanish guns and other armaments, military uniforms, and blueprints for Spanish forts in the Americas, although Castillo San Cristóbal has more extensive and impressive exhibits. There's also a gift shop. The fort is a National Historic Site administered by the U.S. Park Service; it's a World Heritage Site as well. Various tours and a video are available in English. ⊠ *Calle del Morro, Old San Juan* ☎ *787/729–6960* ⊕ *www.nps.gov/saju* ⊠ *$3; $5 includes admission to Castillo San Cristóbal* ☉ *Daily 9–6.*

La Fortaleza. Sitting atop the fortified city walls overlooking the harbor, the Fortaleza was built between 1533 and 1540 as a fortress, but it wasn't a very good one. It was attacked numerous times and was occupied twice, by the British in 1598 and the Dutch in 1625. When El Morro and the city's other fortifications were finished, the Fortaleza became the governor's palace. Numerous changes have been made to the original primitive structure over the past four centuries, resulting in the current eclectic yet eye-pleasing collection of marble and mahogany, medieval towers, and stained-glass galleries. It is still the official residence of the island's governor, and is the Western Hemisphere's oldest executive mansion in continual use. Guided tours are conducted several times a day in English and Spanish; both include a short video presentation. Call ahead to verify the day's schedule, as tours are often canceled because of official functions. Proper attire is required: no sleeveless shirts or very short shorts. The tours begin near the main gate in a yellow building called the Real Audiencia, housing the Oficina Estatal de Preservación Histórica. ⊠ *Western end of Calle Fortaleza, Old San Juan* ☎ *787/721–7000* ⊕ *www.fortaleza.gobierno.pr* ⊠ *$3 suggested donanation* ☉ *Weekdays 9–3:45.*

Paseo de la Princesa. Built in the mid-nineteenth century to honor the Spanish princess of Asturias, this street with a broad pedestrian walkway is spruced up with flowers, trees, benches, and street lamps. Unfurling westward from Plaza del Inmigrante along the base of the fortified city walls, It leads to the Fuente Raíces, a striking fountain depicting the various ethnic groups of Puerto Rico. Take a seat and watch the boats zip across the water. Beyond the fountain is the beginning of Paseo del Morro, a well-paved shoreline path that hugs Old San Juan's walls and leads past the city gate at Calle San Juan and continues to the tip of the headland, beneath El Morro. ⊠ *San Juan.*

17

Alcaldía. San Juan's city hall was built between 1602 and 1789. In 1841 extensive alterations were made so that it would resemble the city hall in Madrid, with arcades, towers, balconies, and an inner courtyard. Renovations have refreshed the facade of the building and some interior rooms, but the architecture remains true to its colonial style. Only the patios are open to public viewings. A municipal tourist information center and an art gallery with rotating exhibits are in the lobby. ⊠ *153 Calle San Francisco, Plaza de Armas, Old San Juan* ☎ *787/480–2548* ✇ *Free* ⊙ *Weekdays 8–4.*

Capilla del Cristo. According to legend, in 1753 a young horseman named Baltazar Montañez got carried away during festivities in honor of San Juan Bautista (St. John the Baptist), raced down Calle Cristo, and plunged over its steep precipice. Historical records maintain the man died, but legend contends that he lived. (Another version of the story has it that the horse miraculously stopped before plunging over the cliff.) Regardless, this chapel was built partly to prevent further calamities. Inside is a small silver altar dedicated to the Christ of Miracles. You can peer in through the wrought-iron gates, which are usually closed. ⊠ *End of Calle Cristo, Old San Juan* ☎ *No phone* ✇ *Free.*

Casa Blanca. The original structure on this site was a wooden house built in 1521 as a home for Ponce de León; he died in Cuba without ever having lived here. His descendants occupied the house's sturdier replacement, a lovely colonial mansion with tile floors and beamed ceilings, for more than 250 years. It was the home of the U.S. Army commander in Puerto Rico from the end of the Spanish-American War in 1898 to 1966. As of this writing, Casa Blanca was closed for a lengthy restoration, but you can still peer in at it through the gates. ⊠ *1 Calle San Sebastián, Old San Juan.*

Catedral de San Juan Bautista. The Catholic shrine of Puerto Rico had humble beginnings in the early 1520s as a thatch-roofed, wooden structure. After a hurricane destroyed the church, it was rebuilt in 1540, when it was given a graceful circular staircase and vaulted Gothic ceilings. Most of the work on the present cathedral, however, was done in the 19th century. The remains of Ponce de León are behind a marble tomb in the wall near the transept, on the north side. The trompe l'oeil work on the inside of the dome is breathtaking. Unfortunately, many of the other frescoes suffer from water damage. ⊠ *151 Calle Cristo, Old San Juan* ☎ *787/722–0861* ⊕ *www.catedralsanjuan.com* ✇ *$1 donation suggested* ⊙ *Mon.–Sat. 8–5, Sun. 8–2:30.*

Galería Nacional. Built by Dominican friars in 1523, this convent—the oldest in Puerto Rico—once served as a shelter during Carib Indian attacks and, more recently, as headquarters for the Antilles command of the U.S. Army. The beautifully restored building contains the Galería Nacional, which showcases the collection of the Institute of Puerto Rican Culture. Arranged chronologically, the museum traces the development of Puerto Rican art over the centuries, from José Campeche and Francisco Oller to Rafael Tufiño and Myrna Báez. You'll also find a good collection of *santos*, traditional wood carvings of saints. ⊠ *98*

Hear your footsteps echo throughout Castillo San Felipe's vast network of tunnels, designed to amplify the sounds of approaching enemies.

Calle Norzagaray, Old San Juan ☎ *787/725–2670* ⊕ *www.icp.gobierno. pr* ✉ *$3* ☉ *Mon.–Sat. 9:30–5.*

Museo de las Américas. On the second floor of the imposing former military barracks, Cuartel de Ballajá, this museum houses four permanent exhibits covering the native people of the Americas, African heritage in Puerto Rico, conquest and colonization, and popular arts in the Americas. You'll also find a number of temporary exhibitions. ⊠ *Calle Norzagaray and Calle del Morro, Old San Juan* ☎ *787/724–5052* ⊕ *www. museolasamericas.org* ✉ *$3* ☉ *Tues.–Sat. 9–noon, 1–4, Sun. 11–4.*

Plaza de Armas. The Old City's original main square was once used as military drilling grounds. Bordered by Calles San Francisco, Rafael Cordero, San José, and Cruz, it has a fountain with 19th-century statues representing the four seasons as well as a bandstand and a small café. The Alcaldía commands the north side. This is one of the most popular meeting places in Old San Juan, so you're likely to encounter lots of bustle: artists sketching caricatures, pedestrians waiting in line at food carts, and hundreds of pigeons waiting for handouts. ⊠ *Old San Juan.*

Plaza de Colón. The tallest statue of Christopher Columbus in the Americas stands atop a soaring column and fountain in this bustling Old San Juan square, kitty-corner to Castillo San Cristóbal. What was once called St. James Square was renamed in 1893 to honor the 400th anniversary of Columbus's arrival in Puerto Rico. Bronze plaques on the statue's base relate various episodes in the life of the explorer. Local artisans often line the plaza, so it's a good place to stop for souvenirs. ⊠ *Old San Juan.*

GREATER SAN JUAN

Taxis, buses, *públicos* (shared vans), or a rental car are needed to reach the points of interest in "new" San Juan. Avenida Muñoz Rivera, Avenida Ponce de León, and Avenida Fernández Juncos are the main thoroughfares that cross Puerta de Tierra, east of Old San Juan, to the business and tourist districts of Santurce, Condado, Ocean Park, and Isla Verde. Dos Hermanos Bridge connects Puerta de Tierra with Miramar, Condado, and Isla Grande. Isla Grande Airport, from which you can take short hops, is on the bay side of the bridge. On the other side, the Condado Lagoon is bordered by Avenida Ashford, which threads past the high-rise Condado hotels and Avenida Baldorioty de Castro Expreso, which barrels east to the airport and beyond. Due south of the lagoon is Miramar, a residential area with fashionable turn-of-the-20th-century homes and a few hotels and restaurants. Isla Verde, with its glittering beachfront hotels, casinos, discos, and public beach, is to the east, near the airport.

WHAT TO SEE

El Capitolio. The white-marble Capitol, a fine example of Italian Renaissance style, dates from 1929. The grand rotunda, which can be seen from all over San Juan, was completed in the late 1990s. Fronted by eight Corinthian columns, it's a very dignified home for the commonwealth's constitution. Although the Senate and the House of Representatives have offices in the more modern buildings on either side, the Capitol is where the legislators meet. You can also watch the legislature in action—note that the action is in Spanish—when it is in session, most often Monday and Thursday. Guided tours, which last about an hour and include visits to the rotunda and other parts of the building, are by appointment only. ⊠ *Av. Constitución, Puerta de Tierra* ☎ *787/724–2030 Ext. 4609* ⊕ *www.olspr.org* ✉ *Free* ☉ *Daily 8–5:30.*

Museo de Arte Contemporáneo de Puerto Rico. This Georgian-style structure, once a public school, displays a dynamic range of works by both established and up-and-coming Latin American artists. Many of the works on display have strong political messages, including pointed commentaries on Puerto Rico's status as a commonwealth. Only a small part of the more than 900 works in the permanent collection is on display at any time, but it might be anything from an exhibit of ceramics to a screening of videos. ⊠ *1220 Av. Ponce de León, at Av. R.H. Todd, Santurce* ☎ *787/977–4030* ⊕ *www.museocontemporaneopr.org* ✉ *$5 donation suggested* ☉ *Tues.–Fri. 10–4, Sat. 11–5, Sun. 11–5.*

FodorśChoice
★

Museo de Arte de Puerto Rico. At 130,000 square feet one of the biggest museums in the Caribbean, this beautiful neoclassical building was once the San Juan Municipal Hospital. The collection of Puerto Rican art starts with works from the colonial era, most of them commissioned for churches. Here you'll find works by José Campeche, the island's first great painter. His *Immaculate Conception,* finished in 1794, is a masterpiece. Also well represented is Francisco Oller y Cestero, who was the first to move beyond religious subjects to paint local scenes. His influence is still felt today: another gallery room is filled with works by artists inspired by Oller. The original building, built in the 1920s,

Continued on page 694

WALKING OLD SAN JUAN

Old San Juan is Puerto Rico's quintessential colonial neighborhood. Narrow streets and plazas are still enclosed by thick fortress walls, and bougainvillea bowers spill over exquisite facades. A walk along streets paved with slate-blue cobblestones leads past colonial mansions, ancient churches, and intriguing museums and galleries. Vivacious restaurants and bars that teem with life young and old are always nearby, making it easy to refuel and reinvigorate anytime during your stroll.

by Christopher P. Baker

left, strolling down Calle del Cristo; top right, a view from El Morro; bottom right, dancers in front of Castillo San Cristóbal

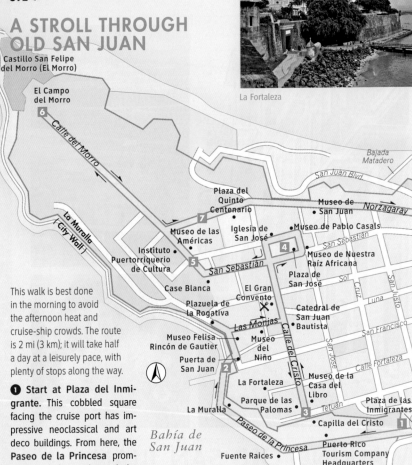

A STROLL THROUGH OLD SAN JUAN

Castillo San Felipe del Morro (El Morro)

El Campo del Morro

La Fortaleza

⑥

Calle del Morro

La Muralla (City Wall)

Bajada Matadero

San Juan Blvd

Plaza del Quinto Centenario

Museo de San Juan

Norzagaray

⑦

Museo de las Américas

Iglesia de San José

Museo de Pablo Casals

San Sebastián

④

Instituto Puertorriqueño de Cultura

⑤

San Sebastián

Museo de Nuestra Raíz Africana

Sol

Cruz

San Justo

Case Blanca

Plaza de San José

Luna

Plazuela de la Rogativa

El Gran Convento

Catedral de San Juan Bautista

San Francisco

Museo Felisa Rincón de Gautier

Las Monjas

Museo del Niño

Calle del Cristo

San José

Calle Fortaleza

Puerta de San Juan

②

La Fortaleza

Museo de la Casa del Libro

Plaza de las Inmigrantes

①

La Muralla

Parque de las Palomas

③

Tetuán

Bahía de San Juan

Paseo de la Princesa

Capilla del Cristo

Fuente Raíces

Puerto Rico Tourism Company Headquarters

This walk is best done in the morning to avoid the afternoon heat and cruise-ship crowds. The route is 2 mi (3 km); it will take half a day at a leisurely pace, with plenty of stops along the way.

❶ Start at Plaza del Inmigrante. This cobbled square facing the cruise port has impressive neoclassical and art deco buildings. From here, the **Paseo de la Princesa** promenade unfurls west beneath the ancient city wall, **La Muralla.** Artisans set up stalls under the palms on weekends. Midway along the brick-paved walkway, stop to admire the **Fuente Ra-**

ices monument and fountain: dolphins cavort at the feet of figures representing Puerto Rico's indigenous, Spanish, and African peoples.

❷ Pass through the Puerta de San Juan. This fortified entrance in La Muralla was built in 1520 and still retains its massive wooden gates, creaky on their ancient hinges. Immediately beyond, turn left and ascend to **Plazuela de la Rogativa,** a tiny plaza where a contemporary statue recalls

the torch-lit procession that thwarted an English invasion in 1797. The harbor views are fantastic. Then, walk east one block to reach the **Catedral de San Juan Bautista,** the neoclassical 19th-century cathedral containing the mausoleum of Ponce de León.

❸ Head south on Calle del Cristo. Sloping gradually, this lovely cobbled street is lined with beautifully restored colonial mansions housing cafés, galleries, and boutiques. Pass-

Puerta de San Juan

astillo San Cristóbal

Calle del Cristo

Catedral de San Juan Bautista

ATLANTIC OCEAN

0   1/8 mi

0   1/8 km

San Miguel

La Muralla (City Wall)

Sol

Luna

O'Donnell

Castillo San Cristóbal

◆Visitors Center

Muñoz Rivera

Plaza de Colón

Ponce de Léon   25

Teatro Tapía

Tanca

8

9

Castillo San Felipe del Morro

ing Calle Fortaleza, note **La Fortaleza**, the official residence of the Puerto Rican Governor at the end of the street. Calle del Cristo ends at **Capilla del Cristo**, a chapel adorned within by silver *milagros* (token requests).

❹ **Return via Calle del Cristo and continue to Plaza de San José.** Catercorner to the cathedral you'll find **El Gran Convento**, a former convent turned hotel, with an excellent restaurant, tapas bar, and café. At **Plaza de San José** visit the **Museo de Pablo Casals**, dedicated to the Spanish cellist, and the **Iglesia de San José**, a simple church dating from 1532.

❺ **Walk west on Calle San Sebastián.** This narrow street with colonial mansions painted in vibrant pastels ends at the gleaming white **Casa Blanca**. The oldest continually occupied residence in the Americas was originally the home of Ponce de León. Today it's a delightful museum furnished with period pieces. The garden is a tranquil spot for contemplation.

❻ **Follow Calle del Morro** north. One block from Casa Blanca you'll emerge upon a broad grassy headland—the Campo del Morro—popular with kite-flying families. It's skewered by an arrow-straight gravel path that aims at the imposing **Castillo San Felipe del Morro** (El

Morro), guarding the harbor entrance. Allow one-hour to roam the small museum, turrets, labyrinthine tunnels, and six levels of ramparts soaring 140 feet above the ocean.

❼ **Retrace your steps and turn left on Calle Norzagaray.** This street runs atop the Atlantic shoreline, offering sweeping ocean vistas. On your right you'll pass the **Plaza del Quinto Centenario**, pinned by an impressive statue: the *Tótem Telúrico*. Beyond, stroll past the Convento de los Dominicos to reach the **Museo de San Juan**. Housed in a former market, it traces the city's history and displays works by Puerto Rico's master painters.

❽ **Continue east to Castillo San Cristóbal.** Spanning 27 acres, this multitiered fortress was completed in 1771 with mighty bulwarks that protected the city from eastern attack by land. It features superb historical exhibits and reenactments by soldiers in period costumes.

❾ **Exit the castle, turn south and walk one block to Plaza de Colón,** This leafy square is lined with excellent cafés and restaurants where you can rest your feet and enjoy a great meal.

proved to be too small to house the museum's collection of Puerto Rican art by itself: the newer east wing here is dominated by a five-story-tall stained-glass window, the work of local artist Eric Tabales.

There's much more to the museum, including a beautiful garden filled with a variety of native flora and a 400-seat theater that's worth seeing for its remarkable hand-crocheted lace curtain. ⊠ *299 Av. José de Diego, Santurce* ☎ *787/977–6277* ⊕ *www.mapr.org* ⊠ *$6; free admission Wed. 2–8* ☉ *Tues.–Sat. 10–5, Sun. 11–6.*

Museo de Historia, Antropología y Arte. The Universidad de Puerto Rico's small Museum of History, Anthropology and Art offers rotating exhibitions in each of these three areas. Its archaeological and historical collection covers the Native American influence on the island and the Caribbean, the colonial era, and the history of slavery. There's also a small collection of Egyptian antiquities. Art holdings include a range of Puerto Rican popular, graphic, folk, and fine art; the museum's prize exhibit is the painting *El Velorio* (*The Wake*), by the 19th-century artist Francisco Oller. If you're looking to see something in particular, call before you go, as only a small portion of the collection is on display at a time. ⊠ *Universidad de Puerto Rico, Av. Ponce de León, Río Piedras* ☎ *787/763–3939 or 787/764–0000 Ext. 5852* ⊕ *www.uprrp. edu* ⊠ *Free* ☉ *Mon.–Tues. and Thurs.–Fri. 9–4:30, Wed. 9–8:30, Sun. 11:30–4:30.*

SAN JUAN ENVIRONS

Casa Bacardí Visitor Center. Exiled from Cuba, the Bacardí family built a small rum distillery here in the 1950s. Today it's the world's largest, with the capacity to produce 100,000 gallons of spirits a day and 21 million cases a year. You can hop on a little tram to take an approximately 45-minute tour of the visitor center, though you don't visit the distillery itself. Yes, you'll be offered a sample. If you don't want to drive, you can reach the factory by taking the ferry from Pier 2 for 50¢ each way and then a *público* (public van service) from the ferry pier to the factory for about $2 or $3 per person. ⊠ *Road 165, Rte. 888, Km 2.6, Cataño* ☎ *787/788–1500* ⊕ *www.casabacardi.org* ⊠ *Free* ☉ *Mon.– Sat. 9–6, last tour at 4:30; Sun. 10–5, last tour at 3:45.*

Parque Histórico Juan Ponce de León (Ruinas de Caparra). In 1508 Ponce de León established the island's first settlement here. The Caparra Ruins— a few crumbling walls—are what remains of an ancient fort. The small **Museo de la Conquista y Colonización de Puerto Rico** (Museum of the Conquest and Colonization of Puerto Rico) contains historical documents, exhibits, and excavated artifacts, though you can see the museum's contents in less time than it takes to say the name. Both the ruins and the museum are maintained by the Puerto Rican Institute of Culture. ⊠ *Rte. 2, Km 6.4, Guaynabo* ☎ *787/781–4795* ⊕ *www.icp. gobierno.pr* ⊠ *Free* ☉ *Weekdays 8:00–4:30.*

EASTERN PUERTO RICO

EL YUNQUE

The more than 100 billion gallons of precipitation that El Yunque receives annually spawns rushing streams and cascades, outsize impatiens and ferns, and 240 tree species. In the evening millions of inch-long coquís (tree frogs) begin their calls. El Yunque is also home to the cotorra, Puerto Rico's endangered green parrot, as well as 67 other types of birds.

El Yunque is the only tropical rain forest in the U.S. National Forest System, spanning 28,000 acres, reaching an elevation of more than 3,500 ft. and receiving an estimated average of 200–240 inches of rain each year. The forest's 13 hiking trails are extremely well maintained; many of them are easy to navigate and less than 1 mile long. It's about 73°F year-round, so weather isn't much of a factor for seasonal planning. For easy parking and fewer crowds, be sure to arrive early in the day, although the park rarely gets crowded by U.S. National Park standards. Expect rain nearly every day, but keep eyes peeled post-showers for the best bird-watching.

Carve out some time to stop at the cathedral-like **El Portal Visitor Center** (⊠ *Rte. 191, Km 4.3, off Rte. 3* ☎ *787/888–1880* ⊕ *www.fs.fed.us/ r8/caribbean* ≊ *$4* ☉ *Daily 9–5*). Enter via an elevated walkway that transports visitors across the forest canopy, 60 feet above the ground. Signs identify and explain the birds, animals, and other treasures seen among the treetops. Below the walkway, find a ground-level nature trail with stunning views of the lower forest and coastal plain. Inside the Center interactive exhibits explain the El Yunque National Forest's history, topography, flora, and fauna. The facility also has a well-stocked bookstore and gift shop.

The 13 official trails throughout El Yunque are well marked, and easy for both beginners and children. The trails on the north side of El Yunque, the park's main tourist hub, tend toward folks with minimal or no hiking experience. There are several short trails (about ½ mile) that are completely paved. On the south side, expect fewer people and moderate to challenging hikes. These trails are not as well maintained as the marked trails found lower in the forest. Regardless of where you go, you'll be immersed in the sounds, smells, and scenic landscape of the park. For avid outdoor adventurers, it's possible to hike between the north and south sides of El Yunque. If you prefer to see the sights from a car, as many people do, simply follow Route 191 as it winds into the mountains and stop at several observation points along the way.

FAJARDO

Founded in 1772, Fajardo has historical notoriety as a port where pirates stocked up on supplies. It later developed into a fishing community and an area where sugarcane flourished. (There are still cane fields on the city's fringes.) Today it's a hub for the yachts that use its marinas; the divers who head to its good offshore sites; and the day-trippers who travel by catamaran, ferry, or plane to the out-islands of Culebra and Vieques. With the most-significant docking facilities on the island's eastern side, Fajardo is often congested and difficult to navigate.

Reserva Natural Las Cabezas de San Juan. The 316-acre reserve on a headland north of Fajardo is owned by the nonprofit Conservation Trust of Puerto Rico. You ride in open-air trolleys and wander down boardwalks through seven ecosystems, including lagoons, mangrove swamps, and dry-forest areas. Green iguanas skitter across paths, and guides identify other endangered species. A half-hour hike down a wooden walkway brings you to the mangrove-lined **Laguna Grande,** where bioluminescent microorganisms glow at night. The restored **Fajardo Lighthouse** is the final stop on the tour; its Spanish colonial tower has been in operation since 1882, making it Puerto Rico's second-oldest lighthouse. The first floor houses ecological displays; a winding staircase leads to an observation deck. The only way to see the reserve is on one of the many guided tours; reservations are required through the Conservation's very comprehensive website. ⊠ *Rte. 987, Km 6* ☎ *787/722–5882 weekdays; 787/860–2560 weekends* ⊕ *www.fideicomiso.org.*

VIEQUES AND CULEBRA

CULEBRA

Culebra is known around the world for its curvaceous coastline. Playa Flamenco, the tiny island's most famous stretch of sand, is considered one of the two or three best beaches in the world. If Playa Flamenco gets too crowded, as it often does around Easter and Christmas, there are many other beaches that will be nearly deserted. There's archaeological evidence that Taíno and Carib peoples lived on Culebra long before the arrival of the Spanish in the late 15th century. The Spanish didn't bother laying claim to it until 1886; its dearth of freshwater made it an unattractive location for a settlement. Although the island now has modern conveniences, its pace seems little changed from a century ago. There's only one town, Dewey, named after U.S. Admiral George Dewey. When the sun goes down, Culebra winds down as well. But during the day it's a delightful place to stake out a spot on Playa Flamenco or Playa Soni and read, swim, or search for shells. So what causes stress on the island? Nada.

VIEQUES

This island off Puerto Rico's east coast is famed for its Playa Sun Bay, a gorgeous stretch of sand with picnic facilities and shade trees. In May 2003 the U.S. Navy withdrew from its military operations and turned over two-thirds of Vieques to the local government, which is transforming it into the Vieques National Wildlife Refuge. Vieques has two communities—Isabel Segunda, where the ferries dock, and the smaller Esperanza. Both have restaurants and hotels that will surprise you with their sophistication.

Fodor'sChoice ★ **Puerto Mosquito Bioluminescent Bay.** East of Esperanza, Puerto Mosquito Bioluminescent Bay is one of the world's best spots to have a glow-in-the-dark experience with undersea dinoflagellates. Local tour operators like Abe's offer kayak trips or excursions on nonpolluting boats to see the bay's microorganisms, which appear to light up when the water around them is agitated. Look behind your boat, and you'll see a twinkling wake. Even the fish that swim through and jump from the water will bear an eerie glow. The high concentration of dinoflagellates sets the bay apart from the other spots around the world (including others in Puerto Rico) that are home to these algae. The bay is at its best when there's little or no moonlight; rainy nights are beautiful, too, because the raindrops splashing in the water produce ricochet sparkles that shimmer like diamonds. ⊠ *Reach via unpaved roads off Rte. 997, Vieques.*

SOUTHERN PUERTO RICO

Bosque Estatal de Guánica (*Guánica State Forest*). The 9,900-acre Bosque Estatal de Guánica, a United Nations Biosphere Reserve, is a great place for hiking expeditions. It's an outstanding example of a tropical dry coastal forest, with some 700 species of plants ranging from the prickly-pear cactus to the gumbo limbo tree. It's also one of the best places on the island for bird-watching, since you can spot more than 100 species, including the pearly-eyed thrasher, the lizard cuckoo, and the nightjar.

One of the most popular hikes is the **Ballena Trail,** which begins at the ranger station on Route 334. This easy 1¼-mile (2-km) walk follows a partially paved road and takes you past a mahogany plantation to a dry plain covered with stunted cactus. A sign reading "Guayacán centenario" leads you to an extraordinary guayacán tree with a trunk that measures 6 feet across. The moderately difficult **Fuerte Trail** takes you on a 3½-mile (5½-km) hike to an old fort built by the Spanish Armada. It was destroyed during the Spanish-American War in 1898, but you can still see the ruins of the old observatory tower.

In addition to going in the main entrance on Route 334, you can enter on Route 333, which skirts the forest's southwestern quadrant. You can also try the less explored western section, off Route 325. ⊠ *Enter along Rte. 334, 333, or 325, Guánica* ☎ *787/821–5706* 🏷 *Free* ☉ *Daily 9–5.*

PONCE

The island's second-largest urban area, Ponce shines in 19th-century style with pink-marble-bordered sidewalks, painted trolleys, and horse-drawn carriages. Stroll around the main square, the Plaza de las Delicias, with its perfectly pruned India-laurel fig trees, graceful fountains, gardens, and park benches. View the Catedral de Nuestra Señora de la Guadalupe (Our Lady of Guadalupe Cathedral), perhaps even attend the 6 am Mass, and walk down Calles Isabel and Cristina to see turn-of-the-20th-century wooden houses with wrought-iron balconies.

Castillo Serrallés. This lovely Spanish-style villa—such a massive house that people in the town below referred to it as a castle—was built in the 1930s for Ponce's wealthiest family, the makers of Don Q rum. Guided tours give you a glimpse into the lifestyle of a sugar baron. The dining room is a highlight, with its original hand-carved furnishings. A permanent exhibit explains the area's sugarcane and rum industries. The extensive garden, with sculptured bushes and a shimmering reflection pool, is considered the best kept on the island. ⊠ *17 El Vigía, El Vigía* ☎ *787/259–1774* ⊕ *home.coqui.net/castserr* 🏷 *$8.50, includes admission to Cruceta El Vigía and Butterfly Garden* ☉ *Thur.–Sun. 9:30–6:30.*

Centro Ceremonial Indígena de Tibes *(Tibes Indian Ceremonial Center).*
This archaeological site, discovered after flooding from a tropical storm
in 1975, is the most important on the island. The ancient ceremonial center dates from AD 300 to 700 and includes nine playing fields
used for a ritual ball game that some think was similar to soccer. The
fields are bordered by smooth stones, some of which are engraved with
petroglyphs that researchers say might have ceremonial or astronomical significance. The most eye-catching part of the site is the *Plaza de
Estrella,* or Plaza of the Star, where the stones are arranged in a pattern that resembles a rising sun. Experts say it might have been used
to chart the seasons. A village with several thatched huts has been
reconstructed in an original setting. Be sure to visit the small museum
before taking a walking tour of the site. ⊠ *Rte. 503, Km 2.5, Barrio
Tibes* ☎ *787/840–2255 or 787/840–5685* ⊕ *ponce.inter.edu/tibes/tibes.
html* ☎ *$3* ☉ *Tues.–Sun. 8–4:30.*

♙ **Hacienda Buena Vista.** Built by Salvador de Vives in 1838, Buena Vista
FodorśChoice   was one of the area's largest coffee plantations. It's a technological
★   marvel—water from the nearby Río Canas was funneled into narrow
brick channels that could be diverted to perform any number of tasks,
including turning the waterwheel. (Seeing the two-story wheel slowly
begin to turn is fascinating, especially for kids.) Nearby is the two-story
manor house, filled with furniture that gives a sense of what it was like
to live on a coffee plantation nearly 150 years ago. Make sure to take a
look in the kitchen, dominated by a massive hearth. In 1987 the plantation was restored by the Puerto Rican Conservation Trust, which leads
four tours a day (one in English). The tours are by reservation only, so
make sure to call several days ahead. After seeing the plantation, you
can buy coffee beans and other souvenirs at the gift shop. Allow yourself an hour to travel the winding road from Ponce. ⊠ *Rte. 123, Km
16.8, Sector Corral Viejo* ☎ *787/722–5882 weekdays; 787/284–7020
weekends* ☎ *$8* ☉ *Wed.–Sun., tours at 8:30, 10:30, 1:30 and 3:30.*

FodorśChoice   **Museo de Arte de Ponce.** This building—designed by Edward Durrell
★   Stone, who also designed the original Museum of Modern Art in New
York City and the Kennedy Center in Washington, D.C.—is easily identified by the hexagonal galleries on the second story. The museum,
which underwent a major renovation in 2010, has one of the best
art collections in Latin America, which is why residents of San Juan
frequently make the trip down to Ponce. The 3,000-piece collection
includes works by famous Puerto Rican artists such as Francisco Oller,
represented by a lovely landscape called *Hacienda Aurora.* There are
plenty of European works on display as well, including paintings by
Peter Paul Rubens and Thomas Gainsborough. The highlight of the
European collection is the Pre-Raphaelite paintings, particularly the
mesmerizing *Flaming June,* by Frederick Leighton, which has become
the museum's unofficial symbol. You can take a break in the museum's
three sculpture gardens, or relax in Restaurant Al Sur. Watch for special exhibits, such as a recent one examining the work of video artists. ⊠ *2325 Av. Las Américas, Sector Santa María* ☎ *787/840–1510*
⊕ *www.museoarteponce.org* ☎ *$6* ☉ *Wed.–Mon. 10–6.*

Today it's a museum, but for more than 100 years Parque de Bombas served as Ponce's main firehouse.

Museo de la Historia de Ponce. Housed in two adjoining neoclassical mansions, this museum includes 10 exhibition halls covering the city's residents, from the Taíno Indians to the Spanish settlers to the mix of the present. Hour-long guided tours in English and Spanish give an overview of the city's history. The descriptions are mostly in Spanish, but displays of clothing from different eras still are interesting to see. ⊠ *53 Calle Isabel, at Calle Mayor, Ponce Centro* ☎ *787/844–7042* ✉ *Free* ⏱ *Tues.–Sun. 8–4:30.*

♺ **Parque de Bombas.** After El Morro in Old San Juan, this distinctive
Fodor'sChoice red-and-black-striped building may be the second-most-photographed
★ structure in Puerto Rico. Built in 1882 as a pavilion for an agricultural and industrial fair, it was converted the following year into a firehouse. Today it's a museum tracing the history—and glorious feats—of Ponce's fire brigade. Kids love the antique fire truck on the lower level. Short tours in English and Spanish are given on the half hour, and you can sign up for free trolley tours of the historic downtown here. The island's most helpful tourism officials staff a small information desk inside the door. ⊠ *Plaza de las Delicias, Ponce Centro* ☎ *787/284–3338* ⊕ *www. visitponce.com* ✉ *Free* ⏱ *Daily 9–5.*

SAN GERMÁN

Around San Germán's (population 39,000) two main squares—Plazuela Santo Domingo and Plaza Francisco Mariano Quiñones (named for an abolitionist)—are buildings done in every conceivable style of architecture found on the island, including Mission, Victorian, Creole, and Spanish colonial. The city's tourist office offers a free, guided trolley tour. Students and professors from the Inter-American University often fill the center's bars and cafés.

★ **Capilla de Porta Coeli** *(Heaven's Gate Chapel).* One of the oldest religious buildings in the Americas, this mission-style chapel overlooks the long, rectangular Plazuela de Santo Domingo. It's not a grand building, but its position at the top of a stone stairway gives it a noble air. Queen Isabel Segunda decreed that the Dominicans should build a church and monastery in San Germán, so a rudimentary building was built in 1609, replaced in 1692 by the structure that can still be seen today. (Sadly, most of the monastery was demolished in 1866, leaving only a vestige of its facade.) The chapel now functions as a museum of religious art, displaying painted wooden statuary by Latin American and Spanish artists. ⊠ *East end of Plazuela Santo Domingo* ☏ *787/892–5845* ⊕ *www. icp.gobierno.pr* ▨ *$3* ⊗ *Wed.–Sun. 8:30–noon and 1–4.*

CENTRAL PUERTO RICO

Fodor's Choice ★ **Arecibo Observatory.** Hidden among pine-covered hills, the Arecibo Observatory is home to the world's largest radar-radio telescope. Operated by the National Astronomy and Ionosphere Center of Cornell University, the 20-acre dish lies in a 563-foot-deep sinkhole in the karst landscape. If the 600-ton platform hovering eerily over the dish looks familiar, it may be because it was featured in the movie *Contact.* You can walk around the viewing platform and explore two levels of interactive exhibits on planetary systems, meteors, and weather phenomena in the visitor center. There's also a gift shop. Note that the trail leading up to the observatory is extremely steep. For those who have difficulty walking or have a medical condition, ask a staff member at the gate about a van that provides courtesy shuttle service to the observatory entrance. ⊠ *Rte. 625, Km 3.0, Arecibo* ☏ *787/878–2612* ⊕ *www.naic. edu* ▨ *$10 adults; $6 children and seniors* ⊗ *Daily 9–4, except closed Mon. and Tues., Jan. 16–May 31 and Aug. 1–Dec. 14.*

Fodor's Choice ★ **Parque de las Cavernas del Río Camuy.** The 268-acre Parque de las Cavernas del Río Camuy contains one of the world's largest cave networks. After watching an introductory film, a tram takes you down a trail shaded by bamboo and banana trees to Cueva Clara, where the stalactites and stalagmites turn the entrance into a toothy grin. Hour long guided tours in English and Spanish lead you on foot through the 180-foot-high cave, which is teeming with wildlife. You're likely to see the blue-eyed river crabs and long-legged tarantulas. More elusive are the bats that make their home here. They don't come out until dark, but you can feel the heat they generate at the cave's entrance. The visit ends with a tram ride to the Tres Pueblos sinkhole, where you can see the third-longest underground river in the world passing from one cave to another. Tours are first-come, first-served; plan to arrive early on weekends, when locals join the crowds. There's a picnic area, cafeteria, and gift shop. ⊠ *Rte. 129, Km 18.9, Camuy* ☏ *787/898–3100* ⊕ *www. parquesnacionalespr.com* ▨ *$15* ⊗ *Wed.–Sun. 8:30–5; last tour at 3:30.*

WESTERN PUERTO RICO

MAYAGÜEZ

With a population of slightly more than 100,000, this is the largest city on Puerto Rico's west coast. Although bypassed by the mania for restoration that has spruced up Ponce and Old San Juan, Mayagüez is graced by some lovely turn-of-the-20th-century architecture, such as the landmark art deco Teatro Yagüez and the Plaza de Colón.

☺ **Zoológico de Puerto Rico.** Puerto Rico's only zoo, the 45-acre Zoológico de Puerto Rico, is just north of downtown. After $13 million in renovations, it's looking pretty spiffy. New on the scene is a 45-foot-tall aviary, which allows you to walk through a rain-forest environment as tropical birds fly freely above your head. There's also a new butterfly park where you can let brilliant blue morphos land on your hand, and an arthropodarium where you can get up close and personal with spiders and their kin. Video monitors are built into the floor to show off the bugs that normally get trampled underfoot. The older section of the park has undergone an extensive renovation, so most of the cages have been replaced by fairly natural-looking environments. One of the most popular residents is Mundi, a female elephant who arrived as a baby more than two decades ago. There are also plenty of lions, tigers—and even bears. There is a $3 charge for parking. ⊠ *Rte. 108, north of Rte. 65, Miradero* ☎ *787/834–8110* ⊕ *www.parquesnacionalespr.com* 🖃 *$13* ⏰ *Wed.–Sun. 8:30–4.*

RINCÓN

Jutting out into the ocean along the rugged western coast, Rincón, meaning "corner" in Spanish, may have gotten its name because it's tucked into a bend of the coastline. Some, however, trace the town's name to Gonzalo Rincón, a 16th-century landowner who let poor families live on his land. Whatever the history, the name suits the town, which is like a little world unto itself.

The most famous hotel in the region is the Horned Dorset Primavera— the only Relais & Chateaux property in Puerto Rico. It's one of the most luxurious resorts on the island, not to mention in the Caribbean. A couple of larger hotels, including the Rincón of the Seas and Rincón Beach Resort, have been built, but Rincón remains a laid-back place. The town is still a mecca for wave-seekers, particularly surfers from the East Coast of the United States, who often prefer the relatively quick flight to Aguadilla airport direct from New York–area airports instead of the long haul to the Pacific. One of Rincón's greatest attractions is the diving and snorkeling at nearby Desecheo Island, but the town continues to cater to all sorts of travelers, from budget-conscious surfers to families to honeymooners seeking romance.

WHERE TO EAT

Your palate will be delighted by the range of dining choices available in Puerto Rico. In cosmopolitan San Juan, European, Asian, Middle Eastern, and chic fusion eateries vie for your attention with family-owned restaurants specializing in seafood or *comida criolla* (creole cooking, or local Puerto Rican food). Many of the most innovative chefs here have restaurants in the city's large hotels, but don't be shy about venturing into stand-alone establishments—many concentrated in Condado and San Sebastián. Old San Juan is also home to a number of notable new restaurants and cafés, offering more artisanal-style cuisine—crop-to-cup coffee, rustic homemade pizzas, and creative vegetarian food—at affordable prices. Throughout the island, there's a radiant pride in what the local land can provide, and enthusiastic restaurateurs are redefining what Puerto Rican food is, bite by tasty bite.

What to Wear: Dress codes vary greatly, though a restaurant's price category is a good indicator of its formality. For less expensive places, anything but beachwear is fine. Ritzier eateries will expect collared shirts for men (jacket and tie requirements are rare) and chic attire for women. When in doubt, do as the Puerto Ricans often do and dress up.

OLD SAN JUAN

$$$ ✕ **Aguaviva.** The name means "jellyfish," which explains why this ultra-
SEAFOOD cool, ultramodern place has dim blue lighting like a tranquil ocean, and lamps shaped like jellyfish floating overhead. Elegantly groomed oysters and clams float on cracked ice along the raw bar. Eating here is like submerging oneself into the ocean. The extensive, regularly changing menu is alive with inventive ceviches, including one with mahimahi, tomato, jicama, and Sriracha hot sauce. For something more filling, try fried snapper stuffed with lobster mofongo, or shrimp in a garlic cream sauce with yuca gnocchi. You could also empty out your wallet for one of the *torres del mar,* or "towers of the sea." This gravity-defying dish comes hot or cold and includes oysters, mussels, shrimp—you name it. Oh, and don't pass up the lobster mashed potatoes. Those alone are worth the trip. ⑤ *Average main: $26 ⊠ 364 Calle Fortaleza, Old San Juan* ☎ *787/722–0665* ⊕ *www.oofrestaurants.com* ☉ *No lunch.*

$$$ ✕ **Barú.** A global menu has earned Barú a solid reputation among san-
ECLECTIC juaneros, so this stylishly contemporary restaurant in a 275-year-old colonial townhouse (the tile floor's original) is often crowded. The dishes, some served in medium-size portions so you can order several and share, range from Middle Eastern to Asian to Caribbean. Favorites include almond-crusted goat cheese with mango sauce and yuca chips. More substantial fare includes risotto with shiitake mushrooms and goat cheese, filet mignon with mashed potatoes and red-wine sauce, and pork ribs with a ginger-tamarind glaze. The dining room is dark and mysterious. You can dine on high stools at the bar. Wine pours here are generous. ⑤ *Average main: $25 ⊠ 150 Calle San Sebastián, Old San Juan* ☎ *787/977–7107* ⊕ *www.barupr.com* ☉ *Closed Mon. No lunch.*

$ ✕ **Cuatro Sombras Torrefacción y Café.** If you want to try locally grown,
CAFÉ single-origin, shade-grown coffee, this micro-roastery and café is the
Fodor'sChoice place to do it. Owners Pablo Muñoz and Mariana Suárez grow their
★ beans in the mountains of Yauco on a recently revived hacienda that has been in Muñoz family since 1846. After years spent learning the best growing practices, they opened this cafe in early 2011 to take the fruits of their labor from "crop to cup." It's been attracting attention ever

since. The wood planks that line the banquette are from repurposed coffee storage pallets, and the red accents that catch your eye throughout the room recall perfectly ripe coffee beans. The name Cuatro Sombras, or "four shades," refers to the four types of trees traditionally used in Puerto Rico to provide shade for coffee plants. And although it's the delicious, medium-bodied brew that steals the show, there's also a small but tasty menu of pastries and sandwiches. ⑤ *Average main: $7* ✉ *259 Calle Recinto Sur, Old San Juan* ☎ *787/724–9955* ⊕ *www.cuatrosombras.com* ❍ *No dinner.*

$$$
LATIN AMERICAN
ASIAN

✕ **Dragonfly.** Dark and sexy, this popular Latin-Asian restaurant, all done up in Chinese red, feels more like a fashionable after-hours lounge than a restaurant. The romantic ambience, created partly through tightly packed tables and low lighting, is a big draw. The small plates, meant to be shared, come in generous portions. Don't miss the calamari, fried with onions and oyster sauce and tossed with a local cilantro-like herb called *recao*. Tuna sushi is turned on its head and served atop a deep-fried rice cake dressed with spicy mayo and seaweed salad. Make sure to try the inventive cocktails that nicely complement the food. Reservations aren't accepted, but we'll let you in on a secret to save yourself a frustrating wait: you can call ahead and get yourself put on the waiting list. ⑤ *Average main: $25* ✉ *364 Calle Fortaleza, Old San Juan* ☎ *787/977–3886* ⊕ *www.oofrestaurants.com* ⊗ *Reservations not accepted* ❍ *No lunch.*

$$$
SPANISH

✕ **El Picoteo.** You could make a meal of the small dishes that dominate the menu at this tapas restaurant on a mezzanine balcony at the Hotel El Convento. You won't go wrong ordering the grilled cuttlefish or the pistachio-crusted salmon with a Manchego-cheese sauce and passing them around the table. If you're not into sharing, there are several kinds of paella that arrive on huge plates. There's a long, lively bar inside; one dining area overlooks a pleasant courtyard, and the other looks out onto Calle Cristo. Even if you have dinner plans elsewhere, consider stopping here for a nightcap or a midday pick-me-up. ⑤ *Average main: $30* ✉ *Hotel El Convento, 100 Calle Cristo, Old San Juan* ☎ *787/723–9202* ⊕ *www.elconvento.com.*

$$
PUERTO RICAN
Fodor'sChoice
★

✕ **La Fonda del Jibarito.** The menus are handwritten and the tables wobble, but sanjuaneros have favored this casual, no-frills, family-run restaurant—tucked away on a quiet cobbled street—for years. The conch ceviche, goat fricassee, and shredded beef stew are among the specialties on the menu of typical Puerto Rican *comida criolla* dishes. The tiny back porch is filled with plants, and the dining room is filled with fanciful depictions of life on the street outside. Troubadors serenade patrons, including plenty of cruise-ship passengers when ships are in dock. ⑤ *Average main: $15* ✉ *280 Calle Sol, Old San Juan* ☎ *787/725–8375* ⊕ *www.eljibaritopr.com.*

$$
PUERTO RICAN

✕ **La Mallorquina.** Dating from 1848, La Mallorquina is thought to be the island's oldest restaurant. It specializes in various versions of *asopao*, a soupy rice dish with chicken or seafood, as well as other Puerto Rican and Spanish-inspired favorites. But it's the old-fashioned atmosphere that really recommends the place. In a room of whirring ceiling fans and antique marble floor tiles, the nattily attired staffers zip between the

17

tables, which are covered in white tablecloths. Note that the restaurant closes during the low-season month of September, and that the servers can be a bit short with tourists. $ *Average main: $20* ⊠ *207 Calle San Justo, Old San Juan* 🕾 *787/722–3261* ⊕ *www.lamallorquinapr.com* ⊗ *Closed Sun.*

$$$$
ECLECTIC
Fodor'sChoice
★

✕**Marmalade.** "Wow!" may well be your first reaction after entering Old San Juan's hippest and finest restaurant. U.S.-born owner-chef Peter Schintler—who apprenticed with Raymond Blanc and Gordon Ramsay—has created a class act that's famous for its ultra-chic lounge bar. The restaurant's sensual and minimalist orange-and-white decor features high-back chairs and cushioned banquettes beneath recessed halogen lights. The menu uses many local, sustainable ingredients prepared California-French fashion, resulting in complex flavors and strong aromas. You might try Kobe beef cheeks with heirloom corn, chanterelles, and barley pilaf, or homemade black truffle tagliatelle with a marsala butter. Schintler also works wonders with vegetables, including the humble parsnip, which is roasted and served with blackberries, Marcona almonds, and an almond milk–rosemary foam. Diners can build their own four- to six-course tasting menu, with or without pairings from the very strong wine list, or order à la carte. In addition, the restaurant is accommodating to vegetarians, those with food allergies, and other dietary restrictions. $ *Average main: $28* ⊠ *317 Calle Fortaleza, Old San Juan* 🕾 *787/724–3969* ⊕ *www.marmaladepr.com* ⊗ *No lunch.*

$$$
SPANISH

✕**Toro Salao.** The name means "Salty Bull," and there's something about this place that makes its moniker entirely appropriate. (And it's not just the bullfighting posters that decorate one of the two-story-high walls.) This popular Spanish-Puerto Rican tapas restaurant was opened by Emilio Figueroa, who helped turn the southern end of Calle Fortaleza into the city's top dining destination. There are plenty of small dishes to share, such as a delicious baked Brie that's served with crostini and topped with a chorizo jam (yes, a sausage jam); crispy mahimahi fritters; and Spanish-style flatbread pizzas, called *cocas*. They also make their own fresh pork sausage. The dining room, with a bar lit up in lusty red, is pleasant enough, but the tables that spill onto the adjacent cobblestone square are even better. Stop by for live music on Thursdays and Saturdays. $ *Average main: $25* ⊠ *367 Calle Tetuán, Old San Juan* 🕾 *787/722–3330* ⊕ *www.oofrestaurants.com* ⊗ *No lunch July–Oct.*

$$
VEGETARIAN
★

✕**Verde Mesa.** For some, the words "healthy," "vegetarian," and "delicious" don't belong in the same sentence, but they all come together at Verde Mesa. With punched-tin ceilings, mason-jar lighting fixtures, and eclectic decor inspired by Versailles' Petit Trianon, the focus at this romantic restaurant is on inspiring beauty and pleasure through the senses. Much of the organic produce used in the regularly changing menu comes from the owners' farm and other local sources. The flavor combinations are anything but accidental. You might try a "potion" drink: one standout is made with tarragon flowers, mixed citrus juices, and ginger. Start with a garlicky "hummus" of local pigeon peas. The signature Verde Mesa rice is a mixture of in-season vegetables and chickpeas that the owners say has turned many a skeptic into further exploring the culinary potential of vegetables. You'll also find quite a few expertly prepared tuna and salmon dishes, if you don't want to go all veggie. ⑤ *Average main: $15 ✉ 254, Calle Tetuán, Old San Juan* ☎ 787/390–4662 ☉ *Closed Sun.–Mon.*

$ ✕ **Waffle-era Tea Room.** The only tearoom in Puerto Rico, this breezy
CAFÉ spot overlooking San Juan Bay has a sort of neo-Victorian, steam-punk feel. Choose from nearly 30 loose teas, ranging from white and black to fruity blends. But you'll probably be even more curious about the coffee setup, which looks like a mad-science experiment. It's a siphon fire-brewing system, a painstaking process popular in Japan. You can sample premium local coffees and other rare brews, like the famous (or infamous?) Kopi Luwak, one of the world's most expensive coffees (on their way to your cup, the beans pass through—what else?—the digestive track of a civet cat). The menu consists of house-made sweet or savory waffles—or smaller "wafflitos." You might also choose a "waffe-izza" with fresh tomato sauce and blowtorch-melted mozzarella. We're still thinking of the decadent crème brûlée wafflito. ⑤ *Average main: $9 ✉ Top of Calle Tetuán and Calle Cristo, Old San Juan* ☎ 787/721–1512 ⚐ *Reservations not accepted* ☉ *Closed Mon.–Wed.*

GREATER SAN JUAN

$$$$ ✕ **Budatai.** You'll feel as if you're entering a secret club when you arrive
ASIAN at this stylish hot spot in Condado's poshest shopping district. The
★ restaurant, on the third floor, is decked out in rich, dark colors, with Chinese lanterns that look as if they were designed by Salvador Dalí. The attentive service and the elegantly dressed crowd, however, never feel stuffy. The brainchild of one of Puerto Rico's best-known chefs, Roberto Treviño, it's a seamless mix of Latin-accented pan-Asian food, including duck fried rice with sweet plantains and halibut sashimi with coconut, yuzu, and toasted garlic. We couldn't get enough of the calamari, fried for a few seconds in hot oil and then quickly sautéed with sweet onions. The upstairs outdoor terrace is a good place for drinks; consider stopping by on the last Sunday evening of the month, when you can enjoy the jazz concert at Ventana al Mar without the crowds. Sunday brunch is also served. ⑤ *Average main: $34 ✉ 1056 Av. Ashford, Condado* ☎ 787/725–6919 ⊕ *www.budatai.com.*

$$$$ ✕ **Il Mulino New York.** You'll want for nothing at the San Juan outpost
ITALIAN of the famed Manhattan restaurant, where a team of tuxedoed waiters
Fodor'sChoice effortlessly coordinates your entire meal experience. The dark-wood-
★ paneled walls and heavy velvet drapes are an odd juxtaposition with the tropical climate, but everything about this place is elegant and tasteful. Garlic bread, fried zucchini, and other antipasti arrive moments after you sit down, though you'll want to pace yourself and leave room for the mammoth entrées to come. Standouts include rigatoni Bolognese, stuffed whole branzino (deboned tableside), and fresh pappardelle with sausage. There's no fusion or haute cuisine here, just solid Italian dishes, painstakingly executed. All this perfection comes at a price, though the shot of homemade grappa they offer at the end might help ease the shock. ⑤ *Average main: $39 ✉ The Ritz-Carlton, San Juan, 6991 Av. de los Gobernadores, Isla Verde* ☎ 787/791–8632 ⊕ *www.ilmulino.com* ⚐ *Reservations essential* ☉ *No lunch.*

17

$$ ✕**Kasalta.** Those who think coffee can never be too strong should make
CAFÉ   a beeline to Kasalta, which has an amazing pitch-black brew that will
knock your socks off. Make your selection from the display cases full
of luscious pastries, particularly the famous *quesito* (cream cheese–filled
puff pastry) and other tempting treats. Walk up to the counter and order
a sandwich, such as the savory Cubano, or other items such as octopus
salad. For dinner there are fish dishes and other, more substantial fare.
Occasionally quality can be uneven, though, and some staff members
are curt with tourists. ⑤ *Average main: $18* ✉ *1966 Calle McLeary,
Ocean Park* ☎ *787/727–7340* ⊕ *www.kasalta.com.*

$$$ ✕**Miró.** Like its namesake, the painter Joan Miró, this restaurant draws
SPANISH   its inspiration from the Catalan region of Spain, where the cuisine is
heavy on seafood and hearty tapas. Start with steamed clams with garlic
or braised chorizo and peppers. (If you're here at the right time, you
might get to try regional favorites like razor clams or baby octopus.)
Main courses include sizzling lamb chops, as well as salmon in a sauce
of Cabrales cheese, or *arroz negro* with mixed shellfish. Prints by the
artist hang on the walls, adding an authentic touch to the maze of tiny
dining rooms. If you prefer, you can also dine on the more casual front
terrace. Daily brunch is available, and there's often live Spanish music
Thursday through Sunday. ⑤ *Average main: $24* ✉ *1214 Av. Ashford,
Condado* ☎ *787/723–9593* ⊕ *www.miroseafood.com.*

$$$ ✕**Pamela's.** If you've always dreamed of fine dining for two right on
CARIBBEAN   the beach, only steps from where crashing waves meet the shore, head
Fodor'sChoice   to this local favorite in Ocean Park. If you prefer air conditioning, an
★   elegant glassed-in solarium awaits, complete with black cobblestone
floors and slow-turning ceiling fans. The menu is a contemporary, cre-
ative mix of Caribbean spices and other tropical ingredients. To start,
try the corn fritters with a spicy cilantro aioli. The restaurant prides
itself on its fresh seafood, so move on to the rainbow trout, stuffed with
crab and coconut and steamed in a banana leaf, or choose the seared
salmon served with an *acerola* (Caribbean cherry) chimichurri. ⑤ *Aver-
age main: $28* ✉ *Numero Uno Guest House, 1 Calle Santa Ana, Ocean
Park* ☎ *787/726–5010* ⊕ *www.numero1guesthouse.com.*

$$$$ ✕**Pikayo.** Celebrity chef and Puerto Rico native Wilo Benet's flagship
ECLECTIC   restaurant makes the most of its elegant surroundings at the Conrad San
Fodor'sChoice   Juan Condado Plaza hotel. Works from local artists line the walls, and
★   the atmosphere is formal but never hushed. The menu offers a twist on
traditional Puerto Rican classics as well as more international flavors.
Start with a glass of Benet's own wine, either a simple *tempranillo* (red)
or an *albariño* (white). Then try some of the starters; particularly good
are the pork belly sliders and the spicy tuna on crispy rice (known here
as *pegao*). For main courses, options include lamb chops with wild
mushrooms and a Dijon mustard demiglace, and jumbo shrimp with
celery root purée and a chorizo emulsion. Don't be surprised if Benet
himself stops by your table to make sure everything is just to your liking.
⑤ *Average main: $35* ✉ *Conrad San Juan Condado Plaza, 999 Av. Ash-
ford, Condado* ☎ *787/721–6194* ⊕ *www.wilobenet.com* ☾ *No lunch.*

EASTERN PUERTO RICO

$$$ ✕ **Calizo.** There's a string of seafood shacks in the village of Las Croabas,
SEAFOOD all serving delicious fried fish. This open-air eatery with tables covered
by straw-topped umbrellas and anchored by a bustling square bar, takes
things up a notch or two. Look for dishes like seafood salad in a spicy
vinaigrette, mahimahi with scallops, a rich seafood paella, and chunks
of lobster sautéed in cilantro butter. Wash it all down with a cold san-
gria. It's almost across from the Balneario Seven Seas, making it a great
place to refuel after a day at the beach. The only drawback is that it's a
bit on the pricey side. $ *Average main: $29* ⊠ *Rte. 987, Las Croabas,
Fajardo* ☎ *787/863–3664.*

$$$ ✕ **Pasión por el Fogón.** Pasión por el Fogón is one of Fajardo's most
CARIBBEAN beloved restaurants. Owner Norma Guadaloupe, who will no doubt
greet you at the door, promises that the service at this perennial favorite can't be beat, while chef Myrta Pérez Toledo possesses a talent for
taking traditional dishes and making them into something special. Succulent cuts of meat and fish are presented in unexpected ways—witness
a perfectly cooked flank steak rolled into a cylinder standing on one
end. But what makes this dish remarkable is the slightly sweet tamarind sauce that brings out the meat's earthy flavors. If you're a seafood
lover, start with the lime-infused red-snapper ceviche, and then move
on to the lobster medallions broiled in butter. For dessert, order the
"Caribbean Sun," a version of an ice cream sundae that blends caramel, cinnamon, and chocolate toppings. $ *Average main: $30* ⊠ *Rte.
987, Km 2.3, Fajardo* ☎ *787/863–3502* ⊕ *www.pasionporelfogon.net*
⌂ *Reservations essential.*

VIEQUES AND CULEBRA

CULEBRA

$ ✕ **Juanita Bananas.** This casual spot is one of the most popular eateries
SUSHI on Culebra. Chef Jennifer Daubon uses only the freshest local pro-
ECLECTIC duce and catch of the day to inspire a menu heavy on appetizers, light
bites, and sushi. The menu changes daily—check the chalkboard—but
chicken wings at happy hour and a variety of unique sushi rolls are
most popular. Order at the bar, and grab a seat inside or on the back
patio to witness the the sights of Culebra. $ *Average main: $10* ⊠ *Hotel
Kokomo, Calle Pedro Marquez, across from the ferry dock, Culebra*
☎ *787/742–1060* ⊕ *www.juanitabananas.com.*

$ ✕ **Mamacita's.** Pull your dinghy up to the dock and watch the resident
CARIBBEAN iguanas plod past at this simple open-air, tin-roofed restaurant on a
rough-plank deck beside the Dewey canal. Tarpon cruise past in the jade
waters below, and the to and fro of boaters also keeps patrons amused.
Doubling as Culebra's favorite local watering hole and gringo hangout,
palm tree trunks litter the space, which is painted in a rainbow of pink,
purple, and green. With a nightly changing menu, Mamacita's down-
home dishes play a part in the appeal. The menu is heavy on burgers and
sandwiches, but seafood dishes include an excellent mahimahi. $ *Av-
erage main: $12* ⊠ *64 Calle Castelar, #66, Dewey* ☎ *787/742–0322*
⊕ *www.mamacitasguesthouse.com.*

17

$ ✕ **Zaco's Tacos.** After spending years in the kitchen of popular hangout
MEXICAN   Mamacita's, chef Zach Sizer decided to open his own joint, a no-frills
Fodor'sChoice   taco spot delivering fresh, flavorful, affordable grub. Good thing he did;
★   Zaco's Tacos is already a runaway success. Arched ceilings are painted
in bright primary colors, lending a warm, festive feel to the cozy space.
An outdoor wood terrace in the back offers open-air dining and Sunday
brunch, though most just prefer to order some delicious beer-battered
fish, *carnitas* (pork), or seared tuna tacos at the bar. For the adventurous, pork belly, beef, and tongue tacos are on the menu, as well as
heartier burritos. Refresh with a light hibiscus tea, or a more obvious
indulgence—one of the many tequila-saturated margaritas. ⑤ *Average
main: $5* ✉ *21 Calle Pedro Marquez, DeweyCulebra* ☏ *787/742–0243*
⊕ *www.zacostacos.com* ⊘ *Closed Thur.*

VIEQUES

$$ ✕ **Conuco.** A mix of locals and gringos frequent excellent newcomer
PUERTO RICAN   Conuco, soft-spoken Puerto Rico native Rebecca Betancourt's homage
Fodor'sChoice   to local food with an upscale twist. Barnlike open windows look out
★   onto one of Isabel Segunda's main streets, and within, the airy room is
simple but cozy, enhanced by bright yellow walls, seafoam chairs, white
table tops, and ceiling fans. A back patio offers alfresco dining. Start
with an sangria rum punch, then move onto *any* of the menu's many
selections; it's all that wonderful. Piping-hot arepas Viequenses are piled
high with pepper and octopus salad, while small *tostones rellenos* (fried
plantains) are shaped into cups filled with a citrusy ceviche. *Sorullitos*
(cheesy corn fritters) and *bacalaítos* (cod fritters) are reimagined with
modern flair. The only thing trumping the flavors of a juicy *churrasco*
(skirt steak) with rice and beans and overflowing seafood *mofongo*
is the wow-factor of Betancourt's presentations. Elevating cooking to
art form, this local spot is one that will have you dreaming about
Vieques long after you've left the island. ⑤ *Average main: $15* ✉ *110
Luis Muñoz Rivera, Isabel SegundaVieques* ☏ *787/741–2500* ⊕ *www.
restauranteconuco.com.*

$$$ ✕ **El Quenepo.** Elegant yet unpretentious, El Quenepo remains the hottest
ECLECTIC   act in town, adding fine dining and a touch of class to the Esperanza
Fodor'sChoice   waterfront. Six stable doors on an inviting powder blue building open
★   to expose ocean views. The menu, which changes yearly, features local
herbs and fruits such as *quenepas* (limes) and breadfruit in the artfully
prepared dishes that owners Scott and Kate Cole call "fun, funky island
food." Scott is the chef, known for his seafood specials highlighting
the daily catch; Kate is the consummate hostess. Start with the popular grilled Caesar salad followed by sensational *mofongo* stuffed with
shrimp and lobster in sweet-and-spicy *criollo* sauce. Oenophiles will
appreciate the large wine list, and the sangria is delicious. Lucky walk-
ins can grab a seat at the more casual high bar tables, but for the true
experience of this gem, make a reservation. ⑤ *Average main: $25* ✉ *148
Calle Flamboyan, EsperanzaVieques* ☏ *787/741–1215* ⌃ *Reservations
essential* ⊘ *Closed Mon.*

$$$$ ✕ **Mix on the Beach.** Local dining reaches new heights courtesy of cel-
ECLECTIC   ebrated chef Alain Ducasse at Mix on the Beach. The multi-Michelin-
decorated restaurant at the W Retreat & Spa—Ducasse's first in the

Caribbean—puts a French twist on Caribbean-Latino cuisine. And although it's some of the priciest cuisine on the island, it's worth the splurge. The bi-level dining terraces overlook a sensational swimming-pool complex that at night is delicately lit to perfection. The rollicking ocean provides the soundtrack to some seriously romantic al fresco dining. To share, the Caribbean paella with local lobster delivers in spades, while server after server can been seen delivering the moist salty cod to neighboring tables. At breakfast, the housemade strawberry jam goes beautifully with flaky, fresh croissants, and for dessert, the Ducasse candy bar–akin to a fancy KitKat–is a must-try. ⑤ *Average main: $30* ⊠ *W Retreat & Spa, Route 200, Km 3.2, Isabel SegundaVieques* ☎ *787/741–4100* ⊕ *www.wvieques.com/mix* ⌕ *Reservations essential.*

SOUTHERN PUERTO RICO

PONCE

$$$ ✕**Archipiélago.** With perhaps the greatest view in all of Puerto Rico, this
LATIN AMERICAN ambitious restaurant has stepped in to fill the city's culinary vacuum.
Fodor'sChoice It sits on the sixth and seventh floors of a building that overlooks the
★ Parque de Bombas and Catedral de Nuestra Señora de Guadalupe. The beautifully designed restaurant and lounge have quickly found their place among the hottest spots in Puerto Rico. Expect a chic crowd that's dressed to impress dining on Puerto Rican fusion dishes as diverse as beer-battered mahimahi, plantain-stuffed pork or steak topped with lemon chimichurri. A terrace has live jazz on the weekends, which pairs well with their renowned mojitos. ⑤ *Average main: $21* ⊠ *76 Calle Cristina, 6th Floor, Ponce Centro, Ponce* ☎ *787/812–8822* ⊕ *www. archipielagopr.com* ۞ *Closed Mon. and Tues.*

$$ ✕**Cabuqui.** On sweltering hot days, it takes a lot to make *ponceños* leave
ECLECTIC their homes. Yet they come out in droves to the tree-shaded courtyard of
★ the Cubuqui. When a breeze shakes the flower-covered branches, things cool down considerably. And if nature doesn't cooperate, there are always the three air-conditioned dining rooms. The menu is extremely well traveled, stopping in Argentina (*churrasco*, or skirt steak, served with homemade chimichurri) and France (veal fillet in a red wine sauce) before heading back to Puerto Rico for such dishes as *masitas de cerdo* (chunks of perfectly seasoned pork). The wine list, which includes many bottles from Spain and Chile, is quite reasonable. There's always live music, whether it's a small band playing jazz or a single accordionist losing himself in a tango. ⑤ *Average main: $20* ⊠ *32 Calle Isabel, Ponce Centro, Ponce* ☎ *787/984–5696* ۞ *Closed Sun.–Tues.*

$$ ✕**El Ancla.** Families favor this laid-back restaurant, whose dining room
SEAFOOD sits at the edge of the sea. The kitchen serves generous and affordable plates of fish, crab, and other fresh seafood with *tostones* (fried plantains), french fries, and garlic bread. Try the shrimp in garlic sauce, salmon fillet with capers, or the delectable mofongo stuffed with seafood. Finish your meal with one of the fantastic flans. The piña coladas—with or without rum—are exceptional. ⑤ *Average main: $20* ⊠ *805 Av. Hostos Final, Ponce Playa, Ponce* ☎ *787/840–2450* ⊕ *www. restauranteelancla.com.*

17

WESTERN PUERTO RICO

$$
SEAFOOD

✕ El Bohío. Watch seagulls dive for their food while you dine on a covered deck extending out into the bay. The long list of seafood is prepared in a variety of ways: Shrimp comes breaded, stewed, or skewered; conch is served as a salad or cooked in a butter-and-garlic sauce; and the lobster can be prepared just about any way you can imagine. This restaurant, on stilts above

the water, is about the most charming setting in Joyuda. ⓢ *Average main: $15* ⊠ *Rte. 102, Km 13.9, Joyuda* ☎ *787/851–2755* ⊕ *www. restauranteelbohiojoyuda.com* ⊗ *Closed Oct.*

$
PUERTO RICAN
CARIBBEAN

✕ Rincón Tropical. Don't be scared off by the cheap plastic tables and chairs. What you should notice is that they are almost always full of locals enjoying the area's freshest seafood. The kitchen keeps it simple, preparing dishes with the lightest touch. Highlights include mahimahi with onions and peppers as well as fried red snapper with rice and beans. Fried plantains make a nice accompaniment to almost anything. Stop by weekdays for the $5 lunch special. ⓢ *Average main: $10* ⊠ *Rte. 115, Km 12, Rincón* ☎ *787/823–2017* ⊕ *www.rinconpr. com/rincontropical.*

$
JAPANESE
Fodor'sChoice
★

✕ The Pool Bar Sushi. One of only a few sushi restaurants on the west coast, the open-air Pool Bar attracts visitors from as far away as San Juan. The menu rivals that of any high-end Japanese restaurant, offering mango tuna rolls, eel maki, dim sum, and wakame seaweed salads. A house favorite is the Starving Surfer Roll of crunchy shrimp and avocado topped with spicy tuna. The relaxed setting is especially popular with surfers drawn by the nightly surf flicks projected on the movie-screen backdrop. Arrive early on Thursday nights to enjoy live jazz. ⓢ *Average main: $9* ⊠ *Pools Beach Cabanas, Rte. 413, Rincón* ☎ *787/823–2583* ⊕ *www.poolsbeach.com* ⊗ *Closed Tues. No lunch.*

$$$$
CARIBBEAN
★

✕ Restaurant Aaron at the Horned Dorset Primavera. People come from all over the island for a meal at this exquisite restaurant. A pair of stone stairways leads up to the elegant dining room, with black-and-white marble floors, chandeliers with ruby-red shades, and a Steinway piano dating back to 1901. Dessert and after-dinner drinks are often served on the terrace, where you'll hear the constant crash of the waves. The 10-course tasting menu, an extravagant meal with a $125 price tag, might include foie gras with maple berry glaze, pan-seared scallops with asparagus risotto, or poached *chillo* (red snapper) with apricot gnocchi. Adding Caribbean accents to classical French cuisine, the à la carte menu changes weekly but might include roasted rack of lamb and wahoo in a pistachio crust. Dress is formal by island standards, except in the downstairs "Blue Room" dining area, where a similar menu is served. ⓢ *Average main: $40* ⊠ *Horned Dorset Primavera, Rte. 429, Km 3, Rincón* ☎ *787/823–4030* ⊕ *www.horneddorset.com* ⌣ *Reservations essential Jacket required* ⊗ *Closed Mon.–Wed. Apr.–Nov.*

$$
CARIBBEAN
✕**Tamboo.** Here is a bar and grill that doesn't fall too far into either category. The kitchen prepares a wide range of unique dishes, from king-crab sandwiches to baby-back ribs brushed with guava sauce. Despite the laid-back atmosphere, the food presentation is fit for a high-end restaurant. The open-air bar serves a mean mojito, recently voted the best on the island. The deck is a great place to watch novice surfers wipe out on the nearby beach. On weekends, you can enjoy live music. ⑤ *Average main: $17* ✉ *Beside the Point, Rte. 413, Km 4.4, Rincón* ☎ *787/823–8550* ⊕ *www.besidethepointe.com* ☾ *Closed Sept.*

WHERE TO STAY

In San Juan, the best beaches are in Isla Verde, though Condado is more centrally located. Old San Juan offers easy access to dining and nightlife. Outside San Juan, particularly on the east coast, you can find self-contained luxury resorts that cover hundreds of acres. Around the island, government-sponsored *paradores* are rural inns, others offer no-frills apartments, and some are large hotels close to either an attraction or beach.

For expanded reviews, facilities, and current deals, visit Fodors.com.

PRIVATE VILLAS AND CONDOS

In the west, southwest, and south—as well as on the islands of Vieques and Culebra—smaller inns and condominiums for short-term rentals are the norm. Villa rentals are increasingly popular.

17

RENTAL CONTACTS

Island West Properties & Beach Rentals. Island West Properties & Beach Rentals can help you rent villas in Rincón by the day, week, or month. The company has been around for years, so it corners the market. ✉ *Rte. 413, Km 0.7* ☎ *787/823–2323* ⊕ *www.islandwestrentals.com.*

Puerto Rico Vacation Apartments. Some 200 properties in Condado and Isla Verde can be rented from this apartment company. ✉ *Calle Marbella del Caribe Oeste S-5, Isla Verde, San Juan* ☎ *787/727–1591, 800/266–3639* ⊕ *www.sanjuanvacations.com.*

Rainbow Realty. A list of rental properties is available from gay-friendly Rainbow Realty. ✉ *278 Calle Flamboyán, Esperanza Vieques* ☎ *787/741–4312* ⊕ *www.viequesrainbowrealty.com.*

OLD SAN JUAN

$$
B&B/INN
🏠 **The Gallery Inn.** Nothing like this rambling, eclectic inn exists anywhere else in San Juan—or Puerto Rico, for that matter. **Pros:** one-of-a-kind lodging; ocean views; wonderful classical music concerts. **Cons:** no elevator; several narrow, winding staircases; an uphill walk from rest of Old San Juan; no sign out front; sometimes raucous pet macaws and cockatoos. **TripAdvisor:** "wonderful romantic site," "unique property," "artistic paradise." ⑤ *Rooms from: $185* ✉ *204–206 Calle Norzagaray, Old San Juan* ☎ *787/722–1808* ⊕ *www.thegalleryinn.com* 🛏 *20 rooms, 5 suites* ⑩ *Breakfast.*

see detail map of
Old San Juan

El Morro

San Cristóbal

Old San Juan

Tourist Information Center

Ferry Terminal

Cruise Ship Docks 1–6

ISLA DE CABRAS

Parque Nacional
Isla de Cabras

Palo Seco

Parque Recreativo
La Esperanza

El Caño Exp.

Ferry Terminal

Bahía de San Juan

Avenida Muñoz Rivera

Parque Muñoz Rivera

Parque Del Nuevo Milenio

Escambrón

Avenida de la Constitución

Canal de San Antonio

Laguna Condado

Miramar

Calle Cerra

Isla Grande Airport
(Fernando L. Rivas
Dominici Airport)

San Juan
Convention Center

Bahía de Puerto Nuevo

Calle Las Cucharillas

Palmas

Catano

Juan Sánchez

Autopista José de Diego

Ave Central Ivanita

Fort Buchanan

Avenida Franklin D Roosevelt

Bosque Estatal
San Patricio

Rafael Nadal Exp.

Avenida San Patricio

Avenida Escorial

Gobernador Pinero

Avenida José de Diego

Pueblo Viejo

Bayamon

Río De Bayamon

Parque de Torrimar

Rio Hondo Exp.

Greater San Juan

Atlantic Ocean

Condado
Avenida Ashford
Santurce
Calle McLeary
Calle Loiza
Comunidad
Ocean Park
Punta las Marías

8 9
11
5
6 7 10
2
3
26
Román Baldorioty de Castro Exp.
37

Calle Del Parque

25
35

1

Avenida Juan Ponce De León

Calle Tapia

Avenida Eduardo Conde

36

Laguna
Los
Corozos

Río
Piedras

12 Isla Verde 14
Avenida Isla Verde 13 15

Avenida Los Governadores

Luis Muñoz Marín
International Airport

26 Marginal Los Angeles

22

18

Calle Teniente César L. Gonzalez

23
41

Hato Rey
Central

Calle Guayama
27

25

Avenida Luis Muñoz Rivera

Oriente

Calle Sicilia

Deportivo
Manuel Perez

Puente Teodoro Moscoso

Laguna
San Jose

Adolfo
Dones

17

Carolina

Canal Suarez

8

Avenida Iturregui

arque
Muñoz
Marín
Parque
Baldrich
Ave. Jesus T Piñero

Universidad de
Puerto Rico
4

Hato Rey Sur

Calle José De Diego
Calle 47

Calle Simon Madera

Calle Zurana

Sabana Llana
Norte

18
El Cinco

847

Avenida Regimiento 65 De Infanteri
3

181

Universidad de
Puerto Rico
Jardín Botánical

1

176

KEY

1	*Exploring Sights*
1	*Restaurants & Hotels*
🚢	*Ferry*
🛈	*Tourist Information*

El Convento Hotel

$$$
HOTEL
Fodor's Choice
★

🏨 **Hotel El Convento.** Carmelite nuns once inhabited this 350-year-old convent, but there's no longer anything austere about it. **Pros:** Lovely building; atmosphere to spare; plenty of nearby dining options. **Cons:** Near some noisy bars; small pool and small bathrooms. **TripAdvisor:** "full of character," "charming," "superb location." ⑤ *Rooms from: $260* ⊠ *100 Calle Cristo, Old San Juan* ☎ *787/723–9020* ⊕ *www. elconvento.com* ➷ *63 rooms, 5 suites* ⍟ *No meals.*

$$$
HOTEL

🏨 **Sheraton Old San Juan Hotel & Casino.** This hotel's triangular shape subtly echoes the cruise ships docked nearby. **Pros:** harbor views; near many dining options; good array of room types. **Cons:** motel feel to guest rooms; noise from casino overwhelms lobby and restaurants; Wi-Fi in public areas only. **TripAdvisor:** "surprisingly convenient," "nice place with a great view," "perfect location to explore." ⑤ *Rooms from: $259* ⊠ *100 Calle Brumbaugh, Old San Juan* ☎ *787/721–5100 or 866/376–7577* ⊕ *www.sheratonoldsanjuan.com* ➷ *200 rooms, 40 suites* ⍟ *No meals.*

GREATER SAN JUAN

$
B&B/INN
★

🏨 **Andalucía.** In a Spanish-style house, this friendly little inn lives up to its name with such details as hand-painted tiles and ceramic pots filled with greenery. **Pros:** terrific value; helpful hosts; gorgeous courtyard. **Cons:** not right on the beach; some rooms are smaller than others. **TripAdvisor:** "comfortable and convenient," "friendly hosts," "charming." ⑤ *Rooms from: $99* ⊠ *2011 Calle McLeary, Ocean Park* ☎ *787/309–3373* ⊕ *www.andalucia-puertorico.com* ➷ *11 rooms* ⍟ *No meals.*

$
B&B/INN

At Wind Chimes Inn. Hidden behind a whitewashed wall covered with bougainvillea, this Spanish-style villa gives the impression of an exclusive retreat. **Pros:** Charming architecture; on the edge of Condado; can use facilities at Acacia Seaside Inn. **Cons:** On a busy street; old-fashioned rooms; only a few rooms have closets. **TripAdvisor:** "small and cozy," "charmingly authentic," "quiet." $ *Rooms from: $120* ⊠ *1750 Av. McLeary, Condado* ☎ *787/727–4153 or 800/946–3244* ⊕ *www.at windchimesinn.com* ⌁ *17 rooms, 5 suites* ⎮⊙⎮ *No meals.*

> **BEST BETS FOR LODGING**
>
> **Best for Romance**
>
> Hotel El Convento, Numero Uno, The Ritz-Carlton, San Juan
>
> **Best Beachfront**
>
> El San Juan Hotel & Casino, The Ritz-Carlton, San Juan
>
> **Best Pool**
>
> El San Juan Hotel & Casino, Gallery Inn, The Ritz-Carlton, San Juan

$
HOTEL

Coral Princess. This Art Deco building—one of the few left in Condado—has personality to spare. **Pros:** good value; friendly staff; comfortable common areas. **Cons:** not directly on the beach; small pool; Wi-Fi is in lobby only. **TripAdvisor:** "quaint," "great small hotel," "the perfect getaway." $ *Rooms from: $125* ⊠ *1159 Av. Magdalena, Condado* ☎ *787/977–7700* ⊕ *www.coralpr.com* ⌁ *25 rooms* ⎮⊙⎮ *Breakfast.*

$$$
RESORT
☾
Fodor's Choice
★

El San Juan Hotel & Casino. For decades this iconic hotel was the don't-miss destination in Isla Verde, and a renovation in 2007 has helped keep everyone's attention. **Pros:** beautiful pool; great dining options in and near hotel; on a fantastic beach. **Cons:** noise in the lobby from bars and casino; self-parking lot is a long walk from the hotel entrance; small bathrooms, without baths. **TripAdvisor:** "everything you need," "classic resort," "gorgeous hotel and facilities." $ *Rooms from: $330* ⊠ *6063 Av. Isla Verde, Isla Verde* ☎ *787/791–1000* ⊕ *www.elsanjuanhotel.com* ⌁ *386 rooms, 57 suites* ⎮⊙⎮ *No meals.*

$
B&B/INN
★

Hostería del Mar. A top-to-bottom renovation in 2011 banished this small inn's formerly drab room decor, and in its place are stylish rooms decorated in bright blues and whites, with brand-new mattresses and plasma-screen televisions. **Pros:** right on the beach; lovely building; good on-site dining. **Cons:** long walk to other restaurants; no pool; Wi-Fi in lobby only. **TripAdvisor:** "cozy spot," "laid-back beach vibe," "intimate." $ *Rooms from: $129* ⊠ *1 Calle Tapia, Ocean Park* ☎ *787/727–3302* ⊕ *www.hosteriadelmarpr.com* ⌁ *23 rooms, 2 suites.*

$$$
RESORT
Fodor's Choice
★

La Concha—A Renaissance Resort. La Concha—an icon of Tropical Modernist architecture—fits the ideal of a chic Caribbean resort. **Pros:** stunning architecture; numerous on-site social activities; beautiful guestrooms. **Cons:** noisy bar/lobby, particularly when there's live music; beach can be narrow during times of high tide and surf advisories. **TripAdvisor:** "beautiful," "wonderful location," "very friendly employees." $ *Rooms from: $300* ⊠ *1077 Av. Ashford, Condado* ☎ *787/721–7500* ⊕ *www.laconcharesort.com* ⌁ *232 rooms, 16 suites; 235 tower suites* ⎮⊙⎮ *No meals.*

17

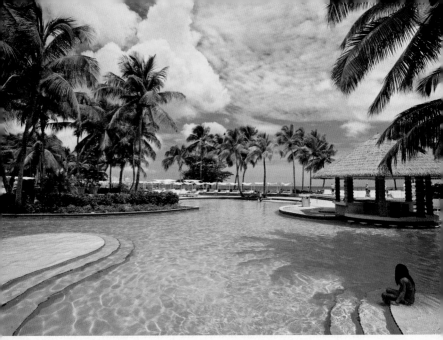

El San Juan Hotel & Casino.

$ **Numero Uno Guest House.** Although the name refers to the hotel's
HOTEL   address, Numero Uno is how guests rate this small hotel. **Pros:** friendly
Fodor'sChoice atmosphere; great restaurant; right on the beach. **Cons:** a long walk
★   to other restaurants; small pool. **TripAdvisor:** "cozy but nice," "very
pleasant," "great people and location." Ⓢ *Rooms from: $129 ✉ 1 Calle
Santa Ana, Ocean Park* ☎ *787/726–5010 or 866/726–5010* ⊕ *www.
numero1guesthouse.com* ↪ *12 rooms, 4 apartments* ⦿*Breakfast.*

$$$$ **The Ritz-Carlton, San Juan.** Elegant marble floors and fountains don't
RESORT undermine the feeling that this is a true beach getaway. **Pros:** top-notch
☾   service; excellent restaurant options; pretty pool area. **Cons:** not much
Fodor'sChoice is within walking distance; extremely expensive for San Juan lodg-
★   ing. **TripAdvisor:** "refined haven," "excellent high-end hotel," "very
relaxing." Ⓢ*Rooms from: $700 ✉ 6961 Av. de los Gobernadores,
Isla Verde* ☎*787/253–1700, 800/241–3333* ⊕ *www.ritzcarlton.com/
sanjuan* ↪ *416 rooms, 11 suites* ⦿*No meals.*

$$$ **San Juan Water & Beach Club.** Stepping into the elevators decked out
HOTEL in black lights at this boutique hotel is almost like entering a nightclub.
★   **Pros:** fun atmosphere; interesting design; great nightlife option. **Cons:**
very dark hallways; small pool. **TripAdvisor:** "excellent staff," "super
relaxing," "hipster hotel." Ⓢ*Rooms from: $269 ✉ 2 Calle Tartak, Isla
Verde* ☎ *787/728–3666 or 888/265–6699* ⊕ *www.waterbeachclubhotel.
com* ↪ *77 rooms, 4 suites* ⦿*No meals.*

EASTERN PUERTO RICO

$$$$
RESORT
★

⌂ **El Conquistador Resort & Golden Door Spa.** Perched on a bluff overlooking the ocean, El Conquistador (The Conqueror) is a sprawling complex that has claimed the northern tip of the island and is one of Puerto Rico's most sought-after destination resorts. **Pros:** bright, spacious rooms; unbeatable views of the nearby islands; good dining options; various meal plans available. **Cons:** must take a boat to reach the beach; long waits at the funicular taking guests between levels; self-parking is far from the hotel entrance; hidden fees like parking ($16/day) and kids club ($70/day). **TripAdvisor:** "breathtaking view," "beautiful," "heaven on Earth." ⑤ *Rooms from: $400* ⌂ *1000 Av. El Conquistador* ☎ *787/863–1000 or 800/468–0389* ⊕ *www.elconresort. com* ⌂ *750 rooms, 15 suites, 234 villas* ⧉ *Some meals.*

$$$$
RESORT

⌂ **Gran Meliá Puerto Rico.** This massive resort, on an enviable stretch of pristine coastline, has an open-air lobby with elegant floral displays that resemble a Japanese garden, and the swimming pool's columns call to mind ancient Greece. **Pros:** beautiful setting; lovely pool area; short walk to the beach. **Cons:** parking spots are scarce; facade is blank and uninviting; though Wi-Fi is free in the lobby, in-room Internet is $14/day. **TripAdvisor:** "stunning," "beautiful grounds," "relaxing." ⑤ *Rooms from: $390* ⌂ *200 Coco Beach Boulevard, Rte. 968, Km 5.8, Coco Beach* ☎ *787/809–1770, 877/476–3542* ⊕ *www.gran-melia-puerto-rico.com* ⌂ *363 junior suites, 123 RedLevel suites, 5 oceanfront villas, 1 two-bedroom Oceanfront Presidential Villa* ⧉ *No meals.*

$$$$
RESORT
Ⓒ

⌂ **Rio Mar Beach Resort & Spa, a Wyndham Grand Resort.** Be it for work or play, guests come to this sprawling 500-acre resort to enjoy a host of outdoor activities, including championship golf and tennis, as well as hiking excursions in the nearby rain forest. **Pros:** expansive beachfront; good restaurants in hotel; plenty of outdoor activities. **Cons:** dark and depressing parking garage; long lines at check-in desk; in-room Wi-Fi costs $15/day, worn grounds. **TripAdvisor:** "great beach," "beautiful property," "friendly staff." ⑤ *Rooms from: $390* ⌂ *6000 Río Mar Blvd.* ☎ *787/888–6000 or 888/4–RIO–MAR* ⊕ *www.wyndhamriomar.com* ⌂ *528 rooms, 72 suites, 59 villas* ⧉ *No meals.*

$$$$
RESORT
Fodor'sChoice
★

⌂ **St. Regis Bahia Beach Resort.** In the lush foothills of El Yunque rain forest where Río Espíritu Santo meets the Atlantic, this luxurious, environmentally-aware property has raised the bar on lodging in Puerto Rico. **Pros:** Privacy, impeccable service, luxury amenities. **Cons:** Isolated location; daily $60 resort fee; slim off-property restaurant selection. **TripAdvisor:** "natural surroundings," "fabulous property," "luxurious and family friendly." ⑤ *Rooms from: $1,000* ⌂ *State Road 187, Km 4.2* ☎ *787/809–8000, 866/961–3326* ⊕ *www.stregisbahiabeach.com* ⌂ *104 rooms, 35 suites* ⧉ *No meals.*

VIEQUES AND CULEBRA

$$
HOTEL

⌂ **Bravo Beach Hotel.** This completely renovated boutique hotel several blocks north of the ferry dock in Isabel Segunda feels more suited to swank South Beach than laid-back Vieques. **Pros:** gorgeous building; beautiful pools; friendly new management. **Cons:** out of the way

17

location in residential neighborhood; can't swim on property's beach. **TripAdvisor:** "bliss," "great service and beautiful location," "lovely guest house." Ⓢ *Rooms from: $175* ⊠ *North Shore Rd., Isabel Segunda Vieques* 🕾 *787/741–1128* ⊕ *www.bravobeachhotel.com* 🖙 *7 rooms, 2 suites, 1 villa* �’❑❙ *Breakfast.*

$$
HOTEL
Fodor'sChoice
★

🔛 **Club Seaborne.** The most sophisticated place to set down roots in Culebra, this cluster of slate-blue plantation-style cottages paints a pretty picture on a hilltop overlooking Fulladoza Bay. **Pros:** Lovely cottages; privacy; lush gardens. **Cons:** Some steps to negotiate; no elevator; spotty Internet and phone reception. **TripAdvisor:** "peaceful and relaxing," "beautiful views," "great accommodation." Ⓢ *Rooms from: $199* ⊠ *Playa Sardinas Ward II, Fulladoza Bay, Culebra* 🕾 *787/742–3169* ⊕ *www.clubseabourne.com* 🖙 *3 rooms, 8 villas, 1 cottage* �’❑❙ *Breakfast.*

$$
HOTEL
★

🔛 **Hacienda Tamarindo.** The 250-year-old tamarind tree rising more than three stories through the center of the main building gives this plantation-style house and former dance hall its name. **Pros:** Beautiful views; nicely designed rooms; excellent breakfasts. **Cons:** Drive to beaches; small parking lot; no full-service restaurant; no elevator. **TripAdvisor:** "paradise found," "very relaxing," "heavenly." Ⓢ *Rooms from: $195* ⊠ *Rte. 996, Km 4.5, Esperanza, Vieques* 🕾 *787/741–8525* ⊕ *www. haciendatamarindo.com* 🖙 *16 rooms, 1 penthouse suite* �’❑❙ *Breakfast.*

$$
HOTEL

🔛 **Inn on the Blue Horizon.** The six Mediterranean-style villas here were the tiny island's first taste of luxury, and it's still a lovely accommodation, to a large extent because of its perch across sprawling lawns that overlook breathtaking ocean. **Pros:** eye-popping view; private accommodations; spacious grounds; free Wi-Fi in public areas. **Cons:** no elevator. **TripAdvisor:** "amazing atmosphere," "beautiful hotel and wonderful staff," "perfect tranquility." Ⓢ *Rooms from: $160* ⊠ *Rte. 996, Km 4.2, Esperanza, Vieques* 🕾 *787/741–3318 or 877/741–BLUE* ⊕ *www.innonthebluehorizon.com* 🖙 *10 rooms, 1 suite* �’❑❙ *Breakfast.*

$$$
B&B/INN
★

🔛 **Malecón House.** Posh boutique spots like this seaside escape in Esperanza are raising the bar on lodging in Vieques. **TripAdvisor:** "perfect location," "awesome lodging," "peaceful." Ⓢ *Rooms from: $175* ⊠ *105 Calle Flamboyan, Esperanza, Vieques* 🕾 *787/741–0663* ⊕ *www. maleconhouse.com* 🖙 *9 rooms, 1 suite* �’❑❙ *Breakfast.*

$$$$
RESORT
Fodor'sChoice
★

🔛 **W Retreat & Spa.** Hovering over two gorgeous beaches, the über-hip W Retreat & Spa opened in November 2009 as the island's hot spot for urbane fashionistas. **Pros:** sensational decor; full-service spa; five-minute drive from the airport. **Cons:** high prices even in low season; $60 daily resort fee. **TripAdvisor:** "wonderful," "perfect mojitos in a perfect setting," "superb rooms and relaxing pools." Ⓢ *Rooms from: $679* ⊠ *Rte. 200, Km 3.2, Isabel Segunda, Vieques* 🕾 *787/741–4100* ⊕ *www.wvieques.com* 🖙 *156 rooms, 21 suites* �’❑❙ *No meals.*

SOUTHERN PUERTO RICO

$$
RESORT
☻

🔛 **Copamarina Beach Resort.** Without a doubt the most beautiful resort on the southern coast, the Copamarina is set on 16 palm-shaded acres facing the Caribbean Sea. **Pros:** Tropical decor; plenty of activities; great dining options. **Cons:** Sand at the beach has a gummy feel; noise from the many kids. **TripAdvisor:** "beautiful place with delicious food," "designed for comfort and beauty," "nearly perfect location." ⑤ *Rooms from: $235* ⊠ *Rte. 333, Km 6.5, Guánica* ☎ *787/821–0505 or 800/468–4553* ⊕ *www.copamarina.com* ⇗ *104 rooms, 2 villas* ⑪ *No meals.*

$$
RESORT
☺
🏨 **Hilton Ponce Golf & Casino Resort.** The south coast's biggest resort sits on a black-sand beach about 4 mi (6 km) south of downtown Ponce. **Pros:** Good golf; large casino; game room and pool for kids. **Cons:** Isolated location; bland rooms. **TripAdvisor:** "can't get enough," "great stay," "wonderful laid-back resort." ⑤ *Rooms from: $179* ⊠ *1150 Av. Caribe, La Guancha* ☎ *787/259–7676 or 800/445–8667* ⊕ *www.hiltoncaribbean.com* ⇗ *242 rooms, 13 suites* ⑪ *No meals.*

$
HOTEL
🏨 **Hotel Meliá.** In the heart of Ponce, this family-owned hotel has been a local landmark for over a century. **Pros:** Great location on the main square; walking distance to downtown sites; good dining options near hotel. **Cons:** Rooms are somewhat outdated; front rooms are a bit noisy; green carpet and curtains make the rooms rather stuffy. **TripAdvisor:** "convenient location," "really nice restored old hotel," "classic old-school charm." ⑤ *Rooms from: $140* ⊠ *75 Calle Cristina, Ponce Centro* ☎ *787/842–0260 or 800/448–8355* ⊕ *www.hotelmeliapr.com* ⇗ *68 rooms, 6 suites* ⑪ *Breakfast.*

$
RENTAL
Fodor's Choice
★
🏨 **Mary Lee's by the Sea.** This meandering cluster of apartments sits upon quiet grounds full of brightly colored flowers. **Pros:** Feels like a home away from home, warm and friendly owner, near pristine beaches and forests. **Cons:** Weekly maid service unless requested daily, no nightlife options, no pool. **TripAdvisor:** "charming property in idyllic setting," "wonderful beaches," "beauty and romance." ⑤ *Rooms from: $120* ⊠ *Rte. 333, Km 6.7 Guánica* ☎ *787/821–3600* ⊕ *www.maryleesbythesea.com* ⇗ *10 apartments* ⑪ *No meals.*

WESTERN AND CENTRAL PUERTO RICO

¢
HOTEL
Fodor's Choice
★
🏨 **Casa Grande Mountain Retreat.** Here you'll come as close as you can to sleeping in a tree house. **Pros:** unspoiled setting with spectacular views; accessible for people with disabilities; outdoor activities. **Cons:** no air-conditioning; long drive to other sights/restaurants. **TripAdvisor:** "seclusion in an untouristed location," "beautiful scenery," "hidden retreat." ⑤ *Rooms from: $110* ⊠ *Rte. 612, Km 0.3, Utuado* ☎ *787/894–3939* ⊕ *www.hotelcasagrande.com* ⇗ *20 rooms* ⑪ *No meals.*

$$
B&B/INN
🏨 **Casa Isleña.** With its barrel-tiled roofs, wall-enclosed gardens, and open-air dining room, Casa Isleña might remind well-traveled souls of a villa on the coast of Mexico. **Pros:** Secluded setting; beautiful beach; great tapas bar; daily yoga offered. **Cons:** Hotel closed September and October; books up quickly; management seldom on-site. **TripAdvisor:** "steps to the ocean," "relaxing atmosphere," "beautiful location." ⑤ *Rooms from: $185* ⊠ *Rte. 413, Km 4.8, Barrio Puntas, Rincón* ☎ *787/823–1525 or 888/289–7750* ⊕ *www.casa-islena.com* ⇗ *9 rooms* ⑪ *Breakfast.*

$$$$
RESORT
Fodor's Choice
★
🏨 **Horned Dorset Primavera.** This is, without a doubt, the most luxurious hotel in Puerto Rico. **Pros:** Unabashed luxury; unmatched meals; lovely setting; yoga "treehouse". **Cons:** On a very slender beach; staff is sometimes haughty; morning light floods through small shadeless windows near the ceiling. **TripAdvisor:** "beautiful spot," "the best

17

Tres Sirenas

romantic vacations ever," "a special place." $ *Rooms from: $1,355* ⊠ *Rte. 429, Km 3, Rincón* ☎ *787/823–4030 or 800/633–1857* ⊕ *www. horneddorset.com* ⤴ *40 villas* ⏷ *Some meals.*

$
HOTEL
🏠 **Lazy Parrot.** Painted in eye-popping tropical hues, this mountainside hotel doesn't take itself too seriously. **Pros:** Economy rooms available; tropical setting; microwaves in rooms. **Cons:** Not on the beach; stairs to climb, some may consider the whimsical style tacky. **TripAdvisor:** "comfortable," "relaxed tropical mood," "very chilled out." $ *Rooms from: $150* ⊠ *Rte. 413, Km 4.1, Rincón* ☎ *787/823–5654 or 800/294–1752* ⊕ *www.lazyparrot.com* ⤴ *21 rooms* ⏷ *Breakfast.*

$$
HOTEL
🏠 **Lemontree Oceanfront Cottages.** Sitting right on the beach, this pair of lemon-yellow buildings holds six apartments named after such fruits as Mango, Cocoa, Banana, and Piña. **Pros:** Far from the crowds; on-call massage therapist; spacious balconies. **Cons:** Beach is very narrow; must drive to shops and restaurants; no elevator. **TripAdvisor:** "isolated," "super charming," "delightful oceanside experience." $ *Rooms from: $197* ⊠ *Rte. 429, Km 4.1* ☎ *787/823–6452* ⊕ *www.lemontreepr.com* ⤴ *6 apartments* ⏷ *No meals.*

$$
RESORT
🏠 **Rincón Beach Resort.** It's a bit off the beaten path, but that's part of the allure of this oceanfront resort. **Pros:** Beautiful pool area; laid-back vibe; children's playground. **Cons:** Far from dining options; lacks Puerto Rican flavor; decor is slightly dated; halls echo. **TripAdvisor:** "nice resort," "absolutely beautiful," "fabulous location." $ *Rooms from: $205* ⊠ *Rte. 115, Km 5.8, Añasco, Rincón* ☎ *787/589–9000* ⊕ *www. rinconbeach.com* ⤴ *112 rooms* ⏷ *No meals.*

$$$
B&B/INN
Fodor's Choice
★
🏠 **Tres Sirenas.** Waves gently lap against the shores at this boutique inn named "Three Mermaids" in honor of the owners' daughters. **Pros:** In-room massages; spotless and tastefully decorated, discounted rates May through October. **Cons:** Usually booked; set breakfast hour, Wi-Fi occasionally drops. **TripAdvisor:** "a villa in paradise," "excellent relaxing stay," "amazing views." ⑤ *Rooms from: $280* ⊠ *26 Seabeach Dr., Rincón* ☎ *787/823–0558* ⊕ *www.tressirenas.com* ↪ *2 rooms, 1 studio, 2 apartments* ⑩ *Breakfast.*

$$$
RESORT
Fodor's Choice
★
🏠 **Villa Montaña.** This secluded cluster of villas, situated on a deserted stretch of beach between Isabela and Aguadilla, feels like a little town. **Pros:** Bikes and playground for children; on a secluded beach; great food. **Cons:** A bit pricey; far from other dining options; airplane noise. **TripAdvisor:** "relaxed beachfront villas," "perfect," "great place to relax." ⑤ *Rooms from: $255* ⊠ *Rte. 4466, Km 1.9, Isabela* ☎ *787/872–9554 or 888/780–9195* ⊕ *www.villamontana.com* ↪ *38 rooms, 41 villas* ⑩ *No meals.*

$$
HOTEL
★
🏠 **Villas del Mar Hau.** One-, two-, and three-bedroom cottages—painted in cheery pastels and trimmed with gingerbread—are the heart of this beachfront hotel. **Pros:** Laid-back vibe; protected swimming cove great for children; good restaurant. **Cons:** Very basic rooms; may be too kitschy for some, 5 pm check-in. **TripAdvisor:** "beautiful tropical setting," "hidden paradise," "like camping on a gorgeous beach." ⑤ *Rooms from: $180* ⊠ *Rte. 466, Km 8.3, Isabela* ☎ *787/872–2045* ⊕ *www.hauhotelvillas.com* ↪ *46 cottages* ⑩ *No meals.*

17

NIGHTLIFE AND THE ARTS

Qué Pasa, the official visitor's guide, has listings of events in San Juan and out on the island. For daily listings, pick up a copy of the English-language edition of the *San Juan Star.* The Thursday edition's weekend section is especially useful. For the gay scene, check out the monthly *Puerto Rico Breeze*; the free newspaper is found in many businesses, especially in the Condado area.

NIGHTLIFE

Wherever you go, dress to impress. Puerto Ricans have flair, and both men and women love getting dressed up to go out. Bars are usually casual, but if you have on jeans, sneakers, and a T-shirt, you may be refused entry at swankier nightclubs and discos.

In Old San Juan, Calle San Sebastián is lined with bars and restaurants. Salsa music blaring from jukeboxes in cut-rate pool halls competes with mellow Latin jazz in top-flight nightspots. Evenings begin with dinner and stretch into the late hours (often until 3 or 4 in the morning) at the bars of the more upscale, so-called SoFo (south of Fortaleza) end of Old San Juan. An eclectic crowd heads to the Plaza del Mercado in Santurce after work to hang out in the plaza or enjoy drinks and food in one of the small establishments skirting the farmers' market. Condado and Ocean Park have their share of nightlife, too. Most are restaurant-and-bar environments.

Just east of San Juan along Route 187, funky Piñones has a collection of open-air seaside eateries that are popular with locals. On weekend evenings many places have merengue combos, Brazilian jazz trios, or reggae bands. In the southern city of Ponce, people embrace the Spanish tradition of the *paseo,* an evening stroll around the Plaza de las Delicias. The boardwalk at La Guancha in Ponce is also a lively scene. Live bands often play on weekends. Elsewhere *en la isla,* nighttime activities center on the hotels and resorts.

OLD SAN JUAN AND GREATER SAN JUAN

BARS AND MUSIC CLUBS

El Batey. This legendary hole-in-the-wall bar won't win any prizes for decor, but still, it has an irresistibly artsy and welcoming vibe. Add your own message to the graffiti-covered walls (they have a B.Y.O.S, or Bring Your Own Sharpie policy), or put your business card alongside the hundreds that cover the lighting fixtures. The ceiling may leak, but the jukebox has the best selection of oldies in town. Join locals in a game of pool. ⌂ *101 Calle Cristo, Old San Juan* ☎ *No phone.*

★ **Nuyorican Café.** There's something interesting happening at this hipper-than-hip, no-frills, wood-paneled performance space nearly every night, be it an early evening play, poetry reading, or talent show or, later on, a band playing Latin jazz, Cuban *son,* Puerto Rican salsa, or rock. During breaks between performances the youthful, creative crowd chats in an alley outside the front door. It's usually closed on Monday. ⌂ *312 Calle San Fransico (entrance on Callejón de la Capilla), Old San Juan* ☎ *787/977–1276* ⊕ *www.nuyoricancafepr.com..*

Wet. On the roof of the San Juan Water & Beach Club Hotel, this sexy spot offers some of the best ocean views anywhere in Isla Verde. On weekends there's a DJ, and locals pack in to relax at the bar or on the leather beds reserved for bottle service. ⌂ *San Juan Water & Beach Club, 2 Calle Tartak, Isla Verde* ☎ *787/725–4664.*

CASINOS

By law, all casinos are in hotels, primarily in San Juan. The government keeps a close eye on them. Dress for the larger casinos is on the formal side, and the atmosphere is refined, particularly in the Isla Verde resorts. Casinos set their own hours but are generally open from noon to 4 am. In addition to slot machines, typical games include blackjack, roulette, craps, Caribbean stud (a five-card poker game), and *pai gow* poker (a combination of American poker and the Chinese game pai gow). Hotels with casinos have live entertainment most weekends, as well as restaurants and bars. The minimum age to gamble (and to drink) is 18.

The Casino at The Ritz-Carlton, San Juan. With its golden columns, turquoise and bronze walls, and muted lighting, the Ritz casino, the largest in San Juan, stays refined by day or night. There's lots of activity, yet everything is hushed. ⌂ *6991 Av. de los Gobernadores, Isla Verde* ☎ *787/253–1700.*

InterContinental San Juan Resort & Casino. A blue neon light envelops you as you enter this casino, which underwent a $2 million renovation in 2009, adding a host of new slot machines and more elegant decor. Live music is usually available on Saturday nights. ✉ *5961 Av. Isla Verde, Isla Verde* ☎ *787/791–6100.*

Sheraton Old San Juan Hotel & Casino. It's impossible to ignore this ground-floor casino, the only place to gamble in Old San Juan. You can see the gaming room from the hotel's main stairway, the balcony above, and the lobby. Light bounces off the Bahía de San Juan and pours through its many windows; passengers bound off their cruise ships and pour through its many glass doors. ✉ *101 Calle Brumbaugh, Old San Juan* ☎ *787/721–5100.*

DANCE CLUBS

Atlantic Beach. The oceanfront-deck bar of this hotel is famed in the gay community for its early-evening happy hours. But the pulsating tropical music, exotic drinks, and ever-pleasant ocean breeze would make it a hit in any case. Good food is also served on deck. ✉ *1 Calle Vendig, Condado, San Juan* ☎ *787/721–6900.*

Brava. A long line of young people can be spotted at the door of this chic club at the El San Juan Hotel. The two-level club, each with its own DJ and dance floor, is one of the best places for dancing. There's a different theme party Thursday through Saturday. ✉ *El San Juan Hotel & Casino, 6063 Av. Isla Verde, Isla Verde, San Juan* ☎ *787/641–3500* ⊕ *www.bravapr.com.*

Club Lazer. This multilevel club has spots for quiet conversation, spaces for dancing to loud music, and a landscaped roof deck overlooking San Juan. The crowd changes every night; Saturday is ladies' night, when male strippers sometimes perform. ✉ *251 Calle Cruz, Old San Juan, San Juan* ☎ *787/725–7581* ⊕ *www.clublazer.com.*

17

THE ARTS

Museo de Arte de Ponce. The Museo de Arte de Ponce occasionally sponsors chamber-music concerts and recitals by members of the Puerto Rico Symphony Orchestra. ✉ *2325 Av. Las Américas, Sector Santa María* ☎ *787/848–0505.*

Teatro La Perla. Check for Spanish-language theater productions and concerts at the Teatro La Perla. ✉ *Calle Mayor and Calle Cristina, Ponce Centro* ☎ *787/843–4322.*

Teatro Tapia. Named for Puerto Rican playwright Alejandro Tapia y Rivera, the theater hosts traveling and locally produced theatrical and musical productions. Matinee performances with family entertainment are also held here, especially around the holidays. ✉ *Calle Fortaleza, Plaza Colón, Old San Juan, San Juan* ☎ *787/480–5004.*

SHOPPING

San Juan has the island's best range of stores, but it isn't a free port, so you won't find bargains on electronics and perfumes. You can, however, find excellent prices on china, crystal, clothing, and jewelry. Shopping for local crafts can also be gratifying: you'll run across a lot that's tacky, but you can also find treasures, and in many cases you can watch the artisans at work. Popular items include *santos* (small carved figures of saints or religious scenes), hand-rolled cigars, handmade *mundillo* lace from Moca, *vejigantes* (colorful masks used during Carnival and local festivals) from Loíza and Ponce, and fancy men's shirts called guayaberas.

In Old San Juan—especially on Calles Fortaleza and Cristo—you can find everything from T-shirt emporiums to selective crafts stores, bookshops, art galleries, jewelry boutiques, and even shops that specialize in made-to-order Panama hats. Calle Cristo has a number of factory-outlet stores, including Coach and Ralph Lauren.

With many stores selling luxury items and designer fashions, the shopping spirit in the San Juan neighborhood of Condado is reminiscent of that in Miami. Avenida Ashford is considered the heart of San Juan's fashion district, and you'll find plenty of high-end clothing stores here.

OLD SAN JUAN AND GREATER SAN JUAN
SPECIALTY STORES

ART ★ **Galería Botello.** The very influential Galería Botello displays the works of the late Angel Botelli, who was hailed as the "Caribbean Gauguin" as far back as 1943. His work, which often uses the bright colors of the tropics, usually depicts island scenes. His paintings hang in the Museo de Arte de Puerto Rico. There are works on display here by other prominent local artists as well. ⊠ *208 Calle Cristo, Old San Juan, San Juan* ☎ *787/723–9987* ⊕ *www.botello.com.*

CLOTHES ★ **Cappalli.** Noted local designer Lisa Cappalli sells her lacy, sensuous designs in this boutique, which specializes in ready-to-wear and custom fashions. ⊠ *207 Calle O'Donnell, Old San Juan, San Juan* ☎ *787/289–6565* ⊕ *www.lisacappalli.net.*

Clubman. With many years spent catering to a primarily local clientele, Clubman remains the classic choice for gentlemen's clothing. ⊠ *263 Calle Fortaleza, Old San Juan, San Juan* ☎ *787/724–5631.*

David Antonio. Prolific designer David Antonio runs a shop that's small but full of surprises. His joyful creations range from updated versions of the men's classic guayabera to fluid chiffon and silk tunics and dresses for women. ⊠ *69 Av. Condado, Condado, San Juan* ☎ *787/725–0600.*

Nativa. The window displays at Nativa are almost as daring as the clothes it sells. ⊠ *55 Calle Cervantes, Condado, San Juan* ☎ *787/724–1396.*

★ **Nono Maldonado.** Nono Maldonado is well known for his high-end, elegant clothes for men and women, particularly those done in linen. He should know a thing or two about style—he worked for many years as the fashion editor of *Esquire* and presents a periodic couture collection. This second-floor store also serves as the designer's studio. ⊠ *1112 Av. Ashford, 2nd floor, Condado, San Juan* ☎ *787/721–0456.*

Otto. In his shop Otto Bauzá stocks international lines of casual and formal wear for younger men. ⊠ *69 Av. Condado, Condado, San Juan* ☎ *787/722–4609.*

GIFTS **Butterfly People.** Exotic *mariposas* cover the walls of Butterfly People. Clear plastic cases hold everything from a pair of common butterflies to dozens of rarer specimens in this serene and lovely shop. The butterflies are gathered only from certified farms once they complete their life spans. ⊠ *257 Calle de la Cruz, Old San Juan, San Juan* ☎ *787/723–2432* ⊕ *www.butterflypeople.com.*

Spicy Caribbee. Kitchen items, cookbooks, and many spices and sauces from around the Caribbean are on offer at Spicy Caribbee. ⊠ *154 Calle Cristo, Old San Juan, San Juan* ☎ *888/725–7259* ⊕ *www. spicycaribbee.com.*

JEWELRY **Bared.** For a good selection of watches and jewelry, visit Bared. Look for the massive clock face on the corner. ⊠ *206 San Justo, Old San Juan, San Juan* ☎ *787/724–4811.*

Joyería Cátala. The oldest jewelery store in San Juan, Joyería Cátala is known for its large selection of necklaces made with pearls and semi-precious stones. ⊠ *Plaza de Armas, 152 Calle Rafael Cordero, Old San Juan, San Juan* ☎ *787/722–3231.*

SOUVENIRS

Mi Pequeño San Juan. You might manage to find the hotel where you're staying reproduced in plaster at this shop, which specializes in tiny ceramic versions of San Juan doorways. The works, all created by hand right in the shop, make a wonderful souvenir. ⊠ *152 Calle Fortaleza, Old San Juan, San Juan* ☎ *787/977–1636 or 787/721–5040* ⊕ *www. mipequenosanjuan.com.*

SPORTS AND ACTIVITIES

17

BOATING AND SAILING

Aqua Frenzy Kayaks. Aqua Frenzy Kayaks also rents sturdy kayaks and arranges comprehensive kayak tours of Puerto Mosquito and other areas if Abe's is booked. Reservations are required for the excursion to the bio bay; the evening kayak trip costs $30. Make reservations at least 24 hours in advance. ⊠ *At dock area below Calle Flamboyán, Esperanza, Vieques* ☎ *787/741–0913* ⊕ *www.aquafrenzy.com.*

East Winds Excursions. At East Winds Excursions catamarans ranging in size from 45 feet to 65 feet take you offshore for snorkeling. Two of the catamarans are powered, and this cuts down tremendously on the travel time to outlying islands. Trips include stops at isolated beaches and a lunch buffet, and begin at $89 per person. All craft are outfitted with swimming decks, freshwater showers, and full-service bars. These vessels are some of the plushest for day sails in the area. ⊠ *Marina Puerto del Rey, Rte. 3, Km 51.4, Fajardo* ☎ *787/860–3434, 877/937–4386* ⊕ *www.eastwindcats.com.*

DIVING AND SNORKELING

The diving is excellent off Puerto Rico's south, east, and west coasts, as well as its nearby islands. Particularly striking are dramatic walls created by a continental shelf off the south coast near La Parguera and Guánica. There's also some fantastic diving near Fajardo and around Vieques and Culebra, two small islands off the east coast. It's best to choose specific locations with the help of a guide or outfitter. Escorted half-day dives range from $65 to $120 for one or two tanks, including all equipment; in general, double those prices for night dives. Packages that include lunch and other extras are more. Snorkeling excursions, which include transportation, equipment rental, and sometimes lunch, start at $50. Equipment rents for about $5 to $10.

Aquatic Adventures. Captain Taz Hamrick takes guests out on snorkeling and PADI-certified scuba trips, as well as charters to the surrounding cayes. ⊠ *Dewey, Culebra* ☏ *787/209–3494* ⊕ *diveculebra.com.*

Culebra Divers. Run by Monika and Walter Rieder, Culebra Divers is the island's premiere dive shop catering to those new to scuba and those adept at underwater navigation. Travel to more than 60 local sites on one of the company's 25-foot cabin cruisers and hope to spot wildlife like spotted eagle rays, octopus, moray eels, and turtles. One-tank dives are $70, and two-tank dives are $98; rental equipment is a flat $15. An additional $25 includes an underwater scooter, which propels you through the sea à la James Bond. You can also rent a mask and snorkel to explore on your own. ⊠ *4 Calle Pedro Marquez, Dewey, Culebra* ☏ *787/742–0803* ⊕ *www.culebradivers.com.*

Sea Ventures Pro Dive Center. At Sea Ventures Pro Dive Center you can get your diving certification, arrange dive trips to 20 offshore sites, or organize boating and sailing excursions. ⊠ *Marina Puerto del Rey, Rte. 3, Km 51.4, Fajardo* ☏ *800/739–DIVE* ⊕ *www.divepuertorico. com* ⌨ *Two-tank dive for certified divers, including equipment, $119.*

FISHING

Puerto Rico's waters are home to large game fish such as marlin, wahoo, dorado, tuna, and barracuda; as many as 30 world records for catches have been set off the island's shores.

Mike Benítez Sport Fishing. Half-day and full-day excursions as well as split charters can be arranged through Mike Benítez Sport Fishing. From the 45-foot *Sea Born* you can fish for yellowfin tuna, mahimahi, white marlin, blue marlin, and others. ⊠ *Club Náutico de San Juan, 480 Av. Fernández Juncos, Puerta de Tierra, San Juan* ☏ *787/723–2292* ⊕ *www. mikebenitezsportfishing.com.*

GOLF

Aficionados may know that Puerto Rico is the birthplace of golf legend Chi Chi Rodríguez—and he had to hone his craft somewhere. Currently, you can find nearly 20 courses on the island, including many championship links. Be sure to call ahead for tee times; hours vary, and several hotel courses give preference to guests. Greens fees start at about $20 and go up as high as $165.

The **Puerto Rican Golf Association** (⊠ *58 Calle Caribe, San Juan* ☏ *787/793–3444* ⊕ *www.prga.org*) is a good source for information on courses and tournaments.

★ **El Conquistador Resort.** The 18-hole, Arthur Hills–designed course at El Conquistador Resort is famous for its 200-foot changes in elevation. From the highest spot, on the 15th hole, you have great views of the surrounding mountains. The trade winds make every shot challenging. Greens fees for resort guests range from $90 to $160 and are even steeper for nonguests. ⊠ *1000 Av. El Conquistador, Fajardo* ☎ *787/863–6784.*

★ **Palmas del Mar Country Club.** Palmas del Mar Country Club has two good golf courses: The Rees Jones–designed Flamboyán course, named for the nearly six dozen flamboyant trees that pepper its fairway, has been rated one of the top five courses in the world. The older Gary Player–designed Palm course has a challenging par 5 that scoots around wetlands. ⊠ *Palmas del Mar, Route 906, Humacao* ☎ *787/656–8548* ⊕ *www.palmaspac.com* ⅄ *Greens fees from $95.*

★ **Río Mar Country Club.** The Río Mar Country Club has a clubhouse with a pro shop, two restaurants between two 18-hole courses, to grab a sit-down lunch or a quick beverage and a bite. The River Course, designed by Greg Norman, has challenging fairways that skirt the Mameyes River. The Ocean Course, designed by Tom and George Fazio, has slightly wider fairways than its sister; iguanas can usually be spotted sunning themselves near its fourth hole. ■ TIP→ If you're not a resort guest, be sure to reserve tee times at least 24 hours in advance. ⊠ *Río Mar Beach Resort & Spa, a Wyndham Grand Resort, 6000 Río Mar Blvd., Río Grande* ☎ *787/888–7060* ⊕ *www.wyndhamriomar.com* ⅄ *Greens fees for hotel guests range from $50 (for 9 holes) to $165 (for 18 holes). Fees for walk-ins range from $60–$180.*

HORSEBACK RIDING

Horseback riding is a well-established family pastime in Puerto Rico, with *cabalgatas* (group day rides) frequently organized on weekends through mountain towns.

★ **Hacienda Carabalí.** Hacienda Carabalí, a family-run operation, is a good place to jump in the saddle and ride one of Puerto Rico's Paso Fino horses. Hour-long rides ($32 adult, $20 kids 3–11) take you around the 600-acre ranch, while two-hour treks take you to a river where you and your horse can take a dip. If you prefer something more high-tech, rent a four-wheeler for an excursion through the foothills of El Yunque. ⊠ *Rte. 992, Km 4, Río Grande* ☎ *787/889–5820* ⊕ *www.haciendacarabalipuertorico.com.*

SURFING

The very best surfing beaches are along the northwestern coast from Isabela south to Rincón, which gained notoriety by hosting the World Surfing Championship in 1968. Today the town draws surfers from around the globe, especially in winter, when the waves are at their best.

East of the city, in Piñones, the Caballo has deep- to shallow-water shelf waves that require a big-wave board known as a gun. Playa La

Pared, near Balneario de Luquillo, is a surfer haunt with medium-range waves. Numerous local competitions are held here throughout the year.

Desecheo Surf & Dive Shop. Desecheo Surf & Dive Shop rents snorkeling equipment ($15 a day), Boogie boards ($20 a day), and a variety of short and long surfboards ($25–$45 a day). The company also has a small shop with swimwear, sandals, sunglasses, and surf gear. ⊠ *Rte. 413, Km 2.5* ☎ *787/823–0390* ⊕ *www.desecheosurfshop.com.*

Mar Azul. Mar Azul has Rincón's best selection of performance surf-boards and stand-up paddleboards to buy or rent. Paddleboard lessons ($40 for 90 minutes) are also available. This is one of the best surf shops on the entire island. ⊠ *Rte. 413, Km 4.4* ☎ *787/823–5692* ⊕ *www. puertoricosurfinginfo.com.*

Saba

WORD OF MOUTH

"Saba is a total gem of an island. Once on it, you can hike/climb Mt. Scenery. I don't know about snorkeling, but [I] understand it's a GREAT place to go scuba diving."

—BellaClaire

WELCOME TO SABA

Great Pt.

ATLANTIC OCEAN

Man of War Shoals

Cave of Rum Bay

Torrens Pt.

Edward S. Arnold Snorkel Trail

Well's Bay

Mary's Point Mtn.

Third Encounter

Ladder Bay

7 Troy Hill

Mt. Scenery ◆

8 6

Great Hill

Maskerhorne Hill

Ladder Pt.

The Bottom

The Road

Ladder Labrynth

9 St. John's

Thais Hill

Tent Pt.

KEY

➤	Beaches
◩	Dive Sites
🚢	Ferry
⛴	Cruise Ship Terminal
1	Restaurants
1	Hotels

Tent Bay

Fort Bay

Fort Bay

Giles Quarter

SABA NATIONALMAR

10 11

To Saba Bank

TO ST. MAARTEN

Mountainous Saba's precipitous terrain allows visitors to choose between the heights and the depths. The Bottom, the island's capital, was once thought to be the crater of a dormant volcano. From here a trail of 400 rough-hewn steps drops to the sea. Divers can take a different plunge to view the pristine reef.

THE UNSPOILED QUEEN

Tiny Saba—an extinct volcano that juts out of the ocean to a height of 2,855 feet—is just 5 square miles (13 square km) in size and has a population of about 1,500. Part of the Dutch Caribbean, it's 28 miles (45 km) south of St. Maarten and surrounded by some of the richest dive sites in the Caribbean.

Restaurants ▼		Hotels ▼	
Bistro del Mare	**1**	Cottage Club	**3**
Brigadoon	**4**	Ecolodge Rendez-Vous	**6**
Deep End Bar & Grill	**10**	El Momo	**4**
Pop's Place	**11**	Juliana's Hotel	**5**
Queen's Garden Restaurant	**9**	Queen's Garden Resort	**7**
Rainforest Restaurant	**8**	Scout's Place	**2**
Restaurant Eden	**6**	Shearwater Resort	**1**
Saba's Treasure	**2**		
Scout's Place	**3**		
Swinging Doors	**7**		
Tropics Café	**5**		

18

SABA

TOP REASONS TO VISIT SABA

1 Diving: Divers flock to Saba because of the clear water and clear ocean life.

2 Hiking: Hikers can climb the island's pinnacle, Mt. Scenery, but the less intense trails offer many sweeping vistas as well.

3 Authenticity: Saba reminds you of what the Caribbean used to be: the locals are genuine, and tourist traps are just about nonexistent.

4 Ecotourism: Several hotels cater to ecotourists, with resident nature pros who can tell you everything about local flora and fauna.

5 Quirkiness: On this unusual island, the airport landing and "the Road" are thrill rides, Wells Bay beach disappears at the end of every summer, and the Bottom is not on the bottom.

By Roberta
Sotonoff

Though Saba (pronounced *say*-ba) is just south of St. Maarten (if you've seen the original *King Kong*, you may recognize its majestic silhouette from the beginning of the film), the islands couldn't be more different. St. Maarten is all beaches, gambling, and duty-free shopping; Saba is ecotourism, diving, and hiking.

Nearly half of Saba's 5 square miles (13 square km) is covered in verdant tropical rain forest; the other half is sprinkled with hamlets composed of white, green-shuttered houses trimmed in gingerbread, roofed in red, and built on grades so steep they seem to defy physics. Flower-draped walls and neat picket fences border narrow paths among the bromeliads, palms, hibiscus, orchids, and Norfolk Island pines. The land dips and climbs à la San Francisco and eventually drops off into sheer cliffs that fall right into the ocean, the fodder for some of the world's most striking dive sites and the primary reason for Saba's cultlike following. Divers seem to relish the fact that they're in on Saba's secret.

But word about this Dutch Caribbean island is slowly getting out. Every year, more tourists are turned on to Saba's charms and make the 11-minute, white-knuckle flight from St. Maarten into the tiny airport with a runway not much larger than an aircraft carrier's. Indeed, traffic jams along the winding, narrow road (yes, there's really just one) are rare, unless the driver in front of you stops to chat. The past few years have seen the opening of more restaurants (big advances, considering around-the-clock electricity was established only in 1970). But don't come expecting a booming metropolis; even as it changes, Saba retains an old-world charm.

A major point of local pride is that many Saban families can be traced all the way back to the island's settlement in 1640 (the surnames Hassell, Johnson, and Peterson fill the tiny phone book). And Sabans hold their traditions dear. Saba lace—a genteel art that dates back to the 1870s—is still hand-stitched by local ladies who, on the side, also distill potent, 151-proof Saba Spice, which is for sale in most of the island's mom-and-pop shops. And islanders like to keep their ancestors close in a very literal sense: in keeping with a generations-old tradition, the dead are buried in local families' neatly tended gardens.

Like the residents of most small towns, the Sabans are a tight-knit group; nothing happens without everyone hearing about it, making crime pretty much a nonissue. That said, they are eager to welcome newcomers and tend to make travelers feel less like tourists and more like old friends. After all, they're proud to show off their home, which they lovingly call "the unspoiled queen."

> ## LOGISTICS
>
> **Getting to Saba:** There are no nonstops from the United States. You have to transfer in St. Maarten for the short flight.
>
> **Hassle Factor:** Medium to High.
>
> **On the Ground:** Taxis can take you around, or you can rent a car. There's just one road, so it's not as if you could get lost. Some people even hitchhike.

PLANNING

WHEN TO GO

High season runs from mid-December through April. The Saba Day long weekend is usually at the end of the first week of December, and Carnival is in the summer (July or August).

GETTING HERE AND AROUND

AIR TRAVEL

All flights arrive in St. Maarten, where you have to transfer for a short flight.

Airport The approach to Saba's tiny airstrip is as thrilling as a roller-coaster ride; luckily, the de Havilland Twin Otter aircraft are built for it. In fact, the pilot needs only half the length of the runway to land properly. (If you're nervous, don't sit on the right. The wing seems almost to scrape against the cliff side on the approach.)

Juancho E. Yrausquin Airport. Once you've touched down on the airstrip, the pilot taxis an inch or two, turns, and deposits you just outside Juancho E. Yrausquin Airport. ☎ *599/545–2568, 800/634–4907, 599/545–4237.*

Airlines Winair. The only airline to fly to Saba (SAB) is Winair; all the flights are from St. Maarten. ☎ *800/634–4907, 599/545–2568, 599/545–4247* ⊕ *www.fly-winair.com.*

BOAT AND FERRY TRAVEL

Dawn II. A 65-foot aluminum vessel that holds 50 people, the *Dawn II* runs on Tuesday, Thursday, and Saturday between Philipsburg and Fort Bay. It leaves Saba at 7 am, arriving at St. Maarten at 9 am, and departs from St. Maarten at 5 pm, arriving at Fort Bay at 7 pm. The fare is $45 one-way plus $5 harbor fee or $68 for same-day return ticket plus an additional $12 harbor fee. Call ahead to check current schedules. ☎ *599/416–2299* ⊕ *www.sabactransport.com.*

18

The Edge. This high-speed ferry leaves St. Maarten's Pelican Marina in Simpson Bay for Fort Bay on Saba every Wednesday through Sunday at 9 am (check in for the trip an hour before). It departs for the return trip about 3:30 pm. The trip, which can be rough, takes just over an hour each way. Round-trip fare is $75 per person for a Saba day trip, plus a $12 port fee, and 5% extra if you pay by credit card. Passports are necessary for travel. ☎ 599/544–2640 ⊕ *www.stmaarten-activities.com.*

CAR TRAVEL

You won't need long to tour the island by car—you can cover the entire circuitous length of the Road in the space of a morning. If you want to shop, have lunch, and do some sightseeing, plan on a full day.

Caja's Car Rental. Rentals from this local firm are about $50 per day. Keep in mind that the gas station in Fort Bay, the only one on the island, closes at 3 pm. ⊠ *The Bottom* ☎ 599/416–2388.

TAXI TRAVEL

Taxis charge a set rate for up to four people per taxi, with an additional cost for each person more than four. The fare from the airport to Hell's Gate is $10, to Windwardside it's $12.50, and to the Bottom it's $20. The fare from the Fort Bay ferry docks to Windwardside is $15. A taxi from Windwardside to the Bottom is $10.

ESSENTIALS

Banks and Exchange Services U.S. dollars are accepted everywhere, but Saba's official currency is the Netherlands Antilles florin (NAf; also called the guilder). The exchange rate is fixed at NAf 1.79 to US$1. Both First Caribbean International Bank and the Royal Bank of Trinidad and Tobago are in Windwardside and provide foreign-exchange services. The Windward Island Bank in the Bottom offers full banking services, weekdays 8:30–3:30.

Electricity 110 volts/60 cycles; visitors from North America should have no trouble using their travel appliances.

Emergencies Ambulance ☎ 599/416–3288, 599/416–3289. **Fire** ☎ 599/416–3710, 599/416–3737. **Police** ⊠ *The Bottom* ☎ 599/416–3237.

Passport Requirements Visitors must carry a valid passport and have an ongoing or return ticket.

Phones Phones take prepaid phone cards, which can be bought at stores throughout the island, or local coins. To call Saba from the United States, dial 011 + 599 + 416, followed by the four-digit number.

Taxes and Service Charges You must pay a $5 departure tax when leaving Saba by plane for St. Maarten or $20 if you're continuing on an international flight, which may already be included in your international ticket. There is a $5 departure tax by boat, which is sometimes covered in the cost of the ticket. Several of the larger hotels will tack on a 10%–15% service charge; others include it in rates. Hotels add a 5% government tax plus a 3% turnover tax to the cost of a room.

ACCOMMODATIONS

There are no big resorts on Saba, just some small hotels and guesthouses, as well as a few rental apartments and villas.

HOTEL AND RESTAURANT PRICES

Prices in the restaurant reviews are the average cost of a main course at dinner or, if dinner is not served, at lunch; taxes and service charges are generally included. Prices in the hotel reviews are the lowest cost of a standard double room in high season, excluding taxes, service charges, and meal plans (except at all-inclusives). Prices for rentals are the lowest per-night cost for a one-bedroom unit in high season.

VISITOR INFORMATION

Contact Saba Tourist Office ☎ 599/416–2231, 599/416-2322 ⊕ www. sabatourism.com.

WEDDINGS

Contact Lt. Governor of Saba. If you want to be married in Saba at somewhere other than the Government Building's courtroom, you must submit a written request to the Lt. Governor of Saba. ☎ 599/416–3497, 599/416-3311, 599/416–3312.

EXPLORING SABA

Getting around the island means negotiating the narrow, twisting roadway that clings to the mountainside and rises from sea level to almost 2,000 feet. Although driving isn't difficult, be sure to go slowly and cautiously. If in doubt, leave the driving to a cabbie so you can enjoy the scenery.

The Bottom. Sitting in a bowl-shaped valley 820 feet above the sea, this town is the seat of government and the home of the lieutenant governor. The gubernatorial mansion, next to Wilhelmina Park, has fancy fretwork, a steeply pitched roof, and wraparound double galleries.

On the other side of town is the Wesleyan Holiness Church, a small stone building with white fretwork. Though it's been renovated and virtually reconstructed over the years, its original four walls date from 1919; go inside and look around. Stroll by the church, beyond a place called the Gap, to a lookout point where you can see the 400 rough-hewn steps leading down to Ladder Bay. This and Fort Bay were the two landing sites from which Saba's first settlers had to haul themselves and their possessions up to the heights. Sabans sometimes walk down to Ladder Bay to picnic. Think long and hard before you do: climbing back requires navigating the same 400 steps.

Cove Bay. Near the airport on the island's northeastern side, this 20-foot-long strip of rocks and pebbles laced with gray sand is really the only place for sunning. There's also a small tide pool here for swimming.

Flat Point. This is the only place on the island where planes can land. The runway here is one of the world's shortest, with a length of approximately 1,300 feet. Only STOL (short takeoff and landing) prop planes dare land here, as each end of the runway drops off more than 100 feet into the crashing surf below.

Fort Bay. The end of the Road is also the jumping-off place for all of Saba's dive operations and the location of the St. Maarten ferry dock. The island's only gas station is here, as is a 277-foot pier that

Engineering Feats

To view Saba from a distance is to be baffled: the island soars out of the Caribbean Sea. Steep, rocky shores, on the conical volcano that formed it, provide a seemingly impassable barrier to the outside world. How anyone saw this land as inhabitable is a mystery. But Sabans are a tenacious lot, and they were bound and determined to make this island theirs.

Among the sheer rock walls that surround Saba, at what is now Fort Bay, settlers found a tiny cove where entrance was possible. They navigated rowboats in between the crashing waves, steadied themselves against the swell, and then, waist-deep in water, pulled their boats to shore. Nothing got onto the island without coming this way, not a person, or a set of dishes, or a sofa. From there, supplies were hauled up a steep path composed of more than 200 steps (all of different heights and widths) in the hands or on the heads of Sabans. The trail had been carved into the mountain and climbed 820 feet above sea level to the Bottom through a grand crevice. Visitors who were unable to climb were carried to the top at a cost of 30 guilders.

For nearly 300 years after Saba was settled, this was how it was done. Then, in the early 1900s, the locals decided to build a road. They first approached the Dutch government for help. Legend has it that the Dutch said the grade was too steep, that it could not be done. But the Sabans, in particular, Josephus Lambert Hassell, would not be deterred. He took a correspondence course in road building, and in 1938, with no trained engineers, road construction began. The road took about 15 years to complete and now climbs 653 feet out of Fort Bay.

The next feat of engineering came in 1956, when the Technical Economic Counsel of Dutch Caribbean deemed tourism Saba's only marketable resource and decided that a pier and an airport had to be built. The airport was built on Flat Point, a solidified lava flow that was the only place that was flat enough. In 1959, the first conventional single-engine aircraft landed on the 1,300-foot aircraft carrier–size strip, the shortest international one in the world. The airport itself opened in 1963. Engineers first tried to build a pier in 1934, but the perpetual waves destroyed it almost immediately. In 1972, the Sabans tried again and were able to build a short, 277-foot-long pier (the sea was simply too deep for anything longer). Unfortunately, it is too small to accommodate cruise ships, a major thorn in the tourism industry's side.

accommodates the tenders from ships. On the quay are a decompression chamber, which at this writing is not in use, and three dive shops. Deep End Bar and Grill and Pop's Place are two good places to catch your breath while enjoying some refreshments and the view of the water.

Saba National Marine Park. Established in 1987 to preserve and manage the island's marine resources, the Saba National Marine Park encircles the entire island, dipping down to 200 feet. It's zoned for diving, swimming, fishing, boating, and anchorage. A unique aspect of Saba's diving is the submerged pinnacles at about the 70-foot depth

Looking down from Mt. Scenery

mark. Here all forms of sea creatures rendezvous. The information center offers talks and slide shows for divers and snorkelers and provides literature on marine life. (Divers are charged $3 a dive to help maintain the park facilities.) Before you visit, call first to see if anyone is around. ⊠ *Saba Conservation Foundation/Marine Park Visitors Center, Fort Bay* ☎ *599/416–3295* ⊕ *www.sabapark.org* ☉ *Weekdays 8–5.*

Hell's Gate. The Road makes 14 hairpin turns up nearly 2,000 vertical feet to Hell's Gate. Holy Rosary Church, on Zion's Hill, is a stone structure that looks medieval but was built in 1962. In the community center behind the church, village ladies sell their intricate lace. The same ladies make the potent rum-based Saba Spice, each according to her old family recipe. The intrepid can venture to Lower Hell's Gate, where the Old Sulphur Mine Walk leads to bat caves (with a sulfuric stench) that can—with caution—be explored.

Fodor'sChoice
★
Mt. Scenery. Stone and concrete steps—1,064 of them—rise to the top of Mt. Scenery. En route to the mahogany grove at the summit, the steps pass giant elephant ears, ferns, begonias, mangoes, palms, and orchids; there are six identifiable ecosystems in all. The staff at the Trail Shop in Windwardside can provide a field guide. Have your hotel pack a picnic lunch, wear sturdy shoes, and take along a jacket and a canteen of water. The round-trip excursion, which takes about three hours, is best begun in the early morning.

Windwardside. The island's second-largest village, perched at 1,968 feet, commands magnificent views of the Caribbean. Here amid the oleander bushes are rambling lanes and narrow alleyways winding through the hills, and clusters of tiny, neat houses and shops as well as the Saba

Tourist Office. At the village's northern end is the Church of St. Paul's Conversion, a colonial building with a red-and-white steeple.

Harry L. Johnson Museum. Small signs mark the way to the Harry L. Johnson Museum. This 160-year-old former sea captain's home is surrounded by lemongrass, clover, and a playground for small chilldren. Period pieces on display include a handsome mahogany four-poster bed, an antique organ, and, in the kitchen, a rock oven. You can also look at old documents, such as a letter a Saban wrote after the hurricane of 1772, in which he sadly says, "We have lost our little all." Don't miss the delightful stroll to the museum down the stone-walled Park Lane, one of the prettiest walks in the Caribbean. ⊠ *Windwardside* ☎ *No phone* ⌚ *$2* ☉ *Weekdays 10–noon and 1–4.*

WHERE TO EAT

The island might be tiny, but there's no shortage of mouthwatering fare, including French dishes, fresh seafood, and Caribbean specialties. Reservations are necessary, as most of the restaurants are quite small. In addition, some places provide transportation.

What to Wear: Restaurants are informal. Shorts are fine during the day, but for dinner you may want to put on slacks or a casual sundress. Just remember that nights in Windwardside can be cool because of the elevation.

$$$
SEAFOOD

╳ **Bistro del Mare.** While dining alongside the pool at the Shearwater Resort, savor the sounds of the sea, soft jazz, and a panorama from 2,000 feet above sea level. The frequently changing, pricey menu offers a good wine selection. Specialties include tomato-basil soup, calamari fritti, and lobster ravioli. Fresh seafood is a given. ⑤ *Average main: $24* ⊠ *Shearwater Resort, Booby Hill, Windwardside* ☎ *599/416–2498* ⊕ *www.shearwater-resort.com* ⌸ *Reservations essential* ☉ *No dinner Sun. and Mon.*

$$$
ECLECTIC
★

╳ **Brigadoon.** The exceptional fare draws just as many people to this local favorite as the entertaining atmosphere, which stars eccentric co-owner Trish Chammaa. She hosts with jokes and brassy banter while her husband toils over supper in the back, and the result is a great experience. Brigadoon's glass-top tables are accented with Caribbean runners. The varied menu includes vegetarian entrées, fresh Saban lobster, sesame- and coriander-encrusted yellowfin tuna, and baby back ribs. Thursday and Saturday are prime rib and sushi nights. As for the decadent desserts, the cheesecake, which comes in a variety of flavors, is a standout. Also worth a try: Madagascar vanilla bean–ginger rum, made in-house. ⑤ *Average main: $22* ⊠ *Windwardside* ☎ *599/416–2380* ⌸ *Reservations essential* ☉ *Closed Sep. and Tue. No lunch.*

$$
AMERICAN

╳ **Deep End Bar and Grill.** The owners of the Saba Deep dive shop run this lively harborside spot, which has a stained-glass window, mahogany bar, and newly refinished furniture and floors. The soups and sandwiches (especially the Reuben) are excellent, and the customers are usually high-spirited—most have just come from a dive. Dinner is served only on holidays. ⑤ *Average main: $15* ✉ *Fort Bay* ☎ *599/416–3438, 599/416–3397* ⊙ *No dinner.*

$
CARIBBEAN
✕**Pop's Place.** You'll find this itty-bitty come-as-you-are, Caribbean-flavor shack directly on the water, overlooking the pier in Fort Bay. Newly remodeled with a bar fashioned to look like a ship, it retains its cozy atmosphere. Chef Vick Phaiton, who has been featured on the Food Network, whips up some mouthwatering dishes, including creole snapper and eggplant "caviar"; among his famed desserts are a chocolate soufflé and a crème brûlée. ⑤ *Average main: $8* ✉ *Fort Bay* ☎ *599/416–3640* ▭ *No credit cards* ⊙ *Closed Mon.*

$$$
ECLECTIC
Fodor'sChoice
★
✕**Queen's Garden Restaurant.** Set in a lovely garden and showcasing sweeping views of the Bottom, this dimly lighted venue is the perfect place for a romantic meal. You can expect superb Saban lobster or some other tasty menu offering, or the chef will create something to your liking. The smoked-duck-breast salad starter is mouthwatering. Service is excellent. Come early for cocktails at the outdoor bar, which overlooks the pool—and, below that, the ocean—then stay late and be awed by the stars above you. Poolside parties, musical events, and theme nights with international flavors spice things up. A jacket is required for dinner only. ⑤ *Average main: $27* ✉ *1 Troy Hill Dr., Troy Hill* ☎ *599/416–3494* ⊕ *www.queensaba.com/theresort* ⌱ *Reservations essential Jacket required* ⊙ *No dinner Mon.*

$$
CARIBBEAN
★
✕**Rainforest Restaurant.** You might need a flashlight for the five-minute hike down the Crispeen Track, by way of the Mt. Scenery Trail, to find this restaurant in the middle of the rain forest. Once you arrive, you'll feel truly away from it all. Fresh seafood is always available, vegetables are picked fresh from the restaurant's own garden, and though the steaks are huge, locals usually opt for red curry shrimp—and apple pie or homemade ice cream for dessert. On Wednesday a slide show depicts the ecological aspects of the island. And every night you are surrounded by music—the lilting sound of the tree frogs. ⑤ *Average main: $20* ✉ *Ecolodge Rendez-Vous, Crispeen Track, Windwardside* ☎ *599/416–3888* ⊙ *Closed Mon.*

$$$
EUROPEAN
Fodor'sChoice
★
✕**Restaurant Eden.** On a rooftop amid a lovely garden setting, Chef Norbert Schippers concocts an eclectic, European-French cuisine menu that might include anything from Italian risotto to seafood and steaks. Sample the Frutti del Mare, pasta with seafood and garden vegetables, which is topped with a lobster cream sauce. The restaurant prides itself on the freshness of its ingredients. ⑤ *Average main: $27* ✉ *Lambee's Place, above Sea Saba Dive Center, Windwardside* ☎ *599/416–2539* ⊕ *www.edensaba.com* ⌱ *Reservations essential* ⊙ *Closed Tue. No lunch.*

$$
PIZZA
✕**Saba's Treasure.** Right in the heart of Windwardside sits this relaxed restaurant whose interior is crafted to look like the inside of a ship. Outside you practically sit on the street (grab one of these chairs for maximum local flavor). Go for a quick meal of stone-oven pizza, the best on the island, or linger over a drink at the tiny bar. ⑤ *Average main: $18* ✉ *Windwardside* ☎ *599/416–2819* ⊕ *www.sabastreasure.com* ⊙ *No dinner Sun.*

$$
CARIBBEAN
✕**Scout's Place.** At this spacious, fun-loving restaurant and bar, you'll find dishes like goat stew and spit-roasted chicken. Theme nights include

Friday fish-and-chips or chicken ($14) and Saturday barbecue ($16). In addition to the good food, a great reason to come here is the atmosphere. Locals flock to Scout's Place on Friday for karaoke, but there's bound to be a group looking for fun every other night of the week. Sit on the outdoor veranda, which has stunning views of the water, the tiny houses, and the lush forest that make Saba so picturesque. $ *Average main: $18* ⊠ *Windwardside* ☎ *599/416–2740, 599/416–2205* ⊕ *www. scoutsplace.com* ⊗ *No dinner Sun.*

$$
BARBECUE
★

✕ **Swinging Doors.** A cross between an English pub and an Old West saloon (yes, there are swinging doors), this lively watering hole serves not-to-be-missed barbecue on Tuesday and Friday nights. Pick from ribs, chicken, or ribs and chicken ($12), and don't forget to ask for peanut sauce—you'll be glad you did. Steak night is Sunday ($16–$18). The rest of the week it's just drinks. Expect plenty of conversation, including some local gossip. $ *Average main: $15* ⊠ *Windwardside* ☎ *599/416–2506* ▬ *No credit cards.*

$$
ECLECTIC

✕ **Tropics Café.** Breakfast, lunch, and dinner are served poolside at Juliana's Hotel in the cabana-style, open-air dining room or in the small dining room, which is dominated by a bar. The café is owned by the same couple who own the hotel. Sandwiches, salads, and fresh fish dominate the menu. Dinner is served only on Wednesday and Sunday, both designated as Grill Night, and on Friday, Movie Night. The movie is projected onto a sheet strung up just beyond the pool—you can get a chicken or burger dinner for just $12. $ *Average main: $20* ⊠ *Windwardside* ☎ *599/416–2469, 888/289–5708* ⊕ *www.sabatropics. com* ⊗ *No lunch Mon. No dinner Mon., Tue., Thu., Sat.*

WHERE TO STAY

Saba's few hotel rooms are primarily in a handful of friendly, tidy inns or guesthouses perched on ledges or tucked into tropical gardens. Because the island is so small, it doesn't much matter where you stay. Among the choices are a couple of delightful small inns and splendid, small ecoresorts. There are also more than a dozen apartments, cottages, and villas for rent. Cable TV is common, but air-conditioning is a rarity.

For expanded reviews, facilities, and current deals, visit Fodors.com.

$
HOTEL
☺

🏠 **Cottage Club.** Form follows function at these gingerbread bungalows, where the price is right and the proximity to downtown is ideal. **Pros:** walking distance to Windwardside; lushly landscaped pool with a gorgeous view; majestic lobby–reception room. **Cons:** stark suites; no on-site dining; some of the walks to the rooms are steep; no a/c. **TripAdvisor:** "private and beautiful view," "the friendliest neighbors," "the very best in quality service." $ *Rooms from: $120* ⊠ *Windwardside* ☎ *599/416–2486* ⊕ *www.cottage-club.com* ⇲ *10 cottages, some wheelchair accessible* ❗◯❘ *No meals.*

$
HOTEL

🏠 **Ecolodge Rendez-Vous.** If you like hiking and getting back to nature, this lodge, a five-minute walk deep in the rain forest, is for you. **Pros:** Candlelit Rainforest Restaurant serves three meals a day; nature-theme cottages. **Cons:** hike to get here; only three cottages have ocean views;

no electricity or Internet; steep climb to rooms. **TripAdvisor:** "peaceful," "perfect place for hiking," "the whole experience was wonderful." $ *Rooms from: $75* ✉ *Crispeen Track, Windwardside* ☎ *599/416–3348, 599/416–7388* ⊕ *www.ecolodge-saba.com* ➦ *12 cottages* ⍥ *No meals.*

$
HOTEL
▦ **El Momo.** If you want to feel as if you're doing your ecological part without giving up every modern convenience, consider these tiny cottages. **Pros:** snack bar–lounge with hammock; cottages buried in the woods; smoke-free property; Wi-Fi. **Cons:** tiny accommodations; strenuous hike to get here; no a/c. **TripAdvisor:** "rustic and beautiful," "wonderful place with an unbeatable view," "great secluded cottages." $ *Rooms from: $65* ✉ *Booby Hill* ☎ *599/416–2265* ⊕ *www.elmomocottages.com* ➦ *7 cottages* ⍥ *No meals.*

$
HOTEL
☺
★
▦ **Juliana's Hotel.** Reasonable, in town, great views, and accommodations from good to luxurious—it's all here. **Pros:** across the street from Tropics Café; outdoor, in-rock shower in Orchid Cottage; two on-site computers with free Internet; full breakfast. **Cons:** close quarters; a hike to get off the property; not all rooms have a/c. **TripAdvisor:** "great place and great owners," "best view ever," "like home in paradise." $ *Rooms from: $120* ✉ *Windwardside* ☎ *599/416–2269* ⊕ *www.julianas-hotel.com* ➦ *9 rooms, 1 apartment, 3 cottages* ⍥ *Breakfast.*

$$
HOTEL
Fodor'sChoice
★
▦ **Queen's Garden Resort.** At this romantic getaway, a quaint stone stairway winds up past the largest pool on the island, all the way to the patio in front of the main building, which houses the lovely Queen's Garden restaurant. **Pros:** pool bar; private Jacuzzis with sweeping views. **Cons:** occasional parties can make things loud and crowded; not wheelchair accessible. **TripAdvisor:** "magical getaway," "amazing property and staff," "wonderful service and location." $ *Rooms from: $230* ✉ *1 Troy Hill Dr., Troy Hill* ☎ *599/416–3494* ⊕ *www.queenssaba.com* ➦ *12 1- or 2-bedroom suites* ⍥ *No meals.*

$
HOTEL
▦ **Scout's Place.** Owned by dive masters Wolfgang and Barbara Tooten, this all-in-one, no-frills dive resort is especially good for the diver on a tight budget. **Pros:** on-site dive shop; multilingual owners; karaoke on Friday. **Cons:** smallish rooms; some don't get much sunlight; karaoke on Friday. **TripAdvisor:** "friendly and fun," "great getaway," "idyllic with a mountain view." $ *Rooms from: $109* ✉ *Windwardside* ☎ *599/416–2740, 599/416–2205, 866/656–7222 for reservations* ⊕ *www.scoutsplace.com* ➦ *10 rooms, 1 2-bedroom cottage* ⍥ *Breakfast.*

$
RESORT
★
▦ **Shearwater Resort.** You may never want to leave this boutique hotel, 2,000 feet above the sea—it's that secluded and peaceful, Rooms are spacious and comfortable, with lots of upscale amenities. **Pros:** upscale; one of the best views on the island. **Cons:** the road is very steep, and it's a schlep to get here. **TripAdvisor:** "the best escape from reality," "top of the line," "amazing views." $ *Rooms from: $195* ✉ *Booby Hill, Windwardside* ☎ *599/416–2498* ⊕ *shearwater-resort.com* ➦ *9 suites or cottage rooms with balcony* ⍥ *Breakfast.*

18

Divers will find spectacular marine life and coral in Saba's 28 dive sites.

NIGHTLIFE

Guido's. There's often dancing on weekends at Guido's. ⊠ *Windwardside* ☏ *599/416–2230.*

Scout's Place. When night rolls around, the convivial bar here can get crowded, and sometimes there's dancing. Go on Friday for karaoke night, when people swarm the spacious dining area. ⊠ *Windwardside* ☏ *599/416–2740.*

SHOPPING

The history of Saba lace, one of the island's most popular goods, goes back to the late 19th century. Gertrude Johnson learned lace making at a Caracas convent school. She returned to Saba in the 1870s and taught the art that has endured ever since. Saban ladies display and sell their creations at the community center in Hell's Gate and from their houses; just follow the signs. Collars, tea towels, napkins, and other small articles are relatively inexpensive; larger ones, such as tablecloths, can be pricey. The fabric requires some care—it's not drip-dry. Saba Spice is another island buy. Although it *sounds* as delicate as lace, and the aroma is as sweet as can be, the base for this liqueur is 151-proof rum.

Helen's Notions & Fabrics. More than a century ago, when Saba men were out fishing, the island ladies learned to tat lace. They still do delicate lacework and add it to blouses, dresses, tablecloths, and napkins. It's available for sale at several locations on the island. The most accessible is Helen's. ⊠ *The Bottom.*

El Momo Folk Art. The shelves here overflow with regional crafts, local postcards, handmade jewelry, knickknacks, and anything else El Momo can find a spot for. ⊠ *Windwardside* ☎ *599/416–2518* ✆ *9–6.*

JoBean Glass. Artist-owner Jo Bean's handmade glass-bead jewelry and sterling silver and gold pieces are delicate and unique. She also offers workshops in beadwork. ⊠ *Windwardside* ☎ *599/416–2490* ⊕ *www. jobeanglassart.com.*

★ **Peanut Gallery.** From watercolors of local houses to ocean-inspired sculpture, the Peanut Gallery offers the island's best selection of local and Caribbean art. Take time to browse through the offerings, and you might just walk away with something better than a refrigerator magnet to remember your trip with. ⊠ *Windwardside* ☎ *599/416–2509.*

★ **Saba Artisan Foundation.** Here you can buy the hand-screened fabrics by the yard or already made into resort clothing. The foundation also serves as a central location for buying the famous Saba lace as well as T-shirts and spices. ⊠ *The Bottom* ☎ *599/416–3260.*

SPORTS AND ACTIVITIES

DIVING AND SNORKELING

Fodor'sChoice
★
Saba is one of the world's premier scuba-diving destinations. Visibility is extraordinary, and dive sites are alive with corals and other sea creatures. Within ½ mile (¾ km) of shore, seawalls drop to depths of more than 1,000 feet. The Saba National Marine Park, which includes shoals, reefs, and seawalls rich with corals and fish, is dedicated to preserving its marine life.

Divers have a pick of 28 sites, including **Third Encounter,** a top-rated pinnacle dive (usually to about 110 feet) for advanced divers, with plentiful fish and spectacular coral; **Man of War Shoals,** another popular pinnacle dive (70 feet), with myriad fish and coral; and **Ladder Labyrinth,** a formation of ridges and alleys (down to 80 feet), where likely sightings include grouper, sea turtles, and sharks.

Snorkelers shouldn't feel left out: the marine park has several marked spots where reefs or rocks sit in shallow water. Among these sites is **Torrens Point** on the northwest side of the island. Waterproof maps are available from the marine park, the Saba Conservation Foundation, or dive shops.

Expect to pay about $50 for a one-tank dive, around $90 for a two-tank dive. There is also a mandatory $3 dive fee imposed by the Saba Marine Park plus a $1 per night nature fee and a $1 charge per dive for the hyperbaric chamber.

Saba Deep. If you're looking for a very personal, one-on-one dive experience, try Saba Deep, which tends to take out smaller groups. The company offers PADI- and/or NAUI-certified instructors. ⊠ *Fort Bay* ☎ *599/416–3347* ⊕ *www.sabadeep.com.*

Saba Divers. Owned by German divers, Saba Divers offers multilingual instruction, making it a great option for anyone interested in meeting

18

international divers or in practicing their language skills. It's the only outfit on the island that allows its customers to dive with Nitrox for free. ⌂ *Windwardside* ☎ *599/416–2740* ⊕ *www.sabadivers.com.*

Sea Saba. All of Sea Saba's excursions are accompanied by at least two dive instructors and can include up to 10 divers on one of two 40-foot boats. The staff is both knowledgeable and jovial, making a day on the boat an illuminating and enjoyable experience for any diver. ⌂ *Windwardside* ☎ *599/416–2246* ⊕ *www.seasaba.com.*

☾ **Sea and Learn.** Every October, local dive operator Lynn Costenaro, of Sea Saba, orchestrates an event that has become an international attraction. Sea and Learn is when pharmacologists, biologists, and other nature experts from all over the world descend on Saba to give presentations, lead field trips, and show off research projects, all of which are designed to increase environmental awareness. Past events have included monitoring undersea octopus checkpoints and studying the medicinal value of indigenous plants. There are even special events for kids. And best of all, it's free. You can sign up online. ☎ *599/416–2246* ⊕ *www.seaandlearn.org.*

GUIDED TOURS

The taxi drivers who meet the planes at the airport or the boats at Fort Bay conduct tours of the island. Tours can also be arranged by dive shops or hotels. A full-day trek costs $50 for one to four passengers and $12.50 per person for groups larger than four. If you're in from St. Maarten for a day trip, you can do a full morning of sightseeing, stop off for lunch (have your driver make reservations before starting), complete the tour afterward, and return to the airport in time to make the last flight back to St. Maarten. Guides are available for hiking; arrangements may be made through the tourist office or the Trail Shop in Windwardside. Or check out the island in a guided boat tour available for groups of up to 10 on Tuesday and Wednesday. In an hour and a half you can circle the island while learning about its history, its indigenous seabird population, and its coral reefs.

HIKING

On Saba you can't avoid hiking, even if you just go to mail a postcard. The big deal, of course, is Mt. Scenery, with 1,064 steps leading to its top.

Saba Conservation Foundation. For information about Saba's 18 recommended botanical hikes, check with the Saba Conservation Foundation, which maintains trails, at its office in Fort Bay or at its shop in Windwardside. Botanical tours are available on request. The charges for trail use are a voluntary $1 per day or $3 per stay. Crocodile James (James Johnson) will explain the local flora and fauna. A guided, strenuous, full-day hike through the undeveloped side of Mt. Scenery costs about $50. ⌂ *Fort Bay* ☎ *599/416–3295* ⌂ *Trail Shop, Windwardside* ☎ *599/416–2630* ⊕ *www.sabapark.org.*

St. Barthélemy

WORD OF MOUTH

"If you've been to France and like the culture then I'm sure you will
enjoy St. Barth. It's France in the tropics."

—Sharona

WELCOME TO ST. BARTHÉLEMY

Ile Chevreau

ATLANTIC OCEAN

Pte. à Colombier

Anse à Colombier

La Petite Anse

Anse des Flamands

Anse à Galets

Ile. Petit Jean

Anse Gros Jean

[19]

[19] [17] [18]

Colombier

Anse des Cayes

Caribbean Sea

Corossol

[18]

[12] [16]

Anse Corossol

Inter-Oceans Museum

St. Jean Airport

Baie de St-Jean

St-Jean

[20]

Public Beach

Gustavia
see detail map

TO ST. MARTIN

Gustavia

Lurin

[9]

Les Petits Saintes

Mt. Lurin

Petite Anse de Galet (Shell Beach)

Grande Pt.

Gustavia

[2]

[7]

Municipal Museum

Carré d'Or

[6]

R. de la République

R. Auguste Nyman

Fort George

[1]

Tourist Office

R. Duquesne

R. de la Paix

R. du Roi Oscar II

R. du Général de Gaulle

R. Jeanne d'Arc

R. Schoelcher

Chanzy

[5]

[4]

[3]

R. du Bord de Mer

R. du Centenaire

R. Lafayette Thiers

R. Jean Bart

R. de la Colline

[2]

R. Samuel Fahlberg

R. Courbet Gambetta

Post Office

R. du Presbytère

R. de l'Église

R. du Bord de Mer

R. I. de Brun

R. des Normands

[1]

[8]

Fort Cart

0   200 yards

0   200 m

0   1/2 mi

0   1/2 km

Chic travelers put aside their cell phones long enough to enjoy the lovely beaches—long, surf-pounded strands; idyllic crescents crowned by cliffs or forests; glass-smooth lagoons perfect for windsurfing. Nothing on St. Barth comes cheap. But on a hotel's awning-shaded terrace St. Barth's civilized ways seem worth every penny.

KEY

🛥 *Ferry*
⤢ *Beaches*
◥ *Dive Sites*
1 *Restaurants*
①	*Hotels*

ST.BARTHÉLEMY

19

LA RIVIERA DES CARAÏBES

Just 8 square miles (21 square km), St. Barth is a hilly island with many sheltered bays. Development is tightly controlled, so you will find no high-rise resorts to spoil your views. The French, who had controlled the island since the late 17th century, gave it to Sweden in 1784 but finally reclaimed it in 1877.

TOP REASONS TO VISIT ST. BARTHÉLEMY

1 The Scene: The island is active, sexy, hedonistic, and hip, and the human scenery is as beautiful as the sparkling-blue sea vistas.

2 Super Chic: St. Barth continues to change and evolve, becoming ever more chic.

3 Great Dining: New restaurants continue to tempt gourmets and gourmands.

4 Shopping Galore: If you're a shopper, you'll find bliss stalking the latest in clothes and accessories in dozens of the Caribbean's best boutiques.

5 Getting Out on the Water: Windsurfing, kitesurfing and other water sports make going to the beach more than just a lounging experience.

ST. BARTHÉLEMY BEACHES

There is a beach in St. Barth to suit every taste. Whether you are looking for wild surf, a dreamy white-sand strand, or a spot at a chic beach club close to shopping and restaurants, you will find it within a 20-minute drive.

(Above) Snorkeling at Anse à Colombier (Bottom right) Anse à Colombier (Top right) Anse des Flamands

There are many *anses* (coves) and nearly 20 *plages* (beaches) scattered around the island, each with a distinctive personality; all are open to the public, even if the beach fronts the toniest of resorts. Because of the variety and number of beaches, even in high season you can find a nearly empty beach, despite St. Barth's tiny size. That's not to say that all the island's beaches are equally good or even equally suitable for swimming, but each beach has something unique to offer. Unless you are having lunch at a beachfront restaurant that has lounging areas set aside for its patrons, you should bring your own umbrella, beach mat, and water (all of which are easily obtainable all over the island if you haven't brought yours with you on vacation). Topless sunbathing is common, but nudism is supposedly forbidden—although both Grande Saline and Gouverneur are de facto nude beaches. Shade is scarce.

THE RIGHT BEACH

For long stretches of talcum-soft pale sand choose La Saline, Gouverneur, or Flamands. For seclusion in nature, pick the tawny grains of Corossol. But the most remarkable beach on the island, Shell Beach, is right in Gustavia and hardly has sand at all! Millions of tiny pink shells wash ashore in drifts, thanks to an unusual confluence of ocean currents, sea-life beds, and hurricane action.

Anse à Colombier. The beach here is the least accessible, thus the most private, on the island; to reach it you must take either a rocky footpath from Petite Anse or brave the 30-minute climb down (and back up) a steep, cactus-bordered trail. Boaters favor this beach and cove for its calm anchorage.

Anse de Grand Cul de Sac. The shallow, reef-protected beach is nice for small children, fly-fishermen, kayakers, and windsurfers—and for the amusing pelicanlike frigate birds that dive-bomb the water fishing for their lunch. You needn't do your own fishing; you can have a wonderful lunch at one of the excellent restaurants.

Anse de Grande Saline. Secluded, with its sandy ocean bottom, this is just about everyone's favorite beach. There can be a bit of wind here, so you can enjoy yourself more if you go on a calm day. In spite of the prohibition, young and old alike go nude. The beach is a 10-minute walk up a rocky dune trail. Although there are several good restaurants for lunch near the parking area, once you get here, the beach is just sand, sea, and sky.

Anse de Lorient. This beach is popular with St. Barth families and surfers, who like its rolling waves and central location. Be aware of the level of the tide, which can come in very quickly. Hikers and avid surfers often walk over the

hill to Point Milou in the late afternoon when the waves roll in.

Anse des Flamands. This is the most beautiful of the hotel beaches—a roomy strip of silken sand. Come here for lunch and then spend the afternoon sunning, taking a long beach walk, and swimming in the turquoise water.

★ **Anse du Gouverneur.** Because it's so secluded, this beach is a popular place for nude sunbathing. It is truly beautiful, with blissful swimming and views of St. Kitts, Saba, and St. Eustatius. Venture here at the end of the day and watch the sun set behind the hills. The road here from Gustavia also offers spectacular vistas. Legend has it that pirates' treasure is buried in the vicinity. There are no restaurants or other services here, so plan accordingly.

Baie de St-Jean. Like a mini–Côte d'Azur—beachside bistros, terrific shopping, bungalow hotels, bronzed bodies, windsurfing, and day-trippers who tend to arrive on BIG yachts—the reef-protected strip is divided by Eden Rock promontory. Except in high season, when the hotels are fully booked, you can rent chaises and umbrellas at La Plage restaurant or at Eden Rock, where you can lounge for hours over lunch.

19

By Elise Meyer   St. Barthélemy blends the respective essences of the Caribbean, France, and *Architectural Digest* in perfect proportions. A sophisticated but unstudied approach to relaxation and respite prevails: you can spend the day on a beach, try on the latest French fashions, and watch the sunset while nibbling tapas over Gustavia Harbor, then choose from nearly 100 excellent restaurants for an elegant or easy evening meal. You can putter around the island, scuba dive, windsurf on a quiet cove, or just admire the lovely views.

A mere 8 square miles (21 square km), St. Barth is a hilly island, with many sheltered inlets providing visitors with many opportunities to try out picturesque, quiet beaches. The town of Gustavia wraps itself around a modern harbor lined with everything from size-matters mega-yachts to rustic fishing boats to sailboats of all descriptions. Red-roofed villas dot the hillsides, and glass-front shops line the streets. Beach surf runs the gamut from kiddie-pool calm to serious-surfer dangerous, beaches from deserted to packed. The cuisine is tops in the Caribbean, and almost everything is tidy, stylish, and up-to-date. French *savoir vivre* prevails throughout the island.

Christopher Columbus discovered the island—called "Ouanalao" by its native Caribs—in 1493; he named it for his brother Bartolomé. The first group of French colonists arrived in 1648, drawn by the ideal location on the West Indian Trade Route, but they were wiped out by the Caribs, who dominated the area. Another small group from Normandy and Brittany arrived in 1694. This time the settlers prospered—with the help of French buccaneers, who took advantage of the island's strategic location and protected harbor. In 1784 the French traded the island to King Gustav III of Sweden in exchange for port rights in Göteborg. The king dubbed the capital Gustavia, laid out and paved streets, built three forts, and turned the community into a prosperous free port. The island thrived as a shipping and commercial center until the 19th century, when earthquakes, fires, and hurricanes brought financial ruin. Many residents fled for newer lands of opportunity, and Oscar II of Sweden decided to return the island to France. After briefly considering selling it to America, the French took possession of St. Barthélemy again on August 10, 1877.

Today the island is a free port, and in 2007 it became a Collectivity, a French-administered overseas territory outside of continental France. Arid, hilly, and rocky, St. Barth was unsuited to sugar production and thus never developed an extensive slave base. Some of today's 3,000 current residents are descendants of the tough Norman and Breton settlers of three centuries ago, but you are more likely to encounter attractive French twenty- and thirtysomethings from Normandy and Provence who are friendly, English speaking, and here for the sunny lifestyle.

PLANNING

WHEN TO GO

High season in St. Barth is typical for the Caribbean, from mid-December through mid-April (or until after Easter). During busy holiday periods prices can shoot up to the highest levels, but in the summer (particularly June and July), there are some remarkable bargains on the island, though some restaurants still close over the summer months, and hotels tend to do their annual maintenance during this time as well.

GETTING HERE AND AROUND

AIR TRAVEL

There are no direct flights to St. Barth. Most North Americans fly first into St. Maarten's Queen Juliana International Airport (⇨ *Chapter 23, St. Maarten/St. Martin for more information)*, from which the island is 10 minutes by air. Winair has regularly scheduled flights from St. Maarten. Tradewind Aviation has regularly scheduled service from San Juan and also does charters. Anguilla Air Services and St. Barth Commuter have scheduled flights and also do charters. You must reconfirm your return interisland flight, even during off-peak seasons, or you may very well lose your reservations. Be certain to leave ample time between your scheduled flight and your connection in St. Maarten—three hours is the minimum recommended (and be aware that luggage frequently doesn't make the trip; your hotel or villa-rental company may be able to send someone to retrieve it). It's a good idea to pack a change of clothes, required medicines, and a bathing suit in your carry-on—or better yet, pack very light and don't check baggage at all.

In business since 2002, Tradewind Aviation, a charter airline, provides convenient scheduled service to St. Barth from San Juan in modern, air-conditioned, turbine-powered aircraft flown by two pilots. Connecting through San Juan affords St. Barth visitors the most nonstop commercial flight options from the U.S. mainland and a convenient, domestic transfer point that is more convenient than St. Maarten.

Airports Aéroport de St-Jean ☎ *0590/27-63-56.*

Local Airline Contacts Anguilla Air Services ☎ *264/498-5922* ⊕ *www. anguillaairservices.com.* **St. Barth Commuter** ☎ *0590/27-54-54* ⊕ *www.*

DID YOU KNOW?

The largest hotel on St. Barth has just over 70 rooms, which means you get a great deal of personal service and attention wherever you stay.

LOGISTICS

Getting to St. Barth: There are no direct flights to St. Barth (SBH). You must fly to another island and then catch a smaller plane for the hop over, or you can take a ferry. Most Americans fly first to St. Maarten, and then take the 10-minute flight to St. Barth, but you can connect through St. Thomas or San Juan as well.

Hassle Factor: Medium–high.

On the Ground: Many hotels offer free airport transfers; before you arrive, they will contact you for your arrival information. Otherwise, there's a taxi stand at the airport; unmetered taxis cost about €10 to €25 to reach most hotels. If you are renting a car, you may pick it up from the airport; if you have a reservation, rental agents will meet you at the ferry if you arrive by boat.

Getting Around the Island: Most people coming to St. Barth rent a car. Taxis are expensive, but some visitors are happy to let an experienced driver negotiate the roads at night. Any restaurant will be happy to call a cab back to your hotel after dinner. Otherwise, there is no other transportation option on the island. It's also possible to rent a motorbike, but steep roads can make driving a stressful experience if you aren't experienced.

stbarthcommuter.com. **Tradewind Aviation** ☎ 800/376–7922, 203/267–3305 in Connecticut ⊕ www.tradewindaviation.com. **Winair** ☎ 0590/27–61–01, 866/466–0410 ⊕ www.fly-winair.com.

BOAT AND FERRY TRAVEL

St Barth can be reached by sea via ferry service or charter boat. There are three companies that provide passenger ferry service between St. Maartin and St. Barth, so check each provider's timetable to determine the most convenient departure. All service is to and from Quai de la République in Gustavia. Voyager offers round-trips for about $100 per person from either Marigot or Oyster Pond. Great Bay Express has several round-trips a day from Bobby's Marina in St. Maarten for €55 if reserved in advance, or €60 for same-day departures. Babou One, a new, stabilized, air-conditioned boat run by West Indies Ferry Express with service between Marigot and Gustavia, takes only 70 minutes. There are three convenient departures daily, at a cost of about €50 for adults, €35 for children under 12 (each way). Private boat charters are also available, but they are very expensive; Master Ski Pilou is one of the companies that offer the service.

Boat and Ferry Contacts Great Bay Express Ferry. This express service provides quick ferry transportation between Phillipsburg and Gustavia two or three times daily. You can now book online. ☎ 690/71–83–01 ⊕ www.sbhferry. com. **Master Ski Pilou.** Master Ski Pilou provides private boat transfers to St. Barth from St. Maarten. ☎ 0590/27–91–79 ⊕ www.masterskipilou.com. **Voyager.** Voyager has several daily departures to Gustavia from Marigot or Oyster Pond in St. Martin ☎ 0590/87–10–68 ⊕ www.voy12.com. **West Indies Ferry Express** ☎ 590/590–29–63–70 ⊕ www.westindiesferry.com.

19

CAR TRAVEL

Roads are sometimes unmarked, so get a map and look for signs pointing to a destination. These will be nailed to posts at all crossroads. Roads are narrow and sometimes very steep, but recent work has improved roads all over the island; even so, check the brakes and gears of your rental car before you drive away. ■ TIP→ Take a careful inventory of existing dents and scrapes on your rental vehicle with pictures on your smartphone or digital camera. Maximum speed on the island is 30 mph (50 kph). Driving is on the right, as in the United States and Europe. Parking is an additional challenge. There are two gas stations on the island, one near the airport and one in Lorient. They aren't open after 5 pm or on Sunday, but the station near the airport has pumps that accept automated payment by chip-and-pin credit card (such as those used throughout Europe), although at this writing most U.S. credit cards don't have the chip required for credit payments. Considering the short distances, a full tank of gas should last you most of a week.

Car Rentals: You must have a valid driver's license and be 25 or older to rent, and in high season there may be a three-day minimum. During peak periods, such as Christmas week and February, be sure to arrange for your car rental ahead of time. When you make your hotel reservations, ask if the hotel has its own cars available to rent; some hotels provide 24-hour emergency road service—something most rental companies don't offer. A tiny but powerful Smart car is a blast to buzz around in, and also a lot easier to park than larger cars. Expect to pay at least $55 per day. A Mini-Cooper convertible makes the most of sunny drives.

Car-Rental Contacts Avis ☎ 0590/27-71-43 ⊕ www.avis-stbarth.com. **Budget** ☎ 0590/27-66-30. **Cool Rental** ☎ 590/27-52-58. **Europcar** ☎ 0590/27-73-33 ⊕ www.st-barths.com/europcar/index.html. **Gumbs** ☎ 0590/27-75-32. **Gust Smart of St-Barth** ☎ 0590/27-95-06. **Hertz** ☎ 0590/27-71-14. **Turbe** ☎ 0590/27-71-42 ⊕ www.saint-barths.com/turbecarrental/.

MOPED, SCOOTER, AND BIKE TRAVEL

Several companies rent motorbikes, scooters, mopeds, and mountain bikes. Motorbikes go for about $30 per day and require a $100 deposit. Helmets are required. Scooter and motorbike rental places are mostly along rue de France in Gustavia and around the airport in St-Jean.

Contacts Barthloc Rental ⊠ Rue de France, Gustavia ☎ 0590/27-52-81 ⊕ www.barthloc.com. **Chez Béranger** ⊠ Rue de France, Gustavia ☎ 0590/27-89-00. **Ets Denis Dufau** ⊠ St-Jean ☎ 0590/27-70-59.

TAXI TRAVEL

Taxis are expensive and not particularly easy to arrange, especially in the evening. There's a taxi station at the airport and another in Gustavia; from elsewhere you must contact a dispatcher in Gustavia or St-Jean. Fares are regulated by the Collectivity, and drivers accept both dollars and euros. If you go out to dinner by taxi, let the restaurant know if you will need a taxi at the end of the meal, and they will call one for you.

Contacts Gustavia taxi dispatcher ☎ 0590/27-66-31. **St-Jean taxi dispatcher** ☎ 0590/27-75-81.

ESSENTIALS

Banks and Exchange Services Legal tender is the euro, but U.S. dollars are widely accepted. ATMs are common and dispense only euros.

Electricity Voltage is 220 AC/60 cycles, as in Europe. You'll need a converter and perhaps a transformer for electronic devices. Most hotels have converters available for guests' use.

Emergency Services Air Ambulance ☎ 545–4744. **Ambulance and Fire** ☎ 0590/18. **Hospital Emergency** ☎ 590/51–19–00. **Police** ☎ 17, 0590/27–66–66.

Language French, but English is widely spoken.

Passport Requirements All visitors must carry a valid passport and have a return or ongoing ticket. A visa is not necessary if for stays of up to a month. Passports must be valid for at least three months from the date of entry to the territory of St. Barthélemy.

Phones Many hotels will provide or rent you a cell phone to use during your stay. Some U.S. cell companies work in St. Barth. The country code for St. Barth is 590. Thus, to call St. Barth from the United States, dial 011 + 590 + 590 and the local six-digit number. Some cell phones use the prefix 690. For calls on St. Barth, you must dial 0590 plus the six-digit local number.

Taxes and Service Charges The island charges a $5 departure tax when your next stop is another French island, $10 to anywhere else payable in cash only (dollars or euros). Some hotels add a 10% service charge. Sometimes it is included in the room rate, so check. There is a 5% room tax on hotels and villa rentals.

Tipping Restaurants include a 15% service charge in their published prices, but it's common French practice to leave 5% to 10% more in cash, even if you have paid by credit card. Most taxi drivers don't expect a tip.

ACCOMMODATIONS

Most hotels on St. Barth are small (the largest has fewer than 70 rooms) and stratospherically expensive, but there are some reasonable options. About half of the accommodations on St. Barth are in private villas. Prices drop dramatically after March, and summer is a great time for a visit. Check hotel websites for updates of discounts and special offers that seem to be becoming more common with the current economy.

HOTEL AND RESTAURANT PRICES

Prices in the restaurant reviews are the average cost of a main course at dinner or, if dinner is not served, at lunch; taxes and service charges are generally included. Prices in the hotel reviews are the lowest cost of a standard double room in high season, excluding taxes, service charges, and meal plans (except at all-inclusives). Prices for rentals are the lowest per-night cost for a one-bedroom unit in high season.

VISITOR INFORMATION

Contact Office du Tourisme ✉ Quai Général-de-Gaulle ☎ 0590/27–87–27 ⊕ www.saintbarth-tourisme.com.

Because of the long legal residency requirement, it's not really feasible to get married on St. Barth unless you're a French citizen.

EXPLORING ST. BARTHÉLEMY

With a little practice, negotiating St. Barth's narrow, steep roads soon becomes fun. Recent infrastructure upgrades and the prevalence of small, responsive cars have improved things a lot. Free maps are everywhere, roads are smooth and well marked, and signs will point the way. The tourist office has annotated maps with walking tours that highlight sights of interest. Parking in Gustavia is still a challenge, especially during busy vacation times.

Corossol. Traces of the island's French provincial origins are evident in this two-street fishing village with a little rocky beach.

Inter Oceans Museum/Museum of Shells. Ingenu Magras's Inter Oceans Museum has more than 9,000 seashells and an intriguing collection of sand samples from around the world. You can buy souvenir shells. ⊠ *Corossol* ☎ *0590/27–62–97* €3 ⊙ *Tues.–Sun. 9–12:30 and 2–5.*

Gustavia. You can easily explore all of Gustavia during a two-hour stroll. Most shops close from noon to 3 or 4, so plan lunch accordingly, but stores stay open past 7 in the evening.

Tourist Office. A good spot to park your car is rue de la République, alongside the catamarans, yachts, and sailboats. The tourist office on the pier can provide maps and a wealth of information. During busier holiday periods, the office may be open all day. ⊠ *Rue de la République, Gustavia* ☎ *0590/27–87–27* ⊕ *www.saintbarth-tourisme.com* ⊙ *Mon. 8:30–12:30, Tues.–Fri. 8–noon and 2–5, Sat. 9–noon*

Le musée territorial de Saint Barthélemy. On the far side of the harbor known as La Pointe is the charming Municipal Museum, where you can find watercolors, portraits, photographs, and historic documents detailing the island's history, as well as displays of the island's flowers, plants, and marine life. ⊠ *La Pointe, Gustavia* ☎ *590/29–71–55* €2 ⊙ *Mon., Tues., Thurs., and Fri. 8:30–12:30 and 2:30–6, Sat. 9–12:30. Closed July 26–August 31.*

Lorient. Site of the first French settlement, Lorient is one of the island's two parishes; a restored church, a school, and a post office mark the spot. Note the gaily decorated graves in the cemetery.

Le Manoir. One of St. Barth's secrets is Le Manoir, a 1610 Norman manor, now a guesthouse, which was painstakingly shipped from France and reconstructed in Lorient in 1984. Look for the entrance by the Ligne de St. Barth building. ⊠ *Lorient* ☎ *0590/27–79–27.*

St-Jean. There is a monument at the crest of the hill that divides St-Jean from Gustavia. Called *The Arawak*, it symbolizes the soul of St. Barth. A warrior, one of the earliest inhabitants of the area (AD 800–2,500), holds a lance in his right hand and stands on a rock shaped like the island; in his left hand he holds a conch shell, which sounds the cry of nature; perched beside him are a pelican (which symbolizes the air and survival by fishing) and an iguana (which represents the earth). The half-mile-long crescent of sand at St-Jean is the island's most popular beach. A popular activity is watching and photographing the hair-raising airplane landings, but be sure to not stand in the area at the beach end of the runway, where someone was seriously injured. You'll also find some of the best shopping on the island here, as well as several restaurants. ⊠ *St-Jean.*

Toiny Coast. Over the hills beyond Grand Cul de Sac is this much-photographed coastline. Stone fences crisscross the steep slopes of Morne Vitet, one of many small mountains on St. Barth, along a rocky shore that resembles the rugged coast of Normandy. Nicknamed the "washing machine" because of its turbulent surf, it is not recommended even to expert swimmers because of the strong undertow.

WHERE TO EAT

Dining on St. Barth compares favorably to almost anywhere in the world. Varied and exquisite cuisine, a French flair in the decor, sensational wine, and attentive service make for a wonderful epicurean experience in almost any of the more than 80 restaurants. On most menus, freshly caught local seafood mingles on the plate with top-quality provisions that arrive regularly from Paris. Interesting selections on the Cartes de Vins are no surprise, but don't miss the sophisticated cocktails whipped up by island bartenders. They are worlds away from cliché Caribbean rum punches with paper umbrellas.

Most restaurants offer a chalkboard full of daily specials that are usually a good bet. But even the pickiest eaters will find something on every menu. Some level of compliance can be paid to dietary restrictions within reason, and especially if explained in French; just be aware that French people generally let the chef work his or her magic. Expect your meal to be costly; however, you can dine superbly and somewhat economically if you limit pricey cocktails, watch wine selections, share appetizers or desserts, and pick up snacks and picnic meals from one of the well-stocked markets. Or you could follow the locals to small *crêperies,* cafés, sandwich shops, and pizzerias in the main shopping areas. Lunch is usually less costly than dinner. *Ti Creux* means "snack" or "small bite."

Lavish publications feature restaurant menus and contacts. Ask at your hotel or look on the racks at the airport for current issues. Reservations are strongly recommended and, in high season, essential. Lots of restaurants now accept reservations by email. Check websites and social media. Except during the Christmas–New Year's season it's not usually necessary to book far in advance. A day's—or even a few hours'—notice is usually sufficient. At the end of the meal, as in France, you must request the bill. Until you do, you can feel free to linger at the table and enjoy the complimentary vanilla rum that's likely to appear.

Check restaurant bills carefully. A *service compris* (service charge) is always added by law, but you should leave the server 5% to 10%

19

extra in cash. You'll usually come out ahead if you charge restaurant meals on a credit card in euros instead of paying with American currency, as your credit card might offer a better exchange rate than the restaurant (though since most credit cards nowadays have conversion surcharges of 3% or more, the benefit of using plastic is rapidly disappearing). Many restaurants serve locally caught *langouste* (lobster); priced by weight, it's usually the most expensive item on a menu and, depending on its size and the restaurant, will range in price from $40 to $60. *In menu prices below, it has been left out of the range.*

What to Wear: A bathing suit and *gauzy top or shift* is acceptable at beachside lunch spots, but not really in Gustavia. Jackets are never required and are rarely worn by men, but most people do dress fashionably for dinner. Casual chic is the idea; women wear whatever is hip, current, and sexy. You can't go wrong in a tank dress or anything clingy and ruffly with white jeans and high sandals. The sky is the limit for high fashion at nightclubs and lounges in high season, when you might (correctly) think everyone in sight is a model. Nice shorts (not beachy ones) at the dinner table may label a man *américain*, but many locals have adopted the habit, and nobody cares much. Wear them with a pastel shirt to really fit in (never tucked in). Pack a light sweater or shawl for the occasional breezy night.

> **BACK-UP FERRY**
>
> Even if you are planning to fly to St. Barth, it's a good idea to keep the numbers and schedules for the three ferry companies handy in case your flight is delayed. An evening ferry could save you having to scramble for a hotel room in St. Maarten. If you are planning to spend time in St. Maarten before traveling on to St. Barth, the ferry is half the cost and somewhat more reliable than the puddle-jumper, and you can leave from Marigot, Oyster Pond, or Philipsburg. Check at the brand-new St. Barth Tourist Information counter at Princess Juliana Airport for specifics if things didn't go according to your plan.

ANSE DE TOINY

$$$$
MODERN FRENCH
Fodor's Choice
★

✕ **Le Gaïac.** Chef Stéphane Mazières is the only person in the Caribbean to share the Grand Chef designation of the Relais & Châteaux organization with the likes of Daniel Boulud and Thomas Keller. The new management of Hôtel Le Toiny (which includes Francophile Lance Armstrong) has fine-tuned the dramatic, tasteful, cliff-side dining porch to showcase his gastronomic art, and this is one dinner that you won't want to miss. Less stuffy than you might remember from seasons past, the food is notable for its innovation and extraordinary presentation, and the warm but consummately professional service sets a glorious standard. Rare ingredients and unique preparations delight: gossamer sheets of beet encase tuna tartare "cannelloni"; tender roasted Iberian pork is served in a potato crust, and a piquant sauce; venison medallions come with tender chestnut blinis. A greenhouse has even been installed on this former pineapple field to grow organic produce for the restaurant, and you can think of it while you savor saffron candied pineapple.

Le Gaïac, Anse de Toiny

The menu changes frequently, evolving and refining ideas. On Tuesday's special Fish Market Night, you choose your own fish to be grilled; there's a €43 buffet brunch on Sunday. This is one restaurant that is a true hedonistic experience, but you're on vacation, after all. $ *Average main: €36* ⊠ *Hôtel Le Toiny, Anse à Toiny* ☎ *0590/29–77–47* ⊕ *www. letoiny.com* ⚭ *Reservations essential* ⊙ *Closed Sept.–mid-Oct.*

FLAMANDS

$$$ ✕ **La Langouste.** This tiny beachside restaurant in the pool courtyard of
SEAFOOD Hôtel Baie des Anges is run by Anny, the hotel's amiable, ever-present proprietor. It lives up to its name by serving fantastic, fresh-grilled lobster at a price that is somewhat gentler than at most other island venues. Simple, well-prepared fish, pastas, and an assortment of refreshing cold soups, including a corn-and-coconut soup perfumed with lemongrass, are also available. Be sure to try the warm goat cheese in pastry served on a green salad with a fruity salsa. $ *Average main: €25* ⊠ *Hôtel Baie des Anges, Anse des Flamands* ☎ *0590/27–63–61* ⊕ *www. hotelbaiedesanges.fr* ⚭ *Reservations essential* ⊙ *Closed May–Oct.*

GRAND CUL DE SAC

$$$$ ✕ **Bar'tô.** The pretty restaurant in the gardens of the Guanahani hotel
ITALIAN showcases the refined cuisine of chef Philippe Masseglia presented beautifully from a menu that ranges from seared sea scallops in a light curry sauce to baby veal with purple artichokes. There is a €75 tasting menu if the whole table is adventurous. Don't miss the amazing soft coconut

cake served with a luscious sauce of spiced passion fruit. $ *Average main: €35* ⊠ *Hotel Guanahani, Grand Cul de Sac* ☎ 590/27–66–60 ⊘ *Closed Mon. and Tues.*

$$$ ✕ **La Gloriette.** For a beachside lunch with your toes in the sand, La
CARIBBEAN Gloriette is a dream. Picnic tables under the cocoloba trees are shady, and everyone is having a great time. Longtime visitors will remember the original creole restaurant here, and will be happy to know that the *accras* (salt-cod fritters with spicy sauce) are as good as ever. There are huge, fresh salads and many daily specials on the blackboard. Super-fresh grilled fish is a great choice, and the sushi-style tatakis are light and delicious. At dinner there are good pizzas for dining in or taking back to your villa. Don't miss the artisanal, island-flavored rums offered after your meal, and available at the tiny shop. $ *Average main: €23* ⊠ *Plage de Grand Cul de Sac, Grand Cul de Sac* ☎ 690/29–85–71 ⊘ *Closed Wed.*

$$$$ ✕ **Restaurant des Pêcheurs.** From fresh, morning beachside brioche to
SEAFOOD a final evening drink in the sexy lounge, you can dine all day in this
★ soaring thatch pavilion that is the epitome of chic. The restaurant at Le Sereno, like the Christian Liaigre–designed resort, is serenity itself. Each menu item is a miniature work of art, beautifully arranged and amiably served. Each day there is a different €44 three-course menu. "Authentic" two-course bouillabaisse *à l'ancienne,* the famous French seafood stew, is served every Friday, and the chef even gives a class in its preparation, but the menu also lists daily oceanic arrivals from Marseille and Quiberon on France's Atlantic coast: roasted, salt-crusted, or grilled to your personal perfection. Fans of Provence will love the aioli special on Wednesday, and Sunday is paella night. This—and sand between your toes—is heaven. $ *Average main: €32* ⊠ *Le Sereno, Grand Cul de Sac* ☎ 0590/29–83–00 ⊕ *www.lesereno.com* ⌨ *Reservations essential.*

GRANDE SALINE

$$$ ✕ **Le Tamarin.** A leisurely lunch here en route to Grande Saline beach is
FRENCH a St. Barth *must.* But new management makes it tops for dinner too. Sit
★ on one of the licorice-colored Javanese couches in the lounge area and nibble excellent sushi, or settle at a table under the wondrous tamarind tree for which the restaurant is named. A unique cocktail each day, ultrafresh fish provided by the restaurant's designated fisherman, and gentle prices accommodate local residents as well as the holiday crowd. The restaurant is open year-round. $ *Average main: €21* ⊠ *Grande Saline* ☎ 0590/27–72–12 ⊘ *Closed Tue.*

$$$ ✕ **Meat and Potatoes.** If you think that St. Barth is sometimes too "girly,"
STEAKHOUSE you will love this new restaurant at the end of the road to Saline Beach. The white interior is lined with banquettes heaped with red, black, and gray pillows; there are almost a dozen different cuts of steak, from tenderloins to T-bones, at least a dozen starchy sides, and some vegetables for good measure. There is also fresh fish for the red-meat averse. Don't miss the Provençal *pommes ratte,* wedges of potatoes cooked in duck fat, fresh rosemary, and sea salt. The wine list is full of complementary bottles, heavy on Bordeaux's best. $ *Average main: €30* ⊠ *Grande Saline* ☎ 590/51–15–98.

$$$$ ✕ **PaCrì.** Recently moved to the Manapany Hotel, an adorable young
ITALIAN husband-and-wife team (she is the chef) serve delicious, huge portions
★ of house-made pasta, wood-oven pizza (at lunch only), and authentic
Italian main courses, including chicken Milanese, and fresh local fish
carpaccios on a breezy open terrace in Anse de Cayes, a popular surfing beach. The menu—handwritten on a chalkboard—changes daily.
Don't miss the softball-size hunk of the best artisanal mozzarella you've
ever had, flown in from Puglia, Italy and garnished with prosciutto or
tomato and basil. The eggplant Parmesan appetizer is delicious and
more than enough for a meal. Like the pastas, the bread and the desserts
are made in-house, and the authentic tiramisu is only one of the winners. $ *Average main: €33* ⊠ *Anse de Cayes* ☎ *0590/27–66–55* ⊕ *www.
pacristbarth.com* ⚏ *Reservations essential.*

GUSTAVIA

$$ ✕ **B4.** Pronounced *before,* this lounge-restaurant occupies the central
FRENCH former location of longtime St. Barth mainstay Le Sapotillier. In addi-
tion to enjoying lighter French cuisine, wok stir-frys, generous salads,
pizzas, and traditional raclette, you can hang out in the lounge with
music, bar, and flat-screen TVs. The restaurant is great to fill up the
pocket time after dinner and *before* you head to your other late-night
activities. $ *Average main: €19* ⊠ *13 rue Samuel Fahlberg, Gustavia*
☎ *590/52–45–31* ☉ *Closed Tue.*

$$$$ ✕ **Bagatelle St Barth.** New in 2012, the sophisticated St. Tropez–inspired
BISTRO interior, right on the harbor, is a pretty place to watch big boats and
enjoy a menu of classic French bistro favorites such as truffled roast
chicken, pastis-flamed shrimp, and steak tartare. There are platters of
charcuterie and fromage for sharing, and a great wine list. Fans of the
popular sister establishments in New York's Meatpacking District and
Los Angeles will recognize the friendly service and lively atmosphere,
and the great music provided by resident DJs. $ *Average main: €32*
⊠ *Rue Samuel Fahlberg, Gustavia* ☎ *590/27–51–51.*

$$$$ ✕ **Bonito.** The former Mandala space has been completely transformed
LATIN AMERICAN into a chic beach house, with big, white, canvas couches in the center,
Fodor's Choice tables around the sides, an open kitchen, and three bar areas. The young
★ Venezuelan owners go to great lengths to see that guests are having as
much fun as they are. The specialty is ceviche with eight different vari-
eties, in combos that are prettily arrayed on poured-glass platters for
culinary experimentation. Try octopus and shrimp, or wahoo garnished
with sweet potatoes and popcorn. Traditionalists might like the fricassee
of escargots, or foie gras served with mango, soy, and preserved lemon.
Carnivores will love the rack of lamb. $ *Average main: €32* ⊠ *Rue de
la Sous-Préfecture, Gustavia* ☎ *590/27–96–96* ⊕ *www.ilovebonito.com*
⚏ *Reservations essential* ☉ *Closed Mon. No lunch.*

$$$$ ✕ **Dõ Brazil.** This restaurant is open every day for lunch and dinner
ECLECTIC and offers live music for sundown cocktail hour on Thursday, Fri-
day, and Saturday evenings, as well as top DJs spinning the latest club
mixes for evening events, which are listed in the local papers. Right on
Gustavia's Shell Beach, you'll find tasty light fare like chilled soups,
fruit-garnished salads with tuna, shrimp, and chicken, plus sandwiches,

19

burgers, pastas, and grilled fresh fish for lunch. Everyone loves the Dõ Brazil hot pot: Mahimahi, shrimps and sea scallops in a sauce of lemongrass and coconut milk. At dinner there is also a €35 three-course prix fixe and some reasonable soups and salads, which can help keep the bill in line. The extensive cocktail menu tempts, but at €12 each, your bar bill can quickly exceed the price of dinner. There is a €20 children's menu. ⑤ *Average main: €33* ⊠ *Shell Beach, Gustavia* ☎ *0590/29–06–66* ⊕ *www.dobrazil.com.*

$$$
ASIAN
✕ **Eddy's.** By local standards, dinner in the pretty, open-air, tropical garden here is reasonably priced. The cooking is French-creole-Asian. Fish specialties, especially the sushi tuna sampler, are fresh and delicious, and there are always plenty of notable daily specials. Just remember some mosquito repellent for your ankles. ⑤ *Average main: €24* ⊠ *Rue du Centenaire, Gustavia* ☎ *0590/27–54–17* ⚐ *Reservations not accepted* ⊘ *Closed Sun. No lunch.*

$$$
CARIBBEAN
★
✕ **Le Palace.** Tucked into a tropical garden, this popular in-town restaurant known for its barbecued ribs, beef fillet, and rack of lamb is consistently one of our absolute favorites. Fish-market specialties like red snapper cooked in a banana leaf or grilled tuna are good here, as are grilled duck with mushroom sauce and a skewered surf-and-turf with a green curry sauce. The blackboard lists daily specials that are usually a great choice, like a salad of tomato, mango, and basil. ⑤ *Average main: €23* ⊠ *Rue Général-de-Gaulle, Gustavia* ☎ *0590/27–53–20* ⚐ *Reservations essential* ⊘ *Closed Sun. and mid-June–July.*

$$
ECLECTIC
☾
★
✕ **Le Repaire.** This friendly brasserie overlooks Gustavia's harbor, and is a popular spot from its opening at noon to its late-night closing. The flexible hours are great if you arrive midafternoon and need a substantial snack before dinner. Grab a cappuccino, pull a captain's chair up to the street-side rail, and watch the pretty girls. The menu ranges from cheeseburgers, which are served only at lunch along with the island's best fries, to simply grilled fish and meat, pastas, and risottos. The composed salads always please. Wonderful ice-cream sundaes round out the menu. ⑤ *Average main: €19* ⊠ *Quai de la République, Gustavia* ☎ *0590/27–72–48* ⊘ *Closed Sun. in June.*

$$$
ITALIAN
Fodor's Choice
★
✕ **L'Isola.** St. Barth's chic sister to the Santa Monica (California) favorite, Via Veneto, is packing in happy guests for Italian classic dishes, dozens of house-made pasta dishes, prime meats, and the huge, well-chosen wine list. Restaurateur Fabrizio Bianconi wants it all to feel like a big Italian party, and with all the celebrating you can hear at dinner in this pretty and romantic room, it sure sounds like he succeeded. Favorite dishes include a hearty veal chop in a sage-butter sauce, and supernal risottos, with wild mushrooms or wild boar, depending on how wild you like it . ⑤ *Average main: €27* ⊠ *Rue du roi Oscar II, Gustavia* ☎ *590/51–00–05* ⊕ *www.lisolastbarth.com* ⚐ *Reservations essential* ⊘ *Closed Sep. and Oct.*

$$$$
FRENCH
✕ **Maya's.** New Englander Randy Gurley and his wife Maya (the French-born chef) provide a warm welcome and a very pleasant dinner on their cheerful dock decorated with big, round tables and crayon-colored canvas chairs, all overlooking Gustavia Harbor. A market-inspired menu of good, simply prepared and garnished dishes like stir-fry scallops and

shrimp, and pepper-marinated beef fillet changes daily, assuring the ongoing popularity of a restaurant that seems to be on everyone's list of favorites. $ *Average main: €39* ⊠ *Public, Gustavia* ☎ *0590/27–75–73* ⊕ *www.mayas-stbarth.com* ⌖ *Reservations essential.*

$$$$
ECLECTIC
Fodor'sChoice
★

✕ **Wall House.** The food is excellent—and the service is always friendly—at this restaurant on the far side of Gustavia Harbor. The light-as-air gnocci with pesto are legendary, and the rotisserie duck marinated in honey from the rotisserie is a universal favorite. Local businesspeople crowd the restaurant for the bargain €11 prix-fixe lunch menu, with classic dishes like duck-leg confit. For €18 the menu includes the main dish or salad of the day, coffee and petits fours, and a glass of wine or beer. An old-fashioned dessert trolley showcases some really yummy sweets—the sugar topping for your crème brûlée is blazed with a mini-torch tableside. $ *Average main: €33* ⊠ *La Pointe, Gustavia* ☎ *0590/27–71–83* ⊕ *www.wallhouserestaurant.com* ⌖ *Reservations essential* ☽ *No lunch Sun.*

POINTE MILOU

$$$$
ECLECTIC
Fodor'sChoice
★

✕ **Le Ti St. Barth Caribbean Tavern.** Chef-owner Carole Gruson captures the funky, sexy spirit of the island in her wildly popular hilltop hot spot. We always come here to dance to great music with the attractive crowd lingering at the bar, lounge at one of the pillow-strewn banquettes, or chat on the torch-lighted terrace. By the time your appetizers arrive, you'll be best friends with the next table. Top-quality fish and meats are cooked on the traditional charcoal barbecue; big spenders will love the Angus beef filet Rossini with truffles, but there are lighter options like wok shrimp with Chinese noodles, and seared tuna with caviar. Provocatively named desserts, such as Nymph Thighs (airy lemon cake with vanilla custard), Daddy's Balls (passion-fruit sorbet and ice cream), and Sweet Thai Massage (kiwi, pineapple, mango, and lychee salad) end the meal on a fun note. Around this time someone is sure to be dancing on top of the tables. There's an extensive wine list. The famously raucous full-moon parties, cabarets, and Monday "Plastic Boots" Ladies' Night are all legendary. $ *Average main: €47* ⊠ *Pointe Milou* ☎ *0590/27–97–71* ⊕ *www.letistbarth.com* ⌖ *Reservations essential.*

19

ST-JEAN

$$$
WINE BAR
Fodor'sChoice
★

✕ **Le Bistroy/Absolutely Wine.** A bit of Bordeaux came to St. Barth in 2012. Sit at a shaded communal table at this lively, modern gastro-pub/wine bar/wine school in St-Jean's Villa Creole shopping enclave any time of the day. Come for first-rate sharing platters of charcuterie, pâté, artisanal cheeses, choose-your-ingredient salads, and fabulous wines. An affable young female sommelier gives daily wine courses and hosts tastings in the wine cellar...delightful! The on-site market sells delicacies to take back to your villa or hotel. $ *Average main: €19* ⊠ *La Villa Créole, St-Jean* ☎ *590/52–20–96* ⊕ *www.absolutely-wine.com.*

CLOSE UP

St. Barth's Spas

Visitors to St. Barth can enjoy more than the comforts of home by taking advantage of any of the myriad spa and beauty treatments that are available on the island. The major hotels, the Isle de France, the Guanahani, and the Carl Gustav, have beautiful, comprehensive, on-site spas. Others, including the Hôtel le Village St-Jean, Le Sereno, and Le Toiny, have added spa cottages, where treatments and services can be arranged on-site.

Depending on availability, all visitors to the island can book services at all of these. In addition, scores of independent therapists will come to your hotel room or villa and provide any therapeutic discipline you can think of, including yoga, Thai massage, shiatsu, reflexology, and even manicures, pedicures, and hairdressing. You can get up-to-date recommendations at the tourist office in Gustavia.

WHERE TO STAY

There's no denying that hotel rooms and villas on St. Barth carry high prices. You're paying primarily for the privilege of staying on the island, and even at $800 a night the bedrooms tend to be small. Still, if you're flexible—in terms of timing and in your choice of lodgings—you can enjoy a holiday in St. Barth and still afford to send the kids to college.

The most expensive season falls during the holidays (mid-December to early January), when hotels are booked far in advance, may require a 10- or 14-day stay, and can be double the high-season rates. At this writing, some properties are reconsidering minimum stays, and there are concessions to the current *crise* (economic downturn). A 5% government tourism tax on room prices (excluding breakfast) is in effect; be sure to ask if it is included in your room rate or added on.

When it comes to booking a hotel on St. Barth, the reservation manager can be your best ally. Rooms within a property can vary greatly. It's well worth the price of a phone call or the time investment of an email correspondence to make a personal connection, which can mean a lot when it comes to arranging a room that meets your needs or preferences. Details of accessibility, views, recent redecorating, meal options, and special package rates are topics open for discussion. Most quoted hotel rates are per room, not per person, and include service charges and airport transfers. Bargain rates found on Internet booking sites can sometimes yield unpleasant surprises in terms of the actual room you get. Consider contacting the hotel about a reservation and mentioning the rate you found. Often they will match it, with a better room.

For expanded reviews, facilities, and current deals, visit Fodors.com.

VILLAS AND CONDOMINIUMS

On St. Barth the term *villa* is used to describe anything from a small cottage to a luxurious, modern estate. Today almost half of St. Barth's accommodations are in villas, and we recommend considering this option, especially if you're traveling with friends or family. Ever more advantageous to Americans, villa rates are usually quoted in dollars, thus bypassing unfavorable euro fluctuations. Most villas have a small private swimming pool and maid service daily except Sunday. They are well furnished with linens, kitchen utensils, and such electronic playthings as CD and DVD players, satellite TV, and broadband Internet. Weekly in-season rates range from $1,400 to "oh-my-gosh." Most villa-rental companies are based in the United States and have extensive websites that allow you to see pictures or panoramic videos of the place you're renting; their local offices oversee maintenance and housekeeping and provide concierge services to clients. Just be aware that there are few beachfront villas, so if you have your heart set on "toes in the sand" and a cute waiter delivering your Kir Royale, stick with the hotels or villas operated by hotel properties.

VILLA RENTAL CONTACTS

Marla. Marla is a local St. Barth villa-rental company that represents more than 100 villas, many of which are not listed with other companies. ☎ *0590/27–62–02* ⊕ *www.marlavillas.com.*

St. Barth Properties, Inc. St. Barth Properties, Inc., owned by American Peg Walsh—a regular on St. Barth since 1986—represents more than 120 properties here and can guide you to the perfect place to stay. Weekly peak-season rates range from $1,400 to $40,000, depending on the property's size, location, and amenities. The excellent website offers virtual tours of most of the villas and even details of availability. An office in Gustavia can take care of any problems you may have and offers some concierge-type services. ☎ *508/528–7727, 800/421–3396* ⊕ *www.stbarth.com.*

Wimco. Wimco, which is based in Rhode Island, oversees bookings for more than 230 properties on St. Barth. Rents range from $2,000 to $10,000 for two- and three-bedroom villas; larger villas rent for $7,000 per week and up. Properties can be previewed and reserved on Wimco's website (which occasionally lists last-minute specials), or you can obtain a catalog by mail. The company will arrange for babysitters, massages, chefs, and other in-villa services for clients, as well as private air charters. ☎ *800/932–3222* ⊕ *www.wimco.com.*

ANSE DE TOINY

$$$$
HOTEL
Fodor's Choice
★

Hôtel Le Toiny. Privacy and serenity are the mission here, but so is sustainability with features such as a water-treatment plant, organic cleaning products, and moves toward using solar energy. **Pros:** extremely private; luxurious rooms; flawless service; environmental awareness. **Cons:** not on the beach; isolated (at least half an hour's drive from town). **TripAdvisor:** "romantic paradise," "very private," "perfection." *$ Rooms from: €1,280* ⊠ *Anse de Toiny* ☎ *0590/27–88–88* ⊕ *www. letoiny.com* ⇆ *14 1-bedroom villas, 1 3-bedroom villa* ☉ *Closed Sept.– late Oct.* ⦿ *Breakfast.*

19

Hotel Guanahani and Spa, Grand Cul de Sac

COLOMBIER

$$
B&B/INN
Le P'tit Morne. Each of the modestly furnished but freshly decorated and painted mountainside studios has a private balcony with panoramic views of the coastline. **Pros:** reasonable rates; great area for hiking. **Cons:** rooms are basic; remote location. **TripAdvisor:** "truly relaxed," "beautiful," "an absolute delight." ⑤ *Rooms from: €195* ⊠ *Colombier* ☎ *0590/52–95–50* ⊕ *www.timorne.com/fr* ⤳ *14 rooms* ⑪ *Breakfast.*

FLAMANDS

$$$
HOTEL
☾
★
Hôtel Baie des Anges. Everyone is treated like family at this casual retreat with 10 clean, spacious rooms. **Pros:** on St. Barth's longest beach; family-friendly; excellent value. **Cons:** the area is a bit remote from the town areas, necessitating a car. **TripAdvisor:** "still a hidden gem," "perfect," "charming beach hotel." ⑤ *Rooms from: €385* ⊠ *Anse des Flamands* ☎ *0590/27–63–61* ⊕ *www.hotelbaiedesanges.fr* ⤳ *10 rooms* ☾ *Closed Sept.* ⑪ *No meals.*

$$$$
RESORT
Fodor's Choice
★
Hotel St-Barth Isle de France. An obsessively attentive management team ensures that this intimate, casual, refined resort remains among the very best accommodations in St. Barth—if not the entire Caribbean. **Pros:** prime beach location; terrific management; great spa; excellent restaurant. **Cons:** garden rooms—though large—can be dark; you will definitely want a car to get around; unfortunately, the day will come when you will have to leave this paradise. **TripAdvisor:** "stunning," "nice hotel in a remote location," "beautiful resort." ⑤ *Rooms from: €695* ⊠ *B.P. 612, Baie des Flamands* ☎ *0590/27–61–81* ⊕ *www.*

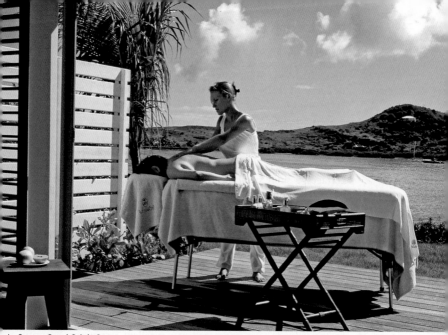

Le Sereno, Grand Cul de Sac

isle-de-france.com 🛏 *32 rooms, 2 villas* ⏱ *Closed Sept.–mid-Oct.*
🍽 *Breakfast.*

GRAND CUL DE SAC

$$$$
RESORT
☾
Fodor's Choice
★

🏨 **Hotel Guanahani and Spa.** The largest full-service resort on the island has lovely rooms and suites (14 of which have private pools) and impeccable personalized service, not to mention one of the island's only children's programs (though it's more of a nursery). **Pros:** fantastic spa; beach-side sports; family-friendly; great service. **Cons:** lots of walking all around the property, and a steep walk to beach. **TripAdvisor:** "relaxing stay," "beautiful grounds," "great staff." ⑤ *Rooms from: €646* ✉ *Grand Cul de Sac* ☎ *0590/27–66–60* ⊕ *www.leguanahani.com* 🛏 *35 suites, 32 rooms* ⏱ *Closed Sept.* 🍽 *Breakfast.*

$$
RENTAL
☾
★

🏨 **Hotel Les Ondines Sur La Plage.** Right on the beach of Grand Cul de Sac, this reasonably priced, intimate gem comprises modern, comfortable apartments with room to really spread out. **Pros:** spacious beachfront apartments; close to restaurants and water sports; pool; airport transfers. **Cons:** not a resort; beach is narrow in front of the property; will need a car to get around. **TripAdvisor:** "perfection," "lovely small hotel," "wonderful location." ⑤ *Rooms from: €350* ✉ *Grand Cul de Sac* ☎ *590/27–69–64* ⊕ *www.stbarth-lesondineshotel.com* 🛏 *6 rooms* 🍽 *Breakfast.*

$$$$
RESORT
Fodor's Choice
★

🏨 **Le Sereno.** Those seeking a restorative, sensous escape will discover true nirvana at the quietly elegant, aptly named Le Sereno. **Pros:** romantic rooms; beach location; superchic comfort; friendly atmosphere; handicap accessible. **Cons:** no a/c in bathrooms; some construction planned for this part of the island over the next few years. **TripAd-visor:** "very good service," "beautiful setting," "muted sophistica-tion." ⑤ *Rooms from: €690* ⊠ *B.P. 19 Grand-Cul-de-Sac, Grand Cul de Sac* ☎ *0590/29–83–00* ⊕ *www.lesereno.com* ⇥ *37 suites and villas* ⑩ *Breakfast.*

GRANDE SALINE

$ ⌂ **Salines Garden Cottages.** Budget-conscious beach lovers who don't
RENTAL   require a lot of coddling need look no further than these petite garden cottages, a short stroll from what is arguably St. Barth's best beach. **Pros:** only property walkable to Salines Beach; quiet; reasonable rates. **Cons:** far from town; not very private; strict cancellation policy. **TripAd-visor:** "comfortable," "a refined silence," "quaint and lovely." ⑤ *Rooms from: €140* ⊠ *Grand Saline* ☎ *0590/51–04–44* ⊕ *www.salinesgarden. com* ⇥ *5 cottages* ☉ *Closed mid-Aug.–mid-Oct.* ⑩ *Breakfast.*

GUSTAVIA

$$$$ ⌂ **Carl Gustaf.** This sophisticated hotel right in Gustavia is the last
HOTEL   word in luxury, and it's within walking distance of everything in town
Fodor's Choice   if you don't mind climbing the hill. **Pros:** luxurious decor; in-town
★   location; loads of in-room gadgets; excellent restaurant; beautiful spa. **Cons:** not on the beach; outdoor space limited to your private plunge pool. **TripAdvisor:** "perfect stay," "spectacular view and great service," "incredible experience." ⑤ *Rooms from: €995* ⊠ *Rue des Normands, Gustavia* ☎ *0590/29–79–00* ⊕ *www.hotelcarlgustaf.com* ⇥ *14 suites* ☉ *Closed May–Oct.* ⑩ *Breakfast.*

$ ⌂ **Sunset Hotel.** Ten simple, utilitarian rooms (one can accommodate
HOTEL   three people) right in Gustavia sit across from the harbor and offer an economical and handy, if not luxurious option for those who want to stay in town. **Pros:** reasonable rates; in town. **Cons:** no elevator; not resortlike in any way. **TripAdvisor:** "beautiful hotel," "wonderful sun-sets," "great location." ⑤ *Rooms from: €110* ⊠ *Rue de la Républic, Gustavia* ☎ *590/27–77–21* ⊕ *www.saint-barths.com/sunset-hotel/* ⇥ *10 rooms* ⑩ *No meals.*

LORIENT

$$$ ⌂ **Hotel La Banane.** Starting in 2012, the nine high-style rooms in this
B&B/INN   small complex are available to groups who reserve at least three units,
★   making it a great choice for a destination wedding. **Pros:** short walk to beach; friendly and social atmosphere at pool areas; great baths. **Cons:** just for weekly group rentals; rooms are small; location of entrance through parking lot is not attractive. **TripAdvisor:** "unforgettable," "a place of luxury," "peaceful tasteful place." ⑤ *Rooms from: €485* ⊠ *Baie de Lorient, Lorient* ☎ *0590/52–03–00* ⊕ *www.labanane.com* ⇥ *9 rooms* ☉ *Closed Sept.–Oct. 15* ⑩ *Breakfast.*

$ ⌂ **Le Normandie.** The immaculate rooms here are small but stylish,
B&B/INN   and there's nothing on the island at this price range compares. **Pros:**
★   friendly management; pleasant atmosphere; good value. **Cons:** tiny

Eden Rock, St-Jean

rooms, small bathrooms. **TripAdvisor:** "chic," "a short stay in heaven," "fantastic service." ⑤ *Rooms from: €155* ⊠ *Lorient* ☎ *0590/27–61–66* ⊕ *www.normandiehotelstbarts.com* ⇨ *8 rooms (7 double, 1 single)* ⑪ *Breakfast.*

$
RENTAL
☺

🏠 **Les Mouettes.** This guesthouse offers clean, simply furnished, and economical bungalows that open directly onto the beach. **Pros:** right on the beach; family-friendly. **Cons:** rooms are basic; right near the road; requirement of 30% prepayment 3 months in advance, which can only be cancelled one month in advance of reservation. No pool, no TV. **TripAdvisor:** "heaven to me," "fabulous budget accommodations," "great value and location." ⑤ *Rooms from: €150* ⊠ *Lorient Beach* ☎ *0590/27–77–91* ⊕ *lesmouetteshotel.com* ⇨ *7 bungalows* ▬ *No credit cards* ⑪ *No meals.*

POINTE MILOU

$$$
RESORT
☺
★

🏨 **Christopher.** This longtime St. Barth favorite of European families is hosted by an experienced management team that delivers a high standard of courteous professionalism and personalized service. **Pros:** comfortable elegance; family-friendly; reasonable price; updated rooms. **Cons:** resort is directly on the water but not on a beach, three-night minimum stay. **TripAdvisor:** "beauty all around," "excellent winter escape," "the staff make the hotel." ⑤ *Rooms from: €450* ⊠ *Pointe Milou* ☎ *590/27–63–63* ⊕ *www.hotelchristopher.com* ⇨ *42 rooms* ☽ *Closed Sept.–mid-Oct.* ⑪ *Breakfast.*

ST-JEAN

$$$$
RESORT
☾
Fodor's Choice
★

▦ **Eden Rock.** St. Barth's first hotel opened in the 1950s on the craggy bluff that splits Baie de St-Jean, and it's evolved into one of the island's top properties. **Pros:** chic clientele; beach setting; great restaurants; can walk to shopping and restaurants. **Cons:** some suites are noisy because of proximity to street. **TripAdvisor:** "unbelievable hotel," "amazing experience," "indulgent." ⑤ *Rooms from: €695* ⊠ *Baie de St-Jean, Baie de St-Jean* ☎ *0590/29–79–99, 877/563–7015 in U.S.* ⊕ *www. edenrockhotel.com* ⤳ *32 rooms, 2 villas* ☾ *Closed Aug. 29 to Oct. 17* ⑩ *Breakfast.*

$$$
HOTEL
☾
★

▦ **Emeraude Plage.** Right on the beach of Baie de St-Jean, this petite resort consists of small but immaculate bungalows and villas with modern, fully equipped outdoor kitchenettes on small patios; nice bathrooms add to the comfort. **Pros:** beachfront and in-town location; good value; cool kitchens on each porch. **Cons:** smallish rooms. **TripAdvisor:** "beautiful beach," "total vacation," "simply perfect." ⑤ *Rooms from: €385* ⊠ *Baie de St-Jean, St-Jean* ☎ *0590/27–64–78* ⊕ *www.emeraudeplage. com* ⤳ *28 bungalows* ☾ *Closed Sept.–mid-Oct.* ⑩ *No meals.*

$
HOTEL
☾
Fodor's Choice
★

▦ **Hôtel le Village St-Jean.** You get the advantages of a villa and the services of a hotel at Hôtel Le Village, where for two generations the Charneau family has offered friendly service and reasonable rates, making guests feel like a part of the family. **Pros:** great value; convenient location; wonderful management, friendly clientele. **Cons:** A walk up a steep hill to the hotel; can be noisy, depending on how close your room is to the street below. **TripAdvisor:** "humble elegance," "perfect island flair," "a bit of paradise." ⑤ *Rooms from: €225* ⊠ *Baie de St-Jean, St-Jean* ☎ *0590/27–61–39, 800/651–8366* ⊕ *www.villagestjeanhotel.com* ⤳ *5 rooms, 20 cottages, 1 3-bedroom villa, 2 2-bedroom villas* ⑩ *Breakfast.*

$$$
RENTAL
☾

▦ **Les Îlets de la Plage.** On the far side of the airport, tucked away at the far corner of Baie de St-Jean, these well-priced, comfortably furnished island-style one-, two-, and three-bedroom bungalows (four right on the beach, seven up a small hill) have small kitchens, pleasant open-air sitting areas, and comfortable bathrooms. **Pros:** beach location; apartment conveniences; front porches. **Cons:** no TV (unless requested), a/c only in bedrooms; right next to the airport, extra charge for Internet. **TripAdvisor:** "lovely location," "peace and relaxation," "secluded and comfortable." ⑤ *Rooms from: €450* ⊠ *Plage de St-Jean, St-Jean* ☎ *0590/27–88–57* ⊕ *www.lesilets.com* ⤳ *11 bungalows* ☾ *Closed Sept.–Nov. 1* ⑩ *No meals.*

$$$
HOTEL

▦ **Le Tom Beach Hôtel.** This chic but casual boutique hotel right on busy St-Jean beach is fun for social types, and the nonstop house party often spills out onto the terraces and lasts into the wee hours. **Pros:** party central at beach, restaurant, and pool; in-town location. **Cons:** trendy social scene is not for everybody, especially light sleepers. **TripAdvisor:** "relaxing time," "the perfect hotel," "great venue." ⑤ *Rooms from: €450* ⊠ *Plage de St-Jean, St-Jean* ☎ *0590/27–53–13* ⊕ *www.tombeach. com* ⤳ *12 rooms* ⑩ *Breakfast.*

NIGHTLIFE

Most of the nightlife in St. Barth is centered in Gustavia, though there are a few places to go outside of town. "In" clubs change from season to season, so you might ask around for the hot spot of the moment, but none really get going until about midnight. Theme parties are the current trend. Check the daily *St. Barth News* or *Le Journal de Saint-Barth* for details. A late (10 pm or later) reservation at one of the club-restaurants will eventually become a front-row seat at a party. *Saint-Barth Leisures* contains current information about sports, spas, nightlife, and the arts.

GUSTAVIA

Bar de l'Oubli. This is where young locals gather for drinks. Bring cash, they don't accept plastic. ⌧ *Rue du Roi Oscar II, Gustavia* ☎ *0590/27–70–06.*

Victoria's Restaurant at the Carl Gustaf. This hotel lures a more sedate crowd, namely those in search of quiet conversation and views of the sunset. The pretty room has tasty bar snacks, and the bartender whips up the best Planter's Punch on the island, digging into the hotel's stash of "Old Rums" from all over the Caribbean. ⌧ *Hotel Carl Gustaf, Rue des Normands, Gustavia* ☎ *0590/27–82–83.*

Le Repaire. This restaurant lures a crowd for cocktail hour and its pool table. ⌧ *Rue de la République, Gustavia* ☎ *0590/27–72–48.*

★ **Le Sélect.** This is St. Barth's original hangout, commemorated by Jimmy Buffett's song, "Cheeseburger in Paradise." The boisterous garden is where the barefoot boating set gathers for a cold Carib beer, at prices somewhat lower than the usual. ⌧ *Rue du Centenaire, Gustavia* ☎ *0590/27–86–87.*

Le Yacht Club. Although ads call it a private club, dress right and you can probably get in to this hot spot anyway. Nothing much happens till midnight, when the terrific DJs get things going. Check the local papers for details of special parties. ⌧ *Rue Jeanne d'Arc, Gustavia* ☎ *0690/49–23–33* ⊕ *www.caroleplaces.com.*

Supper Club The Strand. This suavely white-draped "boite" above Gustavia's Casa Nikki offers tapas and cocktails starting at 7. Dinner is served until about 11 when it turns into a Champagne Lounge with a fun party. Star DJs spin, and, at this writing, on Thursdays wine and champagne is buy one, get one free. ⌧ *Gustavia Harbor, Gustavia* ☎ *0590/27–63–77* ⊕ *www.the-strand.fr.*

19

ST-JEAN

★ **Le Nikki Beach.** This place rocks on weekends during lunch, when the scantily clad young and beautiful lounge on the white canvas banquettes. At night there are beach BBQs, theme parties, fashion shows, and other creative events. The hip and the gorgeous flock here Sunday afternoons for a great beach party. ⊠ *St-Jean* ☏ *0590/27–64–64* ⊕ *www.nikkibeach.com.*

SHOPPING

Fodor'sChoice ★ St. Barth is a duty-free port, and with its sophisticated crowd of visitors, shopping in the island's 200-plus boutiques is a definite delight, especially for beachwear, accessories, jewelry, and casual wear. It would be no overstatement to say that shopping for fashionable clothing, jewels, and designer accessories is better in St. Barth than anywhere else in the Caribbean. New shops open all the time, so there's always something new to discover. Stores close for lunch from noon to 3, and many on Wednesday afternoon as well, but they are open until 7 in the evening. A popular afternoon pastime is strolling about the two major shopping areas in Gustavia and St-Jean.

In Gustavia, boutiques line the three major shopping streets. Quai de la République, which is right on the harbor, rivals New York's Madison Avenue or Paris's avenue Montaigne for high-end designer retail, including shops for **Louis Vuitton, Bulgari, Cartier, Chopard,** and **Hermès.** These shops often carry items that are not available in the United States. The elegant Carré d'Or plaza is great fun to explore. Shops are also clustered in **La Savane Commercial Center** (across from the airport), **La Villa Créole** (in St-Jean), and **Espace Neptune** (on the road to Lorient). It's worth working your way from one end to the other at these shopping complexes—just to see or, perhaps, be seen. Boutiques in all three areas carry the latest in French and Italian sportswear and some haute couture. Bargains may be tough to come by, but you might be able to snag that *Birkin* that has a long waiting-list stateside, and in any case, you'll have a lot of fun hunting around.

Shopping for up-to-the-minute fashions is as much a part of a visit to St. Barth as going to the beach. Shops change all the time, both in ownership and in the lines that are carried. Current listings are just a general guide. The best advice is simply to go for a long stroll in the late afternoon and check out all the shops on the way.

If you are looking for locally made art and handicrafts, call the tourist office, which can provide information, and arrange visits to the studios of some of the island artists, including Christian Bretoneiche, Robert Danet, Nathalie Daniel, Patricia Guyot, Rose Lemen, Aline de Lurin, and Marion Vinot. A few good gallery/craft boutiques are also scattered around Gustavia, and the larger hotels.

GUSTAVIA

CLOTHING

Black Swan. Black Swan has an unparalleled selection of bathing suits for men, women, and children. The wide range of styles and sizes is appreciated. They also have souvenir-appropriate island logo-wear and whatever beach equipment you might require. ✉ *Le Carré d'Or, Gustavia* ☎ *590/52–48–30.*

Boutique Lacoste. This store has a huge selection of the once-again-chic alligator-logo wear, as well as a shop next door with a complete selection of the Petit Bateau line of T-shirts popular with teens. ✉ *Rue du Bord de Mer, Gustavia* ☎ *0590/27–66–90.*

Café Coton. Café Coton is a great shop for men, especially for long-sleeve linen shirts in a rainbow of colors and Egyptian cotton dress shirts. ✉ *Rue du Bord du Mer, Gustavia* ☎ *0590/52–48–42.*

Calypso. Calypso carries sophisticated, sexy resort wear and accessories by Balenciaga, Chloe, and D Squared, among others. ✉ *Le Carré d'Or, Gustavia* ☎ *0590/27–69–74* ⊕ *www.saint-barths.com/calypso/.*

Filles Des Iles. Shop here for high-quality, flattering attire by designers like Shamane, Scooter, Dyrberg Kern, and sophisticated swimwear by Princess Tam Tam, which even women "of a certain" age can wear. The shop also stocks delicious artisanal fragrances and chic accessories. ✉ *8, Villa Creole, St-Jean* ☎ *590/29–04–08.*

Hermès. The Hermès store in St. Barth is an independently owned franchise, and prices are slightly below those in the States. ✉ *Rue de la République, Gustavia* ☎ *0590/27–66–15.*

Kokon. Kokon offers a nicely edited mix of designs for on-island or off, including the bo'em, Lotty B. Mustique, and Day Birger lines, and cute shoes to go with them by Heidi Klum for Birkenstock. ✉ *Rue Fahlberg, Gustavia* ☎ *0590/29–74–48.*

Linde Gallery. Linde sells vintage sunglasses, accessories, vintage ready-to-wear from the 1970s and '80s, as well as books, CDs, and DVDs. ✉ *Les Hauts de Carré d'Or, Gustavia* ☎ *590/29–73–86* ⊕ *www. lindegallery.com.*

Linen. Linen has tailored linen shirts for men in a rainbow of soft colors, and their soft slip-on driving mocs in classic styles are a St. Barth must. ✉ *Rue du Général de Gaulle, Gustavia* ☎ *0590/27–54–26.*

Lolita Jaca. Don't miss this store for trendy, tailored sportswear. ✉ *Le Carré d'Or, Gustavia* ☎ *0590/27–59–98* ⊕ *www.lolitajaca.com.*

Longchamp. Fans of the popular travel bags, handbags, and leather goods will find a good selection at about 20% off stateside prices. ✉ *Rue Général de Gaulle, Gustavia* ☎ *0590/51–96–50.*

Pati de Saint Barth. This is the largest of the three shops that stock the chic, locally made T-shirts, totes, and beach wraps that have practically become the logo of St. Barth. The newest styles have hand-done graffiti-style lettering. The shop also has some handicrafts and other giftable items. ✉ *Rue Du Bord de Mer, Gustavia* ☎ *0590/29–78–04* ⊕ *www. madeinstbarth.com.*

19

Shops on rue de la France, Gustavia

Poupette St. Barth. All the brilliant color-crinkle silk and chiffon batik and embroidered peasant skirts and tops are designed by the owner. There also are great belts and beaded bracelets. ✉ *Rue de la République, Gustavia* ☎ *0590/27–55–78* ⊕ *www.poupettestbarth.com.*

Saint-Barth Stock Exchange. On the far side of Gustavia Harbor is the island's consignment and discount shop. ✉ *La Pointe-Gustavia, Gustavia* ☎ *0590/27–68–12.*

Stéphane & Bernard. This store stocks a well-edited, large selection of superstar French fashion designers, including Rykiel, Missoni, Valentino, Versaci, Ungaro, Christian Lacroix, and Eres beachwear. ✉ *Rue de la République, Gustavia* ☎ *0590/27–65–69* ⊕ *www.stephaneandbernard.com.*

Vanita Rosa. This store showcases beautiful lace and linen sundresses and peasant tops, with accessories galore. ✉ *Rue du Roi Oscar II, Gustavia* ☎ *0590/52–43–25* ⊕ *www.vanitarosa.com.*

Victoire. Classic, well-made sportswear in luxurious fabrics and great colors, with a French twist on preppy, will please shoppers eager for finds that will play as well in Nantucket or Greenwich as they do on St. Barth. ✉ *Rue du général de Gaulle, Gustavia* ☎ *590/29–84–60* ⊕ *www.victoire-paris.com.*

FOODSTUFFS

A.M.C. This supermarket is a bit older than Marché U in St-Jean but able to supply nearly anything you might need for housekeeping in a villa or for a picnic. ✉ *Quai de la République, Gustavia.*

HANDICRAFTS

Fabienne Miot. Look for unusual and artistic jewelry, featuring rare stones and natural pearls at this shop. ☒ *Rue de la République, Gustavia* ☎ *0590/27–73–13.*

Kalinas Perles. Beautiful freshwater pearls are knotted onto the classic St. Barth–style leather thongs by artist Jeremy Albaledejo, who also has a great eye for other artisans' works showcased in a gallery-like setting. ☒ *Rue du Bord de Mer, Gustavia* ☎ *690/65–93–00.*

Le P'tit Collectionneur. Encouraged by his family and friends, André Berry opened his private musuem, "le P'tit Collectionneur," in early 2007 to showcase his lifelong passion for collecting fascinating objects such as 18th-century English pipes and the first phonograph to come to the island. He will happily show you his treasures. ☒ *La Pointe, Gustavia* ☎ *€2* ☉ *Mon.–Sat., 10–noon and 4–6 pm.*

JEWELRY

Bijoux de la Mer. This store carries beautiful and artistic jewelry made of South Sea pearls in wonderful hues strung in clusters on leather to wrap around the neck or arms. ☒ *Rue de la Républic, Gustavia* ☎ *590/52–37–68* ⊕ *www.bijouxdelamerstbarth.com.*

Carat. Carat has Chaumet and a large selection of Breitling watches, plus rarities by Richard Mille, Breguet. ☒ *Quai de la République, Gustavia* ☎ *590/27–67–22 No phone* ⊕ *www.caratsaintbarth.com/.*

Donna del Sol. Next door to Cartier, designer Donna del Sol carries beautiful handmade gold chains, Tahitian pearl pieces, and baubles in multicolor diamonds of her own designs. Have something special in mind? She'll work with clients to design and produce custom items. ☒ *Quai de la République, Gustavia* ⊕ *www.donnadelsol.com.*

Sindbad. This tiny shop, an island favorite since 1977, curates funky, unique couture fashion jewelry by Gaz Bijou of St-Tropez, crystal collars for your pampered pooch, and other reasonably priced, up-to-the-minute styles. Current favorites are the South Sea pearls strung on leather thongs or colorful silky cords. ☒ *Carré d'Or, Gustavia* ☎ *0590/27–52–29* ⊕ *www.sindbad-st-barth.com.*

LIQUOR AND TOBACCO

M'Bolo. Be sure to sample the varieties of infused rums, including lemongrass, ginger, and the island favorite, vanilla. Bring home some in the beautiful hand-blown bottles. Chefs will like the selection of Laguiole knives, and the local spices too. ☒ *Rue Général-de-Gaulle, Gustavia* ☎ *0590/27–90–54.*

LORIENT

COSMETICS

Ligne de St. Barth. Don't miss the superb skin-care products made on-site from local tropical plants by this St. Barth company. ☒ *Rte. de Saline, Lorient* ☎ *0590/27–82–63* ⊕ *www.lignestbarth.com.*

19

FOODSTUFFS

JoJo Supermarché. JoJo is the well-stocked counterpart to Gustavia's large supermarket and gets daily deliveries of bread and fresh produce. JoJoBurger, next door, is the local surfers' favorite spot for a (very good) quick burger. ⊠ *Lorient.*

ST-JEAN

CLOTHING

Black Swan. Black Swan has an unparalleled selection of bathing suits. The wide range of styles and sizes is appreciated. ⊠ *La Villa Créole, St-Jean* ⊕ *www.blackswanstbarth.com.*

Iléna. This boutique has incredible beachwear and lingerie by Chantal Thomas, Sarda, and others, including Swarovski crystal–encrusted bikinis for the young and gorgeous. ⊠ *Villa Creole, St-Jean* ☎ *0590/29–84–05.*

Lili Belle. Check out Lili Belle for a nice selection of wearable and current styles. ⊠ *Pelican Plage, St-Jean* ☎ *0590/87–46–14.*

Morgan. Morgan has a line of popular casual wear in the trendy vein. ⊠ *La Villa Créole, St-Jean* ☎ *0590/27–71–00.*

St. Tropez KIWI. Look to this popular boutique with two branches (one in Gustavia and one in St-Jean) for resort wear. ⊠ *3 Villas Créole, St-Jean* ☎ *0590/27–57–08.*

SUD SUD.ETC.Plage. This store stocks everything for the beach: inflatables, mats, bags, and beachy shell jewelry, as well as bikinis and gauzy cover-ups. ⊠ *Galerie du Commerce, St-Jean* ☎ *0590/27–90–56.*

FOODSTUFFS

Marche U. This fully stocked supermarket across from the airport has a wide selection of French cheeses, pâtés, cured meats, produce, fresh bread, wine, and liquor. There is also a good selection of prepared foods and organic grocery items. ⊠ *St-Jean* ☎ *0590/27–68–16.*

Maya's to Go. This is the place to go for prepared picnics, meals, salads, rotisserie chickens, and more from the kitchens of the popular restaurant in Gustavia. ⊠ *Galleries du Commerce, St-Jean* ☎ *0590/29–83–70* ⊕ *www.mayastogo.com* ⊙ *Closed Mon.*

SPORTS AND ACTIVITIES

BOATING AND SAILING

St. Barth is a popular yachting and sailing center, thanks to its location midway between Antigua and St. Thomas. Gustavia's harbor, 13 to 16 feet deep, has mooring and docking facilities for 40 yachts. There are also good anchorages available at Public, Corosol, and Colombier. You can charter sailing and motorboats in Gustavia Harbor for as little as a half day. Stop at the tourist office in Gustavia, or ask at your hotel for an up-to-the minute list of recommended charter companies.

Jicky Marine Service. Jicky Marine Service offers full-day outings, either on a variety of motorboats, or 42- or 46-foot catamaran, to the uninhabited Île Fourchue for swimming, snorkeling, cocktails, and lunch. The cost starts at about $100 per person; an unskippered motor rental runs about $260 a day. ☒ *Ferry dock, Gustavia* ☎ *0590/27–70–34* ⊕ *www.jickymarine.com.*

🐚 **Yellow Submarine.** Yellow Submarine takes you "six feet under" (the surface of the sea) for a close-up view of St. Barth's coral reefs through large glass portholes. It costs €40 for adults, €25 for children under 12. Trips depart daily, from the Ferry Dock in Gustavia with departures at 11 am and 2 pm, with Night Excursions Wednesday and Friday at 5:45 pm but more often depending on demand, so call first. ☒ *Ferry Dock, Gustavia* ☎ *0590/52–40–51* ⊕ *www.yellow-submarine.fr.*

DIVING AND SNORKELING

Several dive shops arrange scuba excursions to local sites. Depending on weather conditions, you may dive at **Pain de Sucre, Coco Island,** or toward nearby **Saba.** There's also an underwater shipwreck to explore, plus sharks, rays, sea tortoises, coral, and the usual varieties of colorful fish. The waters on the island's leeward side are the calmest. For the uncertified who still want to see what the island's waters hold, there's an accessible shallow reef right off the beach at Anse de Cayes that you can explore if you have your own mask and fins, and a hike down the hill to the beach at Corossol brings you to a very popular snorkeling spot for locals.

Réserve Marine de St-Barth. Most of the waters surrounding St. Barth are protected in the island's Réserve Marine de St-Barth, which also provides information at its office in Gustavia. The diving here isn't nearly as rich as in the more dive-centered destinations like Saba and St. Eustatius, but the options aren't bad either, and none of the smaller islands offer the ambience of St. Barth. ☒ *Gustavia* ☎ *0590/27–88–18.*

🐚 **Plongée Caraïbe.** Plongée Caraïbe is recommended for its up-to-the-minute equipment and dive boat. They also run two-hour group snorkeling trips on the *Blue Cat Catamaran*; a half-day is €40. ☎ *0590/27–55–94* ⊕ *www.plongee-caraibes.com.*

Splash. In Gustavia, Splash offers PADI and CMAS (Confederation Mondiale des Activites Subaquatiques—World Underwater Federation) courses in diver training at all levels. All the instructors speak French and English. Although their boat normally leaves daily at 9 am, 11:30 am, 2 pm, and in the evening for a night dive, they will adjust their times to suit your preferences. ☒ *Gustavia* ☎ *590/54–75–98* ⊕ *www. divestbarth.com.*

West Indies Dive. Marine Service operates the only five-star, PADI-certified diving center on the island, called West Indies Dive. Scuba trips, packages, resort dives, night dives, and certifications start at $90, including gear. ☎ *0590/27–70–34.*

19

FISHING

Most fishing is done in the waters north of Lorient, Flamands, and Corossol. Popular catches are tuna, marlin, wahoo, and barracuda. There's an annual St. Barth Open Fishing Tournament, organized by Océan Must, in mid-July.

Jicky Marine Service. Jicky Marine Service arranges ocean-fishing excursions. ⊠ *Gustavia* ☎ *0590/27–70–34* ⊕ *www.jickymarine.com*.

Océan Must Marina. Océan Must Marina arranges deep-sea fishing expeditions as well as bare boat and staffed boat charters. ⊠ *La Pointe, Gustavia* ☎ *0590/27–62–25* ⊕ *www.oceanmust.com*.

GUIDED TOURS

You can arrange island tours by minibus or car at hotel desks or through any of the island's taxi operators in Gustavia or at the airport. The tourist office runs a variety of tours with varying itineraries that run about €46 for a half day for up to eight people. You can also download up-to-the-minute walking and driving tour itineraries from the Tourist Board's website.

Mat Nautic. Mat Nautic can help you arrange to tour the island by water on a Jet Ski or WaveRunner. ⊠ *Quai du Yacht Club, rue Jeanne d'Arc, Gustavia* ☎ *0690/49–54–72*.

St-Barth Tours & Travel. St-Barth Tours & Travel will customize a tour of the island. They can also book ferry trips. ⊠ *Rue Saint Thomas, Gustavia* ☎ *0590/52–41–38*.

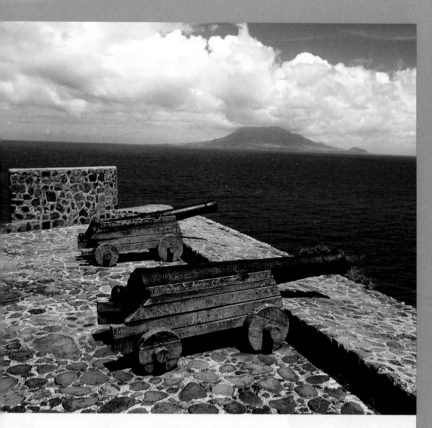

St. Eustatius

WORD OF MOUTH

"Ever considered Saint Eustatius? A real Caribbean island. No high-rise buildings. You [can] get there from St. Martin with an 18-minute flight. A real gem!"

—pechtold

WELCOME TO ST. EUSTATIUS

FRIENDLY TRANQUILITY

A tiny part of the Dutch Caribbean, St. Eustatius (often just called "Statia") is just under 12 square miles (30 square km), which is still twice as large as Saba. The island, which is 38 miles (63 km) south of St. Maarten, has a population of less than 4,000. And although there are three beaches, they are better for strolling than swimming.

Boven Ba

Cocoluch Bay

Jenkins Bay

Boven

Little Mountain

Tumble Down Dick Bay

Signal Hill

Interlopers Pt. ◆ Ft. Royal

Stenara Reef

Smoke Alley Beach (Oranje Beach)

Hotels ▼
Country Inn 1
Statia Lodge 2

Gallows

Crooks Castle

Double Wreck

Barracuda Reef

KEY
↘ Beaches
�ₙ Dive Sites
↑ Rain Forest
① Hotels

Like Saba, tiny Statia is a quiet Caribbean haven for scuba divers and hikers. When the island was called the Emporium of the Western World, warehouses stretched for miles along the quays, and 200 merchant ships could anchor at its docks. These days it's the day-trippers from St. Maarten who walk the quays.

Fontaan Bay

Venus Bay

lboa Hill

Zeelandia

ATLANTIC OCEAN

Zeelandia Beach

Zeelandia Bay

Concordia Bay

1

Great Bay

Franklin Delano Roosevelt Airport

Compagnie Bay

Lynch Bay
Lynch Bay Beach

Fair Play

♦ **Lynch Plantation Museum**

New Ground

English Quarter

Corre Corre Bay

♦ **Behind the Mountain**

Upper Town

Oranjestad
see detail map

Crater

♦ **The Quill**

Lower Town

♦ **Miriam C. Schmidt Botanical Garden**

2

Kay Bay

♦ **Ft. de Windt**

Bucaneers Bay

Back-off Bay

Caribbean Sea

0   1 mile

0   1 km

ST. EUSTATIUS

20

TOP REASONS TO VISIT ST. EUSTATIUS

1 Diving: Visiting the many varied wrecks in Statia's protected waters is a highlight.

2 Hiking: Hiking the Quill, an extinct volcano that holds a primeval rain forest, is the top activity for landlubbers.

3 Welcoming: The genuine friendliness of the people here is overwhelming.

4 History: For anyone interested in 18th-century history, even a day trip from St. Maarten is a satisfying experience.

Updated
by Roberta
Sotonoff

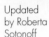

The stars are ablaze, but it's dark on the road between the Blue Bead Bar & Restaurant and the Old Gin House hotel. A chicken running across the road constitutes all the traffic, and except for the sound of crickets, there is silence. The island of St. Eustatius, commonly called Statia (pronounced *stay*-sha), is safe. How safe? The scuttlebutt is that a St. Maarten police officer sent to serve on the island thinks he is being punished because there is nothing for him to do.

With a population of about 3,813, it's difficult for someone to commit a crime—or do most anything else—without everyone finding out. Everyone knows everyone, and that's also a blessing. Statians are friendly; they beep their horns and say hello to anyone they see. Even daytrippers are warmly welcomed as friends. There are no strangers here.

Think of this tiny Dutch Caribbean island for quiet times, strolls through history, and awesome diving and hiking. While many of its neighbors are pursuing the tourist business big-time, Statia just plods along. That's its charm.

During the late 18th century, the island in the Dutch Windward Triangle was a hub for commerce between Europe and the Americas. When ships carrying slaves, sugar, cotton, ammunition, and other commodities crowded its harbor, it was known as the Emporium of the Western World and the Golden Rock.

With an 11-gun salute to the American Stars and Stripes on the brig-of-war the *Andrew Doria* on November 16, 1776, Statia's golden age ended. Statia's noteworthy role as the first country to recognize U.S. independence from Great Britain was not a gesture appreciated by the British. In 1781, British Admiral George Rodney looted and economically destroyed the island. It has never really recovered.

Indeed, chaos ensued between 1781 and 1816 as the Dutch, English, and French vied for control of the island. It changed hands 22 times. The Netherlands finally won out, and Statia has been a Dutch possession since 1816.

Remnants of those bygone days are evident around the island. Hanging off the cliff at the only village, Oranjestad, is the nearly 370-year-old Ft. Oranje, the site from where the famous shots were fired. The original Dutch Reformed Church, built in 1755, sits in its courtyard. Oranjestad itself, on a ridge above the sea, is lush with greenery and bursting with bougainvillea, oleander, and hibiscus. The rest of the island is rather pristine. The eastern side, bordered by the rough waters of the Atlantic, has an untamed quality to it, and extinct volcanoes and dry plains anchor the north end. Statia's crown is the Quill, a 1,968-foot extinct volcano, its verdant crater covered with a primeval rain forest. Hiking to the peak is a popular pastime.

> ## LOGISTICS
>
> **Getting to St. Eustatius:** There are no nonstop flights here from the United States, and the only way to get here is a Winair flight from St. Maarten.
>
> **Hassle Factor:** Medium to High.
>
> **On the Ground:** This is a small place. You can rent a car or scooter for trips out of town, or you can take a taxi.

Beaches on the island come and go as the waters see fit, but first-class dive sites lure most visitors to the island. Wrecks and old cannons are plentiful at archaeological dive sites, and modern ships, such as the cable-laying *Charles L. Brown*, have been sunk into underwater craters. Stingrays, eels, turtles, and barracudas live in the undersea Caribbean neighborhood where giant pillar coral, giant yellow sea fans, and reef fingers abound. The sea has reclaimed the walls of Dutch warehouses that have sunk into the Caribbean over the past several hundred years, but these underwater ruins serve as a day-care center for abundant schools of juvenile fish.

On land, beachcombers hunt for blue beads. The 17th-century baubles, found only on Statia, were used to barter for rum, slaves, tobacco, and cotton. The chance of finding one is slim, though you can see them at the island's museum. Pre-Columbian artifacts, dating back to 500 BC, are also on display there.

Statia is mostly a short-flight day-trip destination from nearby St. Maarten. That might be just enough for some visitors. But those who linger can appreciate the unspoiled island, its history, and its peacefulness. Most of all, it's the locals who make a visit to the island special.

20

PLANNING

GETTING HERE AND AROUND
AIR TRAVEL
Flights to Statia from St. Maarten are timed to coincide with the arrival of international flights. There is no regularly scheduled ferry service. Reconfirm your flight, because schedules can change abruptly. The departure fee from the island is $5.65. If flying out of St. Maarten,

check to see if the international departure fee has already been added into your airline ticket.

Airline Contact Winair. The only way to get to Statia (EUX) is on one of the regularly scheduled Winair flights from Saba or St. Maarten; you'll have to book this flight yourself, directly with Winair, either by phone or online. Winair has six daily flights from St. Maarten to St. Eustatius. The flights range from roughly $110 to $175. ☎ 599/318-3291, 800/634-4907 ⊕ www.fly-winair.com.

Airlport Contact Franklin Delano Roosevelt Airport. The flight from St. Maarten to Statia's Franklin Delano Roosevelt Airport takes 16 minutes. ☎ 599/318-2887.

CAR TRAVEL

Driving in Statia is not difficult, mostly because there are not that many places to go. Street signs are not plentiful, but anyone you ask for directions will be more than happy to help you. The roads are generally in good condition. Daily rates for a car rental begin at $35.

Car Rental Contacts ARC Car Rental ✉ Oranjestad ☎ 599/318-2595. **Brown's** ✉ White Wall Rd. 8, Oranjestad ☎ 599/318-2266. **Rainbow Car Rental** ✉ Statia Mall, Oranjestad ☎ 599/318-2811. **Walter's** ✉ Chapel Piece, Oranjestad ☎ 599/318-2719.

SCOOTER TRAVEL

Zipping around by scooter is another option. Scooter rentals start at $20 per day, including insurance.

Contacts L.P.N. Scooter Rentals ☎ 599/318-1476.

TAXI TRAVEL

You could literally walk from the airport runway into town; one or two taxis are usually waiting for arriving passengers at the airport, and you'll be whisked into Oranjestad for about $8.

ESSENTIALS

Banks and Currency Exchange As of January 1, 2011, the U.S. dollar is the legal tender, replacing the Dutch Caribbean guilder (NAf or ANG).

FirstCaribbean International Bank. This branch in Upper Town provides exchange services. ☎ 599/318-2392 ⊕ www.cibcfcib.com ⊗ Weekdays 8:30–3:30.

Windward Islands Bank. The bank has an ATM at the airport and Mazinga Square, as well as exchange services in town. ☎ 599/318-2846, 599/318-2847 ⊕ www.wib-bank.net ⊗ Weekdays 8–3:30.

Emergencies Ambulance ☎ 912, 599/318-2211. **Fire** ☎ 913, 599/318-2360. **Police** ☎ 911, 599/318-2333. **St. Eustatius School of Medicine (Scuba Emergencies)** ✉ Fort Bay ☎ 599/318-2600.

Mail The post office is on Ruby Hassell Road, Upper Town. Airmail letters to North America and Europe are $1.59, postcards 92¢. When sending letters to the island, be sure to include "Dutch Caribbean" in the address.

Passport Requirements All visitors must present a valid passport and a return or ongoing ticket for entry to Statia.

Phones To call Statia from North America, dial 011 + 599 + 318, followed by the four-digit number. To call the United States using an AT&T card, the access number is 001–800–872–2881. To call within the island, dial only the five-digit number that starts with an 8.

Taxes and Service Charges The departure tax—$10 for flights to Dutch Caribbean islands and foreign destinations—is payable in cash only. Note: when flying home through St. Maarten, list yourself as "in transit" to avoid paying the tax levied in St. Maarten if you will be there for less than 24 hours. Hotels collect a 7% government tax and 3% turnover tax. Restaurants charge a 3% government tax and a 10% service charge.

Tipping Taxi drivers, 10%; housekeeping, a dollar or two per day; waitstaff, an extra 5%–10%.

Visitor Information Tourist Office. There is also a tourist information booth at the airport, open daily. ⊠ *Fort Oranjestraat, Oranjestad* ☎ *599/318-2433, 599/318-2433 Airport Tourism Booth* ⊕ *www.statiatourism.com* ☼ *Mon.–Thurs. 8–noon and 1–5, Fri. 8–noon and 1–4:30.*

ACCOMMODATIONS

Statia has only five hotels with 20 rooms or fewer—and except for Statia Lodge all are within Oranjestad. There are also a handful of bed-and-breakfasts. Nothing on the island could be described as luxurious.

HOTEL AND RESTAURANT PRICES

Prices in the restaurant reviews are the average cost of a main course at dinner or, if dinner is not served, at lunch; taxes and service charges are generally included. Prices in the hotel reviews are the lowest cost of a standard double room in high season, excluding taxes, service charges, and meal plans (except at all-inclusives). Prices for rentals are the lowest per-night cost for a one-bedroom unit in high season.

WEDDINGS

Foreign couples must be at least 21 and Dutch nationals at least 18. Documents should be received 14 days before the wedding date. The application requires notarized original documents, including birth certificates, passports (for non-Dutch people), divorce decrees, and death certificates of deceased spouses. The ceremony can be performed in English, Dutch, Spanish, or Papiamento. For more information, visit ⊕ *www.statiatourism.com.*

20

EXPLORING ST. EUSTATIUS

Statia is an arid island with a valley between two mountain peaks. Most sights lie in the valley, making touring the island easy. From the airport you can rent a car or take a taxi and be in Oranjestad in minutes; to hike the Quill, Statia's highest peak, you can drive to the trailhead in less than 15 minutes from just about anywhere. Other trails with their breathtaking views include Boven, 450 feet elevation, Gilboa, 400 feet, and Venus Bay.

Lynch Plantation Museum. Also known as the Berkel Family Plantation, or the Berkel's Domestic Museum, these two one-room buildings show

St. Eustatius Historical Foundation Museum

what life was like almost 100 years ago. A remarkable collection preserves this family's history—pictures, eyeglasses, original furnishings, and farming and fishing implements—and gives a detailed perspective of life on Statia. Call ahead to arrange a private tour. Since it's on the northeast side of the island, you need either a taxi or a car to get there. ⊠ *Lynch Bay* ☎ *599/318–2338* ✉ *Free* ☉ *By appointment only.*

Ⓒ **Miriam C. Schmidt Botanical Garden.** Relaxation and quiet abound on these 52 acres, where there's a greenhouse, a palm garden, a kitchen garden, and an observation bird trail. Its location, on the Atlantic side of the Quill on a plot called Upper Company, reveals a superb view of St. Kitts. For a picnic, there's no better place, but the only way to get there is by car or taxi, and some of the road is not well paved. ☎ *599/318–2284* ⊕ *www.statiapark.org* ✉ *Suggested donation $5* ☉ *Sunrise–sunset.*

ORANJESTAD

Fodor'sChoice
★
Oranjestad. Statia's only town, Oranjestad sits on the west coast facing the Caribbean. Both Upper Town—with cobblestone streets that designate its historic section—and Lower Town are easy to explore on foot.

Ft. Oranje. Three bastions have clung to these cliffs since 1636. In 1976 Statia participated in the U.S. bicentennial celebration by restoring the fort, and now the black cannons extend beyond the ramparts. In the parade grounds a plaque, presented in 1939 by Franklin D. Roosevelt, reads "Here the sovereignty of the United States of America was first formally acknowledged to a national vessel by a foreign official."

Built in 1775, the partially restored **Dutch Reformed Church**, on Kerkweg (Church Way), has lovely stone arches that face the sea. Ancient tales can be read on the gravestones in the adjacent 18th-century cemetery, where people were often buried atop one another. On Synagogepad (Synagogue Path) off Kerkweg is **Honen Dalim** ("She Who Is Charitable to the Poor"), one of the Caribbean's oldest synagogues. Dating from 1738, its exterior is partially restored.

Lower Town sits below Fort Oranjestraat (Fort Orange Street) and some steep cliffs. It is accessible from Upper Town on foot via the zigzagging, cobblestone Fort Road or by car via Van Tonningenweg. Warehouses and shops that were piled high with European imports in the 18th century are either abandoned or simply used to store local fishermen's equipment. One of them has been restored to become the **Mazinga by the Bay** gift shop.

Along the waterfront is a lovely park with palms, flowering shrubs, and benches—the work of the historical foundation. Peeking out from the shallow waters are the crumbling ruins of 18th-century buildings, reminders of Statia's days as the merchant hub of the Caribbean. The sea has slowly advanced since then, and it now surrounds many of the stone-and-brick ruins, making for fascinating snorkeling.

St. Eustatius Historical Foundation Museum. In the center of Upper Town is the former headquarters of Lord George Rodney, a British admiral during the American Revolution. While here, Rodney confiscated everything from gunpowder to wine in retaliation for Statia's gallant support of the fledgling country. The completely restored house is Statia's most important intact 18th-century dwelling. Exhibits trace the island's history from the pre-Columbian 6th century to the present. At the museum you can also buy a booklet with a self-guided walking tour of the sights. The tour begins in Lower Town at the marina and ends at the museum. ⊠ *Doncker House, 3 Wilhelminaweg, Upper Town, Oranjestad* ☎ *599/318–2288* 🖃 *$3* ⊙ *Weekdays 9–5, weekends 9–noon* .

Fodor's Choice ★   **The Quill.** This extinct, perfectly formed, 1,968-foot volcano has a primeval rain forest in its crater. Hike and be surrounded with giant elephant ears, ferns, flowers, wild orchids, and fruit trees, and maybe if you're lucky, glimpse the elusive and endangered *iguana delicatissima* (a large—sometimes several feet long—greenish-gray lizard with spines down its back). The volcanic cone rises 3 mi (5 km) south of Oranjestad on the main road. Local boys go up to the Quill by torchlight to catch delectable land crabs. The tourist board or Statia Marine Park will help you make hiking arrangements, and you must purchase a $6 permit before beginning the hike. Figure on two to four hours to hike the volcano.

St. Eustatius National Parks. There are three national parks in Statia: National Marine Park, Quill/Boven National Park, and Miriam C. Schmidt Botanical Garden. To hike the Quill or Boven or dive in the marine park you must purchase a $6 permit at the St. Eustatius National Parks, the information booth at the airport, or at your hotel. ⊠ *Gallows Bay, Lower Town* ☎ *599/318–2884* ⊕ *www.statiapark.org.*

20

BEACHES

If you desire a white sandy beach, calm waters, and a place to cool yourself off with a quick dip, you're looking at the wrong island. Statia's beaches are mostly deserted, rocky stretches of pristine shoreline. Many of the beaches on the Caribbean side are here today and reclaimed by the sea tomorrow, and the Atlantic side is an untamed mass of wild swells and vicious undertow. Walking, shelling, and searching for the elusive blue beads are popular pastimes for beachgoers. It's more likely, however, that the only place you will find real blue beads is at the St. Eustatius Historical Foundation Museum.

Lynch Bay Beach. Just two bends north of Corre Corre Bay on the island's Atlantic side, light-brown sand and rock cover this small beach, which is really an extension of Zeelandia Beach. Opt for walking instead of swimming here. There are turbulent swells, and there's a strong undertow. **Amenities:** none. **Best for:** walking. ⊠ *Lynch Bay*.

Smoke Alley Beach (*Oranje Beach*). The color of the sand varies from light beige to black at this beach on the Caribbean side near Gallows Bay. Sometimes much of the beach is claimed by ebb and flow. The waters are sometimes calm, so snorkeling is possible, but it's usually a better place for a swim or sunning. **Amenities:** none. **Best for:** swimming. ⊠ *North end, Oranjestad*.

Zeelandia Beach. Walking, shelling, and sunbathing are popular pastimes on this 2-mile (3-km) stretch of black-and-tan sand. Its Atlantic-side location makes it dangerous for swimming. **Amenities:** none. **Best for:** walking. ⊠ *Oranjestad*.

WHERE TO EAT

As with most everything on the island, low-key and casual is the name of the game when it comes to Statia's restaurants.

$$ ╳ **Blue Bead Bar & Restaurant.** This delightful little blue-and-yellow restaurant, a favorite with locals, is the perfect place to watch the sunset. It is one of those places where everyone talks to everyone. There are always daily specials; the menu includes pizza, seafood, Italian and French food. ⑤ *Average main: $18* ⊠ *Bay Rd., Gallows Bay, Lower Town, Oranjestad* ☏ *599/318–2873* ☉ *Closed Mon. and Tues.*

ECLECTIC
Fodor'sChoice
★

$ ╳ **Chinese Bar & Restaurant.** Unless you're into Formica, don't expect to be wowed by the atmosphere at this simple spot. What you will find are large portions of dishes such as *bami goreng* (Indonesian-style noodles with bits of beef, pork, or shrimp as well as tomatoes, carrots, bean sprouts, cabbage, soy sauce, and spices); or pork chops with a spicy sauce. It's do-it-yourself table hauling if you want to eat outside. ⑤ *Average main: $12* ⊠ *Queen Beatrix Rd., Upper Town, Oranjestad* ☏ *599/318–2389* ▭ *No credit cards*.

CHINESE

$$ ╳ **Golden Era Hotel Restaurant.** Don't pass up this restaurant just because it's completely nondescript. Concentrate instead on the tasty seafood and fine creole fare. It has another thing going for it: it's alongside the water, so the sound of the Caribbean is always playing in the background.

CARIBBEAN

20

$ *Average main: $15* ✉ *Golden Era Hotel, Bay Rd., Lower Town, Oranjestad* ☎ *599/318–2445, 599/318–2345, 599/318–2355.*

$

CHINESE

✕ **Grillhouse/San Yen Chinese Bar & Restaurant.** Short on decor—a few tables and a bar on the verandah—but long on taste, this Chinese restaurant has a special—a dish combining chicken, scallops, shrimp, beef, and sausage with vegetables—that's delicious, filling, and well worth the trip. $ *Average main: $11* ✉ *White Wall* ☎ *599/318–2915* ▭ *No credit cards.*

$

CARIBBEAN

✕ **Ocean View Terrace.** This spot in the courtyard overlooking the historic Ft. Oranje is a favorite for those who like to watch the sunset. It hasn't changed over the years. Owner Lauris Redan serves sandwiches and burgers for lunch and local cuisine—baked snapper with shrimp sauce, spicy chicken, tenderloin steak—at dinner. Every now and then there's a succulent barbecue. $ *Average main: $7* ✉ *Fort Oranjestraat, Upper Town, Oranjestad* ☎ *599/318–2934* ▭ *No credit cards* ☉ *No lunch Sun.*

$$$

FRENCH

✕ **The Old Gin House Main Dining Room.** In a comfortable dining room that borders a flower-filled courtyard, this bistro serves a very basic menu of fish, lobster, and steak. Chocolate Thunder Cake and crème brûlée cheesecake are specialty desserts. High-end private dining for 6 to 12 guests is also available (reservations are necessary). $ *Average main: $27* ✉ *Old Gin House, Bay Rd., Lower Town, Oranjestad* ☎ *599/318–2319* ⊕ *www.oldginhouse.com* ☉ *Closed Wed. No lunch.*

$$$

INTERNATIONAL

✕ **Papaya Restaurant.** This pleasant addition to Statia's restaurant scene serves upscale fare that includes artfully presented steaks, pasta, and seafood. White-tablecloth decor is accented with light pink and beige both inside and on the patio. Don't forget to try the house specialty, a papaya shake. $ *Average main: $29* ✉ *William Plantz #18* ☎ *599/318–0044* ▭ *No credit cards* ☉ *Closed Mon. No dinner Fri. No lunch Sat.*

$

BAKERY

✕ **Sand Box Tree Bakery.** This is the perfect spot for a quick sandwich; to satisfy your sweet tooth; or to order a wedding, birthday, or other special-occasion cake. $ *Average main: $4* ✉ *Kerkweg, Upper Town, opposite the Dutch Reformed Church, Oranjestad* ☎ *599/318–2469* ▭ *No credit cards.*

$$

ECLECTIC

✕ **Seaside Bar & Grill.** This extension of the Gin House faces the water. The simple menu includes great scrambled eggs for breakfast and sandwiches and tasty salads for lunch. Service is slow, but on this island there is no reason to rush. $ *Average main: $13* ✉ *Old Gin House Hotel, Bay Rd., Lower Town, Oranjestad* ☎ *599/318–2319* ☉ *No dinner.*

$$

ECLECTIC

✕ **Smoke Alley Bar & Grill.** Owners Michelle and Manny Balelo cook Tex-Mex, Italian, Caribbean, and American food to order at this beachfront hangout. The open-air eatery, famous for its happy hour, is the only place on the island where you can get draft beer. There's live music and barbecue every Friday night. Tuesday is "two for Tuesday"—you can get two meals for $22. $ *Average main: $14* ✉ *Gallows Bay, Lower Town, Oranjestad* ☎ *599/318–2002* ▭ *No credit cards* ☉ *Closed Sun.*

$

BURGER

☾

✕ **Superburger.** Statia's version of fast food comes from this little hangout, which serves burgers, shakes, and ice cream as well as local West Indian dishes. It's a local favorite for lunch. $ *Average main: $6* ✉ *Graaffweg, Upper Town, Oranjestad* ☎ *599/318–2412* ▭ *No credit cards* ☉ *No dinner weekends.*

WHERE TO STAY

Statia has several basic rental apartments available as alternatives to hotel rooms, and a few are available for $60 or less per night. Don't expect much beyond cable TV, a bathroom, and a kitchenette. Check with the tourist office for options.

For expanded reviews, facilities, and current deals, visit Fodors.com.

$ ▦ **Country Inn.** Facing Zeelandia Bay and close to the airport, this folksy
B&B/INN   little inn is surrounded by a lush tropical garden. **Pros:** very homey; tropical garden is lovely. **Cons:** not on the water and a 15-minute walk to town; a vehicle is recommended. **TripAdvisor:** "can't beat it," "average at best," "somewhere to relax." ⑤ *Rooms from: $60 ⊠ 3 Passionfruit Rd., Concordia* ☎ *599/318–2484* ⤴ *6 rooms* ▤ *No credit cards* ¶◎¶ *Multiple meal plans.*

$ ▦ **Golden Era Hotel.** On the waterfront across the street from the Old
HOTEL   Gin House, this property has a funky, retro-1960s feel. **Pros:** friendly staff; right on the waterfront; dive shop is next door; breakfast included. **Cons:** no-frills rooms are dark. **TripAdvisor:** "good for the price," "golden-era hotel still golden," "great waterfront location." ⑤ *Rooms from: $110 ⊠ Bay Rd., Lower Town, Oranjestad* ☎ *599/318–2545* ⤴ *19 rooms, 1 suite* ¶◎¶ *Breakfast.*

$$ ▦ **Old Gin House.** Built from 17th- and 18th-century cobblestones, this
HOTEL   old cotton warehouse is now a hotel and restaurant. **Pros:** conveniently
★   located; American breakfast at the Seaside Bar is included. **Cons:** rooms are dark; hotel could use some sprucing up. **TripAdvisor:** "historical gem," "a hotel with ambition," "quaint and relaxing." ⑤ *Rooms from: $147 ⊠ Bay Rd., Lower Town, Oranjestad* ☎ *599/318–2319* ⊕ *www. oldginhouse.com* ⤴ *18 rooms, 2 suites* ¶◎¶ *Breakfast.*

$ ▦ **Statia Lodge.** Look out from your cottage patio of the island's best
RENTAL   digs and enjoy drop-dead-gorgeous views of St. **Pros:** the best views
☾   and most modern accommodations on the island; landscaping is lovely;
★   French, English, and German spoken. **Cons:** no a/c; not near the water or town (which is why the car or scooter is necessary); not accessible for people with disabilities. ⑤ *Rooms from: $150 ⊠ White Wall* ☎ *599/318–1900* ⊕ *www.statialodge.com* ⤴ *10 1-bedroom cottages, 2 2-bedroom cottages* ☾ *Closed Sep.* ¶◎¶ *No meals.*

20

NIGHTLIFE

Statia's nightlife consists of local bands playing weekend gigs and quiet drinks at hotel bars.

Kool Korner Bar & Restaurant. The island's oldest bar, the tiny Kool Korner is a lively after-work and weekend hangout. It's across from the St. Eustatius Historical Foundation Museum. ⊠ *Wilhelminaweg, Upper Town, Oranjestad* ☎ *599/318–3386.*

Smoke Alley Bar & Grill. On Friday night you can find live music at Smoke Alley. ⊠ *Lower Town, Gallows Bay* ☎ *599/318–2002.*

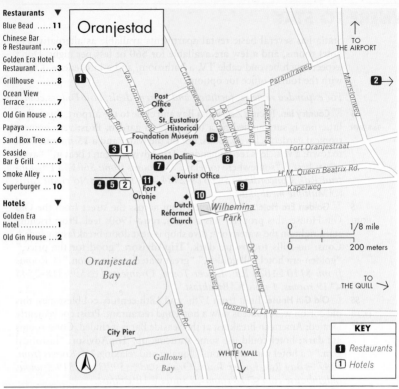

SHOPPING

The limited shopping here is all duty-free. But other than the predictable souvenirs, there's not much to buy. Several shops carry Dutch cheeses and chocolates and an interesting book by Heleen Cornett called *St. Eustatius: Echoes of the Past*.

Mazinga on the Bay. Head to this small store for the basics and for giftier items. It's inside an old seaside warehouse across from the Gin House. ⊠ *Gallows Bay, Upper Town, Oranjestad* ☎ *599/318–3345* ⊕ *www. mazingaonthebay.com*.

Paper Corner. Magazines, a few books, computers, computer accessories, and stationery supplies are on offer here. ⊠ *Van Tonningenweg, Upper Town, Oranjestad* ☎ *599/318–2208*.

SPORTS AND ACTIVITIES

DIVING AND SNORKELING

Fodor's Choice ★ Forget about glitz and nightlife. Statia is the quintessential low-key island. Finding an elusive *iguana delicatissima* on the Quill is probably the most exciting thing you can do on land. Statia's real thrills are underwater.

Long ago the ocean reclaimed the original seawall built by the Dutch in the 1700s. The sunken walls, remnants of old buildings, cannons, and anchors are now part of an extensive reef system populated by reef fingers, juvenile fish, and other sea creatures.

Statia has more than 30 dive sites protected by the Statia Marine Park, which has an office on Bay Road in Lower Town. Barracuda swim around colorful coral walls at **Barracuda Reef,** off the island's southwest coast. At **Double Wreck,** just offshore from Lower Town, you can find two tall-masted ships that date from the 1700s. The coral has taken on the shape of these two disintegrated vessels, and the site attracts spiny lobsters, stingrays, moray eels, and large schools of fish. About 100 yards west of Double Wreck is the Japanese ship Cheng Tong, which sank in 2004. Off the south end of the island, the sinking of the Charles L. Brown, a 1957 cable-laying vessel that was once owned by AT&T, created another artificial reef when it was sunk in a 135-foot underwater crater. Off the island's western shore, **Stenapa Reef** is an artificial reef created from the wrecks of barges, a harbor boat, and other ship parts. Large grouper and turtles are among the marine life you can spot here. For snorkelers, **Crooks Castle** has several stands of pillar coral, giant yellow sea fans, and sea whips just southwest of Lower Town.

There are dive shops along Bay Road in Lower Town that rent all types of gear (including snorkeling gear for about $10 a day), offer certification courses, and organize dive trips. One-tank dives start at $40; two-tank dives are about $80.

Golden Rock Dive Center. Operated by Glenn and Michele Faires, Golden Rock Dive Center has PADI's Gold Palm designation. In addition to certification courses, the shop offers a National Geographic program that emphasizes conservation. ⊠ *Gallows Bay, Lower Town, Oranjestad* ☎ *599/318–2964* ⊕ *www.goldenrockdive.com.*

Scubaqua. Catering to Europeans as well as Americans, Scubaqua has dive courses available in various languages. ⊠ *Gallows Bay, behind Blue Bead Restaurant, Lower Town, Oranjestad* ☎ *599/318–5450* ⊕ *www.scubaqua.com.*

Statia National Parks. Both the Saba Marine Park and Quill/Boven National Park are under the supervision of Statia National Parks. The marine tag fee, which all divers must buy, is used to help offset the costs of preserving the coral and other sea life here; the cost is $4 per day or $30 annually. There are two decompression chambers on the island, and the University of Sint Eustatius School of Medicine offers technical training in undersea and hyperbaric medicine. ☎ *599/318–2884* ⊕ *www.statiapark.org.*

20

GUIDED TOURS

Statia's three taxis and two large buses are available for island tours. A 2½-hour outing costs $40 per vehicle for five people (extra people are $5 each), usually including airport transfer. For one person it is $20. (If you'd rather head out on your own, there's a self-guided walking tour booklet available from the St. Eustatius Historical Foundation Museum.)

HIKING

Trails range from the easy to the "Watch out!" The big thrill here is the Quill, the 1,968-foot extinct volcano with its crater cradling a rain forest. Give yourself two to four hours to complete the hike. The tourist office has a list of 12 marked trails and can put you in touch with a guide. Quill National Park includes a trail into the crater, which is a long, winding but safe walk. Maps and the necessary $6 permit, which is good for a year, are available at the Statia Marine Park headquarters on Bay Road. Wear layers: it can be cool on the summit and steamy in the interior.

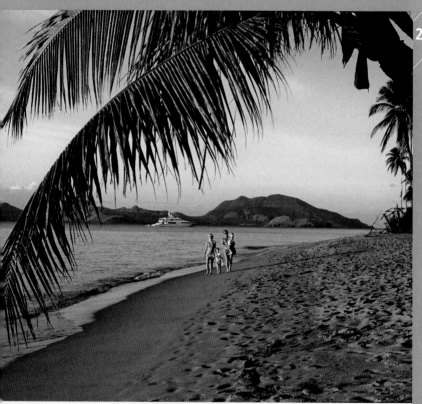

St. Kitts and Nevis

WORD OF MOUTH

"If it's not a beach day, do go to Brimstone Hill. It's a wonderful excursion and is a World Heritage Site. All the islands have beaches but Brimstone Hill is worth the trip, even if it is a beach day."

—CW

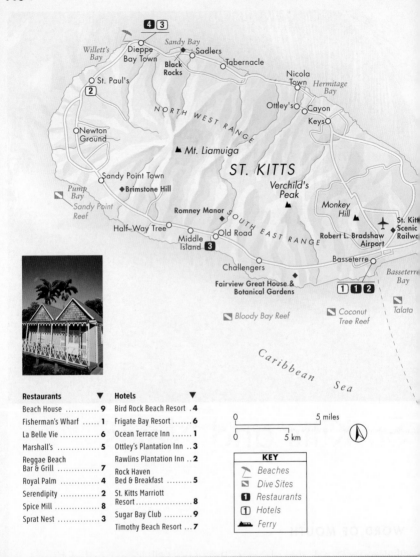

Restaurants ▼

Beach House **9**

Fisherman's Wharf **1**

La Belle Vie **6**

Marshall's **5**

Reggae Beach
Bar & Grill **7**

Royal Palm **4**

Serendipity **2**

Spice Mill **8**

Sprat Nest **3**

Hotels ▼

Bird Rock Beach Resort . **4**

Frigate Bay Resort **6**

Ocean Terrace Inn **1**

Ottley's Plantation Inn .. **3**

Rawlins Plantation Inn .. **2**

Rock Haven
Bed & Breakfast **5**

St. Kitts Marriott
Resort **8**

Sugar Bay Club **9**

Timothy Beach Resort ... **7**

KEY

⌁ Beaches

◹ Dive Sites

1 Restaurants

① Hotels

⛴ Ferry

TOP REASONS TO VISIT ST. KITTS AND NEVIS

1 History: Both St. Kitts and Nevis are steeped in history; Brimstone Hill Fortress is a man-made UNESCO World Heritage site.

2 Luxury: Luxurious, restored plantation inns can be found on both islands.

3 Landscape: Both islands have extinct volcanoes and luxuriant rain forests ideal for hikes, as well as fine diving and snorkeling sites.

4 Unspoiled: You'll find less development—particularly on Nevis—and more cordial and courteous islanders than on more touristy islands.

5 Water Activities: Both islands feature aquatic activities aplenty, with fine sailing, deep-sea fishing, diving (especially off St. Kitts), and windsurfing (especially around Nevis).

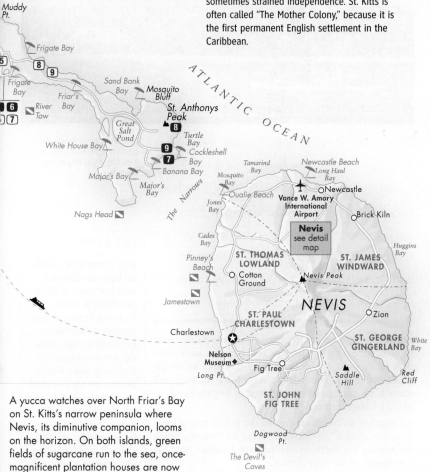

WELCOME TO
ST. KITTS AND NEVIS

THE MOTHER COLONY
AND HER SISTER

St. Kitts, a 65-square-mile (168-square-km)
island, is 2 miles (3 km) from smaller Nevis,
about 40 square miles (121 square km). The
two former British colonies are joined in a
sometimes strained independence. St. Kitts is
often called "The Mother Colony," because it is
the first permanent English settlement in the
Caribbean.

Muddy
Pt.

Frigate Bay

5 **8** **9**

Frigate
Bay

Friar's
Bay

River
Taw

6

7

Sand Bank
Bay

Mosquito
Bluff

St. Anthonys
Peak

8

Great
Salt
Pond

White House Bay

Major's Bay

Major's
Bay

Nags Head

ATLANTIC OCEAN

Turtle
Bay

Cockleshell
Bay

9

7

Banana Bay

The Narrows

Tamarind
Bay

Mosquito
Bay

Oualie Beach

Jones
Bay

Cades
Bay

Pinney's
Beach

Jamestown

Newcastle Beach

Long Haul
Bay

Newcastle

Vance W. Amory
International
Airport

Brick Kiln

Nevis
see detail
map

Huggins
Bay

ST. THOMAS
LOWLAND

Cotton
Ground

Nevis Peak

ST. JAMES
WINDWARD

NEVIS

ST. PAUL
CHARLESTOWN

Charlestown

Nelson
Museum

Long Pt.

Fig Tree

ST. JOHN
FIG TREE

Zion

ST. GEORGE
GINGERLAND

White
Bay

Saddle
Hill

Red
Cliff

Dogwood
Pt.

The Devil's
Caves

A yucca watches over North Friar's Bay
on St. Kitts's narrow peninsula where
Nevis, its diminutive companion, looms
on the horizon. On both islands, green
fields of sugarcane run to the sea, once-
magnificent plantation houses are now
luxurious inns, and lovely stretches of
uncrowded beach stretch before you.

ST. KITTS AND NEVIS BEACHES

St. Kitts and Nevis aren't noted for endless sensuous strands, yet beachcombers will find enough variety during their holiday. The finest beaches are fairly developed (Frigate Beach on the Caribbean side, with one bar after another, is a party-hearty destination on weekends), but both islands offer surf-lashed Atlantic stretches fine for R&R à deux if not swimming.

(Above) Pinney's Beach, Nevis
(Bottom right) Friar's Bay, St. Kitts (Top right) Frigate Bay, St. Kitts

Beaches on St. Kitts are free and open to the public (even those occupied by hotels). The best beaches, with powdery white sand, are in the Frigate Bay area or on the lower peninsula. The Atlantic waters are rougher, and many black-sand beaches northwest of Frigate Bay double as garbage dumps.

All beaches on Nevis are free to the public (the plantation inns cordon off "private" areas on Pinney's Beach for guests), but there are no changing facilities, so wear a swimsuit under your clothes.

THE SAND

Both islands have appealing beige-hue beaches, such as Pinney's or those garlanding St. Kitts's Southeast Peninsula. Many abutting the Atlantic feature earthier colors, ranging from warm mocha to taupe-gray. Some Atlantic beaches are wind-whipped and wilder, such as Conaree, ideal for bodysurfing, though they're not regularly maintained, so otherwise soft sand competes with seaweed, shells, and driftwood.

21

ST. KITTS

Banana/Cockleshell Bays. These twin connected eyebrows of glittering champagne-color sand—stretching nearly 2 miles (3 km) total at the southeastern tip of the island—feature majestic views of Nevis and are backed by lush vegetation and coconut palms. The first-rate restaurant–bar Spice Mill (next to Rasta-hue Lion Rock Beach Bar—order the knockout Lion Punch) and Reggae Beach Bar & Grill bracket either end of Cockleshell. Plans for a 125-room mixed-use Park Hyatt (with additional residential condos and villas), originally slated for development by late 2013, are on hold. The water is generally placid, ideal for swimming. The downside is irregular maintenance, with seaweed (particularly after rough weather) and occasional litter, especially on Banana Bay. Follow Simmonds Highway to the end and bear right, ignoring the turnoff for Turtle Beach. ⊠ *Banana Bay.*

Friar's Bay. Locals consider Friar's Bay, on the Caribbean (southern) side, the island's finest beach. It's a long, tawny scimitar where the water always seems warmer and clearer. Unfortunately, the shelved Marine World development has co-opted nearly half the strand. Still, several happening bars, including Shipwreck, Mongoose, and Sunset Grill, serve terrific, inexpensive local food and cheap, frosty drinks. Chair rentals cost around $3, though if you order lunch,

you can negotiate a freebie. Friar's is the first major beach along Southeast Peninsula Drive (aka Simmonds Highway), approximately a mile (1½ km) southeast of Frigate Bay. ⊠ *Friar's Bay.*

Frigate Bay. The Caribbean side offers talcum-powder-fine beige sand framed by coconut palms and sea grapes, and the Atlantic side (a 15-minute stroll)—sometimes called North Frigate Bay—is a favorite with horseback riders. South Frigate Bay is bookended by Sunset Café and the popular, pulsating Buddies Beach Hut. In between are several other lively beach spots, including Cathy's (fabulous jerk ribs), the Monkey Bar, Elvis Love Shack, and Mr. X Shiggidy Shack. Most charge $3 to $5 to rent a chair, though they'll often waive the fee if you ask politely and buy lunch. Locals barhop late into Friday and Saturday nights. Waters are generally calm for swimming; the rockier eastern end offers fine snorkeling. The incomparably scenic Atlantic side is—regrettably—dominated by the Marriott (plentiful dining options), attracting occasional pesky vendors. The surf is choppier and the undertow stronger here. On cruise-ship days groups stampede both sides. Frigate Bay is easy to find, just less than 3 miles (5 km) from downtown Basseterre. ⊠ *Frigate Bay.*

Sand Bank Bay. A dirt road, nearly impassable after heavy rains, leads to a long mocha crescent on the Atlantic.

About 4 miles long, Pinney's Beach is one of the best on Nevis.

The shallow coves are protected here, making it ideal for families, and it's usually deserted. Brisk breezes lure the occasional windsurfer, but avoid the rocky far left area because of fierce sudden swells and currents. This exceptionally pretty beach lacks shade; Christophe Harbour has constructed several villas and a beach club (which may eventually hold an upscale restaurant open to the public). As you drive southeast along Simmonds Highway, approximately 10 miles (16 km) from Basseterre, look for an unmarked dirt turnoff to the left of the Great Salt Pond. ⊠ *Sand Bank Bay.*

NEVIS

Newcastle Beach. This broad swath of soft ecru sand shaded by coconut palms is near Nisbet Plantation, on the channel between St. Kitts and Nevis. It's popular with snorkelers, but beware stony sections and occasional strong currents that kick up seaweed and roil the sandy bottom. ⊠ *Newcastle.*

Oualie Beach. South of Mosquito Bay and north of Cades and Jones bays, this beige-sand beach lined with palms and sea grapes is where the folks at Oualie Beach Hotel can mix you a drink and fix you up with water-sports equipment. There's excellent snorkeling amid calm water and fantastic sunset views with St. Kitts silhouetted in the background. Several beach chairs and hammocks (free with lunch, $3 rental without) line the sand and the grassy "lawn" behind it. Oualie is at the island's northwest tip, approximately 3 miles (5 km) west of the airport. ⊠ *Oualie Beach.*

Pinney's Beach. The island's showpiece has soft, golden sand on the calm Caribbean, lined with a magnificent grove of palm trees. The Four Seasons Resort is here, as are the plantation inns' beach clubs and casual beach bars such as Sunshine's, Chevy's, and the Double Deuce. Regrettably, the waters can be murky and filled with kelp if the weather has been inclement anywhere within a hundred miles, depending on the currents. ⊠ *Pinney's Beach.*

By Jordan
Simon

These idyllic sister islands, 2 miles (3 km) apart at their closest point, offer visitors a relatively authentic island experience. Both have luxuriant mountain rain forests; uncrowded beaches; historic ruins; towering, long-dormant volcanoes; charming if slightly dilapidated Georgian capitals in Basseterre (St. Kitts) and Charlestown (Nevis); intact cultural heritage; friendly if shy people; and restored 18th-century sugar plantation inns run by elegant, if sometimes eccentric, expatriate British and American owners.

The islands' history follows the usual Caribbean route: Amerindian settlements, Columbus's voyages, fierce colonial battles between the British and French, a boom in sugar production second only to that of Barbados. St. Kitts became known as the mother colony of the West Indies: English settlers sailed from there to Antigua, Barbuda, Tortola, and Montserrat, and the French dispatched colonists to Martinique, Guadeloupe, St. Martin, and St. Barth.

St. Kitts and Nevis, in addition to Anguilla, achieved self-government as an associated state of Great Britain in 1967. Anguillians soon made their displeasure known, separating immediately, whereas St. Kitts and Nevis waited until 1983 to become an independent nation. The two islands, despite their superficial similarities, have taken increasingly different routes regarding tourism. Nevis received an economic boost from the Four Seasons, which helped establish it as an upscale destination. St. Kitts, however, has yet to define its identity at a time when most islands have found their tourism niche. A fierce sibling rivalry has ensued.

Though its comparative lack of development is a lure, the Kittitian government is casting its economic net in several directions. Golf, ecotourism, and scuba diving are being aggressively promoted. And the government hopes the number of available rooms will increase roughly 30% by 2014 to more than 2,000, according to the "build it and they will come" philosophy. But is St. Kitts ready to absorb all this? The island offers a surprisingly diverse vacation experience while retaining its essential Caribbean flavor. Divers have yet to discover all its underwater attractions, and nature lovers will be pleasantly surprised by the hiking. There's now every kind of accommodation, as well as gourmet dining, golf, and gaming.

Meanwhile, Nevis seems determined to stay even more unspoiled (there are still no traffic lights). Its natural attractions and activities certainly rival those of St. Kitts, from mountain biking and ecohiking to windsurfing and deep-sea fishing, though lying in a hammock and dining on romantic candlelit patios remain cherished pursuits. Pinney's Beach, despite occasional hurricane erosion, remains a classic Caribbean strand. Its historic heritage, from the Caribbean's first hotel to Alexander Hamilton's childhood home, is just as pronounced, including equally sybaritic plantation inns that seem torn from the pages of a romance novel.

Perhaps it's a warning sign that many guests call the catamaran trip to Nevis the high point of their stay on St. Kitts—and many Kittitians build retirement and second homes on Nevis. The sister islands' relationship remains outwardly cordial if slightly contentious. Nevis papers sometimes run blistering editorials advocating independence, though one plebiscite has already failed. St. Kitts and Nevis may separate some day, but for now their battles are confined to ad campaigns and political debates. Fortunately, well-heeled and barefoot travelers alike can still happily enjoy the many energetic and easygoing enticements of both blissful retreats.

PLANNING

WHEN TO GO

The high season is relatively short, starting in mid-December and stretching into early or mid-April. The shoulder season (roughly April to mid-June and November to mid-December) offers lower rates. Rates are lower still from mid-June through November, but some establishments close for a month or longer.

GETTING HERE AND AROUND

AIR TRAVEL

Many travelers connect in Antigua, San Juan, St. Maarten, or St. Thomas. To Nevis, it's almost always cheaper to fly into St. Kitts and then take a regularly scheduled ferry, but check the schedules or book a transfer from your resort (if available) in advance.

There are nonstop flights to St. Kitts from Atlanta (Delta), Charlotte (US Airways), Miami (American), and New York–JFK (American). There are no nonstops from the United States to Nevis.

Airline Contacts American/American Eagle. American/American Eagle has daily flights into St. Kitts and thrice-weekly flights to Nevis from San Juan; Miami is another option. ☎ 869/465–2273, 869/469–8995.

LIAT. Other major domestic airlines (US Airways once weekly nonstop from Charlotte and Delta once weekly from Atlanta) fly from their

LOGISTICS

Getting to St. Kitts and Nevis:
Many travelers connect in Antigua, San Juan, St. Maarten, or St. Thomas. When going to Nevis, it's almost always cheaper to fly into St. Kitts and then take a regularly scheduled ferry to Nevis, but check the schedules. Robert L. Bradshaw International Airport on St. Kitts (SKB) and the smaller, simpler Vance W. Armory International Airport on Nevis (NEV) are still fairly sleepy.

Hassle Factor: Low to medium for St. Kitts, medium for Nevis.

On the Ground: Taxis meet every ferry and flight to St. Kitts or Nevis.

The taxis are unmetered, but fixed rates, in EC dollars, are posted at the airport and at the jetty. Note that rates are the same for one to four passengers. On St. Kitts the fares from the airport range from EC$32 to Frigate Bay, to EC$72 for the farthest point. From the airport on Nevis it's EC$27 to Nisbet Plantation, EC$54 to the Four Seasons, and EC$67 to Montpelier. There is a 50% surcharge between 10 pm and 6 am. Before setting off in a cab, be sure to clarify whether the rate quoted is in EC or U.S. dollars.

eastern hubs either into Antigua, St. Maarten, San Juan, or St. Thomas, where connections to St. Kitts (and, less frequently, to Nevis) can be made on LIAT. ☎ *869/465–1330* ⊕ *www.liatairline.com*.

Winair. Nevis connections can also be made from St. Maarten on Winair. ☎ *869/469–5302* ⊕ *www.fly-winair.com*.

Robert L. Bradshaw International Airport. St. Kitts' airport (SKB) is Robert L. Bradshaw International Airport. ⊠ *Golden Rock* ☎ *465–8013*.

Vance W. Amory International Airport. The Nevis airport (NEV) is Vance W. Amory International Airport. ⊠ *Newcastle, Nevis* ☎ *869/469–9343*.

BOAT AND FERRY TRAVEL

There are several ferry services between St. Kitts and Nevis, all with schedules that are subject to abrupt change. Most companies make two or three daily trips. All the ferries take about 30 to 45 minutes and cost $8–$10.

Contacts Leyton Ferry Schedule. Up-to-date information is available at Leyton Ferry Schedule. ☎ *869/466–6734, 869/662–9811, 869/469–0403* ⊕ *boatschedule.leytonms.com*.

Nevis Water Sports. Nevis Water Sports provides sea-taxi service. ☎ *869/469–9060*.

There's an additional EC$1 tax for port security, paid separately upon departure.

CAR TRAVEL

Driving Tips: One well-kept main road circumnavigates St. Kitts and is usually clearly marked, making it difficult to get lost, though the northeast can get a bit bumpy and the access roads to the plantation inns are notoriously rough.

The roads on Nevis are fairly new and generally smooth, at least on the most traveled north, west, and south sides of the island. The east coast has some potholes, and pigs, goats, and sheep still insist on the right-of-way all around the island. Drivers on both islands tend to travel at a fast clip and pass on curves, so drive defensively. Driving is on the left, British-style, though you will probably be given an American-style car.

Renting a Car: You can get by without a car if you are staying in the Frigate Bay–Basseterre area, but elsewhere you'll need to rent a car. On Nevis it's often easier to just take taxis and guided tours. On St. Kitts, present your valid driver's license and $24 at the police station on Cayon Street in Basseterre to get a temporary driving permit (on Nevis the car-rental agency will help you obtain the $24 local license at the police station). The license is valid for three months on both islands. On either island, car rentals start at about $45 per day for a compact; expect to pay a few extra bucks for air-conditioning. Most agencies offer substantial multiday discounts.

Contacts Avis. Avis has the best selection of Suzuki and Daihatsu four-wheel-drive vehicles on St. Kitts, as well as rental exchange on Nevis and complimentary pickup. ⊠ *South Independence Sq., Basseterre* ☎ *869/465–6507* ⊕ *www.avisstkitts.com.*

Delisle Walwyn. Delisle Walwyn provides an excellent selection and the option of a replacement car for one day on Nevis if you rent for three days or more on St. Kitts. ⊠ *Liverpool Row, Basseterre* ☎ *869/465–8449.*

Funky Monkey Tours & Rentals. Funky Monkey Tours & Rentals lets you ride on the wild side in Polaris Ranger and Razor 4x4s; prices start at $115 per half day. You can also rent Vespas for $75 per day, as well as Sea-Doo wave runners. Or follow in their tire tracks, off-roading through the island on a three-hour Funky Monkey tours. ⊠ *Nelson Springs, Nevis* ☎ *869/665–6045, 869/665–6245* ⊕ *www.funkymonkeytours.com.*

Nevis Car Rentals. Nevis Car Rentals is a recommended agency. ⊠ *Newcastle, Nevis* ☎ *869/469–9837.*

Striker's Car Rental. Striker's Car Rental has a good selection of vehicles. ⊠ *Hermitage Rd., Gingerland, Nevis* ☎ *869/469–2654.*

TDC/Thrifty Rentals. TDC/Thrifty Rentals has a wide selection of vehicles and outstanding service; it offers a three-day rental that includes a car on both islands. ⊠ *Central St., West Independence Square, Basseterre* ☎ *869/465–2991* ⊕ *www.tdclimited.com/dept_content.asp?did=8* ⊠ *Bay Rd., Charlestown, Nevis* ☎ *869/469–5430* ⊕ *www.tdclimited.com/dept_content.asp?did=8.*

TAXI TRAVEL

Taxi rates are government regulated and posted at the airport, the dock, and in the free tourist guide. Be sure to clarify whether the fare is in EC or U.S. dollars. There are fixed rates to and from all the hotels and to and from major points of interest.

Airport Transfers: On St. Kitts the fares from the airport range from EC$32 to Frigate Bay, to EC$72 for the farthest point. From the airport on Nevis it's EC$27 to Nisbet Plantation, EC$54 to the Four Seasons, and EC$67 to Montpelier. There is a 50% surcharge between 10 pm and 6 am.

Contacts St. Kitts Taxi Association ☎ 869/465-8487, 869/465-4253, 869/465-7818 after hrs. **Nevis Taxi Service.** ☎ 869/469-5631, 869/469-9790 for the airport, 869/469-5515 after dark.

ESSENTIALS

Banks and Exchange Services Legal tender is the Eastern Caribbean (EC) dollar. The rate of exchange at this writing is EC$2.70 to US$1. U.S. dollars are accepted practically everywhere, but change is usually EC currency. Most large hotels, restaurants, and shops accept major credit cards, but small inns and shops often do not. All banks, including the Royal Bank of St. Kitts and Scotia Bank, have ATMs. There are ATMs on Nevis at the airport, Bank of Nova Scotia, First Caribbean International Bank, and St. Kitts–Nevis National Bank.

Electricity 110 volts, 60 cycles.

Emergency Services Ambulance and Emergencies ☎ 911. **Police** ☎ 869/465-2241 on St. Kitts, 869/469-5391 on Nevis.

Passport Requirements All travelers must have a valid passport and a return or ongoing ticket. Canadian citizens (not connecting through U.S. territory) need either a valid passport or a birth certificate (with a raised seal) accompanied by a government-issue photo ID.

Phones Phone cards, which you can buy in denominations of EC$5, $10, and $20, are handy for making local phone calls, calling other islands, and accessing U.S. direct lines. To call St. Kitts and Nevis from the United States, dial area code 869, then access code 465, 466, 468, or 469 and the local four-digit number.

Taxes The departure tax is US$22, payable in cash only. There's no sales tax on either St. Kitts or Nevis. Hotels collect a 9% government tax.

Tipping Hotels add a 10%–12% service charge to your bill. Restaurants occasionally do the same; ask if it isn't printed on the menu; a 15% tip is appropriate when it isn't included. Taxi drivers typically receive a 10% tip, porters and bellhops $1 per bag; housekeeping staff, $2 to $3 per night.

ACCOMMODATIONS

St. Kitts has a wide variety of places to stay—beautifully restored plantation inns, full-service affordable hotels, simple beachfront cottages, and all-inclusive resorts. One large resort—the Marriott—is more midrange than upscale and attracts large groups and package tourists. Choose St. Kitts if you want a wider choice of activities and accommodations (you can always do Nevis as a day trip). Nevis is a small island with no large resorts, and most accommodations are upscale—primarily plantation inns and the luxurious Four Seasons. It's much quieter than St. Kitts, so choose it if you want to get away from the hectic island scene and simply relax in low-key comfort and surprisingly high style.

Four Seasons Resort Nevis: Really in a class by itself, the Four Seasons is the only sizable, lavish, high-end property on either island. If you can afford it, the resort is certainly one of the Caribbean's finest; recent post-hurricane renovations improved on near-perfection.

Plantation Inns: St. Kitts and Nevis feature renovated, historic plantation houses that have been turned into upscale inns. On Nevis, the inns are the most distinctive form of lodging. They are usually managed by hands-on owner-operators and offer fine cuisine and convivial hospitality; though not usually on a beach, most of these inns have beach clubs with free private shuttle service.

HOTEL AND RESTAURANT PRICES

Prices in the restaurant reviews are the average cost of a main course at dinner or, if dinner is not served, at lunch; taxes and service charges are generally included. Prices in the hotel reviews are the lowest cost of a standard double room in high season, excluding taxes, service charges, and meal plans (except at all-inclusives). Prices for rentals are the lowest per-night cost for a one-bedroom unit in high season.

VISITOR INFORMATION

Contacts St. Kitts Tourism Authority ☎ *212/535–1234 in New York City,* *800/582–6208, 866/556–3847 for Nevis alone* ⊕ *www.stkittstourism.kn.* **St. Kitts–Nevis Hotel and Tourism Association** ✉ *Liverpool Row, Box 438, Basseterre* ☎ *869/465–5304* ⊕ *www.stkittsnevishta.org.*

WEDDINGS

Two-day residency requirement. License is $80, application $20. Valid passport or birth certificate required; if divorced, a divorce decree; if widowed, a death certificate of the deceased spouse.

ST. KITTS

EXPLORING ST. KITTS

You can explore Basseterre, the capital city, in a half hour or so, and should allow four hours for an island tour. Main Road traces the northwestern perimeter of the island through seas of sugarcane and past breadfruit trees and stone walls. Villages with tiny pastel-color houses of stone and weathered wood are scattered across the island, and the drive back to Basseterre around the island's other side passes through several of them. The most spectacular stretch of scenery is on Dr. Kennedy Simmonds Highway, which goes to the tip of the Southeast Peninsula. This modern road twists and turns through the undeveloped grassy hills that rise between the calm Caribbean and the windswept Atlantic, passing the shimmering pink Great Salt Pond, a volcanic crater, and seductive beaches. Major developments are under way, including the Beaumont Park Racetrack near Dieppe Bay. The 6-furlong racetrack and state-of-the-art stables opened in December 2009. Cards include some stakes races with horses from as far afield as France and Ireland competing; admission and parking are free; up to 9,000 spectators converge on the site, enhancing the exciting equine environment. At this writing an entertainment complex with an upscale restaurant as well as polo grounds, go-karts, a retail complex, and bird and butterfly parks are slated to follow by late 2012.

WHAT TO SEE

Basseterre. On the south coast, St. Kitts's walkable capital is graced with tall palms and flagstone sidewalks; although many of the buildings appear run-down, there are interesting shops, excellent art galleries, and some beautifully maintained houses. Duty-free shops and boutiques line the streets and courtyards radiating from the octagonal **Circus**, built in the style of London's famous Piccadilly Circus.

Independence Square. There are lovely gardens on the site of a former slave market at Independence Square. The square is surrounded on three sides by 18th-century Georgian buildings. ⊠ *Off Bank St.*.

St. George's Anglican Church. St. George's Anglican Church is a handsome stone building with a crenellated tower originally built by the French in 1670 and called Nôtre-Dame. The British burned it down in 1706 and rebuilt it four years later, naming it after the patron saint of England. Since then it has suffered a fire, an earthquake, and hurricanes and was once again rebuilt in 1869. ⊠ *Cayon St.*.

Port Zante. Port Zante is an ambitious, ever-growing 27-acre cruise-ship pier and marina in an area that has been reclaimed from the sea. The domed welcome center is an imposing neoclassical hodgepodge, with columns and stone arches, shops, walkways, fountains, and West Indian–style buildings housing luxury shops, galleries, restaurants, and a small casino. A second pier, 1,434 feet long, has a draft that accommodates even leviathan cruise ships. The selection of shops and restaurants (Tiffany Bar and Deli is a find for fantastic local fare, Twist for global fusion cuisine) is expanding as well. ⊠ *Waterfront, behind Circus*.

National Museum. In the restored former Treasury Building, the National Museum presents an eclectic collection reflecting the history and culture of the island. ⊠ *Bay Rd.* ☎ *869/465–5584* ⌨ *EC$1 residents, US$1 nonresidents* ☉ *Weekdays 9–5, Sat. 9–1*.

NEED A BREAK?

Ballahoo. The tropically themed second-floor terrace eatery Ballahoo draws a crowd for breakfast, lunch, and dinner. Specialties include chili shrimp, Madras beef curry, and a toasted rum-and-banana sandwich topped with ice cream. At lunchtime you can watch the bustle of the Circus and enjoy special prices on such dishes as roti bursting with curried chicken or vegetables. Grab fresh local juices (tamarind, guava) if you can. Though the service is lackadaisical bordering on rude, the food is at least plentiful, the daiquiris are killer, the Wi-Fi free, and the people-watching delightful. ⊠ **Fort St.** ☎ **869/465–4197** ⊕ **www.ballahoo.com.**

Black Rocks. This series of lava deposits was spat into the sea ages ago when the island's volcano erupted. It has since been molded into fanciful shapes by centuries of pounding surf. ⊠ *Atlantic coast, outside town of Sadlers, Sandy Bay*.

★ **Brimstone Hill.** This 38-acre fortress, a UNESCO World Heritage Site, is part of a national park dedicated by Queen Elizabeth in 1985. After routing the French in 1690, the English erected a battery here; by 1736 the fortress held 49 guns, earning it the moniker Gibraltar of the West Indies. In 1782, 8,000 French troops laid siege to the stronghold, which was defended by 350 militia and 600 regular troops of the Royal Scots and East Yorkshires. When the English finally surrendered, they were allowed to march from the fort in full formation out of respect for their bravery (the English afforded the French the same honor when they surrendered the fort a mere year later). A hurricane severely damaged the fortress in 1834, and in 1852 it was evacuated and dismantled. The beautiful stones were carted away to build houses.

The citadel has been partially reconstructed and its guns remounted. It's a steep walk up the hill from the parking lot. A seven-minute orientation film recounts the fort's history and restoration. You can see remains of the officers' quarters, redoubts, barracks, ordnance store, and cemetery. Its museum collections were depleted by hurricanes, but some pre-Columbian artifacts, objects pertaining to the African heritage of the island's slaves (such as masks and ceremonial tools), weaponry, uniforms, photographs, and old newspapers remain. The spectacular view includes Montserrat and Nevis to the southeast; Saba and St. Eustatius to the northwest; and St. Barth and St. Maarten to the north. Nature trails snake through the tangle of surrounding hardwood forest and savanna (a fine spot to catch the green vervet monkeys—inexplicably brought by the French and now outnumbering the residents—skittering about). ⊠ *Main Rd., Brimstone Hill* ☎ *869/465–2609* ⊕ *www. brimstonehillfortress.org* ☜ *$8* ⊙ *Daily 9:30–5:30.*

Fairview Great House & Botanical Gardens. Parts of this French colonial great house set on more than 2 lush tropical acres date back to 1701, including original ipe beams. The interior has been impeccably restored in period fashion, with each room painted in different colors from pomegranate to lemon. Furnishings include a 16-seat mahogany dinner table set with china and silver; docents relate fascinating factoids (chaises were broadened to accommodate petticoats—or "can-can skirts," in local parlance). Cross the cobblestone courtyard to the original kitchen, replete with volcanic stone and brick oven, and bathing room (heated rocks warmed spring water in the tub). The fieldstone cellar now contains the gift shop, offering local pottery, art, and honey harvested on-site at the apiary. You can wander meticulously maintained gardens with interpretive signage, filled with chattering birds and monkeys. The Nirvana restaurant offers worthy local food (lunch buffets, creative Mediterranean-tinged fare for dinner); dips in the pool are a bonus. ⊠ *Artist's Level Hill, Boyd's* ☎ *869/465–3141* ☜ *$10* ⊙ *Daily 9–5 (last entrance 4:30).*

Old Road. This site marks the first permanent English settlement in the West Indies, founded in 1624 by Thomas Warner. Take the side road toward the interior to find some Carib petroglyphs, testimony of even earlier habitation. The largest depicts a female figure on black volcanic rock, presumably a fertility goddess. Less than a mile east of Old Road along Main Road is **Bloody Point,** where French and British soldiers joined forces in 1629 to repel a mass Carib attack; reputedly so many Caribs were massacred that the stream ran red for three days. ⊠ *St. Kitts* ✛ *Main Rd. west of Challengers.*

Cannons at Brimstone Hill, a UNESCO World Heritage Site on St. Kitts

★ **Romney Manor.** The ruins of this somewhat restored house (reputedly once the property of Thomas Jefferson) and surrounding replicas of chattel-house cottages are set in 6 acres of glorious gardens, with exotic flowers, an old bell tower, and an enormous, gnarled 350-year-old saman tree (sometimes called a rain tree). Inside, at **Caribelle Batik,** you can watch artisans hand-printing fabrics by the 2,500-year-old Indonesian wax-and-dye process known as batik. Look for signs indicating a turnoff for Romney Manor near Old Road. ⌂ *Old Road* ☎ 869/465–6253 ⊕ *www.caribellebatikstkitts.com* ✉ *Free* ☽ *Daily 9–5.*

St. Kitts Scenic Railway. The old narrow-gauge train that had transported sugarcane to the central sugar factory since 1912 is all that remains of the island's once-thriving sugar industry. Two-story cars bedecked in bright Kittitian colors circle the island in just under four hours. Each passenger gets a comfortable, downstairs air-conditioned seat fronting vaulted picture windows and an upstairs open-air observation spot. The conductor's running discourse embraces not only the history of sugar cultivation but also the railway's construction, local folklore, island geography, even other agricultural mainstays from papayas to pigs. You can drink in complimentary tropical beverages (including luscious guava daiquiris) along with the sweeping rain-forest and ocean vistas, accompanied by an a cappella choir's renditions of hymns, spirituals, and predictable standards like "I've Been Workin' on the Railroad." ⌂ *Needsmust* ☎ 869/465–7263 ⊕ *www.stkittsscenicrailway.com* ✉ *$89, children 4–12 $44.50* ☽ *Departures vary according to cruise-ship schedules (call ahead, but at least once daily Dec.–Apr., usually 8:30 am).*

Beach House

WHERE TO EAT

St. Kitts restaurants range from funky beachfront bistros to elegant plantation dining rooms (most with prix-fixe menus); most fare is tinged with the flavors of the Caribbean. Many restaurants offer West Indian specialties such as curried mutton, pepper pot (a stew of vegetables, tubers, and meats), and Arawak chicken (seasoned and served with rice and almonds on breadfruit leaf).

What to Wear. Throughout the island, dress is casual at lunch (but no bathing suits). Dinner, although not necessarily formal, definitely calls for long pants and sundresses.

$$$$
ECLECTIC
Fodor'sChoice
★

✕ **Beach House.** Executive chef Damien Heaney and staff put the sin in scintillating at this outpost of chic on Turtle Beach. The opening salvo of the überluxurious Christophe Harbour development on the island's Southwest Peninsula, the Beach House preens like an advance scout for the army of chic. The tiered 60-seat restaurant and over-size 30-seat lounge wouldn't be out of place in L.A., featuring a rich color palette, plush yet comfy furnishings, hardwood floors, sea-grass carpets, billowing white draperies forming cozy nooks, and romantically lighted lanterns throughout. Damien's eclectic menu showcases the Caribbean's sultry melting pot of culinary traditions—Spanish, Asian, French, and African, taking the confusion out of fusion cuisine. Stunners such as poached mahimahi with parsnip-cassava mash, wilted zucchini leekoven-dried tomato jam, and wild mushroom-roast garlic sauce provide textbook examples of how to juxtapose textures, flavors, even colors. The island's finest wine list runs from Argentina to Alsace to Australia; bracket your evening with trendy cocktails with *cojones* and the extensive postprandial selection of aged rums and Cuban cigars. $ *Average main: $32* ⊠ *Turtle Beach* ☎ 869/469–5299 ⊕ *www.stkittsbeachhouse.com* ⚖ *Reservations essential* ⊘ *Closed Sun.–Mon.*

$$$ ✕ **Fisherman's Wharf.** Part of the Ocean Terrace Inn, this extremely casual
SEAFOOD waterfront eatery is decorated in swaggering nautical style, with rusty anchors, casks, buoys, and walls splashed with aqua waves and wild, psychedelically hued murals of fishing boats and their catch. Try the excellent conch chowder, followed by fresh grilled lobster or other ship-shape seafood, and finish off your meal with a slice of the memorable banana cheesecake. The place is generally hopping, especially on weekend nights when live bands often jam atop the split-level, breeze-swept bar. $ *Average main: $24* ⊠ *Ocean Terrace Inn, Fortlands, Basseterre* ☎ 869/465–2754 ⊕ *www.oceanterraceinn.com* ⊘ *No lunch.*

$$$ ✕ **La Belle Vie.** This très sympa nod to St. Kitts' French heritage is aptly
FRENCH titled "the good life." The cozy antiques-strewn lobby–bar leads to the semi-enclosed garden dining patio. Everything brims with brio from the brioches baked on-site to Brel and Aznavour on the soundtrack (accompanied by tree frogs). Nantes-born Fabien Richard deftly executes bistro fare at fair prices. You could feast on appetizers alone: salad *chabichoux* (warm goat cheese, *lardons*, mesclun) or velvety tomato *bavarois* with prosciutto. But opt for the bargain $41 three-course prix fixe; main courses might include salmon in aniseed sauce, duck sautéed with honey and lime, or olive-and-balsamic-crusted rack of lamb. Even the old-fashioned veggies delight, including smashing potatoes *dauphinoise*. Save room for an unimpeachable peach sable (tart) with crème anglaise. A few minor complaints include: mosquitoes on still nights, limited wine selection, and the occasional overcooked if tasty entrée. $ *Average main: $30* ⊠ *19 Golf View, Frigate Bay* ☎ 869/465–5216, 869/764–6035 ⊕ *www.labellevie-stkitts.com* ⚖ *Reservations essential* ⊘ *No lunch.*

$$$ ✕ **Marshall's.** The pool area of Horizons Villa Resort is transformed
ECLECTIC into a stylish eatery thanks to smashing ocean views, potted plants, serenading tree frogs, and elegant candlelit tables. Jamaican chef Verral Marshall fuses ultrafresh local ingredients with global influences. Recommended offerings include grilled swordfish with passion-fruit beurre blanc, pan-seared duck breast with raspberry-ginger sauce, or homemade sorbets. Most dishes are regrettably orthodox (rack of lamb in port reduction), and the execution is uneven, especially since Verral opened a branch of Marshall's on Nevis. $ *Average main: $29* ⊠ *Horizons Villa Resort, Frigate Bay* ☎ 869/466–8245 ⊕ *www.marshalls-stkitts.com* ⚖ *Reservations essential* ⊘ *No lunch.*

$$ ✕ **Reggae Beach Bar & Grill.** Treats at this popular daytime watering
ECLECTIC hole include honey-mustard ribs, coconut shrimp, grilled lobster, decadent banana bread pudding with rum sauce, and an array of tempting tropical libations. Business cards and pennants from around the world plaster the bar, and the open-air space is decorated with a variety of nautical accoutrements, from fishnets and turtle shells to painted wooden crustaceans. You can snorkel here, spot hawksbill turtles and the occasional monkey, visit the enormous house pig Wilbur (who once "ate" beer cans whole, then moved to "lite" beers—but feeding is no longer

encouraged), laze in a palm-shaded hammock, or rent a kayak, Hobie Cat or snorkeling gear. Beach chairs are free. Locals come Sunday afternoons for dancing to live bands. ⑤ *Average main: $21* ⌧ *S.E. Peninsula Rd., Cockleshell Beach* ☎ *869/762–5050* ⊕ *www.reggaebeachbar.com* ⊘ *No dinner.*

$$$$
ECLECTIC
★

✕ **Royal Palm.** A 65-foot, spring-fed pool bisects the elegant restaurant at Ottley's Plantation Inn into a semi-enclosed lounge with sea views and a breezy alfresco stone patio. Three-course extravaganzas (dishes are also available à la carte) blend indigenous ingredients with Asian, Mediterranean, Southwestern, and Latin touches: for example, butternut squash–chèvre ravioli in hazelnut brown butter; Malaysian fried lemon sole with roasted tomato–chili sambal (a condiment) over *nasi goreng* (fried rice); or marinated, grilled, flat-iron steak Bayamon with chipotle drizzle, African cream polenta, and avocado salsa. Finish with simple yet sinful indulgences such as coconut-cream cheesecake or mango mousse with raspberry coulis. The combination of superb food, artful presentation, romantic setting, and warm bonhomie is unbeatable. ⑤ *Average main: $66* ⌧ *Ottley's Plantation Inn, Ottley's* ☎ *869/465–7234* ⊕ *www.ottleys.com* ⌇ *Reservations essential.*

$$$
ECLECTIC
★

✕ **Serendipity.** This stylish restaurant occupies an old Creole home whose deck offers lovely views of Basseterre and the bay. As charming as the enclosed patio is, the interior lounge is more conducive to romantic dining, with cushy sofas, patterned hardwood floors, porcelain lamps, and African carvings. The menu reflects co-owner–chef Alexander James's peripatetic postings: you might start with wonderfully crispy fried Brie with sweet-and-sour blackberry sauce or beautifully presented spring rolls with plum-soy dipping sauce. Mahimahi crusted with cheddar, Parmesan, basil, and garlic floating on pools of creole and saffron cream sauces; or prosciutto-wrapped beef tenderloin topped with pâté, prosciutto slice, and Madeira sauce paired with tiger shrimp in garlic sauce typify the ambitious main courses. The wine list is well considered; vegetarians will be delighted by the many creative options; and very affordable lunches feature gargantuan tapas-style selections. ⑤ *Average main: $34* ⌧ *3 Wigley Ave., Fortlands, Basseterre* ☎ *869/465–9999* ⊕ *www.serendipitystkitts.com* ⌇ *Reservations essential* ⊘ *Closed Mon. No lunch weekends.*

$$$$
ECLECTIC
★

✕ **Spice Mill.** This beachfront beauty references the Caribbean's multiethnic cuisine, a melting pot of African, French, English, Iberian, Indian, Chinese, and Dutch influences. But the kitchen also stays home in proper locavore fashion, sourcing as much local produce as possible from Kittitian farmers and fishermen (who might troop through the restaurant with 30 just-caught snapper for "De Bossman"). Spice Mill merrily marries those gastronomic traditions with fresh ingredients, juxtaposing colors, tastes, and textures right from the dips served with scrumptious homemade breads. Panko-crusted crab cake might be served with mango-lemon aioli and green papaya ceviche. Confit of duck leg brilliantly contrasts sweet and savory: pumpkin, braised celery, and orange sauce. The culinary globe-trotting approach also dictates the decor—a mix of regional (coconut-wood-top bar, Carib canoe, and crayfish baskets from Dominica) and cosmopolitan (white beach beds, cushioned couches) elements, making even the bar (open daily and serving light snacks) a barefoot-chic hangout. Lunch is considerably cheaper and more island-flavored. $ *Average main: $33* ⊠ *Cockleshell Beach* ☎ *869/465–6455* ⊕ *www.spicemillrestaurant.com* ⌦ *Reservations essential* ☉ *Closed Sun. No dinner Mon.*

$$
SEAFOOD
★

✕ **Sprat Net.** This simple cluster of picnic tables—sheltered by a brilliant-turquoise corrugated-tin roof and decorated with driftwood, life preservers, photos of coastal scenes, and fishnets—sits on a sliver of sand. Nonetheless, it's an island hot spot. There's nothing fancy on the menu: just grilled fish, lobster, ribs, and chicken served with mountains of coleslaw and peas and rice. But the fish is amazingly fresh: the fishermen–owners heap their catches on a center table from which you choose your own dinner, then watch it grilled to your specification before dining family-style on paper plates. An adjacent hut serves up the final food group: pizza, Wednesday–Sunday. Sprat Net offers old-style Caribbean flavor, with the cheapest drinks and best bands on weekends. No wonder cars line up along the road, creating an impromptu jump-up. $ *Average main: $15* ⊠ *Main Road, Old Road Town* ☎ *869/466–7535* ▭ *No credit cards* ☉ *Closed Sep. No lunch.*

WHERE TO STAY

St. Kitts has an appealing variety of places to stay—beautifully restored plantation inns (where a meal plan including afternoon tea in addition to breakfast and dinner is the norm), full-service, affordable hotels, simple beachfront cottages, and all-inclusive resorts. There are also several guesthouses and self-serve condos. Increasing development has been touted (or threatened) for years. At this writing, the ultraritzy Park Hyatt is still in negotiations to debut its first Caribbean property on Cockleshell Bay, alongside oft-delayed upscale villa compounds such as the culture-oriented, ecocentric Kittitian Hills (architect Bill Bensley designed some of Thailand's most remarkable resorts), several golf courses, and the $17 million Beaumont Park horse-racing venue (itself part of a megadevelopment on the island's northwest end). The island's first large hotel, the St. Kitts Marriott Resort, plans to add 270 condos by late 2012, but any upcoming developments are all fewer than 300 units, including the sparkling 185-unit Ocean's Edge condo complex on Frigate Bay and deluxe properties such as the grand Christophe Harbour development that will sprawl elegantly across the Southeast Peninsula replete with spectacular villas, beach clubs, celebrity restaurants, megayacht marina, Tom Fazio–designed golf course, and boutique hotels (perhaps a Mandarin Oriental).

For expanded reviews, facilities, and current deals, visit Fodors.com.

$
RESORT

⊞ **Bird Rock Beach Resort.** This basic scuba-set resort crowns a bluff above Basseterre, delivering amazing views of the town, sea, and mountains from every vantage point. **Pros:** exuberant, friendly clientele; great diving; excellent value; superb views. **Cons:** small man-made beach; insufficient parking; difficult for physically challenged to maneuver; several rooms leased longterm to students; poor lighting; dilapidated decor. **TripAdvisor:** "great place to stay," "friends for life," "good diving."

⑤ *Rooms from: $105* ✉ *2 miles (3 km) east of Basseterre, Basseterre Bay* ☎ *869/465–8914, 877/244–6285* ⊕ *www.birdrockbeach.com* ↝ *30 rooms, 18 studios* ⎜○⎜ *No meals.*

$
HOTEL
▥ **Frigate Bay Resort.** This cheery property's combination of location, value, and polite service compensates for dowdy decor and dire need for minor repairs throughout. **Pros:** terrific value; easy walk to beaches; pretty pool spanned by gazebo and bridge; plentiful year-round deals; sofa beds and easily combined units ideal for families. **Cons:** no direct beachfront; slightly dilapidated; occasionally noisy; uneven food; Wi-Fi signal intermittent. **TripAdvisor:** "very impressed with the rooms," "wonderful oasis," "holiday in paradise." ⑤ *Rooms from: $145* ✉ *Frigate Bay, St. Kitts* ☎ *869/465–8935, 800/266–2185* ⊕ *www.frigatebay.com* ↝ *40 rooms, 24 studios* ⎜○⎜ *No meals.*

$
HOTEL
▥ **Ocean Terrace Inn.** Referred to by locals as OTI, this is a rarity: a smart, intimate business hotel that nonetheless appeals to vacationers. **Pros:** excellent service; fine facilities for a small hotel; good restaurants; walking distance to Basseterre attractions and restaurants; suites represent excellent value for families. **Cons:** must drive to beaches; sprawling layout; some rooms need sprucing up; difficult for physically challenged to navigate. **TripAdvisor:** "very clean," "surrounded by vegetation and waterfalls," "great views and staff." ⑤ *Rooms from: $135* ✉ *Wigley Ave., Fortlands* ☎ *869/465–2754, 800/524–0512* ⊕ *www.oceanterraceinn.com* ↝ *69 rooms, 8 condos* ⎜○⎜ *Multiple meal plans.*

$$$
HOTEL
Fodor'sChoice
★
▥ **Ottley's Plantation Inn.** You're treated like a beloved relative rather than a commercial guest at this quintessential Caribbean hotel, formerly a sugar plantation, at the foot of Mt. Liamuiga. **Pros:** posh yet unpretentious luxury; wonderfully helpful staff and owners; gorgeous gardens; excellent dining. **Cons:** no beach; bumpy access road; long walk from farthest cottages to office. **TripAdvisor:** "a gracious inn in a priceless location," "the most relaxing holiday ever," "rainforest hospitality." ⑤ *Rooms from: $244* ✉ *Ottley's, southwest of Nicola Town* ☎ *869/465–7234, 800/772–3039* ⊕ *www.ottleys.com* ↝ *24 rooms* ⎜○⎜ *Multiple meal plans.*

$$$
B&B/INN
▥ **Rawlins Plantation Inn.** Civilized serenity awaits at this remote plantation inn between verdant Mt. Liamuiga and the cobalt Caribbean. **Pros:** utter tranquillity; exquisite setting; fine kitchen; no TV. **Cons:** no beach; uneven service; no TV. **TripAdvisor:** "amazingly peaceful," "great getaway," "incredible dining experience." ⑤ *Rooms from: $354* ✉ *St. Paul's, St. Kitts* ☎ *869/465–6221, 888/790–5264* ⊕ *www.rawlinsplantation.com* ↝ *12 rooms* ⊗ *Closed Aug. and Sept.* ⎜○⎜ *Breakfast.*

$
B&B/INN
▥ **Rock Haven Bed & Breakfast.** This restful, cozy bed-and-breakfast, a two-minute drive from Frigate Bay beaches (airport transfers are included), provides true local warmth, courtesy of Judith and Keith Blake. **Pros:** genuine island hospitality; immaculately maintained; delicious breakfasts. **Cons:** long walk to beach; car recommended to get around. **TripAdvisor:** "best in comfort and hospitality," "breathtaking views," "delightful hosts." ⑤ *Rooms from: $179* ✉ *Frigate Bay, St. Kitts* ☎ *869/465–5503* ⊕ *www.rock-haven.com* ↝ *2 rooms* ⎜○⎜ *Breakfast.*

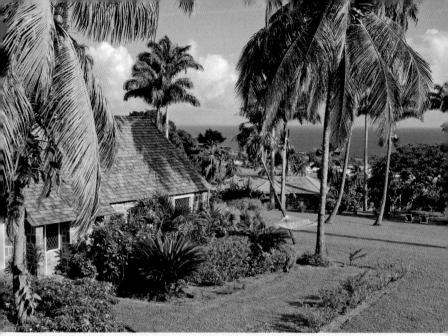

Ottley's Plantation Inn

$$ **St. Kitts Marriott Resort.** Although this big, bustling beachfront resort
RESORT offers something for everyone from families to conventioneers, golfers
to gamblers, it's overscaled for tiny, quiet St. Kitts and almost devoid of
Caribbean charm and flair, save for a jungle mural behind reception, an
odd pirate ship replica, and craft market hidden in the basement. **Pros:**
great range of activities; good bars; plentiful on-site duty-free shopping;
enormous main pool. **Cons:** impersonal, sometimes inefficient service;
surprise extra charges; mostly mediocre food; not enough units feature
ocean views. **TripAdvisor:** "lots of things to do," "a good all-around
resort," "great food." ⑤ *Rooms from: $259* ⊠ *858 Frigate Bay Rd.,
Frigate Bay* ☎ *869/466–1200, 800/223–6388* ⊕ *www.stkittsmarriott.
com* ⋑ *393 rooms, 76 suites* ⦿❙*No meals.*

$ **Sugar Bay Club.** This sprawling property borders Frigate Bay's wild
RESORT Atlantic side, offering varied accommodations in an architectural mish-
mash ranging from Creole-style cottages to cinder-block eyesores. **Pros:**
great value; family-friendly; on a lovely wild Atlantic beach; on-site
mini-mart; complimentary Wi-Fi. **Cons:** inadequate facilities compared
with most hotels its size; rough surf for kids; several units used for
student housing; some facilities shut down when resort isn't full. **Tri-
pAdvisor:** "very nice people," "nice property," "great hotel with a great
staff." ⑤ *Rooms from: $120* ⊠ *Frigate Bay, St. Kitts* ☎ *869/465–8037,
888/930–0055* ⊕ *www.sugarbayclub.com* ⋑ *72 rooms, 6 1-bedroom
cottages, 11 2-bedroom cottages* ⦿❙*No meals.*

$ **Timothy Beach Resort.** The only St. Kitts resort sitting directly on a
RENTAL Caribbean beach is incomparably located and restful, a great bud-
get find thanks to smiling service and simple but sizable apartments.
Pros: unbeatable location; close to the beach action; pleasant on-site

restaurant and bar; plentiful deals. **Cons:** occasionally worn decor; can hear beach bar music weekend nights; no view from most bedrooms. **TripAdvisor:** "excellent location," "nice getaway spot," "so relaxed." Ⓢ *Rooms from: $145* ✉ *1 South Frigate Bay Beach, Frigate Bay* ☎ *869/465–8597, 845/201–0047* ⊕ *www.timothybeach.com* ⤳ *60 apartments* ⦿ *No meals.*

NIGHTLIFE

Most nightlife revolves around the hotels, which host folkloric shows and calypso and steel bands of the usual limbo-rum-and-reggae variety. The growing Frigate Bay "strip" of beach bars, including Monkey Bar, Rainbow, Mr. X Shiggidy Shack, Inon's, Buddies Beach Hut, and Ziggy's, is the place to party hearty on weekend nights.

Bob & Elvis The Party Bus. A wild, wacky evening is promised by Bob & Elvis The Party Bus ("What Happens on the Bus....Stays on the Bus," reads the slogan) as they escort an increasingly raucous crowd via their psychedelically hued bus Wednesday and Friday to four of the island's top liming spots. ✉ *Frigate Bay* ☎ *869/466–8110* ⊕ *www. caribbeanjourneymasters.com/BobElvis.cfm.*

Look for such hard-driving local exponents of soca music as Nu-Vybes, Grand Masters, Small Axe, and Royalton 5; and "heavy dancehall" reggae group House of Judah. The Marriott's large, glitzy casino has table games and slots.

BARS AND CLUBS

Circus Grill. A favorite happy-hour watering hole is the Circus Grill, a second-floor eatery whose veranda offers views of the harbor and the activity on the Circus. ✉ *Bay Rd., Basseterre* ☎ *869/465–0143.*

Club Kactus. Club Kactus is jammed and jamming on most weekend nights, especially when respected Jamaican musical acts perform live. Its kitchen also turns out local fare with surprising flair. ✉ *Lighthouse, outside Basseterre by Bird Rock Beach Resort* ☎ *869/466–9016.*

★ **Keys Cigar Bar.** Keys Cigar Bar is a surprisingly low-key, classy hangout, with jazz-salsa duos, cushy sofas, high-back straw chairs, chess-set tables, and a superlative selection of aged rums and *Cubanos* (as well as top Dominican and Nicaraguan brands). If it's packed, try the hotel's Lobby Bar for tapas on tap and 'tinis with 'tude. ✉ *St. Kitts Marriott Resort, Frigate Bay* ☎ *869/466–1200.*

★ **Mr. X Shiggidy Shack.** Mr. X Shiggidy Shack is known for its sizzling Thursday-night bonfire parties replete with fire-eaters, raucous karaoke Saturday, and Sunday dinners accompanied by the MRT band; it's also a must-stop on locals' unofficial Friday-night liming circuit of Frigate Bay bars. ✉ *Frigate Bay* ☎ *869/762–3983, 869/465–0673* ⊕ *www. mrxshiggidyshack.com.*

SHOPPING

21

St. Kitts has limited shopping, but several duty-free shops offer good deals on jewelry, perfume, china, and crystal. Numerous galleries sell excellent paintings and sculptures. The batik fabrics, scarves, caftans, and wall hangings of Caribelle Batik are well known. British expat Kate Spencer is an artist who has lived on the island for years, reproducing its vibrant colors on everything from silk pareus (beach wraps) to note cards to place mats. Other good island buys include crafts, jams, and herbal teas. Don't forget to pick up some CSR (Cane Spirit Rothschild), which is distilled from fresh wild sugarcane right on St. Kitts. The Brinley Gold company has made a splash among spirits connoisseurs with its coffee, mango, coconut, lime, and vanilla rums (there is a tasting room at Port Zante).

AREAS AND MALLS

Most shopping plazas are in downtown Basseterre, on the streets radiating from the Circus.

All Kind of Tings. All Kind of Tings, a peppermint-pink edifice on Liverpool Row at College Street Ghaut, functions as a de facto vendors' market, where several booths sell local crafts and cheap T-shirts. Its courtyard frequently hosts folkloric dances, fashion shows, poetry readings, and steel-pan concerts. ⊠ *St. Kitts.*

Pelican Mall. The Pelican Mall—a shopping arcade designed to look like a traditional Caribbean street—has 26 stores, a restaurant, tourism offices, and a bandstand near the cruise-ship pier. ⊠ *St. Kitts.*

Port Zante. Directly behind Pelican Mall, on the waterfront, is Port Zante, the deepwater cruise-ship pier where a much-delayed upscale shopping–dining complex is becoming a 25-shop area (including the usual ubiquitous large jewelry concerns like Aboott's, Diamonds International, and Kay Jewelers); the **Amina Market** here is a fine source for cheap local crafts. If you're looking for inexpensive, island-y T-shirts and souvenirs, check out the series of vendors' huts behind Pelican Mall to the right of Port Zante as you face the sea. ⊠ *St. Kitts.*

Shoreline Plaza. Shoreline Plaza is next to the Treasury Building, right on Basseterre's waterfront. ⊠ *St. Kitts.*

TDC Mall. TDC Mall is just off the Circus in downtown, with a few boutiques and Chef's Garden for great local food in the a courtyard setting adorned with gingerbread and sports photos. ⊠ *St. Kitts.*

SPECIALTY ITEMS

ART

Booyork Gallery. Booyork Gallery is the atelier of Dennis Richards, who works in a remarkable range of mediums from pastels to papier-mâché, ceramics to collages: creative Carnival-inspired accessories (incorporating coconut husks, painted ostrich feathers, spangles, and beads), paintings on packed black sand, and wondrous watercolors, both figurative and abstract. Call ahead for appointments. ⊠ *Sir Lee Moore's Bldg., College St., Basseterre* ☎ *869/466–9159* ⊕ *www.booyork.com.*

Spencer Cameron Art Gallery. Spencer Cameron Art Gallery has reproductions of historical Caribbean island charts and prints, in addition to owner Rosey Cameron's popular Carnevale clown prints and a wide selection of exceptional artwork by Caribbean artists. It also showcases the work of Glass Island (exquisite Italianate art glass from frames to plates in sinuous shapes and seductive colors) and various local craftspeople. The gallery will mail anywhere. Rosey and Kate Spencer also run a new offshoot in the Marriott called the Art Cooperative. ⊠ *10 N. Independence Sq., Basseterre* ☎ *869/465–1617.*

HANDICRAFTS

★ **Caribelle Batik.** Caribelle Batik sells gloriously colored batik wraps, kimonos, caftans, T-shirts, dresses, wall hangings, and the like. ⊠ *Romney Manor, Old Road Town* ☎ *869/465–6253.*

Crafthouse. The Crafthouse is one of the best sources for local dolls, wood carvings, and straw work. ⊠ *Bay Rd., Southwell Industrial Site, ½ mile [1 km] east of Shoreline Plaza, Basseterre* ☎ *869/465–7754.*

Island Hopper. This is a good place for island crafts, especially wood carvings, pottery, textiles, and colorful resort wear, as well as humorous T-shirts and trinkets. ⊠ *The Circus, Basseterre* ☎ *869/465–2905.*

Fodor'sChoice **Kate Design.** This boutique showcases the highly individual style of
★ Kate Spencer, whose original paintings, serigraphs, note cards, and other pieces are available from her studio outside Rawlins Plantation. ⊠ *Mount Pleasant House, St. Paul's* ☎ *869/465–7740* ⊕ *www. katedesign.com.*

Potter's House. The atelier-home of Carla Astaphan, whose beautifully glazed ceramics and masks celebrate Afro-Caribbean heritage, also carries marvelous Haitian pieces. ⊠ *Camps Estate House, Camps Village* ☎ *869/465–5947.*

SPORTS AND ACTIVITIES

BOATING AND FISHING

Most operators are on the Caribbean side of Frigate Bay, known for its gentle currents. Turtle Bay offers stronger winds and stunning views of Nevis. Though not noted for big-game fishing, several steep offshore drop-offs do lure wahoo, barracuda, shark, tuna, yellowtail snapper, and mackerel. Rates are occasionally negotiable; figure approximately $350 for a four-hour excursion with refreshments.

Leeward Island Charters. The knowledgeable Todd Leypoldt of Leeward Island Charters takes you out on his charter boats, *Spirit of St. Kitts, Caona* and *Eagle.* He's also available for snorkeling charters, beach picnics, and sunset-moonlight cruises. ⊠ *Basseterre* ☎ *869/465–7474* ⊕ *www.stkittsleewardislandcharters.com.*

Mr. X Watersports. Located within Mr. X Shiggidy Shack *(⇨ see Nightlife above),* this shop rents small craft, including motorboats (waterskiing and jet skiing are available). Paddleboats are $15 per hour, sailboats (with one free lesson) $25 per hour. Deep-sea fishing charters, snorkeling tours, water taxis, sunset dinner cruises, and private charters with captain and crew are available. Mr. X and his cohorts are usually hanging out at the adjacent open-air Monkey Bar. ⊠ *Frigate Bay* ☎ *869/465–0673* ⊕ *www.mrxshiggidyshack.com.*

Reggae Beach Bar & Grill. This establishment rents kayaks from the restaurant, offers sailing lessons, and can also arrange fishing trips. ⊠ *Cockleshell Beach* ☎ *869/762–5050* ⊕ *www.reggaebeachbar.com.*

DIVING AND SNORKELING

Though unheralded as a dive destination, St. Kitts has more than a dozen excellent sites, protected by several new marine parks. The surrounding waters feature shoals, hot vents, shallows, canyons, steep walls, and caverns at depths from 40 to nearly 200 feet. The St. Kitts Maritime Archaeological Project, which surveys, records, researches, and preserves the island's underwater treasures, has charted several hundred wrecks of galleons, frigates, and freighters dating back to the 17th century. **Bloody Bay Reef** is noted for its network of underwater grottoes daubed with purple anemones, sienna bristle worms, and canary-yellow sea fans that seem to wave you in. **Coconut Tree Reef,** one of the largest in the area, includes sea fans, sponges, and anemones, as well as the Rocks, three enormous boulders with impressive multilevel diving. The only drift-dive site, **Nags Head,** has strong currents, but experienced divers might spot gliding rays, lobsters, turtles, and reef sharks. Since it sank in 50 feet of water in the early 1980s, the *River Taw* makes a splendid site for less experienced divers. **Sandy Point Reef** has been designated a National Marine Park and includes Paradise Reef, with swim-through 90-foot sloping canyons, and Anchors Away, where anchors have been encrusted with coral formations. The 1985 wreck of the *Talata* lies in 70 feet of water; barracudas, rays, groupers, and grunts dart through its hull.

Dive St. Kitts. This PADI–NAUI facility offers competitive prices, computers to maximize time below, wide range of courses from refresher to technical, and friendly, laid-back dive masters. The Bird Rock location features superb shore diving (unlimited when you book packages): common sightings 20 to 30 feet out include octopuses, nurse sharks, manta and spotted eagle rays, sea horses, even barracudas George and Georgianna. It also offers kayak and snorkeling tours. ⊠ *2 miles [3 km] east of Basseterre, Frigate Bay* ☎ *869/465–1189, 869/465–8914* ⊕ *www.divestkitts.com.*

Kenneth's Dive Center. Kenneth Samuel, the owner of this a PADI company, takes small groups of divers with C cards to nearby reefs. Rates average $70 for single-tank dives, $95 for double-tank dives; add $10 for equipment. Night dives, including lights, are $80–$90, and snorkeling trips (four-person minimum) are $40, drinks included. After 25 years' experience, former fisherman Samuel is considered an old pro (Jean-Michel Cousteau requested his guidance upon his first visit in the 1990s) and strives to keep groups small and prices reasonable. ⊠ *Bay Rd., Newtown* ☎ *869/465–2670* ⊕ *www.kennethdivecenter.com.*

Pro-Divers. Owned by Auston Macleod, PADI-certified dive master–instructor, this outfitter offers resort and certification courses running $125–$450. Dive computers are included gratis. He offers free introductory scuba courses Sunday–Thursday at 10 am at the Marriott, and a $30 Bubblemaker PADI course for kids eight and younger. He also takes groups to snorkeling sites accessible only by boat via his custom-built

38-foot catamaran. ⊠ *Ocean Terrace Inn, Basseterre* ☎ *869/660–3483* ⊕ *www.prodiversstkitts.com.*

GOLF

St. Kitts hopes to market itself as a golf destination with the remodeling of the Royal St. Kitts Golf Course and two upcoming resort and villa developments that include 18-hole courses, one designed by Tom Fazio (which promises to be one of the Caribbean's most spectacular, with huge elevation drops, ruins, extraordinary sweeping vistas, carries over ravines: "Scottsdale meets Pebble Beach"), another by Ian Woosnam.

Royal St. Kitts Golf Club. This 18-hole, par-71 links-style championship course underwent a complete redesign by Thomas McBroom to maximize Caribbean and Atlantic views and increase the challenge (there are 12 lakes and 83 bunkers). Holes 15 through 17 (the latter patterned after Pebble Beach No. 18) skirt the Atlantic in their entirety, lending new meaning to the term sand trap. The sudden gusts, wide but twisting fairways, and extremely hilly terrain demand pinpoint accuracy and finesse, yet holes such as 18 require pure power. Greens fees are $150 for Marriott guests in high season, $180 for nonguests, with twilight and super-twilight discounts. The development includes practice bunkers, a putting green, a short-game chipping area, and the fairly high-tech Royal Golf Academy. ⊠ *St. Kitts Marriott Resort, Frigate Bay* ☎ *869/466–2700, 866/785–4653* ⊕ *www.royalstkittsgolfclub.com.*

GUIDED TOURS

The taxi driver who picks you up will probably offer to act as your guide to the island. Each driver is knowledgeable and does a three-hour tour of Nevis for $75 or a four-hour tour of St. Kitts for $80. He can also make a lunch reservation at one of the plantation restaurants, and you can incorporate this into your tour.

Kantours. On St. Kitts, Kantours offers comprehensive general island tours, as well as a variety of specialty excursions, including ATV expeditions. ⊠ *St. Kitts* ☎ *869/465–2098, 869/465–3054 in St. Kitts, 869/469–0136 in Nevis* ⊕ *www.kantours.com.*

Tropical Tours. The friendly guides at Tropical Tours can run you around St. Kitts (from $27 per person), arrange kayaking and snorkeling, deep-sea fishing (from $135 per person), and take you to the volcano or rain forest for $52 per person and up. ⊠ *St. Kitts* ☎ *869/465–4167* ⊕ *www.tropicalstkitts-nevis.com.*

HIKING

Trails in the central mountains vary from easy to don't-try-it-by-your-self. Monkey Hill and Verchild's Peak aren't difficult, although the Verchild's climb will take the better part of a day. Don't attempt Mt. Liamuiga without a guide. You'll start at Belmont Estate—at the west end of the island—on horseback, and then proceed on foot to the lip of the crater, at 2,600 feet. You can go down into the crater—1,000 feet deep and 1 mile (1½ km) wide, with a small freshwater lake—clinging to vines and roots and scaling rocks, even trees. Expect to get muddy. There are several fine operators (each hotel recommends its favorite); tour rates generally range from $50 for a rain-forest walk to $95 for a volcano expedition and usually include round-trip transportation from your hotel and picnic lunch.

★ **Duke of Earl's Adventures.** Owner Earl of Duke is as entertaining as his nickname suggests—and his prices are slightly cheaper ($45 for a rainforest tour includes refreshments, $70 volcano expeditions add lunch; hotel pickup and drop-off is complimentary). He genuinely loves his island and conveys that enthusiasm, encouraging hikers to swing on vines or sample unusual-looking fruits during his rain-forest trip. He also conducts a thorough volcano tour to the crater's rim and a drive-through ecosafari tour ($50 with lunch). ⊠ *St. Kitts* ☎ *869/465–1899, 869/663–0994.*

Greg's Safaris. Greg Pereira of Greg's Safaris, whose family has lived on St. Kitts since the early 19th century, takes groups on half-day trips into the rain forest and on full-day hikes up the volcano and through the grounds of a private 18th-century great house. The rain-forest trips include visits to sacred Carib sites, abandoned sugar mills, and an excursion down a 100-foot coastal canyon containing a wealth of Amerindian petroglyphs. The Off the Beaten Track 4x4 Plantation Tour provides a thorough explanation of the role sugar and rum played in the Caribbean economy and colonial wars. He and his staff relate fascinating historical, folkloric, and botanical information. ⊠ *St. Kitts* ☎ *869/465–4121* ⊕ *www.gregsafaris.com.*

HORSEBACK RIDING

Wild North Frigate Bay and desolate Conaree Beach are great for riding, as is the rain forest.

Trinity Stables. Guides from Trinity Stables offer beach rides ($50) and trips into the rain forest ($60), both including hotel pickup. The latter is intriguing, as guides discuss plants' medicinal properties along the way (such as sugarcane to stanch bleeding) and pick oranges right off a tree to squeeze fresh juice. Otherwise, the staffers are cordial but shy; this isn't a place for beginners' instruction. ⊠ *St. Kitts* ☎ *869/465–3226.*

SEA EXCURSIONS

In addition to the usual snorkeling, sunset, and party cruises (ranging in price from $40 to $95), most companies offer whale-watching excursions during the winter migrating season, January through April.

Blue Water Safaris. Blue Water Safaris offers half-day snorkeling trips or beach barbecues on deserted cays, as well as sunset and moonlight cruises on its 65-foot catamarans *Irie Lime* and *Swaliga*, and the smaller *Falcon*. It also runs kayaking tours. ⊠ *Basseterre* ☎ *869/466–4933* ⊕ *www.bluewatersafaris.com.*

Leeward Island Charters. This reliable charter offers day and overnight charters on two catamarans—the 67-foot *Eagle* and 78-foot *Spirit of St. Kitts*. Day sails are from 9:30 to 4:30 and include a barbecue, an open bar, and use of snorkeling equipment. The Nevis trip stops at Pinney's Beach for a barbecue and at Shooting Bay, a tiny cove in the bullying shadow of a sheer cliff, where petrels and frigate birds inspect your snorkeling skills. The crews are mellow, affable, and knowledgeable about island life. ⊠ *Basseterre* ☎ *869/465–7474* ⊕ *www.stkittsleewardislandcharters.com.*

ZIP-LINING

☾ **Sky Safari Tours.** On these popular tours would-be Tarzans and Janes whisk through the "Valley of the Giants" (so dubbed for the towering trees) at speeds up to 50 mph (80 kph along five cable lines); the longest (nicknamed "The Boss") stretches 1,350 feet through towering turpentine and mahogany trees draped thickly with bromeliads, suspended 250 feet above the ground. Following the Canadian-based company's mantra of "faster, higher, safer," it uses a specially designed trolley with secure harnesses attached. Many of the routes afford unobstructed views of Brimstone Hill and the sea beyond. The outfit emphasizes environmental and historical aspects. Guides provide nature interpretation and commentary, and the office incorporates Wingfield Estate's old sugar plantation, distillery, and church ruins, which visitors can explore. Admission is usually $65–$75, depending on the tour chosen. It's open daily 9–6, with the first and last tours departing at 10 and 3. ⊠ *Wingfield Estate* ☎ *869/466–4259, 869/465–4347* ⊕ *www.skysafaristkitts.com.*

NEVIS

Nevis's charm is its rusticity: there are no traffic lights, goats still amble through the streets of Charlestown, and local grocers announce whatever's in stock on a blackboard (anything from pig snouts to beer).

EXPLORING NEVIS

Nevis's Main Road makes a 21-mile (32-km) circuit through the five parishes; various offshoots of the road wind into the mountains. You can tour Charlestown, the capital, in a half hour or so, but you'll need three to four hours to explore the entire island.

Bath Springs. The Caribbean's first hotel, the Bath Hotel, built by businessman John Huggins in 1778, was so popular in the 19th century that visitors, including such dignitaries as Samuel Taylor Coleridge and Prince William Henry, traveled two months by ship to "take the waters" in the property's hot thermal springs. It suffered extensive hurricane and probably earthquake damage over the years and languished in disrepair until recently. Local volunteers have cleaned up the spring and built a stone pool and steps to enter the waters; now residents and visitors enjoy the springs, which range from 104°F to 108°F, though signs still caution that you bathe at your own risk, especially if you have heart problems. The development houses the Nevis Island Administration offices; there's still talk of adding massage huts, changing rooms, a restaurant, and a cultural center and historic exhibit on the original hotel property. Follow Main Street south from Charlestown. ⊠ *Charlestown outskirts* ☎ *No phone.*

★ **Botanical Gardens of Nevis.** In addition to terraced gardens and arbors, this remarkable 7.8-acre site in the glowering shadow of Mt. Nevis has natural lagoons, streams, and waterfalls, superlative bronze mermaids, egrets and herons, and extravagant fountains. You can find a proper rose garden, sections devoted to orchids and bromeliads, cacti, and flowering trees and shrubs—even a bamboo garden. The entrance to the Rain Forest Conservatory—which attempts to include every conceivable Caribbean ecosystem and then some—duplicates an imposing Maya temple. A splendid re-creation of a plantation-style great house contains a café with sweeping sea views, and the upscale Galleria shop selling art, textiles, jewelry, and Indonesian teak furnishings sourced during the owners' world travels. ⊠ *Montpelier Estate* ☎ *869/469–3509* ⊕ *www.botanicalgardennevis.com* ⊠ *$13* ⊙ *Mon.–Sat. 9–4.*

★ **Charlestown.** About 1,200 of Nevis's 10,000 inhabitants live in the capital. If you arrive by ferry, as most people do, you'll walk smack onto Main Street from the pier. It's easy to imagine how tiny Charlestown, founded in 1660, must have looked in its heyday. The weathered buildings still have fanciful galleries, elaborate gingerbread fretwork, wooden shutters, and hanging plants. The stone building with the clock tower (1825, but mostly rebuilt after a devastating 1873 fire) houses the courthouse and second-floor **library** (a cool respite on sultry days). The little park next to the library is Memorial Square, dedicated to the fallen of World Wars I and II. Down the street from the square, archaeologists have discovered the remains of a Jewish cemetery and synagogue (Nevis reputedly had the Caribbean's second-oldest congregation), but there's little to see.

Alexander Hamilton Birthplace. The Alexander Hamilton Birthplace, which contains the Hamilton **Museum**, sits on the waterfront. This bougainvillea-draped Georgian-style house is a reconstruction of what is believed to have been the American patriot's original home, built in 1680 and likely destroyed during a mid-19th earthquake. Born here in 1755, Hamilton moved to St. Croix when he was about 12. He moved to the American colonies to continue his education at 17; he became George Washington's Secretary of the Treasury and died in a duel with political rival Aaron Burr in 1804. The Nevis House of Assembly occupies the second floor; the museum downstairs contains Hamilton memorabilia, documents pertaining to the island's history, and displays on island geology, politics, architecture, culture, and cuisine. The gift shop is a wonderful source for historic maps, crafts, and books on Nevis. ⊠ *Low St., Charlestown* ☎ *869/469–5786* ⊕ *www.nevis-nhcs.org* ⊠ *$5, with admission to Nelson Museum of Nevis History $7* ⊙ *Weekdays 9–4, Sat. 9–noon* ⊠ *Nevis.*

Eden Brown Estate. This government-owned mansion, built around 1740, is known as Nevis's haunted house, or haunted ruins. In 1822 a Miss Julia Huggins was to marry a fellow named Maynard. However, come wedding day, the groom and his best man killed each other in a duel. The bride-to-be became a recluse, and the mansion was closed down. Local residents claim they can feel the presence of "someone" whenever they go near the eerie old house with its shroud of weeds and wildflowers. Though memorable more for the story than the hike or ruins, it's always open, and it's free. ⊠ *East Coast Rd., between Lime Kiln and Mannings, Eden Brown Bay* ☎ *No phone.*

Mt. Nevis rising behind the Botanical Gardens of Nevis

Mansa's Farm. Anyone who wants a real sense of island daily life and subsistence should call Mervin "Mansa" Tyson. He'll take you past his fruit trees and herb gardens through rows of tomatoes, cucumbers, string beans, eggplant, zucchini, sweet pepper, melons, and more. Discussing the needs for at least partial organic growing practices, he passionately explains how he adapted traditional folk pesticides and describes the medicinal properties of various plants, cultivated and wild. He'll prepare a lunch using his produce, including delectable refreshing fruit drinks at his Mansa's Last Stand grocery across from the beach. Weekend barbecues are a highlight. All in all, this agritourism foray redefines food for thought. ⊠ *Cades Bay* ☎ *869/469–8520* ☒ *Varies* ☉ *Call for appointment.*

Nelson Museum of Nevis History. Purportedly this is the Western Hemisphere's largest collection of Lord Horatio Nelson memorabilia, including letters, documents, paintings, and even furniture from his flagship. Nelson was based in Antigua but came on military patrol to Nevis, where he met and eventually married Frances Nisbet, who lived on a 64-acre plantation here. Half the space is devoted to often-provocative displays on island life, from leading families to vernacular architecture to the adaptation of traditional African customs, from cuisine to Carnival. The shop is an excellent source for gifts, from homemade soaps to historical guides. ⊠ *Bath Rd. outside, Charlestown* ☎ *869/469–0408* ⊕ *www.nevis-nhcs. org* ☒ *$5, with Hamilton Museum $7* ☉ *Weekdays 9–4, Sat. 9–noon.*

St. John's Figtree Church. Among the records of this church built in 1680 is a tattered, prominently displayed marriage certificate that reads "Horatio Nelson, Esquire, to Frances Nisbet, Widow, on March 11, 1787." ⊠ *Church Ground* ☎ *No phone.*

WHERE TO EAT

Dinner options range from intimate meals at plantation guesthouses (where the menu is often prix fixe) to casual eateries. Seafood is ubiquitous, and many places specialize in West Indian fare. The island is trying to raise its profile as a fine-dining destination by holding NICHE (Nevis International Culinary Heritage Exposition), a gastronomic festival with guest chefs and winemakers offering cooking seminars and tastings during the second half of October.

What to Wear. Dress is casual at lunch, although beach attire is unacceptable. Dress pants and sundresses are appropriate for dinner.

$$$ ✗ **Bananas.** Peripatetic English owner Gillian Smith has held jobs with
ECLECTIC Disney and Relais & Châteaux, and everything about Bananas (read
★ lovably nuts) borrows from her wildly diverse experiences. Even the setting is delightfully deceptive: the classic stone, brick, and wood plantation great house nestled amid extravagant gardens was painstakingly built by Gillian herself in 2006. Her fun, funky, shabby-chic sensibility informs every aspect of the restaurant. The colonial look (pith helmets, steamer trunks, beamed ceiling, white wicker, chandeliers dangling from the corrugated tin roof) contrasts with Turkish kilims, Moroccan lamps, and whimsical touches like a lighted tailor's dummy and antique tennis rackets. The food is equally eclectic and globe-trotting, running from bourbon-glazed ribs to lobster tails with pineapple-ginger salsa. Despite the improvisational ambience, there's no monkeying around with quality at Bananas. $ *Average main: $26* ✉ *Upper Hamilton Estate* ☎ *869/469–1891* ⊕ *www.bananasrestaurantnevis.com* ⌚ *Reservations essential* ⊘ *Closed Sun. and Thurs.*

$$$$ ✗ **Coconut Grove.** This thatched-palm roof–and–rough timber structure
ECLECTIC sports a sensuous South Seas look, best appreciated on the deck as the
★ sun fireballs across the Caribbean. Inside, handsome teak furnishings are animated by Buddhas, parrot-hue throw pillows, batik hangings, and gauzy curtains. The service is warm, the champagne is properly chilled, and the splendid Pacific Rim–Mediterranean fusion fare seems designed to complement the admirable wine selection—with 8,000 bottles it is second on the sister islands only to that of the Four Seasons—rather than the other way around. Owners Gary and Karin Colt often bring winemaker friends in from Europe for tastings and dinners. Stephen "Chef Steve" Smith, a CIA grad and registered dietitian, introduced heart-healthier options such as curry-scented pumpkin soup with fat-free soy cream, grilled line-catch-of-the-day with pumpkin mash and sour-orange beurre-blanc foam, and a miraculously fiber-licious 100-calorie whole-wheat-flour–and–black-bean brownie sweetened with agave syrup. Nonetheless, Gary (who likes his indulgences) laughs, "We're not the food police"; hence the menu includes the likes of burger en brioche with homemade duck foie gras and baby Camembert baked in pear brandy with cranberry confiture. Happy hour, 11 pm–midnight, often ushers in impromptu dancing, continuing the "Bali high" theme. The downstairs "Coco Beach" is hip-hopping and happening with infinity pool for use, sensational St. Kitts views, affordable, creative, lighter daytime fare (try ceviche made—and caught—by sous chef Matt Lloyd,

or wondrous watermelon gazpacho goosed with basil), and live music many evenings. $ *Average main: $38* ✉ *Nelson's Spring, Pinney's Beach* ☎ *869/469–1020* ⊕ *www.coconutgroverestaurantnevis.com* ⚭ *Reservations essential* ⊘ *Closed Aug.–Oct.*

$$$$
STEAKHOUSE
Fodor'sChoice
★

✕ **Coral Grill.** The most ambitious aspect of the Four Seasons' renovation was the "de-formalizing" of its restaurants, most notably the unlikely but wildly successful conversion of its former haute Dining Room into a stunning steak house. Yet it eschews the genre's typical men's-club decor, lightening and brightening the original's imposing space. The graceful patio, beamed cathedral ceilings, flagstone hearth, and parquet floors remain; yet an open contemporary lounge that wouldn't be out of place in SoHo or Santa Monica now bisects the vast interior. Exquisite, deceptively simple appetizers include popcorn shrimp with red pepper dip or by-the-book beef tartare. But you're here for the grilled items, from Wagyu steak that dissolves in your mouth to intensely flavored yet meltingly tender Berkridge Kurobata pork chops to gossamer lobster tails. Corn-fed USDA prime cuts are Black Diamond–labeled, sourced from select Midwest farms. Meats are served with a choice of Shiraz reduction, béarnaise, or chimichurri; seafood with saffron sauce, lemongrass-coriander vinaigrette, or citrus hollandaise. Or dip into one of several flavored butters. The must extravagance is the Parillada, $65 per person for two (enough to feed a family). The hotel can arrange a unique interactive dive-and-dine experience, plunging you into the deep to pluck lobster and other marine creatures that the chefs will cook for you later. The phone-book-size wine list is admirably comprehensive with some surprisingly fair prices. Friday-night beach barbecues are deliciously hedonistic. $ *Average main: $46* ✉ *Four Seasons Nevis, Pinney's Beach* ☎ *869/469–1111, 869/469–6238* ⊕ *www.fourseasons.com/nevis* ⚭ *Reservations essential* ⊘ *No lunch.*

$$
SEAFOOD
★

✕ **Double Deuce.** Mark Roberts, the former chef at Montpelier, decided to chuck the "five-star lifestyle" and now co-owns this jammed, jamming beach bar, which lures locals with fine, fairly priced fare, creative cocktails, and a Hemingway-esque feel (the shack is plastered with sailing and fishing pictures, as well as Balinese masks, steer horns, license plates, and wind chimes). Peer behind the ramshackle bar and you'll find a gleaming modern kitchen where Mark (and fun-loving firebrand partner Lyndeta) prepare sublime seafood he often catches himself, as well as organic beef burgers, velvety pumpkin soup, creative pastas, and lip-smacking ribs. The "DD" is as cool and mellow as it gets. Stop by for free Wi-Fi and proper espresso, a game of pool, riotous Thursday-night karaoke, or just to hang out with a Double Deuce Stinger (Lyndy's answer to Sunshine's Killer Bee punch). You'll find more than 5,000 songs on the "jukebox"—Akon to ZZ Top, Sarah Vaughan to Van Morrison; if you can't find your favorite, the "DJ" will download it for you while you take a quick dip. Dinner can be arranged for parties of 6 to 10. $ *Average main: $20* ✉ *Pinney's Beach* ☎ *869/469–2222* ⊕ *www.doubledeucenevis.com* ⚭ *Reservations essential* ▬ *No credit cards* ⊘ *Closed Mon.*

$$
SEAFOOD

✕ **Gallipot.** Gallipot attracts locals with ultrafresh seafood at reasonable prices, marvelous views of St. Kitts across the road, and sensational sunsets. Large Sunday lunches with ample portions (musts are lobster eggs Benedict and classic roast beef and Yorkshire pudding) are a big draw. The Fosberys originally built the octagonal bar as an addition to their small beach house down the road, and their daughter and son-in-law, Tracy and Julian Rigby, provide the catch (fishnets and photos from their sportfishing championships grace the bar). Julian built a smoker (Tracy dubs it "the eyesore"), where he cures melt-in-your-mouth wahoo, kingfish, and sailfish carpaccio. Those seeking land specialties can happily tuck into the smoked duck, steak-and-kidney pie, or chicken korma curry, seasoned with herbs from Tracy's garden. $ *Average main: $22* ⊠ *Jones Bay* ☎ *869/469–8230* ⊕ *www.gallipotnevis.com* ⊙ *Closed Mon.–Wed. No dinner Sun.*

$$$
ECLECTIC
★
✕ **Hermitage Plantation Inn.** After cocktails in the inn's antiques-filled parlor (the knockout rum punches are legendary), dinner is served on the veranda. Many ingredients are harvested from the inn's herb garden, fruit trees, piggery, and livestock collection; the scrumptious cured meats, baked goods, preserves, and ice creams are homemade. Sumptuous dishes lovingly prepared by the incomparable (and delightfully named) chef Lovey Boddie and team might include breadfruit-cheddar soufflé, seafood quenelles in gossamer curry cream, lemongrass-lime fish cakes with ginger aioli, lobster with tomato-basil butter and conch stuffing, herb-crusted lamb with rosemary and guava, and passion fruit–ginger cheesecake. A traditional wood-burning oven yields savory items as well. Wednesday night pig roasts are an island must. The ever-growing wine list is exceptionally priced. Bon mots and bonhomie serve as prelude, intermezzo, and coda for a lively evening. $ *Average main: $32* ⊠ *Gingerland* ☎ *869/469–3477* ⊕ *www.hermitagenevis.com* ⚑ *Reservations essential.*

$$$
CARIBBEAN
✕ **Mango.** This casual beach bar at the Four Seasons is a perennial hot spot for locals and visitors, thanks to a gorgeous outdoor deck overlooking the illuminated water, sizzling music, fab drinks, hip decor, and a farm-to-table menu showcasing local ingredients, many grown by the staff. You can savor artfully presented, robustly flavored Caribbean classics such as cornmeal-dusted calamari with curry remoulade, herb-and-cinnamon cured wahoo with mango-soy dressing, Carib beer–battered flying fish with candied red onions and passion-fruit mayonnaise, and mouth- and eye-watering barbecued baby back ribs. The kitchen also delights with updated twists, such as ethereal coconut foam floating in silken, roasted-butternut-squash soup infused with ginger and cinnamon. $ *Average main: $25* ⊠ *Four Seasons Resort, Pinney's Beach* ☎ *869/469–1111, 869/469–6238.*

$$$$
CARIBBEAN
★
✕ **Miss June's Cuisine.** Dinner with Miss June Mestier, a dynamo originally from Trinidad, could never be called ordinary. The all-inclusive experience (held only once weekly, usually Wednesday) begins with cocktails in the ornate living room, followed by dinner in an elegant dining room where tables are set with mismatched china and crystal. Hors d'oeuvres and three courses, including soup and fish, are served. "Now that you've had dinner," Miss June proclaims, "let's have fun," and she presents a grand multidish feast highlighting her Trinidadian curries, local vegetable preparations, and meats. "I invite people into

my home for dinner and then my manager has the audacity to charge them as they leave!" quips Miss June, who joins guests (diners have included Oprah Winfrey, John Grisham, and members of Aerosmith) after dinner for coffee and brandy. Miss June won't kick you out, but she may ask you to turn the lights out as you leave. ⑤ *Average main: $65* ✉ *Jones Bay* ☎ *869/469–5330* ⚖ *Reservations essential* ⊘ *Closed Thurs.–Tues. No lunch.*

$$$$
ECLECTIC
★
╳ **Montpelier Plantation & Beach.** The Hoffman family (Muffin, son Tim, and daughter-in-law Meredith) presides over a scintillating evening, starting with canapés and cocktails in the civilized Great Room. Dinner is served on the breezy west veranda, which gazes serenely upon the lights of Charlestown and St. Kitts. The inventive executive chef, Kosta Staicoff, uses the inn's organic herb gardens and fruit trees to full advantage, while experimenting with molecular gastronomy to create playful foam and froth. The changing three-course menu might present lemongrass consommé with spiny lobster salpicon, braised pork shoulder with onion confit and coconut jus, and guava tartlet with carrot froth. Meredith has crafted an exemplary wine list perfectly matched to the cuisine. The Mill opens nightly with sufficient reservations, offering a different set four-course menu accompanied by champagne and sorbets. Torches light cobblestone steps up to this theatrical faux sugar mill with crystal sconces, floating candles, and an antique mahogany gear wheel suspended from the ceiling. Simpler lunches (order the lobster salad from the constantly changing menu) are served on the refreshing patio, while a tapestry of tapas is on tap for $4 to $15 per dish at the poolside Indigo. ⑤ *Average main: $60* ✉ *Montpelier Estate* ☎ *869/469–3462* ⊕ *www.montpeliernevis.com* ⚖ *Reservations essential* ⊘ *Closed late Aug.–early Oct.*

$$$
ECLECTIC
╳ **Mount Nevis Hotel & Beach Club.** Savor cocktails in the distinctive lounge (accented by sisal rugs, mosaic tiles, towering bamboo stalks, and flowers floating in crystal bowls). Then repair to the sublime open-air dining room, where a pianist holds forth on an illuminated stage by the pool with a splendid view of St. Kitts. The elegant yet light menu deftly blends local ingredients with a cornucopia of Caribbean-continental cuisines, artfully presented by Acapulco-born chef Vicente Zaragoza. Sterling starters on the ever-changing menu might be goat cheese and fire-roasted peppers on jerk foccacia or homemade conch ravioli in tomato-basil sauce. Worthy main courses include roast Cornish hen in caper-lime beurre blanc with polenta and grilled local tomatoes, or blackened red snapper in mango gastrique. There's always a fine vegetarian choice such as fresh mozzarella ovoline and tomato stack over local hydroponic greens. Finish with tropical variations on classics such as ginger crème brûlée or passion-fruit cheesecake. Vicente also runs the new, more affordable alfresco grill whose convection oven turns out marvelous baked goods in minutes. ⑤ *Average main: $28* ✉ *Shaws Rd., Mt. Nevis Estates* ☎ *869/469–9373* ⊕ *www.mountnevishotel.com* ⚖ *Reservations essential.*

$$$
ITALIAN
★
╳ **Neve.** It's difficult for a three-meal all-purpose resort restaurant to provide sophisticated ambience, but come evening Neve triumphantly transforms into a sleek, but not slick, Italian trattoria. The antipasti are

superb, from a classic caprese salad with homemade mozzarella and eggplant roulade to textbook tuna carpaccio. The kitchen scales the heights with its pizzas and pastas: gnocchi in sage butter sauce; black squid risotto with garlic-fried baby squid, pinot grigio reduction, and citrus gremolata; or a perfectly crispy *quattro stagioni* pie (double-smoked ham, marinated artichokes, white anchovies, black olives) that would be the envy of Chicago and Napoli. The fun, hip wine program showcases affordable Italian offerings on a cart: 14 reds, 14 whites, five Proseccos by the bottle, carafe, or glass. Finish with a tiramisu that would bring any Tuscan mamma to tears. $\boxed{S}$ *Average main: $28* ✉ *Four Seasons Nevis, Pinney's Beach* ☏ *869/469–1111, 869/469–6238* ⊕ *www.fourseasons.com/nevis* ⌖ *Reservations essential.*

$$$$ ✕ **Nisbet Plantation Beach Club.** The blissfully air-conditioned great house
ECLECTIC is an oasis of polished hardwood floors, mahogany and cherrywood furnishings, equestrian bronzes, antique hurricane lamps, wicker furnishings, portraits by famed Nevisian artist Eva Wilkin, and stone walls. Tables on the veranda look down the palm-tree-lined fairway to the sea. The four-course menu combines continental, Pacific Rim, and Caribbean cuisines with local ingredients. The more mature clientele dictates less complex options from house-cured gravlax to three-cheese tortellini marinara. But Filipino-born executive chef Antonio Piani might sneak in chicken-and-coconut dumpling soup, lobster ravioli in seafood Nantua sauce, and lemon-and-vanilla mascarpone mousse with hazelnut praline. Enjoy an impressively cosmopolitan selection of cocktails or coffee with silky-soft live music in the civilized front bar. Witty, dapper maître d' Patterson Fleming (his cravat collection, more than 1,000 augmented by guests over the years, is enviable!) ensures a smooth, swank experience. $\boxed{S}$ *Average main: $65* ✉ *Newcastle* ☏ *869/469–9325* ⊕ *www. nisbetplantation.com* ⌖ *Reservations essential.*

$$ ✕ **Riviere House.** Labor of love is redefined at this carefully restored and
ECLECTIC expanded colonial home with stately colonnades, gingerbread trim,
★ and luscious hues from lemon to lavender. Prices remain affordable to entice islanders; 20% of profits go to the local hospital—eat well and feel good about yourself. It doubles as de facto entertainment center, starting with live music on the brick patio. One wall pays tribute to great African(-American) leaders: Bob Marley, Mandela, Marcus Garvey, Martin Luther King Jr. The cinema, decorated with original posters and soundtrack LPs, features fantastic acoustics and regular screenings of classics. Another front room acts as gallery, including recycled-plastic mosaics and magnificent painterly photographs of Namibia by co-owner Annie Lupinacci. Meals are attractively presented, perhaps garnished with edible tarragon florets or swirls of balsamic vinaigrette. Among the standouts are splendidly chunky conch-corn chowder; braised free-range mutton (a revelation) over sautéed forest-grown breadfruit; and wonderfully aromatic portobello mushrooms served with roasted red pepper, polenta, and three-bean ragout, drizzled with cream-cashew sauce. Stewed for five hours, the meaty texture would convert even the most confirmed carnivore. Superlative lunch options range from curried chicken wrap with guacamole to lobster-spinach quiche. $\boxed{S}$ *Av-*

erage main: $21 ✉ *Government Rd., Charlestown* ☎ *869/469–7117* ⌂ *Reservations essential* ⊙ *Closed Sun. and Mon.*

$$$
ECLECTIC
✕ **The Rocks at Golden Rock.** Merely calling this glam eatery's tiered setting dramatic doesn't do justice to a genuine artistic and engineering masterpiece. Glass panels and ceilings (displaying the night sky while reflecting patio lights) open up the existing stone-and–ipe hardwood great house. A series of cascading waterfalls, chutes, limpid pools, lily ponds, and fountains filigree the surrounding civilized jungle with liquid silver. Strategically placed boulders resemble hulking Henry Moore sculpture; even the cut stone was painstakingly joined without mortar. Decor playfully contrasts classic and modern. A stone gazebo recalls an upside-down plantation-era copper boiler (the patio's barrel-vaulting also slyly mimics sugar equipment). Twisted metal chairs provide conversation pieces (not seating); splashes of red, orange, yellow, and slate blue enliven the chairs and long banquette. Contemporary and colonial artworks from Mali and Afghanistan grace the interior. Sadly the kitchen doesn't quite match the setting's splendor or creativity. But the atmosphere more than compensates, and solid choices include jerk pork with pineapple relish or pan-roasted snapper with crispy risotto cake and red-pepper coulis. ⑤ *Average main: $28* ✉ *Gingerland* ☎ *869/469–3346* ⊕ *www.golden-rock.com* ⌂ *Reservations essential* ⊙ *No lunch.*

$$
CARIBBEAN
✕ **Sunshine's.** Everything about this shack overlooking (and spilling onto) the beach is larger than life, including the Rasta man Llewelyn "Sunshine" Caines himself. Flags and license plates from around the world complement the international patrons (including an occasional movie or sports star wandering down from the Four Seasons). Picnic tables are splashed with bright sunrise-to-sunset colors; even the palm trees are painted, though "it gone upscaled," as locals say, with VIP cabanas. Fishermen cruise up with their catch—you might savor lobster rolls or snapper creole. Don't miss the lethal house specialty, Killer Bee rum punch. As Sunshine boasts, "One and you're stung, two, you're stunned, three, it's a knockout." ⑤ *Average main: $20* ✉ *Pinney's Beach* ☎ *869/469–5817.*

WHERE TO STAY

Most lodgings are in restored manor or plantation houses scattered throughout the island's five parishes (counties). The owners often live at these inns, and it's easy to feel as if you've been personally invited down for a visit. Before dinner you may find yourself in the drawing room having a cocktail and conversing with the family, other guests, or visitors who have come for a meal. Meal plans for most inns include breakfast and dinner (plus afternoon tea) and offer a free shuttle service to their "private" stretch of beach. If you require TVs and air-conditioning, you're better off staying at hotels and simply dining with the engaging inn owners. A collection of 24 smart, spacious, two- to four-bedroom units called Nelson Spring Beach Villas & Spa (at the eponymous historic site, just north of Pinney's Beach) is a worthy addition, though rentals are usually by the week. All units include washer/dryer, kitchen, private garage, and modern amenities; the property features a small spa and the reasonably priced, festive Yachtsman Grill

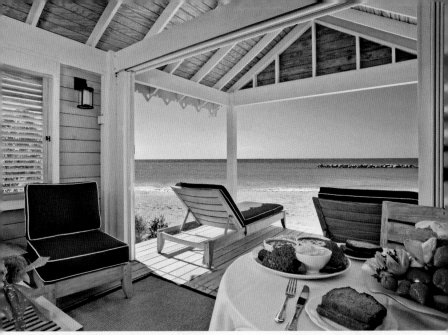

Four Seasons Resort Nevis

restaurant (though ownership squabbles may force it to move). Other small upscale compounds are in various stages of development, including the overhauled Cliffdwellers at Tamarind Bay (site of Marshall's Nevis restaurant) and the Zenith Beach houses, connected with the delightful Chrishi Beach Club on Cades Bay.

For expanded reviews, facilities, and current deals, visit Fodors.com.

$$$$
RESORT
☕
Fodor's Choice
★

Four Seasons Resort Nevis. This beachfront beauty impeccably combines world-class elegance with West Indian hospitality while scrupulously maintaining and upgrading facilities. **Pros:** luxury without attitude; superlative service; marvelous food; dazzling golf and spa; each building block has a washer/dryer, and room amenities include free detergent. **Cons:** pricey; sometimes overrun by conventions, incentive groups (off-season mainly), and families; long walk from farthest rooms to lobby and restaurants; berms added as secondary defense against storm surges impede some beachfront room views; inconveniently placed electrical outlets. **TripAdvisor:** "Caribbean perfection," "heavenly from start to finish," "off the beaten path." ⑤ *Rooms from: $595* ✉ *Pinney's Beach* ☎ *869/469–1111, 869/469–6238, 800/332–3442 in U.S., 800/268–6282 in Canada* ⊕ *www.fourseasons.com* ⤴ *179 rooms, 17 suites, 61 villas* ⑩ *No meals.*

$$
HOTEL
★

Golden Rock Plantation Inn. Pam Barry's great-great-great-grandfather built this hillside estate in the early years of the 19th century; Pam has imbued the inn with her love of Nevisian heritage and nature, and co-owners, acclaimed artists Brice Marden and wife Helen Harrington, have imparted a chic, modernist sensibility. **Pros:** ecofriendly; arty crowd; glorious grounds. **Cons:** no actual beach though there are two beach clubs; lack of air-conditioning can be a problem on still days. **TripAdvisor:** "wonderful garden and warm welcome," "beautiful with terrific service," "tropical garden paradise." ⑤ *Rooms from: $298* ✉ *Gingerland* ☎ *869/469–3346* ⊕ *www.golden-rock.com* ⤢ *16 rooms, 1 suite* ⊗ *Closed mid-Aug.–mid-Oct.* ⦿ *No meals.*

$$$

HOTEL

Fodor's Choice

★

🏠 **Hermitage Plantation Inn.** A snug 1670 great house—reputedly the Caribbean's oldest surviving wooden building—forms the heart of this breeze-swept hillside hideaway. **Pros:** wonderful sense of history; delightful owners and clientele; delicious food. **Cons:** long drive to beach; hillside setting difficult for physically challenged to negotiate. **TripAdvisor:** "authentic," "most relaxing vacation," "old-world charm." ⑤ *Rooms from: $325* ✉ *Gingerland* ☎ *869/469–3477, 800/682–4025* ⊕ *www.hermitagenevis.com* ⤢ *8 rooms, 8 cottages, 1 house* ⦿ *Multiple meal plans.*

$$

RENTAL

🏠 **Hurricane Cove Bungalows.** These dramatically set one-, two-, and three-bedroom bungalows (cleverly designed and imported from Finland) cling like glorified tree houses to a cliff overlooking several glittering beaches. **Pros:** sensational views; good value for one-bedroom cottages; free use of snorkeling equipment. **Cons:** no air-conditioning for the rare stifling day; minuscule pool; hike back up from beach; kitchens need upgrading. **TripAdvisor:** "great family gathering spot," "rustic charm," "a perfect hideaway." ⑤ *Rooms from: $245* ✉ *Hurricane Hill,*

CLOSE UP

Nevis's Day at the Races

21

One of the Caribbean's most festive, endearingly idiosyncratic events is the Nevis Turf and Jockey Club's Day at the Races, held 9 to 12 times a year on the wild and windswept Indian Castle course. I first experienced the event in the mid-1990s, when I met club president Richard "Lupi" Lupinacci, owner of the Hermitage Plantation Inn. Before even introducing himself, Richard sized me up in the driveway: "You look about the right size for a jockey. How's your seat?" His equally effervescent wife, Maureen, then interceded, "Darling, if you loathe horses, don't worry. In fact, Lupi and I have an agreement about the Jerk and Turkey Club. I get major jewels for every animal he buys."

Since my riding skills were rusty, it was decided that I should be a judge (despite questionable vision, even with glasses). "If it's really by a nose, someone will disagree with you either way," I was reassured. The next day presented a quintessential Caribbean scene. Although a serious cadre of aficionados (including the German consul) talked turf, the rest of the

island seemed more interested in liming and enjoying lively music. Local ladies dished out heavenly barbecued chicken and devilish gossip. Sheep and cattle unconcernedly ambled across the course. But when real horses thundered around the oval, the wooden stands groaned under the weight of cheering crowds, and bookies hand-calculated the payouts.

The irregularly scheduled races continue, albeit now on a properly sodded track, as does the equine hospitality.

Hermitage Stables. Here you can opt for everything from horseback riding to jaunts in hand-carved mahogany carriages. ⊠ *Gingerland* ☎ *869/469–3477.*

Nevis Equestrian Centre. The Nevis Equestrian Centre offers leisurely beach rides as well as more demanding canters through the lush hills, starting at $55. ⊠ *Cotton Ground, Pinney's Beach* ☎ *869/662–9118* ⊕ *www.nevishorseback.com.*

—Jordan Simon

Oualie Beach ☎ *869/469–9462* ⊕ *www.hurricanecove.com* ⇆ *13 cottages* ۞ *Closed Sept.* ⦿*No meals.*

$$$$
RESORT
Fodor's Choice
★

⌂ **Montpelier Plantation & Beach.** This Nevisian beauty—a Relais & Châteaux property—epitomizes understated elegance and graciously updated plantation living, courtesy of the congenial, cultured Hoffman family. **Pros:** impeccable service; lovely cuisine; exquisite gardens; trendily minimalist decor. **Cons:** some may find it a little stuffy; no beach on-site. **TripAdvisor:** "redefines escape and relaxation," "simply stunning," "superb experience." ⑤ *Rooms from: $545* ⊠ *Montpelier Estate* ☎ *869/469–3462, 888/334–7609* ⊕ *www.montpeliernevis.com* ⇆ *17 rooms, 2 1-bedroom villas, 1 2-bedroom villa* ۞ *Closed mid-Aug.–early Oct.* ⦿*Multiple meal plans.*

$$$
HOTEL
★

⌂ **Mount Nevis Hotel & Beach Club.** The personable, attentive Meguid family blends the intimacy of the plantation inns, contemporary amenities of the Four Seasons, and typical Nevisian warmth in this hilltop aerie. **Pros:** friendly staff; fantastic views; comforts of home at comparatively affordable prices; complimentary cell phone (pay for card). **Cons:** lacks beach; long drive to many island activities; occasional plane noise. **TripAdvisor:** "spectacular view," "paradise within paradise," "relaxing island gem." ⑤ *Rooms from: $300* ⊠ *Shaw's Rd., Mount Nevis* ☎ *869/469–9373, 800/756–3847* ⊕ *www.mountnevishotel.com* ⪡ *8 rooms, 8 junior suites, 16 suites, 10 villas* ⑩ *Breakfast.*

$$$$ 🛏 **Nisbet Plantation Beach Club.** At this beachfront plantation inn, pale
RESORT yellow cottages face a regal, palm-lined grass avenue that sweeps like
★ a bridal gown's train to the champagne-hue beach. **Pros:** glorious setting; the definition of casual elegance; environmentally conscious practices; plentiful recreational options such as mountain bikes, kayaks, even Vespa scooters; extras such as free use of digital video recorders and handheld GPS locators. **Cons:** long drive to most activities on island; airplanes occasionally whoosh by; food is variable; occasionally dodgy Wi-Fi signal. **TripAdvisor:** "believe the hype," "absolutely perfect," "the Caribbean at its best." ⑤ *Rooms from: $670* ⊠ *Newcastle* ☎ *869/469–9325, 800/742–6008* ⊕ *www.nisbetplantation.com* ⪡ *36 rooms* ⑩ *Some meals.*

$$ 🛏 **Oualie Beach Hotel.** These cozy Creole-style gingerbread cottages
RESORT daubed in cotton-candy colors sit just steps from a hammock-strewn taupe beach overlooking St. **Pros:** fantastic water-sports operations; affordable (especially with recreational packages); appealing beach. **Cons:** showing some wear; not ideal for less active types. **TripAdvisor:** "great location on the beach," "so relaxing and perfect," "a bit of paradise." ⑤ *Rooms from: $270* ⊠ *Oualie Beach* ☎ *869/469–9735* ⊕ *www. oualiebeach.com* ⪡ *32 rooms* ⑩ *Multiple meal plans.*

NIGHTLIFE

In season it's usually easy to find a local calypso singer or a steel or string band performing at one of the hotels, notably the Four Seasons and Oualie Beach (which also features string musicians on homemade instruments Tuesday evening), as well as at the Pinney's bars. Scan the posters plastered on doorways announcing informal jump-ups. Though Nevis lacks high-tech discos, many restaurants and bars have live bands or DJs on weekends.

★ **Chrishi Beach Club.** Though more a daytime hangout (especially Sunday, when Nevisian movers and shakers descend on the lovely beach with their families—and act like overgrown kids themselves), Chrishi Beach Club remains hip and happening through sunset thanks to vivacious Norwegian expats Hedda and Christian "Chrishi" Wienpahl. You can sprawl on comfy chaises and thatched, white, beach waterbeds (exemplifying the couple's wit and whimsy). Enjoy the righteous lounge mix (and mixology) and the glorious St. Kitts views (even the hideous Sea Bridge car ferry looks like an art installation from this vantage point), and what Hedda calls "European café-style" food (salads, pizzas, sandwiches like Brie with sun-dried tomatoes and cranberries). Kids have their own club with fresh-fruit smoothies, and Hedda's fun funky HWD jewelry line (incorporating leather, coins, found objects) is on sale. ✉ *Main St., Cades Bay* ☎ *869/662–3958, 869/662–3959* ⊕ *www. chrishibeachclub.com.*

Water Department Barbecue. The Water Department Barbecue is the informal name for a lively Friday-night jump-up that's run by two fellows from the local water department to raise funds for department trips. Friday afternoons the tents go up and the grills are fired. Cars line the streets and the guys dish up fabulous barbecue ribs and chicken—as certain customers lobby to get their water pressure adjusted. It's a classic Caribbean scene. ✉ *Pump Rd., Charlestown* ☎ *No phone.*

SHOPPING

Nevis is certainly not the place for a shopping spree, but there are some unusual and wonderful surprises, notably the island's pottery, hand-embroidered clothing, and dolls by Jeannie Rigby. Honey is another buzzing biz. Quentin Henderson, the amiable former head of the **Nevis Beekeeping Cooperative,** will even arrange trips by appointment to various hives for demonstrations of beekeeping procedures. Other than a few hotel boutiques and isolated galleries, virtually all shopping is concentrated on or just off Main Street in Charlestown. The lovely old stonework and wood floors of the waterfront Cotton Ginnery Complex make an appropriate setting for stalls of local artisans.

SPECIALTY ITEMS

ART

Eva Wilkin Gallery. Nevis has produced one artist of some international repute, the late Dame Eva Wilkin, who for more than 50 years painted island people, flowers, and landscapes in an evocative art naïf style. Her originals are now quite valuable, but prints are available in some local shops. The Eva Wilkin Gallery occupies her former atelier (hours are very irregular, so call ahead). If the paintings, drawings, and prints are out of your price range, consider buying the lovely note cards based on her designs; the new owners are also promoting promising regional artists. ✉ *Clay Ghaut, Gingerland* ☎ *869/469–2673.*

Robert Humphreys. Humphreys sells his work, flowing bronze sculptures of pirouetting marlins and local birds and animals, at his home, where it's possible to watch the artist at work in his studio. ✉ *Zetlands* ☎ *869/469–3326, 869/469–6217* ⊕ *www.caribbronzes.org.*

CLOTHING

Most hotels have their own boutiques.

Island Fever. The island's classiest shop carries an excellent selection of everything from bathing suits and dresses to straw bags and jewelry. ✉ *Main St., Charlestown* ☎ *869/469–0867.*

HANDICRAFTS

★ **Bocane Ceramics.** Cheryl "Cherrianne" Liburd's Bocane Ceramics stocks beautifully designed and glazed local pottery, which she dubs "functional art," such as platters painted with marine life, pineapple tea sets, and coffee tables topped with mosaic depictions of chattel houses. ✉ *Main St., Stoney Grove* ☎ *869/469–5437* ⊕ *www.bocane-ceramics.com.*

CraftHouse. This marvelous source for local specialties, from vetiver mats to leather moccasins, also has a smaller branch in the Cotton Ginnery. ⊠ *Pinney's Rd., Charlestown* ☎ *869/469–5505.*

Nevis Handicraft Co-op Society. This shop next to the tourist office offers works by local artisans (clothing, ceramic ware, woven goods) and locally produced honey, hot sauces, and jellies (try the guava and soursop). ⊠ *Main St., Charlestown* ☎ *869/469–1746.*

★ **Newcastle Pottery.** This cooperative has continued the age-old tradition of hand-built red-clay pottery fired over burning coconut husks. It's possible to watch the potters and purchase wares at their small Newcastle factory. ⊠ *Main Rd., Newcastle* ☎ *869/469–9746.*

★ **Philatelic Bureau.** Opposite the tourist office, this is the place to go for stamp collectors. St. Kitts and Nevis are famous for their decorative, and sometimes valuable, stamps. Real beauties include the butterfly, hummingbird, and marine-life series. ⊠ *Cotton Ginnery, Charlestown* ☎ *869/469–0617.*

SPORTS AND ACTIVITIES

BIKING

Windsurfing Nevis/Wheel World. This shop offers mountain-bike rentals as well as specially tailored tours on its state-of-the-art Gary Fisher, Trek, and Specialized bikes. The tours ($55–$75), led by Winston Crooke, a master windsurfer and competitive bike racer, encompass lush rain forest, majestic ruins, and spectacular views. Costs vary according to itinerary and ability level but are aimed generally at experienced riders. Winston and his team delight in sharing local knowledge, from history to culture. For those just renting (rates from $25 daily), Winston and Reggie determine your performance level and suggest appropriate routes. ⊠ *Oualie Beach* ☎ *869/469–9682* ⊕ *www.bikenevis.com.*

DIVING AND SNORKELING

The **Devil's Caves** make up a series of grottoes where divers can navigate tunnels, canyons, and underwater hot springs while viewing lobsters, sea fans, sponges, squirrelfish, and more. The village of **Jamestown,** which washed into the sea around Ft. Ashby, just south of Cades Bay, makes for superior snorkeling and diving. Reef-protected Pinney's Beach offers especially good snorkeling. Single-tank dives are usually $70, two-tank dives $100; packages provide deep discounts.

☾ ★ **Scuba Safaris.** This PADI five-star facility and NASDS Examining Station is staffed by experienced dive masters who offer everything from a resort course to full certification to Nitrox. Their equipment is always state-of-the-art, including underwater scooters. It also provides a snorkeling learning experience that enables you not only to see but to listen to sea life, including whales and dolphins, as well as an exhilarating underwater scooter safari, night dives, and kids' bubblemakers. ⊠ *Oualie Beach* ☎ *869/469–9518* ⊕ *www.scubanevis.com.*

FISHING

Fishing here focuses on kingfish, wahoo, grouper, tuna, and yellowtail snapper, with marlin occasionally spotted. The best areas are Monkey Shoals and around Redonda. Charters cost approximately $450–$500 per half day, $850–$1,000 per full day, and usually include an open bar.

Deep Venture. Run by fisherman–chef Matt Lloyd, Deep Venture does day-fishing charters (he keeps the catch), providing a real insight into both commercial fishing and the Caribbean kitchen. ☒ *Oualie Beach* ☎ *869/469–5110.*

Nevis Water Sports. Nevis Water Sports offers sportfishing aboard the 31-foot *Sea Brat* under the supervision of tournament-winning captain Ian Gonzaley. The company helps organize the annual Nevis Yacht Club Sports Fishing Tournament, which reels in competitors from all over the Caribbean. ☒ *Oualie Beach* ☎ *869/469–9060* ⊕ *www.fishnevis.com.*

GOLF

Fodor's Choice ★ **Four Seasons Golf Course.** Duffers doff their hats to the beautiful, impeccably maintained Robert Trent Jones Jr.–designed Four Seasons Golf Course: the virtual botanical gardens surrounding the fairways almost qualify as a hazard in themselves. The front 9 holes are fairly flat until Hole 8, which climbs uphill after your tee shot. Most of the truly stunning views are along the back 9. The signature hole is the 15th, a 660-yard monster that encompasses a deep ravine; other holes include bridges, steep drops, rolling pitches, extremely tight and unforgiving fairways, sugar-mill ruins, and fierce doglegs. Attentive attendants canvas the course with beverage buggies, handing out chilled, peppermint-scented towels and preordered Cubanos that help test the wind. Greens fees per 18 holes are $190 for hotel guests, $290 for nonguests. ☒ *Four Seasons Resort Nevis, Pinney's Beach* ☎ *869/469–1111* ⌕ *18 holes, par 72, 6,766 yd.*

GUIDED TOURS

Fitzroy "Teach" Williams. Guide Fitzroy "Teach" Williams is the former president of the taxi association—even older cabbies call him "the Dean." He's an excellent tour guide. ☎ *869/469–1140.*

TC's Island Tours. TC, a Yorkshire lass who used to drive a double-decker bus in England and has been married to a Nevisian for more than a decade, offers entertaining explorations via TC's Island Tours. ☎ *869/469–2911.*

HIKING

The center of the island is Nevis Peak—also known as Mt. Nevis—which soars 3,232 feet and is flanked by Hurricane Hill on the north and Saddle Hill on the south. If you plan to scale Nevis Peak, a daylong affair, it's highly recommended that you go with a guide. Your hotel can arrange it (and a picnic lunch) for you. The 9-mile (15-km) **Upper Round Road Trail** was constructed in the late 1600s and cleared and restored by the Nevis Historical and Conservation Society. It connects the Golden Rock Plantation Inn, on the east side of the island, with Nisbet Plantation Beach Club, on the northern tip. The trail encompasses numerous vegetation zones, including pristine rain forest, and impressive plantation ruins. The original cobblestones, walls, and ruins are still evident in many places.

★ **Peak Heaven at Herbert Heights.** This tour company is run by the Herbert family, who lead four-hour nature hikes up to panoramic Herbert Heights, where you drink in fresh local juices and the views of Montserrat; the powerful telescope, donated by Greenpeace, makes you feel as if you're staring right into that island's simmering volcano (or staring down whales during their migratory season). The trail formed part of an escape route for runaway slaves, and you can also inspect recent archaeological excavations providing insight into the indigenous peoples. Numerous hummingbirds, doves, and butterflies flit and flutter through the rain forest. The Herberts painstakingly reconstructed thatched cottages that offer a glimpse of village life a century ago, dubbed Peak Heaven, at Nelson's Lookout. These include a small, poignant, history museum; shop selling local crafts; gallery; and massage room. The solar-powered Coal Pot restaurant offers heaping helpings of affordable island fare (try any soup, the thyme-seared snapper, and scrumptious homemade ice creams) alongside the splendid vistas. There's even a small playground at the entrance. Hike prices start at $25. ⊠ *Nevis* ☎ *869/469–2856, 869/665–6926* ⊕ *www.peakheavennevis.com.*

Sunrise Tours. Run by Lynell and Earla Liburd, Sunrise Tours offers a range of hiking trips, but their most popular is Devil's Copper, a rock configuration full of ghostly legends.Hikes range from $20 to $40 per person, and you receive a certificate of achievement. ⊠ *Nevis* ☎ *869/469–2758* ⊕ *www.nevisnaturetours.com.*

Top to Bottom. This tour company offers ecorambles (slow tours) and hikes that emphasize Nevis's volcanic and horticultural heritage (including pointing out bat caves and folkloric herbal and "murderous" medicines). Kayaks are available for rent, and Nikki Johnson conducts tours in Long Haul Bay. Three-hour rambles or hikes are $20 per person (snacks and juice included); it's $40 for more strenuous climbs (two are offered) up Mt. Nevis. ⊠ *Nevis* ☎ *869/469–9080* ⊕ *www.walknevis.com.*

WINDSURFING

★ **Windsurfing Nevis.** Waters are generally calm and northeasterly winds steady yet gentle, making Nevis an excellent spot for beginners and intermediates. Windsurfing Nevis offers top-notch instructors (Winston Crooke is one of the best in the islands) and equipment for $30 per hour. Beginners get equipment and two-hour instruction for $60. Groups are kept small (eight maximum), and the equipment is state-of-the-art from Mistral, North, and Tushingham. It also offers kayak rentals and tours along the coast, stopping at otherwise inaccessible beaches. ⊠ *Oualie Beach* ☎ *869/469–9682.*

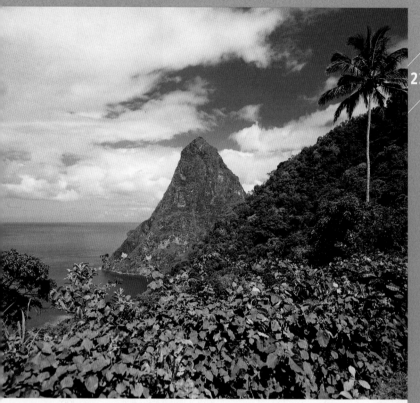

St. Lucia

WORD OF MOUTH

"St. Lucia is very lush, with mountains, flora, fauna, plantations, and waterfalls. Reminded us of Jamaica and Hawaii. Driving can be a little difficult, and everything is quite spread out. The beaches are made up of coarse brownish/beige sand and the water is a dark blue. There are a few black sand beaches also."

—KVR

WELCOME TO ST. LUCIA

THE CARIBBEAN'S TWIN PEAKS

St. Lucia, 27 miles (43.5 km) by 14 miles (22.5 km), is a volcanic island covered to a large extent by a lush rain forest, much of which is protected as a national park. The most notable geological features are the twin Pitons, some 2,600 feet high.

KEY	
⚲	Beaches
◣	Dive Sites
⛴	Ferry
⚓	Cruise Ship Terminal
🟦	Restaurants
①	Hotels
⁂	Rain Forest

Explorers, pirates, soldiers, sugar planters, and coal miners have made their mark on this lovely landfall, and the lush tropical peaks known as the Pitons (Gros and Petit) have witnessed them all. Today's visitors come to snorkel and scuba dive in St. Lucia's calm cobalt-blue waters, sun themselves on its multihued beaches, or sail off tiny Pigeon Island.

TOP REASONS TO VISIT ST. LUCIA

1 The Beauty: Magnificent, lush scenery makes St. Lucia one of the most beautiful Caribbean islands.

2 The Romance: A popular honeymoon spot, St. Lucia is filled with romantic retreats.

3 Indulgent Accommodations: Sybaritic lodging options include an all-inclusive spa resort, a posh dive resort sandwiched between a mountain and the beach, and two resorts with prime locations between the Pitons.

4 The St. Lucia Jazz Festival: Performers and fans come from all over the world for this musical event.

5 The Welcome: The friendly St. Lucians love sharing their island and their cultural heritage with visitors.

ST. LUCIA BEACHES

The sand on St. Lucia's beaches ranges from golden to black, and the island has some of the best off-the-beach snorkeling in the Caribbean — especially along the southwest coast.

(Above) Reduit Beach at Rodney Bay Village (Bottom right) Anse des Pitons on Jalousie Bay (Top right) Marigot Bay

St. Lucia's longest, broadest, and most popular beaches are in the north, which is also the flattest part of this mountainous island and the location of most resorts, restaurants, and nightlife. Many of the island's biggest resorts front the beaches from Choc Bay to Rodney Bay and extending north to Cap Estate. Elsewhere, tiny coves with inviting crescents of sand offer great swimming and snorkeling opportunities. Beaches are all public, but hotels flank many along the northwestern coast. A few secluded stretches of beach on the west coast south of Marigot Bay, accessible primarily by boat, are popular swimming and snorkeling stops on catamaran or powerboat sightseeing trips. Don't swim along the windward (east) coast, as the Atlantic Ocean is too rough—but the views are spectacular. At Coconut Bay Resort, which has a beautiful beach facing the Atlantic at the southernmost tip of the island, the water is too rough for swimming.

GOLDEN SAND

Reduit Beach at Rodney Bay Village is considered St. Lucia's finest, with golden sand and lots of water sports. Farther south, little beaches have sand ranging in color from gold to gray, becoming darker as you head south; one, magnificently located right between the Pitons, has imported white sand on top of the natural black. Marigot Bay, a peninsula of golden sand studded with palm trees, is lovely but very tiny.

Anse Chastanet. In front of the resort of the same name, just north of the city of Soufrière, this palm-studded dark-sand beach has a backdrop of green hills, brightly painted fishing skiffs bobbing at anchor, and the island's best reefs for snorkeling and diving. The resort's gazebos are nestled among the palms; its dive shop, restaurant, and bar are on the beach and open to the public. ⊠ *1 mile (1½ km) north of Soufrière.*

★ **Anse Cochon.** This remote dark-sand beach is reached only by boat or via Ti Kaye Village's mile-long access road. The water and adjacent reef are superb for swimming, diving, and snorkeling. Moorings are free, and boaters can enjoy refreshments at Ti Kaye's beach bar. ⊠ *3 miles (5 km) south of Marigot Bay.*

Anse des Pitons *(Jalousie Beach).* The white sand on this crescent beach, snuggled between the Pitons, was imported and spread over the natural black sand. Accessible through the Jalousie Plantation Sugar Beach resort property or by boat, the beach offers good snorkeling, diving, and breathtaking scenery. ⊠ *1 mile (1½ km) south of Soufrière.*

Marigot Beach *(Labas Beach).* Calm waters rippled only by passing yachts lap a sliver of sand studded with palm trees on the north side of Marigot Bay. The beach is accessible by a ferry that operates continually from one side of the bay to the other, and you can find

refreshments at adjacent restaurants. ⊠ *Marigot Bay.*

Pigeon Point. At this small beach within Pigeon Island National Park ($5 admission), on the northwestern tip of St. Lucia, a restaurant serves snacks and drinks, but this is also a perfect spot for picnicking. ⊠ *Pigeon Island.*

Fodor's Choice | **Reduit Beach.** This long stretch of golden sand frames Rodney Bay and is within walking distance of many hotels and restaurants in Rodney Bay Village. The Rex St. Lucian hotel, which faces the beach, has a watersports center, where you can rent sports equipment and beach chairs and take windsurfing or waterskiing lessons. Many feel that Reduit (pronounced red-wee) is the island's finest beach. ⊠ *Rodney Bay.*

Vigie Beach. This 2-mile (3-km) strand runs parallel to the George F. L. Charles Airport runway in Castries and continues on past the Rendezvous resort, where it is called Malabar Beach. ⊠ *Castries, next to airport, Castries.*

By Jane E. Zarem

A lush, mountainous island between Martinique and St. Vincent, St. Lucia has evolved into one of the Caribbean's most popular vacation destinations—particularly for honeymooners and other romantics enticed by the island's striking natural beauty, its many splendid resorts and appealing inns, and its welcoming atmosphere.

The capital city of Castries and nearby villages in the northwest are home to 40% of the population. This area, along with Rodney Bay farther north and Marigot Bay just south of the capital, are the destinations of most vacationers. In the central and southwestern parts of the island dense rain forest, jungle-covered mountains, and vast banana plantations dominate the landscape. A tortuous road follows most of the coastline, bisecting small villages, cutting through mountains, and passing by fertile valleys. On the southwest coast, Petit Piton and Gros Piton, the island's unusual twin peaks that rise out of the sea to more than 2,600 feet, are familiar landmarks for sailors and aviators alike. Divers are attracted to the reefs found just north of Soufrière, which was the capital during French colonial times. Most of the natural tourist attractions are in this area, along with several more fine resorts and inns.

The pirate François Le Clerc, nicknamed Jambe de Bois (Wooden Leg) for obvious reasons, was the first European "settler" in St. Lucia. In the late 16th century Le Clerc holed up on Pigeon Island, just off the island's northernmost point, and used it as a staging ground for attacking passing ships. Now Pigeon Island is a national park, connected by a causeway to the mainland; today Sandals Grande St. Lucian Spa & Beach Resort, one of the largest resorts in St. Lucia, and The Landings, a luxury villa community, sprawl along that causeway.

Like most of its Caribbean neighbors, St. Lucia was first inhabited by Arawaks and then the Carib Indians. British settlers attempted to colonize the island twice in the early 1600s, but it wasn't until 1651, after the French West India Company suppressed the local Caribs, that Europeans gained a foothold. For 150 years, battles over possession of the island were frequent between the French and the British, with a dizzying

LOGISTICS

Getting to St. Lucia: St. Lucia's primary gateway is Hewanorra International Airport (UVF) in Vieux Fort, on the island's southern tip. Regional airlines fly into George F. L. Charles Airport (SLU) in Castries, commonly called Vigie Airport and more convenient to resorts in the north. The drive between Hewanorra and resorts in the north takes 90 minutes; the trip between Hewanorra and Soufrière takes about 45 minutes.

Hassle Factor: Medium to high, because of the long drive from Hewanorra International Airport.

On the Ground: Taxis are available at both airports, although transfers may be included in your travel package. It's an expensive ride to the north from Hewanorra—at least $75—and about $65 to Soufrière. A helicopter shuttle cuts the transfer time to about 10 minutes, but the cost doubles.

Getting Around the Island: A car is more important if you are staying at a small inn or hotel away from the beach. If you're staying at an all-inclusive beach resort and you don't plan to leave for meals, taxis may be the better bet.

22

14 changes in power before the British finally took possession in 1814. The Europeans established sugar plantations, using slaves from West Africa to work the fields. By 1838, when the slaves were emancipated, more than 90% of the population was of African descent—roughly the same proportion of today's 170,000 St. Lucians.

On February 22, 1979, St. Lucia became an independent state within the British Commonwealth of Nations, with a resident governor-general appointed by the queen. Still, the island appears to have retained more relics of French influence—notably the island patois, cuisine, village names, and surnames—than of the British. Most likely, that's because the British contribution primarily involved the English language, the educational and legal systems, and the political structure, whereas the French culture historically had more influence on the arts—culinary, dance, and music.

PLANNING

WHEN TO GO

The high season runs from mid-December through mid-April and during the annual St. Lucia Jazz Festival and Carnival events; at other times of the year hotel rates can be significantly cheaper. December and January are the coolest months, and June through August are the hottest. Substantial rain (more than just a tropical spritz) is more likely from June through November.

GETTING HERE AND AROUND

AIR TRAVEL

American Airlines flies nonstop from Miami, with connecting service from New York and other major cities via American Eagle from San Juan. Delta flies nonstop from Atlanta. JetBlue flies nonstop from New

York (JFK). US Airways flies nonstop from Philadelphia and Charlotte. Air Caraïbes flies from Guadeloupe and Martinique; LIAT flies from several neighboring islands.

Airports Hewanorra International Airport (*UVF*). Located at the southeastern tip of the island, Hewanorra can accommodate large jets, including all nonstop flights from the U.S. mainland. ⊠ *Vieux Fort* ☎ *758/454–6355.*

George F.L. Charles Airport (*SLU*). Commonly called Vigie Airport, this airport is in the north of the island. It accommodates only small prop aircraft because of its location and runway limitations. ⊠ *Vigie, Castries* ☎ *758/452–1156.*

Airline Contacts: Air Caraïbes ☎ *758/453–0357.* **American Airlines/American Eagle** ☎ *758/459–6500, 758/452–1820, 800/744–0006.* **Delta** ☎ *758/484–5594.* **JetBlue** ☎ *877/766–9614, 888/844–5428.* **LIAT** ☎ *888/844–5428, 758/452–3056.* **US Airways** ☎ *758/454–8186.*

Air Transfers St. Lucia Helicopters. You can considerably reduce travel time to and from the airport by taking St. Lucia Helicopters, but the price is high: $145 per person each way for a 10-minute airport-to-airport shuttle. ⊠ *Castries* ☎ *758/453–6950* ⊕ *www.stluciahelicopters.com.*

BOAT AND FERRY TRAVEL

When cruise ships are in port in Castries, a water taxi shuttles back and forth between Pointe Seraphine (on the north side of the harbor) and La Place Carenage (on the south side) for $2 per person each way.

L'Express des Iles. This fast ferry connects St. Lucia with Martinique, Dominica, and Guadeloupe. The trip between Castries and Fort de France, Martinique, takes 1½ hours; Roseau, Dominica, 3½ hours; and Point-à -Pitre, Guadeloupe, 5½ hours. ☎☎ *758/456–5000* ⊕ *www. express-des-iles.com.*

Rodney Bay Ferry. For those arriving at Rodney Bay Marina, this ferry travels between the marina and the Rodney Bay shopping complex daily on the hour, from 9 to 4, for $5 per person round-trip. ☎ *758/452–8816.*

BUS TRAVEL

Privately owned and operated minivans constitute St. Lucia's bus system, an inexpensive and efficient means of transportation used primarily by local people. Buses are a good way to travel between Castries and the Rodney Bay area. Fares in the north range from EC$1.50 to EC$2.50 (ideally payable in local currency), but you can also travel to Vieux Fort or Soufrière (two-plus hours, EC$8). Wait at a marked stop and hail the passing minivan. Let the conductor or driver know where you need to go, and he'll stop at the appropriate place.

CAR TRAVEL

Roads in St. Lucia are winding and mountainous, except north of Castries, making driving a challenge for timid or apprehensive drivers and exhausting for everyone else. You drive on the left, British-style. Seat belts are required, and speed limits are enforced, especially in Castries.

Car Rentals To rent a car you must be at least 25 years old and provide a valid driver's license and a credit card. If you don't have an international driver's license, you must buy a temporary St. Lucia driving permit ($20 [EC$54]) at the car-rental office, the immigration office at either airport, or the Gros Islet police station. Car-rental rates are usually quoted in U.S. dollars and range from $50 to $80 per day or $300 to $425 per week.

Car-Rental Contacts Avis ✉ *Vide Bouteille, Castries* ☎ *758/452–2700* ⊕ *www. avisstlucia.com* ✉ *Vieux Fort* ☎ *758/454–6325* ✉ *Vigie* ☎ *758/452–2046.* **Cool Breeze Jeep/Car Rental** ✉ *Soufrière* ☎ *758/459–7729* ⊕ *www. coolbreezecarrental.com.* **Courtesy Car Rental** ✉ *Bois d'Orange, Gros Islet* ☎ *758/452–8140* ⊕ *www.courtesycarrentals.com.* **Hertz** ✉ *Cap Estate* ☎ *758/450–0222* ⊕ *www.hertz.com* ✉ *Vieux Fort* ☎ *758/454–9636* ✉ *Vigie* ☎ *758/451–7351.*

TAXI TRAVEL

Taxis are unmetered, although fares are fairly standard. Sample fares for up to four passengers are Castries to Rodney Bay, $20; Rodney Bay to Cap Estate, $10; Castries to Cap Estate, $25; Castries to Marigot Bay, $30; Castries to Anse La Raye, $40; Castries to Soufrière, $90; and Castries to Vieux Forte, $75. Always ask the driver to quote the price *before* you get in, and be sure that you both understand whether it's quoted in EC or U.S. dollars. Drivers are generally careful, knowledgeable, and courteous.

ESSENTIALS

Banks and Exchange Services The official currency is the Eastern Caribbean dollar (EC$), but U.S. dollars (not coins) are accepted nearly everywhere—although you may get your change in local currency. Major credit cards and traveler's checks are also widely accepted. ATMs dispense only local currency. Major banks on the island include Bank of Nova Scotia (Scotiabank), FirstCaribbean International Bank, and Royal Bank of Canada.

Electricity The electric current on St. Lucia is 220 volts, 50 cycles, with a square, three-pin plug (U.K. standard). You'll need a transformer to convert voltage and a plug adapter to use most North American appliances; dual-voltage computer and phone chargers or other appliances will still need a plug adapter, which you can often borrow from the hotel. More and more hotels and resorts have added 110-volt outlets for general use but sometimes only for electric razors. Many hotels and resorts also provide iPod docking stations.

Emergency Services Ambulance and Fire ☎ *911.* **Police** ☎ *999.*

Passport Requirements U.S. and Canadian citizens must have a valid passport to enter St. Lucia and a return or ongoing ticket.

Phones The area code for St. Lucia is 758. You can make direct-dial overseas and interisland calls from St. Lucia, and the connections are excellent. You can charge an overseas call to a major credit card with no surcharge; from public phones and many hotels, dial 811 to charge the call to your credit card. Some hotels charge a small fee (usually about EC$1) for local calls. Many retail outlets sell phone cards to use for either local or international calls from any touch-tone telephone (including pay phones) in St. Lucia. Cell phones may be rented from LIME or Digicel offices in Castries, Gablewoods Mall, Baywalk Mall in

Rodney Bay, and Vieux Fort, or you can purchase a local SIM card for $20 (which includes an $8 call credit) in those same locations. The cards may be topped up at hundreds of business locations around the island.

Safety Although crime isn't a significant problem, take the same precautions that you would at home—lock your door, secure your valuables, and don't carry too much money or flaunt expensive jewelry on the street or at the beach.

Taxes The departure tax of $26 (EC$68) is incorporated into the price of your airfare. A government tax of 8% is added to all hotel and restaurant bills, although a V.A.T. (value-added tax), may replace that tax in the future. (At this writing, the V.A.T. rate and implementation date have not been set.) Most restaurants and some hotels also add a service charge of 10% in lieu of tipping.

ACCOMMODATIONS

Nearly all St. Lucia's resorts and small inns are tucked into lush surroundings on secluded coves, unspoiled beaches, or forested hillsides in three locations along the calm Caribbean (western) coast. They're in the greater Castries area between Marigot Bay, a few miles south of the city, and Labrelotte Bay in the north; in and around Rodney Bay and north to Cap Estate; and in and around Soufrière on the southwest coast near the Pitons. There's only one resort in Vieux Fort, near Hewanorra. The advantage of being in the north is that you have access to a wider range of restaurants and nightlife; in the south, you may be limited to your hotel's offerings and a few other dining options—albeit some of the best—in and around Soufrière.

Beach Resorts: Most people choose to stay in one of St. Lucia's many beach resorts, the majority of which are upscale and fairly pricey. Several are all-inclusive, including three Sandals resorts, two Sunswept resorts (The Body Holiday and Rendezvous), Almond Morgan Bay, East Winds Inn, and Smugglers Cove Resort & Spa. Others may offer an all-inclusive option.

Small Inns: If you are looking for something more intimate and perhaps less expensive, a locally owned inn or small hotel is a good option; it may or may not be directly on the beach.

Villas: Luxury villa communities that operate like hotels are a good alternative for families. Several are in the north in or near Cap Estate.

HOTEL AND RESTAURANT PRICES

Prices in the restaurant reviews are the average cost of a main course at dinner or, if dinner is not served, at lunch; taxes and service charges are generally included. Prices in the hotel reviews are the lowest cost of a standard double room in high season, excluding taxes, service charges, and meal plans (except at all-inclusives). Prices for rentals are the lowest per-night cost for a one-bedroom unit in high season.

VISITOR INFORMATION

Contacts St. Lucia Tourist Board ☎ 212/867–2950 in New York, 800/456–3984 ⊕ www.saintlucianow.com.

22

WEDDINGS

Wedding licenses that cost $125 require a three-day waiting period; those that cost $200 don't require a waiting period. Some resorts offer free weddings.

EXPLORING ST. LUCIA

Except for a small area in the extreme northeast, one main route circles all of St. Lucia. The road snakes along the coast, cuts across mountains, makes hairpin turns and sheer drops, and reaches dizzying heights. It takes at least four hours to drive the whole loop. Even at a leisurely pace with frequent sightseeing stops, and whether you're driving or being driven, the curvy roads make it a tiring drive in a single outing.

The West Coast Road between Castries and Soufrière (a 1½- to 2-hour journey) has steep hills and sharp turns, but it's well marked and incredibly scenic. South of Castries, the road tunnels through Morne Fortune, skirts the island's largest banana plantation (more than 127 varieties of bananas, called "figs" in this part of the Caribbean, grow on the island), and passes through tiny fishing villages. Just north of Soufrière the road negotiates the island's fruit basket, where most of the mangoes, breadfruit, tomatoes, limes, and oranges are grown. In the mountainous region that forms a backdrop for Soufrière, you will notice 3,118-foot Mt. Gimie (pronounced Jimmy), St. Lucia's highest peak. Approaching Soufrière, you'll have spectacular views of the Pitons, and that spume of smoke wafting out of the thickly forested mountainside just east of Soufrière emanates from the so-called "drive-in" volcano.

The landscape changes dramatically between the Pitons and Vieux Fort on the island's southeastern tip. Along the South Coast Road traveling southeasterly from Soufrière, the terrain starts as steep mountainside with dense vegetation, progresses to undulating hills, and finally becomes rather flat and comparatively arid. Anyone arriving at Hewanorra International Airport, which is in Vieux Fort, and staying at a resort near Soufrière will travel along this route, a journey of about 30 minutes.

From Vieux Fort north to Castries, a 1½-hour drive, the East Coast Road twists through Micoud, Dennery, and other coastal villages. It then winds up, down, and around mountains, crosses Barre de l'Isle Ridge, and slices through the rain forest. Much of the scenery is breathtaking. The Atlantic Ocean pounds against rocky cliffs, and acres and acres of bananas and coconut palms blanket the hillsides. If you arrive at Hewanorra and stay at a resort near Castries or Rodney Bay, you'll travel along the East Coast Road.

CASTRIES AND THE NORTH

Castries, the capital city, and the area north and just south of it are the island's most developed areas. The roads are straight, mostly flat, and easy to navigate. The beaches are some of the island's best. Rodney Bay Marina and most of the resorts, restaurants, and nightspots are north of Castries. Pigeon Island, one of the important historical sites, is at

CLOSE UP

Embracing Kwéyòl

English is St. Lucia's official language, but most St. Lucians speak and often use Kwéyòl—a French-based Creole language—for informal conversations among themselves. Primarily a spoken language, Kwéyòl in its written version doesn't look at all like French; pronounce the words phonetically, though—*entenasyonnal* (international), for example, or the word *Kwéyòl* (Creole) itself—and you indeed sound as if you're speaking French.

Pretty much the same version of the Creole language, or patois, is spoken in the nearby island of Dominica. Otherwise, the St. Lucian Kwéyòl is quite different from that spoken in other Caribbean islands that have a French and African heritage, such as Haiti, Guadeloupe, and Martinique—or elsewhere, such as Louisiana, Mauritius, and Madagascar. The Kwéyòl spoken

in St. Lucia and Dominica is mostly unintelligible to people from those other locations—and vice versa.

St. Lucia embraces its Creole heritage by devoting the month of October each year to celebrations that preserve and promote Creole culture, language, and traditions. In selected communities throughout the island, events and performances highlight Creole music, food, dance, theater, native costumes, church services, traditional games, folklore, native medicine—a little bit of everything, or *tout bagay*, as you say in Kwéyòl.

Creole Heritage Month culminates at the end of October with all-day events and activities on Jounen Kwéyòl Entenasyonnal, or International Creole Day, which is recognized by all countries that speak a version of the Creole language.

the island's northwestern tip. About 15 minutes south of Castries lies lovely Marigot Bay, which is both a yacht haven and a picture-pretty destination for landlubbers.

WHAT TO SEE

Bounty Rum Distillery. St. Lucia Distillers, which produces the island's own Bounty and Chairman's Reserve rums, offers 90-minute Rhythm and Rum tours of its distillery, including information on the history of sugar, the background of rum, a detailed description of the distillation process, colorful displays of local architecture, a glimpse at a typical rum shop, Caribbean music, and a chance to sample the company's rums and liqueurs. The distillery is at the Roseau Sugar Factory in the Roseau Valley, on the island's largest banana plantation, a few miles south of Castries and not far from Marigot. Reservations for the tour are essential. ⊠ *Roseau Sugar Factory, West Coast Rd., Roseau* ☎ *758/451–4528* ⊕ *www.saintluciarums.com* ☑ *$10* ⊙ *Weekdays 9–3*.

Castries. The capital, a busy commercial city of about 65,000 people, wraps around a sheltered bay. Morne Fortune rises sharply to the south of town, creating a dramatic green backdrop. The charm of Castries lies in its liveliness rather than its architecture, since four fires that occurred between 1796 and 1948 destroyed most of the colonial buildings. Freighters (exporting bananas, coconut, cocoa, mace, nutmeg, and citrus fruits) and cruise ships come and go frequently, making Castries

Harbour one of the Caribbean's busiest ports. **Pointe Seraphine** is a duty-free shopping complex on the north side of the harbor, about a 20-minute walk or two-minute cab ride from the city center; a launch ferries passengers across the harbor when cruise ships are in port. Pointe Seraphine's attractive Spanish-style architecture houses more than 20 upscale duty-free shops, a tourist information kiosk, a taxi stand, and car-rental agencies. **La Place Carenage,** on the south side of the harbor near the pier and markets, is another duty-free shopping complex with a dozen or more shops and a café. **Derek Walcott Square** (formerly Columbus Square), a green oasis bordered by Brazil, Laborie, Micoud, and Bourbon streets, was renamed to honor the hometown poet who won the 1992 Nobel Prize in Literature—one of two Nobel laureates from St. Lucia (the late Sir W. Arthur Lewis won the 1979 Nobel in economic science). Some of the few 19th-century buildings that survived fire, wind, and rain can be seen on Brazil Street, the square's southern border. On the Laborie Street side there's a huge, 400-year-old samaan (monkeypod) tree with leafy branches that shade a good portion of the square. Directly across Laborie Street from Derek Walcott Square is the Roman Catholic **Cathedral of the Immaculate Conception,** which was built in 1897. Though it's rather somber on the outside, its interior walls are decorated with colorful murals reworked in 1985, just before Pope John Paul II's visit, by St. Lucian artist Dunstan St. Omer. This church has an active parish and is open daily for both public viewing and religious services. ⊠ *Castries.*

★ **Castries Market.** Under a brilliant orange roof, the bustling **Castries Market** is at its liveliest on Saturday morning, when farmers bring their produce and spices to town—as they have for more than a century. Next door to the produce market is the **Craft Market,** where you can buy pottery, wood carvings, and handwoven straw articles. At the **Vendors' Arcade,** across Peynier Street from the Craft Market, you'll find still more handicrafts and souvenirs. ⊠ *Corner of Jeremie and Peynier Sts., Castries* ⊙ *Closed Sun.*

Ft. Charlotte. Begun in 1764 by the French as the Citadelle du Morne Fortune, Ft. Charlotte was completed after 20 years of battling and changing hands. Its old barracks and batteries are now government buildings and local educational facilities, but you can drive around and look at the remains, which include redoubts, a guardroom, stables, and cells. You can also walk up to the Inniskilling Monument, a tribute to the 1796 battle in which the 27th Foot Royal Inniskilling Fusiliers wrested the Morne from the French. At the military cemetery, which was first used in 1782, faint inscriptions on the tombstones tell the tales of French and English soldiers who died here. Six former governors of the island are buried here, as well. From this point atop Morne Fortune, you have a beautiful view of Castries Harbour, Martinique farther north, and the twin peaks of the Pitons to the south. ⊠ *Morne Fortune, Castries.*

Government House. The official residence of the governor-general of St. Lucia, one of the island's few remaining examples of Victorian architecture, is perched high above Castries, halfway up Morne Fortune—the "Hill of Good Fortune"—which forms a backdrop for the capital city. Morne Fortune has also overlooked more than its share of *bad* luck over the years, including devastating hurricanes and four fires that leveled Castries. Within Government House itself is **Le Pavillon Royal Museum,** which houses important historical photographs and documents, artifacts, crockery, silverware, medals, and awards; original architectural drawings of Government House are displayed on the walls. However, you must make an appointment to visit. ⊠ *Morne Fortune, Castries* ☎ *758/452–2481* ⊠ *Free* ☉ *Tues. and Thurs. 10–noon and 2–4, by appointment only.*

Fodor'sChoice **Marigot Bay.** This is one of the prettiest natural harbors in the Caribbean.
★ In 1778 British admiral Samuel Barrington sailed into this secluded bay-within-a-bay and, the story goes, covered his ships with palm fronds to hide them from the French. Today this small community is a favorite anchorage for boaters and a peaceful destination for landlubbers. **Discovery at Marigot Bay**—a luxury resort, marina, and marina village with restaurants, bars, grocery store, bakery, and boutiques—has revitalized the area without marring the beauty or the ecology of Marigot Bay. A 24-hour ferry ($2 round-trip) connects the bay's two shores—a voyage that takes about a minute each way. ⊠ *Marigot Bay.*

☺ **Our Planet Centre.** The only such attraction of its kind, at least to date,
Fodor'sChoice Our Planet Centre is devoted to the many facets of the Earth's environ-
★ ment. It's a fascinating, educational stop for the entire family, and an especially good option on a rainy day. Using cutting-edge technology, the exhibits include an Immersion Tunnel, where you can see how the planet was created and grew into its current state; Hurricane Island, where touch screens allow you to manipulate weather patterns to create a hurricane; Mirrorsphere, which gives a kaleidoscopic view of Earth's plants and animals; Science on a Sphere, installed by NOAA/NASA, which views the Earth from space complete with hurricanes, earthquakes, volcanoes, and tsunamis; and—the best part—a laser show in the Special Effects Theatre, where the lighting, shaking seats, wind, and mist mimic extreme weather events. The personalized guided tour takes about 90 minutes, but you'll probably want to linger longer at some of the exhibits and interactive games—which is fine. A gift shop features locally made recycled, reused, natural products. ⊠ *La Place Carenage, Jeremie St., Castries* ☎ *758/453–0107* ⊕ *www.ourplanetcentre.org* ⊠ *$35* ☉ *Mon.–Sat. 9–4:30 (last booking at 3:30), Sun. by reservation or when a cruise ship is in port.*

☺ **Pigeon Island National Landmark.** Jutting out from the northwest coast,
★ Pigeon Island is connected to the mainland by a causeway. Tales are told of the pirate Jambe de Bois (Wooden Leg), who once hid out on this 44-acre hilltop islet—a strategic point during the French and British struggles for control of St. Lucia. Now it's a national park and a venue for concerts, festivals, and family gatherings. There are two small beaches with calm waters for swimming and snorkeling, a restaurant, and picnic areas. Scattered around the grounds are ruins of barracks, batteries, and garrisons that date from 18th-century French and English battles. In the Museum and Interpretative Centre, housed in the restored British officers' mess, a multimedia display explains the island's ecological and historical significance. Pigeon Island National Landmark is

administered by the St. Lucia National Trust. ⊠ *Pigeon Island, Rodney Bay* ☎ *758/452–5005* ⊕ *www.slunatrust.org* ⊠*$5* ⊗ *Daily 9–5.*

☺ **Rain Forest Sky Rides.** Ever wish you could get a bird's-eye view of the
★ rain forest? Or at least experience it without hiking up and down miles of mountain trails? Here's your chance. Depending on your athleticism and spirit of adventure, choose a two-hour aerial tram ride, a zip-line experience, or both. Either guarantees a magnificent view as you peacefully slip above or actively zip through the canopy of the 3,442-acre Castries Waterworks Rain Forest in Babonneau, 30 minutes east of Rodney Bay. On the tram ride, eight-passenger gondolas glide slowly among the giant trees, twisting vines, and dense thickets of vegetation accented by colorful flowers as a tour guide explains and shares anecdotes about the various trees, plants, birds, and other wonders of nature found in the area. The zip line, on the other hand, is a thrilling experience in which you're rigged with a harness, helmet, and clamps that attach to cables strategically strung through the forest. Short trails connect the 10 lines, so riders come down to earth briefly and hike to the next station before speeding through the forest canopy to the next stop. Bring binoculars and a camera. ⊠ *Chassin, Babonneau* ☎ *758/458–5151* ⊕ *www.rainforestadventure.com* ⊠ *Tram $72, zip line $69, combo $85* ⊗ *Tues.–Sun. 9–4.*

Rodney Bay. This natural bay and an 80-acre man-made lagoon are now surrounded by a huge complex of hotels, popular restaurants, a big mall, and the island's only casino. It's named for Admiral George Rodney, who sailed the British Navy out of Gros Islet Bay in 1780 to attack and ultimately destroy the French fleet. With 232 slips, Rodney Bay Marina is one of the Caribbean's premier yachting centers and the destination of the Atlantic Rally for Cruisers (a transatlantic yacht crossing) each December. Yacht charters and sightseeing day trips can be arranged at the marina. Rodney Bay is about 15 minutes north of Castries; the Rodney Bay Ferry makes hourly crossings between the marina and the mall, as well as daily excursions to Pigeon Island. ⊠ *Rodney Bay.*

SOUFRIÈRE

Soufrière, the site of much of St. Lucia's renowned natural beauty, is the destination of most sightseeing trips. This is where you can get up close to the landmark Pitons and explore the French colonial capital of St. Lucia, with its "drive-in" volcano, botanical gardens, working plantations, waterfalls, and countless other examples of the natural beauty for which St. Lucia is deservedly famous.

WHAT TO SEE

Fodor'sChoice **Diamond Falls Botanical Gardens and Mineral Baths.** These splendid gardens
★ are part of Soufrière Estate, a 2,000-acre land grant presented by King Louis XIV in 1713 to three Devaux brothers from Normandy in recognition of their services to France. The estate is still owned by their descendants; Joan DuBouley Devaux maintains the gardens. Bushes and shrubs bursting with brilliant flowers grow beneath towering trees and line pathways that lead to a natural gorge. Water bubbling to the surface

from underground sulfur springs streams downhill in rivulets to become Diamond Waterfall, deep within the botanical gardens. Through the centuries, the rocks over which the cascade spills have become encrusted with minerals and tinted yellow, green, and purple. Near the falls, mineral baths are fed by the underground springs. King Louis XVI of France provided funds in 1784 for the construction of a building with a dozen large stone baths to fortify his troops against the St. Lucian climate. It's claimed that Joséphine Bonaparte bathed here as a young girl while visiting her father's plantation nearby. During the Brigand's War, just after the French Revolution, the bathhouse was destroyed. In 1930 André DuBoulay had the site excavated, and two of the original stone baths were restored for his use. Outside baths were added later. For a small fee, you can slip into your swimsuit and soak for 30 minutes in one of the outside pools; a private bath costs slightly more. ⊠ *Soufrière Estate, Diamond Rd.* ☎ *758/459–7155* ⊕ *www.diamondstlucia.com* ☞ *$5, public bath $4, private bath $6* ☉ *Mon.–Sat. 10–5, Sun. 10–3.*

Edmund Forest Reserve. Dense tropical rain forest stretches from one side of the island to the other, sprawling over 19,000 acres of mountains and valleys. It's home to a multitude of exotic flowers and plants, as well as rare birds—including the brightly feathered Jacquot parrot. The Edmund Forest Reserve, on the island's western side, is most easily accessible from the road to Fond St. Jacques, which is just east of Soufrière. A trek through the lush landscape, with spectacular views of mountains, valleys, and the sea beyond, can take three or more hours. It takes about 30 minutes from Soufrière and 90 minutes or more from the north end of St. Lucia to reach the reserve by car. It's a strenuous hike, so you need plenty of stamina and sturdy hiking shoes. Permission from the Forest & Lands Department is required to access reserve trails, and the department requires that a naturalist or forest officer guide you because the vegetation is so dense. ☎ *758/450–2231, 758/450–2078 for Forest & Lands Department* ⊕ *www.malff.com* ☞ *Guide for nature trails $10; hiking trails $25; bird-watching $30; guided tours including hotel transfers $55–$85* ☉ *Daily by appointment only.*

☾ ★ **Fond Doux Estate.** One of the earliest French estates established by land grants (1745 and 1763), this plantation still produces cocoa, citrus, bananas, coconut, and vegetables on 135 hilly acres; the restored 1864 plantation house is still in use, as well. A 30-minute walking tour begins at the cocoa fermentary, where you can see the drying process under way. You then follow a trail through the lush cultivated area, where a guide points out various fruit- or spice-bearing trees and tropical flowers. Additional trails lead to old military ruins, a religious shrine, and another vantage point for viewing the spectacular Pitons. Cool drinks and a creole buffet lunch are served at the Jardin Cacao restaurant. Souvenirs, including just-made chocolate sticks, are sold at the boutique. ⊠ *Chateaubelair* ☎ *758/459–7545* ⊕ *www.fonddouxestate.com* ☞ *$10; $25 includes buffet lunch* ☉ *Daily 8–4.*

☾ **La Soufrière Drive-In Volcano.** As you approach, your nose will pick up the strong scent of the sulfur springs—more than 20 belching pools of muddy water, multicolor sulfur deposits, and other assorted minerals baking and steaming on the surface. Despite the name, you don't

DID YOU KNOW?

The Devaux family has owned Diamond Botanical Gardens since 1713; the sulfurous water has stained the surrounding rocks different colors.

actually drive all the way in—you drive up within a few hundred feet of the gurgling, steaming mass and then walk behind your guide—whose service is included in the admission price—around a fault in the substratum rock. It's a fascinating, educational half hour, though it can also be pretty stinky on a hot day. ☏ *758/459–5500* ✉ *$2* ⊙ *Daily 9–5.*

22

⟳ **Morne Coubaril.** On the site of an 18th-century estate, a 250-acre land grant by Louis XIV of France in 1713, the original plantation house has been rebuilt and a farm workers' village has been re-created. It does a good job of showing what life was like for both the owners (a single family owned the land until 1960) and those who did all the hard labor over the centuries producing cotton, coffee, sugarcane, and cocoa. Cocoa, coconuts, and manioc are still grown on the estate using traditional agricultural methods. Guides show how coconuts are opened and roasted for use as oil and animal feed and how cocoa is fermented, dried, crushed by dancing on the beans, and finally, formed into chocolate sticks. Manioc roots (also called cassava) are grated, squeezed of excess water, dried, and turned into flour used in baking. The grounds are lovely for walking or hiking, and the views of mountains and Soufrière Harbour are spellbinding. More adventurous visitors can enjoy Soufrière Hotwire Rides, a zip line excursion with eight stations, taking you under Petit Piton and through the adjacent rain forest. The large, open-air restaurant serves a creole buffet luncheon by reservation only. ✉ *2 miles (3 km) south of town* ☏ *758/459–7340* ⊕ *www. mornecoubarilestate.com; www.stluciaziplining.com* ✉ *$7, with lunch $15; zip line $69* ⊙ *Daily 8–5.*

Fodor's Choice ★ **The Pitons.** Rising precipitously from the cobalt-blue Caribbean Sea just south of Soufrière Bay, these two unusual mountains are a symbol of St. Lucia and also a UNESCO World Heritage Site. Covered with thick tropical vegetation, the massive outcroppings were formed by lava from a volcanic eruption 30 to 40 million years ago. They are not identical twins since—confusingly—2,619-foot Petit Piton is taller than 2,461-foot Gros Piton, though Gros Piton is, as the word translates, broader. It's possible to climb the Pitons, but it's a strenuous trip. Gros Piton is the easier climb, though the trail up even this shorter Piton is still very tough. Either climb requires the permission of the Forest & Lands Department and the use of a knowledgeable guide. ☏ *758/450–2231, 758/450–2078 for St. Lucia Forest & Lands Department* ✉ *Guide services $45* ⊙ *Daily by appointment only.*

Soufrière. The oldest town in St. Lucia and the former French colonial capital, Soufrière was founded by the French in 1746 and named for its proximity to the volcano of the same name. The wharf is the center of activity in this sleepy town (which currently has a population of about 9,000), particularly when a cruise ship anchors in pretty Soufrière Bay. French colonial influences are evident in the second-story verandas, gingerbread trim, and other appointments of the wooden buildings that surround the market square. The market building itself is decorated with colorful murals.

Soufrière Tourist Information Centre. Head here for information about area attractions. Note that souvenir vendors station themselves outside some of the popular attractions in and around Soufrière, and they can be persistent. Be polite but firm if you're not interested. ⊠ *Bay St.* ☎ *758/459–7200.*

VIEUX FORT AND THE EAST COAST

Vieux Fort, on the southeastern tip of St. Lucia, is the location of Hewanorra International Airport, which serves all commercial jet aircraft arriving and departing the island. Although less developed for tourism than the island's north and west, the area around Vieux Fort and points north along the east coast are home to some of St. Lucia's unique ecosystems and interesting natural attractions.

WHAT TO SEE

Barre de l'Isle Forest Reserve. St. Lucia is divided into eastern and western halves by Barre de l'Isle ridge. A mile-long (1½-km-long) trail cuts through the reserve, and four lookout points provide panoramic views. Visible in the distance are Mt. Gimie, immense green valleys, both the Caribbean Sea and the Atlantic Ocean, and coastal communities. The trailhead is about a half-hour drive from Castries; it takes about an hour to walk the trail—an easy hike—and another hour to climb Mt. La Combe Ridge. Permission from the St. Lucia Forest & Lands Department is required to access the trail in Barre de l'Isle; a naturalist or forest officer guide will accompany you. ⊠ *East Coast Rd., midway between Castries and Dennery, Ravine Poisson* ☎ *758/450–2231, 758/450–2078* ⌨ *Guide services $10* ⊙ *Daily, by appointment only.*

Frégate Island Nature Reserve. A mile-long (1½-km) trail encircles the nature reserve, which you reach from the East Coast Road near the fishing village of Praslin. In this area boatbuilders still fashion traditional fishing canoes, called *gommiers* after the trees from which the hulls are made. The Amerindian people, who originally populated the Caribbean, used the ancient design. A natural promontory at Praslin provides a lookout from which you can view the two small islets, Frégate Major and Frégate Minor, and—with luck—the frigate birds that nest here from May to July. The only way to visit is on a guided tour, which includes a ride in a gommier to Frégate Minor for a picnic lunch and a swim; all trips are by reservation only and require a minimum of two people. Arrange visits through your hotel, a tour operator, or the St. Lucia National Trust; many tours include round-trip transportation from your hotel, as well as the tour cost. ⊠ *Praslin* ☎ *758/452–5005, 758/453–7656, 758/454–5014 for tour reservations* ⊕ *www.slunatrust. org* ⌨ *$18* ⊙ *Daily by appointment only.*

Mamiku Gardens. One of St. Lucia's largest and loveliest botanical gardens surrounds the hilltop ruins of the Micoud Estate. Baron Micoud, an 18th-century colonel in the French Army and governor-general of St. Lucia, deeded the land to his wife, Madame de Micoud, to avoid confiscation by the British during one of the many times when St. Lucia changed hands. Locals abbreviated her name to "Ma Micoud," which, over time, became "Mamiku." (The estate did become a British military outpost in 1796 but, shortly thereafter, was burned to the ground by slaves during the Brigand's War.) The estate is now primarily a banana plantation, but the gardens themselves—including several secluded or "secret" gardens—are filled with tropical flowers and plants, delicate orchids, and fragrant herbs. ⊠ *Vieux Fort Hwy., Praslin* ☎ *758/455–3729* ⌨ *$6; guided tour, $8* ☉ *Daily 9–5.*

Maria Islands Nature Reserve. Two tiny islands in the Atlantic Ocean off St. Lucia's southeastern coast make up the reserve, which has its own interpretive center. The 25-acre Maria Major and the 4-acre Maria Minor, its little sister, are inhabited by two rare species of reptiles (the colorful Zandoli Terre ground lizard and the harmless Kouwes grass snake). They share their home with frigate birds, terns, doves, and other wildlife. There's a small beach for swimming and snorkeling, as well as an undisturbed forest, a vertical cliff covered with cacti, and a coral reef for snorkeling or diving. The St. Lucia Trust offers tours, including the boat trip to the islands, by appointment only; bring your own picnic lunch, as there are no facilities. ⊠ *Vieux Fort* ☎ *758/452–5005, 758/453–7656, 758/454–5014 for tour reservations* ⊕ *www.slunatrust. org* ⌨ *$35* ☉ *Aug.–mid-May, Wed.–Sun. 9:30–5, by appointment only.*

22

WHERE TO EAT

Bananas, mangoes, passion fruit, plantains, breadfruit, okra, avocados, limes, pumpkins, cucumbers, papaya, yams, christophenes (also called chayote), and coconuts are among the fresh fruits and vegetables that grace St. Lucian menus. The French influence is strong, and most chefs cook with a creole flair. Resort buffets and restaurant fare include standards like steaks, chops, pasta, and pizza—and every menu lists fresh fish along with the ever-popular lobster.

Caribbean standards include callaloo, stuffed crab back, pepper-pot stew, curried chicken or goat, and *lambi* (conch). The national dish of salt fish and green fig—a stew of dried, salted codfish and boiled green banana—is, let's say, an acquired taste. A runner-up in terms of local popularity is bouyon, a cooked-all-day soup or stew that combines meat (usually pig tail), "provisions" (root vegetables), pigeon peas, dumplings, broth, and local spices. Soups and stews are traditionally prepared in a coal pot, a rustic clay casserole on a matching clay stand that holds the hot coals.

Chicken and pork dishes and barbecues are also popular here. Fresh lobster is available in season, which lasts from August through March. As they do throughout the Caribbean, local vendors set up barbecues along the roadside, at street fairs, and at Friday-night "jump-ups" and do bang-up business selling grilled fish or chicken legs, bakes (fried biscuits), and beer—you can get a full meal for less than $10. Most other meats are imported—beef from Argentina and Iowa, lamb from New Zealand. Piton is the local brew; Bounty, the local rum.

With so many popular all-inclusive resorts, guests take most meals at hotel restaurants—which are generally quite good, and in some cases, exceptional. It's fun when vacationing, however, to try some of the local restaurants, as well—for lunch when sightseeing or for a special night out.

What to Wear: Dress on St. Lucia is casual but conservative. Shorts are usually fine during the day, but bathing suits and immodest clothing are frowned upon anywhere but at the beach. In the evening the mood is casually elegant, but even the fanciest places generally expect only a collared shirt and long pants for men and a sundress or slacks for women.

THE NORTH: RODNEY BAY TO CAP ESTATE

$$$
SEAFOOD

✕ **Buzz.** Opposite the Royal St. Lucian hotel and Reduit Beach, Buzz is in Rodney Bay's "restaurant central." Starting with cool drinks (maybe a Buzz cooler) and warm appetizers (perhaps lobster and crab cakes, crispy calamari, or tempura shrimp) at the friendly bar, diners make their way to the dining room or the garden for some serious seafood or a good steak, baby back ribs, West Indian pepper-pot stew, or spicy lamb shanks. The seared yellowfin tuna, potato-crusted red snapper, and seafood creole are big hits, too. And there's a full vegetarian menu, as well. Fresh lobster is available in season (August–March). ⑤ *Average main: $24* ✉ *Reduit Beach Ave., Rodney Bay* ☎ *758/458–0450* ⊕ *www.buzzstlucia.com* ⌕ *Reservations essential* ⊗ *No lunch. Closed Mon., Apr.–Nov.*

$$$
STEAKHOUSE

✕ **The Charthouse.** Since 1985, The Charthouse has been charcoal broiling U.S. Prime steaks and serving them to hungry St. Lucians and vacationers in an open-air, waterfront location on Rodney Bay. (For those who visit by sea, docking facilities are available at the restaurant.) Some prefer the hickory-smoked baby back ribs or the roast prime rib of beef—or even grilled seafood. In any case, it's all prepared and served by a friendly staff, many of whom have been with the restaurant since it opened. Fresh lobster is delivered daily in season. After dinner, gentlemen (and audacious ladies) can choose from a wide variety of Cuban cigars. Take-out service is also available. ⑤ *Average main: $28* ✉ *Reduit Beach Ave., Rodney Bay* ☎ *758/459–8115* ⊕ *www.charthousestlucia.com* ⌕ *Reservations essential* ⊗ *No lunch.*

$$$$
ECLECTIC
Fodor's Choice
★

✕ **The Edge.** The innovative Swedish chef Bobo Bergstrom, formerly the culinary director at Windjammer Landing and chef de cuisine at the famed Operakallaren in Stockholm, has brought "Eurobbean" cuisine to his own restaurant, which overlooks the harbor at Harmony Suites hotel. St. Lucian locals and visitors alike rave about chef Bobo's culinary feats, the excellent wine list, and the island's first sushi bar. The contemporary fusion style combines the chef's European heritage, Caribbean traditions and ingredients, and a touch of Asian influence. Among the dozen starters is a dreamy lobster bisque seasoned with saffron and paprika. Follow that with snapper braised in fennel bouillon, jerk-marinated-and-grilled beef tenderloin, or spice-glazed rabbit roulade. You might want to consider the five-course tasting menu. There's sure to be a dish on the extensive menu (or at the sushi bar) that suits everyone in your party, but be sure to leave room for a fabulous dessert. ⑤ *Average main: $39* ✉ *Harmony Suites, Reduit Beach Ave., Rodney Bay* ☎ *758/450–3343* ⊕ *www.edge-restaurant.com* ⌕ *Reservations essential.*

$$$ ╳ **Tao.** For exquisite dining, head for Tao at the Body Holiday in Cap
ASIAN   Estate. Perched on a second-floor balcony at the edge of Cariblue Beach,
Fodor'sChoice   you're guaranteed a pleasant breeze and a starry sky while you enjoy
★   fusion cuisine—Asian tastes with a Caribbean touch. Choose from
appetizers such as seafood dumplings, sashimi salad, or miso-eggplant
timbale, followed by tender slices of pork loin teriyaki, twice-cooked
duck, wok-seared calves' liver, or tandoori chicken—the results are
mouthwatering. Fine wines accompany the meal, desserts are extrava-
gant, and service is superb. Seating is limited; hotel guests have prior-
ity, so reserve early. ⑤ *Average main: $30* ✉ *The Body Holiday, Cap
Estate* ☎ 758/457–7800 ⊕ *www.thebodyholiday.com* ⚓ *Reservations
essential* ⊘ *No lunch.*

$$$ ╳ **Ti Bananne.** Poolside at the Coco Palm hotel in Rodney Bay, Ti Bananne
CARIBBEAN   is an open-air Caribbean-style bistro and bar. Breakfast attracts mostly
★   hotel guests, but the elegant yet casual restaurant attacts a wider range
of clientele for lunch and dinner. Lunch is a good bet if you're poking around Rodney Bay, need a break from Reduit Beach, or are just
looking for a good meal in an attractive spot. On Wednesday there's
a special creole lunch buffet; for Sunday brunch, a barbecue buffet. In
the evening the breezy dining room is where the magic really comes
through. The exquisite French-inspired, creole-influenced dishes here
include panfried snapper with orange and butter sauce and green fig
Lyonnaise. Leave room for dessert—the trio of crèmes brûlées (mango
and ginger, coconut, and seamoss and cinnamon) is the showstopper.
And speaking of the show, a live band entertains every evening. ⑤ *Average main: $28* ✉ *Coco Palm, Gros Islet* ☎ 758/456–2828 ⊕ *www.
coco-resorts.com* ⚓ *Reservations essential.*

CASTRIES

$$$$ ╳ **Coal Pot.** Popular since the early 1960s, this tiny (only 10 tables)
FRENCH   waterfront restaurant overlooking pretty Vigie Cove is managed by
Fodor'sChoice   local artist Michelle Elliott and her French husband, Xavier Ribot, who
★   is also the chef. For a light lunch, opt for a bowl of creamy pumpkin
soup, Greek or shrimp salad, or broiled fresh fish with creole sauce. Dinner might start with a divine lobster bisque, followed by fresh seafood
accompanied by one (or more) of the chef's fabulous sauces—ginger,
coconut-curry, lemon-garlic butter, or wild mushroom. Heartier eaters
may prefer duck, lamb, beef, or chicken laced with peppercorns, red
wine, onion, or Roquefort sauce. ⑤ *Average main: $32* ✉ *Vigie Cove
☎ 758/452–5566 ⊕ *www.coalpotrestaurant.com* ⚓ *Reservations essential* ⊘ *Closed Sun. No lunch Sat.*

$$$ ╳ **Jacques Waterfront Dining.** Chef—owner Jacky Rioux creates magical
SEAFOOD   dishes in his open-air garden restaurant, which overlooks Vigie Cove
and was known for years as Froggie Jack's. The cooking style is decid-
edly French, as is Rioux, but fresh produce and local spices create a
fusion cuisine that's memorable at either lunch or dinner. You might
start with a bowl of creamy tomato-basil or pumpkin soup, a grilled
portobello mushroom, or octopus and conch in curried coconut sauce.
Main courses include fresh seafood, such as oven-baked kingfish with
a white wine–and–sweet pepper sauce, or breast of chicken stuffed with

smoked salmon in a citrus-butter sauce. The wine list is also impressive. ⑤ *Average main: $28* ⊠ *Vigie Cove* ☎ *758/458–1900* ⊕ *www.jacques restaurant.com* ⚒ *Reservations essential* ⊘ *Closed Sun.*

MARIGOT BAY

$$
SEAFOOD
☾
★

✗**Chateau Mygo.** Walk down a garden path to Chateau Mygo (a corruption of the word Marigot), pick out a table on the dockside dining deck, pull up a chair, and soak up the waterfront atmosphere of what is arguably the prettiest bay in the Caribbean. The tableau is mesmerizing—and that's at lunch, when you can order a sandwich, burger, fish- or chicken-and-chips, salads, or grilled fish or chicken with peas and rice and vegetables. At dinner, chef–owner Doreen Rambally—whose family has owned and operated this place since the mid-1970s—draws on three generations of East Indian and creole family recipes. Beautifully grilled fresh tuna, red snapper, kingfish, mahimahi, and local lobster are embellished with flavors such as ginger, mango, papaya, or passion fruit, and then dished up with regional vegetables—perhaps callaloo, okra, dasheen, breadfruit, christophene, or yams. You can also have roast pork, beef, a chicken dish, or pizza—and you'll find the only sushi bar on St. Lucia's west coast. This is a very casual restaurant where locals, yachties, and frequent visitors know they'll get a delicious, reasonably priced meal right on the waterfront. And oh, that view! ⑤ *Average main: $20* ⊠ *Marigot Bay* ☎ *758/451–4772.*

$$$$
ECLECTIC
Fodor'sChoice
★

✗**Rainforest Hideaway.** Fusion fare—in this case, the exotic tastes and flavors influencing classical French cuisine—is presented by chef Noel Nugent at this romantic fine-dining hideaway on the north shore of pretty Marigot Bay. It's definitely worth the 20-minute-or-so drive from Castries. A little ferry whisks you to the alfresco restaurant, perched on a dock, where you're greeted with complimentary champagne. You'll be duly impressed by entrées such as balsamic-glazed roast quail, five-spice roast fillet of beef, or citrus-marinated wild salmon, accompanied by rich sauces, exotic vegetables, and excellent wines—not to mention the blanket of stars in the sky overhead and the live jazz several times a week. ⑤ *Average main: $35* ⊠ *Marigot Bay* ☎ *758/286–0511* ⊕ *www. rainforesthideawaystlucia.com* ⚒ *Reservations essential* ⊘ *No lunch; closed Tues.; closed Sept.*

SOUFRIÈRE

$$$
CARIBBEAN

✗**Boucan.** Ahh…chocolate! Here at Boucan on the Rabot Estate, a working cocoa plantation and also home to Hotel Chocolat, you'll find that heavenly flavor infused into just about every dish: cacao gazpacho or citrus salad with white chocolate dressing for starters. The main course might be either red snapper or rib-eye steak marinated with roasted cacao nibs or dorado served with a red wine and cacao sauce. You get the picture. Dessert, of course, is the grand chocolate finale: chocolate tart, meringue floating in a sea of chocolate crème anglaise, dark chocolate mouse…even cacao sorbet. Yum. ⑤ *Average main: $23* ⊠ *Hotel Chocolat, Rabot Estate, West Coast Rd., 3 miles (5 km) south of Soufrière, Soufrière* ☎ *758/457–1624* ⚒ *Reservations essential.*

Amazing views at Dasheene Restaurant in the Ladera Resort

$$$ ╳ **Dasheene Restaurant and Bar.** The terrace restaurant at Ladera resort
CARIBBEAN has breathtakingly close-up views of the Pitons and the sea between
Fodor'sChoice them, especially beautiful at sunset. The ambience is casual by day and
★ magical at night. Executive chef Orlando Satchell describes his creative
West Indian menu as "sexy Caribbean." Appetizers may include grilled
crab claws with a choice of dips or silky pumpkin soup with ginger.
Typical entrées are "fisherman's catch" with a choice of flavored butters
or sauces, shrimp Dasheene (panfried with local herbs), grilled rack of
lamb with coconut risotto and curry sauce, or pan-seared fillet of beef
marinated in lime-and-pepper seasoning. Light dishes, pasta dishes, and
fresh salads are also served at lunch—along with the view. ⑤ *Average
main: $30* ⊠ *Ladera, 2 miles (3 km) south of Soufrière* ☎ *758/459–7323*
⊕ *www.ladera.com.*

$$ ╳ **Lifeline Restaurant at the Hummingbird.** The chef at this cheerful restau-
CARIBBEAN rant-bar in the Hummingbird Beach Resort specializes in French-creole
cuisine, starting with fresh seafood or chicken seasoned with local herbs
and accompanied by vegetables just picked from the Hummingbird's
garden. Sandwiches and salads are also available. If you stop for lunch,
sit outside by the pool for a magnificent view of the Pitons (you can
also take a dip), and be sure to visit the batik studio and art gallery of
proprietor Joan Alexander-Stowe, which is next to the dining room.
⑤ *Average main: $18* ⊠ *Hummingbird Beach Resort, Anse Chastanet
Rd.* ☎ *758/459–7985* ⊕ *www.istlucia.co.uk.*

$$ ╳ **The Still.** When you're visiting Diamond Waterfall and other attrac-
CARIBBEAN tions in Soufrière, this is a great lunch spot. The two dining rooms seat
up to 400 people, so it's also a popular stop for tour groups and cruise
passengers. The emphasis is on local cuisine using vegetables such as

christophene, breadfruit, yam, and callaloo along with grilled fish or chicken, but there are also pork and beef dishes. All fruits and vegetables used in the restaurant are organically grown on the estate. Lunch is a buffet. $ *Average main: $18* ⊠ *The Still Plantation, Sir Arthur Lewis St.* 🕾 *758/459–7261* ⊕ *www.thestillplantation.com* ⊗ *No dinner*.

WHERE TO STAY

Most people—particularly honeymooners—choose to stay in one of St. Lucia's many grand beach resorts, most of which are upscale and pricey. Several are all-inclusive, including the three Sandals resorts, two resorts owned or managed by Sunswept (The Body Holiday and Rendezvous), Almond Morgan Bay, East Winds Inn, and Smugglers Cove Resort & Spa.

If you're looking for lodgings that are smaller and less expensive, St. Lucia has dozens of small inns and hotels that are primarily locally owned and frequently quite charming. They may or may not be directly on the beach. Luxury villa communities and independent private villas are another alternative in St. Lucia. Most of the villa communities are in the north near Cap Estate.

For expanded reviews, facilities, and current deals, visit Fodors.com.

PRIVATE VILLAS AND CONDOS

Luxury villa and condo communities are an important part of the accommodations mix on St. Lucia, as they can be an economical option for families, other groups, or couples vacationing together. Several communities have opened in recent years, and more are on the way. The villa units themselves are privately owned, but non-owners can rent individual units directly from the property managers for a vacation or short-term stay, much like reserving hotel accommodations. Units with fully equipped kitchens, up to three bedrooms, and as many baths run $200 to $2,500 per night, depending on the size and the season.

Local real-estate agencies will arrange vacation rentals of privately owned villas and condos that are fully equipped. Most private villas are in the hills of Cap Estate in the very north of the island, at Rodney Bay or Bois d'Orange, or in Soufrière among St. Lucia's natural treasures. Some are within walking distance of a beach.

All rental villas are staffed with a cook who specializes in local cuisine, and a housekeeper; in some cases, a caretaker lives on the property and a gardener and night watchman are on staff. All properties have telephones, and some have Internet access and fax machines. Telephones may be barred against outgoing overseas calls; plan to use a phone card or calling card. Most villas have TVs, DVDs, and CD players. All private villas have a swimming pool; condos share a community pool. Vehicles are generally not included in the rates, but rental cars can be arranged for and delivered to the villa upon request. Linens and basic supplies (such as bath soap, toilet tissue, and dish-washing detergent) are included. Pre-arrival grocery stocking can be arranged.

Units with one to nine bedrooms and the same number of baths run $200 to $2,000 per night, depending on the size of the villa, the amenities, the number of guests, and the season. Rates include utilities and government taxes. Your only additional cost will be for groceries and staff gratuities. A security deposit is required upon booking and refunded after departure less any damages or unpaid miscellaneous charges.

Rental Contacts Discover Villas of St. Lucia. ✉ *Cap Estate* ☎ *758/484–3066* ⊕ *www.a1stluciavillas.com.* **Island Villas St. Lucia.** ✉ *Gros Islet* ☎ *758/458– 4903, 866/978–8499 in the U.S.* ⊕ *www.island-villas.com/stlucia.php.* **Tropical Villas.** ✉ *Cap Estate* ☎ *758/450-8240* ⊕ *www.tropicalvillas.net.*

THE NORTH: RODNEY BAY TO CAP ESTATE

$$

ALL-INCLUSIVE

☺

🏨 **Almond Morgan Bay Beach Resort.** An all-inclusive resort for singles, couples, and families alike, Almond Morgan Bay offers both quiet seclusion on 22 acres surrounding a stretch of white-sand beach and tons of free sports and activities. **Pros:** family-friendly; lots to do; golf privileges nearby; great dining atmosphere at Morgan's Pier. **Cons:** resort is huge and can be very busy, especially when all rooms are filled; beach is small. **TripAdvisor:** "friendly staff," "good service," "an inclusive holiday to remember." ⑤ *Rooms from: $340* ✉ *Choc Bay, Castries* ☎ *758/450– 2511* ⊕ *www.almondresorts.com* ⤳ *340 rooms* ¶◎¶ *All-inclusive.*

$

RESORT

☺

★

🏨 **Bay Gardens Beach Resort.** One of three Bay Gardens properties in Rodney Bay Village, the family-friendly beach resort has a prime location directly on beautiful Reduit Beach. **Pros:** perfect location on St. Lucia's best beach; excellent value; stay at one, play at three resorts. **Cons:** popular place, so you need to book far in advance in season. **TripAdvisor:** "fabulous," "beautiful beachfront resort," "amazing family vacation." ⑤ *Rooms from: $185* ✉ *Reduit Beach Ave., Rodney Bay* ☎ *758/457– 8500, 877/629–3200 in the U.S.* ⊕ *www.baygardensbeachresort.com* ⤳ *36 rooms, 36 suites* ¶◎¶ *Multiple meal plans.*

$

HOTEL

🏨 **Bay Gardens Hotel.** Independent travelers and regional businesspeople swear by this cheerful, well-run boutique hotel at Rodney Bay Village. **Pros:** excellent service; great value; Croton suites are a best bet. **Cons:** not beachfront; heavy focus on business travelers, so it's not exactly a vacation environment. **TripAdvisor:** "great location," "wonderful people," "really friendly." ⑤ *Rooms from: $96* ✉ *Rodney Bay* ☎ *758/452–8060, 877/620–3200* ⊕ *www.baygardenshotel.com* ⤳ *59 rooms, 28 suites* ¶◎¶ *Multiple meal plans.*

$$$$

ALL-INCLUSIVE

Fodor's Choice

★

🏨 **The Body Holiday.** At this adults-only spa resort on picturesque Cariblue Beach—where daily treatments are included in the rates—you can customize your own "body holiday" onlin even before you leave home. **Pros:** daily spa treatment included; excellent dining; interesting activities such as archery (including free instruction). **Cons:** extremely expensive; unremarkable rooms; small bathrooms; lots of steps to the spa. **TripAdvisor:** "five-star luxury," "the whole package," "a complete rejuvenation experience." ⑤ *Rooms from: $1,162* ✉ *Cariblue Beach, Cap Estate* ☎ *758/457–7800* ⊕ *www.thebodyholiday.com* ⤳ *152 rooms, 3 suites* ¶◎¶ *All-inclusive.*

Cotton Bay Village

$$$$
RESORT
Fodors Choice
★

 Calabash Cove Resort & Spa. The luxurious suites and private cottages at this inviting boutique resort spill gently down a tropical hillside to the secluded beach at Bonaire Bay, just south of Rodney Bay. **Pros:** stylish, sophisticated, and friendly; great food; wedding parties can reserve the entire resort. **Cons:** the long, bone-crunching dirt entrance road; its many steps may be difficult for those with physical challenges. **TripAdvisor:** "most amazing place," "absolute bliss," "very quiet and very nice." ⑤ *Rooms from: $445* ⊠ *Bonaire Estate, Rodney Bay* ☎ *758/456–3500* ⊕ *www.calabashcove.com* ✎ *17 suites; 9 cottages* ⑩ *Multiple meal plans.*

$$$
RESORT
Fodors Choice
★

Cap Maison. This luxurious villa community on a seaside bluff overlooking Smugglers Cove has 22 units that can be configured as up to 49 rooms, junior suites, and oversize one-, two-, or three-bedroom villa suites. **Pros:** private and elegant; golf and tennis privileges nearby; those rooftop plunge pools. **Cons:** a/c in bedrooms only; beach access (the 62 steps) may be a consideration. **TripAdvisor:** "a quiet and relaxing place," "secluded and pretty," "wonderful getaway." ⑤ *Rooms from: $435* ⊠ *Smugglers Cove Dr., Cap Estate* ☎ *758/457–8670, 888/765–4985 in the U.S.* ⊕ *www.capmaison.com* ✎ *10 rooms, 39 suites in 22 villas* ⑩ *Multiple meal plans.*

$
HOTEL
☾
★

Coco Palm. This stylish boutique hotel in Rodney Bay Village also includes Coco Kreole, a cozy guesthouse at the edge of the property, and is right in the middle of the Rodney Bay Village action. **Pros:** excellent value; fabulous swim-up rooms; family suites. **Cons:** not directly on the beach; nightly entertainment can get noisy. **TripAdvisor:** "fabulous pool," "the definition of service," "comfortable hotel with welcoming staff." ⑤ *Rooms from: $156* ⊠ *Reduit Beach Ave., Rodney Bay*

☏ *758/456–2800, 877/655–2626 in the U.S.* ⊕ *www.coco-resorts.com* 🛏 *80 rooms, 12 suites* ❙❂❙ *Multiple meal plans.*

$$
RESORT
☺
★

🏨 **Cotton Bay Village.** Wedged between a quiet ocean beach and the St. Lucia Golf Resort & Country Club, these luxurious, individually designed and decorated colonial-style town houses and château-style villas surround a village center and a free-form lagoon pool. **Pros:** truly luxurious; very private; family-friendly. **Cons:** a/c in bedrooms only; bathrooms have showers only; rental car advised if you plan to leave the property. **TripAdvisor:** "beautiful villas," "spacious accommodation," "a relaxing stay." ⑤ *Rooms from: $313* ✉ *Cap Estate* ☏ *758/456–5700* ⊕ *www.cottonbayvillage.com* 🛏 *206 suites in 74 villas* ❙❂❙ *No meals.*

$$$$
ALL-INCLUSIVE

🏨 **East Winds Inn.** Guests keep returning to East Winds Inn, a small all-inclusive resort on a secluded beach halfway between Castries and Rodney Bay, where 7 acres of botanical gardens surround 13 duplex gingerbread-style cottages, three ocean-view rooms, and a suite. **Pros:** long-established clientele is the best recommendation; lovely beach; excellent dining; peaceful and quiet. **Cons:** not the best choice for families (though children are welcome); very expensive. **TripAdvisor:** "the most relaxing spot," "where everyone knows your name," "a Caribbean gem." ⑤ *Rooms from: $890* ✉ *Labrelotte Bay* ☏ *758/452–8212* ⊕ *www.eastwinds.com* 🛏 *30 rooms* ❙❂❙ *All-inclusive.*

$$$$
RESORT
☺
★

🏨 **The Landings.** On 19 acres along the Pigeon Point Causeway at the northern edge of Rodney Bay, the Landings is so called because the property surrounds a private, 80-slip yacht harbor where residents can dock their own yachts literally at their doorstep. **Pros:** spacious, beautifully appointed units; perfect place for yachties to come ashore; personal chef service. **Con:** additional $30 per day "activities fee." **TripAdvisor:** "beautiful beach," "outstanding resort," "laid-back beauty." ⑤ *Rooms from: $519* ✉ *Pigeon Island Causeway, Gros Islet* ☏ *758/458–7300* ⊕ *www.landings.rockresorts.com* 🛏 *122 units* ❙❂❙ *No meals.*

$$$$
RESORT
★

🏨 **Royal St. Lucia by Rex Resorts.** This luxurious all-suites resort on St. Lucia's best beach caters to every whim—for the whole family. **Pros:** great beachfront; roomy accommodations; family-friendly; convenient to restaurants, clubs, and shops. **Cons:** dated guest rooms and baths; expensive. **TripAdvisor:** "a very special place," "fantastic location and spacious rooms," "excellent service." ⑤ *Rooms from: $789* ✉ *Reduit Beach Ave., Rodney Bay* ☏ *758/452–8351* ⊕ *www.rexcaribbean.com* 🛏 *96 suites* ❙❂❙ *Multiple meal plans.*

$$$$
ALL-INCLUSIVE
Fodor's Choice
★

🏨 **Sandals Grande St. Lucian Spa & Beach Resort.** Grand, yes. And busy, busy, busy. Couples love this place—particularly young honeymooners and those getting married here—the biggest and splashiest of the three Sandals resorts on St. Lucia. **Pros:** excellent beach; lots of activities; dreamy spa; airport shuttle. **Cons:** the really long ride to and from Hewanorra; buffet meals are uninspired. **TripAdvisor:** "beautiful and relaxing," "a week I'll never forget," "all great except the food." ⑤ *Rooms from: $576* ✉ *Pigeon Island Causeway, Gros Islet* ☏ *758/455–2000* ⊕ *www.sandals.com* 🛏 *271 rooms, 11 suites* ❙❂❙ *All-inclusive.*

$$$$
ALL-INCLUSIVE

🏨 **Sandals Halcyon Beach St. Lucia.** This is the most intimate and low-key of the three Sandals resorts on St. Lucia; like the others, though, it's beachfront, all-inclusive, for couples only, and loaded with amenities

Sandals Grande St. Lucian Spa & Beach Resort

and activities. **Pros:** all the Sandals amenities in a more intimate setting; lots of dining and activity choices; exchange privileges (including golf) at two other Sandals properties. **Cons:** it's Sandals, so it's a theme property after all. **TripAdvisor:** "clean and relaxing," "first-class service," "intimate." $ *Rooms from: $485* ⊠ *Choc Bay, Castries* ☎ *758/453–0222, 888/726–3257* ⊕ *www.sandals.com* ⇨ *169 rooms* |○| *All-inclusive.*

$$$$
ALL-INCLUSIVE

🛏 **Sandals Regency St. Lucia Golf Resort & Spa.** One of three Sandals resorts on St. Lucia, this is the second-largest and distinguishes itself with its own 9-hole golf course (for guests only). **Pros:** lots to do; picturesque location; on-site golf; airport shuttle. **Cons:** somewhat isolated; expert golfers will prefer the St. Lucia Golf Resort & Country Club, in Cap Estate. **TripAdvisor:** "amazing from start to finish," "great resort," "be back soon." $ *Rooms from: $491* ⊠ *La Toc Rd., Castries* ☎ *758/452–3081* ⊕ *www.sandals.com* ⇨ *212 rooms, 116 suites* |○| *All-inclusive.*

$$
ALL-INCLUSIVE
�映

🛏 **Smugglers Cove Resort & Spa.** This huge, all-inclusive, village-style resort has more food, fun, and features than you and your family will have time to enjoy in a week. **Pros:** family rooms sleep five; excellent children's program; superlative tennis facilities; nightly entertainment is family-friendly. **Cons:** busy, busy, busy; not the place for a quiet getaway; guest rooms are spread far and wide on the hillside. **TripAdvisor:** "an A+ vacation resort," "great resort for your first time in St. Lucia," "loved the food." $ *Rooms from: $325* ⊠ *Cap Estate* ☎ *758/457–4140, 855/719—321 in the U.S.* ⊕ *www.smugglersresort.com* ⇨ *257 rooms, 100 suites* |○| *All-inclusive.*

Sandals Halcyon Beach, the Pierhouse Restaurant

$$
RESORT

⌚

★

🏨 **Windjammer Landing Villa Beach Resort.** As perfect for families as for a romantic getaway, Windjammer Landing offers lots to do yet still provides plenty of privacy. **Pros:** lovely, spacious units; beautiful sunset views; family-friendly, in-unit dining. **Cons:** some units have living rooms with no a/c; you'll want to rent a car if you plan to leave the property often, as it's far from the main road. **TripAdvisor:** "hospitality A+," "a unique retreat," "beautiful views." ⑤ *Rooms from: $359* ✉ *Trouya Point Rd., Labrelotte Bay* ☎ *758/456–9000, 877/522–0722 in the U.S.* ⊕ *www.windjammer-landing.com* ➳ *41 suites, 72 villas* 🍽 *Multiple meal plans.*

GREATER CASTRIES

$$$$
ALL-INCLUSIVE

★

🏨 **Rendezvous.** Romance is alive and well at this easygoing, all-inclusive couples resort, which stretches along the dreamy white sand of Malabar Beach opposite the George F.L. Charles Airport runway. **Pros:** convenient to Castries and Vigie Airport; great beach; romance in the air; popular wedding venue. **Cons:** no room TVs; occasional flyover noise. **TripAdvisor:** "a relaxing experience," "total bliss," "fantastic staff." ⑤ *Rooms from: $838* ✉ *Vigie, Castries* ☎ *758/457–7900* ⊕ *www.theromanticholiday.com* ➳ *57 rooms, 35 suites, 8 cottages* 🍽 *All-inclusive.*

MARIGOT BAY TO ANSE LA RAYE

$$$$
RESORT
☺
Fodor'sChoice
★

◻ Discovery at Marigot Bay. Five miles (8 km) south of Castries, this chic, ecofriendly villa resort climbs the hillside of what author James Michener called "the most beautiful bay in the Caribbean." **Pros:** peaceful and picturesque, with a stunning bay view; oversize villa accommodations; 12 ground-level units available for those with difficulty negotiating stairs. **Cons:** a/c in bedrooms only; you'll need a rental car to explore beyond Marigot Bay; nearby beach is pretty but tiny. **TripAdvisor:** "beautiful location," "wonderful service," "an oasis of class." ⑤ *Rooms from: $500* ⊠ *Marigot Bay* ☎ *758/458–5300, 877/384–8037 in the U.S.* ⊕ *www.discoverystlucia.com* ↷ *67 rooms, 57 suites* ◎ *Multiple meal plans.*

$$
RESORT
★

◻ Ti Kaye Village. Rustic elegance is not an oxymoron, at least at this upscale cottage community on the hillside up from Anse Cochon beach. **Pros:** perfect for a wedding, honeymoon, or private getaway; love those garden showers; good restaurant; excellent beach for snorkeling; dive shop on-site. **Cons:** far from anywhere; very bumpy 1.5-mile (2-km) dirt access road; all those steps to the beach; not a good choice for anyone with physical challenges; no kids under age 12. **TripAdvisor:** "beautiful resort and surroundings," "great private resort," "relaxing vacation spot." ⑤ *Rooms from: $325* ⊠ *Anse Cochon* ☎ *758/456–8101* ⊕ *www.tikaye.com* ↷ *33 rooms* ◎ *Multiple meal plans.*

SOUFRIÈRE

$$$$
RESORT
★

◻ Anse Chastanet Resort. This resort is magical—spectacular rooms, some with stunning Piton vistas beyond open fourth walls, peek out of the thick rain forest that cascades down a steep hillside to the sea. **Pros:** great for divers; Room 14B, which has a tree growing through the bathroom; the open-air Piton views. **Cons:** no pool; entrance road is difficult to negotiate; steep hillside certainly not conducive to strolling; some may miss in-room TVs, phones, and a/c. **TripAdvisor:** "laid-back friendly staff," "good old-fashioned Caribbean experience," "excellent food and service." ⑤ *Rooms from: $495* ⊠ *Anse Chastanet Rd.* ☎ *758/459–7000, 800/223–1108 in U.S.* ⊕ *www.ansechastanet.com* ↷ *49 rooms* ◎ *Multiple meal plans.*

$$$$
HOTEL

◻ Hotel Chocolat. Anyone who loves chocolate will love this little cottage community just south of Soufrière and within shouting distance of the Pitons. **Pros:** small and sophisticated; chocolate lover's dream hotel; no service charge and no tipping expected. **Cons:** rental car advised; not for anyone allergic or less than thrilled by the idea of all that chocolate. **TripAdvisor:** "eco-friendly luxury," "foodie paradise," "sunny smiles and wonderful food." ⑤ *Rooms from: $550* ⊠ *Rabot Estate, West Coast Rd., 2 miles (3 km) south of town, Soufrière* ☎ *758/457–1624, 800/757–7132 in the U.S.* ⊕ *www.thehotelchocolat.com* ↷ *14 rooms* ◎ *Multiple meal plans.*

$
B&B/INN

◻ Hummingbird Beach Resort. Unpretentious and welcoming, this delightful little inn on Soufrière Harbour has simply furnished rooms—a traditional motif emphasized by four-poster beds and African wood sculptures—in small seaside cabins. **Pros:** local island hospitality;

small and quiet; good food. **Cons:** few resort amenities—but that's part of the charm. **TripAdvisor:** "great restaurant," "breathtaking views," "friendly service." ⑤ *Rooms from: $90 ⊠ Anse Chastanet Rd.* ☎ *758/459–7985, 888/790–5264 in the U.S.* ⊕ *www.istlucia.co.uk* ⇨ *9 rooms, 2 with shared bath; 1 suite; 1 cottage* ⦿*Multiple meal plans.*

$$$$
RESORT
Fodor'sChoice
★

Jade Mountain. This premium-class and premium-priced hotel is a five-level behemoth stuck on the side of a mountain that slopes down to the sea. **Pros:** amazing accommodations; huge in-room pools; incredible Piton views. **Cons:** sky-high rates; lack of in-room communication and a/c; not appropriate for children or anyone with disabilities. **TripAdvisor:** "with view you only dream about," "very special," "absolutely amazing." ⑤ *Rooms from: $1,200 ⊠ Anse Chastanet, Anse Chastanet Rd.* ☎ *758/459–4000* ⊕ *www.jademountainstlucia.com* ⇨ *28 suites* ⦿*Multiple meal plans.*

$$$$
RESORT
☾
Fodor'sChoice
★

The Jalousie Plantation, Sugar Beach. Located on the most dramatic 192 acres in St. Lucia, Jalousie Plantation flows down Val des Pitons—the steep valley smack between the Pitons—on the remains of an 18th-century sugar plantation 2 miles (3 km) south of Soufrière. **Pros:** incomparable scenery, service, and amenities; family-friendly; lots of activities, including complimentary scuba diving. **Cons:** very expensive; fairly isolated, so a meal plan makes sense; cottages are surrounded by thick foliage, so bring mosquito spray. **TripAdvisor:** "exotic and beautiful location," "made to feel welcome," "amazing hotel in a dream setting." ⑤ *Rooms from: $900 ⊠ Val de Pitons, 2 miles (3 km) south of town* ☎ *800/235–4300, 758/456–8000* ⊕ *www.jalousieplantation.com* ⇨ *11 rooms, 42 villas* ⦿*Multiple meal plans.*

$$$$
B&B/INN
Fodor'sChoice
★

Ladera. One of the most sophisticated small inns in the Caribbean, the elegantly rustic Ladera is perched 1,100 feet above the sea directly between the two Pitons. **Pros:** breathtaking Pitons vista; in-room pools; excellent cuisine. **Cons:** the hotel's communal infinity pool is not very big; open fourth walls and steep drops make this inappropriate for children (and also means no a/c); rental car advised. **TripAdvisor:** "more rustic than luxurious," "everything was stunning," "a unique place." ⑤ *Rooms from: $665 ⊠ West Coast Rd., 3 miles (5 km) south of town, Val de Pitons* ☎ *758/459–6600, 866/290–0978 in the U.S.* ⊕ *www. ladera.com* ⇨ *23 suites, 9 villas* ⦿*Multiple meal plans.*

$$$$
RESORT
★

Stonefield Estate Villa Resort & Spa. One 18th-century plantation house and several gingerbread-style cottages dot this 26-acre family-owned estate, a tropical hillside with eye-popping views of Petit Piton. **Pros:** very private; beautiful pool; great sunset views from villa decks; lovely wedding venue. **Cons:** a rental car is recommended; you have to drive to off-site restaurants. **TripAdvisor:** "beautiful location," "super relaxing and very private," "fantastic views." ⑤ *Rooms from: $545 ⊠ West Coast Rd., 1 mile (1½ km) south of Soufrière* ☎ *758/459–7037* ⊕ *www. stonefieldvillas.com* ⇨ *17 villas* ⦿*Multiple meal plans.*

VIEUX FORT

$$$$
ALL-INCLUSIVE
☾

Coconut Bay Beach Resort & Spa. The only resort in Vieux Fort, Coconut Bay is a sprawling (85 acres), family-friendly seaside retreat minutes from St. Lucia's Hewanorra International Airport. **Pros:** great for families; perfect for windsurfers; friendly and sociable atmosphere. **Cons:** bathrooms have showers only; rough surf precludes ocean swimming; close to the airport but far from everything else. **TripAdvisor:** "week in paradise," "great beach and pools," "beautiful location." ⑤ *Rooms from: $659* ⊠ *Vieux Fort* ☎ *758/459–6000* ⊕ *www. cbayresort.com* ⮎ *254 rooms* ❦ *All-inclusive.*

NIGHTLIFE AND THE ARTS

THE ARTS

Fodor's Choice   **St. Lucia Jazz Festival.** Held in early May, the weeklong St. Lucia Jazz
★   Festival is one of the premier events of its kind in the Caribbean. International jazz greats perform at outdoor venues on Pigeon Island and at various hotels, restaurants, and nightspots throughout the island; free concerts are also held at Derek Walcott Square in downtown Castries. ⊠ *Pigeon Island, Gros Islet* ⊕ *www.stluciajazz.org.*

THEATER

Derek Walcott Center Theatre. The small, open-air Derek Walcott Center Theatre, next to The Great House restaurant in Cap Estate, seats 200 people for monthly productions of music, dance, and drama, as well as Sunday brunch programs. The Trinidad Theatre Workshop also presents an annual performance here. For schedule and ticket information, contact The **Great House** restaurant. ⊠ *next to The Great House, Cap Estate* ☎ *758/450–0551, 758/450–0450 for the Great House.*

NIGHTLIFE

Most resort hotels have entertainment—island music, calypso singers, and steel bands, as well as disco, karaoke, and talent shows—every night in high season and a couple of nights per week in the off-season. Otherwise, Rodney Bay is the best bet for nightlife. The many restaurants and bars there attract a crowd nearly every night.

BARS

Jambe de Bois. At this cozy Old English–style pub, there's live jazz on Sunday and violin on Thursday. ⊠ *Pigeon Island, Gros Islet* ☎ *758/450–8166.*

CASINOS

Treasure Bay Casino. St. Lucia opened its first casino in early 2011. You'll find more than 250 slot machines, along with 22 gaming tables (poker, blackjack, roulette, and craps) and a sports bar with 31 television screens. ⊠ *Bay Walk Shopping Mall, Rodney Bay* ☎ *758/459–2901* ⊕ *www.treasurebaystlucia.com* ☉ *Sun.–Thurs. 10 am–3 am, Fri.–Sat., 10 am–4 am.*

DANCE CLUBS

Rodney Bay has the most bars and clubs. Most dance clubs with live bands have a cover charge of $10 to $20 (EC$25 to EC$50), and the music usually starts at 11 pm.

22

Delirius. At Delirius, visitors and St. Lucians alike "lime" over cocktails at the horseshoe-shaped bar and at tables in the garden. The atmosphere is casual, the decor is contemporary, and the music (live bands or DJ) from the 1960s, '70s, and '80s. ⊠ *Reduit Beach Ave., Rodney Bay* ☎ *758/451–3354.*

Doolittle's. The music at Doolittle's changes nightly. Expect live bands and a mix of calypso, soul, salsa, steel band, reggae, limbo, and other music for dancing. ⊠ *Marigot Beach Club, Marigot Bay* ☎ *758/451–4974.*

STREET PARTIES

★ **Anse La Raye "Seafood Friday".** For a taste of St. Lucian village life, head for this street festival, held every Friday night. Beginning at 6:30 pm, the main street in this tiny fishing village—about halfway between Castries and Soufrière—is closed to vehicles, and the residents prepare what they know best: fish cakes, grilled or stewed fish, hot bakes (biscuits), roasted corn, boiled crayfish, and lobster (it's grilled before your eyes). Prices range from a few cents for a fish cake or bake to $10 or $15 for a whole lobster, depending on its size. Walk around, eat, chat with the local people, and listen to live music until the wee hours of the morning. ⊠ *Anse la Raye.*

Fodor's Choice **Gros Islet Jump-Up.** A Friday-night ritual for locals and visitors alike is to head to the Gros Islet Jump-Up, the island's largest street party. Huge speakers set up on the village's main street blast out Caribbean music all night long. Sometimes there are live bands. When you take a break from dancing, you can buy barbecued fish or chicken, rotis, beer, and soda from villagers who set up grills right along the roadside. It's the ultimate "lime" experience. ⊠ *Gros Islet.*

SHOPPING

The island's best-known products are artwork and wood carvings, straw mats, clay pottery, and clothing and household articles made from batik and silk-screened fabrics that are designed and produced in island workshops. You can also take home straw hats and baskets and locally grown cocoa, coffee, spices, sauces, and flavorings.

AREAS AND MALLS

★ **Baywalk Mall,** at Rodney Bay, is a 60-store complex of boutiques, restaurants, banks, a beauty salon, jewelry and souvenir stores, and the island's first casino.

Along the harbor in Castries, rambling structures with bright-orange roofs house several markets that are open from 6 am to 5 pm Monday through Saturday. Saturday morning is the busiest and most colorful time to shop. For more than a century, farmers' wives have gathered at the **Castries Market** to sell produce—which, alas, you can't import to the United States. But you can bring back spices (such as cocoa, turmeric, cloves, bay leaves, ginger, peppercorns, cinnamon sticks, nutmeg, and mace), as well as bottled hot-pepper sauces—all of which cost a fraction of what you'd pay back home. The **Craft Market,** adjacent to the produce market, has aisles and aisles of baskets and other handmade straw work, rustic brooms made from palm fronds, wood carvings, leather work, clay pottery, and souvenirs—all at affordable prices. The **Vendors' Arcade,** across the street from the Craft Market, is a maze of stalls and booths where you can find handicrafts among the T-shirts and costume jewelry.

Gablewoods Mall, on the Gros Islet Highway in Choc Bay, a couple of miles north of downtown Castries, has about 35 shops that sell groceries, wines and spirits, jewelry, clothing, crafts, books and overseas newspapers, music, souvenirs, household goods, and snacks.

Along with 54 boutiques, restaurants, and other businesses that sell services and supplies, a large supermarket is the focal point of each **J.Q.'s Shopping Mall;** one is at Rodney Bay and another is at Vieux Fort.

Marigot Marina Village in Marigot Bay has shops and services for boaters and landlubbers alike, including a bank, grocery store, business center, art gallery, assortment of boutiques, and French bakery and café.

Duty-free shopping areas are at **Pointe Seraphine,** an attractive Spanish-motif complex on Castries Harbour with more than 20 shops, and **La Place Carenage,** an inviting three-story complex on the opposite side of the harbor. You can also find duty-free items at Baywalk Mall, in a few small shops at the arcade at the Royal St. Lucia hotel in Rodney Bay, and, of course, in the departure lounge at Hewanorra International Airport. You must present your passport and airline ticket to purchase items at the duty-free price.

Vieux Fort Plaza, near Hewanorra International Airport in Vieux Fort, is the main shopping center in the southern part of St. Lucia. You'll find a bank, supermarket, bookstore, toy shop, and several clothing stores there.

SPECIALTY ITEMS

ART

Artsibit Gallery. The moderately priced works on display here are made by local painters and sculptors. ⊠ *Brazil and Mongiraud Sts., Castries* ☎ *758/452–7865.*

Caribbean Art Gallery. On offer here are original artwork by local artists, along with antique maps and prints and hand-painted silk. ⊠ *Rodney Bay Marina, Rodney Bay* ☎ *758/452–8071.*

Llewellyn Xavier. World-renowned St. Lucian artist Llewellyn Xavier creates modern art, ranging from vigorous oil abstracts that take up half a wall, to small objects made from beaten silver and gold. Much of his work has an environmental theme and is created from recycled materials. Xavier's work is on permanent exhibit at major museums in New York and Washington, D.C. Others are sold in gift shops throughout the island. Call to arrange a visit to his studio. ⊠ *Mount du Cap, Cap Estate* ☎ *758/450–9155* ⊕ *www.llewellynxavier.com.*

BOOKS AND MAGAZINES

Sunshine Bookshop. In addition to newspapers and magazines, Sunshine Bookshop carries novels and titles of regional interest, including books by the St. Lucian Nobel laureate Derek Walcott and other Caribbean authors. ⊠ *Gablewoods Mall, Castries* ☏ *758/452–3222.*

Valmont Books. This shop carries West Indian literature and picture books, as well as stationery. ⊠ *Jeremie and Laborie Sts., Castries* ☏ *758/452–3817.*

CLOTHES AND TEXTILES

★ **The Bagshaws of St. Lucia.** Using Sydney Bagshaw's original designs, this shop sells clothing and table linens in colorful tropical patterns. The fabrics are silk-screened by hand in the adjacent workroom. You can also find Bagshaw boutiques at Pointe Seraphine and La Place Carenage, as well as a selection of items in gift shops at Hewanorra Airport. Visit the workshop to see how the designs are turned into colorful silk-screened fabrics, which are then fashioned into clothing and household articles. It's open weekdays from 8:30 to 5, Saturday 8:30 to 4, and Sunday 10 to 1. Weekend hours may be extended if a cruise ship is in port. ⊠ *La Toc Rd., La Toc Bay, Castries* ☏ *758/451–9249.*

The Batik Studio. The superb batik sarongs, scarves, and wall panels here are designed and created on-site by Joan Alexander-Stowe. ⊠ *Hummingbird Beach Resort, Anse Chastanet Rd., Soufrière* ☏ *758/459–7985.*

Caribelle Batik. At Caribelle Batik, craftspeople demonstrate the art of batik and silk-screen printing. Meanwhile, seamstresses create clothing and wall hangings, which you can purchase in the shop. The studio is in an old Victorian mansion, high atop Morne Fortune, overlooking Castries. There's a terrace where you can have a cool drink and a garden full of tropical orchids and lilies. Caribelle Batik creations are featured in many gift shops throughout St. Lucia. ⊠ *Howelton House, Old Victoria Rd., Morne Fortune, Castries* ☏ *758/452–3785* ⊕ *www.caribellebatikstlucia.com.*

Sea Island Cotton Shop. High-quality T-shirts, Caribelle Batik clothing and other resort wear, and colorful souvenirs are all for sale here. ⊠ *Baywalk Mall, Rodney Bay* ☏ *758/458–4220* ⊕ *www.seaislandstlucia.com* ⊠ *Gablewoods Mall, Choc Bay, Castries* ☏ *758/451–6946.*

GIFTS AND SOUVENIRS

Caribbean Perfumes. Using exotic flowers, fruits, tropical woods, and spices, Caribbean Perfumes blends a half dozen lovely scents for women and two aftershaves for men. The reasonably priced fragrances, all made in St. Lucia, are available at the perfumery (in the garden adjacent to the restaurant) and at many hotel gift shops. ⊠ *Jacques Waterfront Dining, Vigie Marina, Castries* ☏ *758/453–7249* ⊕ *www.caribbeanperfumes.com.*

HANDICRAFTS

Choiseul Arts & Crafts Centre. You can find locally made clay and straw pieces at the Choiseul Arts & Crafts Centre. It's on the southwest coast, halfway between Soufrière and Vieux Fort; many of St. Lucia's artisans come from this area. ⊠ *La Fargue* ☏ *758/454–3226.*

Eudovic Art Studio. Head to this workshop and studio for trays, masks, and abstract figures sculpted by Vincent Joseph Eudovic from local mahogany, red cedar, and eucalyptus wood. ⊠ *Goodlands, Morne Fortune, Castries* ☎ *758/452–2747* ⊕ *www.eudovicart.com.*

Zaka. At Zaka, you may get a chance to talk with artist and craftsman Simon Gajhadhar, who fashions totems and masks from driftwood and other environmentally friendly sources of wood—taking advantage of all the natural nibs and knots that distinguish each piece. Once the "face" is carved, it is painted in vivid colors to highlight the exaggerated features and provide expression. Each piece is unique. ⊠ *Malgretoute, on the road to Jalousie Plantation, Soufrière* ☎ *758/457–1504* ⊕ *www.zaka-art.com.*

SPORTS AND ACTIVITIES

BIKING

Although the terrain is pretty rugged, two tour operators have put together fascinating bicycle and combination bicycle-hiking tours that appeal to novice riders as well as those who enjoy a good workout. Prices range from $60 to $100 per person.

★ **Bike St. Lucia.** This company takes small groups of bikers on Jungle Biking tours along trails that meander through the remnants of the 18th-century plantation that's part of the Anse Chastanet estate in Soufrière. Stops are made to explore the French colonial ruins, study the beautiful tropical plants and fruit trees, enjoy a picnic lunch, and take a dip in a river swimming hole or a swim at the beach. There's a training area for learning or brushing up on off-road riding skills. If you're staying in the north, you can arrange a tour that includes transportation to the Soufrière area. ⊠ *Anse Mamin Plantation, adjacent to Anse Chastanet, Soufrière* ☎ *758/457–1400* ⊕ *www.bikestlucia.com.*

Palm Services Bike Tours. To start a Palm Services tour, participants first take a jeep or bus across the central mountains to Dennery, on the east coast. After a 3-mile (5-km) ride through the countryside, bikes are exchanged for shoe leather. The short hike into the rain forest ends with a picnic and a refreshing swim next to a sparkling waterfall—then the return leg to Dennery. All gear is included, and the tours are suitable for all fitness levels. ⊠ *Rodney Bay* ☎ *758/458–0908* ⊕ *www.adventuretoursstlucia.com.*

BOATING AND SAILING

Rodney Bay and Marigot Bay are centers for bareboat and crewed yacht charters. Their marinas offer safe anchorage, shower facilities, restaurants, groceries, and maintenance for yachts sailing the waters of the eastern Caribbean. Charter prices range from $400 to $500 per overnight or $1,750 to $10,000 per week, depending on the season and the type and size of vessel, plus $250 extra per day if you want a skipper and cook.

Bateau Mygo. The customized, crewed charters from Bateau Mygo are on a 38-foot catamaran, for either a couple of days or a week. ⊠ *Chateau Mygo Villas, Marigot Bay* ☎ *758/458–3957* ⊕ *www.bateaumygo.com.*

Destination St. Lucia (DSL) Ltd. For its bareboat yacht charters, DSL's vessels include a 42-foot catamaran and monohulls ranging in length from 32 to 50 feet. ⊠ *Rodney Bay Marina, Rodney Bay* ☎ *758/452–8531* ⊕ *www.dsl-yachting.com.*

Moorings Yacht Charters. Bareboat and crewed catamarans and monohulls ranging from Beneteau 39s to Morgan 60s are what you can get from this company. ⊠ *Marigot Bay Marina, Marigot Bay* ☎ *758/451–4357, 800/952–8420* ⊕ *www.moorings.com.*

DIVING AND SNORKELING

Depending on the season and the particular trip, prices range from about $40 to $60 for a one-tank dive to $175 to $260 for a six-dive package over three days and $265 to $450 for a 10-dive package over five days. Dive shops provide instruction for all levels (beginner, intermediate, and advanced). For beginners, a resort course (pool training), followed by one open-water dive, runs from $90 to $120. Snorkelers are generally welcome on dive trips and usually pay $50 to $65, which includes equipment and sometimes lunch and transportation.

Fodor's Choice ★ **Anse Chastanet,** near the Pitons on the southwest coast, is the best beach-entry dive site. The underwater reef drops from 20 feet to nearly 140 feet in a stunning coral wall.

A 165-foot freighter, *Lesleen M,* was deliberately sunk in 60 feet of water near **Anse Cochon** to create an artificial reef; divers can explore the ship in its entirety and view huge gorgonians, black coral trees, gigantic barrel sponges, lace corals, schooling fish, angelfish, sea horses, spotted eels, stingrays, nurse sharks, and sea turtles.

Anse La Raye, midway up the west coast, is one of St. Lucia's finest wall and drift dives and a great place for snorkeling.

Superman's Flight is a dramatic drift dive along the steep walls beneath the Pitons. At the base of **Petit Piton** a spectacular wall drops to 200 feet, where you can view an impressive collection of huge barrel sponges and black coral trees; strong currents ensure good visibility.

At the **Pinnacles,** four coral-encrusted stone piers rise to within 10 feet of the surface.

DIVE OPERATORS

Dive Fair Helen. This PADI center offers half- and full-day excursions to wreck, wall, and marine reserve areas, as well as night dives. ⊠ *Marigot Bay Marina, Marigot Bay* ☎ *758/451–7716, 888/855–2206 in U.S. and Canada* ⊕ *www.divefairhelen.com.*

Scuba St. Lucia. Daily beach and boat dives and resort and certification courses are available from this PADI Five Star facility, and so is underwater photography and snorkeling equipment. Day trips from the north of the island include round-trip speedboat transportation. ⊠ *Anse*

Chastanet Resort, Anse Chastanet Rd., Soufrière ☎ *758/459–7755, 888/465–8242 in the U.S.* ⊕ *www.scubastlucia.com.*

Island Divers. Found at the edge of the Soufriere Marine Park at Anse Cochon, with two reefs and an offshore wreck accessible from shore, Island Divers has a convenient location for boat dives, PADI certification, and specialty courses. A day package includes hotel transfers, lunch at Ti Kaye's beachside bar and grill, a two-tank dive, and the use of snorkel gear for the day. ✉ *Ti Kaye Village, Anse Cochon* ☎ *758/456– 8110* ⊕ *www.islanddiversstlucia.com.*

FISHING

Among the deep-sea creatures you can find in St. Lucia's waters are dolphin (the fish, also called dorado or mahimahi), barracuda, mackerel, wahoo, kingfish, sailfish, and white and blue marlin. Sportfishing is generally done on a catch-and-release basis, but the captain may permit you to take a fish back to your hotel to be prepared for your dinner. Neither spearfishing nor collecting live fish in coastal waters is permitted. Half- and full-day deep-sea fishing excursions can be arranged at either Vigie Marina or Rodney Bay Marina. A half day of fishing on a scheduled trip runs about $85 per person to join a scheduled party for a half day or $500 to $1,000 for a private charter for up to six or eight people, depending on the size of the boat and the length of time. Beginners are welcome.

Captain Mike's. The captain's fleet of Bertram powerboats (31 to 38 feet) accommodate as many as eight passengers for half-day or full-day sportfishing charters; tackle and cold drinks are supplied. ✉ *Vigie Marina, Castries* ☎ *758/452–7044* ⊕ *www.captmikes.com.*

Hackshaw's Boat Charters. In business since 1953, Hackshaw's Boat Charters runs charters on boats that include the 31-foot *Blue Boy* and the 50-foot, custom-built *Lady Hack* and *Lady Anne.* ✉ *Vigie Marina, Castries* ☎ *758/453–0553, 758/452–3909* ⊕ *www.hackshaws.com.*

Mako Watersports. Mako takes fishing enthusiasts out on the well-equipped six-passenger *Annie Baby.* ✉ *Rodney Bay Marina, Rodney Bay* ☎ *758/452–0412.*

GOLF

St. Lucia has only one 18-hole championship course: **St. Lucia Golf Resort & Country Club**, which is in Cap Estate. **Sandals Regency Golf Resort and Spa** has a 9-hole course for its guests.

St. Lucia Golf Resort & Country Club. The island's only public course is at the northern tip, with wide views of both the Atlantic and the Caribbean. The 18-hole championship course is 6,836 yards and par 71. Its clubhouse's fine-dining restaurant, the Cap Grill, serves breakfast, lunch, and dinner; the Sports Bar is a convivial meeting place any time of day. You can rent clubs and shoes and arrange lessons at the pro shop and perfect your swing at the 350-yard driving range. Greens fees are approximately $105 for 9 holes and $145 for 18 holes, including carts, which are required; club and shoe rentals are available. Reservations are essential. Complimentary transportation from your hotel or cruise ship is provided for parties of three or more people. The St. Lucia Golf Open, a two-day spring tournament, is open to amateurs; it's a handicap event, and prizes are awarded. ⊠ *Cap Estate* ☎ *758/452–8523* ⊕ *www. stluciagolf.com.*

GUIDED TOURS

Taxi drivers are well informed and can give you a full tour and often an excellent one, thanks to government-sponsored training programs. From the Castries area, full-day island tours cost $40 to $75 per person for up to four people, depending on the route and whether entrance fees and lunch are included. If you plan your own day, expect to pay the driver $40 per hour plus tip.

Jungle Tours. This company specializes in rain-forest hiking tours for all levels of ability. You're required only to bring hiking shoes or sneakers and have a willingness to get wet and have fun. The cost is $95 per person and includes lunch, fees, and transportation via an open Land Rover truck. ⊠ *Cas en Bas, Gros Islet* ☎ *758/715–3438* ⊕ *www. jungletoursstlucia.com.*

St. Lucia Helicopters. Now you can get a bird's-eye view of the island. A 10-minute North Island tour ($85 per person) leaves from Pointe Seraphine, in Castries, continues up the west coast to Pigeon Island, then flies along the rugged Atlantic coastline before returning inland over Castries. The 20-minute South Island tour ($140 per person) starts at Pointe Seraphine and follows the western coastline, circling beautiful Marigot Bay, Soufrière, and the majestic Pitons before returning inland over the volcanic hot springs and tropical rain forest. A complete island tour combines the two and lasts 30 minutes ($175 per person). ⊠ *Pointe Seraphine, Castries* ☎ *758/453–6950* ⊕ *www.stluciahelicopters.com.*

St. Lucia Heritage Tours. The Heritage Tourism Association of St. Lucia (HERITAS), a volunteer group that represents local sites and institutions, puts together "authentic St. Lucia experiences" that focus on local culture and traditions. Groups are kept small, and the tours can be tailored to your interests. Some of the unusual sites visited include a 19th-century plantation house surrounded by nature trails, a 20-foot waterfall hidden away on private property, and a living museum presenting Creole practices and traditions. Plan on paying $75 per person for a full-day tour. ⊠ *Pointe Seraphine, Castries* ☎ *758/451–6058* ⊕ *www.heritagetoursstlucia.org.*

Sunlink Tours. This huge tour operator offers dozens of land, sea, and combination sightseeing tours, as well as shopping tours, plantation, and rain-forest adventures via jeep safari, deep-sea fishing excursions, and day trips to other islands. Prices range from $35 for a half-day shopping tour to $140 for a full-day land-and-sea jeep safari to Soufrière. ⊠ *Reduit Beach Ave., Rodney Bay* ☎ *758/456–9100* ⊕ *www. sunlinktours.com.*

HIKING

The island is laced with trails, but you shouldn't attempt the more challenging ones—especially those that are deep in the rain forest—on your own.

St. Lucia Forest & Lands Department. Trails under this department's jurisdiction include the Barre de L'Isle Trail, the DesCartiers Rain Forest Trail, and the Edmund Rain Forest Reserve Trail. It also provides guides, who explain the plants and trees you'll encounter and keep you on the right track. Seasoned hikers climb the Pitons, the two volcanic cones rising 2,461 feet and 2,619 feet, respectively, from the ocean floor just south of Soufrière. Hiking is recommended only on Gros Piton, which offers a steep but safe trail to the top. The first half of the hike is moderately difficult; reaching the summit is challenging and should be attempted only by those who are physically fit. The view from the top is spectacular. Tourists are also permitted to hike Petit Piton, but the second half of the hike requires a good deal of rock climbing, and you'll need to provide your own safety equipment. Hiking either Piton requires permission from the St. Lucia Forest & Lands Department and a guide. ☎ 758/468–5649, 758/450–2078.

HORSEBACK RIDING

Creole horses, a breed native to South America and popular on the island, are fairly small, fast, sturdy, and even-tempered animals suitable for beginners. Established stables can accommodate all skill levels. They offer countryside trail rides, beach rides with picnic lunches, plantation tours, carriage rides, and lengthy treks. Prices run about $60 for one hour, $70 for two hours, and $85 for a three-hour beach ride and barbecue. Transportation is usually provided between the stables and nearby hotels. Local people sometimes appear on beaches with their steeds and offer 30-minute rides for $10 to $15; ride at your own risk.

Atlantic Shores Riding Stables. The two-hour trail rides from Atlantic Shores can take place on the beach and through the countryside. Beginners are welcome. ✉ *Savannes Bay, Vieux Fort* ☎ 758/285–1090.

International Pony Club. The beach-picnic ride from the International Pony Club includes time for a swim—with or without your horse. Both English- and Western-style riding are available. ✉ *Beauséjour Estate, Gros Islet* ☎ 758/452–8139, 758/450–8665.

Trim's National Riding Stable. At the island's oldest riding stable, there are four sessions per day, plus beach tours, trail rides, and carriage tours to Pigeon Island. ✉ *Cas-en-Bas, Gros Islet* ☎ 758/450–8273.

SEA EXCURSIONS

Fodor'sChoice
★
A day sail or sea cruise from Rodney Bay or Vigie Cove to Soufrière and the Pitons is a wonderful way to see St. Lucia and a great way to get to the island's distinctive natural sites. Prices for a full-day sailing excursion to Soufrière run about $100 per person and include a land tour to the Diamond Botanical Gardens, lunch, a stop for swimming and

snorkeling, and a visit to pretty Marigot Bay. Two-hour sunset cruises along the northwest coast cost $45 to $60 per person.

↻ **Brig Unicorn.** The 140-foot tall ship *Brig Unicorn*, used in the filming of the TV miniseries *Roots* and the movie *Pirates of the Caribbean,* is a 140-foot replica of a 19th-century sailing ship. Day trips along the coast are fun for the whole family. Several nights each week a sunset cruise, with drinks and a live steel band, sails to Pigeon Point and back. ✉ *Vigie Marina, Castries* ☎ *758/452–8644.*

Captain Mike's. Customized sightseeing or whale-watching trips ($45 per person) can be arranged for small groups (four to six people) through Captain Mike's. ✉ *Vigie Marina, Castries* ☎ *758/452–7044* ⊕ *www. captmikes.com.*

Endless Summer. On *Endless Summer*, a 56-foot "party" catamaran, you can take a day trip along the coast to Soufrière—hotel transfers, tour, entrance fees, lunch, and drinks included—for $100 per person. A half-day swimming and snorkeling trip is also available. For romantics, there's a weekly sunset cruise, with dinner and entertainment. ✉ *Rodney Bay* ☎ *758/450–8651* ⊕ *www.stluciaboattours.com.*

Mystic Man Tours. This company operates glassbottom boat, sailing, snorkeling whale- and dolphin-watching tours—all great family excursions. ✉ *Bay St., Soufrière* ☎ *758/459–7783* ⊕ *www.mysticmantours.com.*

Rodney Bay Ferry. There are two departures daily to Pigeon Island from this company. The cost of $50 per person round-trip includes the entrance fee to the island and lunch; snorkeling equipment can be rented for $12. ✉ *Rodney Bay Marina, Rodney Bay* ☎ *758/452–8816.*

WINDSURFING AND KITEBOARDING

Windsurfers and kiteboarders congregate at Anse de Sables Beach in Vieux Fort, at the southeastern tip of St. Lucia, to take advantage of the blue-water and high-wind conditions that the Atlantic Ocean provides.

Reef Kite and Surf Centre. You can rent equipment or take lessons from certified instructors in windsurfing and kitesurfing at this water-sports center. Windsurfing equipment rental is $45 for a half day; $60 for a full day. Kitesurfing equipment rental is $60 for a half day; $80 for a full day. A three-hour beginning windsurfing course costs $90, including equipment. For kiteboarding, the three-hour starter course costs $180, including equipment and safety gear. Kitesurfing is particularly strenuous, so participants must be excellent swimmers and in good physical health. ✉ *Anse de Sables, near Coconut Bay Beach Resort, Vieux Fort* ☎ *758/454–3418.*

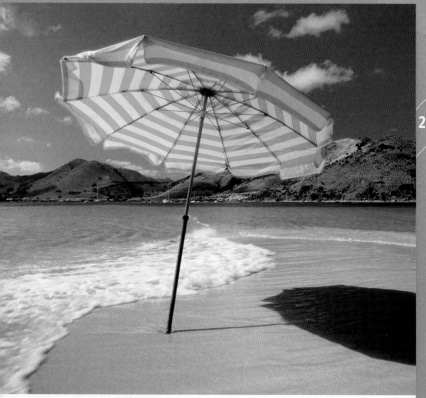

St. Maarten/
St. Martin

WORD OF MOUTH

"[A] don't-miss activity would be an afternoon on Maho Beach watching the planes come in. [It's the o]nly place in the world where planes land and take off so close over your head. There are two bars and chairs to rent on the beach. If you go, I promise that you will always remember it as a high point of your [trip]."

—riverbirch

WELCOME TO ST. MAARTEN/ ST. MARTIN

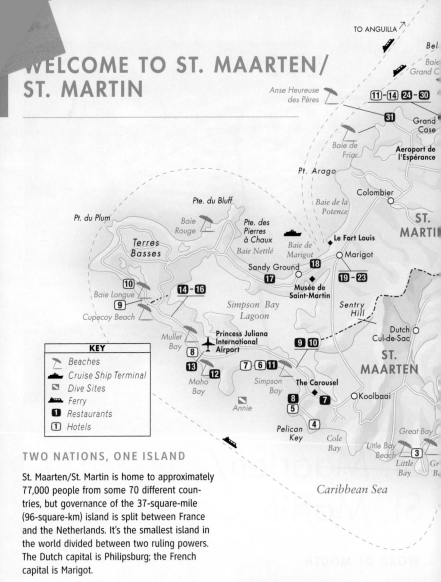

TO ANGUILLA

Bel

Baie
Grand C

Anse Heureuse
des Pères

11 - 14 24 - 30

31

Grand
Case

Aeroport de
l'Espérance

Baie de
Friar

Pt. Arago

Colombier

ST.
MARTI

Baie de la
Potence

Pte. du Bluff

Pt. du Plum

Baie
Rouge

Pte. des
Pierres
à Chaux

Baie Nettlé

Le Fort Louis

Terres
Basses

Baie de
Marigot

18

Marigot

Sandy Ground

17

19 - 23

Baie Longue

10

Musée de
Saint-Martin

Simpson Bay
Lagoon

Sentry
Hill

9

Cupecoy Beach

14 - 16

Dutch
Cul-de-Sac

Mullet
Bay

Princess Juliana
International
Airport

9 10

ST.
MAARTEN

KEY

8

7 6 11

The Carousel

Koolbaai

⤢	Beaches
🚢	Cruise Ship Terminal
◳	Dive Sites
⛴	Ferry
1	Restaurants
①	Hotels

13

12

Maho
Bay

Simpson
Bay

8

7

Annie

8

5

Pelican
Key

4

Cole
Bay

Great Bay

Little Bay
Beach

3

Little
Bay

Gr
B

Caribbean Sea

TWO NATIONS, ONE ISLAND

St. Maarten/St. Martin is home to approximately 77,000 people from some 70 different countries, but governance of the 37-square-mile (96-square-km) island is split between France and the Netherlands. It's the smallest island in the world divided between two ruling powers. The Dutch capital is Philipsburg; the French capital is Marigot.

St. Maarten/St. Martin, a half-Dutch, half-French island, is a place where gastronomy flourishes, where most resorts are large rather than small, where casinos draw gamblers, where sporting opportunities are plentiful, and where the sunning, as on the south end of Orient Beach, is au naturel.

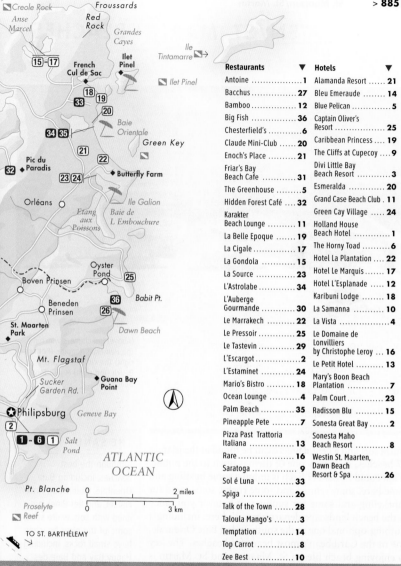

Restaurants ▼		Hotels ▼	
Antoine	1	Alamanda Resort	21
Bacchus	27	Bleu Emeraude	14
Bamboo	12	Blue Pelican	5
Big Fish	36	Captain Oliver's Resort	25
Chesterfield's	6	Caribbean Princess	19
Claude Mini-Club	20	The Cliffs at Cupecoy	9
Enoch's Place	21	Divi Little Bay Beach Resort	3
Friar's Bay Beach Cafe	31	Esmeralda	20
The Greenhouse	5	Grand Case Beach Club	11
Hidden Forest Café	32	Green Cay Village	24
Karakter Beach Lounge	11	Holland House Beach Hotel	1
La Belle Epoque	19	The Horny Toad	6
La Cigale	17	Hotel La Plantation	22
La Gondola	15	Hotel Le Marquis	17
La Source	23	Hotel L'Esplanade	12
L'Astrolabe	34	Karibuni Lodge	18
L'Auberge Gourmande	30	La Samanna	10
Le Marrakech	22	La Vista	4
Le Pressoir	25	Le Domaine de Lonvilliers by Christophe Leroy	16
Le Tastevin	29	Le Petit Hotel	13
L'Escargot	2	Mary's Boon Beach Plantation	7
L'Estaminet	24	Palm Court	23
Mario's Bistro	18	Radisson Blu	15
Ocean Lounge	4	Sonesta Great Bay	2
Palm Beach	35	Sonesta Maho Beach Resort	8
Pineapple Pete	7	Westin St. Maarten, Dawn Beach Resort & Spa	26
Pizza Past Trattoria Italiana	13		
Rare	16		
Saratoga	9		
Sol é Luna	33		
Spiga	26		
Talk of the Town	28		
Taloula Mango's	3		
Temptation	14		
Top Carrot	8		
Zee Best	10		

TOP REASONS TO VISIT ST. MAARTEN/ST. MARTIN

1 Great Food: The island has so many good places to eat that you could eat out for a month and never repeat a restaurant visit.

2 Lots of Shops: Philipsburg is one of the best shopping spots in the Caribbean, and Marigot brings a touch of France.

3 Beaches Large and Small: Thirty-seven picture-perfect beaches are spread out all over the island.

4 Water Sports Galore: The wide range of water sports will satisfy almost any need.

5 Nightlife Every Night: There is a wide variety of nightlife: shows, discos, beach bars, and casinos.

ST. MAARTEN/ST. MARTIN BEACHES

For such a small island, St. Maarten/St. Martin has a wide array of beaches, from the long expanse of Baie Orientale on the French side to powdery-soft Mullet Bay on the Dutch side.

(Above) Beachgoers watching the Heineken Regatta. (Bottom right) The cliffs at Cupecoy Beach (Top right) Mullet Bay Beach

Warm surf and a gentle breeze can be found at the island's 37 beaches, and every one of them is open to the public. What could be better? Each is unique: some bustling and some bare, some refined and some rocky, some good for snorkeling and some for sunning. Whatever you fancy in the beach landscape department, it's here, including a clothing-optional one at the south end of Baie Orientale, one of the Caribbean's most beautiful beaches. The key to enjoying beach life on St. Maarten and St. Martin is to try out several beaches; one quickly discovers that several of the island's gems don't have big hotels lining their shores. Petty theft from cars in beach parking lots is an unfortunate fact of life in St. Maarten and St. Martin. Leave nothing in your parked car, not even in the glove compartment or the trunk.

THE SAND

Although the best beaches, including Baie Orientale, Mullet Bay, Anse Marcel, and Ilet Pinel, are lined with soft, white sand, some of the nicer beaches have small rocks, including Happy Bay and Baie des Péres. Atlantic-facing Le Galion has soft sand and gentle surf because it is protected by a reef, but soft sand (in the case of Guana Bay and Cupecoy) can also be accompanied by heavy surf.

23

DUTCH SIDE

Several of the best Dutch-side beaches are developed and have large-scale resorts. But others, including Simpson Bay and Cupecoy, have little development. You'll sometimes find vendors or beach bars to rent chairs and umbrellas (but not always).

Cupecoy Beach. This picturesque area of sandstone cliffs, white sand, and shoreline caves is a necklace of small beaches that come and go according to the whims of the sea. Even though the western part is more developed, the surf can be rough. It's popular with gay locals and visitors. Break-ins have been reported in cars, so don't leave anything at all in your vehicle. ⊠ *Cupecoy, between Baie Longue and Mullet Bay.*

★ **Dawn Beach.** True to its name, Dawn Beach is the place to be at sunrise. On the Atlantic side of Oyster Pond, just south of the French border, this is a first-class beach for sunning and snorkeling. It's not usually crowded, and there are several good restaurants nearby. To find it, follow the signs to Mr. Busby's restaurant. ⊠ *South of Oyster Pond, Dawn Beach.*

Great Bay. This is probably the easiest beach to find because it curves around Philipsburg. A bustling, white-sand beach, Great Bay is just behind Front Street. Here you'll find boutiques, eateries, and a pleasant boardwalk,

but pollution here can be a problem. Busy with cruise-ship passengers, the beach is best west of Captain Hodge Pier or around Antoine Restaurant. ⊠ *Philipsburg.*

Little Bay. Despite its popularity with snorkelers and divers as well as kayakers and boating enthusiasts, Little Bay isn't usually crowded. Maybe the gravelly sand is the reason. But it does boast panoramic views of St. Eustatius, Philipsburg, the cruise-ship terminal, Saba, and St. Kitts. The beach is west of Fort Amsterdam and accessible via the Divi Little Bay Beach Resort. ⊠ *Little Bay Rd., Little Bay.*

Mullet Bay Beach. Many believe that this mile-long, powdery white-sand beach near the medical school is the island's best. Swimmers like it because the water is usually calm. When the swell is up, the surfers hit the beach. It's also the place to listen for the "whispering pebbles" as the waves wash up. ⊠ *South of Cupecoy, Mullet Bay.*

Simpson Bay Beach. This secluded, half-moon stretch of white-sand beach on the island's Caribbean side is a hidden gem. It's mostly surrounded by private residences. There are no big resorts, no Jet Skiers . . . and no crowds. Southeast of the airport, follow the signs to Mary's Boon and the Horny Toad guesthouses. ⊠ *Simpson Bay.*

Baie Orientale, the island's longest beach

FRENCH SIDE

Almost all the French-side beaches, whether busy Baie Orientale or less busy Baie des Pères (Friar's Bay), have beach clubs and restaurants. For about $25 a couple you get two chaises (*transats*) and an umbrella (*parasol*) for the day, not to mention chair-side service for drinks and food. Only some beaches have bathrooms and showers, so if that is your preference, inquire.

Anse Heureuse (Happy Bay). Not many people know about this romantic, hidden gem. Happy Bay has powdery sand, gorgeous luxury villas, and stunning views of Anguilla. The snorkeling is also good. To get here, turn left on the rather rutted dead-end road to Baie des Pères (Friar's Bay). The beach itself is a 10- to 15-minute walk from the last beach bar. ⊠ *Happy Bay.*

Baie de Grand Case (Grand Case). Along this skinny stripe of a beach bordering the culinary capital of Grand Case, the old-style gingerbread architecture sometimes peeps out between the bustling restaurants. The sea is calm, and there are tons of fun lunch options from bistros to beachside barbecue stands

(called *lolos*). Several of the restaurants rent chairs and umbrellas; some include their use for lunch patrons. In between there is a bit of shopping, certainly for beach necessities but also for the same kinds of handcrafts found in the Marigot market. ⊠ *Grand Case.*

Baie des Péres (Friar's Bay). This quiet cove close to Marigot has beach grills and bars, with chaises and umbrellas, calm waters, and a lovely view of Anguilla. To get to the beach, take National Road 7 from Marigot, go toward Grand Case to the Morne Valois hill, and turn left on the dead-end road at the sign. ⊠ *Friar's Bay.*

Baie Longue (Long Bay). Though it extends over the French Lowlands, from the cliff at La Samanna to La Pointe des Canniers, the island's longest beach has no facilities or vendors. It's the perfect place for a romantic walk. Be aware that car break-ins are a particular problem here. To get here, take National Road 7 south of Marigot. The entrance marked "La Samanna" is the first entrance to the beach. For a splurge, lunch at the resort or sunset drinks are a must. ⊠ *Baie Longue.*

23

Baie Orientale (Orient Bay). ★ **Fodor's Choice** Many consider this the island's most beautiful beach, but its 2 miles (3 km) of satiny white sand, underwater marine reserve, variety of water sports, beach clubs, and hotels also make it one of the most crowded. Lots of "naturists" take advantage of the clothing-optional policy, so don't be shocked. Early-morning nude beach walking is de rigueur for the guests at Club Orient, at the southeastern end of the beach. Plan to spend the day at one of the clubs; each bar has different color umbrellas, and all boast terrific restaurants and lively bars. You can have an open-air massage, try any sea toy you fancy, and stay until dark. To get to Baie Orientale from Marigot, take National Road 7 past Grand Case, past the Aéroport de L'Espérance, and watch for the left turn. ⊠ *Baie Orientale.*

Baie Rouge (Red Bay). At this home to a couple of beach bars, complete with chaises and umbrellas, you can bask with the millionaires renting the big-ticket villas in the "neighborhood" and take advantage of the gorgeous beach they came for. Baie Rouge and its salt ponds make up a nature preserve, the location of the oldest habitations in the Caribbean. This area is widely thought to have the best snorkeling beaches on the island. You can swim the crystal waters along the point and explore a swim-through cave. The beach is fairly popular with gay men in the mornings and early afternoons. There are two restaurants here; only Chez Raymond is open every day, and cocktail hour starts when the conch shell blows, so keep your ears open. There is a sign and a right turn after you leave Baie Nettlé. ⊠ *Baie Rouge.*

Ilet Pinel (Pinel Island). A protected nature reserve, this kid-friendly island is a five-minute ferry ride from French Cul de Sac ($7 per person round-trip). The ferry runs every half hour from midmorning until dusk. The water is clear and shallow, and the shore is sheltered. If you like snorkeling, don your gear and paddle along both coasts of this pencil-shape speck in the ocean. You can rent equipment on the island or in the parking lot before you board the ferry for about $10. Plan for lunch any day of the week at the water's edge at a palm-shaded beach hut at **Karibuni** (except in September, when it's closed) for the freshest fish, great salads, tapas, and drinks—try the frozen mojito for a treat. ⊠ *Ilet Pinel.*

Le Galion. A coral reef borders this quiet beach, part of the island's nature preserve, which is paradise if you are traveling with children. The water is calm, clear, and quite shallow, so it's a perfect place for families with young kids. It's a full-service place, with chair rentals, restaurants, and water-sports operators. Kiteboarders and windsurfers like the trade winds at the far end of the beach. On Sunday there are always groups picnicking and partying. To get to Le Galion, follow the signs to the unmissable Butterfly Farm and continue toward the water. ⊠ *Quartier d'Orleans.*

Baie Rouge, St-Martin

By Elise Meyer   St. Maarten/St. Martin is virtually unique among Caribbean destinations. The 37-square-mile (96-square-km) island is a seamless place (there are no border gates), but it is governed by two nations—the Netherlands and France—and has residents from 70-some different countries. A call from the Dutch side to the French is an international call, currencies are different, and the vibe is even different. Only the island of Hispaniola, which encompasses two distinct countries, Haiti and the Dominican Republic, is in even a similar position in the Caribbean.

Happily for Americans, who make up the majority of visitors to St. Maarten/St. Martin, English works in both nations. Dutch St. Maarten might feel particularly comfortable for Americans: the prices are lower (not to mention in U.S. dollars), the big hotels have casinos, and there is more nightlife. Huge cruise ships disgorge masses of shoppers into the Philipsburg shopping area at midmorning, when roads can quickly become overly congested. But once you pass the meandering, unmarked border into the French side, you will find a bit of the ambience of the south of France: quiet countryside, fine cuisine, and in Marigot, a walkable harbor area with outdoor cafés, outdoor markets, and plenty of shopping and cultural activities.

Almost 4,000 years ago, it was salt and not tourism that drove the little island's economy. Arawak Indians, the island's first known inhabitants, prospered until the warring Caribs invaded, adding the peaceful Arawaks to their list of conquests. Columbus spotted the isle on November 11, 1493, and named it after St. Martin (whose feast day is November 11), but it wasn't populated by Europeans until the 17th century, when it was claimed by the Dutch, French, and Spanish. The Dutch and French finally joined forces to claim the island in 1644, and the Treaty of Concordia partitioned the territory in 1648. According to legend the border was drawn along the line where a French man and a Dutch man, running from opposite coasts, met.

Both sides of the island offer a touch of European culture along with a lot of laid-back Caribbean ambience. Water sports abound—diving, snorkeling, sailing, windsurfing, and in early March, the Heineken Regatta. With soft trade winds cooling the subtropical climate, it's easy to while away the day relaxing on one of the 37 beaches, strolling Philipsburg's boardwalk, and perusing the shops on Philipsburg's Front Street or the *rues* (streets) of the very French town of Marigot. Although luck is an important commodity at St. Maarten's 13 casinos, chance plays no part in finding a good meal at the excellent eateries or after-dark fun in the subtle to sizzling nightlife. Heavy development—especially on the Dutch side—has stressed the island's infrastructure, but slowly some of the more dilapidated roads are showing some signs of improvement. A series of large roundabouts, with the beginnings of some decent signage, and attractive monumental sculptures has improved traffic flow (remember, the cars already in the roundabout have right-of-way). At long last, the eyesore of hurricane-wrecked buildings that line the golf course at Mullet Bay have been demolished, and a particularly rainy 2011 has painted the island a particularly vibrant shade of green.

When cruise ships are in port (and there can be as many as seven at once), shopping areas are crowded and traffic moves at a snail's pace. We suggest spending the days on the beach or the water, and planning shopping excursions for the early morning or at cocktail hour, after "rush hour" traffic calms down. Still, these are minor inconveniences compared with the feel of the sand between your toes or the breeze through your hair, gourmet food sating your appetite, or having the ability to crisscross between two nations on one island.

PLANNING

WHEN TO GO

The high season begins in December and runs through the middle of April. During the off-season, hotel rooms can be had for as little as half the high-season rates.

GETTING HERE AND AROUND

AIR TRAVEL

There are nonstop flights from Atlanta (Delta, seasonal), Charlotte (US Airways), Miami (American), New York–JFK (American, JetBlue), New York–Newark (United), Philadelphia (US Airways), and Boston (Jet-Blue). There are also some nonstop charter flights (including GWV/Apple Vacations from Boston). You can also connect in San Juan, primarily on American. Many smaller Caribbean-based airlines, including Air Caraïbes, Caribbean Airlines, Dutch Antilles Express, Insel, LIAT, and Winair (Windward Islands Airways), offer service from other islands in the Caribbean.

Airports Aéroport de L'Espérance. Aéroport de L'Espérance, on the French side, is small and handles only island-hoppers. ⊠ *SFG Route l'Espérance, Grand*

LOGISTICS

Getting to St. Maarten/St. Martin: There are nonstop flights to St. Maarten from the United States, as well as connecting service through San Juan. Further, St. Maarten is a hub for smaller, regional airlines. The island's main airport is Princess Juliana International Airport (SXM), on the Dutch side. Aeroport de L'Espérance (SFG), on the French side, is small and handles only small planes.

Hassle Factor: Low to medium.

On the Ground: Most visitors rent a car upon arrival, but taxi service is available at the airport with fixed fares to all hotels on the island, and you'll be able to pay the fare in U.S. dollars. Although the island is small, it's still a long drive to many hotels on the French side, and the fares will add up.

Getting Around the Island: Most visitors rent a car because rates are fairly cheap and the island is easy to navigate. It's possible to get by with taxis if you are staying in a major hub such as Philipsburg or Baie Orientale, but you may spend more money than if you rented a car.

Case ☎ 590/27–11–00 ⊕ www.aeroport-saintmartin.com. **Princess Juliana International Airport.** Princess Juliana International Airport on the Dutch side handles all the large jets. ☎ 721/546–7542 ⊕ www.pjiae.com.

Airline Contacts Air Caraïbes ☎ 590/590–87–10–36 ⊕ www.aircaraibes-usa.com. **American Airlines** ☎ 599/545–2040, 800/433–7300. **Caribbean Airlines** ☎ 721/546–7610. **Delta Airlines** ☎ 721/546–7615. **Dutch Antilles Express** ☎ 721/546–7640. **Insel Air** ☎ 721/546–7690. **JetBlue** ☎ 721/546–7664, 721/546–7663. **LIAT** ☎ 721/546–7677. **St. Barths Commuter** ☎ 721/546–7698. **United Airlines** ☎ 721/546–7671. **US Airways** ☎ 721/546–7683. **Winair** ☎ 721/546–7690. **Windward Express Airways** ☎ 721/545–2001.

BOAT AND FERRY TRAVEL

You can take ferries to St. Barth (45–80 minutes, €67–€93 from the Dutch or French side, though you can pay in dollars); to Anguilla (20 minutes, $25 from the French side); and to Saba (one to two hours, $90–$100 from the Dutch side). *Babou One,* a new, stabilized, air-conditioned boat run by West Indies Ferry Express, offers service between Marigot and Gustavia in only 70 minutes, timed to connect with international flights to and from St. Maarten's Princess Juliana Airport.

Contacts *Dawn II.* Service to Saba ✉ Philipsburg, St. Maarten ☎ 599/416–2299 ⊕ www.sabactransport.com. *Edge I and Edge II.* Day-trips to Saba, St. Barth. ✉ Pelican Marina, Simpson Bay, St. Maarten ☎ 599/544–2640, 599/544–2631 ⊕ www.stmaarten-activities.com. **Link Ferries.** Service to Anguilla. ✉ Marigot, St. Martin ☎ 264/497–2231 in Anguilla, 264/497–3290 in Anguilla ⊕ www.link.ai. **Shauna.** Service to Anguilla ✉ Simpson Bay, St. Maarten ☎ 264/772–2031 in Anguilla. *Voyager II.* Service to St. Barth from Marigot. ✉ Marigot, St. Martin ☎ 590/87–10–68 ⊕ www.voy12.com. **West Indies Ferry Express.** Service to St. Barth. ✉ Marigot ☎ 590/590–29–63–70 ⊕ www.westindiesferry.com.

CAR TRAVEL

It's easy to get around the island by car. Most roads are paved and in generally good condition. However, they can be crowded, especially when the cruise ships are in port; you might experience traffic jams, particularly around Marigot and Philipsburg. Be alert for potholes and speed bumps, as well as the island tradition of stopping in the middle of the road to chat with a friend or yield to someone entering traffic. Few roads are identified by name or number, but most have signs indicating the destination. Driving is on the right. There are gas stations in Simpson Bay near the airport.

Car Rentals: You can book a car at Juliana International Airport, where all major rental companies have booths. They provide a shuttle to the rental-car lot. Rates are among the best in the Caribbean, as little as $20–$35 per day. You can rent a car on the French side, but this rarely makes sense for Americans because of the unfavorable exchange rates.

Car-Rental Contacts Avis ☎ 721/545-2847, 590-0690/634-947 *on the French side.* **Budget** ☎ 721/545-4030, 721/55-40-30. **Dollar/Thrifty Car Rental** ☎ 721/545-2393. **Empress Rent-a-Car** ☎ 721/545-2062. **Golfe Car Rental** ☎ 0590/51-94-81 *on the French side* ⊕ www.golfecarrental.com. **Hertz** ☎ 721/545-4541. **Unity** ☎ 721/520-5767 ⊕ www.unitycarrental.com.

SCOOTER TRAVEL

Though traffic can be heavy, speeds are generally slow, so a moped can be a good way to get around. Scooters rent for as low as €25 per day and motorbikes for €37 a day at Eugene Moto, on the French side. The Harley-Davidson dealer, on the Dutch side, rents hogs for $150 a day or $900 per week.

Contacts Eugene Moto ⊠ Sandy Ground Rd., Sandy Ground, St. Martin ☎ 590/87-13-97. **Harley-Davidson** ⊠ 71 Union Rd., Cole Bay, St. Maarten ☎ 721/544-2704 ⊕ www.h-dstmartin.com.

TAXI TRAVEL

There is a government-sponsored taxi dispatcher at the airport and at the harbor. Posted fares are for one or two people. Add $5 for each additional person, $1 to $2 per bag, $1 for a box or bundle. It costs about $18 from the airport to Philipsburg or Marigot, and about $30 to Dawn Beach. After 10 pm fares go up 25%, and after midnight 50%. Licensed drivers can be identified by the "taxi" license plate on the Dutch side and the window sticker on the French. You can hail cabs on the street or call the taxi dispatch to have one sent for you. Fixed fares apply from Juliana International Airport and the Marigot ferry to the various hotels around the island. The Dutch St. Maarten Taxi Association can be reached day or night at its hotline number.

Taxi Contacts Airport Taxi Dispatch ☎ 721/545-4317. **Dutch St. Maarten Taxi Association** ☎ 721/543-7815, 9247 24 Hour Hotline.

ESSENTIALS

Banks and Exchange Services Legal tender on the Dutch side is the Netherlands Antilles florin, but almost everyone accepts dollars. On the French side, the currency is the euro, but most establishments accept dollars. ATMs dispense dollars or euros, depending on where you are.

Electricity Generally, 110 volts AC (60-cycle) on the Dutch side, just as in the United States. The French side operates on 220 volts AC (60-cycle), with round-prong plugs; there, you'll need an adapter (many hotels can supply these for you).

Emergency Services Dutch-side emergencies ☎ *911, 721/542-2222.*
French-side emergencies ☎ *17, 590/52-25-52.*

Language Dutch is the official language of St. Maarten, and French is the official language of St. Martin, but almost everyone speaks English.

Passport Requirements A valid passport is required for all visitors.

Phones Calling from one side of the island to another is an international call. To phone from the Dutch side to the French, you first must dial 00–590–590 for local numbers, or 00–590–690 for cell phones, then the number. To call from the French side to the Dutch, dial 00–721, then the local number. To call a local number on the French side, dial 0590 plus the six-digit number. On the Dutch side, just dial the seven-digit number with no prefix. Any of the local carriers—and most hotel concierges—can arrange for a prepaid rental phone for your use while you are on the island for about $5 a weekday plus a per-minute charge.

Taxes and Service Charges Departure tax from Juliana Airport is $10 to destinations within the Netherlands Antilles and $30 to all other destinations. It is usually included in your air ticket. It will cost you €3 (usually included in the ticket price) to depart by plane from Aéroport de L'Espérance and $5 (the rate can change) by ferry to Anguilla from Marigot's pier. Hotels on the Dutch side add a 15% service charge to the bill as well as a 5% government tax. Hotels on the French side add 10%–15% and generally 5% tax.

Tipping Service charges may be added to hotel and restaurant bills on the Dutch side (otherwise tip 15%–18%). On the French side, a service charge is customary; on top of the included service it is customary to leave an extra 5%–10% *in cash* for the server. Taxi drivers, porters, and maids depend on tips. Give 10% to 15% to cabbies, $1 per bag for porters, and $2 to $5 per night per guest for chambermaids.

ACCOMMODATIONS

The island, though small, is well developed—some say overdeveloped— and offers a wide range of lodging. The larger resorts and time-shares are mostly on the Dutch side; the French side has more intimate properties. Just keep in mind that the popular restaurants around Grand Case, on the French side, are a long drive from most Dutch-side hotels. French-side hotels often charge in euros. Be wary of some of the very lowest-price alternatives, as some of these can be very run-down time-shares, or properties that function as short-term housing for temporary workers or tourists with very low-end tour companies. Additionally, make note of locations of properties very close to the airport, to avoid unpleasant surprises related to noise. In general, the newer a property, the better off you will be.

Resorts and Time-Shares: In general, many of the older properties, especially the time-shares, are suffering from the wear-and-tear of multiple owners, and it is hard to recommend them because of great variances from unit to unit.

Small Inns: Small guesthouses and inns can be found on both sides of the island. It is worth exploring these, especially if you are not the big-resort type.

Villas and Condos: Both sides of the island have a wide variety of villas and condos for every conceivable budget. Some of the resorts offer villa alternatives, which make for a good compromise. In addition, some of the high-end condo developments are offering unsold units as rentals, and some are brand-new and terrific bargains.

HOTEL AND RESTAURANT PRICES

Prices in the restaurant reviews are the average cost of a main course at dinner or, if dinner is not served, at lunch; taxes and service charges are generally included. Prices in the hotel reviews are the lowest cost of a standard double room in high season, excluding taxes, service charges, and meal plans (except at all-inclusives). Prices for rentals are the lowest per-night cost for a one-bedroom unit in high season.

VISITOR INFORMATION

Contacts Dutch-side Tourist Information Bureau ⊠ *Vineyard Park Bldg., 33 W. G. Buncamper Rd., Philipsburg, St. Maarten* ☎ *721/542–2337* ⊕ *www.vacationstmaarten.com.* **French-side Office de Tourisme** ⊠ *Rte. de Sandy Ground, near Marina de la Port-Royale, Marigot, St. Martin* ☎ *590/87–57–21* ⊕ *www.st-martin.org.*

WEDDINGS

There's a three-day waiting period on the Dutch side. Getting married on the French side is not a viable option because of long wait times.

EXPLORING ST. MAARTEN/ST. MARTIN

The best way to explore St. Maarten/St. Martin is by car. Though often congested, especially around Philipsburg and Marigot, the roads are fairly good, though narrow and winding, with some speed bumps, potholes, roundabouts, and an occasional wandering goat herd. Few roads are marked with their names, but destination signs are common. Besides, the island is so small that it's hard to get really lost—at least that is what locals tell you.

If you're spending a few days, get to know the area with a scenic "loop" around the island. Be sure to pack a towel and some water shoes, a hat, sunglasses, and sunblock. Head up the east shoreline from Philipsburg, and follow the signs to Dawn Beach and Oyster Pond. The road winds past soaring hills, turquoise waters, quaint West Indian houses, and wonderful views of St. Barth. As you cross over to the French side, turn into Le Galion for a stop at the calm sheltered beach, the stables, the butterflies, or the windsurfing school, then keep following the road toward Orient Bay, the St-Tropez of the Caribbean. Continue to Anse Marcel, Grand Case, Marigot, and Sandy Ground. From Marigot, the flat island of Anguilla is visible. Completing the loop brings you past

Cupecoy Beach, through Maho and Simpson Bay, where Saba looms in the horizon, and back over the mountain road into Philipsburg.

DUTCH SIDE

WHAT TO SEE

PHILIPSBURG

The capital of Dutch St. Maarten stretches about a mile (1½ km) along an isthmus between Great Bay and the Salt Pond and has five parallel streets. Most of the village's dozens of shops and restaurants are on Front Street, narrow and cobblestone, closest to Great Bay. It's generally congested when cruise ships are in port, because of its many duty-free shops and several casinos. Little lanes called *steegjes* connect Front Street with Back Street, which has fewer shops and considerably less congestion. Along the beach is a ½-mile-long (1-km-long) boardwalk with restaurants and several Wi-Fi hot spots.

Wathey Square (pronounced *watty*) is in the heart of the village. Directly across from the square are the town hall and the courthouse, in the striking white building with the cupola. The structure was built in 1793 and has served as the commander's home, a fire station, a jail, and a post office. The streets surrounding the square are lined with hotels, duty-free shops, fine restaurants, and cafés. The **Captain Hodge Pier,** just off the square, is a good spot to view Great Bay and the beach that stretches alongside.

Sint Maarten Museum. The Sint Maarten Museum hosts rotating cultural exhibits and a permanent historical display called Forts of St. Maarten–St. Martin. Artifacts range from Arawak pottery shards to objects salvaged from the wreck of the HMS *Proselyte.* ⊠ *7 Front St., Philipsburg* ☎ *721/542–4917* ⊕ *www.speetjens.com/museum* ☞ *$1* ☉ *Weekdays 10–4, Sat. 10–2.*

ELSEWHERE IN ST. MAARTEN

☾ **The Carousel.** Ride a beautiful restored Italian carousel and enjoy dozens of flavors of homemade Italian gelato and French pastries. Adults will love the espresso bar with great coffee drinks, and there is even a small cocktail bar. It's a perfect attraction for kids of all ages. ⊠ *60 Welfare Rd, Cole Bay, St. Maarten* ☎ *721/544–3112* ☞ *TK* ☉ *Tues.–Sun. 2–10.*

☾ **St. Maarten Park.** This delightful little enclave houses animals and plants indigenous to the Caribbean and South America, including many birds that were inherited from a former aviary. There are also a few strays from other parts of the world and a snake house with boa constrictors and other slithery creatures. The zoo's lone male collared peccary now has a female to keep him company. A family of cotton-topped tamarins also have taken residence at the zoo. All the animals live among more than 100 different plant species. The Monkey Bar is the zoo's charming souvenir shop, and sells Caribbean and zoo mementos. This is a perfect place to take the kids when they need a break from the sand and sea. ⊠ *Madame Estate, Arch Rd., Philipsburg* ☎ *721/543–2030* ⊕ *www. stmaartenzoo.com* ☞ *$10* ☉ *Daily 9–5.*

Concordia

The smallest island in the world to be shared between two different countries, St. Maarten/St. Martin has existed peacefully in its subdivided state for more than 360 years. The Treaty of Concordia, which subdivided the island, was signed in 1648 and was really inspired by the two resident colonies of French and Dutch settlers (not to mention their respective governments) joining forces to repel a common enemy, the Spanish, in 1644. Although the French were promised the side of the island facing Anguilla and the Dutch the south side of the island, the boundary itself

wasn't firmly established until 1817 and then after several disputes (16 of them, to be exact).

Visitors to the island will likely not even notice that they have passed from the Dutch to the French side unless they notice that the roads on the French side feel a little smoother. In 2003 the population of St. Martin (and St. Barthélemy) voted to secede from Guadeloupe, the administrative capital of the French West Indies. That detachment became official in February 2007, and St. Martin is now officially known as the Collectivité de Saint-Martin.

FRENCH SIDE

WHAT TO SEE

MARIGOT

It is great fun to spend a few hours exploring the bustling harbor, shopping stalls, open-air cafés, and boutiques of St. Martin's biggest town, especially on Wednesday and Saturday, when the daily open-air craft markets expand to include fresh fruits and vegetables, spices, and all manner of seafood. The market might remind you of Provence, especially when aromas of delicious cooking waft by. Be sure to climb up to the fort for the panoramic view, stopping at the museum for an overview of the island. **Marina Port La Royale** is the shopping–lunch-spot central to the port, but rue de la République and rue de la Liberté, which border the bay, have duty-free shops, boutiques, and bistros. The West Indies Mall offers a deluxe (and air-conditioned) shopping experience, with such shops as Lacoste. There's less bustle here than in Philipsburg, but the open-air cafés are still tempting places to sit and people-watch. Marigot is fun into the night, so you might wish to linger through dinnertime. From the harborfront you can catch ferries for Anguilla and St. Barth. Parking can be a real challenge during the business day, and even at night during the high season.

Fort Louis. Though not much remains of the structure itself, Fort Louis, which was completed by the French in 1789, is great fun if you want to climb the 92 steps to the top for the wonderful views of the island and neighboring Anguilla. On Wednesday and Saturday there is a market in the square at the bottom. ⊠ *Marigot.*

Saint Martin Museum. At the southern end of Marigot, next to the Marina Port La Royale, is a museum dedicated to preserving St. Martin's history and culture. A new building houses a variety of pre-Columbian treasures unearthed by the Hope Estate Archaeological Society. ⊠ *Terre Basse Rd., Marigot* ☎ *0690/29–48–36* ⊕ *www.museesaintmartin.com* ☜ *$5* ⊙ *Daily 9–1 and 3–5.*

FRENCH CUL DE SAC

North of Orient Bay Beach, the French colonial mansion of St. Martin's mayor is nestled in the hills. Little red-roof houses look like open umbrellas tumbling down the green hillside. The area is peaceful and good for hiking. From the beach here, shuttle boats make the five-minute trip to **Ilet Pinel,** an uninhabited island that's fine for picnicking, sunning, and swimming. There are full-service beach clubs there, so just pack the sunscreen and head over.

GRAND CASE

The Caribbean's own Restaurant Row is the heart of this French-side town, a 10-minute drive from either Orient Bay or Marigot, stretching along a narrow beach overlooking Anguilla. You'll find a first-rate restaurant for every palate, mood, and wallet. At lunchtime, or with kids, head to the casual lolos (open-air barbecue stands) and feet-in-the sand beach bars. Twilight drinks and tapas are fun. At night, stroll the strip and preview the sophisticated offerings on the menus posted outside before you settle in for a long and sumptuous meal. If you still have the energy, there are lounges with music (usually a DJ) that get going after 11 pm.

ORLÉANS

North of Oyster Pond and the Étang aux Poissons (Fish Lake) is the island's oldest settlement, also known as the French Quarter. You can find classic, vibrantly painted West Indian–style homes with the original gingerbread fretwork, and large areas of the nature and marine preserve that is working to save the fragile ecosystem of the island.

ELSEWHERE IN ST. MARTIN

☺ FodorsChoice ★ **Butterfly Farm.** If you arrive early in the morning when the butterflies first break out of their chrysalis, you'll be able to marvel at the absolute wonder of dozens of butterflies and moths from around the world and the particular host plants with which each evolved. At any given time, some 40 species of butterflies—numbering as many as 600 individual insects—flutter inside the lush screened garden and hatch on the plants housed there. Butterfly art and knickknacks are for sale in the gift shop. In case you want to come back, your ticket, which includes a guided tour, is good for your entire stay. ⊠ *Le Galion Beach Rd., Quartier d'Orléans* ☎ *590/87–31–21* ⊕ *www.thebutterflyfarm.com* ☜ *$12* ⊙ *Daily 9–3:30.*

FodorsChoice ★ **Pic du Paradis.** Between Marigot and Grand Case, "Paradise Peak," at 1,492 feet, is the island's highest point. There are two observation areas. From them, the tropical forest unfolds below, and the vistas are breathtaking. The road is quite isolated and steep, best suited to a four-wheel-drive vehicle, so don't head up here unless you are prepared for the climb. There have also been some problems with crime in this area, so it might be best to go with an experienced local guide.

Loterie Farm. Halfway up the road to Pic du Paradis is Loterie Farm, a peaceful 150-acre private nature preserve opened to the public in

The view from Fort Louis, high above Marigot

1999 by American expat B. J. Welch. There are hiking trails and maps, so you can go on your own (€5) or arrange a guide for a group (€25 for six people). Along the marked trails you will see native forest with tamarind, gum, mango, and mahogany trees, and wildlife including greenback monkeys if you are lucky. In 2011 Loterie opened a lovely spring-fed pool and Jacuzzi area with lounge chairs, great music, and chic tented cabanas called L'Eau Lounge; if you're with a group, consider the VIP package there. Don't miss a treetop lunch or dinner at **Hidden Forest Café** (⇨ *Where to Eat, below*), Loterie Farm's restaurant, where Julie Perkis cooks delicious, healthy meals and snacks. If you are brave—and over 4 feet 5 inches tall—try soaring over trees on one of the longest zip lines in the Western Hemisphere. ⊠ *Rte. de Pic du Paradis 103, Rambaud* ☎ *590/87–86–16, 590/57–28–55* ⊕ *www. loteriefarm.com* ⊠ *€35–€55* ⊘ *Tues.–Sun. 9–4* ⊠ *Rte. de Pic du Paradis, Pic du Paradis.*

WHERE TO EAT

Although most people come to St. Maarten/St. Martin for sun and fun, they leave praising the cuisine. On an island that covers only 37 square miles (96 square km), there are more than 400 restaurants from which to choose. You can sample the best dishes from France, Thailand, Italy, Vietnam, India, Japan, and, of course, the Caribbean.

Many of the best restaurants are in Grand Case (on the French side), but you should not limit your culinary adventures to that village. Great dining thrives throughout the island, from the bistros of Marigot to the

BEST BETS FOR DINING

Fodor's Choice★
Bacchus, Mario's Bistro, La Cigale, L'Astrolabe, Le Pressoir, Le Tastevin, Talk of the Town, Temptation, Bamboo

MOST ROMANTIC
Antoine, Le Pressoir, Sol é Luna, La Samanna, Le Domaine de Lonvilliers, Temptation, La Marrakesh

BEST VIEW
Sol é Luna, La Cigale, Taloula Mango's

BEST LOCAL FOOD
Chesterfield's, Claude Mini-Club

BEST FOR FAMILIES
Taloula Mango's, Lolos

BEST FOR A SPECIAL OCCASION
La Samanna (especially the wine dinner in the cellar)

HIP AND YOUNG
Treelounge/Hidden Forest Café, Palm Beach, Temptation, Karakter, Bamboo, Calmos Café

hopping restaurants of Cupecoy to the low-key eateries of Simpson Bay. Whether you enjoy dining on fine china in one of the upscale restaurants or off a paper plate at the island's many lolos (roadside barbecue stands), St. Maarten/St. Martin's culinary options are sure to appeal to every palate. Loyalists on both "sides" will cheerfully try to steer you to their own favorites, and it's common to cite high euro prices to deter exploration, but some restaurants still offer a one-to-one exchange rate between dollars and euros if you use cash, and main-course portions are often large enough to be shared.

During high season, it's essential to make reservations, and making them a month in advance is advisable for some of the best places. Dutch-side restaurants sometimes include a 15% service charge, so check your bill before tipping. On the French side, service is always included, but it is customary to leave 5% to 10% extra in cash for the server. Don't count on leaving tips on your credit card—it's customary to tip in cash. A taxi is probably the easiest solution to the parking problems in Grand Case, Marigot, and Philipsburg. Grand Case has two lots—each costs $4—at each end of the main boulevard, but they're often packed.

What to Wear: Although appropriate dining attire ranges from swimsuits to sport jackets, casual dress is usually appropriate throughout restaurants on the island. For men, a jacket and khakis or jeans will take you anywhere; for women, dressy pants, a skirt, or even fancy shorts are usually acceptable. Jeans are fine in the less formal eateries.

DUTCH SIDE

CUPECOY

$$$
ITALIAN
✕ **La Gondola.** Owner Davide Foini started out by selling just his homemade pasta, which proved to be so popular that he opened this authentic trattoria that has found its way onto many "best bets" lists of island regulars. The kitchen still rolls out the dough for the dozens of pasta dishes on the encyclopedic Italian menu, which also includes favorites

like veal parmigiana, chicken piccata in marsala sauce, and osso buco Milanese. Save room for desserts like the *fantasia di dessert del Carnevale di Venezia* (a warm chocolate tart and frozen nougat served with raspberry sauce) or tiramisu. The service is professional and high-tech—the waiters take orders with earpieces and handheld computers. $ *Average main: $28* ⊠ *Atlantis World Casino, Rhine Rd. 106, Cupecoy* ☎ *721/544–3938* ⊕ *www.lagondola-sxm.com* ⊗ *No lunch.*

$$$$ ✕ **Rare.** Within an intimate, clubby setting, a guitarist provides back-
STEAKHOUSE ground music while carnivores delight in chef Dino Jagtiani's creative menu. The focus is steak: certified Angus prime cuts topped with chimichurri, béarnaise, horseradish, peppercorn, or mushroom sauce. Not into red meat? You can also choose from seafood, pork, lamb, or veal. Sample some delicious sides like truffled mashed potatoes or cultivated mushroom sauté (a tasty fungi variety). Luscious desserts will make you forget that you will want to look good in your bathing suit tomorrow morning. Check the restaurant's website for specials. $ *Average main: $54* ⊠ *Atlantis World Casino, Rhine Rd. 106, Cupecoy* ☎ *721/545–2254* ⊕ *ww.rareandtemptation.com* ⚐ *Reservations essential* ⊗ *Closed Sept. and Mon. June–Oct. No lunch.*

$$$$ ✕ **Temptation.** Supercreative chef Dino Jagtiani, who trained at the Culi-
ECLECTIC nary Institute of America, is the mastermind behind dishes like seared
★ foie gras PB and J (melted foie gras accented with peanut butter and homemade port-wine fig jam) and herb-crusted Chilean sea bass. The chef, who compares dessert to lovemaking ("both intimate, and not to be indulged in lightly"), offers a crème brûlée tasting, as well as Granny Smith apple tempura with cinnamon ice cream and caramel sauce for the sweet tooth. The wine list is extensive, and features a number of reasonably priced selections. There are also many inventive cocktails, such as the St. Maartini—a refreshing blend of coconut rum, guava puree, passion-fruit juice, and peach schnapps. The dining room is pretty and intimate, in spite of its location behind the casino. There's outdoor seating as well. $ *Average main: $36* ⊠ *Atlantis Casino Courtyard, Rhine Rd. 106, Cupecoy* ☎ *721/545–2254* ⊕ *www.chefdino.com* ⚐ *Reservations essential* ⊗ *Closed Sun. June–Oct. No lunch.*

MAHO

$$$ ✕ **Bamboo.** This dramatic and hip addition to the top level of the Maho
ASIAN central shopping area features red lacquer walls, lounging tables, Indo-
Fodor's Choice nesian art, a first-rate bar, and electro-house tunes. You can get terrific
★ sushi and sashimi, both the classic Japanese varieties and the American-ized ones (California roll, for example). All are good, as are the Asian hot appetizers and bartender Viktor's exotic cocktails like the Tranquillity (citrus vodka and smoky oolong tea). If you're not into Asian fare, try the salmon, ribs, or beef. The young crowd keeps this place hopping way past midnight. If you're solo, you will have a great time hanging and even dining at the bar. There is a sake and sushi happy hour from 5 to 7 nightly. $ *Average main: $20* ⊠ *Sonesta Maho Beach Resort & Casino, 1 Rhine Rd., Maho* ☎ *721/545–3622* ⊕ *www.bamboobernies. net* ⊗ *No lunch weekdays.*

$$$ ✕ **Big Fish.** A chic, white interior, fresh-caught fish, and friendly, if some-
SEAFOOD times relaxed, service, are the draw this Oyster Pond restaurant. The

location is convenient whether you are staying in Oyster Pond or Dawn Beach. Stick with whatever was most recently in the sea, and you will be happy with your food. If offered, grouper in curry-coconut is a yummy option, and the hurricane shrimp is a local favorite. The owners also run a fishing-charter outfit, and they will happily cook up your daily catch here, too. $ *Average main: $28* ⊠ *14 Emerald Merrit Rd., Oyster Pond, St. Maarten* ☎ *721/586–1961.*

$$$
ITALIAN
✕ **Pizza Pasta Trattoria Italiana.** Tucked away on a quiet street near Casino Royale, this Italian eatery is extremely popular with locals. The menu includes favorites like penne Bolognese and eggplant Parmesan, but the real winners are the thin-crust pizzas. The freshly brewed iced tea is great on a hot day. With its laid-back atmosphere and friendly staff, this is a cozy spot for families with small children or a place where you just run in and grab a quick bite. $ *Average main: $22* ⊠ *Maho Shopping Plaza, Maho* ☎ *721/545–4034* ☼ *No lunch Sun.*

PHILIPSBURG

$$$$
FRENCH
✕ **Antoine.** You'd be hard-pressed to find a more enjoyable evening in Philipsburg. Owner Jean Pierre Pomarico's warmth shines through as he greets guests and ushers them into the comfy seaside restaurant. Low-key, blue-accented decor, white bamboo chairs, watercolors lining the walls, and candles—along with the sound of the nearby surf—create a relaxing atmosphere. The lobster thermidor (a succulent tail oozing with cream and Swiss cheese) is a favorite, but other specialties include lobster bisque, seafood linguine, and a beef fillet with béarnaise sauce. The prix-fixe menu is a great deal. $ *Average main: $32* ⊠ *119 Front St., Philipsburg* ☎ *721/542–2964* ⊕ *www.antoinerestaurant.com* ⌂ *Reservations essential.*

$$
CARIBBEAN
✕ **Chesterfield's.** Both locals and tourists seem to love this restaurant at Bobby's Marina. Seafood is the main focus, but steaks, burgers, pasta, and poultry are all on the dinner menu, and you can also get breakfast and lunch. If you love sophisticated cuisine, look elsewhere, but the portions are big and the prices reasonable. Happy hour is every night from 5 to 7. $ *Average main: $19* ⊠ *Great Bay Marina, Philipsburg* ☎ *721/542–3484* ⊕ *www.chesterfields-restaurant.com.*

$$
ECLECTIC
✕ **The Greenhouse.** The famous happy hour is just one of the reasons people flock to the Greenhouse. This waterfront restaurant balances a relaxed atmosphere, reasonable prices, and popular favorites like burgers, prime rib, and steaks. If you're seeking something spicy, try the creole shrimp. The daily specials, like the Friday-night Lobster Mania, are widely popular. $ *Average main: $21* ⊠ *Bobby's Marina, Philipsburg* ☎ *721/542–2941* ⊕ *www.thegreenhouserestaurant.com.*

$$$
FRENCH
✕ **L'Escargot.** The wraparound verandah, the bunches of grapes hanging from the chandeliers, and the Toulouse-Lautrec–style murals add to the colorful atmosphere of this restaurant in a 150-year-old, gingerbread, Creole house. As the name suggests, snails are a specialty, and are offered several ways. But the menu also includes many other French standards like onion soup, crispy duck, and veal cordon bleu. There's a Friday night cabaret show, complete with cancan in the tradition of *La Cage aux Folles.* $ *Average main: $28* ⊠ *96 Front St., Philips-*

burg 🕿 721/542–2483 ⊕ *www.lescargotrestaurant.com* ⊙ *Closed Sun. June–Oct. No lunch weekends.*

$$$ ✕**Ocean Lounge.** An airy modern veranda perched on the Philipsburg
ECLECTIC boardwalk gives Ocean Lounge its distinct South Beach vibe. You'll
want to linger over fresh fish and steaks, as you watch the scene with
tourists of all varieties passing by two-by-two on romantic evening
strolls, or determined cruise-ship passengers surveying the surround-
ing shops by day. The daily tasting menu (one option includes two
glasses of good wine) offers a chance to sample the cuisine. ⑤ *Average
main: $30* ⊠ *Holland House Beach Hotel, 43 Front St., Philipsburg*
🕿 721/542–2572 ⊕ *www.hhbh.com.*

$$ ✕**Taloula Mango's.** Ribs are the specialty at this casual beachfront res-
ECLECTIC taurant, but the jerk chicken and thin-crust pizza, not to mention a few
vegetarian options like the tasty falafel, are not to be ignored. On weekdays lunch is accompanied by live music; every Friday during happy
hour a DJ spins tunes. In case you're wondering, the restaurant got its
name from the owner's golden retriever. ⑤ *Average main: $17* ⊠ *Sint
Rose Shopping Mall, off Front St. on beach boardwalk, Philipsburg*
🕿 721/542–1645 ⊕ *www.taloulamango.com.*

SIMPSON BAY

$$ ✕**Karakter Beach Lounge.** Karakter, a funky and charming modern beach
ECLECTIC bar, is right behind the airport, serving up fun, great music, relaxation,
★ and a lot of style. The vibe is more like St. Tropez than St. Maarten.
Open from 10 am till sunset, the restaurant serves up healthy and tasty
choices for any appetite: fresh fruit smoothies, tropical cocktails, fresh
fruit salads, healthy sandwiches, and tapas. A sign near the shower/
bathhouse invites guest to "come hang out here and shower before
you go to the airport." So this is a place to keep in mind in case your
flight is delayed or if you have a layover between flights, or if you just
want to spend every last second of your vacation on the sand. ⑤ *Av-
erage main: $14* ⊠ *121 Simpson Bay Rd., Simpson Bay, St. Maarten*
🕿 721/523–9983 ⊕ *www.karakterbeach.com.*

$$ ✕**Pineapple Pete.** This popular, casual, and fun place is well located,
SEAFOOD with a game room that includes seven pool tables, four dart boards, an
☺ arcade, and flat-screen TVs tuned to sports. A friendly, efficient staff
will serve you burgers, seafood, and ribs, but for a real treat try one of
the specialties like the tasty crab-stuffed shrimp appetizer. Follow it up
with succulent, herb-crusted rack of lamb. There's free Wi-Fi and live
entertainment Tuesday through Sunday. Its an easy choice for a bite near
the airport, and open nonstop from 11 am through closing. ⑤ *Average
main: $20* ⊠ *56 Welfare Rd., Simpson Bay* 🕿 721/544–6030 ⊕ *www.
pineapplepete.com* ⌕ *Reservations essential.*

$$$ ✕**Saratoga.** At Simpson Bay Yacht Club you can choose to be inside or
ECLECTIC on the waterside terrace. The menu changes daily, but you can never
go wrong with one of chef John Jackson's fish specialties, including red
snapper with white wine reduction or yellowfin tuna "filet mignon"
with miso-roasted veggies. You might start with oysters flown in from
France, or sesame seaweed salad. The wine list includes 150 different
bottles, including many by the glass. ⑤ *Average main: $27* ⊠ *Simp-
son Bay Yacht Club, 68 Welfare Rd., Simpson Bay* 🕿 721/544–2421

www.sxmsaratoga.com ⌕ *Reservations essential* ⊘ *Closed Sun. Closed Aug.–Sept. No lunch.*

$　⨯ **Top Carrot.** Open from 7 am to 6 pm, this café and juice bar is a popular
VEGETARIAN　breakfast and lunch stop. It features vegetarian entrées, sandwiches, salads, homemade pastries, and, more recently, fresh fish. Favorites include
a pastry stuffed with pesto, avocado, red pepper, and feta cheese, or a
cauliflower, spinach, and tomato quiche. The house-made granola and
yogurt are local favorites, but folks also drop in just for espresso and
the large selection of teas. Many also come for the free Wi-Fi service.
Adjacent to the restaurant is a gift shop with Asian-inspired items and
spiritual books. ⑤ *Average main: $8* ⌧ *Airport Rd., near Simpson Bay
Yacht Club, Simpson Bay* ☎ *721/544–3381* ⊘ *Closed Sun. No dinner.*

$　⨯ **Zee Best.** This friendly bistro serves one of the best breakfasts on the
CAFÉ　island. There's a huge selection of fresh-baked pastries—try the almond
croissants—plus sweet and savory crepes, omelets, quiches, and freshly
baked croissants and other treats from the oven. Specialties include the
St. Maarten omelet, filled with ham, cheese, mushrooms, onions, green
peppers, and tomatoes. Best of all, breakfast is served from 7:30 am
until 2 pm. Lunch includes sandwiches, salads, and the chef's famous
spaghetti Bolognese. Grab a table in the dining room or on the terrace;
it's a good place to relax with a newspaper and a cup of cappuccino.
■**TIP**➔ There are also locations near the Airport, and at Port de Plaisance.
⑤ *Average main: $8* ⌧ *Plaza del Lago, Simpson Bay* ☎ *721/544–2477*
▭ *No credit cards.*

FRENCH SIDE

BAIE NETTLÉ

$$$$　⨯ **La Cigale.** On the edge of Baie Nettlé, La Cigale has wonderful views
FRENCH　of the lagoon from its dining room and its open-air patio, but the
Fodor's Choice　charm of the restaurant comes from the devoted attention of adorable
★　owner Olivier, helped by his mother and brother, and various cousins,
too. Stephane Istel's delicious food is edible sculpture: ravioli of lobster
with wild mushrooms and foie gras is poached in an intense lobster
bisque, and house-smoked swordfish and salmon is garnished with goat
cheese and seaweed salad drizzled with dill-lime vinaigrette. ⑤ *Average
main: €37* ⌧ *101 Laguna Beach, Baie Nettlé* ☎ *599/87–90–23* ⊕ *www.
restaurant-lacigale.com* ⌕ *Reservations essential* ⊘ *Closed Sun. in Sept.
and Oct. No lunch.*

BAIE ORIENTALE

$$$$　⨯ **L'Astrolabe.** Chef Stephan Decluseau gets raves for his modern inter-
FRENCH　pretations of classic French cuisine served around the pool at this cozy,
relaxed restaurant in the Esmeralda Resort. Corn soup; foie gras terrine
with apricot and quince jam; an amazing roast duck with pineapple-
ginger sauce; and deliciously fresh fish dishes are just some of the offerings. There are lots of choices for vegetarians, a three-course prix fixe, a
children's menu, and a lobster party with live music every Friday night.
⑤ *Average main: €26* ⌧ *Esmeralda Resort, Baie Orientale* ☎ *0590/87–
11–20* ⊕ *www.esmeralda-resort.com* ⌕ *Reservations essential* ⊘ *No
lunch. No dinner Wed.*

$$$
AMERICAN
★

✕**Palm Beach.** One of the newer additions to the Baie Orientale beach clubs is as stylish as its Florida namesake. Balinese art and furniture, big comfy chaises on the beach, and an active bar set the stage. Pretty girls are the decor. There are three big tree-house-like lounges for lunch or if you are looking for a place to spend the afternoon. The menu of salads, grills, and brochettes is served in a pavilion shaded by sail-like awnings. Take the exit to BooBoo Jam after the gas station. The Sunday night beach party is the place to be for locals and guests alike. ⑤ *Average main: €24 ⊠ Baie Orientale ☎ 690/35–99–06 ⊕ www.palmbeachsxm. net ⊗ No dinner.*

23

FRIAR'S BAY

$$
BISTRO

✕**Friar's Bay Beach Café.** There is a sophisticated vibe at this quiet, rather elegant beach club that may make patrons feel as if they are on a private beach. The decor is not as funky as at some of the other beach-club restaurants, but look out for the red and black signs on the road between Grand Case and Marigot so you'll know where to turn. Drive slow because the road is rough. You can rent lounge chairs and umbrellas and spend the whole day relaxing, drinking, and dining. The restaurant is open from breakfast through the spectacular sunset, offering a menu reminiscent of a French bistro's. Be sure to look at the specials on the blackboard, but carpaccios of meat and fish are sparklingly fresh, and the salads are terrific. Plus, you'll also find French standbys such as tomato and goat cheese tartlets, as well as "international" ones like burgers and sandwiches. On Sunday evenings there is live music until 9 pm. ⑤ *Average main: €18 ⊠ Friar's Bay Rd., Friar's Bay ☎ 590/49–16–87 ⊟ No credit cards.*

FRENCH CUL DE SAC

$$$
CARIBBEAN

✕**Sol é Luna.** Charming and romantic, this restaurant puts its best tables on the balcony, from which you can best appreciate the great views. Begin your meal with an appetizer like curry tuna carpaccio, monkfish spring rolls, or roasted vegetables with goat cheese; then move on to an entrée such as fresh pasta with mixed seafood or beef tenderloin flamed with Cognac. Don't be surprised if you see a proposal or two during your meal, as this is one of the most romantic restaurants on the island. ■TIP➜ Before ordering one of the "specials," ask about the prices; sometimes they can be surprisingly high compared to regular menu items. ⑤ *Average main: €21 ⊠ 61 Rte. de Mont Vernon, French Cul de Sac ☎ 590/29–08–56 ⊕ www.solelunarestaurant.com ⊗ Closed mid-June–early July and Sept.–early Oct.*

GRAND CASE

$$
FRENCH
Fodor's Choice
★

✕**Bacchus.** If you want to lunch with the savviest locals, you have to scrape yourself from the beach and head into the industrial park outside Grand Case, where Benjamin Laurent, the best wine importer in the Caribbean, has built this lively, deliciously air-conditioned reconstruction of a wine cellar. He serves up first-rate starters, salads, and main courses made from top ingredients brought in from France, lovingly prepared by top chefs. Shop here for gourmet groceries for your villa, or hang in the new cigar–rum lounge. The wines are sublime, and you will get an amazing education along with a great lunch. You won't mind eating indoors here—just think of it as the perfect sunblock. Enter at the "Hope Estate" sign in the roundabout across from the road that leads to the Grand Case Airport. $ *Average main: €20* ✉ *18–19 Hope Estate, Grand Case Rd., Grand Case* ☎ *0590/87–15–70* ⊕ *www.bacchussxm.com* ☯ *No dinner. Closed Sun.*

$$$ ✕ **L'Auberge Gourmande.** A fixture of
FRENCH   Boulevard Grand Case, L'Auberge Gourmande is in one of the oldest Creole houses in St. Maarten/St. Martin. The formal dining room is framed by elegant arches. The light Provençal cuisine is a delight, with menu choices like roasted rack of lamb with an herb crust over olive mashed potatoes, Dover sole in lemon butter, and pork filet mignon stuffed with apricots and walnuts. There are vegetarian options, a kids' menu, and a good selection of wines. Ask for an outside table. $ *Average main: €21* ✉ *89 bd. de Grand Case, Grand Case* ☎ *590/87–73–37* ⊕ *www.laubergegourmande.com* ☯ *Closed Sept. No lunch.*

$$$ ✕ **L'Estaminet.** The name of this restaurant is an old-fashioned word for
FRENCH   "tavern" in French, but the food is anything but archaic. The creative, upscale cuisine served in this modern, clean space is fun and surprising, utilizing plenty of molecular gastronomy. This means that intense liquid garnishes might be inserted into your goat-cheese appetizer or perhaps given to you in a tiny toothpaste tube, or even a plastic syringe. The bright flavors, artistic plating, and novelty make for a lively meal that will be remembered fondly. Under no circumstances should you pass up the chocolate tasting for dessert. $ *Average main: €23* ✉ *139 bd. de Grand Case, Grand Case* ☎ *590/29–00–25* ⊕ *www.estaminet-sxm. com* ☯ *Closed Mon. in June–Nov.*

$$$ ✕ **Le Pressoir.** In a carefully restored West Indian house painted in bril-
FRENCH   liant reds and blues, Le Pressoir has charm to spare. The name comes
Fodor'sChoice   from the historic salt press that sits opposite the restaurant, but the thrill
★   comes from the culinary creations of chef Franc Mear and the hospitality of his beautiful wife Melanie. If you are indecisive, or just plain smart, try any (or all) of the degustations (tastings) of four soups, four foie gras preparations, or four fruit desserts, each showcasing sophisticated preparations with adorable presentations. Foie gras is served in a dollhouse-size terrine, with a teensy glass of Sauternes. $ *Average main: €30* ✉ *30 bd. de Grand Case, Grand Case* ☎ *590/87–76–62* ⊕ *www. lepressoir-sxm.com* ⊰ *Reservations essential* ☯ *Closed mid-Sept.–mid-Oct. and Sun. in May–Dec. No lunch.*

$$$ ✕ **Le Tastevin.** In the heart of Grand Case, Le Tastevin is on everyone's
FRENCH   list of favorites. The attractive wood-beamed room is the "real" St. Martin style, and the tasty food is enhanced by Joseph, the amiable owner, who serves up lunch and dinner every day on a breezy porch over a glittering blue sea. Salads and simple grills rule for lunch; at dinner,

try one of the two tasting menus, either a "brasserie" style menu or a more expensive "gourmet" menu that includes excellent wines. $ *Average main: €29* ⊠ *86 bd. de Grand Case, Grand Case* ☎ *590/87–55–45* ⊕ *www.letastevin-restaurant.com* ⌣ *Reservations essential* ⊘ *Closed mid-Aug.–Sept.*

$

CARIBBEAN

Fodor's Choice

★

✕ **Talk of the Town.** Although St. Martin is known for its upscale dining, each town has its roadside barbecue stands, called lolos, including the island's culinary capital of Grand Case. They are open from lunchtime until evening, but earlier in the day you'll find fresher offerings. Locals flock to the square of a half-dozen stands in the middle of Grand Case, on the water side. Not to say that these stands offer haute or fine cuisine, but they are fun, relatively cheap, and offer an iconic St. Martin meal. Talk of the Town is one of the most popular. With plastic utensils and paper plates, it couldn't be more informal. The menu includes everything from succulent grilled ribs to stewed conch, fresh snapper, and grilled lobster at the most reasonable price on the island. Don't miss the johnnycakes and side dishes like plantains, curried rice, beans, and coleslaw that come with your choice. The service is friendly, if a bit slow, but sit back with a beer and enjoy the experience. On weekends there is often live music. **Sky's the Limit** is another iconic lolo, just two picnic tables over. At this writing the lolos are still offering a one-to-one exchange between euros and dollars. $ *Average main: €10* ⊠ *Bd. de Grand Case, Grand Case* ☎ *590/29–63–89* ⌣ *Reservations essential* ▭ *No credit cards.*

MARIGOT

$$$

CARIBBEAN

✕ **Claude Mini-Club.** An island institution, Claude Mini-Club has delighted patrons with its blend of creole and French food since 1969, but it now has new owners and a fresh paint job. The whole place is built tree-house style around the trunks of coconut palms, and the lofty perch means you have great views of Marigot Harbor. The dinner buffet on Wednesday and Saturday nights is legendary. It includes more than 30 dishes, often including conch soup, grilled lobster, roast leg of lamb, Black Angus roast beef, and roast pig. The prix-fixe menus are something of a bargain. There's live music for dancing on Fridays. $ *Average main: €24* ⊠ *49 bd. de France, Marigot* ☎ *590/87–50–69* ⊕ *www.restaurantminiclub.com* ⊘ *Closed Sun.*

$$

CARIBBEAN

✕ **Enoch's Place.** The blue-and-white-striped awning on a corner of the Marigot Market makes this place hard to miss. But Enoch's cooking is what draws the crowds. Specialties include garlic shrimp, fresh lobster, and rice and beans (like your St. Martin mother used to make). Try the saltfish and fried johnnycake—a great breakfast option. The food more than makes up for the lack of decor, and chances are you'll be counting the days until you can return. $ *Average main: €13* ⊠ *Marigot Market, Front de Mer, Marigot* ☎ *590/29–29–88* ⊕ *www.enochsplace. com* ⌣ *Reservations not accepted* ▭ *No credit cards* ⊘ *Closed Sun. No dinner.*

$$

ECLECTIC

✕ **La Belle Epoque.** A favorite among locals, this brasserie is a good choice at the Marigot marina. Whether you stop for a drink or a meal, you'll soon discover that it's a great spot for boat- and people-watching. The menu has a bit of everything: big salads, pizza, and seafood are always good bets. There's also a good wine list. And it's open nonstop seven days a week for breakfast through late dinner. $ *Average main: €16* ✉ *Marina de la Port Royale, Marigot* ☎ 590/87–87–70 ⊕ *www.belle-epoque-sxm.com.*

$$
CONTEMPORARY

✕ **La Source.** Somewhat hidden behind the boutiques in Marina La Royale (look near Vilbrequin), this tiny new "healthy" restaurant features a French seasonal menu as well as sandwiches, salads, soups, fair-trade coffee and teas, and organic pastries. A bargain lunch special includes the special of the day and a drink, and the organic pasta dishes are delicious and inventive. The light choices, which include crab tartare with seaweed, and organic-chicken salad, are terrific. Even the pastries are organic. $ *Average main: €14* ✉ *Port La Royale Marina, Marigot* ☎ 590/27–17–27.

$$$
MOROCCAN
★

✕ **Le Marrakech.** Some twenty years ago, the charming owners renovated this beautifully historic St. Martin *case.* After several other restaurant ventures, they have returned to the original cottage to serve up delicious, authentic Moroccan cuisine in a beautiful and romantic space with an open garden that feels just like Morocco. And it should feel authentic; the decor was created by a Moroccan architect. The food is fragrant and delicious, with portions so huge you will have enough lunch for the next day. The couscous and tagines are authentically spiced and served with professional friendliness by an affable staff in Moroccan serving pieces. The mixed appetizers (*meze*) are delectable, and the royal couscous is justly popular. Kabobs and tajines are a great change of pace from the usual Caribbean and French fare. Lounge in the tented courtyard after dinner—and don't be surprised to be entertained by a talented belly-dancer. The restaurant is on Marigot's main road across from the stadium. $ *Average main: €24* ✉ *169 rue de Hollande, Marigot* ☎ 590/27–54–48 ⏣ *Reservations essential* ⊗ *Closed Sun.*

PIC DU PARADIS

$$
CARIBBEAN
☾
Fodor'sChoice
★

✕ **Hidden Forest Café.** Schedule your trip to Loterie Farm to take advantage of the lovely tree-house pavilions where lunch or dinner has a safari vibe and where the yummy, locally sourced food is inventive and fresh. New in 2012 is L'Eau Lounge, a giant spring-fed pool with Jacuzzis, lounge-cabanas, and a St. Barth-meets-Wet 'n' Wild atmosphere. Curried-spinach chicken with banana fritters is a popular pick, but there are great choices for vegetarians, too, including cumin lentil balls; those with stouter appetites dig into the massive Black Angus tenderloin. Loterie Farm's other eatery, Treelounge, features great cocktails and tapas, is open Monday through Saturday, and stays open late with frequent live music. $ *Average main: €20* ✉ *Loterie Farm, Pic Paradis 103, Rambaud* ☎ 590/87–86–16 ⊕ *www.loteriefarm.com* ⊗ *Closed Mon.*

SANDY GROUND

$$$$
ECLECTIC
Fodor'sChoice
★

✕ **Mario's Bistro.** Don't miss dinner at this romantic eatery, a perennial favorite for its ravishing cuisine, romantic ambience, and most of all the marvelously friendly owners. Didier Gonnon and Martyne Tardif are out front, while chef Mario Tardif is in the kitchen creating ravishing dishes such as bouillabaisse with green Thai curry, a duet of grilled

St. Maarten vs. St. Martin

If this is your first trip to St. Maarten/ St. Martin, you're probably wondering which side will better suit your needs. That's hard to say, because in some ways the difference between the two can seem as subtle as the hazy boundary line dividing them. But there are some major differences.

St. Maarten, the Dutch side, has the casinos, more nightlife, and bigger hotels. St. Martin, the French side, has no casinos, less nightlife, and hotels that are smaller and more intimate. Many have kitchenettes, and most

include breakfast. There are many good restaurants on the Dutch side, but if fine dining makes your vacation, the French side rules.

The biggest difference might be currency—the Netherlands Antilles guilder (also called the florin) on the Dutch side, the euro on the French side. And the relative strength of the euro can translate to some expensive surprises. Many establishments on both sides (even the French) accept U.S. dollars.

23

lamb chops and braised lamb shank shepherd pie, and sautéed jumbo scallops with crab mashed potatoes and leek tempura. Leave room for the heavenly upside-down banana coconut tart with caramel sauce and coconut ice cream. The restaurant is rather strict about reservations for large groups, so be sure to call and get the details. $ *Average main: €31* ✉ *48 Rue Morne Rd, at the Sandy Ground Bridge, Sandy Ground* ☎ *590/87–06–36* ⊕ *www.mariosbistro.com* ⚞ *Reservations essential* ☾ *Closed Sun., Aug., and Sept. No lunch.*

WHERE TO STAY

St. Maarten/St. Martin accommodations range from modern megaresorts such as the Radisson and the Westin St. Maarten to condos and small inns. On the Dutch side many hotels cater to groups, and although that's also true to some extent on the French side, you can find a larger collection of intimate accommodations there. ■ TIP→ Offseason rates (April through the beginning of December) can be as little as half the high-season rates.

For expanded reviews, facilities, and current deals, visit Fodors.com.

TIME-SHARE RENTALS

Time-share properties are scattered around the island, mostly on the Dutch side. There's no reason to buy a share, as these condos are rented out whenever the owners are not in residence. If you stay in one, be prepared for a sales pitch. Most rent by the night, but there's often substantial savings if you secure a weekly rate. Not all offer daily maid service, so make sure to ask before you book. As some properties are undergoing renovations at this writing, be sure to ask about construction conditions, and in any case, ask for a recently renovated unit.

PRIVATE VILLAS

Villas are a great lodging option, especially for families who don't need to keep the kids occupied, or groups of friends who just like hanging out together. Since these are for the most part freestanding houses, their greatest advantage is privacy. These properties are scattered throughout the island, often in gated communities or on secluded roads. Some have bare-bones furnishings, whereas others are over-the-top luxurious, with gyms, theaters, game rooms, and several different pools. There are private chefs, gardeners, maids, and other staffers to care for both the villa and its occupants.

Villas are secured through rental companies. They offer properties with weekly prices that range from reasonable to more than many people make in a year. Check around, as prices for the same property vary from agent to agent. Because of the economy, many villas are now offered by the night rather than by the week, so it's often possible to book for less than a full week's stay. Rental companies usually provide airport transfers and concierge service, and for an extra fee will even stock your refrigerator.

RENTAL CONTACTS

French Caribbean International. French Caribbean International offers rental properties on the French side of the island. ☎ *800/322–2223 in the U.S. ⊕ www.frenchcaribbean.com.*

Island Hideaways. Island Hideaways, the island's oldest rental company, rents villas on both sides. ☎ *800/832–2302 in the U.S., 703/378–7840 ⊕ www.islandhideaways.com.*

Island Properties. Island Properties has properties scattered around the island. ✉ *62 Welfare Rd., Simpson Bay, St. Maarten* ☎ *599/544–4580, 866/978–5852 in the U.S. ⊕ www.remaxislandproperties.com.*

Jennifer's Vacation Villas. Jennifer's Vacation Villas rents villas on both sides of the island. ✉ *Plaza Del Lago, Simpson Bay Yacht Club, Simpson Bay, St. Maarten* ☎ *631/546–7345 in New York, 721/544–3107 in St. Maarten ⊕ www.jennifersvacationvillas.com.*

Pierrescaraïbes. Pierrescaraïbes, owned by American Leslie Reed, has been renting and selling upscale St. Martin villas to satisfied clients for more than a decade. The company's well-designed website makes it easy to get a sense of the first-rate properties available in all sizes and prices. The company is associated with Christie's Great Estates. ✉ *Plaza Caraibes, rue Kennedy, Bldg. A, Marigot, St. Martin* ☎ *590/51–02–85 in St. Martin ⊕ www.pierrescaraibes.com.*

Romac Southeby's International Realty. Romac Southeby's International Realty rents luxury villas, many in gated communities. ✉ *54 Simpson Bay Rd., Simpson Bay, St. Maarten* ☎ *877/537–9282 in the U.S. ⊕ www.caribbeanbestrealestate.com.*

Villas of Distinction. Villas of Distinction is one of the oldest villa-rental companies on the French side of the island. Check their website for special deals. ☎ *800/289–0900 in the U.S. ⊕ www.villasofdistinction.com.*

BEST BETS FOR LODGING

Fodor's Choice★

L'Esplanade, Blue Pelican, the Horny Toad, La Samanna, Palm Court, Westin St. Maarten Dawn Beach Resort & Spa

BEST FOR ROMANCE

La Samanna, Le Domaine de Lonvilliers, Palm Court, Princess Heights

BEST BEACHFRONT

The Horny Toad, La Samanna, Le Domaine de Lonvilliers, Esmeralda, Radisson Blu St. Martin

BEST POOL

Radisson Blu St. Martin, Westin St. Maarten Dawn Beach Resort & Spa

BEST SERVICE

La Samanna, Le Domaine de Lonvilliers

BEST FOR KIDS

Alamanda Resort, Divi Little Bay Beach Resort, Radisson Blu St. Martin, Royal Islander

23

WIMCO. WIMCO has more hotel, villa, apartment, and condo listings in the Caribbean than just about anyone else. ☎ *401/849–8012 in Rhode Island, 866/449–1553 in the U.S.* ⊕ *www.wimco.com.*

DUTCH SIDE

CUPECOY

$$$
RENTAL

The Cliff at Cupecoy Beach. The Cliff at Cupecoy Beach, offers luxurious, high-rise condos, rented out when the owners are not in residence. **Pros:** great views; good for families; close to Maho casinos and restaurants; tight security. **Cons:** it's apartment living, so if you're looking for resort-y or beachy, this is not your place; there is a concierge, but no other hotel services; **TripAdvisor:** "great views," "luxurious property," "beautiful condo." ⑤ *Rooms from: $425* ⊠ *Rhine Rd., Cupecoy, St. Maarten* ☎ *866/978–5839, 721/546–6633* ⊕ *www.cliffsxm.com* ⤳ *72 apartments.*

LITTLE BAY

$
RESORT
☾

Divi Little Bay Beach Resort. Bordering the lovely but sparsely populated Little Bay, this renovated property is well located and is awash with water sports. **Pros:** good location; lovely beach, kids stay and eat free. **Cons:** ongoing renovations; pool areas not great. **TripAdvisor:** "wonderful property," "awesome beach," "tranquil setting." ⑤ *Rooms from: $219* ⊠ *Little Bay Rd., Little Bay* ☎ *721/542–2333, 800/367–3484 in the U.S.* ⊕ *www.divilittlebay.com* ⤳ *218 rooms* ⦿ *No meals.*

MAHO

$$
RESORT
☾

Sonesta Maho Beach Resort and Casino. The island's largest hotel, which is on Maho Beach, isn't luxurious or fancy, but this full-service resort offers everything right on the premises at reasonable rates, and it is located very close to the airport. **Pros:** huge resort complex; lots of shopping; nonstop nightlife. **Cons:** resort is aging; not the place for a personal, quiet getaway, limited dining choices on the all-inclusive plan. **TripAdvisor:** "first class," "beautiful place," "customer service is priority here." $ *Rooms from: $289* ✉ *1 Rhine Rd., Box 834, Maho* ☎ *721/545–2115, 800/223–0757, 800/766–3782* ⊕ *www.sonesta.com/ mahobeach* ↝ *537 rooms* ⎮⊖⎮ *No meals.*

$$ 　 ⛆ **Westin St. Maarten Dawn Beach Resort & Spa.** Straddling the border
RESORT 　between the Dutch and French sides, the modern Westin sits on one
ⵣ 　of the island's best beaches. **Pros:** on Dawn Beach; plenty of activities;
Fodor's Choice 　no smoking allowed. **Cons:** very big; a bit off the beaten track; time-
★ 　share sales people can be bothersome. **TripAdvisor:** "gorgeous pool
and beach," "just beautiful," "peaceful." $ *Rooms from: $322* ✉ *144 Oyster Pond Rd., Oyster Pond* ☎ *599/543–6700, 800/228–3000 in the U.S.* ⊕ *www.westinstmaarten.com* ↝ *310 rooms, 15 suites, 99 1-, 2-, and 3-bedroom condo units* ⎮⊖⎮ *No meals.*

PELICAN KEY

$$ 　 ⛆ **Blue Pelican.** The 13 brand-new apartment units hidden in this private
RENTAL 　enclave in Pelican Key were built by the owners of Hotel L'Esplanade
Fodor's Choice 　and Le Petit Hotel on the French side. **Pros:** gorgeous new residences;
★ 　great pool; excellent, management, and security. **Cons:** Residence, not a
resort; not on the beach; definitely need a car to get around since there
is no restaurant. $ *Rooms from: $290* ✉ *Billy Folly Rd., Pelican Key, St. Maarten* ☎ *590–690/50–60–20* ⊕ *www.bluepelicansxm.com* ↝ *13 apartments* ⎮⊖⎮ *No meals.*

PHILIPSBURG

$ 　 ⛆ **Holland House Beach Hotel.** An ideal location for shoppers and sun
HOTEL 　worshippers, this historic hotel faces the Front Street pedestrian mall; to
the rear are the boardwalk and a long stretch of Great Bay Beach. **Pros:**
excellent location; free Wi-Fi; young, engaging management. **Cons:** in a
busy, downtown location; no pool, not very resort-y. **TripAdvisor:** "nice
food and central location," "friendly staff," "excellent island experi-
ence." $ *Rooms from: $175* ✉ *43 Front St., Philipsburg* ☎ *721/542– 2572* ⊕ *www.hhbh.com* ↝ *48 rooms, 6 suites* ⎮⊖⎮ *Multiple meal plans.*

$ 　 ⛆ **Sonesta Great Bay Beach Resort and Casino.** Location, location, loca-
RESORT 　tion. Away from the docks that are usually crawling with cruise ships,
ⵣ 　but only a 10-minute walk from downtown Philipsburg, this resort
is well positioned even if it doesn't offer the height of luxury. **Pros:**
good location; nice beach and pool; enough activities to keep you busy.
Cons: hallways are white and bare, giving them a hospital-like feel;
Wi-Fi is expensive; although it's beautiful, pollution can be a problem
at the beach. **TripAdvisor:** "fabulous beach," "great view," "friendly
and convenient." $ *Rooms from: $135* ✉ *19 Little Bay Rd., Philips- burg* ☎ *721/542–2446, 800/223–0757 in the U.S.* ⊕ *www.sonesta.com/ greatbay* ↝ *257 rooms* ⎮⊖⎮ *Multiple meal plans.*

SIMPSON BAY

$ 　 ⛆ **The Horny Toad.** Because of its stupendous view of Simpson Bay and
B&B/INN 　the simple, but immaculate and comfortable rooms with creative decor,
Fodor's Choice 　this lovely guesthouse is widely considered the best on this side of
★ 　the island. **Pros:** tidy rooms; friendly vibe; beautiful beach is usually
deserted. **Cons:** rooms are very basic; need a car to get around; no kids
under seven allowed; no pool. **TripAdvisor:** "perfect," "best value on
the beach," "great host." $ *Rooms from: $218* ✉ *2 Vlaun Dr., Simpson*

The Westin Dawn Beach Resort & Spa, St. Maarten

Bay ☎ *721/545–4323, 800/417–9361 in the U.S.* ⊕ *www.thtgh.com* ⇆ *8 rooms* ⊙ *No meals.*

$ ⊞ **La Vista.** Hibiscus and bougainvillea line brick walkways that connect
RENTAL the 32 wood-frame bungalows and beachfront suites of this intimate
and friendly, family-owned time-share resort perched at the foot of
Pelican Key. **Pros:** close to restaurants and bars. **Cons:** no-frills furnishings; not the best beach. **TripAdvisor:** "small gem in a great location," "a visual feast in tranquility," "great stay with beautiful view."
⑤ *Rooms from: $180* ⊠ *53 Billy Folly Rd., Simpson Bay* ☎ *721/544–
3005, 888/790–5264 in the U.S.* ⊕ *www.lavistaresort.com* ⇆ *50 suites,
penthouses, and cottages* ⊙ *No meals.*

$ ⊞ **Mary's Boon Beach Plantation.** A shaded courtyard welcomes guests at
HOTEL this quirky, informal guesthouse on a 3-mi-long stretch of Simpson Bay.
Pros: small and intimate; interesting history. **Cons:** need a car; charge
for Internet; because of airport proximity, it can be quite noisy; mosquitoes abound year-round. **TripAdvisor:** "right on the beach," "awesome
food and view," "great staff." ⑤ *Rooms from: $150* ⊠ *117 Simpson
Bay Rd., Simpson Bay* ☎ *721/545–7000* ⊕ *www.marysboon.com* ⇆ *37
rooms* ⊙ *No meals* ☞ *6-night min. late Dec.–mid-Mar.*

FRENCH SIDE

ANSE MARCEL

$$ ⊞ **Hotel Le Marquis.** If you crave spectacular vistas and intimate sur-
HOTEL roundings and don't mind heights or steep walks, this is a fun property,
★ with a funky St. Barth vibe. **Pros:** romantic honeymoon destination;
doting staff; amazing views. **Cons:** not on the beach; no restaurant; on a

Le Domaine de Lonvilliers

steep hill. **TripAdvisor:** "absolute perfection," "beautiful amenities," "a romantic spot." ⑤ *Rooms from: €245* ⊠ *Pigeon Pea Hill, Anse Marcel* ☎ *590/29–42–30* ⊕ *www.hotel-marquis.com* ⌒ *17 rooms* ⦿ *Breakfast.*

$$$$
RESORT
Fodor's Choice
★

🏨 **Le Domaine de Lonvilliers by Christophe Leroy.** International sophisticates are excited to see what the chic restaurateur-chef of St-Tropez's Table du Marché and superluxe vacation properties in Marrakech and Avoriaz will make of this classic property on 148 acres of lush gardens bordering the exceptionally beautiful and secluded beach in Anse Marcel. **Pros:** excellent restaurant; chic atmosphere; lovely gardens; beachfront setting, great breakfast buffet. **Cons:** some rooms have round bathtubs right in the middle of the room; you will need a car to get around; beach is shared with the busy Radisson Blu. **TripAdvisor:** "beautiful hotel," "very special place," "gorgeous location." ⑤ *Rooms from: €470* ⊠ *Anse Marcel* ☎ *590/52–35–35* ⊕ *www.hotel-le-domaine.com* ⌒ *124 rooms, 5 suites* ⊗ *Closed Sept.* ⦿ *Breakfast.*

$$$
RESORT
☺
Fodor's Choice
★

🏨 **Radisson Blu St. Martin Resort, Marina and Spa.** A $10 million renovation in 2011 has brought a new level of service, design, and comfort to this family-friendly resort with 18 prime acres on one of the island's prettiest beachy coves. **Pros:** newly refurbished resort; attentive service; activities galore; great beach; excellent breakfast buffet. **Cons:** need a car to get around; lots of families at school-vacation times; beach can be busy. **TripAdvisor:** "great staff," "amazing beach," "terrific and memorable stay." ⑤ *Rooms from: €371* ☏ *590/87–67–09, 800/333–3333 in the U.S.* ⊕ *www.radissonblu.com/resort-stmartin* ⌒ *189 rooms, 63 suites* ⦿ *Breakfast.*

BAIE LONGUE

$$$$
RESORT
Fodor'sChoice
★

La Samanna. A long stretch of pretty, white-sand beach borders this venerable resort. **Pros:** great beach; convenient location; romantic; attentive service; excellent spa. **Cons:** rather pricey for standard rooms; small pools; ongoing renovations in some areas. **TripAdvisor:** "a Caribbean gem," "wonderful beach," "idyllic property." Ⓢ *Rooms from: €995 ⊠ Baie Longue* 🕾 *590/87–64–00, 800/854–2252 in the U.S.* ⊕ *www.lasamanna.com* ⇆ *27 rooms, 54 suites* ⊘ *Closed Sept. and Oct.* ⏐⊙⏐ *Breakfast.*

23

BAIE ORIENTALE

$$$
RESORT
☾

Alamanda Resort. One of the few resorts directly on the white-sand beach of Orient Bay, this hotel has a funky feel and spacious, colonial-style suites with terraces that overlook the pool, beach, or ocean. **Pros:** pleasant property; friendly staff; right on Orient Beach. **Cons:** some rooms are noisy; could use some updating. **TripAdvisor:** "fabulous Orient beach," "absolute paradise," "pleasant staff." Ⓢ *Rooms from: €375* ⊠ *Baie Orientale* 🕾 *590/52–87–40, 800/622–7836* ⊕ *www.alamanda-resort.com* ⇆ *42 rooms* ⏐⊙⏐ *Breakfast.*

$$$$
RENTAL
☾
Fodor'sChoice
★

Caribbean Princess. These 12 large, newly decorated, well-equipped, and updated two- and three-bedroom condos have big kitchens and living rooms, lovely balconies over Orient Beach (a few steps away), new furniture, and share a pretty pool. **Pros:** the comforts of home; nice interior design; direct beach access. **Cons:** not a full-service resort. **TripAdvisor:** "perfect room," "it's paradise," "beautiful view." Ⓢ *Rooms from: €500 ⊠ C5 Parc de la Baie Orientale, Baie Orientale* 🕾 *0590/52–94–94* ⊕ *www.hotelcaribbeanprincess.com/* ⇆ *12 condos* ⊘ *Closed Sept.* ⏐⊙⏐ *Breakfast.*

$$
HOTEL
☾
★

Esmeralda Resort. Almost all of these traditional Caribbean-style, kitchen-equipped villas, which can be configured to meet the needs of different groups, have their own private pool, and the fun of Orient Beach, where the hotel has its own private beach club, is a two-minute walk away. **Pros:** beachfront location; private pools; plenty of activities; frequent online promotions. **Cons:** need a car to get around; iffy Wi-Fi service. **TripAdvisor:** "great hotel and location," "staff was outstanding," "awesome accommodations." Ⓢ *Rooms from: €300 ⊠ Baie Orientale* 🕾 *590/87–36–36, 800/622–7836* ⊕ *www.esmeralda-resort.com* ⇆ *65 rooms* ⊘ *Closed Sept. and Oct.* ⏐⊙⏐ *Breakfast.*

$$$$
RENTAL

Green Cay Village. Surrounded by five acres of lush greenery high above Baie Orientale, these villas are perfect for families or groups of friends who are looking for privacy and the comforts of home. **Pros:** beautiful setting; near Baie Orientale; perfect for families with teens or older kids. **Cons:** need a car to get around; beach is a five-minute walk; need to be vigilant about locking doors, as there have been reports of crime in the area. **TripAdvisor:** "beautiful villa," "the best view," "the best for a tropical vacation." Ⓢ *Rooms from: €660 ⊠ Parc de la Baie Orientale, Baie Orientale* 🕾 *590/87–38–63* ⊕ *www.greencay.com* ⇆ *9 villas* ⏐⊙⏐ *Breakfast.*

$
HOTEL

Hotel La Plantation. Perched high above Orient Bay, this colonial-style hotel is a charmer, and guests give high marks to the recent renovations. **Pros:** relaxing atmosphere; eye-popping views. **Cons:** small pool; beach

La Samanna

is a 10-minute walk away. **TripAdvisor:** "very comfortable," "a wonderful small hotel," "charming." $ *Rooms from: €205* ✉ *C5 Parc de La Baie Orientale, Baie Orientale* ☎ *590/29–58–00* ⊕ *www.la-plantation. com* ⌖ *52 rooms* ☉ *Closed Sept.–mid-Oct.* ⦿ *Breakfast.*

$$$
HOTEL
Fodor's Choice
★

⌂ **Palm Court.** The romantic beachfront units of this *hotel de charme* are steps from the fun of Orient Beach yet private, quiet, and stylishly up-to-date. **Pros:** big rooms; fresh and new; nice garden. **Cons:** across from, but not on the beach;. **TripAdvisor:** "great location," "quiet and clean," "perfect." $ *Rooms from: €360* ✉ *Parc de la Baie Orientale, Baie Orientale* ☎ *590/87–41–94* ⊕ *www.sxm-palm-court.com* ⌖ *24 rooms* ☉ *Closed Sept.* ⦿ *Breakfast.*

FRENCH CUL DE SAC

$$
B&B/INN
Fodor's Choice
★

⌂ **Karibuni Lodge.** Lovely in every way, this new, super-chic, yet reasonably-priced, enclave of spacious suites surrounded by gorgeous tropical gardens offer stunning views of tiny Pinel Island. **Pros:** stylish; new; eco-friendly; lushly comfortable; amazing views. **Cons:** removed from the action; definitely need a car; not a resort, and not on the beach. **TripAdvisor:** "quiet and simple elegance," "simply paradise," "exquisite experience." $ *Rooms from: €255* ✉ *29 Terrasses de Cul de Sac, French Cul de Sac* ☎ *690/64–38–58* ⊕ *www.lekaribuni.com* ⌖ *6 suites* ⦿ *Breakfast.*

GRAND CASE

$$$$
RENTAL
♻

⌂ **Bleu Emeraude.** The 11 spacious apartments in this tidy complex sit right on a sliver of Grand Case Beach. **Pros:** brand-new; walk to restaurants; attractive decor. **Cons:** it's not resort-y at all. **TripAdvisor:** "view from our room is amazing," "beautiful hotel," "spacious." $ *Rooms*

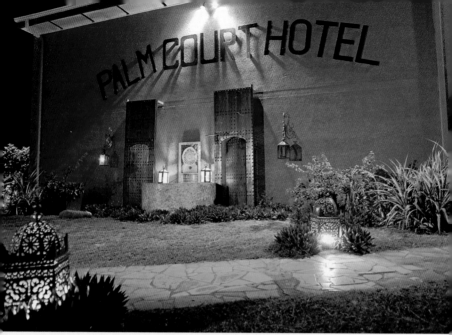
Palm Court Hotel

from: €400 ✉ *240 bd. de Grand Case, Grand Case* ☎ *0590/87–27–71*
⊕ *www.bleuemeraude.com* ⤶ *4 studios, 6 1-bedroom apartments, 1
2-bedroom apartment* ⑩ *Breakfast.*

\$\$
RESORT
☺

🏨 **Grand Case Beach Club.** This beachfront property on a cove at the east
end of Grand Case has a friendly staff and spectacular sunset views.
Pros: reasonably priced; comfortable rooms; walking distance to restaurants. **Cons:** small beach; dated decor and buildings; need a car to
explore island. **TripAdvisor:** "great location outweighs lack of amenities," "total relaxation and beauty," "great restaurant." ⑤ *Rooms from:
€335* ✉ *21 rue de Petit Plage, at north end of bd. de Grand Case, Box
339, Grand Case* ☎ *590/87–51–87, 800/344–3016 in the U.S.* ⊕ *www.
grandcasebeachclub.com* ⤶ *72 apartments* ⑩ *Breakfast.*

\$\$\$
HOTEL
☺
Fodor's Choice
★

🏨 **Hôtel L'Esplanade.** Enthusiasts return again and again to the classy,
loft-style suites in this immaculate boutique hotel. **Pros:** attentive management; very clean; updated room decor; family-friendly feel. **Cons:**
lots of stairs to climb; not on the beach. **TripAdvisor:** "gorgeous sunsets," "beautiful hotel," "pleasant and personable staff." ⑤ *Rooms
from: €425* ✉ *Grand Case* ☎ *590/87–06–55, 866/596–8365 in the U.S.*
⊕ *www.lesplanade.com* ⤶ *24 units* ⑩ *No meals.*

\$\$\$
HOTEL
☺
★

🏨 **Le Petit Hotel.** Surrounded by some of the best restaurants in the Caribbean, this beachfront boutique hotel, sister hotel to Hotel L'Esplanade,
oozes charm and has the same caring, attentive management. **Pros:**
walking distance to everything in Grand Case; friendly staff; clean,
updated rooms. **Cons:** many stairs to climb; no pool. **TripAdvisor:**
"cozy and private," "rooms with a fantastic view," "well conceived
and well executed." ⑤ *Rooms from: €390* ✉ *248 bd. de Grand Case,*

Grand Case ☎ *590/29–09–65* ⊕ *www.lepetithotel.com* ⇆ *9 rooms, 1 suite* ⫿◯⫿ *Breakfast.*

OYSTER POND

$ **⊡ Captain Oliver's Resort.** This cluster of pink bungalows is perched high
HOTEL on a hill above a lagoon. **Pros:** restaurant is reasonably priced; ferry trips leave from the hotel. **Cons:** not on the beach; not fancy or modern. **TripAdvisor:** "good staff," "charming and relaxed," "warm authenticity." ⑤ *Rooms from: €241* ⊠ *Oyster Pond* ☎ *590/87–40–26* ⊕ *www. captainolivers.com* ⇆ *50 suites* ◷ *Closed Sept. and Oct.* ⫿◯⫿ *Breakfast.*

NIGHTLIFE

St. Maarten has lots of evening and late-night action. To find out what's doing on the island, pick up *St. Maarten Nights, St. Maarten Quick Pick Guide,* or *St. Maarten Events,* all of which are distributed free in the tourist office and hotels. The glossy *Discover St. Martin/St. Maarten* magazine, also free, has articles on island history and on the newest shops, discos, and restaurants. Or buy a copy of Thursday's *Daily Herald* newspaper, which lists all the week's entertainment. Insiders will tell you to head to Maho, go first to Bamboo for cocktails and sushi, hit Sky Beach, then finally, go to Tantra.

The island's casinos—all 13 of them—are found only on the Dutch side. All have craps, blackjack, roulette, and slot machines. You must be 18 years or older to gamble. Dress is casual (but excludes bathing suits or skimpy beachwear). Most casinos are found in hotels, but there are also some independents.

DUTCH SIDE

MAHO

BARS AND CLUBS

Bamboo. Bamboo is a sophisticated club-restaurant with soft techno music. ⊠ *Sonesta Maho Beach Resort & Casino, 1 Rhine Rd., Maho* ☎ *721/545–3622* ⊕ *www.bamboobernies.net.*

Bliss. The open-air nightclub and lounge, which is good for dancing, rocks till late. ⊠ *Caravanserai Resort, Maho* ☎ *721/544–3410* ⊕ *www. bliss-sxm.com.*

Cheri's Café. Across from Maho Beach Resort and Casino, Cheri's (you can't miss it—look for pink) features Sweet Chocolate, a lively band that will get your toes tapping and your tush twisting. Snacks and hearty meals are available all day long on a cheerful veranda decorated with thousands of inflatable beach toys. It's closed Tuesdays. ⊠ *45 Rhine Rd., Maho* ☎ *721/545–3361* ⊕ *www.cheriscafe.com.*

Fodor's Choice **Sky Beach.** The Sky Beach Rooftop Beach and Lounge is perfect for visi-
★ tors who don't want to leave the beach vibe after the sun goes down. The elegant rooftop pulses with techno and house music while guests lounge on beds in cabanas. There is sand volleyball for fun and great cocktails at the happening bar. Great views and stargazing come with the territory. In-the-know clubbers come here after a bite of sushi at

Gambling is the most popular indoor activity in St. Maarten.

Bamboo but before Tantra starts to wake up after midnight. Open Wednesday through Sunday til late. There is live jazz on weekends and outdoor movies on Thursdays. ⊠ *Sonesta Maho Resort & Casino, 1 Rhine Rd., Maho, St. Maarten* ☎ *721/545–3547* ⊕ *www.theskybeach. com.*

Soprano's. Starting each night at 8, the pianist at Soprano's takes requests for oldies, romantic favorites, or smooth jazz. Come for Happy Hour from 8 to 9 pm with a full menu that includes pizza. the bar is open until 3 am nightly. ⊠ *Sonesta Maho Beach Resort & Casino, 1 Rhine Rd., Maho* ☎ *721/545–2485* ⊕ *www.sopranospianobar.com.*

Sunset Beach Bar. This popular spot offers a relaxed, anything-goes atmosphere. Enjoy live music Wednesday through Sunday as you watch planes from the airport next door fly directly over your head. Bring your camera for stunning photos. ⊠ *Maho Beach, Maho* ☎ *721/545–3998* ⊕ *www.sunsetsxm.com.*

Tantra Nightclub & Sanctuary. This is definitely the hottest nightclub at the Sonesta Maho. Come late—things don't really get going until after 1 am. On Wednesday nights ladies drink champagne for free, and drinks are $2 for everyone on Fridays. Celebrity DJs spin on Saturdays. Feel free to dress up. ⊠ *Sonesta Maho Beach Resort & Casino, 1 Rhine Rd., Maho Bay* ☎ *721/545–2861* ⊕ *www.tantrasxm.com.*

PHILIPSBURG
BARS AND CLUBS
Axum Art Café and Gallery. This 1960s-style coffee shop offers local cultural activities as well as live jazz and reggae. It's open daily, 11:30 am until the wee hours. ⊠ *7L Front St., Philipsburg* ☎ *721/542–0547.*

Ocean Lounge. Ocean Lounge is the quintessential people-watching venue. Sip a guavaberry colada and point your chair toward the boardwalk. ⊠ *Holland House Hotel, 43 Front St., Philipsburg* ☎ *721/542–2572.*

SIMPSON BAY

BARS AND CLUBS

Buccaneer Bar. Buccaneer Bar is the place to enjoy a BBC (Bailey's banana colada), a slice of pizza, and a nightly bonfire. It's family-friendly and conveniently located. ⊠ *Behind Atrium Beach Resort, 10 Billy Folly Rd., Simpson Bay* ☎ *721/522–9700* ⊕ *www.buccaneerbeachbar.com.*

Pineapple Pete. At Pete's you can groove to live music or visit the game room for a couple of rounds of pool. ⊠ *Airport Rd., Simpson Bay* ☎ *721/544–6030* ⊕ *www.pineapplepete.com.*

Red Piano. The Red Piano has terrific live music and great cocktails every night. ⊠ *Hollywood Casino, Billy Folly Rd., Simpson Bay* ☎ *721/580–1841* ⊕ *www.theredpianosxm.com.*

FRENCH SIDE

BAIE DES PÈRES

BARS AND CLUBS

★ **Kali's Beach Bar.** On the French side, Kali's Beach Bar Restaurant is a happening spot with live music late into the night, and has been since the late 1980s. On the night of the full moon and on every Friday night, the beach bonfire and late-night party here is the place to be, but its a great place to hang out all day long on the chaises you can rent for the day. The Rasta-theme restaurant serves lunch and dinner on bright yellow and red picnic tables shaded by palm-fronds. You can rent a beach kayak and paddle the secluded, relatively tranquil bay. Be sure to ask Kali for some tastes of his homemade fruit-infused rum. ⊠ *Baie des Pères* ☎ *690/49–06–81.*

BAIE ORIENTALE

BARS AND CLUBS

Boo Boo Jam. This beach club on Orient Bay is a jumping joint with a mix of calypso, meringue, salsa, and other beats with parties on Friday and Sunday nights, and every day for lunch. ⚠ As at other beach venues, don't leave any belongings at all in your car. ⊠ *Baie Orientale* ☎ *690/75–21–66.*

GRAND CASE

BARS AND CLUBS

★ **Calmos Café.** Calmos Café draws a young local crowd. Just walk through the boutique and around the back to the sea and pull up a beach chair or park yourself at a picnic table. It's open all day, but the fun really begins at the cocktail hour, when everyone enjoys tapas. The little covered deck at the end is a perfect for romance. On Thursday and Sunday there is often live reggae on the beach. ⊠ *40 bd. de Grand Case, Grand Case* ☎ *590/29–01–85* ⊕ *lecalmoscafe.com.*

La Noche. La Noche may tempt you during your after-dinner stroll in Grand Case; consider continuing your evening at this sexy lounge decorated in red, where the house music starts at 11 (or later) and continues until the last reveler quits. The dress code is "chic and sexy." ⊠ *147 bd. de Grand Case, Grand Case* ☎ *590/29–72–89.*

SHOPPING

It's true that the island sparkles with its myriad outdoor activities—diving, snorkeling, sailing, swimming, and sunning—but shopaholics are drawn to the sparkle in the jewelry stores. The huge array of such stores is almost unrivaled in the Caribbean. In addition, duty-free shops can offer substantial savings—about 15% to 30% below U.S. and Canadian prices—on cameras, watches, liquor, cigars, and designer clothing. It's no wonder that many cruise ships make Philipsburg a port of call. Stick with the big vendors that advertise in the tourist press, and you will be more likely to avoid today's ubiquitous fakes and replicas. On both sides of the island, be alert for idlers. They can snatch unwatched purses. Just be sure to know the U.S. prices of whatever you plan on buying in St. Maarten so you know if you're getting a deal or just getting dealt a bad hand.

Prices are in dollars on the Dutch side, in euros on the French side. As for bargains, there are more to be had on the Dutch side; prices on the French side may sometimes be higher than those you'll find back home, and the fact that prices are in euros doesn't help affordability. Merchandise may not be from the newest collections, especially with regard to clothing, but there are items available on the French side that are not available on the Dutch side. Finally, remember the important caveat about shopping anywhere: if it sounds too good to be true, it usually is.

DUTCH SIDE

MAHO

You'll find a moderately good selection of stores in Maho Plaza, near the Sonesta resort in Maho. Many Americans prefer to shop here since they can pay in U.S. dollars and get better deals than on the French side.

PHILIPSBURG

Philipsburg's **Front Street** has reinvented itself. Now it's mall-like, with a redbrick walk and streets, palm trees lining the sleek boutiques, jewelry stores, souvenir shops, and outdoor restaurants, and the old reliables, such as McDonald's and Burger King. Here and there a school or a church appears to remind visitors there's more to the island than shopping. Back Street is where you'll find the **Philipsburg Market Place**, a daily open-air market where you can haggle for bargains on items such as handicrafts, souvenirs, and beachwear. **Old Street**, near the end of Front Street, has stores, boutiques, and open-air cafés offering French crepes, rich chocolates, and island mementos.

HANDICRAFTS

Guavaberry Emporium. Visitors to the Dutch side of the island come for free samples at the the small factory where the Sint Maarten Guavaberry Company makes its famous liqueur. You'll find a multitude of versions, including one made with jalapeño peppers. Check out the hand-painted bottles. The store also sells the Gourmet BBQ & Hot Sauce Collection and souvenir hats ⊠ *8–10 Front St., Philipsburg* ☎ *721/542–2965* ⊕ *www.guavaberry.com.*

Shipwreck Shop. Shipwreck Shop has outlets all over the island that stock a little of everything: colorful hammocks, handmade jewelry, and lots of the local Guavaberry liqueur, but the main store on Front Street in Philipsburg has the largest selection of wares. ⊠ *42 Front St., Philipsburg* ☎ *721/542–2962, 721/542–6710* ⊕ *www.shipwreckshops.com.*

JEWELRY AND GIFTS

Jewelry is big business on both the French and Dutch sides of the island, and many stores have outlets in both places. The so-called duty-free prices, however, may not give you much savings (if anything) over what you might pay at home, and sometimes prices are higher than you would pay at a shop back home. Compare prices in a variety of stores before you buy, and if you know you want to search for an expensive piece of jewelry or high-end watch, make sure you price your pieces at home and bargain hard to ensure you get a good deal.

Little Europe. Little Europe sells fine jewelry, crystal, and china in its two branches in Philipsburg. ⊠ *80 Front St., Philipsburg* ☎ *721/542–4371* ⊕ *www.littleeuropejewellers.com* ⊠ *2 Front St., Philipsburg* ☎ *721/542–4371* ⊕ *www.littleeuropejewellers.com.*

Little Switzerland. The large Caribbean duty-free chain sells watches, fine crystal, china, perfume, and jewelry. ⊠ *52 Front St., Philipsburg* ☎ *721/542–2523* ⊕ *www.littleswitzerland.com* ⊠ *Harbor Point Village, Pointe Blanche* ☎ *721/542–7785* ⊕ *www.littleswitzerland.com* ⊠ *Westin Dawn Beach Resort & Spa, Dawn Beach* ☎ *721/543–6451* ⊕ *www.littleswitzerland.com.*

Oro Diamante. Oro Diamante carries loose diamonds, jewelry, watches, perfume, and cosmetics. ⊠ *62-B Front St., Philipsburg* ☎ *599/543–0342, 800/635–7950 in the U.S.* ⊕ *www.oro-diamante.com.*

FRENCH SIDE

GRAND CASE
ART GALLERIES
★ **Atelier des Tropismes.** Contemporary Caribbean artists, including Paul Elliot Thuleau, who is a master of capturing the unique sunshine of the islands, are showcased at Atelier des Tropismes. This is a serious gallery with some very good artists. And it's open late, so you can browse before dinner. ⊠ *107 bd. de Grand Case, Grand Case* ☎ *590/29–10–60* ⊕ *tropismesgallery.com.*

MARIGOT
On the French side, wrought-iron balconies, colorful awnings, and gingerbread trim decorate Marigot's smart shops, tiny boutiques, and bistros in the **Marina Port La Royale** complex and on the main streets, **Rue de la Liberté** and **Rue de la République.** Also in Marigot are the pricey **West Indies Mall** and the **Plaza Caraïbes,** which house designer shops, although some shops are closing in the economic downturn.

ART GALLERIES

Gingerbread Galerie. This gallery on the far side of the marina specializes in Haitian art and sells both expensive paintings and more reasonably priced decorative pieces of folk art. ⊠ *Marina Port La Royale, Marigot* ☎ *590/51–94–95* ⊕ *www.gingerbread-gallery.com.*

Vou Deco. Shop here for beautiful modern home accessories with a French flair. ⊠ *Plaza Caraibes, Rue General de Gaulle, Marigot* ☎ *590/29–46–63.*

CLOTHING

On the French side, the best luxury-brand shops are found either in the modern, air-conditioned West Indies Mall or the Plaza Caraïbes center across from Marina Port La Royale in Marigot. There is also a small center in Grand Case, called La Petite Favorite, with four shops and a café.

JEWELRY AND GIFTS

Artistic Jewelers. Artistic Jewelers carries the work of David Yurman, among many others, as well as high-end designer watches, including Chanel, Baum & Mercier, Technomarine, and Chopard. ⊠ *8 rue du Général de Gaulle, Marigot* ☎ *590/52–24–80* ⊕ *www.artisticjewelers. com.*

Manek's. Manek's sells, on two floors, electronics, luggage, perfume, jewelry, Cuban cigars, duty-free liquors, and tobacco products. ⊠ *Rue de la République, Marigot* ☎ *590/87–54–91.*

SPORTS AND ACTIVITIES

BOATING AND SAILING

The island is surrounded by water, so why not get out and enjoy it? The water and winds are perfect for skimming the surf. It'll cost you around $1,200 to $1,500 per day to rent a 28- to 40-foot powerboat, considerably less for smaller boats or small sailboats. Drinks and sometimes lunch are usually included on crewed day charters.

DUTCH SIDE

Random Wind. Random Wind offers full-day sailing and snorkeling trips on a traditional 54-foot clipper. Charter prices depend on the size of the group and whether lunch is served. The regularly scheduled Paradise Daysail costs $95 per person ($50 for kids) and includes food and drink. Departures are on the Dutch side, from Skipjack's at Simpson Bay, at 8:30 am Tuesday through Friday. ⊠ *Ric's Place, Simpson Bay* ☎ *721/587–5742* ⊕ *www.randomwind.com.*

St. Maarten 12-Metre Challenge. Sailing experience is not necessary for the St. Maarten 12-Metre Challenge, one of the island's most popular activities. Participants compete on 68-foot racing yachts, including Dennis Connor's *Stars and Stripes* (the actual boat that won the America's Cup in 1987) and the *Canada II.* Anyone can help the crew grind winches, trim sails, and punch the stopwatch, or you can just sit back and watch everyone else work. The thrill of it is priceless, but book well in advance;

this is the most popular shore excursion offered by cruise ships in the Caribbean. It's offered four times daily; the entire experience lasts about three hours. Only children over 12 are allowed. ⊠ *Bobby's Marina, Philipsburg* ☎ *721/542–0045* ⊕ *www.12metre.com.*

FRENCH SIDE

MP Yachting. MP Yachting rents boats of all sizes, with or without a crew, for short trips and long, and it's located conveniently at Marina Port La Royale in Marigot. ⊠ *Marina Port La Royale, Marigot* ☎ *690/53–37–40* ⊕ *www.mpyachting.com.*

Sun Evasion. Sun Evasion is a charter company with locations all over the world, including St. Martin. You can take a half- or full-day charter to Tintamarre, St. Barth, or Ilet Pinel on a mono- or multihull powerboat, available with or without a skipper. ⊠ *Marina Port La Royale, Marigot* ☎ *690/35–03–18* ⊕ *www.sun-evasion.com.*

FISHING

You can angle for yellowtail snapper, grouper, marlin, tuna, and wahoo on deep-sea excursions. Costs range from $150 per person for a half day to $250 for a full day. Prices usually include bait and tackle, instruction for novices, and refreshments. Ask about licensing and insurance.

DUTCH SIDE

Lee's Deepsea Fishing. Lee's Deepsea Fishing organizes excursions, and when you return, Lee's Roadside Grill will cook your tuna, wahoo, or whatever else you catch and keep. Rates start at $200 per person for a half day. ⊠ *82 Welfare Rd., Cole Bay* ☎ *721/544–4233* ⊕ *www.leesfish.com.*

Natalie Kate Adventures. Captain Paul enjoys helping beginners to catch big sailfish including white, striped, and blue marlin, from a 33-foot Bertram sport fishing vessel. The company also does private charters, transfers, and sunset cruises. ☎ *721/580–0800* ⊕ *www.nataliekateadventures.com.*

Rudy's Deep Sea Fishing. Rudy's Deep Sea Fishing has been around for years, and is one of the more experienced sport-angling outfits. A private charter trip for four people starts at $525 for a half-day excursion. ⊠ *14 Airport Rd., Simpson Bay* ☎ *721/545–2177* ⊕ *www.rudysdeepseafishing.com.*

FRENCH SIDE

Private Yacht Charter. Private Yacht Charter offers deep-sea fishing, snorkeling trips, and catamaran trips including snacks and drinks. ⊠ *Oyster Pond Great House Marina, 14 Emerald Merit Rd, Oyster Pond, St. Maarten* ☎ *690/83–53–05* ⊕ *www.privateyachtcharter-sxm.com.*

GOLF

DUTCH SIDE

Mullet Bay Golf Course. St. Maarten is not a golf destination. Nevertheless, there have been improvements to Mullet Bay Golf Course, on the Dutch side, which is now again an 18-hole course and the island's only choice. But it's still not a major draw or a must-play. ✉ *Airport Rd., north of airport, Mullet Bay* ☎ *721/545–3069.*

HORSEBACK RIDING

Island stables offer riding packages for everyone from novices to experts. A 90-minute ride along the beach costs $50 to $70 for group rides and $70 to $90 for private treks. Reservations are necessary. You can arrange rides directly or through most hotels.

FRENCH SIDE

Bayside Riding Club. Bayside Riding Club, on the French side, is a long-established outfit that can accommodate all levels of riders. Group beach rides of 1 to 1½ hours around a nature preserve are €65–€80 per person. Full moon rides get rave reviews. Other rides can be arranged with prior contact. ✉ *Galion Beach Rd., Baie Orientale* ☎ *590/87–36–64.*

KAYAKING

Kayaking is becoming very popular and is almost always offered at the many water-sports operations on both the Dutch and the French sides. Rental starts at about $15 per hour for a single and $19 for a double.

DUTCH SIDE

TriSports. TriSports organizes kayaking and snorkeling excursions in addition to its biking operation. ✉ *Airport Rd. 14B, Simpson Bay* ☎ *721/545–4384* ⊕ *www.trisportsxm.com.*

FRENCH SIDE

Kali's Beach Bar. On the French side, kayaks are available at Kali's Beach Bar. ✉ *Friar's Bay* ☎ *690/49–06–81* ⊕ *www.kali-beach-bar.com.*

Wind Adventures. Near Le Galion Beach, Wind Adventures offers rentals and instruction in kayaking, kitesurfing, windsurfing, Hobie cats, and stand-up paddle surfing. ✉ *Baie Orientale* ☎ *590/29–41–57* ⊕ *www.wind-adventures.com.*

SCUBA DIVING

Diving in St. Maarten/St. Martin is mediocre at best, but those who want to dive will find a few positives. The water temperature here is rarely below 70°F (21°C). Visibility is often 60 to 100 feet. The island has more than 30 dive sites, from wrecks to rocky labyrinths. Right outside of Philipsburg, 55 feet under the water, is the HMS *Proselyte*, once explored by Jacques Cousteau. Although it sank in 1801, the boat's cannons and coral-encrusted anchors are still visible.

Off the north coast, in the protected and mostly current-free Grand Case Bay, is **Creole Rock.** The water here ranges in depth from 10 feet to 25 feet. Other sites off the north coast include **Ilet Pinel**, with its good shallow diving; **Green Key**, with its vibrant barrier reef; and **Tintamarre**, with its sheltered coves and geologic faults. On average, one-tank dives start at $55; two-tank dives are about $100. Certification courses start at about $400.

The Dutch side offers several full-service outfitters and SSI (Scuba Schools International) and/or PADI certification. There are no hyperbaric chambers on the island.

DUTCH SIDE

Dive Safaris. Dive Safaris has a shark-awareness dive on Friday where participants can watch professional feeders give reef sharks a little nosh. The company also offers a full PADI training program and can tailor dive excursions to any level. ⊠ *La Palapa Marina, Simpson Bay* ☎ *721/545–3213* ⊕ *www.divestmaarten.com.*

Ocean Explorers Dive Shop. Ocean Explorers Dive Shop is St. Maarten's oldest dive shop, and offers different types of certification courses. ⊠ *113 Welfare Rd., Simpson Bay* ☎ *721/544–5252* ⊕ *www.stmaarten diving.com.*

FRENCH SIDE

Neptune. Neptune is a PADI-certified outfit and very popular for its friendly owners Fabien and Sylvie, whose extensive experience thrills happy clients of reef, wreck, and cove dives. There is also an extensive program for beginners. ⊠ *Plage d'Orient Bay, Baie Orientale* ☎ *690/50–98–51* ⊕ *www.neptune-dive.com.*

Octopus. Octopus offers PADI diving certification courses and all-inclusive dive packages, using the latest equipment and a 30-foot power catamaran called *Octopussy.* The company also offers private and group snorkel trips starting at $40, including all necessary equipment. The dive shop also services regulators. ⊠ *15 bd. de Grand Case, Grand Case* ☎ *590/29–11–27* ⊕ *www.octopusdiving.com.*

SEA EXCURSIONS

DUTCH SIDE

Bluebeard II. This 60-foot custom-built day-sail catamaran is specially designed for maximum safety and comfort. *Bluebeard II* sails around Anguilla's south and northwest coasts to Prickly Pear Cay, where there are excellent coral reefs for snorkeling and powdery white sands for sunning. ⊠ *Simpson Bay* ☎ *721/587–5935* ⊕ *www.bluebeardcharters.com.*

Celine. For low-impact sunset and dinner cruises, try the catamaran *Celine.* ⊠ *Skip Jack's Restaurant, Simpson Bay* ☎ *721/526–1170, 721/552–1335* ⊕ *www.sailstmaarten.com.*

☾ **Golden Eagle.** The sleek 76-foot catamaran *Golden Eagle* takes day-sailors to outlying islets and reefs for snorkeling and partying. ⊠ *Bobby's Marina, Philipsburg* ☎ *721/526–1170* ⊕ *www.sailingsxm.com.*

SNORKELING

Some of the best snorkeling on the Dutch side can be found around the rocks below Fort Amsterdam off Little Bay Beach, in the west end of Maho Bay, off Pelican Key, and around the reefs off Oyster Pond Beach. On the French side, the area around Orient Bay—including Caye Verte, Ilet Pinel, and Tintamarre—is especially lovely and is officially classified and protected as a regional underwater nature reserve. Sea creatures also congregate around Creole Rock at the point of Grand Case Bay. The average cost of an afternoon snorkeling trip is about $45 to $55 per person.

DUTCH SIDE

Aqua Mania Adventures. Aqua Mania Adventures offers a variety of snorkeling trips. The newest activity, called Rock 'n Roll Safaris, lets participants not only snorkel, but navigate their own motorized rafts. ⊠ *Pelican Marina, Simpson Bay* ☎ *721/544–2640, 721/544–2631* ⊕ *www.stmaarten-activities.com.*

Eagle Tours. Eagle Tours is geared more to cruise groups, but anyone can sign on for the four-hour power rafting or sailing trips that include snorkeling, a beach break, and lunch. The sailing trips are done aboard a 76-foot catamaran. Some cruises stop in Grand Case or Marigot for a bit of shopping. ⊠ *Bobby's Marina, Philipsburg* ☎ *721/542–3323* ⊕ *www.sailingsxm.com.*

FRENCH SIDE

Kontiki Watersports. Arrange equipment rentals and snorkeling trips through Kontiki Watersports. ⊠ *Northern beach entrance, Parc de la Baie Orientale, Baie Orientale* ☎ *590/87–46–89.*

WINDSURFING

The best windsurfing is on Galion Bay on the French side. From November to May, trade winds can average 15 knots.

FRENCH SIDE

Wind Adventures. Wind Adventures offers rentals and lessons in both windsurfing and kitesurfing. One-hour lessons are about €40. The company offers a fun vacation package that works out to a terrific deal: two hours of activities each day for five days for €199. ⊠ *Northern beach entrance, Baie Orientale* ☎ *590/29–41–57* ⊕ *www.wind-adventures.com.*

Windy Reef. Windy Reef has offered windsurfing lessons and rentals since 1991. ⊠ *Galion Beach, past Butterfly Farm* ☎ *690/34–21–85* ⊕ *www.windyreef.com.*

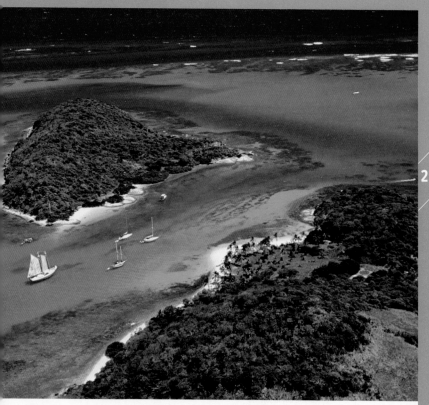

St. Vincent and the Grenadines

WORD OF MOUTH

"Bequia is a great island if you are seeking something small (only seven square miles in area) and somewhat off the beaten path. The main village is located around Admiralty Bay, which is a popular spot for sailboaters. There's not a lot to do on the island, so . . . if you are looking to completely relax and 'get away from it all,' Bequia is the place to do it."

—RoamsAround

WELCOME TO ST. VINCENT AND THE GRENADINES

A STRING OF PEARLS

St. Vincent, which is 18 miles (29 km) long and 11 miles (18 km) wide, is the northernmost and largest of the chain of 32 islands that make up St. Vincent and the Grenadines and extend 45 miles (72 km) southwest toward Grenada. What these islands all have in common is a get-away-from-it-all atmosphere.

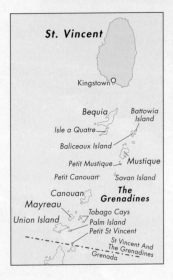

St. Vincent

Kingstown

Bequia Battowia Island
Isle a Quatre
Baliceaux Island
Petit Mustique Mustique
Petit Canouan Savan Island
Canouan **The Grenadines**
Mayreau
Union Island Tobago Cays
Palm Island
Petit St Vincent
St Vincent And The Grenadines
Grenada

Restaurants ▼

Basil's Bar & Restaurant **2**
Cobblestone Roof-Top ... **3**
The French Verandah **6**
Wallilabou Anchorage .. **1**
Vee Jay's
Restaurant & Bar **4**
Young Island Resort **5**

Hotels ▼

Beachcombers Hotel **5**
Buccament Bay Resort .. **1**
Cobblestone Inn **2**
Grand View
Beach Hotel **3**
Mariners Hotel **9**
Rosewood
Apartment Hotel **8**
Sunset Shores
Beach Hotel **6**
Villa Lodge Hotel **4**

KEY	
⌂	Beaches
⛴	Cruise Ship Terminal
◨	Dive Sites
⛴	Ferry
❶	Restaurants
①	Hotels

The 32 Grenadine islands and cays are perfectly shaped, with some of the Caribbean's best anchorages and prettiest beaches.

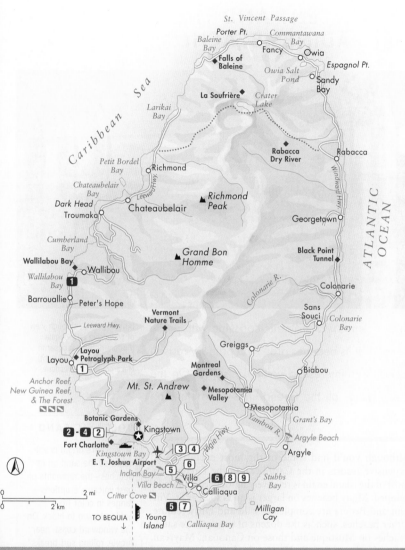

TOP REASONS TO VISIT ST. VINCENT AND THE GRENADINES

1 **Diverse Landscape:** St. Vincent offers a lush landscape, extraordinary hiking trails, remarkable botanical gardens, majestic waterfalls, and intriguing dive sites.

2 **Tranquility:** With few large resorts and no crowds, you're guaranteed peace and quiet.

3 **Sail Away:** Island-hopping sailing charters are the premier way to travel through the beautiful Grenadines.

4 **Beach Paradise:** Grenadine beaches have brilliant-white, powdery-soft sand, washed by gentle waves in several shades of blue.

ST. VINCENT AND THE GRENADINES BEACHES

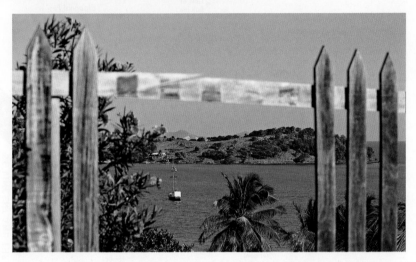

St. Vincent has a dramatic coastline with pretty coves, but its beaches aren't the primary reason to visit this interesting volcanic island. On the other hand, all the Grenadines have stunning beaches.

(Above) A fence-through view of Friendship Bay, Bequia (Bottom right) A sandbar in the Tobago Cays (Top right) Macaroni Beach, Mustique

Although you'll find some of the most exclusive and expensive resorts in the Caribbean in the Grenadines, most of the island chain is relatively untouched and undeveloped. Many beaches on larger islands such as St. Vincent and Bequia are completely wild and fairly remote. Other beaches, such as the dozens of sugar-white sandy beaches on Mustique and those on Canouan, Mayreau, Palm Island, and Petit St. Vincent, look as if they jumped right off the pages of a fashion-magazine photo shoot— and in some cases they have been used as backdrops. But the Grenadines also include the group of uninhabited, completely undeveloped islands known as the Tobago Cays, five islands that make up the Tobago Cays Marine Park, each with a pristine beach. Not all the beaches in the Grenadines are equally beautiful, but none are crowded.

VOLCANIC SAND

St. Vincent's origin is volcanic, so the sand on its beaches—the remnants of past volcanic eruptions— ranges in color from golden brown to black. On the windward coast, near Argyle, rolling surf breaks onto a broad expanse of black-sand beach—a beautiful view but dangerous for swimming. Indian Bay Beach has fairly light sand and is best for swimming.

24

ST. VINCENT

Aside from the beach on private Young Island, just offshore, all beaches on St. Vincent are public. Indian Bay is a popular swimming and snorkeling spot. Villa Beach, on the mainland opposite Young Island, is more of a waterfront area than a beach—except at the northern end, where the sand broadens considerably. The southern end is sometimes so narrow that it becomes nonexistent; nevertheless, boats bob at anchor in the channel, and dive shops, inns, and restaurants line the shore, making this an interesting place to be. On the windward coast, dramatic swaths of broad black sand are strewn with huge black boulders, but the water is rough and unpredictable. On the leeward coast, swimming is recommended only in the lagoons, rivers, and bays.

BEQUIA

Bequia has clean, uncrowded white-sand beaches. Some can be reached with either a healthy trek on foot or a short water-taxi ride from the jetty at Port Elizabeth; others require land transportation.

CANOUAN

Though only 3½ miles (5½ km) long, Canouan faces a mile-long coral reef—one of the longer barrier reefs in the Caribbean—that offers excellent diving and snorkeling opportunities. In addition, the island has four exquisite white-sand beaches. The northern two-thirds of the island is set aside for a luxury resort and golf club. Its proximity to several of the other Grenadines (Mayreau and the Tobago Cays in particular) makes excursions to other beautiful beaches relatively easy.

MAYREAU

Mayreau's primary beach, Saltwhistle Bay, is unique because the calm water of the Caribbean is on one side, and the more powerful Atlantic surf is on the other; a narrow strip of white-sand beach is all that separates them.

MUSTIQUE

Mustique has a number of beautiful white-sand beaches at the foot of each of its lovely green valleys, one reason for its appeal to the rich and famous. Villas are strung out along the northern half of the island, but the best beach, the picture-perfect Macaroni Beach, is on the south side.

PALM ISLAND

The beach on tiny Palm Island is beautiful, white, and powdery. Offshore, between Palm Island and its neighbor Petit St. Vincent, a sandbar with a single palapa offers an isolated spot in mid-ocean for a beach picnic.

PETIT ST. VINCENT

This tiny private resort island has beautiful white-sand beaches on its western end; the sand here is particularly soft

Beautiful Macaroni Bay, Mustique

and free of most rocks, but there's a drop-off in the water. The beaches on the north shore, although beautiful, are fairly rocky. There's also a small, rocky beach on the south shore. Since the island is private, there are never any crowds.

Word of Mouth. "If you're drawn to the idea of private island resorts (and who isn't?),...take a look at Petit St. Vincent, which is not far from Palm."

TOBAGO CAYS

The five uninhabited Tobago Cays are known for their colorful reefs full of tropical fish and many green sea turtles that can be spotted on almost any visit. Four of the five islands—Petit Rameau, Petit Bateau, Jamesby, and Baradal—are enclosed within Horseshoe Reef; the fifth, Petit Tabac, stands separately to the east. All the islands have gorgeous white-sand beaches that are the most pristine in the Grenadines, since they are completely unmarred by development (the Tobago Cays make up a marine sanctuary). A wreck just off the tip of Baradal offers good snorkeling. The Tobago Cays, in fact, are one of the top snorkeling destinations in the Caribbean.

UNION ISLAND

Although it's an important hub for travelers heading to some of the smaller islands in the Grenadines (especially the private retreats such as Petit St. Vincent and Palm Island and also Mayreau, which does not have an airstrip), the hilly, volcanic island has few beaches that compare with those on its closest neighbors. The best beach, Bigsand Beach, is on the north shore and has powdery white sand.

Updated by
Jane E. Zarem

A string of 32 islands and cays makes up the nation of St. Vincent and the Grenadines. St. Vincent is one of the least touristy islands in the Caribbean—an unpretentious and relatively quiet island, where fishermen get up at the crack of dawn to drop their nets into the sea, working people conduct business in town, and farmers work their crops in the countryside.

24

Hotels and inns on St. Vincent are almost all small, locally owned and operated, and definitely not glitzy. So far, there are only two resorts—one on a bay north of Kingstown and another on a separate island, 600 feet from the mainland. Restaurants serve mainly local food—grilled fish, stewed or curried chicken, rice, and root vegetables (called "provisions"). And the beaches are either tiny crescents of black or brown sand on remote leeward bays or sweeping expanses of the same black sand pounded by Atlantic surf.

Independent travelers interested in active, ecofriendly vacations are discovering St. Vincent's natural beauty, its sports opportunities on land and sea, and the richness of its history. They spend their vacation walking or hiking St. Vincent's well-defined jungle trails, catching a glimpse of the rare St. Vincent parrot in the Vermont Valley, exploring exotic flora in the Botanic Gardens and in Montreal Gardens, delving into history at Ft. Charlotte, and climbing the active volcano La Soufrière. Underwater, the snorkeling and scuba landscapes are similarly intriguing.

The Grenadines, on the other hand, dazzle vacationers with amazing inns and resorts, fine white-sand beaches, excellent sailing waters, and a get-away-from-it-all atmosphere.

Bequia, just south of St. Vincent and a pleasant hour's voyage by ferry, has a large complement of inns, hotels, restaurants, shops, and activities; it's a popular vacation destination in its own right. Its Admiralty Bay is one of the prettiest anchorages in the Caribbean. With superb views, snorkeling, hiking, and swimming, the island has much to offer the international mix of backpackers, landlubbers, and luxury-yacht owners who frequent its shores.

South of Bequia, on the exclusive, private island of Mustique, elaborate villas are tucked into lush hillsides. Mustique does not encourage wholesale tourism, least of all to those hoping for a glimpse of the rich and famous who own or rent villas here. The appeal of Mustique is its seclusion.

Boot-shape Canouan, mostly quiet and unspoiled and with only 1,200 or so residents, is nevertheless a busy venue for chartering yachts. It also accommodates the well-heeled guests of the posh, full-service resort that takes up the entire northern third of the island, in part with one of the Caribbean's most challenging and scenic golf courses.

Tiny Mayreau (fewer than 200 residents) has one of the area's most beautiful (and unusual) beaches. At Saltwhistle Bay, the Caribbean Sea is often mirror calm while just yards away, the rolling Atlantic surf washes the opposite shore. Otherwise, Mayreau has a single unnamed village, one road, rain-caught drinking water, and a couple of inns—but no airport, no bank, and no problems!

Union Island, with its dramatic landscape punctuated by Mt. Taboi, is the transportation center of the southern Grenadines. Its small but busy airport serves landlubbers, and its yacht harbor and dive operators serve sailors and scuba divers. Clifton, the quaint main town, has shops, restaurants, and a few guesthouses. Ashton, the second significant town, is mainly residential.

Meanwhile, it took decades to turn the 100-acre, mosquito-infested mangrove swamp called Prune Island into the upscale private resort now known as Palm Island. Today, wealthy vacationers lounge on the island's five palm-fringed white-sand beaches.

Petit St. Vincent is another private, single-resort island that was reclaimed from the overgrowth by the late Hazen K. Richardson II. The luxury resort's cobblestone cottages are so private that, if you wish, you could spend your entire vacation completely undisturbed.

And finally, there are the Tobago Cays, five uninhabited islands south of Canouan and east of Mayreau that draw snorkelers, divers, and boaters. Surrounded by a shallow reef, the tiny islands have rustling palm trees, pristine beaches with powdery sand, the clearest water in varying shades of brilliant blue—and plenty of resident fish and sea turtles.

The various islands of St. Vincent and the Grenadines are fairly close together. Whether you go by boat or by plane, traveling between them is not difficult. And each of them is unique—once there, you'll definitely want to sample more than one.

PLANNING

WHEN TO GO

High season runs from mid-December through mid-April; in the off-season, rates at larger resorts may be reduced by up to 40%. Seasonal discounts vary dramatically by resort and by island, with some of the

LOGISTICS

Getting to St. Vincent and the Grenadines: Until Argyle International Airport opens (scheduled for late 2013), there are no nonstop flights between the United States and St. Vincent and the Grenadines. Travelers from North America arrive at airports in St. Vincent, Bequia, Canouan, Mustique, or Union Island via regional airlines that connect to major airlines serving Barbados, Grenada, Puerto Rico, or St. Lucia. Some of the smaller Grenadines require both a flight and a boat ride. Unless you're on a private jet, it's an exhausting, time-consuming trip (and fairly expensive), yet people still make the effort to reach some of the most wonderful, unspoiled islands in the Caribbean. Once you've landed on St. Vincent, it's also possible to hop to several different islands for a day or longer by air or by an interisland ferry.

Hassle Factor: High, but worth it.

On the Ground: St. Vincent's E.T. Joshua Airport is in Arnos Vale, about halfway between Kingstown and Villa Beach. It's a small but busy airport and accommodates only turboprop passenger aircraft or small private jets. In the Grenadines, Canouan's modern airport has an extended runway that can accommodate jets. Bequia, Mustique, and Union islands each have an airstrip with frequent regional service. Taxis and buses are readily available at the airport on St. Vincent. The taxi fare to Kingstown or the Villa Beach area is $12 (or EC$30). Taxi service is available from the airports on Bequia, Mustique, Canouan, and Union islands.

luxury resorts offering specials periodically throughout the year; the most luxurious resorts, however, are always expensive. The cheaper small hotels and guesthouses have little or no seasonal variation in their rates.

GETTING HERE AND AROUND

AIR TRAVEL

Until Argyle International Airport opens (scheduled for late 2013), there are no nonstop flights between the United States and St. Vincent and the Grenadines. Travelers from North America arrive at E.T. Joshua International Airport (SVD) in St. Vincent or the airports in Bequia (BQU), Canouan (CIW), Mustique (MQS), or Union Island (UNI) via regional airlines that connect with major airlines serving Barbados, Grenada, Puerto Rico, or St. Lucia.

Airport Contacts Grantley Adams International Airport. There is a tourist information desk at the Barbados airport. ✉ *BGI, Barbados* ☎ *246/428-0961, 246/233-8746.*

Airports Canouan Airport. Small and medium jets are able to use Canouan's airport. ✉ *CIW, Canouan* ☎ *784/458-8049.* **E.T. Joshua Airport.** This small, busy airport on St. Vincent can accommodate only turboprop passenger aircraft or small private jets. ✉ *SVD, Arnos Vale, St. Vincent* ☎ *784/458-4685.*

Airline Contacts Grenadine Airways. Operating a shared-charter service, Grenadine Airways links Barbados with the four airports in the Grenadines. It also flies between St. Vincent and the various Grenadines. ☎ *246/418–1654 for shared–charter flights, 784/456–6793 for inter–Grenadine flights.*

LIAT. This airlines's flights connect St. Vincent, Bequia, and Union with Barbados, Grenada, Puerto Rico, and St. Lucia. ☎ *784/458–4841, 888/844–5428 throughout the Caribbean* ⊕ *www.liatairline.com.*

Mustique Airways. This local airline operates scheduled service between Barbados and Mustique (with meet-and-greet service at the Barbados airport for in-transit passengers), as well as private charters between Mustique, St. Vincent, Bequia, Canouan, or Union, and Barbados, St. Lucia, Grenada, or Martinique. ☎ *784/456–4586* ⊕ *www.mustique.com.*

SVG Air. SVG operates daily scheduled flights between St. Vincent and St. Lucia's Hewanorra International, as well as between St. Vincent and the four Grenadine airports. ☎ *784/457–5124, 800/744–7285* ⊕ *www. svgair.com.*

SVG Air (Grenada). SVG Air (Grenada) operates scheduled flights between Grenada and Union Island, continuing on to St. Vincent. ☎ *473/444–3549, 800/744–7285* ⊕ *www.svgair.com/grenada.*

CAR TRAVEL

Car rental is available on St. Vincent, Bequia, or Mustique. Rental cars in St. Vincent and Bequia cost about $55 to $85 per day or $300 to $400 a week. Unless you already have an international driver's license, you'll need to buy a temporary driving permit for $24 (EC$65), valid for six months. To get one, present your valid driver's license at the police station on Bay Street or the Licensing Authority on Halifax Street, both in Kingstown, St. Vincent, or at the Revenue Office in Port Elizabeth, Bequia.

St. Vincent Contacts Avis. Avis is the only international agency on St. Vincent. ✉ *E.T. Joshua International Airport, Arnos Vale, St. Vincent* ☎ *784/456–6861* ⊕ *www.avis.com.*

Ben's Auto Rental. This reliable company offers airport pickup and drop-off service on request. ✉ *Sion Hill, St. Vincent* ☎ *784/456–2907* ⊕ *www.bensautorentals.com.*

David's Auto Clinic. This local agency comes recommended. ✉ *Sion Hill, St. Vincent* ☎ *784/457–4026.*

Star Garage ✉ *Grenville St., Kingstown, St. Vincent* ☎ *784/456–1743.*

Bequia Contacts Bequia Jeep Rentals. This company rents both jeeps, whose four-wheel drive is best for negotiating the island's hilly roads, and much smaller Nissan cars. ✉ *Friendship, Bequia* ☎ *784/458–3760* ⊕ *www. bequiajeeprentals.com.*

Challenger. This local taxi and tour-guide operation also rents four-wheel-drive vehicles. ✉ *Belmont, Bequia* ☎ *784/458–3811.*

Mustique Contacts Mustique Mechanical Services. Head here to rent cars, Mokes (beach buggies), and motor scooters. ✉ *Mustique Company, Britannia Bay, Mustique* ☎ *784/488–8555.*

ST. VINCENT DRIVING TIPS

About 360 miles (580 km) of paved roads wind around St. Vincent's perimeter, except for a section in the far north with no road at all that precludes a circle tour of the island. A few roads jut into the interior a few miles, and only one east–west road (through the Mesopotamia Valley) bisects the island. Roads in the country are often not wide enough for two cars to pass, and people (including schoolchildren), dogs, goats, and chickens often share the roadway with cars, minibuses, and trucks. Outside populated areas, roads can be bumpy and potholed; be sure your rental car

has tire-changing equipment and a spare. Drive on the left, and toot your horn before you enter blind curves out in the countryside, where you'll encounter plenty of steep hills and hairpin turns.

If you're planning an extended stay on St. Vincent and expect to travel frequently between Kingstown and, say, the Villa Beach area, a rental car might be useful although not necessary, as both taxis and buses are inexpensive and readily available. On Bequia, a rental car will be handy if you're staying for several days in a remote location—that is, anywhere beyond Port Elizabeth.

24

FERRY TRAVEL

A one-way trip between St. Vincent and Bequia takes 60 minutes and costs $8 (EC$20) each way or $14 (EC$35) round-trip with the same ferry company.

Contacts Admiralty Transport. This ferry makes several round-trips daily between Kingstown and Bequia. 784/458–3348 ⊕ www.admiralty-transport.com.

M/V Bequia Express. This ferry runs several round-trips between Kingstown and Bequia. 784/458–3472 ⊕ www.bequiaexpress.net.

Jaden Sun. This ferry's reliable, comfortable service goes between mainland St. Vincent and Bequia (25 minutes), Canouan (1½ hours), and Union islands (2 hours), with an "as needed" stop in Mayreau. There is no service on Tuesday and Wednesday afternoons, or public holidays or on Saturday in the low season. The one-way fare between Kingstown and Bequia is $12; between Kingstown and Canouan, $25; between Kingstown and Union, $28. 784/451–2192 ⊕ www.jadeninc.com.

M/V Barracuda. The interisland ferry M/V Barracuda, also known as "the mail boat," operates twice weekly. It leaves St. Vincent on Monday and Thursday mornings, stopping in Canouan, Mayreau, and Union Island. It makes the return trip Tuesdaay and Friday On Saturday it does a round-trip from St. Vincent to each island, returning the same day. 784/527–6135.

M/V Gem Star. This boat takes passengers from Kingstown to Canouan and Union on Tuesday and Friday mornings, returning early Wednesday and Saturday mornings. 784/526–1158.

TAXI TRAVEL

Taxis are not metered. Settle on the price—and the currency—before entering the taxi. Taxis are always available at the airport in St. Vincent; the fare from the airport to Kingstown or Villa is $12 (EC$30). In Bequia, the taxis—usually pickup trucks, with their beds fitted with seats accommodating four to six people under an awning—will take you to Port Elizabeth, to the vari-

ous hotels, or on a day of sightseeing. On Canouan, resorts generally provide airport transfers, although taxis are available. On Mustique, transfers are usually provided, but taxis are available. On Union Island, it's a short walk or jitney ride from the airport to the dock (a two-minute trip) to meet the launch from Palm Island or Petit St. Vincent; taxis are also available for the brief ride into Clifton, the main town.

ESSENTIALS

Banks and Exchange Services ATMs can be found at banks in Kingstown and their branches. U.S. dollars are accepted nearly everywhere, although you'll receive change in Eastern Caribbean currency (EC$), which is the preferred currency. U.S. coins are not accepted anywhere. The exchange rate is fixed at EC$2.67 to US$1. Hotels, car-rental agencies, and most shops and restaurants also accept major credit cards and traveler's checks.

Dress Don't pack camouflage clothing. It is illegal to wear any form of camouflage clothing in St. Vincent and the Grenadines (as it is on most Caribbean islands), as that pattern is reserved for the local police. The law is strictly enforced, and the clothing may be confiscated.

Electricity Electric current is generally 220–240 volts, 50 cycles. Some large resorts, such as Petit St. Vincent, have 110 volts, 60 cycles (U.S. standard); many have 110-volt shaver outlets.

Passports Requirements You need a valid passport and an ongoing or return ticket to enter St. Vincent and the Grenadines.

Phones The area code is 784. If making a collect call to the United States, dial 800/CALLUSA (☎ 800/225–5872). For international credit-card calling, dial 800/744–2000.

Taxes and Service Charges The departure tax from St. Vincent and the Grenadines is $16 (EC$40), payable at the airport in cash in either U.S. or EC currency; children under 12 are exempt. Increasingly, departure taxes are incorporated into the price paid for airfare, although St. Vincent is currently an exception. A government tax of 10% is added to the room cost on hotel bills, a 15% V.A.T. (value-added tax) is added to restaurant checks and other purchases, and a 10% service charge is often added to hotel bills and restaurant checks.

Tipping If a 10% service charge has not been added to your restaurant tab, a gratuity at that rate is appropriate. Otherwise, tipping is expected only for special service. Bellmen and porters, $1 per bag; housekeeping,

$2 per day; taxi drivers and tour guides, 10%.

ACCOMMODATIONS

Mass tourism hasn't come to St. Vincent and the Grenadines, but that could change after the Argyle International Airport opens in late 2013. With one or two exceptions, hotels and inns on St. Vincent are modest. Look to one of the exclusive resorts in the Grenadines if you want luxury and privacy, where both can be found in great abundance. If you have the time, it's easy to island-hop by air or ferry, staying in simple guesthouses to maximize both your budget and experiences.

Luxury Resorts: On Young Island, just a stone's throw from St. Vincent's shore, at Buccament Bay on St. Vincent, and scattered throughout the Grenadines, luxury resorts offer a laid-back vacation experience without sacrificing service, comfort, and privacy.

Simple Resorts and Guesthouses: Most lodgings in St. Vincent are simple, small, and relatively inexpensive. You'll also find small hotels and guesthouses with similarly forgiving rates throughout the Grenadines—on Bequia and Union, in particular.

Villas: Luxurious villas make up the majority of accommodations on Mustique, and they offer every amenity you can imagine. Private villas are also available for rent on St. Vincent, Bequia, and Canouan.

HOTEL AND RESTAURANT PRICES

Prices in the restaurant reviews are the average cost of a main course at dinner or, if dinner is not served, at lunch; taxes and service charges are generally included. Prices in the hotel reviews are the lowest cost of a standard double room in high season, excluding taxes, service charges, and meal plans (except at all-inclusives). Prices for rentals are the lowest per-night cost for a one-bedroom unit in high season.

VISITOR INFORMATION

Contacts St. Vincent and the Grenadines Tourism Authority ☎ 212/687–4981 *in New York City,* 800/729–1726 ⊕ *www.discoversvg.com.* **St. Vincent & The Grenadines Hotel & Tourism Association** ⊕ *www.svghotels.com.*

WEDDINGS

At least a 24-hour residency is required. A special governor-general's marriage license must be obtained in person from the Ministry of Justice at the Registrar's Office in St. Vincent. Bring valid passports, return or ongoing plane tickets, certified and notarized divorce decrees, and an appropriate death certificate if either party is widowed. An official

---

DOLLAR BUSES

"Dollar buses," on St. Vincent are privately owned, brightly painted minivans; fares range from EC$1 to EC$6 (40¢ to $2.25). Routes are indicated on the windshield, and the bus will stop on demand. Just wave from the road or point your finger to the ground as a bus approaches. To get off, signal by tapping your knuckles twice above the window by your seat or ask the conductor, usually a young boy who rides along to open the door and collect fares; it's helpful to have the correct change in EC coins. In Kingstown, the central departure point is the bus terminal at the New Kingstown Fish Market.

24

marriage officer, priest, or minister registered in St. Vincent and the Grenadines must officiate at the ceremony, and two witnesses must be present.

ST. VINCENT

EXPLORING ST. VINCENT

Kingstown's shopping and business district, historic churches and cathedrals, and other points of interest can easily be seen in a half day, with another half day for the Botanic Gardens. The coastal roads of St. Vincent offer spectacular panoramas and scenes of island life. The Leeward Highway follows the scenic Caribbean coastline; the Windward Highway follows the more dramatic Atlantic coast. A drive along the windward coast requires a full day. Exploring La Soufrière or the Vermont Trails is also a major undertaking, requiring a very early start and a full day of strenuous hiking.

Barrouallie. Once an important whaling village, Barrouallie (*bar*-relly) today is home to anglers earning their livelihoods trawling for blackfish, which are actually small pilot whales. The one-hour drive north from Kingstown on the Leeward Highway takes you along ridges that drop to the sea, through small villages and lush valleys, and beside bays with black-sand beaches and safe bathing. ⊠ *Barrouallie.*

Black Point Tunnel. In 1815, under the supervision of British colonel Thomas Browne, Carib and African slaves drilled a 300-foot tunnel through solid volcanic rock—an engineering marvel at the time—to facilitate the transportation of sugar from estates in the north to the port in Kingstown. Today Jasper Rock Tunnel is the centerpiece of Black Point Historic & Recreation Park, which also has an interpretation center, children's playground, and washrooms. The tunnel, just off beautiful black-sand Black Point Beach, links Grand Sable with Byrea Bay, to the north of Colonarie (pronounced con-a-*ree*). ⊠ *Black Point, north of Colonarie.*

⊘ **Botanic Gardens.** A few minutes north of downtown by taxi is the oldest
Fodor'sChoice botanical garden in the Western Hemisphere. It was founded in 1765,
★ after Captain Bligh—of *Bounty* fame—brought the first breadfruit tree to this island for landowners to propagate. The prolific bounty of the breadfruit trees was used to feed the slaves. You can see a direct descendant of this original tree among the specimen mahogany, rubber, teak, and other tropical trees and shrubs in the 20 acres of gardens. Two dozen rare St. Vincent parrots, confiscated from illegal collections, live in the small aviary. Guides explain all the medicinal and ornamental trees and shrubs; they also appreciate a tip (about $5 per person) at the end of the tour. ⊠ *Off Leeward Hwy, northeast of town, Montrose, Kingstown* 🕿 *784/457–1003* 🆓 *Free* ۞ *Daily 6–6.*

★ **Ft. Charlotte.** Started by the French in 1786 and completed by the British in 1806, the fort was named for Queen Charlotte, wife of King George III. It sits on Berkshire Hill, a dramatic promontory 2 miles (3 km) north of Kingstown and 636 feet above sea level, affording a stunning view of the capital city and the Grenadines. Interestingly, cannons face inward—the fear of attack by the French and their Carib allies was far greater than any threat approaching from the sea. In any case, the fort saw no action. Nowadays, the fort serves as a signal station for ships; its ancient cells house historical paintings of the island by Lindsay Prescott. ⊠ *Berkshire Hill, 2 miles north of town, Kingstown.*

Georgetown. St. Vincent's second-largest city (and former capital), halfway up the island's Atlantic coast and surrounded by acres and acres of coconut groves, makes a convenient place to stop for a cool drink or snack or other essential shopping while traveling along the windward coast. A tiny, quiet town—with a few streets, small shops, a restaurant or two, and modest homes—it's completely unaffected by tourism. Georgetown is also the site of the now-defunct Mount Bentinck sugar factory. ⊠ *Georgetown.*

Kingstown. The capital city of St. Vincent and the Grenadines is on the island's southwestern coast. The town of 13,500 residents wraps around Kingstown Bay; a ring of green hills and ridges, studded with houses, forms a backdrop for the city. This is very much a working city, with a busy harbor and few concessions to tourists. Kingstown Harbour is the only deepwater port on the island.

A few gift shops can be found on and around **Bay Street,** near the harbor. Upper Bay Street, which stretches along the bayfront, bustles with daytime activity—workers going about their business and housewives doing their shopping. Many of Kingstown's downtown buildings are built of stone or brick brought to the island in the holds of 18th-century ships as ballast (and replaced with sugar and spices for the return trip to Europe). The Georgian-style stone arches and second-floor overhangs on former warehouses create shelter from midday sun and the brief, cooling showers common to the tropics.

Grenadines Wharf, at the south end of Bay Street, is busy with schooners loading supplies and ferries loading people bound for the Grenadines. The **Cruise-Ship Complex,** just south of the commercial wharf, has a mall with a dozen or more shops, plus restaurants, a post office, communications facilities, and a taxi-minibus stand.

An almost infinite selection of produce fills the **Kingstown Produce Market,** a three-story building that takes up a whole city block on Upper Bay, Hillsboro, and Bedford streets in the center of town. It's noisy, colorful, and open Monday through Saturday—but the busiest times (and the best times to go) are Friday and Saturday mornings. In the courtyard, vendors sell local arts and crafts. On the upper floors, merchants sell clothing, household items, gifts, and other products.

Little Tokyo, so called because funding for the project was a gift from Japan, is a waterfront shopping area with a bustling indoor fish market and dozens of stalls where you can buy inexpensive homemade meals, drinks, ice cream, bread and cookies, clothing, trinkets, and even get a haircut.

St. George's Cathedral, on Grenville Street, is a pristine, creamy yellow Anglican church built in 1820. The dignified Georgian architecture includes simple wooden pews, an ornate chandelier, and beautiful

A waterfall near Waillabou Bay, St. Vincent

stained-glass windows; one was a gift from Queen Victoria, who actually commissioned it for London's St. Paul's Cathedral in honor of her first grandson. When the artist created an angel with a red robe, she was horrified by the color and sent it abroad. The markers in the cathedral's graveyard recount the history of the island. Across the street is **St. Mary's Roman Catholic Cathedral of the Assumption,** built in stages beginning in 1823. The strangely appealing design is a blend of Moorish, Georgian, and Romanesque styles applied to black brick. Nearby, freed slaves built the **Kingstown Methodist Church** in 1841. The exterior is brick, simply decorated with quoins (solid blocks that form the corners), and the roof is held together by metal straps, bolts, and wooden pins. **Scots Kirk** was built from 1839 to 1880 by and for Scottish settlers but became a Seventh-Day Adventist church in 1952. ⊠ *Kingstown.*

La Soufrière. This towering volcano, which last erupted in 1979, is 4,048 feet high and so huge in area that its surrounding mountainside covers virtually the entire northern third of the island. The eastern trail to the rim of the crater, a two-hour ascent, begins at Rabacca Dry River. ⊠ *Rabacca Dry River, Rabacca.*

Layou Petroglyph Park. Just beyond the small fishing village of Layou, about 45 minutes north of Kingstown, are petroglyphs (rock carvings) that were carved into a giant boulder by pre-Columbian inhabitants in the 8th century. For about $2 you can be escorted along the nature trail to the site. ⊠ *Leeward Hwy., Layou* ☎ *784/454–8686* 🖙 *$2* ⊙ *Daily 8–5.*

Mesopotamia Valley. The rugged, ocean-lashed scenery along St. Vincent's windward coast is the perfect counterpoint to the lush, calm leeward coast. In between, the fertile Mesopotamia Valley (nicknamed Mespo) has a view of dense rain forests, streams, and endless banana and coconut plantations. Breadfruit, sweet corn, peanuts, and arrowroot also grow in the rich soil here. Mountain ridges, including 3,181-foot Grand Bonhomme Mountain, surround the valley. ⊠ *Mesopotamia.*

Fodor'sChoice ★ **Montreal Gardens.** Welsh-born landscape designer Timothy Vaughn renovated 7½ acres of neglected commercial flower beds and a falling-down plantation house into a stunning yet informal garden spot. Anthurium, ginger lilies, birds-of-paradise, and other tropical flowers are planted in raised beds; tree ferns create a canopy of shade along the walkways. The gardens are in the shadow of majestic Grand Bonhomme Mountain, deep in the Mesopotamia Valley, about 12 miles (19 km) from Kingstown. ⊠ *Montreal St., Mesopotamia* ☎ *784/458–1198* ⊠ *$2* ☉ *Dec.–Aug., weekdays 9–5.*

Owia. The village of Owia, on the island's far northeast coast and at least a two-hour drive from Kingstown, is the home of many descendants of the Carib people. It's also the home of the **Owia Arrowroot Processing Factory.** Long used to thicken sauces and flavor cookies, arrowroot is now also used in pharmaceutical products and as a finish for high-quality computer paper. St. Vincent produces 90% of the world's supply of arrowroot, but that is only a tiny fraction of the maximum levels exported in the 1960s. Close to the village is the **Owia Salt Pond,** created by the pounding surf of the Atlantic Ocean, which flowed over a barrier reef of lava rocks and ridges. Picnic and take a swim before the long return trip to Kingstown. ⊠ *Owia.*

Rabacca Dry River. This rocky gulch just north of Georgetown was carved from the earth by lava flow from the 1902 eruption of nearby **La Soufrière.** When it rains in the mountains, the riverbed changes from dry moonscape to a trickle to a gushing river within minutes—and then simply dries up again. Before the Rabacca Dry River Bridge opened in March 2007, drivers would often get stranded on one side or the other whenever the river flooded. ⊠ *Rabacca.*

Ⓒ ★ **Wallilabou Bay.** The *Pirates of the Caribbean* movie left its mark at Wallilabou (pronounced wally-la-*boo*), a location used for filming the opening scenes of "The Curse of the Black Pearl" in 2003. Many of the buildings and docks built as stage sets remain, giving the pretty bay (a port of entry for visiting yachts) an intriguingly historic appearance. You can sunbathe, swim, picnic, or buy your lunch at Wallilabou Anchorage. This is a favorite stop for day-trippers returning from the Falls of Baleine and boaters anchoring for the evening. Nearby, at Wallilabou Heritage Park, there's a river with a small waterfall and pool, where you can take a freshwater plunge. ⊠ *Wallilabou.*

BEACHES

Argyle Beach. Though this spectacular black-sand beach on St. Vincent's southeast (windward) coast is not safe for swimming, you'll love to watch the surf crashing here. The new international airport is being built very near the beach. **Amenities:** none. **Best for:** solitude, walking. ⊠ *Argyle.*

Buccament Bay Beach. A long strand of (imported) white sand stretches in front of Buccament Bay Resort, about a half hour northwest of Kingstown. The water is calm, and snorkeling is very good. **Amenities:** food and drink; parking. **Best for:** snorkeling; swimming; walking; sunsets. ⊠ *Buccament Bay.*

Indian Bay Beach. South of Kingstown and separated from Villa Beach by a rocky hill, Indian Bay beach has golden sand but is slightly rocky; it's very good for snorkeling. **Amenities:** food and drink. **Best for:** snorkeling; swimming. ⊠ *Villa, Calliaqua.*

Villa Beach. The long stretch of sand in front of the row of hotels and restaurants along the Young Island Channel varies from 20 to 25 feet wide to practically nonexistent. The broadest, sandiest part is in front of Beachcombers Hotel, which is also the perfect spot for sunbathers to get lunch and liquid refreshments. **Amenities:** food and drink; water sports. **Best for:** swimming. ⊠ *Villa, Calliaqua.*

WHERE TO EAT

Nearly all restaurants in St. Vincent specialize in local West Indian cuisine, although you can find chefs with broad culinary experience at a few hotel restaurants. Local dishes to try include callaloo (similar to spinach) soup, curried goat or chicken, rotis (turnovers filled with curried meat or vegetables), fresh-caught seafood (lobster, kingfish, snapper, and mahimahi), local vegetables (squashlike christophene, also known as chayote; and pumpkin) and "provisions" (roots such as yams and dasheen), and tropical fruit (including avocados, breadfruit, mangoes, soursop, pineapples, and papaya). Fried or baked chicken is available everywhere, often accompanied by "rice 'n' peas" or *pelau* (a stew made with rice, coconut milk, and either chicken or beef seared in caramelized sugar). At Campden Park, just north of Kingstown, the local beer, Hairoun, is brewed in accordance with a German recipe. Sunset is the local rum.

What to Wear. Restaurants are casual. You may want to dress up a little—long pants and collared shirts for gents, summer dresses or dress pants for the ladies—for an evening out at a pricey restaurant, *but none of the establishments listed below require gentlemen to wear a jacket or tie.* Beachwear, however, is never appropriate in restaurants.

$$$
CARIBBEAN

✕ **Basil's Bar and Restaurant.** It's not just the air-conditioning that makes this restaurant cool. Basil's, at street level at the Cobblestone Inn, is owned by Basil Charles, whose Basil's Beach Bar on Mustique is a hangout for the vacationing rich and famous. This is the Kingstown power-lunch venue. Local businesspeople gather for the daily buffet (weekdays) or full menu of salads, sandwiches, barbecued chicken, or fresh seafood platters. Dinner entrées of pasta, local seafood, and chicken are served at candlelit tables. $ *Average main: $20* ⊠ *Cobblestone Inn, Upper Bay St., Kingstown* ☎ *784/457–2713* ⊘ *Closed Sun.*

24

$ ✕ **Cobblestone Roof-Top Bar & Restaurant.** To reach what is perhaps the
CARIBBEAN most pleasant, the breeziest, and the most satisfying breakfast and lunch
★ spot in downtown Kingstown, diners must climb the equivalent of three
flights of interior stone steps within the historic Cobblestone Inn. But
getting to the open-air rooftop restaurant is half the fun, as en route diners get an up-close view of a 19th-century sugar (and later arrowroot)
Georgian warehouse that's now a very appealing boutique inn. A full
breakfast menu is available to hotel guests and the public alike. The luncheon menu ranges from homemade soups, salads (tuna, chicken, fruit,
or tossed), sandwiches, or burgers and fries to full meals of roast beef,
stewed chicken, or grilled fish served with rice, plantains, macaroni pie,
and fresh local vegetables. $ *Average main: $12* ⊠ *Cobblestone Inn,
Upper Bay St., Kingstown* ☎ *784/456–1937* ⊘ *No dinner.*

$$$ ✕ **The French Verandah.** Dining by candlelight on the waterfront terrace of
FRENCH Mariners Hotel means excellent French cuisine with Caribbean flair—
Fodor's Choice and one of the best dining experiences on St. Vincent. Start with a rich
★ soup (traditional French onion, fish with aioli, or callaloo and conch)
or escargots, stuffed crab back, or conch salad. Main courses include
fresh fish and shellfish grilled with fresh herbs, garlic butter and lime,
or creole sauce. Landlubbers may prefer beef bourguignonne, *suprème
de poulet*, grilled lamb chops, or beef tenderloin with béarnaise, Roque-
fort, or mushroom sauce. For dessert, there's the wonderful *mi-cuit*, a
warm chocolate delicacy with vanilla ice cream. Lighter, equally deli-
cious fare is served at lunch. $ *Average main: $26* ⊠ *Mariners Hotel,
Villa Beach, Calliaqua* ☎ *784/453–1111* ⊕ *www.marinershotel.com*
⌂ *Reservations essential.*

$ ✕ **Vee Jay's Restaurant & Bar.** Come here for "authentic Vincy cuisine"
CARIBBEAN specials, which are chalked on the blackboard: mutton or fish stew,
chicken or vegetable rotis, curried goat, souse, and *buljol* (sautéed cod-
fish, breadfruit, and vegetables). Not-so-Vincy sandwiches, fish-and-
chips, and burgers can be authentically washed down with *mauby*, a
bittersweet drink made from tree bark; linseed, peanut, passion-fruit,
or sorrel punch; local Hairoun beer; or cocktails. Lunch is buffet-style.
$ *Average main: $12* ⊠ *Bay St., Kingstown* ☎ *784/457–2845* ⌂ *Reser-
vations essential* ⊘ *Closed Sun.*

$$ ✕ **Wallilabou Anchorage.** Halfway up St. Vincent's Caribbean coast, this
CARIBBEAN is a favorite luncheon stop for folks sailing the Grenadines and for
landlubbers touring the leeward coast. The picturesque view of the bay
is enhanced by the period stage sets left behind by the *Pirates of the
Caribbean* filmmakers. Open all day from 8 am, the bar-and-restaurant
serves snacks, sandwiches, tempting West Indian dishes and lobster
in season. Ice, telephones, business services, and shower facilities are
available to boaters. $ *Average main: $16* ⊠ *Leeward Hwy., Wallilabou*
☎ *784/458–7270.*

$$$$ ✕ **Young Island Resort Restaurant.** Take the ferry (a two-minute ride from
CONTEMPORARY Villa Beach) to Young Island for a delightful lunch or a very special
Fodor's Choice romantic evening. Stone paths lead to candlelit tables, some in breezy,
★ thatch-roof kiosks. Gentle waves lap against the shore. Five-course,
prix-fixe dinners of grilled seafood, roast pork, succulent beef tenderloin, duck breast, and sautéed chicken are accompanied by local

vegetables. Two or three choices are offered for each course, and a board of freshly made breads (coconut, raisin, banana, country white, cinnamon, or whole-grain wheat) is offered. Lunch is à la carte—soups, salads, grilled meats, or fish—and served on the beachfront terrace. ⑤ *Average main: $45* ✉ *Young Island Cut, Young Island* ☎ *784/458–4826* ⊕ *www.youngisland.com* ⚓ *Reservations essential.*

WHERE TO STAY

With a few exceptions—most notably, Buccament Bay Resort northwest of the capital city—tourist accommodations and facilities on St. Vincent are in either Kingstown or the Villa Beach area. All guest rooms have air-conditioning, TV, and phone, unless stated otherwise.

For expanded reviews, facilities, and current deals, visit Fodors.com.

PRIVATE VILLAS AND CONDOS

Because the island's air service is limited to small planes operated by regional carriers, huge villa communities and condo complexes have been late to arrive in St. Vincent—though the international airport set to open in late 2013 will likely change that. The island's first villa community at Buccament Bay opened in summer 2010; many of the one- and two-bedroom town houses are available for vacation rentals.

RECOMMENDED HOTELS AND RESORTS

$
HOTEL
★
Beachcombers Hotel & Spa. Guests come to Beachcombers for the great beachfront, comfortable rooms, friendly service, and lively atmosphere both day and night. **Pros:** great value and location; best beachfront in the area. **Cons:** popular with small groups so book well ahead; standard rooms are very standard (you can upgrade to deluxe or penthouse rooms for not too much more). **TripAdvisor:** "nice and comfortable," "relaxing and very enjoyable," "elegant grounds." ⑤ *Rooms from: $99* ✉ *Villa Beach, Calliaqua* ☎ *784/458–4283* ⊕ *www.beachcombershotel.com* ⚐ *27 rooms, 4 suites* ⑩ *No meals.*

$$$$
ALL-INCLUSIVE
☾
Fodor'sChoice
★
Buccament Bay Resort. This luxury villa community, by far the largest resort in St. Vincent, is on a pretty bay about a half hour northwest of Kingstown. **Pros:** beautiful accommodations; lots of amenities; food and service are very good; great spot for soccer-playing kids. **Cons:** amazingly expensive, even though rates include connecting airfare from Barbados; ongoing construction in phases through 2013, but owners are working hard to minimize any disturbance to guests. **TripAdvisor:** "stunning rooms," "total relaxation," "excellent service." ⑤ *Rooms from: $1,365* ✉ *Buccament Bay* ☎ *784/457–4100* ⊕ *www.buccamentbay.com* ⚐ *150 units* ⑩ *All-inclusive.*

$
B&B/INN
★
Cobblestone Inn. This boutique hotel is cozy, convenient, inexpensive, and loaded with historic charm—but it's nowhere near a beach. **Pros:** convenient for an overnight stay if you're taking an early ferry to the Grenadines; historical atmosphere; fascinating architecture. **Cons:** mostly tiny rooms; wandering around the downtown streets at night is not recommended; not on the beach. **TripAdvisor:** "great restaurant," "superb service," "charming." ⑤ *Rooms from: $75* ✉ *Upper Bay St., Kingstown* ☎ *784/456–1937* ⊕ *www.thecobblestoneinn.com* ⚐ *20 rooms, 6 suites* ⑩ *No meals.*

24

$ \bullet **Grand View Beach Hotel.** The unobstructed view of the Grenadines
HOTEL from this stylish, family-run hotel on a very private promontory is
★ very grand indeed. **Pros:** friendly, family-run boutique vibe; beautiful (grand) sunset views; lots of on-site amenities—including a squash
court. **Cons:** that hike down to the beach; a rental car would be handy;
a few rooms don't have air-conditioning. **TripAdvisor:** "true Caribbean
flavor," "good old-fashioned hospitality," "great ambience and friendly
staff." $ *Rooms from: $115* ✉ *Villa Point, Calliaqua* ☎ *784/458–4811*
⊕ *www.grandviewhotel.com* ➽ *19 rooms, 2 suites* ❑*Multiple meal
plans.*

$ \bullet **Mariners Hotel.** This pleasant, small hotel is on the Villa Beach water-
HOTEL front, opposite Young Island. **Pros:** restaurant's French cuisine; the use
of the lovely Young Island beach; many water sports available nearby.
Cons: rooms are simply decorated; bathrooms have showers, no tubs;
pool small (but refreshing). **TripAdvisor:** "great restaurant and nice
rooms," "nice hotel on the beach," "great service." $ *Rooms from:
$145* ✉ *Villa Beach, Calliaqua* ☎ *784/457–4000* ⊕ *www.marinershotel.
com* ➽ *21 rooms* ❑*No meals.*

$ \bullet **Rosewood Apartment Hotel.** Perched high on a hillside overlooking Villa
RENTAL Beach and Young Island, the view of the Grenadines from the patio or
terrace of every one of these self-contained apartments is mesmerizing—
particularly at sunset. **Pros:** accommodating management, and what
a view! **Cons:** not on the beach; steep driveway and hillside location
may complicate casual strolls. **TripAdvisor:** "very friendly for families,"
"great view," "simply wonderful." $ *Rooms from: $80* ✉ *Rose Cottage, Villa, Calliaqua* ☎ *784/457–5051* ⊕ *www.rosewoodsvg.com* ➽ *9
rooms, 1 suite* ❑*No meals.*

$ \bullet **Sunset Shores Beach Hotel.** Down a long, steep driveway off the main
HOTEL road, this lemon-yellow, low-rise, family-owned hotel faces a narrow
★ curve of Villa beachfront. **Pros:** picturesque location opposite Young
Island; pool–bar area lovely at sundown; the price is right. **Cons:** room
decor is attractive but a bit bland; beach is slim. **TripAdvisor:** "good
location," "friendly atmosphere," "magnificent service." $ *Rooms
from: $150* ✉ *Villa Beach, Calliaqua* ☎ *784/458–4411* ⊕ *www.
sunsetshores.com* ➽ *32 rooms* ❑*Multiple meal plans.*

$ \bullet **Villa Lodge Hotel.** The venerable Villa Lodge has been welcoming
B&B/INN guests since 1961, when a private hillside home was first transformed
into a family-operated inn. **Pros:** good rates; you can catch a minibus at
the door to go to town or Villa Beach; rooms have both 110v and 220v
outlets; restaurant is very good. **Cons:** street noise may be an issue in
front rooms. **TripAdvisor:** "thoughtful and friendly staff," "excellent
customer service," "comfortable." $ *Rooms from: $130* ✉ *Indian Bay,
Calliaqua* ☎ *784/458–4641,* ⊕ *www.villalodgehotel.com* ➽ *11 rooms,
8 apartments* ❑*No meals.*

$$$$ \bullet **Young Island Resort.** One of St. Vincent's two true resorts is actu-
RESORT ally 200 yards offshore (a three-minute ride from Villa Beach by hotel
☯ launch), on its own 35-acre island. **Pros:** St. Vincent's best (white-sand)
Fodor's Choice beach; casually elegant; romantic but also good for families and other
★ groups. **Cons:** pricey; no a/c in some rooms; no phones or TVs in rooms
(though this might be a plus for some). **TripAdvisor:** "very relaxing,"

Young Island Resort

"superb food," "among the very best." $ *Rooms from: $532* ⊠ *Young Island Cut, Young Island* ☎ *784/458–4826* ⊕ *www.youngisland.com* ↬ *23 cottage rooms, 6 cottage suites* ⦿ *Multiple meal plans.*

NIGHTLIFE

Nightlife in St. Vincent consists mostly of once-a-week (in season) hotel barbecue buffets with a steel band or a local string band (usually older gents who play an assortment of string instruments). Jump-ups, so called because the lively calypso music makes listeners jump up and dance, happen around holidays, festivals, and Vincy Mas—St. Vincent's Carnival—which starts in June and is the biggest cultural event of the year. At a couple of nightspots in Kingstown and at Villa Beach, you can join Vincentians for late-night dancing to live or recorded reggae, hip-hop, and soca music.

DANCE AND MUSIC CLUBS

Dance clubs generally charge a cover of $10 (EC$25), slightly more for headliners.

Aquatic Club. Live local music plays on most Friday and Saturday nights here. ⊠ *Villa Beach, Calliaqua* ☎ *784/458–4205.*

SHOPPING

The 12 small blocks that hug the waterfront in **downtown Kingstown** make up St. Vincent's main shopping district. Among the shops that sell goods to fulfill household needs are a few that sell local crafts, gifts, and souvenirs. Bargaining is neither expected nor appreciated. The

cruise-ship complex, on the waterfront in Kingstown, has a collection of a dozen or so boutiques, shops, and restaurants that cater primarily to cruise-ship passengers but welcome all shoppers. The best souvenirs of St. Vincent are intricately woven straw items, such as handbags, hats, slippers, baskets, and grass mats that range in size from place mats to room-size floor mats. If you're inclined to bring home a floor mat, pack (or buy) a few heavy-duty plastic bags and some twine. The mats aren't heavy and roll or fold rather neatly; wrapped securely and tagged, they can be checked or carried on board as luggage for the flight home. Local artwork and carvings are available in galleries, from street vendors, and in shops at the cruise-ship complex.

ANTIQUES AND FURNITURE

At Basil's. Near the Young Island ferry dock and Mariners Hotel stands St. Vincent's only antiques and furniture store. Specializing in 200-year-old Asian pieces and the latest creations from Bali, India, and Africa, Basil's collection appeals to fine-furniture collectors as well as anyone seeking interesting, affordable items for either home or garden. Even if you're just looking, you might be smitten by the French wines, chocolates, and cheeses. ⊠ *Across from Young Island, Villa Beach, Calliaqua* ☎ *784/456–2602.*

DUTY-FREE GOODS

Gonsalves Duty-Free Liquor. Wine and liquor is available at discounts of up to 40% at this airport shop. ⊠ *E.T. Joshua International Airport, Departure Lounge, Arnos Vale* ☎ *784/456–4781.*

Voyager. One of the few duty-free shops in St. Vincent, Voyager has a small selection of cameras, electronics, watches, china, and jewelry. ⊠ *R.C. Enterprises Ltd., Halifax and Bay Sts., Kingstown* ☎ *784/456–1686.*

FOOD

C.K. Greaves Supermarket. Whether you're putting together a picnic, stocking your kitchenette, provisioning a yacht, looking for locally made seasoning sauces, or just want some snacks, C.K. Greaves Supermarket is the main supermarket and your best bet. **Sunrise Supermarket,** in Arnos Vale and across the road from the airport, is owned by the same company. Both can be reached by the same phone number, and either store will deliver your order to the dock. ⊠ *Upper Bay St., Kingstown* ☎ *784/457–1074.*

Gourmet Food. This shop specializes in delicious breads and imported cheeses and meats, as well as a full range of deli items and other tidbits. ⊠ *Calliaqua* ☎ *784/456–2987* ⊕ *www.gourmetfoodsvg.com.*

Market Square. Don't miss visiting Market Square, a three-story enclosed building that really bustles on Friday and Saturday mornings, when vendors bring their produce, meats, and fish to market. ⊠ *Bay and Bedford Sts., Kingstown* ☎ *No phone* ⊙ *Closed Sun.*

LOCAL ART AND HANDICRAFTS

★ **Little Art Gallery.** The gallery's owner, Caroline Sardine, is an accomplished artist and the daughter of the owners of Grand View Beach Hotel. Many of her paintings are on display in the hotel; in the Little Art

Gallery, she sells original art (her own and that of others), along with handcrafted items such as pottery, ceramics, coconut toys, handmade dolls, painted calabashes ("bashees"), goatskin drums, and mahogany carvings. The gallery is in the hotel's beachfront restaurant and is open every day but Monday from 2 pm. ⊠ *Grand View Grill, Indian Bay Beach, Indian Bay, Calliaqua* ☎ *784/458–4811.*

Nzimbu Browne. This self-taught craftsman, artist, musician, and drum maker is best known for his original banana art, which he creates from dried banana leaves, carefully selecting and snipping varicolored bits and arranging them on pieces of wood to depict local scenes. Prices range from $15 or $20 for smaller items to several thousands of dollars for larger works sold in galleries. Browne has a kiosk in front of his home, but sometimes sets up shop on Bay Street, near the Cobblestone Inn. ⊠ *McKie's Hill, Kingstown* ☎ *784/457–1677* ⊕ *www.nzimbu-browne.com.*

St. Vincent Craftsmen's Centre. Locally made grass floor mats, place mats, and other straw articles, as well as batik cloth, handmade West Indian dolls, hand-painted calabashes, and framed artwork are all available at this store that's three blocks from the wharf. No credit cards are accepted. ⊠ *Frenches St., Kingstown* ☎ *784/457–2516.*

Wallilabou Craft Centre. Established in 1986, this local cooperative teaches villagers various techniques for weaving straw and other natural fibers. Workers create baskets, handbags, hats, toys, and other items that are sold in the Kingstown market; they make good souvenirs of a visit to St. Vincent. The store is on the leeward coast, about a half-hour's drive north of Kingstown. ⊠ *Leeward Hwy., Wallilabou* ☎ *784/456–0078.*

SPORTS AND ACTIVITIES

BICYCLING

Bicycles can be rented for about $25 per day, but roads aren't conducive to leisurely cycling. Serious cyclists, however, will enjoy mountain biking in wilderness areas.

Sailor's Wilderness Tours. Individuals or groups can head out for half-day, 16-mile bike tours for $50 per person. The price includes 21-speed mountain-bike rental. ⊠ *Middle St., Kingstown* ☎ *784/457–1712, 784/457–9207 after hours* ⊕ *www.sailortours.com.*

BOATING AND FISHING

Fodor's Choice ★ From St. Vincent you can charter a monohull or catamaran (bareboat or complete with captain, crew, and cook) to weave you through the Grenadines for a day or a week of sailing—or for a full-day fishing trip. One of the most spectacular cruising areas in the world, particularly for sailing, the islands of the Grenadines are close enough to allow landfall at a different island nearly every day, yet some are far enough apart to allow for true blue-water sailing. Bequia and Union Island have excellent yacht services and waterfront activity. Mustique is a dream destination, as is Mayreau. Visitors on yachts can dine at the private Palm Island and Petit St. Vincent resorts. Canouan is a prime yacht-chartering locale, and the Tobago Cays are a don't-miss destination for snorkeling and diving.

Boats of all sizes and degrees of luxury are available. Bareboat charter rates in high season start at about $260 and go up to $1,000 or more per day for monohull sailing yachts and $600-plus per day for catamarans; add $130 per day for a captain and $120 per day for a chef. Rates for a crewed luxury sailing yacht begin at about $5,000 per week for two guests and go up to $20,000 or more for boats that accommodate eight guests. Fishing trips cost about $400 for a half day and $600 for a full day.

Barefoot Yacht Charters. Barefoot's fleet of catamarans and monohulls are in the 32- to 50-foot range. ⊠ *Blue Lagoon, Ratho Mill, Calliaqua* ☎ *784/456–9526* ⊕ *www.barefootyachts.com.*

Crystal Blue Sportfishing Charters. These sportfishing charters are on a 34-foot pirogue and are for both casual and serious fishermen. ⊠ *Indian Bay, Calliaqua* ☎ *784/457–4532.*

Sunsail. The bareboat and crewed yachts from Sunsail range from 30 feet to 50 feet. ⊠ *Blue Lagoon, Ratho Mill, Calliaqua* ☎ *784/458–4308* ⊕ *www.sunsail.com.*

TMM Yacht Charters. The fully equipped yachts and catamarans here range from 38 to 51 feet and are either bareboat or crewed. ⊠ *Blue Lagoon, Ratho Mill, Calliaqua* ☎ *784/456–9608* ⊕ *www.sailtmm.com.*

DIVING AND SNORKELING

Fodor's Choice ★ Novices and advanced divers alike will be impressed by the marine life in the waters around St. Vincent—brilliant sponges, huge deepwater coral trees, and shallow reefs teeming with colorful fish. Many sites in the Grenadines are still virtually unexplored. It can't be emphasized enough, however, that the coral reef is extremely fragile; you must only look and never touch.

Most dive shops offer three-hour beginner "resort" courses, full certification courses, and excursions to reefs, walls, and wrecks throughout the Grenadines. A single-tank dive costs about $75; a two-tank, $135; a 10-dive package, $650. A half-day snorkel trip will cost $60. All prices include equipment.

St. Vincent, "the critter capital of the Caribbean," is ringed by one long, almost continuous reef. The best dive spots are in the small bays along the western coast between Kingstown and Layou; many are within 20 yards of shore and only 20 to 30 feet down. **Anchor Reef** has excellent visibility for viewing a deep-black coral garden, schools of squid, sea horses, and maybe a small octopus. **Critter Corner,** just 600 feet off Indian Bay beach, is St. Vincent's hallmark "muck" dive site—a wealth of marine life lurks in and among the sand, silt, sea grass, and boulders. The **Forest**, although a shallow dive, is still dramatic, with soft corals in pastel colors and schools of small fish. **New Guinea Reef** slopes to 90 feet and can't be matched for its quantity of corals and sponges. The pristine waters surrounding the **Tobago Cays,** in the southern Grenadines, will give you a world-class diving or snorkeling experience.

Dive Fantasea. On offer are dive and snorkeling trips along the St. Vincent coast and to the Tobago Cays. ⊠ *Villa Beach, Calliaqua* 🕾 *784/457–4477.*

Dive St. Vincent. The NAUI- and PADI-certified instructor Bill Tewes and his two certified dive masters offer beginner and certification courses for ages eight and up, advanced water excursions along the St. Vincent coast and to the southern Grenadines for diving connoisseurs, and an introductory scuba lesson for novices. ⊠ *Young Island Dock, Villa Beach, Calliaqua* 🕾 *784/457–4714, 784/457–4928* ⊕ *www. divestvincent.com.*

Indigo Dive. The dives here are tailored to match your experience level. ⊠ *St. Vincent Yacht Club, Blue Lagoon, Ratho Mill, Calliaqua* 🕾 *784/493–9494* ⊕ *www.indigodive.com.*

GUIDED TOURS

Several operators on St. Vincent offer sightseeing tours on land or by sea. Per-person prices range from $30 for a two-hour tour to the Botanic Gardens to $150 for a day sail to the Grenadines. A full-day tour around Kingstown and either the leeward or windward coast, including lunch, will cost about $65 per person. You can arrange for informal land tours through taxi drivers, who double as knowledgeable guides. Expect to pay $20 to $25 per hour for up to four people.

Fantasea Tours. A fleet of powerboats here are ready to take groups of snorkelers on a coastal cruise to the Falls of Baleine, to Bequia and Mustique, or to the Tobago Cays. ⊠ *Villa Beach, Calliaqua* 🕾 *784/457– 4477* ⊕ *www.fantaseatours.com.*

Sailor's Wilderness Tours. Options from this company include a comfortable sightseeing drive (by day or by moonlight), mountain biking on remote trails, or a strenuous hike up La Soufrière volcano—and they're usually under the expert guidance of Trevor "Sailor" Bailey himself. ⊠ *Middle St., Kingstown* 🕾 *784/457–1712* ⊕ *www.sailors wildernesstours.com.*

Sam's Taxi Tours. In addition to half- and full-day tours of St. Vincent, Sam's also offers hiking tours to La Soufrière and scenic walks along the Vermont Nature Trails. Also available: a day trip to Mustique and a tour on Bequia that includes snorkeling at Friendship Bay. ⊠ *Sion Hill, Cane Garden, Kingstown* 🕾 *784/456–4338* ⊕ *www.samstaxiandtours.com.*

HIKING

St. Vincent offers hikers and trekkers a choice of experiences: easy, scenic walks near Kingstown; moderately difficult nature trails in the central valleys; and exhilarating climbs through a rain forest to the rim of an active volcano. Bring a hat, long pants, and insect repellent if you plan to hike in the bush.

Fodor'sChoice **La Soufrière.** La Soufrière, the queen of climbs, is St. Vincent's active
★ volcano (it last erupted in 1979). Approachable from either the windward or leeward coast, this is *not* a casual excursion for the inexperienced—the massive mountain covers nearly the entire northern third of the island. Climbs take all day. You'll need stamina and sturdy shoes to reach the top (at just over 4,000 feet) to peek into the mile-wide

(1½-km-wide) crater. Be sure to check the weather before you leave; hikers have been disappointed to find a cloud-obscured view at the summit. You can arrange for a guide ($25 to $30) through your hotel, the SVG Tourism Authority, or tour operators. The eastern approach is most popular. In a four-wheel-drive vehicle you pass through Rabacca Dry River, north of Georgetown, and the Bamboo Forest; then it's a two-hour, 3½-mile (5½-km) hike to the summit. If you're approaching from the west, near Châteaubelair, the climb is longer—6 miles (10 km)—and rougher, but even more scenic. If you hike up one side and down the other, you must arrange in advance to be picked up at the end. ⊠ *Rabacca.*

Vermont Nature Trails. These two hiking trails start near the top of the Buccament Valley, 5 miles (8 km) north of Kingstown. A network of 1½-mile (2½-km) loops passes through bamboo, evergreen forest, and rain forest. In the late afternoon you may be lucky enough to see the rare St. Vincent parrot, *Amazona guildingii.* ⊠ *Buccament Bay.*

THE GRENADINES

The Grenadine Islands are known for great sailing, excellent scuba diving and snorkeling, magnificent beaches, and unlimited chances to relax with a picnic, watch the sailboats, and wait for the sun to set. Each island has a different appeal. Whether you like quiet relaxation, nonstop activity, or socializing (as long as you're not looking for wild nightlife), the Grenadines just might be your thing.

BEQUIA

Bequia (pronounced *beck*-way) is a Carib word meaning "island of the cloud." Hilly and green, with several golden-sand beaches, Bequia is 9 miles (14½ km) south of St. Vincent's southwestern shore; with a population of 5,000, it's the largest of the Grenadines. Although boat-building, whaling, and fishing have been the predominant industries here for generations, sailing has now become almost synonymous with Bequia. Admiralty Bay is a favored anchorage for both privately owned and chartered yachts. Lodgings range from comfortable resorts and villas to cozy West Indian–style inns. Bequia's airport and the frequent ferry service from St. Vincent make this a favorite destination for day-trippers, as well. The ferry docks in Port Elizabeth, a tiny town with waterfront bars, restaurants, and shops where you can buy handmade souvenirs, including the exquisitely detailed model sailboats that are a famous Bequia export. The Easter Regatta is held during the four-day Easter weekend, when revelers gather to watch boat races and celebrate the island's seafaring traditions with food, music, dancing, and competitive games.

EXPLORING BEQUIA

To see the views, villages, beaches, and boatbuilding sites around Bequia, hire a taxi at the jetty in Port Elizabeth. Several usually line up under the almond trees to meet each ferry from St. Vincent. The driver will show you the sights in a couple of hours, point out a place for

24

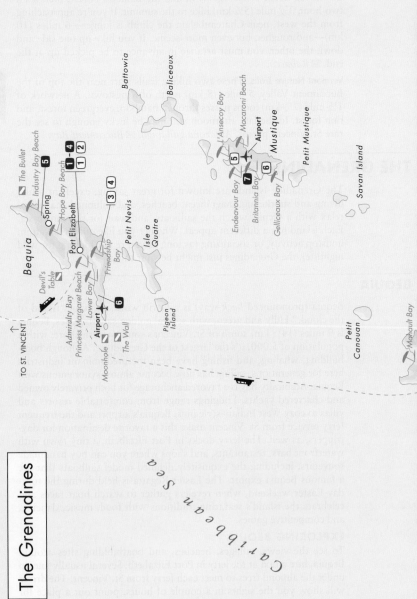

The Grenadines

TO ST. VINCENT →

Bequia

The Bullet

Industry Bay Beach **5**

Hope Bay Beach

Spring

Port Elizabeth   **1 - 4**   **1** **2**

Petit Nevis

Devil's Table

Admiralty Bay

Princess Margaret Beach

Lower Bay

Airport

Moonhole

The Wall   **6**

Friendship Bay

Isle a Quatre

3 **4**

Pigeon Island

Battowia

Baliceaux

L'Ansecoy Bay

Macaroni Beach

Airport

Mustique   **5**   ✈

Endeavour Bay

Britannia Bay   **7**

Gelliceaux Bay   **6**

Petit Mustique

Savan Island

Petit Canouan

Mabauli Bay

Caribbean Sea

24

ATLANTIC OCEAN

Charleston Bay

Godahl Beach

Canouan

Grand Bay

South Glossy Bay Gibralter

Friendship Bay

Airport

North Mayreau Channel

Tobago Cays

Sail Rock

Saltwhistle Bay Beach

Saline Bay Beach

Mayreau

Palm Island

Big Sand

Airport

Clifton

Ashton

Martinique Channel

Chatham Bay

Union Island

Carriacou

Martinique Channel

Petit St. Vincent

TO CARRIACOU

KEY

⚓ Ferry
🏖 Beaches
🤿 Dive Sites
1 Restaurants
1 Hotels

0 — 4 miles
0 — 6 km

Restaurants ▶

Anchorage Yacht Club	8
L'Auberge des Grenadines	4
Basil's Bar	7
Dawn's Creole	5
De Reef	6
Frangipani	1
Gingerbread	2
Lambi's	9
Mac's Pizzeria	3

Hotels ▶

Anchorage Yacht Club	11
Bequia Beachfront Villas	4
Bequia Beach Hotel	3
The Canouan Resort	7
Cotton House	5
Dennis' Hideaway	10
Firefly Mustique	6
Frangipani Hotel	1
Gingerbread Hotel	2
Kings Landing	12
Palm Island Resort	13
Petit St. Vincent Resort	14
Saltwhistle Bay Club	9
Tamarind Beach Hotel & Yacht Club	8

lunch, and drop you (if you wish) at a beach for swimming and snorkeling and pick you up later on. Negotiate the fare in advance, but expect to pay about $25 per hour for the tour. Water taxis are available for transportation between the jetty in Port Elizabeth and the beaches. The cost is $6 (EC$15) per person each way, but keep in mind that most of these operators are not regulated: ride at your own risk.

Admiralty Bay. This huge sheltered bay on the leeward side of Bequia is a favorite anchorage of yachters. Year-round it's filled with boats; in season they're moored cheek by jowl. It's the perfect spot for watching the sun dip over the horizon each evening—either from your boat or from the terrace bar of one of Port Elizabeth's bay-front hotels. ⊠ *Port Elizabeth.*

Hamilton Battery/Ft. Hamilton. Just north of Port Elizabeth, high above Admiralty Bay, is an 18th-century fort that was built to protect the harbor from marauders. Today it's a place to enjoy a magnificent view. ⊠ *Hamilton.*

Mt. Pleasant. Bequia's highest point (at an elevation of 881 feet) is a reasonable goal for a hiking trek. Alternatively, it's a pleasant drive. The reward is a stunning view of the island and the surrounding Grenadines. ⊠ *Mt. Pleasant.*

☾ **Old Hegg Turtle Sanctuary.** In the far northeast of the island, Orton
★ "Brother" King, a retired skin-diving fisherman, tends to more than 200 endangered hawksbill turtles until they can be released back into the sea. He'll be glad to show you around and tell you how his project has increased the turtle population in Bequia. ⊠ *Park Beach, Industry* ☎ *784/458–3245* ⊕ *www.turtles.bequia.net* ✉ *$5 donation requested* ☾ *By appointment only.*

★ **Port Elizabeth.** Bequia's capital, referred to locally as "the harbour," is on the northeastern side of Admiralty Bay. The ferry from St. Vincent docks at the jetty in the center of the tiny town, which is only a few blocks long and a couple of blocks deep. Walk north along Front Street, which faces the water, to the open-air market, where you can buy local fruits and vegetables and some handicrafts; farther along, you can find some of Bequia's famous model-boat shops. Walking south from the jetty, Belmont Walkway meanders along the bay front past shops, cafés, restaurants, bars, and small hotels. ⊠ *Port Elizabeth.*

BEACHES

☾ **Friendship Bay Beach.** This horseshoe-shaped, mile-long (1½-km-long),
Fodor'sChoice protected beach on Bequia's midsouthern coast can be reached by land
★ taxi. Refreshments are available at Bequia Beach Hotel's Bagatelle grill. **Amenities:** food and drink. **Best for:** swimming; snorkeling; walking. ⊠ *Friendship.*

Hope Bay Beach. Getting to this beach facing Bequia's windward side involves a long taxi ride (about $10) and a mile-long (1½-km-long) walk downhill on a semipaved path. Your reward is a magnificent crescent of white sand, total seclusion, and—if you prefer—nude bathing. Be sure to ask your taxi driver to return at a prearranged time. Bring your own lunch and drinks, as there are no facilities. Even though

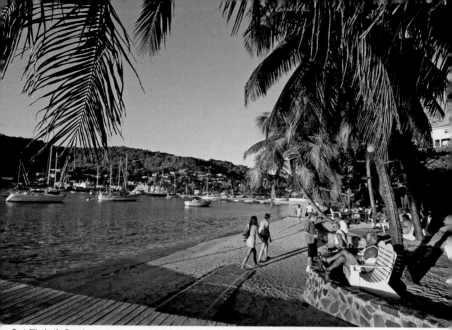

Port Elizabeth, Bequia

the surf is fairly shallow, swimming may be dangerous because of the undertow. **Amenities:** none. **Best for:** solitude; nudists. ✉ *Hope Bay.*

Industry Bay Beach. This nearly secluded beach is fringed with towering palms on the northeastern (windward) side of the island; getting here requires transportation from Port Elizabeth. This beach is good for snorkelers, but there could be a strong undertow. Bring a picnic; the nearest facilities are at Firefly Bequia resort, about a 10- to 15-minute walk. **Amenities:** none. **Best for:** solitude; snorkeling. ✉ *Industry.*

ᑕ **Lower Bay Beach.** This broad, palm-fringed beach south of Port Elizabeth
Fodor's Choice and Princess Margaret Beach is reachable by land or water taxi or a
★ healthy hike from town. It's an excellent beach for swimming and snorkeling. The restaurants here include Mango's Beach Bar and De Reef. **Amenities:** food and drink; toilets; water sports. **Best for:** swimming; snorkeling. ✉ *Lower Bay.*

ᑕ **Princess Margaret Beach.** Quiet and wide, with a natural stone arch at
★ one end, the beach is not far from Port Elizabeth's Belmont Walkway; but you still need a water- or land-taxi ride to get here. When you tire of the water, snoozing under the palm and sea grape trees is always an option. Plan to have lunch at Max's Bar. **Amenities:** food and drink; toilets. **Best for:** swimming; snorkeling; walking. ✉ *between Port Elizabeth and Lower Bay, Port Elizabeth.*

WHERE TO EAT

Dining on Bequia ranges from casual local-style meals to more elaborate cuisine, and both the food and the service are consistently good. Barbecues at Bequia's hotels mean spicy West Indian seafood, chicken, and beef, plus a buffet of side salads, vegetable dishes, and desserts.

$$ ╳**Dawn's Creole Beach Café.** It's worth the trip to Industry for the deli-
CARIBBEAN   cious West Indian food and the view. Lunch options include callaloo
soup, burgers or barbecued chicken wings and fries, lobster sandwich,
and daily specials such as "goat water" (a savory soup with bits of goat
meat and root vegetables), fresh fish, and conch. At dinner (by reserva-
tion only), the five-course creole seafood, lobster, or vegetarian specials
include the christophene (chayote) and breadfruit accompaniments that
Dawn's is known for. Barbecue is always available on request. There's
live music at Sunday brunch; full-moon grill parties feature country
music. ⑤ *Average main: $18* ⊠ *Industry* ☎ *784/458–3400* ⌂ *Reserva-
tions essential.*

$$ ╳**De Reef.** This casual beach bar and restaurant on Lower Bay is the
CARIBBEAN   primary feeding station for long, lazy beach days. When the beach bar
closes at dusk, the restaurant takes over and it starts to fill up with those
who have made reservations. For breakfast (from 7) or a light lunch,
De Reef bakes its own breads, croissants, coconut cake, and cookies—
and blends fresh juices to accompany them. For a full lunch or dinner,
conch, lobster, whelk, and shrimp are treated the West Indian way, and
the curried conch is famous. Every other Saturday in season there's a
seafood buffet dinner accompanied by live music; on Sunday afternoon,
a jam session. ⑤ *Average main: $14* ⊠ *Lower Bay* ☎ *784/458–3958*
⌂ *Reservations essential* ▬ *No credit cards.*

$$$ ╳**Frangipani.** By day, this is perfect for a harborside breakfast or lunch; but
CARIBBEAN   just before sunset the yachting crowd comes ashore to what is arguably
★   the most popular gathering spot in Bequia—the Frangipani Hotel's water-
front bar. After a drink and a chat, the mood turns romantic, with candle-
light and excellent Caribbean cuisine in the open-air dining room. The
à la carte menu emphasizes seafood and local dishes. On Monday night
in high season a local string band plays catchy tunes; on Friday night,
folksingers entertain. The Thursday Frangi barbecue buffet (about $30)
is accompanied by steel-band music and a jump-up. ⑤ *Average main: $25*
⊠ *Frangipani Hotel, Belmont Walkway, Port Elizabeth* ☎ *784/458–3255*
⊕ *www.frangipanibequia.com* ⌂ *Reservations essential.*

$$$ ╳**Gingerbread.** The airy dining veranda at the Gingerbread Hotel offers
CARIBBEAN   all-day dining and a panoramic view of Admiralty Bay and all the
★   waterfront activity. The lunch crowd enjoys barbecued beef kebabs or
chicken with fried potatoes or onions, grilled fish, homemade soups,
salads, and sandwiches. In the evening, steaks, seafood, and curries
are specialties of the house. Save room for warm, fresh gingerbread—
served here with lemon sauce. In season, dinner is often accompanied
by live music. ⑤ *Average main: $22* ⊠ *Gingerbread Hotel, Belmont
Walkway, Port Elizabeth* ☎ *784/458–3800* ⊕ *www.gingerbreadhotel.
com* ⌂ *Reservations essential.*

$$ ╳**L'Auberge des Grenadines.** Owned by the French-born Jacques Thevenot
FRENCH   and his Vincentian wife, Eileen, this fine French restaurant is conve-
★   nient for the yachting crowd, day trippers, and anyone staying awhile.
The extensive menu marries French and West Indian cuisines: seafood
and local vegetables are prepared with a French twist. Lobster is a spe-
cialty; select your own from the lobster pool. Light salads and sand-
wiches are available at lunch. Choose dinner from either the à la carte or

prix-fixe menu. Delicious baguettes and delicate pastries round out any meal. ⑤ *Average main: $22* ✉ *north shore of Admiralty Bay, Hamilton* ☎ *784/458–3555* ⊕ *www.caribrestaurant.com* ⌕ *Reservations essential.*

$$
PIZZA
☾
★

✕ **Mac's Pizzeria.** Overheard at the dock in Mustique: "We're sailing over to Bequia for pizza." The two-hour sunset sail to Admiralty Bay is worth the trip to Mac's, which has been serving brick-oven pizza in Bequia since 1980. Choose from 17 mouthwatering toppings (including lobster), or opt for homemade lasagne, quiche, conch fritters, pita sandwiches, or soups and salads. Mac's home-baked cookies, muffins, and banana bread (by the slice or the loaf) are great for dessert or a snack. Or top off your meal with a scoop or two of Maranne's homemade ice cream in tropical flavors. The outdoor terrace has water views. Takeout is also available. ⑤ *Average main: $16* ✉ *Belmont Walkway, Port Elizabeth* ☎ *784/458–3474* ⌕ *Reservations essential* ◔ *Closed Mon.*

24

WHERE TO STAY

In addition to several small hotels and inns in Port Elizabeth, Friendship Bay, and elsewhere on the island, a number of villas are available for vacation rental in Spring, Friendship Bay, Lower Bay, and other scenic areas of Bequia. They're suitable for two people or as many as a dozen, and the weekly rentals in high season run from as low as $560 a week for a "sweet and simple" villa to $9,000 or more for an elaborate villa with an Italian-style courtyard, gardens, and pool.

For expanded reviews, facilities, and current deals, visit Fodors.com.

RENTAL CONTACT

Grenadine Island Villas ✉ *Belmont Walkway, Port Elizabeth* ☎ *784/457–3739, 784/529–8046 after hours* ⊕ *www.grenadinevillas.com.*

RECOMMENDED HOTELS AND RESORTS

$$
RENTAL
☾

🏨 **Bequia Beachfront Villas.** Perfectly situated on mile-long (1½-km-long) Friendship Bay beach, these self-catering, condo-style suites are an excellent alternative for families and other groups. **Pros:** perfect for small groups; villas are 20 feet from the water; huge accommodations; all the comforts of home. **Cons:** far from town; rent a jeep to get around; steep hill to road might be difficult for those with disabilities. **TripAdvisor:** "great place to getaway," "truly sweet," "idyllic home from home." ⑤ *Rooms from: $311* ✉ *Friendship Bay, Friendship* ☎ *784/457–3423, 800/367–8455 in the U.S.* ⊕ *www.fortrecoverybequia.com* ⬎ *4 villas* ⑩ *No meals.*

$$
HOTEL
☾
Fodor's Choice
★

🏨 **Bequia Beach Hotel.** With an ideal location on pretty Friendship Bay, this sparkling boutique hotel (just finished in 2011) is a great choice for a relaxing beach getaway or family vacation. **Pros:** everything's brand-new; fabulous beach; great for beach lovers and families. **Cons:** lots of steps up to the restaurant and street level from beachfront suites; no TVs except in villas—is that a problem? ⑤ *Rooms from: $275* ✉ *on Friendship Bay, Friendship* ☎ *784/458–1600* ⊕ *www.bequiabeach.com* ⬎ *11 rooms, 26 suites, 6 villas* ⑩ *Breakfast.*

$$$
B&B/INN
★

🏨 **Firefly Plantation Bequia.** This small inn, under the same ownership as Firefly in Mustique, is about 2 miles (3 km) north of Port Elizabeth on a 28-acre sugar plantation that dates back to the late 18th century. **Pros:** secluded location; exquisite contemporary rooms with fabulous views; good restaurant and friendly bar. **Cons:** you'll want to rent a vehicle; negotiating the steep hillside and many steps can be daunting for anyone, and it's not recommended for the elderly or those with disabilities. **TripAdvisor:** "Caribbean paradise," "pure charm," "gorgeous surroundings." ⑤ *Rooms from: $395* ✉ *Spring* 🕾 *784/458–3414* ⊕ *www.fireflybequia.com* ⇆ *8 rooms* ⦿ *Breakfast.*

$
HOTEL
🖾 **Frangipani Hotel.** The venerable Frangipani, once a sea captain's home and also the birthplace of James Mitchell, former prime minister of St. Vincent and the Grenadines, is known for its welcoming waterfront bar and restaurant. **Pros:** great waterfront location; beautiful harbor view from hillside rooms; lively bar and restaurant at night. **Cons:** steep hillside not easy for anyone with disabilities; no air-conditioning in most rooms; "original" rooms—and the cold-watere bath—are basic. **TripAdvisor:** "friendly accommodation," "excellent food," "nice rooms." ⑤ *Rooms from: $75* ✉ *Belmont Walkway, Port Elizabeth* 🕾 *784/458–3255* ⊕ *www.frangipanibequia.com* ⇆ *15 rooms, 10 with bath* ⦿ *No meals.*

$
HOTEL
☾
🖾 **Gingerbread Hotel.** The breezy waterfront suites—each suitable for up to three guests—are large and modern, with bedroom alcoves, adjoining salons, and full kitchens (but no air-conditioning). **Pros:** in the middle of all the action; lovely waterfront suites; good casual restaurant; weekly rates available. **Cons:** you might miss air-conditioning if the breeze isn't brisk; no TV; skip the economy hillside apartments, even though they have a/c. ⑤ *Rooms from: $150* ✉ *Belmont Walkway, Port Elizabeth* 🕾 *784/458–3800* ⊕ *www.gingerbreadhotel.com* ⇆ *7 suites, 3 apartments* ⦿ *No meals.*

SHOPPING

Long renowned for their boatbuilding skills, Bequians have translated that craftsmanship to building model boats. In their workshops in Port Elizabeth you can watch as hair-thin lines are attached to delicate sails or individual strips of wood are glued together for decking. Other Bequian artisans create scrimshaw, carve wood, crochet, or work with fabric—designing or hand-painting it first, then creating clothing and gift items for sale. Bequia's shops are mostly on Front Street and Belmont Walkway, its waterfront extension, just steps from the jetty where the ferry arrives in Port Elizabeth. North of the jetty there's an open-air market; farther along the road, you'll find the model-boat shops. Opposite the jetty, at Bayshore Mall, shops sell ice cream, baked goods, stationery, gifts, and clothing; there's also a grocery, liquor store, pharmacy, travel agent, and bank. On Belmont Walkway, south of the jetty, shops and studios showcase gifts and handmade articles. Shops are open weekdays from 8 to 5, Saturday 8 to noon.

Bequia Bookshop. Head here for Caribbean literature, plus cruising guides and charts, Caribbean flags, beach novels, souvenir maps, and exquisite scrimshaw and whalebone penknives carved by Bequian scrimshander Sam McDowell. ✉ *Belmont Walkway, Port Elizabeth* 🕾 *784/458–3905.*

Claude Victorine. A small roadside sign marks the studio of French artist Claude Victorine. Stop by and admire her delicate, hand-painted, silk wall hangings and scarves—and the watercolors of her daughter,

Louloune. Her studio is open from noon to 7 pm; it's closed Friday. ⊠ *Lower Bay* ☎ *784/458–3150.*

Local Color. This shops stocks an excellent and unusual selection of hand-made jewelry, wood carvings, scrimshaw, and resort clothing. It's above the Porthole restaurant, near the jetty. Note that it's closed in October. ⊠ *Belmont Walkway, Port Elizabeth* ☎ *784/458–3202.*

Fodor's Choice ★ **Mauvin's Model Boat Shop.** At Mauvin's Model Boat Shop you can purchase a Bequia trademark—one of its handmade model boats—or special-order a replica of your own yacht. The models are incredibly detailed and quite expensive—from a few hundred to several thousand dollars. The simplest models take about a week to make. ⊠ *Front St., Port Elizabeth* ☎ *784/458–3669.*

Noah's Arkade. Gifts, souvenirs, and contemporary arts and crafts from all over the Caribbean are available at this hotel shop. ⊠ *Frangipani Hotel, Belmont Walkway, Port Elizabeth* ☎ *784/458–3424.*

Fodor's Choice ★ **Sargeant Brothers Model Boat Shop.** In addition to its handcrafted, expertly rigged, and authentically detailed model boats, Sargeant Brothers also builds custom models on commission. ⊠ *Front St., Port Elizabeth* ☎ *758/458–3344.*

SPORTS AND ACTIVITIES

BOATING AND SAILING

Fodor's Choice ★ With regular trade winds, visibility for 30 miles (48 km), and generally calm seas, Bequia is a big draw for those sailing the Grenadines—which easily rates among the best blue-water sailing anywhere in the world. At Port Elizabeth, you'll find all kinds of options: day sails or weekly charters, bareboat or fully crewed, monohulls or catamarans. Prices for day trips start at about $125 per person.

Friendship Rose. This 80-foot schooner spent its first 25 years ferrying both passengers and mail between Bequia and neighboring islands. In the late 1960s it was refitted, and the *Friendship Rose* now takes passengers on day trips from Bequia to Mustique and the Tobago Cays. ⊠ *Harbour office, Waterfront, Port Elizabeth* ☎☎ *784/457–3888* ☎ *784/457–3739, 784/457–0886* ⊕ *www.friendshiprose.com.*

Nicola IV. Skippered by Nicki Hazell, a native of Bequia, and his Spanish wife Cristina, this 44-foot C&C sailing yacht lets passengers participate. On a day sail to Mustique or a snorkeling trip to the nearby uninhabited island of Isle de Quatre, you can take the helm if you want, or simply sit back and enjoy the view. Longer charters of a week or more are also available. ⊠ *Paget Farm* ☎☎ *784/458–3093* ☎ *784/495–4229 cell* ⊕ *www.bequia.net.*

DIVING AND SNORKELING

About 35 dive sites around Bequia and nearby islands are accessible within 15 minutes by boat. The leeward side of the 7-mile (11-km) reef that fringes Bequia has been designated a marine park. The **Bullet,** off Bequia's northeast point, has limited access because of rough seas, but it's a good spot for spotting rays, barracuda, and the occasional nurse shark. **Devil's Table** is a shallow dive at the northern end of Admiralty Bay that's rich in fish and coral and has a sailboat wreck nearby at 90 feet.

The **Wall** is a 90-foot drop, off West Cay. Expect to pay dive operators $70 for a one-tank and $106 for a two-tank dive, including equipment. Dive boats welcome snorkelers for about $20 per person, but for the best snorkeling in Bequia, take a water taxi to the bay at Moonhole and arrange a pickup time.

Bequia Dive Adventures. This company offers PADI instruction courses and takes small groups on three dives daily; harbor pickup and return is included for customers staying on yachts. ⊠ *Belmont Walkway, Port Elizabeth* ☎ *784/458–3826* ⊕ *www.bequiadiveadventures.com.*

Dive Bequia. Dive and snorkel tours, night dives, and full equipment rental is available from Dive Bequia, and so are resort and certification courses. ⊠ *Gingerbread Hotel, Belmont Walkway, Port Elizabeth* ☎ *784/458–3504* ⊕ *www.bequiadive.com.*

CANOUAN

Halfway down the Grenadines chain, this tiny boot-shape island—3½ miles (5½ km) long and 1¼ miles (2 km) wide—has only about 1,200 residents. But don't let its historically slow pace and quiet ways fool you. Canouan (pronounced *can*-o-wan), which is the Carib word for "turtle," has a modern airport with an extended runway suitable for small to midsize jets. The island boasts one of the region's largest and most exquisite resorts, with a championship golf course and a world-class spa. It also claims four of the most pristine white-sand beaches in the Caribbean, and it's a busy port for yacht charters and diving expeditions to the Tobago Cays. Mt. Royal, the highest point on the island at 900 feet, offers panoramic 360-degree views of St. Vincent, all the Grenadines, and even St. Lucia on a clear day.

BEACHES

Godahl Beach. This lovely stretch of white-sand beach (pronounced *Gud*-ul) is at the southern end of Carenage Bay and surrounded by the Canouan Resort at Carenage Bay property, including the resort's beach bar and restaurant and its spa. To access the beach through the resort, nonguests must purchase a day package at the resort's front office. The pass, which is $130 per person (plus government taxes and service charge), includes round-trip (on-island) transportation to and from the resort, the use of a golf cart to move around the property, the use of beaches and recreational activities (such as water sports and the gym), and a three-course lunch in any of the resort restaurants that are open then. **Amenities:** food and drink; showers; toilets. **Best for:** swimming; walking. ⊠ *Carenage Bay.*

Grand Bay Beach. In the center of Canouan on the leeward coast, Grand Bay is the island's longest beach and the site of Charlestown, the largest town, where ferries dock; it's also called Charlestown Bay beach. **Amenities:** food and drink; toilets. **Best for:** swimming. ⊠ *Charlestown Bay.*

Mahault Bay Beach. This lovely but remote expanse of beach (pronounced *mah*-ho) is at the northern tip of the island, surrounded by Mt. Royal; the beach is accessible through the Canouan Resort at Carenage Bay

Carenage Bay Resort

property or by sea. **Amenities:** none. **Best for:** solitude; swimming. ✉ *Mahault Bay.*

South Glossy Bay Beach. This and other Glossy Bay beaches along the southwest (windward) coast of Canouan are absolutely spectacular. South Glossy Bay is within walking distance of the airport. **Amenities:** none. **Best for:** swimming; walking. ✉ *Glossy Bay.*

WHERE TO STAY

For expanded reviews, facilities, and current deals, visit Fodors.com.

$$$$
RESORT
🖼 **The Canouan Resort at Carenage Bay.** At this full-service beach resort, the roomy villas are sprinkled, amphitheater-style, around 300 acres of the 1,200-acre property. **Pros:** beautiful accommodations; lots of activities for the entire family; and ahh, the spa! **Cons:** very expensive; everything is à la carte (except breakfast). **TripAdvisor:** "excellent service," "paradise does exist," "a diamond in the rough." ⑤ *Rooms from: $950* ✉ *Carenage Bay* ☎ *784/458–8000* ⤴ *30 suites, 13 villas* ⑩ *Multiple meal plans.*

Ⓢ
Fodor's Choice
★

$$
HOTEL
🖼 **Tamarind Beach Hotel & Yacht Club.** Thatched roofs are a trademark of this low-rise beachfront hotel, owned by the same Italian consortium that owns the nearby Canouan Resort at Carenage Bay. **Pros:** good value for Canouan; excellent setting for diving and boating enthusiasts. **Cons:** no pool; standard rooms are small. **TripAdvisor:** "quiet and relaxing," "beautiful location," "courtesy and service." ⑤ *Rooms from: $340* ✉ *Charlestown* ☎ *784/458–8044* ⊕ *www.tamarindbeachhotel. com* ⤴ *32 rooms, 8 suites* ⑩ *Multiple meal plans.*

Ⓢ
★

SPORTS AND ACTIVITIES

Fodor'sChoice **BOATING**
★ The Grenadines have some of the most superb cruising waters in the world. Canouan is at the midpoint of the Grenadines, making for an easy sail north to St. Vincent, Bequia, and Mustique or south to Mayreau, the Tobago Cays, and beyond.

Moorings. Next to the Tamarind Beach Hotel & Yacht Club, Moorings has bareboat and crewed yacht charters of monohulls and catamarans ranging in size from 38 to 52 feet. ⊠ *Tamarind Beach Hotel & Yacht Club, Charlestown* ☎ *784/482–0653* ⊕ *www.moorings.com.*

DIVING AND SNORKELING

The mile-long (1½-km-long) reef and waters surrounding Canouan offer excellent snorkeling as well as spectacular sites for both novice and experienced divers. **Gibraltar,** a giant stone almost 30 feet down, is a popular site; plenty of colorful fish and corals are visible. **Windward Bay,** on Canouan's southeast coast, is a large lagoon protected by a barrier reef, making it perfect for snorkeling. The crystalline waters surrounding the nearby **Tobago Cays** offer marvelous diving and snorkeling.

One-tank dives cost $110 per dive; two-tank dives, $175 per dive; night dives, $130 per dive. A full range of PADI courses are offered; novices can take a Discover Scuba Diving course for $175. Three-hour snorkeling trips to the Tobago Cays cost $110 per person, including equipment.

Canouan Dive Center. Specializing in taking small groups of divers, whether beginners or experts, to the Tobago Cays and other nearby sites, Canouan Dive Center is a full-service PADI facility that also offers resort and certification courses. ⊠ *Tamarind Beach Hotel & Yacht Club, Charlestown* ☎ *784/528–8030* ⊕ *www.canouandivecenter.com.*

GOLF

Grenadines Estate Golf Club, the only 18-hole, championship golf course in St. Vincent and the Grenadines, is also one of the best in the Caribbean.

Fodor'sChoice **The Grenadines Estate Golf Club.** This 18-hole, par-72 championship
★ course is spread over 60 acres. The first 9 holes of the Jim Fazio–designed course, along with holes 10 and 18, are in a pretty, green plain that stretches down to the sea. The rest have been carved into the mountainside, affording spectacular views of Canouan Island, the resort itself, and the surrounding Grenadines. The 13th hole offers a wraparound view of the Grenadines; it's also the most challenging because its unforgiving green is at the edge of a cliff. Greens fees for 18 holes are $220 for resort guests, $300 for nonguests; for 9 holes, $135 (for resort guests only). Greens fees include a golf cart. Golf instruction and rental clubs are available, and a pro shop and lounge are in the resort. ⊠ *The Canouan Resort at Carenage Bay, Carenage Bay* ☎ *784/458–8000.*

MAYREAU

Mayreau (pronounced *my*-row) is minuscule—1½ square miles (4 square km). With the exception of 22 acres at its northern tip that was purchased in 1977 by a German-Canadian family and 21 acres that comprise the island's single (unnamed) village and were acquired by St. Vincent and the Grenadines, Mayreau remains owned by heirs of the original French plantation owners. Only about 250 residents live in the hilltop village, and there are no proper roads. Guests at the resort on Saltwhistle Bay enjoy these natural surroundings in one of the prettiest locations in the Grenadines—one of the few spots where the calm Caribbean is separated from the Atlantic surf by only a narrow strip of beach. It's a favorite stop for boaters as well, who anchor in Saltwhistle Bay and come ashore for lunch or dinner. Except for water sports and hiking, there's not much to do—but everyone prefers it that way. For a day's excursion, you can hike up Mayreau's only hill (wear sturdy shoes) for a stunning view of the Tobago Cays. Then stop for a drink at Dennis' Hideaway and enjoy a swim at Saline Bay beach, where you may be joined by a boatload of cruise-ship passengers. This pretty little island is a favorite stop for small ships that ply the waters of the Grenadines and anchor just offshore for the day. The only access to Mayreau is by boat (ferry, private, or hired), which you can catch or reserve at Union Island.

BEACHES

Saline Bay Beach. This beautiful 1-mile (1½-km) crescent of sand on the southwest coast has no facilities, but you can walk up the hill to Dennis' Hideaway for lunch or drinks. The adjacent dock is where the ferry that travels between St. Vincent and Union Island ties up, and small cruise ships occasionally anchor offshore to give passengers a beach break. **Amenities:** none. **Best for:** swimming. ⌧ *Saline Bay*.

Fodor's Choice ★ **Saltwhistle Bay Beach.** This beach at the northwestern tip of the island takes top honors—it's an exquisite crescent of powdery white sand, shaded by perfectly spaced palms, sea grape trees, and flowering bushes. It's also a popular anchorage for the yachting crowd, who stop for a swim and lunch or dinner at the beachfront Saltwhistle Bay Club. **Amenities:** food and drink; toilets. **Best for:** snorkeling; swimming. ⌧ *Saltwhistle Bay*.

WHERE TO STAY

For expanded reviews, facilities, and current deals, visit Fodors.com.

$
B&B/INN **Dennis' Hideaway.** Each room in this hilltop guesthouse has a private balcony with a perfect view of the sun as it sets over Saline Bay. **Pros:** great value; friendly; good restaurant; good base for boaters and divers. **Cons:** no frills or amenities. **TripAdvisor:** "little gem," "paradise," "cultural perfection." $ *Rooms from: $85* ⌧ *near Saline Bay* ☏ *784/458–8594* ⊕ *www.dennis-hideaway.com* ⇄ *5 rooms* ⊘*❙ Breakfast*.

$$$$
RESORT **Saltwhistle Bay Club.** The little cottages here are so cleverly hidden among the 22 acres of palm and sea grape trees that fringe Saltwhistle Bay that sailors need binoculars to be sure they're there at all. **Pros:** delightfully natural; great anchorage; all-day dining; fabulous beach. **Cons:** extremely remote—especially for landlubbers; cottages need updating. **TripAdvisor:** "amazing location," "superb position," "escape to paradise." $ *Rooms from: $480* ⌧ *on Saltwhistle Bay* ☏ *784/458–8444* ⊕ *www.saltwhistlebay.com* ⇄ *8 units* ⊘ *Closed Sept. and Oct.* ⊘*❙ Some meals*.

SPORTS AND ACTIVITIES

BOATING AND FISHING

Dennis' Hideaway. Yacht charters, drift-fishing trips, dive trips, and day sails can be arranged at Dennis' Hideaway. Expect to pay $40 per person for drift fishing for 1½ hours and $75–$100 per person (depending on the number of passengers) for a full day of sailing, swimming, and snorkeling—lunch included. ⊠ *Near Saline Bay* ☎ *784/458–8594* ⊕ *www.dennis-hideaway.com.*

MUSTIQUE

This upscale haven, 18 miles (29 km) southeast of St. Vincent, is 3 miles (5 km) by 1¼ miles (2 km) at its widest point. The island is hilly and has several green valleys, each with a sparkling white-sand beach facing an aquamarine sea. The permanent population is about 300. Back in the 1960s, Britain's Princess Margaret put this small, private island on the map after owner Colin Tennant (Lord Glenconner) presented her with a 10-acre plot of land as a wedding gift. Tennant had purchased the entire 1,400-acre island in 1958 for $67,500. The Mustique Company—which Tennant formed in 1968 to develop the copra, sea-island cotton, and sugarcane estate into the glamorous hideaway it has become—now manages the privately owned villas, provides housing for all island employees, and operates Mustique Villa Rentals. Arrangements must be made about a year in advance to rent one of the luxury villas that now pepper the northern half of the island.

Sooner or later, stargazers see the resident glitterati at Basil's Bar, the island's social center. Proprietor Basil Charles also runs a boutique crammed with clothes and accessories from Bali. A pair of cotton-candy-color, gingerbread-style buildings, the centerpiece of the tiny village, houses a gift shop and clothing boutique. There's also an antiques shop with fabulous objets d'art and a deli–grocery stocked with Brie and champagne.

The Mustique Blues Festival, held during the first two weeks of February, features artists from North America, Europe, and the Caribbean; shows occur nightly at Basil's Bar. The festival is quite a draw.

BEACHES

Britannia Bay Beach. This beach on the west coast is right next to the Brittania Bay jetty, and Basil's Bar is convenient for lunch. **Amenities:** food and drink; toilets. **Best for:** swimming. ⊠ *Mustique.*

Endeavour Bay Beach. This is the main beach used by guests of the Cotton House. Swimming and snorkeling are ideal, and a dive shop with water-sports equipment rental is available on site. The resort's Beach Café restaurant and bar are convenient for lunch or snacks. **Amenities:** food and drink; toilets; water sports. **Best for:** snorkeling; swimming. ⊠ *Mustique.*

Gelliceaux Bay Beach. This beach on the southwest coast is one of 10 marine conservation areas designated by St. Vincent and the Grenadines. **Amenities:** none. **Best for:** snorkeling. ⊠ *Mustique.*

L'Ansecoy Bay Beach. At the island's very northern tip, this broad crescent of white sand fringes brilliant turquoise water. Just offshore, the French liner *Antilles* went aground in 1971. **Amenities:** none. **Best for:** snorkeling; swimming. ⊠ *Mustique.*

Macaroni Beach. Macaroni is Mustique's most famous stretch of fine white sand—offering swimming (no lifeguards) in moderate surf that's several shades of blue, along with a few palm huts and picnic tables in a shady grove of trees. **Amenities:** parking. **Best for:** swimming. ⊠ *Mustique.*

Fodors Choice ★

WHERE TO EAT

$$$$
SEAFOOD

✕ Basil's Bar. Basil's is *the* place to be—and only partly because it's *the only* place to be in Mustique. It's just a wood deck perched on bamboo stilts over the waves; there's a thatched roof, a congenial bar, and a dance floor that's open to the stars—in every sense. You never know what celebrity may show up at the next table. The food is simple and good—mostly seafood, homemade ice cream, burgers, and salads, great French toast and banana pancakes, the usual cocktails, and unusual wines. Wednesday is Jump Up & Barbecue Night, with live music; Sunday is Locals Night, with a buffet of local dishes. ⑤ *Average main: $34* ⊠ *Britannia Bay* ☏ *784/488–8350* ⊕ *www.basilsmustique.com* ⌂ *Reservations essential.*

WHERE TO STAY

For expanded reviews, facilities, and current deals, visit Fodors.com.

Mustique Villa Rentals. Except for the Cotton House and Firefly hotels, Mustique is an island of villas—74 of them. Rentals must be arranged through Mustique Villa Rentals, even though the villas are privately owned. Villas are all architecturally unique, with two to nine bedrooms. Rentals include a full staff (with a cook), laundry service, and a vehicle or two. Houses range from "rustic" (albeit with en suite bathrooms for every bedroom, phones, pools, and other amenities) to extravagant, expansive mansions with resident butler. All are elegant and immaculately maintained. Weekly rentals run from $5,000 for a two-bedroom villa in the off-season to $55,000 for a palatial seven-bedroom villa in winter. ⊠ *The Mustique Co., Ltd., St. Vincent, St. Vincent and the Grenadines* ☏ *784/458–4621* ⊕ *www.mustique-island.com.*

$$$$
RESORT
Fodors Choice ★

Cotton House. Mustique's grand hotel, the main building of which was once an 18th-century cotton warehouse, has oceanfront rooms and suites with private walkways leading to the beach, a quartet of elegant ocean-view suites, and three poolside cottages. **Pros:** beautiful rooms; great attention to detail; the pillow menu; excellent dining. **Cons:** madly expensive; more sedate than, say, Firefly. **TripAdvisor:** "beautiful setting," "incredible cocoon of tranquility," "perfection as always." ⑤ *Rooms from: $830* ⊠ *Endeavor Bay* ☏ *784/456–4777* ⊕ *www.cottonhouse.net* ⇲ *12 rooms, 5 suites, 3 cottages* ☉ *Closed Sept. and Oct.* ❑ *Multiple meal plans.*

$$$$
ALL-INCLUSIVE ★

Firefly Mustique. Tiny and charming, this three-story aerie is wedged into dense tropical foliage on a steep hillside above Britannia Bay. **Pros:** relaxed and friendly spot; great ocean views from each room; the bar—a hangout for guests and visiting celebrities—features martini

24

Cotton House

and champagne menus. **Cons:** very expensive; house-party atmosphere at the bar can get noisy at night. **TripAdvisor:** "neat upscale inn," "great guest house," "pure magic." $ *Rooms from: $995* ✉ *Britannia Bay* ☎ *784/488–8414* ⊕ *www.mustiquefirefly.com* ⤳ *5 rooms* ⍾ *All-inclusive.*

SPORTS AND ACTIVITIES

Water-sports facilities are available at the Cotton House, and most villas include sports equipment. Four floodlighted tennis courts are near the airport for those whose villa lacks its own; there's a cricket field (matches on Sunday afternoon) and an equestrian center. Motorbikes or "mules" (beach buggies) to ride around the bumpy roads rent for $75 per day.

DIVING AND SNORKELING

Mustique Watersports. Mustique is surrounded by coral reefs, and nearly 20 dive sites are nearby. Mustique Watersports offers PADI instruction and certification and has a 28-foot, fully equipped dive boat. Rates are $110 for an introductory course, $85 for a one-tank dive, and $350 for a five-dive package. A special "bubble maker" introduction-to-diving course for children ages 8–11 costs $40. Snorkelers can rent a mask and fins for $10 per hour or $25 per day; snorkeling trips are $40 per person, with a two-person minimum. ✉ *Cotton House, Endeavour Bay* ☎ *784/456–3486* ⊕ *www.mustique-island.com.*

HORSEBACK RIDING

Mustique Equestrian Centre. Mustique is the only island in the Grenadines where you can find a fine thoroughbred horse or pony to ride. Daily excursions leave from the Mustique Equestrian Centre, which is one block from the airport. Rates are $70 per hour for an island trek; private lessons begin at $60. All rides are accompanied, and children five years or older are allowed to ride. ⊠ *Mustique* 📞 *784/488–8000* ⊕ *www.mustique-island.com.*

PALM ISLAND

A private speck of land (only 135 acres), exquisite Palm Island used to be an uninhabited, mosquito-infested swamp called Prune Island. One intrepid family put heart and soul—as well as muscle and brawn and lots of money—into taking the wrinkles out of the prune and rechristened it Palm Island. The Caldwell family cleaned up the five surrounding beaches, built bungalows, planted palm trees, and irrigated the swamp with seawater to kill the mosquitoes. The rustic getaway existed for 25 years before Palm Island's current owners, Elite Island Resorts, dolled up the property, and now it's one of the finest resorts in the Caribbean. Other than the resort, the island is populated only by a handful of privately owned villas. Access is via Union Island, 1 mile (1½ km) to the west and a 10-minute ride in the resort's launch.

WHERE TO STAY

For expanded reviews, facilities, and current deals, visit Fodors.com.

$$$$
ALL-INCLUSIVE
Fodor's Choice
★

🏨 **Palm Island Resort.** Perfect for a honeymoon, rendezvous, or chic escape, this palm-studded resort offers peace and tranquillity, along with five dazzling white-sand beaches, a calm aquamarine sea for swimming and water sports, nature trails for quiet walks, a pool with waterfall, a 9-hole golf course, sophisticated dining, impeccable service, and exquisite accommodations. **Pros:** private and romantic; fabulous beach; great snorkeling right outside beachfront cottages 15 and 16; free scuba resort course. **Cons:** quiet nights (early to bed and early to rise); fairly isolated; very expensive. **TripAdvisor:** "wonderful trip," "beautiful natural spot," "unwind in paradise." 💲 *Rooms from: $910* ⊠ *Palm Island* 📞 *784/458–8824* ⊕ *www.palmislandcaribbean.com* 🛏️ *33 rooms, 8 suites, 2 villas* 🍽️ *All-inclusive.*

PETIT ST. VINCENT

The southernmost of St. Vincent's Grenadines, tiny (115 acres), private Petit St. Vincent—pronounced "Petty" St. Vincent and affectionately called PSV—is ringed with white-sand beaches and covered with tropical foliage. Hazen Richardson, who passed away in 2008, created the resort in 1968. New owners (as of November 2010) have made extensive renovations (cottage upgrades, a new casual beachside restaurant, an air-conditioned fitness and yoga center, an open-air spa, an air-conditioned library with a TV and Internet access, a new children's center, and landscaping upgrades), with a promise not to change the design and nature of the property. To get to PSV, you fly from Barbados to Union Island, where the resort's motor launch meets you for the 30-minute voyage.

WHERE TO STAY

For expanded reviews, facilities, and current deals, visit Fodors.com.

$$$$
ALL-INCLUSIVE
Fodor'sChoice
★

Petit St. Vincent. No phones, no room TVs, no outside interferences, and no planned activities are particularly appealing when you can indulge your desert-island fantasies without forgoing luxury. **Pros:** beautifully secluded; roomy and comfortable accommodations; excellent cuisine. **Cons:** you're pretty much a captive audience here; some of the beaches are rocky; all this luxury and solitude doesn't come cheap. **TripAdvisor:** "one-of-a-kind place," "stunning in every way," "magical." $ *Rooms from: $1,350* ✉ *Petit St. Vincent* ☎ *784/458–8801, 800/654–9326 in the U.S.* ⊕ *www.psvresort.com* ⇘ *22 cottages* ☉ *Closed Sept. and Oct.* ⦶ *All-inclusive.*

TOBAGO CAYS

Fodor'sChoice
★

Tobago Cays, a small group of five uninhabited islands just east of Mayreau in the southern Grenadines, was declared a wildlife reserve—Tobago Cays Marine Reserve—in 2006 by the St. Vincent and the Grenadines government to preserve the natural beauty and biodiversity of the cays and to allow visitors to experience some of the best snorkeling in the world. The sparkling-clear water is studded with sponges and coral formations and populated by countless colorful fish and turtles. All the major dive operators and sailing and snorkeling day trips go here, sometimes making it a little overcrowded, but the Tobago Cays are everyone's version of a tropical paradise and one unforgettable place.

UNION ISLAND

Union is a popular anchorage for vacationers sailing the Grenadines and a crossroads for others heading to surrounding islands. Clifton, the main town and a port of entry for yachts, is small and commercial, with a bustling harbor, a few simple beachfront inns and restaurants, businesses that cater to yachts, and the regional airstrip—perhaps the busiest in the Grenadines. Hugh Malzac Square, in the center of town, honors the first black man to captain a merchant-marine ship. The ship was the *Booker T. Washington*; the time was 1942. Malzac was from Union Island. Taxis and minibuses are available to get around the island, and water taxis go between islands—including Happy Island, a man-made islet in the harbor where you can get a good stiff rum punch and even some grilled lobster or fish. The Easterval Regatta occurs during the Easter weekend with festivities that include boat races, sports and games, a calypso competition, a beauty pageant, and a cultural show featuring the Big Drum Dance (derived from French and African traditions). Union Island has several small inns and hotels, some directly on the waterfront and others inland.

BEACHES

☉ **Bigsand Beach.** Union has relatively few good beaches, but this one at Richmond Bay on the north shore, a five-minute drive from Clifton, is a pretty crescent of powdery white sand, protected by reefs and with lovely views of Mayreau and the Tobago Cays. **Amenities:** none. **Best for:** solitude; snorkeling; swimming. ✉ *Richmond Bay.*

Continued on page 978

GOLF IN THE CARIBBEAN

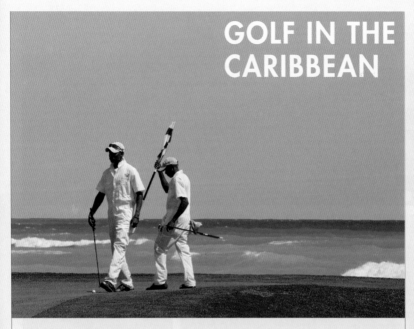

Is there anything better than sinking a 25-foot putt where palm trees sway and turquoise waves meet cerulean sky? Golfers love playing the first-rate Caribbean courses, where stunning views come with comfortable and luxurious resorts. Let the duffers lounge by the pool while you head off for a morning round before the sun gets too hot. You can always meet up on the 19th hole. Mild weather year-round means you can be digging out of a sand trap in the Dominican Republic or Barbados instead of digging out of a snowstorm back home.

With more than three dozen terrific courses from which to choose, golfers of all ages and abilities can find Nirvana, or at least a couple of fun holiday rounds in the Caribbean. The combination of high-end development and advances in lower-maintenance, drought-tolerant turf hybrids has sparked a boom for golf tourism. You will find iconic courses designed by top celebrities like Nicklaus, Player, Norman, Fazio, Dye, and a couple of Joneses. Every course isn't for every player—some are a bit worse for the wear, some are killer-tough, and others are quite costly. Look for golf packages, promotions, all-inclusives, and learning programs that include greens fees and equipment rentals to lessen the bite.

Four Seasons Resort Nevis

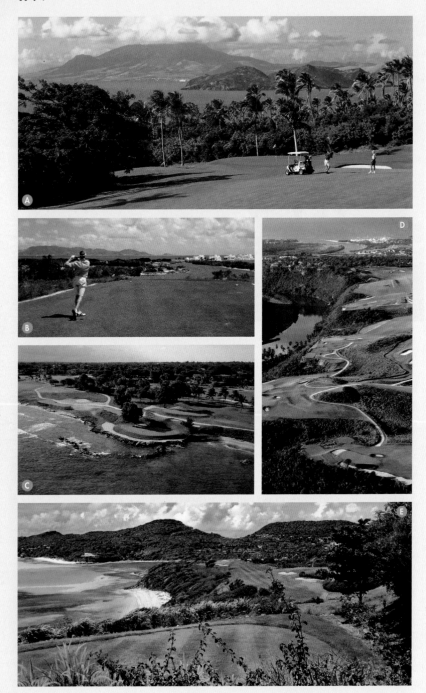

BEST CARIBBEAN GOLF COURSES

(A) Four Seasons Golf Course, Nevis
Majestic scenery, lush landscaping, and a $10 million renovation bring this Robert Trent Jones, Jr. up to par. The wicked layout winds through ravines and sugar mills, and is home to a monkey colony on the back nine, where the land elevates 400 feet to offer views of the 36-square-mile paradise.

(B) Temenos Golf Club, Anguilla
One of the finest golf experiences in the Caribbean has been re-opened and is now managed by Cap Juluca. Anguilla's first and only course, a $50 million creation of golf legend Greg Norman, was first opened in 2006 and offers dramatic elevation changes and water features on 13 holes. In planning the course, significant environmental efforts were undertaken to preserve and to enhance the island's natural habitats, protecting mangroves, salt marshes, dunes and an historic salt pond.

(C) Sandy Lane, Barbados
45 blissful holes on three spectacular courses. There are only 112 guest rooms at this superluxe enclave. The original "Old Nine" winds through the estate gardens, The "Country Club" has five lakes for challenge and pristine fairways, but it's Tom Fazio's famed "Green Monkey" that gets the brag-

ging rights. It's strictly state of the art. The golf carts, included in the green fees of the Country Club and Green Monkey courses, are fitted with a GPS device to show your location on the green. It reveals hazards such as bunkers and provides tips on the best way to play the hole. You can even use it to order light refreshments.

(D) Teeth of the Dog, Casa de Campo, DR
The "teeth" of Teeth of the Dog is a local nickname for the island's jagged-edge coral reefs, visible along the breathtaking beachside holes. *Golf Magazine* calls it the #1 Caribbean Course. Its superstar designer, Pete Dye, calls it a "a masterpiece, with seven holes created by God." Signature Dye challenges and obstacles abound, as do the fans, amateur and pro, of this classic beauty. Pack your camera for this one, at least you will have some shots to show off.

(E) Trump International Golf Club, Grenadines
This was designed by Jim Fazio and has astounding views. Created to be fun for golfers of all levels, the front nine is shorter, flatter and protected from the winds that pick up on the challenging back nine, where the holes get longer, as the course winds its way around

877 ft. high Mount Royal, providing stunning panoramas of the Grenadines and the Blue Caribbean.

Punta Espada Golf Course, Dominican Republic
The first of what will be three Jack Nicklaus—designed courses at the new Cap Cana development in Punta Cana has already hosted one PGA championship event. Stunning bluffs and lush tropical vegetation along three miles of white-sand beach make for a breathtaking par 72 round for golfers at all levels of play. But don't trust us, *Golfweek* named it "Best Course in the Caribbean and Mexico."

Tobago Plantations Golf & Country Club, Trinidad and Tobago
The ocean-side course—the newest on the island—has amazing views, not to mention challenging greens and fairways.

BEST CARIBBEAN TEACHING PROGRAMS

Casa de Campo Resort, Dominican Republic

Let's face it, a shot glass is a far less useful souvenir than a precision chip shot. If you're looking to polish your golf skills along with your tan, there are fine teaching programs offered at some of the premier Caribbean courses.

JAMAICA

Two prime courses in the Montego Bay area provide terrific teaching programs.

The Half Moon Golf Academy (⊕ *www. halfmoongolf.com* ⅄ *from $100/hr. to $150/hr.*)offers a variety of instructional programs individually tailored for beginners through professionals. Individuals or family groups can take hour-long private lessons or multi-lesson introductory clinics focusing on the fundamentals. Seasoned players will enjoy the two-hour lessons to work on club and shot selection as well as course management skills. Head Pro Ewan Peebles, who runs the program, is a PGA player from Scotland with more than 10 years of teaching experience. He is currently Jamaica's top-ranked professional golfer.

At **Kevyn Cunningham's** eponymous **Golf Academy** (⊕ *www.caribbeangolfschool. com* ⅄ *$625 2-day school; $975 3-day school; $175/person for lessons*) at the **Ritz Carlton**, the "classroom" is the famously difficult White Witch course. An effective and popular instructor, he directed the David Leadbetter program in the Caribbean for 10 years before starting his own school. There are one-, two-, and three-day programs focusing on swing mechanics, complete with high-tech computer analysis. Book a full-day private lesson if, perish the thought, you need to shake the yips or the shanks—or just want to spend 8 hours (and $1,500) with a top pro. You'll go home with a complete analysis and a plan for ongoing improvements on a DVD. It's easy to arrange customized programs for families or groups here as well.

THE DOMINICAN REPUBLIC

Casa de Campo is home to the **David Leadbetter Golf Academy** (⊕ *http://davidleadbetter.com* ⅄ *$650 2-day school; $975 3-day school; $225/hr. for lessons*) and its respected teaching curriculum. PGA Pro Tim Vickers, Sr., heads the various workshops, which vary in length and subject matter; but we know more than one golfer who credits his terrific short game (chipping and putting) to a course here. One-, two-, and three-day customized programs include, video analysis, club-fitting, course management, and skills development.

PRACTICAL INFORMATION

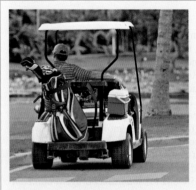

Golf field on the Bavaro area, DR

PACKING

A little forethought will keep you safe and keep expensive resort pro-shop purchases to a minimum. Pack for tropical heat and blazing sun with wicking, breathable golf attire. Seek sun-protective sportswear such as Golfwear with an SPF of up to 50. It blocks more than 90% of the sun's harmful rays. Light colors are cooler, and you will undoubtedly want a brimmed hat and UV-protective sunglasses.

Most clubs maintain strict dress codes. In general: denim, cut-offs, sneakers, gym/running shorts, and tank tops are prohibited. Both men and women are expected to wear soft-spike golf shoes (these can be rented at most courses). Men wear collared shirts with sleeves. Women may wear sleeveless sport shirts (not tank tops) with Bermuda-length shorts, capris, or skirts no shorter than about 5 inches above the knee.

Accessories such as gloves, tees, golf balls, markers, repair tools for greens and the like are available at the pro shops but will prove costly. Don't forget to stash a golf towel or two, insect repellent, and sunscreen. Power bars, Band-aids, and small packets of pain relievers are light to carry and invaluable when you need them.

SHIPPING

Be sure to check with your airline for the latest guidelines, but generally, major carriers allow a passenger to check in one hard-sided golf bag of up to 50 pounds. Heavier than that, and you'll likely incur extra baggage fees. This will be enough for 14 clubs, a dozen balls, a pair of shoes, accessories, and a lightweight stand bag. A soft-sided bag is not advisable; in fact the airline will usually require a damage waiver. Connecting flights can mean lost or delayed luggage, especially on smaller planes. Consider renting equipment at your destination, but keep in mind that new clubs at high-end pro shops can top $60 per round, and older courses may have older equipment.

Golfers (and other sports-enthusiasts too) have good experiences using reliable, if pricy, door-to-door luggage delivery services such as **Golf Bag Shipping** (⊕ *www.golfbagshipping.com*) or **Luggage Forward** (⊕ *www.luggageforward.com*). Prices range from $350 to $500 round trip to Dominican Republic or Barbados. Plan ahead: it takes up to 10 business days. If you are going to Puerto Rico or the U.S. Virgin Islands you can ship by UPS Ground or FedEx for about $200 to $300 each way, depending delivery speed. In any case, include durable identification, insure the delivery, and address it to the hotel concierge, being sure to notify the concierge, also.

Chatham Bay Beach. The desolate but lovely golden-sand beach at Chatham Bay offers good swimming. **Amenities:** none. **Best for:** solitiude; swimming. ⊠ *Chatham Bay.*

WHERE TO EAT

$$$ ✕ **Anchorage Yacht Club.** You can't get much closer to waterfront dining
SEAFOOD than here at the AYC. This is the yachting crowd's favorite stop for
⟳ land-side meals—breakfast, lunch, or dinner. It's also a perfect alternative for guests at Palm Island Resort to get the opposite perspective in terms of the view (and, let's face it, the environment). Freshly baked croissants and other pastries, along with pitchers of fresh-squeezed juice and piping-hot coffee, present the perfect wake-up. At lunch, the sandwiches, salads, burgers, grilled fish, and more are served with a view. And at dinner, the place comes alive with weekend entertainment (more often in season) as you enjoy fresh seafood cooked to order or, perhaps, a lobster prepared to your liking. $ *Average main: $22* ⊠ *waterfront, Clifton* ☎ *784/458–8821* ⊕ *www.anchorage-union.com* ⚓ *Reservations essential.*

WHERE TO STAY

For expanded reviews, facilities, and current deals, visit Fodors.com.

$ ⌂ **Anchorage Yacht Club.** The popular AYC offers convenient, inexpen-
HOTEL sive land-side accommodations to boaters looking for a night or two on dry land, as well as to those beginning or ending a sailing vacation through the Grenadines. **Pros:** two minutes from airport via jitney; convenient for all boating activities, good restaurant; convivial atmosphere **Cons:** rooms are comfortable but definitely not luxurious; entrance into the beach bungalows is through the bathroom. $ *Rooms from: $100* ⊠ *Clifton* ☎ *784/458–8221* ⊕ *www.anchorage-union.com* ⟿ *10 rooms, 1 suite* ⚭ *No meals.*

SPORTS AND ACTIVITIES

BOATING AND SAILING

Union is a major base for yacht charters and sailing trips. At the Union Island airstrip you can arrange a day sail throughout the lower Grenadines: Palm Island, Mayreau, the Tobago Cays, Petit St. Vincent, and Carriacou. A full day of snorkeling, fishing, and swimming costs about $75 per person for a scheduled sail or $750 for up to four passengers on a private charter—lunch and drinks included.

DIVING AND SNORKELING

Grenadines Dive. Glenroy Adams, a Bequia native who claims to know "every dive site in the Grenadines," is the dive master here. The company offers Tobago Cays snorkeling trips and wreck dives at the *Purina,* a sunken World War I English gunboat. Single-tank dives cost $65; multi-tidive packages are discounted. Beginners can take a four-hour resort course, which includes a shallow dive, for $85. Certified divers can rent equipment by the day or week. ⊠ *Kings Landing Hotel, Clifton* ☎ *784/458–8138* ⊕ *www.grenadinesdive.com.*

Trinidad and Tobago

WORD OF MOUTH

"My top [Trinidad] picks are: Mt. Saut D'Eau for great views, day or night....Stay overnight at the Asa Wright Nature Centre for bird watching and a peaceful night's rest.

—superjuliemango

WELCOME TO
TRINIDAD AND TOBAGO

Caribbean Sea

Blanchisseuse Bay

Chupara Pt.

Cyril Bay
Tyrico Bay
Maracas Bay
La Vache Bay

Las Cuevas Bay

Saddle Rd.

El Tucuche

Asa Wrig Nature Cent

Dragon's Mouth

Chaguaramas

[9]

[8]

Tunapuna

Lopin Comp

Port of Spain ★

San Juan

[11]

[1]–[10]
[1]–[7]

Caroni Bird Sanctuary ◆

Piarco Internati Airpo

[10]

Chaguaramas Military History & Aerospace Museum ◆

Chaguanas

Dattareya Yoga Centre ◆

Flanigin Town

California

Couva

Tabaquite

Gulf of Paria

KEY

⛴	*Ferry*
↗	*Beaches*
1	*Restaurants*
[1]	*Hotels*

San Fernando

Princes Town

Ne Gr

Oropuche Lagoon

Irois Bay

La Brea

Penal

Pointe-a-Pierre

0 _____ 10 mi
0 _____ 10 km

Cedros Bay

Point Fortin

Basse Terre

Fullarton

Icacos Pt.

Islote Pt.

Erin Bay

San Francique

Erin Pt.

Moru

The most southerly of the Caribbean islands, Trinidad is also the most colorful. Islanders trace their roots to Africa, India, China, and Madeira, and they speak English, Spanish, Hindi, and French patois. On much quieter Tobago the most exciting event is often the palm trees swaying high above a gentle arc of a beach.

Scarborough

TO TOBAGO

Grande Rivière
Madamas Bay
Matelot
12 · Toco · Sans Souci
Salibea Bay
Galera Pt.
Point Galera Lighthouse
Mt. Oropuche · Redhead
El Cerro del Aripo · Balandra Bay
Matura Main Rd. · Saline Bay
Eastern rima · Valencia
Sangre Grande
Churchill-Roosevelt Hwy. · Matura Bay
Manzanilla Beach
Cocos Bay
Guataro Pt.
leland · Rio Claro · Pierreville
Mayaro Bay
Guayaguayare
Galeota Pt.
Guayaguayare Bay

ATLANTIC OCEAN

BUSINESS AND PLEASURE

The two-island republic is the southernmost link in the Antillean island chain, some 7 miles (11 km) off the coast of Venezuela, but Tobago's Main Ridge and Trinidad's Northern Range are believed to represent the farthest reaches of the Andes Mountains. Trinidad is a large petroleum and natural-gas producer. Tiny Tobago is known more for its quiet atmosphere and gorgeous, wild beaches.

Tobago

Scarborough

25

TRINIDAD AND TOBAGO

Restaurants ▼		Hotels ▼	
Angelo's	5	Asa Wright Nature Centre Lodge	11
Apsara	6	The Carlton Savannah	7
Chaud	9	Coblentz Inn	3
Joseph's	4	Courtyard by Marriott	8
Mélange	8	Crews Inn	9
Prime Restaurant	1	Crowne Plaza	4
Tiki Village	2	Hilton Trinidad	1
Trotters	10	Holiday Inn Express	10
Veni Mangé	3	Hyatt Regency Trinidad	6
The Verandah	7	Kapok Hotel	2
Wings Restaurant	11	Le Grande Almandier	12
		Monique's	5

TOP REASONS TO VISIT TRINIDAD AND TOBAGO

1 Carnival: Trinidad's Carnival is the Caribbean's biggest and best party, but nightlife is hopping the rest of the year, too.

2 Bird-Watching: Both Trinidad and Tobago are major bird-watching destinations; Trinidad itself has more resident species than any other Caribbean island.

3 Culture Sharing: A melding of many cultures means lively festivals year-round and a fabulous mix of cuisines.

4 Music: The steel pan was invented in Trinidad, and excellent bands play all over the island.

TRINIDAD AND TOBAGO BEACHES

Trinidad and Tobago offer two completely different beach experiences. Tobago attracts thousands of international visitors with a choice of white or honey-color beaches. You won't find manicured country-club sand here, but those who enjoy feeling as though they've landed on a desert island will relish the untouched quality of these shores.

(Above) Sarongs for sale on Turtle Beach, Tobago (Bottom right) Manzanilla Beach, Trinidad (Top right) A lifeguard tower at Maracas Bay, Trinidad

Big sister Trinidad has some good beaches for swimming and sunning, particularly on the north coast, though none as picture perfect as those in Tobago. Although popular with some locals, the beaches of the western peninsula (such as Maqueripe) are not particularly attractive, and the water in this area is often polluted by sewage. All beaches on Trinidad are free and open to the public. Many locals are fond of playing loud music wherever they go, and even the most serene beach may suddenly turn into a seaside party.

BAKE AND SHARK

Maracas Bay in Trinidad is famous for its bake and shark (about $5), a deep-fried piece of shark stuffed into fried batter. To this, you can add any of dozens of toppings, such as tamarind sauce and coleslaw. There are dozens of beach huts serving the specialty, as well as stands in the nearby parking lot (Richard's is by far the most popular).

TRINIDAD

Balandra Bay. On the northeast coast, the beige-sand beach—popular with locals on weekends—is sheltered by a rocky outcropping and is a favorite of body-surfers. Much of this beach is suitable for swimming. It can be rather noisy on the weekends. Take the Toco Main Road from the Valencia Road, and turn off at the signs indicating Balandra (just after Salybia). **Amenities:** lifeguards. **Best for:** surfing; swimming. ⊠ *Off Valencia Rd. near Salybia.*

Blanchisseuse Bay. The facilities are non-existent at this narrow, palm-fringed beach, but it's an ideal spot for a romantic picnic. A lagoon and river at the east end of the beach allow you to swim in freshwater, but beware of floating logs in the river, as they sometimes contain mites that can cause a body rash (called *bete rouge* locally). You can haggle with local fishermen to take you out in their boats to explore the coast. This beach is about 14 miles (23 km) after Maracas; just keep driving along the road until you pass the Arima turnoff. The coastal and rain-forest views here are spectacular. **Amenities:** none. **Best for:** swimming; walking. ⊠ *North Coast Rd. just beyond Arima turnoff.*

Grande Riviere. On Trinidad's rugged northeast coast, Grande Riviere is well worth the drive. Swimming is good, and there are several guesthouses nearby for refreshments, but the main attractions

here are turtles. Every year up to 500 giant leatherback turtles come onto the beach to lay their eggs. If you're here at night, run your hand through the black sand to make it glow—a phenomenon caused by plankton. **Amenities:** food and drink. **Best for:** swimming; walking. ⊠ *End of Toco Main Rd.*

Las Cuevas Bay. This narrow, picturesque strip on North Coast Road is named for the series of partially submerged and explorable caves that ring the beach. A food stand offers tasty snacks, and vendors hawk fresh fruit across the road. You can also buy fresh fish and lobster from the fishing depot near the beach. You have to park your car in the small parking lot and walk down a few steps to get to the beach, so be sure to take everything from the car (it will be out of sight once you are on the beach). There are basic changing and toilet facilities. It's less crowded here than at nearby Maracas Bay and seemingly serene, although, as at Maracas, the current can be treacherous. **Amenities:** food and drink; parking; toilets. **Best for:** swimming; walking. ⊠ *North Coast Rd., 7 miles (11 km) east of Maracas Bay.*

Manzanilla Beach. You can find picnic facilities and a pretty view of the Atlantic here, though the water is occasionally muddied by Venezuela's Orinoco River. The Cocal Road running the length of this beautiful beach is lined with stately palms. This is where many well-heeled

25

Beach-goers relaxing on Turtle Beach, Tobago

Trinis have vacation houses. The Nariva River, which enters the sea just south of this beach and the surrounding Nariva Swamp, is home to the manatee and other rare species, including the much-maligned anaconda. To get here take the Mayaro turnoff at the town of Sangre Grande. Manzanilla is where this road first meets the coast. **Amenities:** food and drink; lifeguards. **Best for:** sunrise; walking. ⊠ *Southeast of Sangre Grande.*

Maracas Bay. This stretch of sand has a cove and a fishing village at one end. It's *the* local favorite, so it can get crowded on weekends. Lifeguards will guide you away from strong currents. Parking sites are ample, and there are snack bars selling the famous bake and shark. Take the winding North Coast Road from Maraval (it intersects with Long Circular Road right next to KFC Maraval) over the Northern Range; the beach is about 7 miles (11 km) from Maraval. **Amenities:** food and drink; lifeguards; parking; toilets. **Best for:** partiers; swimming; walking. ⊠ *North Coast Rd.*

Salibea Bay (*Salybia Bay*). This gentle beach has shallows and plenty of shade—perfect for swimming. Snack

vendors abound in the vicinity. Like many of the beaches on the northeast coast, this one is packed with people and music trucks blaring soca and reggae on weekends. It's off the Toco Main Road, just after the town of Matura. **Amenities:** food and drink; parking; toilets. **Best for:** partiers; swimming; walking. ⊠ *Off Toco Main Rd. south of Toco.*

TOBAGO

Bacolet Beach. This dark-sand beach was the setting for the films *Swiss Family Robinson* and *Heaven Knows, Mr. Allison.* If you are not a guest at the Blue Haven Hotel, access is down a track next door to the hotel. The bathroom and changing facilities are for hotel guests only. **Amenities:** food and drink. **Best for:** swimming; walking. ⊠ *Windward Rd., east of Scarborough.*

Englishman's Bay. This mile-long, somewhat wild beach is usually deserted. There are no facilities. **Amenities:** none. **Best for:** solitude; walking. ⊠ *North Side Rd., east of Castara Bay.*

Great Courland Bay. This bay near Ft. Bennett has clear, tranquil waters. Along the sandy beach—one of Tobago's longest—you can find several glitzy hotels. A marina attracts the yachting crowd. **Amenities:** none. **Best for:** swimming; walking. ⊠ *Leeward Rd., northeast of Black Rock, Courland.*

King's Bay. Surrounded by steep green hills, this is the prettiest swimming site off the road from Scarborough to Speyside. The crescent beach is marked by a sign about halfway between the two towns. Just before you reach the bay, there's a bridge with an unmarked turnoff that leads to a parking lot; beyond that, a landscaped path leads to a waterfall with a rocky pool. Locals will likely offer to guide you to the top of the falls; however, you may find the climb not worth the effort. **Amenities:** food and drink; lifeguards; parking; showers. **Best for:** swimming; walking. ⊠ *Delaford.*

Lovers Beach. You have to hire a local to bring you to this isolated retreat of pink sand. Ask one of the fishermen in Charlotteville to arrange a ride for you, but be sure to haggle. It should cost you no more than TT$25 a person roundtrip. **Amenities:** none. **Best for:** solitude; snorkeling. ⊠ *North coast, reachable only by boat from Charlotteville.*

Mt. Irvine Beach. The beach across the street from the Mt. Irvine Bay Hotel has great surfing in July and August, and the snorkeling is excellent, too. It's also ideal for windsurfing in January and April. There are picnic tables surrounded by painted concrete pagodas and a snack bar. **Amenities:** food and drink; showers; toilets. **Best for:** snorkeling; surfing; swimming; windsurfing. ⊠ *Shirvan Rd., Mt. Irvine.*

Parlatuvier. On the north side of the island, the beach is best approached via the road from Roxborough. It's a classic Caribbean crescent, a scene peopled by villagers and fishermen. **Amenities:** none. **Best for:** swimming. ⊠ *Parlatuvier.*

Pigeon Point Beach. This stunning locale is often displayed on Tobago travel brochures. The white-sand beach is lined with swaying coconut trees, and there are changing facilities and food stalls nearby. The beach is public but you must pay admission (about TT$18) to enter the grounds and use the facilities. **Amenities:** food and drink; showers; toilets. **Best for:** partiers; swimming. ⊠ *Pigeon Point.*

Stone Haven Bay. This gorgeous stretch of sand is across the street from the Grafton Beach Resort. **Amenities:** none. **Best for:** swimming. ⊠ *Shirvan Rd., Black Rock.*

Store Bay. The beach, where boats depart for Buccoo Reef, is little more than a small sandy cove between two rocky breakwaters, but the food stands here are amazing: several huts licensed by the tourist board to local ladies who sell roti, *pelau*, and curried crab and dumplings. It's near the airport; just walk around the Crown Point Hotel to the beach entrance. **Amenities:** food and drink; showers; toilets. **Best for:** partiers; swimming. ⊠ *Crown Point.*

Turtle Beach. This beach is named for the leatherback turtles that lay their eggs here at night between February and June. (If you're very quiet, you can watch; the turtles don't seem to mind.) It's 8 miles (13 km) from the airport between Black Rock and Plymouth. **Amenities:** solitude. **Best for:** walking. ⊠ *Southern end of Great Courland Bay between Black Rock and Plymouth.*

Pigeon Point, Tobago

EATING AND DRINKING WELL IN TRINIDAD AND TOBAGO

(Above) Curried crab (Bottom right) Ingredients for a roti (Top right) Creole-style pelau

Food here blends indigenous, British, French, Spanish, African, South American, East Indian, Chinese, and Middle Eastern influences. Referencing the national dish, acclaimed second-generation chef Debra Sardinha-Metivier notes, "We are a callaloo in people form. Maybe you had a Chinese grandmother or Indian grandfather who helped broaden, sophisticate your palate."

Today there's a growing awareness, pun intended, of returning to roots: "Everything comes full circle; organic-farm-to-table sustainability was always a necessity. More people then had a backyard garden . . . and shared. If I had a mango tree, and my neighbor had a coconut, we would barter. . . . Adapting to modern life while creatively meeting the needs of three square meals (including a rushed lunch for workers) began fusion cuisine." It's the fusion (particularly of Indian and Caribbean) that sets Trinidad apart. —Jordan Simon

STREET FOOD

Although much of what you'll find in restaurants and stalls here resembles variations on Caribbean standards, street food, which rules rushed Trini life, stands out. You'll find fresh rotis (akin to wraps) stuffed with curried meat, seafood, or chicken; chicken *geera* (an Indian dish heavily seasoned with cumin); pies—beef, cheese, fish, *aloo* (Hindi for potato); and *pows* (from the Cantonese *pao-tzu*, steamed wrapped buns with savory or sweet filling, typically pork).

CALLALOO

Reflecting the island's pronounced African influence, this hearty stew is the national dish (variants are found throughout the islands). Into the pot go the leaves of the dasheen, which resembles slightly bitter spinach and is also called taro or "callaloo bush," along with okra, chili peppers, coconut milk, *chadon bene* (an herb also known as culantro), garlic, onion, tubers, and sometimes crab. It's often served with macaroni pie (essentially pasta baked with cheese and eggs).

CRAB AND DUMPLING

Tobagonian cuisine mimics Trinidad's, for the most part, but its signature dish is messy, marvelous curried crab with dumpling. The sweet blue crabs and dumplings are simmered in a rich coconut sauce. Tobago is also celebrated for its sumptuously prepared "provisions" (often-starchy vegetables), soups, and stews.

PELAU

Pelau is another mainstay, its roots dating back to 5th-century BC Mesopotamia and brought to Europe by Alexander the Great's army. International variations run from rice pilaf to Spain's paella; Trinidad's version borrows from several cultures. Chicken, beef, pork, or goat is cooked down with rice, pigeon peas, pumpkin, brown sugar, onions, garlic, and often the ubiquitous curry

powder (which Trinis consider a metaphor for the spiciness of their lives).

ROTI

One of the great Indian contributions to Trinidad, this is unleavened flatbread cooked on an iron griddle called a *tawa/tava* and stuffed with a variety of filling fillings. *Sada* roti is the simplest kind, filled with curried lentils, fire-roasted tomato, eggplant, potato, and other vegetables. It's a popular breakfast option, along with *paratha* roti (aka "Buss-Up-Shut"), rubbed with clarified butter to enhance flavor and grilled until crisp, brown, and crumbly, and usually served with fried eggs. The classic roti, *dhalpuri*, is stuffed with ground yellow split peas, garlic, cumin, and pepper; meats are often added.

SWEETS

Guava paste, sticky-sweet but delectable candied tamarind or papaya balls, and Indian snacks like *gulab jamon* (creamy dough fried in sugar syrup scented with cardamom and rosewater) are common. Pone, which is similar to bread pudding, derives its consistency from ground provisions such as cassava (manioc), sweet potato, or pumpkin. Grated cinnamon, nutmeg, raisins, coconut, and sugar are added and baked in a casserole. Tobago chefs often add a pinch of black pepper to provide an edgy counterpoint.

Updated by Vernon O'Reilly-Ramesar

These lush islands lay claim to being the economic power-house of the Caribbean. Vast oil and gas reserves have led to a high standard of living, and tourism is not the mainstay of the economy. Indeed, the word tourist is seldom used here; the preference is for the much friendlier (and perhaps vaguer) visitor. Trinidad's Northern Range is thought to be part of the Andes in South America (it was connected to the mainland as recently as the last Ice Age). This geological history helps explain why the range of flora and fauna is much greater than on other Caribbean islands.

The two islands have very different histories, although both islands' Amerindian populations were virtually wiped out by the arrival of Europeans. After Columbus landed in Trinidad in 1498, the island came under Spanish rule. In an attempt to build the population and provide greater numbers to fend off a potential British conquest, the government at the time encouraged French Catholics from nearby islands to settle in Trinidad. This migration can be seen in the large number of French place-names scattered around the island. Despite this effort, the British conquered the island in 1797.

Tobago had a much more turbulent history. Named after the tobacco that was used by the native Amerindian population, it was settled by the British in 1508. The island was to change hands at least 22 times before eventually returning to Britain in 1814.

The two islands were merged into one crown colony in 1888, with Tobago being made a ward of Trinidad. Independence was achieved in 1962 under the leadership of Dr. Eric Williams, who became the first prime minister. The islands became an independent republic in 1976, with a bicameral Parliament and an appointed president.

Trinidad's capital city, Port of Spain, is home to some 300,000 of the island's 1.3 million inhabitants. Downtown Port of Spain is a bustling commercial center complete with high-rise office buildings and seemingly perpetual traffic. Happily, the northern mountain range rises just behind the city and helps to take much of the edge off the urban clamor.

The majority of Trinidad's population is of either African or East Indian background—the descendants of African slaves and indentured East Indian laborers, who came to work the plantations in the 19th century. The island is always buzzing with a variety of celebrations and arts performances that might include African drumming and classical Indian dance. Although these two groups compose more than 80% of the population, other groups such as the French, Spanish, Chinese, and even Lebanese have left their mark.

Many of the art forms that are considered synonymous with the Caribbean were created on this relatively small island. Calypso was born here, as were soca, limbo, and the steel pan (steel drum). The island can also claim two winners of the Nobel Prize in Literature—V.S. Naipaul (2001), who was born in Trinidad and wrote several of his earlier books about the island, and Derek Walcott (1992), a St. Lucian who moved to Trinidad in 1953. Many tourists make a pilgrimage simply to trace the places mentioned in Naipaul's most famous novel, *A House for Mr. Biswas* (1961), which was partially based on his father's life.

Physically, the island offers an exact parallel to the rain forests of South America, which allows for interesting—and sometimes challenging—adventures. Beach lovers accustomed to the electric blue water and dazzling white sand of coral islands may be disappointed by the beaches on Trinidad. The best beaches are on the north coast, with peach sand, clean blue-green water, and the forest-covered Northern Range as a backdrop. Beaches are almost completely free of hotel development.

Tobago is 23 miles (37 km) northeast of Trinidad. The population here is much less ethnically diverse than that of Trinidad, with the majority being of African descent. Tobagonians have their own dialect and distinct culture. Tourism is much more a part of the island's economy, and you can find excellent resorts and facilities—along with pretty white-sand beaches.

PLANNING

WHEN TO GO

Trinidad is more of a business destination than a magnet for tourists, so hotel rates (particularly in Port of Spain) are fairly stable year-round; nevertheless, you can usually get a price break during the traditional Caribbean low season (from May to December). Carnival (in January, February, or March) brings the highest rates.

Tobago is much more of a tourist destination, but since the island is more popular with Europeans than Americans, its busy periods are sometimes different from those of islands with more of an American presence.

LOGISTICS

Getting to Trinidad and Tobago: You can fly nonstop to Trinidad from several U.S. cities, but there are no nonstop flights to Tobago from the United States; to get to Tobago, you will have to take a short flight from Trinidad on LIAT or Caribbean Airlines. Trinidad's Piarco International Airport (POS), about 30 minutes east of Port of Spain (take Golden Grove Road north to the intersection with the Churchill-Roosevelt Highway and then follow it west for about 10 miles [16 km] to Port of Spain), is a modern facility with 16 air bridges.

Tobago's small Crown Point Airport (TAB) is the gateway to the island.

Hassle Factor: Medium to high.

On the Ground: Few hotels provide airport transfers, but you can always ask when you make your reservations. If you've booked a package, sometimes transfers are included. In Trinidad, taxis are readily available at Piarco Airport; the fare to Port of Spain is set at $50 ($100 after 10 pm). In Tobago the fare from Crown Point Airport to Scarborough or Grafton Beach is about $65.

GETTING HERE AND AROUND

AIR TRAVEL

There are nonstops to Trinidad from Houston (Continental), Miami (American, Caribbean Airlines), New York–JFK (American, Caribbean Airlines), and New York–Newark (Continental). There are no nonstop flights to Tobago from the United States; to get to Tobago, you will have to fly from Trinidad to the A.N.R. Robinson International Airport on Caribbean Airlines or LIAT.

Local Airline Contacts American Airlines ☎ 868/821–6000. **Caribbean Airlines** ☎ 868/625–7200, 868/669–3000. **Continental Airlines** ☎ 800/461–2744. **LIAT** ☎ 868/627–2982, 888/844–5428.

Airports Piarco International Airport. Trinidad's airport is modern, with 14 air bridges. It's about 30 minutes east of Port of Spain (take Golden Grove Road north to the intersection with the Churchill-Roosevelt Highway and then follow it west for about 10 miles [16 km] to Port of Spain). ✉ POS, Trinidad ☎ 868/669–4101 ⊕ www.tntairports.com. **A.N.R. Robinson International Airport** (Crown Point International Airport). ✉ TAB, Tobago ☎ 868/639–0509 ⊕ www.tntairports.com.

FERRY TRAVEL

The seas between Trinidad and Tobago can be very rough, and flights are frequent and only 20 minutes long, so it's better to fly than take a ferry.

Contact Port Authority of Trinidad and Tobago. Trips between Trinidad and Tobago are made on one of the two high-speed CAT ferries and take 2½ hours. The ferries leave twice a day from the jetty at the foot of Independence Square in Port of Spain and three times a day from the cruise-ship complex in Scarborough. The round-trip fare is TT$100. There is also a water-taxi service that travels between Port of Spain and San Fernando in southern Trinidad for TT$15 each way. ☎ ⊕ .

CAR TRAVEL

Don't rent a car if you're staying in Port of Spain, but if you're planning to tour Trinidad, you'll need some wheels, as you will if you end up staying out on the island. In Tobago you're better off renting a four-wheel-drive vehicle than relying on expensive taxi service. On either island, driving is on the left, British style. Be aware that Tobago has very few gas stations—the main ones are in Crown Point and Scarborough. Be cautious driving on either island, because despite the introduction of the breathalyzer, many people still take their chances driving after drinking, and erratic driving is the norm rather than the exception.

Trinidad Car Rentals Auto Rentals ⊠ *Piarco International Airport, Piarco, Trinidad* ☎ *868/669–2277.* **Southern Sales Car Rentals** ⊠ *Piarco International Airport, Piarco, Trinidad* ☎ *868/669–2424, 269 from courtesy phone in airport baggage area.* **Thrifty** ⊠ *Piarco International Airport, Piarco, Trinidad* ☎ *868/669–0602.*

Tobago Car Rentals Baird's Rentals ⊠ *Crown Point Airport, Crown Point, Tobago* ☎ *868/639–7054.* **Rattan's Car Rentals** ⊠ *Crown Point Airport, Crown Point, Tobago* ☎ *868/639–8271.* **Rollock's Car Rentals** ⊠ *Crown Point Airport, Crown Point, Tobago* ☎ *868/639–0328.* **Thrifty** ⊠ *Rex Turtle Beach Hotel, Great Courland Bay, Black Rock, Tobago* ☎ *868/639–8507.*

TAXI TRAVEL

In Trinidad, taxis are readily available at Piarco Airport; the fare to Port of Spain is set at $50 ($100 after 10 pm). In Tobago the fare from Crown Point Airport to Scarborough or Grafton Beach is about $65. Taxis in Trinidad and Tobago are easily identified by their license plates, which begin with the letter *H*. Passenger vans, called Maxi Taxis, pick up and drop off passengers as they travel (like a bus) and are color-coded according to which of the six areas they cover. Rates are generally less than $1 per trip. (Yellow is for Port of Spain, red for eastern Trinidad, green for south Trinidad, and black for Princes Town. Brown operates from San Fernando to the southeast—Erin, Penal, Point Fortin. The only color for Tobago is blue.) They're easy to hail day or night along most of the main roads near Port of Spain. For longer trips you need to hire a private taxi. Cabs aren't metered, and hotel taxis can be expensive.

ESSENTIALS

Banks and Exchange Services At this writing, the exchange rate for the Trinidadian dollar (TT$) is about TT$6.40 to US$1. Most businesses on the islands will accept U.S. currency and credit cards, and ATM cards are almost universally accepted. Cash is necessary only in the smallest neighborhood convenience shops and roadside stalls. There are far fewer bank branches in Tobago than in Trinidad. Trinidad has ATMs in all but the most remote areas. In Tobago there are only a few in Scarborough and at the airport in Crown Point.

Electricity 110 volts/60 cycles (U.S. standard).

Emergency Services Ambulance and Fire ☎ *990.* **Police** ☎ *999.*

Passport Requirements Everyone coming into Trinidad and Tobago must have a valid passport.

Phones The area code for both islands is 868 ("TNT" if you forget). This is also the country code if you're calling to Trinidad and Tobago from another country. From the United States, just dial "1" plus the area code and number. To make a local call to any point in the country simply dial the seven-digit local number. Most hotels and guesthouses will allow you to dial a direct international call. To dial a number in North America or the Caribbean dial "1" and the U.S. or Canadian area code before the number you're calling, but watch out for the hefty surcharge for overseas calls that most hotels add.

Taxes The departure tax is TT$100, but is required by law to be included in the ticket price. All hotels add a 10% government tax. Prices for almost all goods and services include a 15% V.A.T. (value-added tax).

Tipping Almost all hotels will add a 10% to 15% service charge. Most restaurants include a 10% service charge, which is considered standard on these islands. If it isn't on the bill, tip according to service: 10% to 15% is fine. Tip taxi drivers 10%; housekeeping staff $1 to $2 per night.

ACCOMMODATIONS

Trinidad isn't a top tourist destination, so resorts are few and far between, and many are a long drive from Port of Spain and the airport. However, a few eco-conscious options are worth the hassle, particularly if you are a bird-watcher. Tobago has many lodging options, and it's a much smaller island with better beaches, so your choice of resort there is driven more by the amenities you want and your budget than by the resort's location.

Beach Resorts: Tobago has a nice mix of midsize resorts, including several offering a fair degree of luxury, but there are also many choices for budget-oriented tourists, as is the case in Trinidad, where fewer tourists mean better value at the small beach resorts that cater primarily to locals. Few hotels on either island offer anything but room-only rates, though there are now two all-inclusive resorts on Tobago.

Ecoresorts: An especially good option for nature lovers, particularly bird-watchers, is Trinidad's Asa Wright Nature Centre Lodge. Several of Tobago's small resorts are particularly green.

Hotels: Though they have nice pools and other resort-type amenities, Trinidad's hotels are geared more for business travelers. Options for beachgoers are more limited and farther removed from Port of Spain.

HOTEL AND RESTAURANT PRICES

Prices in the restaurant reviews are the average cost of a main course at dinner or, if dinner is not served, at lunch; taxes and service charges are generally included. Prices in the hotel reviews are the lowest cost of a standard double room in high season, excluding taxes, service charges, and meal plans (except at all-inclusives). Prices for rentals are the lowest per-night cost for a one-bedroom unit in high season.

SAFETY

Travelers should exercise caution in Trinidad, especially in the highly populated east–west corridor and downtown Port of Spain, where walking on the streets at night is not recommended unless you're with a group. Trinidad has recorded more than 400 homicides annually for the past few years, but these do not generally involve tourists. As a general rule, Tobago is safer than its larger sister island. There is little visible police presence in most areas of Trinidad. Petty theft occurs on both islands, so don't leave cash or other easy-to-steal valuables in bags that you check at the airport, and use your hotel's safe.

VISITOR INFORMATION

Contacts TDC ⊠ *Maritime Centre, Level 1, 9 10th Ave., Barataria* ☎ *868/638–7962* ⊕ *www.tdc.co.tt* ⊠ *Piarco International Airport, Piarco* ☎ *868/669–5196.* **Tobago Division of Tourism** ⊠ *N.I.B. Mall, Level 3, Wilson St., Scarborough* ☎ *868/639–2125* ⊕ *www.visittobago.gov.tt* ⊠ *A.N.R. Robinson Airport, Crown Point, Tobago* ☎ *868/639–0509.* **Tourism Hotline** ☎ *888/595–4868.* **Trinidad and Tobago Tourism Office** ☎ *800/748–4224* ⊕ *www.gotrinidadandtobago.com.*

WEDDINGS

There is a three-day residency requirement. A passport, airline ticket, and proof of divorce (if you've been married before) are all required, as is a $55 license fee.

Registrar General ⊠ *Jerningham St., Scarborough, Tobago* ☎ *868/639–3210* ⊠ *72–74 South Quay, Port of Spain, Trinidad* ☎ *868/624–1660.*

25

TRINIDAD

EXPLORING TRINIDAD

The intensely urban atmosphere of Port of Spain belies the tropical beauty of the countryside surrounding it. You'll need a car and three to eight hours to see all there is to see. Begin by circling the Queen's Park Savannah to Saddle Road, in the residential district of Maraval. After a few miles the road begins to narrow and curve sharply as it climbs into the Northern Range and its undulating hills of dense foliage. Stop at the lookout on North Coast Road; a camera is a must-have here. You pass a series of lovely beaches, starting with Maracas. From the town of Blanchisseuse there's a winding route to the Asa Wright Nature Centre that takes you through canyons of towering palms, mossy grottoes, and imposing bamboo. In this rain forest keep an eye out for vultures, parakeets, hummingbirds, toucans, and, if you're lucky, maybe red-bellied, yellow-and-blue macaws. Trinidad also has more than 600 native species of butterflies and far more than 1,000 varieties of orchids.

Fodor's Choice ★ **Asa Wright Nature Centre.** Nearly 200 acres here are covered with plants, trees, and multihued flowers, and the surrounding acreage is atwitter with more than 200 species of birds, including the gorgeous blue-crowned motmot and the rare (and protected) nocturnal oilbird. If you stay at the center's inn for two nights or more, take one of the guided hikes (included in your room price if you are staying here) to the oilbirds' breeding grounds in Dunston Cave (reservations for hikes are essential). Those who don't want to hike can relax on the inn's veranda and watch birds swoop about the porch feeders. You are also more than likely to see a variety of other animal species, including agoutis (similar to large guinea pigs) and alarmingly large golden tegu lizards. This

CLOSE UP

East Indians in Trinidad

With the abolition of slavery in the British colonies in 1838, many plantation economies such as Trinidad were left looking for alternative sources of cheap labor. Trinidad tried to draw Europeans, but the heat made them ineffective. Attention finally turned to the Indian subcontinent, and in 1845 the first ship of Indian laborers arrived in Trinidad. These indentured workers came mainly from the poorer parts of Uttar Pradesh. They undertook the three-month journey to the New World with the understanding that after their five-year work stint was over, they could re-indenture themselves or return to India. The system stayed in place until 1917.

The Indians proved effective on the sugarcane and cocoa plantations, helping them return to prosperity. In an effort to discourage the Indians from returning home, the colony eventually offered a land grant as an incentive to stay. Many took up the offer and stayed to make new lives in their adopted homeland. Their descendants still maintain many traditions and, to some extent, language. East Indian culture is a vibrant component of T&T's national culture, and you can find Indian festivals and music sharing center stage at all national events. East Indians compose about half the islands' population.

stunning plantation house looks out onto the lush, untouched Arima Valley. Even if you're not staying over, book ahead for lunch (TT$150), offered Monday through Saturday, or for the noontime Sunday buffet (TT$220). The center is an hour outside Blanchisseuse. ⊠ *Arima Valley* 🕾 *868/667–4655* ⊕ *www.asawright.org* 🖃 *$10* ☉ *Daily 9–5. Guided tours at 10:30 and 1:30.*

☾ **Caroni Bird Sanctuary.** This large swamp with mazelike waterways is bordered by mangrove trees, some plumed with huge termite nests. If you're lucky, you may see lazy caimans idling in the water and large snakes hanging from branches on the banks, taking in the sun. In the middle of the sanctuary are several islets that are home to Trinidad's national bird, the scarlet ibis. Just before sunset the ibis arrive by the thousands, their richly colored feathers brilliant in the gathering dusk, and as more flocks alight, they turn the mangrove foliage a brilliant scarlet. Bring a sweater and insect repellent. The sanctuary's only official tour operator is Winston Nanan *(↪ Bird-watching in Sports and Activities).* ⊠ *½ hr from Port of Spain; take Churchill Roosevelt Hwy. east to Uriah Butler south; turn right and in about 2 mins, after passing Caroni River Bridge, follow sign for sanctuary* 🕾 *868/645–1305* 🖃 *$10* ☉ *Daily dawn–dusk.*

Chaguaramas Military History & Aerospace Museum. Although this museum covers everything from Amerindian history to the Cold War, the emphasis is on the two world wars, and it's a must-see for history buffs. The exhibits, on a former U.S. military base, are in a large hangarlike shed without air-conditioning, so dress appropriately. There's a decidedly charming and homemade feel to the place; in fact, most exhibits were made by the curator and founder, Commander Gaylord Kelshall of

Inside visitor center and lodge at Asa Wright Nature Centre, Trinidad

the T&T Coast Guard. The museum is set a bit off the main road but is easily spotted by the turquoise BWIA L1011 jet parked out front (Trinidad and Tobago's former national airline). ⊠ *Western Main Rd., Chaguaramas* ☎ *868/634–4391* ☜ *TT$20* ⊗ *Mon.–Sat. 9–5.*

🔆 **Dattatreya Yoga Centre.** This impressive temple site was constructed by artisans brought in from India. It is well worth a visit to admire the intricate architectural details of the main temple, learn about Trinidad Hinduism, and marvel at the towering 85-foot statue of the monkey deity, Hanuman. Krishna Ramsaran, the compound manager, is extremely helpful and proud to explain the history of the center and the significance of the various *murtis* (sacred statues). Kids are welcome, so this makes for a pleasant and educational family outing (kids seem especially interested in the giant elephant statues that guard the temple doors). This is a religious site, so appropriate clothing is required (no shorts), and shoes must be left outside the temple door. It's fine to take pictures of the statue and the temple exterior and grounds, but permission is required to take pictures inside, as it's an active place of worship. The temple is half an hour from Port of Spain; take Churchill Roosevelt Highway east to Uriah Butler south; turn right until the Chase Village flyover (overpass); follow the signs south to Waterloo; then follow signs to the temple. ⊠ *Datta Dr. at Orangefield Rd., Carapichaima* ☎ *868/673–5328* ☜ *Free* ⊗ *Daily dawn–dusk, services daily.*

Lopinot Complex. It's said that the ghost of the French count Charles Joseph de Lopinot prowls his former home on stormy nights. Lopinot came to Trinidad in 1800 and chose this magnificent site to plant cocoa. His restored estate house has been turned into a museum—a guide is available from 10 to 6—and a center for *parang,* the Venezuelan-derived folk music. Although worthwhile for those interested in the finer points of Trinidad history, this may not be worth the long and winding drive for most visitors. ⊠ *Take Eastern Main Rd. from Port of Spain to Arouca; look for sign that points north* ☎ *No phone* 💲 *Free* ⊙ *Daily 6–6.*

Point Galera Lighthouse. This essential stop when touring the northeast was constructed in 1897 on a stunning cliff. It's still used to warn ships about the rough waters below, the point where the Atlantic Ocean and Caribbean Sea meet. You can walk out onto a nearby rocky outcropping that marks Trinidad's easternmost point. On most days Tobago is clearly visible from here. A local legend (unprovable) tells that a group of Arawaks jumped off this point to their deaths rather than be captured by the Spanish. You'll pass several beautiful beaches on the drive from Toco to the lighthouse. The journey from Port of Spain takes about two hours; take Churchill Roosevelt Highway east to Valencia Road; follow the road east to Toco Main Road sign; take this road all the way to Toco; from the Toco intersection, follow the sign to Point Galera. ⊠ *Galera Rd., 3 miles (5 km) from triangular Toco intersection* 💲 *Free* ⊙ *Daily dawn–dusk.*

NEED A BREAK?

Kay's Pot. On the long drive to Point Galera, be sure to stop at Kay's Pot for a great meal en route. Many consider it worth the drive all by itself. In a corner of the front parking lot of Arthur's Grocery and Bar, Kay serves an incredible array of local food such as souse (pickled pigs' feet in a lime-and-cucumber sauce), curried crab, and many kinds of grilled and jerk meats. The informal atmosphere, low prices, and music pouring out of the bar make for a fun and unusual dining experience. ⊠ *Toco Main Rd., Rampanalgas* ☎ *No phone.*

Port of Spain. Most organized tours begin at the port. If you're planning to explore on foot, which will take two to four hours, start early in the day; by midday the port area can get very hot and crowded. It's best to end your tour on a bench in the Queen's Park Savannah, sipping a cool coconut water bought from one of the vendors operating out of flatbed trucks. For about 75¢ he'll lop the top off a green coconut with a deft swing of the machete and, when you've finished drinking, lop again, making a bowl and spoon of coconut shell for you to eat the young pulp. Take extra care at night; women should not walk alone. Local police advise tourists and locals to avoid the neighborhoods just east of Port of Spain.

The town's main dock, **King's Wharf,** entertains a steady parade of cruise and cargo ships, a reminder that the city started from this strategic harbor. When hurricanes threaten other islands, it's not unusual to see as many as five large cruise ships taking advantage of the safety of the harbor. It's on Wrightson Road, the main street along the water on the southwest side of town. The previous national government embarked on a massive development plan to turn the area into a vibrant and attractive commercial and tourism zone. Many spanking-new high-rises have already been built, but the current government halted the project because of cost.

Across Wrightson Road and a few minutes' walk from the south side of King's Wharf, the busy **Independence Square** has been the focus of the downtown area's major gentrification. Flanked by government buildings and the familiar twin towers of the Financial Complex (they adorn all T&T dollar bills), the square (really a long rectangle) is a lovely park with trees, flagstone walkways, chess tables, and the Brian Lara Promenade (named after Trinidad's world-famous cricketer). On its south side is the International Waterfront Centre, with its gleaming skyscrapers and fast-ferry dock. On the eastern end of the square is the Cathedral of the Immaculate Conception; it was by the sea when it was built in 1832, but subsequent landfill around the port gave it an inland location. The imposing Roman Catholic structure is made of blue limestone from nearby Laventille.

Frederick Street, Port of Spain's main shopping drag, starting north from the midpoint of Independence Square, is a market street of scents and sounds—perfumed oils sold by sidewalk vendors and CDs (mostly pirated) being played from vending carts.

At Prince and Frederick streets, **Woodford Square** has served as the site of political meetings, speeches, public protests, and occasional violence. It's dominated by the magnificent Red House, a Renaissance-style building that takes up an entire city block. Trinidad's House of Parliament takes its name from a paint job done in anticipation of Queen Victoria's Diamond Jubilee in 1897. The original Red House was burned to the ground in a 1903 riot, and the present structure was built four years later. The building is undergoing a multiyear refurbishment, so the parliament is currently using one of the buildings at the International Waterfront Centre for sittings.

The view of the south side of the square is framed by the Gothic spires of Trinity, the city's Anglican cathedral, consecrated in 1823; its mahogany-beam roof is modeled after that of Westminster Hall in London. On the north are the impressive Public Library, the Hall of Justice, and City Hall.

If the downtown port area is the pulse of Port of Spain, the great green expanse of **Queen's Park Savannah,** roughly bounded by Maraval Road, Queen's Park West, Charlotte Street, and Saddle Road, is the city's soul. You can walk straight north on Frederick Street and get there within 20 minutes. Its 2-mi (3-km) circumference is a popular jogger's track. The northern end of the Savannah is devoted to plants. A rock garden, known as the Hollows, and a fishpond add to the rusticity. In the middle of the Savannah you will find a small graveyard where members of the Peschier family—who originally owned the land—are buried. The Southern end near the National Academy of the Performing Arts turns into a massive food court every evening. Although the perimeter of the Savannah is busy and safe, you should take care when walking across the park, as there have been occasional reports of muggings. The sheer size of the Savannah makes it difficult for local authorities to patrol, so it is best avoided altogether at night.

25

A series of astonishing buildings constructed in several 19th-century styles—known collectively as the **Magnificent Seven**—flanks the western side of the Savannah. Notable are Killarney, patterned (loosely) after Balmoral Castle in Scotland, with an Italian-marble gallery surrounding the ground floor; Whitehall, constructed in the style of a Venetian palace by a cacao-plantation magnate and, until recently, the office of the prime minister; Roomor (named for the Roodal and Morgan families—it's still occupied by the Morgans), a flamboyantly baroque colonial house with a preponderance of towers, pinnacles, and wrought-iron trim that suggests an elaborate French pastry; and the Queen's Royal College, in German Renaissance style, with a prominent tower clock that chimes on the hour. Sadly, several of these fine buildings have fallen into advanced decay.

National Academy for the Performing Arts. Head over to the southeast corner of the Savannah, which is dominated by the shiny National Academy for the Performing Arts. It opened in 2009 in time to host the opening ceremony for the Commonwealth Heads of Government Meeting. The Chinese-built structure looks something like a rounded glass-and-metal version of Sydney's famous opera.

National Museum & Art Gallery. Be sure to walk a few yards farther south to see the National Museum & Art Gallery, especially its Carnival exhibitions, the Amerindian collection and historical re-creations, and the fine 19th-century paintings of Trinidadian artist Cazabon. Tours are free. ⊠ *117 Upper Frederick St., Port of Spain* ☎ *868/623–5941* ⌨ *Free* ☉ *Tues.–Sat. 10–6, Sun. 2–6.*

Emperor Valley Zoo & Botanical Gardens. The cultivated expanse of parkland north of the Savannah is the site of the president's and prime minister's official residences and also the Emperor Valley Zoo & Botanical Gardens A meticulous lattice of walkways and local flora, the parkland was first laid out in 1820 for Governor Ralph Woodford. In the midst of the serene wonderland is the 8-acre zoo, which exhibits mostly birds and animals of the region—including the brilliantly plumed scarlet ibis as well as slithering anacondas and pythons; you can also see (and hear) the wild parrots that breed in the surrounding foliage. The zoo draws a quarter of a million visitors a year. Tours are free. ⊠ *Northern side of Queen's Park Savannah, Port of Spain* ☎ *868/622–3530, 868/622–5343* ⌨ *Zoo TT$20 adults; TT$10 kids under 12, gardens free* ☉ *Daily 9–6* ⊠ *Trinidad.*

WHERE TO EAT

The food on T&T is a delight to the senses and has a distinctively creole touch, though everyone has a different idea about what creole seasoning is (just ask around, and you'll see). Bountiful herbs and spices include bay leaf, chadon bene (aka culantro, and similar in taste to cilantro), nutmeg, turmeric, and different varieties of peppers. The cooking also involves a lot of brown sugar, rum, plantain, and local fish and meat. If there's fresh juice on the menu, be sure to try it. You can taste Asian, Indian, African, French, and Spanish influences, among others, often in a single meal. Indian-inspired food is a favorite: rotis (ample sandwiches

The Steel Pan

25

The sound of a steel pan playing poolside has become emblematic of the Caribbean. What you may not know is that the fascinating instrument has an interesting and humble history that began in Trinidad.

In 1883 the British government banned the playing of drums on the island, fearful that they were being used to carry secret messages. Enterprising Afro-Trinidadians immediately found other means of creating music. Some turned to cut bamboo poles beaten rhythmically on the ground; these were called Tambu Bamboo bands, and they soon became a major musical force on the island. With the coming of industry, new materials such as hubcaps and biscuit tins were added as "instruments" in the bands. These metal additions were collectively known as "pan." Later, after the Americans established military bases on the islands during World War II, empty oil drums became available and were quickly put to musical use.

At some point it was discovered that these drums could be cut down, heated in a fire, and beaten into a

finely tuned instrument. The steel pan as we know it was thus born. Soon there were entire musical bands playing nothing but steel pans. For years the music gestated in the poorer districts of Port of Spain and was seen as being suitable only for the lower classes of society, a reputation not helped by the fact that the loyal followers of early steel bands sometimes clashed violently with their rivals. Eventually, the magical sound of the pan and its amazing ability to adapt to any type of music won it widespread acceptance.

Today the government recognizes the steel pan as the official musical instrument of Trinidad and Tobago. It's played year-round at official functions and social gatherings, but the true time for the steel pan is Carnival. In the annual Panorama festival, dozens of steel bands from around the country compete for the "Band of the Year" title. Some have fewer than a dozen steel pans, whereas others number in the hundreds. The performance of the larger bands creates a thunderous wall of sound.

of soft dough with a filling, similar to a wrap) are served as a fast food; a mélange of curried meat or fish and vegetables frequently makes an appearance, as do vindaloos (spicy meat, vegetable, and seafood dishes). Pelau (rice, peas, and meat stewed in coconut milk), is another local favorite. Crab lovers will find large bluebacks curried, peppered, or in callaloo (Trinidad's national dish), a stew made with green dasheen leaves, okra, and coconut milk. Shark and bake (lightly seasoned, fried shark meat) is the sandwich of choice at the beach.

What to Wear. Restaurants are informal: you won't find any jacket-and-tie requirements. Beachwear, however, is too casual for most places. A nice pair of shorts is appropriate for lunch, and pants or sundresses are probably a better choice for dinner.

$$$$ ✕ **Angelo's.** Calabrian chef Angelo Cofone married a Trinidadian and
ITALIAN soon found himself in the restaurant business. Popular with locals and visiting businesspeople alike, Angelo's has an innovative Italian menu that changes regularly, and there's always a daily special. The restaurant is on Ariapita Avenue, which locals now refer to as the restaurant strip. ⑤ *Average main: $40* ⊠ *38 Ariapita Ave., Woodbrook, Port of Spain* ☎ *868/628–5551.*

$$$$ ✕ **Apsara.** This upscale Indian eatery is one of the few in Trinidad
INDIAN that features genuine Indian cuisine and not the local (though equally tasty) version. The name means "celestial dancer," and the food here is indeed heavenly. The inviting terra-cotta interior is decorated with hand-painted interpretations of Mughal art. Choosing dishes from the comprehensive menu is a bit daunting, so don't be afraid to ask for help. The *Husseini boti kebab* (lamb marinated in poppy seeds and masala) is an excellent choice. Service can be a bit slow at times, and the prices are fairly high. ⑤ *Average main: $45* ⊠ *13 Queen's Park E, Belmont, Port of Spain* ☎ *868/627–7364, 868/623–7659* ⊘ *Closed Sun.*

$$$$ ✕ **Chaud.** Style meets substance at veteran chef Khalid Mohammed's
ECLECTIC restaurant. Set in a restored house opposite the Queen's Park Savannah,
Fodor'sChoice the restaurant offers expansive views of Port of Spain's largest park, and
★ local artwork adorns the walls. Famous for his extravagance, Mohammed presents food that rises off the plate like a Manhattan skyscraper. There is an obsession with freshness here, and satisfaction is virtually guaranteed. Although the prices are high here, it's well worth it for a special romantic evening. ⑤ *Average main: $63* ⊠ *2 Queen's Park W, Port of Spain* ☎ *868/623–0375* ⊕ *www.chaudkm.com* ⚐ *Reservations essential* ⊘ *Closed Sun. No lunch Sat.*

$$$ ✕ **Joseph's.** Lebanese-born chef Joseph Habr has been serving fine cui-
ECLECTIC sine at his Maraval location for over a decade, and has over 20 years
Fodor'sChoice of experience under his belt. The restaurant is a lovely open affair with
★ a dining room that looks out on a lush garden—complete with the sound of flowing water. Joseph visits every table and is always happy to offer helpful advice. The menu is comprehensive, and somehow there seems to be an Arabic element in even seemingly conventional dishes. If in doubt, it's impossible to go wrong with any of the lamb offerings. ⑤ *Average main: $30* ⊠ *3A Rookery Nook; the restaurant is a little out of the way; take Saddle Rd. into Maraval and follow it to RBTT Bank.*

Rookery Nook is on left., Maraval, Port of Spain ☎ 868/622–5557 ⊘ *Closed Sun. No lunch Sat.*

$$$$
ECLECTIC

✕ **Mélange.** Some of the most imaginative food on the island is to be found at this elegant establishment on restaurant row. Chef and owner Moses Ruben uses his years of experience as head chef at the Hilton to create delightfully balanced meals. His imaginative curried-crab-and-dumplings appetizer, which consists of delicately curried crabmeat served on a shell full of miniature dumplings, is exceptional. $ *Average main: $44* ⊠ *40 Ariapita Ave., Woodbrook, Port of Spain* ☎ 868/628–8687 ⊘ *Closed Sun. No lunch Sat. No dinner Mon.*

$$$$
ECLECTIC

✕ **Prime Restaurant.** Occupying the ground floor of the BHP Billiton tower, this upscale establishment caters to businesspeople armed with large expense accounts and demanding tastes. The subtle lighting, understated decor, and attentive staff also make this the ideal spot for a romantic dinner or a special-occasion splurge. Though a variety of options are available, most diners come for the excellent Angus steaks, and not without reason. The wine cellar is one of the best on the island, and a well-chosen vintage may help take some of the edge off the inevitably large bill. The restaurant is behind the Marriott and next door to the Movietowne complex. $ *Average main: $80* ⊠ *Ground fl., BHP Billiton Bldg., Invaders Bay* ☎ 868/624–6238 ⊕ *www.trentrestaurants. com/prime* ⌂ *Reservations essential* ⊘ *Closed Sun.*

$$$$
ASIAN
★

✕ **Tiki Village.** Port of Spainers in the know flock to the eighth floor of the Kapok Hotel, where the views of the city from this teak-lined dining room are simply spectacular, day and night. The solid menu includes the best of Polynesian and Asian fare. The Sunday dim sum—with tasting-size portions of dishes such as pepper squid and tofu-stuffed fish—is very popular. $ *Average main: $37* ⊠ *Kapok Hotel, 16–18 Cotton Hill, St. Clair, Port of Spain* ☎ 868/622–5765 ⌂ *Reservations essential.*

$$
AMERICAN

✕ **Trotters.** Although Trinidad has many American sports-bar chain restaurants, this local version easily beats them at their own game. There is often a lively crowd watching the more than 20 giant screens featuring all the latest in soccer and international sports. The huge square bar in the middle of the restaurant is where folks gather. Dining areas branch off from the bar area, and though some are more isolated than others, it is virtually impossible to escape the cheers of the throng of sports enthusiasts. The food include excellent burgers, hearty salads, and Italian favorites and steaks. The standard is consistently excellent, and the servers, bedecked in pins and wearing safari hats, are efficient and attentive. $ *Average main: $23* ⊠ *Corner of Maraval Rd. and Sweetbriar Rd., St. Clair* ☎ 868/627–8768.

$$$
CARIBBEAN
☕
Fodor's Choice
★

✕ **Veni Mangé.** The best lunches in town are served in this traditional West Indian house. This restaurant is the creation of Rosemary (Roses) Hezekiah and her late sister, Allyson Hennessy—a Cordon Bleu–trained chef who was a local television celebrity. The creative creole menu changes regularly, but there's always an unusual and delicious vegetarian entrée (Roses is vegetarian). Veni's version of Trinidad's national dish, callaloo, is considered one of the best on the island. The *chip chip* (a small local clam) cocktail is deliciously piquant and is a restaurant rarity. The restaurant's signature dish, stewed oxtail with dumplings, is not served every day but is worth ordering if it's available. $ *Average main: $22* ✉ *67A Ariapita Ave., Woodbrook, Port of Spain* ☎ *868/624–4597* ⊕ *www.venimange.com* ۞ *Closed weekends. No dinner Mon., Tues., or Thurs.*

$$$

CARIBBEAN

Fodor'sChoice

★

✕ **The Verandah.** Owner and hostess Phyllis Vieira has been running a restaurant since the 1980s; she prides herself on her "free-style Caribbean" dishes. The open veranda, interior, and courtyard of this beautiful gingerbread-style colonial house provide a suitable setting for the reasonably priced, consistently excellent menu, which changes weekly and is brought to you on a blackboard by the attentive, white-garbed staff. $ *Average main: $30* ✉ *10 Rust St., St. Clair, Port of Spain* ☎ *868/622–6287* ⚐ *Reservations essential* ۞ *Closed Sun. No dinner Mon.–Wed. No lunch Sat.*

$

CARIBBEAN

✕ **Wings Restaurant & Bar.** Rum shops and good food are an intrinsic part of Trinidad life, and both are combined in this colorful eatery, which is open from 10 to 6. Regulars from the nearby university and industrial park flock here at lunchtime to enjoy a wide selection of local Indian food. It can get a bit loud, but at least there are fans to keep the heat under control—just barely. To get here, turn off the Churchill Roosevelt Highway at the FedEx building (north side of the highway) in Tunapuna, and take the first left. $ *Average main: $7* ✉ *16 Mohammed Terr., Tunapuna* ☎ *868/645–6607* ▤ *No credit cards* ۞ *Closed Sun. No dinner.*

WHERE TO STAY

Because Trinidad is primarily a business destination, most accommodations are in or near Port of Spain. Standards are generally good, though not lavish. Port of Spain has a small downtown core—with a main shopping area along Frederick Street—and is surrounded by inner and outer suburbs. The inner areas include Belmont, Woodbrook, Newtown, St. Clair, St. Ann's, St. James, and Cascade. The nearest beach to most hotels is Maracas Bay, which is a half-hour drive over the mountains. Carnival visitors should book many months in advance and be prepared to pay top dollar for even the most modest hotel.

For expanded reviews, facilities, and current deals, visit Fodors.com.

$$$

HOTEL

⛫ **Asa Wright Nature Centre Lodge.** This hotel, designed for serious bird-watchers, is surrounded by 200 acres of wilderness and by streams, waterfalls, and natural pools an hour's drive from the nearest beach or town. **Pros:** best bird-watching on the island; main house has a wonderful colonial feel; peaceful setting. **Cons:** miles from anything else on the island; no dining choices; the lack of entertainment options at night can be unnerving; very expensive. **TripAdvisor:** "paradise for birders," "once-in-a-lifetime experience," "luxury is the view and ambience." $ *Rooms from: $430* ✉ *Arima Valley* ☎ *868/667–4655, 800/426–7781* ⊕ *www.asawright.org* ⇋ *24 rooms* ۞ *All meals.*

$

HOTEL

Fodor'sChoice

★

⛫ **The Carlton Savannah.** Those looking for a boutique hotel without compromising service and quality come to the Carlton, a chic and sleek hotel in the quiet Cascade area has already attracted visiting dignitaries and discerning businessmen. **Pros:** convenient and quiet location; free Wi-Fi;

stylish, modern feeling; excellent restaurants. **Cons:** not within walking distance of shopping. **TripAdvisor:** "great boutique hotel," "excellent service," "especially for Carnival." $ *Rooms from: $169* ✉ *2–4 Coblentz Ave., Cascade* ☎ *868/621–5000* ⊕ *www.thecarltonsavannah. com* ➹ *155 rooms, 10 suites* ¶◎¶ *No meals.*

$ ▦ **Coblentz Inn.** Just a short drive from downtown in the quiet suburb
HOTEL of Cascade, this small boutique hotel offers peace, quiet, and style at a relatively affordable price. **Pros:** rooms have genuine charm; small but attentive staff; common areas are relaxing and great for catching up on reading. **Cons:** restaurant's food can be unreliable; small compound can feel cramped. **TripAdvisor:** "friendly and helpful staff," "charming small place," "unique." $ *Rooms from: $140* ✉ *44 Coblentz Ave., Cascade, Port of Spain* ☎ *868/621–0541* ⊕ *www.coblentzinn.com* ➹ *17 rooms* ¶◎¶ *Breakfast.*

$ ▦ **Courtyard by Marriott.** This large hotel in the capital offers excellent
HOTEL facilities and a great location. **Pros:** excellent location for shopping and
★ dining; large and airy rooms; high service standards. **Cons:** just off busy highway; the many business travelers can make it feel a bit uncomfortable for leisure guests. **TripAdvisor:** "well looked after," "fantastic service," "comfortable and clean." $ *Rooms from: $179* ✉ *Invaders Bay, Audrey Jeffers Hwy., Port of Spain* ☎ *868/627–5555* ⊕ *www.marriott. com* ➹ *116 rooms, 3 suites* ¶◎¶ *No meals.*

$ ▦ **Crews Inn Hotel & Yachting Centre.** On Trinidad's western peninsula, this
HOTEL hotel is in the middle of the island's most popular nightlife area, about 20 minutes from downtown. **Pros:** great view of marina; airy rooms are tastefully decorated; great for yachting enthusiasts. **Cons:** far from Port of Spain; limited shopping and dining nearby. **TripAdvisor:** "relaxing atmosphere," "fabulous scenery," "cozy and relaxing getaway." $ *Rooms from: $224* ✉ *Point Gourde, Chaguaramas* ☎ *868/634–4384* ⊕ *www.crewsinn.com* ➹ *42 rooms, 4 suites* ¶◎¶ *Breakfast.*

$ ▦ **Crowne Plaza Trinidad.** Proximity to the port and Independence Square
HOTEL is both the draw and the drawback here. **Pros:** close to downtown and the business core; revolving restaurant has wonderful views; much cheaper than the Hyatt for a similar downtown location. **Cons:** there's traffic noise by the pool area; hasn't kept pace with the higher standards offered by new hotels on the scene. **TripAdvisor:** "a very interesting and exciting place," "clean," "friendly staff." $ *Rooms from: $159* ✉ *Wrightson Rd., Port of Spain* ☎ *868/625–3361, 800/227–6963* ⊕ *www.ichotelsgroup.com* ➹ *243 rooms, 5 suites* ¶◎¶ *Breakfast.*

$ ▦ **Hilton Trinidad & Conference Centre.** The Hilton was the most upscale
HOTEL hotel on the island before the arrival of the Hyatt Regency, and it still
★ commands a loyal following. **Pros:** great view; newly renovated rooms; full range of hotel services; reliable and consistent service; the thrill of saying you stayed at the hotel where the U.S. president stayed. **Cons:** no longer the best luxury choice on the island; pool area can be very noisy when parties are going on—especially at Carnival time. **TripAdvisor:** "nice renovation," "very nice service," "professional staff." $ *Rooms from: $149* ✉ *Lady Young Rd., Port of Spain* ☎ *868/624–3211, 800/445–8667 in U.S.* ⊕ *www.hiltoncaribbean.com* ➹ *385 rooms, 27 suites* ¶◎¶ *No meals.*

25

Hyatt Regency Trinidad

$ **Holiday Inn Express & Suites Trincity.** Just five minutes from the airport
HOTEL   and with a complimentary shuttle service, this handy hotel is popular
with short-stay travelers. **Pros:** convenient to the airport; close to Trincity Mall. **Cons:** not close to the major urban centers; nearby traffic can
be horrendous; has that bland chain-hotel feeling. **TripAdvisor:** "welcoming staff," "great layover hotel," "not bad." *⑤ Rooms from: $150
⊠ 1 Exposition Dr., Trincity ☎ 868/669–6209 ⊕ www.ichotelsgroup.
com � 62 rooms, 20 suites ⊚ Breakfast.*

$ **Hyatt Regency Trinidad.** Trinidad's only full-service hotel on the water-
HOTEL   front is a striking high-rise structure and part of the government's dra-
Fodor's Choice   matic makeover of the Port of Spain waterfront. **Pros:** easily the most
★   upscale full-service hotel on the island; view from the rooftop pool is
unbeatable; convenient to downtown and shopping. **Cons:** right on the
city's busiest commuter road; waterfront area is usually teeming with
people; the smell of the nearby wharf can be unpleasant. **TripAdvisor:**
"luxury in the sun," "excellent service," "a pleasant stay." *⑤ Rooms
from: $244 ⊠ 1 Wrightson Rd., Port of Spain ☎ 868/623–2222 ⊕ trini-
dad.hyatt.com ⋐ 418 rooms, 10 suites ⊚ No meals.*

$ **Kapok Hotel.** In a good neighborhood just off Queen's Park Savannah,
HOTEL   the Kapok is a good all-around value if you want to stay in the city;
it offers a high level of comfort and service. **Pros:** great location away
from downtown noise; smaller alternative to Hilton and Hyatt; one of
the best restaurants on the island. **Cons:** lacks some of the services of
larger hotels; some rooms are much smaller than others; pool is a bit
small. **TripAdvisor:** "great service," "beautiful small hotel," "comfortable." *⑤ Rooms from: $149 ⊠ 16–18 Cotton Hill, St. Clair, Port of*

Spain ☎ *868/622–5765, 800/344–1212* ⊕ *www.kapokhotel.com* ⤳ *73 rooms, 12 suites, 9 studios* ❍ *No meals.*

$ **⌂ Le Grande Almandier.** This low-priced hotel is on Trinidad's remote and
HOTEL beautiful northeast coast in an area that is a popular weekend escape for
★ locals seeking a lush rain-forest backdrop and expansive beach. **Pros:**
right on the beach; great for turtle-watching in season; small, with a
friendly-family vibe. **Cons:** far from the capital; no bar, and restaurant
serves only wine; limited shopping and dining options; car is definitely
required for any exploring. **TripAdvisor:** "very good local food," "great
getaway," "worth it for the turtles." ⑤ *Rooms from: $136* ✉ *2 Hosang
St., Grande Riviere* ☎ *868/670–1013* ⊕ *www.legrandealmandier.com*
⤳ *10 rooms* ❍ *Breakfast.*

$ **⌂ Monique's.** Spacious but simple rooms and proximity to Port of Spain
B&B/INN ensure the popularity of this guesthouse, which consists of two separate
buildings. **Pros:** huge rooms; in a generally quiet area; family ownership shows in the concern for the comfort of guests; on the main
road to Maracas Beach. **Cons:** room feel dated; no bar; not within
walking distance of shopping or dining. **TripAdvisor:** "needs updating," "great family vacation," "quiet and out of the way." ⑤ *Rooms
from: $90* ✉ *114–116 Saddle Rd., Maraval, Port of Spain* ☎ *868/628–
3334, 868/628–2351* ⊕ *www.moniquestrinidad.com* ⤳ *20 rooms*
❍ *Breakfast.*

NIGHTLIFE AND THE ARTS

NIGHTLIFE

There's no lack of nightlife in Port of Spain, and spontaneity plays a big
role—around Carnival time look for the handwritten signs announcing
the "Panyard," where the next informal gathering of steel-drum bands
is going to be. Gay and lesbian travelers can take advantage of an
increasingly lively gay scene in Trinidad, with parties drawing upward
of 200 people on most weekends. Two of the island's top nightspots
are on a former American army base in Chaguaramas.

★ **51° Lounge.** At this stylish club there's entertainment on most nights,
and Thursday is always packed to the rafters (go after 11 if you want
to avoid the karaoke crowd). Don't even think about showing up in
shorts, as there's a strict "elegant casual" dress code and an age limit
of 25 years and older. Admission is often free, but call ahead to make
sure. ✉ *51 Cipriani Blvd., Woodbrook, Port of Spain* ☎ *868/627–0051.*

Anchorage/Tsunami Beach Club. Good for early-evening cocktails and
snacks. ✉ *Point Gourde Rd., Chaguaramas* ☎ *868/634–4334.*

Coco Lounge. This busy hangout on the popular Ariapita Avenue strip
caters to upscale nightlifers who come to sip cocktails in the elegant,
modern-plantation-style interior or watch the world go by from the huge
veranda. ✉ *35 Carlos St., Woodbrook, Port of Spain* ☎ *868/622–6137.*

Drink! Wine Bar. A large and varied selection of wines makes this cozy
lounge popular with locals and visitors alike. There are snacks on offer
and frequent performances from visiting DJs and musicians. It's a great

place to meet members of the local arts community. ⊠ *63 Rosalino St., Woodbrook, Port of Spain* ☎ *868/622–2895* ⊘ *Closed Mon.*

★ **More Vino.** Young professionals head here to network while sipping one of the more than 100 varieties of wine. Although most people choose to sit outside during the evening, seating is also available in the air-conditioned interior. Inside, you will also find an astonishing number of bottles on display for consumption on the premises or to take away. Cheeses and other items for nibbling are also available. ⊠ *23 O'Connor St., Woodbrook, Port of Spain* ☎ *868/622–8466.*

Pier 1. At Pier 1 you can dance through the night on a large wooden deck jutting into the ocean, with gentle sea breezes to cool you down. It's about 20 minutes west of Port of Spain, so get a party together from your hotel and hire a cab. It opens at 9 pm Wednesday through Sunday, and it keeps going till very late. ⊠ *Western Main Rd., Chaguaramas* ☎ *868/634–4426.*

Trotters. At this sports bar in a two-story atrium are an abundance of TV screens as well as more than 30 varieties of beer from around the globe. It's incredibly popular on weekends—despite the pricey drinks. ⊠ *Maraval and Sweet Briar Rd., St. Clair, Port of Spain* ☎ *868/627–8768.*

Zen. What was once a movie theater now holds a very popular club with a stylish interior and a varied crowd. On the balcony is a VIP area (open to anyone who pays the extra admission charge) where the well-heeled keep track of the action on the dance floor below. The beat goes on until the sun comes up. ⊠ *9–11 Keate St., Port of Spain* ☎ *868/625–9936.*

CARNIVAL

Trinidad always seems to be anticipating, celebrating, or recovering from a festival. Visitors are welcome at these events, which are a great way to explore the island's rich cultural traditions.

Fodor'sChoice
★
Trinidad's version of the pre-Lenten bacchanal may be the oldest in the Western Hemisphere; there are festivities all over the country, but the most lavish are in Port of Spain. Trinidad's Carnival has the warmth and character of a massive family reunion and is billed by locals (not unreasonably) as "The Greatest Show on Earth." The season begins right after Christmas, and the parties, called *fêtes,* don't stop until Ash Wednesday. Listen to a radio station or go online for five minutes, and you can find out where the action is. The Carnival event itself officially lasts only two days, from *J'ouvert* (2 am) on Monday to midnight the following day, Carnival Tuesday. But if you really want to *experience* Carnival, then you need to arrive in Trinidad a week or two early to enjoy the preliminary events. (Hotels fill up quickly, so be sure to make reservations months in advance, and be prepared to pay premium prices for a minimum five-night stay. Even bedrooms in private houses have been known to go for as much as $300 per night.) If you visit during Carnival, try to get tickets to one of the all-inclusive parties where thousands of people eat and drink to the sound of music all night long. And although the festivities are mostly of the adult variety, children can parade in a kiddie carnival that takes place on the Saturday morning the week before the official events.

Carnival is a showcase for performers of calypso, which mixes dance rhythms with social commentary—sung by characters with such evocative names as Shadow, the Mighty Sparrow, and Black Stalin—and soca, which fuses calypso with a driving dance beat. As Carnival approaches, many of these singers perform nightly in calypso tents around the city. Many hotels also have special concerts by popular local musicians. You can also visit the city's "panyards," where steel orchestras such as the Renegades, Desperadoes, Neal and Massy All-Stars, Invaders, and Phase II rehearse their musical arrangements (most can also be heard during the winter season).

From the Sunday before Lent until midnight on Carnival Tuesday, when Port of Spain's exhausted merrymakers finally go to bed, it's basically one big nonstop party. The next day, feet are sore, but spirits have been refreshed. Lent (and theoretical sobriety) takes over for a while.

SHOPPING

25

Good buys in Trinidad include Angostura bitters, Old Oak or Vat 19 rum, and leather goods, all widely available throughout the country. Thanks in large part to the costumes needed for Carnival, there's no shortage of fabric shops. The best bargains for Asian and East Indian silks and cottons can be found in downtown Port of Spain, on Frederick Street and around Independence Square. Recordings of local calypsonians and steel-pan performances as well as *chutney* (local East Indian music) are available throughout the islands and make great gifts. Note that duty-free goods are available only at the airport upon departure or arrival.

AREAS AND MALLS

Downtown Port of Spain, specifically **Frederick, Queen,** and **Henry streets,** is full of fabrics and shoes. **Ellerslie Plaza** is an attractive outdoor mall well worth a browse. **Excellent City Centre** is set in an old-style oasis under the lantern roofs of three of downtown's oldest commercial buildings. Look for cleverly designed keepsakes, trendy cotton clothes, and original artwork. The upstairs food court overlooks bustling Frederick Street. The **Falls at West Mall,** just west of Port of Spain, is a dazzling temple to upscale shopping that could hold its own anywhere in the world. **Long Circular Mall** has upscale boutiques that are great for window-shopping. The **Market at the Normandie Hotel** is a small collection of shops that specialize in indigenous fashions, crafts, jewelry, basketwork, and ceramics. You can also have afternoon tea in the elegant little café.

SPECIALTY ITEMS
CLOTHING

Meiling. This fine designer shop sells classically detailed Caribbean resort clothing. ⊠ *Kapok Hotel, St. Clair Maraval, Port of Spain* ☎ *868/627–6975.*

Radical. T-shirts and original men's and women's casual clothing is what you'll find at Radical. ⊠ *The Falls at West Mall, Western Main Rd., Westmoorings* ☎ *868/632–5800* ⊠ *Long Circular Mall, Long Circular*

Rd., St. James, Port of Spain ☎ 868/628–5693 ✉ *Excellent City Centre, Independence Sq., Port of Spain* ☎ 868/627–6110.

DUTY-FREE GOODS

De Lima's. All the traditional duty-free luxury goods are available from De Lima's. ✉ *Piarco International Airport, Piarco* ☎ 868/669–4738.

Stecher's. The branch at Ellerslie Plaza in Maraval carries only perfumes and cosmetics, but the Stecher's at the airport also carries china, crystal, handcrafted pieces, and jewelry. ✉ *Piarco International Airport, Piarco* ☎ 868/669–4793.

T-Wee Liquor Store. The deals on alcohol here would be hard to find at many other places in the world. ✉ *Piarco International Airport, Piarco* ☎ 868/669–4748.

HANDICRAFTS

★ The tourism office can provide a list of local artisans who sell straw and cane work, miniature steel pans, and other crafts.

Cockey. For painted plates, ceramics, aromatic candles, wind chimes, and carved-wood pieces and instruments, check out Cockey. ✉ *Long Circular Mall, Long Circular Rd., St. James, Port of Spain* ☎ 868/628–6546.

101 Art Gallery. Trinidad's foremost gallery showcases Jackie Hinkson (figurative watercolors), Peter Sheppard (stylized realist local landscapes in acrylic), Sundiata (semi-abstract watercolors), and other local artists. Openings are usually held Tuesday evenings; the gallery is closed Sunday and Monday. ✉ *Art Society of Trinidad and Tobago Bldg., Jamaica Blvd. and St. Vincent Ave., Federation Park, Port of Spain* ☎ 868/628–4081.

Poui Boutique. Stylish handmade batik items, Ajoupa ware (an attractive, local terra-cotta pottery), and many other gift items are availble here. The miniature ceramic houses and local scenes are astoundingly realistic, and are all handcrafted by owners Rory and Bunty O'Connor. ✉ *Ellerslie Plaza, Long Circular Rd., Maraval, Port of Spain* ☎ 868/622–5597.

MUSIC

Just CDs and Accessories. This shop carries a good selection of popular local musicians as well as other music genres. ✉ *Long Circular Mall, Long Circular Rd., St. James, Port of Spain* ☎ 868/622–7516.

Rhyner's. The soca and steel-pan recordings and other local music from this airport store (it's in duty-free) make great last-minute souvenirs. ✉ *Piarco International Airport, Piarco* ☎ 868/669–3064.

SPORTS AND ACTIVITIES

BIRD-WATCHING

★ Trinidad and Tobago are among the top 10 spots in the world in terms of the number of species of birds per square mile—more than 430, many living within pristine rain forests, lowlands and savannas, and fresh- and saltwater swamps. If you're lucky, you might spot the collared trogon, Trinidad piping guan (known locally as the common pawi), or rare white-tailed Sabrewing hummingbird. Restaurants often hang feeders outside on their porches, as much to keep the birds away from your food as to provide a chance to see them. Both the Asa Wright Nature Centre and Caroni Bird Sanctuary (⇨ *Exploring Trinidad*) are major bird-watching destinations.

Point-a-Pierre Wildfowl Trust. This 26-acre haven for rare bird species is within the unlikely confines of a petrochemical complex; you must call in advance for a reservation. ✉ *Petrotrin Complex, Point-a-Pierre* ☎ *868/658–4200.*

Winston Nanan. Nanan, a self-taught ornithologist, knows the local fauna as well as his own children. He will arrange personal tours in his own car anywhere on the island. His business is based at the Caroni Bird Sanctuary, but his expertise makes a trip with him to the Northern Range or the northeast a must for just about any true bird-watcher. It won't be cheap (figure on $400–$500 a day), but the personal attention and his willingness to try to find rare species are well worth the expense. ✉ *Trinidad* ☎ *868/645–1305.*

FISHING

The islands off the northwest coast of Trinidad have excellent waters for deep-sea fishing; you may find wahoo, kingfish, and marlin, to name a few. The ocean here was a favorite angling spot of Franklin D. Roosevelt.

Bayshore Charters. Through Bayshore Charters you can fish for an afternoon or hire a boat for a weekend; the *Melissa Ann* is fully equipped for comfortable cruising, sleeps six, and has an air-conditioned cabin, a refrigerator, cooking facilities, and fishing equipment. Captain Sa Gomes is one of the most experienced charter captains on the islands. ✉ *29 Sunset Dr., Bayshore, Westmoorings* ☎ *868/637–8711.*

Trinidad & Tobago Yacht Club. Members of the Trinidad & Tobago Yacht Club may be willing to arrange a fishing trip for you. ✉ *Western Main Rd., Bayshore, Westmoorings* ☎ *868/637–4260.*

GOLF

St. Andrew's Golf Club. The best course in Trinidad is just outside Port of Spain. Greens fees are approximately $40 for 9 holes, $75 for 18 holes. The most convenient tee times are available on weekdays. Golf shoes with soft spikes are required. ✉ *Moka, Saddle Rd., Maraval, Port of Spain* ☎ *868/629–0066.*

GUIDED TOURS

Although any taxi driver in Trinidad or Tobago can take visitors to the major attractions, using a tour company often makes for a more leisurely and educational adventure. Tour operators are also more mindful of the sensitivities of tourists and are much less likely to subject passengers to breakneck speeds and "creative" driving.

★ **Banwari Experience.** Andrew Welch and his knowledgable staff have numerous, customizable tour packages to serve your needs in T&T. They specialize in cultural experiences that immerse you in island customs, history, nature, and most of all food. A number of their tours reveal the best-kept secrets in Trinidad's dining scene. Mr. Welch has friends all over the island, and these friends are some of Trinidad's best chefs, artists, and adventurers. Individual and group tours as well as family packages are available, all at reasonable rates. ✉ *Bourg Mala-tresse, Santa Cruz* ☎ *868/675–1619, 868/624–8687* ⊕ *www.banwari. com.*

Caribbean Discovery Tours Ltd. Stephen Broadbridge's tours are completely personalized and can include both on- and offshore activities. Tours can range from the strenuous to the leisurely, with prices based on the duration of the expedition and the number of participants. ✉ *9B Fondes Amandes, St. Ann's, Port of Spain* ☎ *868/624–7281, 868/620–1989* ⊕ *www.caribbeandiscoverytours.com.*

Kalloo's. Tours from Kalloo's include a fascinating three-hour tour of Port of Spain as well as an overnight one devoted to turtle-watching. ✉ *Piarco International Airport, Piarco* ☎ *868/669–5673, 868/622–9073* ⊕ *www.kalloos.com.*

Sensational Tours & Transport. Coming highly recommended, this company is probably your best choice for island tours. Owner Gerard Nicholas worked for the tourist board for many years and knows the island intimately. Tour prices are reasonable, too. ✉ *47 Reservoir Rd., La Pastora, Santa Cruz* ☎ *868/702–4129, 868/315–3652.*

TOBAGO

EXPLORING TOBAGO

A driving tour of Tobago, from Scarborough to Charlotteville and back, can be done in about four hours, but you'd never want to undertake this spectacular, and very hilly, ride in that time. The switchbacks can induce nausea as well as awe, so it's a good idea to take some motion-sickness pills along with you. Plan to spend at least one night at the Speyside end of the island, and give yourself a chance to enjoy this largely untouched country and seaside at leisure.

Charlotteville. This delightful fishing village in the northeast is within a series of steep hills. Fishermen here announce the day's catch by sounding their conch shells. A view of Man O' War Bay with Pigeon Peak (Tobago's highest mountain) behind it at sunset is an amazing sight. ✉ *Tobago.*

Flagstaff Hill. One of the highest points on the island sits at the northern tip of Tobago. Surrounded by ocean on three sides and with a view of other hills, Charlotteville, and St. Giles Island, this was the site of an American military lookout and radio tower during World War II. It's an ideal spot for a sunset picnic. The turnoff to the hill is at the major bend on the road from Speyside to Charlotteville. It's largely unpaved, so the going may be a bit rough. ✉ *Tobago.*

Ft. King George. On Mt. St. George, a short drive up the hill from Scarborough, Tobago's best-preserved historic monument clings to a cliff high above the ocean. Ft. King George was built in the 1770s and operated until 1854. It's hard to imagine that this lovely, tranquil spot commanding sweeping views of the bay and landscaped with lush tropical foliage was ever the site of any military action, but the prison, officers'

A cannon at Ft. King George, Tobago

mess, and several stabilized cannons attest otherwise. Just to the left of the tall wooden figures dancing a traditional Tobagonian jig is the former barrack guardhouse, now housing the small **Tobago Museum.** Exhibits include weapons and other pre-Columbian artifacts found in the area; the fertility figures are especially interesting. Upstairs are maps and photographs of Tobago's past. Be sure to check out the gift display cases for the perversely fascinating jewelry made from embalmed and painted lizards and sea creatures; you might find it hard to resist a pair of bright-yellow shrimp earrings. The **Fine Arts Centre** at the foot of the Ft. King George complex shows the work of local artists. ⊠ *84 Fort St., Scarborough* ☎ *868/639–3970* ✉ *Fort free, museum TT$5* ☽ *Weekdays 9–5.*

★ **Kimme Sculpture Museum.** The diminutive and eccentric German-born sculptress Luise Kimme fell in love with the form of Tobagonians and has devoted her life to capturing them in her sculptures. Her pieces can exceed 12 feet in height and are often wonderfully whimsical. Much of her work is done in wood (none of it local), but there are many bronze pieces as well. The museum itself is a turreted structure with a commanding view of the countryside. Most locals refer to it as "The Castle." There are numerous signs in Mt. Irvine directing visitors to the museum. ⊠ *Mt. Irvine* ☎ *868/639–0257* ⊕ *www.luisekimme.com* ✉ *TT$20* ☽ *Sun. 10–2 or by appointment.*

Scarborough. Around Rockley Bay on the island's leeward hilly side, this town is both the capital of Tobago and a popular cruise-ship port, but it feels as if not much has changed since the area was settled two centuries ago. It may not be one of the delightful pastel-color cities of the Caribbean, but Scarborough does have its charms, including several interesting little shops. Whatever you do, be sure to check out the busy Scarborough Market, an indoor and outdoor affair with fresh vegetables, live chickens, and clothing. Note the red-and-yellow Methodist church on the hill, one of Tobago's oldest churches. ⊠ *Tobago.*

NEED A BREAK?

Ciao Café. With more than 20 flavors of gelato, Ciao Café is an essential stop on any visit to the capital. You can also get pizza slices and sandwiches if you're looking for a quick snack. There's seating in the air-conditioned interior and a lovely outdoor perch from which to absorb the downtown action sheltered from the blazing sun. In addition to the usual complement of coffees, cocktails are also available. ⊠ *20 Burnett St., Scarborough* ☎ *868/639–3001.*

Speyside. At the far reach of Tobago's windward coast, this small fishing village has a few lodgings and restaurants. Divers are drawn to the unspoiled reefs in the area and to the strong possibility of spotting giant manta rays. The approach to Speyside from the south affords one of the most spectacular vistas of the island. Glass-bottom boats operate between Speyside and **Little Tobago Island,** an important seabird sanctuary. ⊠ *Tobago.*

St. Giles Island. The underwater cliffs and canyons here off the northeastern tip of Tobago draw divers to this spot, where the Atlantic meets the Caribbean. ⊠ *Take Windward Rd. inland across mountains from Speyside.*

WHERE TO EAT

Curried crab and dumplings is a Sunday-dinner favorite in Tobago. *Oildown*—a local dish—tastes better than it sounds: it's a gently seasoned mixture of boiled breadfruit and salt beef or pork flavored with coconut milk. Mango ice cream or a sweet-and-sour tamarind ball makes a tasty finish. You may want to take home some hot-pepper sauce or chutney to a spice-loving friend or relative.

$$
CARIBBEAN
Fodor's Choice
★

✕ **Blue Crab Restaurant.** The Sardinha family have been serving the best local lunches at their home since the 1980s. The ebullient Alison entertains and hugs diners while her husband, Ken, does the cooking. The food is hearty and usually well seasoned in the creole style. The only bad news here is that the restaurant is rarely open for dinner; the good news is that you may not have room for dinner after lunch. ⑤ *Average main: $20* ⊠ *Robinson and Main Sts., Scarborough* ☎ *868/639–2737* ⊕ *www.tobagobluecrab.com* ☉ *Closed weekends. No dinner.*

$$$
ECLECTIC

✕ **Bonkers.** This restaurant at the Toucan Inn is atmospheric and excellent. Designed by expat British co-owner Chris James, the architecture is a blend of Kenyan and Caribbean styles, executed entirely in local teak and open on all sides. The menu is huge; Chris claims it pains him to remove any items, so he just keeps adding more. You can savor your lobster Rockefeller while enjoying the nightly entertainment. Open for breakfast and lunch seven days a week, this is the busiest eatery on the island. $ *Average main: $21* ⊠ *Toucan Inn, Store Bay Local Rd., Crown Point* ☎ *868/639–7173* ⊕ *www.toucan-inn.com.*

$$$
ECLECTIC
Fodor'sChoice
★

✕ **Café Coco.** This stylish eatery seats 200, but it's divided into multiple levels, so there's still a sense of intimacy. Statuary is strewn about with carefree abandon, and the sound of flowing water permeates the room. The main courses range widely and may include Cuban stewed beef as well as shrimp tempura. The restaurant is seldom full, so getting a table is usually not a problem. $ *Average main: $22* ⊠ *TTEC Substation Rd. off Crown Point Rd., Crown Point* ☎ *868/639–0996* ⊕ *www.cocoreef.com/cafecoco.*

$$$$
ECLECTIC

✕ **Café Iguana.** This funky little restaurant and art gallery is a popular gathering place at night, as it serves some of the best cocktails on the island. The menu is eclectic, but there is a distinct Tobago touch to everything and an emphasis on local ingredients. The crayfish, though messy to eat, is not to be missed. The art on the walls is available for sale—you might want to exercise restraint with the cocktails before deciding to become an art investor. $ *Average main: $41* ⊠ *Store Bay Local Rd. at Milford Rd., Crown Point* ☎ *868/631–8205* ⊕ *www.iguanatobago.com* ⊗ *Closed Wed.*

$$$$
CARIBBEAN
★

✕ **Kariwak Village Restaurant.** Recorded steel-band music plays gently in the background at this romantic, candlelit spot in the Kariwak Village complex. In a bamboo pavilion that resembles an Amerindian round hut, Cynthia Clovis orchestrates a very original menu. Whatever the dish, it will be full of herbs and vegetables picked from her organic garden. Be sure to try the delicious homemade ice cream. Friday and Saturday buffets, with live jazz or calypso, are a Tobagonian highlight. $ *Average main: $31* ⊠ *Crown Point* ☎ *868/639–8442* ⊕ *www.kariwak.com.*

$$$$
ITALIAN

✕ **La Tartaruga.** Milanese owner Gabriele de Gaetano has created the island's most prominent Italian eatery. Sitting on the large patio surrounded by lush foliage with Gabriele rushing from table to table chatting in Italian-laced English is all the entertainment you'll need. Cuisine ranges from basic but tasty pizzas to elaborate Northern Italian pasta dishes. The impressive cellar stocks only Italian wines. $ *Average main: $35* ⊠ *Buccoo Rd., Buccoo* ☎ *868/639–0940* ⌂ *Reservations essential* ⊗ *Closed Sun. No lunch.*

$$$$
ECLECTIC

✕ **MeShell's.** This little restaurant housed in a pink building on the road to Mt. Irvine may not always have food as good as its looks, but it more than makes up for it with atmosphere: most diners head for the covered patio surrounded by a tropical garden. The main focus here is seafood and steaks, and the daily panfried catch of the day in a creole sauce is a popular favorite. Though this is a fairly expensive place, don't expect towering exotic presentations. Regulars rave about the Death by Chocolate dessert. $ *Average main: $34* ⊠ *Corner of Shirvan Rd. and Old Buccoo Rd., Mt. Pleasant* ☎ *868/631–0353* ⊗ *Closed Sun. No lunch.*

$
CAFÉ
Fodor'sChoice
★

✕ **Shore Things Café & Craft.** With a dramatic setting over the ocean on the Milford Road between Crown Point and Scarborough, this is a good spot to stop for a lunch or coffee break. Survey the view from the deck tables while enjoying a variety of freshly prepared juices (the tamarind is particularly refreshing) and nibbling on excellent sandwiches. The

25

whole-wheat pizza is great. While waiting for your meal, you can shop for local crafts in the lovely and comprehensive gift shop. ⑤ *Average main: $6* ⊠ *25 Old Milford Rd., Lambeau* ☎ *868/635–1072* ⊙ *Closed Sun. No dinner.*

$$$$
CARIBBEAN
★

✕ **Shutters on the Bay.** The warm-yellow dining area of this hotel restaurant is on the second floor of a colonial-style building and surrounded by white push-out shutters that frame a magical view of Bacolet Bay. The menu features a variety of dishes, all with a contemporary Caribbean twist. Fish dishes are a standout; don't be afraid to try some of the more exotic local offerings, such as callaloo soup, or some of the local starches (called "ground provisions"), such as dasheen (taro) or breadfruit. ⑤ *Average main: $34* ⊠ *Blue Haven Hotel, Bacolet Bay, Scarborough* ☎ *868/660–7500* ⚖ *Reservations essential.*

$$$$
ECLECTIC

✕ **Tamara's.** At the elegant Coco Reef Resort you can dine on contemporary cuisine with an island twist. The peach walls and whitewashed wooden ceiling make the resort's restaurant feel airy and light, and island breezes waft through the palm-lined terrace. The prix-fixe menu changes seasonally, and the fish dishes are worth special attention. A full tropical buffet breakfast is served daily; dinner is served nightly. There is a prix-fixe choice of one, two, or three courses. ⑤ *Average main: $35* ⊠ *Coco Reef Resort, Crown Point, Scarborough* ☎ *868/639–8571* ⚖ *Reservations essential.*

WHERE TO STAY

Tobago is much more of a tourist destination than Trinidad, and this is reflected in the range of accommodations. Those seeking luxury can find a number of upscale resorts and villas, and the budget-minded can take advantage of several more intimate establishments.

For expanded reviews, facilities, and current deals, visit Fodors.com.

$
HOTEL

▦ **Arnos Vale Hotel.** On 450 hillside acres, this hotel is the perfect retreat for nature lovers and lovers in general. **Pros:** complete peaceful setting; beautifully landscaped grounds; large and immaculate rooms; stay where The Beatles stayed. **Cons:** miles away from dining or shopping; some rooms are quite a hike away from the beach. **TripAdvisor:** "not for the fussy but can't beat location," "shabby and unloved," "could have been so beautiful." ⑤ *Rooms from: $135* ⊠ *Arnos Vale Rd., Scarborough* ☎ *868/639–2881* ⊕ *www.arnosvalehotel.com* ⥱ *29 rooms, 3 suites* ⏐◎⏐ *No meals.*

$
HOTEL
Fodor's Choice
★

▦ **Blue Haven Hotel.** Justifiably celebrated, this 1940s-era luxury hotel overlooks a spectacular secluded beach on Bacolet Bay just outside Scarborough. **Pros:** historic charm; beautiful beach; more European flair than any other hotel on the island. **Cons:** lacks the range of services of the larger hotels; far from the attractions of Crown Point; beach is a short walk down a hillside. **TripAdvisor:** "wonderful staff and beautiful views," "total relaxation," "hotel with charisma and class." ⑤ *Rooms from: $238* ⊠ *Bacolet Bay, Scarborough* ☎ *868/660–7400* ⊕ *www.bluehavenhotel.com* ⥱ *43 rooms, 8 suites, 1 villa* ⏐◎⏐ *Multiple meal plans.*

$ 🏨 **Blue Waters Inn.** A tropical rain forest creeps up behind this eco-
HOTEL friendly hotel, which sits on sheltered, turquoise Batteaux Bay; it's just
★ east of Speyside and a 90-minute drive from Scarborough. **Pros:** rooms
open onto the beach; enthusiastic and friendly staff; simple but delicious food. **Cons:** it's a long drive from Scarborough. **TripAdvisor:**
"sublime meals," "fantastic views and bird watching," "friendly and
relaxed." *⑤ Rooms from: $215 ✉ Batteaux Bay, Speyside ☎ 868/660–
4077 ⊕ www.bluewatersinn.com ⟲ 31 rooms, 3 suites, 4 bungalows
¶❍¶ Breakfast.*

$$$$ 🏨 **Coco Reef Resort.** Although it's just a short distance from the aiport,
RESORT this expansive enclave feels remote, with pink buildings that are
☾ sprawled along a perfect stretch of coast. **Pros:** beautifully appointed
★ rooms; the only private beach on the island; impeccable and understated
service. **Cons:** pool area can get a bit too busy; no Wi-Fi; some rooms
are far from the beach and reception; very expensive. **TripAdvisor:**
"beautiful setting," "relaxed and chilled," "idyllic." *⑤ Rooms from:
$479 ✉ Coconut Bay, Crown Point ☎ 868/639–8571, 800/221–1294
⊕ www.cocoreef.com ⟲ 100 rooms, 27 suites, 8 villas ¶❍¶ Breakfast.*

$ 🏨 **Grafton Beach Resort.** The first all-inclusive in Tobago now only offers
RESORT the package as an $80 per person option—it remains a very popular
☾ choice for young couples. **Pros:** large rooms; lively pool area. **Cons:**
so-so food; the free drinks plan can sometimes make for a rowdy
crowd. **TripAdvisor:** "excellent service," "great view," "decent hotel."
*⑤ Rooms from: $125 ✉ Shirvan Rd., Black Rock ☎ 868/639–0191
⟲ 102 rooms, 4 suites ¶❍¶ Multiple meal plans.*

$ 🏨 **Kariwak Village.** Alan and Cynthia Cloves have created an intimate,
HOTEL tranquil oasis that draws guests who return year after year. **Pros:** cozy
★ and intimate throughout; excellent restaurant; beautiful grounds. **Cons:**
the New Age concept not for everyone (although it isn't imposed on
guests); no beach. **TripAdvisor:** "wonderful food and service," "unique
and wonderful retreat," "tranquility defined." *⑤ Rooms from: $175
✉ Crown Point ☎ 868/639–8442 ⊕ www.kariwak.com ⟲ 24 rooms
¶❍¶ No meals.*

$$$$ 🏨 **Le Grand Courlan Resort & Spa.** This hotel is more upscale than its sister
ALL-INCLUSIVE property, the Grafton Beach Resort, with rooms that have large balconies overlooking one of the best beaches on the island. **Pros:** beautiful
beach; perfect for those who want to get away from screaming children. **Cons:** other hotels offer better rooms and services for the same
price or less; restaurants are mediocre. **TripAdvisor:** "laid-back relaxation," "friendly staff," "romantic." *⑤ Rooms from: $450 ✉ Shirvan
Rd., Black Rock ☎ 868/639–9667 ⊕ www.legrandtobago.com ⟲ 80
rooms, 3 suites ¶❍¶ All-inclusive.*

$ 🏨 **Mt. Irvine Bay Hotel.** Although the hotel lacks some of the fancier ame-
HOTEL nities, there's still something magical about its 1970s shabby gentility
that can't be found at the flashy new resorts. **Pros:** beautiful grounds;
perfect for the golf lover; access to one of the prettiest beaches. **Cons:**
public spaces feel dated; poor restaurant service. **TripAdvisor:** "beautiful location with attentive staff," "peaceful and refreshing," "old-
world ambience." *⑤ Rooms from: $200 ✉ Shirvan Rd., Mt. Irvine*

25

Tobago

TOBAGO

Scarborough

Caribbean Sea

(22 mi/35 km)

Port of Spain

TRINIDAD

VENEZUELA

Englishman's Bay

Castara Bay — Castara

Moriah

Arnos Vale Reef

Les Coteaux

Plymouth

Ft. King George

Great Courland Bay — 4

Turtle Beach — 5

Stone Haven Bay — 7 · 10 · 6

Mt. Irvine Reef

Black Rock

Mt. Irvine Beach — 8

Buccoo Bay — 2

Pigeon Point

Store Bay — 3 · 9 · 4

Sandy Point Beach — 5

Crown Pt. Airport

Crown Point

Canaan

Kimme Sculpture Museum

Little Rockley Bay — 8

Rockley Bay

Scarborough

Hillsborough Bay

9

Bacolet Bay — 1 · 1 — Bacolet Beach

7 · 11

6 · 10

Columbus Pt.

TO TRINIDAD

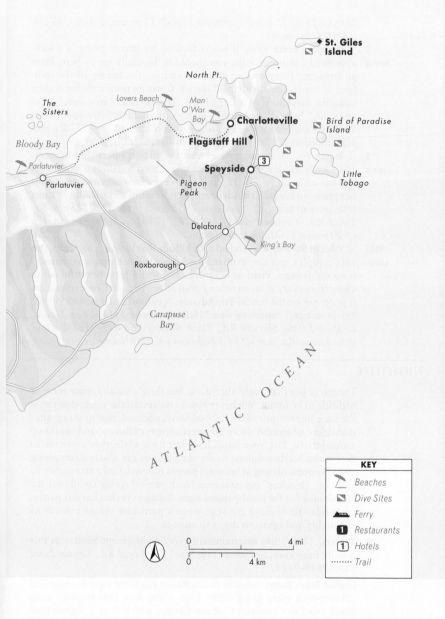

St. Giles
Island

North Pt.

The
Sisters

Lovers Beach

Man
O'War
Bay

Charlotteville

Bird of Paradise
Island

Bloody Bay

Flagstaff Hill

Parlatuvier

Speyside 3

Parlatuvier

Pigeon
Peak

Little
Tobago

Delaford

King's Bay

Roxborough

Carapuse
Bay

ATLANTIC OCEAN

KEY	
⚲	Beaches
◩	Dive Sites
🚢	Ferry
1	Restaurants
1	Hotels
······	Trail

0   4 mi

0   4 km

☎ 868/639–8871 ⊕ *www.mtirvine.com* ➥ *53 rooms, 6 suites, 46 cottages* ⦿ *No meals.*

$ 🏠 **Plantation Beach Villas.** If you're looking for luxury living in a well-
RENTAL appointed Caribbean villa, you should be blissfully happy here. **Pros:** an engaging alternative to a hotel room; on the beach; all the comforts of home, along with maid service. **Cons:** no restaurant for dinner; lacks the diversions of a large hotel. **TripAdvisor:** "wonderful villas and staff," "attentive service," "lovely surroundings." ⑤ *Rooms from: $250* ⊠ *Stone Haven Bay Rd., Black Rock* ☎☎ *868/639–9377* ⊕ *www. plantationbeachvillas.com* ➥ *6 3-bedroom villas* ⦿ *No meals.*

$ 🏠 **Toucan Inn.** This budget hotel near the airport offers simple rooms
HOTEL and a lively social scene. **Pros:** great value; good restaurant. **Cons:** pool and bar area can be a bit raucous on weekends; rooms are serviceable but plain; no beach. **TripAdvisor:** "great location and friendly," "quiet little piece of heaven," "nice staff." ⑤ *Rooms from: $120* ⊠ *Store Bay Local Rd., Crown Point* ☎ *868/639–7173* ⊕ *www.toucan-inn.com* ➥ *20 rooms* ⦿ *Multiple meal plans.*

$$$$ 🏠 **Villas at Stonehaven.** Perched on a hillside overlooking the ocean, this
RENTAL villa complex sets the standard for luxury self-catering accommodations on Tobago. **Pros:** as luxurious as Tobago gets; beautiful ocean views from every villa; an infinity pool all to yourself. **Cons:** restaurant is poor; not on the beach. **TripAdvisor:** "peaceful and spacious villas," "great service," "stunning view." ⑤ *Rooms from: $413* ⊠ *Bon Accord, Grafton Estate, Shirvan Rd., Black Rock* ☎ *868/639–9887* ⊕ *www. stonehavenvillas.com* ➥ *14 3-bedroom villas* ⦿ *No meals.*

NIGHTLIFE

Tobago is not that lively after dark, but there's usually some form of nightlife to be found. Whatever you do the rest of the week, don't miss the huge impromptu party, dubbed Sunday School, that gears up after midnight on Saturday on all the street corners of Buccoo and breaks up around dawn. Pick your band, hang out for a while, then move on. In downtown Scarborough on weekend nights you can also find competing sound systems blaring at informal parties that welcome extra guests. In addition, "blockos" (spontaneous block parties) spring up all over the island; look for the hand-painted signs. Tobago also has harvest parties on Sunday throughout the year, when a particular village extends its hospitality and opens its doors to visitors.

★ **Bonkers.** There's live entertainment every night except Sunday at this usually busy club. ⊠ *Toucan Inn, Store Bay Local Rd., Crown Point* ☎ *868/639–7173.*

Grafton Beach Resort. Grafton Beach Resort has some kind of organized cabaret-style event every night. Even if you hate that touristy stuff, check out Les Couteaux Cultural Group, which does a high-octane dance version of Tobagonian history. ⊠ *Shirvan Rd., Black Rock* ☎ *868/639–0191.*

Kariwak Village. As many locals as visitors frequent Kariwak Village on Friday and Saturday nights, when one of the better local jazz-calypso bands almost always plays. ⊠ *Crown Point* ☎ *868/639–8442.*

Continued on page 1022

CARNIVAL IN TRINIDAD

Vernon O'Reilly Ramesar

The "Greatest Show on Earth" is also the best party in the Caribbean, and it's not brought to you by Barnum & Bailey but by the people of Trinidad. The island's pre-Lenten Carnival is rooted in Trinidad's African and French-Creole cultures and is more spontaneous than similar celebrations in Latin America; its influence reaches as far as Miami, Toronto, and London.

Trinidad's celebration has evolved through the years. What was once a two-day affair has turned into a lengthy party season starting in early January and lasting until Ash Wednesday. The biggest and best parties are held in and around Port of Spain, where locals max out their credit cards and even take out bank loans to finance their costumes and attend as many parties as possible.

On Carnival Monday and Tuesday the traffic lights of Port of Spain are turned off and the streets are turned over to a human traffic jam of costumed revelers.

They jump and dance to the pounding sound of music trucks—featuring huge speakers and either live music or a DJ—and turn Port of Spain into a pulsing celebration of island life that they call the *mas*.

Mas bands—some with thousands of members, others with a mere handful—must follow a route and pass judging points to win a prize, but increasingly, they simply don't bother. They're in it for the fun. To grease the wheels, makeshift bars are set up along all the city's streets.

Children stiltwalkers in colorful Carnival costumes, Queens Park Savannah, Port of Spain

CARNIVAL 101

THE FETE

Huge outdoor parties (called *fetes*) are held in the months before Carnival; during the final week, there are usually several fetes every day. You can get tickets for many of them through the major hotels, but some exclusive fetes may require an invitation from a well-connected Trinidadian.

THE PANORAMA

While fetes are important to Carnival, the Panorama Steelpan Preliminaries and finals are essential. Two weeks before Carnival, the "Prelims" are held, when dozens of steel drum orchestras compete for a place in the finals held on Carnival Saturday. Music lovers go to hear the throbbing sound of hundreds of steelpans beating out a syncopated rhythm, and the rum-fueled party often rivals even the best fetes.

DIMANCHE GRAS

On Carnival Sunday, top calypsonians compete to be Calypso Monarch, and this offers you an especially good opportunity to experience Carnival in one easy shot. The show was once held in Queen's Park Savannah, but the location now varies.

THE COSTUMES

To be a true part of Carnival, you need a costume. Every mas band has its own costumes, which must be reserved months in advance (these days online). You pick up yours at the band's mas "camp" and find out where and when to meet your band. Then all you have to do is jump, walk, or wave in the Carnival procession as the spirit moves you. Drinks and food may be included.

(top) Trinidad Carnival celebrations during Junior Parade of the Bands, (bottom) masquerader in a colorful costume.

MUSIC

Carnival is powered by music, and though the steelpan still plays a big part, it is the *soca* performers who draw the biggest crowds. Some of the big names include Machel Montano, Shurwayne Winchester, and Allyson Hinds. You can hear the most popular performers at the bigger fetes and at the Soca Monarch competition held on Carnival Friday before the more prestigious Calypso Monarch contest.

THE MAS BANDS

Trinis are passionate about their favorite mas band. The most popular have costumes largely comprised of beaded bikinis and feathered headdresses and are called "pretty mas." Very large bands such as Tribe, Island People, and Hart's fall into this category. If you're not willing to show that much skin or want more theater, then choose a band like MacFarlane, which offers more elaborate costumes with a thematic story. As has always been the case, women greatly outnumber men in the bands.

Carnival costumes are usually colorful—and skimpy.

TOP FETES

Safety is an increasing concern in Trinidad, especially at Carnival time. Fetes that attract a better heeled crowd offer more security and sufficient bars to cater to the thousands of revelers who attend. They usually command higher prices but are worth the cost.

Kama Sutra is held at the Trinidad Country Club on the Saturday before Carnival weekend. It is all-inclusive and features a good selection of food and premium drinks.

Eyes Wide Shut is held at The Oval (home of Trinidad cricket) and tends to attract a younger crowd.

Insomnia is an overnight fete held in Chaguaramas, just West of Port of Spain, on Carnival Saturday, and the partying doesn't stop till sunrise.

The Brian Lara and Moka all-inclusive fetes are both held on the afternoon of Carnival Sunday. Tickets for both are highly sought. Brian Lara is considered the most exclusive of all fetes and is the most expensive.

Shade. This sure bet for raucous late-night fun is open from 7 pm to 4 am Wednesday through Saturday. It's near the gas station. ⊠ *Milford Rd. and Robert St., Crown Point* ☎ *868/639–9651.*

SHOPPING

Souvenir seekers will do better in Trinidad than in Tobago, but determined shoppers ought to be able to find a few things to take home. Scarborough has the largest collection of shops, and Burnett Street, which climbs sharply from the port to St. James Park, is a good place to browse.

FOOD

Forro's Homemade Delicacies. Eileen Forrester, wife of the Anglican archdeacon of Trinidad and Tobago, supervises a kitchen full of good cooks who boil and bottle the condiments sold here and pack them in little straw baskets—or even in bamboo. Most of the jars of tamarind chutney, lemon and lime marmalade, hot sauce, and guava and golden-apple jelly are small, easy to carry, and inexpensive. ⊠ *The Andrew's Rectory, Bacolet St., opposite the fire station, Scarborough* ☎ *868/639–2485.*

HANDICRAFTS

Cotton House. This shop is a good bet for jewelry and imaginative batik work, and Paula Young runs it like an art school. You can visit the upstairs studio; if it's not too busy, you can even make a batik square at no charge. ⊠ *Bacolet St., Scarborough* ☎ *868/639–2727.*

Shore Things Café & Crafts. Masks and music are just two of the many kinds of souvenirs you can pick up at Shore Things Café & Crafts. ⊠ *25 Old Milford Rd., Lambeau* ☎ *868/635–1072.*

Store Bay. The stalls at Store Bay sell T-shirts, local handicrafts, and lots of other souvenirs. It's also convenient to the airport for any last-minute purchases. ⊠ *Store Bay, Crown Point.*

SPORTS AND ACTIVITIES

BIRD-WATCHING

★ Some 200 varieties of birds have been documented on Tobago: look for the yellow oriole, scarlet ibis, and the comical motmot—the male of the species clears sticks and stones from an area and then does a dance complete with snapping sounds to attract a mate. The flora is as vivid as the birds. Purple-and-yellow *poui* trees and spectacular orange immortelles splash color over the countryside, and something is blooming virtually every season.

Pioneer Journeys. Pat Turpin and Renson Jack at Pioneer Journeys can give you information about their bird-watching tours of Bloody Bay rain forest and Louis d'Or River valley wetlands. ⊠ *Tobago* ☎ *868/660–4327, 868/660–5175* ✎ *pturpin@tstt.net.tt.*

Rooks Nature Tours. Naturalist and ornithologist David Rooks offers bird-watching walks inland and trips to offshore bird colonies. He's generally considered the best guide on the island. ⊠ *462 Moses Hill, Lambeau* ☎ *868/756–8594.*

BOAT TOURS

Tobago offers many wonderful spots for snorkeling. Although the reefs around Speyside in the northeast are becoming better known, **Buccoo Reef,** off the island's southwest coast, is still the most popular—perhaps too popular. Over the years the reef has been badly damaged by the ceaseless boat traffic and by thoughtless visiting divers who take pieces of coral as souvenirs. Still, it's worth experiencing, particularly if you have children. Daily 2½-hour tours by glass-bottom boats let you snorkel at the reef, swim in a lagoon, and gaze at Coral Gardens—where fish and coral are as yet untouched. Most dive companies in the Black Rock area also arrange snorkeling tours. There's also good snorkeling near the **Arnos Vale Hotel** and the **Mt. Irvine Bay Hotel.**

Hew's Glass Bottom Boat Tours. These tours are perfect for those who want to see sealife but who neither snorkel nor dive. Boats leave daily at 11:30 am. ⊠ *Pigeon Point* ☎ *868/639–9058.*

DIVING

An abundance of fish and coral thrives on the nutrients of Venezuela's Orinoco River, which are brought to Tobago by the Guyana current. Off the west coast is **Arnos Vale Reef,** with a depth of 40 feet and several reefs that run parallel to the shore. Here you can spot French and queen angelfish, moray eels, southern stingrays, and even the Atlantic torpedo ray. Much of the diving is drift diving in the mostly gentle current. **Crown Point,** on the island's southwest tip, is a good place for exploring the Shallows—a plateau at 50 to 100 feet that's favored by turtles, dolphins, angelfish, and nurse sharks. Just north of Crown Point on the southwest coast, **Pigeon Point** is a good spot to submerge. North of Pigeon Point, long, sandy beaches line the calm western coast; it has a gradual offshore slope and the popular **Mt. Irvine Wall,** which goes down to about 60 feet.

A short trip from Charlotteville, off the northeast tip of the island, is **St. Giles Island.** Here are natural rock bridges—London Bridge, Marble Island, and Fishbowl—and underwater cliffs. The **waters off Speyside** on the east coast draw scuba divers who come for the many manta rays in the area. Exciting sites in this area include Batteaux Reef, Angel Reef, Bookends, Blackjack Hole, and Japanese Gardens—one of the loveliest reefs, with depths of 20 to 85 feet and lots of sponges.

Tobago is considered a prime diving destination, as the clear waters provide maximum visibility. Every species of hard coral and most soft corals can be found in the waters around the island. Tobago is also home to the largest-known brain coral. Generally, the best diving is around the Speyside area. Many hotels and guesthouses in this area cater to the diving crowd with basic accommodations and easy access to the water. You can usually get the best deals with these "dive-and-stay" packages.

AquaMarine Dive Ltd. On the northeast coast, AquaMarine is friendly, laid-back, and popular with casual divers. ⊠ *Blue Waters Inn, Batteaux Bay, Speyside* ☎ *868/639–4416* ⊕ *www.aquamarinedive.com.*

CaribStu. World traveler Stuart Sampson decided to settle in Tobago and launch CaribStu, a personalized diving service for individuals or couples. ✉ *On the beach, between the jetty and the gas station, Charlotteville* ☎ *868/733–1298* ⊕ *www.caribstu.com.*

Tobago Dive Experience. Class sizes at Tobago Dive Experience are kept small to ensure that all divers get the attention they need. It has the most comprehensive range of courses, including PADI, NAUI, and BSAC, and prices are very competitive. ✉ *Manta Lodge, Speyside* ☎ *868/639–7034* ⊕ *www.tobagodiveexperience.com.*

FISHING

Dillon's Deep Sea Charters. This company is excellent for full- and half-day trips for kingfish, barracuda, wahoo, mahimahi, blue marlin, and others. A full day on the sea with either a beach stop for lunch or a cruise around the island runs about $700, including equipment. ✉ *Crown Point* ☎ *868/639–9386.*

Hard Play Fishing Charters. The colorful skipper at Hard Play, Gerard "Frothy" De Silva, helps you bag your own marlin. ✉ *13 The Evergreen, Old Grange, Mt. Irvine Bay* ☎ *868/639–7108.*

GOLF

★ **Mt. Irvine Golf Club.** The 18-hole, par-72 course at the Mt. Irvine Golf Club was once ranked among the top courses in the Caribbean and among the top 100 in the world, but course maintenance has suffered over the years. Greens fees are $30 for 9 holes, $48 for 18 holes. ✉ *Mt. Irvine Bay Hotel, Shirvan Rd., Mt. Irvine* ☎ *868/639–8871.*

Tobago Plantations Golf & Country Club. The 18-hole, par-72 course is set on rolling greens. It offers some amazing views of the ocean as a bonus. Greens fees are $60 for one 18-hole round, $100 for two rounds (these rates include a golf cart and taxes). This is the newer of the two main courses on the island and is by far the most popular. The course is well maintained and contains areas of mangrove and forest that are home to many bird species. ✉ *Tobago Plantations Golf & Country Club, Lowlands* ☎ *868/631–0875.*

GUIDED TOURS

Frank's Glass Bottom Boat & Birdwatching Tours. In addition to glass-bottom-boat and snorkeling tours of the shores of Speyside, Frank also conducts guided tours of the rain forest and Little Tobago. As a native of Speyside, he's extremely knowledgeable about the island's flora, fauna, and folklore. ✉ *Speyside* ☎☎ *868/660–5438.*

Tobago Travel. The island's most experienced operator is almost certain to have the perfect tour for you. ✉ *Scarborough* ☎ *868/639–8778.*

Turks and Caicos Islands

WORD OF MOUTH

"One word to describe TCI—stunning! Every morning I would wake up and look out a Grace Bay beach and say 'Wow!'"

—Ocdogsmon

"Diving off Grand Turk was great, the wall is just 10 minutes off-shore and the water visibility was very good."

—fishee

WELCOME TO TURKS AND CAICOS ISLANDS

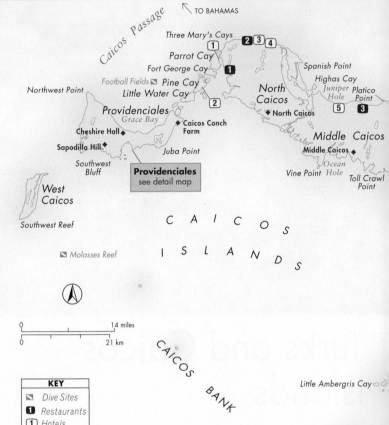

TO BAHAMAS

Caicos Passage

Three Mary's Cays

Parrot Cay

Fort George Cay

Football Fields

Pine Cay

Little Water Cay

Northwest Point

Providenciales

Grace Bay

Cheshire Hall

Sapodilla Hill

Southwest Bluff

Caicos Conch Farm

Juba Point

Providenciales see detail map

Spanish Point

Highas Cay

North Caicos

Juniper Hole

Platico Point

◆ North Caicos

⑤

③

Middle Caicos

Middle Caicos ◆

Ocean Hole

Vine Point

Toll Crawl Point

West Caicos

Southwest Reef

Molasses Reef

C A I C O S

I S L A N D S

0 ─── 14 miles
0 ─── 21 km

C A I C O S   B A N K

Little Ambergris Cay

SEAL CAYS

White Cay

KEY	
Dive Sites	
❶	Restaurants
①	Hotels

Only 8 of these 40 islands between the Bahamas and Haiti are inhabited. Divers and snorkelers can explore one of the world's largest coral reefs. Land-based pursuits don't get much more taxing than teeing off at the Provo Golf and Country Club or sunset-watching from the seaside terrace of a laid-back resort.

GEOGRAPHICAL INFO

Though Providenciales is a major offshore banking center, sea creatures far outnumber humans in this archipelago of 40 islands, where the total population is a mere 25,000. From developed Provo to sleepy Grand Turk to sleepier South Caicos, the islands offer miles of undeveloped beaches, crystal-clear water, and laid-back luxury resorts.

Restaurants ▼	Hotels ▼
Coral Reef Bar & Grill **4**	Blue Horizon Resort **9**
Daniel's Cafe **3**	Castaway Villa **8**
Higgs Cafe **1**	Hollywood
Island Thyme Bistro **5**	Beach Suites.............**3**
Pat's Place **6**	Meridian Club **2**
Silver Palms **2**	Parrot Cay Resort **1**
	Pelican Beach Hotel **4**
	Pirate's Hideaway **10**
	South Caicos Ocean & Beach Resort **6**
	Tradewinds Guest Suites **5**
	Villas of Salt Cay **7**

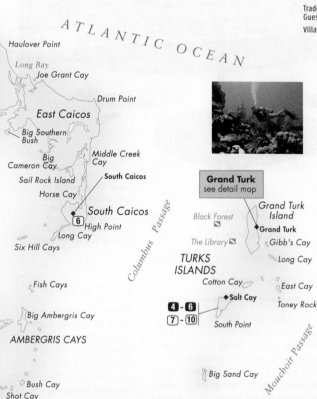

ATLANTIC OCEAN

Haulover Point
Long Bay
Joe Grant Cay
Drum Point
East Caicos
Big Southern Bush
Big Cameron Cay
Middle Creek Cay
Sail Rock Island
South Caicos
Horse Cay
South Caicos
6 High Point
Long Cay
Six Hill Cays
Fish Cays
Big Ambergris Cay
AMBERGRIS CAYS
Bush Cay
Shot Cay

Columbus Passage

Black Forest
The Library
TURKS ISLANDS
Cotton Cay

Grand Turk see detail map

Grand Turk Island
◆Grand Turk
Gibb's Cay
Long Cay

East Cay

◆Salt Cay
Toney Rock
4-**6**
7-**10**
South Point

Big Sand Cay

Mouchoir Passage

26

TURKS AND CAICOS ISLANDS

TOP REASONS TO VISIT TURKS AND CAICOS ISLANDS

1 Beautiful Beaches: Even on Provo, there are miles of deserted beaches without any beach umbrellas in sight.

2 Excellent Diving: The third-largest coral-reef system in the world is among the world's top dive sites.

3 Easy Island-Hopping: Island-hopping beyond the beaten path will give you a feel for the islands.

4 The Jet Set: Destination spas, penthouse suites, and exclusive villas and resorts make celebrity-spotting a popular sport.

5 Exploring on the Sea: You'll find excellent fishing and boating among the uninhabited coves and cays.

TURKS AND CAICOS BEACHES

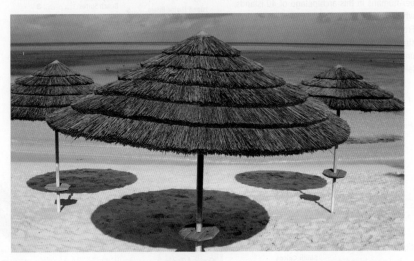

If you're on a quest for the world's best beaches, then Turks and Caicos is your destination. They are blessed with stunning strands and shallow waters protected by outer reefs, a combination that makes for the most amazing turquoise water.

(Above) Beach palapas on Grace Bay, Providenciales (Bottom right) Half Moon Bay at Big Water Cay, off Providenciales (Top right) Sapodilla Bay, Providenciales

Grace Bay Beach in Providenciales has the best of the best, and most of the island's resorts are clustered here. On the rare occasions that storms bring seaweed, it is quickly raked and buried. The water is protected by an outer reef, so it's often as still as glass. There is never an undertow or litter, and there are no beach vendors, so the opportunities for relaxation are optimal. Grand Turk is spoiled for choices when it comes to beach options: sunset strolls along miles of deserted beaches, picnics in secluded coves, beachcombing on the coral-line sands, snorkeling around shallow coral heads close to shore, and admiring the impossibly turquoise-blue waters. There are also great beaches on several other less visited islands.

BEACH LOGISTICS

Although there is no charge for parking at any beach, come prepared. Umbrellas are provided by resorts for guests only, and resorts generally don't share with nonguests, even for a price. Grace Bay has the busiest sections of beachfront, especially at Beaches Resort and Club Med, but there are still plenty of secluded areas if you wish to explore beyond your own resort.

All the beaches of Turks and Caicos have bright white sand that's soft like baby powder. An added bonus is that no matter how hot the sun gets, your feet never burn. The sand is soft and clean, even in the water, so there is no fear of stepping on rocks or corals. Even the beach areas with corals for snorkeling have clear, clean sand for entry until you reach them.

PROVIDENCIALES

★ Fodor's Choice **Grace Bay.** The 12-mile (18-km) sweeping stretch of ivory-white, powder-soft sand on Provo's north coast is simply breathtaking, and home to migrating starfish as well as shallow snorkeling trails. The majority of Provo's beachfront resorts are along this shore, and it's the primary reason the Turks and Caicos is a world-class destination. ⊠ *Grace Bay Rd., on the north shore.*

Half Moon Bay. A natural ribbon of sand linking two uninhabited cays is only inches above the sparkling turquoise waters and one of the most gorgeous beaches on the island. There are limestone cliffs to explore as well as small, private sand coves; there's even a small wreck offshore for snorkeling. It's only a short boat ride away from Provo, and most of the island's tour companies run excursions here or simply offer a beach drop-off. These companies include Silverdeep and Caicos Dream Tours

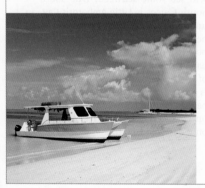

(⇨ Boating and Sailing, in Sports and Activities). ⊠ *15 mins from Leeward Marina, between Pine Cay and Water Cay, accessible only by boat, Big Water Cay.*

Malcolm's Beach. It's one of the most stunning beaches you'll ever see, but you'll need a high-clearance vehicle to reach it. Bring your own food and drinks, because it doesn't have any facilities or food service unless you have made a reservation with Amanyara to eat at the resort. ⊠ *Malcolm's Beach Rd., keep straight after passing the Amanyara turnoff.*

Sapodilla Bay. The best of the many secluded beaches and pristine sands around Provo can be found at this peaceful quarter-mile cove protected by Sapodilla Hill, with its soft strand lapped by calm waves, where yachts and small boats move with the gentle tide. ⊠ *North of South Dock, at end of South Dock Rd.*

GRAND TURK

Governor's Beach. A beautiful crescent of powder-soft sand and shallow, calm turquoise waters front the official British governor's residence, called Waterloo, framed by tall casuarina trees that provide plenty of natural shade. To have it all to yourself, go on a day when cruise ships are not in port. On days when ships are in port, the beach is lined with lounge chairs.

26

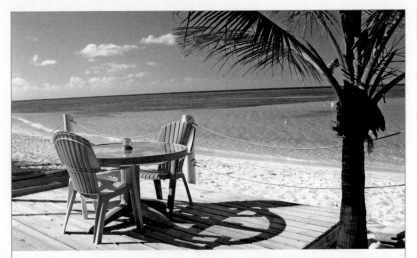

Pillory Beach, Grand Turk.

Little Bluff Point Beach. Just west of the Grand Turk Lighthouse is a low, limestone-cliff-edged, shell-covered beach that offers more of a beachcombing experience and looks out onto shallow waters, mangroves, and often flamingos, especially in spring and summer.

Pillory Beach. With sparkling neon turquoise water, this is the prettiest beach on Grand Turk; it also has great off-the-beach snorkeling.

NORTH CAICOS

The beaches of North Caicos are superb for shallow snorkeling and sunset strolls, and the waters offshore have excellent scuba diving. **Horse Stable Beach** is the main beach for annual events and beach parties. **Whitby Beach** usually has a gentle tide, and its thin strip of sand is bordered by palmetto plants and taller trees.

SALT CAY

Big Sand Cay. Accessible by boat with the on-island tour operators, Big Sand Cay, 7 miles (11 km) south of Salt Cay, is tiny and totally uninhabited; it's also known for its long, unspoiled stretches of open sand.

North Beach. The north coast of Salt Cay has superb beaches, with tiny, pretty shells and weathered sea glass, but North Beach is the reason to visit Salt Cay; it might be the finest beach in Turks and Caicos, if not the world. Part of the beauty lies not just in the soft, powdery sand and bright blue water but in its isolation; it's very likely that you will have this lovely beach all to yourself.

SOUTH CAICOS

The beaches at **Belle Sound** on South Caicos will take your breath away, with lagoonlike waters. Expect the beach to be natural and rustic—after storms you will see some seaweed. Due south of South Caicos is **Little Ambergris Cay**, an uninhabited cay about 14 miles (23 km) beyond the Fish Cays, with excellent bonefishing on the second-largest sandbar in the world. On the opposite side of the ridge from Belle Sound, **Long Bay** is an endless stretch of beach, but it can be susceptible to rough surf; however, on calmer days, you'll feel like you're on a deserted island.

By Ramona Settle

26

With water so turquoise that it glows, you may find it difficult to stray far from the beach in the Turks and Caicos. You may find no need for museums, and no desire to see ruins or even to read books. You may find yourself hypnotized by the water's many neon hues. And since the beaches are among the most incredible you will ever see, don't be surprised if you wake up on your last morning and realize that you didn't find a lot of time for anything else.

Although ivory-white, soft, sandy beaches and breathtaking turquoise waters are shared among all the islands, the landscapes are a series of contrasts, from the dry, arid bush and scrub on the flat, coral islands of Grand Turk, Salt Cay, South Caicos, and Providenciales to the greener, foliage-rich undulating landscapes of Middle Caicos, North Caicos, Parrot Cay, and Pine Cay.

A much-disputed legend has it that Columbus first discovered these islands in 1492. Despite being on the map for longer than most other island groups, the Turks and Caicos Islands (pronounced *kay*-kos) still remain part of the less-discovered Caribbean. More than 40 islands— only 8 inhabited—make up this self-governing British overseas territory that lies just 575 miles (925 km) southeast of Miami on the third-largest coral-reef system in the world.

The political and historical capital island of the country is Grand Turk, but most of the tourism development, which consists primarily of boutique hotels and condo resorts, has occurred in Providenciales, thanks to the 12-mile (18-km) stretch of ivory sand that is Grace Bay. Once home to a population of around 500 people plus a few donkey carts, Provo has become a hub of activity, resorts, spas, restaurants, and water sports. It's the temporary home for the majority of visitors who come to the Turks and Caicos.

Marks of the country's colonial past can be found in the wooden-and-stone, Bermudian-style clapboard houses—often wrapped in deep-red

LOGISTICS

Getting to the Turks and Caicos: Several major airlines fly nonstop to Providenciales from the United States. If you're going to one of the smaller islands, you'll usually need to make a connection in Provo. All international flights arrive at Providenciales International Airport (PLS), but you can hop over to the other islands from there.

Hassle Factor: Low–high, depending on the island and your home airport.

On the Ground: You can find taxis at the airports. Taxi fares are fairly reasonable on Provo and Grand Turk; on the smaller islands transfers can cost more since gas is much more expensive.

Getting Around the Islands: If you are staying on Provo, you may find it useful to have a car, since the island is so large and the resorts are so far-flung, if only for a few days of exploring or to get away from your hotel for dinner. On Grand Turk, you can rent a car, but you probably won't need to.

bougainvillea—that line the streets on the quiet islands of Grand Turk, Salt Cay, and South Caicos. Donkeys roam free in and around the salt ponds, which are a legacy from a time when residents of these island communities worked hard as both slaves and then laborers to rake salt (then known as "white gold") bound for the United States and Canada. In Salt Cay the remains of wooden windmills are now home to large osprey nests. In Grand Turk and South Caicos, the crystal-edge tidal ponds are regularly visited by flocks of rose-pink flamingos hungry for the shrimp to be found in the shallow, briny waters.

In all, only some 45,000 people live in the Turks and Caicos Islands; more than half are "Belongers," the term for the native population, mainly descended from African and Bermudian slaves who settled here beginning in the 1600s. The majority of residents work in tourism, fishing, and offshore finance, as the country is a haven for the overtaxed. Indeed, for residents and visitors, life in "TCI" is anything but taxing. But even though most visitors come to do nothing—a specialty in the islands—it does not mean there's nothing to do.

PLANNING

WHEN TO GO

High season in Turks and Caicos runs roughly from January through March, with the usual extra-high rates during the Christmas and New Year's holiday period. Several hotels on Provo offer shoulder-season rates in April and May. During the off-season, rates are reduced substantially, as much as 40%. With bad world economies, you can find specials even during peak seasons or call resorts directly to negotiate.

GETTING HERE AND AROUND
AIR TRAVEL
You can fly nonstop from Atlanta (Delta), Boston (American and Jet-Blue), Charlotte (US Airways), Miami (American), New York–JFK (American and JetBlue), Newark–EWR (United), and Philadelphia (US Airways).

Although carriers and schedules can vary seasonally, there are many nonstop and connecting flights to Providenciales from several U.S. cities on American, Delta, JetBlue, and US Airways. There are also flights from other parts of the Caribbean on Air Turks & Caicos; this airline also flies to some of the smaller islands in the chain from Provo. There are also flights from Nassau on Bahamas Air, to Canadian cities on WestJet and Air Canada, and to London on British Airways.

Airports: The main gateways into the Turks and Caicos Islands are Providenciales International Airport (PLS) and Grand Turk International Airport (GDT). For private planes, Provo Air Center is a full-service FBO (Fixed Base Operator) offering refueling, maintenance, and short-term storage, as well as on-site customs and immigration clearance, a lounge, and concierge services. There are smaller airports on Grand Turk (GDT), North Caicos (NCS), Middle Caicos (MDS), South Caicos (XSC), and Salt Cay (SLX). All have paved runways in good condition. Even if you are going on to other islands in the chain, you will probably stop in Provo first for customs, then take a domestic flight onward.

Airport Contacts Turks & Caicos Islands Airport Authority. The TCIAA web site publishes an up-to-date, up-to-the-minute list of all flights coming into and out of the islands, along with real-time delay information. ⊕ www.tciairports.com.

Airline Contacts Air Turks & Caicos ☎ 649/941–5481 ⊕ www.airturksandcaicos.com. **American Airlines** ☎ 649/946–4948, 800/433–7300. **Bahamas Air** ☎ 242/377–5505 in Nassau, 800/222–4262 ⊕ up.bahamasair.com. **Caicos Express.** Caicos Express ☎ 649/243–0237. **Delta** ☎ 800/241–4141. **Jet-Blue** ☎ 800/538–2583 ⊕ www.JetBlue.com. **United Airlines** ☎ 800/538–2929 ⊕ www.united.com. **US Airways** ☎ 800/622–1015.

BOAT AND FERRY TRAVEL
Despite the island's relative proximity, ferry service is limited in the Turks and Caicos. You can take a ferry from Provo to North Caicos and from Grand Turk to Salt Cay, and that's about it.

Contacts Caribbean Cruisin' ✉ Walkin Marina, Leeward, Providenciales ☎ 649/946–5406, 649/231–4191 ⊕ www.tciferry.com. **Salt Cay Ferry** ☎ 649/946–6909 ⊕ www.turksandcaicoswhalewatching.com.

CAR TRAVEL
Driving here is on the left side of the road, British style; when pulling out into traffic, remember to look to your right. Give way to anyone entering a roundabout, as roundabouts are still a relatively new concept in the Turks and Caicos; stop even if you are on what appears to be the primary road. The maximum speed is 40 mph (64 kph), 20 mph (30 kph) through settlements, and limits, as well as the use of seat belts, are enforced.

26

If you are staying on Provo, you may find it useful to have a car, since the island is so large and the resorts are so far-flung, if only for a few days of exploring or to get away from your hotel for dinner. On Grand Turk you can rent a car, but you probably won't need to. Car- and jeep-rental rates average $39 to $80 per day on Provo, plus a $15 surcharge per rental as a government tax. Reserve well ahead of time during the peak winter season. Most agencies offer free mileage and airport pickup service. Avis and Budget have offices on the islands. You might also try local Provo agencies such as Grace Bay Car Rentals, Rent a Buggy, Tropical Auto Rentals, and Caicos Wheels—the latter rents scooters, colorful ATVs, cars, and even cell phones. Pelican Car Rentals is on North Caicos.

Contacts Avis ⊠ *Providenciales* ☎ *649/946–4705* ⊕ *www.avis.tc.* **Budget** ⊠ *Providenciales* ☎ *649/946–4079* ⊕ *www.provo.net/budget.* **Caicos Wheels** ⊠ *Grace Bay Court, Grace Bay Rd., Providenciales* ☎ *649/242–6592* ⊕ *www. CaicosWheels.com.* **Grace Bay Car Rentals** ⊠ *Providenciales* ☎ *649/941– 8500* ⊕ *www.gracebaycarrentals.com.* **Pelican Car Rentals** ⊠ *North Caicos* ☎ *649/241–8275.* **Rent a Buggy** ⊠ *Providenciales* ☎ *649/946–4158* ⊕ *www. rentabuggy.tc.* **Scooter Bob's** ⊠ *Turtle Cove, Providenciales* ☎ *649/946–4684* ⊕ *www.Provo.net/Scooter.* **Tony's Car Rental** ⊠ *Grand Turk* ☎ *649/946– 1879* ⊕ *www.TonysCarRental.com.* **Tropical Auto Rentals** ⊠ *Providenciales* ☎ *649/946–5300* ⊕ *www.provo.net/tropicalauto.*

TAXI TRAVEL

You can find taxis at the airports. A trip between Provo's airport and most major hotels runs about $12 per person. On Grand Turk a trip from the airport to Cockburn Town is about $8; it's $8 to $15 to hotels outside town on Grand Turk. Transfers can cost more on the smaller islands, where gas is much more expensive. Taxis (actually large vans) in Providenciales are metered, and rates are regulated by the government at $2 per person per mile traveled. In the family islands, taxis may not be metered, so it's usually best to try to negotiate a cost for your trip in advance. On Grand Turk and South Caicos, it's useful to make advance arrangements with your hotel for an airport pickup.

Taxi Contacts Provo Taxi & Bus Group. In Provo call the Provo Taxi & Bus Group for more information. ☎ 649/946–5481.

ESSENTIALS

Banks and Exchange Services The official currency on the islands is U.S. dollars. On Provo, there are ATMs at all bank branches (Scotiabank and First Caribbean), at the Graceway IGA Supermarket Gourmet, and at Ports of Call shopping center. There are also Scotiabank and First Caribbean branches on Grand Turk.

Electricity Current is suitable for all U.S. appliances (120/240 volts, 60 Hz).

Emergency Services Emergency numbers in the Turks and Caicos are ☎ 999 or 911.

Guided Tours Big Blue Unlimited has taken ecotouring to a whole new level with educational ecotours, including three-hour kayak trips and more-land-based guided journeys around the family islands. Their

Coastal Ecology and Wildlife tour is a kayak adventure through red mangroves to bird habitats, rock iguana hideaways, and natural fish nurseries. The North Caicos Mountain Bike Eco Tour gets you on a bike to explore the island, the plantation ruins, the inland lakes, and a flamingo pond with a stop-off at Susan Butterfield's home for lunch. Package costs range from $85 to $225 per person.

Nell's Taxi offers taxi tours of Provo, priced between $25 and $30 for the first hour and $25 for each additional hour.

Contacts Air Turks & Caicos ☎ 649/946–4999 ⊕ www.flyairtc.com. **Big Blue Unlimited** ✉ Leeward Marina, Leeward, Providenciales ☎ 649/946–5034 ⊕ www.bigblue.tc. **Nell's Taxi** ☎ 649/231–0051.

Passport Requirements A valid passport is required to travel by air to the Turks and Caicos. Everyone must have an ongoing or return ticket.

Phones The country code for the Turks and Caicos is 649. To call the Turks and Caicos from the United States, dial 1 plus the 10-digit number, which includes 649. Be aware that this is an international call. Calls from the islands are expensive, and many hotels add steep surcharges for long distance.

Taxes The departure tax is $35 and is usually included in the cost of your airline ticket. If not, it's payable only in cash or traveler's checks. Restaurants and hotels add an 11% government tax. Hotels also typically add 11% to 15% for service.

ACCOMMODATIONS

The Turks and Caicos can be a fairly expensive destination. Most hotels on Providenciales are pricey, but there are some moderately priced options; most accommodations are condo-style, but not all resorts are family-friendly. You'll find several upscale properties on the outer islands—including the famous Parrot Cay—but the majority of places are smaller inns. What you give up in luxury, however, you gain back tenfold in island charm. Though the smaller islands are relatively isolated, that's arguably what makes them so attractive in the first place.

Resorts: Most of the resorts on Provo are upscale; many are condo-style, so at least you will have a well-furnished kitchen for breakfast and a few quick lunches. There are three all-inclusive resorts on Provo. A handful of other luxury resorts are on the smaller islands.

Small Inns: Aside from the exclusive, luxury resorts, most of the places on the outlying islands are smaller, modest inns with relatively few amenities. Some are devoted to diving.

Villas and Condos: Villas and condos are plentiful, particularly on Provo, and usually represent a good value for families. However, you need to plan a few months in advance to get one of the better choices, less if you want to stay in a more developed condo complex.

HOTEL AND RESTAURANT PRICES

Prices in the restaurant reviews are the average cost of a main course at dinner or, if dinner is not served, at lunch; taxes and service charges are generally included. Prices in the hotel reviews are the lowest cost of a standard double room in high season, excluding taxes, service charges, and meal plans (except at all-inclusives). Prices for rentals are the lowest per-night cost for a one-bedroom unit in high season.

VISITOR INFORMATION

The tourist offices on Grand Turk and Providenciales are open daily from 9 to 5.

Contacts Turks & Caicos Islands Tourist Board ✉ *Front St., Cockburn Town, Grand Turk* ☎ *649/946–2321* ✉ *Stubbs Diamond Plaza, The Bight, Providenciales* ☎ *649/946–4970* ⊕ *www. turksandcaicostourism.com.*

WEDDINGS

The residency requirement is 24 hours, after which you can apply for a marriage license to the registrar in Grand Turk. You must present a passport, original birth certificate, and proof of current marital status, as well as a letter stating both parties' occupations, ages, addresses, and fathers' full names. No blood tests are required. License fee is $50.

Nila Destinations Wedding Planning ☎ *649/941–4375* ⊕ *www.nilavacations. com.*

PROVIDENCIALES

Passengers typically become oddly silent when their plane starts its descent, mesmerized by the shallow, crystal-clear turquoise waters of Chalk Sound National Park. This island, nicknamed Provo, was once called Blue Hills after the name of its first settlement. Just south of the airport and downtown area, Blue Hills still remains the closest thing you can get to a more typical Caicos island settlement on this, the most developed of the islands in the chain. Most of the modern resorts, exquisite spas, water-sports operators, shops, business plazas, restaurants, bars, cafés, and the championship golf course are on or close by the 12-mile (18-km) stretch of Grace Bay beach. In spite of the ever-increasing number of taller and grander condominium resorts—many have popped up in the past 10 years—it's still possible to find deserted stretches on this priceless, ivory-white shoreline. For guaranteed seclusion, rent a car and go explore the southern shores and western tip of the island, or set sail for a private island getaway on one of the many deserted cays nearby.

Progress and beauty come at a price: with plenty of new visitors arriving each year, the country's charms are no longer a secret, but don't worry—you'll still enjoy the gorgeous beaches and wonderful dinners. Although you may start to believe that every road leads to a big resort development, there are, happily, plenty of sections of beach where you can escape the din.

Although you may be kept quite content enjoying the beachscape and top-notch amenities of Provo itself, it's also a great starting point for island-hopping tours by sea or by air as well as fishing and diving trips.

Resurfaced roads should help you get around and make the most of the main tourism and sightseeing spots.

EXPLORING PROVIDENCIALES

☺ **Caicos Conch Farm.** On the northeast tip of Provo, this is a major mariculture operation, where mollusks are farmed commercially (more than 3 million conch are here). It's a popular tourist attraction, too, offering guided tours and a small gift shop selling conch-related souvenirs, jewelry, and freshwater pearls. You can even meet Jerry and Sally, the residence conch that come out on demand. ⊠ *Leeward-Going-Through, Leeward* ☎ *649/946–5330* ⊠ *$6* ⊗ *Mon.–Sat. 9–4.*

Cheshire Hall. Standing eerily just west of downtown Provo are the remains of a circa-1700 cotton plantation owned by Loyalist Thomas Stubbs. A trail weaves through the ruins, where a few inadequate interpretive signs tell the story of the island's doomed cotton industry with very little information about the plantation itself. A variety of local plants are also identified. The lack of context can be disappointing for history buffs; a visit to North Caicos Wades Green plantation or the Turks & Caicos National Museum could well prove a better fit. ⊠ *Leeward Hwy., behind Ace Hardware, Providenciales* ☎ *649/941–5710 for National Trust* ⊕ *www.tcinationaltrust.org* ⊠ *$5* ⊗ *Mon.–Sat. 8:30–4:30 (guided tour required).*

☺ **Sapodilla Hill.** On this cliff overlooking the secluded Sapodilla Bay, you can discover rocks carved with the names of shipwrecked sailors and dignitaries from TCI's maritime and colonial past. There are carvings on the rocks that some claim are secret codes and maps to hidden treasures; many have tried in vain to find these treasures. The hill is known by two other names, Osprey Rock and Splitting Rock. The less adventurous can see molds of the carvings at Provo's International Airport. It's best to go by boat with Captain Bill's Adventures, as cars in the parking area are occasionally broken into. ⊠ *Off South Dock Rd., west of South Dock, Providenciales.*

WHERE TO EAT

There are more than 50 restaurants on Provo, from casual to elegant, with cuisine from Asian to European (and everything in between). You can spot the islands' own Caribbean influence no matter where you go, exhibited in fresh seafood specials, colorful presentations, and a tangy dose of spice. Some restaurants do close during the slow season, with dates fluctuating yearly; usually closings are from late August through late October.

Pick up a free copy of *Where When How's Dining Guide*, which you will find all over the island; it contains menus, websites, and pictures of all the restaurants.

GRACE BAY

$$$$ ✕ **Anacaona.** At the Grace Bay Club, this palapa-shaded (thatch-roof)
ECLECTIC restaurant has become a favorite of the country's chief minister. But despite the regular presence of government bigwigs, the restaurant

26

Providenciales

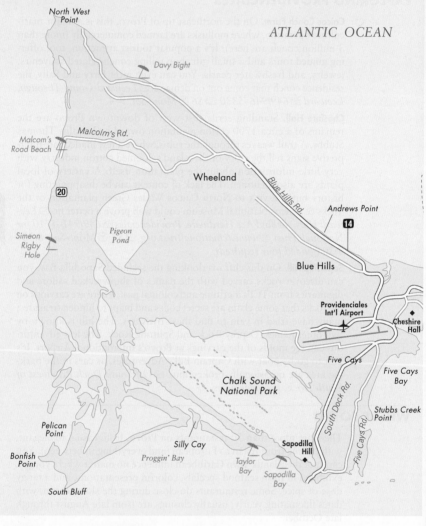

ATLANTIC OCEAN

North West Point

Davy Bight

Malcom's Road Beach

Malcolm's Rd.

Wheeland

Blue Hills Rd.

Andrews Point

Simeon Rigby Hole

Pigeon Pond

Blue Hills

Providenciales Int'l Airport

Cheshire Hall

Five Cays

Five Cays Bay

Chalk Sound National Park

South Dock Rd.

Five Cays Rd.

Stubbs Creek Point

Pelican Point

Silly Cay

Proggin' Bay

Taylor Bay

Sapodilla Hill

Sapodilla Bay

Bonfish Point

South Bluff

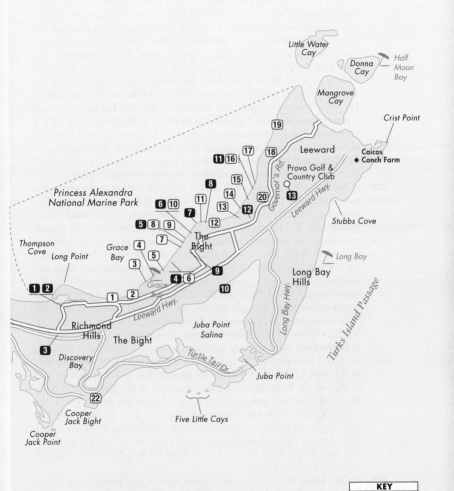

Water Cay

Little Water Cay

Donna Cay

Half Moon Bay

Mangrove Cay

Crist Point

Leeward

Caicos Conch Farm

19

17 **18**

11 **16**

Provo Golf & Country Club

15

Princess Alexandra National Marine Park

8

14

6 **10**

11

13

20

13

Governor's Rd.

Leeward Hwy.

Stubbs Cove

7

12

12

Thompson Cove

5 **8**

9

The Bight

Long Bay

Long Point

7

Grace Bay

4

Long Bay Hills

3

5

Grace Bay

4 **6**

9

10

Turks Island Passage

1 **2**

1

2

Leeward Hwy.

Juba Point Salina

Long Bay Hwy.

Richmond Hills

The Bight

Discovery Bay

Turtle Tail Dr.

Juba Point

22

Cooper Jack Bight

Five Little Cays

Cooper Jack Point

KEY

0   2 miles

0   2 km

Beaches

1 Restaurants

1 Hotels

continues to offer a memorable dining experience minus the tie, the air-conditioning, and the attitude. Start with a bottle of fine wine; then enjoy the light and healthful Mediterranean-influenced cuisine. The kitchen uses the island's bountiful seafood and fresh produce. Oil lamps on the tables, gently revolving ceiling fans, and the murmur of the trade winds add to the Edenic environment. The entrancing ocean view and the careful service make it an ideal choice when you want to be pampered. It's a good thing the setting is amazing; portions are tiny, so you're paying for ambience. Check out the world's first infinity bar, which seems to spill right into the ocean. The lighted menus are a huge plus—no more squinting in the dark to read—yet they do not take away from the romantic experience. Children under 12 are not allowed. Long pants and collared shirts are required. $ *Average main:* $34 ⊠ *Grace Bay Club, Grace Bay, Providenciales* ☎ 649/946–5050 ⊕ *www.gracebayresorts.com* ⚄ *Reservations essential* ⊙ *Sept.*

$$$$
ECLECTIC
☪
Fodor's Choice
★

✕ **Bay Bistro.** You simply can't eat any closer to the beach than here, the only restaurant in all of Provo that is built directly on the sand. You dine on a covered porch surrounded by palm trees and the sound of lapping waves. The spring-roll appetizer is delicious, and the oven-roasted chicken is the best on the island. Junior, one of Provo's top bartenders, might bring your drink balanced on the top of his head. Brunch on weekends includes such favorites as eggs Benedict with mimosas (included) and is very popular; lines can be long if you don't have a reservation. Around the time of the full moon, ask about the memorable beach barbecue: all-you-can-eat ribs, pig roast, and bonfire on the sand. $ *Average main:* $31 ⊠ *Sibonné, Princess Dr., Grace Bay, Providenciales* ☎ 649/946–5396 ⊕ *sibonne.com/grace-bay-bistro/.*

$$$
ITALIAN

✕ **Caicos Café.** New owners have also brought a new menu focusing on island food with an Italian twist. The bruschetta that everyone gets at the start of the meal is delicious enough that you may ask for seconds, and the bread is baked fresh every day at the bakery next door. Blackened fish and jerk chicken on top of pasta are popular with the locals. Ravioli with cream sauce is the tastiest dish. On windy nights, the inland setting offers protection from the breezes. Be sure to wear bug spray at night. $ *Average main:* $27 ⊠ *Caicos Café Plaza, Grace Bay Rd., Grace Bay, Providenciales* ☎ 649/946–5278 ⚄ *caicoscafe@ tciway.tc* ⊙ *Closed Sun.*

$$$$
INTERNATIONAL
Fodor's Choice
★

✕ **Coco Bistro.** With tables under palm trees, Coco Bistro has a divine setting, and the food is just as good. Though not directly on the beach, the location under the tropical tree grove still reminds you that you are on vacation. Main courses are complemented by both French flourishes (served au poivre, for example) and West Indian (such as with mango chutney) and are accompanied by fried plantains and mango slaw to maintain a Caribbean flair. Consider conch soup, soft-shell-crab tempura, and sun-dried tomato pasta from the internationally influenced menu. This is the best of the best in Grace Bay. $ *Average main:* $37 ⊠ *Grace Bay Rd., Grace Bay, Providenciales* ☎ 649/946–5369 ⊕ *www. CocoBistro.tc* ⚄ *Reservations essential* ⊙ *Closed Mon. No lunch.*

$$$$ ✕ **Coyaba Restaurant.** Directly behind Grace Bay Club and next to Carib-
ECLECTIC bean Paradise Inn, this posh eatery serves nostalgic favorites with tempt-
Fodor's Choice ing twists in conversation-piece crockery and in a palm-fringed setting.
★ Chef Paul Newman uses his culinary expertise for the daily-changing
main courses, which include exquisitely presented dishes such as crispy,
whole, yellow snapper fried in Thai spices. One standout is lobster
Thermidor in a Dijon-mushroom cream sauce. Try several different
appetizers instead of a single more expensive entrée for dinner; guava-
and-tamarind barbecue ribs and coconut-shrimp tempura are two good
choices if you go that route. If you enjoy creative menus, this is the
place for you. Chef Paul, who won the 2011 Canadian *Iron Chef* competition, keeps the resident expat crowd happy with traditional favorites such as lemon meringue pie, albeit with his own tropical twist.
Don't skip dessert; Paul makes the most incredible chocolate fondant
you will ever have. $ *Average main: $42* ✉ *Off Grace Bay Rd., beside
Caribbean Paradise Inn, Grace Bay, Providenciales* ☎ 649/946–5186
⊕ *www.coyabarestaurant.com* ⊜ *Reservations essential* ☉ *Closed Tues.
No lunch.*

$$$$ ✕ **Fairways Steakhouse.** If you're a steak lover, there is no better steak
STEAKHOUSE to be found on the island. Located at the golf course, during the day it
Fodor's Choice serves casual fare; at night it converts to fine dining. Rib eyes are aged
★ different dates, you pick the aging. Pick a special chef's butter and
accompanied sauce such as béarnaise, port wine, or peppercorn. Start
with the amazing avacado bruschetta, add the delectable onion soup
(do not miss!) and you will not have room for dessert. The weekend
brunch is one of the best on the island. Lauren, the executive chef, can
also host private event parties. $ *Average main: $35* ✉ *Grace Bay Rd.,
Grace Bay* ☎ 649/946-5833 ⊜ *fairways@tciway.tc.*

$$$$ ✕ **Grace's Cottage.** At one of the prettiest dining settings on Provo, tables
ECLECTIC are artfully set under wrought-iron cottage-style gazebos and around
the wraparound veranda, which skirts the gingerbread-covered main
building. In addition to such tangy and exciting entrées as panfried
red snapper with roasted-pepper sauce or melt-in-your-mouth grilled
beef tenderloin with truffle-scented mashed potatoes, the soufflés are
well worth the 15-minute wait and the top-tier price tag. Portions are
small, but the quality is amazing. Service is impeccable (ladies are given
a small stool so that their purses do not touch the ground). $ *Average
main: $34* ✉ *Point Grace, Grace Bay, Providenciales* ☎ 649/946–5096
⊜ *concierge@pointgrace.com* ⊜ *Reservations essential* ☉ *No lunch.*

$$$ ✕ **Hemingway's.** A casual and gorgeous setting, with a patio and deck
ECLECTIC offering views of Grace Bay, makes this one of the most popular res-
taurants that cater to tourists. At lunch do not miss the best fish tacos
with mango chutney. For dinner there is an excellent kids' menu and
something for everyone, including vegetarians. Order the popular "Old
Man of the Sea," which features the freshest fish of the day. It's known
for great sauces such as the wine reduction for the filet mignon, the
creole for fish dishes, and a delicious curry for chicken. If you're on a
budget, go right before 6 pm, when you can still order the less expensive
lunch menu items. Go on a Thursday or Friday night when there's live

26

music while you dine. $ *Average main: $25* ⊠ *The Sands at Grace Bay, Grace Bay* ☎ 649/946–5199.

$$$ ✕ **Mango Reef.** This is arguably the most popular restaurant of vacation-
ECLECTIC   ers on the island. It's very reasonably priced (by Provo standards) and even has an ever-popular three-course dinner for $42. Although food quality can be inconsistent, try the lobster ravioli, which is reliably quite good. Try to go on a Tuesday or Friday night when NaDa performs easy-listening tunes while you dine (check ahead for music schedule). $ *Average main: $23* ⊠ *Princess Rd., Grace Bay* ☎ 649/946–8200.

$$$$ ✕ **O'Soleil.** Located at the Somerset, this is one of Provo's few indoor,
ECLECTIC   air-conditioned restaurants, though you can also eat outside on the terrace. White-on-white decor under vaulted ceilings gives it a Miami-chic ambience. The executive chef mixes international styles, including influences from the Caribbean, Asia, and Europe. Some of the standouts include the miso-honey-marinated sea bass, roasted New Zealand rack of lamb, and excellent risotto. You could easily make a meal out of a selection of appetizers, too. Ask for simpler off-the-menu options for the children. $ *Average main: $35* ⊠ *The Somerset Princess Dr., Grace Bay, Providenciales* ☎ 649/946–5900 ⊕ *www.thesomerset.com.*

TURTLE COVE

$ ✕ **Angela's Top o' the Cove New York Style Delicatessen.** Order deli sand-
DELI   wiches, salads, enticingly rich desserts, and freshly baked pastries at this island institution on Leeward Highway, just south of Turtle Cove. From the deli case you can buy the fixings for a picnic; the shelves are stocked with an eclectic selection of fancy foodstuffs, as well as beer and wine. It's open at 6:30 am for a busy trade in coffees and cappuccinos. This is a cheesesteak comparable to what you get in Philly, but the location isn't where most tourists stay–it's worth the drive, though. $ *Average main: $9* ⊠ *Leeward Hwy., Turtle Cove, Providenciales* ☎☎ 649/946–4694 ⊕ *www.provo.net/topofthecove* ⊗ *No dinner.*

$$$ ✕ **Magnolia Wine Bar and Restaurant.** Restaurateurs since the early 1990s,
ECLECTIC   hands-on owners Gianni and Tracey Caporuscio make success seem
★   simple. Expect well-prepared, uncomplicated choices that range from European to Asian to Caribbean. You can construct an excellent meal from the outstanding appetizers; do not miss the spring rolls and the grilled-vegetable-and-fresh-mozzarella stack. Finish your meal with the mouthwatering molten chocolate cake. The atmosphere is romantic, the presentations are attractive, and the service is careful. It's easy to see why the Caporuscios have a loyal following. The adjoining wine bar includes a handpicked list of specialty wines, which can be ordered by the glass. The marine setting is a great place to watch the sunset. $ *Average main: $25* ⊠ *Miramar Resort, Turtle Cove, Providenciales* ☎ 649/941–5108 ⊕ *www.magnoliaprovo.com* ⊗ *Closed Mon. No lunch.*

$$ ✕ **Tiki Hut.** From its location overlooking the marina, the ever-popular
AMERICAN   Tiki Hut continues to serve consistently tasty, value-priced meals in a
☺   fun atmosphere. Locals take advantage of the Wednesday night $14 chicken-and-rib special, and the lively bar is a good place to sample local Turks Head brew. There's a special family-style menu (the best kids' menu in Provo) and kids' seating. Don't miss pizzas made with the signature white sauce, or the jerk wings, coated in a secret barbecue

sauce and then grilled—they're out of this world! The restaurant can be busy, with long waits for a table, and you can reserve only with five people or more. ⑤ *Average main: $15* ⊠ *Turtle Cove Marina, Turtle Cove, Providenciales* ☎ 649/941–5341 ⊕ *www.tikihuttci.com/.*

ELSEWHERE ON PROVIDENCIALES

$$ ✕**Da Conch Shack.** An institution in Provo for many years, this brightly
CARIBBEAN   colored beach shack is justifiably famous for its conch and seafood. The legendary specialty, conch, is fished fresh out of the shallows and broiled, spiced, cracked, or fried to absolute perfection. This is the freshest conch anywhere on the island, as the staff dive for it only after you've placed your order, but if you don't like seafood, there is chicken on the menu. Go on a Tuesday night when jerk chicken, peas and rice, and slaw are only $10.99, or a Thursday night when there's live music on the sand. The restaurant has been featured on the Travel Channel on numerous shows. ⑤ *Average main: $15* ⊠ *Blue Hills Rd., Blue Hills, Providenciales* ☎ 649/946–8877 ⊕ *www.conchshack.tc/* ⊟ *No credit cards.*

WHERE TO STAY

26

Most of the resorts on Providenciales are on Grace Bay, but a few are more isolated or even off the beach.

For expanded reviews, facilities, and current deals, visit Fodors.com.

PRIVATE VILLA RENTALS

On Provo you can rent a self-catering villa or private home. For the best villa selection, make your reservations three to six months in advance, or you may not get your first choice. Most villas can be rented on multiple villa-rental sites, which act as booking agents, and most have property managers or owners on island to assist you.

RENTAL CONTACTS

Coldwell Banker TCI. The hardworking agents at Coldwell Banker list some of the most beautiful vacation homes in Provo. ⊠ *Grace Bay* ☎ 649/946–4969 ⊕ *www.coldwellbankertci.com.*

Prestigious Properties. Prestigious Properties offers a wide selection of modest to magnificent villas in the Leeward, Grace Bay, and Turtle Cove areas of Providenciales. ⊠ *Grace Bay* ☎ 649/946–5355 ⊕ *www. prestigiousproperties.com.*

T.C. Safari. T.C. Safari handles booking for numerous properties around Provo. ⊠ *Providenciales* ☎ 649/941–5043, 828/625–9992 ⊕ *www. tcsafari.tc.*

GRACE BAY

$$$ 🏨 **The Alexandra Resort.** Situated on the most popular stretch of Grace
RESORT   Bay Beach, the Alexandra is within walking distance of shops, Coral
🐾   Garden's snorkeling, and excellent restaurants. **Pros:** luxury for less; all rooms have ocean views. **Cons:** A small temporary reception gives a lesser first impression; rooms have only queen beds. **TripAdvisor:** "calm quiet property," "for beach lovers," "total relaxation." ⑤ *Rooms from: $320* ⊠ *Princess Dr., Grace Bay, Providenciales* ☎ 649/946–5807, 800/704–9424 ⊕ *www.alexandraresort.com* ⇆ *88 rooms* ⦿ *No meals.*

$$$$
ALL-INCLUSIVE
☪
★
☒ **Beaches Turks and Caicos Resort and Spa.** The largest resort in the Turks and Caicos Islands can satisfy families as eager to spend time apart as together. **Pros:** great place for families; all-inclusive. **Cons:** with an all-inclusive plan you miss out on the island's other great restaurants; construction next door to the east side of the property. **TripAdvisor:** "fabulous beach," "first class," "great family vacation spot." ⑤ *Rooms from: $884 ☒ Lower Bight Rd., Grace Bay, Providenciales ☎ 649/946–8000, 800/726–3257 ⊕ www.beaches.com ⇋ 359 rooms, 103 suites* ¶◎¶ *All-inclusive.*

$$$$
RESORT
☒ **Club Med Turkoise.** Guests still fly in from the United States, Europe, and Canada to enjoy the scuba diving, windsurfing, and waterskiing on the turquoise waters at the doorsteps of the area's first major resort. **Pros:** all-inclusive; active; good value; adults only; numerous languages spoken. **Cons:** even with some renovations, the rooms are dormlike and need updates and TLC; food has gone downhill. **TripAdvisor:** "hooked for life," "awesome service and activities," "close to heaven." ⑤ *Rooms from: $554 ☒ Grace Bay Rd., Grace Bay, Providenciales ☎ 649/946–5500, 888/932–2582 ⊕ www.clubmed.com ⇋ 293 rooms* ¶◎¶ *Multiple meal plans.*

$$$$
RESORT
☒ **Gansevoort Turks and Caicos, A Wymara Resort.** South Beach Miami chic meets island time at this gorgeous new resort with modern, comfortable furnishings. **Pros:** service is pleasant and eager to please; gorgeous heated pool and beautiful rooms; great ambience. **Cons:** since this is one of Provo's few nightlife venues, Friday and Saturday nights can get a little too lively. **TripAdvisor:** "best service," "incredible beach," "classy and hip." ⑤ *Rooms from: $349 ☒ Lower Bight Rd., Providenciales, Turks and Caicos Islands, BWI, Grace Bay, Providenciales ☎ 649/941–7555 ⊕ www.GansevoortTurksandCaicos.com ⇋ 55 rooms, 32 suites, 4 penthouses* ¶◎¶ *Breakfast.*

$$$$
RESORT
☪
★
☒ **Grace Bay Club.** This stylish resort retains a loyal following because of its helpful, attentive staff and unpretentious elegance. **Pros:** gorgeous pool and restaurant lounge areas with outdoor couches, daybeds, and fire pits; all guests receive a cell phone to use on the island. **Cons:** no children allowed at Anacaona restaurant. **TripAdvisor:** "great hotel," "perfect service," "a true relaxation destination." ⑤ *Rooms from: $796 ☒ Grace Bay Rd., behind Grace Bay Court, Grace Bay, Providenciales ☎ 649/946–5050, 800/946–5757 ⊕ www.gracebayclub.com ⇋ 59 suites* ¶◎¶ *Breakfast.*

$$
RENTAL
☒ **Harbour Club Villas.** Although not on the beach, this small complex of villas is by the marina, making it a good base for scuba diving and bonefishing. **Pros:** nice value, great base for divers, personable and friendly hosts. **Cons:** need a car to get around island, not close to the better beaches, accommodations are a bit rustic. **TripAdvisor:** "very memorable," "perfect relaxing island villa," "wonderful hospitality." ⑤ *Rooms from: $245 ☒ 36 Turtle Tail Dr., Turtle Tail ☎ 649/941–5748, 866/456–0210 ⊕ www.harbourclubvillas.com ⇋ 6 villas* ¶◎¶ *No meals.*

$$$
RESORT
☪
★
☒ **Ocean Club Resorts.** Enormous, locally painted pictures of hibiscus make a striking first impression as you enter the reception area at one of the island's most well-established condominium resorts. **Pros:** family-friendly resort with shuttles between the two shared properties; screened

CLOSE UP

What Is a Potcake?

Potcakes are indigenous dogs of the Bahamas and Turks and Caicos Islands. Traditionally, the stray dogs would be fed from the leftover scraps of food that formed at the bottom of the pot; this is how they got their name. Much is being done these days to control the stray dog population. The TCSPCA and Potcake Place are two agencies working to adopt out the puppies. You can "travel with a cause" by adopting one of these gorgeous pups; they come with all the shots and all the papers required to bring them back home to the United States. Even if you don't adopt, you can help by volunteering as a carrier—bringing one back to its adopted family. Customs in the States is actually easier when you are bringing back a potcake! For more information on how you can help, check out the website for Potcake Place (⊕ *www. potcakeplace.com*).

balconies and porches allow a respite from incessant air-conditioning. Cons: both resorts are showing their age. **TripAdvisor:** "beautiful beach," "heaven on Earth," "peace and quiet." ⑤ *Rooms from: $289* ⊠ *Grace Bay, Providenciales* ☎ *649/946–5880, 800/457–8787* ⊕ *www.oceanclubresorts.com* ⇨ *174 suites: 86 at Ocean Club East, 88 at Ocean Club West* ⑩ *No meals.*

$$$$
RESORT

Point Grace. Asian-influenced rooftop domes blend with Romanesque stone pillars and wide stairways in this plush resort, which offers spacious beachfront suites and romantic cottages surrounding the centerpiece: a turquoise infinity pool with perfect views of the beach. **Pros:** relaxing environment; beautiful pool. **Cons:** can be stuffy (signs around the pool remind you to be quiet). **TripAdvisor:** "absolutely beautiful," "perfect place for relaxing," "private." ⑤ *Rooms from: $656* ⊠ *Grace Bay, Providenciales* ☎ *649/946–5096, 888/924–7223* ⊕ *www.pointgrace.com* ⇨ *23 suites, 9 cottage suites, 2 villas* ⊘ *Closed Sept.* ⑩ *Breakfast.*

$$$$
RESORT
☾

Regent Palms. High on luxury and glitz, this is a place to see and be seen. **Pros:** great people-watching; lively atmosphere; one of the best spas in the Caribbean. **Cons:** some would say busy not lively; a little formal and stuffy (people dress up to be "seen" at the pool). **TripAdvisor:** "great features," "elegant," "gorgeous." ⑤ *Rooms from: $850* ⊠ *Grace Bay, Providenciales* ☎ *649/946–8666, 866/630-5890* ⊕ *www. regenthotels.com* ⇨ *72 suites* ⑩ *Breakfast.*

$$$
RESORT
★

Royal West Indies Resort. With a contemporary take on colonial architecture and the outdoor feel of a botanical garden, this unpretentious resort has plenty of garden-view and beachfront studios and suites for moderate self-catering budgets. **Pros:** the best bang for the buck on Provo; on one of the widest stretches of Grace Bay Beach. **Cons:** Club Med next door can be noisy. **TripAdvisor:** "amazing personalized resort," "absolutely beautiful," "relaxing trip." ⑤ *Rooms from: $310* ⊠ *Grace Bay, Providenciales* ☎ *649/946–5004, 800/332–4203* ⊕ *www. royalwestindies.com* ⇨ *99 suites* ⑩ *No meals.*

26

$$$$
RESORT
☺

☒ **Sands at Grace Bay.** Spacious gardens and winding pools set the tone for one of Provo's most popular family resorts. **Pros:** one of the best places for families; central to shops and numerous restaurants; screened balconies and porches give an escape from incessant air-conditioning. **Cons:** a new wooden pool deck can cause splinters, so keep an eye on the kids; avoid courtyard rooms, which are not worth the price. **TripAdvisor:** "pleasant stay," "beautiful room," "a lovely atmosphere." ⑤ *Rooms from: $360* ☒ *Grace Bay, Providenciales* ☎ *649/941–5199, 877/777–2637* ⊕ *www.thesandstc.com* ⌁ *118 suites* ⑩ *No meals.*

$$$$
RESORT
☺
Fodor's Choice
★

☒ **Seven Stars.** The tallest property on the island also sets a high mark for luxury. **Pros:** gorgeous inside and out; walking distance to everything in Grace Bay; terrific deck bar by the beach. **Cons:** some find the giant scale of the resort too big for the rest of the island. **TripAdvisor:** "beautiful location," "fantastic resort," "service beyond compare." ⑤ *Rooms from: $618* ☒ *Grace Bay Rd., Providenciales* ☎ *649/941–3777, 866/570–7777* ⊕ *www.sevenstarsgracebay.com* ⌁ *143 suites* ⑩ *Breakfast.*

$$
HOTEL

☒ **Sibonné.** Dwarfed by most of the nearby resorts, the smallest hotel on Grace Bay Beach has snug (by Provo's spacious standards) but pleasant rooms with Bermuda-style balconies and a completely circular but tiny pool. **Pros:** closest property to the beach; the island's best bargain directly on the beach. **Cons:** pool is small and dated. **TripAdvisor:** "perfect place to stay," "charming," "beautiful beach." ⑤ *Rooms from: $175* ☒ *Princess Dr., Grace Bay, Providenciales* ☎ *649/946–5547, 800/528–1905* ⊕ *www.sibonne.com* ⌁ *29 rooms, 1 apartment* ⑩ *Breakfast.*

$$$$
RESORT
Fodor's Choice
★

☒ **The Somerset.** This luxury resort has the "wow" factor, starting with the architecture, followed by the service, and ending in your luxuriously appointed suite. **Pros:** the most beautiful architecture on Provo; terrific service; Tuesday night beach BBQ bonfires. **Cons:** the cheapest lock-out rooms are not worth the cost—they can get noisy. **TripAdvisor:** "lovely property," "a great resort," "beautiful but sadly lacking service." ⑤ *Rooms from: $900* ☒ *Princess Dr., Grace Bay, Providenciales* ☎ *649/946–5900, 877/887–5722* ⊕ *www.thesomerset.com* ⌁ *53 suites* ⑩ *Breakfast.*

$$$$
RESORT

☒ **The Tuscany.** This self-catering, quiet, upscale resort is the place for independent travelers to unwind around one of the prettiest pools on Provo. **Pros:** luxurious; all condos have ocean views; beautiful pool. **Cons:** no restaurant and far from the best restaurants; very expensive for self-catering. **TripAdvisor:** "very friendly and helpful staff," "a beautiful relaxing spot," "superb hospitality and setting." ⑤ *Rooms from: $775* ☒ *Grace Bay, Providenciales* ☎ *649/941–4667, 866/359–6466* ⊕ *www.thetuscanyresort.com* ⌁ *30 condos* ⑩ *No meals.*

$$$$
ALL-INCLUSIVE

☒ **Veranda Resort.** And now for something completely different for Provo: an upscale, quiet, ultraluxury, all-inclusive resort. **Pros:** excellent service; top-shelf spirits included; unique clapboard architecture. **Cons:** included meals mean you may miss out on excellent independent restaurants; only two restaurants can mean a wait for a table at prime times. **TripAdvisor:** "wonderful escape," "the most beautiful beach,"

West Bay Club

"perfect in every way." ⑤ *Rooms from: $775* ✉ *Princess Dr., Providenciales* ☎ *649/339–5050* ⊕ *www.VerandaTCI.com* ↩ *168 rooms* ⑩ *All-inclusive.*

$$$
HOTEL
🏨 **Villa Del Mar.** This resort, which opened in 2008, offers some tremendous features for the price, even though it is not directly on Grace Bay Beach. **Pros:** close to the best restaurants on the island; within walking distance of Casablanca Casino; continental breakfast included in rate. **Cons:** no on-site restaurant; no views from most floors; not directly on the beach. ⑤ *Rooms from: $320* ✉ *Cresent Rd., Grace Bay* ☎ *649/941–5160* ⊕ *www.YourVillaDelMar.com* ↩ *18 rooms, 24 suites* ⑩ *Breakfast.*

$$$$
RENTAL
🏨 **Villa Renaissance.** Modeled after a Tuscan villa, this luxury property is for the self-catering tourist. **Pros:** luxury for less; one of the prettiest courtyards in Provo. **Cons:** the pool bar is not consistenly manned; not a full-service resort. **TripAdvisor:** "wonderful beach and accommodations," "great staff," "understated luxury." ⑤ *Rooms from: $725* ✉ *Grace Bay, Providenciales* ☎ *649/941–5300, 877/285–8764* ⊕ *www. villarenaissance.com* ↩ *20 suites* ⑩ *No meals.*

$$$
RESORT
Fodor's Choice
★
🏨 **West Bay Club.** One of Provo's newest resorts has a prime location on a pristine stretch of Grace Bay Beach just steps away from the best off-the-beach snorkeling. **Pros:** all rooms have a beach view; new, clean, and sparkling; contemporary architecture makes it stand out from other resorts. **Cons:** a car is needed to go shopping and to the best restaurants. **TripAdvisor:** "quiet and relaxing," "amazing dream escape," "exceptional in every way." ⑤ *Rooms from: $345* ✉ *Lower Bight Rd., Lower Bight, Providenciales* ☎ *649/946–8550* ⊕ *www.TheWestBayClub.com* ↩ *46 suites* ⑩ *No meals.*

$$$$
RESORT
Fodor's Choice
★

⊞ **Windsong Resort.** On a gorgeous beach lined with several appealing resorts, Windsong stands out for two reasons: the Sail Provo program and a magnificent pool. **Pros:** the pool is the coolest; Sail Provo on property; gorgeous new resort. **Cons:** resort is experiencing some growing pains, so service can be lacking; studios have only a refrigerator and microwave; thinner stretch of beachfront here. **TripAdvisor:** "low key and wonderful," "great beach," "stunning views and accommodations." ⑤ *Rooms from: $390* ⊠ *Stubbs Rd., Lower Bight, Providenciales* ☎ *649/941–7700, 800/946-3766* ⊕ *www.windsongresort.com* ➴ *16 studios, 30 suites* ⑩ *No meals.*

ELSEWHERE ON PROVIDENCIALES

$$$$
RESORT
Fodor's Choice
★

⊞ **Amanyara.** If you seek seclusion, peace, and tranquillity in a Zenlike atmosphere, this is your place. **Pros:** on one of the best beaches on Provo; resort is quiet and secluded. **Cons:** isolated; far from restaurants, excursions, and other beaches. **TripAdvisor:** "breathtaking," "great getaway," "a perfect vacation experience." ⑤ *Rooms from: $1,650* ⊠ *Northwest Point* ☎ *649/941–8133* ⊕ *www.amanresorts.com* ➴ *40 pavilions* ⑩ *No meals.*

NIGHTLIFE

Although Provo is not known for its nightlife, there are some live bands and bars. Popular singers such as NaDa, JustSpliff, Corey Forbes, and Quiton Dean perform at numerous restaurants and barbecue bonfires. Danny Buoy's, where you can always watch the latest game on big video screens, gets going late at night. Be sure to see if any ripsaw bands—aka rake-and-scrape—are playing while you're on island; this is one of the quintessential local music types and is popular at local restaurants in Blue Hills.

Late-night action can be found at Gansevoort Turks + Caicos (*see hotel review*), where DJs play until the wee hours on weekends, and Casablanca Casino, where everyone ends the night. The best ambience is wherever Daniel and Nadine are singing; this crowd-pleasing couple has a following—even among tourists. Now there's a reason to go out on Tuesday; a barbecue bonfire at The Somerset offers live music while you dine on the sand.

On nights with major sports on TV, head to Gansevoort's beach bar to watch on a huge TV in the sand.

Keep abreast of events and specials by checking **TCI eNews** (⊕ *www. tcienews.com*).

BARS AND CLUBS

Danny Buoy's. A popular Irish pub, Danny Buoy's has pool tables, darts, and big-screen TVs. It's a great place to watch sports from anywhere in the world. ⊠ *Grace Bay Rd., across from Carpe Diem Residences, Grace Bay, Providenciales* ☎ *649/946–5921.*

Stelle. Bringing South Beach Miami chic to the beach, this is one of the few places that are "happening" on a Saturday night. Live bands, DJs, and celebrity sightings make the action. ⊠ *Gansevoort Wymara Resort, The Bight, Providenciales* ☎ *649/941–7555* ⊕ *www.*

Best Spas in Provo and Beyond

A Turks Island Salt Glow, where the island's sea salt is mixed with gentle oils to exfoliate, smooth, and moisturize the skin, is just one of the treatments you can enjoy in one of the island spas. Being pampered spa-style has become as much a part of a Turks and Caicos vacation as sunning on the beach. Marine-based ingredients fit well with the Grace Bay backdrop at the Thalasso Spa at **Point Grace,** where massages take place in two simple, bleached-white cottages standing on the dune line, which means you have a spectacular view of the sea-blue hues—if you manage to keep your eyes open. The Regent Spa at the **Regent Palms** offers individual treatments, with a water feature by day, a fire feature at night. The signature body scrub uses hand-crushed local conch shells to smooth the skin. But the widest choice of Asian-inspired treatments (and the most unforgettable scenery) can be found at the 6,000-square-foot Como Shambhala Spa at the **Parrot Cay Resort,** which has outdoor whirlpools and a central beechwood lounge overlooking the shallow turquoise waters and mangroves.

Spa Tropique. Provo also has a note-worthy day spa that's not in one of the Grace Bay resorts. Manager Terri Tapper blends Swedish, therapeutic, and reflexology massage techniques using oils made from natural plants and products produced locally and within the Caribbean region. The Turks Island Salt Glow has become one of her most popular treatments. ⊠ *Ports of Call, Grace Bay Rd., Grace Bay, Providenciales* ☎ *649/941–5720* ⊕ *www.spatropique.com.*

26

gansevoortturksandcaicos.com/gansevoort-bagatelle-bistrot-beach-club.php.

Somewhere . . . On The Beach. A Tex-Mex alternative that gives the wallet a break from fine dining becomes the hot spot on Thursday nights with live music. Three levels of outdoor decks add to the fun. ⊠ *Coral Gardens on Grace Bay, The Bight, Providenciales* ☎ *649/231–0590.*

CASINOS

Casablanca Casino. This casino has brought slots, blackjack, American roulette, poker, craps, and baccarat back to Provo. Open from 7 pm until 4 am, this is the last stop for the night. Grace Bay Club has introduced the infinity bar, the only one of its kind in the world, which gives the impression that it goes directly into the ocean. ⊠ *Grace Bay Rd., Grace Bay, Providenciales* ☎ *649/941–3737.*

SHOPPING

Handwoven straw baskets and hats, polished conch-shell crafts, paintings, wood carvings, model sailboats, handmade dolls, and metalwork are crafts native to the islands and nearby Haiti. The natural surroundings have inspired local and international artists to paint, sculpt, print, craft, and photograph; most of their creations are on sale in Providenciales.

SHOPPING AREAS

There are several main shopping areas in Provo: Grace Bay has the newer **Saltmills** complex and **La Petite Place** retail plaza, the new **Regent Village**, and the original **Ports of Call** shopping village. Two markets on the beach near the Ocean Club and the Beaches Turks & Caicos Resort & Spa allow for barefoot shopping.

RECOMMENDED STORES

ART AND CRAFTS GALLERIES

★ **Anna's Art Gallery and Studio.** Anna's sells original artworks, silk-screen paintings, sculptures, and handmade sea-glass jewelry. ⊠ *The Saltmills, Grace Bay* ☎ *649/231–3293.*

ArtProvo. ArtProvo is the island's largest gallery of designer wall art; also shown are native crafts, jewelry, handblown glass, candles, and other gift items. Featured artists include Trevor Morgan, from Salt Cay, and Dwight Outten. ⊠ *Regent Village, Grace Bay* ☎ *649/941–4545.*

Greensleeves. This boutique offers paintings and pottery by local artists, baskets, jewelry, and sisal mats and bags. The proceeds from sales of works in the Potcake Corner help fund the Potcake Place rescue center for the islands' stray dogs. ⊠ *Central Sq., Leeward Hwy., Turtle Cove* ☎☎ *649/946–4147.*

FOOD

Graceway IGA Supermarket Gourmet. With a large fresh produce section, bakery, gourmet deli, and extensive meat counter, Provo's largest supermarket, is likely to have what you're looking for, and it's the most consistently well-stocked store on the island. It's got a good selection of prepared foods, including rotisserie chicken, pizza, and potato salad. But prices can be much higher than at home. ⊠ *Grace Bay Rd., Grace Bay* ☎ *649/941–5000.*

LIQUOR

Wine Cellar. Visit this store for its large selection of duty-free liquor at the best prices ⊠ *Leeward Hwy., east of Suzie Turn Rd., Turtle Cove* ☎ *649/946–4536.*

SPORTS AND ACTIVITIES

BOATING AND SAILING

Provo's calm, reef-protected seas combine with constant easterly trade winds for excellent sailing conditions. Several multihulled vessels offer charters with snorkeling stops, food and beverage service, and sunset vistas. Prices range from $39 per person for group trips (subject to passenger minimums) to $600 or more for private charters.

Caicos Tours. For sightseeing below the waves, try the semisubmarine Undersea Explorer operated by Caicos Tours. You can stay dry within the small, lower observatory as it glides along on a one-hour tour of the reef, with large viewing windows on either side. The trip costs $55. ⊠ *Turtle Cove Marina, Turtle Cove* ☎ *649/231–0006* ⊕ *www.caicostours.com.*

☾ **Island Vibes.** Shaun Dean makes these excursions stand out since he grew
Fodor'sChoice up on these waters. If conditions are right, he'll have you snorkel the
★ "abyss," where the reef drops 6,000 feet. The sight is amazing. His boat
is also the best on Provo, including a diving board on the roof. ✉ *Turtle
Cove* ☎ *649/231–8423* ⊕ *www.islandvibestours.com.*

Sail Provo. Located at Windsong Resort, Sail Provo runs 52-foot and
48-foot catamarans on scheduled half-day, full-day, sunset, and kid-
friendly glowworm cruises, where underwater creatures light up the
sea's surface for several days after each full moon. They are extremely
popular for private charters. ✉ *Providenciales* ☎ *649/946–4783*
⊕ *www.sailprovo.com.*

DIVING AND SNORKELING

Fodor'sChoice The island's many shallow reefs offer excellent and exciting snorkel-
★ ing relatively close to shore. Try **Smith's Reef**, over Bridge Road east of
Turtle Cove.

Scuba diving in the crystalline waters surrounding the islands ranks
among the best in the Caribbean. The reef and wall drop-offs thrive
with bright, unbroken coral formations and lavish numbers of fish and
marine life. Mimicking the idyllic climate, waters are warm all year,
averaging 76°F to 78°F in winter and 82°F to 84°F in summer. With
minimal rainfall and soil runoff, visibility is usually good and frequently
superb, ranging from 60 feet to more than 150 feet. An extensive system
of marine national parks and boat moorings, combined with an ecocon-
scious mind-set among dive operators, contributes to an uncommonly
pristine underwater environment.

Dive operators in Provo regularly visit sites at **Grace Bay** and **Pine Cay** for
spur-and-groove coral formations and bustling reef diving. They make
the longer journey to the dramatic walls at **North West Point** and **West
Caicos** depending on weather conditions. Instruction from the major
diving agencies is available for all levels and certifications, even Technical diving. An average one-tank dive costs $45; a two-tank dive, $90.
There are also two live-aboard dive boats available for charter working out of Provo.

☾ **Big Blue Unlimited.** Big Blue Unlimited has taken ecotouring to a whole
new level with educational ecotours, including three-hour kayak trips
and land-focused guided journeys around the family islands. Its Coastal
Ecology and Wildlife tour is a kayak adventure through red mangroves
to bird habitats, rock iguana hideaways, and natural fish nurseries. The
Middle Caicos Bicycle Adventure gets you on a bike to explore the
island, touring limestone caves in Conch Bar with a break for lunch
with the Forbes family in the village of Bambarra. Packages are $255 for
adults. No children under 12 are allowed. ✉ *Leeward Marina, Leeward*
☎ *649/946–5034* ⊕ *www.bigblue.tc.*

Caicos Adventures. Caicos Adventures, run by friendly Frenchman Fifi
Kuntz, offers daily trips to West Caicos, French Cay, and Molasses
Reef. ✉ *Regent Village, Grace Bay Rd., Grace Bay* ☎ *649/941–3346*
⊕ *www.tcidiving.com.*

26

Diving with stingrays

☾ Caicos Dream Tours. Caicos Dream Tours, at the Alexandra Resort, offers several snorkeling trips, including one that has you diving for conch before lunch on a gorgeous beach. The company also offers private charters. ⊠ *Providenciales* ☎ *649/231–7274* ⊕ *www.caicosdreamtours. com.*

Fodor's Choice
★

Dive Provo. Dive Provo is a PADI five-star operation that runs daily one- and two-tank dives to popular Grace Bay sites as well as West Caicos. ⊠ *Ports of Call, Grace Bay* ☎ *649/946–5040, 800/234–7768* ⊕ *www. diveprovo.com.*

Provo Turtle Divers. Provo Turtle Divers, which also operates satellite locations at the Ocean Club East and Ocean Club West, has been on Provo since the 1970s. The staff is friendly, knowledgeable, and unpretentious. ⊠ *Turtle Cove Marina, Turtle Cove* ☎ *649/946–4232, 800/833–1341* ⊕ *www.provoturtledivers.com.*

FISHING

The islands' fertile waters are great for angling—anything from bottom- and reef-fishing (most likely to produce plenty of bites and a large catch) to bonefishing and deep-sea fishing (among the finest in the Caribbean). Each July the Caicos Classic Catch & Release Tournament attracts anglers from across the islands and the United States who compete to catch the biggest Atlantic blue marlin, tuna, or wahoo. For any fishing activity, you are required to purchase a $15 visitor's fishing license; operators generally furnish all equipment, drinks, and snacks. Prices range from $100 to $375, depending on the length of trip and size of boat.

Diving the Turks and Caicos Islands

Scuba diving was the original water sport to draw visitors to the Turks and Caicos Islands in the 1970s. Aficionados are still drawn by the abundant marine life, including humpback whales in winter, sparkling clean waters, warm and calm seas, and the coral walls and reefs around the islands. Diving in the Turks and Caicos—especially off Grand Turk, South Caicos, and Salt Cay—is still considered among the best in the world.

Off Providenciales, dive sites are along the north shore's barrier reef. Most sites can be reached in anywhere from 10 minutes to 1½ hours. Dive sites feature spur-and-groove coral formations atop a coral-covered slope. Popular stops such as **Aquarium, Pinnacles,** and **Grouper Hole** have

large schools of fish, turtles, nurse sharks, and gray reef sharks. From the south side, dive boats go to **French Cay, West Caicos, South West Reef,** and **Northwest Point.** Known for typically calm conditions and clear water, the West Caicos Marine National Park is a favorite stop. The area has dramatic walls and marine life, including sharks, eagle rays, and octopus, with large stands of pillar coral and huge barrel sponges.

Off Grand Turk, the 7,000-foot coral wall **drop-off** is actually within swimming distance of the beach. Buoyed sites along the wall have swim-through tunnels, cascading sand chutes, imposing coral pinnacles, dizzying vertical drops, and undercuts where the wall goes beyond the vertical and fades beneath the reef.

26

Grandslam Fishing Charters. For deep-sea fishing trips in search of marlin, sailfish, wahoo, tuna, barracuda, and shark, look up Grandslam Fishing Charters. ⊠ *Turtle Cove Marina, Turtle Cove* ☎ *649/231–4420* ⊕ *www.GSFishing.com.*

Gwendolyn Fishing Charters. For deep-sea fishing trips in search of marlin, sailfish, wahoo, tuna, barracuda, and shark, look up Gwendolyn Fishing Charters. ⊠ *Turtle Cove Marina, Turtle Cove* ☎ *649/946–5321* ⊕ *www.fishtci.com.*

Silverdeep. Captain Arthur Dean at Silverdeep is said to be among the Caribbean's finest bonefishing guides. ⊠ *Leeward Marina, Leeward* ☎ *649/946–5612* ⊕ *www.silverdeep.com.*

GOLF

Fodor'sChoice
★
Provo Golf and Country Club. The par-72, 18-hole championship course at Provo Golf and Country Club is a combination of lush greens and fairways, rugged limestone outcroppings, and freshwater lakes, and is ranked among the Caribbean's top courses. Fees are $160 for 18 holes with shared cart. Premium golf clubs are available. ⊠ *Governor's Rd., Grace Bay* ☎ *649/946–5991* ⊕ *www.provogolfclub.com.*

HORSEBACK RIDING

Provo's long beaches and secluded lanes are ideal for trail rides on horseback.

Provo Ponies. Provo Ponies offers morning and afternoon rides for all levels. A 60-minute ride costs $75; a 90-minute ride is $90. Reservations are required, and there is a 200-pound weight limit. It's closed on week-ends. ⊠ *Long Bay* ☎ *649/946–5252* ⊕ *www.provoponies.com.*

LITTLE WATER CAY

☾ This small, uninhabited cay is a protected area under the Turks &
★ Caicos National Trust and just a stone's throw away from Walkin and
Leeward marinas. On a private boat, the trip takes five minutes; an
excursion boat takes 5 to 15 minutes once you leave the Grace Bay
area. On these 150 acres are two trails, small lakes, red mangroves,
and an abundance of native plants. Boardwalks protect the ground,
and interpretive signs explain the habitat. The small island is home to
about 2,000 rare, endangered rock iguanas. Experts say the iguanas
are shy, but these creatures actually seem rather curious. They waddle
right up to you, as if posing for a picture. Several water-sports operators
from Provo and North Caicos include a stop on the island as part of a
snorkel or sailing excursion (it's usually called Iguana Island). There's a
$5 permit fee to visit the cay, and the proceeds go toward conservation
in the islands. ⚠ Unless you're a woman who loves to get a pedicure the
hard way, watch your toes when you are standing in sand near the iguanas—
they have been known to mistake partially buried colored nails for grapes!

PARROT CAY

Once said to be a hideout for pirate Calico Jack Rackham and his lady
cohorts Mary Read and Anne Bonny, the 1,000-acre cay, between Fort
George Cay and North Caicos, is now the site of an ultraexclusive
hideaway resort.

WHERE TO STAY

For expanded reviews, facilities, and current deals, visit Fodors.com.

$$$$ 🖬 **Parrot Cay Resort.** This private paradise, on its own island, combines
RESORT minimalist tranquillity with the best service in Turks and Caicos. **Pros:**
Fodor's Choice impeccable service; gorgeous, secluded beach; the spa is considered
★ one of the best in the world. **Cons:** only two restaurants on the entire
island; it can be costly to get back and forth to Provo for excursions,
as there is only private ferry service. **TripAdvisor:** "quiet paradise,"
"great service," "tranquil getaway." ⑤ *Rooms from: $700* ⊠ *Parrot
Cay* ☎ *649/946–7788, 877/754–0726* ⊕ *www.parrotcay.como.bz* ⇆ *42
rooms, 4 suites, 14 villas* ❦ *Breakfast.*

PINE CAY

15 to 20 minutes by boat from Provo.

Pine Cay's 2½-mile-long (4-km-long) beach is among the most beautiful
in the archipelago. The 800-acre private island, which is in the string
of small cays between Provo and North Caicos, is home to a secluded
resort and almost 40 private residences. The beach alone is reason to

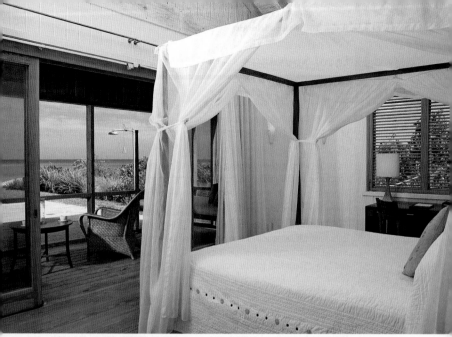

Parrot Cay Resort

stay here: the sand seems a little whiter, the water a little brighter than beaches on the other cays. Nonguests of the Meridien Club can make reservations for lunch, which will include the private boat transfer. Expect to pay between $100 and $150 for the day; there are themed buffets on Sunday.

WHERE TO STAY

For expanded reviews, facilities, and current deals, visit Fodors.com.

$$$$
RESORT
Fodor's Choice
★

⊡ **Meridian Club.** A private club atmosphere on the prettiest beach in Turks and Caicos is *the* place to de-stress, with no phones, no TVs, no a/c, no worries. **Pros:** the finest beach in Turks and Caicos; rates include some of the best food in the Turks and Caicos as well as snorkeling trips. **Cons:** no TVs or phones, so you are really unplugged here; costly to get back to Provo for shopping or other Provo-based excursions or activities. **TripAdvisor:** "relaxing and beautiful," "great food and staff," "stunning empty beach." ⑤ *Rooms from: $1,060* ⊠ *Pine Cay* ☎ *649/946–7758, 866/746–3229* ⊕ *www.meridianclub.com* ⊅ *12 rooms, 1 cottage, 7 villas* ⊘ *Closed Aug.–Oct.* ⑩ *All meals.*

NORTH CAICOS

Thanks to abundant rainfall, this 41-square-mile (106-square-km) island is the lushest in the Turks and Caicos chain. With an estimated population of only 1,500, the expansive island allows you to get away from it all. Bird lovers can see a large flock of flamingos here, anglers

Local Souvenirs

What should you bring home after a fabulous vacation in the Turks and Caicos Islands? Here are a few suggestions, some of which are free!

If you comb Pelican Beach or go on a conch-diving excursion, bring two conch shells (the maximum number allowed) home. Remember, only the shell, no living thing, is allowed.

The Middle Caicos Coop shop in Blue Hills sells carved wooden boats from Middle Caicos, and local straw hats and bags. You'll find locally made ceramics at Art Provo and at Turks & Caicos National Trust (at Town Center Mall or next to Island Scoop Ice Cream).

There are two cultural centers, one between Ocean Club East and Club Med, and the other next to Beaches Resort (there's a third one under construction between Aquamarine Beach Houses and Gansevoort). Here you'll find batik clothing and locally made jewelry. Custom-made pieces can be ordered.

The Conch Farm sells beautiful, affordable jewelry made from conch shells and freshwater pearls.

One of the best souvenirs is the hardcover coffee-table cookbook from the Red Cross. Not only is it gorgeous, featuring recipes from all the great chefs of the Turks and Caicos, but the proceeds help the Red Cross.

The best free souvenir—besides your phenomenal tan—is a potcake puppy. The puppy you adopt comes with carrier, papers, and all the shots—and will remind you year after year of your terrific vacation.

---

can find shallow creeks full of bonefish, and history buffs can visit the ruins of a Loyalist plantation. Although there's little traffic, almost all the roads are paved, so bicycling is an excellent way to sightsee. Even though it's a quiet place, you can find some small eateries around the settlements and in Whitby, giving you a chance to try local and seafood specialties, sometimes served with homegrown okra or corn. The beaches are more natural here, and they are sometimes covered with seaweed and pine needles, as there are no major resorts to rake them daily. Nevertheless, some of these secluded strands are breathtaking, even if not as manicured as those of the upscale resorts on Provo.

North Caicos is definitely rustic, especially in comparison with shiny new Provo. Accommodations are clean but fairly basic. Locals are consistently friendly, and life always seems to move slowly.

Photography Tip. Don't you hate finding that your pictures lack the bright colors you saw at the beach and on the water? Brightly lighted water reflects on the lens and causes the pictures to look washed out. Solution? Use a circular polarizer—it's like sunglasses for your camera, reducing glare and saturating colors so your pictures look professional.

EXPLORING NORTH CAICOS

Flamingo Pond. This is a regular nesting place for the beautiful pink birds. They tend to wander out into the middle of the pond, so bring binoculars to get a better look. ⊠ *North Caicos.*

Kew. This settlement has a small post office, a school, a church, and ruins of old plantations—all set among lush tropical trees bearing limes, papayas, and custard apples. Visiting Kew will give you a better understanding of the daily life of many islanders. ⊠ *North Caicos.*

Wades Green. Visitors can view well-preserved ruins of the greathouse, overseer's house, and surrounding walls of one of the most successful plantations of the Loyalist era. A lookout tower provides views for miles. Contact the National Trust for tour details. ⊠ *Kew* ☎ *649/941–5710 for National Trust* 🔖 *$5* 🕙 *Daily, by appointment only.*

WHERE TO STAY

For expanded reviews, facilities, and current deals, visit Fodors.com.

$$$
RENTAL
🏠 **Hollywood Beach Suites.** With 7 miles of secluded beaches and few others to share them with, this property with four self-contained units is completely relaxing. **Pros:** secluded, tranquil, upscale furnishings. **Cons:** might feel a little quiet if you're wanting a busy vacation or active social scene. **TripAdvisor:** "serenity at its best," "perfect remote getaway," "absolutely amazing view." ⑤ *Rooms from: $325* ⊠ *Hollywood Beach Dr., Whitby* ☎ *649/231–1020, 800/551–2256* ⊕ *www.Hollywoodbeachsuites.com* 🛏 *4 suites* 🍴 *No meals.*

$$
HOTEL
🏠 **Pelican Beach Hotel.** North Caicos islanders Susan and Clifford Gardiner built this small, palmetto-fringed hotel in the 1980s on the quiet, mostly deserted Whitby Beach. **Pros:** the beach is just outside your room, linens are crisp and clean. **Cons:** location may be too remote and sleepy for some people; beach is in a "natural" state, meaning seaweed and pine needles. **TripAdvisor:** "get away from it all," "great place for quiet relaxing," "serene and comfortable." ⑤ *Rooms from: $165* ⊠ *Whitby* ☎ *649/946–7112, 877/774–5486* ⊕ *www.pelicanbeach.tc* 🛏 *14 rooms, 2 suites* 🕙 *Closed Aug. 15–Sept. 15* 🍴 *Some meals.*

MIDDLE CAICOS

At 48 square miles (124 square km) and with fewer than 300 residents, this is the largest and least developed of the inhabited islands in the Turks and Caicos chain. A limestone ridge runs to about 125 feet above sea level, creating dramatic cliffs on the north shore and a cave system farther inland. Middle Caicos has rambling trails along the coast; the **Crossing Place Trail,** maintained by the National Trust, follows the path used by the early settlers to go between the islands. Inland are quiet settlements with friendly residents. North Caicos and Middle Caicos are linked by a causeway; since they are now linked by a road, it's possible to take a ferry from Provo to North Caicos, rent a car, and explore both North Caicos and Middle Caicos.

26

EXPLORING MIDDLE CAICOS

☾ **Conch Bar Caves.** These limestone caves have eerie underground lakes and milky-white stalactites and stalagmites. Archaeologists have discovered Lucayan Indian artifacts in the caves and the surrounding area. The caves are inhabited by some harmless bats. If you visit, don't worry—they don't bother visitors. It's best to get a guide. If you tour the caves, be sure to wear sturdy shoes, not sandals. ⊠ *Middle Caicos.*

WHERE TO EAT AND STAY

$$
RENTAL
📷 **Blue Horizon Resort.** At this property, undulating cliffs skirt one of the most dramatic beaches in the Turks and Caicos. **Pros:** breathtaking views of Mudjin Harbour from the rooms; lack of development makes you feel like you're away from it all. **Cons:** only one restaurant on Middle; may be too isolated for some. **TripAdvisor:** "beautiful place," "total relaxation and isolation," "deserted pristine beach for yourself." ⑤ *Rooms from: $175* ⊠ *Mudjin Harbour, Conch Bar* ☎ *649/946–6141* ⊕ *www.bhresort.com* ⟿ *5 cottages, 2 villas* ⑩ *No meals.*

SPORTS AND ACTIVITIES

CAVE TOURS
Cardinal Arthur. Taxi driver and fisherman Cardinal Arthur can give you a good cave tour. ⊠ *Middle Caicos* ☎ *649/946–6107.*

SOUTH CAICOS

This 8½-square-mile (21-square-km) island was once an important salt producer; today it's the heart of the fishing industry. Nature prevails, with long, white beaches, jagged bluffs, quiet backwater bays, and salt flats. Diving and snorkeling on the pristine wall and reefs are a treat enjoyed by only a few.

In 2008 Hurricanes Hanna and Ike gave South Caicos a one-two punch, and many of the buildings at Cockburn Harbour sustained substantial damage; island residents had to wait more than a month to have power restored. Although the island has recovered, the few dive operators have disappeared. The best way to dive (other than independently) is through Sea Crystal Divers from Salt Cay, which requires spending the night at Salt Cay.

The major draw for South Caicos is its excellent diving and snorkeling on the wall and reefs (with an average visibility of 100 feet). It's practically the only thing to do on South Caicos other than to lie on the lovely beaches. Several local fishermen harvest spiny lobsters for the Turks and Caicos and for export. Making up the third-largest reef in the world, the coral walls surrounding South Caicos are dramatic, dropping dramatically from 50 feet to 6,000 feet in the blink of an eye.

EXPLORING SOUTH CAICOS

At the northern end of the island are fine white-sand beaches; the south coast is great for scuba diving along the drop-off, and there's excellent snorkeling off the windward (east) coast, where large stands of elkhorn and staghorn coral shelter several varieties of small tropical fish. A huge, sunken plane broken in pieces makes an excellent site. Spiny lobster and queen conch are found in the shallow Caicos Bank to the west and are harvested for export by local processing plants. The bonefishing here is some of the best in the West Indies.

Cockburn Harbour. The best natural harbor in the Caicos chain hosts the South Caicos Regatta, held each year in May. ⊠ *South Caicos.*

WHERE TO EAT AND STAY

Restaurant choices on South Caicos are limited, and no one takes credit cards, so bring cash. Except for the Dolphin Pub at the South Caicos Ocean & Beach Resort, the three best places are operated directly out of the owners' homes. **Love's** restaurant (on Airport Road) offers a daily changing menu of fresh seafood priced from $8 to $15. **Darryl's** (on Stubbs Road) is another casual restaurant that offers whatever is brought in for the day; expect to pay $10 to $20. Ask around to find out when (or if) these local favorites will be open; neither has a phone.

$$ 🏨 **South Caicos Ocean & Beach Resort.** Rustic and basic—though perfectly
HOTEL acceptable—this is your only lodging option in South Caicos. **Pros:** each room has stunning views of the Caicos Banks; the best scuba diving off South Caicos is in front of the hotel; it has the only real restaurant on the island. **Cons:** you need to bring cash to pay for everything but your room; not on the beach. ⑤ *Rooms from: $160* ⊠ *Turker Hill* ☏ *649/946–3810* ⊕ *www.southcaicos.oceanandbeachresort.com* ⌗ *24 rooms, 6 apartments* ⑪ *No meals.*

GRAND TURK

Just 7 miles (11 km) long and a little more than 1 mile (1½ km) wide, this island, the capital and seat of the Turks and Caicos government, has been a longtime favorite destination for divers eager to explore the 7,000-foot-deep pristine coral walls that drop down only 300 yards out to sea. On shore, the tiny, quiet island is home to white-sand beaches, the National Museum, and a small population of wild horses and donkeys, which leisurely meander past the white-walled courtyards, pretty churches, and bougainvillea-covered colonial inns on their daily commute into town. A cruise-ship complex that opened at the southern end of the island in 2006 brings about 600,000 visitors per year. Despite the dramatic changes this could make to this peaceful tourist spot, the dock is self-contained and is about 3 miles (5 km) from the tranquil, small hotels of Cockburn Town, Pillory Beach, and the Ridge and far from most of the western-shore dive sites. The influx has also pushed Grand Turk to open up a few new historic sites, including Grand Turk's Old Prison, and the Lighthouse.

26

All in the Family

Belongers, from the taxi driver meeting you to the chef feeding you, are often connected. "Oh, him?" you will hear. "He my cousin!" As development has been mercifully slow, such family connections, as well as crafts, bush medicine, ripsaw music, storytelling, and even recipes, have remained constant. But where do such traditions come from? Recently, researchers came closer to finding out. Many Belongers had claimed that their great-great-grandparents told them their forebears came directly from Africa. For decades their stories were ignored. Indeed, most experts believed that Belongers were descendants of mostly second-generation Bermudian and Caribbean slaves.

In 2005 museum researchers continued their search for a lost slave ship called *Trouvadore*. The ship, which wrecked off East Caicos in 1841, carried a cargo of 193 Africans, captured to be sold into slavery, almost all of whom miraculously survived the wreck. As slavery had been abolished in this British territory at the time, all the Africans were found and freed in the Turks and Caicos Islands. Since there were only a few thousand inhabitants in the islands at the time, these first-generation African survivors were a measurable minority (about 7% of the population then). Researchers have concluded that all the existing Belongers may be linked by blood or marriage to this one incident.

During one expedition, divers found a wrecked ship of the right time period. If these remains are *Trouvadore*, the Belongers may finally have a physical link to their past to go with their more intangible cultural traditions. So while you're in the islands, look closely at the intricately woven baskets, listen carefully to the African rhythms in the ripsaw music, and savor the stories you hear. They may very well be the legacy of *Trouvadore* speaking to you from the past. For more information, check out the website ⊕ *www. trouvadore.org.*

EXPLORING GRAND TURK

Pristine beaches with vistas of turquoise waters, small local settlements, historic ruins, and native flora and fauna are among the sights on Grand Turk. Fewer than 5,000 people live on this 7½-square-mile (19-square-km) island, and it's hard to get lost, as there aren't many roads.

COCKBURN TOWN

The buildings in the colony's capital and seat of government reflect a 19th-century Bermudian style. Narrow streets are lined with low stone walls and old street lamps, which are now powered by electricity. The once-vital *salinas* (natural salt pans, where the sea leaves a film of salt) have been restored, and covered benches along the sluices offer shady spots for observing wading birds, including flamingos that frequent the shallows. Be sure to pick up a copy of the tourist board's *Heritage Walk* guide to discover Grand Turk's rich architecture.

Her Majesty's Prison. This prison was built in the 19th century to house runaway slaves and slaves who survived the wreck of the *Trouvadore* in 1841. After the slaves were granted freedom, the prison housed

Grand Turk

Restaurants ▼

Birdcage
Restaurant **4**

Guanahani
Restaurant
& Bar **1**

Mookie Pookie
Pizza Palace **2**

Sand Bar **3**

Secret Garden ...**5**

Hotels ▼

Bohio Drive
Resort **2**

Island House **1**

Osprey Beach
Hotel **4**

Salt Raker Inn ...**3**

Northwest
Point

Little Bluff Point

**Grand Turk
Lighthouse**

NORTH
WELLS

North Creek

*Corktree
Beach*

CORK-
TREE

RIDGE

Flamingo Cove Marina

1

North Salina

1 **2**

*Pillory
Beach*

BREEZY
BRAE

Town Pond

2

**Turks & Caicos
National Museum**

Her Majesty's Prison — Victoria Library

St. Mary's Church

Pillory Salina

3

3

Cockburn
Town

5

4 **4**

Osprey Beach

ATLANTIC OCEAN

Red Salina

Grand Turk
International
Airport

South Creek

Gibbs
Cay

WATERLOO

*Hawks
Pond*

Hawks Nest
Plantation

Former U.S.
A.F.B.

Governor's Beach

White Sands Beach

*Hawks
Nest
Salina*

Round
Cay

Columbus' Landfall

KEY

⚓ *Cruise Ship Terminal*

⩘ *Beaches*

◨ *Dive Sites*

1 *Restaurants*

1 *Hotels*

0   1/2 mi

0   1/2 km

criminals and even modern-day drug runners until it closed in the 1990s. The last hanging here was in 1960. Now you can see the cells, solitary-confinement area, and exercise patio. The prison is open only when there is a cruise ship at the port. ⊠ *Pond St.* ☎ *No phone.*

Turks and Caicos National Museum. In one of the oldest stone buildings on the islands, the national museum houses the Molasses Reef wreck, the earliest shipwreck—dating to the early 1500s—discovered in the Americas. The natural-history exhibits include artifacts left by Taíno, African, North American, Bermudian, French, and Latin American settlers. The museum has a 3-D coral reef exhibit, a walk-in Lucayan cave with wooden artifacts, and a gallery dedicated to Grand Turk's little-known involvement in the Space Race (John Glenn made landfall here after being the first American to orbit the Earth). An interactive children's gallery keeps knee-high visitors "edutained." The museum also claims that Grand Turk was where Columbus first landed in the New World. The most original display is a collection of messages in bottles that have washed ashore from all over the world. ⊠ *Duke St.* ☎ *649/946–2160* ⊕ *www.tcmuseum.org* ⊠ *$5* ⊗ *Mon., Tues., Thurs., and Fri. 9–4, Wed. 9–5, Sat. 9–1.*

BEYOND COCKBURN TOWN

Grand Turk Lighthouse. More than 150 years old, the lighthouse, built in the United Kingdom and transported piece by piece to the island, used to protect ships in danger of wrecking on the northern reefs. Use this panoramic landmark as a starting point for a breezy cliff-top walk by following the donkey trails to the deserted eastern beach. ⊠ *Lighthouse Rd., North Ridge.*

WHERE TO EAT

Conch in every shape and form, fresh grouper, and lobster (in season) are the favorite dishes at the laid-back restaurants that line Duke Street. Away from these more touristy areas, smaller and less expensive eateries serve chicken and ribs, curried goat, peas and rice, and other native island specialties. Prices are more expensive than in the United States, as most of the produce has to be imported.

COCKBURN TOWN

$$$ ✕ **Birdcage Restaurant.** At the top of Duke Street, this has become the
CARIBBEAN place to be on Sunday and Wednesday nights, when a sizzling barbe-
★ cue of ribs, chicken, and lobster combines with live "rake-and-scrape" music from a local group called High Tide to draw an appreciative crowd. Arrive before 8 pm to secure beachside tables and an unrestricted view of the band; the location around the Osprey pool is lovely. The rest of the week, enjoy more elegant and eclectic fare accompanied by an increasingly impressive wine list. ⑤ *Average main: $24* ⊠ *Osprey Beach Hotel, Duke St., Cockburn Town* ☎ *649/946–2666* ⊕ *www. ospreybeachhotel.com/dining.*

$ ✕ **Mookie Pookie Pizza Palace.** Local husband-and-wife team "Mookie"
ECLECTIC and "Pookie" have created a wonderful backstreet parlor that has gained well-deserved popularity over the years as much more than a pizza place. At lunchtime the tiny eatery is packed with locals ordering

specials such as steamed beef, curried chicken, and curried goat. You can also get burgers and omelets, but stick to the specials if you want fast service, and dine in if you want to get a true taste of island living. By night, the place becomes Grand Turk's one and only pizza takeout and delivery service, so if you're renting a villa or condo, put this spot on speed dial. $ *Average main: $12* ⊠ *Hospital Rd., Cockburn Town* ☎ *no phone* ▬ *No credit cards* ⊘ *Closed Sun.*

$$ ✕ **Sand Bar.** Run by two Canadian sisters, this popular beachside bar is
AMERICAN a good value, though the menu is limited to fish-and-chips, quesadillas, and similarly basic bar fare. The tented wooden terrace jutting out onto the beach provides shade during the day, making it an ideal lunch spot, but it's also a great place to watch the sunset. The service is friendly, and the local crowd often spills into the street. $ *Average main: $14* ⊠ *Duke St., Cockburn Town* ☎ *No phone.*

$$ ✕ **Secret Garden.** Hurricanes Hannah and Ike inflicted some serious dam-
SEAFOOD age on this local favorite, but now it's back and better than ever. Simply prepared garlic shrimp or grilled grouper are among the more popular dishes. It lives up to its name, located behind Salt Raker Inn in a pretty courtyard garden. Friday nights feature live music by rake-and-scrape bands. $ *Average main: $17* ⊠ *Cockburn Town* ☎ *649/946–2260.*

ELSEWHERE ON GRAND TURK

$$$ ✕ **Guanahani Restaurant and Bar.** Off the town's main drag, this restaurant
ECLECTIC sits on a stunning but quiet stretch of beach. The food goes beyond the
★ usual Grand Turk fare, thanks to the talents of Canadian-born chef Zev Beck, who takes care of the evening meals. His pecan-crusted mahimahi and crispy sushi rolls are to die for. For lunch, Middle Caicos native Miss Leotha makes juicy jerk chicken to keep the crowd happy. The menu changes daily. The food is some of the best in Grand Turk. $ *Average main: $26* ⊠ *Bohio Dive Resort & Spa, Pillory Beach* ☎ *649/946–2135* ⊕ *www.bohioresort.com.*

WHERE TO STAY

Accommodations include original Bermudian inns, more modern but small beachfront hotels, and very basic to well-equipped self-catering suites and apartments. Almost all hotels offer dive packages, which are an excellent value.

For expanded reviews, facilities, and current deals, visit Fodors.com.

COCKBURN TOWN

$$ 🏨 **Osprey Beach Hotel.** Grand Turk veteran hotelier Jenny Smith has
HOTEL transformed this two-story oceanfront hotel with her artistic touches:
Fodor'sChoice palms, frangipani, and deep green azaleas frame it like a painting. **Pros:**
★ best hotel on Grand Turk; walking distance to Front Street, restaurants, and excursions. **Cons:** three-night minimum; rocky beachfront. **TripAdvisor:** "comfortable lodging," "excellent place to stay," "pleasant." $ *Rooms from: $175* ⊠ *Duke St., Cockburn Town* ☎ *649/946–2666* ⊕ *www.ospreybeachhotel.com* ⊃ *11 rooms, 16 suites* ⊘ *No meals* ⊃ *3-night minimum.*

$ 🏨 **Salt Raker Inn.** A large anchor on the sun-dappled pathway marks the
B&B/INN entrance to this 19th-century house, which is now an unpretentious

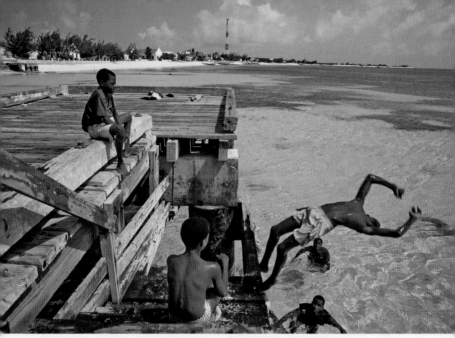

Cockburn Town, Grand Turk

inn. **Pros:** excellent location that is an easy walk to Front Street, restaurants, and excursions. **Cons:** no no-smoking rooms. **TripAdvisor:** "relaxation," "charming and perfect," "great historic place." ⑤ *Rooms from: $115 ⊠ Duke St., Cockburn Town ☎ 649/946–2260 ⊕ www. hotelsaltraker.com ↝ 10 rooms, 3 suites* ⏀ *No meals.*

ELSEWHERE ON GRAND TURK

$$ ⊡ **Bohio Dive Resort and Spa.** Completely restored after two hurricanes
RESORT in 2008, this basic yet comfortable hotel is the choice of divers. **Pros:** has the best restaurant in Grand Turk; on a gorgeous beach; steps away from awesome snorkeling. **Cons:** three-night minimum doesn't allow for quick getaways from Provo. **TripAdvisor:** "total relaxation," "a wonderful oasis," "great food." ⑤ *Rooms from: $225 ⊠ Pillory Beach ☎ 649/946–2135 ⊕ www.bohioresort.com ↝ 12 rooms, 4 suites* ⏀ *No meals ⌁ 3-night minimum.*

$$ ⊡ **Island House.** Years of business-travel experience helped Colin
RENTAL Brooker create the comfortable, peaceful suites that overlook North
  ⏁ Creek. **Pros:** full condo units feel like a home away from home. **Cons:** not on the beach; you need a car to get around. **TripAdvisor:** "spacious and modern," "wonderful host," "very relaxed." ⑤ *Rooms from: $150 ⊠ Lighthouse Rd. ☎ 649/232–1439 ⊕ www.islandhouse.tc ↝ 8 suites* ⏀ *No meals ⌁ 2-night minimum.*

NIGHTLIFE

Grand Turk is a quiet place where you come to relax and unwind, so most of the nightlife consists of little more than happy hour at sunset so you have a chance to glimpse the elusive green flash. Most restaurants turn into gathering places where you can talk with the new friends you have made that day, but there a few more nightlife-oriented places that will keep you busy after dark. On some evenings, you'll be able to catch Mitch Rollings of Blue Water Divers; he often headlines the entertainment at the island's different restaurants.

SPORTS AND ACTIVITIES

BICYCLING

Oasis Divers. The island's mostly flat terrain isn't very taxing, and most roads have hard surfaces. Take water with you: there are few places to stop for refreshments. Most hotels have bicycles available, but you can also rent them for $10 to $15 a day from Oasis Divers. They now offer fun Segway tours. ⊠ *Duke St., Cockburn Town* 🖼🖼 *649/946–1128* ☎ *800/892–3995* ⊕ *www.oasisdivers.com.*

26

DIVING AND SNORKELING

★ In these waters you can find undersea cathedrals, coral gardens, and countless tunnels, but note that you must carry and present a valid certificate card before you'll be allowed to dive. As its name suggests, the **Black Forest** offers staggering black-coral formations as well as the occasional black-tip shark. In the **Library** you can study fish galore, including large numbers of yellowtail snapper. At the Columbus Passage separating South Caicos from Grand Turk, each side of a 22-mile-wide (35-km-wide) channel drops more than 7,000 feet. From January through March, thousands of Atlantic humpback whales swim through en route to their winter breeding grounds. **Gibb's Cay,** a small cay a couple of miles off of Grand Turk, where you can swim with stingrays, makes for a great excursion.

Blue Water Divers. Blue Water Divers has been in operation on Grand Turk since 1983 and is the only PADI Gold Palm five-star dive center on the island. Owner Mitch will undoubtedly put some of your underwater adventures to music in the evenings when he plays at the Osprey Beach Hotel or Salt Raker Inn. ⊠ *Duke St., Grand Turk, Cockburn Town* 🖼🖼 *649/946–2432* ⊕ *www.grandturkscuba.com.*

Oasis Divers. Oasis Divers specializes in complete gear handling and pampering treatment. It also supplies Nitrox and rebreathers. ⊠ *Duke St., Cockburn Town* 🖼🖼 *649/946–1128* ⊕ *www.oasisdivers.com.*

SALT CAY

Fewer than 100 people live on this 2½-square-mile (6-square-km) dot of land, maintaining an unassuming lifestyle against a backdrop of stucco cottages, stone ruins, and weathered wooden windmills standing sentry in the abandoned salinas. The beautifully preserved island is bordered by beaches where weathered green and blue sea glass and pretty shells often wash ashore. Beneath the waves, 10 dive sites are minutes from shore.

There are big plans for Salt Cay, which will change the small island forever, though probably not for several years. Gone will be the donkeys and chickens roaming the streets; in their place will be a luxurious resort and new golf course. If you want to see how the Caribbean was when it was laid-back, sleepy, and colorful, visit the island now before it changes.

EXPLORING SALT CAY

Salt sheds and salinas are silent reminders of the days when the island was a leading producer of salt. Now the salt ponds attract abundant birdlife. Island tours are often conducted by motorized golf cart. From January through April, humpback whales pass by on the way to their winter breeding grounds.

What little development there is on Salt Cay is found in its main community, Balfour Town. It's home to several small hotels and a few cozy stores, as well as the main dock and the Coral Reef Bar & Grill, where locals hang out with tourists to watch the sunset and drink a beer.

White House. The grand stone house, which once belonged to a wealthy salt merchant, is testimony to the heyday of Salt Cay's eponymous industry. Still privately owned by the descendants of the original family, it's sometimes opened up for tours. Ask Tim Dunn, an actual descendant of the original owners, as he may give you a personal tour to see the still-intact, original furnishings, books, and medicine cabinet that date back to the early 1800s. ⊠ *Victoria St., Balfour Town* ☒ *Free.*

WHERE TO EAT

$$$ ✕ **Island Thyme Bistro.** Owner Porter Williams serves potent alcoholic
ECLECTIC   creations as well as fairly sophisticated local and international cuisine.
★   Try steamed, freshly caught snapper in a pepper-wine sauce with peas and rice, or spicy-hot chicken curry served with tangy chutneys. Don't forget to order the "Porter" house steak. You can take cooking lessons from the chef, enjoy the nightly Filipino fusion tapas during happy hour, and join the gang for Friday-night pizza. This is a great place to make friends and the best place to catch up on island gossip. The airy, trellis-covered spot overlooks the salinas. There's a small shop with gifts and tourist information; you can also get a manicure or pedicure here. ⑤ *Average main: $26* ⊠ *North District* ☎ *649/946–6977* ⊕ *www. islandthyme.tc/* ⚠ *Reservations essential* ⊗ *Closed Wed. mid-May–June and Sept.–late Oct.*

$$ ✕ **Pat's Place.** Island native Pat Simmons can give you a lesson in the
CARIBBEAN   medicinal qualities of her garden plants and periwinkle flowers, as well as provide excellent native cuisine for a very reasonable price in her typical Salt Cay home. Home cooking doesn't get any closer to home than this. Try conch fritters for lunch and steamed grouper with okra rice for dinner. Be sure to call ahead, as she cooks only when there's someone to cook for. Pat also has a small grocery shop selling staples.

Ⓢ *Average main: $15* ✉ *South District* ☎ *649/946–6919* ⚓ *Reservations essential* ▭ *No credit cards.*

WHERE TO STAY

For expanded reviews, facilities, and current deals, visit Fodors.com.

$$$ 🏠 **Castaway.** This only dwelling on stunning 3-mile (5-km) North Beach
RENTAL might just be what the doctor ordered if you're in need of total relaxation—it can be hard to fathom having one of the world's most beautiful beaches all to yourself. **Pros:** on a spectacular beach; perfect for relaxing. **Cons:** it's a dark, secluded road into town at night. **TripAdvisor:** "beautiful place and big hearts," "simplistic beauty," "relaxing place on the beach." Ⓢ *Rooms from: $265* ✉ *North Beach* ☎ *649/946–6977* ⊕ *www.castawayonsaltcay.com* ⛵ *4 suites* 🍴❌ *No meals.*

$$ 🏠 **Pirates Hideaway and Blackbeard's Quarters.** Owner Candy Herwin—
RENTAL true to her self-proclaimed pirate status—has smuggled artistic treasures across the ocean and created her own masterpieces to deck out this lair. **Pros:** artist workshops are offered during peak season. **Cons:** rocky beachfront. Ⓢ *Rooms from: $200* ✉ *Victoria St., South District* ☎ *649/946–6909* ⊕ *www.saltcay.tc* ⛵ *2 suites, 1 house* 🍴❌ *No meals.*

$$ 🏠 **Tradewinds Guest Suites.** Yards away from Dean's Dock, a grove of
RENTAL whispering casuarina trees surrounds these five single-story, basic apartments, which offer a moderate-budget option on Salt Cay with the option of dive packages. **Pros:** walking distance to diving, fishing, dining, and dancing. **Cons:** a/c costs extra; some may feel isolated with few nighttime activities and no TV. Ⓢ *Rooms from: $190* ✉ *Victoria St., Salt Cay, Balfour Town* ☎ *649/946–6906* ⊕ *www.tradewinds.tc* ⛵ *5 apartments* 🍴❌ *No meals.*

$$$$ 🏠 **Villas of Salt Cay.** One of the nicest places to stay in Salt Cay is cen-
RENTAL trally located on Victoria Street, in the middle of everything. **Pros:** bedrooms are set up for extra privacy; on Victoria Street within walking distance of everything; on a private stretch of beach. **Cons:** not all rooms have a/c; cabanas don't have kitchens; shared pool. Ⓢ *Rooms from: $395* ✉ *Victoria St., Balfour Town* ☎ *649/946–6909* ⊕ *www.thevillasofsaltcay.com* ⛵ *1 2-bedroom villa, 1 1-bedroom cottage, 3 cabanas* 🍴❌ *No meals.*

SPORTS AND ACTIVITIES

DIVING AND SNORKELING
Scuba divers can explore the wreck of the *Endymion,* a 140-foot wooden-hull British warship that sank in 1790; you can swim through the hull and spot cannons and anchors. It's off the southern point of Salt Cay.

Salt Cay Divers. Salt Cay Divers conducts daily dive trips and rents all the necessary equipment. In season, they run whale-watching trips. They can also help get you to Salt Cay from Provo or Grand Turk, and stock your villa with groceries. ✉ *Balfour Town* ☎ *649/946–6906* ⊕ *www.saltcaydivers.tc.*

WHALE-WATCHING

During the winter months (January through April), Salt Cay is a center for whale-watching, when some 2,500 humpback whales pass close to shore. Whale-watching trips can most easily be organized through your inn or guesthouse.

Fodor's Choice ★ **Crystal Seas Adventures.** Proprietor Tim Dunn, whose family descends from the original owners of Salt Cay's historic White House, knows these waters as well as anybody. His company offers a variety of excursions: diving with stingrays at Gibbs Cay, and trips to Grand Turk and secluded beaches, such as Great Sand Cay. Whale-watching is also very popular, and Dunn is the only outfitter with diving trips to South Caicos, reputed to be one of the best places in the world for this. ✉ Balfour Town ☎ 649/243–9843 ⊕ www.crystalseasadventures.com.

United States Virgin Islands

WORD OF MOUTH

"If you hope to do a lot of snorkeling, stay on St. John and rent a jeep to explore the island. A regular car will not do. You and your kids could visit two beaches every day and return to a beautiful villa nicely exhausted . We are returning to the Coral Bay area for the third time. We love the 'quieter' side of the island and are taking our young adult kids with us this time."

—Kathva

WELCOME TO UNITED STATES VIRGIN ISLANDS

ATLANTIC

Big Hans
Lollick

Inner
Brass

Picara Pt.

Santa
Maria
Bay

Botany
Bay

Stumpy
Bay

Magens
Bay

Lovelund Bay

Thatch
Cay

Dorothea

Fortuna

David Pt.

Brewers
Bay

Charlotte
Amalie

ST. THOMAS

Pillsbury
Sound

St. Thomas
see detail
map

Cyril E. King
International
Airport

Hassel
Island

Nadir

Red
Hook

Great
St. James
Island

Water
Island

Frenchman
Bay

Bovoni
Bay

Long Pt.

Little St. James
Island

← TO
PUERTO RICO

Cane
Bay

Hams Bay

Davis
Bay

Frederiksted

Henry E. Rohlsen
International
Airport

West End
Salt Pond

Krause Pt.

Long Pt.
Bay

Long Pt.

Sandy
Pt.

AMERICA'S CARIBBEAN

About 1,000 miles (1,600 km) from the southern tip of Florida, the U.S. Virgin Islands were acquired from Denmark in 1917. St. Croix, at 84 square miles (218 square km), is the largest of the islands; St. John, at 20 square miles (52 square km), is the smallest. Together, they have a population of around 110,000, half of whom live on St. Thomas.

A perfect combination of the familiar and the exotic, the U.S. Virgin Islands are a little bit of home set in an azure sea. With hundreds of idyllic coves and splendid beaches, chances are that on one of the three islands you'll find your ideal Caribbean vacation spot.

TOP REASONS TO VISIT UNITED STATES VIRGIN ISLANDS

1 Incomparable Sailing: St. Thomas is one of the Caribbean's major sailing centers.

2 Great Hiking: Two-thirds of St. John is a national park that's crisscrossed by excellent hiking trails.

3 Beaches: Though Magens Bay on St. Thomas and Trunk Bay on St. John are two of the most perfect beaches you'll ever find,

St. Croix's West End beaches are fetching in their own way.

4 Shopping: Shopping on both St. Thomas and St. Croix is stellar.

5 Deep-Sea Fishing: St. Thomas is one of the best places to catch Atlantic blue marlin between the months of June and October.

U.S. VIRGIN ISLANDS BEACHES

The beaches of the USVI are like pearly white smiles that outline the curve of the bays on both the Atlantic Ocean to the north and the Caribbean Sea to the south. The brilliant sand provides a beaming contrast to the deep turquoise seas and the lush green palms and sea grape trees that line the shores.

(Above) Trunk Bay, St. John (Bottom right) Coki Beach, St. Thomas (Top right) Magens Bay, St. Thomas

The three main islands of the USVI offer a wide range of beach experiences and activities. St. Thomas and St. John are widely known for having the best beaches, but there is one more island that you shouldn't miss if you're also visiting St. Thomas. Water Island, a half-mile ferry ride from Crown Bay Marina on St. Thomas, has Honeymoon Beach, one of the most perfect powdery beaches you'll find (though some say that Sprat Beach, which is much farther away from the ferry dock, is better). There are restrooms on Honeymoon Beach as well as a restaurant that serves lunch, but it's a half-mile hike from the ferry dock (some of it up a rather steep hill).

DON'T MISS

St. Thomas is the busiest and most developed of the U.S. Virgin Islands. Don't miss watching the planes land from Brewer's Beach, eating fish and fungi (a polenta-like side dish) at Coki Beach, renting a paddleboat at Magens Bay, bodysurfing in the winter at Hull Bay, and enjoying a rum and Coke from beachside bar service at Morningstar Beach.

For complete information on these beaches see individual beach sections within the chapter.

ST. THOMAS

All 44 St. Thomas beaches are open to the public, although you can reach some of them only by walking through a resort. Hotel guests frequently have access to lounge chairs and floats that are off-limits to nonguests; for this reason you may feel more comfortable at one of the beaches not associated with a resort, such as **Magens Bay** (which charges an entrance fee to cover beach maintenance) or **Coki Beach**, the latter abutting Coral World Ocean Park and offering the island's best off-the-beach snorkeling. **Morningstar Beach** sits between the twin Marriott Resorts on St. Thomas's south shore. **Sapphire Beach** is another of the island's better beaches, and it offers soft, silky sand as well as access to a good reef for snorkeling.

ST. JOHN

St. John is blessed with many beaches, and all of them fall into the good, great, and don't-tell-anyone-else-about-this-place categories. Some are more developed than others—and many are crowded on weekends, holidays, and in high season—but by and large they're still pristine. Beaches along the south and eastern shores are quiet and isolated.

Two of the island's standout beaches can be found in the national park. **Trunk Bay** is the beach that's often pictured on postcards from the Virgin Islands; a long, white sandy beach is fronted by a coral reef that makes waves smooth and steady. **Cinnamon Bay**, which is next to the national park campground, has a water-sports center and fantastic snorkeling; there are also a couple of hiking trails that start at the beach. St. John's other excellent beach is **Hawksnest Bay**. Close to Cruz Bay, it's often busy with locals and tourists alike, but it's a great spot for offshore snorkeling.

ST. CROIX

St. Croix's beaches aren't as spectacular as those on St. John or St. Thomas. But that's not to say you won't find some good places to spread out for a day on the water. The best beach is on nearby **Buck Island**, a national monument where a marked snorkeling trail leads you through an extensive coral reef while a soft, sandy beach beckons a few yards away. Other great beaches are the unnamed **west end beaches** both south and north of Frederiksted. You can park yourself at any of the handful of restaurants north of Frederiksted. Some rent loungers, and you can get food and drinks right on the beach.

27

Updated by
Carol M.
Bareuther and
Lynda Lohr

The U.S. Virgin Islands—St. Thomas, St. John, and St. Croix—may fly the American flag, but "America's Paradise" is in reality a mix of the foreign and familiar that offers something for everyone to enjoy. The history, beautiful beaches, myriad activities, good food, and no-passport-required status make the Virgin Islands an inviting beach destination for many Americans.

With three islands to choose from, you're likely to find your piece of paradise. Check into a beachfront condo on the east end of St. Thomas; then eat burgers and watch football at a beachfront bar and grill. Or stay at an 18th-century plantation great house on St. Croix, go horseback riding at sunrise, and then dine that night on local seafood classics. Rent a tent or a cottage in the pristine national park on St. John; then take a hike, kayak off the coast, read a book, or just listen to the sounds of the forest. Or dive deep into "island time" and learn the art of limin' (hanging out, Caribbean-style) on all three islands.

History books give credit to Christopher Columbus for discovering the New World. In reality, the Virgin Islands, like the rest of the isles in the Caribbean chain, were populated as long ago as 2000 BC by nomadic waves of seagoing settlers as they migrated north from South America and eastward from Central America and the Yucatàn Peninsula.

Columbus met the descendants of these original inhabitants during his second voyage to the New World, in 1493. He anchored in Salt River, a natural bay west of what is now Christiansted, St. Croix, and sent his men ashore in search of fresh water. Hostile arrows rather than welcoming embraces made for a quick retreat, but Columbus did have time to name the island Santa Cruz (Holy Cross) before sailing north. He eventually claimed St. John, St. Thomas, and what are now the British Virgin Islands for Spain and at the same time named this shapely silhouette of 60-some islands Las Once Mil Virgenes, for the 11,000 legendary virgin followers of St. Ursula. Columbus believed the islands barren of the costly spices he sought, so he sailed off, leaving more than a century's gap in time before the next Europeans arrived.

Pioneers, planters, and pirates from throughout Europe ushered in the era of colonization. Great Britain and the Netherlands both claimed St. Croix in 1625. This peaceful coexistence ended abruptly when the Dutch governor killed his English counterpart, thus launching years of battles for possession that would see seven flags fly over this southernmost Virgin isle. Meanwhile, St. Thomas's sheltered harbor proved a magnet for pirates such as Blackbeard and Bluebeard. The Danes first colonized the island in 1666, naming their main settlement Taphus for its many beer halls. In 1691 the town received the more respectable name of Charlotte Amalie in honor of Danish king Christian V's wife. It wasn't until 1718 that a small group of Dutch planters raised their country's flag on St. John. As on its the other Virgin Islands, a plantation economy soon developed.

Plantations depended on slave labor, and the Virgin Islands played a key role in the triangular route that connected the Caribbean, Africa, and Europe in the trade of sugar, rum, and human cargo. By the early 1800s a sharp decline in cane prices because of competing beet sugar and an increasing number of slave revolts motivated Governor-General Peter von Scholten to abolish slavery in the Danish colonies on July 3, 1848. This holiday is now celebrated as Emancipation Day.

After emancipation, the island's economy slumped. Islanders owed their existence to subsistence farming and fishing. Meanwhile, during the American Civil War the Union began negotiations with Denmark for the purchase of the Virgin Islands in order to establish a naval base. However, the sale didn't happen until World War I, when President Theodore Roosevelt paid the Danes $25 million for the three largest islands; an elaborate Transfer Day ceremony was held on the grounds of St. Thomas's Legislature Building on March 31, 1917. A decade later, Virgin Islanders were granted U.S. citizenship. Today the U.S. Virgin Islands is an unincorporated territory, meaning that citizens govern themselves and vote for their own governors, but cannot vote for president or congressional representation.

Nowadays, Virgin Islanders hail from more than 60 nations. Descendants of African slaves are the largest segment of the population, so it's not surprising that they also provide the largest percentage of workers and owners of restaurants, resorts, and shops. The Danish influence is still strong in architecture and street names. Americana is everywhere, too, most notably in recognizable fast-food chains, familiar shows on cable TV, and name-brand hotels. Between this diversity and the wealth that tourism brings, Virgin Islanders struggle to preserve their culture. Their rich, spicy West Indian–African heritage comes to full bloom at Carnival time, when celebrating and playing *mas* (with abandon) take precedence over everything else.

Although the idyllic images of a tropical isle are definitely here, there's evidence, too, of growing pains. Traffic jams are common, a clandestine drug trade fuels crime, and—particularly on St. Thomas—there are few beaches left that aren't fronted by a high-rise hotel. Despite fairly heavy

LOGISTICS

Getting to the USVI: There are many nonstop flights to St. Thomas from the United States, and there are a few nonstops to St. Croix; often, you'll have to change planes in Miami, San Juan, or St. Thomas to reach St. Croix. There are no flights at all to St. John; you have to take a ferry from St. Thomas.

Hassle Factor: Low to high, depending on your flight schedule.

On the Ground: Many travelers do just fine without a car in St. Thomas, but it's much harder if you are renting a villa; also be aware that taxis

can be expensive when used every day. In St. John you must rent a car if you are staying in a villa or in Coral Bay, but you might be able to get by without one if you are staying elsewhere. A car is more of a necessity in St. Croix, regardless of where you stay.

Getting Around the Islands: Frequent, convenient ferries connect St. Thomas and St. John. St. Croix is farther removed, so a flight from St. Thomas is the most common mode of transport, but there is a ferry from St. Thomas several days a week.

development, wildlife has found refuge here. The brown pelican is on the endangered list worldwide but is a common sight in the USVI. The endangered native boa tree is protected, as is the hawksbill turtle, whose females lumber onto the beaches to lay eggs.

PLANNING

WHEN TO GO

High season coincides with that on most other Caribbean islands, from December through April or May; before and after that time, rates can drop by as much as 25% to 50%, depending on the resort.

GETTING HERE AND AROUND

AIR TRAVEL

Fly nonstop to St. Thomas from Atlanta (Delta), Boston (American, seasonal; US Airways; JetBlue via San Juan, seasonal), Charlotte (US Airways), Chicago (United), Detroit (Delta, seasonal), Fort Lauderdale (Spirit), Miami (American), New York–JFK (American; Delta), New York–Newark (United), Philadelphia (US Airways), Toronto (Air Canada, seasonal), or Washington, D.C.–Dulles (United). Fly nonstop to St. Croix from Atlanta (Delta) or Miami (American).

If you can't fly nonstop, then you can connect in San Juan; American Eagle has several daily nonstops. You can also take a seaplane between St. Thomas and St. Croix. The only option for St. John is a ferry from either Red Hook or Charlotte Amalie in St. Thomas. Both Caneel Bay and the Westin have private ferries.

Airports Cyril E. King Airport (*STT*). ⊠ *70 Lindbergh Bay, St. Thomas* ☎ *340/774-5100.* **Henry Rohlsen Airport** (*STX*). St. Croix's airport is on the southwestern side of the island, near Christiansted. ⊠ *RR #2 Kingshill, St. Croix* ☎ *340/778-1012.*

Airline Contacts Air Canada. ☎ *888/247–2262* ⊕ *www.aircanada.com.*
American Airlines/American Eagle. ☎ *800/474–4884* ⊕ *www.aa.com.* **Delta
Airlines.** ☎ *800/221–1212* ⊕ *www.delta.com.* **JetBlue.** ☎ *800/538–2583*
⊕ *www.jetblue.com.* **Seaborne.** ☎ *340/773–6442* ⊕ *www.seaborneairlines.
com.* **Spirit Airlines.** ☎ *800/772–7117* ⊕ *www.spiritair.com.* **United Airlines.**
☎ *800/241–6522, 340/774–9190 in St. Thomas* ⊕ *www.united.com.* **US Airways.** US ☎ *800/622–1015* ⊕ *www.usairways.com.*

BOAT AND FERRY TRAVEL

There's frequent service between St. Thomas and St. John and their
neighbors, the BVI. Check with the ferry companies for the current
schedules. The **Virgin Islands Vacation Guide & Community** (⊕ *www.vinow.
com*) publishes current ferry schedules on its website.

There's frequent daily service from both Red Hook and Charlotte Amalie to Cruz Bay, St. John. About every hour there's a car ferry; you
should arrive at least 25 minutes before departure.

Ferry Contacts Inter-Island Boat Service. Inter-Island has daily and weekly
service between St. John and the British Virgin Islands of Jost Van Dyke, Tortola,
Virgin Gorda, and Anegada. ☎ *340/776–6597 in St. John.*

Native Son. Ferries operate daily between Charlotte Amalie and Red
Hook, in St. Thomas, and West End and Road Town, in Tortola.
☎ *340/774–8685 in St. Thomas* ⊕ *www.nativesonferry.com.*

Smith's Ferry. Smith's operates multiple trips daily between Charlotte
Amalie and Red Hook in St. Thomas, and West End and Road Town,
in Tortola. ☎ *340/775–7292 in St. Thomas* ⊕ *www.smithsferry.com.*

Speedy's. Speedy's offers weekly ferry service to Virgin Gorda. The company also runs seasonal three-day weekend trips to Fajardo, Puerto
Rico. ☎ *284/495–5235 in Tortola* ⊕ *www.speedysbvi.com.*

CAR TRAVEL

Driving is on the left, British-style. The law requires that *everyone* wear
a seat belt. Traffic can be bad during rush hour on all three islands.

Car Rentals in St. Thomas: Avis, Budget, and Hertz all have counters at
Cyril E. King Airport, but there are some other offices as well; in addition, there are local companies.

Car Rentals in St. John: All the car-rental companies in St. John are locally
owned. Most companies are just a short walk from the ferry dock.
Those a bit farther away will pick you up.

Car Rentals in St. Croix: There are both local and national companies on
St. Croix; if your company doesn't have an airport location, you'll be
picked up or a car will be delivered to you.

St. Thomas Car Rental Contacts Avis ☎ *340/774–1468.* **Budget** ☎ *340/776–
5774.* **Dependable Car Rental** ☎ *340/774–2253, 800/522–3076.* **Discount Car
Rental** ☎ *340/776–4858.* **Hertz** ☎ *340/774–1879.*

St. John Car Rental Contacts Best ☎ *340/693–8177.* **Cool Breeze**
☎ *340/776–6588* ⊕ *www.coolbreezecarrental.com.* **Courtesy** ☎ *340/776–6650*
⊕ *www.courtesycarrental.com.* **Delbert Hill Taxi & Jeep Rental Service**
☎ *340/776–6637.* **Denzil Clyne** ☎ *340/776–6715.* **O'Connor Car Rental**
☎ *340/776–6343* ⊕ *www.oconnorcarrental.com.* **St. John Car Rental**

27

☎ *340/776–6103* ⊕ *www.stjohncarrental.com.* **Spencer's Jeep** ☎ *340/693–8784, 888/776–6628* ⊕ *www.spencerjeeprentals.com.*

St. Croix Car Rental Contacts Avis ☎ *340/778–9355, 800/230-4898* ⊕ *www.avis.com.* **Budget** ☎ *340/778–9636, 888/264–8894.* **Hertz** ☎ *340/778–1402, 888/248–4261* ⊕ *www.rentacarstcroix.com.* **Judi of Croix** ☎ *340/773–2123, 877/903–2123* ⊕ *www.judiofcroix.com.* **Midwest** ☎ *340/772–0438, 877/772–0438* ⊕ *www.midwestautorental.com.* **Olympic** ☎ *340/773–8000, 888/878–4227* ⊕ *www.stcroixcarrentals.com.*

TAXI TRAVEL

USVI taxis don't have meters; fares are per person, set by a schedule, and drivers usually take multiple fares, especially from the airport, ferry docks, and cruise-ship terminals. Many taxis are open safari vans, but some are air-conditioned vans.

St. Thomas East End Taxi ☎ *340/775–6974.* **Islander Taxi and Tour Services** ☎ *340/774–4077.* **V.I. Taxi Association** ☎ *340/774–4550.*

St. John Paradise Taxi ☎ *340/714–7913.*

St. Croix Antilles Taxi Service ☎ *340/773–5020.* **St. Croix Taxi Association** ☎ *340/778–1088, 866/778–1045* ⊕ *www.stcroixtaxi.com.*

ESSENTIALS

Banks and Exchange Services The U.S. dollar is used throughout the U.S. Virgin Islands. All major credit cards are accepted by most hotels, restaurants, and shops. ATMs are common on St. Thomas. Banks on St. Thomas include Banco Popular, Scotia Bank, and First Bank. St. John has two banks in Cruz Bay. St. Croix has branches of Banco Popular in the Orange Grove and Sunny Isle. V.I. Community Bank is in Sunny Isle, Frederiksted, Estate Diamond, Orange Grove, and Christiansted. Scotia Bank has branches in Sunny Isle, Frederiksted, Christiansted, and Sunshine Mall.

Electricity Electricity is the U.S. standard.

Emergency Services Dial 911 for all emergencies.

Safety Keep your hotel or vacation villa door locked at all times, and stick to well-lighted streets at night. Keep your rental car locked wherever you park, and lock possessions in the trunk. Don't leave valuables lying on the beach while you snorkel. Don't wander the streets of the main towns alone at night, whether you are in Charlotte Amalie, Cruz Bay, Christiansted, or Frederiksted.

Although crime is not as prevalent in St. John as it is on St. Thomas and St. Croix, it does exist. There are occasional burglaries at villas, even during daylight hours. Lock doors even when you're lounging by the pool. It's not a good idea to walk around Cruz Bay late at night. If you don't have a car, plan on taking a taxi. Since it can be hard to find a taxi in the wee hours of the morning, arrange in advance for a driver to pick you up.

ACCOMMODATIONS

St. Thomas is the most developed of the Virgin Islands; choose it if you want extensive shopping opportunities and a multitude of activities and restaurants. St. John, the least developed of the three, has a distinct following; it's the best choice if you want a small-island feel and easy access to great hiking. However, most villas there aren't directly on the beach. St. Croix is a sleeper. The diversity of the accommodations means that you can stay in everything from a simple inn to a luxury resort, but none of the beaches is as breathtaking as those on St. Thomas and St. John.

Resorts: Whether you are looking for a luxury retreat or a moderately priced vacation spot, there's going to be something for you in the USVI. St. Thomas has the most options. St. John has only two large resorts, both upscale; others are small, but it has some unique eco-oriented camping options. St. Croix's resorts are more midsize.

Small Inns: Particularly on St. Croix, you'll find a wide range of attractive and accommodating small inns; if you can live without being directly on the beach, these friendly, homey places are a good option. St. Thomas also has a few small inns in the historic district of Charlotte Amalie.

Villas: Villas are plentiful on all three islands, but they are especially popular on St. John, where they represent more than half the available lodging. They're always a good bet for families who can do without a busy resort environment.

HOTEL AND RESTAURANT PRICES

Prices in the restaurant reviews are the average cost of a main course at dinner or, if dinner is not served, at lunch; taxes and service charges are generally included. Prices in the hotel reviews are the lowest cost of a standard double room in high season, excluding taxes, service charges, and meal plans (except at all-inclusives). Prices for rentals are the lowest per-night cost for a one-bedroom unit in high season.

VISITOR INFORMATION

Contacts USVI Department of Tourism ☎ *340/774–8784, 800/372–8784* ⊕ *www.visitusvi.com.*

WEDDINGS

Apply for a marriage license at the Superior Court. There's a $50 application fee and $50 license fee. You have to wait eight days after the clerk receives the application to get married, and licenses must be picked up in person weekdays or on weekends for an additional $150, though you can apply by mail. A marriage ceremony at the Superior Court costs $200.

St. Croix Superior Court ✉ *U.S. Virgin Islands* ☎ *340/778–9750.* **St. Thomas Superior Court** ✉ *5400 Veteran's Dr., St. Thomas* ☎ *340/774–6680.*

ST. THOMAS

By Carol M. Bareuther

If you fly to the 32-square-mile (83-square-km) island of St. Thomas, you land at its western end; if you arrive by cruise ship, you come into one of the world's most beautiful harbors. Either way, one of your first sights is the town of Charlotte Amalie. From the harbor you see an idyllic-looking village that spreads into the lower hills. If you were expecting a quiet hamlet with its inhabitants hanging out under palm trees, you've missed that era by about 300 years. Although other islands in the USVI developed plantation economies, St. Thomas cultivated its harbor, and it became a thriving seaport soon after it was settled by the Danish in the 1600s.

The success of the naturally perfect harbor was enhanced by the fact that the Danes—who ruled St. Thomas with only a couple of

HOP ON THE BUS

On St. Thomas the island's large buses make public transportation a very comfortable—though slow—way to get from east and west to Charlotte Amalie and back (service to the north is limited). Buses run about every 30 minutes from stops that are clearly marked with "vitran" signs. Fares are $1 between outlying areas and town and 75¢ in town.

short interruptions from 1666 to 1917—avoided involvement in some 100 years' worth of European wars. Denmark was the only European country with colonies in the Caribbean to stay neutral during the War of the Spanish Succession in the early 1700s. Thus, products of the Dutch, English, and French islands—sugar, cotton, and indigo—were traded through Charlotte Amalie, along with the regular shipments of slaves. When the Spanish wars ended, trade fell off, but by the end of the 1700s Europe was at war again, Denmark again remained neutral, and St. Thomas continued to prosper. Even into the 1800s, while the economies of St. Croix and St. John foundered with the market for sugarcane, St. Thomas's economy remained vigorous. This prosperity led to the development of shipyards, a well-organized banking system, and a large merchant class. In 1845 Charlotte Amalie had 101 large importing houses owned by the English, French, Germans, Haitians, Spaniards, Americans, Sephardim, and Danes.

Charlotte Amalie is still one of the world's most active cruise-ship ports. On almost any day at least one and sometimes as many as eight cruise ships are tied to the docks or anchored outside the harbor. Gently rocking in the shadows of these giant floating hotels are just about every other kind of vessel imaginable: sleek sailing catamarans that will take you on a sunset cruise complete with rum punch and a Jimmy Buffett soundtrack, private megayachts for billionaires, and barnacle-bottom sloops—with laundry draped over the lifelines—that are home to world-cruising gypsies. Huge container ships pull up in Sub Base, west of the harbor, bringing in everything from breakfast cereals to tires. Anchored right along the waterfront are down-island barges that ply the waters between the Greater Antilles and the Leeward Islands, transporting goods such as refrigerators, VCRs, and disposable diapers.

The waterfront road through Charlotte Amalie was once part of the harbor. Before it was filled in to build the highway, the beach came right up to the back door of the warehouses that now line the thoroughfare. Two hundred years ago those warehouses were filled with indigo, tobacco, and cotton. Today the stone buildings house silk, crystal, and diamonds. Exotic fragrances are still traded, but by island beauty queens in air-conditioned perfume palaces instead of through

Fort Christian (1672–80) is the oldest surviving structure in St. Thomas.

open market stalls. The pirates of old used St. Thomas as a base from which to raid merchant ships of every nation, though they were particularly fond of the gold- and silver-laden treasure ships heading to Spain. Pirates are still around, but today's versions use St. Thomas as a drop-off for their contraband: illegal immigrants and drugs.

EXPLORING ST. THOMAS

To explore outside Charlotte Amalie, rent a car or hire a taxi. Your rental car should come with a good map; if not, pick up the pocket-size "St. Thomas–St. John Road Map" at a tourist information center. Roads are marked with route numbers, but they're confusing and seem to switch numbers suddenly. Roads are also identified by signs bearing the St. Thomas–St. John Hotel and Tourism Association's mascot, Tommy the Starfish. More than 100 of these color-coded signs line the island's main routes. Orange signs trace the route from the airport to Red Hook, green signs identify the road from town to Magens Bay, Tommy's face on a yellow background points from Mafolie to Crown Bay through the north side, red signs lead from Smith Bay to Four Corners via Skyline Drive, and blue signs mark the route from the cruise-ship dock at Havensight to Red Hook. These color-coded routes are not marked on most visitor maps, however. Allow yourself a day to explore, especially if you want to stop to take pictures or to enjoy a light bite or refreshing swim. Most gas stations are on the island's more populated eastern end, so fill up before heading to the north side. And remember to drive on the left!

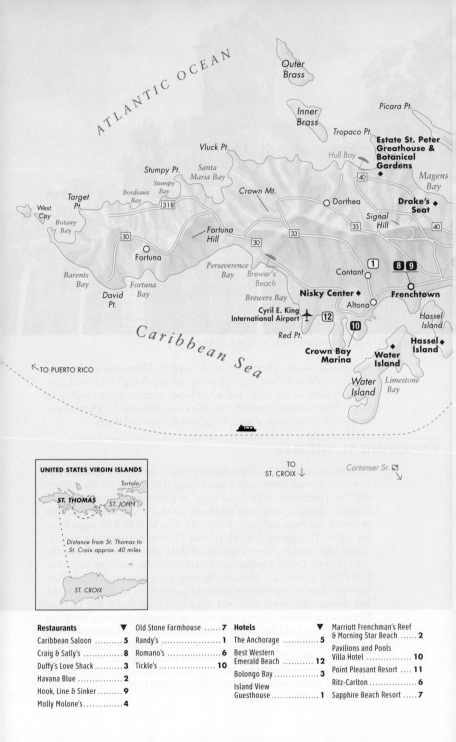

ATLANTIC OCEAN

Outer Brass

Inner Brass

Picara Pt.

Tropaco Pt.

Vluck Pt.

Hull Bay

Estate St. Peter Greathouse & Botanical Gardens

Magens Bay

Stumpy Pt.

Santa Maria Bay

Stumpy Bay

Bordeaux Bay

40

Drake's Seat

Crown Mt.

Dorthea

Signal Hill

33

40

Target Pt.

318

West Cay

Botany Bay

Fortuna Hill

33

30

Fortuna

Perseverance Bay

Brewer's Beach

30

Contant

1

8 9

Barents Bay

Fortuna Bay

David Pt.

Brewers Bay

Nisky Center ◆

Altona

Frenchtown

Cyril E. King International Airport

12

10

Hassel Island

Red Pt.

Crown Bay Marina

Water Island

Hassel Island

Caribbean Sea

Water Island

Limestone Bay

← TO PUERTO RICO

TO ST. CROIX ↓

Cartanser Sr.

TO ST. CROIX ↓

UNITED STATES VIRGIN ISLANDS

Tortola

ST. THOMAS

ST. JOHN

Distance from St. Thomas to St. Croix approx. 40 miles

ST. CROIX

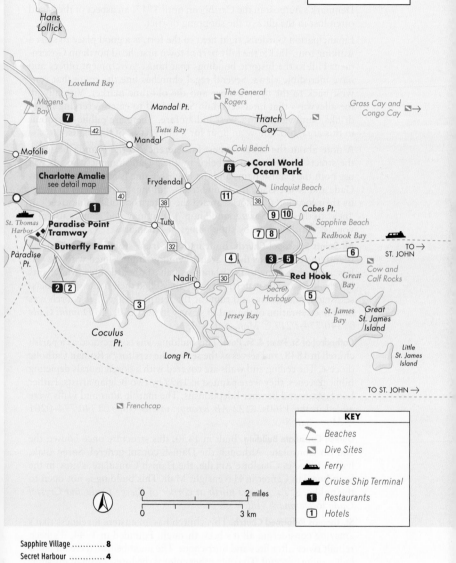

St. Thomas

Hans Lollick

Lovelund Bay

Magens Bay **7**

Mafolie

Mandal Pt.

Mandal

Tutu Bay

42

The General Rogers

Thatch Cay

Grass Cay and Congo Cay →

Charlotte Amalie
see detail map

40

1

Frydendal

38

Coki Beach

6 ◆ **Coral World Ocean Park**

Lindquist Beach

11

38

Cabes Pt.

9 **10**

Sapphire Beach

St. Thomas Harbor

Paradise Point Tramway

Butterfly Famr

Paradise Pt.

Tutu

32

7 **8**

Redhook Bay

TO ST. JOHN →

Nadir

30

4

3 ■ **5**

Red Hook

6

Cow and Calf Rocks

2 **2**

3

Jersey Bay

Secret Harbour

5

Great Bay

St. James Bay

Great St. James Island

Coculus Pt.

Long Pt.

Little St. James Island

TO ST. JOHN →

◢ Frenchcap

KEY

☂	Beaches
◣	Dive Sites
⛴	Ferry
⛴	Cruise Ship Terminal
1	Restaurants
1	Hotels

0 ___ 2 miles
0 ___ 3 km

CHARLOTTE AMALIE

Look beyond the pricey shops, T-shirt vendors, and bustling crowds for a glimpse of the island's history. The city served as the capital of Denmark's outpost in the Caribbean until 1917, an aspect of the island often lost in the glitz of the shopping district.

Emancipation Gardens, right next to the fort, is a good place to start a walking tour. Tackle the hilly part of town first: head north up Government Hill to the historic buildings that house government offices and have incredible views. Several regal churches line the route that runs west back to the town proper and the old-time market. Virtually all the alleyways that intersect Main Street lead to eateries serving frosty drinks, sandwiches, and West Indian fare. There are public restrooms in this area, too. Allow an hour for a quick view of the sights.

A note about the street names: In deference to the island's heritage, the streets downtown are labeled by their Danish names. Locals will use both the Danish name and the English name (such as Dronningens Gade and Norre Gade for Main Street), but most people refer to things by their location ("a block toward the waterfront off Main Street" or "next to the Little Switzerland Shop"). You may find it more useful if you ask for directions by shop names or landmarks.

All Saints Episcopal Church. Built in 1848 from stone quarried on the island, the church has thick, arched window frames lined with the yellow brick that came to the islands as ballast aboard ships. Merchants left the brick on the waterfront when they filled their boats with molasses, sugar, mahogany, and rum for the return voyage. The church was built in celebration of the end of slavery in the USVI. ⊠ *3 Domini Gade* ☎ *340/774–0217* ⊙ *Mon.–Sat. 9–3.*

Cathedral of St. Peter & St. Paul. This building was consecrated as a parish church in 1848, and serves as the seat of the territory's Roman Catholic diocese. The ceiling and walls are covered with a dozen murals depicting biblical scenes; they were painted in 1899 by two Belgian artists, Father Leo Servais and Brother Ildephonsus. The marble altar and walls were added in the 1960s. ⊠ *22-AB Kronprindsens Gade* ☎ *340/774–0201* ⊙ *Mon.–Sat. 8–5.*

Danish Consulate Building. Built in 1830, this structure once housed the Danish Consulate. Although the Danish consul general, Søren Blak, has an office in Charlotte Amalie, the Danish Consulate is now in the Scandinavian Center in Havensight Mall. This building is not open to the public. ⊠ *Take stairs north at corner of Bjerge Gade and Crystal Gade to Denmark Hill.*

St. Thomas Reformed Church. This church has an austere loveliness that's amazing considering all it's been through. Founded in 1744, it's been rebuilt twice after fires and hurricanes. The unembellished cream-color hall is quite peaceful. The only other color is the forest green of the shutters and the carpet. Call ahead if you wish to visit at a particular time, as the doors are sometimes locked. ⊠ *5 Crystal Gade* ☎ *340/776–8255* ⊙ *Weekdays 9–5.*

Educators Park. A peaceful place amid the town's hustle and bustle, the park has memorials to three famous Virgin Islanders: educator Edith

Charlotte Amalie

KEY

■ *Exploring*

① *Restaurants & Hotels*

Williams, J. Antonio Jarvis (a founder of the *Daily News*), and educator and author Rothschild Francis. The last gave many speeches here. ⊠ *Main St., across from post office.*

☾ **Emancipation Garden.** A bronze bust of a freed slave blowing a conch shell commemorates slavery's end, in 1848—the garden was built to mark emancipation's 150th anniversary, in 1998. The gazebo here is used for official ceremonies. Two other monuments show the island's Danish-American connection—a bust of Denmark's King Christian and a scaled-down model of the U.S. Liberty Bell. ⊠ *Between Tolbod Gade and Ft. Christian.*

Enid M. Baa Public Library. Like so many other structures on the north side of Main Street, this large yellow building is a typical 18th-century town house. The library was once the home of merchant and landowner Baron von Bretton. He and other merchants built their houses (stores downstairs, living quarters above) across from the brick warehouses on the south side of the street. This is the island's first recorded fireproof building, meaning it was built of ballast brick instead of wood. Its interior of high ceilings and cool stone floors is the perfect refuge from the afternoon sun. You can browse through historic papers or just sit in the breeze by an open window reading the paper. ⊠ *20 Dronningens Gade* ☎ *340/774–0630* ☾ *Weekdays 9–6, Sat. 10–4.*

☾ **Ft. Christian.** St. Thomas's oldest standing structure, this remarkable building was built between 1672 and 1680 and now has U.S. National Landmark status. Over the years, it was used as a jail, governor's residence, town hall, courthouse, and church. In 2005, a multimillion-dollar renovation was started to stabilize the structure and halt centuries of deterioration. Delays—including the discovery of human skeletal remains buried in the walls from when the structure was used as a Lutheran church—have plagued the project, and the fort remains closed to the public. You can see from the outside the four renovated faces of its famous 19th-century clock tower. ⊠ *Waterfront Hwy. east of shopping district* ☎ *340/776–8605.*

Frederick Lutheran Church. This historic church has a massive mahogany altar, and its pews—each with its own door—were once rented to families of the congregation. Lutheranism is the state religion of Denmark, and when the territory was without a minister, the governor—who had his own elevated pew—filled in. ⊠ *7 Norre Gade* ☎ *340/776–1315* ☾ *Mon.–Sat. 9–4.*

Government House. Built in 1867, this neoclassical white brick-and-wood structure houses the offices of the governor of the Virgin Islands. Inside, the staircases are of native mahogany, as are the plaques, hand-lettered in gold with the names of the governors appointed and, since 1970, elected. Brochures detailing the history of the building are available, but you may have to ask for them. ⊠ *Government Hill, 21–22 Kongens Gade* ☎ *340/774–0001* ☜ *Free* ☾ *Weekdays 8–5.*

Haagensen House. This lovingly restored house was built in the early 1800s by Danish entrepreneur Hans Haagensen. It's surrounded by an equally impressive cookhouse, outbuildings, and terraced gardens. A lower-level banquet hall showcases antique prints and photographs.

Guided tours begin at the nearby Hotel 1829, then continue here. The tour includes stops at two other restored 19th-century houses, a rum factory, amber museum, and finally the lookout tour at Blackbeard's Castle. Tours are given between 9 am and 3 pm on days a cruise ship is in port. Self-guided tours are also available. ⊠ *Behind Hotel 1829 on Government Hill, 29–30 Kongens Gade* ☎ *340/776–1234, 340/776– 1829* ⧉ *Tours $20 guided, $15 self-guided* ⊙ *Oct.–May, daily 9–3; June–Sept., by appointment only.*

Hassel Island. East of Water Island in Charlotte Amalie harbor, Hassel Island is part of the Virgin Islands National Park. On it are the ruins of a British military garrison (built during a brief British occupation of the USVI during the 1800s) and the remains of a marine railway (where ships were hoisted into dry dock for repairs). Daily guided kayak tours to the island are in the works for late 2012, although that may change. ⊠ *Charlotte Amalie harbor* ☎ *340/776–6201* ⊕ *www.nps.gov/viis.*

Hotel 1829. As its name implies, the hotel was built in 1829, but back then it was the private residence of a prominent merchant named Alexander Lavalette. The building's coral-color facade is accented with fancy wrought-iron railings, and the interior is paneled in dark wood, which makes it feel delightfully cool. From the terrace there's an exquisite view of the harbor framed by brilliant orange bougainvillea. You can combine a visit to this hotel with a walking tour of Haagensen House, Villa Notman, Britannia House, the rum factory, the amber museum, and the lookout tower at Blackbeard's Castle just above the hotel. ⊠ *Government Hill, 29–30 Kongens Gade* ☎ *340/776–1829, 340/776–1234* ⊕ *www.hotel1829.com* ⧉ *Tour $20 guided, $15 self-guided* ⊙ *Oct.– May, daily 9–3; June–Sept., by appointment only.*

Legislature Building. Its pastoral-looking lime-green exterior conceals the vociferous political wrangling of the Virgin Islands Senate. Constructed originally by the Danish as a police barracks, the building was later used to billet U.S. Marines, and much later it housed a public school. You're welcome to sit in on sessions in the upstairs chambers. ⊠ *Waterfront Hwy. across from Ft. Christian, Route 30* ☎ *340/774–0880* ⊙ *Daily 8–5.*

Memorial Moravian Church. Built in 1884, this church was named to commemorate the 150th anniversary of the Moravian Church in the Virgin Islands. ⊠ *17 Norre Gade* ☎ *340/776–0066* ⊙ *Weekdays 8–5.*

99 Steps. This staircase "street," built by the Danes in the 1700s, leads to the residential area above Charlotte Amalie and to Blackbeard's Castle, a U.S. national historic landmark. The castle's tower, built in 1679, was once used by the notorious pirate Edward Teach. Today it's home to life-size pirates crafted out of bronze and copper, the largest such collection in the world. If you count the stairs as you go up, you'll discover, as thousands have before you, that there are more than the name implies. ⊠ *Look for steps heading north from Government Hill.*

Pissarro Building. Housing several shops and an art gallery, this was the birthplace and childhood home of the acclaimed 19th-century impressionist painter Camille Pissarro, who lived for most of his adult life in France. The art gallery contains three original pages from Pissarro's sketchbook and two pastels by Pissarro's grandson, Claude. ⊠ *Main St. between Raadets Gade and Trompeter Gade, 14 Dronningens Gade.*

🕙 **Roosevelt Park.** The former Coconut Park was renamed in honor of Franklin D. Roosevelt in 1945. It's a great place to put your feet up and people-watch. A 2007 renovation added five granite pedestals representing the five branches of the military, bronze urns that can be lighted to commemorate special events, and bronze plaques inscribed with the names of the territory's veterans who died defending the United States. There's also a children's playground. ⊠ *Norre Gade, Intersection of Norre Gade and Route 35.*

★ **Seven Arches Museum and Gallery.** This restored 18th-century home is a striking example of classic Danish–West Indian architecture. There seem to be arches everywhere—seven to be exact—all supporting a "welcoming arms" staircase that leads to the second floor and the flower-framed front doorway. The Danish kitchen is a highlight: it's housed in a separate building away from the main house, as were all cooking facilities in the early days (for fire prevention). Inside the house you can see mahogany furnishings and gas lamps and colorful abstract canvases painted by the museum's curator, a local artist. ⊠ *Government Hill, 3 buildings east of Government House, 18A–B Dronningens Gade* ☎ *340/774–9295* ⊕ *www.sevenarchesmuseum.com* ⊠ *$5 donation* ☉ *By appointment only.*

Synagogue of Beracha Veshalom Vegmiluth Hasidim. The synagogue's Hebrew name translates as the Congregation of Blessing, Peace, and Loving Deeds. The small building's white pillars contrast with rough stone walls, as does the rich mahogany of the pews and altar. The sand on the floor symbolizes the exodus from Egypt. Since the synagogue first opened its doors in 1833, it has held a weekly service, making it the oldest synagogue building in continuous use under the American flag and the second-oldest (after the one on Curaçao) in the Western Hemisphere. Guided tours can be arranged. Brochures detailing the key structures and history are also available. Next door the Weibel Museum showcases Jewish history on St. Thomas. ⊠ *15 Crystal Gade* ☎ *340/774–4312* ⊕ *www.onepaper.com/synagogue* ☉ *Weekdays 9–4.*

U.S. Post Office. While you buy stamps, contemplate the murals of waterfront scenes by *Saturday Evening Post* artist Stephen Dohanos. His art was commissioned as part of the Works Project Administration in the 1930s. ⊠ *Tolbod Gade and Main Street, 5046 Norre Gade.*

🕙 **Vendors Plaza.** Here merchants sell everything from T-shirts to African attire to leather goods. Look for local art among the ever-changing selections at this busy market. ⊠ *Waterfront, west of Ft. Christian* ☉ *Weekdays 8–6, weekends 9–1.*

Weibel Museum. In this museum next to the synagogue, 300 years of Jewish history on St. Thomas are showcased. The small gift shop sells a commemorative silver coin celebrating the anniversary of the Hebrew congregation's establishment on the island in 1796. There are also tropically inspired items, such as menorahs painted to resemble palm trees. ⊠ *15 Crystal Gade* ☎ *340/774–4312* ⊠ *Free* ☉ *Weekdays 9–4.*

Coral World Ocean Park offers interactive sea-life encounters.

EAST END

Although the eastern end has many major resorts and spectacular beaches, don't be surprised if a cow or a herd of goats crosses your path as you drive through the relatively flat, dry terrain. You can pick up sandwiches from a deli in the Red Hook area if you want a picnic lunch.

ⓒ
Fodor's Choice
★

Coral World Ocean Park. This interactive aquarium and water-sports center lets you experience a variety of sea life and other animals. There are several outdoor pools where you can pet baby sharks, feed stingrays, touch starfish, and view endangered sea turtles. During the Sea Trek Helmet Dive, you walk along an underwater trail wearing a helmet that provides a continuous supply of air. You can try "snuba," a cross between snorkeling and scuba diving. Swim with a sea lion and have a chance at playing ball or getting a big, wet, whistered kiss. You can also buy a cup of nectar and let the cheerful lorikeets perch on your hand and drink. The park also has an offshore underwater observatory, an 80,000-gallon coral reef exhibit (one of the largest in the world), and a nature trail with native ducks and tortoises. Daily feedings take place at most exhibits. ✉ *Coki Point north of Rte. 38, Estate Fryden-dal* ☎ *340/775–1555* ⊕ *www.coralworldvi.com* ✆ *$19, Sea Lion Swim $105, Sea Lion Encounter $65, Sea Trek $58, Snuba $52, Shark and Turtle Encounters $32, Nautilus $20* ☉ *Daily 9–4. Off-season (May–Oct.) hrs may vary, so call to confirm.*

Red Hook. The IGY American Yacht Harbor marina here has fishing and sailing charter boats, a dive shop, and powerboat-rental agencies. There are also several bars and restaurants, including Molly Molone's, Duffy's Love Shack, and the Caribbean Saloon. One grocery store has a deli that offers sliced meats and cheeses, rotisserie-roasted chickens, prepared salads, freshly baked breads, and other picnic fixings. Ferries depart from Red Hook en route to St. John and the British Virgin Islands. ⊠ *Intersection of Rtes. 38 and 32.*

SOUTH SHORE

⏱ **Butterfly Garden.** Step into this 10,000-square-foot mesh enclosure and watch hundreds of colorful, exotic butterflies flutter all around you. A 25-minute tour takes you through their life cycle. Outside the enclosure, you can wander a garden of native plants designed to attract local butterflies and hummingbirds. There's also a bird show with cockatoos and parrots riding bicycles and engaging in other antics. The butterflies are most active in the morning. If you're a photographer, you'll probably prefer the afternoon, when the butterflies move more slowly and are more easily captured in a picture. ⊠ *Havensight Mall, adjacent to West Indian Company cruise-ship dock, Havensight* ☎ *340/715–3366* ⊕ *www.butterflygardenvi.com* ⊠ *$15* ⊙ *Daily 8:30–4. Off-season (May–Oct.) hrs may vary, so call to confirm.*

Frenchtown. Popular for its bars and restaurants, Frenchtown is also the home of descendants of immigrants from St. Barthélemy (St. Barth). You can watch them pull up their brightly painted boats and display their equally colorful catch of the day along the waterfront. If you chat with them, you can hear speech patterns slightly different from those of other St. Thomians. Get a feel for the residential district of Frenchtown by walking west to some of the town's winding streets, where tiny wooden houses have been passed down from generation to generation.

French Heritage Museum. Next to Joseph Aubain Ballpark, the museum houses fishing nets, accordions, tambourines, mahogany furniture, photographs, and other artifacts illustrating the lives of the French descendants during the 18th through 20th centuries. Admission is free, but donations are accepted. ⊠ *Rue de St. Anne and rue de St. Barthélemy* ☎ *340/774–2320* ⊠ *Free* ⊙ *Mon.–Sat. 9–6* ⊠ *Turn south off Waterfront Hwy. (Rte. 30) at post office.*

⏱ ★ **St. Thomas Skyride.** Fly skyward in a gondola to Paradise Point, an overlook with breathtaking views of Charlotte Amalie and the harbor. You'll find several shops, a bar, a restaurant, a wedding gazebo, and a Ferris wheel. A ¼-mile (½-km) hiking trail leads to spectacular views of St. Croix. Wear sturdy shoes, as the trail is steep and rocky. You can also skip the gondola and taxi to the top for $4 per person from the Havensight Dock. ⊠ *Rte. 30, across from Havensight Mall, 9617 Estate Thomas, Havensight* ☎ *340/774–9809* ⊠ *$21* ⊙ *Thurs.–Tues. 9–5, Wed. 9–9.*

⏱ **Water Island.** This island, the fourth-largest of the U.S. Virgin Islands, floats about ¼ mile (½ km) out in Charlotte Amalie harbor. A ferry between Crown Bay Marina and the island operates several times daily from 6:30 am to 6 pm Monday through Saturday, and from 8 am to 5 pm on Sunday and holidays at a cost of $10 round-trip. (On cruise-ship days, a ferry goes direct from the West India Company dock, but only for those passengers on the bike trip.) From the ferry dock, it's a hike of less than a half-mile to Honeymoon Beach (though you have to go up a big hill), where Brad Pitt and Cate Blanchett filmed a scene of the movie *The Curious Case of Benjamin Button.* Get lunch from a food truck that pulls up on weekends. ⊠ *Charlotte Amalie harbor* ☎ *340/690–4159 for ferry information.*

WEST END

Drake's Seat. Sir Francis Drake is supposed to have kept watch over his fleet and looked for enemy ships from this vantage point. The panorama is especially breathtaking (and romantic) at dusk, and if you arrive late in the day, you can miss the hordes of day-trippers on taxi tours who stop here to take a picture. ⊠ *Rte. 40, Estate Zufriedenheit.*

Estate St. Peter Greathouse and Botanical Gardens. This unusual spot is perched on a mountainside 1,000 feet above sea level, with views of more than 20 islands and islets. You can wander through a gallery displaying local art, sip a complimentary rum punch while looking out at the view, or follow a nature trail that leads you past nearly 70 varieties of tropical plants, including 17 varieties of orchids. ⊠ *Rte. 40, 6A St. Peter Mountain Road, Estate St. Peter* ☎ *340/774–4999* ☑ *$10.*

☾ ★ **Mountain Top.** Head out to the observation deck—more than 1,500 feet above sea level—to get a bird's-eye view that stretches from Puerto Rico's out-island of Culebra in the west all the way to the British Virgin Islands in the east. There's also a restaurant, restrooms, and shops that sell everything from Caribbean art to nautical antiques, ship models, and touristy T-shirts. Kids will like talking to the parrots—and hearing them answer back. ⊠ *Head north off Rte. 33, look for signs, Mountain Top* ☑ *Free* ☾ *Daily 8–5.*

27

BEACHES

Remember to remove all your valuables from the car and keep them out of sight when you go swimming. Break-ins are possible on all three of the U.S. Virgin Islands; most locals recommend leaving your windows down and leaving absolutely nothing in your car.

EAST END

☾ Fodor's Choice ★ **Coki Beach.** Funky beach huts selling local foods such as pâtés (fried turnovers with a spicy ground-beef filling), picnic tables topped with umbrellas sporting beverage logos, quaint vendor kiosks, and a brigade of hair braiders and taxi men make this beach overlooking picturesque Thatch Cay feel like an amusement park. But this is the best place on the island to snorkel and scuba dive. Fish, including grunts, snappers, and wrasses, are like an effervescent cloud you can wave your hand through. Major renovations in late 2011 added a new bathhouse and boardwalk. There are also beefed-up security and regular police patrols in the area after a shooting incident in 2010. **Amenities:** food and drink; lifeguards; watersports. **Best for:** partyers; snorkeling. ⊠ *Rte. 388, next to Coral World Ocean Park.*

Lindquist Beach. The newest of the Virgin Islands' public beaches has a serene sense of wilderness that isn't found on the more crowded beaches. A lifeguard is on duty between 8 am and 5 pm. Picnic tables are available. Try snorkeling over the offshore reef. **Amenities:** lifeguards;

parking (no fee); toilets. **Best for:** solitude; snorkeling. ⊠ *Rte. 38, at end of a bumpy dirt road* ⊟ *$2 per person.*

★ **Sapphire Beach.** A steady breeze makes this beach a boardsailor's paradise. The swimming is great, as is the snorkeling, especially at the reef near Pettyklip Point. Beach volleyball is big on the weekends. Sapphire Beach Resort and Marina has a snack shop, bar, and water-sports rentals. **Amenities:** food and drink; water sports. **Best for:** snorkeling; swimming; windsurfing. ⊠ *Rte. 38, Sapphire Bay.*

Secret Harbour. Placid waters make it easy to stroke your way out to a swim platform offshore from the Secret Harbour Beach Resort & Villas. Nearby reefs give snorkelers a natural show. There's a bar and restaurant, as well as a dive shop. **Amenities:** food and drink; water sports. **Best for:** snorkeling; sunset; swimming. ⊠ *Rte. 32, Red Hook.*

Vessup Beach. This wild, undeveloped beach is lined with sea grape trees and century plants. It's close to Red Hook harbor, so you can watch the ferries depart. The calm waters are excellent for swimming. West Indies Windsurfing is here, so you can rent Windsurfers, kayaks, and other water toys. There are no restrooms or changing facilities. It's popular with locals on weekends. **Amenities:** water sports. **Best for:** swimming. ⊠ *Off Rte. 322, Vessup Bay.*

SOUTH SHORE

Brewer's Beach. Watch jets land at the Cyril E. King Airport as you dip into the usually calm seas. Rocks at either end of the shoreline, patches of grass poking randomly through the sand, and shady tamarind trees 30 feet from the water give this beach a wild, natural feel. Civilization has arrived, in the form of one or two mobile food vans park on the nearby road. Buy a fried-chicken leg and johnnycake or burgers and chips to munch on at the picnic tables. **Amenities:** food and drink; toilets. **Best for:** sunset; swimming. ⊠ *Rte. 30, west of University of the Virgin Islands.*

Morningstar Beach. Nature and nurture combine at this ¼-mi-long (½-km-long) beach between Marriott Frenchman's Reef and Morning Star Beach Resorts, where the amenities include beachside bar service. A concession rents floating mats, snorkeling equipment, sailboards, and Jet Skis. Swimming is excellent; there are good-size rolling waves year-round, but do watch the undertow. If you're feeling lazy, rent a lounge chair with umbrella and order a libation from one of two full-service beach bars. At 7 am and again at 5 pm, you can catch the cruise ships gliding majestically out to sea from the Charlotte Amalie harbor. **Amenities:** food and drink; water sports. **Best for:** partiers; surfing; swimming. ⊠ *Rte. 315, 2 miles (3 km) southeast of Charlotte Amalie, past Havensight Mall and cruise-ship dock.*

WEST END

○ **Magens Bay.** Deeded to the island as a public park, this heart-shape
Fodor'sChoice stretch of white sand is considered one of the most beautiful in the
★ world. The bottom of the bay is flat and sandy, so this is a place for sunning and swimming rather than snorkeling. On weekends and holidays the sounds of music from groups partying under the sheds fill the air. There's a bar, snack shack, and beachwear boutique; bathhouses

with restrooms, changing rooms, and saltwater showers are close by. Sunfish and paddleboats are the most popular rentals at the water-sports kiosk. East of the beach is Udder Delight, a one-room shop that serves a Virgin Islands tradition—a milk shake with a splash of Cruzan rum. (Kids can enjoy virgin versions, which have a touch of soursop, mango, or banana flavoring). If you arrive between 8 am and 5 pm, you pay an entrance fee of $4 per person, $2 per vehicle; it's free for children under 12. **Amenities:** food and drink; parking (fee); water sports. **Best for:** partiers; swimming; walking. ⊠ *Rte. 35, at end of road on north side of island* ☎ *340/777–6300.*

WHERE TO EAT

The beauty of St. Thomas and its sister islands has attracted a cadre of professionally trained chefs who know their way around fresh fish and local fruits. You can dine on terrific cheap local dishes such as goat water (a spicy stew) and fungi (a cornmeal side dish that's similar to polenta) as well as imports that include hot pastrami sandwiches and raspberries in crème fraîche.

Restaurants are spread all over the island, although fewer are found on the west and northwest parts of the island. Most restaurants out of town are easily accessible by taxi and have ample parking. If you dine in Charlotte Amalie, take a taxi. Parking close to restaurants can be difficult to find, and walking around after dark isn't always safe.

If your accommodations have a kitchen and you plan to cook, there's good variety in St. Thomas's mainland-style supermarkets. Just be prepared for grocery prices that are about 20% to 30% higher than those in the United States. As for drinking, a beer in a bar that's not part of a hotel will cost between $3 and $4 and a piña colada $6 or more.

What to Wear: Dining on St. Thomas is informal. Few restaurants require a jacket and tie. Still, at dinner in the snazzier places shorts and T-shirts are inappropriate; men would do well to wear slacks and a shirt with buttons. Dress codes on St. Thomas rarely require women to wear skirts, but you can never go wrong with something flowing.

CHARLOTTE AMALIE

$$$$
ECLECTIC
Fodor'sChoice
★

✕**Banana Tree Grille.** The eagle's-eye view of the Charlotte Amalie harbor from this breeze-cooled restaurant is as fantastic as the food. Linen tablecloths, china, and silver place settings combine with subdued lighting to make an elegant space. To start, try the seafood cocktail of lobster, shrimp, scallops, and squid marinated in a savory herb vinaigrette. The signature dish here—and worthy of its fame—is a New York sirloin seasoned simply with olive oil and garlic and grilled to order. Arrive before 6 pm to watch the cruise ships depart from the harbor while you enjoy a drink at the bar. ⑤ *Average main: $36* ⊠ *Bluebeard's Castle, Bluebeard's Hill, 1331 Estate Taamburg* ☎ *340/776–4050* ⊕ *www.bananatreegrille. com* ⌑ *Reservations essential* ⊘ *Closed Mon. No lunch.*

$$$
CARIBBEAN

✕**Cuzzin's Caribbean Restaurant and Bar.** In a 19th-century livery stable on Back Street, this restaurant is hard to find but well worth it if you want to sample bona fide Virgin Islands cuisine. For lunch, order tender slivers of conch stewed in a rich onion-and-butter sauce, savory braised oxtail, or curried chicken. At dinner the island-style mutton, served in thick gravy and seasoned with locally grown herbs, offers a tasty treat that's deliciously different. Side dishes include peas and rice, boiled green bananas, fried plantains, and potato stuffing. $ *Average main: $24 ☒ 7 Wimmelskafts Gade, also called Back St.* ☎ 340/777–4711.

$$
CARIBBEAN
Fodor'sChoice
★

✕ **Gladys' Cafe.** Even if the local specialties—conch in butter sauce, salt fish and dumplings, hearty red bean soup—didn't make this a recommended café, it would be worth coming for Gladys's smile. Her cozy alleyway restaurant is rich in atmosphere with its mahogany bar and native stone walls, making dining a double delight. While you're here, pick up a $5 or $10 bottle of her special hot sauce. There are mustard-, oil and vinegar–, and tomato-based versions; the tomato-based sauce is the hottest. Only Amex is accepted. $ *Average main: $16 ☒ Waterfront at Royal Dane Mall, 28A Dronningens Gade* ☎ 340/774–6604 ☽ *No dinner.*

$$
AMERICAN
☾

✕ **Greenhouse Bar and Restaurant.** Fun-lovers come to this waterfront restaurant to eat, listen to music, and play games, both video and pool. Even the most finicky eater should find something to please on the eight-page menu that offers burgers, salads, and pizza served all day long, along with peel-and-eat shrimp, Maine lobster, Alaskan king crab, and Black Angus prime rib for dinner. This is generally a family-friendly place, though the Two-for-Tuesdays happy hour and Friday-night live reggae music that starts thumping at 10 pm draw an occasionally rambunctious young-adult crowd. $ *Average main: $19 ☒ Waterfront Hwy. at Storetvaer Gade* ☎ 340/774–7998 ⊕ *www.thegreenhouserestaurant.com.*

$$$$
ITALIAN
★

✕ **Virgilio's.** For the island's best northern Italian cuisine, don't miss this intimate, elegant hideaway that's on a quiet side street. Eclectic art covers the two-story brick walls, and the sound of opera sets the stage for a memorable meal. Come here for more than 40 homemade pastas topped with superb sauces—capellini with fresh tomatoes and garlic or peasant-style spaghetti in a rich tomato sauce with mushrooms and prosciutto. House specialties include osso buco and tiramisu, which are expertly crafted by chef Ernesto Garrigos, who has prepared these two dishes on the Discovery Channel's *Great Chefs of the World* series. $ *Average main: $41 ☒ 18 Main St.* ☎ 340/776–4920 ☖ *Reservations essential* ☽ *Closed Sun.*

EAST END

$$$
AMERICAN

✕ **Caribbean Saloon.** Sports on wide-screen TVs and and live music on weekends are two added attractions at this hip sports bar that's in the center of the action in Red Hook. The menu ranges from finger-licking barbecue ribs to more sophisticated fare, such as the signature filet mignon wrapped in bacon and smothered in melted Gorgonzola cheese. There's always a catch of the day; the fishing fleet is only steps away. A late-night menu is available from 10 pm until 4 am. $ *Average main: $28 ☒ Rte. 32 at American Yacht Harbor, Bldg B., Red Hook* ☎ 340/775–7060 ⊕ *www.caribbeansaloon.com.*

$$
ECLECTIC

✕ **Duffy's Love Shack.** If the floating bubbles don't attract you to this zany eatery, the lime-green shutters, loud rock music, and fun-loving waitstaff just might. It's billed as the "ultimate tropical drink shack," and the bartenders shake up such exotic concoctions as the Love Shack

Where to Shop for Groceries

High food prices in Virgin Islands supermarkets are enough to dull anyone's appetite. Food is significantly more expensive than on the mainland.

Although you'll never match the prices back home, you can shop around for the best deals. If you're traveling with a group, it pays to stock up on the basics at warehouse-style stores such as Pricesmart (membership required) and Cost-U-Less. Even the nonbulk food items here are sold at lower prices than in the supermarkets or convenience stores. Good buys include beverages, meats, produce, and spirits.

After this, head to supermarkets such as Plaza Extra, Pueblo, and Food Center. Although the prices aren't as good

as at the big-box stores, the selection is better.

Finally, if you want to splurge on top-quality meats, exotic produce, imported cheeses, exotic spices, and imported spirits, finish off your shopping at high-end shops such as Marina Market or Gourmet Gallery.

The Fruit Bowl is the place for fresh produce. The prices and selection are unbeatable.

For really fresh tropical fruits, vegetables, and seasoning herbs, visit the farmers' markets in Smith Bay (daily), at Market Square (daily), at Yacht Haven Grande (first and third Sunday of the month), and in Estate Bordeaux (last Sunday of every month).

27

Volcano—a 50-ounce flaming extravaganza. The menu has a selection of burgers, tacos, burritos, and salads. Try the grilled mahimahi taco salad or jerk Caesar wrap. ⑤ *Average main: $15* ⊠ *Red Hook Shopping Center, Rte. 32, Red Hook* ☎ *340/779–2080* ⊕ *www.duffysloveshack. com* ▤ *No credit cards.*

$$$ ✕**Molly Molone's.** This dockside eatery has a devoted following among
IRISH   local boaters, who swear by the traditional American and Irish fare. Opt
☺   for eggs Benedict or rashers of Irish sausages and eggs for breakfast, or
fork into fish-and-chips, Irish stew, or bangers and mash (sausage and mashed potatoes) for lunch or dinner. Beware: the resident iguanas will beg for table scraps—bring your camera. ⑤ *Average main: $24* ⊠ *American Yacht Harbor, Bldg. D, Rte. 32, Red Hook* ☎ *340/775–1270.*

$$$$ ✕**Old Stone Farmhouse.** Dine in the splendor of a beautifully restored
ECLECTIC   plantation house. Come early and sidle up to the beautiful mahogany
Fodor's Choice bar, where you can choose from an extensive wine list. Then, start with
★   French onion soup , move on to osso buco with a lobster risotto; and finish with a house-made passion-fruit sorbet. Personalized attention makes dining here a delight. ⑤ *Average main: $36* ⊠ *Rte. 42, 1 mile (1½ km) west of entrance to Mahogany Run Golf Course, Estate Lovenlund* ☎ *340/777–6277* ⊕ *www.oldstonefarmhouse.com* ⚠ *Reservations essential* ☉ *Closed Mon.*

$$$$ ✕**Romano's Restaurant and Art Gallery.** The dining rooms in this huge
ITALIAN   old stucco house are lined with whimsical works of art painted by
★   doubly talented owner–chef Tony Romano, who also creates superb northern Italian cuisine. Try the pastas, either with a classic ragout or with one of Tony's more unique creations, such as a cream sauce

with mushrooms, prosciutto, pine nuts, and Parmesan. There's classic osso buco and veal scaloppini, too. If you like the food here, keep in mind that Romano also offers his personal chef services at villas and condos. ⑤ *Average main: $39* ✉ *Rte. 388 at Coki Point, Estate Fryden-dal* ☎ *340/775–0045* ⊕ *www.romanosrestaurant.com* ⌂ *Reservations essential* ⊘ *Closed Sun. No lunch.*

SOUTH SHORE

$$$$ ✗ **Havana Blue.** The cuisine here is described as Cuban-Asian, but what-
ECLECTIC ever you call it, the dining experience is outstanding. A glowing wall
Fodor'sChoice of water meets you as you enter, and then you're seated at a table laid
★ with linen and silver that's illuminated in a soft blue light radiating from above. Be sure to sample the mango mojito, made with fresh mango, crushed mint, and limes. Entrées include coconut-chipotle ceviche, sugarcane-glazed pork tenderloin medallions, and the signature dish, miso sea bass. Hand-rolled cigars and aged rums finish the night off in true Cuban style. For something really special, request an exclusive table for two set on Morning Star Beach—you get a seven-course tast-ing menu, champagne, and your own personal waiter, all for $350 for two. ⑤ *Average main: $36* ✉ *Marriott Morningstar Beach Resort, Rte. 315, Estate Bakkeroe* ☎ *340/715–2583* ⊕ *www.havanabluerestaurant. com* ⌂ *Reservations essential* ⊘ *No lunch.*

$$$$ ✗ **Randy's Bar and Bistro.** There's no view here—even though you're at
ECLECTIC the top of a hill—but the somewhat hidden location has helped to
★ keep this one of the island's best dining secrets. This wine shop and deli caters to a local lunch crowd. At night you forget you're tucked into a nearly windowless building. The tableside bread for starters is a thick, crusty focaccia flavored with nearly 10 different vegetables. Try the Brie-stuffed filet mignon or the rack of lamb. After-dinner cigars and wine complete the experience. ⑤ *Average main: $34* ✉ *Al Cohen's Plaza, atop Raphune Hill, ½ mile (¾ km) east of Charlotte Amalie* ☎ *340/777–3199.*

WEST END

$$$$ ✗ **Craig and Sally's.** In the heart of Frenchtown, culinary wizard Sally
ECLECTIC Darash shows off her tasty creativity by never duplicating a menu. Her
Fodor'sChoice inspiration is pure local; it may start when a French fisherman shows
★ up on her doorstep with a fish wiggling at the end of his speargun or when a community matriarch brings by bunches of fresh basil and thyme. The result may be a yellowfin tuna ceviche or roasted eggplant cheesecake with a basil chiffonade. Husband Craig, who has a wry humor, maintains a 300-bottle wine list that's won accolades. ⑤ *Average main: $34* ✉ *22 Honduras St., Frenchtown* ☎ *340/777–9949* ⊕ *www. craigandsallys.com* ⊘ *Closed Mon. and Tues. No lunch weekends.*

$$$ ✗ **Hook, Line and Sinker.** Anchored on the breezy Frenchtown waterfront
SEAFOOD and close to the pastel-painted boats of the local fishing fleet, this har-
ᗡ bor-view eatery serves high-quality fish dishes. The almond-crusted yel-lowtail snapper is a house specialty. Spicy jerk-seasoned swordfish and grilled tuna topped with a yummy mango-rum sauce are also good bets. This is one of the few independent restaurants serving Sunday brunch.

$ *Average main: $24* ⊠ *Frenchtown Mall, 2 Honduras St., Frenchtown* ☏ *340/776–9708* ⊕ *www.hooklineandsinkervi.com.*

$$ ✕ **Tickle's Dockside Pub.** Nautical types as well as the local working crowd
AMERICAN come here for casual fare with homey appeal: chicken-fried steak, meat
Ⓒ loaf with mashed potatoes, and baby back ribs. Hearty breakfasts feature eggs and pancakes, and lunch is a full array of burgers, salads, sandwiches, and soups. From November through April the adjacent marina is full of enormous yachts, which make for some great eye candy while you dine. $ *Average main: $17* ⊠ *Crown Bay Marina, Rte. 304, Estate Contant* ☏ *340/776–1595* ⊕ *ticklesdocksidepub.com.*

WHERE TO STAY

Of the USVI, St. Thomas has the most rooms and the greatest number and variety of resorts. You can let yourself be pampered at a luxurious resort—albeit at a price of $300 to more than $600 per night, not including meals. For much less, there are fine hotels (often with rooms that have a kitchen and a living area) in lovely settings throughout the island. There are also guesthouses and inns with great views and great service at about half the cost of what you'll pay at the beachfront pleasure palaces. Many of these are east and north of Charlotte Amalie or overlooking hills—ideal if you plan to get out and mingle with the locals. There are also inexpensive lodgings (most right in town) that are perfect if you just want a clean room to return to after a day of exploring or beach-bumming.

East End condominium complexes are popular with families. Although condos are pricey (winter rates average $350 per night for a two-bedroom unit, which usually sleeps six), they have full kitchens, and you can definitely save money by cooking for yourself—especially if you bring some of your own nonperishable foodstuffs. (Virtually everything on St. Thomas is imported, and restaurants and shops pass shipping costs on to you.) Though you may spend some time laboring in the kitchen, many condos ease your burden with daily maid service and on-site restaurants; a few also have resort amenities, including pools and tennis courts. The East End is convenient to St. John, and it's a hub for the boating crowd, with some good restaurants. The prices *below* reflect rates in high season, which runs from December 15 to April 15. Rates are 25% to 50% lower the rest of the year.

For expanded reviews, facilities, and current deals, visit Fodors.com.

PRIVATE VILLAS AND CONDOMINIUMS

St. Thomas has a wide range of private villas. Most will require that you book for seven nights during high season, five in low season. A minimum stay of up to two weeks is often required during the Christmas season. The agents who represent villa owners usually have websites and brochures that show photos of the properties they represent. Some villas are suitable for travelers with disabilities, but be sure to ask specific questions about your own needs.

27

RENTAL CONTACTS

Calypso Realty. *St. Thomas* ☎ *340/774–1620, 800/747–4858* ⊕ *www.calypsorealty.com.*

McLaughlin-Anderson Luxury Caribbean Villas. Handling rental villas throughout the U.S. Virgin Islands, British Virgin Islands, and Grenada, McLaughlin-Anderson has a good selection in complexes on St. Thomas's East End. ✉ *1000 Blackbeard's Hill, Suite 3* ☎ *340/776–0635, 800/537–6246* ⊕ *www.mclaughlinanderson.com.*

CHARLOTTE AMALIE

Accommodations in and near town mean that you're close to the airport, shopping, and a number of restaurants. The downside is that this is the most crowded and noisy area of the island. Crime can also be a problem. Don't go for a stroll at night in the heart of town. Use common sense and take the same precautions you would in any major city. Properties along the hillsides are less likely to have crime problems, and they also get a steady breeze from the cool trade winds. This is especially important if you're visiting in summer and early fall.

$ **The Green Iguana.** Atop Blackbeard's Hill, this value-priced small hotel
HOTEL   offers the perfect mix of gorgeous harbor views, proximity to shopping (five-minute walk), and secluded privacy provided by the surrounding showy trees and bushy hibiscus. **Pros:** personalized service; near the center of town; laundry on premises. **Cons:** need a car to get around; neighborhood is sketchy at night. **TripAdvisor:** "quirky boutique style hotel," "great view and spectacular people," "tree house living at its finest." ⑤ *Rooms from: $140* ✉ *37B Blackbeard's Hill* ☎ *340/776–7654, 800/484–8825* ⊕ *www.thegreeniguana.com* ➔ *6 rooms* ⑩ *No meals.*

$ **Hotel 1829.** Antique charm—though some may simply call it old—is
B&B/INN   readily apparent in this rambling 19th-century merchant's house, from the hand-painted Moroccan tiles to a Tiffany window. **Pros:** close to attractions; good prices; breakfast served on the veranda. **Cons:** some small rooms; tour groups during the day; neighborhood dicey at night. **TripAdvisor:** "great bar," "charming and fun," "authentically Caribbean." ⑤ *Rooms from: $105* ✉ *Government Hill, 29-30 Kongens Gade* ☎ *340/776–1829, 800/524–2002* ⊕ *www.hotel1829.com* ➔ *15 rooms* ⑩ *Breakfast.*

$ **Villa Santana.** Built by exiled General Antonio López Santa Anna of
HOTEL   Mexico, this 1857 landmark provides a panoramic view of the harbor
Fodor'sChoice   and plenty of West Indian charm, which will make you feel as if you're
★   living in a charming slice of Virgin Islands history. **Pros:** historic charm; plenty of privacy. **Cons:** not on a beach; no restaurant; need a car to get around. **TripAdvisor:** "a unique and charming location," "away from the crowds," "has something for everyone." ⑤ *Rooms from: $150* ✉ *2D Denmark Hill* ☎ *340/776–1311* ⊕ *www.villasantana.com* ➔ *6 rooms* ⑩ *No meals.*

$ **Windward Passage Hotel.** Business travelers, tourists on their way to
HOTEL   the British Virgin Islands, and laid-back vacationers who want the convenience of being able to walk to duty-free shopping, sights, and restaurants, stay at this harborfront hotel. **Pros:** walking distance to Charlotte Amalie; nice harbor views. **Cons:** basic rooms; on a busy street; no water sports, but dive shop is on property. **TripAdvisor:** "great overnight

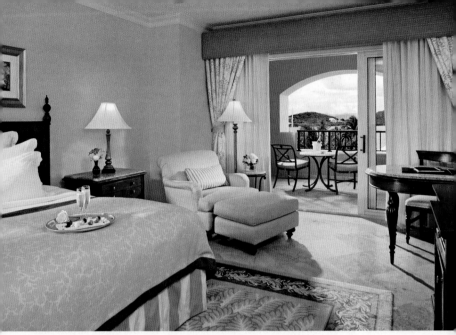

The Ritz-Carlton St. Thomas

hotel," "clean remodeled rooms," "incredible service." $ *Rooms from: $220* ✉ *Waterfront Hwy.* ☎ *340/774–5200, 800/524–7389* ⊕ *www. windwardpassage.com* 🛏 *140 rooms, 11 suites* ❘◎❘ *No meals.*

EAST END

You can find most of the large, luxurious beachfront resorts on St. Thomas's East End. The downside is that these properties are about a 30-minute drive from town and a 45-minute drive from the airport (substantially longer during peak hours). On the upside, they tend to be self-contained, plus there are a number of good restaurants, shops, and water-sports operators in the area. Once you've settled in, you don't need a car to get around.

$$
RENTAL
The Anchorage Beach Resort. A beachfront setting and homey conveniences that include full kitchens and washer–dryer units are what attract families to these two- and three-bedroom suites on Cowpet Bay next to the St. Thomas Yacht Club. **Pros:** on the beach; good amenities. **Cons:** small pool; noisy neighbors; need a car to get around. **TripAdvisor:** "relaxing stay," "good headquarters for exploring," "nice condo." $ *Rooms from: $375* ✉ *Rte. 317, Estate Nazareth* ☎ *800/874–7897* ⊕ *www.antillesresorts.com* 🛏 *11 suites* ❘◎❘ *No meals.*

$$
RENTAL
Pavilions and Pools Villa Hotel. Although the rates might lead you to believe you're buying resort ambience, the reality is that you get fairly basic accommodations here. **Pros:** intimate atmosphere; friendly host; private pools. **Cons:** some small rooms; on a busy road; long walk to beach. **TripAdvisor:** "cute and funky place," "privacy galore," "secluded paradise." $ *Rooms from: $325* ✉ *6400 Rte. 38, Estate Smith Bay* ☎ *340/775–6110, 800/524–2001* ⊕ *www.pavilions*

andpools.com 🔄 *25 1-bedroom villas* ¶◎¶ *Breakfast.*

$$
RESORT
🔲 **Point Pleasant Resort.** Hilltop suites give you an eagle's-eye view of the East End and beyond, and those in a building adjacent to the reception area offer incredible sea views. **Pros:** lush setting; convenient kitchens; pleasant pools. **Cons:** steep climb from beach; need a car to get around; some rooms need refurbishing. **TripAdvisor:** "beautiful view," "nice and very helpful staff," "quiet and relaxing atmosphere." $ *Rooms from: $300* ⊠ *6600 Rte. 38, Estate Smith Bay* ☎ *340/775–7200, 800/524–2300*

⊕ *www.pointpleasantresort.com* 🔄 *128 suites* ¶◎¶ *No meals.*

$$$$
RESORT
♨
Fodor's Choice
★
🔲 **Ritz-Carlton, St. Thomas.** Everything sparkles at the island's most luxurious resort, from the in-room furnishings and amenities to the infinity pool, white-sand beach, and turquoise sea beyond. **Pros:** gorgeous views; great water-sports facilities; beautiful beach; airport shuttle. **Cons:** service can sometimes be spotty for such an upscale (and pricey) hotel; food and drink can lack flair and are expensive ($17 hamburger, $9.75 piña colada); half-hour or more drive to town and airport. **TripAdvisor:** "great venue to fully relax," "beautiful resort," "picturesque property." $ *Rooms from: $610* ⊠ *Rte. 317, Estate Great Bay* ☎ *340/775–3333, 800/241–3333* ⊕ *www.ritzcarlton.com* 🔄 *255 rooms, 20 suites, 2 villas, 81 condos* ¶◎¶ *No meals.*

$$
RENTAL
🔲 **Sapphire Beach Condominium Resort and Marina.** A beautiful half-mile-long white-sand beach is the real ace here, because accommodations can be hit-or-miss, depending on whether you book with a private condo owner (hit) or the management company (miss). **Pros:** beachfront location; water sports abound; near ferries. **Cons:** some rooms need refurbishing; restaurant fare limited; some construction noise. **TripAdvisor:** "best beach on island," "relaxing," "a nice quiet place to stay." $ *Rooms from: $335* ⊠ *6720 Estate Smith Bay* ☎ *800/524–2090, 340/775–6100, 800/874–7897* ⊕ *www.antillesresorts.com* 🔄 *171 condos* ¶◎¶ *No meals.*

$
RENTAL
🔲 **Sapphire Village.** These high-rise towers feel more like apartment buildings than luxury resorts, so if you're looking for a home away from home, this might be the place. **Pros:** within walking distance of Red Hook; nice views; secluded feel. **Cons:** small rooms; limited dining options; noisy neighbors. **TripAdvisor:** "beautifully situated," "beautiful condo with great views," "a pleasant stay." $ *Rooms from: $210* ⊠ *Rte. 38, Sapphire Bay* ☎ *340/779–1540, 800/874–7897* ⊕ *www.antillesresorts.com* 🔄 *15 condos* ¶◎¶ *No meals.*

$$
RENTAL
🔲 **Secret Harbour Beach Resort.** There's not a bad view from these low-rise studios and one- and two-bedroom condos, which are either beachfront or perched on a hill overlooking an inviting cove. **Pros:** beautiful

beach and great snorkeling; good restaurant; secluded location. **Cons:** some rooms are small; car needed to get around; condo owners are territorial about beach chairs. **TripAdvisor:** "great beach," "amazing restaurants," "great place to snorkel and relax." ⑤ *Rooms from: $355* ✉ *Rte. 317, Estate Nazareth* ☎ *340/775–6550, 800/524–2250* ⊕ *www. secretharbourvi.com* ↰ *69 suites* ⦿ *No meals.*

$$$$
ALL-INCLUSIVE
✿
⌂ **Sugar Bay Resort & Spa.** The only completely all-inclusive resort on St. Thomas, this terra-cotta high-rise is surrounded by palm trees and lush greenery, but the rooms and the walkways between them feel a little generic. **Pros:** gorgeous pool area; full-service spa; on-site casino. **Cons:** some steps to climb; small beach; limited dining options. **TripAdvisor:** "beautiful setting and great staff," "vacation of a lifetime," "excellent service." ⑤ *Rooms from: $525* ✉ *38 Smith Bay, Estate Smith Bay* ☎ *340/777–7100, 800/927–7100* ⊕ *www.sugarbayresortandspa.com* ↰ *294 rooms, 7 suites* ⦿ *All-inclusive.*

SOUTH SHORE

The South Shore of St. Thomas connects town to the east end of the island via a beautiful road that rambles along the hillside with frequent peeks between the hills for a view of the ocean and, on a clear day, of St. Croix some 40 miles (64 km) to the south. The resorts here are on their own beaches. They offer several opportunities for water sports, as well as land-based activities, fine dining, and evening entertainment.

$$
RESORT
⌂ **Bolongo Bay Beach Resort.** All the rooms at this family-run resort tucked along a 1,000-foot-long palm-lined beach have balconies with ocean views; down the beach are 12 studio and two-bedroom condos with full kitchens. **Pros:** family-run property; on the beach; water sports abound. **Cons:** a bit run-down; on a busy road; need a car to get around. **TripAdvisor:** "nice atmosphere," "paradise away from hustle and bustle," "very pleasant." ⑤ *Rooms from: $365* ✉ *Rte. 30, Estate Bolongo* ☎ *340/775–1800, 800/524–4746* ⊕ *www.bolongobay.com* ↰ *65 rooms, 12 condos* ⦿ *Multiple meal plans.*

$$$
RESORT
✿
⌂ **Marriott Frenchman's Reef and Morning Star Beach Resorts.** Set majestically on a promontory overlooking the east side of Charlotte Amalie's harbor, Frenchman's Reef is the high-rise full-service superhotel; Morning Star is the even more upscale boutique property that's closer to the fine white-sand beach. **Pros:** beachfront location; good dining options; plenty of activities. **Cons:** musty smell on lower levels; long walk between resorts; a crowded-cruise-ship feel. **TripAdvisor:** "million-dollar view," "great service and friendly hotel staff," "awesome beach." ⑤ *Rooms from: $410* ✉ *Rte. 315, Estate Bakkeroe* ☎ *340/776–8500, 800/233–6388* ↰ *479 rooms, 27 suites; 220 2- and 3-bedroom time-share units* ⦿ *No meals.*

WEST END

A few properties are in the hills overlooking Charlotte Amalie to the west or near French Town, which is otherwise primarily residential.

$
HOTEL
⌂ **Best Western Emerald Beach Resort.** You get beachfront ambience at this reasonably priced miniresort tucked beneath the palm trees, but the tradeoff is that it's directly across from a noisy airport runway. **Pros:** beachfront location; good value; great Sunday brunch. **Cons:**

27

airport noise until 10 pm; on a busy road; limited water sports. **TripAdvisor:** "great views and rooms," "a convenient place to stay," "best beach in St. Thomas." $ *Rooms from: $240* ✉ *8070 Lindberg Bay* ☎ *340/777–8800, 800/780–7234* ⊕ *www.emeraldbeach.com* ➷ *90 rooms* ⦿ *Breakfast.*

$ ▥ **Island View Guesthouse.** Perched 545 feet up the face of Crown
B&B/INN Mountain, this small, homey inn has hands-on owners who can book tours or offer tips about the best sightseeing spots. **Pros:** spectacular views; friendly atmosphere; good value. **Cons:** small pool; need a car to get around. **TripAdvisor:** "dinner is good," "the nicest people and view," "great hosts." $ *Rooms from: $115* ✉ *Rte. 332, Estate Contant* ☎ *340/774–4270, 800/524–2023* ⊕ *www.islandviewstthomas.com* ➷ *12 rooms, 10 with bath* ⦿ *Breakfast.*

NIGHTLIFE AND THE ARTS

On any given night, especially in season, you can find steel-pan bands, rock and roll, piano music, jazz, broken-bottle dancing (actual dancing atop broken glass), disco, and karaoke. Pick up a free copy of the bright yellow *St. Thomas–St. John This Week* magazine (⊕ *www. virginislandsthisweek.com*) when you arrive (it can be found at the airport, in stores, and in hotel lobbies). The back pages list who's playing where. The Friday edition of the *Daily News* carries complete listings for the upcoming weekend.

NIGHTLIFE

CHARLOTTE AMALIE

Greenhouse Bar and Restaurant. Once this popular eatery puts away the salt-and-pepper shakers after 10 pm, it becomes a rock-and-roll club with a DJ or live reggae bands bringing the weary to their feet six nights a week. ✉ *Waterfront Hwy. at Storetvaer Gade, Charlotte Amalie* ☎ *340/774–7998.*

EAST END

Duffy's Love Shack. At this island favorite, a live band and dancing under the stars are the big draws for locals and visitors alike. ✉ *Red Hook Plaza, Red Hook* ☎ *340/779–2080.*

SOUTH SHORE

Epernay Bistro. Sometimes you need nothing more than small tables for easy chatting, wine and champagne by the glass, and a spacious dance floor. You can also mix and mingle with island celebrities here. The action at this intimate nightspot runs from 4 pm until the wee hours Monday through Saturday. ✉ *Frenchtown Mall, 24-A Honduras St., Frenchtown* ☎ *340/774–5348.*

Iggies Beach Bar. Bolongo Bay's beachside bar offers karaoke on Saturday nights, so you can sing along to the sounds of the surf or the latest hits here. There are live bands on weekends, and you can dance inside or kick up your heels under the stars. Wednesday it's Carnival Night, complete with steel-pan music, a limbo show and West Indian buffet. ✉ *Bolongo Bay Beach Club & Villas, Rte. 30, Estate Bolongo* ☎ *340/775–1800.*

THE ARTS
SOUTH SHORE

Pistarkle Theater. This theater in the Tillett Gardens complex is air-conditioned and has more than 100 seats; it hosts a dozen or more productions annually, plus a children's summer drama camp. ✉ *Tillett Gardens, Rte. 38, across from Tutu Park Shopping Mall, Estate Tutu* ☎ *340/775–7877* ⊕ *pistarckletheater.com.*

Reichhold Center for the Arts. St. Thomas's major performing arts center has an amphitheater, and its more expensive seats are covered by a roof. Throughout the year there's an entertaining mix of local plays, dance exhibitions, and music of all types. ✉ *Rte. 30, across from Brewers Beach, Estate Lindberg Bay* ☎ *340/693–1559* ⊕ *www.reichholdcenter.com.*

SHOPPING

Fodor'sChoice ★ St. Thomas lives up to its billing as a duty-free shopping destination. Even if shopping isn't your idea of how to spend a vacation, you still may want to slip in on a quiet day (check the cruise-ship listings—Monday and Sunday are usually the least crowded) to browse. Among the best buys are liquor, linens, china, crystal (most stores will ship), and jewelry. The amount of jewelry available makes this one of the few items for which comparison shopping is worth the effort. Local crafts include shell jewelry, carved calabash bowls, straw brooms, woven baskets, and dolls. The local doll maker Gwendolyn Harley makes costumed West Indian market women and other creations who have become little goodwill ambassadors, bought by visitors from as far away as Asia. Spice mixes, hot sauces, and tropical jams and jellies are other native products.

On St. Thomas stores on Main Street in Charlotte Amalie are open weekdays and Saturday 9 to 5. The hours of the shops in the Havensight Mall (next to the cruise-ship dock) and the Crown Bay Commercial Center (next to the Crown Bay cruise-ship dock) are the same, though occasionally some stay open until 9 on Friday, depending on how many cruise ships are anchored nearby. You may also find some shops open on Sunday if cruise ships are in port. Hotel shops are usually open evenings, as well.

There's no sales tax in the USVI, and you can take advantage of the $1,200 duty-free allowance per family member (remember to save your receipts). Although you can find the occasional salesclerk who will make a deal, bartering isn't the norm.

CHARLOTTE AMALIE

The prime shopping area in **Charlotte Amalie** is between Post Office and Market Squares; it consists of two parallel streets that run east–west (Waterfront Highway and Main Street) and the alleyways that connect them. Particularly attractive are the historic **A.H. Riise Alley, Royal Dane Mall, Palm Passage,** and pastel-painted **International Plaza.**

Vendors Plaza, on the waterfront side of Emancipation Gardens in Charlotte Amalie, is a central location for vendors selling handmade earrings, necklaces, and bracelets; straw baskets and handbags; T-shirts;

27

Made in St. Thomas

Date-palm brooms, frangipani-scented perfume, historically clad dolls, sun-scorched hot sauces, aromatic mango candles: these are just a few of the handicrafts made in St. Thomas.

Justin Todman, aka the Broom Man, keeps the art of broom making alive. It's a skill he learned at the age of six from his father. From the fronds of the date palm, Todman cuts, strips, and dries the leaves. Then he weaves them into distinctively shaped brooms with birch-berry wood for handles. There are feather brooms, cane brooms, multicolor-yarn brooms, tiny brooms to fit into a child's hand, and tall, long-handled brooms to reach cobwebs on the ceiling. Some custom-ers buy Todman's brooms—sold at the **Native Arts & Crafts Coopera-tive**—not for cleaning but rather for celebrating their nuptials. It's an old African custom for the bride and groom to jump over a horizontally laid broom to start their new life.

Gail Garrison puts the essence of local flowers, fruits, and leaves into perfumes, powders, and body splashes. Her Island Fragrances line includes frangipani-, white ginger–, and jasmine-scented perfumes; aro-matic mango, lime, and coconut body splashes; and bay rum aftershave for men. Garrison compounds, mixes, and bottles the products herself in second-floor offices on Charlotte Amalie's

Main Street. You can buy the products in the **Tropicana Perfume Shop**.

Gwendolyn Harley preserves Virgin Islands culture in the personalities of her hand-sewn, softly sculptured historic dolls for sale at the Native Arts & Crafts Cooperative. There are quadrille dancers clad in long, colorful skirts; French women with their neat peaked bonnets; and farmers sporting handwoven straw hats. Each one-of-kind design is named using the last three letters of Harley's first name; the dolls have names like Joycelyn, Vitalyn, and Iselyn.

Cheryl Miller cooks up ingredients such as sun-sweetened papayas, fiery Scotch bonnet peppers, and aromatic basil leaves into the jams, jellies, and hot sauces she sells under her Cheryl's Taste of Paradise line. Five of Miller's products—Caribbean Mustango Sauce, Caribbean Sunburn, Mango Momma Jam, Mango Chutney, and Hot Green Pepper Jelly—have won awards at the National Fiery Foods Show in Albuquerque, New Mexico. You can buy her products at Cost-U-Less, the Native Arts & Crafts Cooperative, and the farmers' market at Yacht Haven Grande on the first and third Sunday of each month.

Jason Budsan traps the aromas of the islands, such as ripe mango and night jasmine, into sumptuous candles he sells at his **Tillett Gardens** workshop.

fabrics; African artifacts; and local fruits. Look for the many brightly colored umbrellas.

ART

Camille Pissarro Art Gallery. This second-floor gallery, at the birthplace of St. Thomas's famous artist, offers a fine collection of original paint-ings and prints by local and regional artists. ⊠ *14 Main St., Charlotte Amalie* ☎ *340/774–4621.*

Gallery St. Thomas. The gallery in this charming space has a nice collection of fine art and collectibles, including paintings, wood sculpture, glass, and jewelry that are from or inspired by the Virgin Islands. ⊠ *Palm Passage, Charlotte Amalie* ☎ *340/777–6363.*

CAMERAS AND ELECTRONICS

Boolchand's. This store sells brand-name cameras, audio and video equipment, and binoculars. ⊠ *31 Main St., Charlotte Amalie* ☎ *340/776–0794* ⊕ *www.boolchand.com.*

Royal Caribbean. The two branches of this shop are near each other; they stock a wide selection of cameras, camcorders, stereos, watches, and clocks. ⊠ *23 Main St., Charlotte Amalie* ☎ *340/776–5449* ⊕ *www.royalcaribbeanvi.com* ⊠ *33 Main St., Charlotte Amalie* ☎ *340/776–4110.*

CHINA AND CRYSTAL

Little Switzerland. This popular Caribbean chain carries crystal from Baccarat, Waterford, and Orrefors; and china from Kosta Boda, Rosenthal, and Wedgwood. There's also an assortment of Swarovski cut-crystal animals, gemstone globes, and many other affordable collectibles. It also does a booming mail-order business. ⊠ *5 Dronningens Gade, across from Emancipation Garden, Charlotte Amalie* ☎ *340/776–2010* ⊕ *www.littleswitzerland.com* ⊠ *3B Main St., Charlotte Amalie* ☎ *340/776–2010.*

CLOTHING

Fresh Produce. This clothing store doesn't sell lime-green mangoes, peachy-pink guavas, or sunny-yellow bananas, but you will find these fun, casual colors on its clothing for children and adults. This is one of only 16 stores to stock all of the California-created, tropical-feel line of women's separates. The dresses, shirts, slacks, and skirts are in small to plus sizes, and bags and hats and other accessories are also available. ⊠ *Riise's Alley, Charlotte Amalie* ☎ *340/774–0807.*

♻ **Local Color.** This St. Thomas chain has clothes for men, women, and children among its brand names, which include Jams World, Fresh Produce, and Urban Safari. You can also find St. John artist Sloop Jones's colorful, hand-painted island designs on cool dresses, T-shirts, and sweaters. The tropically oriented accessories include big-brimmed straw hats, bold-color bags, and casual jewelry. ⊠ *Waterfront Hwy, at Raadets Gade, Charlotte Amalie* ☎ *340/774–2280.*

HANDICRAFTS

Native Arts and Crafts Cooperative. This crafts market is made up of a group of more than 40 local artists—including schoolchildren, senior citizens, and people with disabilities—who create the handcrafted items for sale here: African-style jewelry, quilts, calabash bowls, dolls, carved-wood figures, woven baskets, straw brooms, note cards, and cookbooks. This is also the site of the Virgin Islands Welcome Center. ⊠ *48B Tolbod Gade, across from Emancipation Garden, Charlotte Amalie* ☎ *340/777–1153.*

JEWELRY

Cardow Jewelry. You can get gold in several lengths, widths, sizes, and styles, along with jewelry made of diamonds, emeralds, and other precious gems from this small chain's main store. You're guaranteed 40% to 60% savings off U.S. retail prices, or your money will be refunded within 30 days of purchase. ☒ *33 Main St., Charlotte Amalie* ☎ *340/776–1140* ⊕ *www.cardow.com.*

Diamonds International. At this large chain with several outlets on St. Thomas, just choose a diamond, emerald, or tanzanite gem and a mounting, and you can have your dream ring set in an hour. Famous for having the largest inventory of diamonds on the island, this shop welcomes trade-ins, has a U.S. service center, and includes diamond earrings with every purchase. ☒ *31 Main St., Charlotte Amalie* ☎ *340/774–3707* ☒ *3 Drakes Passage, Charlotte Amalie* ☎ *340/775–2010* ☒ *7AB Drakes Passage, Charlotte Amalie* ☎ *340/774–1516.*

H. Stern Jewelers. The World Collection of jewels set in modern, fashionable designs and an exclusive sapphire watch have earned this Brazilian jeweler a stellar reputation. ☒ *8 Main St., Charlotte Amalie* ☎ *340/776–1939* ⊕ *www.hstern.net.*

Jewels. This jewelry store sells name-brand jewelry and watches in abundance. Designer jewelry lines include David Yurman, Bulgari, Chopard, and Penny Preville. The selection of watches includes Jaeger le Coultre, Tag Heuer, Breitling, Movado, and Gucci. ☒ *Main St. at Riise's Alley, Charlotte Amalie* ☎ *340/777–4222* ⊕ *www.jewelsonline.com* ☒ *Waterfront at Hibiscus Alley, Charlotte Amalie* ☎ *340/777–4222.*

Rolex Watches at A. H. Riise. A.H. Riise is the Virgin Islands' official Rolex retailer, and this shop offers one of the largest selections of these fine timepieces in the Caribbean. An After Sales Service Center helps you keep your Rolex ticking for a lifetime. ☒ *37 Main St., at Riise's Alley, Charlotte Amalie* ☎ *340/776–2303* ⊕ *www.ahriise.com.*

LEATHER GOODS

Coach Boutique at Little Switzerland. This designer leather store has a full line of fine leather handbags, belts, gloves, and more for women, plus briefcases and wallets for men. Accessories for both sexes include organizers, travel bags, and cell-phone cases. ☒ *5 Main St., Charlotte Amalie* ☎ *340/776–2010.*

Zora's. This store specializes in fine, made-to-order leather sandals. There's also a selection of locally made backpacks, purses, and briefcases in durable, brightly colored canvas. ☒ *34 Norre Gade, across from Roosevelt Park, Charlotte Amalie* ☎ *340/774–2559* ⊕ *www.zoraofstthomas.com.*

LINENS

Fabric in Motion. Fine Italian linens share space with Liberty London's silky cottons, colorful batiks, cotton prints, ribbons, and accessories in this small shop. ☒ *7 Store Tvaer Gade, Charlotte Amalie* ☎ *340/774–2006.*

Mr. Tablecloth. This store has prices to please, and the friendly staff here will help you choose from the floor-to-ceiling selection of linens, which include Tuscan lace tablecloths and Irish linen pillowcases. ✉ *6–7 Main St., Charlotte Amalie* ☎ *340/774–4343* ⊕ *mrtablecloth-vi.com.*

LIQUOR AND TOBACCO

A.H. Riise Liquors and Tobacco. This giant duty-free liquor outlet carries a large selection of tobacco (including imported cigars), as well as cordials, wines, and rare vintage Armagnacs, cognacs, ports, and Madeiras. It also stocks fruits in brandy and barware from England. Enjoy rum samples at the tasting bar. The prices are among the best in St. Thomas. ✉ *37 Main St., at Riise's Alley, Charlotte Amalie* ☎ *340/776–2303* ⊕ *www.ahriise.com.*

EAST END

Red Hook has **American Yacht Harbor,** a waterfront shopping area with a dive shop, a tackle store, clothing and jewelry boutiques, a bar, and a few restaurants.

ART

The Color of Joy. This gallery offers locally made arts and crafts, including pottery, batik, hand-painted linen-and-cotton clothing, glass plates and ornaments, and watercolors by owner Corinne Van Rensselaer. There are also original prints by many local artists. ✉ *Rte. 322, about 100 yards west of Ritz-Carlton, Red Hook* ☎ *340/775–4020* ⊕ *www. thecolorofjoyvi.com.*

FOODSTUFFS

Food Center. This supermarket sells fresh produce, meats, and seafood. There's also an on-site bakery and deli with hot and cold prepared foods, which are the big draw here, especially for those renting villas, condos, or charter boats in the East End area. ✉ *Rte. 32, Estate Frydenhoj* ☎ *340/777–8806.*

Marina Market. This market near the ferry to St. John has the best fresh meat and seafood on the island. ✉ *Rte. 32, Red Hook* ☎ *340/779–2411.*

HANDICRAFTS

Ⓒ **Dolphin Dreams.** This crafts store has gaily painted Caribbean-theme Christmas ornaments, art glass from the Mitchell-Larsen studio, and jewelry made from recycled coral. Signature clothing lines include Bimini Bay and Rum Reggae. This boutique is the exclusive Red Hook source for the famous Caribbean Hook Bracelet, originated by the Caribbean Bracelet Company on St. Croix. ✉ *American Yacht Harbor, Bldg. C, Rte. 32, Red Hook* ☎ *340/775–0549* ⊕ *www.dolphindreamsvi.com.*

JEWELRY

Diamonds International. As at others branches of this major jewelry chain, you can choose a diamond or other gem and a mounting and have your ring ready in an hour. The stores have the largest inventory of diamonds on St. Thomas. ✉ *Wyndham Sugar Bay Beach Club & Resort, Rte. 38, Estate Smith Bay* ☎ *340/714–3248* ⊕ *www.diamondsinternational.com.*

Jewels. Designer jewelry available in this major chain include David Yurman, Bulgari, Chopard, and Penny Preville. The selection of watches is also extensive. ✉ *Ritz-Carlton St. Thomas, Rte. 322, Estate Nazareth* ☎ *340/776–7850* ⊕ *www.jewelsonline.com.*

27

SOUTH SIDE

West of Charlotte Amalie, the pink-stucco **Nisky Center,** on Harwood Highway about ½ mile (¾ km) east of the airport, is more of a home-town shopping center than a tourist area, but there's a bank, clothing store, and Radio Shack.

At the Crown Bay cruise-ship pier, the **Crown Bay Center,** off the Harwood Highway in Sub Base about ½ mile (¾ km), has quite a few shops.

Havensight Mall, next to the cruise-ship dock, may not be as charming as downtown Charlotte Amalie, but it does have more than 60 shops. It also has an excellent bookstore, a bank, a pharmacy, a gourmet grocery, and smaller branches of many downtown stores. The shops at **Port of $ale,** adjoining Havensight Mall (its buildings are pink instead of brown), sell discount goods. Next door to Port of $ale is the **Yacht Haven Grande** complex, a stunning megayacht marina with beautiful, safe walkways and many upscale shops.

East of Charlotte Amalie on Route 38, **Tillett Gardens** (⊕ *www. tillettgardens.com*) is an oasis of artistic endeavor. The late Jim and Rhoda Tillett converted this Danish farm into an artists' retreat in 1959. Today you can watch artisans produce silk-screen fabrics, candles, pottery, and other handicrafts. Something special is often happening in the gardens as well, including concerts and an arts-and-crafts fair, held in November and May.

Tutu Park Shopping Mall, across from Tillett Gardens, is the island's only enclosed mall. More than 50 stores and a food court are anchored by Kmart and the Plaza Extra grocery store. Archaeologists have discovered evidence that Arawak Indians once lived near the grounds.

ART

Mango Tango. This gallery sells and displays works by popular local artists—originals, prints, and note cards. There's a one-person show at least one weekend a month, and the store also has the island's largest humidor and a brand-name cigar gallery. ⊠ *Al Cohen's Plaza, ½ mile [¾ km] east of Charlotte Amalie* ☎ *340/777–3060.*

BOOKS

🔥 **Dockside Bookshop.** This Havensight store is packed with books for children, travelers, cooks, and history buffs, and there's also a good selection of paperback mysteries, best sellers, art books, calendars, and prints. It also carries a selection of books written in and about the Caribbean and the Virgin Islands. ⊠ *Havensight Mall, Bldg. VI, Rte. 30, Havensight* ☎ *340/774–4937.*

CAMERAS AND ELECTRONICS

Boolchand's. This store sells brand-name cameras, audio and video equipment, and binoculars. ⊠ *Havensight Mall, Bldg. II, Rte. 30, Havensight* ☎ *340/776–0302* ⊕ *www.boolchand.com.*

CHINA AND CRYSTAL

Scandinavian Center. The Center carries the best of Scandinavia, including Royal Copenhagen, Georg Jensen, Kosta Boda, and Orrefors. Owners Søren and Grace Blak make regular buying trips to northern Europe and are a great source of information on crystal. Online ordering is available if you want to add to your collection once home. ⊠ *Havensight Mall, Bldg. III, Rte. 30, Havensight* ☎ *340/777–8620, 877/454–8377* ⊕ *www.scandinaviancenter.com* ⊠ *Crown Bay Commercial Center, Rte. 30, Crown Bay* ☎ *340/777–8620.*

FOODSTUFFS

Fruit Bowl. This grocery store is the best place on the island to go for fresh fruits and vegetables. There are many ethnic, vegetarian, and health-food items as well as a fresh meat and seafood department. ⊠ *Wheatley Center, intersection of Rtes. 38 and 313, Charlotte Amalie* ☎ *340/774–8565* ⊕ *www.thefruitbowlvi.com.*

Gourmet Gallery. This is where visiting megayacht owners (or their staff) go to buy their caviar. There's also an excellent and reasonably priced wine selection, as well as specialty ingredients for everything from tacos to curries to chow mein. A full-service deli offers imported meats, cheeses, and in-store prepared foods that are perfect for a picnic. ⊠ *Crown Bay Marina, Rte. 304, Estate Contant* ☎ *340/776–8555* ⊠ *Havensight Mall, Bldg. VI, Rte. 30, Havensight* ☎ *340/774–4948.*

HANDICRAFTS

Caribbean Marketplace. This is a great place to buy handicrafts from the Caribbean and elsewhere. Also look for Sunny Caribee spices, teas from Tortola, and coffee from Trinidad. ⊠ *Havensight Mall, Rte. 30, Havensight* ☎ *340/776–5400.*

JEWELRY

H. Stern Jewelers. This Brazilian jeweler is known for the modern settings and designs of its offerings. ⊠ *Havensight Mall, Bldg. II, Rte. 30, Havensight* ☎ *340/776–1223* ⊕ *www.hstern.net.*

Jewels. Head here for name-brand jewelry and watches in abundance. ⊠ *Havensight Mall, Bldg. II, Rte. 30, Havensight* ☎ *340/776–8590* ⊕ *www.jewelsonline.com* ⊠ *Yacht Haven Grande, Rte. 38, Havensight* ☎ *340/776–1908* ⊕ *www.jewelsonline.com.*

LIQUOR AND TOBACCO

Al Cohen's Discount Liquor. This warehouse of a store holds an extremely large wine and liquor selection. ⊠ *Rte. 30, across from Havensight Mall, Havensight* ☎ *340/774–3690.*

Tobacco Discounters. This duty-free outlet carries a full line of discounted brand-name cigarettes, cigars, and tobacco accessories. ⊠ *Port of $ale Mall, Rte. 30, next to Havensight Mall, Havensight* ☎ *340/774–2256.*

MUSIC

Music Shoppe II. This is a good place to buy CDs of the latest Caribbean releases—steel pan, reggae, and calypso. ⊠ *Havensight Mall, Bldg. III, Rte. 30, Havensight* ☎ *340/774–1900.*

TOYS

Kmart. This giant discount chain store has five aisles of toys for boys and girls: Barbie dolls, hula hoops, computer games, dollhouses, talking teddies, and more. ⊠ *Tutu Park Shopping Mall, Rte. 38, Estate Tutu* ☎ *340/714–5839* ⊠ *Lockhart Gardens, Rte. 38, Estate Long Bay* ☎ *340/774–4046.*

27

SPORTS AND ACTIVITIES

AIR TOURS

Caribbean Buzz Helicopters. On the Charlotte Amalie waterfront next to Tortola Wharf, Caribbean Buzz Helicopters offers a minimum 30-minute tour that includes St. Thomas, St. John, and Jost Van Dyke. It's a nice ride if you can afford the splurge (tours are $425 for up to three people), but in truth, you can see most of the aerial sights from Paradise Point, and there's no place you can't reach easily by car or boat. ⊠ *Waterfront, Charlotte Amalie* ☎ *340/775–7335* ⊕ *www.caribbean-buzz.com.*

BOATING AND SAILING

Calm seas, crystal waters, and nearby islands (perfect for picnicking, snorkeling, and exploring) make St. Thomas a favorite jumping-off spot for day- or weeklong sails or powerboat adventures. With more than 100 vessels from which to choose, St. Thomas is the charter-boat center of the U.S. Virgin Islands. You can go through a broker to book a sailing vessel with a crew or contact a charter company directly. Crewed charters start at approximately $2,800 per person per week, and bareboat charters can start at $1,900 per person for a 50- to 55-foot sailboat (not including provisioning), which can comfortably accommodate up to six people. If you want to rent your own boat, hire a captain. Most local captains are excellent tour guides.

Single-day charters are also a possibility. You can hire smaller boats for the day, including the services of a captain if you wish to have someone take you on a guided snorkeling trip around the islands.

Awesome Powerboat Rentals. The 26-foot twin-engine catamarans from this company are available for day charters. Rates range from $345 to $385 for a half or full day, and a captain can be hired for $125 for a day. ⊠ *6100 Red Hook Quarter, Dock P, Red Hook* ☎ *340/775–0860* ⊕ *www.powerboatrentalsvi.com.*

Island Yachts. The sailboats and powerboats from Island Yachts are available with or without crews. ⊠ *6100 Red Hook Quarter, 18B, Red Hook* ☎ *340/775–6666, 800/524–2019* ⊕ *www.iyc.vi.*

Magic Moments. *Luxury* is the word at Magic Moments, where the crew of a 45-foot Sea Ray offers a pampered island-hopping snorkeling cruise for $475 per person (children ages 2–10 are half price). Nice touches include a wine-and-lobster lunch and icy-cold eucalyptus-infused washcloths for freshening up. ⊠ *American Yacht Harbor, Docks B and C, Red Hook* ☎ *340/775–5066* ⊕ *www.yachtmagicmoments.com.*

Nauti Nymph. A large selection of 25- to 31-foot powerboats and power catamarans is available from this company. Rates, which vary from $445 to $640 a day, include snorkeling gear, water skis, and outriggers, but not fuel. You can hire a captain for $115 more. ⊠ *American Yacht Harbor, Dock B and C, Red Hook* ☎ *540/775–5066, 800/734–7345* ⊕ *www.nautinymph.com.*

Stewart Yacht Charters. Run by longtime sailor Ellen Stewart, this company is skilled at matching clients with yachts and crews for week-

Continued on page 1120

BELOW THE WAVES
By Lynda Lohr

Colorful reefs and wrecks rife with corals and tropical fish make the islands as interesting underwater as above. Brilliantly colored reef fish vie for your attention with corals in wondrous shapes. Scuba diving gets you up close and personal with the world below the waves.

Bright blue tangs and darting blue-headed wrasses. Corals in wondrous shapes—some look like brains, others like elk antlers. Colorful, bulbous sponges. All these and more can be spotted along the myriad reefs of the U.S. and British Virgin Islands. You might see a pink conch making its way along the ocean bottom in areas with seagrass beds. If you're really lucky, a turtle may swim into view, or a lobster may poke its antennae out of a hole in the reef or rocks. If you do a night dive, you might run into an octopus. But you may be surprised at how much you can see by simply hovering just below the surface, with nothing more than a mask and snorkel. It's a bird's-eye view, but an excellent one. Whether scuba diving or snorkeling, take along an underwater camera to capture memories of your exciting adventure. You can buy disposable ones at most dive shops or bring one from home.

DIVE AND SNORKELING SITES IN BRITISH VIRGIN ISLANDS

TORTOLA

Although a major base for dive operations in the BVI (due to its proximity to so many exceptional dive sites), Tortola itself doesn't have as much to offer divers. However, there are still some noteworthy destinations. The massive **Brewer's Bay Pinnacles** grow 70 feet high to within 30 feet of the surface; the rock mazes are only for advanced divers because of strong currents and they are not always acces-

sible. Abundant reefs close to shore make **Brewer's Bay** popular with snorkelers, as are **Frenchman's Cay** and **Long Bay Beef Island. Diamond Reef,** between Great Camanoe and Scrub Island, is a small wall about 200 yards long. **Shark Point,** off the northeast coast of Scrub Island, does have resident sharks. Though isolated in open ocean, the wreck of the *Chikuzen,* a Japanese refrigerator ship, is a popular site.

THE ISLANDS OF THE SIR FRANCIS DRAKE CHANNEL

Southeast of Tortola lie a string of islands with some of the BVI's finest dive sites, some world famous. The wreck of the royal mail ship *Rhone* is between Peter and Salt islands and is, perhaps, the most famous dive site in the BVI. **Wreck Alley,** consisting of three sunken modern ships, is between Salt and Cooper islands. At **Alice in Wonderland,** south of

Ginger Island, giant, mushroom-shaped corals shelter reef fish, moray eels, and crustaceans. **Alice's Backside,** off the northwestern tip of Ginger Island, is usually smooth enough for snorkeling and shallow enough so that beginner divers can get a good look at the myriad sealife and sponges.

The Chikuzen

North Bay

Green Cay

Brewer's Bay Pinnacles

Trunk Bay

Josiah's Bay

Great Harbour

Little Harbour

Brewer's Bay

East End

White Bay

Great Harbour

JOST VAN DYKE

Cane Garden Bay

Todman Pk.

Fort Shirley

Road Town

Carrot Bay

Mt. Sage

Road Town Harbour

Long Bay

Great Thatch Island

West End

TORTOLA

Frenchman's Cay

SIR FRANCIS DRAKE

Great Harbour

ST. JOHN

Peter Island

White Bay

Big Reef Bay

Peter Island

The Indians

Norman Island

Peter Island Bluff

Privateer Bay

Caves Norman Island

Money Bay

KEY

Dive Sites

Snorkel

Ferry

0 ——— 2 miles
0 ——— 2 km

Bones
Bight

Loblolly Bay

Flash of
Beauty
Channel

The
Settlement ○

Flamingo
Pond

Red
Pond

Lower
Bay

Budrock
Pond

ANEGADA
(15 miles north of Necker Is.)

Wreck
of the
Rokus

White
Bay

0 ——— 3 miles
0 ——— 3 km

Necker
Island

Eustatia
Island

Berchers
Bay

Long
Bay

North
Sound

Cockroach
Island

DOG ISLANDS

The Chimney

Coral
Gardens

Great Dog
Island

Virgin
Gorda
Peak

South
Sound

VIRGIN
GORDA

Anegada Passage

North Bay

Shark
Point

Kitto
Ghut

Scrub
Island

Pond
Bay

Diamond
Reef

Beef Island
International Airport

The Aquarium

Virgin Gorda
Airport

Handsome
Bay

Spring
Bay

Spanish
Town

Fat Hogs
Bay

The Baths

Long Bay Beef
Island

C H A N N E L

Alice's
Backside

Ginger
Island

Ginger
Island

Manchioneel
Bay

Cooper
Island

Alice in
Wonderland

Rhone

Wreck
Alley

Salt
Island

VIRGIN GORDA

The Baths, though busy, offers some of the best snorkeling in the Virgin Islands among giant boulders and the resulting grottoes. Nearby is **Spring Bay,** with fewer visitors and similar terrain. **The Aquarium,** close to Spanish Town and a good novice site, is so called because of the abundance of reef fish that swim around the submerged granite boulders that are similar to those of The Baths. Further west of Virgin Gorda, the Dog Islands have some in-

Virgin Gorda

teresting and popular sites, including **The Chimney,** a natural opening covered by sponges off Great Dog. South of Great Dog, **Coral Gardens** has a large coral reef with a submerged airplane wreck nearby. Fish are drawn to nearby **Cockroach Island.**

ANEGADA

Surrounded by the third-largest barrier reef in the world, Anegada has great snorkeling from virtually any beach on the island. But there are also some notable dive sites as well. The **Flash of**

Beauty Channel on the north shore is a great open-water dive, but only suitable for experienced divers. But even novices can enjoy diving at the **Wreck of the Rokus,** a Greek cargo ship off the island's southern shore.

DIVE AND SNORKELING SITES IN U.S. VIRGIN ISLANDS

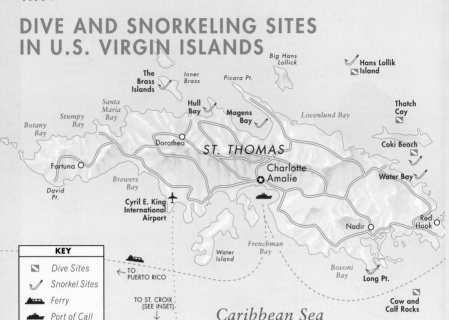

ST. THOMAS

St. Thomas has at least 40 popular dive sites, most shallow. Favorite reef dives off St. Thomas include **Cow and Calf Rocks,** which barely break water off the southeast coast of St. Thomas; the coral-covered pinnacles of **Frenchcap** south of St. Thomas; and tunnels where you can explore undersea from the Caribbean to the Atlantic at **Thatch Cay** (where the Coast Guard cutter *General Rogers* rests at 65 feet). **Grass Cay** and **Mingo Cay** between St. Thomas

and St. John are also popular dive sites. **Coki Beach** offers the best off-the-beach snorkeling in St. Thomas. Nearby Coral World offers a dive-helmet walk for the untrained, and Snuba of St. Thomas has tethered shallow dives for non-certified divers. **Magens Bay,** the most popular beach on St. Thomas, provides lovely snorkeling if you head along the edges. You're likely to see some colorful sponges, darting fish, and maybe even a turtle if you're lucky. This is a stop on every island tour.

ST. JOHN

St. John is particularly known for its myriad good snorkeling spots—certainly more than for its diving opportunities, though there are many dive sites within easy reach of Cruz Bay. **Trunk Bay** often receives the most attention because of its underwater snorkeling trail created by the National Park Service; signs let you know what you're seeing in terms of coral and other underwater features. And the beach is easy to reach since taxis leave on demand from Cruz Bay.

A patchy reef just offshore means good snorkeling at **Hawksnest Beach.** Additionally, **Cinnamon Bay** and **Leinster Bay** also get their fair share of praise as snorkeling spots. That's not to say that you can't find good dive sites near St. John. **Deaver's Bay** is a short boat ride around the point from Cruz Bay, where you can see angelfish, southern stingrays, and triggerfish feeding at 30 to 50 feet. **The Leaf** is a large coral reef off St. John's southern shore.

TORTOLA

Great Thatch Island

West End

Grass Cay

Mingo Cay

Mary Pt.

Leinster Bay

The Narrows

Cinnamon Bay

Trunk Bay

Hawksnest Beach

Cinnamon Bay

Haulover Bay

Honeymoon Beach

East End Pt.

Pillsbury Sound

Lind Point

Coral Harbor

Cruz Bay

ST. JOHN

Long Pt.

Privateer Pt.

Christmas Cove

Great St. James Island

Reef Bay

Flanagan Island

Deaver's Bay

The Leaf

Salt Pond

Little St. James Island

Salt Pond Bay

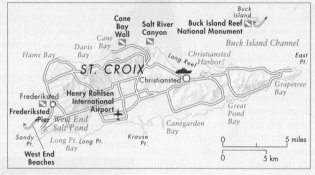

Buck Island

Cane Bay Wall

Salt River Canyon

Buck Island Reef National Monument

Cane Bay

Buck Island Channel

Davis Bay

Hams Bay

ST. CROIX

Long Reef

Christiansted Harbor

East Pt.

Christiansted

Grapetree Bay

French Cap

Frederiksted

Henry Rohlsen International Airport

Great Pond Bay

Frederiksted Pier

West End Salt Pond

Canegarden Bay

Sandy Pt.

Long Pt. Bay

Long Pt.

Krause Pt.

5 miles

5 km

West End Beaches

27

IN FOCUS BELOW THE WAVES

Coral near St. Croix

ST. CROIX

The largest of the U.S. Virgin Islands is a favorite of both divers and snorkelers and offers something for everyone. Snorkelers are often fascinated by the marked snorkeling trail at **Buck Island Reef,** which is a short boat ride from the island's east end; it's a U.S. national monument. Divers are drawn to the north shore, especially the **Cane Bay Wall,** a spectacular drop-off that's reachable from the beach, though usually reached by boat. Another north-shore site is the **Salt River Canyon,** where you can float downward through a canyon filled with colorful fish and coral. On the island's west end, **Frederiksted Pier** is home to a colony of sea horses, creatures seldom seen in the waters of the Virgin Islands. Casual snorkelers would also enjoy snorkeling at the **West End Beaches.**

SCUBA DIVING

St.Croix

If you've never been diving, start with an introductory lesson—often called a "resort course"—run by any one of the Virgin Islands' dive shops. All meet stringent safety standards. If they didn't, they'd soon be out of business. If you're staying at a hotel, you can often find the dive shop on-site; otherwise, your hotel probably has an arrangement with one nearby. If you're on a cruise, cruise-ship companies offer shore excursions that include transportation to and from the ship as well as the resort course. Certification requires much more study and practice, but it is required to rent air tanks, get air refills, and join others on guided dives virtually anywhere in the world.

The number one rule of diving is safety. The basic rules for safe diving are simple, and fools ignore them at their own peril. Serious diving accidents are becoming increasingly rare these days, thanks to the high level of diver training. However, they do still occur occasionally. Surfacing too rapidly without exhaling—or going too deep for too long—can result in an air embolism or a case of the bends. Roy L. Schneider Hospital in St. Thomas has a decompression chamber that serves all the Virgin Islands. If you get the bends, you'll be whisked to the hospital for this necessary treatment.

Fauna is another concern. Though sharks, barracuda, and moray eels are on the most-feared list, more often it's sea urchins and fire coral that cause pain when you accidentally bump them. Part of any scuba-training program is a

Divers learn how to jump in from a boat

St.Croix

review of sea life and the importance of respecting the new world you're exploring. Dive professionals recognize the value of protecting fragile reefs and ecosystems in tropical waters, and instructors emphasize look-don't-touch diving (the unofficial motto is: take only pictures, leave only bubbles). Government control and protection of dive sites is increasing, especially in such heavily used areas as the Virgin Islands.

While you can scuba dive off a beach—and you can find shops renting scuba equipment and providing airfills at the most popular beaches—a trip aboard a dive boat provides a more extensive glimpse into this wonderful undersea world. Since the dive shops can provide all equipment, there's no need to lug heavy weights and a bulky BC in your luggage. For the most comfort, you might want to bring your own regulator if you have one. The dive-boat captains and guides know the best dive locations, can find alternatives when the seas are rough, and will help you deal with heavy tanks and cumbersome equipment. Trips are easy to organize. Dive shops on all islands make frequent

excursions to a wide variety of diving spots, and your hotel, villa manager, or cruise-ship staff will help you make arrangements.

If you fly too soon after diving, you're at risk for decompression sickness, which occurs when nitrogen trapped in your bloodstream doesn't escape. This creates a painful and sometimes fatal condition called the bends, not a sickness you want to develop while you're winging your way home after a fun-filled beach vacation. Opinions vary, but as a rule of thumb, wait at least 12 hours after a single dive to fly. However, if you've made multiple dives or dived several days in a row, you should wait at least 18 hours. If you've made dives that required decompression stops, you should also wait at least 24 hours before flying. To be safe, consult with your physician.

The Virgin Islands offer a plethora of dive sites, and you'll be taken to some of the best if you sign on to a dive trip run by one of the many dive operations scattered around the islands.

27

IN FOCUS BELOW THE WAVES

DIVER TRAINING

Good to know: Divers can become certified through PADI *(www.padi.com)*, NAUI *(www.naui.org)*, or SSI *(www.divessi.com)*. The requirements for all three are similar, and if you do the classroom instruction and pool training with a dive shop associated with one organization, the referral for the open water dives will be honored by most dive shops. Note that you should not fly for at least 24 hours after a dive, because residual nitrogen in the body can pose health risks upon decompression. While there are no rigid rules on diving after flying, make sure you're well-hydrated before hitting the water.

Cost: The four-day cost for classroom dive training can range from $300 to $500, but be sure to ask if equipment, instruction manuals, and log books are extra. Some dive shops have relationships with hotels, so check for dive/stay packages. Referral dives (a collaborative effort among training agencies) run from $400 to $300 and discover scuba runs around $120 to $200.

SNUBA

Beyond snorkeling or the requirements of scuba, you also have the option of "Snuba." The word is a trademarked portmanteau or combo of snorkel and scuba. Marketed as easy-to-learn family fun, Snuba lets you breathe underwater via tubes from an air-supplied vessel above, with no prior diving or snorkel experience required.

NOT CERTIFIED?

Not sure if you want to commit the time and money to become certified? Not a problem. Most dive shops and many resorts will offer a discover scuba day-long course. In the morning, the instructor will teach you the basics of scuba diving: how to clear your mask, how to come to the surface in the unlikely event you lose your air supply, etc. In the afternoon, instructors will take you out for a dive in relatively shallow water—less than 30 feet. Be sure to ask where the dive will take place. Jumping into the water off a shallow beach may not be as fun as actually going out to the coral. If you decide that diving is something you want to pursue, the open dive may count toward your certification.

■TIP→ You can often book discover dives at the last minute. It may not be worth it to go out on a windy day when the currents are stronger. Also the underwater world looks a whole lot brighter on sunny days.

(top) Underwater shot of tropical reef, (bottom) Diver silhouette, Cane Bay, St Croix

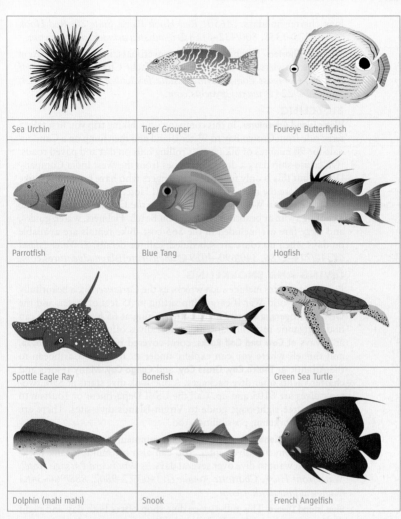

Sea Urchin	Tiger Grouper	Foureye Butterflyfish
Parrotfish	Blue Tang	Hogfish
Spottle Eagle Ray	Bonefish	Green Sea Turtle
Dolphin (mahi mahi)	Snook	French Angelfish

REEF CREATURES IN THE VIRGIN ISLANDS

From the striped sergeant majors to bright blue tangs, the reefs of the Virgin Islands are teeming with life, though not nearly as many as in eons past. Warming waters and pollution have taken their toll on both coral and fish species. But many reefs in the Virgin Islands still thrive; you'll also see sponges, crustaceans, perhaps a sea turtle or two, and bigger game fish like grouper and barracuda; sharks are seen but are rarely a problem for divers. Beware of fire corals, which are not really corals but rather a relative of the jellyfish and have a painful sting; if you brush up against a fire coral, spread vinegar on the wound as soon as possible to minimize the pain.

long charter holidays. ⊠ *6501 Red Hook Plaza, Suite 20, Red Hook* ☎ *340/775–1358, 800/432–6118* ⊕ *www.stewartyachtcharters.com.*

VIP Yacht Charters. Bareboat sail- and powerboats, including a selection of stable trawlers, are available at VIP Yacht Charters. ⊠ *South off Rte. 32, Compass Point Marina, Estate Frydenhoj* ☎ *340/774–9224, 866/847–9224* ⊕ *www.vipyachts.com.*

BICYCLING

Water Island Adventures. In this company's fun biking trip you first take a ferry ride from Crown Bay to Water Island and then jump on a Cannondale for 90 minutes of biking over rolling hills on dirt and paved roads. (On cruise-ship days a direct ferry goes from the West India Company Docks, but this is only for cruise passengers who have booked the bike tour.) Explore the remains of the Sea Cliff Hotel, reputedly the inspiration for Herman Wouk's book *Don't Stop the Carnival,* and then take a cooling swim at beautiful Honeymoon Beach. Helmets, water, guides, and ferry fare are included in the $65 cost. Bike rentals are available on days when no tours are scheduled: call for details. ⊠ *Water Island* ☎ *340/714–2186, 340/690–4019* ⊕ *www.waterislandadventures.com.*

DIVING AND SNORKELING

Popular dive sites include such wrecks as the *Cartanser Sr.,* a beautifully encrusted World War II cargo ship sitting in 35 feet of water, and the *General Rogers,* a Coast Guard cutter resting at 65 feet. Here you can find a gigantic resident barracuda. Reef dives offer hidden caves and archways at **Cow and Calf Rocks,** coral-covered pinnacles at **Frenchcap,** and tunnels where you can explore undersea from the Caribbean to the Atlantic at **Thatch Cay, Grass Cay,** and **Congo Cay.** Many resorts and charter yachts offer dive packages. A one-tank dive starts at $90; two-tank dives are $105 and up. Call the USVI Department of Tourism to obtain a free eight-page guide to Virgin Islands dive sites. There are plenty of snorkeling possibilities, too.

Admiralty Dive Center. Boat dives, rental equipment, and a retail store are available from this dive center. You can also get multiple-tank packages if you want to dive over several days. ⊠ *Windward Passage Hotel, Waterfront Hwy., Charlotte Amalie* ☎ *340/777–9802, 888/900–3483* ⊕ *www.admiraltydive.com.*

Blue Island Divers. This full-service dive shop offers both day and night dives to wrecks and reefs and specializes in custom dive charters. ⊠ *Crown Bay Marina, Rte. 304, Estate Contant* ☎ *340/774–2001* ⊕ *www.blueislanddivers.com.*

B.O.S.S. Underwater Adventure. As an alternative to traditional diving, try an underwater motor scooter called BOSS, or Breathing Observation Submersible Scooter. A 3½-hour tour, including snorkel equipment, rum punch, and towels, is $120 per person. ⊠ *Crown Bay Marina, Rte. 304, Charlotte Amalie* ☎ *340/777–3549* ⊕ *www.bossusvi.com.*

♻ **Coki Dive Center.** Snorkeling and dive tours in the fish-filled reefs off Coki Beach are available from this PADI five-star outfit, as are classes, including one on underwater photography. It's run by the avid diver Peter

Jackson. ⊠ *Rte. 388, at Coki Point, Estate Frydendal* ☎ *340/775–4220* ⊕ *www.cokidive.com.*

Snuba of St. Thomas. In snuba, a snorkeling and scuba-diving hybrid, a 20-foot air hose connects you to the surface. The cost is $74. Children must be eight or older to participate. ⊠ *Rte. 388, at Coki Point, Estate Smith Bay* ☎ *340/693–8063* ⊕ *www.visnuba.com.*

St. Thomas Diving Club. This PADI five-star center offers boat dives to the reefs around Buck Island and nearby offshore wrecks as well as multiday dive packages. ⊠ *Bolongo Bay Beach Resort, Rte. 30, Estate Bolongo* ☎ *340/776–2381* ⊕ *www.stthomasdivingclub.com.*

FISHING

★ Fishing here is synonymous with blue marlin angling—especially from June through October. Four 1,000-pound-plus blues, including three world records, have been caught on the famous North Drop, about 20 miles (32 km) north of St. Thomas. A day charter for marlin with up to six anglers costs $1,800 for the day. If you're not into marlin fishing, try hooking sailfish in winter, dolphin (the fish that's also known as mahimahi, not the mammal) in spring, and wahoo in fall. Inshore trips for four hours start at $600. To find the trip that will best suit you, walk down the docks at either American Yacht Harbor or Sapphire Beach Marina in the late afternoon and chat with the captains and crews.

Abigail III. Captain Red Bailey's *Abigail III* specializes in marlin fishing. It operates out of the Sapphire Beach Resort & Marina. ⊠ *Rte. 38, Sapphire Bay* ☎ *340/775–6024* ⊕ *www.visportfish.com.*

Charter Boat Center. The Charter Boat Center is a major source for sail and powerboat as well as sportfishing charters. Sportfishing charters offered include full-day trips for marlin as well as full, three-quarter, and half days for offshore and inshore species. ⊠ *6300 Smith Bay 16-3, Red Hook* ☎ *340/775–7990* ⊕ *www.charterboat.vi.*

⏱ **Double Header Sportfishing.** This company offers trips out to the North Drop on its 40-foot sportfisher and half-day reef and bay trips aboard its two speedy 35-foot center consoles. ⊠ *Sapphire Bay Marina, Rte. 38, Sapphire Bay* ☎ *340/775–5274* ⊕ *www.doubleheadersportfishing.net.*

Marlin Prince. Captain Eddie Morrison, one of the most experienced charter operators in St. Thomas, specializes in fly-fishing for blue marlin from his 45-foot Viking boat. ⊠ *American Yacht Harbor, Red Hook* ☎ *340/693–5929* ⊕ *www.marlinprince.com.*

GOLF

★ **Mahogany Run Golf Course.** The Mahogany Run Golf Course attracts golfers who are drawn by its spectacular view of the British Virgin Islands and the challenging three-hole Devil's Triangle. At this Tom and George Fazio–designed, par-70, 18-hole course, there's a fully stocked pro shop, snack bar, and open-air clubhouse. Greens fees and half-cart fees for 18 holes are $165 in the winter season. The course is open daily, and there are frequently informal weekend tournaments. It's the only course on St. Thomas. ⊠ *Rte. 42, Estate Lovenlund* ☎ *340/777–6006, 800/253–7103* ⊕ *www.mahoganyrungolf.com.*

27

GUIDED TOURS

VI Taxi Association Tropical Paradise St. Thomas Island Tour. Aimed at cruise-ship passengers, this two-hour tour for two people is done in an open-air safari bus or enclosed van. The $29 tour includes stops at Drake's Seat and Mountain Top. Other tours include a three-hour trip to Coki Beach with a shopping stop in downtown Charlotte Amalie for $35 per person, a three-hour trip to the Coral World Ocean Park for $45 per person, and a five-hour beach tour to St. John for $75 per person. For $35 to $40 for two, you can hire a taxi for a customized three-hour drive around the island. Make sure to see Mountain Top, as the view is wonderful. ⊠ *St. Thomas* ☎ *340/774–4550* ⊕ *www.vitaxi.com.*

SEA EXCURSIONS

Landlubbers and seafarers alike can experience wind in their hair and salt spray in the air while exploring the waters surrounding St. Thomas. Several businesses can book you on a snorkel-and-sail to a deserted cay for a half day that starts at $85 per person or a full day (at least $125 per person). An excursion over to the British Virgin Islands starts at $125 per person, not including customs fees. A luxury daylong motor-yacht cruise complete with lunch is $375 or more per person.

Adventure Center. For a soup-to-nuts choice of sea tours, contact the Adventure Center. ⊠ *Marriott's Frenchman's Reef Hotel, Rte. 315, Estate Bakkeroe* ☎ *340/774–2992, 866/868–7784* ⊕ *www. adventurecenters.net.*

Charter Boat Center. The specialty here is day trips to the British Virgin Islands and day- or weeklong sailing charters. ⊠ *6300 Smith Bay 16-3, Red Hook* ☎ *340/775–7990* ⊕ *www.charterboat.vi.*

Limnos Charters. This company's popular day trip to the British Virgin Islands comes with lunch, an open bar, and snorkeling gear. Destinations include the Baths in Virgin Gorda and the sparsely inhabited island of Jost Van Dyke. ⊠ *Compass Point Marina, Rte. 32, Estate Frydenhoj* ☎ *340/775–3203* ⊕ *www.limnoscharters.com.*

Treasure Isle Cruises. Jimmy Loveland at Treasure Isle Cruises can set you up with everything from a half-day sail to a seven-day U.S. and British Virgin Islands trip that combines sailing with accommodations and sightseeing trips onshore. ⊠ *Rte. 32, Estate Nadir* ☎ *340/775–9500* ⊕ *www.treasureislecruises.com.*

SEA KAYAKING

🐾 Fish dart, birds sing, and iguanas lounge on the limbs of dense mangrove trees deep within a marine sanctuary on St. Thomas's southeast shore.

Virgin Islands Ecotours. Virgin Islands Ecotours rents its two-person sit-atop ocean kayaks and inflatable boats for self-guided exploring as well as for a three-hour guided tour to historic Hassel Island, which includes a visit to some of the historic forts and military structures on the island, a short hike to a breathtaking vista and swim off a deserted beach. The cost is $89 per person. In addition, many resorts on St. Thomas's East End also rent kayaks. ⊠ *Rte. 32, Estate Nadir* ☎ *340/779–2155* ⊕ *www.viecotours.com.*

WINDSURFING

Expect some spills, anticipate the thrills, and try your luck clipping through the seas. Most beachfront resorts rent Windsurfers and offer one-hour lessons for about $120.

Island Sol. If you want to learn to windsurf, try Paul Stoeken's Island Sol. The two-time Olympic athlete charges $120 per hour for private lessons, $85 per hour for group lessons. There's a free clinic every Tuesday at 9:30 am. ✉ *Ritz-Carlton St. Thomas, Rte. 317, Estate Nazareth* ☎ *340/776–9463* ⊕ *www.islandsol.net.*

West Indies Windsurfing. At West Indies, one of the island's best-known independent windsurfing companies, a private kiteboarding lesson costs $125 per hour for the land portion and $250 for a two-hour private lesson on the water. The company also rents stand-up paddleboards (SUP) for $40 per hour, or $200 to $225 per day based on the quality of the board. There's usually calm water—perfect for SUPs—right off Vessup Beach or around the peninsula in Great Bay. ✉ *Vessup Beach, No. 9, Estate Nazareth* ☎ *340/775–6530.*

ST. JOHN

By Lynda Lohr

St. John's heart is Virgin Islands National Park, a treasure that takes up a full two-thirds of St. John's 20 square miles (53 square km). The park helps keep the island's interior in its pristine and undisturbed state, but if you go at midday, you'll probably have to share your stretch of beach with others, particularly at Trunk Bay.

The island is booming (its population of 5,000 is joined by more than 800,000 visitors each year), and it can get crowded at the ever-popular Trunk Bay Beach during the busy winter season; parking woes plague the island's main town of Cruz Bay, but you won't find traffic jams or pollution. It's easy to escape from the fray, however: just head off on a hike or go early or late to the beach. The sun won't be as strong, and you may have that perfect crescent of white sand all to yourself.

St. John doesn't have a major agrarian past like her sister island, St. Croix, but if you're hiking in the dry season you can probably stumble upon the stone ruins of old plantations. The less adventuresome can visit the repaired ruins at the park's Annaberg Plantation and Caneel Bay Resort.

In 1675 Jorgen Iverson claimed the unsettled island for Denmark. By 1733 there were more than 1,000 slaves working more than 100 plantations. In that year the island was hit by a drought, hurricanes, and a plague of insects that destroyed the summer crops. With famine a real threat and the planters keeping them under tight rein, the slaves revolted on November 23, 1733. They captured the fort at Coral Bay, took control of the island, and held it for six months. During this period, about 20% of the island's total population was killed, the tragedy affecting both black and white residents in equal percentages. The rebellion was eventually put down with the help of French troops from Martinique. Slavery continued until 1848, when slaves in St. Croix marched on Frederiksted to demand their freedom from the Danish government.

27

Sugar Mill ruins at Annaberg Plantation

This time it was granted. After emancipation, St. John fell into decline, with its inhabitants eking out a living on small farms. Life continued in much the same way until the national park opened in 1956 and tourism became an industry.

Of the three U.S. Virgin Islands, St. John has the strongest sense of community, which is primarily rooted in a desire to protect the island's natural beauty. Despite the growth, there are still many pockets of tranquillity. Here you can truly escape the pressures of modern life for a day, a week—perhaps forever.

EXPLORING ST. JOHN

St. John is an easy place to explore. One road runs along the northern shore, another across the center of the mountains. There are a few roads that branch off here and there, but it's hard to get lost. Pick up a map at the visitor center before you start out and you'll have no problems. Few residents remember the route numbers, so have your map in hand if you stop to ask for directions. Bring along a swimsuit for stops at some of the most beautiful beaches in the world. You can spend all day or just a couple of hours exploring, but be advised that the roads are narrow and wind up and down steep hills, so don't expect to get anywhere in a hurry. There are lunch spots at Cinnamon Bay and in Coral Bay, or you can do what the locals do—find a secluded spot for a picnic. The grocery stores in Cruz Bay sell Styrofoam coolers just for this purpose.

If you plan to do a lot of touring, renting a car will be cheaper and will give you much more freedom than relying on taxis; on St. John taxis are shared safari vans, and drivers are reluctant to go anywhere until they have a full load of passengers. Although you may be tempted by an open-air Suzuki or Jeep, a conventional car will let you lock up your valuables. You can get just about everywhere on the paved roads without four-wheel drive unless it rains. Then four-wheel drive will help you get up the wet, hilly roads. You may be able to share a van or open-air vehicle (called a safari bus) with other passengers on a tour of scenic mountain trails, secret coves, and eerie bush-covered ruins.

WHAT TO SEE
CRUZ BAY

St. John's main town may be compact (it consists of only several blocks), but it's definitely a hub: the ferries from St. Thomas and the British Virgin Islands pull in here, and it's where you can get a taxi or rent a car to travel around the island. There are plenty of shops, a number of watering holes and restaurants, and a grassy square with benches where you can sit back and take everything in. Look for the current edition of the handy, amusing "St. John Map," featuring Max the Mongoose.

Elaine Ione Sprauve Library. On the hill just above Cruz Bay is the Enighed Estate great house, built in 1757. *Enighed* is Danish for "concord" (unity or peace). The great house and its outbuildings (a sugar factory and horse-driven mill) were destroyed by fire and hurricanes, and the house sat in ruins until 1982. The library offers Internet access for $2 an hour. ⊠ *Rte. 104, make a right past St. Ursula's Church* ☏ *340/776–6359* ⬜ *Free* ⊙ *Weekdays 9–5.*

V.I. National Park Visitors Center. To pick up a useful guide to St. John's hiking trails, see various large maps of the island, and find out about current Park Service programs, including guided walks and cultural demonstrations, stop by the park visitor center. ⊠ *Near baseball field* ☏ *340/776–6201* ⊕ *www.nps.gov/viis* ⊙ *Daily 8–4:30.*

NORTH SHORE

Fodor's Choice ★ **Annaberg Plantation.** In the 18th century, sugar plantations dotted the steep hills of this island. Slaves and free Danes and Dutchmen toiled to harvest the cane that was used to create sugar, molasses, and rum for export. Built in the 1780s, the partially restored plantation at Leinster Bay was once an important sugar mill. Although there are no official visiting hours, the National Park Service has regular tours, and some well-informed taxi drivers will show you around. Occasionally you may see a living-history demonstration—someone making johnnycake or weaving baskets. For information on tours and cultural events, contact the V.I. National Park Visitors Center. ⊠ *Leinster Bay Rd., Annaberg* ☏ *340/776–6201* ⊕ *www.nps.gov/viis* ⬜ *Free* ⊙ *Daily dawn–dusk.*

Peace Hill. It's worth stopping here, just past the Hawksnest Bay overlook, for great views of St. John, St. Thomas, and the BVI. On the flat promontory is an old sugar mill. ⊠ *Off Rte. 20, Denis Bay.*

MID ISLAND

★ **Bordeaux Mountain.** St. John's highest peak rises to 1,277 feet. Route 10 passes near enough to the top to offer breathtaking vistas. Don't stray into the road here—cars whiz by at a good clip along this section. Instead, drive nearly to the end of the dirt road that heads off next to the

27

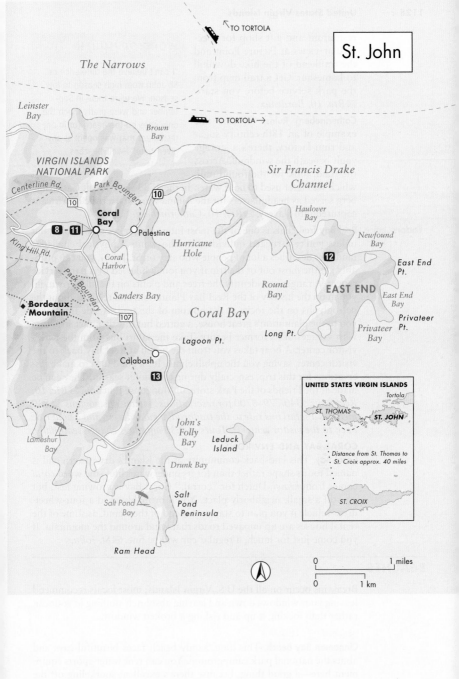

St. John

restaurant and gift shop for spectacular views at Picture Point and the trailhead of the hike downhill to Lameshur. Get a trail map from the park service before you start. ✉ *Rte. 10, Bordeaux.*

Catherineberg Ruins. At this fine example of an 18th-century sugar and rum factory, there's a storage vault beneath the windmill. Across the road, look for the round mill, which was later used to hold water. In the 1733 slave revolt Catherineberg served as headquarters for the Amina warriors, a tribe of Africans captured into slavery. ✉ *Rte. 10, Catherineberg.*

Fodor's Choice ★

Reef Bay Trail. This is one of the most interesting hikes on St. John, but unless you're a rugged individualist who wants a physical challenge (and that describes a lot of people who stay on St. John), you can probably get the most out of the trip if you join a hike led by a park service ranger. A ranger can identify the trees and plants on the hike down, fill you in on the history of the Reef Bay Plantation, and tell you about the petroglyphs on the rocks at the bottom of the trail. A side trail takes you to the plantation's great house, a gutted but mostly intact structure with vestiges of its former beauty. Take the safari bus from the park's visitor center. A boat takes you from the beach at Reef Bay back to the visitor center, saving you the uphill climb. It's a good idea to make reservations for this trip, especially during the winter season. They can be made at the Friends of the Park store, in Mongoose Junction. ✉ *Rte. 10, Reef Bay* ☎ *340/779–8700 for reservations* ⊕ *www.nps.gov/viis* ✉ *$30 includes a safari bus ride to the trailhead, a guided tour, and a boat ride back to the visitor center* ⊘ *Tours at 9:30 am; days change seasonally.*

CORAL BAY AND ENVIRONS

Coral Bay. This laid-back community at the island's dry eastern end is named for its shape rather than for its underwater life—the word *coral* comes from *krawl*, Dutch for "corral." Coral Bay is growing fast, but it's still a small, neighborly place. You'll probably need a four-wheel-drive vehicle if you plan to stay at this end of the island, as some of the rental houses are up unpaved roads that wind around the mountain. If you come just for lunch, a regular car will be fine. ✉ *St. John.*

BEACHES

Break-ins occur on all the U.S. Virgin Islands; most locals recommend leaving your windows down and leaving absolutely nothing in your car, rather than locking it up and risking a broken window.

NORTH SHORE

Cinnamon Bay Beach. This long, sandy beach faces beautiful cays and abuts the national park campground. You can rent water-sports equipment here—a good thing, because there's excellent snorkeling off the point to the right; look for the big angelfish and large schools of purple triggerfish. Afternoons on Cinnamon Bay can be windy—a boon for

St. John Archaeology

Archaeologists continue to unravel St. John's past through excavations at Trunk Bay and Cinnamon Bay, both prime tourist destinations within Virgin Islands National Park.

Work began back in the early 1990s, when the park wanted to build new bathhouses at the popular Trunk Bay. In preparation for that project, the archaeologists began to dig, turning up artifacts and the remains of structures that date to AD 900. The site was once a village occupied by the Taíno, a group that lived in the area until AD 1500. A similar but slightly more recent village was discovered at Cinnamon Bay.

By the time the Taíno got to Cinnamon Bay, roughly a century later, their society had developed to include chiefs, commoners, workers, and slaves. The location of the national park's busy Cinnamon Bay campground was once a Taíno temple that belonged to a king or chief. When archaeologists began digging in 1998, they uncovered several dozen *zemis*, which are small clay gods used in ceremonial activities, as well as beads, pots, and many other artifacts.

Near the end of the Cinnamon Bay dig archaeologists turned up another less ancient but still surprising discovery. A burned layer indicated that a plantation slave village had also stood near Cinnamon Bay campground; it was torched during the 1733 revolt because its slave inhabitants had been loyal to the planters. Since the 1970s, bones from slaves buried in the area have been uncovered at the water's edge by beach erosion.

27

windsurfers but an annoyance for sunbathers—so arrive early to beat the gusts. The Cinnamon Bay hiking trail begins across the road from the beach parking lot; ruins mark the trailhead. There are actually two paths here: a level nature trail (signs along it identify the flora) that loops through the woods and passes an old Danish cemetery, and a steep trail that starts where the road bends past the ruins and heads straight up to Route 10. Restrooms are on the main path from the commissary to the beach and scattered around the campground. **Amenities:** food and drink; parking; showers; toilets; water sports. **Best for:** snorkeling; swimming, walking; windsurfing. ☒ *North Shore Rd., Rte. 20, about 4 miles (6 km) east of Cruz Bay, Cinnamon Bay* ⊕ *www.nps.gov/viis.*

Francis Bay Beach. Because there's little shade, this beach gets toasty warm in the afternoon when the sun comes around to the west, but the rest of the day it's a delightful stretch of white sand. The only facilities are a few picnic tables tucked among the trees and a portable restroom, but folks come here to watch the birds that live in the swampy area behind the beach. The park offers bird-watching hikes here on Friday morning; sign up at the visitor center in Cruz Bay. To get here, turn left at the Annaberg intersection. **Amenities:** parking; toilets. **Best for:** snorkeling, swimming, walking. ☒ *North Shore Rd., Rte. 20, ¼ mile (½ km) from Annaberg intersection, Francis Bay* ⊕ *www.nps.gov/viis.*

★ **Hawksnest Beach.** Sea grape and waving palm trees line this narrow beach, and there are restrooms, cooking grills, and a covered shed for picnicking. A patchy reef just offshore means snorkeling is an easy swim away, but the best underwater views are reserved for ambitious snorkelers who head farther to the east along the bay's fringes. Watch out for boat traffic—a channel guides dinghies to the beach, but the occasional boater strays into the swim area. It's the closest drivable beach to Cruz Bay, so it's often crowded with locals and visitors. **Amenities:** parking; toilets. **Best for:** snorkeling, swimming. ⊠ *North Shore Rd., Rte. 20, about 2 miles (3 km) east of Cruz Bay, Hawksnest Bay* ⊕ *www.nps.gov/viis.*

Maho Bay Beach. St. John sports two Maho Bay Beaches. The first is a gorgeous strip of sand that sits right along the North Shore Road. It's a popular place, particularly on weekends, when locals come out in droves to party at the picnic tables at the south end of the beach. Snorkeling along the rocky edges is good, but the center is mostly sea grass. If you're lucky, you'll cross paths with a turtle. The second Maho Bay Beach sits below Maho Bay Camps, a wonderful hillside enclave of tent cabins that offers breakfast and dinner at its Pavilion Restaurant and water-sports equipment rentals at the beach. Turn left at the Annaberg intersection and follow the signs about 1 mile (1½ km) for Maho Bay Camps. It's a five-minute hike down a long, steep flight of stairs to the beach. **Amenities:** food and drink; parking; toilets; water sports. **Best for:** snorkeling; swimming. ⊠ *North Shore Rd., Rte. 20, Maho Bay* ⊕ *www.nps.gov/viis.*

Fodor'sChoice ★ **Trunk Bay Beach.** St. John's most-photographed beach is also the preferred spot for beginning snorkelers because of its underwater trail. (Cruise-ship passengers interested in snorkeling for a day flock here, so if you're looking for seclusion, arrive early or later in the day.) Crowded or not, this stunning beach is one of the island's most beautiful. There are changing rooms with showers, bathrooms, a snack bar, picnic tables, a gift shop, phones, lockers, and snorkeling-equipment rentals. The parking lot often overflows, but you can park along the road as long as the tires are off the pavement. **Amenities:** food and drink; lifeguards, parking; toilets; water sports. **Best for:** snorkeling; swimming, windsurfing ⊠ *North Shore Rd., Rte. 20, about 2½ miles (4 km) east of Cruz Bay, Trunk Bay* ⊕ *www.nps.gov/viis* ☞ *$4.*

CORAL BAY AND ENVIRONS

Lameshur Bay Beach. This sea grape–fringed beach is toward the end of a partially paved road on the southeast coast. The reward for your long drive is solitude, good snorkeling, and a chance to spy on some pelicans. The beach has a couple of picnic tables, rusting barbecue grills, and a portable restroom. The ruins of the old plantation are a five-minute walk down the road past the beach. The area has good hiking trails, including a trek (more than a mile) up Bordeaux Mountain before an easy walk to Yawzi Point. **Amenities:** parking; toilets. **Best for:** solitude; snorkeling; swimming; walking. ⊠ *Off Rte. 107, about 1½ miles (2½ km) from Salt Pond, Lameshur Bay* ⊕ *www.nps.gov/viis.*

Salt Pond Bay Beach. If you're adventurous, this rocky beach on the scenic southeastern coast—next to Coral Bay and rugged Drunk Bay—is worth exploring. It's a short hike down a hill from the parking lot, and the only facilities are an outhouse and a few picnic tables scattered about. Tide pools are filled with all sorts of marine creatures, and the snorkeling is good, particularly along the bay's edges. A short walk takes you to a pond where salt crystals collect around the edges. Hike farther uphill past cactus gardens to Ram Head for see-forever views. Leave nothing valuable in your car, as thefts are common. **Amenities:** parking; toilets. **Best for:** snorkeling; swimming; walking. ⊠ *Rte. 107, about 3 miles (5 km) south of Coral Bay, Salt Pond Bay* ⊕ *www. nps.gov/viis.*

WHERE TO EAT

The cuisine on St. John seems to get better every year, with chefs vying to see who can come up with the most imaginative dishes, whether you're at one of the elegant establishments at Caneel Bay Resort (where men may be required to wear a jacket at dinner) or a casual joint near Cruz Bay. For quick lunches, try the West Indian food stands in Cruz Bay Park and across from the post office. The cooks prepare fried chicken legs, p t s (meat- and fish-filled pastries), and callaloo.

Some restaurants close for vacation in September and even October. If you have your heart set on a special place, call ahead to make sure it's open during these months.

CRUZ BAY AND ENVIRONS

$$$$
ASIAN
★
✕ **Asolare.** Contemporary Asian cuisine dominates the menu at this elegant open-air eatery in an old St. John house. Come early and relax over drinks while you enjoy the sunset lighting up the harbor. Start with an appetizer such as Peking pork belly with a five-spice waffle and scallion cream sauce, then move on to entrées such as duck confit with salad and shoestring potatoes, shiitake mushrooms, and duck aioli, or the Thai-style hanger steak with a green-curry pistou. If you still have room for dessert, try the mimosa-poached pears with honey. ⑤ *Average main: $40* ⊠ *Rte. 20 on Caneel Hill, Estate Lindholm* ☎ *340/779–4747* ⊕ *www.asolarestjohn.com* ⊗ *No lunch.*

$$$
ITALIAN
☾
✕ **Café Roma.** This second-floor restaurant in the heart of Cruz Bay is *the* place for traditional Italian cuisine: lasagna, spaghetti and meatballs, and three-cheese manicotti. Small pizzas are available at the table, but larger ones are for takeout or at the bar. Rum-caramel bread pudding is a dessert specialty. This casual place can get crowded in winter, so show up early. ⑤ *Average main: $24* ⊠ *Vesta Gade* ☎ *340/776–6524* ⊕ *www.stjohn-caferoma.com* ⊗ *No lunch.*

$
ECLECTIC
✕ **Deli Grotto.** At this air-conditioned (but no-frills) sandwich shop you place your order at the counter and wait for it to be delivered to your

27

table or for takeout. The portobello panino with savory sautéed onions is a favorite, but the other sandwiches, such as the smoked turkey and artichoke, also get rave reviews. Order a brownie or cookie for dessert. ⑤ *Average main: $9* ⊠ *Mongoose Junction Shopping Center, North Shore Rd.* ☎ *340/777–3061* ▭ *No credit cards* ⊘ *No dinner.*

$$$$
AMERICAN
♺ ✕ **Fish Trap Restaurant and Seafood Market.** The main dining room here is open to the breezes and buzzes with a mix of locals and visitors, but the back room has air-conditioning. Start with a tasty appetizer such as conch fritters or fish chowder (a creamy combination of snapper, white wine, paprika, and spices). You can always find steak and chicken dishes, as well as the interesting fish of the day. ⑤ *Average main: $32* ⊠ *Bay and Strand Sts., next to Our Lady of Mount Carmel Church* ☎ *340/693–9994* ⊕ *www.thefishtrap.com* ⊘ *Closed Mon. No lunch.*

$$$$
MEDITERRANEAN
✕ **La Plancha del Mer.** Cooked on a searing-hot iron grill called a *plancha*, the food here takes its cues from Spain and southern France. The house specialty is steak with mashed potatoes and spicy cilantro sauce. Locals and visitors come for the bargain-price appetizers at the bar during happy hour, and brunch (Sunday only) is also popular. ⑤ *Average main: $34* ⊠ *Mongoose Junction Shopping Center, Rte. 104, Cruz Bay* ☎ *340/777–7333* ⊕ *www.laplanchadelmar.com* ⊘ *Closed Wed. No lunch Mon.–Sat.*

$$
ECLECTIC
✕ **Lime Inn.** The vacationers and mainland transplants who call St. John home like to flock to this alfresco spot for the congenial hospitality and good food, including all-you-can-eat shrimp on Wednesday night. Fresh lobster is the specialty, and the menu also includes shrimp-and-steak dishes and rotating chicken and pasta specials. ⑤ *Average main: $28* ⊠ *Lemon Tree Mall, King St.* ☎ *340/776–6425* ⊕ *www.limeinn.com* ⊘ *No lunch Sat. Closed Sun.*

$$$$
ITALIAN
Fodor's Choice
★ ✕ **Zozo's Ristorante.** Creative takes on old standards coupled with lovely presentations draw the crowds to this restaurant at Gallows Point Resort. Start with crispy fried calamari served with a pesto mayonnaise. The chef dresses up roasted mahimahi with a pistachio crust and serves it with a warm goat cheese–and–arugula salad. The slow-simmered osso buco comes with prosciutto-wrapped asparagus and saffron risotto. The sunset views will take your breath away. ⑤ *Average main: $39* ⊠ *Gallows Point Resort, Bay St.* ☎ *340/693–9200* ⊕ *www.zozos.net* ⊘ *No lunch.*

MID ISLAND

$$
ECLECTIC
★ ✕ **Chateau Bordeaux.** Your hamburgers and sweet-potato fries come with a side of fabulous views of Coral Bay and the British Virgin Islands. Located at the popular Bordeaux overlook, this restaurant also serves salads made with local greens, and fish sandwiches. The adjacent ice-cream shop blends up some delicious fruit smoothies. ⑤ *Average main: $15* ⊠ *Rte. 10, Bordeaux* ☎ *340/776–6611* ⊕ *www.chateaubordeauxvi.com* ⊘ *No dinner Fri.–Mon.*

CORAL BAY AND ENVIRONS

$$
AMERICAN
✕ **Donkey Diner.** In an odd combination that works well for Coral Bay visitors and residents, this tiny spot along the main road through Coral Bay sells tasty breakfasts and pizza. Breakfasts can be as ordinary or

as innovative as you like, with the menu running from fried eggs with bacon to blueberry pancakes to scrambled tofu served with home fries. Pizzas are equally eclectic, with toppings that include everything from the usual pepperoni and mushrooms to more exotic corn, raisins, and Kalamata olives, but they are only available Wednesday through Friday and Sunday, when the restaurant remains open until 8 pm. $ *Average main: $16* ✉ *Rte. 10* ☎ *340/693–5240* ⊕ *www.donkeydiner.com* ⊟ *No credit cards.*

$$$
CARIBBEAN
★

✕ **Miss Lucy's Restaurant.** Sitting seaside at remote Friis Bay, Miss Lucy's dishes up Caribbean food with a contemporary flair. Dishes such as tender conch fritters, a spicy West Indian stew called callaloo, and fried fish make up most of the menu, but you also find a generous paella filled with seafood, sausage, and chicken on the menu. Sunday brunches are legendary, and if you're around when the moon is full, stop by for the monthly full-moon party. The handful of small tables near the water is the nicest, but if they're taken or the mosquitoes are swarming, the indoor tables do nicely. $ *Average main: $25* ✉ *Rte. 107, Friis Bay* ☎ *340/693–5244* ⊕ *www.misslucysrestaurant.com* ⊙ *Closed Mon. No dinner Sun.*

$
AMERICAN
★

✕ **Skinny Legs Bar and Restaurant.** Sailors who live aboard boats anchored offshore and an eclectic coterie of residents gather for lunch and dinner at this funky spot in the middle of a boatyard and shopping complex. If owner Moe Chabuz is around, take a gander at his gams; you'll see where the restaurant got its name. It's a great place for burgers, fish sandwiches, and whatever sports are on the satellite TV. $ *Average main: $11* ✉ *Rte. 10* ☎ *340/779–4982* ⊕ *www.skinnylegs.com.*

$$
CARIBBEAN
☘

✕ **Sweet Plaintains.** The food here is a sophisticated take on Caribbean cuisine. The fish of the day—it could be mahimahi or grouper—is always especially good. Or try one of the curries if you don't want seafood. For a real local taste, start with the saltfish cakes served with shredded cabbage and mango puree. The coconut flan for dessert is another Caribbean favorite. $ *Average main: $26* ✉ *Rte. 107* ☎ *340/777–4653* ⊕ *www.sweetplantains-stjohn.com* ⊙ *Closed Sun.*

$
CARIBBEAN
★

✕ **Vie's Snack Shack.** Stop by Vie's when you're out exploring the island. Although it's just a shack by the side of the road, Vie's serves up some great cooking. The garlic chicken legs are crisp and tasty, and the conch fritters are really something to write home about. Plump and filled with fresh herbs, a plateful will keep you going for the rest of the afternoon. Save room for a wedge of coconut pie—called a tart in this neck of the woods. When you're finished eating, a spectacular white-sand beach down the road beckons. $ *Average main: $10* ✉ *Rte. 10, Hansen Bay* ☎ *340/693–5033* ⊕ *www.hansenbaycampground.com* ⊟ *No credit cards* ⊙ *Closed Sun. and Mon. No dinner.*

WHERE TO STAY

St. John doesn't have many beachfront hotels, but that's a small price to pay for all the pristine sand. However, the island's two excellent resorts—Caneel Bay Resort and the Westin St. John Resort & Villas—*are* on the beach. Sandy, white beaches string out along the north coast, which is popular with sunbathers and snorkelers and is where you can find the Caneel Bay Resort and Cinnamon and Maho Bay campgrounds. Most villas are in the residential south-shore area, a 15-minute drive from the north-shore beaches. If you head east, you come to the laid-back community of Coral Bay, where there are growing numbers of villas and cottages. Bands sometimes play at a couple of Coral Bay's nightspots, so if you're renting a villa in the hills above the village, you may hear music later than you'd like. A stay outside of Coral Bay will be peaceful and quiet.

If you're looking for West Indian village charm, there are a few inns in Cruz Bay. Keep in mind that when bands play at any of the town's bars (some of which stay open until the wee hours), the noise can be a problem. Your choice of accommodations also includes condominiums and cottages near town; two campgrounds, both at the edges of beautiful beaches (bring bug repellent); ecoresorts; and luxurious villas, often with a pool or a hot tub (sometimes both) and a stunning view.

If your lodging comes with a fully equipped kitchen, you'll be happy to know that St. John's handful of grocery stores sell everything you're likely to need—though the prices will take your breath away. If you're on a budget, consider bringing some staples (pasta, canned goods, paper products) from home. Hotel rates throughout the island are fairly expensive, but they do include endless privacy and access to most water sports.

Many of the island's condos are just minutes from the hustle and bustle of Cruz Bay, but you can find more scattered around the island. St. John also has a handful of camping spots ranging from the basic Cinnamon Bay Campground to the more comfortable Maho Bay Camps. They appeal to those who don't mind bringing their own beach towels from home or busing their own tables at dinner. If you want your piña colada delivered beachside by a smiling waiter, you'd be better off elsewhere—and ready to pay for the privilege.

For expanded reviews, facilities, and current deals, visit Fodors.com.

PRIVATE CONDOS AND VILLAS

Here and there between Cruz Bay and Coral Bay are about 500 private villas and condos (prices range from $ to $$$$). With pools or hot tubs, full kitchens, and living areas, these lodgings provide a fully functional home away from home. They're perfect for couples and extended groups of family or friends. You need a car, since most lodgings are in the hills and very few are at the beach. Villa managers usually pick you up at the dock, arrange for your rental car, and answer questions upon arrival as well as during your stay. Prices drop in the summer season, which is generally after April 15. Some companies begin off-season pricing a week or two later, so be sure to ask.

If you want to be close to Cruz Bay's restaurants and boutiques, a villa in the Chocolate Hole and Great Cruz Bay areas will put you a few minutes away. The Coral Bay area has a growing number of villas, but you'll be about 20 minutes from Cruz Bay. Beaches lie out along the North Shore, so you won't be more than 15 minutes from the water no matter where you stay.

RENTAL CONTACTS

Book-It VI. ⊠ *5000 Estate Enighed, PMB 15, Cruz Bay* ☎ *340/693–8555, 800/416–1205* ⊕ *www.bookitvi.com.*

Carefree Get-Aways. This company manages vacation villas on the island's southern and western edges. ⊠ *Cruz Bay* ☎ *340/779–4070, 888/643–6002* ⊕ *www.carefreegetaways.com.*

Caribbean Villas & Resorts. Caribbean handles condo rentals for Cruz Views and Gallow's Point Resort, as well as for many private villas. ⊠ *Cruz Bay* ☎ *340/776–6152, 800/338–0987* ⊕ *www.caribbeanvilla. com.*

Caribe Havens. Specializing in the budget market, Caribe Havens has properties scattered around the island. ⊠ *Cruz Bay* ☎ *340/776–6518* ⊕ *www.caribehavens.com.*

Catered to Vacation Homes. Specializing in luxury villas, this company has listings mainly in the middle of the island and on the western edge. ⊠ *Marketplace Suite 206, 5206 Enighed, Cruz Bay* ☎ *340/776–6641, 800/424–6641* ⊕ *www.cateredto.com.*

Cloud 9 Villas. Most of Cloud 9 Villas' offerings are in the Gifft Hill and Chocolate Hole area. ⊠ *Cruz Bay* ☎ *340/774–9633* ⊕ *www. cloud9villas.com.*

Great Caribbean Getaways. This firm handles private villas from Cruz Bay to Coral Bay. ⊠ *Cruz Bay* ☎ *340/693–8692, 800/341–2532* ⊕ *www. greatcaribbeangetaways.com.*

Island Getaways. Options from Island Getaways are mainly villas in the Great Cruz Bay–Chocolate Hole area, with a few others scattered around the island. ⊠ *Cruz Bay* ☎ *340/693–7676, 888/693–7676* ⊕ *www.islandgetawaysinc.com.*

On-Line Vacations ⊠ *Emmaus* ☎ *340/776–6036, 888/842–6632* ⊕ *www. onlinevacations.com.*

Private Homes for Private Vacations ⊠ *7605 Mamey Peak, Coral Bay* ☎☎ *340/776–6876* ⊕ *www.privatehomesvi.com.*

Seaview Vacation Homes. As the name implies, this company's specialty are houses with views of the ocean: they are in the Chocolate Hole, Great Cruz Bay, and Fish Bay areas. ⊠ *Cruz Bay* ☎ *340/776–6805, 888/625–2963* ⊕ *www.seaviewhomes.com.*

Star Villas. Star has cozy villas just outside Cruz Bay. ⊠ *1202 Gallows Point, Cruz Bay* ☎ *340/776–6704* ⊕ *www.starvillas.com.*

St. John Ultimate Villas ⊠ *Cruz Bay* ☎ *340/776–4703, 888/851–7588* ⊕ *www.stjohnultimatevillas.com.*

Vacation Vistas. This company's villas are mainly in the Chocolate Hole, Great Cruz Bay, and Rendezvous areas. ⊠ *Cruz Bay* ☎ *340/776–6462* ⊕ *www.vacationvistas.com.*

Windspree. Windspree's stock is mainly in and around Coral Bay. ⊠ *7924 Emmaus, Cruz Bay* ☎ *340/693–5423, 888/742–0357* ⊕ *www. windspree.com.*

27

Caneel Bay Resort

CRUZ BAY AND ENVIRONS

$$
RENTAL

🏨 **Coconut Coast Villas.** This small condominium complex with studio, two-, and three-bedroom apartments is a 10-minute walk from Cruz Bay, but is insulated from the town's noise in a sleepy suburban neighborhood. **Pros:** good snorkeling; full kitchens; walk to Cruz Bay. **Cons:** small beach; some uphill walks; nearby utility plant can be noisy. **TripAdvisor:** "great staff," "a perfect retreat," "paradise found." ⑤ *Rooms from: $289* ✉ *Turner Bay* 📞 *340/693–9100, 800/858–7989* ⊕ *www.coconutcoast.com* 🛏 *9 units* 🍽 *No meals.*

$$
B&B/INN

🏨 **Estate Lindholm Bed and Breakfast.** Built among old stone ruins on a lushly planted hill overlooking Cruz Bay, Estate Lindholm has an enchanting setting. **Pros:** lush landscaping; gracious host; pleasant decor. **Cons:** can be noisy; some uphill walks; on a busy road. **TripAdvisor:** "a beautiful place to stay," "cozy lodging," "quaint and clean." ⑤ *Rooms from: $340* ✉ *Rte. 20 on Caneel Hill, Estate Lindholm* 📞 *340/776–6121, 800/322–6335* ⊕ *www.estatelindholm.com* 🛏 *14 rooms* 🍽 *Breakfast.*

$$$$
RESORT

🏨 **Gallows Point Resort.** You're a short walk from restaurants and shops at this waterfront location just outside Cruz Bay, but once you step into your condo, the hustle and bustle are left behind. **Pros:** walk to shopping; excellent restaurant; comfortably furnished rooms. **Cons:** some rooms can be noisy; mediocre beach; insufficient parking. **TripAdvisor:** "beautifully landscaped," "romantic and relaxing," "peaceful in paradise." ⑤ *Rooms from: $495* ✉ *Gallows Point, Bay St., Cruz Bay* 📞 *340/776–6434, 800/323–7229* ⊕ *www.gallowspointresort.com* 🛏 *60 units* 🍽 *No meals.*

$
B&B/INN

🏨 **Garden by the Sea Bed and Breakfast.** Located in a middle-class residential neighborhood, this cozy bed-and-breakfast is an easy walk from

Cruz Bay. **Pros:** homey atmosphere; great breakfasts; breathtaking view from deck; near a bird-filled salt pond. **Cons:** noise from nearby power substation; some uphill walks; basic amenities. **TripAdvisor:** "wonderful and lovely," "perfect place for relaxing hospitality," "like staying with a friend." ⑤ *Rooms from: $250* ✉ *Enighed* ☎☎ *340/779–4731* ⊕ *www. gardenbythesea.com* ↴ *3 rooms* ▭ *No credit cards* ¶◯| *Breakfast.*

$
RENTAL

⌬ **Serendip.** This complex offers modern apartments on lush grounds with lovely views and makes a great pick for a budget stay in a residential locale. **Pros:** comfortable accommodations; good views; nice neighborhood. **Cons:** no beach; need car to get around; nearby construction. **TripAdvisor:** "breathtaking views," "the best accommodation on St. John," "beautiful and relaxing." ⑤ *Rooms from: $225* ✉ *Off Rte. 104, Enighed* ☎ *340/776–6646, 888/800–6445* ⊕ *www.serendipstjohn.com* ↴ *10 apartments* ¶◯| *No meals.*

$$$$
RESORT

⌬ **Westin St. John Resort and Villas.** The island's largest resort provides a nice beachfront location and enough activities to keep you busy. **Pros:** entertaining children's programs; pretty pool area; many activities. **Cons:** mediocre beach; long walk to some parts of the resort; need car to get around. **TripAdvisor:** "relaxing atmosphere," "beautiful resort," "lay back and be amazed." ⑤ *Rooms from: $495* ✉ *Rte. 104, Great Cruz Bay* ☎ *340/693–8000, 800/808–5020* ⊕ *www.westinresortstjohn. com* ↴ *174 rooms, 194 villas* ¶◯| *No meals.*

NORTH SHORE

27

$$$$
RESORT
Fodor'sChoice
★

⌬ **Caneel Bay Resort.** Well-heeled honeymooners, couples celebrating anniversaries, and extended families all enjoy Caneel Bay Resort's laid-back luxury. **Pros:** lovely beaches; gorgeous rooms; lots of amenities. **Cons:** staff can be chilly; isolated location; pricey. **TripAdvisor:** "so much to do," "gorgeous beaches," "pure relaxation." ⑤ *Rooms from: $495* ✉ *Rte. 20, Caneel Bay* ☎ *340/776–6111, 888/767–3966* ⊕ *www. caneelbay.com* ↴ *166 rooms* ¶◯| *Breakfast.*

$
RESORT

⌬ **Harmony Studios.** An ecologically correct environment is one of the draws at these condominium-style units that sit hillside at Maho Bay. **Pros:** convivial atmosphere; near beach; comfortable units. **Cons:** lots of stairs; no air-conditioning; need car to get around. **TripAdvisor:** "view unbeatable," "like flying over the Caribbean," "exceptional stay." ⑤ *Rooms from: $225* ✉ *Maho Bay* ☎ *340/776–6240, 800/392–9004* ⊕ *www.maho.org* ↴ *12 units* ¶◯| *No meals.*

$
RESORT
♺
Fodor'sChoice
★

⌬ **Maho Bay Camps.** Tucked into the greenery along the island's North Shore, the eco-conscious Maho Bay Camps attracts a sociable crowd that likes to explore the undersea world off the campground's beach or attend on-site seminars. **Pros:** friendly atmosphere; tasty food; real eco-resort. **Cons:** many stairs to climb; can be buggy; need a car to get around. **TripAdvisor:** "relaxing vacation," "tree houses for grown-ups," "pristine setting." ⑤ *Rooms from: $140* ✉ *Maho Bay* ☎ *340/776–6240, 800/392–9004* ⊕ *www.maho.org* ↴ *114 tent cottages with shared baths* ¶◯| *No meals.*

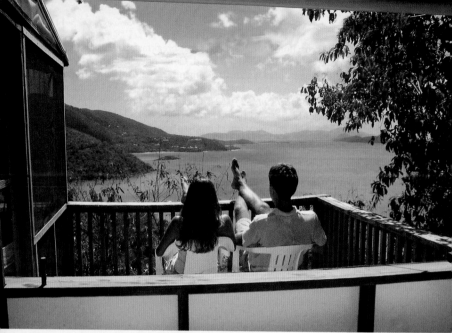

Taking in the views from Maho Bay Camps

CORAL BAY AND ENVIRONS

$
RENTAL

Estate Zootenvaal. Comfortable and casual, this small cottage colony gives you the perfect place to relax. **Pros:** quiet beach; private; near restaurants. **Cons:** some traffic noise; no air-conditioning. ⑤ *Rooms from: $275* ✉ *Rte. 10, Hurricane Hole, Zootenvaal* ☎ *340/776–6321* ⊕ *www. estatezootenvaal.com* ⤴ *4 units* ⊟ *No credit cards* ⦿ *No meals.*

NIGHTLIFE

St. John isn't the place to go for glitter and all-night partying. Still, after-hours Cruz Bay can be a lively little town in which to dine, drink, dance, chat, or flirt. Notices posted on the bulletin board outside the Connections telephone center—up the street from the ferry dock in Cruz Bay—or listings in the island's two small newspapers, the *St. John Sun Times* (⊕ *www.stjohnsuntimes.com*) and *Tradewinds* (⊕ *www. stjohntradewindsnews.com*) will keep you apprised of special events, comedy nights, movies, and the like.

CRUZ BAY

Tap Room. A rotating selection of distinctive brews make the Tap Room popular with locals and visitors. ✉ *Mongoose Junction, Cruz Bay* ☎ *340/715–7775.*

Woody's. Young folks like to gather here, where the sidewalk tables provide a close-up view of Cruz Bay action. ✉ *Near ferry dock and First Bank, Cruz Bay* ☎ *340/779–4625* ⊕ *www.woodysseafood.com.*

Zozo's Ristorante. After a sunset drink at this restaurant, which is up the hill from Cruz Bay, you can stroll around town (much is clustered around the small waterfront park). Many of the young people from the U.S. mainland who live and work on St. John will be out sipping and socializing, too. ⊠ *Gallows Point Resort, Bay St., Cruz Bay* ☎ *340/693–9200* ⊕ *www.zozos. net.*

CORAL BAY AND ENVIRONS

Skinny Legs Bar and Restaurant. Landlubbers and old salts listen to music and swap stories at this popular casual restaurant and bar on the far side of the island. ⊠ *Rte. 10, Coral Bay* ☎ *340/779–4982* ⊕ *www.skinnylegs.com.*

Shipwreck Landing. Live rock, bluegrass, and more are on tap several nights a week at this restaurant. ⊠ *Rte. 107, Freemans Ground, Coral Bay* ☎ *340/693-5640.*

WORD OF MOUTH

"St. John is really laid-back and really casual. There isn't a restaurant on the island that you couldn't go in with flip-flops on. Nightlife is maybe some live entertainment at a bar. Lots of hiking because of the huge National Park, but go early morning because it gets hot and it's hilly. Snorkeling is wonderful." —wliwl

FREE PARKING

Cruz Bay's parking problem is maddening. Your best bet is to rent a car from a company that allows you to park in its lot. Make sure you ask before you sign on the dotted line if you plan to spend time in Cruz Bay.

27

SHOPPING

CRUZ BAY

Luxury goods and handicrafts can be found on St. John. Most shops carry a little of this and a bit of that, so it pays to poke around. The Cruz Bay shopping district runs from **Wharfside Village,** just around the corner from the ferry dock, to **Mongoose Junction,** an inviting shopping center on North Shore Road. (The name of this upscale shopping mall, by the way, is a holdover from a time when those furry island creatures gathered at a nearby garbage bin.) Out on Route 104, stop in at the **Marketplace** to explore its gift and crafts shops. On St. John, store hours run from 9 or 10 to 5 or 6. Wharfside Village and Mongoose Junction shops in Cruz Bay are often open into the evening.

ART

Fodor's Choice ★ **Bajo el Sol.** This gallery sells works by owner Livy Hitchcock, plus pieces from a roster of the island's best artists. You can also shop for oil and acrylics, sculptures, and ceramics. ⊠ *Mongoose Junction Shopping Center, North Shore Rd., Cruz Bay* ☎ *340/693–7070* ⊕ *www. bajoelsolgallery.com.*

Caravan Gallery. Caravan sells unusual jewelry that its owner, Radha Speer, has traveled the world to find. The more you look, the more you see—wood carvings, tribal art, and masks for sale cover the walls and tables, making this a great place to browse. ⊠ *Mongoose Junction Shopping Center, North Shore Rd., Cruz Bay* ☎ *340/779–4566* ⊕ *www. caravangallery.com.*

Coconut Coast Studios. This waterside shop, a five-minute walk from the center of Cruz Bay, showcases the work of Elaine Estern. She specializes in undersea scenes. ⊠ *Frank Bay, Cruz Bay* ☎ *340/776–6944* ⊕ *www.coconutcoast.com.*

BOOKS

National Park Headquarters Bookstore. The bookshop at Virgin Islands National Park Headquarters sells several good histories of St. John, including *St. John Backtime: Eyewitness Accounts From 1718 to 1956*, by Ruth Hull Low and Rafael Lito Valls, and, for intrepid explorers, longtime resident Pam Gaffin's *St. John Feet, Fins and Four-Wheel Drive*, a "complete guide to all of the islands beaches, trails, and roads." ⊠ *Cruz Bay* ☎ *340/776–6201* ⊕ *www.nps.gov/viis.*

CLOTHING

Big Planet Adventure Outfitters. You knew when you arrived that someplace on St. John would cater to the outdoor enthusiasts who hike up and down the island's trails. This store sells flip-flops and Reef footwear, along with colorful and durable cotton clothing and accessories by Billabong. The store also sells children's clothes. ⊠ *Mongoose Junction Shopping Center, North Shore Rd., Cruz Bay* ☎ *340/776–6638* ⊕ *www.big-planet.com.*

Bougainvillea Boutique. This store is your destination if you want to look as if you've stepped out of the pages of the resort-wear spread in an upscale travel magazine. Owner Susan Stair carries very chic men's and women's clothes, straw hats, leather handbags, and fine gifts. ⊠ *Mongoose Junction Shopping Center, North Shore Rd., Cruz Bay* ☎ *340/693–7190.*

St. John Editions. This boutique specializes in swimsuits and nifty cotton dresses that go from beach to dinner with a change of shoes and accessories. Owner Molly Soper also carries attractive straw hats and inexpensive jewelry. ⊠ *North Shore Rd., Cruz Bay* ☎ *340/693–8444.*

FOOD

If you're renting a villa, condo, or cottage and doing your own cooking, there are several good places to shop for food; just be aware that prices are much higher than those at home.

★ **Starfish Market.** The island's largest store usually has the best selection of meat, fish, and produce. ⊠ *The Marketplace, Rte. 104, Cruz Bay* ☎ *340/779–4949* ⊕ *www.starfishmarket.com.*

GIFTS

Bamboula. This multicultural boutique carries unusual housewares, rugs, bedspreads, accessories, and men's and women's clothes and shoes that owner Jo Sterling has found on her world travels. ⊠ *Mongoose Junction*

Shopping Center, North Shore Rd., Cruz Bay ☎ *340/693–8699* ⊕ *www. bamboulastjohn.com.*

Best of Both Worlds. Pricey metal sculptures and attractive artworks hang from the walls of this gallery; the nicest are small glass decorations shaped like mermaids and sea horses. ⊠ *Mongoose Junction Shopping Center, North Shore Rd., Cruz Bay* ☎ *340/693–7005* ⊕ *www. bestofstjohn.com.*

Donald Schnell Studio. You'll find unusual handblown glass, wind chimes, kaleidoscopes, fanciful fountains, and pottery bowls here. Your purchases can be shipped worldwide. ⊠ *Amore Center, Rte. 104, near roundabout, Cruz Bay* ☎ *340/776–6420* ⊕ *www.donaldschnell.com.*

Every Ting. As its name implies, the store at Gallows Point Resort has a bit of this and a bit of that. Shop for Caribbean books and CDs, picture frames decorated with shells, and T-shirts with tropical motifs. Residents and visitors also drop by for a cup of coffee. ⊠ *Gallows Point Resort, Bay St., Cruz Bay* ☎ *340/693–5820* ⊕ *www. stjohnadventures.com.*

Fabric Mill. There's a good selection of women's clothing in tropical brights, as well as lingerie, sandals, and batik wraps here. Or take home several yards of colorful batik fabric to make your own dress. ⊠ *Mongoose Junction Shopping Center, North Shore Rd., Cruz Bay* ☎ *340/776–6194.*

Nest and Company. This small shop carries perfect take-home gifts in colors that reflect the sea. Shop here for soaps in tropical scents, dinnerware, and much more. ⊠ *Mongoose Junction Shopping Center, North Shore Rd., Cruz Bay* ☎ *340/715–2552* ⊕ *www.nestvi.com.*

★ **Pink Papaya.** Head to this shop and art gallery for the work of longtime Virgin Islands resident Lisa Etre. There's also huge collection of one-of-a-kind gifts, including bright tableware, trays, and tropical jewelry. ⊠ *Lemon Tree Mall, King St., Cruz Bay* ☎ *340/693–8535* ⊕ *www. pinkpapaya.com.*

JEWELRY

Free Bird Creations. This is your on-island destination for special handcrafted jewelry—earrings, bracelets, pendants, chains—as well as a good selection of water-resistant watches. ⊠ *Dockside Mall, next to ferry dock, Cruz Bay* ☎ *340/693–8625* ⊕ *www.freebirdcreations.com.*

Jewels. A branch of the St. Thomas store, Jewels carries emeralds, diamonds, and other jewels in attractive yellow- and white-gold settings, as well as strings of creamy pearls, watches, and other designer jewelry. ⊠ *Mongoose Junction Shopping Center, North Shore Rd., Cruz Bay* ☎ *340/776–6007* ⊕ *www.jewelsonline.com.*

R&I Patton Goldsmiths. This store is owned by Rudy and Irene Patton, who design most of the lovely silver and gold jewelry on display. The rest comes from various designer friends. Sea fans (those large, lacy plants that sway with the ocean's currents) in filigreed silver, starfish and hibiscus pendants in silver or gold, and gold sand-dollar-shape charms and earrings are choice selections. ⊠ *Mongoose Junction Shop-*

27

ping Center, North Shore Rd., Cruz Bay ☎ *340/776–6548* ⊕ *www. pattongold.com.*

St. Johnimals. Pampered pets are the ultimate consumers for the goods in this cozy store. The shelves are stocked with carriers made of buttery soft leather, leashes and collars made with crystals, handpainted pet bowls, and toys of all sorts. ✉ *Wharfside Village shopping center, Cruz Bay* ☎ *340/777–9588* ⊕ *www.stjohnimals.com.*

Verace. This store is filled with jewelry from such well-known designers as Toby Pomeroy and Patrick Murphy. Murphy's stunning gold sailboats with gems for hulls will catch your eye. ✉ *Wharfside Village, Strand St., Cruz Bay* ☎ *340/693–7599* ⊕ *www.verace.com.*

CORAL BAY AND ENVIRONS

CLOTHING

Jolly Dog. Head here for the stuff you forgot to pack. Sarongs in cotton and rayon, beach towels with tropical motifs, and hats and T-shirts sporting the "Jolly Dog" logo fill the shelves. ✉ *Skinny Legs Shopping Complex, Rte. 10, Sanders Bay* ☎ *340/693–5900* ⊕ *www.thejollydog. com* ✉ *Skinny Legs Shopping Complex, Rte. 10, Coral Bay* ☎ *340/693– 5900* ⊕ *www.thejollydog.com.*

Sloop Jones. This store is worth the trip all the way out to the island's east end to shop for made-on-the-premises clothing and pillows, in fabrics splashed with tropical colors. Fabrics are in cotton and linen, and are supremely comfortable. ✉ *Off Rte. 10, East End* ☎ *340/779–4001* ⊕ *www.sloopjones.com.*

FOOD

Lily's Gourmet Market. This small store in Coral Bay carries the meat, fish, produce, and staples. ✉ *Cocoloba Shopping Center, Rte. 107, Coral Bay* ☎ *340/777–3335.*

Love City Mini Mart. The store may not look like much from the road, but it's one of the very few places to shop in Coral Bay and has a surprising selection. ✉ *Off Rte. 107, Coral Bay* ☎ *340/693–5790.*

GIFTS

Mumbo Jumbo. With what may be the best prices in St. John, Mumbo Jumbo carries tropical clothing, stuffed sea creatures, and other gifty items in a cozy little shop. ✉ *Skinny Legs Shopping Complex, Rte. 10, Coral Bay* ☎ *340/779–4277.*

SPORTS AND ACTIVITIES

BOATING AND SAILING

If you're staying at a hotel or campground, your activities desk will usually be able to help you arrange a sailing excursion aboard a nearby boat. Most day sails leaving Cruz Bay head out along St. John's north coast. Those that depart from Coral Bay might drop anchor at some remote cay off the island's east end or even in the nearby British Virgin Islands. Your trip usually includes lunch, beverages, and at least one snorkeling stop. Keep in mind that inclement weather could interfere with your plans, though most boats will still go out if rain isn't too heavy.

★ **St. John Concierge Service.** The capable staff can find a charter sail or power boat that fits your style and budget. The company also books fishing and scuba trips. ⊠ *Across from post office, Cruz Bay* ☎ *340/777–2665, 866/504–3331* ⊕ *www.stjohnconciergeservice.com.*

Ocean Runner. For a speedier trip to the cays and remote beaches off St. John, you can rent a powerboat from Ocean Runner. The company rents one- and two-engine boats for $375 to $705 per day. Gas and oil will run you $100 to $300 a day extra, depending on how far you're going. It's a good idea to have some skill with powerboats for this self-drive adventure, but if you don't, you can hire a captain for $120 extra a day. ⊠ *Waterfront, Cruz Bay* ☎ *340/693–8809* ⊕ *www.oceanrunnerusvi.com.*

Sail Safaris. Even novice sailors can take off in a small sailboat from Cruz Bay Beach with Sail Safaris to one of the small islands off St. John. Guided half-day tours on small or large boats start at $70 per person. Rentals run $47 per hour. ⊠ *Waterfront, Cruz Bay* ☎ *340/626–8181, 866/820–6906* ⊕ *www.sailsafaris.net.*

DIVING AND SNORKELING

Although just about every beach has nice snorkeling—Trunk Bay, Cinnamon Bay, and Waterlemon Cay at Leinster Bay get the most praise—you need a boat to head out to the more remote snorkeling locations and the best scuba spots. Sign on with any of the island's water-sports operators to get to spots farther from St. John. If you use the one at your hotel, just stroll down to the dock to hop aboard. Their boats will take you to hot spots between St. John and St. Thomas, including the tunnels at **Thatch Cay,** the ledges at **Congo Cay,** and the wreck of the *General Rogers.* Dive off St. John at **Stephens Cay,** a short boat ride out of Cruz Bay, where fish swim around the reefs as you float downward. At **Devers Bay,** on St. John's south shore, fish dart about in colorful schools. **Carval Rock,** shaped like an old-time ship, has gorgeous rock formations, coral gardens, and lots of fish. It can be too rough here in winter, though. Count on paying $75 for a one-tank dive and $90 for a two-tank dive. Rates include equipment and a tour. If you've never dived before, try an introductory course, called a resort course. Or if certification is in your vacation plans, the island's dive shops can help you get your card.

Cruz Bay Watersports. The owners of Cruz Bay, Marcus and Patty Johnston, offer regular reef, wreck, and night dives and USVI and BVI snorkel tours. The company holds both PADI five-star and NAUI-Dream-Resort status. ⊠ *Lumberyard Shopping Complex, Cruz Bay* ☎ *340/776–6234* ⊕ *www.divestjohn.com* ⊠ *Westin St. John, Rte. 104, Great Cruz Bay* ☎ *340/776–6234.*

Low Key Watersports. Low Key Watersports offers two-tank dives and specialty courses. It's certified as a PADI five-star training facility. ⊠ *1 Bay St., Cruz Bay* ☎ *340/693–8999, 800/835–7718* ⊕ *www.divelowkey.com.*

FISHING

Well-kept charter boats—approved by the U.S. Coast Guard—head out to the north and south drops or troll along the inshore reefs, depending on the season and what's biting. The captains usually provide bait, drinks, and lunch, but you need to bring your own hat and sunscreen. Fishing charters run about $1,100 for the full-day trip.

Captain Byron Oliver. Captain Oliver takes you out to the north and south drops. ⊠ *St. John* ☎ *340/693–8339.*

☾ **Captain Rob Richards.** An excellent choice for fishing charters, Captain Rob Richards is patient with beginners—especially kids—but also enjoys going out with more experienced anglers. He runs the 32-foot center console *Mixed Bag I* and 40-foot Luhrs Express *Mixed Bag II.* Although he's based in St. John, he will pick up parties in St. Thomas. ⊠ *Westin, St. John, Great Cruz Bay* ☎ *340/513–0389* ⊕ *www. sportfishingstjohn.com.*

GUIDED TOURS

In St. John, taxi drivers provide tours of the island, making stops at various sites, including Trunk Bay and Annaberg Plantation. Prices run around $15 a person. The taxi drivers congregate near the ferry in Cruz Bay. The dispatcher will find you a driver for your tour.

V.I. National Park Visitors Center. Along with providing trail maps and brochures about Virgin Islands National Park, the Park Service gives several guided tours, both on- and offshore. Some are offered only during particular times of the year, and some require reservations. ⊠ *Cruz Bay* ☎ *340/776–6201* ⊕ *www.nps.gov/viis.*

HIKING

Although it's fun to go hiking with a Virgin Islands National Park guide, don't be afraid to head out on your own. To find a hike that suits your ability, stop by the park's visitor center in Cruz Bay and pick up the free trail guide; it details points of interest, trail lengths, and estimated hiking times, as well as any dangers you might encounter. Although the park staff recommends long pants to protect against thorns and insects, most people hike in shorts because it can get very hot. Wear sturdy shoes or hiking boots even if you're hiking to the beach. Don't forget to bring water and insect repellent.

Fodor's Choice ★ **Virgin Islands National Park.** Head to the park for more than 20 trails on the north and south shores, with guided hikes along the most popular routes. A full-day trip to Reef Bay is a must; it's an easy hike through lush and dry forest, past the ruins of an old plantation, and to a sugar factory adjacent to the beach. It can be a bit arduous for young kids, however. The park runs a $30 guided tour to Reef Bay that includes a safari bus ride to the trailhead and a boat ride back to the Visitors Center. The schedule changes from season to season; call for times and to make reservations, which are essential. ⊠ *1300 Cruz Bay Creek, St. John* ☎ *340/776–6201* ⊕ *www.nps.gov/viis.*

HORSEBACK RIDING

Carolina Corral. Clip-clop along the island's byways for a slower-pace tour of St. John. Carolina Corral offers horseback trips and wagon rides down scenic roads with owner Dana Barlett. She has a way with horses and calms even the most novice riders. Rates start at $65 for a one-hour ride. ✉ *St. John* ☎ *340/693–5778* ⊕ *www.carolinacorral.com.*

SEA KAYAKING

Poke around the clear bays here and explore undersea life from a sea kayak. Rates run about $70 for a full day in a double kayak. Tours start at $65 for a half day.

Arawak Expeditions. This company's guides use traditional and sit-on-top kayaks for exploring Cruz Bay's waters. The company also rents single and double kayaks, so you can head independently to nearby islands such as Stephen's Cay. ✉ *Mongoose Juction Shopping Center, North Shore Rd., Cruz Bay* ☎ *340/693–8312, 800/238–8687* ⊕ *www. arawakexp.com.*

Crabby's Watersports. Explore Coral Bay Harbor and Hurricane Hole on the eastern end of the island in a sea kayak from Crabby's Watersports. If you don't want to paddle into the wind to get out of Coral Bay Harbor, the staff will drop you off in Hurricane Hole so you can paddle downwind back to Coral Bay. Crabby's also rents snorkel gear, beach chairs, umbrellas, coolers, and floats. ✉ *Rte. 107, next to Cocoloba shopping center, Coral Bay* ☎ *340/714–2415* ⊕ *www.crabbyswatersports.com.*

Hidden Reef EcoTours. Coral reefs, mangroves, and lush sea-grass beds filled with marine life are what you can see on Hidden Reef's two- and three-hour, full-day and full-moon kayak tours through Coral Reef National Monument and its environs. ✉ *Rte. 10, Round Bay* ☎ *340/513–9613, 877/529–2575* ⊕ *www.kayaksj.com.*

WINDSURFING

Cinnamon Bay Campground. Steady breezes and expert instruction make learning to windsurf a snap. Try Cinnamon Bay Campground, where rentals are $40 to $100 per hour. Lessons are available right at the waterfront; just look for the Windsurfers stacked up on the beach. The cost for a one-hour lesson starts at $60, plus the cost of the board rental. You can also rent kayaks, stand-up paddle boards, Boogie boards, small sailboats, and surfboards. ✉ *Rte. 20, Cinnamon Bay* ☎ *340/693–5902, 340/626–4769* ⊕ *www.windnsurfingadventures.com.*

27

ST. CROIX

History is a big draw in St. Croix: planes are filled with Danish visitors who come mainly to explore the island's colonial history. Of course, like the rest of us, they also make sure to spend some time sunning at the island's powdery beaches, getting pampered at the hotels, and dining at interesting restaurants.

Until 1917 Denmark owned St. Croix and her sister Virgin Islands, a fact reflected in street names in the main towns of Christiansted and Frederiksted as well as the surnames of many island residents. In the

18th and 19th centuries, some of those early Danish settlers, as well as other Europeans, owned plantations, all of them worked by African slaves and white indentured servants lured to St. Croix to pay off their debt to society. Some of the plantation ruins—such as the Christiansted National Historic Site, Whim Plantation, the ruins at St. George Village Botanical Garden, and those at Estate Mount Washington and Judith's Fancy—are open for easy exploration. Others are on private land, but a drive around the island reveals the ruins of 100 plantations here and there on St. Croix's 84 square miles (218 square km). Their windmills, great houses, and factories are all that's left of the 224 plantations that once grew sugarcane, tobacco, and other crops at the island's height.

The downturn began in 1801, when the British occupied the island. The end of the slave trade in 1803, an additional British occupation (from 1807 to 1815), droughts, the development of the sugar-beet industry in Europe, political upheaval, and an economic depression all sent the island into a downward spiral.

St. Croix never recovered. The end of slavery in 1848, followed by labor riots, fires, hurricanes, and an earthquake during the last half of the 19th century, brought what was left of the island's economy to its knees. In the 1920s, the start of prohibition in the United States ended the island's rum industry, further crippling the economy. The situation remained dire—so bad that President Herbert Hoover called the territory an "effective poorhouse" during a 1931 visit—until the rise of tourism in the late 1950s and 1960s. With tourism came economic improvements coupled with an influx of residents from other Caribbean islands and the mainland: St. Croix also depends on industries such as the huge oil refinery outside Frederiksted to provide employment.

Today suburban subdivisions fill the fields where sugarcane once waved in the tropical breeze. Condominium complexes line the beaches along the north coast outside Christiansted. Large houses dot the rolling hillsides. Modern strip malls and shopping centers sit along major roads, and it's as easy to find a McDonald's as it is Caribbean fare.

Although St. Croix sits definitely in the 21st century, with only a little effort you can easily step back into the island's past.

EXPLORING ST. CROIX

Although there are things to see and do in St. Croix's two towns, Christiansted and Frederiksted (both named after Danish kings), there are lots of interesting spots in between them and to the east of Christiansted. Just be sure you have a map in hand (pick one up at rental-car agencies, or stop by the tourist office for an excellent one that's free). Many secondary roads remain unmarked; if you get confused, ask for help. Locals are always ready to point you in the right direction.

CHRISTIANSTED

In the 1700s and 1800s Christiansted was a trading center for sugar, rum, and molasses. Today law offices, tourist shops, and restaurants occupy many of the same buildings, which start at the harbor and go up the gently sloped hillsides.

Your best bet to see the historic sights in this Danish-style town is in the morning, when it's still cool. Break for lunch at an open-air restaurant before spending as much time as you like exploring the shopping opportunities. You can't get lost, since all streets lead back downhill to the water.

St. Croix Visitor Center. Friendly advice as well as useful maps and brochures are available from the visitor center. ⊠ *Government House, King St.* ☎ *340/773–1404* ⊕ *www.visitusvi.com* ☺ *Weekdays 8–5.*

Danish Customs House. Built in 1830 on foundations that date from a century earlier, the historic building, which is near Ft. Christiansvaern, originally served as both a customshouse and a post office. In 1926 it became the Christiansted Library, and it's been a national park facility since 1972. It's closed to the public, but the sweeping front steps make a nice place to take a break. ⊠ *King St.* ☎ *340/773–1460* ⊕ *www.nps. gov/chri.*

Ft. Christiansvaern. The large yellow fortress dominates the waterfront. Because it's so easy to spot, it makes a good place to begin a walking tour. In 1749 the Danish built the fort to protect the harbor, but the structure was repeatedly damaged by hurricane-force winds and had to be partially rebuilt in 1771. It's now a national historic site, the best preserved of the few remaining Danish-built forts in the Virgin Islands. The park's visitor center is here. Rangers are on hand to answer questions. ⊠ *Hospital St.* ☎ *340/773–1460* ⊕ *www.nps.gov/chri* ⌨ *$3 (includes Steeple Bldg.* ☺ *Weekdays 8–4:30, weekends 9–4:30.*

Fodor's Choice ★

Government House. One of the town's most elegant structures was built as a home for a Danish merchant in 1747. Today it houses offices. If you're here weekdays from 8 to 4:30, slip into the peaceful inner courtyard to admire the still pools and gardens. A sweeping staircase leads you to a second-story ballroom, still used for official government functions. ⊠ *King St.* ☎ *340/773–1404.*

Post Office Building. Built in 1749, Christiansted's former post office was once the Danish West India & Guinea Company warehouse. It now serves as the park's administrative building. ⊠ *Church St..*

Scale House. Constructed in 1856, this was once the spot where goods passing through the port were weighed and inspected. The park staffers here have on offer a good selection of books about St. Croix history and its flora and fauna. ⊠ *King St.* ☎ *340/773–1460* ⊕ *www.nps.gov/ chri* ☺ *Weekdays 8–4:30, weekends 9–4:30.*

Steeple Building. The first Danish Lutheran church on the island when it was built in 1753, the Steeple Building is now used as a museum. It's worth the short walk to see the archaeological artifacts and exhibits on plantation life, the architectural development of Christiansted, the island's Indian inhabitants, and Alexander Hamilton, who grew up in

27

St. Croix

↑
TO
ST. THOMAS

Cane Bay

Hams Bluff
Hams Bay
Estate Mt. Washington Plantation
North Star
Davis Bay
80
Salt River Bay National Historical Park and Ecological Preserve
Judith's Fancy
Mount Victory Camp
Rain Forest
St. Croix Leap
Annaly
18
Blue Mt.
Mt. Eagle
Northside Rd.
West End Beaches
Mahogaby Rd.
69
Midland Rd.
72
Sunny Isle
Frederiksted
63
St. George Hill
76
Kingshill
70
Frederiksted Pier
Carl & Marie Lawaetz Museum
St. George Village Botanical Gardens
69
Henry E. Rohlsen Airport
Hess Oil Refinery
14 - 16
Centerline Rd.
Canegarden Bay
West End Salt Pond
17 19
Whim Plantation Museum
Melvin H. Evans Hwy.
66
Krause Pt.
Long Pt. Bay
Long Pt.

KEY

⟋	Beaches
⬉	Dive Sites
⛴	Cruise Ship Terminal
🌴	Rain Forest
1	Restaurants
1	Hotels

Buck
Island

Buck Island Reef
National Monument

1 - 7
1 - 2

Green
Cay

6 **10** **11**

Long
Reef

10

Tamarind Reef
Beach

5

*Christiansted
Harbor*

Pull
Pt.

7

*Coakley
Bay*

82

East End Rd.

Cramer's
Park

Cottongarden Pt.

*Teague
Bay*

8

Sugarloaf Hill

3

8

Gallow's Bay

Christiansted

▲
*Recovery
Hill*

4

▲
*Prospect
Hill*

9

South Side Rd.

9

60

Isaacs Bay

*Grapetree
Bay*

Grassy Pt.

◆ Point Udall

*Robin
Bay*

62

South Side Rd.

*Milord
Pt.*

*Great Pond
Bay*

*Manchenil
Bay*

Caribbean Sea

UNITED STATES VIRGIN ISLANDS

Tortola

ST. THOMAS   ST. JOHN

*Distance from St. Thomas to
St. Croix approx. 40 miles*

ST. CROIX

0 ————————— 2 miles

0 ————————— 3 km

Fort Christiansvaern is a national historic site.

St. Croix. Hours are irregular, so ask at the visitor center. ✉ *Church St.* ☎ *340/773–1460* ✉ *$3 (includes Ft. Christiansvaern).*

EAST END

An easy drive along flat, well-marked roads to St. Croix's eastern end takes you through some choice real estate. Ruins of old sugar estates dot the landscape. You can make the entire loop on the road that circles the island in about an hour, a good way to end the day. If you want to spend a full day exploring, you can find some nice beaches and easy walks with places to stop for lunch.

★ **Buck Island Reef National Monument.** Buck Island has pristine beaches that are just right for sunbathing, but there's also some shade for those who don't want to fry. The snorkeling trail set in the reef allows close-up study of coral formations and tropical fish. Overly warm seawater temperatures have led to a condition called coral bleaching that has killed some of the coral. The reefs are starting to recover, but how long it will take is anyone's guess. There's an easy hiking trail to the island's highest point, where you can be rewarded for your efforts by spectacular views of St. John. Charter-boat trips leave daily from the Christiansted waterfront or from Green Cay Marina, about 2 miles (3 km) east of Christiansted. Check with your hotel for recommendations. ✉ *Off North Shore of St. Croix* ☎ *340/773–1460* ⊕ *www. nps.gov/buis.*

Point Udall. This rocky promontory, the easternmost point in the United States, is about a half-hour drive from Christiansted. A paved road takes you to an overlook with glorious views. More adventurous folks can hike down to the pristine beach below. On the way back, look for

Turtles on St. Croix

Green, leatherback, and hawksbill turtles crawl ashore during their annual April-to-November nesting season to lay their eggs. They return from their life at sea every two to seven years to the beach where they were born. Since turtles can live for up to 100 years, they may return many times to nest in St. Croix.

The leatherbacks like Sandy Point National Wildlife Refuge and other spots on St. Croix's western end, but the hawksbills prefer Buck Island and the East End. Green turtles are also found primarily on the East End.

All are endangered species that face numerous predators, some natural, some the result of the human presence. Particularly in the Frederiksted area, dogs and cats prey on the nests and eat the hatchlings. Occasionally

a dog will attack a turtle about to lay its eggs, and cats train their kittens to hunt at turtle nests, creating successive generations of turtle-egg hunters. In addition, turtles have often been hit by fast-moving boats that leave large slices in their shells if they don't kill them outright.

The leatherbacks are the subject of a project by the Earthwatch conservation group. Each summer, teams arrive at Sandy Point National Wildlife Refuge to ensure that poachers, both natural and human, don't attack the turtles as they crawl up the beach. The teams also relocate nests that are laid in areas prone to erosion. When the eggs hatch, teams stand by to make sure the turtles make it safely to the sea, and scientists tag them so they can monitor their return to St. Croix.

27

the Castle Aura, an enormous Moorish-style mansion. It was built by Nadia Farber, the former Contessa de Navarro, who's an extravagant local character. Point Udall is sometimes a popular spot for thieves, so don't leave anything valuable in your car, and leave it unlocked. ⊠ *Rte. 82, Et Stykkeland.*

MID ISLAND

A drive through the countryside between these two towns takes you past ruins of old plantations, many bearing whimsical names (Morningstar, Solitude, Upper Love). The traffic moves quickly—by island standards—on the main roads, but you can pause and poke around if you head down some side lanes. It's easy to find your way west, but driving from north to south requires good navigation. Don't leave your hotel without a map. Allow an entire day for this trip, so you'll have enough time for a swim at a north-shore beach. Although you can find lots of casual eateries on the main roads, pick up a picnic lunch if you plan to head off the beaten path.

Cruzan Rum Distillery. A tour of the company's factory, which was established in 1760, culminates in a tasting of its products, all sold here at good prices. It's worth a stop to look at the distillery's charming old buildings even if you're not a rum connoisseur. ⊠ *West Airport Rd., Estate Diamond* ☎ *340/692–2280* ⊕ *www.cruzanrum.com* ☜ *$5* ☉ *Weekdays 9–4.*

St. George Village Botanical Garden. At this 17-acre estate, fragrant flora grows amid the ruins of a 19th-century sugarcane plantation. There are miniature versions of each ecosystem on St. Croix, from a semiarid cactus grove to a verdant rain forest. The small museum is also well worth a visit. ⊠ *Rte. 70, turn north at sign, St. George* ☎ *340/692–2874* ⊕ *www.sgvbg.org* ⊠ *$8* ☉ *Daily 9–5.*

Estate Whim Museum. The lovingly restored estate, with a windmill, cook house, and other buildings, gives a sense of what life was like on St. Croix's sugar plantations in the 1800s. The oval-shape great house has high ceilings and antique furniture and utensils. Notice its fresh, airy atmosphere—the waterless stone moat around the great house was used not for defense but for gathering cooling air. If you have kids, the grounds are the perfect place for them to run around, perhaps while you browse in the museum gift shop. It's just outside of Frederiksted. ⊠ *Rte. 70, Estate Whim* ☎ *340/772–0598* ⊕ *www.stcroixlandmarks. com* ⊠ *$10* ☉ *Wed.–Sat. 10–4 and cruise-ship days.*

FREDERIKSTED AND ENVIRONS

St. Croix's second-largest town, Frederiksted, was founded in 1751. Just as Christiansted is famed for its Danish buildings, Frederiksted is known for its Victorian architecture. A stroll around its historic sights will take you no more than an hour. Allow a little more time if you want to duck into the few small shops. One long cruise-ship pier juts into the sparkling sea. It's the perfect place to start a tour of this quaint city.

Caribbean Museum Center for the Arts. Sitting across from the waterfront in a historic building, this small museum hosts an always-changing roster of exhibits. Many are cutting-edge multimedia efforts that you might be surprised to find in such an out-of-the-way location. The openings are popular events. ⊠ *10 Strand St.* ☎ *340/772–2622* ⊕ *www.cmcarts. org* ⊠ *Free* ☉ *Tues.–Thurs. and weekends (and any cruise-ship day) 10–4; Fri. 10–7.*

Estate Mount Washington Plantation. Several years ago, while surveying the property, the owners discovered the ruins of a sugar plantation beneath the rain-forest brush. The grounds have since been cleared and opened to the public. You can take a self-guided walking tour of the mill, the rum factory, and other ruins. ⊠ *Rte. 63, Mount Washington* ☉ *Daily dawn–dusk.*

Fort Frederik. On July 3, 1848, 8,000 slaves marched on this fort to demand their freedom. Danish governor Peter von Scholten, fearing they would burn the town to the ground, stood up in his carriage parked in front of the fort and granted their wish. The fort, completed in 1760, houses an art gallery and a number of interesting historical exhibits, including some focusing on the 1848 Emancipation and the 1917 transfer of the Virgin Islands from Denmark to the United States. It's within earshot of the Frederiksted Visitor Center. ⊠ *Waterfront* ☎ *340/772–2021* ⊠ *$3* ☉ *Weekdays (and any cruise-ship day) 8:30–4.*

Frederiksted Visitor Center. Head here for brochures from numerous St. Croix businesses, as well as a few exhibits about the island. ⊠ *Pier* ☎ *340/773-0495* ☉ *Weekdays 8–5.*

Fodor's Choice
★

Lawaetz Family Museum. For a trip back in time, tour this circa-1750 farm, in a valley at La Grange. It's been owned by the prominent Lawaetz family since 1896, which is just after Carl Lawaetz arrived from Denmark. A Lawaetz family member shows you around the lovely two-story house and the farm, noting the four-poster mahogany bed Carl shared with his wife, Marie, the china Marie painted, the family portraits, and the fruit trees that fed the family for several generations. Initially a sugar plantation, the farm was subsequently used to raise cattle and grow produce. ⊠ *Rte. 76, Mahogany Rd., Estate Little La Grange* ☎ *340/772–1539* ⊕ *www.stcroixlandmarks.com* ✑ *$10* ☻ *Wed., Thurs. and Sat. 10–4.*

St. Croix Leap. This workshop sits in the heart of the rain forest, about a 15-minute drive from Frederiksted. It sells mirrors, tables, breadboards, and mahogany jewelry boxes crafted by local artisans. ⊠ *Rte. 76, Brooks Hill* ☎ *340/772–0421* ☻ *Weekdays 9–5, Sat. 10–5.*

West End Salt Pond. A bird-watcher's delight, this salt pond attracts a large number of winged creatures, including flamingos. ⊠ *Veteran's Shore Dr., Hesselberg.*

NORTH SHORE

Judith's Fancy. In this upscale neighborhood are the ruins of an old great house and tower of the same name, both remnants of a circa-1750 Danish sugar plantation. The "Judith" comes from the first name of a woman buried on the property. From the guardhouse at the neighborhood entrance, follow Hamilton Drive past some of St. Croix's loveliest houses. At the end of Hamilton Drive the road overlooks Salt River Bay, where Christopher Columbus anchored in 1493. On the way back, make a detour left off Hamilton Drive onto Caribe Road for a close look at the ruins. The million-dollar villas are something to behold, too. ⊠ *Turn north onto Rte. 751, off Rte. 75, Judith's Fancy.*

27

Mt. Eagle. At 1,165 feet, this is St. Croix's highest peak. Leaving Cane Bay and passing North Star Beach, follow the coastal road that dips briefly into a forest; then turn left on Route 69. Just after you make the turn, the pavement is marked with the words "The Beast" and a set of giant paw prints. The hill you're about to climb is the famous Beast of the St. Croix Half Ironman Triathlon, an annual event during which participants must cycle up this intimidating slope. ⊠ *Rte. 69.*

Salt River Bay National Historical Park and Ecological Preserve. This joint national and local park commemorates the area where Christopher Columbus's men skirmished with the Carib Indians in 1493 on his second visit to the New World. The peninsula on the bay's east side is named for the event: Cabo de las Flechas (Cape of the Arrows). Although the park is still developing, it has several sights with cultural significance. A ball court, used by the Caribs in religious ceremonies, was discovered at the spot where the taxis park. Take a short hike up the dirt road to the ruins of an old earthen fort for great views of Salt River Bay. The area also encompasses a coastal estuary with the region's largest remaining mangrove forest, a submarine canyon, and several endangered species, including the hawksbill turtle and the roseate tern. A visitor center, open winter only, sits just uphill to the west. The water at the beach can be on the rough side, but it's a nice place for sunning. ⊠ *Rte. 75 to Rte. 80, Salt River* ☎ *340/773–1460* ⊕ *www.nps.gov/sari* ☉ *Nov.–June, Tues.–Thurs. 9–4.*

BEACHES

Remember to remove all your valuables from the car and keep them out of sight when you go swimming. Break-ins happen on all three of the U.S. Virgin Islands, and most locals recommend leaving your windows down and leaving nothing in your car.

EAST END

Fodor's Choice   **Buck Island.** Part of Buck Island Reef National Monument, this is a
★   must-see for anyone in St. Croix. The beach is beautiful, but its finest treasures are those you can see when you plop off the boat and adjust your mask, snorkel, and fins to swim over colorful coral and darting fish. Don't know how to snorkel? No problem—the boat crew will have you outfitted and in the water in no time. Take care not to step on those black-pointed spiny sea urchins or touch the mustard-color fire coral, which can cause a nasty burn. Most charter-boat trips start with a snorkel over the lovely reef before a stop at the island's beach. An easy 20-minute hike leads uphill to an overlook for a bird's-eye view of the reef below. Find restrooms at the beach. **Amenities:** toilets. **Best for:** snorkeling; swimming ⊠ *5 miles (8 km) north of St. Croix* ☎ *340/773–1460* ⊕ *www.nps.gov/buis.*

NORTH SHORE

Cane Bay. On the island's breezy North Shore, Cane Bay does not always have gentle waters, but there are seldom many people around, and the scuba diving and snorkeling are wondrous. You can see elkhorn and brain corals, and less than 200 yards out is the drop-off called Cane Bay Wall. Cane Bay can be an all-day destination. You can rent kayaks and snorkeling and scuba gear at water-sports shops across the road, and a couple of casual restaurants beckon when the sun gets too hot. **Amenities:** food and drink; water sports. **Best for:** solitude; snorkeling; swimming. ⊠ *Rte. 80, about 4 miles (6 km) west of Salt River, Cane Bay.*

FREDERIKSTED

West End beaches. There are several unnamed beaches along the coast road north of Frederiksted, but it's best if you don't stray too far from civilization. For safety's sake, most vacationers plop down their towel near one of the casual restaurants spread out along Route 63. The beach at the Rainbow Beach Club, a five-minute drive outside Frederiksted, has a bar, a casual restaurant, water sports, and volleyball. If you want to be close to the cruise-ship pier, just stroll on over to the adjacent sandy beach in front of Ft. Frederik. On the way south out of Frederiksted, the stretch near Sandcastle on the Beach hotel is also lovely. **Amenities:** food and drink; water sports. **Best for:** snorkeling, swimming, walking. ⊠ *Rte. 63, north and south of Frederiksted.*

Some of St. Croix's best beaches are on the west end of the island north and south of Frederiksted.

WHERE TO EAT

Seven flags have flown over St. Croix, and each has left its legacy in the island's cuisine. Fresh local seafood is plentiful and always good; wahoo, mahimahi, and conch are most popular. Island chefs often add Caribbean twists to familiar dishes. For a true island experience, stop at a local restaurant for goat stew, curried chicken, or fried pork chops. Regardless of where you eat, your meal will be an informal affair. As is the case everywhere in the Caribbean, prices are higher than you'd pay on the mainland. Some restaurants may close for a week or two in September or October, so if you're traveling during these months, it's best to call ahead.

CHRISTIANSTED

$
ECLECTIC

✕ **Avocado Pitt.** Locals gather at this Christiansted waterfront spot for the breakfast and lunch specials as well as for a bit of gossip. Breakfast runs to stick-to-the-ribs dishes like oatmeal and pancakes. Lunches include such basics as a crispy chicken-breast sandwich. The yellowfin tuna sandwich is made from fresh fish and gives a new taste to a standard lunchtime favorite. $ *Average main: $11* ⊠ *King Christian Hotel, 59 Kings Wharf* ☎ *340/773–9843* ⊘ *No dinner.*

$$
FRENCH
★

✕ **Café Christine.** At this favorite with the professionals who work in downtown Christiansted the presentations are as dazzling as the food. The small menu changes daily, but look for dishes such as shrimp-and-asparagus salad drizzled with a lovely vinaigrette or a vegetarian plate with quiche, salad, and lentils. Desserts are perfection. If the pear pie topped with chocolate is on the menu, don't hesitate. This tiny restaurant has tables in both the air-conditioned dining room and on the outside porch that overlooks historic buildings. $ *Average main: $15* ⊠ *Apothecary Hall Courtyard, 4 Company St.* ☎ *340/713–1500* ▭ *No credit cards* ☉ *Closed weekends and July–mid-Nov. No dinner.*

$$
CARIBBEAN

✕**Harvey's.** The dining room is plain, even dowdy, and plastic lace table-cloths constitute the sole attempt at decor—but who cares? The food is delicious. Daily specials, such as mouthwatering goat stew and tender conch in butter, served with big helpings of rice and vegetables, are listed on the blackboard. Genial owner Sarah Harvey takes great pride in her kitchen, bustling out from behind the stove to chat and urge you to eat up. $ *Average main: $16* ⊠ *11B Company St.* ☎ *340/773–3433* ☉ *Closed Sun. No dinner.*

$$$$
INTERNATIONAL
★

✕**Kendricks.** The chef at this elegant open-air restaurant—a longtime favorite among locals—conjures up creative contemporary cuisine. To start, try the Alaskan snow-crab cakes with habanero aioli or the warm chipotle pepper with a garlic and onion soup. Move on to the house specialty: herb-crusted rack of lamb with roasted garlic and fresh thyme sauce. $ *Average main: $34* ⊠ *Company St. and King Cross St.* ☎ *340/773–9199* ⊕ *www.kendricksdining.com* ☉ *Closed Sun. No lunch.*

$$$$
INTERNATIONAL
★

✕**Restaurant Bacchus.** On the chic side, this restaurant is as notable for its extensive wine list as it is for its food. The menu changes regu-larly, but often includes favorites such as chopped tuna in a soy-sesame dressing served over crispy wontons. Such entrées as local lobster and fresh fish, steak swimming in mushroom truffle butter, and the filet mignon with Gorgonzola and a foie gras butter are always popular. For dessert, try the rum-drenched sourdough bread pudding. $ *Average main: $37* ⊠ *Queen Cross St. off King St.* ☎ *340/692–9922* ⊕ *www. restaurantbacchus.com* ☉ *Closed Mon. No lunch.*

$$$
ECLECTIC
☾
Fodor's Choice
★

✕**Rum Runners.** The view is as stellar as the food at this highly popu-lar local standby. Sitting right on the Christiansted boardwalk, Rum Runners serves a little bit of everything, including a to-die-for salad of crispy romaine lettuce and tender grilled lobster drizzled with lem-ongrass vinaigrette. More hearty fare includes baby back ribs cooked with the restaurant's special spice blend and Guinness stout. $ *Average main: $23* ⊠ *Hotel Caravelle, 44A Queen Cross St.* ☎ *340/773–6585* ⊕ *www.rumrunnersstcroix.com.*

$$$
ECLECTIC
★

✕**Savant.** Savant is one of those small but special spots that locals love. The cuisine is a fusion of Mexican, Thai, and Caribbean—an unusual combination that works surprisingly well. You can find anything from fresh fish to Thai curry with chicken to maple-teriyaki pork tenderloin coming out of the kitchen. With 20 tables crammed into the indoor dining room and small courtyard, this little place can get crowded. Call early for reservations. $ *Average main: $27* ⊠ *4C Hospital St.* ☎ *340/713–8666* ⊕ *www.savantstx.com* ☉ *Closed Sun. No lunch.*

$$$
ITALIAN

✕**Tutto Bene.** With murals on the walls, brightly striped cushions, and painted trompe-l'oeil tables, Tutto Bene looks more like a sophisticated Mexican cantina than an Italian *cucina*. One bite of the food, however, will clear up any confusion. The menu includes such specialties as veal saltimbocca and medallions of veal with prosciutto and sage. Among the desserts are a decadent tiramisu. Tutu Bene also offers a takeout lunch Tuesday through Friday. ⑤ *Average main: $29* ✉ *Boardwalk Shopping Center, Hospital St., Gallows Bay* ☎ *340/773–5229* ⊕ *www. tuttobenerestaurant.com.*

WEST OF CHRISTIANSTED

$$$ ✕ **Breezez.** This aptly named restaurant is poolside at the Club St. Croix
ECLECTIC condominiums. Visitors and locals are drawn by its reasonable prices
☾ and good food. This is *the* place on the island to be for Sunday brunch. Locals gather for lunch, when the menu includes everything from burgers to blackened prime rib with a horseradish sauce. For dessert, try the Amaretto cheesecake with either chocolate or fruit topping. ⑤ *Average main: $23* ✉ *Club St. Croix, 3220 Golden Rock, off Rte. 752, Golden Rock* ☎ *340/718–7077.*

EAST END

$$ ✕ **The Deep End.** A favorite with locals and vacationers, this poolside
ECLECTIC restaurant serves up terrific crab-cake sandwiches, London broil with onions and mushrooms, and delicious pasta dishes. To get here from Christiansted, take Route 82 and turn left at the sign for Green Cay Marina. ⑤ *Average main: $15* ✉ *Tamarind Reef Hotel, Annas Hope* ☎ *340/713–7071.*

$$$ ✕ **The Galleon.** This popular dockside restaurant is always busy. Start
ECLECTIC with the Caesar salad or perhaps a duck-liver pâté with cherry compote and arugula. The chef's signature dish is a tender filet mignon topped with fresh local lobster. Fish lovers should try the grilled wahoo over creamy Parmesan polenta in a mushroom-thyme sauce. Take Route 82 out of Christiansted, and then turn left at the sign for Green Cay Marina. ⑤ *Average main: $30* ✉ *Green Cay Marina, Annas Hope* ☎ *340/773–9949* ⊕ *www.galleonrestaurant.com* ⊗ *No lunch Mon.–Sat.*

NORTH SHORE

$$ ✕ **Off the Wall.** Divers fresh from a plunge at the North Shore's popular
AMERICAN Cane Bay Wall gather at this breezy spot on the beach. If you want to sit a spell before you order, a hammock beckons. Deli sandwiches, served with delicious chips, make up most of the menu. Pizza and salads are also available. ⑤ *Average main: $17* ✉ *Rte. 80, Cane Bay* ☎ *340/778–4771* ⊕ *www.otwstx.com.*

FREDERIKSTED

$$$ ✕ **Beach Side Café.** Sunday brunch is big, but locals and visitors also
ECLECTIC flock to this oceanfront bistro at Sandcastle on the Beach resort for lunch and dinner. Both menus include burgers and flatbread pizza, but at dinner the grilled pork tenderloin with a tomato-tamarind sauce shines. For lunch, the hummus plate is a good bet. ⑤ *Average main: $27* ✉ *Sandcastle on the Beach, 127 Smithfield* ☎ *340/772–1205* ⊕ *www. sandcastleonthebeach.com* ⊗ *Closed Tues.–Thurs.*

$$$ ✕ **Blue Moon.** This terrific little bistro, which has a loyal local following,
AMERICAN offers a changing menu that draws on Cajun and Caribbean flavors.
Fodor's Choice Try the spicy gumbo with andouille sausage or crab cakes with a spicy
★ aioli for your appetizer. A grilled chicken breast served with spinach and artichoke hearts and topped with Parmesan and cheddar cheeses

27

makes a good entrée. The Almond Joy sundae should be your choice for dessert. There's live jazz on Wednesday and Friday. ⑤ *Average main: $29* ⊠ *7 Strand St.* ☎ *340/772–2222* ⊘ *Closed Mon.*

$ ✕**Polly's at the Pier.** With an emphasis on fresh ingredients, this very
ECLECTIC   casual spot right on the waterfront serves yummy fare. The gourmet grilled-cheese sandwich comes with your choice of three cheeses as well as delicious additions like basil, fresh Bosc pears, and avocado. Salads are a specialty, and many are made with local greens like Bibb lettuce and organic mixed greens. ⑤ *Average main: $12* ⊠ *3 Strand St.* ☎ *340/719–9434* ⊘ *No dinner.*

$ ✕**Turtles Deli.** You can eat outside at this tiny spot just as you enter
DELI   downtown Frederiksted. Lunches are as basic as a corned beef on rye
🐢   or as imaginative as the Raven (turkey breast with bacon, tomato, and melted cheddar cheese on French bread). Also good is the Beast, named after the grueling hill that challenges bikers in the annual triathlon. It's piled high with hot roast beef, raw onion, and melted Swiss cheese with horseradish and mayonnaise. Early risers stop by for cinnamon buns and espresso. ⑤ *Average main: $10* ⊠ *38 Strand St., at Prince Passage* ☎ *340/772–3676* ⊕ *www.turtlesdeli.com* ▭ *No credit cards* ⊘ *Closed Sun. No dinner.*

WHERE TO STAY

If you sleep in either the Christiansted or Frederiksted area, you'll be closest to shopping, restaurants, and nightlife. Most of the island's other hotels will put you just steps from the beach. St. Croix has several small but special properties that offer personalized service. If you like all the comforts of home, you may prefer to stay in a condominium or villa. Room rates on St. Croix are competitive with those on other islands, and if you travel off-season, you can find substantially reduced prices. Many properties offer money-saving honeymoon and dive packages. Whether you stay in a hotel, a condominium, or a villa, you'll enjoy up-to-date amenities. Most properties have room TVs, but at some bed-and-breakfasts there might be only one, in the common room.

Although a stay right in historic Christiansted may mean putting up with a little urban noise, you probably won't have trouble sleeping. Christiansted rolls up the sidewalks fairly early, and humming air conditioners drown out any noise. Solitude is guaranteed at hotels and inns outside Christiansted and those on the outskirts of sleepy Frederiksted.

For expanded reviews, facilities, and current deals, visit Fodors.com.

PRIVATE CONDOMINIUMS AND VILLAS

Most of the villas in St. Croix are in the center or on the East End. Renting a villa gives you the convenience of home as well as top-notch amenities. Many have pools, hot tubs, and deluxe furnishings. Most companies meet you at the airport, arrange for a rental car, and provide helpful information about the island.

If you want to be close to the island's restaurants and shopping, look for a condominium or villa in the hills above Christiansted or on either side of the town. An East End location gets you out of Christiansted's hustle and bustle, but you're still only 15 minutes from town. North Shore locations are lovely, with gorgeous sea views and lots of peace and quiet.

RENTAL CONTACTS

Vacation St. Croix. ✉ *400 La Grande Princess, Christiansted* ☎ *340/718–0361, 877/788–0361* ⊕ *www.vacationstcroix.com.*

CHRISTIANSTED

$ ⚏ **Hotel Caravelle.** A stay at the Caravelle, which is near the harbor,
HOTEL puts you at the waterfront end of a pleasant shopping arcade and steps from shops and restaurants. **Pros:** good restaurant; convenient location; convenient parking. **Cons:** no beach; busy in-town neighborhood. **TripAdvisor:** "stay here if you want convenience," "perfect colonial style getaway," "the friendliest hotel in St. Croix." ⑤ *Rooms from: $170* ✉ *44A Queen Cross St.* ☎ *340/773–0687, 800/524–0410* ⊕ *www.hotelcaravelle.com* ⌁ *43 rooms, 1 suite* ⑩ *No meals.*

$ ⚏ **Hotel on the Cay.** Hop on the free ferry to reach this peaceful lodging
RESORT in the middle of Christiansted Harbor. **Pros:** quiet; convenient location; lovely beach. **Cons:** accessible only by ferry; no parking available; Wi-Fi in upstairs terrace only. **TripAdvisor:** "convenient small beach," "great staff," "barefoot paradise." ⑤ *Rooms from: $120* ✉ *Protestant Cay* ☎ *340/773–2035, 855/654–0301* ⊕ *www.hotelonthecay.com* ⌁ *53 rooms* ⑩ *No meals.*

$ ⚏ **King Christian Hotel.** A stay at the King Christian puts you right in
HOTEL the heart of Christiansted's historic district. **Pros:** rooms have ocean views; car rental in lobby; convenient location. **Cons:** no beach; need to take a taxi at night; no parking lot. **TripAdvisor:** "quaint lovely hotel," "helpful staff," "great location." ⑤ *Rooms from: $105* ✉ *57 King St.* ☎ *340/773–6330, 800/524–2012* ⊕ *www.kingchristian.com* ⌁ *39 rooms* ⑩ *Breakfast.*

WEST OF CHRISTIANSTED

$ ⚏ **Carringtons Inn.** Hands-on owners Claudia and Roger Carrington
B&B/INN are the real reason to stay here, and they serve delicious breakfasts—
Fodor's Choice rum-soaked French toast is a house specialty—dole out advice, and
★   make you feel right at home. **Pros:** welcoming hosts; tasteful rooms; great breakfasts. **Cons:** no beach; need car to get around. **TripAdvisor:** "warm hospitality," "beautiful view," "so comfortable and friendly." ⑤ *Rooms from: $125* ✉ *4001 Estate Hermon Hill, Christiansted* ☎ *340/713–0508, 877/658–0508* ⊕ *www.carringtonsinn.com* ⌁ *5 rooms* ⑩ *Breakfast.*

$ ⚏ **Club St. Croix.** Sitting beachfront just outside Christiansted, this mod-
RENTAL ern condominium complex faces a lovely sandy beach. **Pros:** beach-
☾   front location; good restaurant; full kitchens. **Cons:** need car to get around; sketchy neighborhood. **TripAdvisor:** "sweet and sour," "you've got a friend in paradise," "nice condo." ⑤ *Rooms from: $215* ✉ *Rte. 752, Estate Golden Rock* ☎ *340/718–9150, 800/524–2025* ⊕ *www.antillesresorts.com* ⌁ *53 apartments* ⑩ *No meals.*

$ ⚏ **Colony Cove.** In a string of condominium complexes, Colony Cove
RENTAL lets you experience comfortable beachfront living. **Pros:** beachfront
☾   location; comfortable units; good views. **Cons:** sketchy neighborhood; need car to get around. **TripAdvisor:** "friendly and fabulous," "little

27

piece of paradise," "excellent pool area." $ *Rooms from: $255* ✉ *Rte. 752, Estate Golden Rock* ☎ *340/718–1965, 800/524–2025* ⊕ *www. antillesresorts.com* ⤳ *62 apartments* ⫯⊚⫯ *No meals.*

$
RESORT **🏨 Hibiscus Beach Hotel.** This hotel's lovely beach is the best reason to stay here. **Pros:** nice beach; good restaurant; close to Christiansted. **Cons:** dated decor; sketchy neighborhood; need car to get around. **TripAdvisor:** "nice location and helpful staff," "home again," "great getaway." $ *Rooms from: $200* ✉ *4131 Estate La Grande Princesse, off Rte. 752, La Grande Princesse* ☎ *340/718–4042, 800/442–0121* ⊕ *www. hibiscusbeachresort.com* ⤳ *38 rooms* ⫯⊚⫯ *Breakfast.*

$
RENTAL
☾ **🏨 Sugar Beach.** With all the conveniences of home, Sugar Beach's apartments are immaculate and breezy. **Pros:** pleasant beach; full kitchens; space to spread out. **Cons:** sketchy neighborhood; need car to get around. **TripAdvisor:** "the best of everything," "sugary perfection," "gorgeous privately owned condo." $ *Rooms from: $160* ✉ *Rte. 752, Estate Golden Rock* ☎ *340/718–5345, 800/524–2049* ⊕ *www. sugarbeachstcroix.com* ⤳ *46 apartments* ⫯⊚⫯ *No meals.*

EAST END

$$$$
RESORT
☾ **🏨 The Buccaneer.** Aimed at travelers who want everything at their fingertips, this resort has sandy beaches, swimming pools, and extensive sports facilities. **Pros:** beachfront location; numerous activities; nice golf course. **Cons:** pricey rates; insular environment; need car to get around. **TripAdvisor:** "great place to unwind," "beautiful beaches," "relaxing." $ *Rooms from: $495* ✉ *Rte. 82, Shoys* ☎ *340/712–2100, 800/255–3881* ⊕ *www.thebuccaneer.com* ⤳ *138 rooms* ⫯⊚⫯ *Breakfast.*

$
RESORT
☾ **🏨 Chenay Bay Beach Resort.** The seaside setting and complimentary tennis and water-sports equipment make this resort a real find, particularly for families with active kids. **Pros:** beachfront location; good children's program; wide array of water sports. **Cons:** need car to get around; lacks pizzazz; Wi-Fi in lobby and restaurant only. **TripAdvisor:** "recommended for seasoned travelers," "unbeatable views," "beautiful and buggy." $ *Rooms from: $177* ✉ *Rte. 82, Green Cay* ☎ *340/773–2918, 800/548–4457* ⊕ *www.chenaybay.com* ⤳ *50 rooms* ⫯⊚⫯ *No meals.*

$$$
ALL-INCLUSIVE **🏨 Divi Carina Bay Resort.** An oceanfront location, the island's only casino, and plenty of activities make this resort a good bet. **Pros:** spacious beach; good restaurant; on-site casino. **Cons:** need car to get around; many stairs to climb; staff can seem chilly. **TripAdvisor:** "great little getaway," "a return to barefoot elegance," "ocean view was beautiful." $ *Rooms from: $450* ✉ *25 Rte. 60, Estate Turner Hole* ☎ *340/773– 9700, 877/773–9700* ⊕ *www.divicarina.com* ⤳ *174 rooms, 2 suites, 20 villas* ⫯⊚⫯ *All-inclusive.*

$
HOTEL **🏨 Tamarind Reef Resort.** Spread out along a sandy beach, these low-slung buildings offer casual comfort. **Pros:** good snorkeling; tasty restaurant; rooms have kitchenettes. **Cons:** need car to get around; motel-style rooms. **TripAdvisor:** "spectacular view from every room," "ideal escape," "slow and chill." $ *Rooms from: $275* ✉ *5001 Tamarind Reef, off Rte. 82, Annas Hope* ☎ *340/773–4455, 800/619–0014* ⊕ *www.tamarindreefresort.com* ⤳ *38 rooms* ⫯⊚⫯ *No meals.*

CAMPING IN ST. CROIX

If you really want to commune with nature, you'll be hard-pressed to find a better way to do it on St. Croix than with a stay at **Mount Victory Camp** (⊠ *Creque Dam Rd., Frederiksted* ☎ *340/772-1651 or 866/772-1651* ⊕ *www.mtvictorycamp.com*). Out on the west end, where few tourists stay, this out-of-the-way spread is on 8 acres in the island's rain forest. Hosts Bruce and Mathilde Wilson are on hand to explain the environment. You sleep in remarkable quietude in screened-in tent-cottages ($95–$125), which are perched on a raised platform and covered by a roof. Each has electricity and a rudimentary outdoor kitchen. There are also some bare tent sites for $30 per night. The shared, spotlessly clean bathhouse is an easy stroll away. The location feels remote, but a lovely sand beach and the Sunset Grill restaurant are a 2-mile (3-km) drive down the hill. In another 10 minutes you're in Frederiksted. Reservations are essential, and this is a cash-only place.

$$
RENTAL
★

⊞ **Villa Madeleine.** If you like privacy and your own private pool, you'll like Villa Madeleine. **Pros:** pleasant decor; full kitchens; private pools. **Cons:** lower units sometimes lack views; need car to get around; no beachfront. **TripAdvisor:** "beautiful view," "perfect stay," "exceeded my expectations." ⑤ *Rooms from: $285* ⊠ *Off Rte. 82, Teague Bay* ☎ *340/718-0361, 877/788-0361* ⊕ *www.vacationstcroix.com* ⋑ *43 villas* ⦶ *No meals.*

FREDERIKSTED

$
RESORT

⊞ **Sandcastle on the Beach.** Right on a gorgeous stretch of white beach, Sandcastle has a tropical charm that harks back to a simpler time in the Caribbean; its nearness to Frederiksted's interesting dining scene is also a plus. **Pros:** lovely beach; close to restaurants; gay-friendly vibe. **Cons:** neighborhood sketchy at night; need car to get around; no children's activities. **TripAdvisor:** "two weeks in paradise," "a Caribbean dream," "relaxing and beautiful." ⑤ *Rooms from: $159* ⊠ *127 Smithfield, Rte. 71* ☎ *340/772-1205, 800/524-2018* ⊕ *www. sandcastleonthebeach.com* ⋑ *12 rooms, 8 suites, 3 villas* ⦶ *Multiple meal plans.*

NORTH SHORE

$
B&B/INN

⊞ **Arawak Bay: The Inn at Salt River.** With stellar views of St. Croix's North Shore and an affable host, this small inn allows you to settle into island life at a price that doesn't break the bank. **Cons:** no beach nearby; can be some road noise. **TripAdvisor:** "become a part of the family," "beautiful view," "great local charm and hospitality." ⑤ *Rooms from: $150* ⊠ *Rte. 80, Salt River* ☎ *340/772-1684* ⊕ *www.arawakbaysaltriver.co.vi* ⋑ *12 rooms* ⦶ *Breakfast.*

$$$
RESORT
★

⊞ **Renaissance St. Croix Carambola Beach Resort and Spa.** We like this resort's stellar beachfront setting and peaceful ambience. **Pros:** lovely beach; relaxing atmosphere; close to golf. **Cons:** isolated location; need car to get around. **TripAdvisor:** "beautiful restaurant," "nice beach," "great place for relaxation." ⑤ *Rooms from: $379* ⊠ *Rte. 80, Davis*

27

Villa Greenleaf

Bay ☎ *340/778–3800, 888/236–2427* ⊕ *www.carambolabeachresort.com* 🔁 *151 rooms* ❍ *No meals.*

$ 🏠 **Villa Margarita.** This quiet retreat provides a particularly good base if
RENTAL you want to admire the dramatic views of the windswept coast. **Pros:**
friendly host; great views; snorkeling nearby. **Cons:** isolated location;
need car to get around; limited amenities. **TripAdvisor:** "great views
and great rooms," "St. Croix seclusion," "perfection in paradise."
⑤ *Rooms from: $165* ✉ *Off Rte. 80, Salt River* ☎ *340/713–1930*
⊕ *www.villamargarita.com* 🔁 *3 units* ❍ *No meals.*

$ 🏠 **Waves at Cane Bay.** St. Croix's famed Cane Bay Wall is just offshore
HOTEL from this hotel, giving it an enviable location. **Pros:** great diving; restaurants nearby; beaches nearby. **Cons:** need car to get around; on main
road; bland decor. **TripAdvisor:** "exquisite food," "laid-back atmosphere," "superior service." **⑤** *Rooms from: $175* ✉ *Rte. 80, Cane Bay*
☎ *340/718–1815* ⊕ *www.canebaystcroix.com* 🔁 *12 rooms* ❍ *No meals.*

MID ISLAND

$ 🏠 **Villa Greenleaf.** This spacious B&B is all about the details—four-
B&B/INN poster beds with elegant duvets, towels folded just so, hand-stenciled
Fodor's Choice trim on the walls, and carefully planted gardens. **Pros:** tasteful decor;
★ convivial atmosphere. **Cons:** no beach; no restaurants nearby; need
car to get around. **TripAdvisor:** "the perfect getaway," "luxury and
service," "no better accommodations." **⑤** *Rooms from: $275* ✉ *Is-
land Center Rd., Montpelier* ☎ *340/719–1958, 888/282–1001* ⊕ *www.
villagreenleaf.com* 🔁 *5 rooms* ❍ *Breakfast.*

NIGHTLIFE AND THE ARTS

Christiansted has a lively and eminently casual club scene near the waterfront. Frederiksted has a couple of restaurants and clubs offering weekend entertainment. To find out what's happening in St. Croix's ever-changing nightlife and eclectic arts scene, check out the local newspapers—*V.I. Daily News* (⊕ *virginislandsdailynews.com*) and *St. Croix Avis.*

CHRISTIANSTED

Fort Christian Brew Pub. Locals and visitors come to listen to live music here Wednesday, Friday, and Saturday. ⊠ *Boardwalk at end of Kings Alley, Christiansted* ☎ *340/713–9820* ⊕ *www.fortchristianbrewpub. com.*

Hotel on the Cay. This off-shore resort hosts a West Indian buffet on Tuesday night in the winter season, when you can watch a broken-bottle dancer (a dancer who braves a carpet of shattered glass) and mocko jumbie (stilt-dancing) characters. ⊠ *Protestant Cay, Christiansted* ☎ *340/773–2035* ⊕ *www.hotelonthecay.com.*

EAST END

Divi Carina Bay Resort. Although you can gamble at the island's only casino, it's really the nightly music that draws big crowds to this resort. ⊠ *25 Rte. 60, Estate Turner Hole* ☎ *340/773–7529* ⊕ *www.divicarina. com.*

MID ISLAND

Whim Plantation Museum. The museum outside Frederiksted hosts classical music concerts in winter. ⊠ *Rte. 70, Estate Whim* ☎ *340/772–0598* ⊕ *www.stcroixlandmarks.com.*

FREDERIKSTED

Fodor's Choice ★ **Blue Moon.** Blue Moon is a popular waterfront restaurant in Frederiksted, and it's the place to be for live jazz on Wednesday and Friday, one of the few nightlife options on this end of the island. ⊠ *7 Strand St., Frederiksted* ☎ *340/772–2222* ⊕ *www.bluemoonstcroix.com.*

Fodor's Choice ★ **Sunset Jazz.** This outdoor event is a hot ticket in Frederiksted, drawing crowds of visitors and locals at 6 pm on the third Friday of every month to watch the sun go down and hear good music. ⊠ *Waterfront, Frederiksted* ☎ *340/690–0617.*

SHOPPING

Although the shopping on St. Croix isn't as varied or extensive as that on St. Thomas, the island does have several small stores with unusual merchandise. St. Croix shop hours are usually Monday through Saturday 9 to 5, but there are some shops in Christiansted open in the evening. Stores are often closed on Sunday.

CHRISTIANSTED

In Christiansted the best shopping areas are the **Pan Am Pavilion** and **Caravelle Arcade,** off Strand Street, and along **King** and **Company streets.** These streets give way to arcades filled with boutiques. **Gallows Bay** has a blossoming shopping area in a quiet neighborhood.

27

BOOKS

Undercover Books. This well-stocked independent bookseller sells Caribbean-themed books as well as the latest good reads. The store is in the Gallows Bay shopping area. ⊠ *5030 Anchor Way, across from the post office, Gallows Bay* ☎ *340/719–1567* ⊕ *www.undercoverbooksvi.com.*

CLOTHING

Fodor'sChoice
★ **Coconut Vine.** This is a great place to pop into at the start of your vacation. You'll leave with enough comfy cotton or rayon batik men's and women's clothes to make you look like a local. Although the tropical designs and colors are from Indonesia, they're perfect for the Caribbean. ⊠ *1111 Strand St., Christiansted* ☎ *340/773–1991.*

From the Gecko. This store sells the hippest island-style clothes on St. Croix, as well as other items. ⊠ *1233 Queen Cross St., Christiansted* ☎ *340/778–9433* ⊕ *www.fromthegecko.com.*

Hot Heads. This small store sells hats, hats, and more hats, which are often perched on top of cotton shifts, comfortable shirts, and other tropical wear. If you forgot your bathing suit, this store has a good selection. ⊠ *Kings Alley Walk, Christiansted* ☎ *340/773–7888.*

Pacificotton. Shifts, tops, and pants in Caribbean colors as well as bags and hats fill the racks at Pacificotton. ⊠ *1110 Strand St., Christiansted* ☎ *340/773–2125.*

GIFTS

★ **Gone Tropical.** On her travels about the world, Margo Meacham keeps an eye out for special delights for her shop—gifty items that include tablecloths and napkins in bright Caribbean colors as well as unique fashion accessories. ⊠ *5 Company St., Christiansted* ☎ *340/773–4696* ⊕ *www.gonetropical.com.*

Many Hands. This shop sells pottery in bright colors, paintings of St. Croix and the Caribbean, prints, and maps. They are all made by local artists, and they all make for perfect take-home gifts. The owners ship all over the world. ⊠ *21 Pan Am Pavilion, Strand St., Christiansted* ☎ *340/773–1990.*

Mitchell-Larsen Studio. This glass gallery offers an interesting amalgam of carefully crafted glass plates, sun-catchers, and more. The pieces, all made on-site by a St. Croix glassmaker, are often whimsically adorned with tropical fish, flora, and fauna. ⊠ *58 Company St., Christiansted* ☎ *340/719–1000* ⊕ *www.mitchelllarsenstudio.com.*

Fodor'sChoice
★ **Royal Poinciana.** The attractive Royal Poinciana is filled with island seasonings and hot sauces, West Indian crafts, bath gels, and herbal teas. Shop here for tablecloths and paper goods in tropical brights. ⊠ *1111 Strand St., Christiansted* ☎ *340/773–9892.*

Tesoro. Among the colorful and bold merchandise here are metal sculptures made from retired steel pans, mahogany bowls, and hand-painted place mats in bright tropical colors. ⊠ *36C Strand St., Christiansted* ☎ *340/773–1212.*

HOUSEWARES

Designworks. This store and gallery carries furniture as well as one of the largest selections of local art, along with Caribbean-inspired bric-a-brac in all price ranges. If a mahogany armoire or cane-back rocker catches your fancy, the staff can have it shipped to your home at no charge from its mainland warehouse. ⊠ *6 Company St., Christiansted* ☎ *340/713–8102.*

JEWELRY

Crucian Gold. St. Croix native Brian Bishop's trademark piece is the Turk's Head ring (a knot of interwoven gold strands), but his jewelry made of shards of plantation-era china set in gold are just lovely. ⊠ *1112 Strand St., Christiansted* ☎ *340/773–5241* ⊕ *www.cruciangold.com.*

Gold Worker. This shop specializes in handcrafted jewelry in silver and gold that will remind you of the Caribbean. Hummingbirds dangle from silver chains, and sand dollars adorn gold necklaces. The sugar mills in silver and gold speak of St. Croix's past. ⊠ *3 Company St., Christiansted* ☎ *340/514–6042.*

ib designs. This small shop showcases the handcrafted jewelry of local craftsman Whealan Massicott. Whether in silver or gold, the designs are simply elegant. ⊠ *Company St. at Queen Cross St., Christiansted* ☎ *340/773–4322* ⊕ *www.islandboydesigns.com.*

Nelthropp and Low. The jewelers at Nelthropp and Low can create one-of-a-kind pieces to your design. The shop specializes in gold jewelry but also carries diamonds, emeralds, rubies, and sapphires. ⊠ *1102 Strand St., Christiansted* ☎ *340/773–0365, 800/416–9078* ⊕ *www. nelthropp-low.com.*

Sonya's. This store is owned and operated by Sonya Hough, who invented the popular hook bracelet. She has added an interesting decoration to these bracelets: the swirling symbol used in weather forecasts to indicate hurricanes. ⊠ *1 Company St., Christiansted* ☎ *340/778–8605* ⊕ *www.sonyaltd.com.*

LIQUOR AND TOBACCO

Baci Duty Free Liquor and Tobacco. The walk-in humidor here has a good selection of Arturo Fuente, Partagas, and Macanudo cigars. Baci also carries sleek Swiss-made watches and fine jewelry. ⊠ *1235 Queen Cross St., Christiansted* ☎ *340/773–5040* ⊕ *www.bacidutyfree.com.*

WEST OF CHRISTIANSED

FOOD

Pueblo. This market is similar to stores back in the mainland. ⊠ *Orange Grove Shopping Center, Rte. 75, Christiansted* ☎ *340/773–0118.*

EAST END

FOOD

Schooner Bay Market. Although it's on the smallish side, this market has good-quality deli items. ⊠ *Rte. 82, Mount Welcome* ☎ *340/773–3232* ⊕ *www.schoonerbaymarket.com.*

MID ISLAND

FOOD

Cost-U-Less. This warehouse-type store is great for visitors because it doesn't charge a membership fee. It's east of Sunny Isle Shopping Center. ⊠ *Rte. 70, Sunny Isle* ☎ *340/719–4442* ⊕ *www.costuless.com.*

Plaza Extra. This supermarket chain has a good selection of Middle Eastern foods in addition to the usual grocery-store items. ⊠ *United Shopping Plaza, Rte. 70, Sion Farm* ☎ *340/778–6240* ⊕ *www.plazaextra.com* ⊠ *Rte. 70, Mount Pleasant* ☎ *340/719–1870* ⊕ *www.plazaextra.com.*

Pueblo. This stateside-style market has another branch west of Christiansed. ⊠ *Villa La Reine Shopping Center, Rte. 75, La Reine* ☎ *340/778–1272.*

LIQUOR AND TOBACCO

Kmart. The U.S. discount chain has two branches on St. Croix, both of which carry a huge line of deep discounted, duty-free liquor, among many other items. ⊠ *Sunshine Mall, Rte. 70, Frederiksted* ☎ *340/692–5848* ⊠ *Sunny Isle Shopping Center, Rte. 70, Sunny Isle* ☎ *340/719–9190.*

FREDERIKSTED

The best shopping in Frederiksted is along **Strand Street** and in the side streets and alleyways that connect it with **King Street.** Most stores close on Sunday, except when a cruise ship is in port. Keep in mind that Frederiksted has a reputation for muggings, so it's best to stick to populated areas of Strand and King streets, where there are few—if any—problems.

SPORTS AND ACTIVITIES

BOAT TOURS

Almost everyone takes a day trip to Buck Island aboard a charter boat. Most leave from the Christiansted waterfront or from Green Cay Marina and stop for a snorkel at the island's eastern end before dropping anchor off a gorgeous sandy beach for a swim, a hike, and lunch. Sailboats can often stop right at the beach; a larger boat might have to anchor a bit farther offshore. A full-day sail runs about $100, with lunch included on most trips. A half-day sail costs about $68.

Big Beard's Adventure Tours. From catamarans that depart from the Christiansted waterfront you'll head to Buck Island for snorkeling before dropping anchor at a private beach for a barbecue lunch. ⊠ *Christiansted* ☎ *340/773–4482* ⊕ *www.bigbeards.com.*

Caribbean Sea Adventures. With craft leaving from the Christiansted waterfront, Caribbean Sea Adventures has both half- and full-day trips. ⊠ *Christiansted* ☎ *340/773–2628* ⊕ *www.caribbeanseaadventures.com.*

Teroro Charters. These charters are on two trimarans, *Teroro II* and *Dragonfly*, which leave Green Cay Marina for full- or half-day sails. Bring your own lunch. ⊠ *Green Cay Marina, Annas Hope* ☎ *340/773–3161* ⊕ *www.gotostcroix.com/heinz/index.php.*

Deep-sea fishing in St. Croix's costal waters

DIVING AND SNORKELING

At **Buck Island**, a short boat ride from Christiansted or Green Cay Marina, the reef is so nice that it's been named a national monument. You can dive right off the beach at **Cane Bay**, which has a spectacular drop-off called the Cane Bay Wall. Dive operators also do boat trips along the Wall, usually leaving from Salt River or Christiansted. **Frederiksted Pier** is home to a colony of sea horses, creatures seldom seen in the waters of the Virgin Islands. At **Green Cay,** just outside Green Cay Marina in the east end, you can see colorful fish swimming around the reefs and rocks. Two exceptional North Shore sites are **North Star** and **Salt River,** which you can reach only by boat. At Salt River you can float downward through a canyon filled with colorful fish and coral.

The island's dive shops take you out for one- or two-tank dives. Plan to pay about $65 for a one-tank dive and $100 for a two-tank dive, including equipment and an underwater tour. All companies offer certification and introductory courses called resort dives for novices.

Which dive outfit you pick usually depends on where you're staying. Your hotel may have one on-site. If so, you're just a short stroll away from the dock. If not, other companies are close by. Where the dive boat goes on a particular day depends on the weather, but in any case, all St. Croix dive sites are special. All shops are affiliated with PADI, the Professional Association of Diving Instructors.

Anchor Dive Center. Folks staying in the Judith's Fancy area are closest to Anchor Dive Center. The company also has facilities at the Buccaneer hotel. Anchor takes divers to more than 35 sites, including the

Wall at Salt River Canyon. ⊠ *Salt River Marina, Rte. 80, Salt River* ☎ *340/778–1522, 800/532–3483* ⊕ *www.anchordivestcroix.com.*

Cane Bay Dive Shop. This is the place if you want to do a beach dive or boat dive along the North Shore. The famed Cane Bay Wall is 200 yards from the PADI five-star facility. This company also has shops at Pan Am Pavilion in Christiansted, on Strand Street in Frederiksted, at the Carambola Beach Resort, and at the Divi Carina Bay Resort. ⊠ *Rte. 80, Cane Bay* ☎ *340/718–9913, 800/338–3843* ⊕ *www.canebayscuba.com.*

Dive Experience. Handy for those staying in Christiansted, Dive Experience runs trips to the North Shore walls and reefs in addition to offering the usual certification and introductory classes. It's a PADI five-star facility. ⊠ *1111 Strand St., Christiansted* ☎ *340/773–3307, 800/235–9047* ⊕ *www.divexp.com.*

N2 the Blue. N2 takes divers right off the beach near Coconuts restaurant, on night dives off the Frederiksted Pier, or on boat trips to wrecks and reefs. ⊠ *Frederiksted Pier, Rte. 631, Frederiksted* ☎ *340/772–3483, 877/579–0572* ⊕ *www.n2theblue.com.*

St. Croix Ultimate Bluewater Adventures. This company can take you to your choice of more than 75 sites; it also offers a variety of packages that include hotel stays. ⊠ *Queen Cross St., Christiansted* ☎ *340/773–5994, 877/567–1367* ⊕ *www.stcroixscuba.com.*

FISHING

Since the early 1980s, some 20 world records—many for blue marlin—have been set in these waters. Sailfish, skipjack, bonito, tuna (allison, blackfin, and yellowfin), and wahoo are abundant. A charter runs about $500 for a half day (for up to six people), with most boats going out for four-, six-, or eight-hour trips.

Caribbean Sea Adventures. This charter company can take you out on a 38-foot powerboat. ⊠ *59 Kings Wharf, Christiansted* ☎ *340/773–2628* ⊕ *www.caribbeanseaadventures.com.*

Gone Ketchin'. Captain Grizz, a true old salt, heads these trips. ⊠ *Salt River Marina, Rte. 80, Salt River* ☎ *340/713–1175* ⊕ *www.goneketchin.com.*

GOLF

Fodor's Choice
★ **Buccaneer Golf Course.** This 18-hole course is close to Christiansted. Greens fees are $90, with an additional $20 for cart rental. ⊠ *Rte. 82, Shoys* ☎ *340/712–2144* ⊕ *www.thebuccaneer.com.*

★ **Carambola Golf Club.** This spectacular 18-hole course in the northwest valley was designed by Robert Trent Jones Sr. The greens fees, $135 for 18 holes, include the use of a golf cart. ⊠ *Remaissance St. Croix Carambola Resort, Rte. 18, Davis Bay* ☎ *340/778–5638* ⊕ *www. golfcarambola.com.*

The Links at Divi St. Croix. This attractive minigolf course is just across from the Divi Carina Bay Resort. ⊠ *Rte. 60, Turner Hole* ☎ *340/773–9700* ⊕ *www.divicarina.com* ⌨ *$8* ☾ *Daily noon–8.*

Reef Golf Course. This public course on the island's east end has 9 holes. Greens fees are $20, and cart rental is $15. ⊠ *Teague Bay* ☎ *340/773–8844.*

Horseback riding in the island's rain forest

GUIDED TOURS

St. Croix Safari Tours. These van tours of St. Croix depart from Christiansted and last about five hours. Costs run from $65 per person, including admission fees to attractions. ✉ *St. Croix* ☎ *340/773–6700* ⊕ *www.gotostcroix.com/safaritours.*

St. Croix Transit. Departing from Carambola Beach Resort, St. Croix Transit's three-hour van tours cost from $65 per person, which includes the admission fees to all attractions. ✉ *St. Croix* ☎ *340/772–3333.*

HIKING

Although you can set off by yourself on a hike through a rain forest or along a shore, a guide will be able to point out what's important and tell you why.

Ay-Ay Eco Hike and Tours Association. Run by Ras Lumumba Corriette, the association takes hikers up hill and down dale in some of St. Croix's most remote places, including the rain forest and Mt. Victory. Some hikes include stops at places such as the Lawaetz Museum and old ruins. The cost is $60 per person for a three- or four-hour hike. There's a three-person minimum. A full-day jeep tour through the rain forest runs $120 per person. ✉ *Kingshill* ☎ *340/772–4079.*

HORSEBACK RIDING

Paul and Jill's Equestrian Stables. From Sprat Hall, just north of Frederiksted, co-owner Jill Hurd will take you through the rain forest, across the pastures, along the beaches, and through valleys—explaining the flora, fauna, and ruins on the way. A 1½-hour ride costs $90. ✉ *Rte. 58, Frederiksted* ☎ *340/772–2880, 340/772–2627* ⊕ *www. paulandjills.com.*

KAYAKING

Caribbean Adventure Tours. These kayak tours take you on trips through Salt River Bay National Historical Park and Ecological Preserve, one of the island's most pristine areas. All tours run $45. ⊠ *Salt River Marina, Rte. 80, Salt River* ☎ *340/778-1522* ⊕ *www.stcroixkayak.com.*

Virgin Kayak Tours. Virgin runs guided kayak trips on the Salt River and rents kayaks so you can tour around the Cane Bay area by yourself. Tours start at $45, and kayak rentals are $40 for the entire day. ⊠ *Rte. 80, Cane Bay* ☎ *340/778-0071* ⊕ *www.virginkayaktours.com.*

INDEX

Index > **1179**

PHOTO CREDITS

Department of Tourism. 324, Corbis. 331, DurdenImages/iStockphoto. Chapter 9 Curaçao: 341, Philip Coblentz/Digital Vision. 342 (bottom), Fotoconcept Inc./ age fotostock. 342 (top), Curaçao Tourism. 344, Philip Coblentz/Digital Vision. 345 (left), Stuart Pearce / age fotostock. 345 (right), Curaçao Tourism. 346, Angels at Work/shutterstock. 347, Curaçao Tourism. 351, Walter Bibikow / age fotostock. 354, Curacao Tourist Board. 357, Walter Bibikow / age fotostock. Chapter 10 Dominica: 375, Xavier Font/age fotostock. 376, Dominica Tourist Office. 377 (top), John Anderson/istockphoto. 377 (bottom), Dominica Tourist Office. 378, Greg Johnston / age fotostock. 379 (left), Antoine Hubert/Flickr. 379 (right), Hans Hillewaert/wikipedia.org. 380, Buddy Mays / Alamy. 381 (left), John Gabriel Stedman/wikipedia.org. 381 (right), J.E. (Julius Eduard) Muller/Tropenmuseum (http://collectie.tropenmuseum.nl/default.aspx?idx=ALL&field=*&search=60008905) (Creative Commons Attribution-Share Alike 3.0 Unported license), via Wikimedia Commons. 382, Winston Davidian/istockphoto. 388, John A. Anderson/istockphoto. 395, Fort Young Hotel Dominica. 403, Reinhard Dirscherl / age fotostock. Chapter 11 Dominican Republic: 405, Doug Scott/age fotostock. 406 (bottom), Doug Scott/age fotostock. 406 (top), Guy Thouvenin/age fotostock. 408, RIEGER Bertrand / age fotostock. 409 (top and bottom), The Dominican Republic Ministry of Tourism. 410, The Dominican Republic Ministry of Tourism. 411, The Dominican Republic Ministry of Tourism. 419, Harry Pujols/Flickr. 425, The Dominican Republic Ministry of Tourism. 438, tedmurphy/Flickr. 441, Sanctuary Cap Cana Golf & Spa. 447 (background photo), Sailorr/Shutterstock. 447 (pirate flag), wikipedia.org. 448 (left), rj lerich/Shutterstock. 448 (top right), Photos 12 / Alamy. 448 (bottom right), Anguilla Tourist Board. 449 (left), Lonely Planet Images / Alamy. 449 (center), Nevis Pirate Festival. 449 (right), unforth/Flickr. 450 (top left), The Print Collector / age fotostock. 450 (top and bottom right), wikipedia.org. 451 (left and center), wikipedia.org. 451 (right), Public domain. Chapter 12 Grenada: 467, Doug Scott/age fotostock. 468 (top and bottom), Grenada Board of Tourism. 470, PetePhipp/Travelshots / age fotostock. 471 (left), shaggyshoo/Flickr. 471 (right), Steven Allan/iStockphoto. 472, Grenada Board of Tourism. 482, Haltner Thomas / age fotostock. 499, Grenada Board of Tourism. Chapter 13 Guadeloupe: 501, Bruno Morandi/age fotostock. 502, Bruno Morandi/age fotostock. 504, Walter Bibikow / age fotostock. 505 (left), Ingolf Pompe 8 / Alamy. 505 (right), Walter Bibikow / age fotostock. 506, wikipedia.org. 507, Tristan Deschamps/F1 Online/age fotostock. 508, Susanne Kischnick / Alamy. 509 (left), wikipedia.org. 509 (right), Photocuisine / Alamy. 510, Holger W./shutterstock. 525, Philippe Michel / age fotostock. 533, La Toubana Hotel and Spa. 534, Philippe Giraud. 539, Sylvain Grandadam / age fotostock. Chapter 14 Jamaica: 547, Island Outpost. 548 (bottom), Torrance Lewis/Jamaica Tourist Board/Fotoseeker.com. 548 (top), Julian Love/Jamaica Tourist Board/Fotoseeker.com. 550, Steve Sanacore/Sandals Resorts. 551 (left), Chee-Onn Leong/Shutterstock. 551 (right), newphotoservice/shutterstock. 552, Miranda van der Kroft/Shutterstock. 553, Chee-Onn Leong/shutterstock. 554, Brian Nejedly. 555 (left), LarenKates/Flickr. 555 (right), Jamaica Inn. 556, Jamaica Tourist Board. 565, Franz Marc Frei / age fotostock. 575, Torrance Lewis/Jamaica Tourist Board/Fotoseeker.com. 582, Sandals Resorts. 597, Tramonto / age fotostock. 598 (top and center), TimDuncan/wikipedia.org. 598 (bottom), wbrisco.skyrock.com. 599, Dave Saunders / age fotostock. 600, Doug Pearson / age fotostock. 601 (left), NawlinWiki/wikipedia.org. 601 (center), Philippe Jimenez/wikipedia.org. 601 (right), wikipedia.org. 607, Sergio Pitamitz / age fotostock. Chapter 15 Martinique: 609, P. Narayan / age fotostock. 610, Philip Coblentz/Medioimages. 611, Maison de la France/LEJEUNE Nicole. 612, Guy Thouvenin / age fotostock. 613 (left), Luc Olivier for the Martinique Tourist Board. 613 (right), Pack-Shot/Shutterstock. 614, BarbachaINicolas BOUTHORS/wikipedia.org. 615, Luc Olivier for the Martinique Tourist Board. 623, GARDEL Bertrand / age fotostock. 627, ATOUT FRANCE/Patrice Thébault. 630, Walter Bibikow / age fotostock. 633, Luc Olivier for the Martinique Tourist Board. 643, Frameme/wikipedia.org. 649, Luc Olivier for the Martinique Tourist Board. Chapter 16 Montserrat: 653, John Cole. 654 (left), Igor Kravtchenko / KiMAGIC Photo and Design. 654 (right), Wailunip/wikipedia.org. 656, David Mac Gillivary -Montserrat Tourist Board. Chapter 17 Puerto Rico: 671, Katja Kreder / age fotostock. 672 (bottom), John Rodriguez/iStockphoto. 672 (top), Morales/age fotostock. 674, Julie Schwietert. 675 (left), Pavelsteidl/wikipedia.org. 675 (right), blucolt/Flickr. 676, Marlise Kast. 677, Katja Kreder / age fotostock. 678, steve bly / Alamy. 679 (left), Christian Sumner/iStockphoto. 679 (right), Steve Manson/iStockphoto. 680, Lori Froeb/Shutterstock. 689, Tomás Fano/Flickr. 691 (left), Franz Marc Frei/age fotostock. 691 (top right), Lawrence Robert/Shutterstock. 691 (bottom right), Franz Marc Frei/age fotostock. 692 (left) oStockphoto. 692 (right), Oquendo/Flickr. 693 (top left) runneralan2004/Flickr. 693 (bottom left), runneralan2004/Flickr. 693 (top center) Franz Marc Frei/age fotostock. 693 (top right), Prknlot/Flickr. 699, Franz Marc Frei / age fotostock. 714, Hotel El Convento. 716, Thomas Hart Shelby. 720, Tres Sirenas Beach Inn. Chapter 18 Saba: 729, Michael S. Nolan/age fotostock. 730 (top), Simon Wong/wikipedia.org. 730 (bottom), Edwin van Wier/Shutterstock. 732, Rutger Geerling / age fotostock. 737, Rutger Geerling / age fotostock. 742, Rutger Geerling / age fotostock. Chapter 19 St.

ABOUT OUR WRITERS

St. Thomas–based writer and dietitian Carol M. Bareuther writes for several regional and national magazines, such as *Destinations, Discover St. Thomas-St. John,* and *St. Thomas-St. John This Week.* She's the author of two books, including *Virgin Islands Cooking.*

Long-time St. John resident Lynda Lohr lives above Coral Bay and writes for numerous publications as well as travel websites. She prefers swimming at Great Maho Bay and hiking the island's numerous trails. An inveterate traveler, she's logged many miles to beautiful spots around the world.

Originally from the Isle of Mull in Scotland, Catherine MacGillivray now enjoys island living in Jamaica, where she works as a full-time professional writer. Catherine contributes to a number of regional and international publications on subjects ranging from travel and fine living to food and architecture.

As a life-long resident of New England, Elise Meyer has always considered her trips to the Caribbean to be a wintertime necessity. St. Barth and Anguilla have been favored destinations for more than 20 years. Now that the two kids are off on their own adventures, she's been enjoying longer and more exotic trips with a husband who shares her wanderlust, as well as a firm resolve to never check in luggage. She maintains a blog at www.elisemeyer.blogspot.com.

Susanna Henighan Potter, who updated our coverage of Anegada and Jost Van Dyke, lives in Tortola and writes often about the Virgin Islands as well as her native Tennessee and other destinations.

Vernon O'Reilly-Ramesar is a broadcaster and writer who divides his life between Trinidad and Canada. He spends much of his time exploring the wonders of the Southern Caribbean in his quest for the perfect beachside gin-martini.

Heather Rodino traded the island of Manhattan for the island of Puerto Rico, leaving behind a career in book publishing that included editorial positions at Barnes & Noble's publishing division and the Times Books imprint of Henry Holt. Now a freelance editor and writer, she has contributed to Fodor's *Puerto Rico* (6th and 7th eds.) and *Caribbean* (2011–2013). She lives in the Condado neighborhood of San Juan and doesn't miss those long New York winters.

Jordan Simon has written about nearly every Caribbean island for numerous national publications, including *Cooking Light, Art & Antiques, Condé Nast Traveler, Modern Bride, Town & Country, American Way, Diversion,* Caribbean Travel & Life, and *Hamptons,* and serves as weekly columnist for AOL Travel and as Lifestyle Editor for *Caribbean Living.* He has authored several books, including Fodor's *Colorado,* Fodor's *InFocus Cayman Islands,* and the *Gousha/USA Today Ski Atlas.*

Eileen Robinson Smith has lived in four of the Virgin Islands and is the former managing editor of the *Virgin Islander.* She has written about food and travel for many national magazines. A Fodor's veteran, she has written on the Dominican Republic for more than 15 years and on Martinique and Guadeloupe for more than a decade.

Chicago native Roberta Sotonoff is a confessed travel junkie who writes to support her habit. Her work has appeared in more than 75 domestic and international publications, websites, and guidebooks. She writes frequently about the Caribbean.

Jane E. Zarem travels frequently to the Caribbean from her Connecticut home. She has contributed to numerous Fodor's guides in addition to Caribbean, among them *New England, USA, Cape Cod, and Bahamas,* and most recently authored *In Focus Barbados and St. Lucia.*